Contents

How to Use This Book

ABOUT THE TRAIL PROFILES

Each hike in this book is listed in a consistent, easy-to-read format to help you choose the ideal hike. From a general overview of the setting to detailed driving directions, the profile will provide all the information you need. Here is a sample profile:

Map number and hike number →

1 SOMEWHERE USA HIKE

Round-trip mileage (unless otherwise noted) and the approximate amount of time needed to complete the hike (actual times can vary widely, especially on longer hikes) →

9.0 mi/5.0 hrs

👣3 ⛰8 ← Difficulty and quality ratings

at the mouth of the Somewhere River ← General location of the trail, named by its proximity to the nearest major town or landmark

Map 1.2, page 24 **BEST ☾** ← Symbol indicating that the hike is listed among the author's top picks

Map on which the trailhead can be found and page number on which the map can be found →

Each hike in this book begins with a brief overview of its setting. The description typically covers what kind of terrain to expect, what might be seen, and any conditions that may make the hike difficult to navigate. Side trips, such as to waterfalls or panoramic vistas, in addition to ways to combine the trail with others nearby for a longer outing, are also noted here. In many cases, mile-by-mile trail directions are included.

User Groups: This section notes the types of users that are permitted on the trail, including hikers, mountain bikers, horseback riders, and dogs. Wheelchair access is also noted here.

Permits: This section notes whether a permit is required for hiking, or, if the hike spans more than one day, whether one is required for camping. Any fees, such as for parking, day use, or entrance, are also noted here.

Maps: This section provides information on how to obtain detailed trail maps of the hike and its environs. Whenever applicable, names of U.S. Geologic Survey (USGS) topographic maps and national forest maps are also included; contact information for these and other map sources are noted in the Resources section at the back of this book.

Directions: This section provides mile-by-mile driving directions to the trail head from the nearest major town.

Contact: This section provides an address and phone number for each hike. The contact is usually the agency maintaining the trail but may also be a trail club or other organization.

ABOUT THE ICONS

The icons in this book are designed to provide at-a-glance information on the difficulty and quality of each hike.

The difficulty rating (rated **1–5** with **1** being the lowest and **5** the highest) is based on the steepness of the trail and how difficult it is to traverse

The quality rating (rated **1–10** with **1** being the lowest and **10** the highest) is based largely on scenic beauty, but also takes into account how crowded the trail is and whether noise of nearby civilization is audible

ABOUT THE DIFFICULTY RATINGS

Trails rated 1 are very easy and suitable for hikers of all abilities, including young children.

Trails rated 2 are easy-to-moderate and suitable for most hikers, including families with active children 6 and older.

Trails rated 3 are moderately challenging and suitable for reasonably fit adults and older children who are very active.

Trails rated 4 are very challenging and suitable for physically fit hikers who are seeking a workout.

Trails rated 5 are extremely challenging and suitable only for experienced hikers who are in top physical condition.

MAP SYMBOLS

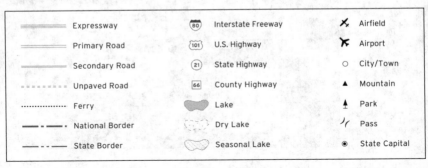

▓▓▓▓▓ Expressway	🛣 Interstate Freeway	✗ Airfield	
═══ Primary Road	🛡 U.S. Highway	✗ Airport	
▬▬ Secondary Road	Ⓔ State Highway	○ City/Town	
▪▪▪▪ Unpaved Road	🛡 County Highway	▲ Mountain	
▬▪▬▪ Ferry	Lake	♣ Park	
▬▪▬▪ National Border	Dry Lake	)(Pass	
▬▪▪▬ State Border	Seasonal Lake	◉ State Capital	

ABOUT THE MAPS

This book is divided into chapters based on major regions in the state; an overview map of these regions precedes the table of contents. Each chapter begins with a map of the region, which is further broken down into detail maps. Trailheads are noted on the detail maps by number.

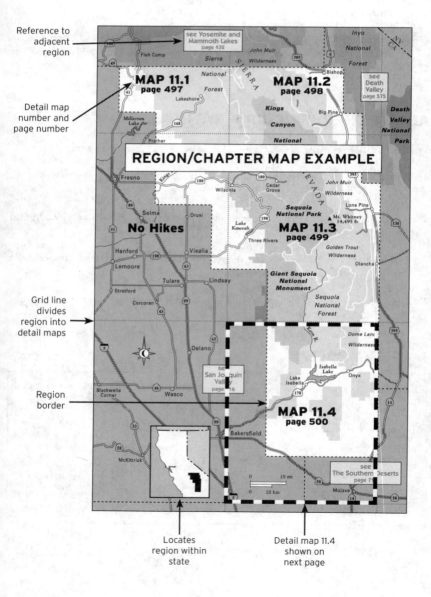

Reference to adjacent region

Detail map number and page number

REGION/CHAPTER MAP EXAMPLE

Grid line divides region into detail maps

Region border

Locates region within state

Detail map 11.4 shown on next page

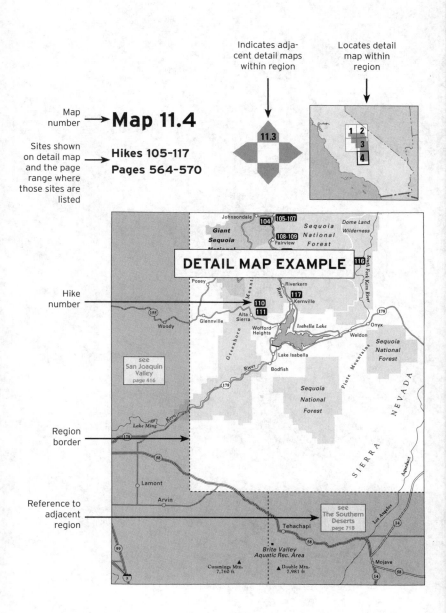

Indicates adjacent detail maps within region

Locates detail map within region

Map number → **Map 11.4**

Sites shown on detail map and the page range where those sites are listed → **Hikes 105–117**
Pages 564–570

11.3

1 2
3
4

DETAIL MAP EXAMPLE

Hike number

Region border

Reference to adjacent region

INTRODUCTION

Author's Note

If the great outdoors is so great, then why don't people enjoy it more? The answer is because of the time trap, and I will tell you exactly how to beat it.

For many, the biggest problem is finding the time to go, whether it is hiking, backpacking, camping, fishing, boating, biking, or even just for a good drive in the country. The solution? Believe it or not, the answer is to treat your fun just as you treat your work, and I'll tell you how.

Consider how you treat your job: Always on time? Go there every day you are scheduled? Do whatever it takes to get there and get it done? Right? No foolin' that's right. Now imagine if you took the same approach to the outdoors. Suddenly your life would be a heck of a lot better.

The secret is to schedule all of your outdoor activities. For instance, I go fishing every Thursday evening, hiking every Sunday morning, and on an overnight trip every new moon (when stargazing is best). No matter what, I'm going. Just like going to work, I've scheduled it. The same approach works with longer adventures. The only reason I have been able to complete hikes ranging from 200 to 300 miles was that I scheduled the time to do it. The reason I spend 125 to 150 days a year in the field is that I schedule them. In my top year, I had nearly 200 days where at least part of the day was enjoyed taking part in outdoor recreation.

If you get out your calendar and write in the exact dates you are going, then you'll go. If you don't, you won't. Suddenly, with only a minor change in your life plan, you can be living the life you were previously dreaming about.

—Tom Stienstra

Author's Note

A wise person once said that a culture can be measured by the resources it chooses to preserve. If that's true, then the state of California is an immense credit to our culture. The Golden State is blessed with an abundance of parks and preserves, including more than 20 units of the National Park System, 18 national forests, 137 federally designated wilderness areas, 275 state parks, and thousands of county and regional parks.

This huge mosaic of parklands celebrates California's diverse landscape, which includes the highest peak in the contiguous United States (Mount Whitney at 14,495 feet) and the lowest point in the western hemisphere (Badwater in Death Valley at 282 feet below sea level). Our state contains 20,000 square miles of desert, nearly 700 miles of Pacific coastline, an unaccountable wealth of snow-capped peaks and alpine lakes, a smattering of islands, and even a handful of volcanoes.

California also boasts its share of the world's tallest living things, the towering coast redwoods. And we are the only state that is home to the world's largest living trees (by volume), the giant sequoias. Also within California's borders are groves of the planet's oldest living things, the ancient bristlecone pines.

Quite simply, we live in a land of superlatives. California's public lands are some of my favorite places on earth, and I believe that everyone should have the chance to see them, and be awed and humbled by their wonders. But this wish comes with a caveat attached: We must tread lightly and gently on our parks, with great respect and care for the land. And we must do whatever is required to ensure the protection of these beautiful places for future generations.

I wish you many inspiring days on the trail.

—Ann Marie Brown

Best Hikes

Can't decide where to hike this weekend? Here are our picks for the best hikes in California in 17 different categories listed from north to south throughout the state:

◖ Best Beach and Coastal Walks

Rim Loop Trail, Patrick's Point State Park, Redwood Empire, page 56.

Lost Coast Trail/Mattole Trailhead, King Range National Conservation Area, Redwood Empire, page 62.

Lost Coast Trail/Sinkyone Trailhead, Sinkyone Wilderness State Park, Mendocino and Wine Country, page 177.

Coast Trail, Point Reyes National Seashore, San Francisco Bay Area, page 304.

Old Landing Cove Trail, Wilder Ranch State Park, Monterey and Big Sur, page 452.

Point Lobos Perimeter, Point Lobos State Reserve, Monterey and Big Sur, page 459.

Montaña de Oro Bluffs Trail, Montaña de Oro State Park, Santa Barbara and Vicinity, page 664.

Razor Point and Beach Trail Loop, Torrey Pines State Reserve, San Diego and Vicinity, page 765.

Bayside Trail, Cabrillo National Monument, San Diego and Vicinity, page 768.

Cabrillo Tidepools, Cabrillo National Monument, San Diego and Vicinity, page 769.

◖ Best for Bird-Watching

Arcata Marsh Trail, Arcata Marsh and Wildlife Sanctuary, Redwood Empire, page 57.

Abbotts Lagoon Trail, Point Reyes National Seashore, San Francisco Bay Area, page 296.

Audubon Canyon Ranch Trail, Marsh Griffin Preserve, San Francisco Bay Area, page 319.

Arrowhead Marsh, Martin Luther King Regional Shoreline, San Francisco Bay Area, page 386.

Elkhorn Slough South Marsh Loop, Moss Landing, Monterey and Big Sur, page 455.

Chester, Sousa, and Winton Marsh Trails, San Luis National Wildlife Refuge, San Joaquin Valley, page 485.

Carrizo Plain and Painted Rock, Carrizo Plains National Monument, San Joaquin Valley, page 489.

Mono Lake South Tufa Trail, Mono Lake Tufa State Reserve, Yosemite and Mammoth Lakes, page 530.

Silverwood Wildlife Sanctuary, San Diego and Vicinity, page 777.

◖ Best Butt-Kickers

Devils Punchbowl (via Doe Flat Trail), Siskiyou Wilderness, Shasta and Trinity, page 77.

Shasta Summit Trail, Shasta-Trinity National Forest, Shasta and Trinity, page 94.

Beacroft Trail, Tahoe National Forest, Tahoe and Northern Sierra, page 234.

Rooster Comb Loop (Long Version), Henry W. Coe State Park, San Francisco Bay Area, page 442.

Half Dome, Yosemite Valley, Yosemite and Mammoth Lakes, page 548.

◖ Best Desert Hikes

◖ Best for Fall Colors

◖ Best Hikes with a View

Moro Rock, Sequoia National Park, Sequoia and Kings Canyon, page 612.

Needles Lookout, Giant Sequoia National Monument, Sequoia and Kings Canyon, page 630.

Devils Slide Trail to Tahquitz Peak, San Jacinto Wilderness, Los Angeles and Vicinity, page 750.

Aerial Tramway to San Jacinto Peak, Mount San Jacinto State Park and Wilderness, California Deserts, page 813.

◖ Best for Kids

Rainbow and Lake of the Sky Trails, Tahoe National Forest, Tahoe and Northern Sierra, page 251.

Angora Lakes Trail, Tahoe National Forest, Tahoe and Northern Sierra, page 254.

Tomales Point Trail, Point Reyes National Seashore, San Francisco Bay Area, page 295.

Fitzgerald Marine Reserve, Moss Beach, San Francisco Bay Area, page 354.

Año Nuevo Trail, Año Nuevo State Reserve, San Francisco Bay Area, page 416.

Pinecrest Lake National Recreation Trail, Stanislaus National Forest, Yosemite and Mammoth Lakes, page 497.

Devils Postpile and Rainbow Falls, Devils Postpile National Monument, Yosemite and Mammoth Lakes, page 538.

Tokopah Falls, Sequoia National Park, Sequoia and Kings Canyon, page 607.

Cabrillo Tidepools, Cabrillo National Monument, San Diego and Vicinity, page 769.

Desert Tortoise Discovery Loop, Desert Tortoise Natural Area, California Deserts, page 799.

◖ Best Meadow Hikes

Haypress Meadows Trailhead, Marble Mountain Wilderness, Shasta and Trinity, page 80.

Gray Butte, Mount Shasta Wilderness, Shasta and Trinity, page 96.

Carson Pass to Echo Lakes Resort (PCT), Tahoe and Northern Sierra, page 268.

Eagle Meadow to Dardanelle, Tahoe and Northern Sierra, page 281.

Grass Valley Loop, Anthony Chabot Regional Park, San Francisco Bay Area, page 388.

McGurk Meadow and Dewey Point, Yosemite National Park, Yosemite and Mammoth Lakes, page 551.

Zumwalt Meadow Loop, Kings Canyon National Park, Sequoia and Kings Canyon, page 597.

Casa Vieja Meadow, Golden Trout Wilderness, Sequoia and Kings Canyon, page 641.

Manter Meadow Loop, Dome Land Wilderness, Sequoia and Kings Canyon, page 648.

◖ Best for Redwoods

Boy Scout Tree Trail, Jedediah Smith Redwoods State Park, Redwood Empire, page 46.

Tall Trees Trail, Redwood National Park, Redwood Empire, page 52.

Redwood Creek Trail, Redwood National Park, Redwood Empire, page 55.

Bull Creek Flats, Humboldt Redwoods State Park, Redwood Empire, page 60.

Main Trail, Muir Woods National Monument, San Francisco Bay Area, page 330.

Shadow of the Giants, Sierra National Forest, Yosemite and Mammoth Lakes, page 559.

General Grant Tree Trail, Kings Canyon National Park, Sequoia and Kings Canyon, page 591.

Redwood Canyon, Kings Canyon National Park, Sequoia and Kings Canyon, page 599.

Congress Trail Loop, Sequoia National Park, Sequoia and Kings Canyon, page 608.

Trail of 100 Giants, Giant Sequoia National Monument, Sequoia and Kings Canyon, page 631.

◖ Best Self-Guided Nature Walks

McCloud Nature Trail, Shasta-Trinity National Forest, Shasta and Trinity, page 114.

Rainbow and Lake of the Sky Trails, Tahoe National Forest, Tahoe and Northern Sierra, page 251.

Trail of the Gargoyles, Stanislaus National Forest, Tahoe and Northern Sierra, page 282.

Shadow of the Giants, Sierra National Forest, Yosemite and Mammoth Lakes, page 559.

Methuselah Trail, Inyo National Forest, Yosemite and Mammoth Lakes, page 566.

Unal Trail, Sequoia National Forest, Sequoia and Kings Canyon, page 646.

Piño Alto Trail, Los Padres National Forest, Santa Barbara and Vicinity, page 674.

McGrath State Beach Nature Trail, McGrath State Beach, Santa Barbara and Vicinity, page 687.

Ponderosa Vista Nature Trail, San Bernardino National Forest, Los Angeles and Vicinity, page 744.

Inaja Memorial Trail, Cleveland National Forest, San Diego and Vicinity, page 772.

◖ Best Short Backpack Trips

Taylor Lake Trail, Russian Wilderness, Shasta and Trinity, page 99.

Toad Lake Trail, Shasta-Trinity National Forest, Shasta and Trinity, page 105.

Echo and Twin Lakes, Lassen Volcanic National Park, Lassen and Modoc, page 153.

Winnemucca Lake from Woods Lake, Mokelumne Wilderness, Tahoe and Northern Sierra, page 270.

Coast Trail, Point Reyes National Seashore, San Francisco Bay Area, page 304.

Black Mountain, Monte Bello Open Space Preserve, San Francisco Bay Area, page 367.

May Lake and Mount Hoffman, Yosemite National Park, Yosemite and Mammoth Lakes, page 513.

Glen Aulin and Tuolumne Falls, Yosemite National Park, Yosemite and Mammoth Lakes, page 520.

Ladybug Trail, Sequoia National Park, Sequoia and Kings Canyon, page 624.

Gabrielino National Recreation Trail to Bear Canyon, Angeles National Forest, Los Angeles and Vicinity, page 706.

◖ Best Summit Hikes

Preston Peak, Siskiyou Wilderness, Shasta and Trinity, page 75.

Grizzly Lake, Trinity Alps Wilderness, Shasta and Trinity, page 88.

Shasta Summit Trail, Shasta-Trinity National Forest, Shasta and Trinity, page 94.

Lassen Peak Trail, Lassen Volcanic National Park, Lassen and Modoc, page 154.

East Peak Mount Tamalpais, Mount Tamalpais State Park, San Francisco Bay Area, page 323.

Mount Dana, Yosemite National Park, Yosemite and Mammoth Lakes, page 526.

White Mountain Peak Trail, Inyo National Forest, Yosemite and Mammoth Lakes, page 566.

Mount Whitney Trail, John Muir Wilderness, Sequoia and Kings Canyon, page 635.

Mount Baldy, Angeles National Forest, Los Angeles and Vicinity, page 731.

Vivian Creek Trail to Mount San Gorgonio, San Gorgonio Wilderness, Los Angeles and Vicinity, page 747.

☖ Best for Swimming Holes

McClendon Ford Trail, Smith River National Recreation Area, Redwood Empire, page 49.

Deer Creek Trail, Lassen National Forest, Lassen and Modoc, page 162.

Paradise Creek Trail, Sequoia National Park, Sequoia and Kings Canyon, page 613.

Alder Creek Trail, Giant Sequoia National Monument, Sequoia and Kings Canyon, page 632.

Big Falls, Santa Lucia Wilderness, Santa Barbara and Vicinity, page 667.

Little Falls, Santa Lucia Wilderness, Santa Barbara and Vicinity, page 667.

Cedar Creek and the Fishbowls, Sespe Wilderness, Santa Barbara and Vicinity, page 682.

Santa Paula Canyon to Big Cone Camp, Los Padres National Forest, Santa Barbara and Vicinity, page 686.

Green Valley Falls, Cuyamaca Rancho State Park, San Diego and Vicinity, page 778.

☖ Best for Waterfalls

Burney Falls Loop Trail, McArthur-Burney Falls Memorial State Park, Lassen and Modoc, page 139.

Feather Falls Loop, Plumas National Forest, Sacramento and Gold Country, page 202.

Grouse Falls, Tahoe National Forest, Tahoe and Northern Sierra, page 237.

McWay Falls Overlook, Julia Pfeiffer Burns State Park, Monterey and Big Sur, page 471.

Waterwheel Falls, Yosemite National Park, Yosemite and Mammoth Lakes, page 519.

Devils Postpile and Rainbow Falls, Devils Postpile National Monument, Yosemite and Mammoth Lakes, page 538.

Upper Yosemite Fall, Yosemite Valley, Yosemite and Mammoth Lakes, page 543.

Mist Trail and John Muir Loop to Nevada Fall, Yosemite Valley, Yosemite and Mammoth Lakes, page 546.

Bridalveil Fall, Yosemite Valley, Yosemite and Mammoth Lakes, page 550.

Tokopah Falls, Sequoia National Park, Sequoia and Kings Canyon, page 607.

☖ Best Wheelchair-Accessible Trails

Taylor Lake Trail, Russian Wilderness, Shasta and Trinity, page 99.

Kangaroo Lake Trailhead, Klamath National Forest, Shasta and Trinity, page 103.

Lake Cleone Trail, MacKerricher State Park, Mendocino and Wine Country, page 179.

South Yuba Independence Trail, Nevada City, Sacramento and Gold Country, page 203.

Sierra Discovery Trail, PG&E Bear Valley Recreation Area, Tahoe and Northern Sierra, page 229.

Abbotts Lagoon Trail, Point Reyes National Seashore, San Francisco Bay Area, page 296.

McWay Falls Overlook, Julia Pfeiffer Burns State Park, Monterey and Big Sur, page 471.

Lower Yosemite Fall, Yosemite Valley, Yosemite and Mammoth Lakes, page 545.

Roaring River Falls, Kings Canyon National Park, Sequoia and Kings Canyon, page 597.

Salt Creek Interpretive Trail, Death Valley National Park, California Deserts, page 794.

C Best for Wildflowers

Lake Margaret, Eldorado National Forest, Tahoe and Northern Sierra, page 263.

Chimney Rock Trail, Point Reyes National Seashore, San Francisco Bay Area, page 300.

Grass Valley Loop, Anthony Chabot Regional Park, San Francisco Bay Area, page 388.

Rocky Ridge and Soberanes Canyon Loop, Garrapata State Park, Monterey and Big Sur, page 459.

Path of the Padres, San Luis Reservoir State Recreation Area, San Joaquin Valley, page 487.

Lundy Canyon Trail, Hoover Wilderness, Yosemite and Mammoth Lakes, page 502.

Hite Cove Trail, Sierra National Forest, Yosemite and Mammoth Lakes, page 543.

Whitney Portal to Lake Thomas Edison (JMT/PCT), Sequoia and Kings Canyon, page 637.

Montaña de Oro Bluffs Trail, Montaña de Oro State Park, Santa Barbara and Vicinity, page 664.

Antelope Valley Poppy Reserve Loop, California Deserts, page 800.

C Best for Wildlife

Note: Seeing wildlife is not guaranteed and is often seasonally influenced.

Coastal Trail (Fern Canyon/Ossagon Section), Prairie Creek Redwoods State Park, Redwood Empire, page 54.

Spirit Lake Trail, Marble Mountain Wilderness, Shasta and Trinity, page 81.

Captain Jack's Stronghold, Lava Beds National Monument, Lassen and Modoc, page 135.

Tomales Point Trail, Point Reyes National Seashore, San Francisco Bay Area, page 295.

Pescadero Marsh, San Francisco Bay Area, page 370.

Año Nuevo Trail, Año Nuevo State Reserve, San Francisco Bay Area, page 416.

Tule Elk State Reserve, San Joaquin Valley, page 490.

Desert Tortoise Discovery Loop, Desert Tortoise Natural Area, California Deserts, page 799.

Hiking Tips

HIKING ESSENTIALS

Aside from the shoes on your feet, it doesn't take much equipment to go day hiking. Whereas backpackers must concern themselves with tents, sleeping pads, pots and pans, and the like, day hikers have an easier time of it. Still, too many day hikers set out carrying too little and get into trouble as a result. Here's our list of essentials:

Food and Water

Water is even more important than food, although it's unwise to get caught without a picnic, or at least some edible supplies for emergencies. If you don't want to carry the weight of a couple water bottles, at least carry a purifier or filtering device so you can get water from streams, rivers, or lakes. It goes without saying, but never, ever drink water from a natural source without purifying it. The microscopic organisms *Giardia lamblia* and *Cryptosporidium* are found in backcountry water sources and can cause a litany of terrible gastrointestinal problems. Only purifying or boiling water from natural sources will eliminate giardiasis.

The new water bottle–style purifiers, such as those made by Bota, Sawyer, or Katadyn Exstream, are as light as an empty plastic bottle and eliminate the need to carry both a filter and a bottle. You simply dip the bottle in the stream, screw on the top (which has a filter inside it), and squeeze the bottle to drink. The water is filtered on its way out of the squeeze top.

Another great new invention is a purifier called SteriPEN, which uses ultraviolet light rays instead of chemicals to purify water. It's small, light, runs on AA batteries, and purifies 32 ounces of water in about 90 seconds.

Of course, in many areas, you won't find a natural water source to filter from, so carrying water is still necessary. Remember that trails that cross running streams in the winter and spring months may cross dry streams in the summer and autumn months.

What you carry for food is up to you. Some

© ANN MARIE BROWN

A brief stop along the trail to examine a map can save you time and frustration.

people go gourmet and carry the complete inventory of a fancy grocery store. If you don't want to bother with much weight, stick with high-energy snacks like nutrition bars, nuts, dried fruit, turkey or beef jerky, and crackers. Our rule is always to bring more than you think you can eat. You can always carry it back out with you, or give it to somebody else on the trail who needs it.

If you're hiking in a group, each of you should carry your own food and water just in case someone gets too far ahead or behind.

Trail Maps

A map of the park or public land you're visiting is essential. Never count on trail signs to get you where you want to go. Signs get knocked down or disappear with alarming frequency, due to rain, wind, or park visitors looking for souvenirs. Many hikers think that carrying a GPS device eliminates the need for a map, but this isn't always true. If you get lost, a map can show you where you are (via landmarks such as peaks, lakes, ridges, etc.) and can show you where the nearest trail is located. It can also show alternate routes if you decide not to go the way you originally planned.

Always obtain a map from the managing agency of the place you're visiting. Their names and phone numbers are listed in this book. For national forest maps, USGS topographical maps, and maps from commercial services, such as Tom Harrison Maps

Extra Clothing

On the trail, conditions can change at any time. Not only can the weather suddenly turn windy, foggy, or rainy, but your own body conditions also change: You'll perspire as you hike up a sunny hill and then get chilled at the top of a windy ridge or when you head into shade. Because of this, cotton fabrics don't function well in the outdoors. Once cotton gets wet, it stays wet. Generally, polyester-blend fabrics dry faster. Some high-tech fabrics will actually wick moisture away from your skin. Invest in a few items of clothing made from these fabrics and you'll be more comfortable when you hike.

Always carry a lightweight jacket with you, preferably one that is waterproof and also wind-resistant. If your jacket isn't waterproof, pack along one of the $2, single-use rain ponchos that come in a package the size of a deck of cards (available at outdoors stores and drug stores). If you can't part with two bucks, carry an extra-large garbage bag, which can be converted into a waterproof vest. In cooler temperatures, or when heading to a mountain summit (even on a hot day), carry gloves and a hat as well.

Flashlight

Just in case your hike takes a little longer than you planned, bring at least one flashlight. Mini flashlights are available everywhere, weigh almost nothing, and can save the day—or night. We especially like the tiny squeeze flashlights, about the size and shape of a quarter, that you can clip on to any key ring. Some turn on and off with a small switch, so you don't have to squeeze them for extended periods. (The Photon Micro-Light is a popular brand.) Whatever kind of flashlight you carry, make sure the batteries work before you set out on the trail. Always take along an extra set of batteries and an extra bulb, or simply an extra flashlight or two. You never know when the darn things will run out of juice.

Sunglasses and Sunscreen

You know the dangers of the sun. Wear sunglasses to protect your eyes and sunscreen with a high SPF on any exposed skin. Put on your sunscreen 30 minutes before you go outdoors so it has time to take effect. In addition, protect the skin on your face with a good wide-brimmed hat. Wearing lip balm with a high SPF is also a smart idea.

Insect Repellent

Several kinds of insect repellent now come with sunscreen, so you can put on one lotion instead of two. Many types of insect repellent have an ingredient called DEET, which is extremely effective but also quite toxic. Children should not use repellent with high levels of DEET, although it seems to be safe for adults. Many other types of repellent are made of natural substances, such as lemon oil. What works best? Everybody has his or her opinion. If you visit the High Sierra in the middle of a major mosquito hatch, it often

THE JOHN MUIR TRAIL AND THE PACIFIC CREST TRAIL

You can have a foothold in the sky with every step on the John Muir Trail (JMT). The trail starts at practically the tip-top of North America – Mount Whitney – and takes you northward across a land of 12,000-foot passes and Ansel Adams-style vistas, then eventually pours you into nature's showpiece of the world, Yosemite Valley.

How could you top that? There is only one way: to hike the Pacific Crest Trail (PCT), of which the JMT partially overlaps. The PCT extends from the Mexico border for 1,700 miles north to Oregon, and then beyond all the way to its end, at the Canadian border – a total distance of 2,650 miles.

The JMT and the PCT are the two premier expeditions in North America. The JMT usually takes about three weeks to complete, covering about 250 miles, including side trips for food drops and other forays. Some swear that the trip should be hiked from north to south, but most prefer south to north, starting with the awesome climb from Whitney Portal to the Whitney Summit, a climb of more than 5,000 feet. Three weeks later, the trip ends with a spectacular descent into Yosemite Valley, past hundreds of gawking tourists on the final three miles on the Mist Trail. Some cheat by starting at Tuolumne Meadows, thus avoiding a 4,000-foot climb out of Yosemite Valley, then heading south, but that is a hollow victory, having technically not completed the trip.

John Muir called the Sierra Nevada the "Range of Light." The trail that tra-verses it has become America's greatest hike – officially 211 miles from the Whitney Summit to Happy Isles in Yosemite Valley. It is a land spiked by 13,000-foot granite spires, untouched sapphire lakes loaded with trout, and canyons that drop as if they were the edge of the earth. There are many highlights, including the Mount Whitney Wilderness, John Muir Wilderness, Kings Canyon National Park, crossing the ice cut at Forester Pass, topping Muir Pass at Muir Hut, the incredible pyramidlike ridgeline near Selden Pass, catching golden trout where a cast can be like tossing a dog a bone, crossing the headwaters of Rush Creek, and finally dropping over Donohue Pass down to Lyell Fork and Tuolumne Meadows.

Yet the PCT goes far beyond this scope. It crosses through 37 wilderness areas, 20 national forests, and seven national parks, topping out at 13,180 feet at Forester Pass in the south Sierra. It also features the worst parts of the entire 2,700-mile route, the Hat Creek Rim (30 miles without water) and across the Mojave, where a siege of hot weather can have you praying for a sip of water out of a cow's hoof print.

All of the JMT and many of the PCT routes are detailed in this book, including how to get wilderness permits, directions to trailheads, maps, contacts, and trail highlights. Many hikers choose not to hike the entire JMT or PCT in one shot. Rather, they use a PCT trailhead, then head up to the crest, taking off on side trips as they choose.

seems like nothing works except covering your entire body in mosquito netting. For typical summer days outside of a hatch period, find a repellent you like and carry it with you.

First-Aid Kit

Nothing major is required here unless you're fully trained in first aid, but a few supplies for treating blisters, an antibiotic ointment, and an anti-inflammatory medicine (such as ibuprofen) can be valuable tools in minor and major emergencies. (For details on taking care of and preventing blisters, see *Shoes and Socks*.) If anyone in your party is allergic to bee stings or anything else in the outdoors, carry their medication.

Swiss Army-Style Pocket Knife

Be sure to carry one with several blades, a can opener, scissors, and tweezers. The latter is useful for removing slivers or ticks.

Compass

A compass can be a real lifesaver. Just be sure that you know how to use it.

Emergency Supplies

Ask yourself this question, "What would I need to have if I had to spend the night out here?" Aside from food, water, and other items previously listed, here are some basic emergency supplies that will get you through an unplanned night in the wilderness:

- Lightweight space blanket or sleeping bag made of foil-like mylar film, designed to reflect radiating body heat. These make a great emergency shelter and weigh and cost almost nothing.
- A lighter or a couple packs of matches in a waterproof container (or sealable plastic bag) and a candle, just in case you ever need to build a fire in a serious emergency.
- Whistle. If you ever need help, you can blow a whistle for a lot longer than you can shout.
- Small signal mirror. It could be just what you need to get found if you ever get lost.

HIKING GEAR

Shoes and Socks

Every hiker eventually conducts a search for the perfect boot. This means looking for something that will provide ideal foot and ankle support and won't cause blisters. Although there are dozens of possibilities—in fact so many that it can be confusing—you *can* find the perfect boot.

For advice on selecting boots, two of the nation's preeminent long-distance hikers, Brian Robinson of Mountain View (7,200 miles in 2001) and Ray Jardine of Oregon (2,700 miles of Pacific Crest Trail in three months), weighed in on the discussion. Both believe that the weight of a boot is the defining factor when selecting hiking footwear. They both go as light as possible, believing that heavy boots will eventually tire you out. Arch support is also vital, especially to people who hike less frequently and thus have not developed great foot strength.

To stay blister-free, the most important factors are clean feet, good socks, and the flexibility of a boot. If there is any foot slippage from a too-thin or compressed sock, accumulated dirt, or a stiff boot, you can rub up a blister in minutes. Wearing two pairs of socks can sometimes do the trick—try two fresh sets of SmartWool socks ($14 a pop), or try one pair over the top of a lightweight wicking liner sock. If you still get a blister or two, know how to treat them fast so they don't turn your walk into a sore-footed endurance test.

SELECTING THE RIGHT BOOTS

In addition to finding boots with the proper flexibility, comfort, and arch support, you'll need to consider the types of terrain you'll be covering and the number of miles (or number of days) you'll be hiking. Investing in the correct shoes will take some time and research, but your feet will thank you for it.

There are three basic kinds of hiking footwear, ranging from lightweight to midweight to heavyweight. Select the right one for you or

ADDING TO THE PACK

If you're setting out on a long-distance adventure, it pays to add these two lightweight items to your backpack: an Ace elastic bandage and a pair of gaiters.

For sprained ankles and twisted knees, an Ace bandage can be like an insurance policy to get you back on the trail and out of trouble. There have been many cases where hikers with a twisted ankle or a sprained knee have relied on a good wrap with a four-inch bandage for the added support to get them home. Always buy the Ace bandage that comes with the clips permanently attached, so you don't have to worry about losing them.

Gaiters are leggings made of water-repellent fabric (Gore-Tex is a popular brand) that fit from just below your knees, over your calves, and attach under your boots. They are of particular help when walking in damp areas or in places where rain is common. As your legs brush against ferns or low-lying plants, gaiters will deflect the moisture. Without them, your pants will be soaking wet in short order.

Should your boots become wet, never try to force them to dry. Some well-meaning folks will try to dry them quickly at the edge of a campfire or actually put the boots in an oven. Although this may dry the boots, it can also loosen the glue that holds them together, ultimately weakening them until one day they fall apart in a heap. A better bet is to treat the leather so the boots become water repellent. Silicone-based liquids are the easiest to use and the least greasy of the treatments available.

A final tip is to have another pair of lightweight shoes or moccasins that you can wear around after a trip. This will give your feet the rest they deserve.

---

pay the consequences. One great trick when on a hiking vacation is to bring a couple different pairs, and then for each hike, wear different footwear. By changing boots, you change the points of stress on your feet and legs, greatly reducing soreness and the chance of creating a hot spot on a foot. This also allows you to go lightweight on flat trails with a hard surface, and heavyweight on steep trails with loose footing, where additional boot weight can help traction in downhill stretches.

LIGHTWEIGHT HIKING BOOTS

In the first category, lightweight hiking boots (or even very sturdy athletic shoes) are designed for day-hiking and short and easy backpacking trips. For those with strong feet and arches, they are popular even on multiday trips. Some of the newer models are like rugged athletic shoes, designed with a Gore-Tex top for lightness and a Vibram sole for traction. These are perfect for people who like to hike but rarely carry a heavy backpack. Because these boots are flexible, they are easy to break in, and with fresh socks they rarely cause blister problems. Because they are lightweight and usually made of a breathable fabric, hiking fatigue is greatly reduced. For day-hiking, they are the footwear of choice for most.

On the negative side, because these boots are so light, traction is not always good on steep, slippery surfaces, and you can lose your footing and fall. In addition, lightweight boots provide less than ideal ankle and arch support, which can be a problem on rocky or steep trails. Turn your ankle and your trip can be ruined. Lightweight hiking boots often are not very durable, either. If you hike a lot, you may wear a pair out in one summer.

MIDWEIGHT HIKING BOOTS OR BACKPACKING BOOTS

These boots are designed for both on- and off-trail hiking, and are constructed to meet

© SABRINA YOUNG

Lightweight hiking shoes are perfect for short treks and day-long trips.

the demands of carrying a light to moderately heavy pack. They usually feature high ankle support, a deep Vibram lug sole, built-in orthotics, arch support, and often a waterproof exterior. They can stand up to hundreds of miles of wilderness use, even if they are banged against rocks and walked through streams.

On the negative side, midweight or backpacking boots can be quite hot, as they are often made of leather and are not breathable. If the boots get wet, they can take days to dry. They weigh a fair amount and can tire you out, especially if you are not accustomed to having weight on your feet. This may reduce the number of miles you are capable of hiking in a day.

MOUNTAINEERING BOOTS OR HEAVYWEIGHT BACKPACKING BOOTS
Like midweight boots, these shoes are designed for both on- and off-trail hiking, but they can stand up to the rigors of carrying a much heavier load. They are designed to be worn on multiday backpacking trips (four days or more with substantial miles hiked each day). Mountaineering boots are identified by

midrange tops, laces that extend almost as far as the toes, and ankle areas that are as stiff as a board. The lack of "give" is what endears them to mountaineers. Their stiffness is preferred when rock climbing, walking off-trail on craggy surfaces, or hiking down the edge of streambeds. Because these boots don't yield on rugged terrain, they can reduce ankle and foot injuries and provide better traction. Some are made so that they can accept crampons for travel on snow and ice.

The drawback to stiff boots is that if you don't have the proper socks and your foot starts slipping around in the boot, you will get a set of blisters that require so much tape and moleskin you will end up looking like a mummy. Also, heavyweight boots must be broken in for weeks or even months before taking them out on the trail.

AT THE STORE
Hiking shoes come in a wide range of styles, brands, and prices. If you wander about comparing all their many features, you will get as confused as a kid in a toy store. Instead, go into the store with your mind clear about what

you want. For the best quality, expect to spend $60–150 for lightweight hiking boots, $100–200 for midweight boots, and $150–250 for mountaineering boots. If you go much cheaper, the quality of the boot—and the health of your feet—will likely suffer. This is one area where you don't want to scrimp.

If you plan on using the advice of a shoe salesperson, first look at what kind of boots he or she is wearing. If the salesperson isn't even wearing boots, then take whatever he or she says with a grain of salt. Most people who own quality boots, including salespeople, will wear them almost daily if their job allows, since boots are the best footwear available.

Enter the store with a precise use and style in mind. Rather than fish for suggestions, tell the salesperson exactly what type of hiking you plan to do. Try two or three brands of the same category of shoe (lightweight, midweight, or heavyweight/mountaineering). Try on both boots in a pair simultaneously so you know exactly how they'll feel. Always try them on over a good pair of hiking socks (see *Socks,* below), not regular everyday socks. If possible, walk up and down a set of stairs, or up and down an incline, while wearing the boots. Your feet should not slide forward easily, and your heel should not move from side to side. Also, your heel should not lift more than one-quarter inch when you walk around. Are the boots too stiff? Are your feet snug yet comfortable, or do they slip? Do they feel supportive on the inside of your foot? Is there enough room in the toe box so that your toes can spread or wiggle slightly? If your toes touch the front of your boot, count on blisters.

Socks

People can spend so much energy selecting the right kind of boot that they virtually overlook wearing the right kind of socks. One goes with the other.

Your socks should be thick enough to cushion your feet and should fit snugly. Without good socks you might fasten the bootlaces too tight, and that's like putting a tourniquet on your feet. On long trips of a week or more, you should have plenty of clean socks on hand, or plan on washing what you have during your trip. As socks become worn, they also become compressed, dirty, and damp. If they fold over, you'll get a blister.

Do not wear cotton socks. Your foot can get damp and mix with dirt, which can cause a hot spot to start on your foot. Instead, start with a sock made of a synthetic composite, such as those made by SmartWool. These will partially wick moisture away from the skin.

If you choose to wear two pairs, or a pair of socks over a sock liner, the exterior sock should be wool or its synthetic equivalent. This will cushion your feet, create a snug fit in your boot, and provide some additional warmth and insulation in cold weather. It is critical to keep socks clean. If you wear multiple socks, you may need to go up a boot size to accommodate the extra layers around your feet.

Blisters

In almost all cases, blisters are caused by the simple rubbing of skin against the rugged interior of a boot. It can be worsened by several factors:

- A very stiff boot or one that allows your foot to move independently inside it as you walk, instead of it flexing along with your foot.
- Thin, ragged, or dirty socks, which are the fastest route to blisters. Thin socks allow your feet to move inside your boots, ragged socks allow your skin to chafe directly against the boot's interior, and dirty socks wrinkle and fold, also rubbing against your feet instead of cushioning them.
- Soft feet. By themselves, soft feet will not cause blisters, but in combination with a stiff boot or thin socks, they can cause terrible problems. One way to cushion your soles is to keep a fresh foot pad made of sponge rubber in your boot. But note that brand-new foot pads are often slippery for a few days, and that can cause blisters. The pads need to be broken in before an expedition, just as with a new boot. Another cure

for soft feet is to get out and walk or jog on a regular basis prior to your hiking trip. In addition, going barefoot regularly can be the best way to build up foot strength and arch support, and to toughen up the bottom of your feet.

The key to treating blisters is to work fast at the first sign of a hot spot. If you feel a hot spot, never keep walking, figuring the problem will go away. Stop immediately and remedy the situation. Before you remove your socks, check to see if the sock is wrinkled—a likely cause of the problem. If so, either change socks or pull them tight, removing the tiny folds, after taking care of the blister.

To take care of the blister, cut a piece of moleskin to cover the offending spot, securing the moleskin with white medical tape. Even better than moleskin is a product called Spenco Second Skin, which helps to heal the blister as well as protect it, and will stick to your skin without tape.

SAFETY IN THE OUTDOORS
Insects and Plants

Ticks, poison oak, and stinging nettles can be far worse than a whole convention of snakes, mountain lions, and bears. But you can avoid them with a little common sense, and here's how:

TICKS

The easiest way to stay clear of ticks is to wear long pants and long sleeves when you hike, and tuck your pant legs into your socks. But this system isn't fail-proof. The darn things sometimes find their way on to your skin no matter what you do. Always check yourself thoroughly when you leave the trail, looking carefully for anything that's crawling on you. Check your clothes, and also your skin underneath. A good friend can be a useful assistant in this endeavor.

Remember that if you find a tick on your skin, the larger brown ones are harmless. Of the nearly 50 varieties of ticks present in California,

only the tiny brown-black ones, called the western black-legged tick, can carry Lyme disease.

Most tick bites cause a sharp sting that will get your attention. But rarely, ticks will bite you without you noticing. If you've been in the outdoors, and then a few days or a week later start to experience flu-like symptoms like headaches, fever, muscle soreness, neck stiffness, or nausea, see a doctor immediately. Tell the doctor you are concerned about possible exposure to ticks and Lyme disease. Another early tell-tale symptom is a slowly expanding red rash near the tick bite, which appears a week to a month after the bite. Caught in its early stages, Lyme disease is easily treated with antibiotics, but left untreated, it can be severely debilitating.

The best way to remove a tick is by grasping it as close to your skin as possible, then pulling it gently and slowly straight out, without twisting or jerking it. Tweezers work well for the job, and many Swiss Army knives include tweezers.

POISON OAK

That old Boy Scout motto holds true: Leaves of three, let them be. Learn to recognize and avoid *Toxicodendron diversilobum,* which produces an itching rash that can last for weeks. The shiny-leaved shrub grows with maddening exuberance in California coastal and mountain canyons below 5,000 feet. If you can't readily identify poison oak, stay away from vinelike plants that have three leaves. Remember that in spring and summer, poison oak looks a little like wild blackberry bushes and often has red colors in its leaves, as well as green. In late fall and winter, poison oak goes dormant and loses its leaves, but it's still potent.

Avoid poison oak by staying on the trail and wearing long pants and long sleeves in areas that are encroached by it. If you prefer to wear shorts when you hike, try a pair of the convertible pants that are found at most outdoor stores. These are lightweight pants with legs that zip off to convert to shorts. Put the pant legs on when you come to an area that is rife with poison oak. If you accidentally

poison oak

touch the plant with your bare skin, wash off the area as soon as possible. Waiting until you get home five hours later may be too late, so wash as best as you can, using stream water or whatever is available. Hikers who are highly allergic to poison oak should consider carrying packages of Technu, a poison oak wash-off treatment that is sold in bottles or individual foil packs. Carrying one little package could save you weeks of scratching.

Remember that if poison oak touches your clothes, your pack, or even your dog, and then you handle any of those items, the oils can rub off onto your skin. Wash everything thoroughly as soon as you get home.

If you do develop poison oak rash, a few relatively new products on the market can help you get rid of it. One product is called Zanfel, and although it costs a small fortune (about $30–40 a bottle), it is available at pharmacies without a prescription. You simply pour it on the rash and the rash vanishes, or at least greatly diminishes. Another lotion, called Büji, works well. If you get a severe case of poison oak, the only recourse is a trip to the doctor for prednisone pills.

STINGING NETTLES

Ouch! This member of the nettle family is bright green, can grow to six feet tall, and is covered with tiny stinging hairs. When you brush against one, it zaps you with its poison, which feels like a mild bee sting. The sting can last for up to 24 hours. Stinging nettles grow near creeks or streams, and they're usually found in tandem with deer ferns and sword ferns. If the nettles zing you, grab a nearby fern leaf and rub the underside of it against the stinging area. It sounds odd, but it sometimes helps to take the sting out. If it doesn't help, you're out of luck, and you just have to wait for the sting to go away.

Wildlife

Snakes, mountain lions, and bears—these creatures deserve your respect, and you should understand a little bit about them.

RATTLESNAKES

Eight rattlesnake species are found in California. These members of the pit viper family have wide triangular heads, narrow necks, and rattles on their tales. Rattlesnakes live where it's warm, usually at elevations below 6,000 feet. Most snakes will slither off at the sound of your footsteps; if you encounter one, freeze or move back slowly so that it can get away without feeling threatened. They will almost always shake their tails and produce a rattling or buzzing noise to warn you off. The sound is unmistakable, even if you've never heard it before.

If you're hiking on a nice day, when rattlesnakes are often out sunning themselves on trails and rocks, keep your eyes open for them so you don't step on one or place your hand on one. Be especially on the lookout for rattlesnakes in the spring, when they leave their winter burrows and come out in the sun. Morning is the most common time to see them, as the midday sun is usually too hot for them.

Although rattlesnake bites are painful, they are very rarely fatal. More than 100 people in California are bitten by rattlesnakes each year, resulting in only one or two fatalities on average. About 25 percent of rattlesnake bites are dry, with no venom injected. Symptoms of bites that do contain venom usually include tingling around the mouth, nausea and vomiting, dizziness, weakness, sweating, and/or chills. If you should get bitten by a rattlesnake, your car key—and the nearest telephone—are your best first aid. Call 911 as soon as you can, or have someone drive you to the nearest hospital. Don't panic or run, which can speed the circulation of venom through your system.

Except for a handful of rattlesnake species, all other California snakes are not poisonous. Just give them room to slither by.

MOUNTAIN LIONS

The mountain lion (also called cougar or puma) lives in almost every region of California but is rarely seen. Most habitats that are wild enough to support deer will support mountain lions, which typically eat about one deer per week. When the magnificent cats do show themselves, they receive a lot of media attention. The few mountain lion attacks on California hikers have been widely publicized. Still, the vast majority of hikers never see a mountain lion, and those who do usually report that the cat vanished into the brush at the first sign of nearby humans.

FACTS ABOUT MOUNTAIN LIONS

Mountain lion expert Steve Torres of the Department of Fish and Game (DFG) provided the following list of truths regarding mountain lions:

1. Mountain lions are very shy and wary of humans. Attacks on people are extremely rare, which is why any threatening encounter can make the news – it is an anomaly.

2. Mountain lions are rarely seen; they are masters of stealth. That is why repeat sightings are alarming and should be reported to the DFG headquarters in Sacramento (916/445-0411).

3. Mountain lions are known for their silence and are rarely vocal. If you hear the cry or roar of a lion, your experience is likely a once-in-a-lifetime event.

4. Mountain lions are not threatened or endangered in any way. Populations are stable to increasing. The biggest threat to mountain lions is loss of habitat to development.

5. Mountain lions are not afraid of dogs. Whereas packs of trained hounds are capable of putting a lion in a tree, solitary pets of all kinds, including dogs, are fair game for mountain lions. In areas with documented mountain lion habitat, dogs should be kept inside at night.

If you're hiking in an area where mountain lions or their tracks have been spotted, remember to keep children close to you on the trail, and your dog leashed. If you see a mountain lion and it doesn't run away immediately, make yourself appear as large as possible (raise your arms, open your jacket, wave a big stick) and speak loudly and firmly or shout. If you have children with you, pick them up off the ground, but try to do it without crouching down or leaning over. (Crouching makes you appear smaller and less aggressive, more like prey.) Don't turn your back on the cat or run from it, but rather back away slowly and deliberately, always retaining your aggressive pose and continuing to speak loudly. Mountain lions are far more likely to attack a fleeing mammal than one that stands its ground. Even after attacking, lions have been successfully fought off by adult hikers and even children who used rocks and sticks to defend themselves.

Bears

The only bears found in California are black bears (even though they are usually brown in color). A century ago, our state bear, the grizzly, roamed here as well, but the last one was shot and killed in the 1930s. Black bears almost never harm human beings—although you should never approach or feed a bear, or get between a bear and its cubs or its food. Black bears weigh between 250 and 400 pounds, can run up to 30 miles per hour, and are powerful swimmers and climbers. When they bound, the muscles on their shoulders roll like ocean breakers. If provoked, a bear could cause serious injury.

There's only one important fact to remember about bears: They love snacks. The average black bear has to eat as much as 30,000 calories a day, and since their natural diet is made up of berries, fruits, plants, fish, insects, and the like, the high-calorie food of human beings is very appealing to them. Unfortunately, too many California campers have trained our state's bears to crave the taste of corn chips, hot dogs, and soda pop.

Any time you see a bear, it's almost a given that it is looking for food, preferably something sweet. Bears have become specialists in the food-raiding business. As a result, you must be absolutely certain that you keep your food away from them. This is best accomplished with a bear-proof food canister, required equipment when backpacking in parts of Yosemite National Park, Sequoia and Kings Canyon National Parks, and much of the rest of the Sierra Nevada. At car campgrounds at these areas, metal bear-proof food storage lockers must be used. Never leave your food unattended or in your vehicle. Tickets are commonly issued for either of these violations. In addition, get an update from the rangers in your park about suitable bear precautions.

Bears are sometimes encountered on trails, although not as frequently as in campgrounds. If you're hiking, bears will most likely hear you coming and avoid you. If one approaches you, either on the trail or in camp, yell loudly, throw small rocks or pine cones in the vicinity, and try to frighten the bear away. A bear that is afraid of humans is a bear that will stay wild and stay alive.

Backpackers should always use bear-proof canisters to store their food for overnight trips. Hanging food from a tree is largely ineffective when done improperly, and the practice is now banned in much of the Sierra Nevada where bear-proof food canisters are required by law. You can rent or buy a bear canister from most outdoor stores, or from many ranger stations in national parks and national forests. For more information, or to rent a canister, contact Yosemite National Park at 209/372-0200, Sequoia and Kings Canyon National Parks at 559/565-3341, or Inyo National Forest at 760/873-2400.

If you are backpacking in an area where bear canisters are not required, or where bears aren't as bold as they are in the heavily visited areas of the Sierra Nevada, you can substitute a food hang for a bear canister. This is where you place your food in a plastic or canvas garbage bag (always double bag your food), then suspend it from a rope in midair, 10 feet from the trunk of a tree and 20 feet off the ground. Counterbalancing two bags with a rope thrown over a tree limb is very effective, but finding an appropriate limb can be difficult.

This is most easily accomplished by tying a rock to a rope, then throwing it over a high but sturdy tree limb. Next, tie your food bag to the rope and hoist it in the air. When you are satisfied with the position of the food bag, tie off the end of the rope to another tree.

Once a bear gets his mitts on your food, he considers it his. There is nothing you can do. If this happens to you once, you will learn never to let food sit unattended.

First Aid
HYPOTHERMIA
A leading cause of death in the outdoors is hypothermia, which occurs when your body's core temperature drops low enough that your vital organs can no longer function. Most cases of hypothermia occur at temperatures in the 50s, not below freezing, as you might expect. Often the victim has gotten wet, and/or is fatigued from physical exertion.

Initial symptoms of hypothermia include uncontrollable shivering, often followed by a complete stop in shivering, extreme lethargy, and an inability to reason. A hypothermic person will often want to lie down and rest or sleep. His or her hiking partners must jump into action to get the victim warm and dry immediately. Remove all wet clothes and put on dry ones. Cover his or her head with a warm hat. If someone in the group has an emergency space blanket (see *Hiking Gear Checklist*), wrap it around the victim. Get the hypothermic person to eat some quick-energy food, even candy, and drink warm beverages—this helps the body produce heat. Do not give the person alcohol, as this encourages heat loss.

HEAT STROKE
Usually the result of overexposure to the sun and dehydration, symptoms of heat stroke include headache, mental confusion, and cramps throughout the body. Immediate action must be taken to reduce the body's core temperature. Pour water on the victim's head. Have him or her sit in a cool stream if possible. Make the person drink as much liquid as possible. Heat stroke is easily avoided by staying adequately hydrated and wearing a large-brimmed hat for protection from the sun.

ALTITUDE SICKNESS AND ADJUSTMENT
Many hikers experience a shortness of breath when hiking only a few thousand feet higher than the elevation where they live. If you live on the California coast, you may notice slightly labored breathing while hiking at an elevation as low as 5,000 feet. As you go higher, it gets worse, sometimes leading to headaches and nausea. It takes a full 72 hours to acclimate to major elevation changes, although most people acclimatize after only 24 to 48 hours. The best preparation for hiking at a high elevation is to sleep at that elevation, or as close to it as possible, the night before. If you are planning a strenuous hike at 7,000 feet or above, spend a day or two before doing easier hikes at the same elevation. Also, get plenty of rest and drink plenty of fluids. Lack of sleep, and alcohol, can contribute to your susceptibility to "feeling the altitude."

Serious altitude sickness typically occurs above 10,000 feet. It is generally preventable by simply allowing enough time for acclimation. But how do you acclimate for a climb to the top of Mount Whitney or Shasta, at more than 14,000 feet? The answer is you can't, at least not completely. Spending a few days beforehand hiking at 10,000 feet and above will help tremendously. Staying fueled with food and fully hydrated will also help. But if you've never hiked above a certain elevation— say 13,000 feet—you don't know how you are going to feel until you get there. If you start to feel ill (nausea, vomiting, severe headache), you are experiencing altitude sickness. Some people can get by with taking aspirin and trudging onward, but if you are seriously ill, the only cure is to descend as soon as possible. If the altitude has gotten to you badly enough, you may need someone to help you walk. Fatigue and elevation sickness can cloud your judgment in the same manner than hypothermia does, so take action before your symptoms become too severe.

Safety on the Trail
NAVIGATIONAL TOOLS

For some hikers, it is quite easy to become lost. If you don't get your bearings, getting found is the difficult part. If you're hiking with a family or group, make sure everybody stays together. If anyone decides to split off from the group for any reason, make sure they have a trail map with them and that they know how to read it. Also, ensure that everyone in your group knows the rules regarding what to do if they get lost:

• Whistle or shout loudly at regular intervals.
• "Hug" a tree. Or a big rock or a bush. That means find a noticeable landmark, sit down next to it, and don't move. Continue to

Rock cairns act as directional signals on the trail.

whistle or shout loudly. A lost person is easier to find if they stay in one place.

In areas above tree line or where the trail becomes faint, some hikers will mark the route with piles of small rocks to act as directional signs for the return trip. But if an unexpected snow buries these piles of rocks, or if you get well off the track, all you are left with is a moonscape. That is why every hiker should understand the concept of orienteering. In the process, you become a mountaineer.

When lost, the first step is to secure your present situation—that is, to make sure it does not get any worse. Take stock of your food, foul-weather gear, camp fuel, clothes, and your readiness to spend the night. Keep in mind that this is an adventure, not a crisis.

Then take out your topographic map, compass, and altimeter. What? Right: Never go into the unknown without them. Place the map on the ground, then set the compass atop the map and orient it north. In most cases, you will easily be able to spot landmarks, such as prominent mountaintops. In cases with a low overcast, where mountains are obscured in clouds, you can take this adventure one step further by checking your altimeter. By scanning the elevation lines on the map, you will be able to trace your near-exact position.

Always be prepared to rely on yourself, but also file a trip plan with the local ranger station, especially if hiking in remote wilderness areas. Carry plenty of food, fuel, and a camp stove. Make sure your clothes, weather gear, sleeping bag, and tent will keep you dry and warm. Always carry a compass, altimeter, and map with elevation lines, and know how to use them, practicing in good weather to get the feel of it.

With enough experience, you will discover that you can "read" the land so well that you will hardly even need to reference a map to find your way.

LIGHTNING

If you see or hear a thunderstorm approaching, avoid exposed ridges and peaks. This is disheartening advice when you're only a mile from the summit of Half Dome, but follow it anyway. If you're already on a mountain top, stay out of enclosed places, such as rock caves or recesses. Confined areas are deadly in lightning storms; hikers seeking refuge from lightning have been killed inside the stone hut on top of Mount Whitney. Do not lean against rock slopes or trees; try to keep a few feet of air space around you. Squat low on your boot soles, or sit on your day pack, jacket, or anything that will insulate you in case lightning strikes the ground.

Safety on the Road

When you start your car and then head down the road for a winter vacation—or in the high Sierra year-round—you may wonder, "What did I forget this time?"

The answer for some might be "plenty."

Car trouble, tires and chains, road conditions, verified directions, and personal safety are all factors in road trips. Many people think they can handle whatever is thrown at them on a vacation. But what actually happens is that they are rewarded or punished for their level of preparation. To ensure you experience the former, rather than the latter, follow these simple tips before you head out on the road:

- **Verify directions:** Just because MapQuest provides directions does not mean they are correct. Get independent verification of every destination and carry a detailed road map.
- **Check road conditions and weather:** Just as pilots do, obtain all available information before taking off on your trip. In California, that starts by calling the CalTrans road condition hot line at 800/427-7623 or checking the website at www.dot.ca.gov/hq/roadinfo. Detailed weather reports and forecasts are available through the *San Francisco Chronicle* website at www.sfgate.com.
- **Determine snow levels:** If you're driving into the mountains in a storm, you can calculate the snow levels by subtracting 3.5 degrees for every 1,000 feet you gain in elevation. The magic number when snow starts

to stick is usually 34°F. So if you're heading to Tahoe, it's raining in Sacramento (elevation 25 feet), and the temperature is 50°F, you will hit snow at an elevation of roughly 4,500 feet as you head up the Sierra.
- **Tires and chains:** Never hope your way through a storm. Make sure your tires are in good condition and inflated properly (they typically lose two to three pounds of pressure per month). Carry the correct chains for your vehicle and know how to put them on so that doing so is fast and easy—to the point where you look forward to driving through a blizzard. If you have four-wheel-drive, don't think you can whip through anything. Be sure you have mud and snow tires (they are labeled M&S) with some tread bite to handle snow and ice. Even then, accelerate very cautiously uphill (when most spinouts occur), and brake very slowly; skids are the product of torque, not speed.
- **Get your vehicle checked:** People often put undeserved trust in their vehicles these days, with the broad-brush assumption that paying a high price guarantees flawless operation. Unfortunately not. The California State Automobile Association provides a vehicle checklist for road travelers. At the minimum, make sure your battery and oil are fresh, and brakes in perfect condition. (Hah! Back in the day, we didn't trust anything to work right and it seemed everybody had a coat hanger and duct tape to keep things together.)
- **Fuel up:** Never set out at night or into bad weather without a full tank of gas. Every winter, the worst traffic jams of the year on I-80 near Truckee are caused when someone in a line of cars runs out of gas in a blizzard, then leaves their car parked in the road and walks to town.
- **Emergency road equipment:** Check to make sure you have complete tire-changing equipment (and know how to use it), emergency flashers, spotlight and cell phone, and that your spare tire is inflated. Other musts: a flashlight, a knife, and duct tape.

- **Emergency overnight gear:** It's always wise to carry a sleeping bag, a six-pack of bottled water or a cooler (it'll keep water from freezing if you get stuck overnight in extremely cold weather) packed with drinks, plus trail food–type snacks. Others may add a thermos with hot coffee, tea, or chocolate milk to that list. Also, keep a source of heat and light in your car, such as a candle in a can.
- **Never split up:** Families should always stay together. According to a wise gent named Aristotle, "When two go upon journey, one sees before the other." If two adults split up, an individual, on their own, might not see the way out of trouble, and in addition, each adult might lose half of their reasoning power.
- **Personal safety:** Don't put yourself in position for something bad to happen. If you feel that an area might be dangerous, then leave. Do not expect yourself to rise to the occasion. You will instead default to your level of training.
- **Ask directions:** Nobody can explain this, but a lot of guys simply will not ask for directions. A key is to never ask directions at a gas station or a convenience store. The best bet is to stop at a restaurant, order dinner, and let the waitress work on your question.
- **File a trip plan:** Again, just as pilots do, leave a trip plan and itinerary with a friend or family member back home. Then, if a search is necessary, they have a locator and timeline to shorten the search.

Note: There are networks of Forest Service roads in California, many of which close in winter, that lead to backcountry camps. For out-of-towners looking at a detailed map, it might appear that these roads could provide a route to the coast. While a joy to drive and explore on a clear summer day, they could become a nightmare after a wrong turn at night for those unfamiliar with the area.

And that leads to the most important lesson of all: Don't be a prisoner of hope.

Survival in the Outdoors

When facing hardship in the outdoors, there are three critical rules of survival:

1. **Stop and stay put:** People often tend to meander around, trying to find a familiar road or rock; they don't want to deal with the thought that they are lost. The first step in a survival scenario is to stop and stay where you are. This is important because when the search-and-rescue team comes looking for you, they're going to be looking at your last known location. The more you wander around, the farther you get away from them.

2. **Identify survival needs:** People get confused sometimes, but survival needs don't change, no matter where you are. You have to identify your survival needs and prioritize them:
   - **Personal protection:** clothing (dry clothes, protective layers, water-repellent shell, hat or ski cap), shelter (sleeping bag or space blanket), fire (lighter, matches, tinder), and meet them in that order. Stay warm, dry, and hydrated.
   - **Signaling:** It can be a flasher you purchase in a store or you can improvise (cell phone, whistle, signal mirror, flares, smoke devices, fresh batteries).
   - **Sustenance:** Water (or water purification tablets) and food (nutrition bars or equivalent). Water is extremely important; food not so important. (Everybody talks about food, but that is the least important of the survival essentials—you can live longer without food than without water.)
   - **Travel:** Only leave if the area you're in isn't meeting your needs or a rescue does not appear imminent. Ensure that you have maps, a compass, and a watch.
   - **Health:** Mental, psychological, and environmental—these are a constant. The only thing that changes might be how you improvise to meet them. In addition to a first-aid kit, consider including a family photo, spiritual material, or a book.

3. **Improvise:** You have to know how to improvise because it's doubtful everything will
be at your disposal to meet your needs. Use
manufactured materials as well as what nature provides—a car offers tons of improvis-
ing equipment: a mirror can be ripped off as
a signaling device; seat cushions can be cut
up for insulation; a spare tire can be burned
as a smoke signal—but only if you know the
search-and-rescue teams are close.

HIKING ETHICS
Hiking with Dogs

Dogs are wonderful friends and great companions. But dogs and nature do not mix well.
Bless their furry little hearts, most dogs can't
help but disturb wildlife, given half a chance.
Even if they don't chase or bark at wildlife,
dogs leave droppings that may intimidate
other mammals into changing their normal
routine. But kept on a leash, a dog can be the
best hiking companion you could ask for.

Dogs are allowed on some trails in

Check to make sure your dog is allowed on
a trail.

California and not on others. For many dog
owners, it's confusing. When using this book,
check the *User Groups* listing under each trail
listing to see whether or not dogs are permitted. Always call the park or public land in
advance if you are traveling some distance
with your dog.

Here's a general guideline to park rules
about dogs:

If you are visiting a national or state park,
99 percent of the time, your dog will not be
allowed to hike with you. There are only a few
exceptions to this rule within the national and
state park systems. Dogs are usually allowed
in campgrounds or picnic areas, but they are
not allowed on trails in these parks. If you
are planning to visit a national or state park,
consider leaving your dog at home.

At other types of parks (county parks, regional parks, and so on), dogs may or may not
be allowed on trails. Always follow and obey a
park's specific rules about dogs. Oftentimes, if
dogs are allowed, they must be on a six-foot or
shorter leash. Don't try to get away with carrying the leash in your hand while your dog runs
free; rangers may give you a ticket.

In national forest or wilderness lands,
dogs are usually permitted off leash, except
in special wildlife management areas or other
special-use areas. Understand that your dog
should still be under voice control—for his
or her safety more than anything. The outdoors presents many hazards for dogs, including mountain lions, porcupines, black bears,
ticks, rattlesnakes, and a host of other potential problems. Dogs are frequently lost in national forest areas. Keeping your dog close to
your side or on a leash in the national forests
will help you both have a worry-free trip and
a great time.

Avoiding the Crowds

Although many regions of California exist
where you can hike without seeing another soul, even on holiday weekends, some of
our better-known parks and public lands are
notorious for crowds. No matter where in

TRAIL ETIQUETTE

Hiking is a great way to get out of the concrete jungle and into the woods and the wild, to places of natural beauty. Unfortunately, this manner of thinking is shared by millions of people. Following some basic rules of etiquette will ensure that we all get along and keep the outdoors a place we can enjoy . . . together.

1. **Enjoy the silence and let nature's sounds prevail.** Keep your voice low and avoid making loud noises. You will increase your chances of encountering wildlife, plus help others enjoy their quiet time in the outdoors.

2. **Be aware of other trail users and yield appropriately.** If you hear someone coming up behind you who is clearly traveling faster than you, stand aside and let them pass. On narrow trails, hikers going downhill should always yield to hikers going uphill. Get out of the way so uphill hikers can keep their momentum as they climb. Also, large groups of hikers should always yield to smaller groups or solo travelers.

3. **Be friendly and polite to other trail users.** A smile or a "hello" as you pass others on the trail is always a good idea. And it may seem obvious, but if someone steps aside to allow you to pass, say "thank you."

4. **Obey all posted signs and trail closures.** Only hike where it's legal. Do not invent "shortcuts" or hike across private property without the express permission of the owner.

5. **Hike only on established trails.** As soon as you walk off a trail, you trample vegetation. Never cut switchbacks; hillside trails are built with switchbacks to keep the slope from eroding. Just a few people cutting the switchbacks can destroy a hillside.

6. **Yield to equestrians.** Horses can be badly spooked by just about anything. Always give them plenty of room. If horses are approaching you, stop alongside the trail until they pass. If horses are traveling in your direction and you need to pass them, call out politely to the rider and ask permission. If the horse and rider moves off the trail and the rider tells you it's okay, then pass.

California you want to hike, there's no reason to subject yourself to packed parking lots, long lines of people snaking up and down switchbacks, and trail destinations that look like Times Square on New Year's Eve. If you take a few simple steps, you can avoid the crowds almost anywhere, even in well-traveled parks near urban areas and in our famous national parks.

- **Hike in the off-season.** For most public lands, the off-season is any time other than summer, or any time when school is in session. Late September through mid-May is an excellent period of time for hiking trips (except during the week between Christmas and New Year's and Easter week). Try to avoid periods near holidays; many people try to beat the crowds by traveling right before or after a holiday, and the result is more crowds.
- **Time your trip for midweek.** Tuesday, Wednesday, and Thursday are always the quietest days of the week in any park or public land.
- **Get up early.** Even Yosemite Valley is serene and peaceful until 8 or 9 A.M. In most parks, if you arrive at the trailhead before 9 A.M., you'll have the first few hours on the trail all to yourself. As an insurance policy, get to the trailhead even earlier.
- **If you can't get up early, stay out late.** When the days are long in summer, you can hike shorter trails from 4 P.M. to 7:30 P.M. or even later. You may see other hikers in the first hour or so, but they'll soon disperse. Trailhead parking lots are often packed at 1 P.M., then nearly empty at 5 P.M. Note that if you hike in the late afternoon or evening, you should always carry a flashlight with you (at least one per person), just in case it gets dark sooner than you planned.
- **Get out and hike in foul weather.** Don your favorite impermeable layer, and go where fair-weather hikers dare not go. Some of the best memories are made on rainy days, cloudy days, foggy days, and days when the wind blows at gale force. The fact is, the vast majority of hikers only hike when the sun is out. Witness nature in all its varied moods, and you may be surprised at how much fun you have.

Tips for Getting Along

When hiking with others, and especially over several days, it pays to do a little planning and a lot of communicating. Here are some tips to having a successful trip:

- **The destination and activities must be agreed upon.** A meeting of the minds gives everybody an equal stake in the trip.
- **If backpacking, guarantee yourself refreshing sleep.** Make certain that your sleeping bag, pillow, pad, and tent are clean, dry, warm, and comfortable.
- **Develop technical expertise.** Test all gear at home before putting it to use on the trail.
- **Guarantee yourself action.** Pick a destination with your favorite activity: adventuring, wildlife watching, swimming, fishing . . .
- **Guarantee yourself quiet time.** Savor the views and the sound of a stream running free, and reserve time with people you care for, and your soul will be recharged.
- **Accordance on food.** Always have complete agreement on the selections for each meal, and check for allergies.
- **Agree on a wake-up time.** Then when morning comes, you will be on course from the start.
- **Equal chances at the fun stuff.** Many duties can be shared over the course of a trip, such as navigating and preparing meals.
- **Be aware, not self-absorbed.** Live so there can be magic in every moment, with an awareness of the senses: sight, sound, smell, touch, taste, and how you feel inside. Have an outlook that alone can promote great satisfaction.
- **No whining.** You can't always control your surroundings, only your state of mind.

Wilderness Ethics

Take good care of this beautiful land you're hiking on. The basics are simple: Leave no

HIKING GEAR CHECKLIST

Backpack

Cell phone
Compass or navigational device
Extra clothing (lightweight jacket, rain poncho, gloves, hat)
First-aid kit
Flashlight or head lamp
Food (energy bars, nuts, dried fruit, jerky)
Insect repellent
Pocket knife
Sunglasses
Sunscreen
Trail map
Watch
Water or water filter

Emergency Supplies

Extra shoelaces
Matches in a waterproof container
Mylar blanket
Signal mirror
Whistle

Long Distance Trails

Ace bandage
Bandana
Bear canister
Extra pair of socks
Eyeglass cleaner or saline solution (for contacts)
Gaiters
Lighweight shoes or moccasins
Toilet paper and zippered plastic bag
Trekking poles

Fun Stuff

Binoculars
Book, including wildflower or bird identification guides
Camera (with extra battery and memory card)
Deck of cards
Fishing license and equipment
Picnic gear

trace of your visit. Pack out all your trash. Do your best not to disturb animal or plant life. Don't collect specimens of plants, wildlife, or even pine cones. Never, ever carve anything into the trunks of trees. If you're following a trail, don't cut the switchbacks. Leave everything in nature exactly as you found it, because each tiny piece has its place in the great scheme of things.

You can go the extra mile, too. Pick up any litter that you see on the trail. Teach your children to do this as well. Carry an extra bag to hold picked-up litter until you get to a trash receptacle, or just keep an empty pocket for that purpose in your day pack or fanny sack.

If you have the extra time or energy, join a trail organization in your area or spend some time volunteering in your local park. Anything you do to help this beautiful planet will be repaid to you, many times over.

REDWOOD EMPIRE

© SABRINA YOU

BEST HIKES

Visitors come from around the world to the

Redwood Empire for one reason: to see the groves of giant redwoods, the tallest trees in the world. On a perfect day in the redwoods here, refracted sunlight beams through the forest canopy, creating a solemn, cathedral-like effect. It feels as if you are standing in the center of the earth's pure magic.

But the redwood forests are only one of the attractions in this area. The Smith River Canyon, Del Norte and Humboldt coasts, and the remote edge of the Siskiyou Wilderness in Six Rivers National Forest all make this region like none other in the world.

On sunny days in late summer, some first-time visitors are incredulous that so few people live in the Redwood Empire. The reason it's not very populated also happens to explain why the trees grow so tall: With few exceptions, the weather consists of rain in the winter – often for weeks at a time – and fog in the summer. If the sun does manage to appear, it's an event almost strange enough to warrant calling the police to say you've spotted a round, yellow UFO. So most folks are content to just visit.

For outstanding days of adventure, three stellar areas should be on your must-see list: the redwood parks from Trinidad to Klamath River, the Smith River National Recreation Area, and the Lost Coast.

The hikes from Trinidad to the Klamath River feature some of the best adventuring day trips in Northern California. A good place to start is Prairie Creek Redwoods State Park, where you can see fantastic herds of Roosevelt elk. Then head over to the beach by hiking Fern Canyon for 20 minutes along the bottom of a canyon, past vertical walls covered with ferns. Then continue north on Coastal Trail, where pristine woodlands and fantastic expanses of untouched beaches await. All the trails through the redwoods north of the Klamath River are winners; it's just a matter of matching up your level of ambition to the right hike.

The Smith River National Recreation Area is equally gorgeous. The Smith is one of the last major free-flowing rivers in America. Wild, unsullied, and beautiful, it's set in a series of gorges and bordered by national forest. The centerpiece is Jedediah Smith Redwoods State Park and its grove of monster-sized redwoods. South Fork Road provides an extended tour into Six Rivers National Forest along the South Fork Smith River, with the option of visiting many of the largest trees in Jedediah Smith Redwoods State Park. The best turnoff is located on U.S. 199 just northeast of the town of Hiouchi. Turn right, cross two bridges, and you will arrive at a fork in the road. Turning left at the fork will take you along the South Fork Smith River and deep into Six Rivers National Forest. Turning right at the fork will take you to a series of trailheads for hikes into redwoods – of these, the best is Boy Scout Tree Trail.

The Lost Coast is often overlooked by visitors because it's difficult to reach. Access is only via a slow, curvy road through the Mattole River Valley, past Petrolia, and out to a piece of coast. The experience is like being in suspended animation – peaceful surroundings with a striking lack of people. One of the best ways to capture the sensation is to drive out near the mouth of the Mattole, then hike south on Coastal Trail long enough to get a feel for the area.

Compared to other regions in California, this corner of the state is somewhat one dimensional. The emphasis here is primarily on exploring the redwoods and the coast, and to some extent, the Smith River. Most of the campgrounds here are designed with those things in mind. There are many private campgrounds set on US 101, as well as near the mouths of the Smith and Klamath Rivers. These make fine base camps for fishing trips when the salmon are running. The state and national park campgrounds in the redwoods are in high demand, and reservations are often necessary during the peak summer vacation season. On the opposite end of the spectrum are primitive and remote settings in Six Rivers National Forest and the Lost Coast – and there are even a few surprise nuggets in Redwood National Park.

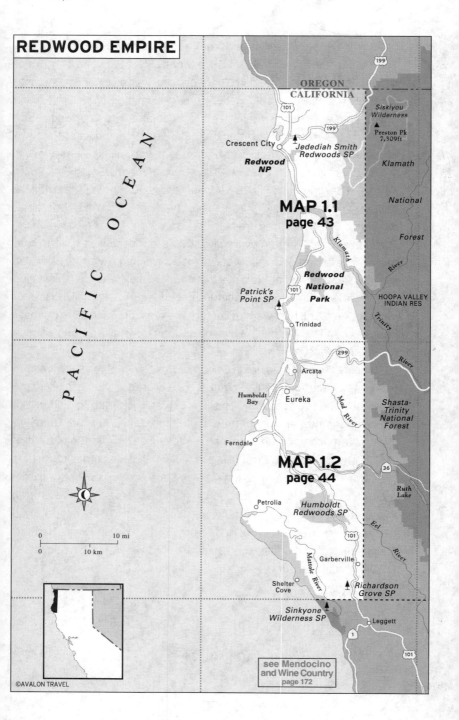

REDWOOD EMPIRE

OREGON
CALIFORNIA

199

Siskiyou
Wilderness

Preston Pk
7,309ft

Crescent City

Jedediah Smith
Redwoods SP

Redwood
NP

Klamath

National

**MAP 1.1
page 43**

Forest

Redwood
National
Park

Patrick's
Point SP

HOOPA VALLEY
INDIAN RES

Trinidad

299

Arcata

Mad River

Shasta-
Trinity
National
Forest

Humboldt
Bay

Eureka

Ferndale

**MAP 1.2
page 44**

36

Ruth
Lake

Petrolia

Humboldt
Redwoods SP

101

Garberville

Eel
River

Shelter
Cove

Mattole River

Richardson
Grove SP

Sinkyone
Wilderness SP

Leggett

1

101

PACIFIC OCEAN

0   10 mi
0   10 km

©AVALON TRAVEL

see Mendocino
and Wine Country
page 172

Map 1.1

Hikes 1-23
Pages 45-57

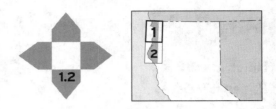

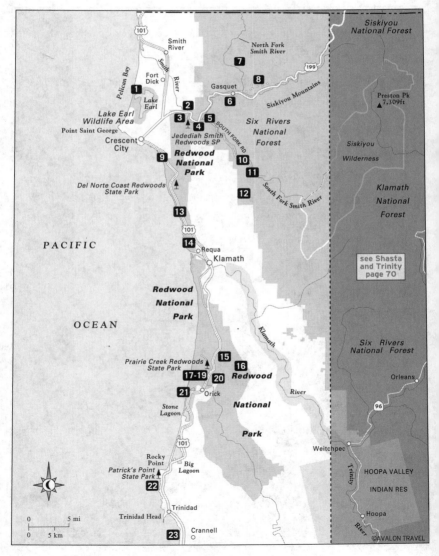

Map 1.2

Hikes 24-38
Pages 57-66

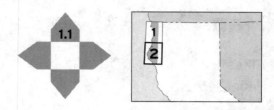

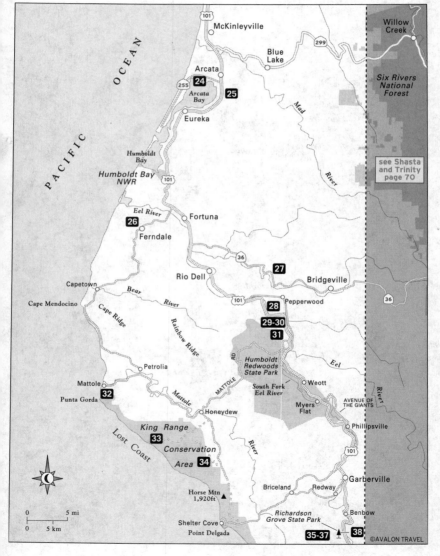

©AVALON TRAVEL

■ WILDLIFE DUNE AREA
2.5 mi / 1.0 hr 🚶1 ⛰7

on the coast of Del Norte County north of Crescent City

Map 1.1, page 43

The Pelican Bay Sand Dunes seem to sweep on forever, spanning more than 10 miles from the mouth of the Smith River south along the Pacific Ocean, nearly reaching Crescent City. After parking at Kellogg Beach, walk north or south for five minutes or five hours—take your pick. Either way, you will feel like a solitary speck against the enormous backdrop of untouched sand dunes and ocean. Only rarely will you see other people. The area is known by several names, including Fort Dick Beach, Kellogg Beach, and Pelican Bay Sand Dunes, but by any name, it's a good place to escape to nothing but wide-open beach for miles.

User Groups: Hikers, dogs, and horses. Mountain bikes permitted but not recommended. No wheelchair facilities.

Permits: No permits are required. Parking and access are free.

Maps: For a free brochure and map, write to Tolowa Dunes State Park. For topographic maps, ask the USGS for Crescent City and Smith River.

Directions: Take US 101 to Crescent City and Northcrest Drive. Turn northwest on Northcrest Drive and drive 1.5 miles to Old Mill Road. Turn left on Old Mill Road and drive 1.25 miles to the end of Old Mill Road and the junction with Sand Hill Road. Turn left on Sand Hill Road (at the Department of Fish and Game office) and drive 0.25 mile to the parking lot and the trailhead.

For trail and walk-in beach access: Take US 101 to Crescent City and Northcrest Drive. Turn northwest on Northcrest Drive and drive six miles (it becomes Lake Earl Drive) to Lower Lake Road. Turn left on Lower Lake Road and drive 2.5 miles to Kellogg Road. Turn left and drive 0.5 mile to the trailhead.

Alternative access: Follow the above access directions, but after turning left on Lower Lake Road, drive five miles to Pala Road. Turn left and drive 0.5 mile to the trailhead.

Contact: Tolowa Dunes State Park, c/o Redwood National and State Parks, 1375 Elk Valley Road, Crescent City, CA 95531, 707/464-6101, www.parks.ca.gov.

■ MYRTLE CREEK TRAIL
2.0 mi / 0.75 hr 🚶3 ⛰7

in the Smith River National Recreation Area

Map 1.1, page 43

This interpretive trail follows year-round Myrtle Creek. The stream drainage runs along a geological boundary between typical local soils (which support redwood and Douglas fir forests) and dry, reddish, iron- and magnesium-rich serpentine soil (where rarer native species grow, such as Bolander's and Vollmer's lilies). It's an easy hike with a lot to look at and learn about, including the remains of an extensive hydraulic mining operation, dating back to 1853, when gold was discovered here. Hikers are asked to respect this vulnerable habitat by keeping to the trail. Collecting artifacts or plants is prohibited.

User Groups: Hikers and dogs. No horses or mountain bikes.

Permits: Campfire permits (free) are required for overnight use. Parking and access are free.

Maps: For a free brochure and hiking guide, write to Smith River National Recreation Area. For a topographic map, ask the USGS for Hiouchi.

Directions: From Crescent City, drive north on US 101 for three miles to U.S. 199. Bear right (east) on U.S. 199 and drive seven miles to the parking area and trailhead. Park on the south side of U.S. 199 and cross the road to access the trailhead.

Contact: Smith River National Recreation Area, P.O. Box 228, Gasquet, CA 95543, 707/457-3131, www.fs.fed.us/r5.

🔳 BOY SCOUT TREE TRAIL

7.0 mi / 3.5 hr   🏃1 ⛰10

**in Jedediah Smith Redwoods State Park
northeast of Crescent City**

Map 1.1, page 43   **BEST** ◗

This is the kind of place where a nature lover can find religion; where the beauty is pure and untouched. The trail is a soft dirt path—often sprinkled with redwood needles—that allows hikers to penetrate deep into an old-growth redwood forest, complete with a giant fern understory and high-limbed canopy. The centerpiece is the Boy Scout Tree, the largest tree on the trail, but what you will remember the most is the serenity of a forest of old redwoods.

This is an easy hike, nearly flat and with only small hills—yet it's extremely rewarding. Just walk into the forest, and a few hours later, walk out. Those few hours can change how you feel about the world. A bonus known to relatively few is Fern Falls, a 40-foot waterfall. Reaching it requires a 3.5-mile hike one-way, making it a 7-mile round-trip hike.

User Groups: Hikers only. No dogs, horses, or mountain bikes. No wheelchair facilities.

Permits: No permits are required. Parking and access are free, $8 at main park entrance.

Maps: A trail map is available for a fee from Jedediah Smith Redwoods State Park. For a topographic map, ask the USGS for Hiouchi.

Directions: From US 101 in Crescent City, turn east on Elk Valley Road and drive one mile to Howland Hill Road. Turn right and drive 3.5 miles to the trailhead, on the left. The last two miles are unpaved.

Note: If you plan to camp at Jedediah Smith Redwoods State Park, use these directions: From Crescent City, drive north on US 101 for three miles to U.S. 199. Bear right (east) on U.S. 199 and drive east past the main entrance to Jedediah Smith Redwoods State Park and continue just past Hiouchi to South Fork Road. Turn right on South Fork Road (County Road 427) and cross two bridges.

At the junction, turn right on Howland Hill Road and drive about five miles to a small parking area and the signed trailhead, on the right side of the road.

Contact: Jedediah Smith Redwoods State Park, 1375 Elk Valley Road, Crescent City, CA 95531, 707/458-3018, www.parks.ca.gov.

🔳 STOUT GROVE TRAIL

0.6 mi / 0.5 hr   🏃1 ⛰8

**in Jedediah Smith Redwoods State Park
northeast of Crescent City**

Map 1.1, page 43

Visiting giant old redwood trees can affect people for a long time. The Stout Tree, the largest redwood in Jedediah Smith Redwoods State Park, is the attraction on this hike. It is so old that it can make your stay on earth seem mighty brief. The wide, level trail is a 10-minute walk that takes an easy course to the Stout Grove and then on to the Stout Tree. Most people take longer than 10 minutes, of course, because they're not used to seeing anything this size, and they take their time, absorbing the surroundings. The Stout Tree is being "loved to death" by people who touch it or trample the undergrowth, and rangers make a special request that you take a picture and leave it at that. Most everybody makes the mandatory stroll to the nearby Smith River, located a few minutes' walk beyond the Stout Tree. A trail that ran alongside the river once started here, but it was washed out by erosion from floodwaters.

User Groups: Hikers and wheelchairs. No dogs, horses, or mountain bikes.

Permits: No permits are required. Parking and access are free, $8 at main park entrance.

Maps: A trail map is available for a fee from Jedediah Smith Redwoods State Park. For a topographic map, ask the USGS for Hiouchi.

Directions: From Crescent City, drive north on US 101 for three miles to U.S. 199. Bear right (east) on U.S. 199 and drive east past the main entrance to Jedediah Smith Redwoods State Park and continue just past Hiouchi to South Fork Road. Turn right on South Fork Road (County Road 427) and cross two bridges. At the junction, turn right on Howland Hill Road and drive about two miles to a small parking area (on the right) and the signed trailhead.

Contact: Jedediah Smith Redwoods State Park, 1375 Elk Valley Road, Crescent City, CA 95531, 707/458-3018, www.parks.ca.gov.

5 CRAIG'S CREEK TRAIL
7.4 mi / 4.25 hr 👥3 ⛰7

in Smith River National Recreation Area northeast of Crescent City

Map 1.1, page 43

An old miners' pack route, vintage 1800s, has been converted into this hiking trail, an obscure path that is overlooked by most visitors. It starts along the South Fork Smith River, loops up the slopes of Craig's Creek Mountain and back down to the river, and ends where Craig's Creek enters the South Fork. In the process, it rises above the river and passes through forest, including old-growth redwoods and Douglas fir. Because of the contour of the mountain, the hike includes a good climb. The starting and ending elevations are the same (200 feet). Most of the time, you can have the entire trail to yourself. The South Fork Smith is very pretty here—a clear, free-flowing stream that drains a huge expanse of the Siskiyou Wilderness. The trail was last cleared in 2007.

User Groups: Hikers, dogs, horses, and mountain bikes. No wheelchair facilities.

Permits: For overnight use, a campfire permit (free) is required. Parking and access are free.

Maps: For a free brochure and hiking guide, write to Smith River National Recreation Area. For a map, ask the U.S. Forest Service for Six Rivers National Forest. For a topographic map, ask the USGS for Hiouchi.

Directions: From Crescent City, drive north on US 101 for three miles to U.S. 199. Bear right (east) on U.S. 199 and drive east past the main entrance to Jedediah Smith Redwoods State Park and continue just past Hiouchi to South Fork Road. Turn right on South Fork Road (County Road 427) and drive approximately one-third mile. Park in the boat-access facility area.

Contact: Smith River National Recreation Area, P.O. Box 228, Gasquet, CA 95543, 707/457-3131, www.fs.fed.us/r5.

6 FRENCH HILL TRAIL
5.6 mi / 3.25 hr 👥3 ⛰6

in Smith River National Recreation Area northeast of Crescent City

Map 1.1, page 43

This trail was created originally as part of the route to transport supplies to build the Camp Six fire lookout station. It is fairly steep, and some use it for an aerobic workout. It passes through old-growth Douglas fir and sugar pines, a forest that has thrived from so much moisture. The beauty and quality of the trail are poor to fair compared to that of other nearby areas. The significance that rates making this book is that while the lookout has long been retired, a high-tech automatic rain gauge was positioned in its place. In 1983, this rain gauge documented the most rain ever recorded in the continental United States for one season: 257 inches. You can drive right to this site.

User Groups: Hikers, dogs, horses, and mountain bikes. No wheelchair facilities.

Permits: No permits are required. Parking and access are free.

Maps: For a free brochure and hiking guide, write to Smith River National Recreation Area. For a map, ask the U.S. Forest Service for Six Rivers National Forest. For a topographic map, ask the USGS for Gasquet.

Directions: From Crescent City, drive north on US 101 for three miles to U.S. 199. Bear right (east) on U.S. 199 and drive 14 miles to Gasquet. Park at the Smith River National Recreation Area Visitor Center (on the left). The trail is located directly across the highway.

Contact: Smith River National Recreation Area, P.O. Box 228, Gasquet, CA 95543, 707/457-3131, www.fs.fed.us/r5.

7 STONY CREEK TRAIL
1.0 mi / 0.5 hr 🏃1 ⛺8

in Smith River National Recreation Area
northeast of Crescent City

Map 1.1, page 43

This easy walk in an unblemished river setting will take hikers to the mouth of Stony Creek, right where it pours into the North Fork Smith River. It's the kind of special place where you just sit and listen to the flow of moving water as it gurgles and pops its way over stones smoothed by years of river flows. The hike is easy, with a few ups and downs as it follows a bluff adjacent to the North Fork Smith (a designated Wild and Scenic River), then is routed right out to the mouth of Stony Creek. You're surrounded by woods, water, and in the spring, wildflowers.

Note: For years, there has been an ongoing disagreement on how to spell it, either Stony or Stoney. The creek itself is spelled "Stony," so it only makes sense to spell it the same.

User Groups: Hikers and dogs. No horses or mountain bikes. No wheelchair facilities.

Permits: Campfire permits (free) are required. Parking and access are free, but parking space is very limited.

Maps: For a free brochure and hiking guide, write to Smith River National Recreation Area. For a map, ask the U.S. Forest Service for Six Rivers National Forest. For a topographic map, ask the USGS for Gasquet.

Directions: From Crescent City, drive north on US 101 for three miles to U.S. 199. Bear right (east) on U.S. 199 and drive 14 miles to Gasquet. Turn left on Middle Fork/Gasquet

Road and drive about 100 feet to North Fork Road. Turn right and drive another mile. Then turn right on Stony Creek Road and drive a short distance to the trailhead.

Contact: Smith River National Recreation Area, P.O. Box 228, Gasquet, CA 95543, 707/457-3131, www.fs.fed.us/r5.

8 ELK CAMP RIDGE TRAIL
7.5-16.4 mi / 3.5 hr-2 days 🏃3 ⛺8

in Smith River National Recreation Area
northeast of Crescent City

Map 1.1, page 43

This trail is like a walk through history. It was originally part of a pack trail between Crescent City and the gold mines in southern Oregon, and the memories of the old days can shadow your hike much of the way. The trailhead is at 1,200 feet, but the route climbs right up to the ridge, reaching more than 3,000 feet. Once you reach the ridge, you have excellent views of surrounding peaks (Preston Peak is the big one) and the Smith River Canyon. Hikers may also notice that much of the vegetation along the trail is stunted, a result of the high mineral content in the serpentine rocks. The trail keeps climbing and ends at 3,400 feet. From start to finish, the trail covers 8.2 miles, although most hikers only make it halfway before they return. Since most of the route traces a ridgeline, there are no suitable camping areas. There is some evidence of the 2002 and 1996 forest fires. The trail was last cleared in 2003.

User Groups: Hikers, dogs, horses, and mountain bikes. No wheelchair facilities.

Permits: Campfire permits (free) are required. Parking and access are free.

Maps: For a free brochure and hiking guide, write to the Smith River National Recreation Area. For a map, ask the U.S. Forest Service for Six Rivers National Forest. For topographic maps, ask the USGS for Gasquet and High Plateau Mountain.

Directions: From Crescent City, drive north

on US 101 for three miles to U.S. 199. Bear right (east) on U.S. 199 and drive 14 miles to Gasquet. Turn left on Middle Fork/Gasquet Road and drive 100 feet; bear right as the road forks. Drive 0.5 mile, turn right on Old Gasquet Toll Road (County Road 314), and drive 2.3 miles. Turn left at the sign for the trailhead, and drive 1.4 steep and rough miles to the trailhead.

Contact: Smith River National Recreation Area, P.O. Box 228, Gasquet, CA 95543, 707/457-3131, www.fs.fed.us/r5.

9 COASTAL TRAIL (LAST CHANCE SECTION)
15.0 mi one-way/ 1 day   🏃3 ⛰8

in Del Norte Redwoods State Park south of Crescent City

Map 1.1, page 43

You get a little bit of heaven on this hike. It's one of the feature trips on the Del Norte coast, coursing through virgin forest and meadows (with beautiful wildflowers in the spring) and granting great coastal views in several spots. The best part of the hike is after the first crossing of US 101 before reaching the historic DeMartin home. (This 15-mile suggested route is to the second crossing of U.S 101.) The trail starts along the coast, veers up sharply into coastal spruce and fir, and then dips into dense, old-growth forest. That's the heaven. The climb required a gain of 1,400 feet. Ever wonder why the trees are so big? It's because with heavy rain in the winter and ponderous fog in summer, they are dripping with moisture. Like many coastal hikes, hitting good weather is the key. Note that when you're crossing meadows, ticks can be a common problem.

User Groups: Hikers and mountain bikes (restricted to first six miles only). No dogs or horses. No wheelchair facilities.

Permits: No permits are required. Parking and access are free, $8 at main park entrance.

Maps: A trail guide is available for a fee from

Redwood National and State Parks, c/o Redwood and State National Parks, 1111 2nd Street, Crescent City, CA 95531, 707/464-6101. For a topographic map, ask the USGS for Sister Rocks.

Directions: From Crescent City, drive south on US 101 for about 2.5 miles to Milepost 23.03 and Enderts Beach Road. Turn right (west) onto Enderts Beach Road and drive for 2.5 miles to the trailhead at the end of the road.

Contact: California State Parks, North Coast Redwoods District, 1375 Elk Valley Road, Crescent City, CA 95531, c/o Redwood National and State Parks, 707/464-6101, www.parks.ca.gov.

10 MCCLENDON FORD TRAIL
3.0 mi / 1.5 hr   🏃1 ⛰8

in Smith River National Recreation Area east of Crescent City

Map 1.1, page 43   BEST (

This is a perfect trail for a hot summer day, complete with a swimming hole. Hike 0.5 mile on the South Kelsey Trail, then one mile on the McClendon Ford Trail to the river. It's an easy hike through a large forest of Douglas fir. The trail crosses Horse Creek, a small tributary, and then leads to a pretty beach on the South Fork Smith River. The starting elevation is 1,000 feet, and the ending elevation is 200 feet. Get the idea? Right, this trail follows an easy descent to the river, taking about 45 minutes to get there. The swimming hole on the river is secluded and out of the way of most vacationers, so most often, you have the place completely to yourself.

Note: This is also the trailhead for South Kelsey Trail. If you are unfamiliar with the area, be sure to have a map of Six Rivers National Forest to reach the trailhead.

User Groups: Hikers, dogs, horses, and mountain bikes. No wheelchair facilities.

Permits: No permits are required. Parking and access are free.

Maps: For a free brochure and hiking guide,

write to Smith River National Recreation Area. For a map, ask the U.S. Forest Service for Six Rivers National Forest. For a topographic map, ask the USGS for Ship Mountain.

Directions: From Crescent City, drive north on US 101 for three miles to U.S. 199. Bear right (east) on U.S. 199 and drive east past the main entrance to Jedediah Smith Redwoods State Park and continue just past Hiouchi to South Fork Road. Turn right on South Fork Road (County Road 427), cross two bridges and bear left on South Fork Road and drive 14 miles to Forest Road 15. Turn right on Forest Road 15 and drive 3.5 more miles to a sign indicating the South Kelsey Trailhead. Turn left and drive two miles to the parking area for South Kelsey Trail. Hike on South Kelsey Trail for 0.5 mile before connecting with McClendon Ford Trail.

Contact: Smith River National Recreation Area, P.O. Box 228, Gasquet, CA 95543, 707/457-3131, www.fs.fed.us/r5.

11 SOUTH KELSEY TRAIL
3-9.0 mi / 1.5 hr- 2 days 🥾2 ⛰️9

in Smith River National Recreation Area east of Crescent City

Map 1.1, page 43

Back before cars, trains, and planes, Kelsey Trail spanned 200 miles from Crescent City eastward to Fort Jones near Yreka. It was built in the mid-19th century by Chinese laborers as a mule-train route. Today the trail consists of 4.5 miles (cleared in 2011) of maintained terrain. The rest of the trail lies in Six Rivers National Forest, and it is a mess—buried by fallen trees and overgrown vegetation, and difficult to even locate. The good news is the maintained section is on a beautiful piece of the South Fork Smith River. The trailhead is near Horse Creek, on the South Fork Smith River, at a 1,200-foot elevation. The trail initially drops down along the South Fork and continues south for 4.5 miles. A few camps are here along

the river, including the Buck Creek shelter (rebuilt in 2001), which is heaven during a heavy rainstorm. The route then rises above the river, and at this point, degenerates into oblivion if you try to follow it out of the canyon. Maps show the route extending to Baldy Peak and Harrington Lake.

User Groups: Hikers, dogs, and horses. Mountain bikes are permitted only to the wilderness boundary. No wheelchair facilities.

Permits: A campfire permit (free) is required. Parking and access are free.

Maps: For a free brochure and hiking guide, write to Smith River National Recreation Area. For a map, ask the U.S. Forest Service for Six Rivers National Forest. For a topographic map, ask the USGS for Summit Valley.

Directions: From Crescent City, drive north on US 101 for three miles to U.S. 199. Bear right (east) on U.S. 199 and drive east past the main entrance to Jedediah Smith Redwoods State Park and continue just past Hiouchi to South Fork Road. Turn right on South Fork Road (County Road 427), cross two bridges and bear left on South Fork Road and drive 14 miles to Forest Road 15. Turn right on Forest Road 15 and drive 3.5 more miles to a sign indicating the South Kelsey Trailhead. Turn left and drive two miles to parking area for South Kelsey Trail.

Contact: Smith River National Recreation Area, P.O. Box 228, Gasquet, CA 95543, 707/457-3131, www.fs.fed.us/r5.

12 SUMMIT VALLEY TRAIL
16.2 mi / 2 days 🥾4 ⛰️7

in Smith River National Recreation Area east of Crescent City

Map 1.1, page 43

This hike is best taken in the early summer—when the wildflowers are blooming; the Smith River is running with a fresh, ample flow; and the temperature is not too warm. The latter becomes a factor on the return trip, which is a killer climb. But at least you have great views of the Siskiyous and Mount Shasta to keep you company. Or, since this trail ends at the South Kelsey Trail near Elkhorn Bar, you could do this as a one-way hike (8.1 miles) with a shuttle car at the South Kelsey trailhead and avoid the terrible climb back.

The trailhead is set on a ridge at 4,600 feet, and the first mile of the hike is on an old jeep road. It then becomes a hiking path as it travels through meadows, where the wildflowers are spectacular in early summer. But then the trail drops, plunging into a canyon and landing hikers along the South Fork Smith River at Elkhorn Bar, a beautiful spot at an elevation of 1,160 feet. Here it junctions with South Kelsey Trail, where you'll find a few primitive campsites along the river. Well, when it comes to hiking, what goes down must come up, and you got it: The return trip is a death march—a 3,500-foot climb over the span of eight miles. Your car waiting at the trailhead will never look so good.

User Groups: Hikers, dogs, and horses. Mountain bikes are permitted only to the wilderness boundary. No wheelchair facilities.

Permits: A campfire permit (free) is required. Parking and access are free.

Maps: Write to Smith River National Recreation Area for a free brochure and hiking guide. For a map, ask the U.S. Forest Service for Six Rivers National Forest. For a topographic map, ask the USGS for Summit Valley.

Directions: From Crescent City, drive north on US 101 for three miles to U.S. 199. Bear right (east) on U.S. 199 and drive east past the main entrance to Jedediah Smith Redwoods State Park and continue just past Hiouchi to South Fork Road. Turn right on South Fork Road (County Road 427), cross two bridges and bear left on South Fork Road and drive 14 miles to Forest Road 15. Turn right on Forest Road 15 and drive 15 miles to the trailhead, on the left. Park on the side of the road.

Contact: Smith River National Recreation Area, P.O. Box 228, Gasquet, CA 95543, 707/457-3131, www.fs.fed.us/r5.

🔢 YUROK LOOP
1.0 mi / 0.5 hr

in Redwood National and State Parks south of Crescent City

Map 1.1, page 43

The Yurok Loop is a great short loop hike that starts right next to pretty Lagoon Creek Pond in Redwood National and State Parks. Here's the deal: From the trailhead, it's a 10-minute walk above a beautiful beach with lots of driftwood, and a gentle climb to a great coastal overlook. From here you can scan miles of ocean and many rocky stacks. After enjoying the view, head south, and when you reach a junction, turn left and enter a forest where the trail burrows almost like a tunnel, heading gently downhill. It then emerges from the forest and leads back to the parking lot, making it a delightful and easy walk that is a perfect break for highway drivers.

Special note: The Hidden Beach section of Coastal Trail (see the following listing) junctions with this trail.

User Groups: Hikers only. No dogs, horses, or mountain bikes.

Permits: No permits are required. Parking and access are free.

Maps: A trail guide is available for a fee from Redwood National and State Parks Headquarters. For a topographic map, ask the USGS for Requa.

Directions: From Crescent City, drive south on US 101 for approximately 14 miles. Turn right at the sign for the Lagoon Creek Parking Area. The trailhead is adjacent to the parking lot (on the ocean/north side).

Contact: Redwood National and State Parks, 1111 2nd Street, Crescent City, CA 95531, 707/465-7335 or 707/464-6101, www.nps.gov/redw/.

14 COASTAL TRAIL (HIDDEN BEACH SECTION)
8.0 mi / 5.0 hr 🏃2 ⛰8

in Redwood National Park south of
Crescent City

Map 1.1, page 43

One of the greatest lookouts anywhere in the hemisphere is available at the Klamath Overlook, where you can scan the vast ocean-blue horizon and actually see the curvature of the earth. This is also an excellent place to see the spouts of passing whales in winter and early spring. After parking, enjoy the view and then head off. It's only a three-mile round-trip to Hidden Beach and back. But you can continue to near False Klamath Rock, making it an eight-miler. The trail runs along coastal bluffs and rocky cliffs, with sweeping views of the ocean. Pray for a clear day.

User Groups: Hikers only. No dogs, horses, or mountain bikes.

Permits: No permits are required. Parking and access are free.

Maps: A trail guide is available for a fee from Redwood National and State Parks Headquarters. For a topographic map, ask the USGS for Requa.

Directions: From Eureka, drive north on US 101 for about 60 miles to the Klamath River. Continue two miles north of the Klamath River Bridge to Requa Road. Turn west on Requa Road and drive 2.5 miles to the Klamath Overlook, at the end of the road. The trailhead is at the south end of the parking area. Head north on Coastal Trail.

Contact: Redwood National and State Parks, 1111 2nd Street, Crescent City, CA 95531, 707/465-7335 or 707/464-6101, www.nps.gov/redw/.

15 LOST MAN CREEK TRAIL
2.0 mi / 1.0 hr 🏃1 ⛰8

in Redwood National Park south of Klamath

Map 1.1, page 43

Lost Man Creek is very pretty, with many rock pools and lots of lush vegetation. It's also a destination that is easy to reach. The trail heads southeast, the first 1.5 miles nearly flat, then starts to climb moderately, and then nearly levels out along the creek. Bring your camera, because it is rare to reach such a pristine setting with such a short walk. The trail is actually a wide gravel roadbed—an old logging road that the park service plans on reclaiming and turning into a more low-key setting. Although the two-mile round-trip is as far as most hikers take it, the trail actually continues for 10 miles, all the way back down to Bald Hills Road. But only the deranged make the 20-mile round-trip—it's so steep that you'll be howling at the moon like a lone wolf.

User Groups: Hikers only. No dogs, horses, or mountain bikes.

Permits: No permits are required. Parking and access are free.

Maps: A trail guide is available for a fee from Redwood National and State Parks Headquarters. For a topographic map, ask the USGS for Orick.

Directions: From Eureka, drive north on US 101 for 41 miles to Orick. Continue north for 3.5 miles just past Davison Road to Lost Man Creek Road. Turn right and drive 0.75 mile to the parking area and trailhead. Trailers and RVs are not permitted on Lost Man Creek Road.

Contact: Redwood National and State Parks, 1111 2nd Street, Crescent City, CA 95531, 707/465-7335 or 707/464-6101, www.nps.gov/redw/.

16 TALL TREES TRAIL
3.2 mi / 1.5 hr 🏃2 ⛰9

in Redwood National Park south of Klamath

Map 1.1, page 43 **BEST (**

This hike is routed into a grove of tall and ancient redwoods of cathedral-like beauty, with the trail shaded and surrounded by a lush fern understory. Your mission here is to reach Tall Trees Grove, home of a 357-foot-high redwood estimated to be 600 years old. According to rangers, this tree has lost about 10 feet of height because of drying. In the summer, Tall Trees Trail is popular, with visitors from all over the United States arriving to see the giant old-growth redwoods. The hike to the grove is just over a mile, and if you want to extend the adventure, you can return cross-country along Redwood Creek or head off toward Emerald Ridge (which is more of a cross-country route, not a designated trail). Warning: There is poison oak off the trail in this area.

User Groups: Hikers only. No dogs, horses, or mountain bikes. No wheelchair facilities.

Permits: A permit is required if you want to drive to the trailhead, with only a limited number of cars allowed per day. Permits are free and can be obtained at the Redwood Information Center starting at 9 A.M. Just pick it up, get the gate combination, and then enjoy your trip.

Maps: A trail guide is available for a fee from Redwood National and State Parks Headquarters. For a topographic map, ask the USGS for Orick.

Directions: From Eureka, drive north on US 101 for 40 miles. About a mile before reaching Orick, stop at the Redwood Information Center, at the west side of the highway. Here you secure a permit number, which is actually a gate combination number you'll need. Drive north on US 101 through Orick and continue 0.25 mile to Bald Hills Road. Turn right on Bald Hills Road. Look for the Tall Tree Access sign and drive seven miles to a locked gate, on the right. Open the gate using your permit/combination number, drive through, close and lock the gate, and then drive six miles down the gravel road (C-Line Road) to the trailhead. No RVs or trailers are permitted.

Contact: Redwood National and State Parks, 1111 2nd Street, Crescent City, CA 95531, 707/465-7335 or 707/464-6101, www.nps.gov/redw/.

17 JAMES IRVINE TRAIL
7.5 mi / 3.0 hr   👫2   ⛰10

in Prairie Creek Redwoods State Park

Map 1.1, page 43

Of the trails that provide access to old-growth in California, the James Irvine Loop is one of the best. It's easy enough that anyone can get a feel for ancient forest within a quick 0.5 mile, yet long enough that the entire loop delivers a sense of discovery and awe with each grove.

This 7.5-mile loop travels past a succession of redwood giants. From the trailhead, it's a 0.6-mile hike to the junction with the James Irvine Trail. Within a few steps, you'll know you're walking in history. The James Irvine Trail contours in and out of lush ravines filled with big trees for 2.6 miles. In one ravine, old-growth 300-foot mammoths rise up with a canopy that blots out the sky, while a sloping wall of ferns and sorrel create an understory that extends 150 yards to the canyon bottom. These are joined on the trail by occasional Douglas firs, Western hemlocks, and Sitka spruce, also in the 300-foot range.

To complete the loop, turn left on the Clintonia Trail and hike 1.4 miles past two more groves to the Miners Ridge Trail. Follow the Miners Ridge Trail 2.7 miles back to the visitors center and enjoy the good, clean feeling that comes with hiking a few hours in a pristine landscape. This hike can also be linked to Fern Canyon.

Permits: No permits are required. There is a state park day-use fee of $8 per vehicle.

Maps: Trail maps are available at the park visitors center for a fee. For a topographic map, ask the USGS for Fern Canyon.

Directions: From Eureka, drive north on US 101 for 41 miles to Orick. Continue north for five miles past Orick and exit at Newton B. Drury Scenic Parkway. Travel west on the parkway for 1 mile to park entrance on left. Turn left and drive a short distance to the visitors center and trailhead on right.

Contact: Prairie Creek Redwoods State

Park, 127011 Newton B. Drury Scenic Parkway, Orick, CA 95555, 707/465-7347, www.parks.ca.gov.

18 COASTAL TRAIL (FERN CANYON/ OSSAGON SECTION)

5.4 mi / 3.0 hr   👫 2   ⛰ 10

in Prairie Creek Redwoods State Park south of Klamath

Map 1.1, page 43   **BEST (**

This is a great hike, once one of the best coastal hikes anywhere. There is a good chance of seeing Roosevelt elk (about a dozen roam at Prairie Creek Redwoods State Park at the meadow and often along Davison Road), Fern Canyon (see listing in this chapter), a dense forest (quiet and pretty), and a series of hidden waterfalls. In addition, there is a huge beach that's spotless—that's right, not even a single piece of litter. Start from the parking area by crossing a shallow stream, and then take the near-level walk on the trail north as far as your heart desires. Most visitors enjoy the waterfalls and the beach, stopping for a picnic before returning. Elk are common here, and while they are accustomed to seeing people, be sure to give them plenty of room anyway. Note that there is a great trail camp about three miles in, but because overnight parking is forbidden at the trailhead, access is best from the east side of Prairie Creek Redwoods State Park, with a one-way hike of 7.5 miles.

User Groups: Hikers and mountain bikes. No dogs or horses. No wheelchair facilities.

Permits: No permits are required. There is a state park day-use fee of $8 per vehicle. Overnight parking is not permitted.

Maps: Trail maps are available at the park visitors center for a fee. For a topographic map, ask the USGS for Fern Canyon.

Directions: From Eureka, drive north on US 101 for 41 miles to Orick. Continue north for 2.5 miles to Davison Road. Turn west on

Davison Road and drive eight miles to Fern Canyon Trailhead. No trailers or RVs are permitted.

Contact: Prairie Creek Redwoods State Park, 127011 Newton B. Drury Scenic Parkway, Orick, CA 95555, 707/465-7347, www.parks.ca.gov.

19 FERN CANYON LOOP TRAIL

0.8 mi / 0.5 hr   👫 1   ⛰ 10

in Prairie Creek Redwoods State Park south of Klamath

Map 1.1, page 43

The Fern Canyon Loop might just be the most inspiring short hike in California. When you walk along the bottom of Fern Canyon, you'll be surrounded by 50-foot-high walls covered with giant ferns—a dramatic setting that isn't duplicated anywhere in the state. Also adding to the beauty is a small waterfall, pouring in through a chasm in the canyon wall and gushing into Home Creek. But it is Home Creek, which runs through the bottom of the canyon, that can cause the one serious problem here. In winter this creek can flood, making the trail impassable. Although bridges are provided from June through September, wear waterproof footwear—hikers often have to hop back and forth across the stream in order to reach the back of the canyon. At the end of the canyon, turn left and climb the trail to the canyon rim, and then continue through the forest back to the trailhead. A bonus is the adjacent beach, which is wide open and spans for miles. It is also common to see Roosevelt elk on the drive in. Note that this trail is recommended and well known by many, so it can get a lot of use during the summer months, yet it is in the winter when it really glows.

User Groups: Hikers only. No dogs, horses, or mountain bikes. No wheelchair facilities.

Permits: No permits are required. There is a state park day-use fee of $8 per vehicle.

Maps: Trail maps are available at the park visitors center for a fee. For a topographic map, ask the USGS for Fern Canyon.

Directions: From Eureka, drive north on US 101 for 41 miles to Orick. Continue north for 2.5 miles to Davison Road. Turn west on Davison Road and drive eight miles to Fern Canyon Trail. No trailers or RVs are permitted.

Contact: Prairie Creek Redwoods State Park, 127011 Newton B. Drury Scenic Parkway, Orick, CA 95555, 707/465-7347, www.parks.ca.gov.

20 REDWOOD CREEK TRAIL
1-16.0 mi / 0.5 hr-1 day   👫2 ⛰8

in Redwood National Park south of Klamath

Map 1.1, page 43   BEST ☾

The Redwood Creek Trail has become a feature hike in Redwood National Park. Though most visitors cut the trip short, it still provides exceptional beauty even in short pieces, with a chance to see elk near the parking area. The trail is routed along Redwood Creek, a pretty stream that flows out to sea near Orick. As you hike into the interior, you'll notice the diversity of the forest, with spruce, alder, redwoods, and maples, as well as lush fern beds in some areas. Stinging nettles are also abundant here, so stay on the trail. The stream attracts a diversity of wildlife, with ducks, herons, and hawks the most common sightings, and ruffed grouse and eagles are occasionally seen. In the summer, the first mile or two of the trail can be quite crowded, but just keep on going. The farther you go, the fewer people you'll see. Note that during the winter, the creek can flood the trail in some areas, making it impassable.

User Groups: Hikers only. No dogs, horses, or mountain bikes. No wheelchair facilities.

Permits: No permits are required. Parking and access are free.

Maps: A trail guide is available for a fee from Redwood National and State Parks

Headquarters. For a topographic map, ask the USGS for Orick.

Directions: From Eureka, drive north on US 101 for approximately 41 miles to Orick and then about 0.25 mile north of Orick to Bald Hills Road. Turn right on Bald Hills Road and drive 0.25 mile to the access road. Turn right and drive 0.5 mile to the parking area and trailhead.

Contact: Redwood National and State Parks, 1111 2nd Street, Crescent City, CA 95531, 707/465-7335 or 707/464-6101, www.nps.gov/redw/.

21 SKUNK CABBAGE TRAIL
5.6 mi / 3.0 hr   👫2 ⛰7

in Redwood National Park south of Klamath

Map 1.1, page 43

Few places anywhere cast such an aura as that found here on the Skunk Cabbage Trail in Redwood National Park, set near the little town of Orick. Every step is filled with the sense that this is an ancient place for old souls and youthful spirits. The trail is routed 2.8 miles amid a stunning forest understory out to a coastal bluff that towers over the Pacific Ocean. Hidden in the Redwood Empire, this rainforest looks like a jungle right out of *Jurassic Park*. You might even swear that a T-Rex must be lurking amid the massive vegetation, spruce, and redwoods. Instead of dinosaurs, you might see black bear, endangered northern spotted owls, or marbled murrelets. We've seen spots where bears have chewed the bark on trees here, too

From the parking area, the trail quickly enters a dense redwood and spruce forest, where the canopy is often completely enclosed by towering tree limbs. The trail meanders along a small watershed, Skunk Cabbage Creek; set beneath is a luxuriant forest floor filled with huge sword ferns, sorrel, and the giant skunk cabbage. The latter is a herbaceous plant with massive stalks, a perennial that reaches its full growth from May through June. It is called skunk cabbage because of its strong scent when taken in, up close and personal; it's even considered by some to be rank. But the smell isn't a factor in this trip; rather, it's about how the lavish growth of the plant adds a sense of age-old mystery to this quiet jungle. The trail eventually winds its way through redwoods as you near the coastal bluffs, which is a good picnic site and turnaround spot.

Try this trail from May through July. In fall and winter, the skunk cabbage dies off, and this hike becomes just another pretty hike in the redwoods.

User Groups: Hikers only. No mountain bikes, dogs, or horses. No wheelchair facilities.

Permits: Parking and access are free.

Maps: Trail maps are available at the park visitors center for a fee. For a topographic map, ask the USGS for Fern Canyon.

Directions: From Eureka, take US 101 north for 41 miles to the signed exit for Redwood Information Center (if you reach Orick, you have gone one mile too far) and get in left turn lane. Turn left and go 150 yards to the parking area. After obtaining trail and park materials at the center, then turn left (north) on US 101 and drive two miles (through Orick) to the trailhead entrance road on the left (comes up suddenly), signed Skunk Cabbage Trail. Turn left and drive 0.25 mile to a parking area.

Contact: Redwood National and State Parks, 1111 2nd Street, Crescent City, CA 95531, 707/465-7335 or 707/464-6101, www.nps.gov/redw/.

22 RIM LOOP TRAIL
5.0 mi / 2.5 hr   🏃1   ⛰9

at Patrick's Point State Park north of Eureka

Map 1.1, page 43   **BEST (**

Patrick's Point State Park is set on a coastal headland lush with ferns, spruce, and wildflowers. It's bordered by the Pacific, which means visitors can go tidepooling or whale-watching. That means that with this trail, you get the best of two worlds. At times it tunnels through thick vegetation, and at other times it opens up to sweeping ocean views. Along the way, several spur trails provide access to many features, including Mussel Rocks, Wedding Rock, Agate Beach, Rocky Point, Patrick's Point, Abalone Point, and Palmer's Point. The views are sensational at every one of these spots. The elevation of the trail is 200 feet and is nearly level its entire length. Each of the spur trails thus drops 200 feet to the beach. The spur trails, while short (they add just 1.5 miles to the hike), will make this a two- to three-hour trip, since you just won't want to rush through it. In addition, Octopus Tree Trail offers a short hike that starts just across from the northern end of Rim Loop Trail. This bonus trail provides a chance to see many spruce trees with roots that have straddled downed logs (hence the name Octopus Trees).

The only downers here are the fog and the heavy tourist traffic, both of which are common during the summer.

User Groups: Hikers only. No dogs, horses, or mountain bikes. The best wheelchair-accessible hiking trail in this park is from the visitors center to the Sumeg Village.

Permits: No permits are required. A state park day-use fee of $8 per vehicle is charged.

Maps: A park map and brochure are available for a fee from Patrick's Point State Park. For a topographic map, ask the USGS for Trinidad.

Directions: From Eureka, drive north on US 101 for 22 miles to Trinidad and continue north for 5.5 miles to Patrick's Point Drive exit. Take that exit and at the stop sign, turn left and drive 0.5 mile to the entrance station. Continue to the Agate Beach parking area.

Contact: Patrick's Point State Park, 4150 Patrick's Point Drive, Trinidad, CA 95570, 707/677-3570, www.parks.ca.gov.

23 TSURAI LOOP
1.5 mi / 1.0 hr   🚶2 ⛰9

on Trinidad Head on the Humboldt coast
north of Eureka

Map 1.1, page 43

The Tsurai Loop is a great, easy walk with coast-al vistas, unique terrain, and a nearby restaurant. The terrain includes the 300-foot miniature mountain at Trinidad Head, the pretty beach-front to the north of the Trinidad Head area, and the Trinidad Pier. The trip is best done in a counterclockwise loop. It starts by hiking up for beautiful views to the north, eventually reaching this perfectly situated rock lookout of the ocean. On clear days it can be an ideal spot to watch for the puff-of-smoke spouts on the ocean surface (made by migrating whales). The trail circles the mountain and then climbs to the top, a flat summit, where the views are only fair. The views are actually a lot better just 50 yards to the south, looking south toward Eureka and Humboldt Bay. As you head back down, you get more views of the rocky Trinidad Harbor and coast. The restaurant? It's called Seascape, and you can get a crab or shrimp omelet (in season) for breakfast that'll have your mouth watering every time you start driving north of Eureka on US 101. If there's a wait at the restaurant, don't hesitate to line up anyway.

User Groups: Hikers and dogs. Mountain bikes permitted but not recommended. No horses. No wheelchair facilities.

Permits: No permits are required. Parking and access are free.

Maps: For a topographic map, ask the USGS for Trinidad.

Directions: From Eureka, drive north on US 101 for 28 miles to Trinidad. Take the Trini-dad exit, turn left at the stop sign, and drive under the US 101 overpass to Main Street. Continue on Main Street to Trinity Street. Turn left and drive a short distance to Edwards Street. Turn right on Edwards Street and drive to the parking area at the foot of the harbor.

Contact: There is no managing agency for information.

24 ARCATA MARSH TRAIL
2-4.5 mi / 1-2.0 hr   🚶1 ⛰8

in Arcata Marsh and Wildlife Sanctuary on the
northern edge of Humboldt Bay

Map 1.2, page 44   **BEST (**

The 307-acre Arcata Marsh is the most popu-lar bird-watching area in Northern Califor-nia, and it's best explored by walking the loop. It is set on a levee above the marsh; the trail is short, flat, and routed in a loop for perfect viewing possibilities. The loop is two miles, but it can be extended on other trails for a longer trip. Several wooden photogra-phy blinds are available on the route, where you can hide yourself to view the ponds up close and take pictures of the birds. The set-ting is unique, with the coast, saltwater bay, brackish-water marsh, pond, foothills, and streams all nearby. This diversity means that an outstanding variety of species (more than 250) are attracted to the area, with sight-ings often including belted kingfishers, ospreys, peregrine falcons, black phoebes, and song and savannah sparrows. In other words, birds from nearly all habitats are rep-resented, which explains why the Audubon Society gives guided tours every Saturday at 8:30 A.M. A lot of people drive here to eat a picnic lunch, and just like Pavlov's dogs, tons of birds show up in the parking lot daily at noon for handouts. The rangers request that you don't feed the birds.

Also of interest is the Arcata Marsh Inter-pretive Center, located at the southwest cor-ner of the parking area, where activities for children are held. The interpretive center is open daily and has free maps, literature, and a posted list of recent bird sightings.

User Groups: Hikers, dogs, and mountain bikes. No horses.

Permits: No permits are required. Parking and access are free.

Maps: For a free, detailed trail map, contact the City of Arcata and ask for the Marsh and Wildlife Trail map. For a topographic map, ask the USGS for Arcata South.

Directions: From Eureka, drive north on US 101 for five miles to Arcata and the Samoa Boulevard exit. Take that exit and turn west onto Samoa Boulevard; drive to I Street. Turn left (south) and continue to the parking area.

Contact: Arcata Marsh Interpretive Center, 707/826-2359, www. arcatamarshfriends.org.

25 REDWOOD LOOP
6.2 mi / 3.0 hr   👣3 ⛰8

in Arcata Redwood Park in the Arcata foothills

Map 1.2, page 44

Arcata Redwoods Park provides a respite for students at nearby Humboldt State and for locals who want to wander amid a beautiful second-growth forest. A network of 18 trails covering about 10 miles in all is here, and the Redwood Loop connects several of them. For newcomers a map is an absolute necessity. Mountain bikes are prohibited at about 50 percent of the trails in the Arcata redwoods, although these rules are occasionally broken.

Start at the sign noting Redwood Park Trail (mountain bikes are not allowed at this trailhead) and take Nature Trail, which will take you by many huge stumps, a small creek, and a forest of redwoods and spruce. The complete route features a 1,200-foot elevation gain and then loss, making it a steep trail both on the way up and on the way down. On weekends, kamikaze mountain bikers tearing downhill can turn this hike into an extremely unpleasant experience.

User Groups: Hikers, dogs, horses, and mountain bikes. Certain sections of the trail are off-limits to horses and mountain bikes; check the trail map for details. No wheelchair facilities.

Permits: No permits are required. Parking and access are free.

Maps: For a free, detailed trail map, contact the City of Arcata and ask for the Community Forest Trail map. A free mountain bike trail map is also available. For topographic maps, ask the USGS for Arcata North and Arcata South.

Directions: From Eureka, drive north on US 101 to Arcata and the 14th Street exit. Take the 14th Street exit and drive east for about one mile into the parking area (look for the Redwood Park Trails sign). No mountain bikes are permitted here. Bikers and equestrians should use the Meadow trailhead, located where 14th Street enters the park.

Contact: City of Arcata, Environmental Services Department, 736 F Street, Arcata, CA 95521, 707/822-7091, www.cityofarcata.org/departments/parks-recreation.

26 RUSS CITY PARK DOUBLE LOOP
2.2 mi / 2.0 hr   👣2 ⛰7

in Russ City Park in Ferndale south of Eureka

Map 1.2, page 44

Russ City Park is Humboldt County's backyard wilderness. Covering just 105 acres, the park has been retained in its primitive state for wildlife, birds, and hikers. Though there's no posted, official name to this recommended route, we call the trail Double Loop, because it's set in the shape of a figure eight, which is quite rare. The trail includes a climb up Lytel Ridge, passing Francis Creek, with sections routed through heavy fern beds and large firs, and offering views of a small pond and the Eel River floodplain. Although the trip is relatively short and easy enough, the terrain is steep in spots, and the trail is challenging, complete with switchbacks. Heavy fog or rain can make it slippery here. Since it's a city park, Russ is little known by outsiders and can provide quiet, secluded hiking.

User Groups: Hikers and dogs. No horses or mountain bikes. No wheelchair facilities.

Permits: No permits are required. Parking and access are free.

Maps: A free map and brochure can be obtained by contacting the City of Ferndale.

For a topographic map, ask the USGS for Ferndale.

Directions: From Eureka, drive south on US 101 for 11 miles to the Ferndale/Fernbridge exit. Take that exit and drive straight about 0.75 mile. Turn right and drive west five miles through town to Ocean Avenue. Turn left on Ocean Avenue and drive 0.75 mile to the park, on the right.

Contact: City of Ferndale, P.O. Box 1095, Ferndale, CA 95536, 707/786-4224, http://ci.ferndale.ca.us/.

27 RATHERT GROVE/ GRIZZLY CREEK TRAIL

1.8 mi / 1.0 hr 🥾1 ⛰️10

at Grizzly Creek Redwoods State Park near Bridgeville

Map 1.2, page 44

This pretty hike is an easy walk through the redwoods. It crosses a small bridge at Grizzly Creek and tunnels under the redwood forest canopy into Rathert Grove, one of four relatively small yet pristine old-growth redwood groves protected in this park. There is nothing difficult about this or the other hikes in the park. In fact, stairs are provided in many of the few, short, steeper spots. What makes this hike special is that on a weekday, you can have an entire old-growth redwood grove all to yourself. Where else can you do that?

Grizzly Creek Redwoods State Park is one of the most overlooked redwood state parks in California, receiving fewer than 25,000 visitors per year—and most of those in July and August. It is often overlooked because it is not located on US 101, but rather Highway 36, a curvy two-laner that provides access to some of the state's most remote areas. Many discover the park by accident, usually heading up to fish, canoe, or kayak the Van Duzen River; the state park provides an excellent river access point, as well as a campground.

The park covers 390 acres. It was spared the chainsaws of loggers by the Georgia-Pacific Corporation, and in return, founder Owen R. Cheatham had one of the park's magnificent old-growth groves named for him.

Note: This park is on the closure list developed by the California Department of Parks, pending final state budget decisions or the possible transfer of park management to other park agencies or volunteer groups.

User Groups: Hikers only. No dogs, horses, or mountain bikes are permitted. Some facilities are wheelchair accessible, but there is no trail access for wheelchairs.

Permits: No permits are required. A fee of $8 per vehicle is charged for parking.

Maps: For a free brochure and map, write Grizzly Creek Redwoods. For a topographic map, ask the USGS for Redcrest Quad.

Directions: From Eureka, drive south on US 101 to the junction of Highway 36 at Alton. Turn east on Highway 36 and drive 17.2 miles to the park entrance, on the right.

Contact: Grizzly Creek Redwoods State Park, 707/777-3683, www.parks.ca.gov.

28 5 ALLENS' TRAIL

2.2 mi / 1.5 hr 🥾4 ⛰️10

in Humboldt Redwoods State Park south of Eureka

Map 1.2, page 44

The 5 Allens' Trail will provide a lasting impression of Humboldt Redwoods State Park for one reason: If you're unprepared, the trail is short but always sweet. It is well worth the effort in exchange for quiet wonders.

From the trailhead near the Eel River, walk under the highway and then start the climb. Up, up, and up it goes, ascending 1,200 feet. The trail passes through a forest of mixed conifers; the tree canopy provides needed shade in the summer. Even though the hike is quite short, few people make it to the end. But if you want a quiet, peaceful spot—and are willing to pay to get it—you'll find it at the end.

A great short side trip from the trailhead

is to instead hike north, along the Eel River to High Rock, one of the better shoreline fishing spots for steelhead during the winter migrations.

User Groups: Hikers only. No dogs, horses, or mountain bikes. No wheelchair facilities.

Permits: No permits are required. Parking and access are free, $8 at main park entrance.

Maps: A map can be obtained for a fee from Humboldt Redwoods State Park. For a topographic map, ask the USGS for Weott.

Directions: From Eureka, drive south on US 101 to the Redcrest exit. Take that exit and turn left, drive under the overpass, and continue a short distance to Avenue of the Giants. Turn right on Avenue of the Giants and drive south three miles (past High Rock Conservation Camp) to the 5 Allens' trailhead parking lot, on the left.

For an alternate route from Garberville, drive north on US 101 to the Founders Tree/ Rockefeller Forest exit. Take that exit (north), turn right, and drive about 200 yards to Avenue of the Giants. Turn left on Avenue of the Giants, cross over the South Fork Eel River, and then bear right at the intersection in order to stay on Avenue of the Giants. Drive a short distance to the 5 Allens' trailhead parking lot, on the right.

Contact: Humboldt Redwoods State Park, Box 100, Weott, CA 95571, 707/946-2409, www.parks.ca.gov.

29 FOUNDERS GROVE NATURE TRAIL
0.5 mi / 0.5 hr 　　　🥾1 ⛰8

in Humboldt Redwoods State Park
south of Eureka

Map 1.2, page 44

There's some irony on this hike. What was once the tallest redwood tree in the park is now the longest redwood tree in the park. What? That's because the Dyerville Giant fell, so this massive redwood is now in prone position. It still is an attraction among the 100 miles of trails at Humboldt Redwoods State Park. Little 0.5-mile Founders Grove Nature Trail provides the shortest and most easily accessible walk in the park. The trail also gives the quickest payoff, which explains why it's the park's most popular hike. The trail's location, near US 101, makes it easy to reach. At the trailhead you'll find a small box with brochures describing each element of the self-guided nature trail. All the while you'll be surrounded by old-growth redwoods— a great reward for such a small physical investment.

Note: This park is on the closure list developed by the California Department of Parks, pending final state budget decisions or the possible transfer of park management to other park agencies or volunteer groups.

User Groups: Hikers only. There is wheelchair access, although the trail is a bit uneven. No dogs, horses, or mountain bikes.

Permits: No permits are required. There is a fee of $8 per vehicle.

Maps: A map is available for a fee from Humboldt Redwoods State Park. For a topographic map, ask the USGS for Weott.

Directions: From Garberville, drive north on US 101 about 20 miles to the Founder Tree/Rockefeller Forest exit. Take that exit and drive a short distance to Avenue of the Giants. Drive 100 yards (crossing Avenue of the Giants) to the Founders Grove Parking Area/Trailhead (it's well signed).

Contact: Humboldt Redwoods State Park, Box 100, Weott, CA 95571, 707/946-2409, www.parks.ca.gov.

30 BULL CREEK FLATS
9.0 mi / 5.25 hr 　　　🥾2 ⛰8

in Humboldt Redwoods State Park
south of Eureka

Map 1.2, page 44　　　　　　　BEST (

This trail offers a streamside walk complete with giant redwoods and a babbling brook. Starting at the trailhead at Bull Creek Flats (a short walk to the Federation Grove), the trail ventures west along Bull Creek, an easy but steady grade as you hike upstream. All the while you're surrounded by forest, both redwoods and fir in a variety of mixes. Most people cross the seasonal bridge at the Big Tree and head back toward the beginning of the trail, at Bull Creek Flats, to make a loop. The feature hike of the route is the Big Tree Area and the giant tree, which you'll reach after four miles of hiking. There are many redwoods here that range from 5 to 10 feet in diameter. The big attraction for years was the Flat Iron Tree, a huge leaning redwood that grew in strange dimensions in order to support itself. Well, it's not leaning anymore, because it fell down and went boom. On the broad side, the Flat Iron Tree measures more than 15 feet. After the trail passes the Big Tree Area, it's routed to the mouth of Albee Creek, ending at Mattole Road. The trailhead here (at Mattole Road), by the way, provides a shorter hike of about a mile to the seasonal bridge at the Big Tree Area.

Note: This park is on the closure list developed by the California Department of Parks, pending final state budget decisions or the possible transfer of park management to other park agencies or volunteer groups.

User Groups: Hikers only. No dogs, horses, or mountain bikes. No wheelchair facilities.

Permits: No permits are required. Parking and access are free, $8 at main park entrance.

Maps: A map is available for a fee from Humboldt Redwoods State Park. For a topographic map, ask the USGS for Weott.

Directions: From Garberville, drive north on US 101 about 20 miles to the Founder Tree/Rockefeller Forest exit. Take that exit and turn left and drive a short distance to Avenue of the Giants. Turn left and drive a short distance to Mattole Road (the sign will say Rockefeller Forest/Honeydew, not Mattole Road). Turn left and drive 1.3 miles to the Lower Bull Creek Flats trailhead.

Contact: Humboldt Redwoods State Park, Box 100, Weott, CA 95571, 707/946-2409, www.parks.ca.gov.

🔢 31 WILLIAMS GROVE TRAIL
3.5 mi / 2.0 hr   🥾1 ⛰️8

in Humboldt Redwoods State Park
south of Eureka

Map 1.2, page 44

This trail makes an ideal, easy trip for campers staying at the Hidden Springs Campground in Humboldt Redwoods State Park. The camp is set in forest just above a big bend in the South Fork Eel River, with the trailhead on the southwest side of the camp. The trail starts out nearly flat, then turns right and parallels the highway. It's easy walking all the way, amid redwoods both young and old. Then the trail crosses under the highway and down the hill to Williams Grove, which has a picnic area and restrooms. Williams Grove Picnic Area can also be reached by car and then used as a trailhead to hike this route in reverse.

Note: This park is on the closure list developed by the California Department of Parks, pending final state budget decisions or the possible transfer of park management to other park agencies or volunteer groups.

User Groups: Hikers only. No dogs, horses, or mountain bikes. No wheelchair facilities.

Permits: No permits are required. A parking fee of $8 is charged per vehicle; parking is free for campers.

Maps: A map is available for a fee from Humboldt Redwoods State Park. For topographic maps, ask the USGS for Weott and Myers Flat.

Directions: From Garberville on US 101, drive to the Myers Flat exit (north of Garberville). Take that exit to Avenue of the Giants. Turn right and drive one mile northwest to Williams Grove parking area. Note: Hidden Springs Campground (open only during the summer) is located one mile south from the US 101 turnoff.

Contact: Humboldt Redwoods State Park, Box 100, Weott, CA 95571, 707/946-2409, www.parks.ca.gov.

32 LOST COAST TRAIL/ MATTOLE TRAILHEAD
25.0 mi one-way / 3 days 🏃2 ⛰10

on the Humboldt coast south of Eureka in King Range National Conservation Area

Map 1.2, page 44   **BEST (**

It's called the Lost Coast because of the isolation of the area, which is shielded on all sides by natural boundaries. For a first visit and a great day hike, take the abandoned jeep trail from the campground at Lighthouse Road and head south three miles to the Punta Gorda Lighthouse. You'll get a glimpse of the greatness here, and you'll probably get the inspiration to continue on Lost Coast Trail, one of California's greatest weekend trips. Set primarily on bluffs and beaches, the trail spans 25 miles from the mouth of the Mattole River south to Shelter Cove. Along the way it traces some of California's most remote portions of coastline. With two vehicles, one parked at each end of the trail, hikers can set up their own shuttle, then hike the trail one-way. A paid shuttle service is available as well (see the *Contact* section, below). This hike is best done from north to south because of winds out of the north; you want them at your back, not in your face. Firm-fitting waterproof boots with good, gripping soles are a necessity: they should be firm fitting because some of the walking is in soft sand, waterproof because there are several small creek crossings, and good gripping because some scrambling over wet boulders is required.

Special note: Several large landslides cover the beach between Shipman and Buck Creeks. These slides are still moving, rocks continue to roll down the beach, and the slides contain numerous large trees. High tides and/or large swells wash against the base of these slides. During high tides and/or large swells, passing through this landslide zone may be hazardous, if not impossible. Consult your tide book, keep an eye on ocean conditions, and plan to pass through this area at as low tide as possible, particularly if ocean swells

are large. Be cautious: This is an extremely isolated area. In many parts, there is no trail, and there is a lot of boulder hopping, where it is possible to twist an ankle.

User Groups: Hikers, dogs, horses, and mountain bikes. No wheelchair facilities.

Permits: Day-use permits are required for organized groups only. A campfire permit (free) is required for overnight use. Parking and access are free.

Maps: A detailed trail map is available for a fee, and a free map and brochure can be obtained from the Bureau of Land Management. Specify the King Range Conservation Area map. For topographic maps, ask the USGS for Petrolia, Cooskie Creek, Shubrick Peak, and Shelter Cove.

Directions: From US 101 in Garberville, drive north to the South Fork-Honeydew exit. Take that exit, drive west on Bull Creek Road, and continue 23 miles to Honeydew and Mattole Road. Turn right on Mattole Road and drive 14 miles (toward Petrolia). At the second bridge over the Mattole Road (one mile before Petrolia), turn left on Lighthouse Road. Drive west on Lighthouse Road to its end. The trailhead is just past Mattole Campground.

Contact: King Range National Conservation Area, 707/986-5400; Bureau of Land Management, Arcata Field Office, 1695 Heindon Road, Arcata, CA 95521-4573, 707/825-2300, www.ca.blm.gov/arcata/king_range.html; Lost Coast Trail Transport Service, 707/986-9909, www.lostcoasttrail.com.

33 KING CREST TRAIL
10.6 mi / 6.5 hr 🏃3 ⛰8

in King Range National Conservation Area south of Eureka

Map 1.2, page 44

King's Peak is one of the most prized destinations in the King Range. At 4,087 feet it's the highest point on the Northern California coast, and from it you get a view that can make you feel that you're perched on top of the world. The ocean seems to stretch on forever to the west, and on a perfect day you can make out the top of Mount Lassen behind the ridgeline of the Yolla Bolly Wilderness, to the east.

Reaching King's Peak requires a 5.3-mile hike from the Northslide Peak trailhead on Smith-Etter Road, and in the process, you climb about 700 feet. Making the trip on a clear day is an absolute necessity, since the climb is buffered by the reward of the sweeping views. Trail signs are very poor, and water supplies at trail camps are from dubious sources, so it's also essential to have a good map and a double-canteen water supply. The entire King Crest Trail extends 10 miles one-way, starting from the trailhead listed in this hike to Saddle Mountain trailhead; then it descends four miles to the beach. That makes a one-way overnight trip with a shuttle vehicle at the end of the trail an ideal alternative. Note that the portion that heads down to the beach is called Buck Creek Trail and that it is very steep, with portions difficult to follow—this is considered an advanced hike; for some hikers, orienteering with a map and compass may be required.

User Groups: Hikers, dogs, horses, and mountain bikes. No wheelchair facilities.

Permits: A campfire permit (free) is required for overnight use. Parking and access are free.

Maps: A detailed trail map is available for a fee, and a free map and brochure can be obtained from the Bureau of Land Management; ask for the King Range Conservation Area map. For a topographic map, ask the USGS for Shubrick Peak.

Directions: On US 101, drive to the South Fork-Honeydew exit (just north of Garberville). Take that exit to Wilder Ridge Road and turn southwest. Drive one mile to Smith-Etter Road and turn west. Drive six miles to the trailhead (this is a primitive, four-wheel-drive road and is closed from November 1 to March 31).

Contact: King Range National Conservation

Area, 707/986-5400; Bureau of Land Management, Arcata Field Office, 1695 Heindon Road, Arcata, CA 95521-4573, 707/825-2300, www.ca.blm.gov/arcata/king_range.html.

34 SPANISH RIDGE TRAIL
9.6 mi / 1 day   👣3 ⛰️8

in King Range National Conservation Area south of Eureka

Map 1.2, page 44

In just a few miles, you can gain access to some of the most remote sections of the California coast. But there's a price (and we'll get to that).

From the Spanish Ridge trailhead, hike 1.8 miles along Cooskie Creek Trail and climb an easy 200 feet before reaching the junction with Spanish Ridge Trail. You then descend 2,300 feet in three miles en route to the coast. Know what that means? Right. Going back, you'll climb 2,300 feet in three miles, and unless you can get a helicopter ride back, you're looking at some serious grunt work—but it's worth it.

The King Range is very rugged, primitive, and isolated. Thanks to that bumpy access road and the climb on the return trip, it's rare to see other people here. And because there are no water sources along this trail, each hiker should carry two canteens of water. This trail is for experienced hikers only, and as with several of the hikes in the King Range, you should bring a map and a compass.

User Groups: Hikers, dogs, mountain bikes, and horses. No wheelchair facilities.

Permits: A campfire permit (free) is required for overnight use. Parking and access are free.

Maps: A detailed trail map is available for a fee, and a free map and brochure can be obtained from the Bureau of Land Management; ask for the King Range Conservation Area map. For topographic maps, ask the USGS for Cooskie Creek and Shubrick Peak.

Directions: On US 101, drive to the South Fork-Honeydew exit (just north of

Garberville). Take that exit to Wilder Ridge Road and turn southwest. Drive one mile to Smith-Etter Road and turn west. Drive 10 miles (this is a primitive, four-wheel-drive road and is closed from November 1 to March 31) to Telegraph Ridge Road. Turn northwest on Telegraph Ridge Road and drive eight miles to the trailhead gate. In summer, continue driving two miles to the trailhead. When the gate is locked, the trailhead is accessible only by a two-mile walk.

Contact: King Range National Conservation Area, 707/986-5400; Bureau of Land Management, Arcata Field Office, 1695 Heindon Road, Arcata, CA 95521-4573, 707/825-2300, www.ca.blm.gov/arcata/king_range.html.

35 LOOKOUT POINT LOOP TRAIL

1.7 mi / 1.0 hr   2   8

in Richardson Grove State Park south of Garberville

Map 1.2, page 44

Big woods. Big water. That's what Lookout Point Loop Trail supplies, with a tour through giant redwoods culminating at the canyon rim over the South Fork Eel River. Giant redwoods approaching 300 feet tall and estimated to be 1,000 years old are the highlight of Richardson Grove, while younger redwoods, fir, and tan oak fill out the forest. To be honest, if you look close, there's actually more tan oak and fir than redwoods. The trail passes through forest and rises to Lookout Point, where there's an excellent view of the South Fork. You can also see the Oak Flat Campground from here. As a free-flowing river, the South Fork Eel River can seem like a small trickle in late summer or a howling torrent during peak flows in winter. When looking down from Lookout Point during summer, it may seem hard to imagine how high the Eel has risen in high-water years. In 1955, 1963, 1986, 1997, and 1998, the river actually flooded its banks and wiped out several campgrounds in the state park. This is an easy and popular hike, both for daytime park visitors and for overnighters at Madrone Campground.

User Groups: Hikers only. No dogs, horses, or mountain bikes. No wheelchair facilities.

Permits: No permits are required. A state park entrance fee of $8 is charged per vehicle.

Maps: For a trail guide and brochure (free), write Richardson Grove State Park. For a topographic map, ask the USGS for Garberville.

Directions: From Santa Rosa, drive north on US 101 to Leggett. Continue north on US 101 about 17 miles to the park entrance, on the west side of the highway. Follow the signs to the Redwood Day-Use Parking Area. Access to the trailhead is at the parking area and also out of Madrone Campground.

Contact: Richardson Grove State Park, c/o California State Parks, North Coast Redwoods District, Piercy Sector, 1600 U.S. Highway 101, No. 8, Garberville, CA 95542, 707/247-3318, www.parks.ca.gov.

36 DURPHY CREEK LOOP

4.0 mi / 3.0 hr   3   7

in Richardson Grove State Park south of Garberville

Map 1.2, page 44

Be ready for a good climb, have a full canteen of water, and note that no whiners are allowed. Why? Because this loop trail is the most challenging hike in Richardson Grove State Park. It starts easily enough, routed right along the left side of Durphy Creek at a tolerable grade. But when the trail turns left and starts to climb up the canyon, all tolerance is forgotten. The trail climbs 800 feet in less than 0.5 mile, with a short cutoff to Tan Oak Springs, then onward to the ridge at 1,400 feet. On the way back down, the route descends through a dense forest of tan oak and is quite steep in the last 0.5 mile, which includes some switchbacks. To complete the loop, turn left at Lookout Point Trail and hike back toward Madrone Campground.

User Groups: Hikers only. No dogs, horses, or mountain bikes. No wheelchair facilities.

Permits: No permits are required. A fee of $6 per vehicle is charged for parking.

Maps: For a trail guide and brochure (free), write Richardson Grove State Park. For a topographic map, ask the USGS for Garberville.

Directions: From Santa Rosa, drive north on US 101 to Leggett. Continue north on US 101 about 17 miles to the park entrance, on the west side of the highway. Follow the signs to the Redwood Day-Use Parking Area. Walk 0.25 mile to Madrone Campground and to the trailhead.

Contact: Richardson Grove State Park, c/o California State Parks, North Coast Redwoods District, Piercy Sector, 1600 U.S. Highway 101, No. 8, Garberville, CA 95542, 707/247-3318, www.parks.ca.gov.

37 WOODLANDS LOOP TRAIL
1.6 mi / 1.0 hr   🏃1 ⛰7

in Richardson Grove State Park south of Garberville

Map 1.2, page 44

You want easy? You get easy. You want forest? You get forest. You want a campground trailhead? You get a campground trailhead. The Woodlands Loop, an easy, pretty trail that starts at the Huckleberry Campground, does all that and more. The trail crosses North Creek and then goes through both redwoods and tan oak that are dense at times. It also includes a gentle uphill portion, rising about 250 feet. The trail and camp are set on the west side of US 101, and with the South Fork Eel River on the east side of the highway, there's no direct river access from this trail or the nearby campground.

User Groups: Hikers only. No dogs, horses, or mountain bikes. No wheelchair facilities.

Permits: No permits are required. A fee of $6 per vehicle is charged for parking.

Maps: For a trail guide and brochure (free), write Richardson Grove State Park. For

a topographic map, ask the USGS for Garberville.

Directions: From Santa Rosa, drive north on US 101 to Leggett. Continue north on US 101 about 17 miles to the park entrance, on the west side of the highway. The trailhead is accessible from the parking lot just inside the entrance.

Contact: Richardson Grove State Park, c/o California State Parks, North Coast Redwoods District, Piercy Sector, 1600 U.S. Highway 101, No. 8, Garberville, CA 95542, 707/247-3318, www.parks.ca.gov.

38 TOUMEY GROVE TRAIL
3.8 mi / 2.75 hr   🏃2 ⛰9

in Richardson Grove State Park south of Garberville

Map 1.2, page 44

The Toumey Trail is one of Richardson Grove State Park's feature summer hikes. It includes walking over the South Fork Eel River on the summer bridge, through a majestic stand of old redwoods, up to Kauffman Springs, and beyond to the Panorama Point Lookout. The trailhead is located between campsite Nos. 123 and 126 at Oak Flat Campground. The trail crosses the river and enters the redwoods; take your time and enjoy the surroundings. The trail climbs 300 feet, rising quickly with a few switchbacks, and arrives at Panorama Point, with excellent views of the Eel River Canyon and Richardson Grove redwoods.

Special note: This trail can be accessed only in the summer months.

User Groups: Hikers only. No dogs, horses, or mountain bikes. No wheelchair facilities.

Permits: No permits are required. A fee of $6 per vehicle is charged for parking.

Maps: For a trail guide and brochure (free), write Richardson Grove State Park. For a topographic map, ask the USGS for Garberville.

Directions: From Santa Rosa, drive north on US 101 to Leggett. Continue north on US 101 about 17 miles to the park entrance, on the west side of the highway. Follow the signs to Oak Flat Campground. The trailhead is located between campsite Nos. 123 and 126. **Contact:** Richardson Grove State Park, c/o California State Parks, North Coast Redwoods District, Piercy Sector, 1600 U.S. Highway 101, No. 8, Garberville, CA 95542, 707/247-3318, www.parks.ca.gov.

SHASTA AND TRINITY

© TOM STIENST

BEST HIKES

At 14,162 feet, Mount Shasta rises like a diamond in a field of coal. Its sphere of influence spans a radius of 125 miles, and its shadow is felt everywhere in the region. Not surprisingly, climbing its mammoth face is the number one activity in the region. It is a truly awe-inspiring half-hike, half-climb on California's most beautiful mountain.

In addition, there are several remarkable backpacking destinations hidden in the western sector of this region: Preston Peak, Young's Valley, Wilderness Falls, and Devils Punchbowl.

But to focus solely on hiking would be a disservice. In fact, this is one of the best areas in North America for an outdoor adventure – especially one involving fishing, powerboating, rafting, and exploring. The region offers giant Shasta Lake, the Sacramento River above and below the lake, the McCloud River, the Trinity Alps, Marble Mountain Wilderness, Russian Wilderness, Castle Crags State Park, Whiskeytown-Shasta-Trinity National Recreation Areas, and the Klamath Mountains. There are also several hundred miles of Pacific Crest Trail (PCT) that are routed across the best of it.

At the charmed center of this beautiful region is the Trinity Alps, where lakes are sprinkled everywhere. It's also home to the headwaters for feeder streams to the Trinity River, Klamath River, New River, Wooley Creek, and others.

The neighboring Klamath Mountains are well known as Bigfoot Country by locals. If you drive up the Forest Service road at Bluff Creek, just off Highway 96 upstream of Weitchpec, you can even find the spot where the famous Bigfoot film clip, once believed to be genuine, was shot with an 8mm camera in the 1960s by a hiker. Well, we haven't seen Bigfoot, but we have discovered tons of outdoor recreation. This remote region features miles of the Klamath and Salmon Rivers, as well as the Marble Mountain Wilderness. Options include canoeing, rafting, and fishing for steelhead on the Klamath River, or hiking into your choice of more than 100 wilderness lakes.

Castle Crags and the Trinity Divide feature hikes to Mount Eddy, the Crags, Grey Rocks, and dozens of pristine lakes, many with fantastic campsites. There are also hikes along portions of rivers, including stellar easy walks along the McCloud River.

Shasta Lake is one of America's top recreation lakes. It is the one destination that is big enough to handle all who love it. The massive reservoir boasts 370 miles of shoreline, 1,200 campsites, 21 boat launches, 11 marinas, 35 resorts, and numerous houseboat and cabin rentals. A remarkable 22 species of fish live in the lake. Many of the campgrounds feature lake views. In addition, getting here is easy — it's a straight shot off of I-5. Hidden here is the boat-in Greens Creek trailhead, as well as several others that offer pretty spots with lake views.

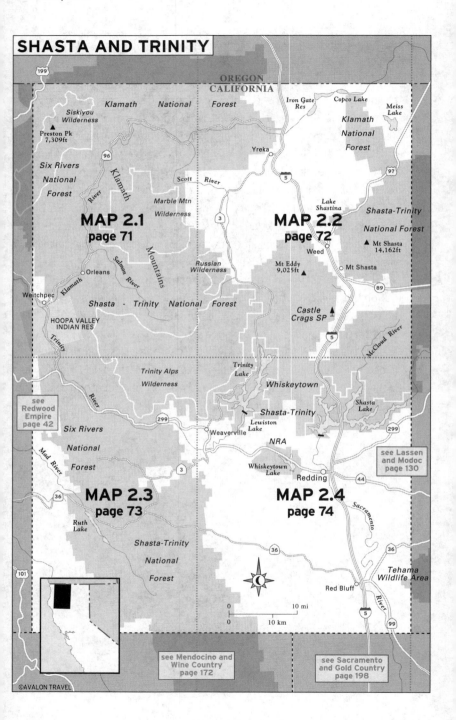

SHASTA AND TRINITY

OREGON
CALIFORNIA

199

Klamath National Forest

Siskiyou
Wilderness

Preston Pk
7,309ft

Six Rivers
National
Forest

96

Klamath

River

Scott River

Marble Mtn
Wilderness

MAP 2.1
page 71

Salmon River

Orleans

Weitchpec

Klamath

Mountains

Russian
Wilderness

Shasta - Trinity National Forest

HOOPA VALLEY
INDIAN RES

Trinity

Iron Gate
Res

Copco Lake

Meiss
Lake

Yreka

Klamath

National

Forest

5

97

Lake
Shastina

Shasta-Trinity

National Forest

MAP 2.2
page 72

Weed

▲ Mt Shasta
14,162ft

Mt Eddy
9,025ft ▲

Mt Shasta

89

Castle
Crags SP

5

McCloud River

3

Trinity Alps
Wilderness

Trinity
Lake

Whiskeytown

Shasta
Lake

see
Redwood
Empire
page 42

Six Rivers

National

Forest

Mad River

299

Weaverville

Lewiston
Lake

Shasta-Trinity

NRA

299

see Lassen
and Modoc
page 130

3

Whiskeytown
Lake

Redding

44

MAP 2.3
page 73

36

Ruth
Lake

Shasta-Trinity

National

Forest

Sacramento

36

36

Tehama
Wildlife Area

MAP 2.4
page 74

101

Red Bluff

0   10 mi

0   10 km

5

99

River

©AVALON TRAVEL

see Mendocino and
Wine Country
page 172

see Sacramento
and Gold Country
page 198

Map 2.1

Hikes 1-22
Pages 75-88

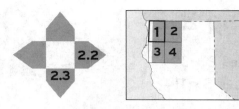

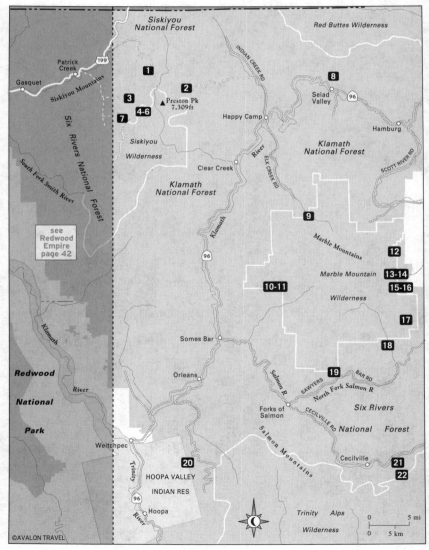

Map 2.2

Hikes 23-59
Pages 89-114

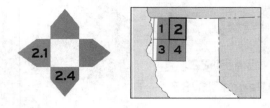

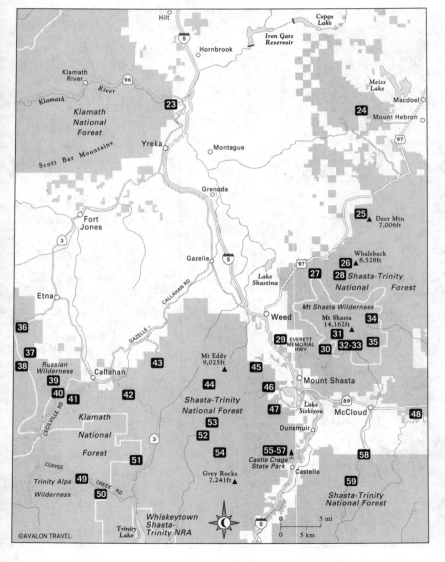

©AVALON TRAVEL

Map 2.3

Hikes 60-66
Pages 115-118

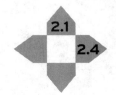

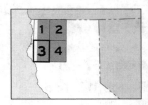

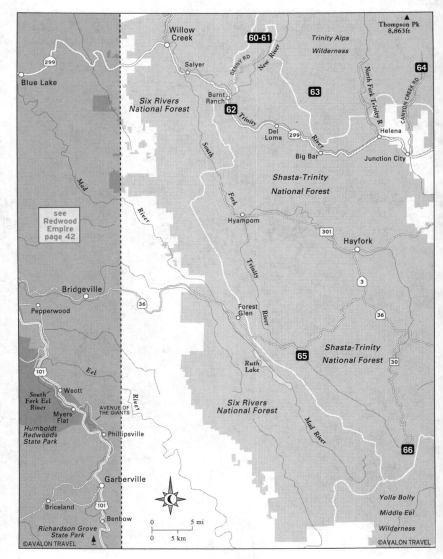

see Redwood Empire page 42

Map 2.4

Hikes 67-78
Pages 118-125

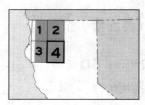

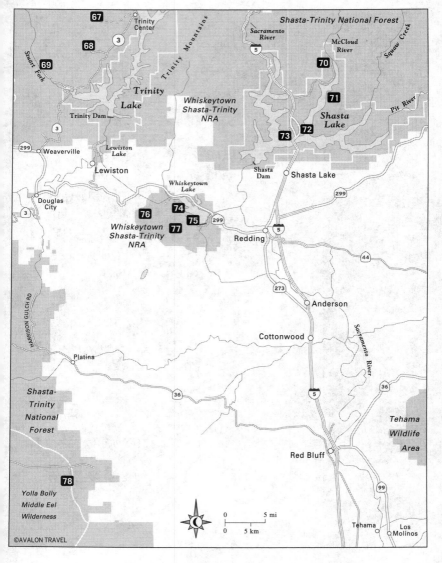

1 YOUNGS VALLEY TRAIL
13.0 mi / 1 day 🚶2 ⛰8

in the Siskiyou Wilderness east of Crescent City

Map 2.1, page 71

The 6.5-mile trip from Youngs Valley down Clear Creek to Youngs Meadow is a beautiful and rewarding trip. Youngs Meadow, set at an elevation of 4,500 feet on the western slope of Preston Peak, is very pretty and makes an excellent picnic area and campsite.

The drive to the trailhead is long and circuitous. It's long just to get to U.S. 199, and from there, you face more than an hour on forest roads. The trailhead is located near Sanger Lake and some camp there the first night in. You start the trip by hiking on a decommissioned Forest Service road. It turns to trail then you start dropping down into Youngs Valley and Clear Creek. The hike features a 600-foot descent into the canyon and to Clear Creek.

From here the ambitious can take this trip farther—much farther. The Youngs Valley Trail is a great first leg of a multiday trip, ultimately heading either farther down Clear Creek to Wilderness Falls, which is an awesome setting (see the listing in this chapter), or to Rattlesnake Meadows, on the slopes of Preston Peak—a short but rugged climb.

User Groups: Hikers, dogs, and horses. No mountain bikes. No wheelchair facilities.

Permits: No permits are required. A campfire permit (free) is required for overnight use. Parking and access are free.

Maps: For a map, ask the U.S. Forest Service for Klamath National Forest. For a topographic map, ask the USGS for Devils Punchbowl.

Directions: From Crescent City, drive north on US 101 for three miles to U.S. 199. Bear right (east) on U.S. 199 and drive 32 miles to Forest Road 18N07. Turn right and drive five miles to a signed junction for Forest Road 18N07. Continue on Forest Road 18N07 for 10 miles (twisty) toward Sanger Lake. Just before Sanger Lake, bear right on Forest Road 4803 (signed Youngs Valley Trail) and drive one mile to the end of the road and the trailhead.

Contact: Smith River National Recreation Area, P.O. Box 228, Gasquet, CA 95543, 707/457-3131, www.fs.fed.us/r5; Klamath National Forest, Happy Camp-Oak Knoll Ranger District, P.O. Box 377, 63822 Highway 96, Happy Camp, CA 96039-0377, 530/493-2243, www.fs.fed.us/r5.

2 PRESTON PEAK
19.0 mi / 2 days 🚶5 ⛰10

in the Siskiyou Wilderness east of Crescent City

Map 2.1, page 71 **BEST ☾**

Only mountaineers need sign up for this trip. The last mile to reach the summit of Preston Peak is steep, rough, and primitive; it can be scary and dangerous for newcomers to mountaineering. With no marked trail on top, hikers must have the ability to scramble cross-country and recognize any dangerous spots—and then avoid them. That done, you'll gain the top—7,309 feet and by far the highest spot in the region, with fantastic surrounding views. Even Mount Shasta, way off to the southeast, comes clearly into view, along with the famous peaks in the Trinity Alps and Marble Mountain Wilderness.

The best route to climb Preston Peak is to hike Youngs Valley Trail (see details about Youngs Valley Trail in this chapter) to Youngs Meadow (an easy five miles). Then head down the Clear Creek Trail (another easy mile) to a somewhat faint junction with the Rattlesnake Meadow Trail. Turn left on Rattlesnake Meadow Trail, where you start to climb, including two very steep, rough, and primitive miles to the flank of Preston Peak. At the end of Rattlesnake Meadow Trail, hikers must go cross-country for another mile or so to the Preston Peak Summit. The last mile is a scramble. Pick your route very carefully and make no climbing mistakes. Although this is a nontechnical climb, there is one difficult spot that can be dangerous. You will see it: a mix of shale, loose gravel, and boulders, with no discernible trail. Take your time and pick your way up one step at a time.

Special note: Always stay off this mountain in wet weather, because the route near the top is very slippery. Always avoid routes that cross through loose shale, which can be extremely dangerous. A fall here can kill you.

User Groups: Hikers only. Dogs are permitted but are strongly not recommended above tree line at Preston Peak. No horses or mountain bikes. No wheelchair facilities.

Permits: A campfire permit is required for overnight use. Parking and access are free.

Maps: For maps, ask the U.S. Forest Service for Six Rivers and Klamath National Forest. For a topographic map, ask the USGS for Devils Punchbowl.

Directions: From Crescent City, drive north on US 101 for three miles to U.S. 199. Bear right (east) on U.S. 199 and drive 32 miles to Forest Road 18N07. Turn right and drive five miles to Forest Road 18N07. Continue on Forest Road 18N07 for 10 miles (twisty) toward Sanger Lake. Just before Sanger Lake, bear right on Forest Road 4803 (signed Youngs Valley Trail) and drive one mile to the trailhead, at the end of the road.

Contact: Klamath National Forest, Happy Camp-Oak Knoll Ranger District, P.O. Box 377, 63822 Highway 96, Happy Camp, CA 96039-0377, 530/493-2243, www.fs.fed.us/r5; Smith River National Recreation Area, P.O. Box 228, Gasquet, CA 95543, 707/457-3131, www.fs.fed.us/r5.

3 DOE FLAT TRAIL
3.5 mi / 2.0 hr

in Smith River National Recreation Area east of Crescent City

Map 2.1, page 71

Doe Flat is the best backpacking jump-off point for the Siskiyou Wilderness. There are several excellent destinations from Doe Flat.

The best are Buck Lake, Devils Punchbowl, Clear Creek, and Wilderness Falls.

It is 1.5 miles from the parking area to the intersection of the Buck Lake Trail (see listing in this chapter), and then another 0.25 mile to Doe Flat. The first 0.75 mile of this easy hike is on a closed forest service road. After that, a trail is routed through forest and then intersects with Buck Lake Trail. To reach Buck Lake, turn right (it's only 0.1 mile to the lake). To reach Doe Flat and its campsite, turn left and continue 0.25 mile. The area is well wooded, with some huge Jeffrey pines and cedars. For late arrivals, a bonus at the trailhead is a small, primitive camping area with three sites and a vault toilet.

User Groups: Hikers, dogs, and horses. No mountain bikes. No wheelchair facilities.

Permits: No permits are required. A campfire permit (free) is required for overnight use. Parking and access are free.

Maps: For a free brochure and hiking guide, write to Smith River National Recreation Area. For a map, ask the U.S. Forest Service for Klamath National Forest. For a topographic map, ask the USGS for Devils Punchbowl.

Directions: From Crescent City, drive north on US 101 for three miles to U.S. 199. Bear right (east) on U.S. 199 and drive 25 miles to Little Jones Creek Road. Turn right on Little Jones Creek Road/Jawbone Road (Forest Road 16) and drive south 9.6 miles to a fork with Forest Road 16N02. When the road forks, turn sharply left on Forest Road 16N02 and drive four miles to the trailhead, at the end of the road.

Contact: Smith River National Recreation Area, P.O. Box 228, Gasquet, CA 95543, 707/457-3131, www.fs.fed.us/r5.

4 BUCK LAKE TRAIL
3.2 mi / 2.0 hr   🏃2 ⛰8

in the Siskiyou Wilderness east of Crescent City

Map 2.1, page 71

Set in the heart of a wilderness forest at an elevation of 4,300 feet, Buck Lake is a little crystal lake surrounded by old-growth firs. After parking, the first 0.75 mile of this easy hike is on a closed forest service road. After that, a trail is routed through forest and then intersects with Buck Lake Trail. Turn right on Buck Lake Trail and hike 0.1 mile to the lake. There are plenty of deer and bear in the area, and the brook trout at the lake are abundant, though small. Traveling to the primitive campground at nearby Doe Flat, you'll cross through beautiful meadows and forest, including Douglas, white, and red firs, along with some maples. In the fall, the changing colors of the maples add a pretty touch to the trip. There is an excellent backpacker's campsite at Doe Flat. The first time we saw Buck Lake was a Memorial Day weekend, the opening day of trout season here, and there were so many rising brook trout that all the dimples on the lake surface looked like rain drops.

User Groups: Hikers, dogs, and horses. No mountain bikes. No wheelchair facilities.

Permits: No permits are required. A campfire permit (free) is required for overnight use. Parking and access are free.

Maps: For a free brochure and hiking guide, write to Smith River National Recreation Area. For a map, ask the U.S. Forest Service for Six Rivers and Klamath National Forest. For a topographic map, ask the USGS for Devils Punchbowl.

Directions: From Crescent City, drive north on US 101 for three miles to U.S. 199. Bear right (east) on U.S. 199 and drive 25 miles to Little Jones Creek Road/Jawbone Road (Forest Road 16). Turn right on Little Jones Creek Road/Jawbone Road (Forest Road 16) and drive south 9.6 miles to a fork with Forest Road 16N02. When the road forks, turn sharply left on Forest Road 16N02 and drive four miles to the trailhead at the end of the road. Take Doe Flat trailhead.

Contact: Smith River National Recreation Area, P.O. Box 228, Gasquet, CA 95543, 707/457-3131, www.fs.fed.us/r5.

5 DEVILS PUNCHBOWL (VIA DOE FLAT TRAIL)
12.2 mi / 1.5 days   🏃5 ⛰10

in the Siskiyou Wilderness east of Crescent City

Map 2.1, page 71   **BEST (**

You'll be wondering if you're afflicted with a hex or a charm when you take the trip to Devils Punchbowl, set at an elevation of 4,800 feet. The hex? The trail includes a climb of 1,500 feet in two miles that'll have you wheezing like a donkey low on hay. The charm? The first view of Devils Punchbowl is not only drop-dead gorgeous but is a sight you will never forget. It's small but pristine, set in a mountain granite bowl, framed by an imposing back wall—a shrine.

After parking, the first 0.75 mile is easy, a downhill glide on a closed forest service road. After that, a trail is routed through forest and then intersects with Buck Lake Trail (Buck Lake is only 0.1 mile off to the right). Bear left so you stay on Doe Flat Trail, and you will quickly reach Doe Flat and its campsite. Continue past Doe Flat. The trail crosses Doe Creek and continues along the side of Bear Mountain, where you will see the signed junction on your right for Devils Punchbowl. From here, you start the first of several switchbacks up Bear Mountain—a long, forbidding butt-kicker that rises virtually straight up the mountain, roughly 100 switchbacks in all. When you finally top the ridge, the route crosses Devils Creek and leaves the forest behind, crossing bare granite domes. The trail is marked by small stacks of rocks, known as trail ducks. You pass a smaller lake, cross a rise, and then the beautiful, gem-like lake awaits. This place is something of a legend but is visited only by those willing to pay the price of the terrible climb to reach it.

Special note: The entire region surrounding Devils Punchbowl consists of sheets of bare granite. The few campsites here are merely small, flat sleeping spaces on rock. There is no firewood available, so bring a backpacking stove for cooking. Bring sealable plastic bags to carry out waste.

User Groups: Hikers and dogs. No horses or mountain bikes. No wheelchair facilities.

Permits: No permits are required. A campfire permit (free) is required for overnight use. Parking and access are free.

Maps: For a free brochure and hiking guide, write to Smith River National Recreation Area. For a map, ask the U.S. Forest Service for Six Rivers and Klamath National Forest. For a topographic map, ask the USGS for Devils Punchbowl.

Directions: From Crescent City, drive north on US 101 for three miles to U.S. 199. Bear right (east) on U.S. 199 and drive 25 miles to Little Jones Creek Road/Jawbone Road (Forest Road 16). Turn right on Little Jones Creek Road (Forest Road 16) and drive south 9.6 miles. When the road forks, turn sharply left on Forest Road 16N02 and drive five miles to the trailhead, at the end of the road.

Contact: Smith River National Recreation Area, P.O. Box 228, Gasquet, CA 95543, 707/457-3131, www.fs.fed.us/r5; Klamath National Forest, Happy Camp-Oak Knoll Ranger District, P.O. Box 377, 63822 Highway 96, Happy Camp, CA 96039-0377, 530/493-2243, www.fs.fed.us/r5.

6 WILDERNESS FALLS
18.0 mi / 2 days

in the Siskiyou Wilderness east of Crescent City

Map 2.1, page 71

Wilderness Falls is one of the great secrets of northwestern California. It's a true hidden jewel, dramatic and pure, and not only untouched, but largely unseen. This bubbling tower of water, created by Clear Creek, crashes down about 35

feet into a boulder then pounds its way down into a foaming pool that's 100 feet across.

The recommended route is to start on Clear Creek National Recreation Trail out of Youngs Valley (see *Youngs Valley Trail* in this chapter). Follow Clear Creek Trail for about nine miles to the waterfall. The trail features a 600-foot descent to the stream, then a gentle descent the rest of the way. There is an excellent campsite about a quarter of a mile upstream from the falls. It's an easy hike to the waterfall, but the trip back is up all the way and is best started very early in the morning, when the temperature is the coolest.

Wilderness Falls can also be accessed out of Doe Flat (see *Doe Flat Trail* in this chapter), and we've also tried it that way. In late May and June, this route includes a wet, cold, and slippery ford of Clear Creek. In summer, it is a much easier river crossing.

User Groups: Hikers, dogs, and horses. No mountain bikes. No wheelchair facilities.

Permits: A campfire permit (free) is required for overnight use. Parking and access are free.

Maps: For a map, ask the U.S. Forest Service for Six Rivers and Klamath National Forest. For a topographic map, ask the USGS for Devils Punchbowl.

Directions: From Crescent City, drive north on US 101 for three miles to U.S. 199. Bear right (east) on U.S. 199 and drive 32 miles to Forest Road 18N07. Turn right and drive five miles to Forest Road 18N07. Continue on Forest Road 18N07 for 10 miles (twisty) toward Sanger Lake. Just before Sanger Lake, bear right on Forest Road 4803 (signed Youngs Valley Trail) and drive one mile to the trailhead, at the end of the road.

Contact: Klamath National Forest, Happy Camp-Oak Knoll Ranger District, P.O. Box 377, 63822 Highway 96, Happy Camp, CA 96039-0377, 530/493-2243, www.fs.fed.us/r5; Smith River National Recreation Area, P.O. Box 228, Gasquet, CA 95543, 707/457-3131, www.fs.fed.us/r5.

7 ISLAND LAKE TRAIL

12.0 mi / 2 days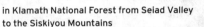

in Smith River National Recreation Area east of Crescent City

Map 2.1, page 71

Island Lake is a mountain bowl framed by the back wall of Jedediah Mountain, a wild, primitive area where threatened spotted owls are more common than hikers. The trailhead is at the Bear Basin area. The hike starts with a walk on a portion of trail that is routed down to the South Fork Smith River, where you'll enter the untouched Siskiyou Wilderness. Enjoy the stream; the hike that follows can have some begging for the memory. The trail intersects with the old route and then rises along a mountain spine, climbing up, up, and up for what seems like an endless three miles. It finally tops a ridge and turns around a bend, where little Island Lake comes into view. A great sense of relief will wash over you.

There are two excellent camps at the lake, set in trees near the lake's shore. The trout are eager to bite, but most are very small, dinker-sized brook trout. A great afternoon side trip is to hike the rim around the lake, which is most easily done in a counterclockwise direction to the top of Jedediah Mountain—a perfect picnic site and a great lookout.

If you hiked to Island Lake back in the day, you will note that the trailhead has been moved a few miles, lengthening the distance to the lake from four miles to six miles. The purpose of this trailhead change is to keep vehicles away from the wilderness, because a fungus that is most commonly introduced from tires on vehicles threatens Port Orford cedars.

User Groups: Hikers, dogs, and horses. No mountain bikes. No wheelchair facilities.

Permits: A campfire permit is required. Parking and access are free.

Maps: For a free brochure and hiking guide, write to Smith River National Recreation Area. For a map, ask the U.S. Forest Service for Six Rivers and Klamath National Forest.

For a topographic map, ask the USGS for Devils Punchbowl.

Directions: From Crescent City, drive north on US 101 for three miles to U.S. 199. Bear right (east) on U.S. 199 and drive 25 miles to Little Jones Creek Road/Jawbone Road (Forest Road 16). Turn right and drive eight miles to Forest Road 16N02. Turn left and drive 2.5 miles to Forest Road 16N10. Turn right. The trailhead is located on your immediate right.

Contact: Smith River National Recreation Area, P.O. Box 228, Gasquet, CA 95543, 707/457-3131, www.fs.fed.us/r5; Klamath National Forest, Happy Camp-Oak Knoll Ranger District, P.O. Box 377, 63822 Highway 96, Happy Camp, CA 96039-0377, 530/493-2243, www.fs.fed.us/r5.

8 SEIAD VALLEY TO OREGON BORDER (PCT)

36.0 mi one-way / 3 days

in Klamath National Forest from Seiad Valley to the Siskiyou Mountains

Map 2.1, page 71

Not many people hike this section of the Pacific Crest Trail (PCT), the northernmost segment in California. But it's a great chunk of trail, whether for a day hike or for the whole duration—all the way to Wards Fork Gap, on the edge of the Rogue Wilderness, in southern Oregon. The ambitious few will head up from the trailhead to the junction of the Boundary National Recreation Trail, a seven-mile trip one-way. The first five miles are a steep climb out of the Klamath River Valley, rising to Upper Devils Peak, which has an elevation of 6,040 feet. This features sensational views to the south of Mount Shasta.

This hike marks the final steps of the 1,700-mile Pacific Crest Trail in California, an epic journey for all, but always classic, even if only sections are enjoyed. If you decide to attempt the south-to-north route, see the *Grider Creek to Seiad Valley (PCT)* hike in this chapter.

User Groups: Hikers, dogs, and horses. No mountain bikes. No wheelchair facilities.

Permits: No permits are required. Parking and access are free.

Maps: A trail information sheet can be obtained by contacting the Happy Camp-Oak Knoll Ranger District. For a map, ask the U.S. Forest Service for Klamath National Forest. For a topographic map, ask the USGS for Seiad Valley.

Directions: From Yreka, take I-5 north to Highway 96. Turn west on Highway 96 and drive approximately 50 miles to Seiad Valley. Continue another mile west on Highway 96 to the trailhead, on the north (right) side. Parking is minimal; park across the highway.

Contact: Klamath National Forest, Happy Camp-Oak Knoll Ranger District, P.O. Box 377, 63822 Highway 96, Happy Camp, CA 96039-0377, 530/493-2243, www.fs.fed.us/r5.

🄴 GRIDER CREEK TO SEIAD VALLEY (PCT)

7.0 mi one-way / 1 day 🏃2 ⛰7

in Klamath National Forest, southeast of Happy Camp to the Grider Creek Trailhead

Map 2.1, page 71

Most hikers use this trailhead to head south into the Marble Mountain Wilderness, not north. For PCT hikers heading south to north, the trail is seven miles one-way, with an additional five miles of road to Seiad Valley on Highway 96. This is an excellent place for PCT hikers to pick up a food stash and dump garbage. You could walk the road, but most try to hitch a ride. The trail here follows Grider Creek, an easy descent northward as the stream pours toward the Klamath River. The only downer is that the last three miles are on a dirt Forest Service road, but for PCT hikers, it's a sign that the next restaurant is not far off. The area features magnificent stands of virgin timber—a mixed conifer forest of cedar, pine, and fir. A good Forest Service campground (Grider Creek Camp) is available about three miles before reaching Seiad Valley.

To pick up the next trail heading for the Oregon border, see the *Seiad Valley to Oregon Border (PCT)* hike in this chapter. If you are hiking this trail in reverse, see the *Etna Summit to Grider Creek (PCT)* hike in this chapter to continue south.

User Groups: Hikers, dogs, and horses. No mountain bikes. No wheelchair facilities.

Permits: A campfire permit (free) is required. Parking and access are free.

Maps: A trail information sheet can be obtained by contacting the Happy Camp-Oak Knoll Ranger District. For a map, ask the U.S. Forest Service for Klamath National Forest. For a topographic map, ask the USGS for Seiad Valley.

Directions: From Yreka, take I-5 north to Highway 96. Turn west on Highway 96 and drive approximately 40 miles to Walker Creek/Grider Creek Road (Forest Road 46N64), located one mile before Seiad Valley. Turn left on Walker Creek Road and drive 50 feet (staying to the left as it runs adjacent to the Klamath River) to Grider Creek Road. Turn right and drive two miles to the trailhead.

Contact: Klamath National Forest, Happy Camp-Oak Knoll Ranger District, P.O. Box 377, 63822 Highway 96, Happy Camp, CA 96039-0377, 530/493-2243, www.fs.fed.us/r5.

🄰 HAYPRESS MEADOWS TRAILHEAD

29.0 mi / 3 days 🏃3 ⛰8

in the Marble Mountain Wilderness near Somes Bar

Map 2.1, page 71   **BEST (**

The Cuddihy Lakes basin is one of the prettiest sections of the Marble Mountain Wilderness. It also is home to one of the largest concentrations of bears anywhere in California. This is a great trip, leading out to One Mile Lake and the Cuddihy Lakes. This area is perfect for backpacking, with beauty, lookouts, and good trail access.

Park at the trailhead (at 4,500 feet), then begin the first two miles of trail, up and across a fir-covered slope of a small peak (a little butt-kicker of a climb). Then the trail descends into Haypress Meadows, a major junction. Turn right and head up Sandy Ridge, which is a long, steady climb. Plan to top the ridge and then camp at Monument Lake, Meteor Lake, One Mile Lake, or Cuddihy Lakes. The view from Sandy Ridge is a sweeping lookout of the Marble Mountains to the east and the Siskiyous to the west, with mountaintop glimpses of Mount Shasta and the Marble Rim.

User Groups: Hikers, dogs, and horses. No mountain bikes. No wheelchair facilities.

Permits: A campfire permit (free) is required for overnight use. Parking and access are free.

Maps: A trail information sheet can be obtained by contacting the Ukonom Ranger District. For a map, ask the U.S. Forest Service for Klamath National Forest or Marble Mountain Wilderness. For a topographic map, ask the USGS for Somes Bar.

Directions: From Willow Creek, at the junction of Highways 299 and 96, take Highway 96 north (twisty at first) for 42 miles to Orleans. Continue eight miles to Somes Bar and Salmon River Road. Turn right on Salmon River Road (Highway 93) and drive 100 feet to a sign that says Camp 3/Haypress Trailhead and Forest Road 15N17 (Offield Mountain Road). Turn left and drive 14.6 miles to Forest Road 15N17E. Turn left and drive 1.5 miles to the access road for Haypress trailhead. Turn left and drive one mile to the trailhead.

Contact: Six Rivers National Forest, Orleans Ranger District, P.O. Box 410, Orleans, CA 95556-0410, 530/627-3291, www.fs.fed.us/r5.

11 SPIRIT LAKE TRAIL

34.0 mi / 4 days   🥾3   ⛰10

in the Marble Mountain Wilderness near Somes Bar

Map 2.1, page 71   **BEST (**

We've hiked to hundreds and hundreds of mountain lakes, and Spirit Lake is one of the prettiest we've ever seen. It sits at the bottom of a mountain bowl encircled by old-growth trees, with a few campsites set at the side of the lake. The Karuk tribe considers this a sacred place. The abundance of wildlife can be remarkable. The far side of the lake is a major deer migration route, an osprey makes regular trips to pluck trout out of the lake for dinner, and the fishing is quite good, especially early in the summer.

Spirit Lake can be the feature destination for a week-long backpack loop, beginning on Haypress Meadows Trail and leading up to Sandy Ridge and then out to the lake, about 17 miles one-way. Most hikers will stop for the night at One Mile or the Cuddihy Lakes on the way out, and that is why those two areas get so much use. Spirit Lake is best visited during the first week of June, when the nights are still cold, the people are few, and the area abounds with fish and deer.

User Groups: Hikers, dogs, and horses. No mountain bikes. No wheelchair facilities.

Permits: A campfire permit (free) is required for overnight use. Parking and access are free.

Maps: A trail information sheet can be obtained by contacting the Ukonom Ranger District. For a map, ask the U.S. Forest Service for Klamath National Forest or Marble Mountain Wilderness. For a topographic map, ask the USGS for Somes Bar.

Directions: From Willow Creek, at the junction of Highways 299 and 96, take Highway 96 north (twisty at first) for 42 miles to Orleans. Continue eight miles to Somes Bar and Salmon River Road. Turn right on Salmon River Road (Highway 93) and drive 100 feet to a sign that says Camp 3/Haypress Trailhead and Forest Road 15N17 (Offield Mountain Road). Turn left and drive 14.6 miles to Forest Road 15N17E. Turn left and drive 1.5 miles to the access road for Haypress trailhead. Turn left and drive one mile to the trailhead.

Contact: Six Rivers National Forest, Orleans Ranger District, P.O. Box 410, Orleans, CA 95556-0410, 530/627-3291, www.fs.fed.us/r5.

12 KELSEY CREEK TRAIL
18.0 mi / 2 days 🥾3 ⛰9

in the Marble Mountain Wilderness
west of Yreka

Map 2.1, page 71

This section of the Kelsey Creek Trail offers many miles of beautiful streamside travel, with Paradise Lake basin as the intended destination for most hikers on this route. The trailhead for this section is set near the confluence of Kelsey Creek and the Scott River, and from there, the trail follows Kelsey Creek upstream. Wildflowers are abundant in the meadows. After four miles and two creek crossings, you'll reach Maple Falls, one of the few waterfalls in the region. The trail continues up the canyon, finally rising to intersect with the Pacific Crest Trail, just below Red Rock. From this junction, hikers have many options. The closest lake is secluded Bear Lake, a pretty spot but, alas, with some tules and mosquitoes. To reach it from the junction requires a short but steep drop into the basin to the immediate west.

User Groups: Hikers, dogs, and horses. No mountain bikes. No wheelchair facilities.

Permits: A campfire permit (free) is required for overnight use. Parking and access are free.

Maps: A trail information sheet can be obtained by contacting the Scott River Ranger District. For a map, ask the U.S. Forest Service for Klamath National Forest or Marble Mountain Wilderness. For topographic maps, ask the USGS for Scott Bar and Grider Valley.

Directions: From Redding, take I-5 to Yreka and the exit for Highway 3/Fort Jones. Take that exit to the stop sign, turn left, and drive a short distance to the lighted intersection. Turn left on Highway 3 and drive 16.5 miles to Fort Jones and Scott River Road. Turn right on Scott River Road and drive 16.8 miles to the Scott River Bridge. Cross it and then turn left immediately, following the road for 0.3 mile. Bear right on another dirt road (do not continue to a second bridge) and drive 0.25 mile to the trailhead.

Contact: Klamath National Forest, Salmon/Scott River Ranger District, 11263 North Highway 3, Fort Jones, CA 96032-9702, 530/468-5351, www.fs.fed.us/r5.

13 PARADISE LAKE TRAIL
4.0 mi / 2.75 hr 🥾3 ⛰8

in the Marble Mountain Wilderness
west of Yreka

Map 2.1, page 71

Paradise Lake, set at an elevation of 5,920 feet, is the easiest lake to reach of the 79 lakes in the Marble Mountain Wilderness. The pretty hike is short enough for a day trip, and it has good lakeside campgrounds if you want to turn your trip into an overnighter. There are also some excellent side trips, including climbing Kings Castle (see the following hike), which tops the mountain rim on the back side of the lake.

From the trailhead (at 4,880 feet), the route quickly enters the designated wilderness, then climbs for nearly two miles (steeply in some areas) and switches back and forth through an old, untouched forest. It then emerges from the trees and rises to a saddle. On the other side is Paradise Lake. It is nestled in a mountain pocket, emerald green and peaceful. Paradise Lake is a mostly shallow lake with few trout, but it does have one deep area. Because the hike to the lake takes only two hours, there are usually campers here all summer long.

User Groups: Hikers, dogs, and horses. No mountain bikes. No wheelchair facilities.

Permits: No permits are required. A campfire permit (free) is required for overnight use. Parking and access are free.

Maps: A trail information sheet can be obtained by contacting the Scott River Ranger District. For a map, ask the U.S. Forest Service for Klamath National Forest or Marble Mountain Wilderness. For topographic maps, ask the USGS for Scott Bar and Marble Mountain.

Directions: From Redding, take I-5 to Yreka and the exit for Highway 3/Fort Jones. Take that exit to the stop sign, turn left, and drive a short distance to the lighted intersection. Turn left on Highway 3 and drive 16.5 miles to Fort Jones. Turn right on Scott River Road and drive 16.8 miles to the turnoff for Indian Scotty Campground. Cross the concrete bridge, bear left on Forest Road 44N45, and drive about five miles. Turn right on an unmarked forest road and drive six miles (signed Paradise Lake) to the trailhead, near the wilderness border.

Contact: Klamath National Forest, Salmon/Scott River Ranger District, 11263 North Highway 3, Fort Jones, CA 96032-9702, 530/468-5351, www.fs.fed.us/r5.

14 KINGS CASTLE TRAIL
5.5 mi / 5.0 hr   🥾4 ⛰10

**in the Marble Mountain Wilderness
west of Yreka**

Map 2.1, page 71

Kings Castle is the imposing perch that sits on the back side of Paradise Lake. From the lake, a half-mile climb tops out at the summit at 7,405 feet. It's a great hike with unforgettable views. You look down at little Paradise Lake as well as far beyond to Northern California's most famous mountain peaks. From the trailhead of Paradise Lake Trail (see previous detailed hike), you make the 1,040-foot climb up to Paradise Lake. From the foot of Paradise Lake, bear to the left and cross the lake's inlet, on the left side. Here you will pick up the route. It climbs up out of the basin to a ridge (great views start here). The trail bears to the left up the back side of the rock monolith. You then gain the peak of Kings Castle by climbing a series of switchbacks up the back side. It is a special trip every step of the way. It's a climb of 2,525 feet from the trailhead. Although not a maintained trail, the route is worn well enough to follow. On the first trip here, this guy didn't see the trail and instead scrambled up the face, bushwhacking it—a difficult ascent, steep all the way, and scrambling up the face. On the top, he was congratulating himself for being such an intrepid

mountaineer, when right then, these two Girl Scouts came bounding up to the summit, easy and happy. "How'd you get here?" he asked. "We just took the trail," one answered. "Trail? What trail?" Guess who the misled guy was: Yep, you guessed it.

User Groups: Hikers only. No dogs, horses, or mountain bikes. No wheelchair facilities.

Permits: No permits are required. A campfire permit (free) is required for overnight use. Parking and access are free.

Maps: A trail information sheet can be obtained by contacting the Scott River Ranger District. For a map, ask the U.S. Forest Service for Klamath National Forest or Marble Mountain Wilderness. For topographic maps, ask the USGS for Scott Bar and Marble Mountain.

Directions: From Redding, take I-5 to Yreka and the exit for Highway 3/Fort Jones. Take that exit to the stop sign, turn left, and drive a short distance to the lighted intersection. Turn left on Highway 3 and drive 16.5 miles to Fort Jones. Turn right on Scott River Road and drive 16.8 miles to the turnoff for Indian Scotty Campground. Cross the concrete bridge, bear left on forest road 44N45, and drive about five miles. Turn right on an unmarked forest road and drive six miles (signed Paradise Lake) to the trailhead near the wilderness border. Hike 1.9 miles to Paradise Lake; bear right and continue another 0.5 mile to Kings Castle.

Contact: Klamath National Forest, Salmon/Scott River Ranger District, 11263 North Highway 3, Fort Jones, CA 96032-9702, 530/468-5351, www.fs.fed.us/r5.

15 MARBLE MOUNTAIN RIM
16.0 mi / 2 days   🥾3 ⛰9

**in the Marble Mountain Wilderness
west of Yreka**

Map 2.1, page 71

Marble isn't usually thought of as a precious stone, but it's gemlike for hikers on this trail. With Marble Valley nearby, climbing the Marble Mountain Rim can be a perfect weekend trip and is easily extended into a longer one. The trailhead at Lovers Camp is probably the most popular in the entire wilderness, especially for packers going by horse into Marble Mountain Wilderness (corrals are available at the trailhead). The route heads up Canyon Creek, a moderate climb, then intersects the Pacific Crest Trail at Marble Valley. This area is very scenic, with lots of deer and wildflowers. Turn left, and the trail crosses the flank of Marble Mountain itself. Once you've arrived, a side trip to the Marble Rim is mandatory. The views are stunning, sweeping in both directions, with steep drop-offs adding to the quiet drama. The rock itself is unlike anything else in Northern California—a mix of black, red, and tan marble, something you'll never forget.

User Groups: Hikers only. No dogs, horses, or mountain bikes. No wheelchair facilities.

Permits: A campfire permit (free) is required for overnight use. Parking and access are free.

Maps: A trail information sheet can be obtained by contacting the Scott River Ranger District. For a map, ask the U.S. Forest Service for Klamath National Forest or Marble Mountain Wilderness. For topographic maps, ask the USGS for Scott Bar and Marble Mountain.

Directions: From Redding, take I-5 to Yreka and the exit for Highway 3/Fort Jones. Take that exit to the stop sign, turn left, and drive a short distance to the lighted intersection. Turn left on Highway 3 and drive 16.5 miles to Fort Jones. Turn right on Scott River Road and drive 16.8 miles to the turnoff for Indian Scotty Campground. Cross the concrete bridge, bear left on Forest Road 44N45, and drive 5.4 miles to Forest Road 43N45. Turn left and drive 1.7 miles to Lovers Camp. Bear right and drive 0.1 mile to the trailhead.

Contact: Klamath National Forest, Salmon/Scott River Ranger District, 11263 North Highway 3, Fort Jones, CA 96032-9702, 530/468-5351, www.fs.fed.us/r5.

16 SKY HIGH LAKES

14.0 mi / 2 days

in the Marble Mountain Wilderness
west of Yreka

Map 2.1, page 71

The Sky High Lakes make for a great overnighter, a seven-mile hike each day, or an inspired one-day in-and-outer. The trip starts at the Canyon Creek trailhead near Lovers Camp. For this trip, take Canyon Creek Trail for about a mile up to a fork, and continue straight (do not turn left and cross Canyon Creek). From here the trail continues to climb, skirting below Marble Mountain, and eventually to Lower Sky High Lake. This is your destination, set below a monster of a rock, Peak 6817. Upper Sky High Lake provides a side jaunt. Note that the trail continues to climb up to the rim and hooks up with the Pacific Crest Trail, making an 18-mile loop trip possible.

User Groups: Hikers, dogs, and horses. No mountain bikes. No wheelchair facilities.

Permits: A campfire permit is required only for hikers planning to camp in the wilderness. Parking and access are free.

Maps: A trail information sheet can be obtained by contacting the Scott River Ranger District. For a map, ask the U.S. Forest Service for Klamath National Forest or Marble Mountain Wilderness. For a topographic map, ask the USGS for Marble Mountain.

Directions: From Redding, take I-5 to Yreka and the exit for Highway 3/Fort Jones. Take that exit to the stop sign, turn left, and drive a short distance to the lighted intersection. Turn left on Highway 3 and drive 16.5 miles to Fort Jones. Turn right on Scott River Road and drive 16.8 miles to the turnoff for Indian Scotty Campground. Cross the concrete bridge, bear left on Forest Road 44N45, and drive 5.4 miles to Forest Road 43N45. Turn left and drive 1.7 miles to Lovers Camp. Bear right and drive 0.1 mile to the Canyon Creek trailhead.

Contact: Klamath National Forest, Salmon/Scott River Ranger District, 11263 North

Highway 3, Fort Jones, CA 96032-9702, 530/468-5351, www.fs.fed.us/r5.

17 SHACKLEFORD CREEK TRAIL

13.0 mi / 2 days 🏃4 ⛰8

in the Marble Mountain Wilderness
west of Yreka

Map 2.1, page 71

Campbell, Cliff, and Summit Lakes are three pretty lakes in the Marble Mountain Wilderness. It is only 5.5 miles to Campbell Lake, reachable via the Shackleford Trail, which makes this a popular destination all summer long. The trail is routed up Shackleford Creek to a basin set just below the Pacific Crest Trail. Here you'll find the series of small mountain lakes.

Note that ambitious trekkers traveling off-trail, cross-country style, can create routes to little Gem, Jewel, and Angel Lakes. Trekking is not for everybody, however, which is why this trip rates a 4. If you want to extend the trip into a loop, you can hike up to the rim of the Pacific Crest Trail, then turn right and go three miles to the Sky High Lakes.

User Groups: Hikers, dogs, and horses. No mountain bikes. No wheelchair facilities.

Permits: A campfire permit is required only for hikers planning to camp in the wilderness. Parking and access are free.

Maps: A trail information sheet can be obtained by contacting the Scott River Ranger District. For a map, ask the U.S. Forest Service for Klamath National Forest or Marble Mountain Wilderness. For a topographic map, ask the USGS for Boulder Peak.

Directions: From Redding, take I-5 to Yreka and the exit for Highway 3/Fort Jones. Take that exit to the stop sign, turn left, and drive a short distance to the lighted intersection. Turn left on Highway 3 and drive 16.5 miles to Fort Jones and Scott River Road. Turn right on Scott River Road and drive seven miles to Quartz Valley Road. Turn left on Quartz Valley Road and drive about four miles to the

sign for Shackleford trailhead and Forest Road 43N21. Turn right and drive 6.5 miles to the trailhead, at the end of the road.

Contact: Klamath National Forest, Salmon/Scott River Ranger District, 11263 North Highway 3, Fort Jones, CA 96032-9702, 530/468-5351, www.fs.fed.us/r5.

18 MULE BRIDGE TRAILHEAD

28.0 mi / 4 days 🏃5 ⛰8

in the Marble Mountain Wilderness
west of Etna

Map 2.1, page 71

The trailhead at Mule Bridge is set alongside the Salmon River, and once you've tightened your backpack, get ready for a long climb up the river drainage. The trail follows the Salmon River all the way up to its headwaters, gaining about 3,500 feet in the process. Plan on climbing for 14 or 15 miles along the river until you start reaching the higher country, where there are many lakeside camps. The trail forks eight miles from the trailhead. The right-hand fork leads to Shelly Meadows and the Pacific Crest Trail.

The main trail continues north for access to Upper Abbotts Camp and many lakes in the upper drainage. This trail ties in with Little North Fork Trail near Hancock Lake. The prettiest glacial-formed lakes in this region are Lake of the Island (12-mile hike), Abbott Lake (13-mile hike), and Lake Ethel (14-mile hike). Even more remote lakes are Wooley Lake, Milne Lake, and Osprey Lake. All of these are hard to reach and require cross-country travel. Several other lakes are in the region, allowing this trek to be extended by several days.

User Groups: Hikers, dogs, and horses. No mountain bikes. No wheelchair facilities.

Permits: A campfire permit (free) is required for campfires and stoves. Parking and access are free.

Maps: A trail information sheet can be obtained by contacting the Salmon Ranger District. For a map, ask the U.S. Forest Service for

Klamath National Forest or Marble Mountain Wilderness. For a topographic map, ask the USGS for Sawyers Bar.

Directions: From Redding, take I-5 to Yreka and the exit for Highway 3/Fort Jones. Take that exit to the stop sign, turn left, and drive a short distance to the lighted intersection. Turn left on Highway 3 and drive southwest 28 miles to Etna. Turn west on Etna-Somes Bar Road (which is Main Street in town) and drive 21 miles to Idlewild Campground. As you enter the campground, take the left fork in the road and continue two miles to the trailhead.

Contact: Klamath National Forest, Salmon/Scott River Ranger District, 11263 North Highway 3, Fort Jones, CA 96032-9702, 530/468-5351, www.fs.fed.us/r5.

19 LITTLE NORTH FORK TRAILHEAD
16.0 mi / 2-3 days

in the Marble Mountain Wilderness near Sawyers Bar

Map 2.1, page 71

Your destination options from this trailhead? There are many: Chimney Rock, Clear Lake, Lily Lake, and Chimney Rock Lake. This trail provides an excellent trip—as long as you don't mind the long grind of a climb to reach the lakes. Like a lot of trails on the edge of the wilderness, this one starts with a long haul out of a river canyon. From the Little North Fork trailhead, start by climbing out toward Chimney Rock, grunting out a rise of about 4,000 feet as you leave the river lowlands and reach the Marble Mountain Wilderness. It's about an eight-mile trip to Clear Lake, a good first day's destination. Although you can simply return the next day, most people will take several days to venture deeper into the wilderness, with 13 lakes and 20 miles of stream in the Upper Abbotts Camp and English Peak areas.

User Groups: Hikers, dogs, and horses. No mountain bikes. No wheelchair facilities.

Permits: A campfire permit (free) is required for campfires and stove. Parking and access are free.

Maps: A trail information sheet can be obtained by contacting the Salmon Ranger District. For a map, ask the U.S. Forest Service for Klamath National Forest or Marble Mountain Wilderness. For a topographic map, ask the USGS for Sawyers Bar.

Directions: From Redding, take I-5 to Yreka and the exit for Highway 3/Fort Jones. Take that exit to the stop sign, turn left, and drive a short distance to the lighted intersection. Turn left on Highway 3 and drive southwest 28 miles to Etna at Sawyers Bar Road. Turn west on Sawyers Bar Road and drive about 25 miles to Sawyers Bar. Continue west on the same road for four miles to Little North Fork Road (Forest Road 40N51). Turn right (north) and drive two miles to the trailhead, at the end of the road.

Contact: Klamath National Forest, Salmon/Scott River Ranger District, 11263 North Highway 3, Fort Jones, CA 96032-9702, 530/468-5351, www.fs.fed.us/r5.

20 HORSE TRAIL RIDGE NATIONAL RECREATION TRAIL
13.0 mi one-way / 2 days

in Six Rivers National Forest on the western edge of the Trinity Alps Wilderness east of Hoopa

Map 2.1, page 71

This is one of the lesser-known national recreation trails in the western United States, but it has many excellent features, and, alas, a few negative ones as well. The six-mile trip to Mill Creek Lakes is set in the least-explored western sector of the Trinity Alps. Although some of the region has been burned severely by wildfire, the Mill Creek Lakes area remains untouched by fire, like an island of green, and makes for a good overnighter.

From the trailhead (at 4,800 feet), the

grades are gradual, with relatively easy elevation climbs and descents. A majority of the forest along the trail was burned in the 1999 Megram fire. While there are many continuous stretches of burned areas, there are also pockets of greenery that the fire missed and ground-level vegetation is making a good comeback. In all, the fire affects 10 miles of this route.

Special note: Do not drink the water available here without first treating it with the best filtration system you can afford.

User Groups: Hikers, dogs, and horses. No mountain bikes. No wheelchair facilities.

Permits: A wilderness permit is required for hikers planning on camping. Parking and access are free.

Maps: For a map, ask the U.S. Forest Service for Six Rivers National Forest. For topographic maps, ask the USGS for Tish Tang Point and Trinity Mountain.

Directions: From the Arcata area, take Highway 299 east to Willow Creek and Highway 96. Turn north on Highway 96 and drive about 12 miles into Hoopa Valley to Big Hill Road. Turn right (east) on Big Hill Road and drive 11 miles to the Six Rivers National Forest border (the road becomes Forest Road 8N01). Continue for 4.5 miles (the road becomes Forest Road 10N02) to the Redcap Trailhead (once off Hoopa reservation land, stay on the chip-seal road).

Contact: Six Rivers National Forest, Lower Trinity Ranger District, P.O. Box 68, Willow Creek, CA 95573, 530/629-2118, www.fs.fed.us/r5.

21 LITTLE SOUTH FORK LAKE TRAIL

13.0 mi / 2 days   🥾 5   ⛰ 10

in the Trinity Alps Wilderness near Cecilville

Map 2.1, page 71

You have to be a little bit crazy to try this trip, and that's why we signed up. This is one of the most difficult lakes to reach in California. Yet

Little South Fork Lake has two idyllic campsites, excellent swimming, and large trout. This route is largely off trail and requires skirting around a big waterfall, but there's no better way in—we've tried three different routes. If you want an easy, clearly marked trail, this is not the hike for you.

From the South Fork trailhead, the trip starts out easy enough. Start by hiking four miles along the Salmon River until reaching the Little South Fork Creek. Turn up the trail upstream along Little South Fork Creek. The trail quickly becomes faint and starts to resemble a game trail—this is where so many people give up. The route eventually dead-ends into Little South Fork Creek. (A faint route on the other side of the creek, the north side, climbs through brush and up the canyon, and we came in that way once from the Caribou Lakes. It is a spiderweb of brush and should be avoided.) From here, there is no trail available; the best route, though still steep and very difficult, is to lateral across the slope on the right side of the stream. It is 1.25 miles upstream to a beautiful, pristine waterfall. Michael Furniss, the world-renown hydrologist, named it Crystal Falls.

To get around the waterfall, loop back and circle it to the right; if you go to the left (which we've tried), you'll add several dreadful hours to the trip scrambling on all fours straight up the slope. Remember that there is no trail and no marked route; this is a cross-country scramble and very slow going. It's another 1.25 miles to the lake, which can take hours of scrambling up and across the wooded slope until you emerge from the forest onto granite plates. Ahead is the lake, beautifully set in a rock bowl framed by a high back wall. There are excellent campsites at each end of the lake.

We hiked into this lake once from Caribou Lakes by climbing the Sawtooth Ridge and dropping down into the basin—the entire route, also off trail, but that creates a potentially hazardous proposition, with some rock climbing and descents with packs. On another trip from Caribou Lakes, we dropped down into Little South Fork Canyon, losing thousands of feet in altitude and in the process getting caught in a brush field like bugs in a spider web. Neither of these other two routes is recommended. In fact, the suggested route is not recommended either. One ranger said we were crazy to include it in the book. He was right, of course.

User Groups: Hikers only. Dogs are permitted but strongly advised against. No horses or mountain bikes. No wheelchair facilities.

Permits: A free wilderness permit is required for hikers planning to camp.

Maps: For a map, ask the U.S. Forest Service for Klamath National Forest or Trinity Alps Wilderness. For a topographic map, ask the USGS for Thompson Peak.

Directions: From Redding, drive north on I-5 for 70 miles. Just past Weed, take the Edgewood exit. At the stop sign, turn left and drive through the underpass to another stop sign. Turn right on Old Highway 99 and drive about six miles to Gazelle. Turn left on Gazelle-Callahan Road and drive 27 miles to Callahan. From Callahan on Highway 3, turn west on Cecilville Road and drive 28 miles to Caribou Road/County Road 1E003 (across from East Fork Campground). Turn left (south) on Caribou Road and drive 3.5 miles to a fork. Bear left at the fork and drive 2.5 miles to the South Fork trailhead.

Contact: Klamath National Forest, Salmon/Scott River Ranger District, 11263 North Highway 3, Fort Jones, CA 96032-9702, 530/468-5351, www.fs.fed.us/r5.

22 GRIZZLY LAKE

**12.0 mi / 2 days
or 38.0 mi / 5 days** 🏃5 ⛰10

in the Trinity Alps Wilderness north of Junction City

Map 2.1, page 71   BEST (

This is a butt-kicker climb to Grizzly Lake, the signature lake in the Trinity Alps. The lake is gorgeous (and we'll get to that), the trek is just plain hard (we'll get to that, too), but the surprise is that despite the extreme difficulty there always seem to be folks here in the summer. You only seem to get it to yourself in the fall, when the nights are cold.

Grizzly Lake is set below awesome Thompson Peak (8,863 feet), with one of the most beautiful wilderness waterfalls anywhere, 80-foot Grizzly Falls, set at the lake's cliff outfall. The lake is so pristine that you can spend hours just looking at it.

There are two ways to get in. Take your pick: From the China Creek trailhead, a butt-kicking six-mile climb with a 5,000-foot elevation gain (with a 1,500-foot canyon descent included on the way); or from the Hobo Gulch trailhead, a moderate grade over the course of 19 miles to make the lake.

Given a choice, most people take the short, butt-kicker route, then cuss at themselves on the way in for doing so. There is almost nothing rewarding about it, and most complete the trip with head down, trying to think about something else. Before you race off to this destination, think long and hard if you really are ready to pay a terrible physical toll to get there. Surprisingly, many do this regardless of the price, and the place gets fairly heavy use.

Or, on the other hand, you could take the longer but more gradual climb from the Hobo Gulch trailhead, set deep in the national forest along Backbone Ridge. On this route, Grizzly Lake is 19 miles away. There's also some forest fire damage along the route. So instead of camping along lakes, hikers camp along pretty streams and flats, taking days to reach the promised land at Grizzly Lake. The trail from Hobo Gulch starts by heading straight north about five miles along the North Fork Trinity River to Rattlesnake Camp, climbing very gently. Cross Rattlesnake Creek, and continue another three miles past the old Morrison Cabin (from the mining days) and on to Pfeiffer Flat. Here the North Fork

Trinity is joined by Grizzly Creek, an attractive backpacking destination. From Pfeiffer Flat, the trail follows Grizzly Creek, rising high toward the Trinity Sawtooth Ridge and requiring an uphill pull to beautiful Grizzly Meadows and then to Grizzly Lake; the final mile is a scramble over a clear hiking route amid rock.

For rock climbers, climbing the lake bowl in a clockwise direction makes for an exciting scramble to Thompson Peak and a perch just below the rock summit; to reach the tip-top of the mountain requires a technical climb.

User Groups: Hikers, dogs, and horses. No mountain bikes. No wheelchair facilities.

Permits: A wilderness permit is required for hikers planning to camp.

Maps: For a map, ask the U.S. Forest Service for Shasta-Trinity National Forest or Trinity Alps Wilderness. For a topographic map, ask the USGS for Thurston Peaks.

Directions: To reach the China Creek trailhead from Redding, drive north on I-5 for 70 miles. Just past Weed, take the Edgewood exit. At the stop sign, turn left and drive through the underpass to another stop sign. Turn right on Old Highway 99 and drive about six miles to Gazelle. Turn left on Gazelle-Callahan Road and drive 27 miles to Callahan and Cecilville Road. Turn west on Cecilville Road and drive 27 miles to Forest Road 37N24. Turn south and drive 3.8 miles to Forest Road 37N07 (it's well signed). Take Forest 37N07 and drive six miles to the trailhead.

To reach the Hobo Gulch trailhead from Weaverville, drive 13 miles west on Highway 299 to Helena and East Fork Road. Turn north on East Fork Road (County Road 421) and drive 3.9 miles to Hobo Gulch Road. Turn left on Hobo Gulch Road (Forest Road 34N07Y) and drive 12 miles to the Hobo Gulch trailhead, located at Hobo Gulch Campground, at the end of the road.

Contact: Shasta-Trinity National Forest, Weaverville Ranger Station, P.O. Box 1190, 210 Main Street, Weaverville, CA 96093, 530/623-2121, www.fs.fed.us/r5.

23 TREE OF HEAVEN TRAIL
0.5 mi / 0.5 hr   👫1 ⛰8

on the Klamath River in Klamath National Forest northwest of Yreka

Map 2.2, page 72

The trail out of the Tree of Heaven Campground provides one of the few streamside trails anywhere along the Klamath River. It once extended 2.5 miles to a fishing spot at the west end of the campground, but has since become completely overgrown. This level, wheelchair-accessible trail heads downstream along the Klamath, and is also an interpretive trail on neo-tropical bird migrations. Visit in fall for berry picking. The Tree of Heaven River access is also a good take-out point for rafters and drift boaters making the all-day run down from Iron Canyon Dam.

User Groups: Hikers, dogs, horses, and mountain bikes. No wheelchair facilities.

Permits: No permits are required. Parking and access are free.

Maps: For a map, ask the U.S. Forest Service for Klamath National Forest. For a topographic map, ask the USGS for Badger Mountain.

Directions: From Yreka, drive north on I-5 for 10 miles to the Highway 96 exit. Turn west on Highway 96 and drive about five miles. Look for the Tree of Heaven Campground, on the left. The trailhead is located at the west end of the campground.

Contact: Klamath National Forest, Headquarters, 1312 Fairlane Road, Yreka, CA 96097 530/842-6131, www.fs.fed.us/r5.

24 JUANITA LAKE TRAIL
1.75 mi / 1.0 hr   👫1 ⛰7

in Klamath National Forest east of Yreka

Map 2.2, page 72

Not many people know about Juanita Lake, including many Siskiyou County residents, but once they find out, on their first visit, they often will take this easy loop trail around the lake to get a feel for the place. The lake is set in a mixed conifer forest, though few trees here are large. Wildlife in the area includes osprey and bald eagles. In the last hour of light during summer, both osprey and eagles occasionally make a fishing trip to the lake. Juanita Lake is a small lake that provides lakeside camping and fishing for brook trout—it's stocked with 2,000 per year. The small fishing piers are wheelchair accessible.

A good side trip is driving on the forest road up to Ball Mountain, about two miles southwest of the lake, for great views of Mount Shasta from the 7,786-foot summit.

User Groups: Hikers and leashed dogs. No mountain bikes or horses. The fishing piers are wheelchair accessible.

Permits: No permits are required. Parking and access are free.

Maps: For a map, ask the U.S. Forest Service for Klamath National Forest. For a topographic map, ask the USGS for Panther Rock.

Directions: From Redding, take I-5 north about 60 miles to the exit for Central Weed/Klamath Falls (Highway 97). Take that exit to the stop sign, turn right and drive 0.5 mile to the intersection with Highway 97. Bear right (north) on Highway 97 and drive 35 miles to Ball Mountain Road. Turn left and drive two miles to a signed turnoff for Juanita Lake. Turn right and drive about three miles to the lake (it's well signed). The trailhead is near the boat dock at the campground.

Contact: Klamath National Forest, Goosenest Ranger District, 37805 Highway 97, Macdoel, CA 96058, 530/398-4391, www.fs.fed.us/r5.

25 DEER MOUNTAIN
4.0 mi / 2.25 hr   🥾2   ⛰️7

in Klamath National Forest north of Mount Shasta

Map 2.2, page 72

Deer Mountain is the second in a line of small peaks set on the north side of Mount Shasta that extend all the way to the Medicine Lake wildlands. North from Shasta, the first peak is the Whaleback, at an elevation of 8,528 feet,

and the second is Deer Mountain, at 7,006 feet. Starting elevation at the parking area is 6,200 feet, and from here you climb 800 feet through forest consisting of various pines and firs to gain the summit. This route gets very little use, even though it's easy to reach and the destination is a mountaintop. Most out-of-towners visiting this area are attracted to the trails on Mount Shasta instead, and most locals just plain overlook it. These slopes get heavy use by hunters, usually from late September through late October.

User Groups: Hikers, dogs, horses, and mountain bikes. No wheelchair facilities.

Permits: No permits are required. Parking and access are free.

Maps: For a map, ask the U.S. Forest Service for Klamath National Forest. For a topographic map, ask the USGS for Whaleback.

Directions: From Redding, take I-5 north about 60 miles to the exit for Central Weed/Klamath Falls (Highway 97). Take that exit to the stop sign, turn right and drive 0.5 mile to the intersection with Highway 97. Bear right (north) on Highway 97 and drive about 15 miles to Deer Mountain Road/Forest Road 19 (Forest Road 42N12). Turn right and drive four miles to Deer Mountain Snowmobile Park and Forest Road 44N23. Turn left on Forest Road 44N23 and drive about two miles. There is no designated trailhead; park off the road and hike cross-country to the top of the mountain. Forest Road 43N69 loops around the base of the mountain; you may also hike from anywhere along that road.

Contact: Klamath National Forest, Goosenest Ranger District, 37805 Highway 97, Macdoel, CA 96058, 530/398-4391, www.fs.fed.us/r5.

26 THE WHALEBACK
3.0 mi / 2.5 hr   🥾3   ⛰️8

in Klamath National Forest north of Mount Shasta

Map 2.2, page 72

After you pass Mount Shasta on I-5, driving north, look off to your right and you'll see a large, humplike mountain that sits directly north of Shasta. It looks like a huge volcanic bump that was born when Shasta was active. That's because it is. This is the Whaleback, 8,528 feet high. It provides a hike with a pay-off view at the top, and a surprise: a large crater. The Whaleback Summit is actually a volcanic cinder cone with a collapsed center. This interesting geology, along with the unsurpassed view of Mount Shasta to the south, makes this a first-rate hike. Yet almost nobody tries it, most likely because they don't realize how near you can drive to the top, or because there is no formal trail. After parking at the gate, you just hike cross-country style up to the rim; it's steep all the way. The 1.5-mile hike is a scramble only in a few places. In the process, you'll climb 1,100 feet, from a starting elevation of 7,400 feet, to Whaleback Rim.

User Groups: Hikers, dogs, horses, and mountain bikes. No wheelchair facilities.

Permits: No permits are required. Parking and access are free.

Maps: For a map, ask the U.S. Forest Service for Klamath National Forest. For a topographic map, ask the USGS for Whaleback.

Directions: From Redding, take I-5 north about 60 miles to the exit for Central Weed/Klamath Falls (Highway 97). Take that exit to the stop sign, turn right and drive 0.5 mile to the intersection with Highway 97. Bear right (north) on Highway 97 and drive 15 miles to Deer Mountain Road. Turn right on Deer Mountain Road and drive four miles to Deer Mountain Snowmobile Park. Drive east on Deer Mountain Road/Forest Road 19 (Forest Road 42N12) for three miles to Forest Road 42N24. Turn right on Forest Road 42N24 and drive three miles to a gate. Park and hike in. There is no designated trail; you must hike cross-country from the road. The peak is about 1.5 miles from the gate.

Contact: Klamath National Forest, Goosenest Ranger District, 37805 Highway 97, Macdoel, CA 96058, 530/398-4391, www.fs.fed.us/r5.

27 WHITNEY FALLS TRAILHEAD

3.4 mi / 2.5 hr

on the northwest slope of Mount Shasta

Map 2.2, page 72

Mount Shasta, at 14,179 feet, is the most prominent landmark in Northern California, and it's well known for its outstanding summit routes on its southern slopes. What is less known, however, is that there are four trailheads set on Shasta's northern and eastern foothills that grant hikers choice day walks and mountaineers a starting point for difficult climbs over glaciers to the top. Those four forgotten trailheads are at Whitney Falls, North Gate, Brewer Creek, and Clear Creek.

The Whitney Falls trailhead is at about 5,600 feet, and from it, the trail heads uphill (for the most part, something of a nightmare). This trailhead and first mile were buried under a flow of mud and debris from a flash flood. Although interesting to geologists, it requires hikers to negotiate rocks, boulders, logs, and deep erosion channels. Look for the faint trail on the right side of the flow. Follow this trail uphill until you pass through a small gorge, then look for the trail heading out of the drainage. The trail spans 1.6 miles to a fork at 6,400 feet, and for day hikers the best bet is turning right and climbing partially up the treeless slope for a fantastic lookout and picnic site. Here you'll discover hidden Whitney Falls, a 250-foot waterfall, with its thin, silvery wisp tumbling through a narrow chute in a dramatic ashen gorge. It takes perfect timing to see this waterfall at anything more than a trickle. The view to the north of Shasta Valley is outstanding, highlighted by the series of hummocks, which are actually chunks of Shasta's former summit that were carried here like miniature hilltops in a massive lava flow after Shasta's last eruption, 600 years ago.

Special notes: If you turn left at the fork instead, you'll venture through forest, then up through another gutted stream drainage. The trail ends, and mountaineers will have to pass Coquette Falls, and then near the peak at the Bolam Glacier, in order to make the summit. Safety gear and expert climbing skills are required. Also note that this trailhead was long called the Bolam Creek trailhead. That was changed in 2002. A new Bolam Creek Trail and route up the north flank of Shasta is planned when funds and manpower become available.

User Groups: Hikers only. No dogs, horses, or mountain bikes. No wheelchair facilities.

Permits: Parking and access are free. A free wilderness permit is required for both day use and overnight use; $30 summit permit required for hikers climbing over 10,000 feet in elevation. All climbers are required to pack out waste and must bring a pack-out bag.

Maps: For a map, ask the U.S. Forest Service for Shasta-Trinity National Forest or Mount Shasta Wilderness. For a topographic map, ask the USGS for Mount Shasta.

Directions: From I-5, drive to the Central Weed/Klamath Falls (Highway 97) exit. Take that exit and drive through Weed to Highway 97. Turn right and drive 11 miles to Bolam Road (Forest Road 43N21), which is usually unsigned. (If you reach County Road A12 on the left, you have gone 0.25 mile too far.) Drive on Bolam Road for four miles toward the mountain (Mount Shasta), crossing the railroad tracks and continuing to the trailhead, at the end of the road. A high-clearance vehicle is required.

Contact: Shasta-Trinity National Forest, Mount Shasta Ranger District, 204 West Alma, Mount Shasta, CA 96067, 530/926-4511, www.fs.fed.us/r5; Fifth Season Climbing Report, 530/926-5555; Mount Shasta Avalanche and Climbing Hotline, 530/926-9613 or www.shastaavalanche.com; Shasta Mountain Guides, 530/926-9613 or www.shastaguides.com.

28 NORTH GATE TRAILHEAD
4.0 mi / 2.75 hr   👣 3   ⛰ 8

on the north slope of Mount Shasta

Map 2.2, page 72

The North Gate trailhead, set at about 7,000 feet, is one of Mount Shasta's most obscure and least-used trails. It sits on the north flank of Shasta, just below a mountain mound called North Gate. The route skirts this mound, following a small stream uphill for 1.6 miles; then farther along, the trail deteriorates and disappears as it nears tree line at 8,400 feet. From here, most day hikers will climb another 400 feet to the source of the creek, a small spring, and have lunch while enjoying the view to the north.

Special note: Mountain climbers who use this route to climb to the Shasta Summit will discover the going is quite easy at first after leaving tree line. The trip then becomes very steep, difficult, and dangerous, whether via Bolam or Hotlum Glacier. This route is only for experienced mountain climbers who are aware of the extreme risks of crossing steep, sheer glaciers.

User Groups: Hikers only. No dogs, horses, or mountain bikes. No wheelchair facilities.

Permits: Parking and access are free. A free wilderness permit is required for both day use and overnight use; $30 summit permit required for hikers climbing over 10,000 feet in elevation. All climbers are required to pack out waste and must bring a pack-out bag.

Maps: For a map, ask the U.S. Forest Service for Shasta-Trinity National Forest or Mount Shasta Wilderness. For a topographic map, ask the USGS for Mount Shasta.

Directions: From I-5, drive to the Central Weed/Klamath Falls (Highway 97) exit. Take that exit and drive through Weed to Highway 97. Turn right and drive 13.5 miles to Military Pass Road (Forest Road 19). Turn right and drive 4.5 miles to a fork with Forest Road 42N16 (Andesite Logging Road). Bear right and drive four miles to the parking area, at the end of the road.

Contact: Shasta-Trinity National Forest, Mount Shasta Ranger District, 204 West Alma, Mount Shasta, CA 96067, 530/926-4511, www.fs.fed.us/r5; Fifth Season Climbing Report, 530/926-5555; Mount Shasta Avalanche and Climbing Hotline, 530/926-9613 or www.shastaavalanche.com; Shasta Mountain Guides, 530/926-9613 or www.shastaguides.com.

²⁹ BLACK BUTTE TRAIL
5.0 mi / 3.5 hr   🏃4 ⛰8

in Shasta-Trinity National Forest between I-5 and Mount Shasta

Map 2.2, page 72

Anybody who has cruised I-5 north to Oregon and gawked in astonishment at Mount Shasta has inevitably seen Black Butte right alongside the highway. That's right, it's that barren cinder cone set between the highway and Mount Shasta, and it can pique a traveler's curiosity. The trail is routed right to the top and can answer all of your questions. But you may not like all of the answers. Over the course of 2.5 miles, you'll climb 1,845 feet—much of it steep, most of it rocky, and in the summer, all of it hot and dry. Shade is nonexistent. There are only two rewards. One is claiming the summit, at 6,325 feet, where you'll find the foundation of an old U.S. Forest Service lookout and great 360-degree views; the other is that the hike is an excellent warm-up for people who are planning to climb Mount Shasta. (That is, providing you don't need a week to recover.) This trip is actually best done on a warm summer night under a full moon.

User Groups: Hikers and dogs. No horses or mountain bikes. No wheelchair facilities.

Permits: No permits are required.

Maps: A trail information sheet is available by contacting the Mount Shasta Ranger District. For a map, ask the U.S. Forest Service for Shasta-Trinity National Forest. For a topographic map, ask the USGS for Mount Shasta city.

Directions: From Redding, take I-5 north to the exit for Central Mount Shasta. Take that exit to the stop sign. Turn right and drive one mile east on Lake Street, and then bear left on Washington Drive (it merges, and then Washington Drive becomes Everitt Memorial Highway). Continue on Washington/Everitt Memorial Highway (past the high school) for about two miles, and look for the sign for Spring Hill Plantation (on the right) and Forest Road 41N18 (on the left). Turn left on Forest Road 41N18/Ash Flat (a gravel road), drive about 200 yards, and bear right, continuing on Forest Road 41N18 for 2.5 miles. After the road crosses under the overhead power line, turn left on Forest Road 41N18A (Black Butte Road) and drive 0.75 mile to the trailhead. Parking is very limited; be sure to park off the road.

Contact: Shasta-Trinity National Forest, Mount Shasta Ranger District, 204 West Alma, Mount Shasta, CA 96067, 530/926-4511, www.fs.fed.us/r5.

³⁰ SAND FLAT TRAILHEAD
3.4 mi / 2.75 hr   🏃3 ⛰8

on the southern slope of Mount Shasta

Map 2.2, page 72

The hike from Sand Flat to Horse Camp, a distance of 1.7 miles, will give you a good taste of the Mount Shasta experience, and you're likely to savor the flavors. Many who make this day hike are compelled to return to climb all the way to the top.

Sand Flat provides a good shaded parking area to start from, at a 6,800-foot elevation. The trail immediately takes off uphill—gradually at first, but then it becomes quite steep. At 7,360 feet, it intersects with Bunny Flat Trail and then continues rising through the forest. Along the way are amazing examples of how avalanches have knocked down entire sections of forest. When you reach Horse Camp, at 7,800 feet, nearing timberline, you'll find many rewards. The first is springwater flowing continuously out of a piped fountain near the Sierra Hut; it's perhaps the best-tasting water in the world. The second is the foreboding view of Red Bank, which forms the mountain rim above Horse Camp. The third is the opportunity to hike up a short way above tree line for the sweeping views to the south of Castle Crags and Lake Siskiyou. After taking the first steps on Summit Trail, you'll likely yearn to keep going all the way to the very top of this magic mountain. If you wish to hike Summit Trail, see the following hike out of Bunny Flat trailhead.

User Groups: Hikers only. No dogs, horses, or mountain bikes. No wheelchair facilities.

Permits: Parking and access are free. A free wilderness permit is required for both day use and overnight use; a $30 summit permit is required for hikers climbing over 10,000 feet in elevation. All climbers are required to pack out waste and must bring a pack-out bag.

Maps: For a map, ask the U.S. Forest Service for Shasta-Trinity National Forest or Mount Shasta Wilderness. For a topographic map, ask the USGS for Mount Shasta.

Directions: From Redding, take I-5 north to the exit for Central Mount Shasta. Take that exit to the stop sign. Turn right and drive one mile east on Lake Street, and then bear left on Washington Drive (it merges, and then Washington Drive becomes Everitt Memorial Highway). Continue on Washington/Everitt Memorial Highway (past the high school) for eight miles to Sand Flat Loop (Forest Road 41N60). Turn left and drive a short distance to the trailhead.

Contact: Shasta-Trinity National Forest, Mount Shasta Ranger District, 204 West Alma, Mount Shasta, CA 96067, 530/926-4511, www.fs.fed.us/r5; Fifth Season Climbing Report, 530/926-5555; Mount Shasta Avalanche and Climbing Hotline, 530/926-9613 or www.shastaavalanche.com; Shasta Mountain Guides, 530/926-9613 or www.shastaguides.com.

31 SHASTA SUMMIT TRAIL

14 mi / 1.5 days 🚶5 ⛰10

on the southern slope of Mount Shasta in the Shasta-Trinity National Forest

Map 2.2, page 72 | BEST (

The hike to the top of Mount Shasta is a great challenge, an ascent of 7,000 feet over ice, snow, and rock while trying to suck what little oxygen you can out of the thin air. It may be the greatest adventure in the West that most people have an honest chance of achieving. The primary dangers are from tumbling boulders and bad weather (which stops half the people who try the climb), including high winds on top in May and June. Yet most hikers in good condition who start the trip very early and have the proper equipment can summit, especially from mid-July through August, when the weather is benign. Early? You should depart from Bunny Flat by 3 A.M., or hike in a day early, set up a base camp at Horse Camp (at tree line), and start no later than 4 A.M. Equipment? A daypack with warm clothes, a windbreaker, two canteens of water, food, and an ice ax and crampons are mandatory. Refill your canteen wherever you find a rivulet of water (it's occasionally possible at Red Bank); rangers recommend using a water filter.

It's an absolute must to make an early start. In the hot summer months, towering cumulus clouds sometimes form on Mount Shasta during the afternoon, and by then you'll want to be making the trip down. If towering cumulonimbus begin forming by noon, intense thunderstorms are possible by mid-afternoon.

The trip starts out of Bunny Flat at 6,900 feet, leads through a forest of Shasta red firs, climbs to where the trail intersects with the route out of Sand Flat, then turns right and rises to Horse Camp, at an elevation of 7,800 feet and a distance of 1.8 miles. It is a must to fill your canteens here. After filling your canteens at the spring, start hiking Summit Trail. Make your first steps across a series of large stones called Olberman's Causeway. From here, the trail quickly rises above timberline, gaining 1,000 feet per mile for six miles, and after a short time, it becomes a faint path. Often this is where the snow and ice start, and you must stop and strap your crampons onto your boots. The walking is easy with crampons. The trail climbs up Avalanche Gulch, and some people stop to make trail camps at a flat spot called Helen Lake, at 10,440 feet. Hikers not acclimated to high altitudes may begin experiencing some dizziness, but there's no relief in sight. At this point, the hike gets steeper (about a 35-degree slope), and some give up before reaching Red Bank—a huge, red, volcanic outcrop at about 12,500 feet. At Red Bank you'll need your ice ax in order to pull your way through a narrow and steep rock/ice chute, where a slip is certain without crampons.

When you emerge atop Red Bank, you are nearly 13,000 feet high, at the foot of a glacier field and Misery Hill, named so because it's a long, slow climb—through snow in spring and scree in summer. It's a myth that a lot of people actually mistake it for the peak—if you were that off base, you'd never make it this far. Once atop Misery Hill, you'll see the true Shasta Summit, a massive pinnacle of lava that seems to jut straight up into the air. Cross a sun-cupped glacier field to reach the pinnacle and there you will see the trail routed up to the top. With a final push, follow the trail, grabbing rocks to help pull you up and sucking the thin air, and with a few last steps, you'll be on top, at 14,179 feet. On clear days you can see hundreds of miles in all directions, and the sky is a deeper cobalt blue than you ever imagined. On top, you'll sign your name in a logbook in an old rusted metal box, then take in the grand wonders surrounding you. It's a remarkable trip, one that can inspire some people to keep their bodies in good enough shape to make the trip every year.

All hikers must pack out their waste. Special waste pack-out bags are available at no charge at the trailhead and at the Mount Shasta Ranger Station in Mount Shasta.

The biggest danger and largest number of injuries on Mount Shasta come not from falling, but from being hit by tumbling boulders. In fact, our former research assistant, Robyn Brewer, was struck in the foot by a boulder in her first attempt at climbing Shasta. She was hit so hard that it knocked her hiking boot off, breaking her foot and requiring an emergency helicopter airlift out for medical treatment. Always keep a good distance between you and your hiking partners, don't hike in a vertical line, and if a rock comes bouncing down, always shout, "Rock! Rock!" Some guides recommend wearing helmets. By the way, Robyn returned to Mount Shasta the following two years and made it to the top on both trips.

The mountain is best hiked when it still has a good coating of snow and ice, which provide excellent footing with crampons. When the snow and ice melt off in late fall, tromping through the small volcanic rocks is like slogging in mushy sand.

Drink lots of water. In high altitudes, dehydration is a common problem and can result in early exhaustion and extreme vulnerability to mountain sickness.

User Groups: Hikers only. No dogs, horses, or mountain bikes. No wheelchair facilities.

Permits: Parking and access are free. A free wilderness permit is required for both day use and overnight use; a $30 summit permit required for hikers climbing over 10,000 feet in elevation. All climbers are required to pack out waste and must bring a pack-out bag.

Maps: For a map, ask the U.S. Forest Service for Shasta-Trinity National Forest or Mount Shasta Wilderness. For a topographic map, ask the USGS for Mount Shasta.

Directions: From Redding, take I-5 north to the exit for Central Mount Shasta. Take that exit to the stop sign. Turn right and drive one mile east on Lake Street, and then bear left on Washington Drive (it merges, and then Washington Drive becomes Everitt Memorial Highway). Continue on Washington/Everitt Memorial Highway (past the high school) for

10 miles to Bunny Flat. As you drive in, the trailhead is on the left.

Contact: Shasta-Trinity National Forest, Mount Shasta Ranger District, 204 West Alma, Mount Shasta, CA 96067, 530/926-4511, www.fs.fed.us/r5; Fifth Season Climbing Report, 530/926-5555; Mount Shasta Avalanche and Climbing Hotline, 530/926-9613 or www.shastaavalanche.com; Shasta Mountain Guides, 530/926-9613 or www.shastaguides.com.

32 GRAY BUTTE

2.8 mi / 1.75 hr 🏃2 △10

from Ski Bowl on the southern slope of Mount Shasta in Mount Shasta Wilderness

Map 2.2, page 72   **BEST (**

This is a great day hike—easy, unique, and with a great pay-off for those who don't mind a short rock climb to a perch atop Gray Butte. Start at the old Ski Bowl, on the right of the road at the Squaw Creek Trailhead (a mile past Panther Meadows and near the end of paved, two-lane Everitt Memorial Highway). This hike is a short one, from Ski Bowl to Gray Butte and back.

From the trailhead, head southeast on a clear route across a volcanic scree, just above tree line. You'll see a sculpted volcanic valley called The Gate. Some mountain visitors consider this to be the mountain's sacred portal to the spiritual dimension. Gray Butte looms above your right. Reaching the top (at 8,119 feet) requires a scramble over sharp-edged volcanic rock (if you wear rings on your fingers, they will scuff the exposed bottom side). But it is well worth it: There is a perfect lookout to the south, with Castle Crags, Mount Lassen, and the drop-off in the Sacramento Valley all prominent.

User Groups: Hikers only. Dogs are allowed at Gray Butte, but not beyond and are not advised. No horses or mountain bikes. No wheelchair facilities.

Permits: Parking and access are free. A free wilderness permit is required for both day use and overnight use; $30 summit permit required for hikers climbing over 10,000 feet in elevation. All climbers are required to pack out waste and must bring a pack-out bag.

Maps: For a map, ask the U.S. Forest Service for Shasta-Trinity National Forest or Mount Shasta Wilderness. For a topographic map, ask the USGS for Mount Shasta.

Directions: From Redding, take I-5 north to the exit for Central Mount Shasta. Take that exit to the stop sign. Turn right and drive one mile east on Lake Street, and then bear left on Washington Drive (it merges, and then Washington Drive becomes Everitt Memorial Highway.) Continue on Washington/Everitt Memorial Highway (past the high school) for 13.5 miles (past Bunny Flat and Panther Meadows) to the trailhead on the right.

Contact: Shasta-Trinity National Forest, Mount Shasta Ranger District, 204 West Alma, Mount Shasta, CA 96067, 530/926-4511, www.fs.fed.us/r5; Fifth Season Climbing Report, 530/926-5555; Mount Shasta Avalanche and Climbing Hotline, 530/926-9613 or www.shastaavalanche.com; Shasta Mountain Guides, 530/926-9613 or www.shastaguides.com.

33 OLD SKI BOWL TO GREEN BUTTE

2.5 mi / 2.0 hr 🏃3 △9

on the southern slope of Mount Shasta

Map 2.2, page 72

One of the great hikes on Mount Shasta is climbing from the Old Ski Bowl lodge site up to Green Butte. At 7,800 feet and set just above timberline, it's the highest drive-to trailhead on Mount Shasta. That means the entire route crosses a volcanic slope, with great views every step of the way and leading to a unique destination as well. Green Butte, a huge rock outcrop set at 9,193 feet, is a perfect perch.

At the parking area, there's a clear route (though it's unsigned) that leads up toward

Green Butte, which is also clearly obvious just a mile away. But while the trip is short, it's very steep, with a 1,300-foot elevation gain. Along the way, a great bonus is a natural spring set about halfway up the butte; be sure to find it and fill your canteen with this sweet-tasting springwater. Although Green Butte is the destination of most visitors here, the hiking route continues to 9,600 feet before disintegrating in the lava rubble and snow. The Old Ski Bowl is one of the legendary spots on Shasta. It was here that a developer desecrated Shasta wildlands by building a ski area above tree line. Well, nature gives, and nature takes back. With no trees to hold snow in place, the old mountain wiped out the ski lifts with an avalanche. Ironically, in the mid-1990s, a new ski area was proposed at the same spot. The week before the decision was made, another avalanche pounded through, clearing a giant swath of trees and wiping out an area right where the lodge had been proposed. Now again, the Shasta Wilderness is untouched by the hand of mankind, rising like a diamond in a field of coal.

User Groups: Hikers only. Dogs are permitted in Old Ski Bowl, but not beyond into Mount Shasta Wilderness. No horses or mountain bikes. No wheelchair facilities.

Permits: Parking and access are free. A free wilderness permit is required for both day use and overnight use; $30 summit permit required for hikers climbing over 10,000 feet in elevation. All climbers are required to pack out waste and must bring a pack-out bag.

Maps: For a map, ask the U.S. Forest Service for Shasta-Trinity National Forest or Mount Shasta Wilderness. For a topographic map, ask the USGS for Mount Shasta.

Directions: From Redding, take I-5 north to the exit for Central Mount Shasta. Take that exit to the stop sign. Turn right and drive one mile east on Lake Street, and then bear left on Washington Drive (it merges, and then Washington Drive becomes Everitt Memorial Highway). Continue on Washington/Everitt Memorial Highway (past the high school) for 13.5 (past Bunny Flat) to parking and the trailhead.

Contact: Shasta-Trinity National Forest, Mount Shasta Ranger District, 204 West Alma, Mount Shasta, CA 96067, 530/926-4511, www.fs.fed.us/r5; Fifth Season Climbing Report, 530/926-5555; Mount Shasta Avalanche and Climbing Hotline, 530/926-9613 or www.shastaavalanche.com; Shasta Mountain Guides, 530/926-9613 or www.shastaguides.com.

34 BREWER CREEK TRAILHEAD
4.2 mi / 3.0 hr   👣 3   ⛰ 9

on the northeast slope of Mount Shasta

Map 2.2, page 72

It's so quiet here that you can practically hear the wildflowers bloom. We've hiked the north slope of Shasta out of the Brewer Creek trailhead several times and have never seen another person. The trip is a perfect day hike. The trailhead is set near Brewer Creek (at 7,200 feet), hence the name. After a short walk through a section of forest that was selectively logged many years ago, you'll enter the Shasta Wilderness and be surrounded by old-growth firs, many scraggly from enduring harsh winters and the short growing season. Here the trail climbs more. It's a steady climb up through forest, with gradual switchbacks as it goes. When you near tree line, at 7,700 feet, the trail turns to the left and begins to lateral across the mountain. It's 2.1 miles to timberline from the trailhead, and most people hike to this point, then turn back. However, you can add an easy mile or two by climbing a wide, volcanic slope with good footing all the way, and rising to 9,500 feet. This is a great spot for a picnic, providing nice views to the north and also perhaps inspiring dreams of the day you'll next climb all the way to the top of Shasta.

Special note: Mountaineers who try to climb Shasta from this trailhead have only one good route from the point where the trail meets tree line, which is to head to the right up and over Hotlum Glacier. This route is extremely difficult, very steep, and dangerous.

User Groups: Hikers only. No dogs, horses, or mountain bikes. No wheelchair facilities.

Permits: Parking and access are free. A free wilderness permit is required for both day use and overnight use; $30 summit permit required for hikers climbing over 10,000 feet in elevation. All climbers are required to pack out waste and must bring a pack-out bag.

Maps: For a map, ask the U.S. Forest Service for Shasta-Trinity National Forest or Mount Shasta Wilderness. For a topographic map, ask the USGS for Mount Shasta.

Directions: From Redding, take I-5 north for 47 miles to the Highway 89/McCloud-Reno exit. Bear right on Highway 89 and drive nine miles to McCloud, then continue for another 2.8 miles to Pilgrim Creek Road. Turn left on Pilgrim Creek Road (Forest Road 13) and drive 7.1 miles to Forest Road 19 (Sugar Pine Butte Road). Turn left and drive 0.9 mile to Forest Road 42N02. Turn left and drive two miles to Forest Road 42N10. Turn left and drive two miles to the trailhead parking area.

Contact: Shasta-Trinity National Forest, Mount Shasta Ranger District, 204 West Alma, Mount Shasta, CA 96067, 530/926-4511, www.fs.fed.us/r5; McCloud Ranger District, 530/964-2184. A 24-hour climbing report is available by calling 530/926-5555.

35 MUD CREEK FALLS
2.0 mi / 1.5 hr   👤3 ⛰8

on the southeast slope of Mount Shasta

Map 2.2, page 72

A short walk on the remote southeast flank of Mount Shasta can provide entry to a land of enchantment. It features deep canyons, views of glaciers and Mount Shasta's prettiest waterfall. The drive in is circuitous but well signed, and it's a surprise to ever find other cars parked at the trailhead. The hike starts on an old overgrown jeep road. It slowly emerges from a sparse forest of Shasta red fir and then climbs to the eastern edge of the dramatic Mud Creek Canyon, at about 7,000 feet in elevation. From here, most hikers climb on for another 15 minutes, arriving at an overlook viewpoint of the waterfall at the bottom of the canyon. The waterfall, best viewed with binoculars, is perhaps 125 feet high. It's wide, and silver, but distant. This area is rich in natural history—the canyon was carved by a glacier and is still fed with water from the towering, fractured Konwakiton Glacier, which runs the color of volcanic silt.

User Groups: Hikers only. No dogs, horses, or mountain bikes. No wheelchair facilities.

Permits: Parking and access are free. A free wilderness permit is required for both day use and overnight use; $30 summit permit required for hikers climbing over 10,000 feet in elevation. All climbers are required to pack out waste and must bring a pack-out bag.

Maps: For a map, ask the U.S. Forest Service for Shasta-Trinity National Forest or Mount Shasta Wilderness. For a topographic map, ask the USGS for Mount Shasta.

Directions: From Redding, take I-5 north for 47 miles to the Highway 89/McCloud-Reno exit. Bear right on Highway 89 and drive nine miles to McCloud, then continue for another 2.8 miles to Pilgrim Creek Road. Turn left on Pilgrim Creek Road (Forest Road 13) and drive five miles (paved) to Forest Road 41N15 (Widow Springs Road). Turn left and drive about five miles to Forest Road 31 (McKenzie Butte). Cross this road and drive straight on Forest Road 41N61 (Cold Creek Road), a dirt and gravel road, for about a mile. Turn left on Forest Road 41N25Y (Clear Creek Road) and drive about three miles to the parking area for the Clear Creek trailhead. The road is well signed.

Contact: Shasta-Trinity National Forest, Mount Shasta Ranger District, 204 West Alma, Mount Shasta, CA 96067, 530/926-4511, www.fs.fed.us/r5; McCloud Ranger District, 530/964-2184. A 24-hour climbing report is available by calling 530/926-5555 or 530/926-9613.

36 ETNA SUMMIT TO GRIDER CREEK (PCT)
49.0 mi one-way / 4 days 🏃3 ⛰10

from Etna Summit north into the Marble
Mountain Wilderness west of Etna

Map 2.2, page 72

The Etna Summit is one of the major access
points for the Pacific Crest Trail in Northern
California. There is a good, safe parking area
(with a nice view), and at an elevation of 5,492
feet, you don't have to start your hike with a
wicked climb that is demanded at so many
other wilderness trailheads. From Etna Summit, the trail starts by crossing rugged, dry,
and often hot terrain that is best dealt with in
the morning. You'll reach Shelly Lake about
eight miles in. Note that there is no water
available along this route until Shelly Lake.
The campground at Shelly Meadows is a good
first-night stopover. From there, an excellent
second-day destination is the Marble Valley,
about another 10 miles north, with camping
in the nearby Sky High Lakes Basin. The next
20 miles of trail cross through and out of the
Marble Mountains. You'll pass Marble Mountain (a side trip to Marble Rim is mandatory),
Paradise Lake (many visitors will make camp
here), and Kings Castle. Most of the trail here
is above tree line, with outstanding lookouts
at several points, including a great vista from
Marble Rim. Moving onward, the trail follows Big Ridge to Buckhorn Mountain (6,908
feet), continues past Huckleberry Mountain
(6,303 feet), and then drops down to the
headwaters of Grider Creek, the next major
trailhead-access point. As you head north, the
trail becomes less and less traveled.

To pick up the next trail heading north,
see the *Grider Creek to Seiad Valley (PCT)*
hike in this chapter. If you are walking this
trail in reverse, see the *Cecilville Road to Russian Wilderness (PCT)* hike in this chapter to
continue south.

User Groups: Hikers, dogs, and horses. No
mountain bikes. No wheelchair facilities.

Permits: Campfire permits (free) are required

for campfires and stoves. Parking and access
are free.

Maps: A trail information sheet can be obtained by contacting the Salmon River Ranger
District. For a map, ask the U.S. Forest Service
for Klamath National Forest or Marble Mountain Wilderness. For a topographic map, ask
the USGS for Eaton Peak.

Directions: From Redding, take I-5 to Yreka
and the exit for Highway 3/Fort Jones. Take
that exit to the stop sign, turn left, and drive
a short distance to the lighted intersection.
Turn left on Highway 3 and drive 28 miles
to Etna. Turn west on Etna-Somes Bar Road
(called Main Street in town) and drive 10.5
miles to Etna Summit. The parking area is
along the road.

Contact: Klamath National Forest, Salmon/
Scott River Ranger District, 11263 North
Highway 3, Fort Jones, CA 96032-9702,
530/468-5351, www.fs.fed.us/r5.

37 TAYLOR LAKE TRAIL
1.0 mi / 0.5 hr 🏃1 ⛰7

from Etna Summit into the Russian Wilderness
west of Etna

Map 2.2, page 72   **BEST (**

Taylor Lake is proof that wilderness-like lakes
can be accessible by wheelchair. The trail is
made of hard-packed dirt and is wheelchair accessible, though wheelchairs with wide wheels
are recommended. For those with boots instead of wheels, it's about a 10-minute walk
to Taylor Lake, a long, narrow lake set on the
northern end of the Russian Wilderness. Trout
fishing is often very good here, and the walk is
short enough for hikers to bring along a small
raft or float tube. The only downer here is that
the Forest Service occasionally permits cows
to graze, and they stomp the grass at the far
end of the lake—and sometimes even walk in
the shallows. Although cows are still permitted, the Forest Service has rerouted the trail
so that hikers won't be walking amid them
at the meadow.

For a side-trip option, the Pacific Crest Trail runs east just above the lake. There is a very steep cut-off trail that climbs from the lake up to the PCT.

User Groups: Hikers, wheelchairs, dogs, and horses. No mountain bikes.

Permits: No permits are required for day use. A campfire permit (free) is required for campfires and stoves. Parking and access are free.

Maps: A trail information sheet can be obtained by contacting the Salmon Ranger District. For a map, ask the U.S. Forest Service for Klamath National Forest or Marble Mountain Wilderness. For a topographic map, ask the USGS for Eaton Peak.

Directions: From Redding, take I-5 to Yreka and the exit for Highway 3/Fort Jones. Take that exit to the stop sign, turn left, and drive a short distance to the lighted intersection. Turn left on Highway 3 and drive 28 miles southwest to Etna. Turn west on Etna-Somes Bar Road (called Main Street in town) and drive 10.25 miles just past Etna Summit to Forest Road 41N18 (a signed access road). Turn left and continue to the trailhead.

Contact: Klamath National Forest, Salmon/Scott River Ranger District, 11263 North Highway 3, Fort Jones, CA 96032-9702, 530/468-5351, www.fs.fed.us/r5.

38 STATUE LAKE
6.0 mi / 4.0 hr 🏃3 ⛰9

in the Russian Wilderness west of Etna

Map 2.2, page 72

Statue Lake earned its name from the unique granite sculptures that frame the back wall of the lake. When you first arrive at the small lake, it's a gorgeous yet solemn sight, one of nature's mountain temples. No place else looks like this. Some of the granite outcrops look like fingers sculpted with a giant chisel. There is a small primitive campsite on a granite overlook, from which you can often see small brook trout rising to feed in the lake.

After parking at the Music Creek trailhead, start the trip by hiking up a moderate grade and climbing about a mile to the Pacific Crest Trail. Turn right and hike on the PCT for about 1.5 miles, an easy walk in the forest. When you reach a small spring creek, stop and fill your canteens, then leave the trail and head uphill. It's about a 30-minute, cross-country hike to the lake, and the last 10 minutes is over a large field of boulders.

User Groups: Hikers only. Dogs are permitted but not advised because of the route crossing a boulder field. No horses or mountain bikes. No wheelchair facilities.

Permits: No permits are required for day use. A campfire permit (free) is required for campfires and stoves. Parking and access are free.

Maps: A trail information sheet can be obtained by contacting the Salmon Ranger District. For a map, ask the U.S. Forest Service for Klamath National Forest or Marble Mountain Wilderness. For a topographic map, ask the USGS for Sawyers Bar.

Directions: From Redding, take I-5 to Yreka and the exit for Highway 3/Fort Jones. Take that exit to the stop sign, turn left, and drive a short distance to the lighted intersection. Turn left on Highway 3 and drive 28 miles southwest to Etna. Turn west on Etna-Somes Bar Road (called Main Street in town), drive over Etna Summit, and continue down the other side to Forest Road 40N54 (just before the Salmon River Bridge). Turn left on Forest Road 40N54 and drive eight miles to the Music Creek trailhead. (A sign that says Pacific Crest Trail is usually posted. The sign for Music Creek trailhead is repeatedly stolen.)

Contact: Klamath National Forest, Salmon/Scott River Ranger District, 11263 North Highway 3, Fort Jones, CA 96032-9702, 530/468-5351, www.fs.fed.us/r5.

39 TRAIL CREEK TRAIL

7.0 mi / 2 days   🥾3 ⛰️6

in the Russian Wilderness west of Callahan

Map 2.2, page 72

Trail Creek Trail is no longer an official trail. (Apparently no one but us tried hiking it.) The Forest Service has decommissioned it, which means no trail maintenance is performed. It is now more of a route, one leading into the Russian Wilderness. The Trail Creek Trail (or route) starts out as more of an old jeep road, involving a steep climb and drop, and then a short cross-country jaunt. (When you finish, you could always write the book, *My Life as a Jeep*.) From Trail Creek Campground to the PCT, you are unlikely to see anybody but your companions, and that's a plus. This is also a good route with dogs, because you won't see a soul.

For most hikers, the trailhead for the Pacific Crest Trail off the Cecilville-Callahan Road is by far preferable. This provides a much easier route into the southern portion of the Russian Wilderness, but it will add 10 miles to your round-trip. That's the attraction of starting here instead.

The trailhead is located a short distance up a gravel road across from Trail Creek Campground, which is on Cecilville-Callahan Road. For the first 1.5 miles, the trail ventures steeply up on an old fire lane. It continues to climb, and as you near the crest, you'll junction with the Pacific Crest Trail. Turn left on the PCT, and then just five minutes later, turn at a signed junction to Syphon Lake. This is a good first night's camp. Russian or Waterdog Lakes are good second-day destinations.

Once you hit the high country, the lakes are very beautiful, especially Russian Lake, which is excellent for swimming. Because the wilderness here is small, it does not take many people hiking in to take up the campsites. Expect occasional cow sightings in midsummer near Syphon Lake. The Russian Wilderness is a place so pristine and so small that it just can't handle many visitors. If you go, walk softly, and treat the fragile area with care.

User Groups: Hikers, dogs, and horses. Mountain bikes allowed only outside of the wilderness border. No wheelchair facilities.

Permits: A wilderness permit is required for hikers planning to camp. Parking and access are free.

Maps: For a map, ask the U.S. Forest Service for Klamath National Forest. For topographic maps, ask the USGS for Deadman Peak and Eaton Peak.

Directions: From Redding, drive north on I-5 for 70 miles. Just past Weed, take the Edgewood exit. At the stop sign, turn left and drive through the underpass to another stop sign. Turn right on Old Highway 99 and drive six miles to Gazelle. Turn left at Gazelle on Gazelle-Callahan Road and drive about 20 miles to Callahan. From Callahan on Highway 3, turn west on County Road 402 (Cecilville Road) and drive 17 miles to Trail Creek Campground. The trail heads north from a gravel road located across from the campground.

Contact: Klamath National Forest, Salmon/Scott River Ranger District, 11263 North Highway 3, Fort Jones, CA 96032-9702, 530/468-5351, www.fs.fed.us/r5.

40 CECILVILLE ROAD TO RUSSIAN WILDERNESS (PCT)

3.0 mi one-way / 1 day   🥾3 ⛰️7

from Cecilville Road west of Callahan to the southern border of the Russian Wilderness

Map 2.2, page 72

This section of the trail is rarely used—it's estimated that less than 1,000 people a year hike here. Most hikers use this as a jump-off spot to the Russian Wilderness. This involves a long, steady climb up to the southern border of the Russian Wilderness. A good destination to the south is the short hike to Hidden Lake or South Fork Lakes.

Those venturing onward along the PCT enter a complex habitat web that includes the headwaters of the Scott, Salmon, and Trinity Rivers, along with the beautiful scenery that such diversity creates.

Either way, you start from the bottom of the canyon at the North Fork Scott River, so you'll face a climb no matter what your destination.

To pick up the next trail heading north (actually, in this case, heading west), see the *Etna Summit to Grider Creek (PCT)* hike in this chapter. If you are walking this trail in reverse, see the *Scott Mountain to Cecilville Road (PCT)* hike in this chapter to continue east.

User Groups: Hikers, dogs, and horses. No mountain bikes. No wheelchair facilities.

Permits: No permits are required for this section. Parking and access are free.

Maps: For topographic maps, ask the USGS for Deadman Peak and Eaton Peak.

Directions: From Redding, drive north on I-5 for 70 miles. Just past Weed, take the Edgewood exit. At the stop sign, turn left and drive through the underpass to another stop sign. Turn right on Old Highway 99 and drive six miles to Gazelle. Turn left at Gazelle on Gazelle-Callahan Road and drive about 20 miles to Callahan. From Callahan, turn west on Cecilville Road (County Road 402, narrow at times) and drive 11.5 miles to the Cecilville Summit. Parking is limited here; a larger parking area is located just past Cecilville Summit at the Carter Meadows trailhead (it will add 0.25 mile to your hike).

Contact: Klamath National Forest, Salmon/ Scott River Ranger District, 11263 North Highway 3, Fort Jones, CA 96032-9702, 530/468-5351, www.fs.fed.us/r5.

41 TRAIL GULCH

4.5 mi / 3.25 hr

in the Trinity Alps Wilderness west of Callahan

Map 2.2, page 72

The Trail Gulch Trail rises along Trail Gulch Creek, steeply at times, but in just 2.25 miles, you'll arrive at Trail Gulch Lake. That makes

it close enough to go in and out in a day, or better yet, you can make it a good weekend overnighter without tremendous strain. It is set northeast of Deadman Peak (7,741 feet) in the Trinity Alps Wilderness. The fishing at Trail Gulch Lake is often good for small trout. Another bonus is how simple it is to extend your trip either to other mountain lakes or deep into the Trinity Alps Wilderness. Long Gulch Lake is just another three miles from Trail Gulch Lake, making it a good side trip.

Note: If you choose to extend into the Trinity Alps, the trail is routed along North Fork Coffee Creek to Kickapoo Waterfall, about nine miles from Trail Gulch Lake. This trip is crowded on summer weekends. Experienced hikers may note that on many maps, Trail Gulch Lake is misidentified as Long Gulch Lake, and vice versa.

User Groups: Hikers, dogs, and horses. No mountain bikes. No wheelchair facilities.

Permits: A wilderness permit is required for hikers planning to camp. Parking and access are free.

Maps: For a map, ask the U.S. Forest Service for Klamath National Forest or Trinity Alps Wilderness. For topographic maps, ask the USGS for Deadman Peak and Billys Peak.

Directions: From Redding, drive north on I-5 for 70 miles. Just past Weed, take the Edgewood exit. At the stop sign, turn left and drive through the underpass to another stop sign. Turn right on Old Highway 99 and drive about six miles to Gazelle. Turn left on Gazelle-Callahan Road and drive about 20 miles to Callahan. From Callahan, turn west on County Road 402 (Cecilville Road) and drive 11 miles. Turn left on Forest Road 39N08 and drive 1.5 miles to the trailhead.

Contact: Klamath National Forest, Salmon/ Scott River Ranger District, 11263 North Highway 3, Fort Jones, CA 96032-9702, 530/468-5351, www.fs.fed.us/r5.

42 SCOTT MOUNTAIN TO CECILVILLE ROAD (PCT)

18.0 mi one-way / 2 days 🏃4 ⛰10

from Highway 3 at Scott Mountain Campground to Cecilville Road near the northern border of the Trinity Alps Wilderness

Map 2.2, page 72

What makes this section of the PCT appealing is that there are a number of wilderness lakes along the way that can be reached by side-trip hikes. From the camp at Scott Mountain, the trail is routed west for five miles, where the first of a series of lakes is within 0.5 mile of the trail. They include Upper Boulder, East Boulder, Mid Boulder, and Telephone Lakes—all quite pretty and accessible from the main trail. After hiking past Eagle Peak, set at 7,789 feet, you'll pass additional short cutoffs that are routed to West Boulder, Mavis, and Fox Creek Lakes. Hikers often camp at one of these lakes before the steep drop down to the South Fork Scott River and heading north into the Russian Wilderness.

To pick up the next trail heading north (actually, in this case, heading west), see the *Cecilville Road to Russian Wilderness (PCT)* hike in this chapter. If you are walking this trail in reverse, see the *Mumbo Basin to Scott Mountain (PCT)* hike in this chapter to continue south.

User Groups: Hikers, dogs, and horses. No mountain bikes. No wheelchair facilities.

Permits: A wilderness permit is required for camping in the Trinity Alps Wilderness. Contact the Weaverville Ranger District for information.

Maps: For topographic maps, ask the USGS for Scott Mountain, Tangle Blue Lake, Billys Peak, and Deadman Peak.

Directions: From Callahan, drive south on Highway 3 about seven miles to the trailhead, at Scott Mountain Campground.

Contact: Shasta-Trinity National Forest, Weaverville Ranger Station, P.O. Box 1190, 210 Main Street, Weaverville, CA 96093, 530/623-2121, www.fs.fed.us/r5.

43 KANGAROO LAKE TRAILHEAD

3.0 mi / 2.25 hr 🏃3 ⛰9

in Klamath National Forest east of Callahan

Map 2.2, page 72   **BEST** ☾

Kangaroo Lake is one of the most easily reached pristine mountain lakes, with a campground, wheelchair-accessible fishing, and a trailhead located near the campground. The remote, but paved Rail Creek Road leads to a parking area set adjacent to the walk-in campground and trailhead for the short walk to the lake.

From the lake, a spur trail rises steeply to the Pacific Crest Trail. Turn left and the PCT rises steeply to the rim overlooking the lake. A nearby scramble to Cory Peak, at 7,737 feet, provides a 360-degree view. This is a great picnic site. All of Northern California's prominent mountain peaks are in view here, and immediately below you, to the west, is Kangaroo Lake, like a large sapphire. The lake covers only 21 acres but often produces large brook trout, most of them 12- to 14-inchers. Backpackers can extend this trip eastward four miles on the Pacific Crest Trail past Robbers Meadow to Bull Lake, a small lake in a relatively sparse setting. In an unsolved conflict, most hikers call this the Kangaroo Lake trailhead, while some Forest Service rangers refer to it as the Fen trailhead.

User Groups: Hikers, dogs, horses, and mountain bikes. Fishing is wheelchair accessible.

Permits: No permits are required. Parking and access are free.

Maps: A trail guide can be obtained by contacting Klamath National Forest. For a map, ask the U.S. Forest Service for Klamath National Forest. For a topographic map, ask the USGS for Scott Mountain.

Directions: From Redding, drive north on I-5 for 70 miles. Just past Weed, take the Edgewood exit. At the stop sign, turn left and drive through the underpass to another stop sign. Turn right on Old Highway 99 and drive about six miles to Gazelle. Turn left on Gazelle-

Callahan Road and drive over the summit. Continue down the other side of the mountain about five miles to Rail Creek Road. Turn left on Rail Creek Road and drive seven miles to where the road dead-ends, at the parking area for Kangaroo Lake. As you drive up, look for the trail to the right of the campground.

Contact: Klamath National Forest, Salmon/ Scott River Ranger District, 11263 North Highway 3, Fort Jones, CA 96032-9702, 530/468-5351, www.fs.fed.us/r5.

44 DEADFALL LAKES- MOUNT EDDY TRAIL

5.0-11.0 mi / 3.0-5.0 hr 👣3 ⛰10

at Parks Creek Trailhead in Shasta-Trinity National Forest west of Mount Shasta

Map 2.2, page 72   **BEST (**

This is one of the best all-around mountain hikes in California. You can do it easy, a 2.5-mile (one-way) hike to Middle Deadfall Lake. Or you can do it hard, an 11-mile round-trip with a climb of 2,500 feet to the 9,025-foot summit. Either way, this hike is a 10.

The sight of Middle Deadfall Lake is always a happy shock to newcomers. Here, tucked away on the west side of Mount Eddy, are three wilderness lakes, the prize being Middle Deadfall. At 25 acres, it's far larger than one might expect—and far prettier, too. Because the parking area and trailhead are at the ridgeline, the hike to this lake is much easier than to other wilderness lakes, often flat or with a very slight grade, making it an excellent day hike.

Start the trip by taking the Pacific Crest trailhead at the south end of the parking lot. The trail is routed through a mixed conifer forest, with views of the Trinity Alps off to the west and with a very gentle rising grade most of the way. You'll cross a logging road, and if you have a dog, make sure they do not veer off up or down the road, but stay with you straight ahead on the trail. As you near the lake, you'll cross a shallow stream (protruding

rocks will keep you dry) and come to a junction (the Pacific Crest Trail bears to the right; the Mount Eddy Summit Trail turns to the left). Continue straight ahead (many people walk past a winter-snow survey marker) up a short rise, and then suddenly below you is Middle Deadfall Lake, at 7,300 feet—one of the highlights along the Pacific Crest Trail in the north state. The best and most secluded campsite here is around the backside of the lake. There are two other lakes nearby: tiny and rarely visited Upper Deadfall, at 7,800 feet, and even smaller Lower Deadfall, at 7,150 feet, which covers five acres and is overlooked in the shadow of its nearby big brother.

From Middle Deadfall, the summit climb is irresistible. Facing the ridge, you can pick the trail back up to your left. The climb becomes steeper, climbing 900 feet past the two small Upper Deadfall Lakes and then up to the ridge overlooking the Deadfall Lakes Basin. The long distance views to the west are breathtaking, and the ridge-top makes for a natural rest stop to soak them up. From here the trail bears to the left (north), rising above tree line, and then climbs another 900 feet in less than a mile, with seven switchbacks routed up a barren slope, providing a steady march up. There is no hint of a view of Mount Shasta. Then, suddenly, just as you gain the top of Mount Eddy, the entire western exposure of Mount Shasta comes into view, a stunning moment with an additional 125 miles of scenic points stretching into the distance. Looking down to the east, you can see how the giant Shasta rises 11,000 feet from the 3,000-foot elevations of the valley below. We put a new notebook and pen in a Ziploc bag in a can here so hikers can sign in.

There is one continuing problem on this route. On a regular basis, mountain bikers illegally ride the Pacific Crest Trail here (which overlaps this route for three miles) between the trailhead above Gumboot Lake, to the north, and the Parks Creek trailhead, to the south. Bikes are banned from the entire length of the PCT, of course.

User Groups: Hikers, dogs, and horses. No mountain bikes. No wheelchair facilities.
Permits: A campfire permit (free) is required for overnight use. Parking and access are free.
Maps: For a map, ask the U.S. Forest Service for Shasta-Trinity National Forest. For a topographic map, ask the USGS for Mount Eddy.
Directions: From Redding, drive north on I-5 for 70 miles. Just past Weed, take the Edgewood exit. At the stop sign, turn left and drive through the underpass to another stop sign. Turn right on Old Highway 99 and drive 0.5 mile to Stewart Springs Road. Turn left on Stewart Springs Road and drive to the road's end, at Stewart Springs Resort. Bear right on Forest Road 17 (Parks Creek Road) and drive nine miles to the Deadfall Lakes parking area, at the summit. The trailhead is at the south side of the parking area. Take the Pacific Crest Trail, heading south.
Contact: Shasta-Trinity National Forest, Mount Shasta Ranger District, 204 West Alma, Mount Shasta, CA 96067, 530/926-4511, www.fs.fed.us/r5.

45 TOAD LAKE TRAIL
1.5 mi / 2 days
in Shasta-Trinity National Forest west of Mount Shasta

Map 2.2, page 72 **BEST**

You might be wondering why a 1.5-mile round-trip hike, with a difficulty rating of only one, is projected as a two-day trip. The reason is the drive to the trailhead. It's an endless, twisting road that winds its way up the Middle Fork drainage of the Sacramento River, rising up along the west flank of Mount Eddy. No one should go up and back in a day. (And keep your tongue in your mouth, because the ride is so jarring that you might bite off the end of it when you hit a big pothole.) But once parked, you'll immediately notice the perfect calm, and then, with a 15-minute walk to the lake (at 6,950 feet), you'll be furnished with a picture-perfect lakeside campsite.

The lake covers 23 acres, provides excellent swimming, fair fishing for small trout (sometimes a bit weedy in late summer), and great side trips. The best is the one-mile hike from Toad Lake to Porcupine Lake, an idyllic spot for a picnic or a walk along the shore. To get there from Toad Lake, look for an unsigned route (it looks kind of like a game trail) located on the backside of the lake. Follow that route upslope to the Pacific Crest Trail. Turn left and then walk south for 0.25 mile on the PCT to the Porcupine Lake cutoff, on the right. Gorgeous.
User Groups: Hikers, dogs, and horses. No mountain bikes allowed on the Pacific Crest Trail. No wheelchair facilities.
Permits: No permits are required. Parking and access are free.
Maps: For a map, ask the U.S. Forest Service for Shasta-Trinity National Forest. For a topographic map, ask the USGS for Mount Eddy.
Directions: From Redding, take I-5 north to the exit for Central Mount Shasta. Take that exit to the stop sign. At the stop sign, turn left and drive 0.5 mile to Old Stage Road. Turn left on Old Stage Road and drive 0.25 mile to a fork with W. A. Barr Road. Stay to the right at the fork and drive two miles, cross Box Canyon Dam at Lake Siskiyou, and continue around the lake on W. A. Barr Road (which becomes Forest Road 26/South Fork Road). Continue four miles past the Lake Siskiyou Camp resort, cross an unnamed concrete bridge, and look for a dirt road on the right (signed Toad Lake/Morgan Meadows). Turn right and drive 0.2 mile to the first fork, bear left, and drive 11 miles to the lake trailhead parking area. The road is very rough and twisting, and for the last 0.5 mile, a high-clearance, four-wheel-drive vehicle is recommended. It is a 0.5-mile walk from the parking area to the lake.
Contact: Shasta-Trinity National Forest, Mount Shasta Ranger District, 204 West Alma, Mount Shasta, CA 96067, 530/926-4511, www.fs.fed.us/r5.

46 SISSON-CALLAHAN
14.0 mi one-way / 2 days 🏃5 ⛰️8

in Shasta-Trinity National Forest near Lake
Siskiyou west of Mount Shasta

Map 2.2, page 72

The Sisson-Callahan Trail is something of a
legend in the Mount Shasta area, yet almost
nobody makes this trek. Long ago, it was a
well-traveled route up the east flank of Mount
Eddy, over the top (through a saddle below
the summit) and down to Deadfall Lakes.
But with a much easier route long available
from the Deadfall Lakes trailhead, this trail
is passed over. Still, we included as something
of a historic landmark.

This route is long, steep, and hot, climbing
5,000 feet over the course of nine miles to the
top of Mount Eddy (at 9,025 feet), then down
nearly 2,000 feet in two miles to Deadfall Lakes
for the nearest campsite. In addition, the great
scenic beauty doesn't start until you've climbed
several thousand feet, and by then you'll care
more about how much water is left in your canteen than about the incredible sweeping view of
Mount Shasta to the east. Alas, you'll then killer
switchbacks to reach the Eddy Ridge. As you
reach the Eddy crest, look close and you will
find an old sign for a former route for the Pacific
Crest Trail; it might be 50 or 60 years old (best
we could gauge). From here it is mandatory to
hike the switchbacks up to the Mount Eddy
Summit. After that, it's a 1,750-foot descent to
Middle Deadfall Lake, where you make camp.
Your hiking reward comes the next morning,
when after lounging around at Lower Deadfall
Lake, you walk out three nearly level miles to
the Park Creek/PCT trailhead, then catch your
shuttle ride back to Mount Shasta. All in all,
this is a genuine butt-kicker of a trail. Unless
you want to do a hike that no one else does, a
much better route to the Deadfall Lakes and
Mount Eddy is from the Parks Creek trailhead,
listed in this chapter as *Deadfall Lakes–Mount
Eddy Trail*.

User Groups: Hikers, dogs, and horses. No
mountain bikes. No wheelchair facilities.

Permits: No permits are required. Parking
and access are free.

Maps: For a map, ask the U.S. Forest Service
for Shasta-Trinity National Forest. For topographic maps, ask the USGS for Mount Shasta
city and Mount Eddy.

Directions: From Redding, take I-5 north to
the exit for Central Mount Shasta city. Take
that exit to the stop sign. Turn left and drive
0.5 mile to Old Stage Road. Turn left on Old
Stage Road and drive 0.25 mile to a fork with
W. A. Barr Road. Stay to the right at the fork
and drive two miles to North Shore Road
(if you cross the dam at Lake Siskiyou, you
have gone too far). Turn right on North Shore
(which becomes Forest Road 40N27/Deer
Creek Road) and drive four miles, across the
bridge on Deer Creek to the next major junction, Forest Road 40N27C. Turn left on Forest
Road 40N27C and park along the edge of the
road before the ford on the North Fork Sacramento. (The water here is sometimes deeper
than it looks; don't be tempted to drive it.) The
Sisson-Callahan Trail (which first appears as
a road) starts on the other side of the ford, on
an old logging skid road that goes to the right.
Within 0.5 mile, it turns into a trail.

Contact: Shasta-Trinity National Forest,
Mount Shasta Ranger District, 204 West
Alma, Mount Shasta, CA 96067, 530/926-
4511, www.fs.fed.us/r5.

47 HEART LAKE TRAIL
3.0 mi / 2.25 hr 🏃2 ⛰️10

at Castle Lake in Shasta-Trinity National
Forest west of Mount Shasta

Map 2.2, page 72

If you scramble up the back wall of little Heart
Lake, you'll get a breathtaking view of Mount
Shasta with the heart-shaped pond in the
foreground. This is one of the best spots for a
calendar-quality photo of Mount Shasta. (Also
note that the best drive-to spot anywhere for
photographs of Mount Shasta is on Castle Lake
Road at a turnout about one mile downhill from

the Castle Lake parking area). Funny thing is, a lot of people can't find little Heart Lake.

The trailhead is on the left side of the lake, just across the outlet stream. From here, the trail rises up along the slope just left of the lake. Below to your right is Castle Lake, a pretty sight that's set in a rock bowl with a high back wall. The trail rises up to a saddle at 5,900 feet. At the saddle, bear uphill to the right on the faint trail. If you have the ability to envision wild landscapes, look for the wall and terrace above you, a bit to the right. It's an easy scramble up over a lip at 6,050 feet, where little Heart Lake is tucked away. Because the lake is small, the water warms up by midsummer, making it great for wading or a quick dip (but it's too small to really swim). The view is a real stunner.

The tale of Castle Lake, set at an elevation of 5,450 feet, is that the water is like none other in the world, which has led some people to jump into the lake for complete renewal. In reality, the water is so pure, containing few nutrients of any kind, that UC Davis has a water-sampling station here in an ongoing comparison study with Lake Tahoe.

User Groups: Hikers and dogs. Not suitable for horses or mountain bikes. No wheelchair facilities.

Permits: No permits are required. Parking and access is free.

Maps: For a map, ask the U.S. Forest Service for Shasta-Trinity National Forest or Castle Crags Wilderness. For a topographic map, ask the USGS for Mount Shasta city.

Directions: From Redding, take I-5 north to the exit for Central Mount Shasta city. Take that exit to the stop sign. Turn left and drive 0.5 mile to Old Stage Road. Turn left on Old Stage Road and drive 0.25 mile to a fork with W. A. Barr Road. Stay to the right at the fork and drive two miles, cross Box Canyon Dam at Lake Siskiyou, and continue 0.5 mile to Castle Lake Road. Turn left and drive 7.5 miles to the parking area at the end of the road, at Castle Lake. The trailhead begins on the eastern end of the parking lot.

Contact: Shasta-Trinity National Forest, Mount Shasta Ranger District, 204 West Alma, Mount Shasta, CA 96067, 530/926-4511, www.fs.fed.us/r5.

48 MIDDLE FALLS TRAIL
0.5–3.0 mi / 0.5–1.5 hr   🚶1 ⛰10

at Fowler's Camp in Shasta-Trinity National Forest east of McCloud

Map 2.2, page 72

Middle Falls, on the McCloud River, is one of the prettiest waterfalls in Northern California. It is a wide and tall cascade of water that pours over a 50-foot cliff into a deep pool in a rock bowl. This hike is an easy walk on a paved trail. You can start at an overlook above Middle Falls (parking nearby), at a trailhead near the restroom at Fowlers Campground, or at the parking lot for Lower Falls. We suggest you start at Lower Falls and skirt the left side of the McCloud River to enjoy the full exposure the river, all three waterfalls, and the experience of it.

Lower Falls is a chut-type waterfall, visible with a short walk from the paved parking area. From here, hike up the trail and enjoy the beautiful McCloud River. When you pass Fowlers Campground, the trail routes into forest with the gorgeous river off to your right. You'll round a bend, probably hearing the waterfall before you see it, and then suddenly, there it is, this wide sheet of falling water. It's something like a miniature Niagara Falls. The trail runs near a boulder field on the outer reaches of the plunge pool. On summer weekends, teenagers climb to the rim above the falls, then plunge 50 feet into the pool like human missiles. It's a dangerous venture that we don't recommend. (At high flow, we've also seen kayakers run over the top.)

The trail switchbacks up to the rim overlooking Middle Falls, then extends upstream to staircase-like Upper Falls. There is only one good spot to see Upper Falls. Instead, the trail runs near its brink, where water shoots past. It is also possible to drive to a parking area near the brink of the falls, reducing the hike to about 50 yards. A restroom is available at the parking area.

There is one frustrating element. Because the falls have become easy to reach, you get the bad with the good—visitors litter this spot, or worse, they discard cigarette butts on the trail. We try to reverse this offensive practice by packing out any trash that we see.

User Groups: Hikers and dogs. No horses or mountain bikes. The paved path from Lower Falls to Middle Falls is wheelchair accessible.

Permits: No permits are required. Parking and access are free.

Maps: For a map, ask the U.S. Forest Service for Shasta-Trinity National Forest. For a topographic map, ask the USGS for McCloud.

Directions: From Redding, take I-5 north for 47 miles to the Highway 89/McCloud-Reno exit. Bear right on Highway 89 and drive nine miles to McCloud. Continue southeast on Highway 89 for five miles to the sign for Fowler's Campground and Forest Road 39N28. Turn right and drive one mile to a fork.

To reach Lower Falls: At the fork, turn right and drive to the parking area and overlook.

To reach Middle Falls Trailhead: Bear left at the fork for Fowler's Campground, drive through the campground to the restroom, and park. The trailhead is across the road from the restroom.

Contact: Shasta-Trinity National Forest, McCloud Ranger District, P.O. Box 1620, 2019 Forest Road, McCloud, CA 96057, 530/964-2184, www.fs.fed.us/r5.

49 CARIBOU LAKES TRAIL
18.0 mi / 2 days   🥾3 ⛰️9

in the Trinity Alps Wilderness northwest of Trinity Lake

Map 2.2, page 72

The Caribou Lakes Basin provides the classic Trinity Alps scene: three high mountain lakes, beautiful and serene, with the back wall of the Sawtooth Ridge casting a monumental backdrop on one side, and on the other side, a drop-off and great views of a series of mountain peaks and ridgelines. Sunsets are absolutely remarkable when viewed from here. The centerpiece is Caribou Lake, the largest lake in the Trinity Alps Wilderness. Because it's a nine-mile hike to the Caribou Lakes Basin, this makes a good first-day destination for backpackers exploring this section of the Trinity Alps Wilderness.

The trail starts at the bottom of the Salmon River, however, and like all trails that start at the bottom of canyons, it means you begin the trip with a terrible climb that never seems to end, especially on hot summer afternoons. Plan on drinking a full canteen of water, and be certain not to miss the natural spring located near the crest, just off to the right. (Look for the spur-like footpath to it.) After reaching the crest, the trail travels counterclockwise around the mountain, several hours en route, and then drops into the Caribou Lakes Basin. Ignore your urge to stop at the first lake, because the best campsites, swimming, and views are from Caribou Lake, the last and largest lake you'll reach in this circuit. Because this is a popular destination, fishing is often poor. The lake is stocked, but these fish are very smart from the relatively large number of people making a cast over the course of a summer.

User Groups: Hikers and dogs. Horses are permitted but not recommended. No mountain bikes. No wheelchair facilities.

Permits: A wilderness permit is required for camping.

Maps: For a map, ask the U.S. Forest Service for Klamath National Forest or Trinity Alps Wilderness. For a topographic map, ask the USGS for Caribou Lakes.

Directions: From Weaverville, take Highway 3 north past Trinity Lake and continue to Coffee Creek Road/County Road 104 (located near the Coffee Creek Ranger Station). Turn left and drive 17 miles to the trailhead at the end of the road, at Big Flat Campground.

Contact: Shasta-Trinity National Forest,

Weaverville Ranger Station, P.O. Box 1190, 210 Main Street, Weaverville, CA 96093, 530/623-2121, www.fs.fed.us/r5; Klamath National Forest, Salmon/Scott River Ranger District, 11263 North Highway 3, Fort Jones, CA 96032-9702, 530/468-5351, www.fs.fed.us/r5.

50 UNION LAKE TRAIL
12.0 mi / 2 days 3 ▲ 7

in the Trinity Alps Wilderness northwest of Trinity Lake

Map 2.2, page 72

Union Lake sits in a granite basin below Red Rock Mountain. The hike in and out is a good weekend affair, but most visitors are backpackers who are using the camp at the lake as a first-day destination for a multiday trip. Of the trailheads on Coffee Creek Road, this one is often overlooked. The trail starts near an old sawmill along Coffee Creek, heads south (to the left), and in less than a mile starts the climb adjacent to Union Creek (on your right). Like most hikes that start at a streambed, you pay for your pleasure, going up, not down. After about two miles, the trail crosses Union Creek and continues on for a few miles, now with the stream on the left. You'll pass a trail junction for Bullards Basin, and about 0.5 mile later, turn right on the cutoff trail to Union Lake.

User Groups: Hikers, dogs, and horses. No mountain bikes. No wheelchair facilities.

Permits: A wilderness permit is required for hikers planning to camp.

Maps: For a map, ask the U.S. Forest Service for Shasta-Trinity National Forest or Trinity Alps Wilderness. For a topographic map, ask the USGS for Caribou Lakes.

Directions: From Weaverville, take Highway 3 north past Trinity Lake and continue to Coffee Creek Road/County Road 104 (located near the Coffee Creek Ranger Station). Turn left and drive about 10 miles to the trailhead, on the left.

Contact: Shasta-Trinity National Forest, Weaverville Ranger Station, P.O. Box 1190,

210 Main Street, Weaverville, CA 96093, 530/623-2121, www.fs.fed.us/r5.

51 BIG BEAR LAKE TRAIL
8.0 mi / 2 days 👫 3 ▲ 8

in the Trinity Alps Wilderness south of Callahan

Map 2.2, page 72

The four-mile hike up to Big Bear Lake, a large, beautiful lake by wilderness standards, can make for a weekend backpack trip. If there's a negative to this trip, it's this: The trail ends at the lake, so if the lakeside campsites are already taken when you arrive, you're out of luck for a quality place to camp. The trailhead is easy to reach, located just off Highway 3 north of Trinity Lake. The route is simple but not easy. It follows Bear Creek for the entire route, with one stream crossing, but climbing all the way. Once you reach the lake, a bonus is the side trip to Little Bear Lake, which takes about a mile of scrambling cross-country to reach. The trail is steep, popular, and beautiful.

User Groups: Hikers and dogs. Horses are allowed but not recommended. No mountain bikes. No wheelchair facilities.

Permits: A wilderness permit is required for hikers planning to camp in the wilderness.

Maps: For a map, ask the U.S. Forest Service for Shasta-Trinity National Forest. For a topographic map, ask the USGS for Tangle Blue Lake.

Directions: From Redding, take I-5 to Yreka and the exit for Highway 3/Fort Jones. Take that exit to the stop sign, turn left, and drive a short distance to the lighted intersection. Turn left on Highway 3 and drive about 40 miles to Callahan. Continue south on Highway 3 for about 13 miles to Bear Creek Loop Road. Turn right and drive a short distance (on an unpaved road) to the signed trailhead (located near the Bear Creek road crossing).

Contact: Shasta-Trinity National Forest, Weaverville Ranger Station, P.O. Box 1190,

210 Main Street, Weaverville, CA 96093, 530/623-2121, www.fs.fed.us/r5.

52 MUMBO BASIN TO SCOTT MOUNTAIN (PCT)
35.0 mi one-way / 4 days 🏃3 ⛰10

in Shasta-Trinity National Forest from Gumboot trailhead to Scott Mountain

Map 2.2, page 72

The PCT starts at a popular trailhead but quickly jumps northward into remote, beautiful country. The first highlight, only a mile up the trail, is the view below, to the left of secluded Picayune Lake. The trail then heads on, passing little yet pristine Porcupine Lake. A short spur trail provides access to this must-see spot. Back on the PCT, the trail heads over the rim and down to Deadfall Lakes, an excellent camping spot. From the ridge, an irresistible side trip is the 4-mile (one-way) trek to the top of Mount Eddy (at 9,025 feet), with its incomparable view of Mount Shasta. From Deadfall Lakes, the trail continues down to the Parks Creek Trailhead and crosses a paved road. It then eventually descends and curves around the headwaters of the Trinity River, then climbs back up Chilcoot Pass and Bull Lake. From here, it's a 10-mile pull to the Scott Mountain Summit trailhead (see the *Cecilville Road to Russian Wilderness (PCT)* hike in this chapter).

If you are walking this trail in reverse, see the *Castle Crags to Mumbo Basin (PCT)* hike in this chapter to continue south.

User Groups: Hikers, dogs, and horses. No mountain bikes. No wheelchair facilities.

Permits: No permits are required. Parking and access are free.

Maps: For topographic maps, ask the USGS for Mumbo Basin, South China Mountain, and Scott Mountain.

Directions: From Redding, take I-5 north to the exit for Central Mount Shasta city. Take that exit to the stop sign. Turn left and drive 0.5 mile to Old Stage Road. Turn left on Old Stage Road and drive 0.25 mile to a fork with

W. A. Barr Road. Stay to the right at the fork and drive two miles, cross Box Canyon Dam at Lake Siskiyou, and continue around the lake on W. A. Barr Road (which becomes Forest Road 26/South Fork Road). Continue four miles past the Lake Siskiyou Camp resort and continue up the canyon for 12.5 miles to Gumboot Lake Road. Bear right, staying on Forest Road 26, and continue 2.5 miles to the ridge and the parking area and trailhead.

Contact: Shasta-Trinity National Forest, Mount Shasta Ranger District, 204 West Alma, Mount Shasta, CA 96067, 530/926-4511, www.fs.fed.us/r5.

53 GUMBOOT LAKE TRAILHEAD
1.5 mi / 1.5 hr 🏃4 ⛰10

in Shasta-Trinity National Forest west of Mount Shasta

Map 2.2, page 72

This is an off-trail trek for people who like to scramble to ridges for views. If you must always have a trail to hike on, well, this trip is not for you. But if you don't mind a little cross-country scramble to a mountain rim then a short cutoff to a peak, with spectacular views of Gumboot Lake and Mount Shasta beyond, then sign up for this hike.

The trip starts at Gumboot Lake (6,050 elevation), which is pretty and has good trout fishing. You circle the lake on the right side, where there's a good trail. At the back of the lake, break off to the right of the trail and start climbing the slope, heading up toward the ridge that circles the back of the lake. A little less than halfway to the top, you'll pass Little Gumboot Lake and after that, you will scramble your way to the ridge, where you'll intersect with the Pacific Crest Trail. Head to the left for a short distance, then again break off the trail, this time to the left, heading on the mountain spine toward the peak that towers over Gumboot Lake, with Mount Shasta as the backdrop off to the east. This peak is your destination. The world may not be perfect, but from this lookout, it comes close.

User Groups: Hikers and dogs only. No horses or mountain bikes. No wheelchair facilities.

Permits: No permits are required. Parking and access are free.

Maps: For a map, ask the U.S. Forest Service for Shasta-Trinity National Forest. For a topographic map, ask the USGS for Mumbo Basin.

Directions: From I-5 at Mount Shasta city, take the Central Mount Shasta exit. At the stop sign, turn west and drive 0.5 mile to Old Stage Road. Turn left on Old Stage Road and drive 0.25 mile to a fork with W. A. Barr Road. Stay to the right at the fork and drive two miles, cross Box Canyon Dam at Lake Siskiyou, and continue around the lake on W. A. Barr Road (which becomes Forest Road 26/South Fork Road). Continue four miles past the Lake Siskiyou Camp resort and continue up the canyon to Gumboot Lake Road (Forest Road 40N37). Bear left on Gumboot Lake Road and drive 0.5 mile to the parking area near the shore of the lake.

Contact: Shasta-Trinity National Forest, Mount Shasta Ranger District, 204 West Alma, Mount Shasta, CA 96067, 530/926-4511, www.fs.fed.us/r5.

54 TAMARACK LAKE TRAILHEAD
5.0 mi / 4.0 hr 　　　　5 　10

in Shasta-Trinity National Forest southwest of Mount Shasta

Map 2.2, page 72

This is sacred country for some hikers, set high in the Trinity Divide at 5,900 feet. Tamarack is a beautiful alpine lake and a place of remarkable serenity. If you can pull yourself away from it, there's a rugged, cross-country route to the north that approaches the summit of Grey Rocks, a series of dark, craggy peaks. This route is steep and difficult, but the view of Castle Crags, Mount Shasta, the ridges of the Trinity Divide, and the Sacramento River

Canyon will have you thanking a higher power for the privilege of breathing the air here.

User Groups: Hikers and dogs. Not suitable for horses or mountain bikes. No wheelchair facilities.

Permits: No permits are required.

Maps: For a map, ask the U.S. Forest Service for Shasta-Trinity National Forest. For a topographic map, ask the USGS for Chicken Hawk Hill.

Directions: From Redding, take I-5 north for about 50 miles to the exit for Castella/Castle Crags State Park. Take that exit to the stop sign, turn left and drive west on Castle Creek Road. Continue past the park (the road becomes Forest Road 25/Whalen Road) and continue 12.5 miles on to Forest Road 38N17 (Tamarack Road). Turn left on Forest Road 38N17 and drive about six miles to the trailhead. The end of this road is extremely rough, with the last mile passable only to four-wheel-drive vehicles with large tires and high clearance. For other vehicles, before this bad section of road, there is a primitive parking area on the right side.

Contact: Shasta-Trinity National Forest, Mount Shasta Ranger District, 204 West Alma, Mount Shasta, CA 96067, 530/926-4511, www.fs.fed.us/r5.

55 ROOT CREEK TRAIL
2.3 mi / 1.75 hr 　　　　1 　7

in Castle Crags State Park south of Mount Shasta

Map 2.2, page 72

Castle Crags State Park features a series of huge granite spires that tower over the Sacramento River Canyon, the kind of sight that can take your breath away the first time you see it from I-5. That sight inspires a lot of people to take one of the hikes at the park, and while most don't have the time, energy, or body conditioning to complete Castle Crags Trail, Root Creek Trail is a good second choice.

As you drive up the access road, look for the signed trailhead to the left, just as you arrive at the parking area. The elevation is 2,500 feet at the trailhead. Start at this trailhead, which is signed for Castle Crags Trail, and walk 0.25 mile to a trail junction. Turn right on Root Creek Trail. From here, the trail is routed through a thick, cool forest, an easy walk that most visitors overlook. It continues to Root Creek, a pretty, babbling stream. There's a hidden waterfall upstream from here that almost nobody knows about.

Note: This park is on the closure list developed by the California Department of Parks, pending final state budget decisions or the possible transfer of park management to other park agencies or volunteer groups.

User Groups: Hikers only. No dogs, horses, or mountain bikes. No wheelchair facilities.

Permits: No permits are required. A state park entrance fee of $8 is charged for each vehicle.

Maps: A trail map can be obtained for a fee by contacting Castle Crags State Park. For a topographic map, ask the USGS for Dunsmuir.

Directions: From Redding, take I-5 north for about 50 miles to the exit for Castella/Castle Crags State Park. Take that exit to the stop sign, turn left and drive west on Castle Creek Road. Drive 0.25 mile to the park entrance, on the right. Turn right and drive to the kiosk. Just past the kiosk, bear right and drive two miles (past the campground) to the parking area for Vista Point. The signed trailhead is at the west edge of the parking area.

Contact: Castle Crags State Park, P.O. Box 80, Castella, CA 96017, 530/235-2684, www.parks.ca.gov.

56 CASTLE CRAGS TO MUMBO BASIN (PCT)

25.0 mi one-way / 2 days 4 ▲10

from Castle Crags State Park west into Shasta-Trinity National Forest

Map 2.2, page 72

This is a key juncture for the PCT, where the trail climbs out of a river canyon and back to high ridgelines. It's in a classic region, the Trinity Divide, known for lakes sculpted in granite and sweeping views of Mount Shasta. From the start, the trail runs beneath the spires of Castle Crags, a setting that can astonish newcomers. From the Sacramento River at Castle Crags, at an elevation of 2,000 feet, the trail laterals up the north side of Castle Creek Canyon, rising just below the base of the awesome crags. It finally hits the rim at the back side of Castle Ridge. Then it follows the rim in a half circle to the west, to the Seven Lakes Basin and beyond to the Mumbo Basin and the Gumboot Lake trailhead. The final five miles of this segment pass by a dozen pristine mountain lakes, but most are well off the trail.

To continue north on the PCT, see the *Mumbo Basin to Scott Moutain (PCT)* hike in this chapter. If you are walking this trail in reverse, see the *Ash Camp to Castle Crags Wilderness (PCT)* hike in this chapter to continue south.

User Groups: Hikers only. No dogs, horses, or mountain bikes. No wheelchair facilities.

Permits: No permits are required. A state park entrance fee of $8 is charged for each vehicle if you drive through the park entrance.

Maps: A trail map can be obtained for a fee by contacting Castle Crags State Park. For topographic maps, ask the USGS for Dunsmuir, Seven Lakes Basin, and Mumbo Basin.

Directions: From Redding, take I-5 north for about 50 miles to the exit for Castella/Castle Crags State Park. Take that exit to the stop sign, turn left and drive west on Castle Creek Road. Drive 0.25 mile to the park entrance, on the right. Turn right and drive to the kiosk. Just past the kiosk is a special parking area for PCT hikers. For day hikers, continue by bearing right, and then drive two miles to the end of the road, where there is a parking area for Vista Point. From the Vista Point parking area, the signed trailhead is back down the road about 50 yards.

Contact: Castle Crags State Park, P.O. Box 80, Castella, CA 96017, 530/235-2684, www.parks.ca.gov.

57 CRAGS TRAIL TO CASTLE DOME

5.7 mi / 4.0 hr

in Castle Crags State Park south of Mount Shasta

Map 2.2, page 72

From Vista Point in Castle Crags State Park, hikers can gaze up at the fantastic crags and spot Castle Dome (at 4,966 feet), the leading spire on the crags' ridge. This high, rounded, missile-shaped piece of rock is your destination on Castle Crags Trail. If you're out of shape, be warned: This climb is a butt-kicker, gaining in elevation all the way.

As you drive up to the parking area, you will see the signed trailhead on your left just as you reach the parking area. The elevation is 2,500 feet. Start by taking Castle Crags Trail for 0.25 mile; when you reach a three-trail junction, continue on Castle Crags Trail. Here the trail launches off, rising through a thick forest. It climbs steeply at times before eventually turning to the right, emerging from the forest, and winding through the lower crags. Once above tree line, the views get better with each rising step. In spring, snow and ice fields are common this high. An excellent picnic spot is at Indian Springs (at 3,600 feet), and many hikers get no farther than this point. But the trail goes onward, always climbing, then getting quite steep before finally reaching a saddle at the foot of Castle Dome, where a few trees have somehow gained toeholds. When you set foot on this divine perch and gaze north at Mount Shasta, it will be a moment you'll prize forever.

It isn't quite pristine, unfortunately, because of highway noise emerging from the canyon, as well as the inevitable freight train. Regardless, the views and photographs are eye-popping, making it a must-do for those who rate their hikes based on the lookouts.

Note: This park is on the closure list developed by the California Department of Parks, pending final state budget decisions or the possible transfer of park management to other park agencies or volunteer groups.

User Groups: Hikers only. No dogs, horses, or mountain bikes. No wheelchair facilities.

Permits: No permits are required. A state park entrance fee of $8 is charged for each vehicle.

Maps: A trail map can be obtained for a fee by contacting Castle Crags State Park. For a topographic map, ask the USGS for Dunsmuir.

Directions: From Redding, take I-5 north for about 50 miles to the exit for Castella/Castle Crags State Park. Take that exit to the stop sign, turn left and drive west on Castle Creek Road. Continue 0.25 mile to the park entrance, on the right. Turn right and drive to the kiosk. Just past the kiosk, bear right and drive two miles to its end, at the parking area for Vista Point. The signed trailhead is back down the road about 50 yards.

Contact: Castle Crags State Park, P.O. Box 80, Castella, CA 96017, 530/235-2684, www.parks.ca.gov.

58 ASH CAMP TO CASTLE CRAGS WILDERNESS (PCT)

30.0 mi one-way / 2 days

from Ash Camp on the McCloud River west into Castle Crags State Park

Map 2.2, page 72

Of the hundreds of rivers along the Pacific Crest Trail, it's the McCloud River that often seems most vibrant with life. This segment of the PCT starts right alongside the lush McCloud River at Ash Camp, set at about 3,000 feet. The trail is then routed downstream above the McCloud for 2.5 miles, one of the most prized sections of trail in this region. At Ah-Di-Na Camp, the trail starts to rise, eventually turning up Squaw Valley Creek and climbing steeply to top Girard Ridge (at 4,500 feet), a long, tiring, and dry climb. But when you top the ridge, Mount Shasta, Black Butte, and Castle Crags suddenly pop into view. After traversing the ridge for a few miles, the trail suddenly drops and cascades down to the Sacramento River Canyon. Your toes will be jamming into your boots as you head downhill. At the river you might stop to soak your feet before picking up and heading west into Castle Crags State Park.

To continue north on the PCT, see the *Castle Crags to Mumbo Basin (PCT)* hike in this chapter. If you are walking this trail in reverse, see the *McArthur-Burney Falls Memorial State Park to Ash Camp (PCT)* hike, in the *Lassen and Modoc* chapter, to continue south.

User Groups: Hikers, dogs, and horses. No mountain bikes. No wheelchair facilities.

Permits: Wilderness permits are required only in Castle Crags Wilderness.

Maps: For topographic maps, ask the USGS for Shoeinhorse Mountain, Yellowjacket Mountain, and Dunsmuir.

Directions: From Redding, take I-5 north for 47 miles to the Highway 89/McCloud-Reno exit. Bear right on Highway 89 and drive nine miles to McCloud and Squaw Valley Road. Turn right on Squaw Valley Road, and drive about five miles. (Squaw Valley Road becomes Forest Road 11/Hawkins Creek Road.) Continue on Forest Road 11, keeping right past the McCloud boat ramp, and continue over the McCloud Dam. Turn right (still Forest Road 11) and drive down the canyon for one mile. At the turnoff for Ash Camp, bear right and drive a short distance to the parking area.

Contact: Shasta-Trinity National Forest, McCloud Ranger District, 2019 Forest Road, P.O. Box 1620, McCloud, CA 96057, 530/964-2184, www.fs.fed.us/r5.

59 MCCLOUD NATURE TRAIL
4.5 mi / 2.5 hr   🥾1 ⛰9

at Nature Conservancy on the McCloud River south of McCloud

Map 2.2, page 72   **BEST (**

Have you ever yearned for a place where old trees are left standing, deer and bobcat roam without fear, and a crystal-perfect river flows free in an untouched canyon? The McCloud River Preserve is such a place, and because it's managed by the Nature Conservancy, it will always remain that way. Although the lower McCloud River is best known for its fly-fishing for trout, there's an excellent hiking trail that runs alongside the river, spanning more than two miles from the parking area on downstream. It's an easy yet beautiful walk among woods and water, requiring a bit of boulder hopping in a few spots. It's well worth it to hike out to the end, where the river plunges into a series of deep holes and gorges. Note that an angler's trail also runs upstream from Ah-Di-Na Campground, but while pretty, this is not the feature walk here. The trailhead for this hike is another one-mile drive at road's end, at the Nature Conservancy section of land.

User Groups: Hikers only. No dogs, horses, or mountain bikes. No wheelchair facilities.

Permits: No permits are required. Parking and access are free.

Maps: For a map, ask the U.S. Forest Service for Shasta-Trinity National Forest. For a topographic map, ask the USGS for Lake McCloud.

Directions: From Redding, take I-5 north for 47 miles to the Highway 89/McCloud-Reno exit. Bear right on Highway 89 and drive nine miles to McCloud at Squaw Valley Road. Turn right on Squaw Valley Road and drive 11.5 miles (at 5 miles, the road passes from Siskiyou County into Shasta County and becomes Forest Road 11. It then crosses a cattle guard and continues to McCloud Reservoir. At the reservoir, turn right and continue) to Battle Creek Cove and Forest Road 38N53/Ah-Di-Na Road (a dirt road) on the right. Turn right and drive seven miles (dusty, often bumpy, continue past Ah-Di-Na Campground) to the road's end, at Fisher Creek and trailhead. The Nature Conservancy boundary is 0.5 mile downstream.

Contact: Shasta-Trinity National Forest, McCloud Ranger District, P.O. Box 1620, 2019 Forest Road, McCloud, CA 96057, 530/964-2184, www.fs.fed.us/r5.

60 NEW RIVER TRAILHEAD
24.0 mi / 3 days

in the Trinity Alps Wilderness east of Willow Creek

Map 2.3, page 73

Most backpackers in the Trinity Alps Wilderness like high mountain lakes, but here is a trail that features small streams. The highlights are the headwaters of the New River (a tributary to the Trinity River), the history of the area, and Mary Blaine Meadow. Because this is a river trail, not a lake trail, it gets very little use.

The trail starts right along the New River, one of California's last runs of summer steelhead. You'll hike about three miles before the junction with the Slide Creek Trail. Slide Creek Trail is 9.5 miles and passes Mary Blaine Meadow, the final destination of this hike (just a half mile before Slide Creek Trail ends at Salmon Summit Trail). The meadow is set below Mary Blaine Mountain, and to the north, Dees Peak. The whole region is cut with small streams in crevices and canyons.

It is set in the relative vicinity of the Megram burn area of 1999, which at the time cut a mosaic-like swath, leaving patches of green amid blackened scars. It is largely recovered, not bad at all anymore.

User Groups: Hikers, dogs, and horses. No mountain bikes. No wheelchair facilities.

Permits: A wilderness permit is required for hikers planning to camp.

Maps: For a map, ask the U.S. Forest Service for Shasta-Trinity National Forest or Trinity Alps Wilderness. For topographic maps, ask the USGS for Jim Jam Ridge, Dees Peak, and Trinity Mountain.

Directions: From Weaverville, take Highway 299 west 45 miles to Denny Road. Turn north (right) on County Road 402 (Denny Road) and drive about 21 miles. Turn left on Forest Road 7N15 and drive four miles north to the trailhead parking area. The trailhead is at Hawkins Bar.

Contact: Shasta-Trinity National Forest, Weaverville Ranger Station, P.O. Box 1190, 210 Main Street, Weaverville, CA 96093, 530/623-2121, www.fs.fed.us/r5.

61 EAST FORK LOOP
20.0 mi / 3 days

in the Trinity Alps Wilderness east of Willow Creek

Map 2.3, page 73

Where else can you hike 20 miles with a chance of not seeing anybody? The East Fork trailhead provides access to one of the more primitive, less-traveled regions of the Trinity Alps Wilderness. It's an area known for streams and forests in the lower reaches and bare limestone ridges in the higher reaches. The trip starts at East Fork trailhead, adjacent to the East Fork New River. It climbs along this watershed and, after two miles, turns before coming to Pony Creek. In the next six miles, which include sections that are quite steep, the trail climbs to Limestone Ridge, near little Rattlesnake Lake. At Limestone Ridge, turn right on New River Divide Trail and head south for six miles, passing Cabin Peak at 6,870 feet and arriving at White Creek Lake.

To complete the loop, turn right on the trail at White Creek Lake and start the trip back, descending most of the way. The trail goes past Jakes Upper Camp and Jakes Lower Camp before linking up again with East Fork Trail for the jog back to the parking area.

User Groups: Hikers, dogs, and horses. No mountain bikes. No wheelchair facilities.

Permits: A wilderness permit is required for hikers planning to camp.

Maps: For a map, ask the U.S. Forest Service for Shasta-Trinity National Forest or Trinity Alps Wilderness. For a topographic map, ask the USGS for Jim Jam Ridge.

Directions: From Weaverville, turn west on Highway 299 and drive 45 miles to Denny Road. Turn north on County Road 402 (Denny Road) and drive 22 miles (the last four miles of the road become unpaved Forest

Road 7N01) to the trailhead parking area. The trailhead is at Hawkins Bar.

Contact: Shasta-Trinity National Forest, Weaverville Ranger Station, P.O. Box 1190, 210 Main Street, Weaverville, CA 96093, 530/623-2121, www.fs.fed.us/r5.

62 BURNT RANCH FALLS
1.25 mi / 1.0 hr

in Shasta-Trinity National Forest on Highway 299 east of Willow Creek

Map 2.3, page 73

Burnt Ranch Falls isn't a spectacular cascade of water like other, more famous waterfalls, but it is the center of a very pretty, easy-to-reach scene on the Trinity River. It's a relatively small but wide waterfall, comprised of about 10 feet of rock that creates a natural barrier for migrating salmon and steelhead during low-water conditions. Thus the highlight comes when river flows rise a bit in the fall, so that you can watch the spectacular sight of salmon and steelhead jumping and sailing through the air to get over and past the falls.

The trail is a short but steep 0.75-mile jaunt down from the Burnt Ranch Campground. When you arrive at the river, walk out a short way on the rocky spot to watch the fish jump. The setting, in an area along Highway 299, has a magnificent natural landscape. From the river, the Trinity Canyon walls look like they ascend into the sky. Unlike most waterfalls, Burnt Ranch Falls is a far less compelling scene at high water. During high, turbid flows, it becomes much more difficult to see fish jumping past the falls.

User Groups: Hikers and dogs. No horses or mountain bikes. No wheelchair facilities.

Permits: No permits are required.

Maps: For a map, ask the U.S. Forest Service for Shasta-Trinity National Forest. For a topographic map, ask the USGS for Ironed Mountain.

Directions: From Weaverville, drive west on Highway 299 to Burnt Ranch. From Burnt

Ranch, continue 0.5 mile west on Highway 299 to the trailhead at Burnt Ranch Campground, on the right.

Contact: Shasta-Trinity National Forest, Weaverville Ranger Station, P.O. Box 1190, 210 Main Street, Weaverville, CA 96093, 530/623-2121, www.fs.fed.us/r5.

63 NEW RIVER DIVIDE TRAIL
30.0 mi / 3 days

in the Trinity Alps Wilderness north of Trinity River's Big Bar

Map 2.3, page 73

The New River Divide Trail provides access to the Limestone Ridge of the Trinity Alps, taking a ridgeline route most of the way. This is an area known for having lookouts from mountain rims, the headwaters of many small feeder streams, and few people. The trip starts at the Green Mountain trailhead, at an elevation of 5,052 feet, and in the first three miles, the route skirts the southern flank of Brushy Mountain, past Panther Camp and Stove Camp, and along the eastern flank of Green Mountain. As the trail climbs toward the Limestone Ridge, you'll find yourself perched on a divide, where the streams on each side pour into different watersheds. Eventually the trail rises all the way to Cabin Peak (at 6,870 feet) and beyond to little Rattlesnake Lake, a one-way distance of about 15 miles. Note that the Megram fire of 1999 consumed a huge area of acreage at the headwaters of the New River, off to the northwest from this ridge route.

User Groups: Hikers, dogs, and horses. No mountain bikes. No wheelchair facilities.

Permits: A wilderness permit is required. Parking and access are free.

Maps: For a map, ask the U.S. Forest Service for Shasta-Trinity National Forest or Trinity Alps Wilderness. For a topographic map, ask the USGS for Del Loam.

Directions: From Weaverville, drive west on Highway 299 for 28 miles to French Creek Road (Forest Road 5913). Turn north (right)

and drive seven miles (the road becomes Forest Road 5N04). Continue straight for four miles to the trailhead, at the Green Mountain parking area.

Contact: Shasta-Trinity National Forest, Big Bar Ranger Station, Star Route 1, Box 10, Big Bar, CA 96010, 530/623-6106, www.fs.fed.us/r5.

64 CANYON CREEK LAKES TRAILHEAD
16.0 mi / 2 days

in the Trinity Alps Wilderness north of Weaverville

Map 2.3, page 73

This is the kind of place where wilderness lovers think they can find religion. But what they find, guaranteed, are tons of other people: Expect about 50 other hikers on weekdays and 200 to 300 on weekends. The destination is Canyon Creek Lakes, set high in a mountain canyon, framed by Sawtooth Mountain to the east and a series of high granite rims to the north. The route in is no mystery; it's a climb of 3,100 feet over the course of eight miles. The trail heads straight upstream along Bear Creek for about 0.25 mile, crossing Bear Creek before continuing along Canyon Creek. Four miles out, you'll reach the first of four waterfalls. The first is the smallest, then they get progressively taller, and all are gorgeous. After the last waterfall, walk 0.5 mile to reach Lower Canyon Creek Lake, seven miles out from the trailhead. From this place, which is now largely above tree line, cross Stonehouse Gulch to reach the first of two lakes. The trail skirts the left side of the first of the Canyon Creek Lakes, then in 0.5 mile, it arrives at the head of the larger one. They are like jewels set in the bottom of a gray, stark, high mountain canyon, and once you've seen them, you'll have their picture branded permanently in your mind. This has become a special weekend favorite for hikers from Eureka and Redding.

User Groups: Hikers, dogs, and horses. No mountain bikes. No wheelchair facilities.

Permits: A wilderness permit is required for hikers planning to camp.

Maps: For a map, ask the U.S. Forest Service for Shasta-Trinity National Forest or Trinity Alps Wilderness. For a topographic map, ask the USGS for Dedrick.

Directions: From Weaverville, drive west on Highway 299 for eight miles to Junction City and Canyon Creek Road. Turn north on Canyon Creek Road and drive 13 miles to the trailhead, at the end of the road (.75 mile past Ripstein Campground).

Contact: Shasta-Trinity National Forest, Weaverville Ranger Station, P.O. Box 1190, 210 Main Street, Weaverville, CA 96093, 530/623-2121, www.fs.fed.us/r5.

65 SOUTH FORK NATIONAL RECREATION TRAIL
20.0 mi / 2 days

in Shasta-Trinity National Forest east of Ruth Lake on Highway 36

Map 2.3, page 73

This remote trail is best known for following along the South Fork Trinity River, heading south toward the Yolla Bolly Wilderness. This is an early-season trail, accessible when so many other mountain routes are still snowbound. And because of that, mountain bikers and equestrians often share the trail on warm spring weekends. There are no lakes anywhere near the trail, and for the most part, the trail just meanders along, with that stream nearby providing a constant point of reference.

Even the trailhead, a short drive out of the Hell Gate Campground, is remote and obscure. Immediately, the trail picks up the stream, and in less than an hour, you might even feel as if you've discovered your own private little universe. The temperatures can really smoke out here in the summer, and the stream is your savior. How far might you go? For many, an hour in, an hour out is plenty. Hikers can keep going to St. Jacques Place, an abandoned camp about 10 miles farther one-way, or even another five miles to the trail's end at Double Cabin site, where you can leave a shuttle car and make this a one-way trip. Note that the trail crosses private property several times; stay on the trail, respect property rights, and help keep this trail open.

User Groups: Hikers and dogs. No horses or mountain bikes. No wheelchair facilities.

Permits: Campfire permits are required for overnight use. Parking and access are free.

Maps: For a map, ask the U.S. Forest Service for Shasta-Trinity National Forest. For a topographic map, ask the USGS for Forest Glen.

Directions: From Red Bluff, take Highway 36 (very twisty) west and drive 47 miles to Platina and continue to the junction with Highway 3. Continue west on Highway 36 for 10 miles to the Hell Gate Campground (on the left) and Forest Road 1526. Turn left on Forest Road 1526 and drive to the trailhead.

Contact: Shasta-Trinity National Forest, Hayfork Ranger Station, P.O. Box 159, Hayfork, CA 96041, 530/628-5227, www.fs.fed.us/r5.

66 BLACK ROCK LAKE TRAIL
4.5 mi / 3.0 hr   👣2 ⛰️8

on the northern boundary of the Yolla Bolly Wilderness west of Red Bluff

Map 2.3, page 73

This 2.25-mile hike from the Stuart Gap trailhead to Black Rock Lake is one of the best day hikes in the Yolla Bolly Wilderness. One of the highlights comes in mid- to late June, when the wildflower blooms are absolutely beautiful. From the trailhead at the northern tip of the wilderness, at 5,600 feet, start by hiking about a mile on the Pettyjohn Trail. It is set along the northwestern flank of North Yolla Bolly Mountain (7,863 feet) and is routed toward Pettyjohn Basin. When you reach the Black Rock Lake Trail, turn right on it and tromp another 1.25 miles to the lake. The trail contours through open stands of pine and fir and some small meadows. Small Black Rock Lake is set just below Black Rock Mountain (7,755

feet), is ideal for swimming, and is stocked with trout by air every other year.

There are many other excellent day hikes from this trailhead: Yolla Bolly Lake (stocked with trout every other year), Black Rock Mountain (great views), North Yolla Bolly Mountain (more sweeping vistas), and Cedar Basin (several creeks). Any of these make for classic days, remote and quiet. The trailhead can also be used as a jump-off spot for a hike straight south on Pettyjohn Trail into the wilderness interior. Note that this trail is usually impassable prior to Memorial Day.

User Groups: Hikers, dogs, and horses. No mountain bikes. No wheelchair facilities.

Permits: A campfire permit is required for hikers planning to camp.

Maps: For a map, ask the U.S. Forest Service for Shasta-Trinity National Forest or Yolla Bolly Wilderness. For a topographic map, ask the USGS for North Yolla Bolly.

Directions: From Red Bluff, take Highway 36 (very twisty) west and drive 47 miles to Platina. Continue west on Highway 36 for 11 miles to Forest Road 30 (Wildwood–Mad River Road). Turn left (south) and drive nine miles to Forest Road 35. Turn left (east) on Forest Road 35 and drive 10 miles to the intersection of several roads. Take the signed fork for Stuart Gap trailhead and drive 1.8 miles (unpaved) to the trailhead parking area. Hike on Pettyjohn Trail for one mile to reach Black Rock Lake Trail.

Contact: Shasta-Trinity National Forest, Yolla Bolly and Hayfork Ranger Station, Hayfork, 530/628-5227, www.fs.fed.us/r5.

67 SWIFT CREEK TRAIL TO GRANITE LAKE
12.0 mi / 2 days   👣4 ⛰️9

in the Trinity Alps Wilderness west of Trinity Center

Map 2.4, page 74

When hikers scan wilderness maps, they often search for trails that are routed a short distance to a beautiful lake for a first night's camp.

That's exactly what you get at Granite Lake, but although the trip in is only about six miles, it's anything but easy. From the trailhead, start by tracing the right side of Swift Creek. Don't be fooled. Just beyond the confluence of Swift and Granite Creeks, you must cross the stream to the left and then pick up Granite Lake Trail. This trail runs along the right side of Granite Creek for four miles and includes a very steep section in the final mile that will have you wondering why you ever thought this was going to be such a short, easy trip.

Two notes on the way in: 1. For the most part, the creek is not accessible as a water source, so monitor your canteen level. 2. There is a series of tumbling, churning waterfalls on Swift Creek—that is, no great free falls, but lots of whitewater.

Finally you'll rise to Gibson Meadow and just beyond, Granite Lake, a gorgeous sight below Gibson Peak. For a natural mountain lake, it's a fair size, with good swimming during the day and trout fishing in the evening. This is a popular spot, so plan on company.

User Groups: Hikers, dogs, and horses. No mountain bikes. No wheelchair facilities.

Permits: A wilderness permit is required for hikers planning to camp.

Maps: For a map, ask the U.S. Forest Service for Shasta-Trinity National Forest or Trinity Alps Wilderness. For topographic maps, ask the USGS for Covington Mill and Trinity Center.

Directions: From Weaverville, take Highway 3 north for 28 miles to Trinity Center and Swift Creek Road. Turn left and drive 6.8 miles to the parking area, at the wilderness border.

Contact: Shasta-Trinity National Forest, Weaverville Ranger Station, P.O. Box 1190, 210 Main Street, Weaverville, CA 96093, 530/623-2121, www.fs.fed.us/r5.

68 LONG CANYON TRAILHEAD

16.0 mi / 2 days

in the Trinity Alps Wilderness northwest of Trinity Lake

Map 2.4, page 74

Your mission, should you choose to accept it, is the 6.5-mile largely uphill hike to the west side of Gibson Peak, where Deer Lake, Summit Lake, Luella Lake, Diamond Lake, and Siligo Peak can provide days of side-trip destinations. From the trailhead, the trip starts by tracing along the East Fork Stuart Fork, a feeder creek to Trinity Lake. After two miles you'll arrive at a fork in the trail. Take the right fork (the left fork is routed to Bowerman Meadows and little Lake Anna), which climbs farther along the stream and then traces the southern flank of Gibson Peak. At times the trail is steep in this area, but finally you'll pass Gibson Peak, and Siligo Peak will come into view. The trail also intersects a loop trail that circles Siligo Peak and provides access to four high mountain lakes. Summit Lake is the favorite.

User Groups: Hikers, dogs, and horses. No mountain bikes. No wheelchair facilities.

Permits: A wilderness permit is required for hikers planning to camp.

Maps: For a map, ask the U.S. Forest Service for Shasta-Trinity National Forest or Trinity Alps Wilderness. For a topographic map, ask the USGS for Covington Mill.

Directions: From Weaverville, take Highway 3 north to Covington Mill and Forest Road 115. Turn left and drive for 2.5 miles to the trailhead.

Contact: Shasta-Trinity National Forest, Weaverville Ranger Station, P.O. Box 1190, 210 Main Street, Weaverville, CA 96093, 530/623-2121, www.fs.fed.us/r5.

69 STUART FORK TRAILHEAD

28.0 mi / 4 days   5 ▲10

in the Trinity Alps Wilderness northwest of Trinity Lake

Map 2.4, page 74

Don't say we didn't warn you: This trail doesn't have a difficulty rating of five for nothing. The hike requires an endless climb—very steep at times, particularly as you near the Sawtooth Ridge—spanning nearly 14 miles to Emerald Lake. The first nine miles are easy, and it will have you thinking that this hike is a piece of cake—long, but easy. But surprise! The last five miles from Morris Meadows are the killer. But after arriving and resting up for a night, you'll find that ecstasy follows. Emerald Lake is one of three lakes set in line in a canyon below the Sawtooth Ridge; the others on this side of the ridge are Sapphire and Mirror. The surroundings are stark and prehistoric, and the lakes are gemlike, blue, and clear, with big rainbow trout and water that is perfect for refreshing swims. The trail continues a mile past Emerald Lake to Sapphire Lake, and from there, it's an off-trail scramble, often across big boulders, as you climb another mile to reach Mirror Lake. The entire scene is surreal.

Special note: On the way to Emerald Lake, you might notice a cutoff trail to the right. On your trail map, you'll notice that it crosses the Sawtooth Ridge and leads in to the acclaimed Caribou Lakes Basin. On the map it appears to be a short, easy trip, but in reality, it involves a terrible climb with more than 100 switchbacks. Don't say you weren't warned.

User Groups: Hikers, dogs, and horses. No mountain bikes. No wheelchair facilities.

Permits: A wilderness permit is required for hikers planning to camp.

Maps: For a map, ask the U.S. Forest Service for Shasta-Trinity National Forest or Trinity Alps Wilderness. For a topographic map, ask the USGS for Covington Mill.

Directions: From Weaverville, take Highway 3 north to Trinity Lake and Trinity Alps Road.

Turn left on Trinity Alps Road and drive 2.5 miles to the trailhead at Bridge Camp.

Contact: Shasta-Trinity National Forest, Weaverville Ranger Station, P.O. Box 1190, 210 Main Street, Weaverville, CA 96093, 530/623-2121, www.fs.fed.us/r5.

70 HIRZ BAY TRAIL

3.2 mi / 1.75 hr   1 ▲8

on the McCloud arm of Shasta Lake north of Redding

Map 2.4, page 74

Most people discover this trail by accident, usually while camping at Hirz Bay Group Camp. That is because this trail, routed along the west side of the beautiful McCloud arm of Shasta Lake, is a natural hike from that camp. The trail traces the shoreline of the lake, in and out along small coves and creek inlets. Straight across the lake are pretty views of the deep coves at Campbell Creek and Dekkas Creek, of unique limestone outcrops, and of Minnesota Mountain (at 4,293 feet). Easy and beautiful, this hike is best in May, when the lake reaches full levels.

User Groups: Hikers and leashed dogs. No mountain bikes or horses. No wheelchair facilities.

Permits: No permits are required. A parking fee of $6 per vehicle is charged if parking at the Hirz Bay boat launch.

Maps: For a map, ask the U.S. Forest Service for Shasta-Trinity National Forest. For a topographic map, ask the USGS for O'Brien.

Directions: From Redding, take I-5 north to Shasta Lake and the exit for Salt Creek/Gilman Road. Take that exit and drive east on Gilman Road/County Road 7H009 for 10 miles to the access road for Hirz Bay boat launch and campground. Turn right and drive to the parking area.

Contact: Shasta-Trinity National Forest, Shasta Lake Ranger District, 14225 Holiday Road, Redding, CA 96003, 530/275-1587; Shasta Lake Visitor Center, 530/275-1589, www.fs.fed.us/shastatrinity.

71 GREENS CREEK BOAT-IN TRAIL
1.0-12.0 mi / 0.5-7.0 hr 👫3 ⛰8

on the McCloud arm of Shasta Lake north of Redding

Map 2.4, page 74

Almost no one hikes this entire trail. Almost no one hikes part of this trail. Almost no one even knows about this trail. Why? Because even with two million people estimated to visit Shasta Lake every year, the only way to access this trail is from a boat-in campsite at Greens Creek, on the east side of the McCloud arm of the lake. At the back of the cove at Greens Creek, you'll find a small U.S. Forest Service billboard posted with recreation guide sheets, and behind it are the campground and trailhead.

There are many fascinating side trips on the steep climb up toward a saddle between Town Mountain, at 4,325 feet, and Horse Mountain, at 4,025 feet. The trail enters an oak and madrone forest that is interspersed with limestone formations. The latter are worth exploring, and if you spend enough time hiking and investigating, you may find some small caves. Most people are inspired to hike just high enough to get a good clear view of the lake below, but not much farther.

User Groups: Hikers and leashed dogs. No horses or mountain bikes. No wheelchair facilities.

Permits: No permits are required. A parking fee of $8 per vehicle is charged at boat ramps.

Maps: For a map, ask the U.S. Forest Service for Shasta-Trinity National Forest. For a topographic map, ask the USGS for O'Brien.

Directions: Load your boat and, from Redding, drive on I-5 north to Shasta Lake and the exit for Salt Creek/Gilman Road. Take that exit and drive east on Gilman Road/County Road 7H009 for 10 miles to the access road for Hirz Bay boat launch. Launch your boat, drive out in the McCloud arm of Shasta Lake toward the Shasta Caverns. Turn left at Greens Creek Cove and land your boat at Greens Creek Boat-In Campground.

Other nearby boat ramps are located to the south, at Lakeview Marina Resort (off Shasta Caverns Road) and at Bailey Cove.

Contact: Shasta-Trinity National Forest, Shasta Lake Ranger District, 14225 Holiday Road, Redding, CA 96003, 530/275-1587; Shasta Lake Visitor Center, 530/275-1589, www.fs.fed.us/shastatrinity.

72 BAILEY COVE LOOP TRAIL
2.8 mi / 1.5 hr 👫2 ⛰8

on the McCloud arm of Shasta Lake north of Redding

Map 2.4, page 74

This hike is best done in May and June, when the lake is full and at its highest levels. In late summer or fall, when the levels are down, you'll be looking out at a lot of red dirt. A favorite part of Shasta Lake is the McCloud arm, where the mountain canyon features limestone formations and the lake's clear, emerald waters. This trail provides a great view of these phenomena, as well as a close-to-the-water loop hike on one of the lake's peninsulas.

From the trailhead, start by hiking on the left fork, which travels out along Bailey Cove. As you continue, the loop trail heads in a clockwise direction, first along the McCloud arm of the lake, then back to the parking area along John's Creek Inlet. When you reach the mouth of Bailey Cove, stop and enjoy the view. Directly across the lake are the limestone formations, featuring North Gray Rocks (at 3,114 feet) and topped by Horse Mountain (at 4,025 feet). The famous Shasta Caverns are located just below North Gray Rocks. And hey, watch out for the poison oak just off the trail.

User Groups: Hikers and leashed dogs. No mountain bikes or horses. No wheelchair facilities.

Permits: No permits are required. A parking fee of $8 per vehicle is charged.

Maps: For a map, ask the U.S. Forest Service for Shasta-Trinity National Forest. For a topographic map, ask the USGS for O'Brien.

Directions: From Redding, take I-5 north to Shasta Lake and the exit for O'Brien/Shasta Caverns. Take that exit and turn east on Shasta Caverns Road and drive 0.1 mile to the sign for Bailey Cove Boat Ramp. Bear right at the sign and drive 0.5 mile to the day-use parking area.

Contact: Shasta-Trinity National Forest, Shasta Lake Ranger District, 14225 Holiday Road, Redding, CA 96003, 530/275-1587; Shasta Lake Visitor Center, 530/275-1589, www.fs.fed.us/shastatrinity.

73 WATERS GULCH OVERLOOK

3.8 mi / 2.0 hr

at Packers Bay on Shasta Lake north of Redding

Map 2.4, page 74

Shasta Lake is so big—the biggest reservoir in California—that it can be difficult to know where to start in your mission to explore it. A good answer is right here on the Waters Gulch Loop. It connects to the Overlook Trail, a cutoff of 0.8 mile that climbs atop a small mountain and furnishes a view of the main lake. The trailhead is at Packers Bay, which is easily accessible off I-5. From the trailhead at the parking area, walk down the road and start hiking the trail from the Packer's Bay boat-ramp parking lots, and then finish back at the trailhead parking areas. This provides the best loop hike. Highlights of this trip include a route that extends onto one of the lake's peninsulas; Waters Gulch; a cove on the main Sacramento River arm of the lake; and several lookout points. Although there are many drive-to areas with lake views, you can get a little seclusion here as well.

User Groups: Hikers and leashed dogs. No horses or mountain bikes. No wheelchair facilities.

Permits: No permits are required. Parking and access are free.

Maps: For a map, ask the U.S. Forest Service for Shasta-Trinity National Forest. For a topographic map, ask the USGS for O'Brien.

Directions: From Redding, take I-5 north to Shasta Lake and the exit for Packers Bay. Take the exit and drive southwest on Packers Bay Road for one mile to the trailhead, on the right (.25 mile before the boat ramp).

Contact: Shasta-Trinity National Forest, Shasta Lake Ranger District, 14225 Holiday Road, Redding, CA 96003, 530/275-1587; Shasta Lake Visitor Center, 530/275-1589, www.fs.fed.us/shastatrinity.

74 BOULDER CREEK FALLS

6.4 mi / 3.5 hr

at Whiskeytown Lake National Recreation Area west of Redding

Map 2.4, page 74

Boulder Creek Falls is 138 feet tall and unique from top to bottom. At the top, the waterfall starts as a narrow cascade where the water builds speed. It then widens into a 28-foot cataract, a gentler rush of water over boulders. As you approach the waterfall, there are several spur trails where people have searched for a lookout. Ignore these side routes. Take the main trail, on the steps on the left, which leads to a perch with the best view. This part of the hike starts out as a dud on a wide logging road, but gets good once you reach the creek about a mile in.

When you reach the creek, the landscape gets a lot prettier—a mix of pine, fir and oak. From here, follow along the creek upstream and cross it three times. After the third crossing, look for a fork a bit up the trail. Take the right fork, keep on for another crossing, and then look for the signed spur trail for the water (3 miles total). This short spur leads to several faint paths, where others have tried to find the best vantage point. Ignore these paths and walk up the steps on the left, leading to a rock perch for the best view of the main falls.

User Groups: Hikers, mountain bikes, dogs, and horse. No wheelchair facilities.

Permits: A parking fee of $5 per vehicle is charged.

Maps: For a detailed trail map, contact

Whiskeytown National Recreation Area. For a topographic map, ask the USGS for Igo.

Directions: From Redding, turn west on Highway 299 and drive 10 miles to the Whiskeytown Visitors Center on the left. Continue west on 299 for seven miles to Carr Powerhouse Road. Turn left and drive 0.5 mile to Carr Powerhouse Road and South Shore Road. Continue straight on South Shore Road for 2.7 miles to the trailhead.

Contact: Whiskeytown National Recreation Area, P.O. Box 188, 14412 J. F. Kennedy Memorial Drive, Whiskeytown, CA 96095, 530/246-1225, www.nps.gov/whis.

75 DAVIS GULCH TRAIL
3.3 mi one-way / 3.5 hr 👣1 ⛰7

at Whiskeytown Lake National Recreation Area west of Redding

Map 2.4, page 74

The Davis Gulch Trail is Whiskeytown Lake's easiest hike. This meandering route along the southwest end of the lake starts out at 1,414 feet (at an information billboard along an access road) and winds its way down to the Brandy Creek Picnic Area, at 1,240 feet. It is a moderate descent on a wide, flat footpath surrounded mostly by oak and manzanita. Along the way, there are many good views of Whiskeytown Lake. The trail spans 3.3 miles and dead-ends. With two vehicles, it is possible to make it a one-way hike with a shuttle and then (better yet) hike the whole route downhill.

User Groups: Hikers and dogs. No horses or mountain bikes. No wheelchair facilities.

Permits: A parking fee of $5 per vehicle is charged.

Maps: For a detailed trail map, contact Whiskeytown National Recreation Area. For a topographic map, ask the USGS for Igo.

Directions: From Redding, turn west on Highway 299 and drive 10 miles to the Whiskeytown Visitors Center on the left. Turn left at the visitors center and drive on J. F. Kennedy Memorial Drive for three miles to the Davis

Gulch trailhead, on the right. To reach the Brandy Creek Picnic Area (and end of the trail), continue three more miles on J. F. Kennedy Memorial Drive.

Contact: Whiskeytown National Recreation Area, P.O. Box 188, 14412 J. F. Kennedy Memorial Drive, Whiskeytown, CA 96095, 530/246-1225, www.nps.gov/whis.

76 WHISKEYTOWN FALLS
3.4 mi / 2.5 hr 👣3 ⛰9

at Whiskeytown Lake National Recreation Area west of Redding

Map 2.4, page 74 **BEST (**

This trail to Whiskeytown Falls features a stunning route next to the falls where a staircase has been cut into rock, with a piped hand rail for safety. Hold on tight and enjoy a series of waterfall lookouts called "Photographer's Ledge" and, up near the top, "Artist's Ledge." The waterfall is estimated at 220 feet tall, top to bottom.

From the parking area, the hike starts on the James K. Carr Trail and leads down an old logging road to Crystal Creek. You cross a bridge, and then start the climb. At one spot, known as Cougar Rock, you will see some unique granite boulders that look like they've been stacked up. Look for the signed trailhead up a ways to the right and continue as the trail keeps climbing up through pretty, shaded Steep Ravine. It's aptly named, so be prepared and ignore the logging spurs off to the sides. In fall, the leaves come alive in golds and yellows. Eventually, the old logging road trail levels out, and after the viewpoint at Wintu View, you'll arrive at a picnic area where bikes and horses must be left. The final piece of trail runs along the creek for 0.25 mile and leads to the base of the falls.

Here, it only gets better. Climb the stone staircase to the left for the best views of the Whiskeytown Falls.

This "secret" waterfall was "unknown" for many years, was "discovered" in 2004, and "revealed to the public" in 2005. The truth is a small number of people have known about it for more than 50 years, but didn't tell anybody. I've seen this "hidden" waterfall, and about 15 others, from my airplane for many years.

User Groups: Hikers, mountain bikes, and horses are permitted up to picnic area. Hikers only allowed after this point. No dogs. No wheelchair facilities.

Permits: A parking fee of $5 per vehicle is charged.

Maps: For a detailed trail map, contact Whiskeytown National Recreation Area. For a topographic map, ask the USGS for Igo.

Directions: From Redding, turn west on Highway 299 and drive 10 miles to the Whiskeytown Visitors Center on the left. Continue west on 299 for eight miles to Crystal Creek Road. Turn left and drive 2.75 miles to reach Mill Creek Trailhead. Look here for the signed James K. Carr trailhead for Whiskeytown Falls.

Contact: Whiskeytown National Recreation Area, P.O. Box 188, 14412 J. F. Kennedy Memorial Drive, Whiskeytown, CA 96095, 530/246-1225, www.nps.gov/whis.

77 BRANDY CREEK FALLS
3.0 mi / 2.0 hr   🏃3 ⛰9

at Whiskeytown Lake National Recreation Area west of Redding

Map 2.4, page 74

Brandy Creek Falls is a cascade chute with a series of pool-and-drops that pour into a big pool. It is spectacular at high water, a cataract where all the waterfall pools are connected into a massive whitewater flow. At low water, it splits into two thin cascades with a series of small drops. This is not a Yosemite-like freefall and the trailhead is still fairly obscure.

From the trailhead, you'll cross a creek in 0.5 mile. There is a large debris field of logs and boulders in the creek, the result of the 1977 flood. Continue on and in another 0.25 mile, you will reach a junction with the Rich Gulch Trail. Though you pass this by and continue

ahead, note that the trail narrows here and is accessible only for hikers. From here to the falls, the trail enters the Brandy Creek Canyon with fern grottoes and clifflike dropoffs. It can be slippery, but the route heads right along the cascade. As you forge on, you will find steps cut in rock that will lead you past five pools and falls that run about 50 feet. Very special stuff.

User Groups: Hikers only. No mountain bikes, dogs, or horses. No wheelchair facilities.

Permits: A parking fee of $5 per vehicle is charged.

Maps: For a detailed trail map, contact Whiskeytown National Recreation Area. For a topographic map, ask the USGS for Igo.

Directions: From Redding, turn west on Highway 299 and drive 10 miles to the Whiskeytown Visitors Center on the left. Turn left at the visitors center, and continue south on Kennedy Memorial Drive to a fork. Bear right at the fork, cross over the dam, and continue past the Brandy Creek area to Shasta Bally Road. Turn left and drive 2.5 miles on the dirt road to a junction. Turn left and drive 0.75 mile to a small parking area. The signed trailhead is 150 feet up the road.

Contact: Whiskeytown National Recreation Area, P.O. Box 188, 14412 J. F. Kennedy Memorial Drive, Whiskeytown, CA 96095, 530/246-1225, www.nps.gov/whis.

78 SYD CABIN RIDGE TRAIL
8.0 mi / 2 days   🏃3 ⛰7

on the eastern boundary of the Yolla Bolly Wilderness west of Red Bluff

Map 2.4, page 74

Not many people hike into the Yolla Bolly Wilderness, set up a camp, then hike back out the next day. But here is a chance to do exactly that. The trailhead is at the Tomhead Saddle, located just west of Tomhead Mountain, at an elevation of 6,757 feet. From here, hike past Tomhead Spring on Syd Cabin Ridge Trail, then drop down into Hawk Camp. Set just below the confluence of three feeder streams,

Hawk Camp is a spot to overnight. On the way back, expect a steady climb with no water between Tomhead Spring and Hawk Camp. If you plan on extending your trip for several days into the wilderness, a network of trails intersects just beyond Hawk Camp, but note that a stream crossing is required.

User Groups: Hikers, dogs, and horses. No mountain bikes. No wheelchair facilities.

Permits: A campfire permit is required for hikers planning to camp.

Maps: For a map, ask the U.S. Forest Service for Shasta-Trinity National Forest or Yolla Bolly Wilderness. For a topographic map, ask the USGS for North Yolla Bolly.

Directions: From Red Bluff, turn west on Highway 36 (twisty) and drive about 13 miles to Cannon Road. Turn left (south) on Cannon Road and go approximately five miles to Pettyjohn Road. Turn right (west) on Pettyjohn Road and drive to Forest Road 27N06. Turn left (south) on Forest Road 27N06 and continue three miles to the parking area at Tomhead Saddle Campground. From Highway 36, this route is a dirt road all the way in. A high-clearance vehicle is recommended. It can also be slippery when wet.

Contact: Shasta-Trinity National Forest, Yolla Bolly and Hayfork Ranger Station, Hayfork, 530/628-5227, www.fs.fed.us/r5.

LASSEN AND MODOC

© NATIONAL PARK SERVICE, LASSEN VOLCANIC NATIONAL PA

BEST HIKES

Mount Lassen and its awesome volcanic past

seem to cast a shadow everywhere you go in this region. At 10,457 feet, the mountain's domed summit is visible for more than 100 miles in all directions. The volcanic-based landscape in the surrounding terrain is a reminder that Lassen blew its top in 1914, with occasional releases after that through 1917.

The hike to Lassen Peak is one of the top day hikes in California — it's challenging enough to provide an aerobic reward, yet easy enough for ambitious children. Lassen Volcanic National Park is easily explored along the main route, the Lassen Park Highway. Along the way, you can pick a few trails for adventure. The best hikes are the Lassen Peak Trail (moderate to challenging), which is best done first thing in the morning, and Bumpass Hell (easy and great for kids), to see the sulfur vents and boiling mud pots. Another favorite for classic alpine beauty is Shadow Lake Trail. This area is often off the radar of mainstream vacationers, making it one of the few national parks where hikers can enjoy the wilderness in relative solitude. Unique features of the region include its pumice boulders, volcanic rock, and spring-fed streams from the underground lava tubes.

Nearby is McArthur-Burney Falls Memorial State Park, along with the Pit River and Lake Britton, which together make up one of Northern California's best recreation destinations for families. This is also one of the best areas for fly-fishing, especially at Hat Creek, Pit River, Burney

Creek, and Manzanita Lake. For more beautiful settings, you can visit Lake Almanor and Eagle Lake, both of which provide lakeside campgrounds and excellent fishing and boating recreation.

And there's more. In remote Modoc County, you'll find Lava Beds National Monument and the South Warner Wilderness. Lava Beds is a stark, pretty, and often lonely place. It's sprinkled with small lakes full of trout, it is home to large-antlered deer that migrate in after the first snow (and after the hunting season has closed), and it features a unique volcanic habitat with huge flows of obsidian (dark, smooth, natural glass formed by the cooling of molten lava) and dacite (gray, craggy volcanic flow). Lava Beds National Monument is home to 445 caves and lava tubes, including the 6,000-foot Catacomb Tunnel. Nearby is pretty Medicine Lake, formed in a caldera, which provides good trout fishing, hiking, and exploring.

This area includes the Hat Creek Rim section of the Pacific Crest Trail, where PCT through-hikers are challenged by almost 30 miles without a water stop. It is by far the worst section of the 2,650-mile PCT – even worse than stretches of the Mojave Desert. Yet when you hear people talk about having completed this hike, if you listen close, it's difficult to distinguish whether they are complaining or bragging.

It seems no matter where you go, there are so many great hikes in this area that you can always find a match for what you desire.

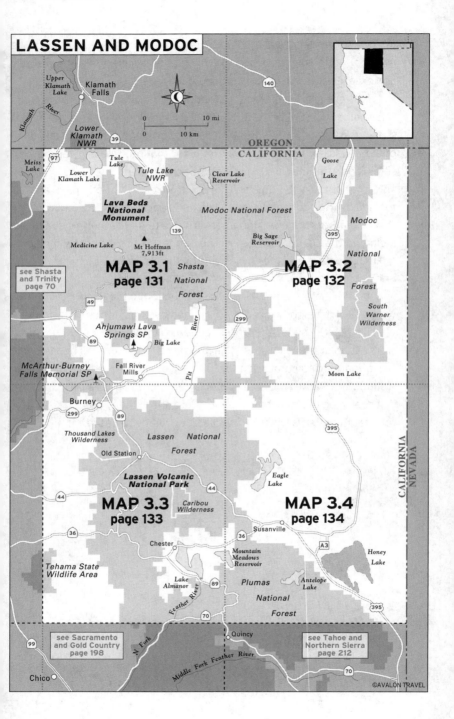

LASSEN AND MODOC

Upper Klamath Lake

Klamath Falls

Klamath River

140

0   10 mi
0   10 km

Lower Klamath NWR

OREGON
CALIFORNIA

Meiss Lake

97

Lower Klamath Lake

Tule Lake

Tule Lake NWR

Clear Lake Reservoir

Goose Lake

Lava Beds National Monument

Modoc National Forest

139

Big Sage Reservoir

395

Modoc

Medicine Lake

Mt Hoffman 7,913ft

MAP 3.1 page 131

Shasta

National

National

Forest

see Shasta and Trinity page 70

49

Forest

299

South Warner Wilderness

MAP 3.2 page 132

Ahjumawi Lava Springs SP

89

Big Lake

River

McArthur-Burney Falls Memorial SP

Fall River Mills

Pit

Moon Lake

Burney

299

89

Thousand Lakes Wilderness

Lassen   National

395

Old Station

Forest

Eagle Lake

Lassen Volcanic National Park

44

MAP 3.3 page 133

Caribou Wilderness

MAP 3.4 page 134

44

36

Susanville

A3

Honey Lake

36

Chester

Mountain Meadows Reservoir

Tehama State Wildlife Area

Lake Almanor

Feather River

Plumas

Antelope Lake

National

CALIFORNIA NEVADA

70

Forest

see Sacramento and Gold Country page 198

99

Quincy

see Tahoe and Northern Sierra page 212

N Fork

70

Chico

Middle Fork Feather River

©AVALON TRAVEL

Map 3.1

Hikes 1-11
Pages 135-140

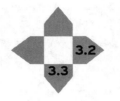

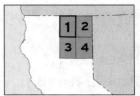

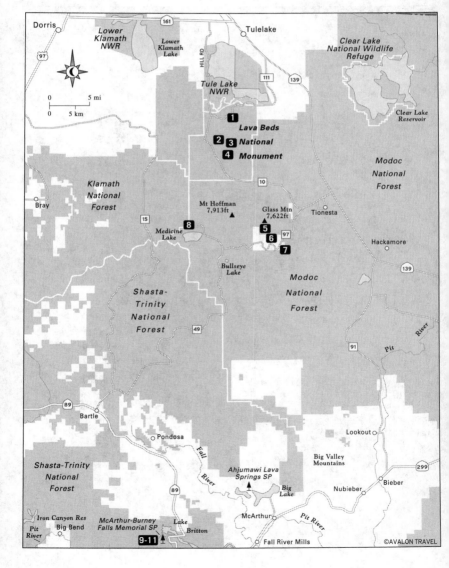

Map 3.2

**Hikes 12-21
Pages 141-146**

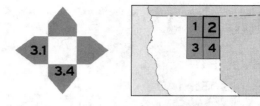

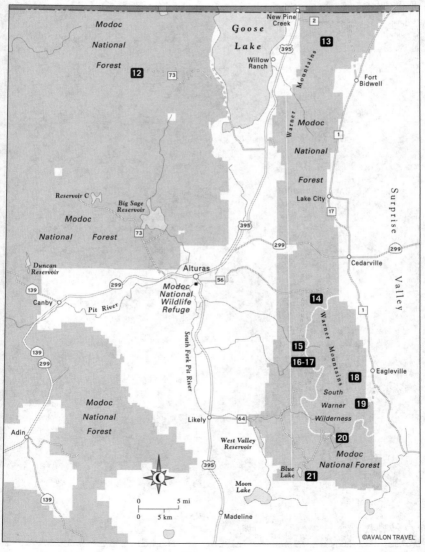

Map 3.3

Hikes 22-54
Pages 147-166

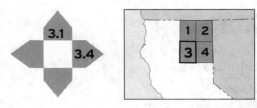

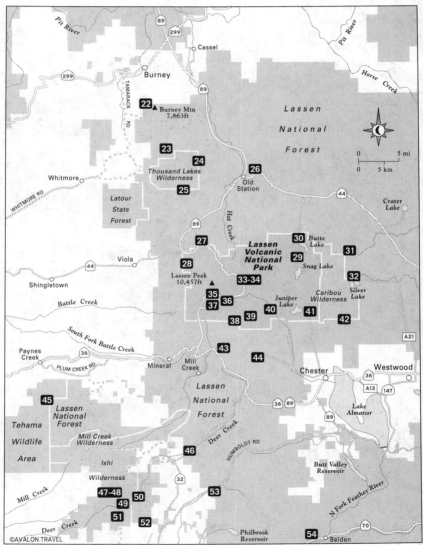

Pit River

89
299
Cassel

299
Burney

89

TAMARACK RD

22 ▲ Burney Mtn
7,863ft

Lassen

National

Forest

Horse Creek

Pit River

23

Whitmore

24

Thousand Lakes
Wilderness

25

26
Old
Station

44

Crater
Lake

WHITMORE RD

Latour
State
Forest

89

27

28

Lassen Peak
10,457ft ▲

Viola

44

Shingletown

Battle Creek

South Fork Battle Creek

Paynes
Creek

36

PLUM CREEK RD

Mineral

Mill
Creek

Hat Creek

Lassen
Volcanic
National
Park

30 Butte
Lake

31

29

Snag Lake

33-34

35

37

36

38   39

40

Juniper
Lake

Caribou
Wilderness

41

32
Silver
Lake

42

A21

43

44

Chester

Westwood

36

A13 147

45

Tehama

Wildlife

Area

Lassen
National
Forest

Mill Creek
Wilderness

Ishi

Wilderness

47-48 50

49

51   52

Mill Creek

Deer Creek

Deer Creek

32

HUMBOLDT RD

53

36 89

Lake
Almanor

89

Butt Valley
Reservoir

Philbrook
Reservoir

N Fork Feather River

54
Belden

70

©AVALON TRAVEL

3.1

3.4

1 2

3 4

0   5 mi

0   5 km

Map 3.4

Hike 55
Pages 167

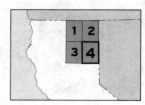

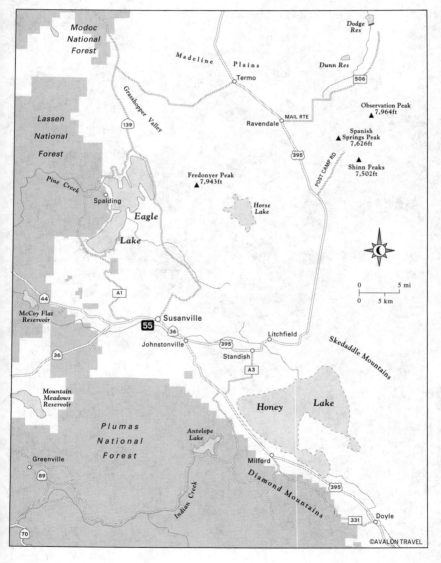

1 CAPTAIN JACK'S STRONGHOLD
1.7 mi / 1.5 hr   🏃1 ⛰7

in Lava Beds National Monument south of
Klamath Wildlife Refuge

Map 3.1, page 131   **BEST (**

Captain Jack's Stronghold provides a history
lesson and an introduction to the Lava Beds
National Monument. It's an easy walk on a
clear trail amid a volcanic plateau, with a few
trenches, dips, and rocks. From this trailhead,
there are actually two loop trails available,
including a shorter route that is just 0.5 mile
long. The general terrain is level, with a trailhead elevation of 4,047 feet and a high point
of 4,080 feet.

Captain Jack was a Modoc warrior who
fought U.S. troops attempting to relocate
Native Americans off their lands and onto a
reservation. His hiding place in this natural
lava fortress was betrayed by his own troops,
and in 1873, Captain Jack was finally captured
and hanged, and this site was later named for
him.

Note that during the winter, this is an outstanding area to see mule deer. Many of the
famous photographs of big bucks in California
were taken in this area. The wildlife viewing is
best at the onset of winter, after the first inch
or two of snow has fallen. In addition, a good
nearby side trip is Tule Lake, a favorite wintering area for waterfowl and bald eagles.

User Groups: Hikers only. No dogs, horses, or
mountain bikes. No wheelchair access.

Permits: No permits are required. A park
entrance fee of $10, good for seven days, is
charged per vehicle.

Maps: A free brochure is available by contacting Lava Beds National Monument. For
a topographic map, ask the USGS for Captain
Jack's Stronghold.

Directions: From Redding, take I-5 north
for 68 miles to the exit for Central Weed/
Highway 97–Klamath Falls. Take that exit
to the stop sign, turn right and drive one mile
through town to the junction with Highway

97. Bear right on Highway 97 and drive 54
miles to Highway 161. Turn right (east) on
Highway 161 and drive 20 miles to Hill Road.
Turn right (south), drive 18 miles to the visitors center, and look for the main road of
the Lava Beds National Monument (it's unnamed). Turn north and drive 13 miles on the
main monument road to the Captain Jack's
Stronghold access road. Turn right and drive
to the trailhead.

Contact: Lava Beds National Monument,
1 Indian Well Headquarters, Tulelake, CA
96134, 530/667-8113, www.nps.gov/labe.

2 WHITNEY BUTTE TRAIL
6.8 mi / 4.0 hr   🏃2 ⛰8

in Lava Beds National Monument south of
Klamath Wildlife Refuge

Map 3.1, page 131

The Whitney Butte Trail is one of three wilderness trails in Lava Beds National Monument, and for many, it's the best of the lot.
From the trailhead at Merrill Cave, set at
4,880 feet, the trail goes west for 3.4 miles,
skirting the northern flank of Whitney Butte
(5,004 feet) and ending at the edge of the
Callahan Lava Flow, on the park's southwest
boundary. Be sure to climb Whitney Butte.
This area bears a resemblance to the surface
of the moon, and skilled photographers who
know how to use sunlight to their advantage
can take black-and-white pictures that can fool
most people into thinking they are looking at
a lunar surface. Most people arrive just to see
the Merrill Ice Cave (which is actually a lava
tube) at the beginning of the hike. If you plan
to explore the cave, bring plenty of flashlight
power, a hard hat, and kneepads.

User Groups: Hikers and horses. No dogs or
mountain bikes. No wheelchair facilities.

Permits: No permits are required. A park
entrance fee of $10, good for seven days, is
charged per vehicle.

Maps: A free brochure is available by contacting Lava Beds National Monument. For

a topographic map, ask the USGS for Schon-chin Butte.

Directions: From Redding, take I-5 north for 68 miles to the exit for Central Weed/Highway 97–Klamath Falls. Take that exit to the stop sign, turn right and drive one mile through town to the junction with Highway 97. Bear right on Highway 97 and drive 54 miles to Highway 161. Turn right (east) on Highway 161 and drive 20 miles to Hill Road. Turn right (south), drive 18 miles to the visitors center, and look for the main road of the Lava Beds National Monument (it's unnamed). Turn north and drive two miles north on the monument main road to the turnoff for Merrill Ice Cave. Turn left and drive 0.75 mile to parking lot and trailhead, at the end of the road.

Contact: Lava Beds National Monument, 1 Indian Well Headquarters, Tulelake, CA 96134, 530/667-8113, www.nps.gov/labe.

3 THOMAS WRIGHT TRAIL
2.2 mi / 1.0 hr   👣1 ⛰7

in Lava Beds National Monument south of Tulelake Wildlife Refuge

Map 3.1, page 131

After just 0.25 mile on this trail, hikers reach the awesome Black Crater. In the world of volcanic geology, this is a spatter cone. It feels as if you are looking into the bowels of the earth. In time, as you continue on, you might even get the sense that ghosts are shadowing your footsteps. That is because some say this area is haunted by the ghosts of Modoc Indians, who fought troops in several violent battles for custody of the land. Though the Modoc warriors eventually lost that war, some say they actually won in the long run, since their spirits haunt modern-day visitors. At the end of the trail are interpretive signs that explain the Thomas Wright battlefield site. For an excellent side trip from here, continue off trail, clambering up to the Hardin Butte, a 130-foot climb, for a view. The butte sits on the western edge of the huge Schonchin Lava Flow.

User Groups: Hikers only. No dogs, horses, or mountain bikes. No wheelchair facilities.

Permits: No permits are required. A park entrance fee of $10, good for seven days, is charged per vehicle.

Maps: A free brochure is available by contacting Lava Beds National Monument. For a topographic map, ask the USGS for Captain Jack's Stronghold.

Directions: From Redding, take I-5 north for 68 miles to the exit for Central Weed/Highway 97–Klamath Falls. Take that exit to the stop sign, turn right and drive one mile through town to the junction with Highway 97. Bear right on Highway 97 and drive 54 miles to Highway 161. Turn right (east) on Highway 161 and drive 20 miles to Hill Road. Turn right (south) and drive five miles to the trailhead on the left (the visitors center is another five miles south).

Contact: Lava Beds National Monument, 1 Indian Well Headquarters, Tulelake, CA 96134, 530/667-8113, www.nps.gov/labe.

4 SCHONCHIN BUTTE TRAIL
1.8 mi / 1.0 hr   👣3 ⛰8

in Lava Beds National Monument south of Tulelake Wildlife Refuge

Map 3.1, page 131

This is a short hike, but for many, it's a butt-kicker. A portion of it is quite steep—enough to get most folks wheezing like old steam locomotives. The trail climbs 600 feet, from a trailhead elevation of 4,700 feet to the lookout at 5,300 feet. There are benches along the trail in case you need to catch your breath. Schonchin Butte has an old fire lookout, and the views are spectacular, of course, especially of the Schonchin Lava Flow to the northeast. Because of the proximity to the visitors center, as well as the short distance involved, many visitors make the tromp to the top. After completing this trip, always explore some of the caves in the matrix of underground lava tubes. You need a hard hat and flashlight to do it (available for a fee at the visitors center). For extensive caving, always wear kneepads. There are more than 700 caves in a five-mile radius, including 15 with signed entrances on the Cave Loop.

User Groups: Hikers only. No dogs, horses, or mountain bikes. No wheelchair facilities.

Permits: No permits are required. A park entrance fee of $10, good for seven days, is charged per vehicle.

Maps: A free brochure is available by contacting Lava Beds National Monument. For a topographic map, ask the USGS for Schonchin Butte.

Directions: From Redding, take I-5 north for 68 miles to the exit for Central Weed/Highway 97–Klamath Falls. Take that exit to the stop sign, turn right and drive one mile through town to the junction with Highway 97. Bear right on Highway 97 and drive 54 miles to Highway 161. Turn right (east) on Highway 161 and drive 20 miles to Hill Road. Turn right (south), drive 18 miles to the visitors center, then look for the main (unnamed) road for the Lava Beds National Monument. Turn north and drive 2.3 miles to the turnoff for Schonchin Butte. Turn right at the sign for Schonchin Butte and drive about one mile on a gravel road to the trailhead.

Contact: Lava Beds National Monument, 1 Indian Well Headquarters, Tulelake, CA 96134, 530/667-8113, www.nps.gov/labe.

⑤ MEDICINE LAKE LOOP
0.5-4.5 mi / 0.5-2.5 hr 🏃1 ⛰8

in Modoc National Forest northeast of Mount Shasta

Map 3.1, page 131

When you stand on the shore of Medicine Lake, it might be difficult to believe that this was once the center of a volcano. The old caldera is now filled with water and circled by conifers, and the lake is clear and crisp. Set at 6,700 feet, it's a unique and popular destination for camping, boating, and fishing. At

some point in their stay, most campers will take a morning or afternoon to walk around the lake. Although there is no specific trail, the route is clear enough. There is a sense of timelessness here. Although its geology is comparable to Crater Lake in Oregon, Medicine Lake is neither as deep nor as blue. But a bonus here is the good shore fishing for large brook trout, often in the 12- to 14-inch class, buoyed by the largest stocks of trout of any lake in the region (30,000 per year). There are also many excellent nearby side trips—including ice caves (along the access road on the way in); a great mountaintop lookout from Little Mount Hoffman, just west of the lake; and nearby little Bullseye and Blanche Lakes.

User Groups: Hikers, dogs, horses, and mountain bikes. There are wheelchair facilities at the beach and the boat ramp.

Permits: No permits are required. Parking and access are free unless you're camping.

Maps: A free brochure on the Medicine Lake Highlands is available by contacting the Doublehead Ranger District. For a map, ask the U.S. Forest Service for Modoc National Forest. For a topographic map, ask the USGS for Medicine Lake.

Directions: From Redding, take I-5 north for 57 miles to the exit for Highway 89/McCloud. Bear right on Highway 89 and drive 28 miles east to Bartle. Just past Bartle, turn left (northeast) on Powder Hill Road (Forest Road 49), and drive 31 miles (it becomes Medicine Lake Road) to the campground and lake access road. Turn left and drive 0.25 mile to the lake.

Contact: Modoc National Forest, Doublehead Ranger District, P.O. Box 369, Tulelake, CA 96134, 530/667-2246, www.fs.fed.us/r5.

6 GLASS MOUNTAIN

2.5 mi / 1.5 hr

in Modoc National Forest east of Medicine Lake

Map 3.1, page 131

Glass Mountain, a glass flow that covers 4,210 acres, is one of the most unusual settings in the Medicine Lake Highlands. It was created when glassy dacite and rhyolitic obsidian flowed from the same volcanic vent without mixing, creating a present-day phenomenon that exhibits no modification from weather, erosion, or vegetation. There are no designated trails on Glass Mountain, so visitors just wander about, inspecting the geologic curiosities as they go. Take care to stay clear of the obsidian, which is quite slippery and can have arrowhead-sharp edges. Don't walk on it, and don't handle it. Be sure to stay on the gray-colored dacite instead. Got it? Stay on the gray stuff. Stay off the black stuff.

User Groups: Hikers and dogs. The terrain is not suitable for horses or mountain bikes. No wheelchair facilities.

Permits: No permits are required. Parking and access are free.

Maps: A free brochure on the Medicine Lake Highlands is available by contacting the Doublehead Ranger District. For a map, ask the U.S. Forest Service for Modoc National Forest. For a topographic map, ask the USGS for Medicine Lake.

Directions: From Redding, take I-5 north for 57 miles to the exit for Highway 89/McCloud. Bear right on Highway 89 and drive 28 miles to Bartle. Just past Bartle, turn left (northeast) on Powder Hill Road (Forest Road 49) and drive about 29 miles (it becomes Medicine Lake Road) to County Road 97. Turn right on County Road 97 and drive about six miles to Forest Road 43N99. Turn north on Forest Road 43N99 and drive to the southern border of Glass Mountain.

Contact: Modoc National Forest, Doublehead Ranger District, P.O. Box 369, Tulelake, CA 96134, 530/667-2246, www.fs.fed.us/r5.

7 BURNT LAVA FLOW

2.5 mi / 1.5 hr

in Modoc National Forest south of Medicine Lake

Map 3.1, page 131

When you walk across the Burnt Lava Flow, a land of "rocks that float and mountains of glass," it may seem as if you're exploring some prehistoric area that resembles the moon. But get this: The lava formation is only about 200 years old, the youngest flow in the Medicine Lake Highlands. It's located south of Glass Mountain and covers some 8,760 acres, with little islands of forest amid the bare, jet-black lava flow. When we took an aerial survey of the area, the Burnt Lava Flow was one of the most fascinating portions of the entire region. On foot, it's even stranger. There is no trail, so pick any direction—most visitors go from tree island to tree island. There are a few weird spots where the ground can be like quicksand when dry and like wet concrete when wet. Just walk around those spots, staying on the hard, black lava flow.

User Groups: Hikers and dogs. The terrain is not suitable for mountain bikes or horses. No wheelchair facilities.

Permits: No permits are required. Parking and access are free.

Maps: For a map, ask the U.S. Forest Service for Modoc National Forest. For a topographic map, ask the USGS for Porcupine Butte.

Directions: From Redding, take I-5 north for 57 miles to the exit for Highway 89/McCloud. Bear right on Highway 89 and drive 28 miles to Bartle. Just past Bartle, turn left on Powder Hill Road (Forest Road 49) and drive 24 miles (the road becomes Medicine Lake Road) to Forest Road 42N25. Turn right and drive (the road becomes Forest Road 56) to the Burnt Lava Flow Geologic Area.

Contact: Modoc National Forest, Doublehead Ranger District, P.O. Box 369, Tulelake, CA 96134, 530/667-2246, www.fs.fed.us/r5.

8 MEDICINE LAKE LAVA FLOW
2.0 mi / 2.0 hr 👣1 ⛰7

in Modoc National Forest north of Medicine Lake

Map 3.1, page 131

The Medicine Lake Lava Flow covers 570 acres but has no designated trails. You can explore in any direction you wish, investigating the ancient, stony-gray dacite, which runs 50 to 150 feet deep. This is part of the Medicine Lake Highlands, located just a mile north of Medicine Lake, where there are "rocks that float and mountains of glass" (a poetic description from Forest Service geologists). Before the first lunar landing, many originally believed this area to resemble the surface of the moon. That is why this area was selected by the Manned Spacecraft Center in 1965 for study by astronauts preparing for the first manned trip to the moon. Most people will just poke around for an hour or two, take a few pictures, and leave, saying they've never seen anything like it.

User Groups: Hikers and dogs. The terrain is not suitable for mountain bikes or horses. No wheelchair facilities.

Permits: No permits are required. Parking and access are free.

Maps: A free brochure on the Medicine Lake Highlands is available by contacting the Doublehead Ranger District. For a map, ask the U.S. Forest Service for Modoc National Forest. For a topographic map, ask the USGS for Medicine Lake.

Directions: From Redding, take I-5 north for 57 miles to the exit for Highway 89/Mc-Cloud. Bear right on Highway 89 and drive 28 miles to Bartle. Just past Bartle, turn left (northeast) on Powder Hill Road (Forest Road 49) and drive 31 miles (it becomes Medicine Lake Road) to the Medicine Lake turnoff. Continue ahead (do not turn) for 2.5 miles, and look for the glass flow, on the left side of the road. Park and go for it.

Contact: Modoc National Forest, Doublehead Ranger District, P.O. Box 369, Tulelake, CA 96134, 530/667-2246, www.fs.fed.us/r5.

9 BURNEY FALLS LOOP TRAIL
1.2 mi / 0.5 hr 👣1 ⛰10

in McArthur-Burney Falls Memorial State Park north of Burney

Map 3.1, page 131 BEST (

Visitors from across the West are attracted to this state park by the chance to see spectacular Burney Falls. At 129 feet high, the waterfall plunges over a cliff in two pieces, split at the rim by a small bluff, where two trees have managed toeholds (although the river flows over the top of them during high water from the spring snowmelt). Underground lava tubes also transport water to the site; water seems to ooze right from the surrounding moss. From the park entrance station, it's a 100-foot walk to the rocky falls overlook, a perfect place for photographs of the waterfall. This spot also marks the start of Burney Falls Loop Trail, an easy 1.2-mile loop around the waterfall and back that was was completely renovated in 2010.

There is a 200-foot drop at the start of the trail, where you skirt the plunge pool of the waterfall. Then the trail is routed downstream along Burney Creek and crosses a wood bridge. Then hike upstream back to the waterfall for more fantastic views. The trail climbs up past the brink of the falls and continues upstream along Burney Creek. It then crosses another bridge and loops back to the Falls Overlook. It's a self-guided nature trail, but rather than having to carry a brochure with you, you can just read the small signs that explain the featured sites. To celebrate the expedition, the next destination is the park's snack bar, where visitors often go for an ice-cream cone. All in all, this is an easy, fun, beautiful, and memorable walk.

User Groups: Hikers only. No dogs, horses, or mountain bikes. There is paved wheelchair access at the falls overlook point, at the beginning of the trail.

Permits: No permits are required. A state park day-use fee of $8 is charged for each vehicle.

Maps: A trail guide is available for a fee at the state park. For a topographic map, ask the USGS for Burney Falls.

Directions: From Redding, take Highway 299 east for 50 miles to Burney and continue five miles to the junction with Highway 89. Turn left (north) and drive 5.8 miles to the state park entrance on the left. At the entrance station, continue straight for a short distance and park in the main lot on the right. The trailhead is across the road at the falls overlook.

Contact: McArthur-Burney Falls Memorial State Park, 24898 Highway 89, Burney, CA 96013, 530/335-2777, www.parks.ca.gov.

🔟 RIM TRAIL
3.0 mi / 1.75 hr

at Lake Britton in McArthur-Burney Falls Memorial State Park north of Burney

Map 3.1, page 131

The Rim Trail provides an ideal hike for campers at Burney Falls State Park. The trail starts at the campground and is routed to the rim of Lake Britton, a distance of 1.5 miles. It's an easy walk, and pretty too, heading first through forest, then emerging with a good lookout of the lake. The total elevation gain and loss is less than 250 feet. An easy side trip takes you down to the beach. The lake, set in a gorge, seems to have special qualities, sometimes shimmering with effervescence. The fishing is good, too—especially for crappie, but bass, bluegill, and trout are plentiful as well.

User Groups: Hikers only. No dogs, horses, or mountain bikes. No wheelchair facilities.

Permits: No permits are required. A state park day-use fee of $8 is charged for each vehicle.

Maps: A trail guide is available for a fee at the state park. For a topographic map, ask the USGS for Burney Falls.

Directions: From Redding, take Highway 299 east for 50 miles to Burney and continue five miles to the junction with Highway 89. Turn left (north) and drive 5.8 miles to the state park entrance on the left. At the entrance station, continue straight for a short distance and park in the main lot on the right. The trailhead is across the road at the falls overlook.

Contact: McArthur-Burney Falls Memorial State Park, 24898 Highway 89, Burney, CA 96013, 530/335-2777, www.parks.ca.gov.

11 MCARTHUR-BURNEY FALLS MEMORIAL STATE PARK TO ASH CAMP (PCT)
52.0 mi one-way / 4 days   🥾5 ⛰5

from McArthur-Burney Falls Memorial State Park west into Ash Camp in Shasta-Trinity National Forest

Map 3.1, page 131

It may be difficult to leave the woods, waters, and aura of Burney Falls, but off you go, facing dry country and some of Northern California's least-used portions of the Pacific Crest Trail. Typically the only hikers who complete this section are the ones hiking the entire route from Mexico to Canada; they're virtually forced to endure it, often at great hardship.

From Burney Falls, the PCT heads west, touching the Pit River arm of Lake Britton, and then continues forward into Lassen Volcanic National Park, crossing into Shasta-Trinity National Forest and up to Grizzly Peak. Much of this route is across dry, hot, exposed slopes, where the trail has deteriorated in many spots due to the encroachment of brush and the zero trail maintenance by the U.S. Forest Service. Knowing you're smack between the lush beauty of Burney Falls (behind you) and the McCloud River (ahead of you) can make dealing with the present brush-infested landscape a frustrating encounter. Always fill your canteens with water wherever you find it, and don't hesitate to make a camp if, late in the day, you find even a small flat spot with water nearby. In extremely dry years it's possible to travel this entire stretch without finding any water.

After the hot, beastly climb near Grizzly Peak, most hikers will want to make a lightning-fast descent to the Eden of the McCloud River at Ash Camp. But hold your horses. As long as you've come this far, make the short side trip up to Grizzly Peak, and while you're looking at the incredible view of Mount Shasta and the McCloud flats, congratulate yourself for completing such a terrible hike. Considering the PCT is the feature national recreation trail in America, this stretch is an embarrassment to the U.S. Forest Service and an abomination to hikers.

To continue north on the PCT, see the *Ash Camp to Castle Crags Wilderness (PCT)* hike in the *Shasta and Trinity* chapter. If you are walking this trail in reverse, see the *Hat Creek Rim to McArthur-Burney Falls Memorial State Park (PCT)* hike in this chapter to continue south.

User Groups: Hikers, dogs (except in the state park boundaries), and horses. No mountain bikes. No wheelchair facilities.

Permits: A campfire permit (free) is required. A fee of $8 is charged per vehicle at the state park.

Maps: For USGS topographic maps, ask for Burney Falls, Skunk Ridge, and Grizzly Peak.

Directions: From Redding, take Highway 299 east for 50 miles to Burney and continue five miles to the junction with Highway 89. Turn left (north) and drive 5.8 miles to the state park entrance on the left. At the entrance station, continue straight for a short distance and park in the main lot on the right.

Contact: McArthur-Burney Falls Memorial State Park, 24898 Highway 89, Burney, CA 96013, 530/335-2777, www.parks.ca.gov.

12 JANES RESERVOIR
1.0 mi / 0.75 hr

in Modoc National Forest north of Alturas

Map 3.2, page 132

A dirt road leads from the southwest corner of Janes Reservoir to Huffman Butte, about a two-mile drive. If your car can't handle the road, you can hike it. The best strategy is to park at the base of the butte and make the easy climb to the top of it. The reward is a nice view of the lake and the surrounding stark terrain.

This is sagebrush country, the high-plateau land of Modoc County. You're likely to see cattle, possibly wild mustangs, and—with the number of wetlands in the area—lots of waterfowl, particularly Canada geese. However, you're unlikely to see people. Even though it's very remote for a drive-to area, a bonus is that there are a number of side trips possible to other lakes. The best are the Alphabet Lakes (Reservoir C has the best trout fishing) and Big Sage Reservoir, on Crowder Flat Road.

User Groups: Hikers, dogs, horses, and mountain bikes. No wheelchair facilities.

Permits: No permits are required. Parking and access are free.

Maps: For a map, ask the U.S. Forest Service for Modoc National Forest. For a topographic map, ask the USGS for South Mountain.

Directions: From Redding, take Highway 299 east for 144 miles (17 miles past Canby) to Crowder Flat Road. Turn left on Crowder Flat Road and continue about 30 miles to the reservoir.

Contact: Modoc National Forest, Devil's Garden Ranger District, 800 West 12th Street, Alturas, CA 96101, 530/233-5811, www.fs.fed.us/r5.

13 HI GRADE NATIONAL RECREATION TRAIL

1.1 mi / 0.5 hr 🥾2 ⛰7

in Modoc National Forest east of Goose Lake

Map 3.2, page 132

The Hi Grade National Recreation Trail is actually 5.5 miles long, but only 1.1 miles are specifically designed for hiking. The remainder of this trail is designated for four-wheel-drive use, one of the only national four-wheel-drive trails in the state. Of course, you can still hike all of it, but it's better to use four-wheeling to get out there, then hike the final mile to get way out there. As you go, watch for signs of old, abandoned mining operations, because gold was discovered here. They never found enough to cause any outpouring of gold miners, though, and the result is a sparsely populated county, with this area being abandoned completely. The surrounding habitat is a mix of high desert and timber, although the trees tend to be small.

A good side trip from the nearby Buck Creek Ranger Station is to Fandango Pass, where there are nice views to the east of Surprise Valley and the Nevada Mountains. This is where a group of immigrants arrived, topped the ridge, looked west, saw Goose Lake, and shouted, "Aha! The Pacific Ocean! We have arrived!" So they started dancing the fandango. That's how the mountain pass got its name. (As lore has it, Native Americans killed them).

User Groups: Hikers, dogs, horses, and mountain bikes. No wheelchair facilities.

Permits: No permits are required. Parking and access are free.

Maps: For a map, ask the U.S. Forest Service for Modoc National Forest. For topographic maps, ask the USGS for Mount Bidwell and Willow Ranch.

Directions: From Redding, take Highway 299 east for 146 miles to Alturas and the junction with U.S. 395. Turn north on U.S. 395 and drive about 35 miles to Forest Road 9. Turn right on Forest Road 9 and drive 4.5 miles to Buck Creek Ranger Station. At the Buck Creek Ranger Station, turn left on Forest Road 47N72 and drive about six miles to the trailhead. Four-wheel-drive vehicles are required.

Contact: Modoc National Forest, Warner Mountain Ranger District, P.O. Box 220, Cedarville, CA 96104, 530/279-6116, www.fs.fed.us/r5.

14 PEPPERDINE TRAILHEAD

12.0 mi / 2 days 🥾3 ⛰9

on the northern boundary of the South Warner Wilderness east of Alturas

Map 3.2, page 132

The six-mile trip on Summit Trail to Patterson Lake is the most popular hike in the South Warner Wilderness. That still doesn't mean you'll run into other people or horses, because the Warners are a remote, lonely place rarely visited by hikers from the Bay Area, Sacramento, or Los Angeles. Patterson Lake is set in a rock basin at 9,000 feet, just below Warren Peak (9,718 feet), the highest lake in the wilderness and the highlight destination for most visitors. The Pepperdine trailhead (at 6,900 feet) is located just beyond Porter Reservoir, where a primitive campground and a horse corral are available. The hike is a sustained climb, gaining 2,100 feet, passing to the right of Squaw Peak (8,646 feet) and then tiny Cottonwood Lake. From Squaw Peak, looking east, you'll feel as if you're looking across hundreds of miles of a stark, uninhabited landscape.

User Groups: Hikers, dogs, and horses. No mountain bikes. No wheelchair facilities.

Permits: A campfire permit (free) is required. Parking and access are free.

Maps: For a map, ask the U.S. Forest Service for Modoc National Forest or South Warner Wilderness. For a topographic map, ask the USGS for Warren Peak.

Directions: From U.S. 395 at the south end of Alturas, turn east on County Road 56 and drive 13 miles to the Modoc National Forest boundary and Parker Creek Road. Turn left and drive six miles on Parker Creek Road, to the sign for Pepperdine Campground. Turn right and drive to the trailhead.

Contact: Modoc National Forest, Warner Mountain Ranger District, P.O. Box 220, Cedarville, CA 96104, 530/279-6116, www.fs.fed.us/r5.

15 PINE CREEK TRAILHEAD
4.0 mi / 3.0 hr   🏃3 ⛰8

on the northwestern boundary of the South Warner Wilderness east of Alturas

Map 3.2, page 132

This is one of the great short hikes anywhere. The Pine Creek Trail is a magnificent traipse into the beautiful South Warner Wilderness.

The trail starts along the south fork of Pine Creek, about 6,800 feet in elevation, then heads straight east into the wilderness, climbing the lush western slopes. In the course of two miles, the trail rises 1,000 feet to the Pine Creek Basin. Along the trail are several small lakes, the largest being the two set right along the trail as you enter the basin. Above you is a stark, volcanic-faced rim with few trees, where the headwaters of eight small creeks start from springs, pour down the mountain, join, and then flow into several small lakes. To lengthen the hike, go on to Patterson Lake, a gorgeous mountain lake surrounded by towering rock walls; the round-trip is 11 miles.

Modoc County is the least-populated and least-known region of California, with only 10,000 residents sprinkled across a huge area. Yet there are many outstanding adventures available here.

User Groups: Hikers, dogs, and horses. No mountain bikes. No wheelchair facilities.

Permits: No permits are required. Parking and access are free.

Maps: For a map, ask the U.S. Forest Service for Modoc National Forest or South Warner Wilderness. For a topographic map, ask the USGS for Eagle Peak.

Directions: On U.S. 395 at the south end of Alturas, turn east on County Road 56 and drive 13 miles to the Modoc National Forest boundary and West Warner Road. Turn right (south) on West Warner Road and go about 10 miles to the sign for the Pine Creek trailhead. Turn left (east) and head 1.75 miles to the parking area. The road is unpaved for the last 12 miles.

Contact: Modoc National Forest, Warner Mountain Ranger District, P.O. Box 220, Cedarville, CA 96104, 530/279-6116, www.fs.fed.us/r5.

16 SOUP SPRING TRAILHEAD
3.0 mi / 2.0 hr   🏃2 ⛰8

on the western boundary of the South Warner Wilderness east of Alturas

Map 3.2, page 132

Mill Creek is a small, pristine trout stream that brings the lonely Warner Mountains to life. It's a short hike to get here, up a hill and then down, heading into a valley. On this valley floor, you'll find Mill Creek, only a 1.5-mile walk out of the Soup Spring trailhead. Mill Creek is a great spot for a picnic lunch or a high-finesse fishing trip. The trout are extremely sensitive, so anything clumsy—like letting your shadow hit the water or clanking your boots on the shore—will spook them off the bite. The trout are small, dark, and chunky, unlike any seen elsewhere.

Some hikers use Slide Creek Trail as a way of climbing up near the Warner Rim and to the intersection with the Summit Trail, the feature hike in the South Warner Wilderness. That makes sense, as there is a primitive campground and corral at the trailhead; then it's a four-mile romp uphill to the Summit Trail junction. It includes a 1,000-foot climb on the way, with the trail routed up the Slide Creek Canyon over the last two miles.

User Groups: Hikers, dogs, and horses. No mountain bikes. No wheelchair facilities.

Permits: No permits are required. Parking and access are free.

Maps: For a map, ask the U.S. Forest Service for Modoc National Forest or South Warner Wilderness. For a topographic map, ask the USGS for Eagle Peak.

Directions: From Alturas, take U.S. 395 south for 18.5 miles to Likely and Jess Valley Road (County Road 64). Turn east on Jess Valley Road and drive nine miles to West Warner Road (Forest Road 5). Turn left on West Warner Road (Forest Road 5) and drive 4.5 miles to Soup Loop Road (Forest Road 40N24). Turn right and drive six miles (a gravel road) to the campground parking lot, on the right.

Contact: Modoc National Forest, Warner Mountain Ranger District, P.O. Box 220, Cedarville, CA 96104, 530/279-6116, www.fs.fed.us/r5.

17 MILL CREEK FALLS TRAILHEAD
0.5 mi / 0.5 hr　　🏃‍1 ⛰‍9

on the southwestern boundary of the South Warner Wilderness east of Alturas

Map 3.2, page 132

The short, easy walk from the Mill Creek Falls trailhead to Clear Lake leads to one of the prettiest spots in Modoc County. It's 0.5 mile to Mill Creek Falls and another 0.5 mile to Clear Lake. At the fork, bear left for the waterfalls, or bear right for the lake. Most hikers will take in both. The trail skirts along the perimeter of a pretty lake set at 6,000 feet. Of the lakes and streams in the Warners, it's Clear Lake that has the largest fish, with brown and rainbow trout ranging to more than 10 pounds. There just aren't many of them. Backpackers can head onward from Clear Lake on Poison Flat Trail, but expect a very steep howler of a climb before intersecting with Mill Creek Trail.

User Groups: Hikers, dogs, and horses. Some wheelchair-accessible facilities are available at the nearby campground, but there is no wheelchair access on this trail. No mountain bikes.

Permits: No permits are required. Parking and access are free.

Maps: For a map, ask the U.S. Forest Service for Modoc National Forest or South Warner Wilderness. For a topographic map, ask the USGS for Eagle Peak.

Directions: From Alturas, take U.S. 395 south for 18.5 miles to Likely and Jess Valley Road (County Road 64). Turn east on Jess Valley Road and drive nine miles to a fork. At the fork, bear left on Forest Road 5 and drive 2.5 miles to Forest Road 40N46. Turn right and drive two miles to the trailhead.

Contact: Modoc National Forest, Warner Mountain Ranger District, P.O. Box 220, Cedarville, CA 96104, 530/279-6116, www.fs.fed.us/r5.

18 EMERSON TRAILHEAD
7.0 mi / 2 days　　🏃‍5 ⛰‍9

on the eastern boundary of the South Warner Wilderness east of Alturas

Map 3.2, page 132

Don't be yelpin' about the dreadful climb up to North Emerson Lake, because we're warning you right here, loud and clear, that it qualifies as a first-class butt-kicker. If you choose to go anyway, well, you asked for it. The trail climbs 2,000 feet in 3.5 miles, but much of that is in a hellish 0.5-mile stretch that'll have you howling for relief. Your reward is little North Emerson Lake at 7,800 feet, a wonderland in a rock bowl with a high sheer back wall.

The Emerson trailhead, the most remote of those providing access to the Warners, is located on the east side of the mountain rim, near stark, dry country. A primitive campground is available at the trailhead. Out of camp, take North Emerson Trail. And while you're at it, get yourself in the right frame of mind to cheerfully accept that you'll be getting your butt kicked. But rest assured that North Emerson Lake is worth every step. You also get incredible long-distance views across the desert to the east.

User Groups: Hikers, dogs, and horses. No mountain bikes. No wheelchair facilities.

Permits: A campfire permit (free) is required. Parking and access are free.

Maps: For a map, ask the U.S. Forest Service for Modoc National Forest or South Warner Wilderness. For a topographic map, ask the USGS for Emerson Peak.

Directions: From Alturas, take Highway 299 east for 22 miles to Cedarville and County Road 1. Turn right (south) on County Road 1 and go about 16 miles to Eagleville and continue another 1.5 miles south on County Road 1 to Emerson Road. Turn right on Emerson Road and go three miles to the trailhead. Emerson Road is very steep and is slippery when wet or icy.

Contact: Modoc National Forest, Warner Mountain Ranger District, P.O. Box 220, Cedarville, CA 96104, 530/279-6116, www.fs.fed.us/r5.

🔟9 EAST CREEK LOOP

15.0 mi / 2 days   🏃3 ⛰7

on the southern boundary of the South Warner Wilderness east of Alturas

Map 3.2, page 132

The East Creek Loop is a favorite loop hike in the Warner Mountains. It can be completed in a weekend, not including driving time, and provides a capsule look at the amazing contrasts of the Warners. The hike includes small, seemingly untouched streams, as well as high, barren mountain rims.

To start this trip, take the East Creek Trail, elevation 7,100 feet. It is routed 5.5 miles north into the wilderness. Just before the junction with Poison Flat Trail, a spring is located on the left side of the trail. Don't miss it—you'll need the water for the upcoming climb. Turn right at the junction with Poison Flat Trail to make the 800-foot climb above tree line, and turn right again on Summit Trail. The loop is completed by taking Summit Trail back south, crossing high, stark country—most

of it more than 8,000 feet in elevation. In the last two miles, the trail drops sharply, descending 1,000 feet on the way to Patterson Campground, which marks the end of the loop trail. Reaching the parking area at the East Creek trailhead requires a 0.5-mile walk on the forest road.

User Groups: Hikers, dogs, and horses. No mountain bikes. No wheelchair facilities.

Permits: A campfire permit (free) is required. Parking and access are free.

Maps: For a map, ask the U.S. Forest Service for Modoc National Forest or South Warner Wilderness. For a topographic map, ask the USGS for Emerson Peak.

Directions: From Alturas, take U.S. 395 south for 18.5 miles to Likely and Jess Valley Road (County Road 64). Turn east on Jess Valley Road and drive nine miles to South Warner Road (Forest Road 64). Turn right and drive southeast (heading toward Patterson Campground) to the access road for East Creek Trail. Turn left and drive a short distance to the parking area.

Contact: Modoc National Forest, Warner Mountain Ranger District, P.O. Box 220, Cedarville, CA 96104, 530/279-6116, www.fs.fed.us/r5.

2️⃣0 SUMMIT LOOP

45.0 mi / 4 days   🏃3 ⛰10

on the southern boundary of the South Warner Wilderness east of Alturas

Map 3.2, page 132

The Summit Loop is the backpacking trek that most hikers yearn to take someday. If you are one of the lucky few to get here, you'll find this hike traverses both sides of the Warner ridge, providing an intimate look at a diverse place. The west side of the Warner Mountains is a habitat filled with small pine trees, meadows, and the headwaters of many small streams. The east side, however, is stark and rugged, with great long-distance lookouts to the east across high desert and miles of sagebrush and juniper.

Start the trip at the Patterson Camp trailhead (at 7,200 feet). From here the trail climbs quickly, rising to 8,200 feet in two miles, accessing high, barren country. Great views abound from here as hikers head north. Then, to reach the north end of the wilderness, take the turn at Owl Creek Trail and hike to Linderman Lake, set at the foot of Devils Knob (8,776 feet). Continue past Squaw Peak (8,646 feet). To return in a loop, make the hairpin left turn at Summit Trail and walk back on the mostly lush western slopes of the Warners. Highlights on the return loop segment include Patterson Lake, 9,000 feet, the headwaters of Mill Creek and North Fork East Creek, and many beautiful and fragile meadows. The trail ends at the East Creek parking area, a 0.5-mile walk from the Patterson Camp trailhead.

Savor every moment of this trip—it's one of the greatest little-known hikes anywhere in the United States. The Warner Mountains have a mystique about them, a charm cultivated by the thoughts of hikers who dream of an area where the landscape is remote and untouched, and the trails are empty. However, only rarely do they get around to it. For most, the Warners are just too remote and too far away, and the trip requires too much time.

User Groups: Hikers, dogs, and horses. No mountain bikes. No wheelchair facilities.

Permits: A campfire permit (free) is required. Parking and access are free.

Maps: For a map, ask the U.S. Forest Service for Modoc National Forest or South Warner Wilderness. For a topographic map, ask the USGS for Emerson Peak.

Directions: From Alturas, take U.S. 395 south for 18.5 miles to Likely and Jess Valley Road (County Road 64). Turn east on Jess Valley Road and drive nine miles to South Warner Road (Forest Road 64). Turn right and drive 16 miles to Patterson Campground. The trailhead is at the camp.

Contact: Modoc National Forest, Warner Mountain Ranger District, P.O. Box 220, Cedarville, CA 96104, 530/279-6116, www.fs.fed.us/r5.

21 BLUE LAKE LOOP NATIONAL RECREATION TRAIL
2.0 mi / 1.25 hr 1 7

at Blue Lake in Modoc National Forest southeast of Alturas

Map 3.2, page 132

Blue Lake, shaped like an egg and rimmed with trees, is one of the prettiest lakes you can reach by driving. That's what sets apart the easy two-mile loop hike around the lake on Blue Lake Loop National Recreation Trail. With a campground at the lake, this trail makes a good side trip for overnight visitors. In addition, a fishing pier and wheelchair-accessible restroom are available. A bonus is that there are some huge trout in this lake—brown trout in the 10-pound class—and they provide quite a treasure hunt amid good numbers of foot-long rainbow trout. Some of the surrounding forest has evidence of a past fire in the area.

User Groups: Hikers and dogs. The fishing pier and restroom are wheelchair accessible. No horses or mountain bikes.

Permits: No permits are required. Parking and access are free.

Maps: For a map, ask the U.S. Forest Service for Modoc National Forest. For a topographic map, ask the USGS for Jess Valley.

Directions: From Alturas, take U.S. 395 south for 18.5 miles to Likely and Jess Valley Road (County Road 64). Turn east on Jess Valley Road (County Road 64) and drive nine miles to a fork. When the road forks, bear right on Blue Lake Road (Forest Road 64) and drive seven miles to Forest Road 39N30 (signed for Blue Lake). Turn right and drive to the parking area.

Contact: Modoc National Forest, Warner Mountain Ranger District, P.O. Box 220, Cedarville, CA 96104, 530/279-6116, www.fs.fed.us/r5.

22 BURNEY MOUNTAIN SUMMIT

0.25–8.0 mi / 0.25–3.0 hr   👣1 ⛰9

in Lassen National Forest south of Burney

Map 3.3, page 133

The view is just so good from the top of Burney Mountain (elevation 7,863 feet) that the trip had to be included in this book. If you drive to the summit, the "hike" consists of just moseying around and gazing off in all directions. There is a fire lookout on top of the mountain. Occasionally, tours are available. Burney Mountain often gets lost in the shadow of its big brothers, Mount Lassen and Mount Shasta, but of the three, the view just might be best from Burney. That's because a view of Lassen or Shasta offers impressive panoramas that just can't be duplicated.

If you show up in the winter or after 6 P.M., when the access road is gated, or if you simply want the exercise, it's a four-mile hike up the road to the top of the mountain.

User Groups: Hikers, dogs, horses, and mountain bikes. No wheelchair facilities.

Permits: No permits are required. Parking and access are free.

Maps: For a map, ask the U.S. Forest Service for Lassen National Forest. For topographic maps, ask the USGS for Burney Mountain West and Burney Mountain East.

Directions: From Redding, take Highway 299 east for 50 miles to Burney and continue five more miles east to Highway 89. Turn south (right) on Highway 89 and drive 10.5 miles to Forest Road 26/Forest Road 34N19 (signed). Turn right on Forest Road 26 and drive 10 miles to Forest Road 34N23. Turn right and drive seven miles to the mountain summit. Note that the summit access road is blocked by a gate at 6 P.M. each day and throughout winter. You can park at the gate and hike to the top.

Contact: Lassen National Forest, Hat Creek Ranger District, 43225 East Highway 299, P.O. Box 220, Falls River Mills, CA 96028, 530/336-5521, www.fs.fed.us/r5.

23 CYPRESS TRAILHEAD

6.0 mi / 1 day   👣3 ⛰8

on the north boundary of the Thousand Lakes Wilderness north of Lassen Volcanic National Park

Map 3.3, page 133

The relocation of the Tamarack Trailhead means that the Cypress Trailhead is no longer the top starting point for the Thousand Lakes Wilderness. The wilderness is located at 5,400 feet, with many small lakes sprinkled about in a radius of just two miles. But getting here involves a climb of more than 1,000 feet. The primary destination is Lake Eiler, a round-trip of six miles, though it is 9.9 miles if you also hike around the lake and return to the trailhead. It is the largest lake in this region, set just below Eiler Butte. But a network of trails here connects to other lakes, so an option is to keep on going for an overnighter. From the south side of Eiler Lake, the trail loops deeper into the wilderness in a clockwise arc. It passes near several other lakes, including Box and Barrett Lakes. Both of these provide good fishing for small trout.

This wilderness is not called "Thousand Lakes" because there are a lot of lakes. After heavy rains or snowmelt, there are thousands of little pockets of water-breeding mosquitoes here in spring. And *that* is how it was named.

User Groups: Hikers, dogs, and horses. No mountain bikes. No wheelchair facilities.

Permits: No permits are required. Parking and access are free.

Maps: For a map, ask the U.S. Forest Service for Lassen National Forest. A wilderness trail map is available for a fee from the Hat Creek Ranger District. For topographic maps, ask the USGS for Thousand Lakes Valley and Jacks Backbone.

Directions: From Redding, take Highway 299 east for 50 miles to Burney and continue east five miles to Highway 89. Turn right (south) on Highway 89 and drive 10.5 miles to Forest Road 26 (Forest Road 34N19). Turn west on

Forest Road 26 (Forest Road 34N19) and drive 8.5 miles to Forest Road 34N60. Turn left and drive 2.5 miles to the parking area.

Contact: Lassen National Forest, Hat Creek Ranger District, 43225 East Highway 299, P.O. Box 220, Falls River Mills, CA 96028, 530/336-5521, www.fs.fed.us/r5.

24 TAMARACK TRAILHEAD
6.5 mi / 3.5 hr   🏃2 ⛰8

on the east boundary of the Thousand Lakes Wilderness north of Lassen Volcanic National Park

Map 3.3, page 133

The big news is that Tamarack Trailhead has a new location that makes it far preferable to the Cypress Trailhead. Those familiar with the area will remember that you used to need a high-clearance four-wheel-drive to reach the former Tamarack Trailhead (the road passed through private property and the owner would not allow the Forest Service to maintain it). The new trailhead is significant because instead of having to hike/climb more than 1,000 feet to reach Lake Eiler, it's now more like 400 feet. The new location adds only about 0.25-mile hiking distance to the trip.

From the new Tamarack Trailhead, your first destination is Lake Eiler, a three-mile hike. Have a picnic, swim, or fish, and then return. If you are setting out on a multiday backpacking trek, then go onward to several other wilderness lakes. The trail is then routed into the northwestern interior of the Thousand Lakes Wilderness. After two miles, you'll reach a fork in the trail; turn left (south) to reach Barrett Lake in just another mile of hiking.

Note that there is a complex trail network in this area with many junctions, creating a situation in which backpackers can invent their own multiday route. From Barrett Lake, other attractive destinations include Durbin Lake, 0.5 mile to the south, and Everett and Magee Lakes, another (very challenging) 2.7 miles away.

User Groups: Hikers, dogs, and horses. No mountain bikes. No wheelchair facilities.

Permits: No permits are required. Parking and access are free.

Maps: For a map, ask the U.S. Forest Service for Lassen National Forest. A wilderness trail map is available for a fee from the Hat Creek Ranger District. For topographic maps, ask the USGS for Thousand Lakes Valley and Jacks Backbone.

Directions: From Redding, take Highway 299 east for 50 miles to Burney and continue east five miles to Highway 89. Turn right (south) on Highway 89 and drive about 14 miles to Forest Road 33N25. Turn west on Forest Road 33N25 and drive 7.5 miles to a Y junction. Turn right and drive just about 1.5 miles to the trailhead (the new route is well signed).

Contact: Lassen National Forest, Hat Creek Ranger District, 43225 East Highway 299, P.O. Box 220, Falls River Mills, CA 96028, 530/336-5521, www.fs.fed.us/r5.

25 BUNCHGRASS TRAILHEAD
8.0 mi / 2 days   🏃2 ⛰7

on the south boundary of the Thousand Lakes Wilderness north of Lassen Volcanic National Park

Map 3.3, page 133

This trailhead is obscure and difficult to reach, and because of that, few visitors choose it as a jump-off spot for their treks. The destination is Durbin Lake, a four-mile hike one-way, making an easy weekend backpack trip. The trailhead elevation is 5,680 feet, and from here, it's a fair walk in, up, and down. If you're not in shape, you'll know it well before you reach the lake. You'll come to Hall Butte (at 7,187 feet) and then Durbin Lake. A side-trip option is to climb Hall Butte. Break off the trail at three miles in, for a 0.5-mile tromp to the top with no trail.

User Groups: Hikers, dogs, and horses. No mountain bikes. No wheelchair facilities.

Permits: A campfire permit (free) is required. Parking and access are free.

Maps: For a map, ask the U.S. Forest Service for Lassen National Forest. A wilderness trail map is available for a fee from the Hat Creek Ranger District. For topographic maps, ask the USGS for Thousand Lakes Valley and Jacks Backbone.

Directions: From Redding, take Highway 299 east for 50 miles to Burney and continue east five miles to Highway 89. Turn right (south) on Highway 89 and drive 31 miles to Forest Road 16 (Forest Road 33N16). Turn right on Forest Road 16 and drive seven miles to Forest Road 32N45. Turn right on Forest Road 32N45 and drive two miles to Forest Road 32N42Y (which is very steep). Turn left and head to the parking area, at the end of the road.

Contact: Lassen National Forest, Hat Creek Ranger District, 43225 East Highway 299, P.O. Box 220, Falls River Mills, CA 96028, 530/336-5521, www.fs.fed.us/r5.

26 HAT CREEK RIM TO MCARTHUR-BURNEY FALLS MEMORIAL STATE PARK (PCT)

40.0 mi one-way / 3 days 🏃3 ⛰8

from the Highway 44 parking area north to McArthur-Burney Falls Memorial State Park

Map 3.3, page 133

This section of the PCT includes the infamous 27-mile section without water. Unless you are through-hiking the entire PCT, there is no reason to suffer this ignominy. Yet this 40-mile section also features Hat Creek, Baum Lake, Crystal Lake, and spectacular Burney Falls.

From the trailhead at Highway 44, the trail passes through the wooded watershed of Hat Creek to a long, shadeless section that will have you counting the drops of water in your canteen. This is the Hat Creek Rim section of the PCT, the roughest section of the entire route from Mexico to Canada, with no water

available for 27 miles of trail. A single drop of water will be valued more than a $10,000 bill. A lot of PCT hikers cheat this section by leaving the trail for the highway, and some will even hitch a ride in the backs of pick-up trucks.

After departing from Hat Creek, the PCT heads past Baum and Crystal Lakes. You cross Highway 299, and from there, it's an eight-mile romp to McArthur-Burney Falls State Park and its breathtaking 129-foot waterfall.

To continue north on the PCT, see the *McArthur-Burney Falls Memorial State Park to Ash Camp (PCT)* hike in this chapter. If you are walking this trail in reverse, see the *Lassen Volcanic National Park to Highway 44 (PCT)* hike in this chapter to continue south.

User Groups: Hikers, dogs (except in the state park boundaries), and horses. No mountain bikes. No wheelchair facilities.

Permits: A campfire permit (free) is required. A state park entrance fee of $8 is charged per vehicle.

Maps: For topographic maps, ask the USGS for Cassel, Dana, Old Station, Murken Bench, Hogback Ridge, and Burney Falls.

Directions: From Redding, take Highway 44 east for 60 miles to Highway 89/44. Turn left (north) on Highway 89/44 and drive 13 miles to Old Station and continue a short distance to Highway 44. Turn right (east) on Highway 44 and drive 0.25 mile beyond the Old Station Post Office to Forest Road 32N20. Turn right on Forest Road 32N20. The trail crosses the road about 0.5 mile from the junction of Highway 44 and Forest Road 32N20. If you have horses and need to park a horse trailer, use Mud Lake trailhead, located three miles from the junction of Highway 89 and Highway 44.

Contact: Lassen National Forest, Hat Creek Ranger District, 43225 East Highway 299, P.O. Box 220, Falls River Mills, CA 96028, 530/336-5521, www.fs.fed.us/r5.

27 NOBLES EMIGRANT TRAIL
2.0-10.0 mi / 1.0 hr-1 day 🏃1 ⛰8

from the Manzanita Lake Trailhead in Lassen
Volcanic National Park east of Red Bluff

Map 3.3, page 133

The most difficult part of this hike is the first
two steps. Why? Because the trailhead is set
near the northern park entrance amid a number of small roads and a maintenance area, and
despite a trail sign, many visitors can't find
it and give up. It's worth the search, because
it's a great day hike for campers staying at
Manzanita Lake.

The trail, with its easy, moderate grade,
passes first through an old forest with towering firs, cedars, and pines. About 2.5 miles in,
you'll arrive at Lassen's strange Dwarf Forest.
Not only will you be surrounded by stunted
trees, but you also get views of Chaos Crags,
a jumble of pinkish rocks constituting what's
left of an old broken-down volcano. Many visitors hike to this point, then turn around and
return to the campground. The trail follows
part of a historical route that was originally
an east–west portion of the California Trail,
used by emigrants in the 1850s. There is no
water available on the trail, so be sure to have
at least one filled canteen per hiker. Because of
the moderate slope, this trail is an ideal cross-
country ski route in the winter months. Key
note: No campfires are allowed in the park.

User Groups: Hikers and horses. No dogs or
mountain bikes. No wheelchair facilities.

Permits: A wilderness permit (free) is required
for hikers planning to camp in the backcountry. A park entrance fee of $10, good for seven
days, is charged for each vehicle.

Maps: Trail maps are available for a fee from
park visitors stations and at Lassen Loomis
Museum Association. For a map, ask the U.S.
Forest Service for Lassen National Forest. For
a topographic map, ask the USGS for Manzanita Lake.

Directions: From Redding, take Highway 44
east for 46 miles to the junction with Highway 89. Turn right (south) on Highway 89

and drive one mile to the park entrance station. Continue on the main park road (Lassen
Park Highway/Highway 89) for 0.5 mile to the
turnoff for Manzanita Lake. The trailhead is
across the road from Manzanita Lake, just
past the Loomis Museum.

Contact: Lassen Volcanic National Park, P.O.
Box 100, Mineral, CA 96063, 530/595-4480,
www.nps.gov/lavo; Lassen Loomis Museum
Association, P.O. Box 220, Mineral, CA 96063,
530/595-3399, www.lassenloomis.info.

28 MANZANITA LAKE TRAIL
1.6 mi / 1.0 hr 🏃1 ⛰8

at the northern entrance to Lassen Volcanic
National Park on Highway 44

Map 3.3, page 133

There's no prettier lake that you can reach
by car in Lassen Park than Manzanita Lake.
That is why many consider the campground
here a perfect destination. With 179 sites, it's
the largest camp in the park, and it's easy to
reach, located just beyond the entrance station
at the western boundary of the park. The trail
simply traces the shoreline of this pretty lake at
a 5,950-foot elevation and is easily accessible
from either the parking area just beyond the
entrance station or from the campground. A
good side trip is across the road to Reflection
Lake, a small and also very pretty lake, which
adds about 0.5 mile to the trip. Note that the
fishing at Manzanita Lake is catch-and-release
only with the use of artificials—do not use
bait, and do pinch down your barbs.

User Groups: Hikers only. No dogs, horses, or
mountain bikes. No wheelchair facilities.

Permits: No permits are required. A $10 park
entrance fee, good for seven days, is charged
for each vehicle.

Maps: Trail maps are available for a fee from
park visitors stations and at Lassen Loomis
Museum Association. For a map, ask the U.S.
Forest Service for Lassen National Forest. For
a topographic map, ask the USGS for Manzanita Lake.

Directions: From Redding, take Highway 44 east for 46 miles to the junction with Highway 89. Turn right (south) on Highway 89 and drive one mile to the park entrance station. Continue on the main park road (Lassen Park Highway/Highway 89) for 0.5 mile, to the turnoff for Manzanita Lake Campground. Turn right and drive 0.5 mile to the day-use parking area.

Contact: Lassen Volcanic National Park, P.O. Box 100, Mineral, CA 96063, 530/595-4480, www.nps.gov/lavo; Lassen Loomis Museum Association, P.O. Box 220, Mineral, CA 96063, 530/529-3450, www.lassenassociation.org.

29 CINDER CONE TRAIL
4.0 mi / 3.0 hr   🥾3 ⛰️8

from Butte Lake Trailhead in Lassen Volcanic National Park

Map 3.3, page 133

Huge chunks of Lassen Volcanic National Park are overlooked by visitors simply because access is not off the park's main roadway (Lassen Park Highway/Highway 89). Butte Lake and Cinder Cone Trail, set in the northeastern corner of the park, are such areas. When you arrive by car, you'll find large, attractive Butte Lake, quite a surprise for newcomers. The trailhead for Nobles Emigrant Trail/Cinder Cone Trail is set at an elevation of 6,100 feet, at the northwest corner of the lake. The trail starts out easy. It heads southwest through forest. But don't be fooled. After 1.5 miles, you'll reach the Cinder Cone cutoff, and there, everything suddenly changes. The last 0.5 mile rises to the top of the Cinder Cone, a short but very intense climb of 800 feet to the summit, at 6,907 feet. The views are unforgettable, especially south to the Painted Dunes and Fantastic Lava Beds. This is a classic volcanic landscape.

User Groups: Hikers only. No dogs, horses, or mountain bikes. No wheelchair facilities.

Permits: No permits are required. A park entrance fee of $10, good for seven days, is charged for each vehicle.

Maps: Trail maps are available for a fee from park visitors stations and at Lassen Loomis Museum Association. For a map, ask the U.S. Forest Service for Lassen National Forest. For a topographic map, ask the USGS for Prospect Peak.

Directions: From Redding, take Highway 44 east for 60 miles to Highway 89/44. Turn left (north) on Highway 89/44 and drive 13 miles to Old Station and continue a short distance to Highway 44. Turn right (east) on Highway 44 and drive 10 miles to Butte Lake Road (Forest Road 32N21). Turn right (south) on Butte Lake Road (Forest Road 32N21) and drive six miles to Butte Lake. The trailhead is located near the boat ramp.

Contact: Lassen Volcanic National Park, P.O. Box 100, Mineral, CA 96063, 530/595-4480, www.nps.gov/lavo; Lassen Loomis Museum Association, P.O. Box 220, Mineral, CA 96063, 530/595-3399, www.lassenloomis.info.

30 PROSPECT PEAK TRAIL
6.6 mi / 4.5 hr   🥾4 ⛰️10

at Butte Lake in Lassen Volcanic National Park

Map 3.3, page 133

Hiking to the top of most mountains requires a long, grinding climb. Gaining the summit of Prospect Peak is somewhat different. Long? No. Grinding? Yep. Your reward is some of the best views in Lassen Volcanic National Park and a trail that gets little use when compared to the others in the park.

The trailhead (Nobles Emigrant Trail), at 6,100 feet, is adjacent to Butte Lake. After less than 0.5 mile, you'll turn right at the junction with Prospect Peak Trail. The trail immediately starts to climb. Get used to it, because there's no respite for several hours. It climbs more than 2,200 feet over the course of just 3.3 miles. It finally tops the summit at 8,338 feet. From here, hikers can see most of the prominent peaks in the park. This includes Lassen Peak, Mount Hoffman, and Crater Butte, along with thousands and thousands of acres of national forest to the north. Since the snowmelt occurs earlier here than in the rest of the park, this trip makes a perfect hike in the early to mid-spring, when the air is still cool. If you wait until summer, you'll find this a dry, forsaken place.

User Groups: Hikers only. No dogs, horses, or mountain bikes. No wheelchair facilities.

Permits: No permits are required. A park entrance fee of $10, good for seven days, is charged for each vehicle.

Maps: Trail maps are available for a fee from park visitors stations and at Lassen Loomis Museum Association. For a map, ask the U.S. Forest Service for Lassen National Forest. For a topographic map, ask the USGS for Prospect Peak.

Directions: From Redding, take Highway 44 east for 60 miles to Highway 89/44. Turn left (north) on Highway 89/44 and drive 13 miles to Old Station and continue a short distance to Highway 44. Turn right (east) on Highway 44 and drive 10 miles to Forest Road 32N21. Turn right (south) on Forest Road 32N21 and drive seven miles to Butte Lake and the parking area near the boat ramp. Look for Nobles Emigrant trailhead (on the west side of the parking lot), and hike 0.5 mile to Prospect Peak Trail, on the right.

Contact: Lassen Volcanic National Park, P.O. Box 100, Mineral, CA 96063, 530/595-4480, www.nps.gov/lavo; Lassen Loomis Museum Association, P.O. Box 220, Mineral, CA 96063, 530/595-3399, www.lassenloomis.info.

31 CONE LAKE TRAILHEAD
4.0 mi / 2.5 hr   👫 2   ⛰ 8

on the northern boundary of the Caribou Wilderness east of Lassen Volcanic National Park

Map 3.3, page 133

The prize destination on this excellent day hike is Triangle Lake, a pretty spot set in the northern Caribou Wilderness near Black Butte. The trailhead is located at tiny Cone Lake, just outside the wilderness. From here, you walk for nearly a mile before passing the wilderness boundary, which is clearly marked. At that point, you can sense the change in features, as the land becomes wild and untouched. Continue one mile south to Triangle Lake, which provides good fishing during the evening for pan-sized trout. If you want more, you can get more.

Here the trail forks. The right fork is routed right into Lassen Volcanic National Park, a distance of only 1.5 miles, from which you can access Widow Lake. A free wilderness permit is required from Lassen Volcanic National Park for overnight use. The left fork, on the other hand, leads to Twin Lakes over the course of just 0.5 mile.

User Groups: Hikers, dogs, and horses. No mountain bikes. No wheelchair facilities.

Permits: No permits are required for day use. Campfire permits are required for overnight use. Parking and access are free.

Maps: A trail map is available for a fee from the Almanor Ranger District. For a map, ask the U.S. Forest Service for Lassen National Forest or Caribou Wilderness. For a topographic map, ask the USGS for Bogard Buttes.

Directions: From Redding, take Highway 44 east for 60 miles to Highway 89/44. Turn left (north) on Highway 89/44 and drive 13 miles to Old Station and continue a short distance to Highway 44. Turn right (east) on Highway 44 and drive 30 miles to Bogard Work Station and nearby Forest Road 10. Turn right on Forest Road 10 and drive six miles to Forest Road 32N09. Turn right on Forest Road

32N09 and drive three miles to the Cone Lake trailhead. Note that the roads are unpaved from Highway 44 to the trailhead.

Contact: Lassen National Forest, Almanor Ranger District, P.O. Box 767, Chester, CA 96020, 530/258-2141, www.fs.fed.us/r5.

32 CARIBOU LAKE TRAILHEAD
12.0 mi / 2 days

on the eastern boundary of the Caribou Wilderness east of Lassen Volcanic National Park

Map 3.3, page 133

The Caribou Lake trailhead provides a hiking trip that is a parade past mountain lakes. Rarely are so many wilderness lakes this close to a trailhead. The trip starts at Caribou Lake, heading west. In no time you pass all kinds of tiny lakes. The first one, Cowboy Lake, is only 0.25 mile down the trail. In another 15 minutes, you'll come to Jewel Lake. This procession of lakes never seems to stop. Eleanor Lake is next. Then, two miles in, turn left at the fork and you pass Black Lake, North and South Divide Lakes, and, farther on, Long Lake. This lake, six miles from the trailhead, should be your destination, since it makes a great two-day backpacking adventure. The Caribou Wilderness is quite small, just nine miles from top to bottom, and only five miles across, with elevations ranging from 5,000 to 7,000 feet. This trip will provide a visit to the best of it.

User Groups: Hikers, dogs, and horses (a horse corral is available at the trailhead). No mountain bikes. No wheelchair facilities.

Permits: A campfire permit (free) is required. Parking and access are free.

Maps: A trail map is available for a fee from the Almanor Ranger District. For a map, ask the U.S. Forest Service for Lassen National Forest or Caribou Wilderness. For a topographic map, ask the USGS for Red Cinder.

Directions: From Red Bluff, take Highway 36 east and drive 83 miles to Westwood (east of Lake Almanor) and County Road A21. Turn north on County Road A21 and go 14.1 miles to Silver Lake Road. Turn left on Silver Lake Road and drive five miles to a Y with Forest Road 10. Turn right on Forest Road 10 and drive 0.25 mile to a fork. Turn left and drive 0.25 mile to the trailhead.

Contact: Lassen National Forest, Almanor Ranger District, 900 East Highway 36, P.O. Box 767, Chester, CA 96020, 530/258-2141, www.fs.fed.us/r5.

33 ECHO AND TWIN LAKES
8.0 mi / 5.5 hr

in Lassen Volcanic National Park east of Red Bluff

Map 3.3, page 133   **BEST (**

You get it all on this hike to Lower Twin Lake: beautiful lakes, forest, meadows, and wildflowers. The route provides testimony to the beauty of the Lassen Wilderness. The trailhead elevation is 7,000 feet. The trail starts on the north side of Summit Lake. Right off, the trail climbs 500 feet in the first mile. After this climb, the rest of the hike will be a breeze. You'll arrive at Echo Lake in just another mile and at Upper Twin and Lower Twin in the next two miles, dropping 500 feet on your way. It's all very pretty and is a great bonus for Summit Lake campers. It makes an outstanding day hike for campers staying at Summit Lake Campground or an easy overnighter for backpackers.

Special note: No campfires are permitted at any time in the wilderness at Lassen Volcanic National Park.

User Groups: Hikers and horses. No dogs or mountain bikes. No wheelchair facilities.

Permits: No permits are required. A park entrance fee of $10, good for seven days, is charged for each vehicle.

Maps: Trail maps are available for a fee at park visitors stations and at Lassen Loomis Museum Association. For a map, ask the U.S. Forest Service for Lassen National Forest. For a topographic map, ask the USGS for Reading Peak.

Directions: From Redding, take Highway 44 east for 46 miles to the junction with Highway 89. Turn right (south) on Highway 89 and drive one mile to the park entrance station. Continue on the main park road (Lassen Park Highway/Highway 89) for 12 miles to the turnoff for Summit Lake North Campground. Turn left and park in the day-use area near the lake. Look for the boardwalk that leads to a trail sign, then turn left and start your hike.

Contact: Lassen Volcanic National Park, P.O. Box 100, Mineral, CA 96063, 530/595-4480, www.nps.gov/lavo; Lassen Loomis Museum Association, P.O. Box 220, Mineral, CA 96063, 530/595-3399, www.lassenloomis.info.

34 SUMMIT LAKE LOOP
0.5 mi / 0.5 hr
🥾1 ⛰️8

in Lassen Volcanic National Park east of Red Bluff

Map 3.3, page 133

Summit Lake is a beautiful spot where deer visit almost every summer evening. Nearby campgrounds on both sides of the lake (north and south) are set in conifers, with a pretty meadow just south of the lake along Kings Creek. This hike is a simple walk around Summit Lake. It is best taken at dusk, when the changing evening colors reflect a variety of tints across the lake surface. Though no lakes in Lassen Volcanic National Park are stocked with trout and the fishing is terrible, you may still see a rising trout or two. The best place to see wildlife, especially deer, is in the meadow adjacent to Kings Creek, the lake's outlet stream. The elevation is 7,000 feet.

User Groups: Hikers and horses. No dogs or mountain bikes. No wheelchair facilities.

Permits: No permits are required. A park entrance fee of $10, good for seven days, is charged for each vehicle.

Maps: Trail maps are available for a fee at park visitors stations and at Lassen Loomis Museum Association. For a map, ask the U.S. Forest Service for Lassen National Forest. For a topographic map, ask the USGS for Reading Peak.

Directions: From Redding, take Highway 44 east for 46 miles to the junction with Highway 89. Turn right (south) on Highway 89 and drive one mile to the park entrance station. Continue on the main park road (Lassen Park Highway/Highway 89) for 12 miles to the turnoff for Summit Lake North Campground. Turn left and park in the day-use area near the lake.

Contact: Lassen Volcanic National Park, P.O. Box 100, Mineral, CA 96063, 530/595-4480, www.nps.gov/lavo; Lassen Loomis Museum Association, P.O. Box 220, Mineral, CA 96063, 530/595-3399, www.lassenloomis.info.

35 LASSEN PEAK TRAIL
5.0 mi / 4.0 hr
🥾4 ⛰️10

in Lassen Volcanic National Park east of Red Bluff

Map 3.3, page 133   BEST (

Lassen Peak crowns the horizon at 10,457 feet. It's a huge volcanic flume with hardened lava flows, craters, outcrops, and extraordinary views in all directions. The peak is a perfect example of a lava pinnacle plug dome. Exploring Lassen Peak has become a popular hike—perhaps the best introduction to mountain climbing a hiker could desire. The trail was rebuilt and reinforced in the summer of 2011.

The trailhead (at 8,500 feet) is adjacent to a large parking area, set at the base of the summit along the main park road (Lassen Park Highway/Highway 89). Looking up from the parking lot, you can see most of the trail to the rim. The climb to the top is a 2.5-mile zigzag on a hard, flat trail, ascending just over 2,000 feet in the process. There are several spots with awesome vistas, looking down into sculpted bowls and to lakes both near and far.

On the rim, you get spectacular views without reaching the true plug-dome peak—Mount Shasta, 100 miles north, appears close enough to reach out and grab. To the east are hundreds of miles of forests and lakes, and to the west, the land drops off to several small volcanic cones and the northern Sacramento Valley. To crown the hike, continue on the trail north, which crosses a volcanic crag for 0.25 mile and then is routed on a path to the summit peak. Fantastic!

In summer, start early, preferably by 8 A.M. Bring a lunch and a canteen or two of water. In the morning, with the air still cool, it's about a two-hour walk to the top, with a 15 percent grade most of the way. This is an exceptional first climb for youngsters, providing for plenty of encouragement and rest stops.

Special note: Winds are common at Lassen Peak, especially on summer afternoons. Hikers should stash a windbreaker in their daypacks. In addition, if you see cumulus clouds starting to form on the rim, common on summer afternoons, don't go. Quick-forming thunderstorms with lightning are also common on hot afternoons. It's always a mistake to suddenly climb the summit without planning the trip. Stay at lower elevations if there's any chance of lightning activity.

User Groups: Hikers only. No dogs, horses, or mountain bikes. No wheelchair facilities.

Permits: No permits are required. A park entrance fee of $10, good for seven days, is charged for each vehicle.

Maps: Trail maps are available for a fee at park visitors stations and at Lassen Loomis Museum Association. For a map, ask the U.S. Forest Service for Lassen National Forest. For a topographic map, ask the USGS for Lassen Peak.

Directions: From Red Bluff, take Highway 36 east and drive 47 miles to the junction with Highway 89. Turn north (left) on Highway 89 and continue 4.5 miles to the park entrance. Continue seven miles on the main park road (Lassen Park Highway/Highway 89) to the parking area and store on the left.

The trailhead is at the west end of the parking lot.

Contact: Lassen Volcanic National Park, P.O. Box 100, Mineral, CA 96063, 530/595-4480, www.nps.gov/lavo; Lassen Loomis Museum Association, P.O. Box 220, Mineral, CA 96063, 530/595-3399, www.lassenloomis.info.

36 SHADOW LAKE TRAIL
1.6 mi / 1.0 hr   🥾2 ⛰8

in Lassen Volcanic National Park east of Red Bluff

Map 3.3, page 133

A hike of less than a mile on this trail will take you past little Terrace Lake (7,800 feet) and then shortly after to Shadow Lake (7,600 feet). It's rare to reach such a pretty lake surrounded by wildlands in such a short distance. The trail involves a short, steep climb to Terrace Lake, and then a 0.25-mile junket to skirt the southeast shoreline of Shadow Lake (which is at least three times the size of Terrace Lake). The lakes are set just north of Reading Peak, 8,701 feet. The trailhead is at 8,000 feet, and because of the altitude, some hikers may experience shortness of breath when making the climb to the lakes. But if you're still feeling good, then by all means continue 0.75 mile to Cliff Lake (7,250 feet), a beautiful spot that's well worth the extra hour.

User Groups: Hikers only. No dogs, horses, or mountain bikes. No wheelchair facilities.

Permits: No permits are required. A park entrance fee of $10, good for seven days, is charged for each vehicle.

Maps: Trail maps are available for a fee at park visitors stations and at Lassen Loomis Museum Association. For a map, ask the U.S. Forest Service for Lassen National Forest. For a topographic map, ask the USGS for Reading Peak.

Directions: From Red Bluff, take Highway 36 east and drive 47 miles to the junction with Highway 89. Turn north (left) on Highway 89 and continue 4.5 miles to the park entrance. Continue nine miles on the main park road (Lassen Park Highway/Highway 89) to the parking area and trailhead, on the left (two miles past the parking area for Lassen Summit).

Contact: Lassen Volcanic National Park, P.O. Box 100, Mineral, CA 96063, 530/595-4480, www.nps.gov/lavo; Lassen Loomis Museum Association, P.O. Box 220, Mineral, CA 96063, 530/595-3399, www.lassenloomis.info.

37 BUMPASS HELL TRAIL
3.0 mi / 2.0 hr   🏃2 ⛰10

in Lassen Volcanic National Park east of Red Bluff

Map 3.3, page 133

This is the most popular trail in Lassen Volcanic National Park. Bumpass Hell is like a walk into the land of perdition, complete with steam vents, boiling mud pots, and natural furnaces. It's all set amid volcanic rock and is prehistoric looking and a bit creepy, as if at any moment a T-Rex might charge around the bend and munch a few tourists. The trip to Bumpass Hell is the most popular hike in the park, and it makes sense, because it's not only the park's largest thermal area but also an excellent morning walk. The elevation at the trailhead is 8,200 feet.

The trail starts with a gradual 500-foot climb. You pass an excellent interpretive sign at an overlook that explains the origin and size of the gigantic Tehama Volcano. (Be sure to stop at the park information sign; the steel map shows just how big the Tehama Volcano was, all the way to Mount Brokeoff.) The trail continues in the first mile to a ridge overlooking the thermal area. You then descend 250 feet into the thermal basin. It sits in a pocket just below Bumpass Mountain (8,753 feet). Exhibits explain the area. There are usually large numbers of tourists at Bumpass Hell, but you can get beyond them by extending your trip to Cold Boiling Lake, another 1.5

miles (one-way), which includes two steep portions of trail.

Special note: For obvious reasons, it's important to stay on the trail or boardwalk near hydrothermal areas.

It is called "Bumpass" Hell because back in the old days, a guy named Bumpass slipped into the boiling water, scalded his feet, and in the ensuing newspaper report, the writer called the place "Bumpass's Hell," and the name stuck.

User Groups: Hikers only. No dogs, horses, or mountain bikes. No wheelchair facilities.

Permits: No permits are required. A park entrance fee of $10, good for seven days, is charged for each vehicle.

Maps: Trail maps are available for a fee from park visitors stations and at Lassen Loomis Museum Association. For a topographic map, ask the USGS for Lassen Peak.

Directions: From Red Bluff, take Highway 36 east and drive 47 miles to the junction with Highway 89. Turn north (left) on Highway 89 and drive 4.5 miles to the park entrance. Continue six miles on the main park road (Lassen Park Highway/Highway 89) to the trailhead, on the right.

Contact: Lassen Volcanic National Park, P.O. Box 100, Mineral, CA 96063, 530/595-4480, www.nps.gov/lavo; Lassen Loomis Museum Association, P.O. Box 220, Mineral, CA 96063, 530/595-3399, www.lassenloomis.info.

38 DRAKE LAKE TRAIL
4.5 mi / 2.75 hr   🏃3 ⛰6

at Drakesbad in Lassen Volcanic National Park

Map 3.3, page 133

Drake Lake is a somewhat swampy sub-alpine lake that brightens a largely dry hillside, where deer are often more plentiful than people. It is set in a remote forested pocket, very secluded, and just difficult enough of a climb that many take a pass on the trip. From the trailhead at Drakesbad, at about 5,650 feet, it's about an 800-foot climb over the course of two miles to Drake Lake (6,482 feet). Midway up the grade, the hike becomes steep and stays that way for nearly 45 minutes.

The lake is the payoff—emerald green and circled by firs. After you catch your breath, you may feel like jumping in and cooling off, particularly if it's a hot summer day. Well, we've got news for you: In early summer, the water is still ice cold, and just when you realize that, a battalion of mosquitoes will show up and start feasting on all your bare, sumptuous flesh. Then what? Jump in and freeze your buns? Stand there and get devoured? Heck no, you'll have your clothes back on in record time.

User Groups: Hikers only. Horses are allowed on a portion of the trail. No dogs or mountain bikes. No wheelchair facilities.

Permits: No permits are required. A park entrance fee of $10, good for seven days, is charged for each vehicle.

Maps: Trail maps are available for a fee from park visitors stations and at Lassen Loomis Museum Association. For a topographic map, ask the USGS for Reading Peak.

Directions: From Red Bluff, take Highway 36 east and drive 47 miles to the junction with Highway 89. Do not turn. Continue east on Highway 36 toward Lake Almanor and to Chester and Feather River Drive. Turn left on Feather River Drive and drive 0.75 mile. Bear left for Drakesbad and Warner Valley, and drive six miles to Warner Valley Road. Turn right and drive 11 miles to Warner Valley Campground. Continue for 0.5 mile to the trailhead, on the left. The last 3.5 miles is unpaved, and there is one steep hill that can be difficult for trailers or RVs.

Contact: Lassen Volcanic National Park, P.O. Box 100, Mineral, CA 96063, 530/595-4480, www.nps.gov/lavo; Lassen Loomis Museum Association, P.O. Box 220, Mineral, CA 96063, 530/595-3399, www.lassenloomis.info.

39 DEVILS KITCHEN TRAIL

4.4 mi / 2.5 hr   🏃2 ⛰8

at Drakesbad in Lassen Volcanic National Park

Map 3.3, page 133

Drakesbad is the undiscovered Lassen—beautiful, wild, and remote. It gets missed by nearly everybody because access is obscure and circuitous—on the way out of Chester en route to the Warner Valley Campground and nearby trailhead—rather than via Lassen's main park highway. There's no way to get here when entering from either of the main Lassen park entrances. But those who persevere will find a quiet paradise, along with this easy trip to Devils Kitchen, a unique geologic thermal area. The trail is an easy hike, heading west above Hot Springs Creek. The elevation at the trailhead is 5,650 feet, with a gradual climb of 300 feet. After two miles it ventures into this barren pocket of steaming vents, boiling mud pots, and fumaroles. You'll immediately see why it was tagged Devils Kitchen. It is dangerous to walk off trail in this area.

User Groups: Hikers only. Horses are allowed on a portion of the trail. No dogs or mountain bikes. No wheelchair facilities.

Permits: No permits are required. A park entrance fee of $10, good for seven days, is charged for each vehicle.

Maps: Trail maps are available for a fee from park visitors stations and at Lassen Loomis Museum Association. For a topographic map, ask the USGS for Reading Peak.

Directions: From Red Bluff, take Highway 36 east and drive 47 miles to the junction with Highway 89. Do not turn. Continue east on Highway 36 toward Lake Almanor and to Chester and Feather River Drive. Turn left on Feather River Drive and drive 0.75 mile. Bear left for Drakesbad and Warner Valley, and drive six miles to Warner Valley Road. Turn right and drive 11 miles to Warner Valley Campground. Continue 0.5 mile to the trailhead, on the left. The last 3.5 miles are unpaved, and there is one steep hill that can be difficult for trailers or RVs.

Contact: Lassen Volcanic National Park, P.O. Box 100, Mineral, CA 96063, 530/595-4480, www.nps.gov/lavo; Lassen Loomis Museum Association, P.O. Box 220, Mineral, CA 96063, 530/595-3399, www.lassenloomis.info.

40 LASSEN VOLCANIC NATIONAL PARK TO HIGHWAY 44 (PCT)
32.0 mi one-way / 3 days

from Warner Valley Campground in Lassen Volcanic National Park

Map 3.3, page 133

Every step on the Pacific Crest Trail in Lassen Volcanic National Park is a pleasure. Start at the wooded Warner Valley (at 5,680 feet), at Hot Springs Creek, and then head north into the park's most remote terrain. The trail is routed across Grassy Swale, past Swan Lake, and on to Lower Twin Lake (seven miles in), a pretty lake circled by conifers.

From here, the trail heads north through a strange but compelling volcanic area. It skirts the western flank of Fairfield Peak (7,272 feet) and then heads onward. It turns west past Soap Lake and Badger Flat, and continues out past the park's boundary. As you hike toward Highway 44, you'll be lateraling Badger Mountain (6,973 feet) to your right, with the Hat Creek drainage off to your immediate left. In this latter stretch of trail, you'll cross no major lakes or streams (plan your water well). You forge on through the national forest, which is mostly second-growth, crossing a few roads along the way. In the spring, wildflowers are exceptional near the Hat Creek area. Several primitive U.S. Forest Service campgrounds are located on the trail about 10 miles north of the border of Lassen Volcanic National Park. Note that no campfires are permitted at any time in the wilderness at Lassen Volcanic National Park.

To continue north on the PCT, see the *Hat Creek Rim to McArthur-Burney Falls Memorial State Park (PCT)* hike in this chapter. If you are walking this trail in reverse, see the *Domingo Springs to Lassen Volcanic National Park (PCT)* hike in this chapter to continue south.

User Groups: Hikers and horses. No dogs or mountain bikes are allowed in the Lassen Volcanic National Park section of the hike. No wheelchair facilities.

Permits: A wilderness permit (free) is required for hikers planning to camp in the Lassen Volcanic National Park backcountry and for equestrians. You may not camp with horses in the national park's backcountry, but a horse corral is available by reservation for overnighters at Summit Lake and Juniper Lake, and a small corral is located near the park's northern boundary for exclusive use by those on the Pacific Crest Trail. A park entrance fee of $10, good for seven days, is charged for each vehicle.

Maps: For topographic maps, ask the USGS for Reading Peak, West Prospect Peak, and Old Station.

Directions: From Red Bluff, take Highway 36 east and drive 47 miles to the junction with Highway 89. Do not turn. Continue east on Highway 36 toward Lake Almanor and to Chester and Feather River Drive. Turn left (north) and drive 0.75 mile to Warner Valley Road (signed to Juniper Lake and Drakesbad). Turn left and drive six miles to Warner Valley Road. Turn right and drive 11 miles (on an improved dirt road) to the Warner Valley Campground and trailhead, on the right.

Contact: Lassen Volcanic National Park, P.O. Box 100, Mineral, CA 96063, 530/595-4480, www.nps.gov/lavo; Lassen National Forest, Hat Creek Ranger District, 43225 East Highway 299, Falls River Mills, CA 96028, 530/336-5521, www.fs.fed.us/r5.

41 JUNIPER LAKE LOOP
7.5 mi / 4.0 hr   🏃3 ⛰10

in Lassen Volcanic National Park north of Lake Almanor

Map 3.3, page 133

The Juniper Lake Loop explores Lassen Volcanic National Park's least-known yet most beautiful backcountry. It features many lakes, many lookouts, and because there are pretty trail camps along the route, the chance to turn the trip into an overnighter. The adventure starts at the trailhead adjacent to the Juniper Lake Ranger Station, which requires a long bumpy ride out of Chester just to reach it. If you arrive late, a campground is available at the lake, at an elevation of 6,792 feet. At the north end of Juniper Lake, the trail heads straight north, and though it has plenty of ups and downs, along with a fairly level stretch through Cameron Meadow, it's mostly down, descending 800 feet to Snag Lake, at an elevation of 6,076 feet. The best advice is to turn south at Snag Lake and take the trail along Grassy Creek to Horseshoe Lake. This section is the prettiest of the hike.

On the second day, you'll skirt the south flank of Crater Butte (7,267 feet), head past Horseshoe Lake, and then continue on to the starting point. Alas, this trip is not flawless. The fishing is poor, mosquitoes are rampant in the early summer, and nights are very cold in the fall.

If you want to extend your trip, on the first day hike from Snag Lake out into the backcountry to Rainbow Lake; a mile later to Lower Twin Lake (6,537 feet); and another mile farther to Swan Lake (6,628 feet). Any of these can make for a good trail camp.

Note: From the north end of Juniper Lake, the 400-foot climb to Inspiration Point provides a lookout for the park's backcountry, but trees partially block the view. No campfires are permitted at Lassen Volcanic National Park.

User Groups: Hikers and horses. No dogs or mountain bikes. No wheelchair facilities.

Permits: For overnight use, a wilderness permit (free) is required. A park entrance fee of $10, good for seven days, is charged for each vehicle.

Maps: Trail maps are available for a fee from park visitors stations and at Lassen Loomis Museum Association. For a topographic map, ask the USGS for Mount Harkness.

Directions: From Red Bluff, take Highway 36 east and drive 47 miles to the junction with Highway 89. Do not turn. Continue east on Highway 36 toward Lake Almanor and to Chester and Feather River Drive. Turn left on Feather River Drive and drive 0.75 mile to a Y. Bear right at the Y to Juniper Lake Road and drive 13 miles to the Snag Lake trailhead, near the ranger station. The access road is rough. Trailers and RVs are not recommended.

Contact: Lassen Volcanic National Park, P.O. Box 100, Mineral, CA 96063, 530/595-4480, www.nps.gov/lavo; Lassen Loomis Museum Association, P.O. Box 220, Mineral, CA 96063, 530/595-3399, www.lassenloomis.info.

42 HAY MEADOW TRAIL
6.0 mi / 2 days   🏃2 ⛰10

on the southern boundary of the Caribou Wilderness north of Lake Almanor

Map 3.3, page 133

Hidden between South Caribou Peak and Black Cinder Rock is a little alpine pocket where dozens of small lakes are sprinkled about the southern Caribou Wilderness. It's a slice of paradise that some hikers call the Hidden Lakes. The trail out of Hay Meadow is a loop that crosses right through these lakes: Beauty, Long, Posey, and Evelyn.

After arriving at the trailhead at Hay Meadow, the trip starts easily enough, first crossing Hay Meadow. In another mile, you'll reach Beauty Lake, the first of the four lakes on this loop hike. They are all good for swimming, although a bit cold, and Beauty and Posey have the best trout fishing.

Although the trip can be made in a day, you likely won't feel like leaving, and planning an easy overnight backpacking trip is recommended. Another bonus of an overnight trip is that you can take the side trip up to Hidden Lakes, a series of several small but pretty waters, set just below South Caribou Mountain.

Note that although the Caribou Wilderness abuts Lassen Volcanic National Park, it's often overlooked in the big park's shadow. That's to your benefit, as long as you know about this trail.

User Groups: Hikers, dogs, and horses (a horse corral is available at the trailhead). No mountain bikes. No wheelchair facilities.

Permits: A campfire permit (free) is required. Parking and access are free.

Maps: A trail map is available for a fee from the Almanor Ranger District. For a map, ask the U.S. Forest Service for Lassen National Forest or Caribou Wilderness. For a topographic map, ask the USGS for Red Cinder.

Directions: From Red Bluff, take Highway 36 east and drive 47 miles to the junction with Highway 89. Do not turn. Continue east on Highway 36 toward Lake Almanor and to Chester. In Chester, continue east on Highway 36 for five miles to Forest Road 10. Turn north on Forest Road 10 and drive 9.5 miles to Forest Road 30N25. Turn left on Forest Road 30N25 and drive to the trailhead.

Contact: Lassen National Forest, Almanor Ranger District, P.O. Box 767, Chester, CA 96020, 530/258-2141, www.fs.fed.us/r5.

43 SPENCER MEADOW TRAIL

10.0 mi / 1 day 🚶3 ⛰7

in Lassen National Forest just south of Lassen Volcanic National Park

Map 3.3, page 133

Spencer Meadow is a pretty mountain meadow on the southern flank of Mount Conrad. Here explorers can discover an effervescent spring pouring forth, one source of Mill Creek and the creation of the headwaters of a Sacramento River tributary. Hiking access is easy; the

trailhead is located at a parking area just off Highway 36.

Start the trip by taking the trail straight north toward Lassen on the Spencer Meadow Trail. Over the course of five miles, the trail passes a small spring (about halfway in, look for the faint spur trail on the left), then tiny Patricia Lake (on the right, hidden), and finally Spencer Meadow and Mill Creek Spring. Note that fishing at Mill Creek is restricted to catch-and-release and the use of artificials with single barbless hooks.

Special note: There is a trailhead closer to Spencer Meadow on Forest Road 29N40, but reaching it involves a long, rough drive.

User Groups: Hikers, dogs, horses, and mountain bikes. No wheelchair facilities.

Permits: No permits are required for day use. Campfire permits are required for overnight use. Parking and access are free.

Maps: A trail map is available for a fee from the Almanor Ranger District. For a map, ask the U.S. Forest Service for Lassen National Forest. For a topographic map, ask the USGS for Childs Meadows.

Directions: From Red Bluff, take Highway 36 east for 43 miles to Mineral, then continue east on Highway 36 for about seven miles to the trailhead parking area on the left.

Contact: Lassen National Forest, Almanor Ranger District, P.O. Box 767, Chester, CA 96020, 530/258-2141, www.fs.fed.us/r5.

44 DOMINGO SPRINGS TO LASSEN VOLCANIC NATIONAL PARK (PCT)

11.0 mi one-way / 1 day 🚶2 ⛰7

at the Domingo Springs Trailhead in Lassen National Forest west of Lake Almanor

Map 3.3, page 133

From Domingo Springs, the Pacific Crest Trail runs straight north through Lassen National Forest. The Little North Fork of the North Fork Feather River is located 0.25 mile to the west and is a good side trip, both for swimming and for fishing for large brown trout. As you enter Lassen Volcanic National Park, you'll pass Little Willow Lake, and two miles later, you'll arrive at Boiling Springs Lake and the Warner Valley Campground. This is a good layover spot, and a side trip to Devils Kitchen is recommended.

To continue north on the PCT, see the *Lassen Volcanic National Park to Highway 44 (PCT)* hike in this chapter. If you are walking this trail in reverse, see the *Feather River to Humboldt Summit (PCT)* hike in this chapter to continue south.

User Groups: Hikers, dogs, and horses. No mountain bikes. No wheelchair facilities.

Permits: A campfire permit (free) is required. Parking and access are free.

Maps: For a map, ask the U.S. Forest Service for Lassen National Forest. For a topographic map, ask the USGS for Stover Mountain.

Directions: From Red Bluff, take Highway 36 east and drive 47 miles to the junction with Highway 89. Do not turn. Continue east on Highway 36 toward Lake Almanor and to Chester and Feather River Drive. Turn left (north) and drive 0.75 mile to Warner Valley Road (signed Juniper Lake and Drakesbad). Turn left and drive to Old Red Bluff Road (County Road 311) and go three miles to the parking area at Domingo Springs.

Contact: Lassen National Forest, Almanor Ranger District, P.O. Box 767, Chester, CA 96020, 530/258-2141, www.fs.fed.us/r5.

45 MCCLURE TRAIL
9.0 mi / 1 day

in the Tehama Wildlife Area east of Red Bluff

Map 3.3, page 133

At first glance, the Tehama Wildlife Area might appear to be nothing more than rolling oak woodlands. But this is a habitat managed expressly for wildlife, and it includes a beautiful stream, abundant vegetation, and plenty of birds and animals.

This trail accesses the best of the wildlife area. From the McClure trailhead, hike down a steep canyon to Antelope Creek. The canyon is buffered by riparian vegetation. In late winter and spring, the canyon's adjoining hillsides come alive in green, and all wildlife seems to prosper. The stream is very pretty, and fishing is catch-and-release only with the use of artificials.

The area is huge, covering 44,862 acres, and is popular in the fall during hunting season for deer and wild pigs. Deer are rampant in late fall and migrate in after the hunting season is over. There are also lots of squirrels, hawks, and rattlesnakes. Low numbers of wild pigs roam the canyons but are never seen from trails. This area is also very popular with turkey hunters in season.

User Groups: Hikers and dogs. Mountain bikes and horses permitted but not recommended because of terrain. No wheelchair facilities.

Permits: A campfire permit (free) is required for overnight use. Parking and access are free.

Maps: For a free map, contact the Tehama Wildlife Area. For a map, ask the U.S. Forest Service for Lassen National Forest. For a topographic map, ask the USGS for Dewitt Peak.

Directions: From Red Bluff, take Highway 36 east and drive 20 miles to Paynes Creek and Plum Creek Road. Turn right (south) on Plum Creek Road and go to Ishi Conservation Camp and continue about 2.5 miles south to High Trestle Road and follow it to Hogsback Road. Park across from the intersection of High Trestle and Hogsback Roads, and walk about 0.25 mile on the dirt road to the trailhead.

Access note: Access to the Tehama Wildlife Area is closed to the public from February to the first Saturday in April. Access is also restricted for a short period during deer season in late September. There are no closures on U.S. Forest Service trails.

Contact: Lassen National Forest, Almanor Ranger District, 900 East Highway 36, P.O.

Box 767, Chester, CA 96020, 530/258-2141, www.fs.fed.us/r5; Department of Fish and Game, Tehama Wildlife Area, P.O. Box 188, Paynes Creek, CA 96075, 530/597-2201; Department of Fish and Game, Region 1 Headquarters, 530/225-2300, www.dfg.ca.gov.

46 DEER CREEK TRAIL

1.0-8.0 mi / 1 day   🏃2 🏔9

in Lassen National Forest along Highway 32 west of Lake Almanor

Map 3.3, page 133   BEST (☾

The Deer Creek Trail has all the ingredients to make it ideal for a trout angler, an explorer, or somebody just looking for a dunk on a hot day. The gorgeous stream runs right alongside the trail, with good access throughout and fish (often plenty of them) in the summer months.

From the parking area, look for the trail on the left side of the road. Start by hiking downstream. The trail is routed downstream along the river for about 10 miles. Rarely does anybody ever walk all the way to the end. Instead they take their time, perhaps fishing or swimming along the way.

In summer, Deer Creek is cold and clear, tumbling its way over rocks and into pools, with trout seemingly in every one. California Department of Fish and Game rules mandate catch-and-release fishing with artificials with a single barbless hook for most of the river. This trail has also become popular among mountain bikers. Most are courteous to hikers, and on a single-track trail, that's important. An interesting note is that the canyon rim is made up of a series of volcanic crags and basalt spires.

User Groups: Hikers, dogs, and horses. Mountain bikes aren't advised. No wheelchair facilities.

Permits: No permits are required. Parking and access are free.

Maps: A trail map is available for a fee from Almanor Ranger District. For a map, ask the U.S. Forest Service for Lassen National Forest. For a topographic map, ask the USGS for Onion Butte.

Directions: From Chico, take Highway 32 northeast for 40 miles (it becomes narrow and twisty). Just after crossing a small, red, metal bridge (locals call it the Red Bridge) that crosses Deer Creek, park on the right (south) side of the road, where there's a dirt pullout. The trailhead is just up from the bridge, on the left (north) side of the road.

Contact: Lassen National Forest, Almanor Ranger District, P.O. Box 767, Chester, CA 96020, 530/258-2141, www.fs.fed.us/r5.

47 TABLE MOUNTAIN TRAIL

3.2 mi / 2.5 hr   🏃3 🏔8

in the Ishi Wilderness east of Red Bluff

Map 3.3, page 133

This trail may be short, but it's anything but sweet. Except, that is, from the top of Table Mountain, at 2,380 feet, where you're supplied with a sweeping view of the Sacramento Valley and the surrounding Land of Ishi. This is where Ishi, the last survivor of the Yahi Yana tribe, escaped from a band of white settlers who exterminated the rest of the Yahis. The Indians had lived here for 3,000 years before being killed off, another stellar moment in the history of the western frontier.

The trail starts from the northwest corner of the wilderness at the Table Mountain trailhead, and then goes 1.6 miles to the summit. It's very steep and challenging, and most hikers will be wheezing like worn-out donkeys before making the top. Because of the hot summers, it's absolutely critical either to start the trip very early in the morning or to time it so that it's done during cool weather. Bring plenty of water for your built-in radiator.

Special note: A wilderness trail map is strongly advised for those hiking in the Ishi Wilderness.

User Groups: Hikers, dogs, and horses. No mountain bikes. No wheelchair facilities.

Permits: A campfire permit is required for hikers planning to camp. Parking and access are free.

Maps: A trail map is available for a fee from Almanor Ranger District. For a map, ask the U.S. Forest Service for Lassen National Forest or Ishi Wilderness. For topographic maps, ask the USGS for Panther Spring and Butte Meadows.

Directions: From Red Bluff, take Highway 36 east and drive about 20 miles to Paynes Creek and then continue to Little Giant Mill Road. Turn right (south) on Little Giant Mill Road (Road 202) and drive about seven miles until you reach Ponderosa Way. Turn south at Ponderosa Way and drive about 10 miles to Forest Road 28N57. Turn right (west) on Forest Road 28N57 and follow Peligreen Jeep Trail for six miles to the trailhead. The last five miles of road are suitable only for four-wheel-drive vehicles.

Contact: Lassen National Forest, Almanor Ranger District, P.O. Box 767, Chester, CA 96020, 530/258-2141, www.fs.fed.us/r5.

48 RANCHERIA TRAIL
4.0 mi / 2.75 hr   🏃4 ⛰9

in the Ishi Wilderness east of Red Bluff

Map 3.3, page 133

On a map, the Rancheria trailhead looks like the closest and easiest trailhead to reach into the Ishi Wilderness from Red Bluff. And the trail also appears short as well. But when you go there, a completely different picture comes into focus. First off, the trailhead access road is quite rough, impassable for most cars, and that's just a prelude to what lies ahead.

The trail starts by following an old jeep road, then leaves the road at a fence line off to the right. If it's hot, which is typical here most of the year, you'll already be reaching for your canteen. The trail then drops like a cannonball for 1,000 feet into the Mill Creek Canyon. This canyon is a surprising and awesome habitat with some of the prettiest areas

of the Ishi Wilderness. The fishing is often good. Rules mandate catch-and-release with the use of artificials. Shadowing your trek and enjoyment of the Mill Creek Canyon is the knowledge that you have to climb back out of that canyon. To make it out before sunset, that climb will likely be during the hottest part of the day. By the time you reach the car, your butt will be thoroughly kicked.

Special note: A trail map is strongly advised for those hiking in the Ishi Wilderness.

User Groups: Hikers, dogs, and horses. No mountain bikes. No wheelchair facilities.

Permits: A campfire permit (free) is required for overnight use. Parking and access are free.

Maps: A trail map is available for a fee from Almanor Ranger District. For a map, ask the U.S. Forest Service for Lassen National Forest or Ishi Wilderness. For topographic maps, ask the USGS for Panther Spring and Butte Meadows.

Directions: From Red Bluff, take Highway 36 east and drive 20 miles to Paynes Creek and continue to Little Giant Mill Road. Turn right (south) on Little Giant Mill Road (Road 202) and drive seven miles to Ponderosa Way. Turn south and drive about 10 miles to Forest Road 28N57. Turn right (west) and follow the Peligreen Jeep Trail for two miles to the Rancheria trailhead. The last two miles of road are suitable only for four-wheel-drive vehicles.

Contact: Lassen National Forest, Almanor Ranger District, P.O. Box 767, Chester, CA 96020, 530/258-2141, www.fs.fed.us/r5.

49 LOWER MILL CREEK
13.0 mi / 1 day   🏃2 ⛰9

in the Ishi Wilderness east of Red Bluff

Map 3.3, page 133

If you have time for only one trail in the Ishi Wilderness, Mill Creek Trail is the one to pick. That goes whether you want to invest just an hour or a full day, because any length of trip can be a joy here. The trail parallels Mill Creek for 6.5 miles to its headwaters, at Papes Place, with magnificent scenery and many good fishing and swimming holes along the way. This is a dramatic canyon, and as you stand along the stream, the walls can seem to ascend into heaven. It's a land shaped by thousands of years of wind and water.

Directly across from the trailhead, on Ponderosa Way, is another trailhead, this one for a route that follows Upper Mill Creek into Lassen National Forest. Although not as spectacular as Lower Mill Creek, it provides a good option for hiking, fishing, and swimming. Note that fishing is restricted to catch-and-release and the use of artificials.

Special note: A trail map is strongly advised for those hiking in the Ishi Wilderness.
User Groups: Hikers, dogs, and horses. No mountain bikes. No wheelchair facilities.
Permits: A campfire permit (free) is required for overnight use. Parking and access are free.
Maps: A trail map is available for a fee from Almanor Ranger District. For a map, ask the U.S. Forest Service for Lassen National Forest or Ishi Wilderness. For topographic maps, ask the USGS for Panther Spring and Butte Meadows.
Directions: From Red Bluff, take Highway 36 east and drive 20 miles to Paynes Creek, and continue to Little Giant Mill Road. Turn right (south) on Little Giant Mill Road (Road 202) and drive seven miles to Ponderosa Way. Turn south at Ponderosa Way and drive about 17 miles to the Mill Creek trailhead. The access road is a slow go.
Contact: Lassen National Forest, Almanor Ranger District, P.O. Box 767, Chester, CA 96020, 530/258-2141, www.fs.fed.us/r5.

50 MOAK TRAIL
14.0 mi / 1.5 days

in the Ishi Wilderness east of Red Bluff
Map 3.3, page 133

Hit it right in the spring, and Moak Trail could be the best overnight hike in California's foothill country. Hit it wrong in the summer, and you'll wonder what you did to deserve such a terrible fate. In the spring, the foothill country is loaded with wildflowers and tall, fresh grass, and the views of the Sacramento Valley are spectacular. The trail includes a poke-and-probe section over a lava-rock boulder field, and there are good trail camps at Deep Hole (2,800 feet) and Drennan. It's an excellent weekend trip, including a loop route by linking Moak Trail with Buena Vista Trail, most of it easy walking. Alas, if you try this trip in the summer or fall, you'll need to have your gray matter examined at Red Bluff General. No wildflowers, no shade, 100-degree temperatures, and as for water, you're dreamin'.

Special note: A trail map is strongly advised for those hiking in the Ishi Wilderness.
User Groups: Hikers, dogs, and horses. No mountain bikes. No wheelchair facilities.
Permits: A campfire permit (free) is required for overnight use. Parking and access are free.
Maps: A trail map is available for a fee from Almanor Ranger District. For a map, ask the U.S. Forest Service for Lassen National Forest or Ishi Wilderness. For topographic maps, ask the USGS for Panther Spring and Butte Meadows.
Directions: From Red Bluff, take Highway 36 east and drive 20 miles to Paynes Creek, and continue to Little Giant Mill Road. Turn right (south) on Little Giant Mill Road (Road 202) and drive seven miles to Ponderosa Way. Turn south at Ponderosa Way and drive about 24 miles to the Moak trailhead.
Contact: Lassen National Forest, Almanor Ranger District, P.O. Box 767, Chester, CA 96020, 530/258-2141, www.fs.fed.us/r5.

51 DEER CREEK TRAIL
14.0 mi / 1.5 days 🥾2 ⛰9

in the Ishi Wilderness east of Red Bluff

Map 3.3, page 133

It's no accident that Deer Creek Trail is the most popular hike in the Ishi Wilderness. Not only are hikers rewarded with striking surroundings, but the hike is a pleasurable romp even if you cut the trip short to just an hour or two. That's because the trail runs midway up naked slopes, offering spectacular views of Deer Creek Canyon's basaltic cliffs and spires, and of the stream below.

The trailhead is at the southeast border of the wilderness. Right from the start, it's routed along the north shore of Deer Creek. Iron Mountain (at 3,274 feet) is located to the immediate north. The trail continues along the stream into the wilderness interior. It skirts past the northern edge of what is called the Graham Pinery, a dense island of ponderosa pine growing on a mountain terrace. A bonus is good bird-watching for hawks, eagles, and falcons at the rock cliffs, and looking for a large variety of wildlife, including rattlesnakes (here's your warning) and lots of squirrels and quail. Note that the stream is stocked with rainbow and brook trout near Potato Patch and Alder Creek Campgrounds. Below Potato Patch Campground, fishing is catch-and-release only with the use of artificials.

Special note: A trail map is strongly advised for those hiking in the Ishi Wilderness.

User Groups: Hikers, dogs, and horses. No mountain bikes. No wheelchair facilities.

Permits: A campfire permit (free) is required for overnight use. Parking and access are free.

Maps: A trail map is available for a fee from Almanor Ranger District. For a map, ask the U.S. Forest Service for Lassen National Forest or Ishi Wilderness. For topographic maps, ask the USGS for Panther Spring and Butte Meadows.

Directions: From Red Bluff, take Highway 36 east and drive 20 miles to Paynes Creek, and continue to Little Giant Mill Road. Turn right (south) on Little Giant Mill Road (Road 202) and drive seven miles to Ponderosa Way. Turn south at Ponderosa Way and drive about 26 miles to the Deer Creek trailhead.

Contact: Lassen National Forest, Almanor Ranger District, P.O. Box 767, Chester, CA 96020, 530/258-2141, www.fs.fed.us/r5.

52 DEVILS DEN TRAIL
9.0 mi / 1 day 🥾4 ⛰8

in the Ishi Wilderness east of Red Bluff

Map 3.3, page 133

The Devils Den trailhead is less than 0.5 mile from the Deer Creek trailhead, but that is where the similarities between the two end. This trail includes a rough climb that's beastly in summer. Always bring a water filtration pump to fill your canteen at Deer Creek. The main attractions here are: 1) nobody else is usually around; 2) the trail is routed through a series of habitat zones over the course of the first 3.5 miles, providing a number of striking contrasts; and 3) nobody else is usually around. Getting the drift, eh?

The trail starts easy. It is routed along Deer Creek for the first mile. Note that fishing here is restricted to catch-and-release and the use of artificials. Enjoy yourself, because what follows is not exactly a picnic. The trail turns left and climbs up Little Pine Creek all the way to the ridge top, with the last mile on an old, hot, and chunky abandoned road. Along the way, the vegetation changes from riparian along the creek to woodland on the slopes, then chaparral on the ridge. The Deer Creek Rim is spiked by small volcanic spires and formations that, in some cases, look like they are from another planet. In addition, an island of conifers, the Graham Pinery, is available for viewing with a 0.25-mile side trip.

Special note: A trail map is strongly advised for those hiking in the Ishi Wilderness.

User Groups: Hikers, dogs, and horses. No mountain bikes. No wheelchair facilities.

Permits: A campfire permit (free) is required for overnight use. Parking and access are free.

Maps: A trail map is available for a fee from Almanor Ranger District. For a map, ask the U.S. Forest Service for Lassen National Forest or Ishi Wilderness. For topographic maps, ask the USGS for Panther Spring and Butte Meadows.

Directions: From Red Bluff, take Highway 36 east and drive about 20 miles to Paynes Creek and then continue to Little Giant Mill Road. Turn right (south) on Little Giant Mill Road (Road 202) and drive seven miles to Ponderosa Way. Turn south at Ponderosa Way and drive 32.5 miles to the Devils Den trailhead (just south of the Deer Creek trailhead).

Contact: Lassen National Forest, Almanor Ranger District, P.O. Box 767, Chester, CA 96020, 530/258-2141, www.fs.fed.us/r5.

53 HUMBOLDT SUMMIT TO DOMINGO SPRINGS (PCT)
28.0 mi one-way / 2 days 🚶3 ⛰6

at Humboldt Summit in Lassen National Forest southwest of Lake Almanor

Map 3.3, page 133

The idea of back-to-back 14-mile days to get through this chunk of trail may not appeal to many hikers, especially while carrying full-weight expedition packs. But that's standard for most hikers on this stretch of PCT, with little here to tarry for and with Lassen Volcanic National Park beckoning ahead. The trail starts just below Humboldt Peak, at 7,087 feet, and heads north along the ridgeline. For the most part, the trail is routed past Butt Mountain (7,866 feet) and down to Soldier Meadows. A spring and stream make this a delightful stop before crossing Highway 36, forging onward another three miles to the Stove Springs Campground. The trail then skirts around the western flank of North Stover Mountain and drops down to Domingo Springs, where another campground is available.

To continue north on the PCT, see the *Domingo Springs to Lassen Volcanic National Park (PCT)* hike in this chapter. If you are walking this trail in reverse, see the *Feather River to Humboldt Summit (PCT)* hike in this chapter to continue south.

User Groups: Hikers, dogs, and horses. No mountain bikes. No wheelchair facilities.

Permits: A campfire permit (free) is required. Parking and access are free.

Maps: For a map, ask the U.S. Forest Service for Lassen National Forest. For topographic maps, ask the USGS for Humboldt Peak and Stover Mountain.

Directions: From Red Bluff, take Highway 36 east and drive 47 miles to the junction with Highway 89. Turn south on Highway 89 and drive four miles to County Road 308 (Humboldt Road). Turn right and drive 15 miles to the trailhead parking area.

Contact: Lassen National Forest, Almanor Ranger District, P.O. Box 767, Chester, CA 96020, 530/258-2141, www.fs.fed.us/r5.

54 FEATHER RIVER TO HUMBOLDT SUMMIT (PCT)
26.0 mi one-way / 2 days 🚶4 ⛰6

at the Belden Trailhead on Highway 70 in Plumas National Forest

Map 3.3, page 133

The trail is not only rough from Belden to Humboldt Summit, it's not particularly pretty either, especially compared to the nearby wilderness. The climb is a mighty dry slice of rattlesnake country. From the North Fork Feather River at Belden (elevation 2,310 feet), the PCT climbs 4,777 feet over the course of this two-day thumper to Humboldt Summit, at 7,087 feet. There are no lakes along this trail, only a few small water holes requiring short side trips. Instead, the prettiest sections are along streams, the first being Chips Creek, which runs adjacent to the trail for eight miles. Then later, there's a short crossing over the headwaters of Willow Creek. Some might prefer to take three days instead of two to hike this section, but with the stunning Lassen Volcanic National Park looming ahead, most hikers are willing to put in long days to get through this area.

To continue north on the PCT, see the *Humboldt Summit to Domingo Springs (PCT)* hike in this chapter. If you are walking this trail in reverse, see the *Bucks Summit to Feather River (PCT)* hike, in the *Sacramento and Gold Country* chapter, to continue south.

User Groups: Hikers, dogs, and horses. No mountain bikes. No wheelchair facilities.

Permits: A campfire permit (free) is required. Parking and access are free.

Maps: For a map, ask the U.S. Forest Service for Plumas National Forest. For topographic maps, ask the USGS for Belden and Humboldt Peak.

Directions: From Quincy, drive west on Highway 70 about 26 miles to the trailhead, at the roadside rest area at Belden.

Contact: Plumas National Forest, Mount Hough Ranger District, 39696 State Highway 70, Quincy, CA 95971, 530/283-0555, www.fs.fed.us/r5.

55 BIZZ JOHNSON
1.0–25.0 mi one-way / 0.5 hr–3 days

west of Susanville

Map 3.4, page 134

In the 1960s, when Shasta legend John Reginato heard that Southern Pacific was going to abandon a rail line between Westwood and Susanville, he urged that it be converted to a hiking trail. It took many years, but the idea eventually struck home, and the Bureau of Land Management worked with the U.S. Forest Service to develop and refine it.

The Bizz Johnson Trail can be okay for day trips, with trailhead access spaced five to seven miles apart. People can hike or bike different portions of the trail. You don't have to complete the entire route, of course. The seven-mile stretch west of Susanville is the most popular stretch of the 25-mile route. The biggest problem is your trip can feel like the endless hike to nowhere.

The trailhead is at 4,200 feet, and the high point of the route is at 5,600 feet at Westwood Junction. The trail traces the old Fernley and Lassen railroad line, a branch line of the South Pacific Railroad. It is routed in the Susan River Canyon along the Susan River for 15 miles, then from the Susanville Railroad Depot to the Mason Station trailhead five miles north of Westwood. The surface is a mixture of compacted dirt and small gravel. The trail features beautiful views in many areas and passes through two old railroad tunnels and 11 old railroad bridges. You won't cross any developed areas.

In the winter, it makes a great trip on cross-country skis or on a snowmobile (snowmobiling is allowed on the western half of the trail, from Mason Station to just beyond Westwood Junction).

The one negative: Like most rails-to-trails projects, it's way too wide.

The future: The trail could eventually be extended all the way to Alturas for a distance of 100 miles. That would be a significant bike trip.

User Groups: Hikers, dogs (must be leashed near Susanville), horses, and mountain bikes. Wheelchair-accessible from Susanville and Hobo Camp trailhead.

Permits: No permits are required. Parking and access are free.

Maps: For a free brochure, contact the Bureau of Land Management. For a map, ask the U.S. Forest Service for Lassen National Forest. For topographic maps, ask the USGS for Westwood East, Fredonyer Pass, and Susanville.

Directions: From Susanville, take Highway 36 to Weatherlow Street. Turn on Weatherlow (it becomes Richmond Road) and drive 0.5 mile to the Susanville Depot Visitor Center (open May–early October) and the trailhead, on the right.

Alternate trailhead: From Westwood, take Highway 36 to County Road A21. Turn north and drive three miles to a signed trailhead access road (dirt). Turn right and drive 0.4 mile to the trailhead, on the left.

Contact: Historic Susanville Railroad Depot Visitor Center, 530/257-3252, www.bizzjohnsontrail.com; Lassen National Forest, Eagle Lake Ranger District, 477-050 Eagle Lake Road, Susanville, CA 96130, 530/257-4188, www.fs.fed.us/r5; Bureau of Land Management, Eagle Lake Field Office, 2950 Riverside Drive, Susanville, CA 96130, 530/257-0456, www.ca.blm.gov.

MENDOCINO AND WINE COUNTRY

© ANN MARIE BRO...

BEST HIKES

For many people, this region offers the best possible

combination around in terms of geography, weather, and outdoor activities. The Mendocino coast is dramatic and remote, with several stellar state parks for hiking, while Sonoma Valley, in the heart of the wine country, produces some of the most popular wines in the world. Add in the self-indulgent options of mud baths and hot springs in Calistoga and a dash of mainstream recreation at Clear Lake, Lake Berryessa, or any other lake, and you have a capsule summary of why the Mendocino coast and the wine country have turned into getaway favorites.

The coast features excellent adventuring and hiking, including some of the best year-round day hikes in California. The Fort Bragg area alone has three state parks, MacKerricher, Van Damme, and Russian Gulch, all with outstanding recreation, including several easy hikes – many amid redwoods and along pretty streams. If you want a campsite at a state park on a summer weekend, make reservations far in advance. The weather is most agreeable in spring and fall, when your chances of blue skies and temperatures in the 60s are best. In summer, it is often foggy, with mist common at daybreak – so much of it that the forest canopy can be dripping with moisture by midmorning. In winter, it can be very wet; the streams and waterfalls are brought to life, ferns and forests are lush and fresh, and yet visitors are relatively few. On weekdays, it is common to have trails all to yourself.

The driving tour of Highway 1 along the coast is the fantasy of many, and it can live up to that fantasy if you don't mind the twists and turns of the road. Along the way, there are dozens of hidden beaches and untouched coastline, where you can stop, explore, and play tag with the waves. Some of the prize spots are Salt Point State Park and Gualala.

As you venture inland, the landscape changes in a dramatic fashion. The terrain consists of rolling foothills peppered with oaks and hot, dry weather in summer. Yet there are still pockets of redwoods hidden in canyons in a few surprise spots, including at Armstrong Redwoods, near Guerneville, and Hendy Woods, near Philo. This region is bordered to the east by the Yolla Bolly Mountains. This is where you will find the Yolla Bolly Wilderness, a landscape that features many small streams that eventually join to form the headwaters of the Eel River. Outside the wilderness boundary, loggers have heavily cut the area.

One of the best lookouts in Northern California is from the top of Mount St. Helena, a great all-day tromp. Bothe-Napa Valley State Park, near Calistoga, has a surprise redwood grove and a beautiful stream under forest canopy. Nearby Sugarloaf Ridge State Park is known for wide-open views from its ridges, yet it also hides a pretty waterfall in a wooded canyon that in winter transforms into a gorgeous easy hike and picnic setting.

Between the beautiful coastal state parks and the surprises in the inland foothills, you get the best of two worlds.

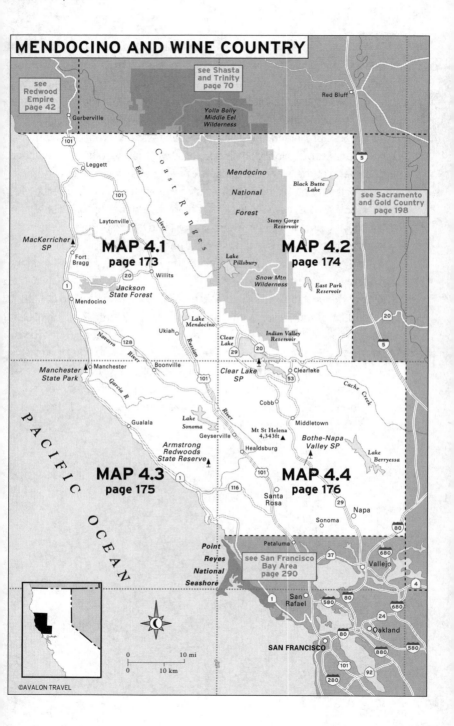

MENDOCINO AND WINE COUNTRY

see Redwood Empire page 42

see Shasta and Trinity page 70

Red Bluff

Yolla Bolly Middle Eel Wilderness

Garberville

101

Leggett

101

Mendocino

National

Forest

Black Butte Lake

see Sacramento and Gold Country page 198

5

Laytonville

Stony Gorge Reservoir

MAP 4.1
page 173

MAP 4.2
page 174

MacKerricher SP

Fort Bragg

20

Willits

Lake Pillsbury

Snow Mtn Wilderness

East Park Reservoir

20

1

Jackson State Forest

Mendocino

Navarro

128

Ukiah

Lake Mendocino

River

Clear Lake

Indian Valley Reservoir

5

29

20

Manchester State Park

Manchester

Boonville

101

Clear Lake SP

Clearlake

Cache Creek

20

Garcia R

53

Cobb

River

Gualala

Lake Sonoma

Geyserville

Mt St Helena 4,343ft ▲

Middletown

Bothe-Napa Valley SP

Lake Berryessa

MAP 4.3
page 175

Armstrong Redwoods State Reserve

Healdsburg

MAP 4.4
page 176

1

116

101

Santa Rosa

29

Napa

Sonoma

80

Point Reyes National Seashore

Petaluma

37

see San Francisco Bay Area page 290

680

Vallejo

4

San Rafael

1

580

80

24

680

Oakland

880

580

SAN FRANCISCO

101

92

280

0   10 mi

0   10 km

©AVALON TRAVEL

PACIFIC OCEAN

Coast Ranges

Eel River

Russian River

Map 4.1

Hikes 1-10
Pages 177-182

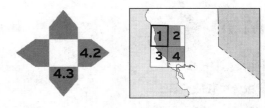

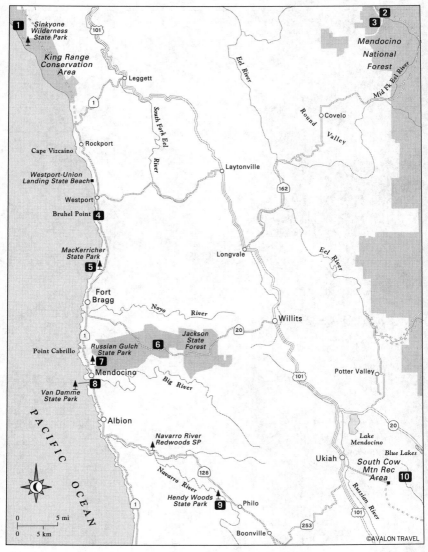

Map 4.2

Hikes 11-16
Pages 183-185

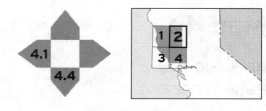

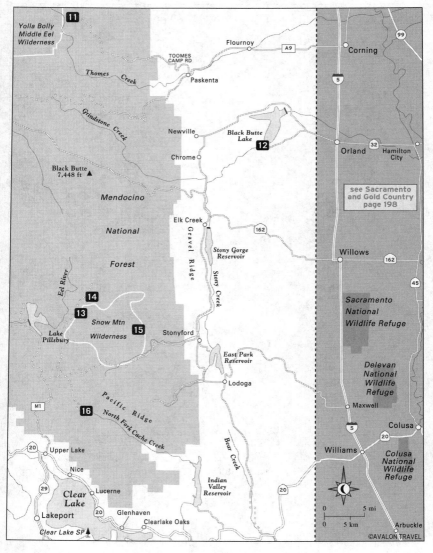

Yolla Bolly Middle Eel Wilderness

11

Flournoy

A9

Corning

99

TOOMES CAMP RD

Thomes Creek

Paskenta

5

Grindstone Creek

Newville

Black Butte Lake

12

Orland

32

Hamilton City

Chrome

Black Butte 7,448 ft

Mendocino

National

Forest

see Sacramento and Gold Country page 198

Elk Creek

162

Stony Gorge Reservoir

Willows

162

Gravel Ridge

Eel River

14

13

Snow Mtn

15

Stony Creek

Lake Pillsbury

Wilderness

Stonyford

Sacramento National Wildlife Refuge

45

East Park Reservoir

Lodoga

Delevan National Wildlife Refuge

M1

16

Pacific Ridge

North Fork Cache Creek

Maxwell

5

Colusa

20

20

Upper Lake

Bear Creek

Williams

Colusa National Wildlife Refuge

Nice

29

Lucerne

Clear Lake

Glenhaven

20

Indian Valley Reservoir

20

Lakeport

Clearlake Oaks

Clear Lake SP

0   5 mi

0   5 km

Arbuckle

©AVALON TRAVEL

Map 4.3

Hikes 17-22
Pages 186-189

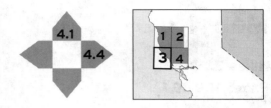

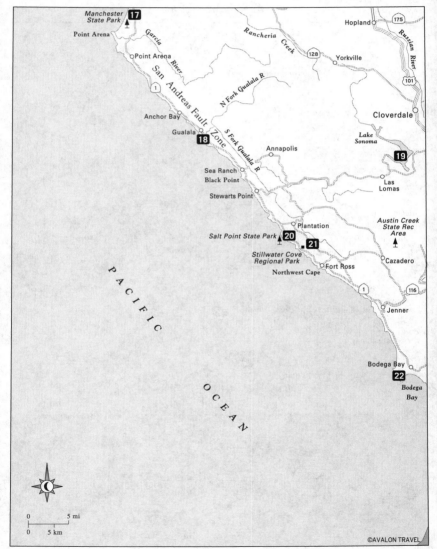

Map 4.4

Hikes 23-30
Pages 189-194

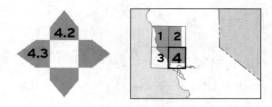

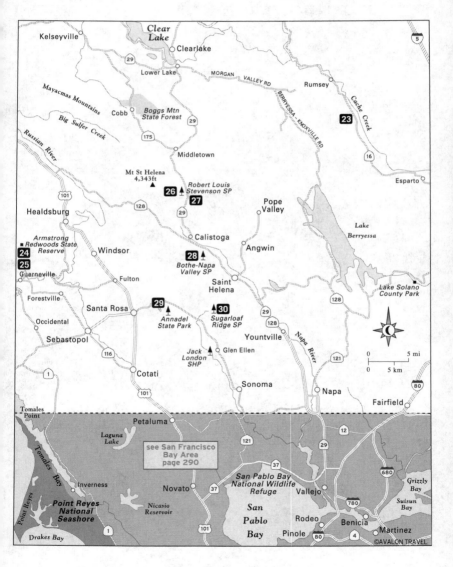

Kelseyville

Clear Lake

Clearlake

29

Lower Lake

MORGAN VALLEY RD

Rumsey

Mayacmas Mountains

Big Sulfer Creek

Cobb

Boggs Mtn State Forest

29

175

BERRYESSA - KNOXVILLE RD

Cache Creek

23

Russian River

Middletown

16

Esparto

Mt St Helena 4,343ft

Robert Louis Stevenson SP

26 **27**

101

128

29

Pope Valley

Lake Berryessa

Healdsburg

Calistoga

Angwin

Armstrong Redwoods State Reserve

24

25

Windsor

28

Bothe-Napa Valley SP

Lake Solano County Park

Guerneville

Fulton

Saint Helena

Forestville

Santa Rosa

29

Annadel State Park

30

Sugarloaf Ridge SP

128

128

Napa River

Occidental

Sebastopol

116

Jack London SHP

Glen Ellen

Yountville

0   5 mi

0   5 km

Cotati

101

Sonoma

121

Napa

80

Fairfield

Tomales Point

Petaluma

see San Francisco Bay Area page 290

121

12

Laguna Lake

37

29

680

Tomales Bay

Inverness

Novato

37

San Pablo Bay National Wildlife Refuge

Vallejo

780

Grizzly Bay

Suisun Bay

Point Reyes National Seashore

Nicasio Reservoir

San Pablo Bay

Rodeo

Benicia

Martinez

Drakes Bay

1

101

Pinole

80

4

©AVALON TRAVEL

1 LOST COAST TRAIL/ SINKYONE TRAILHEAD

16.7 mi one-way / 2 days 🏃3 ⛰10

in Sinkyone Wilderness State Park and on the Mendocino coast

Map 4.1, page 173 **BEST (**

This remote and rugged wilderness of Northern California coastline, covering more than 7,000 acres, is now protected forever as Sinkyone Wilderness State Park. It was once one of the least traveled jewels of California. No more. It has become fairly popular for trekkers looking for the wild side, despite few directional signs along roads, no highways leading here, and virtually no park promotion. The primitive, steep, and unforgiving terrain provides a rare coastal wilderness experience. The best way to explore it is on Lost Coast Trail, which is best hiked north to south to keep the north winds out of your face. A shuttle service is available for a fee through Lost Coast Trail Transport Service.

Day 1: From the northern trailhead at Orchard Camp, Lost Coast Trail starts out flat and pleasant, arcing around Bear Harbor Cove. From here the trail climbs 800 feet and then back down, passing through a redwood grove and also breaking out for sweeping coastal views. Enjoy them, because the hike gets more difficult, including a steep climb up, over, and down a mountain. The trail finally descends into Little Jackass Creek Camp, which is set beside a small stream 10.5 miles from your start.

Day 2: The closeout of a two-day hike should always be as enjoyable as possible, and so it is here, with divine views in many spots along the 6.5-mile route. Alas, there's usually payment for views, and that comes in the form of several rugged climbs in the park's most remote sections. After climbing to nearly 1,000 feet, the trail ends with an 800-foot downgrade over the last mile, descending to the Usal Campground parking area.

Special notes: All food must be bear-proofed. Dogs are permitted only at car camps. At the northern boundary of the Sinkyone Wilderness, this trail continues north into the King Range

National Conservation Area, where it's routed for another 30 miles to the mouth of the Mattole River (see the listing for *Lost Coast Trail/Mattole Trailhead* in the *Redwood Empire* chapter).

User Groups: Hikers only. Horses allowed only on the section of trail between the trailhead at the park entrance and Wheeler Camp. No dogs or mountain bikes. No wheelchair facilities.

Permits: No permits are required. Parking and access are free unless you plan to camp.

Maps: A trail map and brochure is available for a fee from Sinkyone Wilderness State Park. For a topographic map, ask the USGS for Bear Harbor.

Directions: From Garberville, take US 101 north to the exit for Redway. Take that exit to Briceland Road. Turn left (west) on Briceland Road and drive 17 miles to Whitethorn, and continue ahead six miles to the Four Corners Fork. Continue straight again for six miles (the road turns to gravel) to the Needle Rock Ranger Station. Continue past the ranger station to the visitors center and park at Orchard Camp. Be aware that the access road is unpaved, that it may close unexpectedly in the winter, and that four-wheel-drive vehicles are often required in wet weather. There are few signs pointing the way to the park, and when they are posted, they are often stolen. Trailers and RVs are not recommended.

Contact: Sinkyone Wilderness State Park, 707/986-7711, www.parks.ca.gov; Lost Coast Trail Transport Service, 707/986-9909, www.lostcoasttrail.com.

2 SOLDIER RIDGE TRAIL

11.2 mi / 2 days 🏃3 ⛰8

on the southern boundary of the Yolla Bolly Wilderness west of Red Bluff

Map 4.1, page 173

This wilderness trail features three linked segments: Soldier Ridge Trail, Minnie Lake Trail, and Kingsley Lake Trail. In the process, this combines for a 5.6-mile walk to your destination, Kingsley Lake. The rugged climb on

Soldier Ridge Trail to get there, along with the charm of this little lake, usually compels hikers to stay overnight. Actually, it's a long drive in the middle of nowhere just to reach the trail-head, and then when you get there, you'll face a daunting 3.5-mile climb up the spine of Soldier Ridge toward the Yolla Bolly Crest. At the crest are three mountains lined in a row: Sugarloaf Mountain (elevation 7,367 feet), Solomon Peak (7,581 feet), and Hammerhorn Mountain (7,567 feet). The trail crosses a saddle between Sugarloaf Mountain and Solomon Peak, then drops down to little Kingsley Lake, which is created from the headwaters of Thomes Creek. All is quiet and peaceful here.

User Groups: Hikers, dogs, and horses. No mountain bikes. No wheelchair facilities.

Permits: A campfire permit is required for hikers planning to camp. Parking and access are free.

Maps: For a map, ask the U.S. Forest Service for Mendocino National Forest or Yolla Bolly Wilderness. For a topographic map, ask the USGS for South Yolla Bolly.

Directions: From Willits, drive north on US 101 for 13 miles to Longvale and Highway 162. Turn east on Highway 162 and drive 30 miles to the turnoff for Highway 162 East. Turn right and drive nine miles to the Eel River Bridge and Forest Road M1 (Indian Dick Road). At the bridge, turn left (north) onto Forest Road M1 and drive 27 miles to the trailhead, at the end of the road.

Contact: Mendocino National Forest, Covelo Ranger District, 78150 Covelo Road, Covelo, CA 95428, 707/983-6118, www.fs.fed.us/r5.

3 WRIGHTS VALLEY TRAIL
8.0 mi / 4.5 hr   👣2 ⛰️7

on the southern boundary of the Yolla Bolly Wilderness west of Red Bluff

Map 4.1, page 173

The Rock Cabin Trail (also known as the River Trail) extends north into the Yolla Bolly Wilderness and up, over, and down a short ridge before pouring into Wrights Valley. About halfway in, River Trail jumps to Wrights Valley Trail. It's about a four-mile trip one-way to your destination. Here you'll find the headwaters of the Middle Fork Eel River, one of the prettiest streams in the wilderness. The trail is well marked and includes two creek crossings. Whereas the Yolla Bollys provide few lakes, the Middle Fork awaits you. In order to protect endangered steelhead, no fishing is allowed.

Special note: Map-gazing hikers will likely notice small Henthorne Lake, complete with two wilderness cabins, set just 2.5 miles from the Rock Cabin trailhead. Resist the urge to visit. This is maintained as private property, a nature reserve for some lucky soul. Hikers are often tempted to hike in via a very faint cowboy trail (with a river crossing) and camp here illegally.

User Groups: Hikers, dogs, and horses. No mountain bikes. No wheelchair facilities.

Permits: A campfire permit is required for hikers planning to camp. Parking and access are free.

Maps: For a map, ask the U.S. Forest Service for Mendocino National Forest or Yolla Bolly Wilderness. For a topographic map, ask the USGS for South Yolla Bolly.

Directions: From Willits, drive north on US 101 for 13 miles to Longvale and Highway 162. Turn east on Highway 162 and drive 30 miles to the turnoff for Highway 162 East. Turn right and drive nine miles to the Eel River Bridge and Forest Road M1 (Indian Dick Road). At the bridge, turn left (north) onto Forest Road M1 and drive 24 miles to Forest Road 25N15C. Turn left on Forest Road 25N15C and drive 0.75 mile to the turnoff for the Rock Cabin trailhead. Turn left and drive 0.25 mile to the trailhead, at the end of the road.

Contact: Mendocino National Forest, Covelo Ranger District, 78150 Covelo Road, Covelo, CA 95428, 707/983-6118, www.fs.fed.us/r5.

◳ BRUHEL POINT TIDEPOOLS
0.5 mi / 0.5 hr   🏃2 🔺8

on the Mendocino coast north of Fort Bragg

Map 4.1, page 173

Some of the best tidepools on the Pacific Coast can be found in Mendocino. One of the best of the best is here, located just south of Bruhel Point. When you first arrive, you'll find a Cal-Trans roadside vista point (no overnight parking), restrooms, and a beach access trail. This is your calling. The trail is routed north toward Bruhel Point. And much of it is set along the edge of ocean bluffs. Do not make your own descent down the bluff. Instead take only the cutoff trails, which lead to the best tidepool areas. Time your trip during a low tide, or better yet, a minus low tide. That is when the ocean pulls back, leaving a series of holes and cuts in a rock basin that remain filled with water, providing the perfect habitat and viewing areas for all kinds of tiny marine life.

User Groups: Hikers and dogs. Not suitable for mountain bikes or horses. No wheelchair facilities.

Permits: No permits are required. Parking and access are free.

Maps: For a topographic map, ask the USGS for Inglenook.

Directions: From Westport, drive south on Highway 1 about two miles to milepost marker 74.09 and park at the CalTrans Vista Point parking lot. The tidepools are a short walk.

Contact: No managing agency for contact.

◳ LAKE CLEONE TRAIL
1.2 mi / 0.5 hr   🏃1 🔺9

in MacKerricher State Park on the Mendocino coast north of Fort Bragg

Map 4.1, page 173   **BEST (**

MacKerricher State Park is filled with many enticing highlights. It is also one of the few state parks with free day-use access. The loop trail around Lake Cleone is not only easy but also definitely something special. Mrs.

MacKerricher aptly named the trail Cleone, which means "gracious" or "beautiful" in Greek. The route includes several sections on raised wooden walkways, which provide routes through marshy areas. In the winter months, the southern part of the trail (without the boardwalk) can be flooded. Be sure to wear your high boots in the rainy season.

In some spots, the trail burrows like a tunnel through a variety of trees and lush vegetation. At others, it provides many glimpses of pretty Lake Cleone. It loops all the way around the lake, which is almost always full. The beautiful Pacific Ocean looms just beyond to the west, a cypress grove is to the south, and a marsh is to the east. Historically the lake is stocked with trout by the Department of Fish and Game three times before Memorial Day weekend. The boardwalk is wheelchair accessible.

Special note: From the parking lot adjacent to the lake, you can walk under the built-up foundation of an old railroad line (now a bicycle trail called Old Haul Road) and connect to Headlands Trail. This is a must-do. It's an easy short walk, much of it on a raised walkway, that leads to a series of tidepools and the best seal- and whale-watching station on the coast.

User Groups: Hikers, leashed dogs, and wheelchairs (the trail is partially wheelchair accessible). No horses or mountain bikes. Horse trails and mountain bike routes are available elsewhere in the state park.

Permits: No permits are required. Parking and access are free.

Maps: A brochure and trail map is available for a fee at MacKerricher State Park. For a topographic map, ask the USGS for Inglenook.

Directions: From Fort Bragg drive north on Highway 1 for three miles to the park entrance. Turn left and drive to the parking area beside the lake. The trailhead is on the east side of the parking lot.

Contact: MacKerricher State Park, c/o California State Parks, Mendocino District, P.O. Box 440, Mendocino, CA 95460, 707/964-9112, or district office at 707/937-5804, www.parks.ca.gov.

6 CHAMBERLAIN CREEK WATERFALL TRAIL

0.5 mi / 0.5 hr   🚶2 ⛰10

in Jackson State Forest east of Fort Bragg

Map 4.1, page 173

Chamberlain Creek Falls is a surprise—a 50-foot waterfall set in a canyon framed by redwoods, well secluded in Jackson State Forest. Set back off an old logging road, the trail is short, little known to outsiders, and beautiful. This access road (gravel/dirt), by the way, can get muddy in the winter and extremely dusty in the summer. After parking, you'll find the trail routed a short distance down the canyon to the stream, starting with a short series of steps. The trail simply heads down the canyon directly to the base of the waterfall. Jackson State Forest is overlooked by most visitors, despite the beauty of the area and the popularity of the Mendocino coast. That means you'll most likely have the place to yourself.

User Groups: Hikers and dogs. No horses or mountain bikes. No wheelchair facilities.

Permits: No permits are required. Parking and access are free.

Maps: For a free trail map, contact Jackson Demonstration State Forest. For a topographic map, ask the USGS for Northspur.

Directions: From Willits, take Highway 20 west for 17 miles to Forest Road 200, a dirt road just before the Chamberlain Creek bridge. Turn right on Road 200 and drive one mile to a fork. Bear left and drive 3.5 miles. Look for a parking pullout and park on the side of the road. The trailhead is on the left. In the heaviest rainy season, note that State Forest Road 200 is sometimes closed due to weather; call ahead for the status.

Contact: Jackson Demonstration State Forest, 802 North Main Street, Fort Bragg, CA 95437, 707/964-5674, www.fire.ca.gov.

7 FALLS LOOP TRAIL

7.0 mi / 4.0 hr   🚶2 ⛰10

in Russian Gulch State Park on the Mendocino coast south of Fort Bragg

Map 4.1, page 173

A 35-foot waterfall in deep forest makes this walk one of the prettiest on the Mendocino coast. Most of the year, this waterfall is a narrow silvery stream that pours atop and across a boulder. In winter it can build into a more powerful chute and land in the rock basin with surging splashes. It's way better at high flows, of course.

The route is simple. Take North Trail for 2.5 miles out to its junction with Falls Loop Trail (see special note for bikers). This seems nearly flat, with only a slight grade. At that junction, turn left and hike less than a mile, some of it a 150-foot climb, to reach the falls. Even in the summer months, this is a pretty, if narrow, silver cascade, streaming 20 feet across a granite boulder and down into a pool. The entire trip has very little elevation gain. It's an easy walk out to Falls Loop Trail, then only a 200-foot gain to reach the waterfall. As you go, you'll delve deeper and deeper into dense forest, and although a lot of the old growth was taken a long time ago, much is still divine.

Special note: A paved bicycle trail runs parallel to North Trail and makes a great bike trip. But please note that bikes are not permitted on the dirt Falls Loop Trail. Bike racks are available at the intersection of these two trails, meaning bikers can make the trip to the falls with only a one-mile hike. In other words, ride to the Falls Loop Trail junction, park your bike, and walk one mile from there. This bike trail is also wheelchair accessible. A large number of people also walk the bike trail, a five-mile round-trip.

Note: This park is on the closure list developed by the California Department of Parks, pending final state budget decisions or the possible transfer of park management to other park agencies or volunteer groups.

User Groups: Hikers only. No mountain bikes, dogs, or horses. However, a paved trail for bicycles and wheelchairs is routed 2.5 miles to the trailhead of Falls Loop Trail.

Permits: No permits are required. A state park entrance fee of $8 is charged for each vehicle.

Maps: A brochure and trail map is available for a fee at Russian Gulch State Park. For a topographic map, ask the USGS for Mendocino.

Directions: From Fort Bragg, take Highway 1 south for six miles to the Russian Gulch State Park entrance. Turn right and drive a very short distance to the state park entrance. After passing the kiosk, travel down the hill and to the bridge. Turn left and drive past the campsites to the trailhead.

Contact: Russian Gulch State Park, c/o California State Parks, Mendocino District, P.O. Box 440, Mendocino, CA 95460, 707/937-5804, www.parks.ca.gov.

8 FERN CANYON TRAIL
8.1 mi / 5.0 hr

in Van Damme State Park on the Mendocino coast south of Mendocino

Map 4.1, page 173

This beautiful streamside walk amid coastal redwoods is one of the most popular trails on the Mendocino coast. The trail starts at the bottom of a canyon along the Little River and heads upstream, rising gently along the way, with a series of little bridges that crisscross the water. The creek is pretty and often clear, the forest canopy is towering, and the understory of fern and sorrel is lush. Most people hike 2.3 miles (paved all the way) out to the junction of Loop Trail and then turn around and head back. Visitors can add on a three-mile loop, including a visit to the Pygmy Forest. This is where an elevated wood walkway is routed amid this unusual setting. Some people love this, for others, it's no big deal, and there is a closer trailhead to the Pygmy Forest that you can drive to.

Note that heavy rains can flood out the trail and wash out the bridges. Also note that

if you're a cheapskate, you can avoid paying the park entrance fee by parking in the beach parking lot next to the park entrance and walking in.

Special note: Do not get this Fern Canyon Trail confused with the Fern Canyon Loop Trail on the Humboldt County coast, which is listed in the *Redwood Empire* chapter.

User Groups: Hikers only. No dogs or horses. Wheelchairs and mountain bikes are allowed only on the first 2.3 miles of the trail.

Permits: No permits are required. A state park entrance fee of $8 is charged for each vehicle. Beach parking is free.

Maps: A brochure and trail map is available for a fee at Van Damme State Park. For a topographic map, ask the USGS for Mendocino.

Directions: From Mendocino, take Highway 1 south for 2.5 miles to the park entrance. Turn left and drive 0.75 mile (signed) to the trailhead parking near the campground. For campers, start near campsite No. 26.

Contact: Van Damme State Park, c/o California State Parks, Mendocino District, P.O. Box 440, Mendocino, CA 95460, 707/937-5804, www.parks.ca.gov.

9 GLEN EDEN TRAIL
3.0-10.5 mi / 1.0-5.0 hr

in Cow Mountain Recreation Area east of Ukiah

Map 4.1, page 173

This trail will have you sweating like Charles Manson's cellmate. The Glen Eden Trail is not only difficult to find (follow the directions precisely), but has several steep sections and is typically quite hot from late spring through summer and fall. The Glen Eden Trail eventually crosses Mendo Rock Road (this provides another trailhead possibility) and continues up to a series of great overlooks of Clear Lake. The views of Clear Lake and the Mayacmas Range are outstanding. To return, retrace your route. Few make the entire trip, but instead they just hike out to a good lookout and then

return. The chaparral-covered slopes are peppered with pine and oak, with many miles of
trails and fire roads. But it's extremely rare
to see other hikers. No off-road vehicles are
allowed, unlike the southern portion of the
Cow Mountain Recreation Area.

The 52,000-acre Cow Mountain Recreation
Area is named for the longhorn cattle that
once roamed wild.

User Groups: Hikers, dogs, and horses. Mountain bikes are prohibited on the first 2.5 miles
of trail, after which public property starts and
bicycles are allowed. Bikers should access Glen
Eden Trail from other trailheads on Bureau of
Land Management (BLM) land.

Permits: No permits are required. Parking
and access are free.

Maps: For a free trail map of the Cow Mountain Recreation Area, contact the Bureau of
Land Management. For a topographic map,
ask the USGS for Cow Mountain.

Directions: From Ukiah, take Highway 20
east to Scotts Valley Road (near Blue Lakes).
Turn right (south) on Scotts Valley Road and
drive 2.5 miles to trailhead parking on the
left. The Glen Eden trailhead is directly across
the road.

To Mendo Rock Road trailhead, located at
mid-trail: Take US 101 to Ukiah and the exit
for Talmage Road. Take that exit to Tamalge
Road, turn east and drive 1.5 miles to Eastside
Road. Turn right and drive 0.3 mile to Mill
Creek Road. Turn left and drive three miles
to Mendo Rock Road. Turn left (sharp, signed
North Cow Mountain), and drive 5.5 miles
(steep, narrow) to a T-intersection. Turn right
and drive three miles to where Glen Eden
Trail crosses the road.

Contact: Bureau of Land Management, Ukiah
Field Office, 2550 North State Street, Ukiah,
CA 95482, 707/468-4000, www.ca.blm.gov/
ukiah/cowmtn.html.

⓾ BIG HENDY GROVE / HERMIT'S HUT TRAIL

1.0 mi / 0.5 hr   🏃1 ⛰7

in Hendy Woods State Park in Mendocino
National Forest

Map 4.1, page 173

This easy and short walk through an ancient
redwood forest can have you smiling for days.
Hendy Woods is located in the redwood-
filled canyon of the Navarro River, which
flows to the sea on the Mendocino coast.
Although the park covers 845 acres, the two
old-growth redwood groves, Little Hendy
(20 acres) and Big Hendy (80 acres), are most
compelling.

When you first arrive, you'll be stunned at
the sudden interface of the foothill grasslands
with redwoods. At Big Hendy, start by taking
the 0.5-mile Discovery Trail, which leaves the
grasslands and enters the redwood grove on a
dirt path. Suddenly you'll be walking among
towering redwoods, moss-covered stumps, and
a sprinkling of giant fallen trees, all set amid
ferns and sorrel. A great side trip is to walk
uphill on the cutoff trail to the old hermit's
hut in a hollowed-out tree stump, where one
of the last of the real hermits lived for years. A
newspaper clipping here details the old hermit's
strange life, kind of like that of an outdoors
writer.

Note: This park is on the closure list developed by the California Department of Parks,
pending final state budget decisions or the
possible transfer of park management to other
park agencies or volunteer groups.

User Groups: Hikers and wheelchairs. No
dogs, horses, or mountain bikes.

Permits: No permits are required. A state park
entrance fee of $8 is charged for each vehicle.

Maps: A brochure and trail map is available
for a fee at Hendy Woods State Park. For a
topographic map, ask the USGS for Philo.

Directions: From Mendocino, take Highway
1 south for about five miles to Highway 128.
Turn east on Highway 128 and drive about 20
miles to Philo Greenwood Road. Turn south

(right) and drive 0.5 mile to the entrance of Hendy Woods State Park, on the left. The trailhead begins just off the parking area.
Contact: Hendy Woods State Park, c/o California State Parks, Mendocino District, P.O. Box 440, Mendocino, CA 95460, 707/895-3141, www.parks.ca.gov.

11 IDES COVE NATIONAL RECREATION TRAIL
10.5 mi / 5.5 hr 🥾3 ⛰️7

on the southeastern boundary of the Yolla Bolly Wilderness west of Red Bluff

Map 4.2, page 174

At 8,092 feet, South Yolla Bolly Mountain is the highest point in this wilderness. The Ides Cove National Recreation Trail skirts this mountain as part of one of the top one-day loop trails available in the Yolla Bollys. A bonus is that a shorter loop hike (3.5 miles) is also convenient here. From the Ides Cove trailhead, the trail drops down to the headwaters of Slide Creek and heads out to the foot of Harvey Peak, at 7,361 feet. This is the halfway point and a good spot for lunch. The trail turns sharply and is routed back along the flank of the South Yolla Bolly Mountains. On the way, it passes both Long and Square Lakes, which are both tiny water holes stocked with brook trout.

A free campground is available at the trailhead. Horse facilities are nearby, but not at the trailhead. Despite these things, the trail gets only light use.
User Groups: Hikers, dogs, and horses. No mountain bikes. No wheelchair facilities.
Permits: A campfire permit is required for hikers planning to camp.
Maps: For a map, ask the U.S. Forest Service for Mendocino National Forest or Yolla Bolly Wilderness. For a topographic map, ask the USGS for South Yolla Bolly.
Directions: From Redding, take I-5 south to Corning and the exit for Corning Road/Paskenta Road. Take that exit, turn west on Paskenta Road and drive about 20 miles to Paskenta. In

the town of Paskenta, Corning/Paskenta Road will split, becoming Round Valley Road on the left and County Road M2/Toomes Creek Road straight ahead. Continue straight on County Road M2/Toomes Creek Road for 20 miles to Cold Springs Ranger Station and County Road M22. Turn right on County Road M22 and drive about 15 miles to the trailhead.
Contact: Mendocino National Forest, Stonyford Work Center, 5171 Stonyford-Elk Creek Road, P.O. Box 160, Stonyford, CA 95979, 530/963-3128, www.fs.fed.us/r5.

12 BIG OAK TRAIL
1.0 mi / 0.5 hr 🥾1 ⛰️6

at the head of Black Butte Reservoir west of Orland

Map 4.2, page 174

The Big Oak Trail is routed through a riparian area in the Stony Creek drainage above the head of Black Butte Reservoir. The habitat is constantly changing here based on creek flows and temperatures. The route is an easy jaunt. The riparian habitat here is in a protected state, making it an excellent area to see wildlife in the sparse foothills of the Sacramento Valley. It has become part of California's Watchable Wildlife system. The best time for hiking is at dusk, when wildlife viewing is at its best. This hike is not without a few potential problems. The weather is close to intolerable in the summer—a real temperature tantrum—and very hot in spring and fall as well, and that's when most people have time to visit the area.
User Groups: Hikers, dogs, and mountain bikes. No horses. No wheelchair facilities.
Permits: No permits are required. Parking and access are free.
Maps: For a topographic map, ask the USGS for Julian Rocks.
Directions: Take I-5 to Orland and the exit for Black Butte Lake. Take that exit, turn west on Newville Road (County Road 200) and drive 10 miles to County Road 206. Turn left on County Road 206 and drive to County Road

200A. Bear left on County Road 200A and drive to the trailhead.

Contact: U.S. Army Corps of Engineers, Black Butte Lake, 19225 Newville Road, Orland, CA 95963-8901, 530/865-4781, www.spk.usace.army.mil.

13 WATERFALL LOOP TRAIL
13.0 mi / 1 day   👫3 ⛰10

on the northwestern boundary of the Snow Mountain Wilderness in Mendocino National Forest

Map 4.2, page 174

Very few people know about the Snow Mountain Wilderness, and far fewer know about this loop trail that traverses the region's most treasured areas. Double-peaked Snow Mountain itself is the big ridge located about midway between I-5 at Willows and US 101 at Willits.

This trail starts at the northern boundary of the wilderness at the West Crockett trailhead (just west of Crockett Peak). Start by hiking two miles to get into Middle Fork Creek. The trail connects there with a spur trail to the waterfall. Take that spur 0.2 mile to the waterfall.

To turn this into a major loop, take the main trail uphill, a significant climb, to reach a small loop set between East Snow Mountain (7,056 feet) and West Snow Mountain (7,038 feet). To return, take North Ridge Trail, which drops down from Snow Mountain and traces the Middle Fork of Stony Creek for a good portion of the route back to the parking area.

This is a great late winter hike, but much of this area can be quite dry and hot in midsummer, especially on the North Ridge. From late spring through fall, rattlesnakes are common. Hikers should always be certain to carry a lot of water here, twice as much as usual for you.

User Groups: Hikers, dogs, and horses. No mountain bikes. No wheelchair facilities.

Permits: A campfire permit is required for hikers planning to camp. Parking and access are free.

Maps: For a map, ask the U.S. Forest Service for Mendocino National Forest. For topographic maps, ask the USGS for Crockett Peak and St. John Mountain.

Directions: Take I-5 to Willows and the exit for Highway 162. Take that exit, turn west on Highway 162 and drive 21 miles to a T junction (signed Elk Creek). Turn left and drive one mile through the town of Elk Creek to Ivory Mill Road. Turn right on Ivory Mill Road (Road 308) and drive 15 miles to Forest Road M3. Turn left on Forest Road M3 and drive 15.5 miles to the signed turnoff for West Crockett trailhead. Turn left and drive 0.5 mile to the trailhead.

Contact: Mendocino National Forest, Stonyford Work Center, 5171 Stonyford–Elk Creek Road, P.O. Box 160, Stonyford, CA 95979, 530/963-3128, www.fs.fed.us/r5.

14 WINDY POINT TRAILHEAD
3.25 mi / 1.75 hr   👫2 ⛰7

on the northern boundary of the Snow Mountain Wilderness in Mendocino National Forest

Map 4.2, page 174

Every wilderness has secret spots. So it is here in the Snow Mountain Wilderness. On a hot summer day when every drop of water is counted as if it were liquid gold, you'll find a simple paradise on this short walk to the headwaters of a tiny fork of Bear Wallow Creek.

The hike starts at Windy Point, the northernmost trailhead in the Snow Mountains. The trail is routed straight east on Bear Wallow Trail for a little more than a mile across very dry country. About 1.5 miles in, start looking for a spur trail on the right side, and when you see it, take it. This spur drops a short distance down to the source of the north fork of Bear Wallow Creek, a truly secret little spot. If you think there are too many people in the world, just come here and look around.

User Groups: Hikers, dogs, and horses. No mountain bikes. No wheelchair facilities.

Permits: A campfire permit is required for hikers planning to camp. Parking and access are free.

Maps: For a map, ask the U.S. Forest Service for Mendocino National Forest. For topographic maps, ask the USGS for Crockett Peak and St. John Mountain.

Directions: Take I-5 to Willows and the exit for Highway 162. Take that exit, turn west on Highway 162 and drive 21 miles to a T junction (signed Elk Creek). Turn left and drive one mile through the town of Elk Creek to Ivory Mill Road. Turn right on Ivory Mill Road (Road 308) and drive 15 miles to Forest Road M3. Turn left on Forest Road M3 and drive 13 miles to the trailhead.

Contact: Mendocino National Forest, Stonyford Work Center, 5171 Stonyford–Elk Creek Road, P.O. Box 160, Stonyford, CA 95979, 530/963-3128, www.fs.fed.us/r5.

15 BEAR WALLOW TRAILHEAD

4.0 mi / 2.5 hr   🏃2 ⛰7

on the eastern boundary of the Snow Mountain Wilderness in Mendocino National Forest

Map 4.2, page 174

Your destination is a pretty section of Bear Wallow Creek, a small feeder stream to the middle fork of Stony Creek. The hike starts at the Bear Wallow trailhead. From here the Bear Wallow Trail is routed north. After about two miles, start looking for a trail junction on the left side. Be sure not to miss it. Turn left and take the 0.25-mile traipse down to Bear Wallow Creek, a pretty spot and a decent destination for a day's walk. Typically you'll have the place all to yourself. But if you miss the turn, the Bear Wallow Trail continues all the way to Windy Point trailhead, and with no water available, you'll be chanting, "Beam me up, Scotty." In summer, temperatures can be scorching and fire danger is a perpetual problem. Make this hike in late winter or early spring.

User Groups: Hikers, dogs, and horses. No mountain bikes. No wheelchair facilities.

Permits: A campfire permit is required for hikers planning to camp. Parking and access are free.

Maps: For a map, ask the U.S. Forest Service for Mendocino National Forest. For a topographic map, ask the USGS for Fouts Springs.

Directions: Take I-5 to the exit for Maxwell (north of Williams, south of Willows). Take that exit to Maxwell-Sites Road, turn west, and drive to Sites and Sites-Lodoga Road. Turn left on Sites-Lodoga Road and drive to Lodoga and Lodoga-Stonyford Road. Turn left and loop around East Park Reservoir to reach Stonyford and Fouts Spring Road (Road M10). Turn west and drive eight miles to Forest Road 18N06. Turn right and drive nine miles (four-wheel drive is necessary) to the parking area for the trailhead, on the left.

Contact: Mendocino National Forest, Stonyford Work Center, 5171 Stonyford–Elk Creek Road, P.O. Box 160, Stonyford, CA 95979, 530/963-3128, www.fs.fed.us/r5.

16 OVERLOOK LOOP

8.5 mi / 1 day   🏃4 ⛰9

on the southwestern boundary of the Snow Mountain Wilderness in Mendocino National Forest

Map 4.2, page 174

Do you yearn for the passion of the mountain experience? Do you crave the zest of life when you have a bad case of dry mouth and discover a mountain spring? Is the price of a climb worth it for the mountaintop payoff? Are you nuts? You need to answer yes, yes, yes, and yes to be ready for this loop hike. This is not a trail for the indifferent. It includes two killer climbs, a wonderful little spring along the trail, and the ascent of West Snow Mountain, at 7,038 feet. Still interested? Then read on.

The trail starts at the Summit Spring trailhead, and in the first two miles, it includes a no-fun clamber up to High Rock. At the trail junction here, turn right on Box Spring Loop Trail and hike past the headwaters of Trout Creek to Box Spring, located just to the right of the trail, near another trail junction. In hot weather (typically all summer), this spot is paradise. Turn left and make the three-mile climb up West Snow Mountain. You will grunt and thump it out every step of the way. At the top, enjoy this victory for a while before dropping back down for the final three miles to the trailhead and parking area. This is an excellent loop hike, one that furnishes several rewards but makes you earn every one of them.

User Groups: Hikers, dogs, and horses. No mountain bikes. No wheelchair facilities.

Permits: A campfire permit is required for hikers planning to camp. Parking and access are free.

Maps: For a map, ask the U.S. Forest Service for Mendocino National Forest. For a topographic map, ask the USGS for Fouts Springs.

Directions: Take I-5 to the exit for Maxwell (north of Williams, south of Willows). Take that exit to Maxwell-Sites Road, turn west, and drive to Sites and Sites-Lodoga Road. Turn left on Sites-Lodoga Road and drive to Lodoga and Lodoga-Stonyford Road. Turn left and loop around East Park Reservoir to reach Stonyford and Fouts Spring Road (Road M10). Turn west and drive 25 miles to a signed access road for Summit Spring trailhead. Turn right and drive 1.5 miles to the parking area and trailhead, at the end of the road.

Contact: Mendocino National Forest, Stonyford Work Center, 5171 Stonyford–Elk Creek Road, P.O. Box 160, Stonyford, CA 95979, 530/963-3128, www.fs.fed.us/r5.

is routed past Lake Davis to the beach, then continues north along the beach to the mouth of Alder Creek. This is an attractive coastal lagoon, known for many species of birds, including whistling swans. It's also the area where the San Andreas Fault heads off from land into the sea.

Time it right here, and all can seem perfect. Manchester State Park has two moods: one is sweet and one is foul. In late summer, fall, and late winter, radiant sunbeams set the Mendocino coast aglow, making for flawless beach walks. But in early summer, winds often blast out of the northwest and it can feel as if your head could blow off. Good thing it's attached at the neck (well at least for most people). In mid-summer, fog smothers the coast about every morning.

Note: This park is on the closure list developed by the California Department of Parks, pending final state budget decisions or the possible transfer of park management to other park agencies or volunteer groups.

User Groups: Hikers and horses. No dogs. The terrain isn't suitable for mountain bikes. No wheelchair facilities.

Permits: No permits are required. Parking and access are free.

Maps: A brochure and trail map is available for a fee at Manchester State Park. For a topographic map, ask the USGS for Point Arena.

Directions: From Point Arena, take Highway 1 north for five miles to Kinney Lane. Turn left and drive one mile to the park entrance, on the right.

Contact: Manchester State Park, 707/882-2463, c/o California State Parks, Mendocino District, P.O. Box 440, Mendocino, CA 95460, 707/937-5804, www.parks.ca.gov.

🔢17 ALDER CREEK TRAIL
4.0 mi / 1.75 hr 🏃1 ⛰8

in Manchester State Park on the Mendocino coast north of Point Arena

Map 4.3, page 175

The Alder Creek Trail starts by the park headquarters for Manchester State Park. The trail

🔢18 HEADLANDS LOOP
1.5 mi / 0.75 hr 🏃1 ⛰8

in Gualala Point Regional Park on the Sonoma coast

Map 4.3, page 175

The Headlands (to beach) Loop is an easy, short walk. It provides coastal views with a short cutoff on a spur trail. It also furnishes a lookout over the Gualala River and a route amid giant coastal cypress trees. From the visitors center, the trail is routed along the Gualala River and then turns and loops to the left. Here you can take the short cutoff trail that leads to the beach. On the way back, the trail traces the ocean bluffs for a short spell. For coastal views, take the spur trail to a lookout. Then the main trail turns inland and returns to the visitors center. Bonuses here include excellent whale-watching during the winter and good wildflower blooms on the grassy hillsides in spring. It is mostly level. The trailhead elevation is 250 feet.

User Groups: Hikers and dogs. No horses.

Permits: No permits are required. There is a parking fee of $4 per vehicle.

Maps: For a topographic map, ask the USGS for Gualala.

Directions: From Gualala, drive south on Highway 1 for 0.25 mile (over the Gualala River) and turn west into the park entrance. Continue to the visitors center.

Contact: Gualala Point Regional Park, P.O. Box 95, Gualala, CA 95445, 707/785-2377, www.sonomacountyparks.org.

19 SOUTHLAKE TRAIL

5.2 mi / 2.0 hr

at Lake Sonoma northwest of Healdsburg

Map 4.3, page 175

This trail provides the best introduction to Lake Sonoma, unless that is, you have a boat and take advantage of the boat-in campsites. The Southlake Trail starts off of Stewart's Point Road below the Overlook. The short trail at the Overlook provides spectacular views of the lake. But, that's what you get on this trail almost the entire way. The trail winds along the southwestern portion of Warm Springs Arm through gray pine and madrone woodlands. It traces alongside the lake, enters and exits a series of small groves, and extends along the lake's

fingers. At 2.7 miles, you'll reach Quicksilver Campground—it's the easiest hike to any lakeside campground at Lake Sonoma. A few trails bisect the route and extend into more-remote surrounding country, allowing ambitious hikers to create longer adventures. When you've had enough, just turn back.

The trail is not very steep, but does have some changes in elevation. It features sun exposure, making it great for wildflowers in the spring but very hot on summer afternoons. Most of the habitat is oak grasslands, and on rare occasion you may see wild pigs, deer, or rattlesnakes.

User Groups: Hikers, dogs, and horses. No mountain bikes. No wheelchair facilities.

Permits: No permits are required. Parking and access are free.

Maps: For a free map, go to the visitors center or contact the U.S. Corps of Engineers. For a topographic map, ask the USGS for Warm Springs Dam.

Directions: From Santa Rosa, take US 101 north for 12 miles to the exit for Healdsburg and Dry Creek Road. Take that exit, turn left on Dry Creek Road and drive about 11 miles (crossing Dry Creek; Dry Creek Road becomes Skaggs Springs Road; continue past visitors center) to Skaggs Springs–Stewarts Point Road. Turn left and drive 0.25 to a trailhead spur road. Turn right and drive a short distance to the trailhead on the left.

Contact: U.S. Army Corps of Engineers, Lake Sonoma, 3333 Skaggs Springs Road, Geyserville, CA 95441, 707/431-4590; Visitor Center 707/433-9483, www.corpslakes.us/sonoma.

20 SALT POINT BLUFF TRAIL

3.5 mi / 1.5 hr

in Salt Point State Park north of Jenner

Map 4.3, page 175

The dramatic, rocky shoreline of Salt Point State Park is memorable to anyone who has seen it. This trail provides the best look at it, including some simply awesome views from a 100-foot-high ocean bluff. The trailhead is at the parking area set near the tip of Salt Point. From here, hike north over Warren Creek, a seasonal stream, and then continue across the bluffs. You can practically feel the crashing of ocean breakers below you, the spray rocketing skyward. The trail eventually winds around and down to Stump Beach Cove, a pretty, sandy beach where the calm waters are in sharp contrast to the nearby mauling ocean breakers. Salt Point State Park is known for excellent sport abalone diving in season, and also for providing a marine reserve, Gerstle Cove, where no form of marine life may be taken or disturbed. This park is stellar.

User Groups: Hikers only. Horses are allowed on designated trails only, and mountain bikes are allowed only on fire roads. One trail (Gerstle Cove) is paved for wheelchairs for 100 yards out to Salt Point. No dogs.

Permits: No permits are required. A state park day-use fee of $8 is charged per vehicle.

Maps: A trail map is available for a fee from Salt Point State Park. For a topographic map, ask the USGS for Plantation.

Directions: From Santa Rosa, take US 101 north to the exit for River Road. Take that exit, turn left on River Road and drive 13 miles to Highway 116 and Guerneville. Turn right on Highway 116 and drive to Highway 1 at Jenner. Turn north on Highway 1 and drive 20 miles (nine miles past Fort Ross) to the park entrance. Turn left (west) and drive to the entrance kiosk. The trailhead is at the Salt Point parking area.

Contact: Salt Point State Park, 25050 Coast Highway 1, Jenner, CA 95450, 707/847-3221, www.parks.ca.gov.

21 STOCKOFF CREEK LOOP
1.25 mi / 0.75 hr　　　🏃1 ⛰8

in Stillwater Cove Regional Park north of Jenner

Map 4.3, page 175

Highway 1 is one of the top tourist drives in the United States, which explains why the coastal state parks get such heavy use in the summer months. This little regional park, however, is sometimes overlooked by out-of-state traffic. The trailhead is located at the day-use parking lot, and after starting the walk, you'll almost immediately enter a surprising forest comprised of firs and redwoods. You then come to the Loop Trail junction, where you turn right (another good idea is to take Schoolhouse Trail, a spur trail that is routed a short distance to a historic schoolhouse, and then return). The trail is routed along the creek, crosses a few bridges, and eventually rises above the watershed and loops back through forest to the parking area. It's an easy, pretty, and secluded loop hike. The trailhead elevation is 100 feet; elevation changes on this hike amount to 140 feet. A bonus is visiting Stillwater Cove, which requires crossing Highway 1 and then dropping down to the beach, a dramatic rock-strewn shore.

User Groups: Hikers and dogs. No horses or mountain bikes. No wheelchair facilities.

Permits: No permits are required. A day-use fee of $6 is charged for each vehicle.

Maps: For a free brochure, contact Stillwater Cove Regional Park. For a topographic map, ask the USGS for Plantation.

Directions: From Santa Rosa, take US 101 north to the exit for River Road. Take that exit, turn left on River Road and drive 13 miles to Highway 116 and Guerneville. Go right on Highway 116 and drive to Highway 1. Turn right and head north, past the town of Jenner, for 16 miles to the park entrance, on the right at mile marker 37.01.

Contact: Stillwater Cove Regional Park, County of Sonoma, 2300 County Center Drive, Suite 120, Santa Rosa, CA 95403, 707/847-3245; Regional Parks Department, 707/565-2041, www.sonomacountyparks.org.

22 BODEGA HEAD LOOP
1.5 mi / 1.0 hr   🥾1   ⛰9

on the Sonoma coast west of Bodega Bay

Map 4.3, page 175

The view here at sunset can be so beautiful that it can break your heart at all the things you've let slip through your fingers. That aside, the short loop hike at Bodega Head will provide an introduction to one of California's great coastal areas for an easy hike and views that can set off feelings that you will never forget. The trail starts at the east parking lot, and in just 1.5 miles, it takes hikers into a wonderland. Views of cliffs and untouched beaches are the first highlights, and then it is on southward for views of the sea and beyond. For a side trip, take a short tromp on a spur trail to the tip-top of Bodega Head for 360-degree views. Rarely does the ocean seem so vast as it does from here. Note that in spring and early summer, the wind can really howl. In late summer, fall, or late winter, Bodega Bay gets its warmest, and often, most wind-free weather. Whale-watching is great from January through April. But it's the sunsets here that you'll never forget.

User Groups: Hikers only. No horses, dogs, or mountain bikes. No wheelchair facilities.

Permits: No permits are required. Parking and access are free.

Maps: A trail map and brochure are available for a fee from Sonoma Coast State Beach.

Directions: Take US 101 to Petaluma and the exit for East Washington. Take that exit to East Washington. Turn west and drive through Petaluma (it becomes Bodega Avenue) for about 10 miles to Valley Ford Road. Bear right and drive 7.5 miles to Highway 1. Turn north on Highway 1 and drive nine miles to Bodega Bay and continue to East Shore Road. Turn left on East Shore Road and drive less than 0.5 mile to a stop sign at Bay Flat Road. Turn right and drive five miles around Bodega Bay (the road turns into West Side Road). Continue past Spud Point Marina and drive to the Bodega Head parking area.

Contact: Sonoma Coast State Beach, 3095 Highway 1, Bodega Bay, CA 94923, 707/875-3483, www.parks.ca.gov.

23 BLUE RIDGE TRAIL
1.0-17.0 mi / 1 day   🥾5   ⛰9

north of Lake Berryessa

Map 4.4, page 176

The Blue Ridge Trail provides a unique glimpse of the southern portion of the Cache Creek Natural Area and well beyond. Of course, there is a price. The Blue Ridge Trail includes a stretch with a 2,000-foot elevation gain in just over three miles, as well as many pieces of trail that are very steep, rocky, and dry.

The trail starts on the western foothills of the Capay Valley. From here, it climbs up to Blue Ridge, the hilltop rim that splits Yolo and Napa Counties and overlooks Lake Berryessa below to the west. The trail follows the ridge for five miles. Most folks don't last anywhere near that long; you'd better be fit to try it. In spring this can be a sensational hike, with wildflowers ablaze and bushes and trees in full bloom, and clear skies providing sweeping views. You'll see songbirds, swallows, falcons, and eagles flitting, hovering, and soaring. There are also a good share of lizards and rattlesnakes. The views are exceptional in all directions, with the Sutter Buttes and Snow Mountain most prominent, but with even Shasta and Lassen in view on clear days. In fact, the area has just about everything—everything that is, except water. You either bring at least two or three quarts per person, or you surrender, swearing never to hike here again.

User Groups: Hikers and dogs. Horses and mountain bikes, while allowed, aren't recommended because of the steep, rocky terrain. No wheelchair facilities.

Permits: No permits are required. Parking and access are free.

Maps: For a free primitive trail map, contact the Bureau of Land Management. For a topographic map, ask the USGS for Glascock.

Directions: From Sacramento, take I-5 north to Woodland and the exit for Highway 16. Take that exit, turn west on Highway 16 and drive about 45 miles (into the Capay Valley along Cache Creek) to County Road 40 (near Yolo County Park). Turn left on County Road 40 (a gravel road) and drive 0.25 mile and look for a concrete bridge (low water crossing). Continue over the bridge and drive 200 yards and look for the trailhead on the left. Park in the unpaved area near Cache Creek and walk down the dirt road through a meadow to the trailhead. In the winter, the dirt road is blocked by a locked gate; park instead at Lower Yolo County Park and walk down to the trailhead. Note that during the winter, the bridge is at times impassable due to high water.

Contact: Bureau of Land Management, Ukiah Field Office, 2550 North State Street, Ukiah, CA 95482, 707/468-4000, www.ca.blm.gov.

24 GILLIAM CREEK TRAIL
8.9 mi / 1 day   🥾3 ⛰8

in Austin Creek State Recreation Area north of Guerneville

Map 4.4, page 176

The Gilliam Creek Trail starts at 1,100 feet. You contour across the slope, then drop down to the headwaters of Schoolhouse Creek, at 400 feet. The trail then follows the stream, past the confluence with Gilliam Creek, extending 3.7 miles into the backcountry, all the way down to an elevation of 200 feet. At the confluence of East Austin Creek, turn right and hike deeper into wild, hilly country along the stream. Then return on the loop on East Austin Creek Trail, a fire road with a—yep, by now you should have figured this out—a long climb. At this point, you may ask, "Are we having fun yet?" Visitors who love Armstrong Redwoods tend not to speak of the adjoining Austin Creek Recreation Area with any terms of endearment.

The rolling hills, open forests, and streamside riparian habitat in Austin Creek State Recreation Area can seem a million miles away from

the forests of Armstrong Redwoods. Yet the two parks together actually form 6,488 acres of contiguous parkland. While most tourists are walking around the redwoods at Armstrong, this trail offers a quieter, more ambitious alternative.

Note: This park is on the closure list developed by the California Department of Parks, pending final state budget decisions or the possible transfer of park management to other park agencies or volunteer groups.

User Groups: Hikers and horses (no horses permitted during wet weather). Mountain bikes permitted on fire roads. No dogs. No wheelchair facilities.

Permits: No permits are required. A state park day-use fee of $8 is charged for each vehicle. A senior discount is available.

Maps: A trail map is available for a fee from Armstrong Redwoods State Reserve. For a topographic map, ask the USGS for Guerneville.

Directions: From Santa Rosa, take US 101 north to the exit for River Road. Take that exit, turn left on River Road and drive 13 miles to Highway 116 and Guerneville. Go right on Highway 116 and drive a short distance to Armstrong Woods Road. Turn right (north) on Armstrong Woods Road and drive 2.5 miles to the Armstrong Redwoods State Reserve entrance. Continue about four miles to the trailhead. No trailers or vehicles more than 20 feet long are permitted in Austin Creek State Recreation Area.

Contact: Armstrong Redwoods State Reserve, 17000 Armstrong Redwoods Road, Guerneville, CA 95446, 707/869-2015, www.parks.ca.gov.

25 EAST RIDGE TRAIL
6.8 mi / 4.0 hr   🥾3 ⛰7

in Armstrong Redwoods State Reserve north of Guerneville

Map 4.4, page 176

The East Ridge Trail rises 1,400 feet over the course of 3.4 miles. It offers lookouts below into a sea of redwood tops. The trailhead is at a

200-foot elevation, adjacent to Fife Creek. The route climbs gradually at first, then in the first 0.5 mile rises to cross the headwaters of Fife Creek, at an elevation of 600 feet. Your climb has only just begun, and if you're already running out of gas, you'd best head back. The trail continues climbing all the way, contouring its way up toward McCray Mountain (1,940 feet), topping out at a service road at 1,600 feet.

Instead of this more ambitious trip, if you want something short and sweet, take the Discovery Trail or Armstrong Nature Trail in Armstrong Redwoods. Both are very short and beautiful strolls through the park's grove of huge redwoods. But after that taste, your appetite will likely be whetted for something more inspiring. This hike provides it.

Note: This park is on the closure list developed by the California Department of Parks, pending final state budget decisions or the possible transfer of park management to other park agencies or volunteer groups.

User Groups: Hikers and horses. No dogs or mountain bikes. No wheelchair facilities.

Permits: No permits are required. A state park day-use fee of $8 is charged for each vehicle. A senior discount is available. It is possible to park outside the entrance kiosk and walk in without paying a fee.

Maps: A trail map is available for a fee from Armstrong Redwoods State Reserve. For a topographic map, ask the USGS for Guerneville.

Directions: From Santa Rosa, take US 101 north to the exit for River Road. Take that exit, turn left on River Road and drive 13 miles to Highway 116 and Guerneville. Go right on Highway 116 and drive a short distance to Armstrong Woods Road. Turn right (north) on Armstrong Woods Road and drive 2.5 miles to the Armstrong Redwoods State Reserve entrance. The trailhead is adjacent to the visitors center.

Contact: Armstrong Redwoods State Reserve, 17000 Armstrong Redwoods Road, Guerneville, CA 95446, 707/869-2015, www.parks.ca.gov.

26 MOUNT ST. HELENA TRAIL
10.6 mi / 4.5 hr 🚶3 ⛰9

in Robert Louis Stevenson State Park north of Calistoga

Map 4.4, page 176

Mount St. Helena is Sonoma County's highest mountain. This is the peak that strikes such a memorable silhouette when viewed from the Bay Area. This trail climbs to the 4,343-foot summit and requires an ascent of 2,068 feet over the course of five miles. The Mount St. Helena trail starts along Highway 29 at the ridge above the Calistoga Valley. From here, the route follows a moderate grade for the most part, then rises above the forest and includes two steep sections, one at the very end of your climb.

Visibility is best in spring, when north winds clear the air, showcasing remarkable views in all directions. Bill Grummer, a ranger pal, claims that on the best days visitors can see Mount Shasta (192 miles away), but so far we haven't had that experience. However, it is documented that in the late 19th century, surveyors sent signals back and forth between here and Mount Shasta, setting a record for longest signal distance. On other stellar days, you can see the Farallon Islands, 25 miles offshore from San Francisco, and a glimpse of the city itself (but not the Golden Gate Bridge).

In the summer, the hike can be pure hell: Much of the trail is actually a fire road with little shade, there's no water anywhere along the route, and the heat commonly blazes in the 90s and 100s out here. Most visitors make the trip when temperatures are more tolerable, of course, which makes the gradient feel pretty moderate. No matter when you hike, be certain to bring plenty of water, a day pack with high-energy food, a windbreaker, and a change of shirts (so you won't be making the return downhill trip with a cold, wet shirt).

After logging weather records for years, we have found the most likely time for Mount St. Helena to receive snow is just before a full moon in February.

User Groups: Hikers only on single-track trail. Mountain bikes allowed on a nearby fire road 0.25 mile north on Highway 29. No dogs or horses. No wheelchair facilities.

Permits: No permits are required. Parking and access are free.

Maps: A brochure and map are available at the park for a fee. For topographic maps, ask the USGS for Detert Reservoir and Mount St. Helena.

Directions: From Calistoga, take Highway 29 north for eight miles to the parking area at the highway summit, signed Robert Louis Stevenson State Park. The trailhead is next to the parking area. You can park on the east or west side of the road. The trail is located on the west side of the road (the trailhead is not signed from the road).

Contact: Robert Louis Stevenson State Park, c/o Bothe–Napa Valley State Park, 3801 St. Helena Highway North, Calistoga, CA 94515, 707/942-4575, www.parks.ca.gov.

27 PALISADES TRAIL
4.0-9.5 mi one-way / 2.0-4.0 hr
🥾3 ⛰9

near Calistoga

Map 4.4, page 176

The Palisades? Aren't the Palisades a glacier-carved series of 14,000-foot peaks in the Sierra Nevada? Well, yep, but Napa County's Palisades are nearly as dramatic and accessible year-round: It's a stunning, mile-long volcanic wall set along a ridge that overlooks Calistoga and the Napa Valley. The Palisades is dramatic up close and personal, and provides gorgeous long-distance views. In addition, this trail is one of the best near Calistoga for seeing raptors, including a chance to spot peregrine falcons, and also for wildflowers, particularly bitterroot.

From Calistoga, it's a twisty, eight-mile drive up Highway 29 to the parking area and trailhead, the same staging area used for the Mount St. Helena Trail. It is signed Robert

Louis Stevenson State Park. To hike to Table Rock and the Palisades, the trailhead is on the right (southeast) side of the road.

This trip can be done three ways: A 4-mile round-trip to Table Rock and back, an 8-mile round-trip to the southern edge of the Palisades and back (recommended), or a wild 9.5-mile one-way trek (with a shuttle car) down to the valley. The best time for this getaway is from mid-March through mid-May, when the foothills are green, the skies are often crystal-clear, and the morning air is still cool.

From the southeast side of the parking area (elevation 2,250 feet), you start this hike on the Table Rock Trail. It's about two miles to Table Rock (2,465 feet), just enough of a climb to get you above the canyon woodlands. Some enjoy the views from atop Table Rock, have a picnic, and then head back to the car. But the trip gets better by continuing on the Palisades Trail. This drops down to Lasky Point (2,045 feet), and then climbs back up for about two miles along the base of the Palisades (2,930 feet). The trail is spectacular, set just beneath the sheer volcanic cliffs along the ridge. At 3.9 miles in, you will reach the junction of Historic Oat Hill Mine Road, a long-abandoned, rocky jeep road. Most people turn around and head back from here.

Oat Hill Mine Road is the route down to the valley for a one-way hike with a shuttle. But it plummets 2,000 feet over 4.5 miles, some of it rocky, and can be a thigh-burning, knee-wrenching, toe-jamming experience that's only for the deranged (like us, for instance).

Calistoga is one of the best decompression chambers designed by mankind. But after a day or two of getting turned into Jell-O by soaks in steaming mineral water, massages, and mud baths, you can be brought back to life by the electrifying hike to the Palisades.

Note: There is no drinking water available anywhere on the trail. Rangers warn not to leave valuables in your car (covering them with a jacket or blanket isn't enough either).

User Groups: Hikers only. No dogs, horses, or mountain bikes. No wheelchair facilities.

Permits: Parking and access are free.

Maps: A brochure and map are available for a fee at the park or by mail. For topographic maps, ask the USGS for Detert Reservoir and Mount St. Helena.

Directions: From Calistoga, take Highway 29 north for eight miles to the parking area at the highway summit, signed Robert Louis Stevenson State Park. The trailhead is on the right (southeast) side of the road.

Contact: Robert Louis Stevenson State Park, c/o Bothe–Napa Valley State Park, 3801 St. Helena Highway North, Calistoga, CA 94515, 707/942-4575, www.parks.ca.gov.

28 COYOTE PEAK / REDWOOD TRAIL LOOP
4.4 mi / 3.0 hr

in Bothe–Napa Valley State Park south of Calistoga

Map 4.4, page 176

The best way to see the surprise redwoods and pretty creek at Bothe–Napa Valley State Park is on the Coyote Peak/Redwood Trail Loop. Start just past the Ritchey Creek Campground turnoff, near the picnic area. The first 0.5 mile is on the Ritchey Canyon Trail, a very pretty stretch of trail along beautiful Ritchey Creek. Then bear left on the Redwood Trail. You'll be surrounded by some of the park's highest stands of redwoods. The trail continues along Ritchey Creek for 0.25 mile, then connects to the Coyote Peak Trail. Take the Coyote Peak Trail, which rises quickly, skirting the northern flank of Coyote Peak. (A short spur trail will take you all the way to the top, elevation 1,170 feet.) Then the trail drops down the other side of the hill and intersects with South Fork Trail, which heads all the way back down to Ritchey Creek. From the trailhead to the end of the hike, the elevation gain is roughly 800 feet, totaling the up-and-downs.

Who ever heard of redwoods in the Napa Valley? Who ever heard of a mountain peak there, too? Only those who also know of

Bothe–Napa Valley State Park, which is like an island of wildland in a sea of winery tourist traffic. Bothe-Napa has some of the most easterly stands of coastal redwoods, plus Douglas fir and an excellent lookout from Coyote Peak, all quite a surprise for newcomers. Note that temperatures can be extremely hot in the summer—as high as 105 degrees in unshaded areas—but you'll find a cool paradise along Ritchey Creek.

Note: This park is on the closure list developed by the California Department of Parks, pending final state budget decisions or the possible transfer of park management to other park agencies or volunteer groups.

User Groups: Hikers only. Horses permitted on some designated trails. Mountain bikes allowed on fire roads and designated trails but not on most of this described loop. No dogs. No wheelchair facilities.

Permits: No permits are required. A state park fee of $8 is charged per vehicle.

Maps: A brochure and trail map are available for $1 at the park or $1.60 by mail. For a topographic map, ask the USGS for Calistoga.

Directions: From Calistoga, take Highway 29 south for about five miles to the park entrance on the right side of the road. Turn right and drive past the entrance station to just past the Ritchey Creek Campground turnoff (near the picnic area), where there is trailhead parking.

Contact: Bothe–Napa Valley State Park, 3801 St. Helena Highway North, Calistoga, CA 94515, 707/942-4575, www.parks.ca.gov.

29 SPRING LAKE TRAIL
2.0 mi / 1.0 hr

in Spring Lake Regional Park in eastern Santa Rosa

Map 4.4, page 176

Spring Lake is Santa Rosa's backyard fishing hole, a popular place for trout fishing, an evening picnic, or a short hike. For newcomers, we suggest you take the walk along the west shore of Spring Lake. From the parking area, start this trip by walking along the shore to Spring Lake's west dam. Then turn left and head into adjoining Howarth Park and on to Lake Ralphine. It's an easy, enjoyable stroll. The lake is stocked with trout in winter and spring, and it provides a fair warm-water fishery in the summer. The lake is fun and quiet, with boats restricted to electric motors; no gas motors are allowed. The elevation is 300 feet, and the trail is mostly level.

User Groups: Hikers and dogs. Horses are allowed only on designated trails. The park has 2.3 miles of trail that are paved for wheelchair and bicycle use.

Permits: No permits are required. There is a parking fee of $7 per vehicle, and $6 in offseason.

Maps: A free trail map is available from Spring Lake Regional Park. For a topographic map, ask the USGS for Santa Rosa.

Directions: From Santa Rosa, take Highway 12 east (it becomes Hoen Avenue) to Newanga Avenue. Turn left on Newanga Avenue and drive 0.5 mile to the park entrance. The various trailheads are well marked and easily accessible from the parking area at the lake.

Contact: Spring Lake Regional Park, c/o Sonoma County Regional Parks, 2300 Country Center Drive, Santa Rosa, CA 95403, 707/539-8092; Sonoma County Regional Parks Department, 707/565-2041, www.sonomacountyparks.org.

30 BALD MOUNTAIN LOOP
8.2 mi / 1 day　　　　🏃3 ⛰8

in Sugarloaf Ridge State Park north of Sonoma

Map 4.4, page 176

Bald Mountain, elevation 2,729 feet, overlooks the Napa Valley, with Mount St. Helena to the north. The old mountain is the centerpiece of Sugarloaf Ridge State Park, a 4,020-acre park featuring redwoods in the Sonoma Creek watershed, open meadows peppered with oaks on the hilltops, and some chaparral on ridges. On clear days from the summit, you can see portions of the San Francisco Bay Area and then be thankful you're here instead.

The most ambitious hike in the park is the Bald Mountain Loop, an 8.2-mile trek. The trail starts at the parking lot and then is routed into a loop by linking the Bald Mountain, Gray Pine, Brushy Peaks, and Meadow Trails. Many less-demanding hikes are available in the park, but this route will give hikers the greatest sense of the park's wildest lands. It's best hiked in the spring, when the air is still cool, the hills are green, and the wildflowers are in bloom.

There's a bonus as well: When Sonoma Creek is really flowing, a 25-foot waterfall set in a wooded canyon tumbles downstream from the campground; a short trail is available from the park's entrance road, located at an unsigned turnout on the road's shoulder. A more formal route to the waterfall is on Canyon Trail.

Note: This park is on the closure list developed by the California Department of Parks, pending final state budget decisions or the possible transfer of park management to other park agencies or volunteer groups.

User Groups: Hikers only. Horses are allowed on trails in summer and on fire roads in the park in winter. No dogs. No wheelchair facilities.

Permits: No permits are required. A state park day-use fee of $8 is charged for each vehicle.

Maps: A trail map and brochure are available for a fee from Sugarloaf Ridge State Park. For a topographic map, ask the USGS for Kenwood.

Directions: From Santa Rosa, take Highway 12 east through Kenwood to Adobe Canyon Road. Turn left on Adobe Canyon Road and drive 3.5 miles to the main park entrance at the end of the road.

Contact: Sugarloaf Ridge State Park, 2605 Adobe Canyon Road, Kenwood, CA 95452, 707/833-5712, www.parks.ca.gov.

SACRAMENTO AND GOLD COUNTRY

© ANN MARIE BROW

BEST HIKES

From a distance, this section of the Sacramento

Valley looks like flat farmland extending into infinity, with a sprinkling of cities and towns interrupting the view, edged by the foothills of the northern Sierra. But a closer look reveals a landscape filled with Northern California's most significant rivers – the Sacramento, Feather, Yuba, American, and Mokelumne. All of these provide water recreation (in both lakes and rivers), as well as serve as the lifeblood for a series of wildlife refuges.

This is an area for California-history buffs: Malakoff Diggins State Historic Park, Auburn State Recreation Area, and Spenceville Wildlife Area are all here, the center of the extraordinary gold rush era. This region also features the canyons and peaks of Plumas National Forest, and, of course, the 32-mile American River Parkway, stretching from Sacramento on upstream along the American River to Rancho Cordova and Fair Oaks.

The highlight of the foothill country is a series of rivers and lakes that provide great hiking and water sports. Every canyon has a river, and every river has a trail. Some of these trails lead to fantastic waterfalls, such as Feather Falls and Shingle Falls. The lakes include Camanche, Collins, Oroville, Bucks, and many others, and several of these lakes provide trails along their shores.

In love and the great outdoors, timing is everything, and so it is in the Central Valley and the nearby foothills. Spring and fall are gorgeous here, along with many summer evenings. But there are always periods of 100-plus temperatures in the summer. But that's what gives the lakes and rivers such appeal, and in turn, it's why they are treasured. On a hot day, there is nothing quite like hiking deep into a remote canyon, then jumping into a cool river. It can make water seem more valuable than gold and a cold drink on ice worth more than silver.

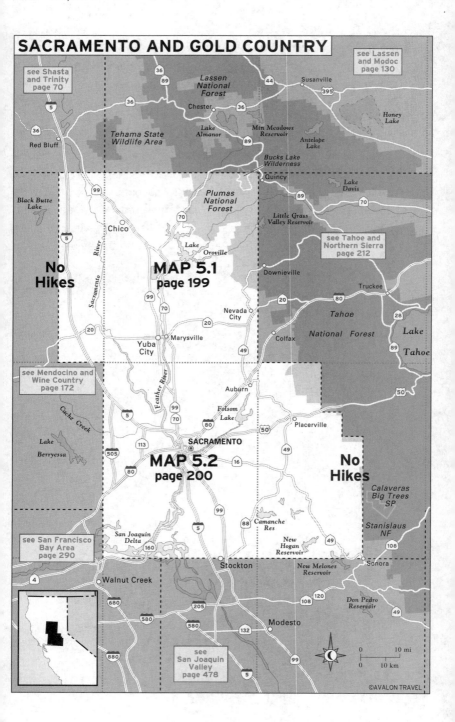

SACRAMENTO AND GOLD COUNTRY

see Shasta
and Trinity
page 70

see Lassen
and Modoc
page 130

Lassen
National
Forest

Susanville

Chester

Lake
Almanor

Mtn Meadows
Reservoir

Honey
Lake

Red Bluff

Tehama State
Wildlife Area

Antelope
Lake

Bucks Lake
Wilderness

Black Butte
Lake

Plumas
National
Forest

Quincy

Lake
Davis

Little Grass
Valley Reservoir

see Tahoe and
Northern Sierra
page 212

Chico

Lake
Oroville

**No
Hikes**

**MAP 5.1
page 199**

Downieville

Truckee

Sacramento River

Nevada
City

Tahoe

National   Forest

Lake

Yuba
City

Marysville

Colfax

Tahoe

see Mendocino and
Wine Country
page 172

Auburn

Cache Creek

Folsom
Lake

Placerville

Lake
Berryessa

Feather River

SACRAMENTO

**MAP 5.2
page 200**

**No
Hikes**

Calaveras
Big Trees
SP

see San Francisco
Bay Area
page 290

San Joaquin
Delta

Camanche
Res

New
Hogan
Reservoir

Stanislaus
NF

Sonora

Walnut Creek

Stockton

New Melones
Reservoir

Don Pedro
Reservoir

Modesto

see
San Joaquin Valley
page 478

0   10 mi
0   10 km

©AVALON TRAVEL

Map 5.1

Hikes 1-7
Pages 201-204

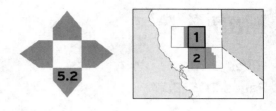

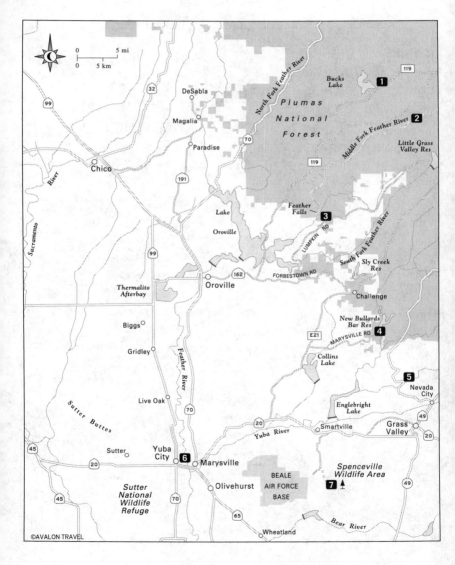

Map 5.2

Hikes 8-10
Pages 205-207

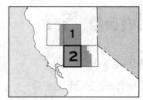

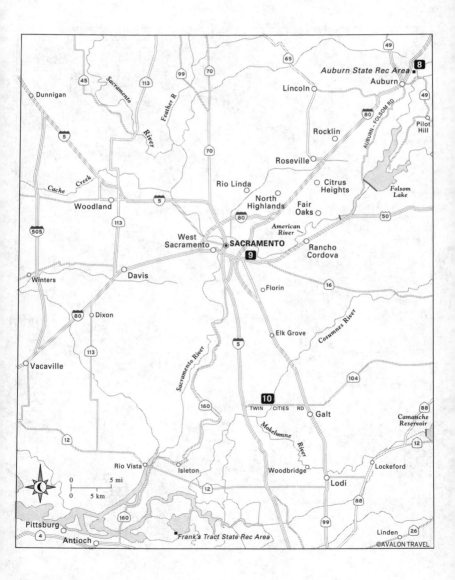

©AVALON TRAVEL

◼ BUCKS SUMMIT TO FEATHER RIVER (PCT)

20.0 mi one-way / 2 days 🏃3 ⛰8

at Bucks Summit Trailhead at the southern boundary of the Bucks Lake Wilderness west of Quincy

Map 5.1, page 199

It's 20 miles from Bucks Summit to Belden, all of it on the Pacific Crest Trail through the Bucks Lake Wilderness. The trail passes across a granitic-based alpine area, where forest is interspersed with glacier-smoothed rock peaks. The trailhead is at Bucks Summit (elevation 5,531 feet), and from here, the route generally follows the ridgeline for many miles, climbing to the southern flank of Mount Pleasant, at 6,924 feet. Along the way, a short spur trail to little Rock Lake provides a good side trip. The trail heads past Three Lakes, where another spur trail provides another option, this one to Kellogg Lake. From here, the trail begins descending and then drops very sharply all the way down to 2,310 feet, to the North Fork Feather River at Belden. Your big toes will be sore for days from jamming into the front of your boots.

To continue north on the Pacific Crest Trail (PCT), see the *Feather River to Humboldt Summit (PCT)* hike, in the *Lassen and Modoc* chapter. If you are walking this trail in reverse, see the *Fowler Peak to Bucks Summit (PCT)* hike, in the *Tahoe and Northern Sierra* chapter, to continue south.

User Groups: Hikers, dogs, and horses. No mountain bikes. No wheelchair access.

Permits: A wilderness permit (free) is required. Parking and access are free.

Maps: For a map, ask the U.S. Forest Service for Plumas National Forest. For a topographic map, ask the USGS for Bucks Lake.

Directions: Take Highway 89 to Quincy and Bucks Lake Road. Turn west on Bucks Lake Road and drive about 11 miles to the trailhead, at Bucks Summit.

Contact: Plumas National Forest, Mount Hough Ranger District, 39696 State Highway 70, Quincy, CA 95971, 530/283-0555, www.fs.fed.us/r5.

◼ HARTMAN BAR NATIONAL RECREATION TRAIL

4.4 mi / 3.0 hr 🏃5 ⛰8

in Plumas National Forest east of Lake Oroville

Map 5.1, page 199

Hikers often pay for their pleasure. This hike involves two installments. The trail descends from the Hartman Ridge down the canyon to Hartman Bar Ridge, on the Middle Fork Feather River. Going down will have your toes jamming into your boots, and the trip back can have your heart firing off like cannon shots. But waiting is the Middle Fork Feather, one of the prettiest streams around, and with some of the best trout fishing as well. In fact, of the hundreds of trout streams in California, the Middle Fork Feather is clearly in the top five. If you don't like to fish but would rather explore farther, a footbridge crosses the stream and climbs the other side of the canyon, meeting Catrell Creek at 0.5 mile. If you want to split the trip in two, the primitive Dan Beebe Camp is available along the river.

User Groups: Hikers, dogs, and horses. A horse corral is at the trailhead. Mountain bikes not recommended. No wheelchair facilities.

Permits: No permits are required. Parking and access are free.

Maps: For a map, ask the U.S. Forest Service for Plumas National Forest. For topographic maps, ask the USGS for Cascade and Haskins Valley.

Directions: From Oroville, drive east on Highway 162 for eight miles to Highway 174/ Forbestown Road (and a junction signed Challenge/LaPorte). Turn right on Forbestown Road and drive east to Highway 120 (Quincy-LaPorte Road). Turn left and drive past LaPorte to Little Grass Valley Road. Turn left and drive a short distance to Black Rock Campground. Turn left on Forest Road 94 and drive 10 miles to Forest Road 22N42Y.

Turn right and drive 0.25 mile to the parking area, at the end of the road.

Contact: Plumas National Forest, Feather River Ranger District, 875 Mitchell Avenue, Oroville, CA 95965-4699, 530/534-6500, www.fs.fed.us/r5.

❸ FEATHER FALLS LOOP
9.5 mi / 4.0 hr 🏃3 ⛰10

in Plumas National Forest east of Lake Oroville

Map 5.1, page 199   BEST (

The viewing deck for 640-foot Feather Falls is spectacular—a platform perched on a knife-edge outcrop for a full frontal view of the falls. The silver plume of water shoots over the brink and free falls into a granite canyon. It's the kind of sight that can leave you feeling refreshed for weeks, imprinted for life. In the spring, it's wide and powerful, and in years when there is a big snowpack in the Sierra, it stays that way well into July. But it runs all year and is beautiful even in the fall.

The trail used to be a loop route best completed in a clockwise direction. In 2011, the bridge on the left fork portion of the loop was destroyed yet again. So, until further notice, the trip is now an in-and-out hike that we still love to do.

From the trailhead, this hike starts through forest and then quickly arrives at a fork in the trail. If the bridge has *not* been replaced, turn right. The route extends in a half-moon curve for 4.5 miles. It's easy going as you stroke your way through forests and across small streams with bridged crossings. The trail laterals across to the edge of the main canyon. At one spot, there are awesome canyon and mountain views.

The trail continues toward the falls. Look for a cut-off spur trail to the left. Take a left at this fork and, at the next fork, bear left to head to the viewing area. This is the best waterfall viewing deck in California. Most hikers spend at least an hour here, enjoying a picnic, getting hydrated, and soaking in the view.

Note: If the bridge has been replaced, then turn left. As you hike, immediately look for the sandstone outcrops up on the left—you can find Indian grinding mortars here. The trail then descends for a mile and crosses a stream on the bridge. In late winter, there can be millions of ladybugs at this spot, an extraordinary sight. The trail then climbs out of the canyon, and laterals across toward the canyon, linking up with the main trail that continues out to Feather Falls.

After enjoying the view from the deck, continue on the main trail and hike to the brink of the falls. The view is nowhere as good as from the deck; as a result, some people climb out on the boulders right at the brink. Fences have been erected here to try and stop this, but people keep doing it. Big mistake: You can easily die doing this. Remember, Darwin rules.

User Groups: Hikers and dogs. Horses and mountain bikes permitted but not recommended. No wheelchair facilities.

Permits: No permits are required. Parking and access are free.

Maps: For a map, ask the U.S. Forest Service for Plumas National Forest. For a topographic map, ask the USGS for Brush Creek.

Directions: From Oroville, drive east on Highway 162 (Oroville Dam Boulevard) about eight miles to Forbestown Road. Turn right (east) on Forbestown Road east and drive six miles to Lumpkin Road. Turn left on Lumpkin Road and drive 10.5 miles to the sign for Feather Falls Trail. Turn left and drive 1.5 miles to the parking area, at the end of the road.

Contact: Plumas National Forest, Feather River Ranger District, 875 Mitchell Avenue, Oroville, CA 95965-4699, 530/534-6500, www.fs.fed.us/r5.

4 BULLARDS BAR TRAIL

1-13.5 mi / 0.5 hr-1 day   🏃1 ⛰7

on Bullards Bar Reservoir in Tahoe National Forest

Map 5.1, page 199

Don't be spooked by the seven-mile length of this trail (13.5 if you include the two loops). Most folks just saunter along for a few miles—maybe take a dunk in the water or cast out a fishing line and sit a spell—then turn back. From the trailhead at the Dark Day Picnic Area, the trail leads west and east along the shore of Bullards Bar Reservoir to Vista Point, overlooking the dam. The path is nearly flat, ranging between 2,243 and 2,250 feet in elevation. Along the way, there are many good fishing and swimming spots, as well as a sprinkling of huge ponderosa pines and Douglas firs. A bonus attraction is that the trail links up with a network of other trails that make up 23 miles of trails in this area. These include Rebel Ridge Trail, 7-Ball Trail, and 8-Ball Trail—all good. Because of the summer heat, this area is best hiked in spring; use then drops off in summer.

User Groups: Hikers, dogs, horses, and mountain bikes. No wheelchair facilities.

Permits: No permits are required. Parking and access are free.

Maps: For a map, ask the U.S. Forest Service for Tahoe National Forest. For topographic maps, ask the USGS for Camptonville and Challenge.

Directions: From Marysville, take Highway 20 east for 12 miles to Marysville Road. Turn left on Marysville Road (signed for Bullards Bar Reservoir) and drive 10 miles to Old Marysville Road. Turn right and drive 14 miles, over the dam, and continue four miles to Dark Day Road. Turn left and drive to the picnic area and trailhead.

Contact: Tahoe National Forest, Nevada City/Downieville Ranger Districts, North Yuba Ranger Station, 15924 Highway 49, Camptonville, CA 95922, 530/288-3231, www.fs.fed.us/r5.

5 SOUTH YUBA INDEPENDENCE TRAIL

1.0-9.0 mi / 0.5-3.0 hr   🏃1 ⛰8

near Nevada City

Map 5.1, page 199   **BEST (**

This is a pleasant, virtually flat trail that is routed along Rush Creek Canyon with pretty views of the stream. A waterfall with a nearby water flume is a unique side attraction. From the trailhead, hike to the west (go right) to visit Rush Creek Falls and spectacular Flume 28, one mile from the trailhead. The entire trail is routed for 4.5 miles through beautiful forest along the Yuba River Canyon. It is loved by both hikers and wheelchair users. The path was originally a canal route, built in 1859 to carry water from the Yuba to a hydraulic mining site in Smartville. This is considered the nation's first wheelchair-accessible wilderness trail; the wheelchair-accessible portion is a seven-mile round-trip. Guided nature walks for groups of six or more are offered by Sequoya Challenge, but reservations are required (see *Contact*, below). Note that this trailhead is set at midtrail along Highway 49, which gives you the option of hiking either direction. There are also other access points to the river and trail. Occasionally, guided walks and gold panning demonstrations are available.

User Groups: Hikers, dogs, and wheelchairs. No horses or mountain bikes.

Permits: No permits are necessary. Parking and access are free.

Maps: A brochure and map are available at the trailhead or from the Bridgeport Ranger Station. For a topographic map, ask the USGS for Nevada City.

Directions: From Auburn, drive north on Highway 49 for 27 miles to Nevada City. Continue on Highway 49 for six miles past Nevada City to the trailhead parking area, along the highway. The parking area is a paved pull-out located just before the South Yuba River Bridge. If you reach the bridge, you have gone too far. Parking is limited.

Contact: South Yuba River State Park, 530/432-2546, www.parks.ca.gov.

6 NORTH BUTTE / SUTTER BUTTES

3.0 mi / 2.0 hr 🚶3 ⛰10

at Sutter Buttes near Yuba City

Map 5.1, page 199

From a lava pinnacle atop the Smallest Mountain Range in the World, you get a hawk's-eye view of land few have seen. This is at the Sutter Buttes, located about an hour north of Sacramento, one of California's last lands of mystery. Since it is surrounded by private land, few have trekked the Sutter Buttes and almost no one has seen Peace Valley, new state land that could become a park.

The best trip is a three-mile round-trip hike to the North Butte. It starts as an easy walk, meandering up through a valley to a sub-ridge, with a 1,000-foot climb off-trail in the last 0.5 mile. A short way in, you will see an Indian grinding rock along a dry creek bed where ancient mortars had been hollowed out in the stone. From here, hike up the valley. It's common to spot red-tailed hawks, vultures, harriers, and deer. The lucky few see fox, bobcat, owls, or golden eagles. There is no trail amid the volcanic crags, scree, and brush for the final 0.5-mile push to the summit. Instead, pick your way up to the 1,863-foot North Butte summit. From the top, you can scan across the multiple peaks, crowned by the South Butte at 2,117 feet. Despite some 37 million people living in California, only a scant few know this experience.

Note: There is no drive-up public access. The only trail access is through guided trips with the Middle Mountain Foundation, and it is very much worth it. (The Maidu called the Sutter Buttes "Esto Yamini," which means "Middle Mountain," and that's how the Foundation got its name.) Trips are best in fall, winter, and early spring.

Some may also wonder how the Sutter Buttes qualifies as "The Smallest Mountain Range in the World." Topographically, land has to have an elevation of at least 2,000 feet to qualify as a mountain. At 2,117 feet, the Sutter Buttes just barely qualify as a mountain range.

User Groups: Hikers only. No dogs, horses, or mountain bikes. No wheelchair facilities.

Permits: Advance reservations for guided group hikes are required at 530/671-6116. Most trips cost $35 (suggested donation). Up to 20 participants are allowed on most hikes.

Maps: A brochure and map are available from trip leaders upon meeting at the Sutter County Museum.

Directions: Hiking groups meet at the Sutter County Museum in Yuba City. Directions are provided when the reservation is confirmed. After orientation, drivers will lead the route past several locked gates to the trailhead in Sutter Buttes.

Contact: Middle Mountain Foundation, P.O. Box 3359, Yuba City, CA 95992-3359, 530/755-3568, www.middlemountain.org.

7 SHINGLE FALLS

5.0 mi / 2.5 hr 🚶2 ⛰7

in Spenceville Wildlife Area near Smartville

Map 5.1, page 199

This is a pretty spot of surprise in the foothills of the Sacramento Valley. Many people call this place Dry Creek Falls. But the real name is Shingle Falls, named decades ago after a military officer from nearby Beale Air Force Base. Your destination, of course, is Shingle Falls, which is easily reached by a five-mile round-trip hike. From the parking area and trailhead, walk across a worn-out bridge, and start hiking to your right on the fire road on the other side. After walking nearly a mile, you'll bear right and hike south on another dirt road. Then, after about 0.25 mile, you can turn left at the cattle guard and, after another 0.1 mile, take any of the three paths veering right. Keep alert, because wild turkeys are common here. At 2.5 miles from the trailhead, you'll come to the road's end, and in turn, to the creek, gorge, and waterfalls. The bigger one is about 60 feet, with steep cliffs walled off by a fence. If you follow a path downstream along the creek, you'll find a smaller waterfall after about 100 yards. Both make fine spots for a springtime visit. Most of the trail here is on a gravel road set amid an oak-and-grassland country in the Sacramento Valley. The stream supports a surprising variety of creekside vegetation, including various oaks, willows, and alders. Wild turkeys are common sightings. Best time to hike the trail? December through April, when the hills are saturated, the aquifer is flushed, and the waterfall is pumping. In turkey season, the Department of Fish and Game conducts a permit system for turkey hunting and hiking is not permitted. Seasonal hunting may be permitted for other species September–January.

User Groups: Hikers and dogs. Horses and mountain bikes not allowed on this trail. Horses allowed on marked trails and service roads. Mountain bikes are allowed only on service roads. No wheelchair facilities.

Permits: No permits are necessary. Parking and access are free. Organized groups must obtain a free permit.

Maps: Free maps of Spenceville Wildlife Area are available at information signposts in the refuge. For a topographic map, ask the USGS for Camp Far West.

Directions: From Marysville, take Highway 20 east for 15 miles to Smartville Road (just east and opposite a CDF fire station). Turn right (south) on Smartville Road and enter the wildlife area. At 0.9 mile, bear left at a fork (the road is signed Chuck Yeager) and continue about 4 miles to Waldo Road (gravel). Turn left on Waldo Road and drive 2.1 miles to Spenceville Road. Turn left and drive two miles to the end of the road, at a closed bridge. Park, walk carefully across the bridge, and begin the hike.

Contact: Spenceville Wildlife Area, c/o Oroville Wildlife Area, Department of Fish and Game, 945 Oro Dam Boulevard West, Oroville, CA 95965, 530/538-2236, www.dfg.ca.gov.

8 CODFISH CREEK TRAIL
3.0 mi / 1.5 hr   👫2 ⛰7

in Auburn State Recreation Area

Map 5.2, page 200

A little-known route along the North Fork American River, Codfish Creek Trail follows an old mining route downstream along its edge, then cuts up the canyon of Codfish Creek. The highlight here is Codfish Falls, but you should then hike up for canyon views. The lowlights are hot summer temperatures—too hot on summer afternoons for enjoyment. The trail begins at the north side of the bridge, on Ponderosa Way, and heads downstream on sunny and exposed slopes. The path brings visitors to a series of cascades on Codfish Creek. If you can, plan your trip for March, April, or May, when you get the double bonus of a full-flowing waterfall and lots of blooming wildflowers. At 1.2 miles, the trail turns right and leads upstream along Codfish Creek, heading away from the river.

User Groups: Hikers and dogs. No horses or mountain bikes. No wheelchair facilities.

Permits: No permits are necessary. Parking and access are free most areas, $10 parking in some areas.

Maps: For a national forest map, which includes Auburn State Recreation Area lands, ask the U.S. Forest Service for Tahoe National Forest. For a topographic map, ask the USGS for Colfax.

Directions: From Sacramento, take I-80 east for 40 miles to Weimar and the Weimar Crossroad exit. Take that exit, then a right at the fork off the off-ramp, and a right onto Ponderosa Way after about 50 feet. Drive 5.5 miles (the road turns to dirt, becomes extremely narrow, and can be deeply rutted after winter rains, so drive slowly and with caution) to a bridge at the American River. Park near the bridge on the south side of the road (the side closest to the river) and look for the trailhead, on the north side of the bridge, with the trail heading downstream past the beach area.

Contact: Auburn State Recreation Area, 501 El Dorado Street, Auburn, CA 95603, 530/885-4527, www.parks.ca.gov.

9 AMERICAN RIVER PARKWAY / JEDEDIAH SMITH MEMORIAL TRAIL
0.25–32.0 mi one-way / 0.5 hr–2 days 　🥾1 　⛰7

along the American River from Sacramento to Folsom

Map 5.2, page 200	BEST (

The idea for the American River Parkway sounded good in concept, and it works even better in practice: A route along the American River that links Sacramento upstream past Rancho Cordova and Fair Oaks. This multi-use trail runs 32 miles from Discovery Park, in Sacramento, up to Folsom. There are actually two parallel trails, one paved for bicyclists and in-line skaters only, and a dirt trail for horses (note that there is no shoulder on the horse trail). Walkers and joggers should stay off the paved portion, and should instead use the dirt trail or the shoulder of the bike trail. The trail connects to Folsom Lake State Recreation Area, off Hazel Avenue (near Nimbus Dam), and continues for another nine miles one-way up to Beals Point, at Folsom Lake. Almost no one hikes, bikes, or skates the entire length, of course. Most simply enjoy short sections, usually on evening walks, jogs, or rides.

Spring and fall are when the American River is prettiest. In spring, the trees and grass are green, the water is rolling fresh, and by May, schools of shad are swimming upstream. Come autumn, the leaves of the adjacent trees turn bright colors, lighting up the river. In the intervening summer months, 100-degree temperatures keep trail use low during the day, but when evening shade emerges, so do joggers and walkers.

Special Note: In-line skates or roller skates are allowed on the state park and county park portions of trail. The state park portion is two separate trails most of the route, but a 0.5 mile section is shared. All nine miles of state trail are paved, and wheelchairs are allowed. Elsewhere, wheelchairs are allowed on the actual trail, and wheelchair-accessible restrooms, fishing areas, and picnic grounds are available along the way.

User Groups: Hikers, dogs, mountain bikes, in-line skates, roller skates, and horses allowed, but horses are not advised. See the *Special Note* about restrictions for mountain bikes and hikers, above.

Permits: No permits are required. Folsom Lake State Recreation Area at the head of the Parkway charges a fee of $10 per vehicle for developed parking and $6 per vehicle for undeveloped parking.

Maps: A trail map is available for a fee at the county parks department. For topographic maps, ask the USGS for Sacramento East, Carmichael, Citrus Heights, and Folsom.

Directions: The trail begins at Folsom Lake Recreation Area and ends at Discovery Park in Sacramento. From Sacramento, take U.S. 50 east for 18.4 miles to Exit 23 for Folsom Boulevard. Take that exit, go 0.2 mile, then bear left to take the ramp toward Folsom and Folsom Boulevard. Turn left on Folsom Boulevard and drive 3.6 miles, then continue straight (becomes Folsom-Auburn Boulevard) and go 2.0 miles to the park entrance.

Contact: County of Sacramento, Parks and Recreation Division, Park Ranger Section, 4040 Bradshaw Road, Sacramento, CA 95827, 916/875-6961, www.sacparks.net; Folsom Lake State Recreation Area, 916/988-0205, www.parks.ca.gov.

10 COSUMNES RIVER TRAIL
3.3 mi / 2.0 hr 　🥾1 　⛰8

in Cosumnes River Preserve near Galt

Map 5.2, page 200

The Cosumnes River Preserve is a wildlife preserve that is just remote enough to be overlooked by many who would love the place. This 3.3-mile hike is a lollipop loop and the preserve also has a paved and wheelchair-accessible one-mile loop with a 0.25-mile boardwalk. The preserve is located in the east Delta near I-5 in the town of Galt. From the visitors center, simply walk on the path along the river. This is a great getaway for bird- and wildlife- watching (stay alert for bird and wildlife sightings), driving tours, easy walks, and hand-powered boating—either bring your own kayak or canoe, or book a kayak trip with an outfitter. Free, guided walking tours are also available.

The best tour watches the marsh come alive at dawn. The Cosumnes River flows through one of the richest landscapes in the Delta, a mix of wetlands, riparian woodlands, river cuts, and sloughs that provides habitat for thousands of waterfowl, songbirds, hawks, and falcons. Coyote, fox, raccoon, otters, rabbits, and deer are common sightings.

User Groups: Hikers only. No mountain bikes, dogs, or horses. No wheelchair facilities.

Permits: No permits are necessary. Parking and access are free; donations accepted.

Maps: A brochure and map are available at the visitors center.

Directions: From Sacramento/I-5 heading south: Take I-5 to the Twin Cities Road exit (marked with a binoculars sign for wildlife viewing, about midway between Stockton and Sacramento). Take the Twin Cities Road exit and go east for exactly one mile, to the first stop sign at Franklin. Turn right on Franklin and drive 1.7 miles. Look for the visitors center on the left side of Franklin and park in the parking lot just past the visitor center.

From Stockton/I-5 North: Take I-5 north to the Thornton–Walnut Grove Road exit. Take that exit and go east to Thornton Road (just after a gas station). Turn left on Thornton and drive two miles (it becomes Franklin Boulevard) and continue over the Thornton-Franklin Bridge to parking and the visitors center on your right.

Contact: Cosumnes River Preserve, 13501 Franklin Boulevard, Galt, CA 95632, 916/684-2816, www.cosumnes.org.

TAHOE AND NORTHERN SIERRA

© TOM STIENST[

BEST HIKES

❰ Butt-Kickers
Beacroft Trail, page 234

❰ Fall Colors
Fallen Leaf Lake Trail, page 254

❰ Hikes with a View
Rubicon Trail, page 246

❰ Kids
Rainbow and Lake of the Sky Trails, page 251
Angora Lakes Trail, page 254

❰ Meadow Hikes
Carson Pass to Echo Lakes Resort (PCT),
    page 268
Eagle Meadow to Dardanelle, page 281

❰ Self-Guided Nature Walks
Rainbow and Lake of the Sky Trails, page 251
Trail of the Gargoyles, page 282

❰ Short Backpack Trips
Winnemucca Lake from Woods Lake, page 270

❰ Waterfalls
Grouse Falls, page 237

❰ Wheelchair-Accessible Trails
Sierra Discovery Trail, page 229

❰ Wildflowers
Lake Margaret, page 263

Mount Tallac affords a view across Lake Tahoe

like no other: a cobalt-blue expanse of water bordered by mountains that span miles of Sierra wildlands. The beauty is stunning. Lake Tahoe is one place where people feel an emotional response just by looking at it. Being here often strikes a deep chord that can resonate inside you for weeks, even after a short visit.

"What about all the people?" you ask. It's true that people come here in droves. But there are many spots that you'll share only with the chipmunks. You can enjoy these spots too – if you're willing to read our books, hunt a bit, and most important, time your trip to span Monday through Thursday.

Tahoe and the Northern Sierra feature hundreds of lakes, including dozens you can drive to. Many provide outstanding launch points for hikes. The best for scenic beauty are Tahoe, Echo Lakes, Donner, and Fallen Leaf in the immediate Tahoe region; Sardine, Gold Lake, and Salmon Lake in the Lakes Basin Recreation Area (also called the Gold Lakes Basin); Union Valley, Loon, and Wrights in the Crystal Basin; Carr, Feely, Lindsey, and Faucherie in the Bowman Lakes Recreation Area; and Caples, Woods, and Burnside near Carson Pass. This list could go on and on. If you haven't figured it out by now, this is one of the most beautiful regions anywhere on earth.

The north end of the Sierra starts near Bucks Lake, a great lake for trout fishing, and extends to Bear River Canyon (and Caples Lake, Silver Lake, and Bear River Reservoir). In between are the Lakes Basin Recreation Area (containing Gold, Sardine, Packer, and other lakes), in southern Plumas County; the Crystal Basin (featuring Union Valley Reservoir and Loon Lake, among others), in the Sierra foothills west of Tahoe; Lake Davis (with the highest catch rates for trout), near Portola; and the Carson River Canyon and Hope Valley, south of Tahoe.

You could spend weeks exploring any of these places, having the time of your life, and still not get to Tahoe's magic. But it is Tahoe where the adventure starts for many, especially in the surrounding Tahoe National Forest, Desolation Wilderness, and Granite Chief Wilderness.

One of California's greatest day trips from Tahoe is to Echo Lakes, where you can take a hiker's shuttle boat across the two lakes to the Pacific Crest Trail, then hike a few miles into Desolation Wilderness and Lake Aloha. Yet with so many wonderful ways to spend a day in this area, this day trip is hardly a blip on the radar scope.

With so many places and so little time, this region offers what can be the ultimate adventureland.

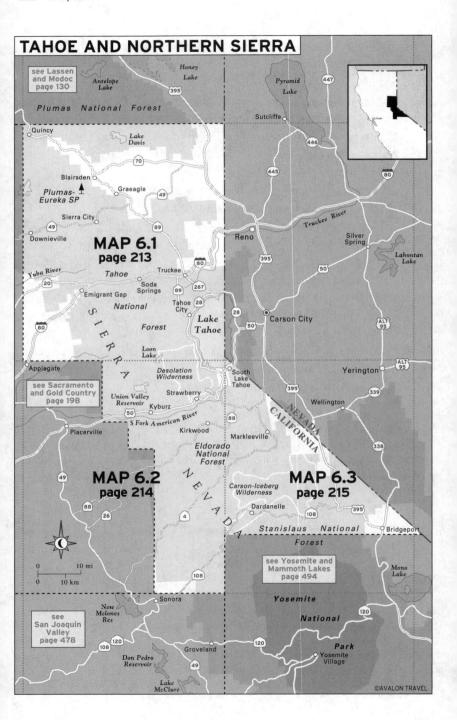

TAHOE AND NORTHERN SIERRA

see Lassen and Modoc page 130

Honey Lake

Antelope Lake

395

Pyramid Lake

447

Plumas National Forest

Sutcliffe

446

Quincy

Lake Davis

70

445

80

Blairsden

Plumas-Eureka SP

Graeagle

49

Truckee River

Sierra City

89

Reno

Silver Spring

Lahontan Lake

Downieville

49

MAP 6.1
page 213

80

Yuba River

Tahoe

Truckee

395

50

20

Soda Springs

89

267

S

Emigrant Gap

National

Tahoe City

28

Carson City

ALT 95

80

Forest

28

50

I
E
R
R
A

Loon Lake

Lake Tahoe

ALT 95

Applegate

Desolation Wilderness

South Lake Tahoe

Yerington

see Sacramento and Gold Country page 198

Union Valley Reservoir

Strawberry

395

Wellington

339

50

Kyburz

S Fork American River

88

N
E
V
A
D
A

338

Placerville

Kirkwood

Markleeville

C
A
L
I
F
O
R
N
I
A

49

Eldorado National Forest

MAP 6.2
page 214

88

26

Carson-Iceberg Wilderness

MAP 6.3
page 215

N

4

Dardanelle

108

395

Bridgeport

Stanislaus National

0   10 mi
0   10 km

Forest

108

see Yosemite and Mammoth Lakes page 494

Sonora

New Melones Res

Mono Lake

see San Joaquin Valley page 478

Yosemite

108

120

120

National

120

Groveland

49

Park

Don Pedro Reservoir

Yosemite Village

Lake McClure

©AVALON TRAVEL

Map 6.1

**Hikes 1-51
Pages 216-245**

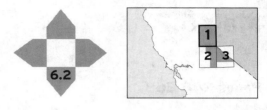

6.2

1
2 3

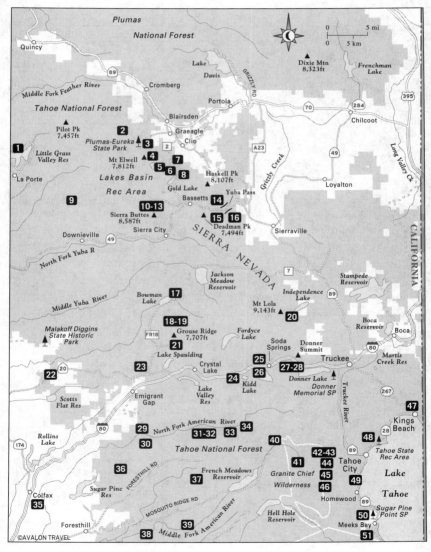

Plumas

National Forest

Quincy

Middle Fork Feather River

Tahoe National Forest

Pilot Pk
7,457ft

1

Little Grass
Valley Res

La Porte

9

Downieville

22

Scotts
Flat Res

Rollins
Lake

Colfax

35

Foresthill

©AVALON TRAVEL

Lake
Davis

Cromberg

Portola

Blairsden

Graeagle
Clio

Plumas-Eureka
State Park

Mt Elwell
7,812ft

Lakes Basin

Rec Area

Gold Lake

Bassetts

10-13

Sierra Buttes
8,587ft

Sierra City

North Fork Yuba R

Middle Yuba River

Bowman
Lake

17

18-19

FR18

Grouse Ridge
7,707ft

21

Lake Spaulding

23

Crystal
Lake

Lake
Valley
Res

24

Kidd
Lake

Emigrant
Gap

29

30

North Fork American River

31-32

Tahoe National Forest

36

Sugar Pine
Res

FORESTHILL RD

French Meadows
Reservoir

37

MOSQUITO RIDGE RD

39

38

Middle Fork American River

2

3

2

4

7

5 **6**

8

Haskell Pk
8,107ft

14

Yuba Pass

15 **16**

Deadman Pk
7,494ft

Jackson
Meadow
Reservoir

Mt Lola
9,143ft

20

Fordyce
Lake

Soda
Springs

25

26

27-28

Donner
Summit

Donner Lake

Donner
Memorial SP

33

34

40

41

42-43

44

45

Granite Chief

Wilderness

46

Hell Hole
Reservoir

Meeks Bay

51

GRIZZLY RD

Dixie Mtn
8,323ft

Frenchman
Lake

70

284

Chilcoot

395

Grizzly Creek

49

Loyalton

SIERRA NEVADA

Sierraville

7

Independence
Lake

89

Stampede
Reservoir

Boca
Reservoir

Boca

80

Martis
Creek Res

Truckee

Truckee River

267

47

Kings
Beach

28

48

Tahoe State
Rec Area

89

Tahoe
City

49

Homewood

89

Lake

Tahoe

Sugar Pine
Point SP

50

Malakoff Diggins
State Historic
Park

20

22

174

89

A23

A23

49

Loyalton

CALIFORNIA

Long Valley Ck

0   5 mi
0   5 km

Map 6.2

Hikes 52-84
Pages 246-268

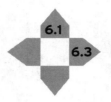

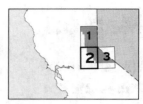

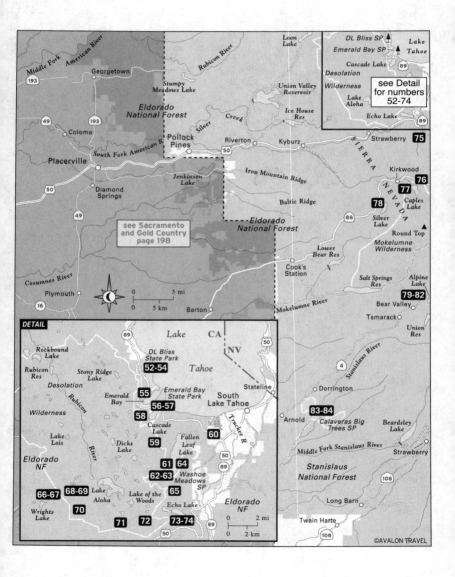

©AVALON TRAVEL

Map 6.3

Hikes 85-111
Pages 268-285

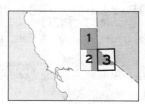

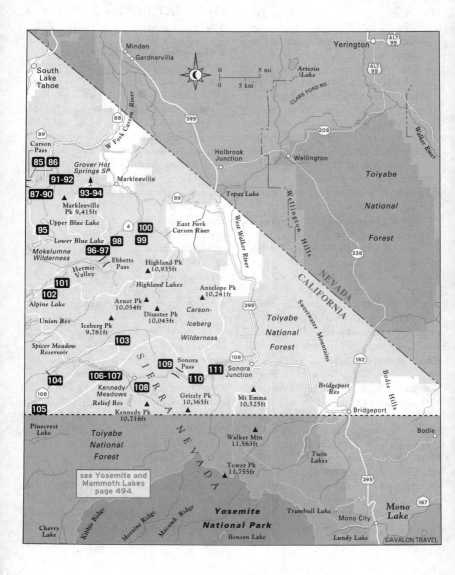

① FOWLER PEAK TO BUCKS SUMMIT (PCT)

26.0 mi one-way / 3 days 🏃4 ◺6

at Fowler Peak north of Little Grass Valley Reservoir in Plumas National Forest

Map 6.1, page 213

Most Pacific Crest Trail (PCT) hikers will want to sprint through this section of trail. From Fowler Peak trailhead, it passes through Plumas National Forest country until reaching the southern border of the Bucks Lake Wilderness. It starts quite nicely, dropping down to the Middle Fork Feather River (3,180 feet), a great trout stream with an excellent footbridge to get you across a gorge. We suggest you linger here and soak it in. Enjoy it, because the rest of this route won't exactly have you writing postcards home. It climbs from the Middle Fork Feather to 6,955-foot Lookout Rock, a long, dry pull, and then drops down to Bucks Creek. Most of this region is dry rattlesnake country, so watch your step, and time your water stops.

To continue north on the PCT, see the *Bucks Summit to Feather River (PCT)* hike in the *Sacramento and Gold Country* chapter. If you are walking this trail in reverse, see the *Yuba River to Fowler Peak (PCT)* hike in this chapter to continue south.

User Groups: Hikers, dogs, and horses. No mountain bikes. No wheelchair access.

Permits: A wilderness permit (free) is required. Parking and access are free.

Maps: For a map, ask the U.S. Forest Service for Tahoe and Plumas National Forests. For topographic maps, ask the USGS for Onion Valley, Dogwood Peak, and Bucks Lake.

Directions: From Oroville, take Highway 162 east for eight miles to Highway 174 (Forbestown Road and the junction signed Challenge/LaPorte). Turn right on Forbestown Road and drive east to Highway 120/Quincy-LaPorte Road. Turn left and drive past LaPorte to Little Grass Valley Road. Turn left on Little Grass Valley Road and drive to Black Rock Campground and Forest Road 94. Bear left on Forest Road 94 and drive three miles to Forest Road 22N27. Turn right and drive four miles to the parking area.

Contact: Plumas National Forest, Feather River Ranger District, 875 Mitchell Avenue, Oroville, CA 95965-4699, 530/534-6500, www.fs.fed.us/r5.

② EUREKA PEAK LOOP

3.0 mi / 2.0 hr 🏃3 ◺10

in Plumas-Eureka State Park east of Quincy

Map 6.1, page 213

The panoramic view of the Sierra Nevada from Eureka Peak (elevation 7,447 feet) includes all the peaks of the Gold Lakes Basin. Mount Elwell (7,818 feet) is the most prominent to the south. Plumas National Forest to the north and west is crowned by Blue Nose Mountain (7,290 feet), Stafford Mountain (7,019 feet), and Beartrap Mountain (7,232 feet). It's the vista that compels people to make the climb—a serious three-mile loop, and the first half is a grunt to the top. The trailhead starts at Eureka Lake, (elevation 6,300 feet). It then climbs 1,150 feet—a good, hard pull to the top. Many people start this trail by accident after seeing the trailhead sign while visiting the lake. That's a mistake. The trip should be planned. Bring plenty of water and snacks to enjoy from the summit.

Note: This park is on the closure list developed by the California Department of Parks, pending final state budget decisions or the possible transfer of park management to other park agencies or volunteer groups.

User Groups: Hikers only. No dogs, horses, or mountain bikes. No wheelchair facilities.

Permits: No permits are required, $8 day-use and parking.

Maps: A brochure and trail map is available for a fee from Plumas-Eureka State Park. For a topographic map, ask the USGS for Johnsville.

Directions: From Sacramento, take I-80 east to Truckee and the exit for Highway 89 North. Turn north on Highway 89 and go past the town of Clio to County Road A14 (Graeagle-Johnsonville Road). Turn left (west) and drive six miles to the park entrance. Continue several miles to Eureka Lake (the road is rough, and high-clearance vehicles are recommended). The trailhead is located at the north end of Eureka Lake.

Contact: Plumas-Eureka State Park, 310 Johnsville Road, Blairsden, CA 96103, 530/836-2380, www.parks.ca.gov.

❸ UPPER JAMISON TRAIL
8.2 mi / 1.0-2 days 👥3 ⛰9

in Plumas-Eureka State Park on the northern boundary of Gold Lakes Basin, east of Quincy

Map 6.1, page 213

There's no reason to rush your way through this trail, which passes Grass, Jamison, and Rock Lakes. Rather, take your time at it, stopping to enjoy the lakes along the way. A good option is to take this route and turn it into an overnight backpacking trip. The trail provides a glimpse of the beauty of the northern section of Lakes Basin Recreation Area, a country of alpine lakes and beveled granite mountains.

From the trailhead at the Jamison Mine building, start the trip by taking Grass Lake Trail. It follows along Little Jamison Creek. Note that a 100-foot cutoff trail provides a route to Little Jamison Falls. Back on the trail, you will climb 1.75 miles (from the parking area) to Grass Lake, with the trail skirting the east side of the lake. For those on a day hike, this is far enough. However, we urge you to forge onward. It's another two miles to Jamison Lake, with the trail climbing more steeply, then crossing the creek twice before arriving at the outlet of Jamison Lake. Another 0.25 mile will route you over to Rock Lake, a pretty sight below Mount Elwell (elevation 7,818 feet). Several good trail campsites are available at Rock, Jamison, and Grass Lakes and are usually occupied on weekends. Note that the first half mile of trail is located in the state park, and the remainder is in Plumas National Forest.

Note: This park is on the closure list developed by the California Department of Parks, pending final state budget decisions or the possible transfer of park management to other park agencies or volunteer groups.

User Groups: Hikers, dogs, horses, and mountain bikes. No wheelchair facilities.

Permits: No permits are required. $8 day-use and parking.

Maps: A brochure and trail map is available for a fee from Plumas-Eureka State Park. For a topographic map, ask the USGS for Johnsville.

Directions: From Sacramento, take I-80 east to Truckee and the exit for Highway 89 North. Take that exit, turn north on Highway 89, and drive past the town of Clio to County Road A14 (Graeagle-Johnsonville Road). Turn left (west) and drive 4.5 miles to a dirt road that is signed Jamison Mine–Grass Lake Mine Complex (before reaching the Jamison Creek Bridge). Turn left and drive on the dirt road for 1.5 miles to the Jamison Mine Complex. The trailhead starts at the far end of the parking lot.

Contact: Plumas-Eureka State Park, 310 Johnsville Road, Blairsden, CA 96103, 530/836-2380, www.parks.ca.gov.

❹ MOUNT ELWELL TRAIL
6.0 mi / 3.5 hr 👥3 ⛰10

at Smith Lake in Gold Lakes Basin south of Quincy

Map 6.1, page 213

This is one of the truly great hikes in the north Sierra. From atop Mount Elwell (7,818 feet), you're surrounded by the Gold Lakes Basin, a wildland filled with alpine lakes and granite mountains. You'll find yourself dreaming of the days when you might visit them. This trail is a good way to start. It begins at the Smith Lake trailhead and passes near Smith Lake (6,079 feet) on Smith Lake Trail, climbing all the way—2,018 feet over the course of three miles—to the top of Mount Elwell. It makes a great day trip for folks staying at the Gray Eagle Lodge. Though few go onward from Mount Elwell, the trip can be extended simply enough. The trail continues past Mount

Elwell, descending 0.75 mile to the Long Lake Trail junction, then another mile to a four-wheel-drive route. From this junction, you can also make a loop back to the Smith Lake trailhead by descending to Long Lake and continuing north three miles on Long Lake Trail.

User Groups: Hikers, dogs, mountain bikes, and horses. No wheelchair facilities.

Permits: No permits are required. Parking and access are free.

Maps: A trail map is available for a fee at the Beckwourth Ranger District. For a map, ask the U.S. Forest Service for Plumas National Forest. For a topographic map, ask the USGS for Gold Lake.

Directions: From Sacramento, take I-80 east to Truckee and the exit for Highway 89 North. Take that exit, turn north on Highway 89, and drive to Clio and continue a short distance north on Highway 89 to Forest Road 24 (Gold Lake Highway). Turn left (west) on Gold Lake Highway and drive five miles to the sign for Gray Eagle Lodge. Turn right and drive 0.5 mile to the Smith Lake trailhead.

Contact: Plumas National Forest, Beckwourth Ranger District, P.O. Box 7, Mohawk Road, Blairsden, CA 96103, 530/836-2575, www.fs.fed.us/r5.

🔢5 BEAR LAKES LOOP

5.6 mi / 3.0 hr   👣3 ⛰10

north of Sierra City

> **Map 6.1, page 213**

Long Lake is one of the celestial settings in the heavenly Gold Lakes Basin. It's the feature destination of this hike, a good tromp that includes some steep, rocky portions. The trailhead is just past the Lakes Basin Campground (elevation 6,300 feet). From here, the trail is clear and well maintained but requires a huff and a puff of a mile. Here you'll see the turnoff for 0.25-mile spur trail to Long Lake, one mile to little Silver Lake, 0.75 mile to Cub Lake, and another 0.5 mile to Little Bear and Big

Bear Lakes, and then 0.75 mile back to the trailhead. Long Lake is always a surprise to newcomers, since it's much larger than most high-country lakes and is very pretty. The trail skirts along the southeast shoreline.

Special Note: Camping is permitted only at the Lakes Basin Campground. No camping is permitted at either Long or Silver Lakes.

User Groups: Hikers, dogs, mountain bikes, and horses. No wheelchair facilities.

Permits: No permits are required. Parking and access are free.

Maps: A trail map is available for a fee at the Beckwourth Ranger District. For a map, ask the U.S. Forest Service for Plumas National Forest. For a topographic map, ask the USGS for Gold Lake.

Directions: From Sacramento, take I-80 east to Truckee and the exit for Highway 89 North. Take that exit, turn north on Highway 89, and drive to Clio and continue a short distance north on Highway 89 to Forest Road 24 (Gold Lake Highway). Turn left on Gold Lake Highway and proceed about six miles until you see the sign for the Long Lake trailhead and Lakes Basin Campground, on the left (west) side of the road.

Contact: Plumas National Forest, Beckwourth Ranger District, P.O. Box 7, Mohawk Road, Blairsden, CA 96103, 530/836-2575, www.fs.fed.us/r5.

🔢6 ROUND LAKE TRAILHEAD

1.4 mi / 1.0 hr   👣1 ⛰8

on the southern boundary of Gold Lakes Basin north of Sierra City

> **Map 6.1, page 213**

The 0.7-mile hike to Big Bear Lake is an easy, popular, and pretty walk. It is most commonly taken by visitors staying at Gold Lake Lodge. The trailhead is located alongside the parking lot next to the road to the lodge, and the trail itself is actually a closed road to Round Lake. It becomes a trail within a few hundred yards when routed west to Big Bear Lake, the first in a series of beautiful alpine lakes in the Gold Lakes Basin. Although most day users return after a picnic at Big Bear Lake, the trip can easily be extended, either west to Round Lake or Silver Lake or north to Long Lake. Most of this country is in the 6,000- to 7,000-foot elevation range and is high granite filled with alpine lakes.

User Groups: Hikers, dogs, mountain bikes, and horses. No wheelchair facilities.

Permits: No permits are required. Parking and access are free.

Maps: A trail map is available for a fee from Beckwourth Ranger District. For a map, ask the U.S. Forest Service for Plumas National Forest. For a topographic map, ask the USGS for Gold Lake.

Directions: From Sacramento, take I-80 east to Truckee and the exit for Highway 89 North. Take that exit, turn north on Highway 89, and drive to Clio and continue a short distance north on Highway 89 to Forest Road 24 (Gold Lake Highway). Turn left (west) on the Gold Lake Highway and drive seven miles until you see the sign for Round Lake Trail. Turn right and continue to the parking area.

Contact: Plumas National Forest, Beckwourth Ranger District, P.O. Box 7, Mohawk Road, Blairsden, CA 96103, 530/836-2575, www.fs.fed.us/r5.

▢ FRAZIER FALLS TRAIL
1.0 mi / 1.0 hr 🚶1 ⛰10

north of Sierra City

Map 6.1, page 213

Frazier Falls is a 178-foot, silver-tasseled waterfall that tumbles out of a chute into a rocky basin. It is like a miniature version of Feather Falls that is located near Lake Oroville. The trail is completely wheelchair-accessible and is a breeze, a 0.5-mile romp on a gentle route that leads to the scenic, fenced overlook of the falls. The best time to visit is early summer, when snowmelt from the high country is peaking, filling Frazier Falls like a huge

fountain. In addition, wildflowers along the trail in early summer add a splash of color, with violet lupine the most abundant. The road to the trailhead is paved all the way, the hike is easy, the falls are beautiful, and as you might expect, thousands of people make the trip every summer.

User Groups: Hikers, wheelchairs, and dogs. No ATVs, mountain bikes, or horses. Wheelchair facilities are available.

Permits: No permits are required. Parking and access are free.

Maps: A trail map is available for a fee from Beckwourth Ranger District. For a map, ask the U.S. Forest Service for Plumas National Forest. For a topographic map, ask the USGS for Gold Lake.

Directions: From Sacramento, take I-80 east to Truckee and the exit for Highway 89 North. Take that exit, turn north on Highway 89, and drive to Clio and continue a short distance north on Highway 89 to Forest Road 24 (Gold Lake Highway). Turn left (west) on the Gold Lake Highway and drive until you see the sign for Frazier Falls. Turn left and drive four miles to the trailhead, on the left.

Note: If you continue west on Gold Lake Highway for several miles, you will see another trailhead sign for Frazier Falls; it can also be reached on this route, but the road is rough and unpaved.

Contact: Plumas National Forest, Beckwourth Ranger District, P.O. Box 7, Mohawk Road, Blairsden, CA 96103, 530/836-2575, www.fs.fed.us/r5.

▣ HASKELL PEAK TRAIL
3.0 mi / 2.0 hr 🚶3 ⛰10

north of Highway 49 in Tahoe National Forest

Map 6.1, page 213

Haskell Peak is one of the great but unknown lookouts. On clear days, visitors can see many mountains both nearby and distant, including Mount Shasta and Mount Lassen, in Northern California; Mount Rose, in Nevada; and the closer Sierra Buttes. To get this view requires a 1,100-foot climb over the course of 1.5 miles, topping out at the 8,107-foot summit. The trail climbs at a decent, steady grade through heavy forest for the first mile. It then flattens and reaches an open area, where Haskell Peak comes into view. From here it's only a 0.25-mile (but very steep) climb to the top. You'll discover that Haskell Peak is the flume of an old volcano and has many unusual volcanic-rock formations. You'll also discover that just about nobody knows about this great hike. A fire lookout was once perched here, but it's gone now. Elevations range from 7,000 feet to 8,107 feet.

User Groups: Hikers, dogs, horses, and mountain bikes. No wheelchair facilities.

Permits: No permits are required. Parking and access are free.

Maps: For a map, ask the U.S. Forest Service for Tahoe National Forest. For a topographic map, ask the USGS for Clio.

Directions: From Sacramento, take I-80 east to Truckee and the exit for Highway 89 North. Take that exit, turn north on Highway 89, and drive to Sierraville and Highway 49. Turn left on Highway 49 and drive 10 miles to Bassetts and the Gold Lake Highway. Turn right on Gold Lake Highway and drive 3.7 miles to Forest Road 9 (Haskell Peak Road). Turn right and drive 8.4 miles. The trailhead is on the left; parking is available on either side of the road.

Contact: Yuba River?Ranger District, 15924 Highway 49, Camptonville, CA 95922, 530/288-3231 or 530/478-6253, www.fs.fed.us/r5.

9 CHIMNEY ROCK TRAIL
5.0 mi / 2.5 hr 🥾 2 ⛰️ 5

north of Downieville in Tahoe National Forest

Map 6.1, page 213

Chimney Rock is a huge volcanic cone that's 12 feet in diameter at its base, and it rises nearly straight up for 25 feet. The great views from the top are well worth the trip. The elevations are roughly 6,400 to 6,800 feet. Yet brace yourself, because this little patch of land has undergone considerable change. First, the trail surface was hardened in 1999. In turn, off-highway-vehicle (OHV) users started showing up in force, especially with dirt bikes. Now nearly 50 percent of the trail users are OHV users, and 50 percent are mountain bikers—and between them, they have driven out the hikers. The Downieville area in general has been taken over by mountain bikes, and hikers looking for a natural, harmonious experience often encounter a pack of bikes. When that happens, it's "Adios, never to return." This trip was once a quiet spectacle, with side ventures around Needle Point and Rattlesnake Peak. Now you cringe when you hear the thunder of oncoming fast traffic. It's like all the problems of city driving have been transported to a mountain trail.

User Groups: Hikers, dogs, mountain bikes, horses, and OHVs (primarily motorcycles). No wheelchair facilities.

Permits: No permits are required. Parking and access are free.

Maps: A trail map is available for a fee at the Downieville Ranger District. For a map, ask the U.S. Forest Service for Tahoe National Forest. For a topographic map, ask the USGS for Mount Fillmore.

Directions: From Sacramento, take I-80 east to Auburn and Highway 49. Turn north on Highway 49 and drive to Nevada City and continue on Highway 49 (it jogs to the left in Nevada City, then narrows) for about 40 miles to an old cannon displayed on the right side of the road (.25 mile before reaching Downieville). Turn right at the cannon onto an unsigned road, make a U-turn back to Highway 49, and drive a short distance back to Saddleback Road. Turn right on Saddleback Road. (Note: When driving on Highway 49 toward Downieville, do not attempt to turn left across traffic to reach Saddleback Road. It is dangerous and illegal.) Continue north on Saddleback Road for eight miles to a five-way intersection. Drive straight through to Road 25-23-1 and continue for 2.6 miles to Road 25-23-1-2 (look for the Chimney Rock Trail sign). Bear right on Road 25-23-1-2 and drive 0.5 mile to an intersection and head straight through. Continue another mile to a turnout on the left side of the road. Park here and hike in 0.6 mile to the trailhead. The total mileage from Downieville is 13 miles.

Note: The last sections of the road are quite rough.

Contact: Yuba River Ranger District, 15924 Highway 49, Camptonville, CA 95922, 530/288-3231 or 530/478-6253, www.fs.fed.us/r5.

10 BUTCHER RANCH TRAIL
8.0 mi / 5.0 hr   👣4 ⛺6

west of Packer Lake in Tahoe National Forest

Map 6.1, page 213

This used to be a great hike, a picture of harmony and beauty. It still is for the few who are here at dawn and get it done before all the mountain bikes show up. The place is overrun now by mountain bikes and motorcycles and weekends are often intolerable. Hikers have virtually been driven out to the point that hiker usage is down below 10 percent of users. This place was once a place of peace and harmony, a mountain canyon paradise where wildflowers were abundant, fishing was good, and a side trip would take hikers to a pristine stream with gorgeous deep pools. No more.

Elevations range from 6,200 to 4,320 feet. The trail follows the contour of Butcher Creek for 1.5 miles to the confluence of Pauley and Butcher Ranch Creeks. You then parallel Pauley Creek, with its deep and beautiful pools. On the way down, you'll drop nearly 2,000 feet over the course of four miles. Try not to laugh on your way down; what goes down must come up, and on the return, you'll be wondering why you ever talked yourself into this trip, especially if you run into a few motorcycles or a pack of mountain bikes heading downhill.

User Groups: Off-highway vehicles, mountain bikes, hikers, dogs, and horses. No wheelchair facilities.

Permits: No permits are required. Parking and access are free.

Maps: A trail map is available for a fee at the Downieville Ranger District. For a map, ask the U.S. Forest Service for Tahoe National Forest. For a topographic map, ask the USGS for Sierra City.

Directions: From Sacramento, take I-80 east to Truckee and the exit for Highway 89 North. Take that exit, turn north on Highway 89, and drive to Sierraville and Highway 49. Turn left on Highway 49 and drive 10 miles to Bassetts and Gold Lake Highway. Turn right (north) on Gold Lake Highway and drive 1.4 miles to Sardine Lake Road. Turn left on Sardine Lake Road and drive a short distance. Cross the Salmon Creek Bridge and continue 0.3 mile to Packer Lake Road. Turn right on Packer Lake Road and drive 2.5 miles to a fork (near Packer Lake). Take the left fork (Packer Saddle Road/ Forest Road 93), drive 2.1 miles, and look for the sign for Sierra Buttes Lookout. Turn left, drive 0.5 mile, and bear right; then continue 0.5 mile to a fork and sign for Butcher Ranch. Take the right fork (Forest Road 93-3) and drive 0.7 mile to a sign for the trailhead. Note: The road is quite steep and is only recommended for high-clearance or four-wheel-drive vehicles. Otherwise, park at the sign for the trailhead and hike 0.5 mile to the trailhead.

Contact: Yuba River Ranger District, 15924 Highway 49, Camptonville, CA 95922, 530/288-3231 or 530/478-6253, www.fs.fed.us/r5.

11 PAULEY CREEK TRAIL
12.0 mi / 2 days   👣4 ⛺8

west of Packer Lake in Tahoe National Forest

Map 6.1, page 213

The Pauley Creek Trail encompasses a land where there are streamside camps, spectacular wildflowers in early summer, and good trout fishing. Pauley Creek is a beautiful stream, and this trail is the best way to see it. Wildlife is also abundant in this watershed. The trailhead is difficult to reach, and the return hike out of the canyon back to the trailhead involves a 1,800-foot climb. Elevations range from 6,200 to 4,400 feet.

Warning: Weekends are horrendous for dealing with high-speed mountain bikes and noisy motorcycles. We've received numerous complaints regarding inconsiderate trail sharing with hikers, so consider timing your trip during the week instead.

User Groups: Hikers, dogs, horses, mountain bikes, and off-highway vehicles. No wheelchair facilities.

Permits: No permits are required. Parking and access are free.

Maps: A trail map is available for a fee at the Downieville Ranger District. For a map, ask the U.S. Forest Service for Tahoe National Forest. For topographic maps, ask the USGS for Downieville, Sierra City, and Gold Lake.

Directions: From Sacramento, take I-80 east to Truckee and the exit for Highway 89 North. Take that exit, turn north on Highway 89, and drive to Sierraville and Highway 49. Turn left on Highway 49 and drive 10 miles to Bassetts and Gold Lake Highway. Turn right (north) on Gold Lake Highway and drive 1.4 miles to Sardine Lake Road. Turn left on Sardine Lake Road and drive a short distance. Cross the Salmon Creek Bridge and continue 0.3 mile to Packer Lake Road. Turn right on Packer Lake Road and drive 2.5 miles to a fork (near Packer Lake). Take the left fork (Packer Saddle Road/Forest Road 93), drive 2.1 miles, and look for the sign for Sierra Buttes Lookout. Turn left, drive 0.5 mile, bear right, and drive 0.5 mile to Forest Road 93-3. Bear right and drive 2.5 miles to a sign that says Gold Valley OHV Route. Turn left and drive 1.5 miles to an intersection. Bear left and cross Pauley Creek, then drive 0.25 mile to a Y-intersection. Bear left and drive 0.25 mile to the trailhead, at the end of the road.

Note: The access road is quite steep and is only recommended for high-clearance or four-wheel-drive vehicles. Otherwise, park at the sign for the trailhead and hike 0.5 mile to the trailhead.

Contact: Yuba River Ranger District, 15924 Highway 49, Camptonville, CA 95922, 530/288-3231 or 530/478-6253, www.fs.fed.us/r5.

12 DEER LAKE TRAIL
5.0 mi / 3.5 hr 🥾3 ⛰8

west of Packer Lake in Tahoe National Forest

Map 6.1, page 213

Most lakes are green, but Deer Lake is the deepest azure blue you can imagine, and with the spectacular Sierra Buttes in the background, it's easy to understand why this trip is so popular. It gets some of the heaviest use of any trail in this section of Tahoe National Forest. It's a 2.5-mile hike to the lake, climbing 1,000 feet and topping out at 7,110 feet. Elevations range from 6,080 to 7,110 feet.

From the trailhead, you'll climb through a basin and get a sweeping view of the massive Sierra Buttes and the surrounding forested slopes. As you head on, you'll cross a signed spur trail, a 0.25-mile route to Grass Lake. It's well worth the short detour, but approach quietly, because deer are common here. Then it's onward, over the ridge and down to Deer Lake. On warm evenings, the brook trout leave countless circles while feeding on surface insects. This hike has it all and that's why it often includes so many other people. Good news for hikers: Mountain bikes are few, and off-highway vehicle use is prohibited.

User Groups: Hikers, dogs, horses, and mountain bikes. No wheelchair facilities.

Permits: No permits are required. Parking and access are free.

Maps: A trail map is available for a fee at the Downieville Ranger District. For a map, ask the U.S. Forest Service for Tahoe National Forest. For a topographic map, ask the USGS for Sierra City.

Directions: From Sacramento, take I-80 east to Truckee and the exit for Highway 89 North. Take that exit, turn north on Highway 89, and drive to Sierraville and Highway 49. Turn left on Highway 49 and drive 10 miles to Bassetts and Gold Lake Highway. Turn right (north) on to Gold Lake Highway and drive 1.4 miles to Sardine Lake Road. Turn left on Sardine Lake Road and drive a short distance. Cross the Salmon Creek Bridge and continue 0.3 mile to Packer Lake Road. Turn right on Packer Lake Road and drive 2.5 miles to the trailhead. Parking is available in the Packsaddle camping area just opposite the trailhead.

Contact: Yuba River Ranger District, 15924 Highway 49, Camptonville, CA 95922, 530/288-3231 or 530/478-6253, www.fs.fed.us/r5.

13 SIERRA BUTTES TRAIL
5.0 mi / 3.5 hr

near Packer Lake in Tahoe National Forest

Map 6.1, page 213

The Sierra Buttes Lookout Station, sitting at 8,587 feet and with a railed stairway to its top, provides a destination for one of California's best day hikes and greatest viewpoints. Stand here one time, and you'll never forget it the rest of your life. The trip starts above Packer Lake, at 6,220 feet. The trail starts by climbing through a series of shaded switchbacks to 6,700 feet, tracing the ridge that eventually leads to the summit, crowned by a series of jagged crags. On the way, you will rise to the rim of a mountain bowl that frames Sardine Lake off to the east. You will climb 2,367 feet to reach the top. The trail traces this rim to the lookout and is capped by three stairways that seem to project into wide-open space. Climbing it is an astounding sensation, almost like climbing the cable at Half Dome. The lookout itself also juts out into space with a grated deck. You scan miles and miles of Sierra mountain country, from Mount Lassen in the north all the way to the Tahoe Rim to the south, with a highlight being Union Valley Reservoir. Because the walkway around the lookout is grated, when you look straight down, you can see past your boots to open air. A bizarre sensation for many, this can even cause spatial disorientation.

User Groups: Hikers, dogs, and horses. No mountain bikes (except on jeep trail). No wheelchair access.

Permits: No permits are required. Parking and access are free.

Maps: A trail map is available for a fee from the Downieville Ranger District. For a map, ask the U.S. Forest Service for Tahoe National Forest. For a topographic map, ask the USGS for Sierra City.

Directions: From Sacramento, take I-80 east to Truckee and the exit for Highway 89 North. Take that exit, turn north on Highway 89, and drive to Sierraville and Highway 49. Turn left on Highway 49 and drive 10 miles to Bassetts and Gold Lake Highway. Turn right on Gold Lake Highway and drive 1.4 miles to Sardine Lake/Packer Lake Road. Turn left, cross a small bridge, and bear right on Packer Lake Road. Continue past Packer Lake and bear left at a fork, following the signs to a trailhead for the Pacific Crest Trail (do not bear right at a jeep road). Continue to a small parking area. The trail starts as a jeep trail next to the parking area (then becomes trail on the ridge).

Contact: Yuba River Ranger District, 15924 Highway 49, Camptonville, CA 95922, 530/288-3231 or 530/478-6253, www.fs.fed.us/r5.

14 CHAPMAN CREEK TRAIL
3.0 mi / 2.0 hr

east of Sierra City in Tahoe National Forest

Map 6.1, page 213

Chapman Creek is a babbling brook that you can walk alongside, or you can stop to picnic near it, fish a little in it, or do absolutely nothing. That's right, nothing. It's that kind of place. The trailhead, elevation 5,840 feet, is set at a campground, providing easy access. Outside of campers, few others know of it. The trail winds easily along the contours of Chapman Creek under the canopy of a dense forest, rising gently along the way. It climbs to 6,400 feet, 560 feet in a span of 1.5 miles. The river is the lifeblood for a variety of birds and wildlife, but few visitors make the trip for that reason. Rather they come to stroll and let their minds wander and be free.

User Groups: Hikers, dogs, horses, and mountain bikes. No wheelchair facilities.

Permits: No permits are required. Parking and access are free.

Maps: For a map, ask the U.S. Forest Service for Tahoe National Forest. For a topographic map, ask the USGS for Sierra City.

Directions: From Sacramento, take I-80 east to Truckee and the exit for Highway 89 North. Take that exit, turn north on Highway 89, and drive to Sierraville and Highway 49. Turn left on Highway 49 and drive over Yuba Pass and continue for four miles to the Chapman Creek Campground, on the right. The trailhead and a parking area are located at the north end of the campground.

Contact: Yuba River Ranger District, 15924 Highway 49, Camptonville, CA 95922, 530/288-3231 or 530/478-6253, www.fs.fed.us/r5.

15 WILD PLUM LOOP / HAYPRESS CREEK

6.0 mi / 1 day   🥾3 ⛰️8

east of Sierra City in Tahoe National Forest

Map 6.1, page 213

For the properly inspired, a canyon with a hidden stream and a waterfall that's surrounded by old-growth red fir make this a wonderful day hike. Why must you be properly inspired? Because the trail climbs from 4,400 feet up Haypress Creek to 5,840 feet, a 1,440-foot rise over just three miles. The trail starts out almost flat for the first 0.5 mile, and then it crosses over Haypress Creek on a footbridge. There's an excellent view of the Sierra Buttes in this area. Continue on Haypress Creek Trail, where you rise past a rocky area and into forest. You pass evidence of logging activity where the trail turns to road for a short spell. Don't despair. The trail soon enters an old-growth forest. It then contours along Haypress Canyon, and then passes by a lovely waterfall. This

hike makes a great day trip with a picnic lunch, and trail use is typically quite light. Note that on the return trip, you turn right on the Pacific Crest Trail to complete the loop. Walk 0.5 mile and turn left at the Wild Plum Loop sign to return.

User Groups: Hikers, dogs, and horses. No mountain bikes. No wheelchair facilities.

Permits: No permits are required. Parking and access are free.

Maps: For a map, ask the U.S. Forest Service for Tahoe National Forest. For a topographic map, ask the USGS for Haypress Valley.

Directions: From Sacramento, take I-80 east to Truckee and the exit for Highway 89 North. Take that exit, turn north on Highway 89, and drive to Sierraville and Highway 49. Turn left on Highway 49 and drive 12 miles (past Bassetts) to Wild Plum Road (near the eastern end of Sierra City) at the sign for Wild Plum Campground. Drive one mile on this road to the Wild Plum trailhead parking area. Walk through the campground to its upper loop, walk around a locked gate, and continue up the road 0.25 mile to the Wild Plum Loop Trail Sign. Walk 0.25 mile to the intersection with the Pacific Crest Trail, turn left, and cross a bridge over Haypress Creek. Continue for 200 yards to the trailhead, on the right.

Contact: Yuba River Ranger District, 15924 Highway 49, Camptonville, CA 95922, 530/288-3231 or 530/478-6253, www.fs.fed.us/r5.

16 YUBA RIVER TO FOWLER PEAK (PCT)

51.0 mi one-way / 4 days   🥾4 ⛰️9

in Tahoe National Forest, off Highway 49 east of Sierra City

Map 6.1, page 213

Pristine alpine lakes and high mountain lookouts highlight this section of the Pacific Crest Trail. Although nearly as beautiful as the section of trail south near Tahoe, this stretch gets far less use. It starts at the Yuba River, and in the first two miles, it climbs an endless series of switchbacks up the back side of the Sierra Buttes. This is a long, grueling climb on exposed terrain with a great reward. Note that the spur trail up to the Sierra Buttes Fire Lookout is an additional 1,400-foot climb, but it furnishes one of the top lookouts in California. The trail then heads north. It skirts past the western border of the Gold Lakes Basin, where a dozen high alpine lakes make for easy side trips and camps. With some terrible switchbacks, the PCT passes Mount Gibraltar (7,343 feet), Stafford Mountain (7,019 feet), and Mount Etna (7,163 feet), and flanks below Pilot Peak (7,457 feet). It then heads along the western slope, eventually reaching the Fowler Peak trailhead.

To continue north on the PCT, see the *Fowler Peak to Bucks Summit (PCT)* hike in this chapter. If you are walking this trail in reverse, see the *Donner Pass to the Yuba River (PCT)* hike in this chapter.

User Groups: Hikers, dogs, and horses. No mountain bikes. No wheelchair access.

Permits: A wilderness permit (free) is required. Parking and access are free.

Maps: For a map, ask the U.S. Forest Service for Tahoe National Forest. For topographic maps, ask the USGS for Haypress Valley, Sierra City, Mount Fillmore, and Onion Valley.

Directions: From Sacramento, take I-80 east to Truckee and the exit for Highway 89 North. Take that exit, turn north on Highway 89, and drive to Sierraville and Highway 49. Turn left on Highway 49 and drive 12 miles (passing Bassetts) to the eastern end of Sierra City. Look for the Pacific Crest Trail access sign and park on the right (north) side of the road.

Contact: Yuba River Ranger District, 15924 Highway 49, Camptonville, CA 95922, 530/288-3231 or 530/478-6253, www.fs.fed.us/r5.

17 GROUSE RIDGE TRAIL (SAWMILL TO EAGLE LAKES)
6.0-16.5 mi / 1.0-2 days 3 9

in Tahoe National Forest north of Emigrant Gap

Map 6.1, page 213

This is a gorgeous hike. The Grouse Ridge Trail weaves up and down from a mountain crest, connecting Sawmill Lake to the north with the Eagle Lakes, for a one-way distance of 8.25 miles. The beauty of this hike is the number of side trips along the way that you can take to make your choice of visits at a half dozen lakes. In fact, we often use Grouse Ridge Trail as a jump-off point to take short and spectacular day hikes. The elevation varies from 6,160 to 6,400 feet, with the ups and downs coming in short yet serious spurts. From Sawmill Lake, climb up a timbered slope to a ridge and a turnoff for Rock Lake, which is worth a visit itself. You then pass Shotgun Lake (it's actually a wet meadow) and continue to Middle Lake, Crooked Lakes, and Milk Lake (gorgeous!). The views are divine much of the way.

Special Note: At Sawmill Lake, the trail crosses the spillway of the dam, which may be impassable in late spring when high water spills into Canyon Creek.

User Groups: Hikers, dogs, horses, and mountain bikes. No wheelchair facilities.

Permits: A campfire permit (free) is required for overnight use. Parking and access are free.

Maps: For a map, ask the U.S. Forest Service for Tahoe National Forest. For topographic maps, ask the USGS for Cisco Grove and English Mountain.

Directions: From Auburn, take I-80 east for 45 miles to the Highway 20 exit. Take that exit, head west, and drive four miles to Bowman Lake Road (Forest Road 18). Turn right on Bowman Lake Road and drive 16 miles to Bowman Lake. Turn right and drive along Bowman Lake to Faucherie Lake Road. Turn right on Faucherie Lake Road and drive 0.5 mile to the north end of

Sawmill Lake and the trailhead. A four-wheel-drive, high-clearance vehicle is required.

Contact: Nevada City Ranger District, 530/265-4531, www.fs.fed.us/r5; Big Bend Visitors Center, Tahoe National Forest, 530/426-3609.

18 LINDSEY LAKES TRAIL
7.0 mi / 3.0 hr

in Tahoe National Forest north of Emigrant Gap

Map 6.1, page 213

The highlight of Lindsey Lakes Trail is that it intersects with other trails, including the beautiful Grouse Ridge Trail, and is set in a gorgeous landscape that features Sierra alpine beauty. But the trail itself from Lindsey Lakes to Rock Lake is a service road closed to public vehicle traffic, so you're hiking up a road. This 3.5-mile trail dead-ends after climbing past the three Lindsey Lakes, and it offers a great optional side trip. From the trailhead at Lower Lindsey Lake (elevation 6,160 feet), hike up to the other lakes on a short trail (it's quite steep in several places) before topping out at 6,400 feet. The route gets medium use and accesses good swimming holes with cold water, but the fishing is poor. The best fishing in this basin is at nearby Culbertson Lake, where you can make a wonderful side trip by hiking out to Rock Lake and up to Bullpen Lake. Another side trip from Lindsey Lakes Trail is Crooked Lakes Trail.

User Groups: Hikers, dogs, and horses. Mountain bikes not advised. No wheelchair facilities.

Permits: No permits are required. Parking and access are free.

Maps: For a map, ask the U.S. Forest Service for Tahoe National Forest. For topographic maps, ask the USGS for English Mountain and Graniteville.

Directions: From Auburn, take I-80 east for 45 miles, then take the Highway 20 exit and drive four miles to Bowman Lake Road (Forest Road 18). Turn right and drive 8.5 miles north

until you see a sign that says Lindsey Lake, Feely Lake, Carr Lake. Turn right and follow the signs to the parking area for Lindsey Lake. The road can be rough for the last 0.5 mile; high-clearance vehicles are advised.

Contact: Nevada City Ranger District, 530/265-4531, www.fs.fed.us/r5; Big Bend Visitors Center, Tahoe National Forest, 530/426-3609.

19 PENNER LAKE
4.5 mi / 3.0 hr

at Carr Lake in Tahoe National Forest north of Emigrant Gap

Map 6.1, page 213

The Round Lake Trail accesses a series of Sierra lakes (including Island Lake and Penner Lake), and is extremely beautiful, but it is also very popular, even crowded at the trailhead on weekends. From the trailhead at Feely Lake (elevation 6,720 feet), the route heads east, climbing first to Island Lake. This lake, named for the little rocky islands sprinkled about, has several good campsites. Turn left when you reach Island Lake and walk 1.5 miles on Crooked Lakes Trail through a fir forest to Penner Lake. The last half mile is uphill, but nothing serious. Penner Lake is one of the crown jewels of the Grouse Ridge area. Along with Island Lake, it has the most scenic beauty, is great for swimming, and is ideal for picnics or just gazing and taking in the mountain panorama. It is best experienced on an early weekday summer morning.

User Groups: Hikers, dogs, mountain bikes, and horses. No wheelchair facilities.

Permits: No permits are required. Parking and access are free.

Maps: For a map, ask the U.S. Forest Service for Tahoe National Forest. For topographic maps, ask the USGS for English Mountain and Graniteville.

Directions: From Auburn, take I-80 east for 45 miles, then take the Highway 20 exit and drive four miles to Bowman Lake Road (Forest Road 18). Turn right and drive 8.5 miles north until you see a sign that says Lindsey Lake, Feely Lake, Carr Lake. Turn right and follow the signs to the parking area at Carr Lake. Continue on foot to the trailhead at Feely Lake. Sections of the road can be rough; four-wheel-drive vehicles are advised.

Contact: Nevada City Ranger District, 530/265-4531, www.fs.fed.us/r5; Big Bend Visitors Center, Tahoe National Forest, 530/426-3609.

20 DONNER PASS TO THE YUBA RIVER (PCT)
38.0 mi one-way / 3 days   👥3   ⛰7

from Highway 80 to Highway 49 in Tahoe National Forest

Map 6.1, page 213

Though not one of the more glamorous sections of the Pacific Crest Trail, this stretch is hardly a stinker. For the most part, it follows a crest connecting a series of small mountaintops before dropping down to Jackson Meadow Reservoir and Highway 49. Some good views are to be had on the first leg of the trail, so many that some PCT hikers begin to take them for granted after awhile. Here the trail is routed past Castle Peak (elevation 9,103 feet), Basin Peak (9,015 feet), and Lacey Mountain (8,214 feet). Covering this much terrain makes for an ambitious first day, perhaps with stops at Paradise Lake or White Rock Lake. As the trail drops to Jackson Meadow Reservoir, the views end, but in time you'll catch sight of the lake; surrounded by firs, it is quite pretty. The PCT then skirts the east side of the reservoir, passes several drive-to campgrounds, heads through Bear Valley (not *the* Bear Valley), and drops steeply to Milton Creek and four miles beyond that to Loves Falls at Highway 49.

To continue north on the PCT, see the *Yuba River to Fowler Peak (PCT)* hike in this chapter. If you are walking this trail in reverse, see the *Barker Pass to Donner Pass (PCT)* hike in this chapter.

User Groups: Hikers, dogs, and horses. No mountain bikes. No wheelchair facilities.

Permits: A campfire permit (free) is required for overnight use. Parking and access are free.

Maps: For a map, ask the U.S. Forest Service for Tahoe National Forest. For topographic maps, ask the USGS for Norden, Soda Springs, Webber, Haypress Valley, Independence Lake, and English Mountain.

Directions: From Auburn, take I-80 east to the Boreal/Donner Summit and the signed exit for Pacific Crest trailhead parking area. Take that exit to parking. There is no hiker parking in the Donner Summit rest area.

Contact: Tahoe National Forest, Sierraville Ranger District, 317 South Lincoln Street, P.O. Box 95, Sierraville, CA 96126, 530/994-3401, www.fs.fed.us/r5.

21 GLACIER LAKE
10.0 mi / 1 day   👥3   ⛰10

in Tahoe National Forest north of Emigrant Gap

Map 6.1, page 213

In just a few hours you can be transported to heaven. Some people, however, call it Glacier Lake. It is only a five-mile hike to get here, a pristine and peaceful high Sierra setting that can make you feel as if you're three days out on a backpacking expedition. The small lake is set in a rockbound bowl with the Black Buttes looming nearby. The tree cover is sparse, and the rock cover is abundant. To get there, start your hike by heading east on Round Lake Trail at Carr Lake, and hike almost three miles. You will pass a series of lakes, including Feely Lake, Island Lake, Round Lake, and Milk Lake. Then you'll drop down into forest and meadow landscape and reach a trail junction. Continue east on Glacier Lake Trail and continue through a meadow and some forest. Here you start a gradual climb, passing a small lake before entering a rocky area and then dropping down to the pretty lake. Several backpacking campsites are available.

Note that the map of Tahoe National Forest does not show the direct route to Glacier Lake. Our suggested unmapped route climbs up through a beautiful canyon. The map, on the other hand, shows the trail routed up a hot, exposed route on Sandy Ridge.

Another note is that cows are often present in the lower meadow portions of the route, near the trail junction. A certain black-and-white cow is known to adopt female hikers, following for up to a mile, staring with lonely brown eyes as if saying, "Momma." Whatever you do, don't wear a cowbell around your neck.

Great side trips are also available. It is a one-mile hike north to the Five Lakes Basin and a 1.5-mile hike south to Beyers Lake. The elevations here range from 5,500 to 7,000 feet.

User Groups: Hikers, dogs, and horses. Mountain bikes not advised. No wheelchair facilities.

Permits: No permits are required. Parking and access are free.

Maps: For a map, ask the U.S. Forest Service for Tahoe National Forest. For topographic maps, ask the USGS for Cisco Grove and English Mountain.

Directions: From Auburn, take I-80 east for 45 miles, then take the Highway 20 exit and drive four miles to Bowman Lake Road (Forest Road 18). Turn right and drive 8.5 miles north until you see a sign that says Lindsey Lake, Feely Lake, Carr Lake. Turn right and follow the signs to the parking area at Carr Lake. Continue on foot to the trailhead at Feely Lake. Sections of the road can be rough; four-wheel-drive vehicles are advised.

Contact: Nevada City Ranger District, 530/265-4531, www.fs.fed.us/r5; Big Bend Visitors Center, Tahoe National Forest, 530/426-3609.

22 PIONEER TRAIL
1.0–24.0 mi / 0.5 hr–2 days

🥾2 ⛰️6

east of Nevada City, off of Highway 20 in Tahoe National Forest

Map 6.1, page 213

Hiking the Pioneer Trail is like taking a history lesson as you trace the route of the first wagon road, opened by emigrants and gold seekers in 1850. Along the way are three campgrounds for backpackers, but the trail is better suited for mountain biking. In fact, it has become almost an exclusive biking trip, but its historical significance still merits inclusion in this book.

From the trailhead at Five Mile House (elevation 3,500 feet), the trail heads east for 15 miles to Bear Valley, gaining 2,000 feet. You will pass Central House (once a stagecoach stop); White Cloud and Skillman Flat (former mill sites, one burned down); and the Omega Overlook, which provides a view of a huge hydraulic gold-mining operation. The CalTrans Omega rest area has a parking area, a restroom, and a viewing platform perched over the South Yuba River Canyon. From the Omega Overlook, you will get dramatic views of the Yuba River and the surrounding granite cliffs.

Note: The mountain bike traffic is high on this trail. While we admire bikers who make the round-trip, it seems a high percentage use the one-way trip downhill from Omega rest area to Five Mile House. When encountering other trail users, remember to demonstrate the utmost courtesy: Bikers should always dismount and walk when passing hikers.

User Groups: Hikers, dogs, mountain bikes, and horses. No wheelchair facilities.

Permits: A campfire permit (free) is required for overnight use. Parking and access are free.

Maps: For a map, ask the U.S. Forest Service for Tahoe National Forest. For a topographic map, ask the USGS for Washington.

Directions: From Nevada City, drive about seven miles east on Highway 20 to the trailhead, across from Lone Grave. If the parking lot there is full, additional parking and trail access are available at Skillman Flat, Upper Burlington Ridge, Harmony Ridge Market, the Omega rest area, and the Washington Overlook trailhead—all located to the east of Highway 20.

Contact: Nevada City Ranger District, 530/265-4531, www.fs.fed.us/r5; Big Bend Visitors Center, Tahoe National Forest, 530/426-3609.

23 SIERRA DISCOVERY TRAIL
1.0 mi / 0.5 hr   🏃1   ⛰8

off Highway 20 near Lake Spaulding

Map 6.1, page 213   BEST (

The waterfall at Bear River is your destination on this easy, short, and nearly flat trail that is accessible to wheelchair users (with a bit of assistance). This is not the wilderness. Much of the trail is pavement, soil cement, or compressed gravel. It is designed as an interpretive loop walk, with information about ecosystems, wildlife, geology, and cultural history available as the trail winds through a forest of pines and incense cedars. This is an ideal mountain walk for seniors, youngsters, or the physically challenged. Bear River Falls is short but wide and is well framed by a forest canopy.

User Groups: Hikers, dogs, and wheelchairs (with assistance). No horses or mountain bikes. Dogs permitted, but rangers strongly discourage bringing them on this trail.

Permits: No permits are necessary. Parking and access are free.

Maps: For a topographic map, ask the USGS for Blue Canyon.

Directions: From Auburn, drive east on I-80 for 45 miles. Take the Highway 20 exit heading west and drive four miles to Bowman Lake Road. Turn right and drive 0.6 mile to the Sierra Discovery Trail parking lot, on the left side of the road.

Contact: Pacific Gas & Electric, 800/743-5000, www.pge.com.

24 LOCH LEVEN LAKES
7.2 mi / 4.0 hr   🏃3   ⛰7

south of Cisco Grove in Tahoe National Forest

Map 6.1, page 213

Most people would like to know what heaven is like but are not very willing to sign up for the trip. This trip to Loch Leven Lakes, however, won't be your final resting place, yet it provides a glimpse of what heaven might resemble. The 3.5-mile hike to Loch Leven Lakes provides sweeping vistas of ridges and valleys, gorgeous high alpine meadows, and glaciated mountain terrain with a series of perfect lakes. As hikers get deeper into the wildlands here, the lakes become progressively more beautiful and pristine. The lakes themselves are clear and blue, set in granite, and speckled with boulders—the perfect picnic site.

The trail starts at 5,680 feet then works its way upward on a moderate grade to the southwest. Granite outcrops are numerous, and huge boulders (deposited by receding glaciers) lie sprinkled among Jeffrey pine and lodgepole pine. The trail crosses a creek and railroad tracks, then climbs through a cool forest. Here the trail becomes steeper, climbing 800 feet in 1.25 miles. It then tops the summit and descends gently to Lower Loch Leven Lake (2.5 miles from the trailhead). Many people stop here, content to just take in the surroundings. But you can forge on for another mile, circling Middle Loch Leven Lake (2.8 miles from the trailhead) and heading east up to High Loch Leven Lake (3.6 miles from the trailhead), at 6,800 feet. At the south end of Lower Loch Leven Lake, turn left at the trail junction to see Middle and High Loch Leven Lakes (turning right at the junction will route you to Salmon Lake, a less-crowded alternative). Once you've come this far, beautiful High Loch Leven is an easy trip and a must-do.

But this hike is not without frustration: The first hour involves a continuous climb with the echo of I-80 traffic in the background. You do not escape the noise until you top the ridge. Elevations range 5,680–6,850 feet at the ridge, a gain of 1,070 feet. With access so easy off I-80, the area can become inundated with people on summer weekends. With no trailhead quota, the numbers can affect the sense of wilderness.

Fishing is fair during the evening bite, and there are backcountry campgrounds at each lake. Restrooms are available at the trailhead (a plus). The trail is generally open for hiking from early June to November, weather permitting; it's not marked for winter use and can be difficult to find in snow conditions.

User Groups: Hikers, dogs, and horses. Mountain bikes not advised. No wheelchair facilities.

Permits: No permits are required. Parking and access are free.

Maps: For a map, ask the U.S. Forest Service for Tahoe National Forest. For a topographic map, ask the USGS for Cisco Grove.

Directions: From Sacramento, take I-80 east into the Sierra Nevada and to the Big Bend exit. Take that exit and then turn left on Hampshire Rocks Road. Follow the signs to the Big Bend Visitors Center, located adjacent to the highway. The parking area and trailhead are about 0.2 mile east of the visitors center. The trailhead is on the opposite side of the road from the parking area.

From Reno, take I-80 west to the Cisco Grove exit. Take that exit and turn right on Hampshire Rocks Road. Continue as above.

Contact: Big Bend Visitor Center, 49685 Hampshire Rocks Road, Soda Springs, CA 95631, 530/426-3609, www.fs.fed.us/r5.

25 LOWER LOLA MONTEZ LAKE

6.0 mi / 3.0 hr 🚶2 ⛰8

in Tahoe National Forest near Soda Springs

Map 6.1, page 213

The hike to Lower Lola Montez Lake is a bad choice for a July or August weekend afternoon. That is because it's so easy, partly because it's right off the highway, and partly because the trail is favored by mountain bikers. So get this one in focus: For hikers who enjoy peace and quiet, this is definitely an off-season trail, best left for the days of autumn, when the vacationers have abandoned Lake Tahoe. The path cuts through Toll Mountain Estates, a private community, and is a mix of wide dirt roads and single-track trails. The first 0.25 mile is on single track; then you reach a dirt road and turn right, cross Castle Creek, and continue until the road becomes single track again. And so it goes. Luckily, the route is marked all the way, and with all the people who visit here, it's unlikely you'll get lost and not be found. The good news is that the Lower Lola Montez Lake is popular for a reason; it's a beautiful alpine lake set at 7,200 feet but shallow enough to warm up for swimming. Fishing is half decent but is best early in the year.

User Groups: Hikers, dogs, horses, and mountain bikes. No wheelchair facilities.

Permits: No permits are required. Parking and access are free.

Maps: For a map, ask the U.S. Forest Service for Tahoe National Forest. For topographic maps, ask the USGS for Soda Springs and Norden.

Directions: From Auburn, take I-80 east for 55 miles to Soda Springs. Take the Soda Springs/Norden exit and cross over the overpass to the north side of the freeway. Follow the paved road east, past the fire station for 0.3 mile to the trailhead parking area.

Contact: Truckee Ranger District, 10811 Stockrest Springs Road, Truckee, CA 96161, 530/587-3558, www.fs.fed.us/r5; Big Bend Visitors Center, Tahoe National Forest, 530/426-3609.

26 PALISADE CREEK TRAIL TO HEATH FALLS
10.0 mi / 6.0 hr   🥾3   ⛰10

in Tahoe National Forest near Soda Springs

Map 6.1, page 213

The hike to Heath Falls is like going on vacation on your credit card. You can have all the fun you want, but when you return home, you have to pay up. That's because the trip to the Heath Falls Overlook is downhill nearly all the way, dropping 1,700 feet over five miles, through stunning alpine scenery that will have you smiling the whole time. The return trip is a long and steady five-mile climb back uphill, so be sure you have plenty of food, water, and energy left for it.

The trail begins at the dam between the two Cascade Lakes, the first of many lakes you'll see on this trip. The big hunk of imposing rock you have to walk around is 7,704-foot Devils Peak. Take the right fork signed for the North Fork American River, and get ready for a steady diet of granite, lakes, and vistas. At 2.2 miles, the trail leaves the rocks behind and enters the forest, switchbacking downhill for two miles to the Palisade Creek Bridge. Look for an unsigned junction 300 yards beyond it, where Heath Falls Overlook Trail heads east. Follow it for 0.5 mile to the trail's end, at a vista of the American River's Heath Falls. Camping is prohibited along this trail because much of it runs through private property, so after enjoying the falls overlook, you've got to make the long climb home. Hope you have at least one Power Bar left.

User Groups: Hikers, dogs, and horses. No mountain bikes. No wheelchair facilities.

Permits: No permits are required. Parking and access are free.

Maps: For a map, ask the U.S. Forest Service for Tahoe National Forest. For topographic maps, ask the USGS for Soda Springs and Norden.

Directions: From Auburn, drive east on I-80 for 55 miles to Soda Springs. Take the Soda Springs/Norden exit and follow Old Highway 40 east for 0.8 mile to Soda Springs Road. Turn south (right) and drive for another 0.8 mile to Pahatsi Road. Turn right. Pahatsi Road turns to dirt in 0.2 mile, and its name changes to Kidd Lakes Road. At 1.5 miles, you'll reach a fork. Continue straight for 2.3 more miles, passing Kidd Lake on your left and the Royal Gorge Devils Lookout Warming Hut on your right. Take the left fork after the warming hut and drive 0.5 mile farther. The trailhead, signed as Palisade Creek Trail, is on the north side of Cascade Lakes.

Contact: Truckee Ranger District, 10811 Stockrest Springs Road, Truckee, CA 96161, 530/587-3558, www.fs.fed.us/r5; Big Bend Visitors Center, Tahoe National Forest, 530/426-3609.

27 WARREN LAKE
14.0 mi / 2 days   🥾4   ⛰9

in Tahoe National Forest near Donner Summit

Map 6.1, page 213

The first 1.6 miles of this trail follow the same route as the Summit Lake Trail (see listing in this chapter), along the PCT access trail and underneath I-80. But Warren Lake hikers will take the left fork where Summit Lake hikers go right. Whereas Summit Lake Trail is an easy stroll in the park, Warren Lake Trail climbs 1,500 feet and then drops 1,500 feet, which you must repeat on the return trip. The elevation change means you part company with most casual hikers. The route climbs through lodgepole pine and red fir forest to a saddle at three miles, where there are excellent views (you can see where you're going to be hiking next). Then the trail drops gently over the next 3.5 miles, into a wide valley basin that has a mix of volcanic and glaciated rocks. Wildflowers abound on the valley floor. After a brief climb to a ridge, the final mile is a steep descent, dropping 1,000 feet to Warren Lake, where you'll find many campsites on the lake's west and south sides. Note that just before you reach the top of the ridge, about 1.3 miles from

Warren Lake, there is a left spur trail that leads to Devils Oven Lake. It's a good day hike for the following day.

User Groups: Hikers, dogs, horses, and mountain bikes. No wheelchair facilities.

Permits: No permits are required. Parking and access are free.

Maps: For a map, ask the U.S. Forest Service for Tahoe National Forest. For a topographic map, ask the USGS for Norden.

Directions: From Auburn, take I-80 east for 60 miles to the Castle Peak Area/Boreal Ridge Road exit just west of Donner Summit. Exit the freeway; turn right and then immediately left. Drive 0.4 mile to the trailhead for Donner Summit and the Pacific Crest Trail.

Contact: Truckee Ranger District, 10811 Stockrest Springs Road, Truckee, CA 96161, 530/587-3558, www.fs.fed.us/r5; Big Bend Visitors Center, Tahoe National Forest, 530/426-3609.

28 SUMMIT LAKE TRAIL
4.0 mi / 2.0 hr

🚶2 ⛰9

in Tahoe National Forest near Donner Summit

Map 6.1, page 213

The Summit Lake Trail is a quick and easy leg-stretcher and a great hike for families, leading two miles to a pretty alpine lake at 7,400 feet. It is crowded on weekends and those who are not fit complain the little climb is harder than they expected. Start hiking from the PCT trailhead, heading east and roughly paralleling the freeway. Watch carefully for an intersection 0.5 mile in. You must turn left and follow the PCT Access Trail north (signed for Castle Pass and Peter Grubb Hut), through a tunnel underneath I-80. (This is not the most scenic part of the trip, but it's not as bad as it sounds.) Once you're on the north side of the freeway, you'll reach a trail fork. Bear right for Summit Lake and Warren Lake, then start to climb a bit. The trail alternates through fir forest and occasional open ridges, with some excellent views to the south and east. At 1.6 miles, you'll

see another trail fork: Warren Lake to the left, and Summit Lake to the right. Bear right, and finish out your walk to the lake's edge, where you can drop in a fishing line if you wish.

User Groups: Hikers, dogs, horses, and mountain bikes. No wheelchair facilities.

Permits: No permits are required. Parking and access are free.

Maps: For a map, ask the U.S. Forest Service for Tahoe National Forest. For a topographic map, ask the USGS for Norden.

Directions: From Auburn, take I-80 east for 60 miles to the Castle Peak Area/Boreal Ridge Road exit just west of Donner Summit. Exit the freeway, turn right, and then immediately left. Drive 0.4 mile to the trailhead for Donner Summit and the Pacific Crest Trail.

Contact: Truckee Ranger District, 10811 Stockrest Springs Road, Truckee, CA 96161, 530/587-3558, www.fs.fed.us/r5; Big Bend Visitors Center, Tahoe National Forest, 530/426-3609.

29 EUCHRE BAR TRAIL
6.0 mi / 3.5 hr

 🚶3 ⛰8

on the North Fork American River near Baxter in Tahoe National Forest

Map 6.1, page 213

A river runs through almost every Sierra gulch and canyon, and so it is with this portion of the North Fork American River. From the trailhead, the route winds steeply down to the river and Euchre Bar, where a suspension footbridge crosses the water. The trail then leads upriver for 2.4 miles, along an excellent stretch of water for fishing, camping, panning for gold, and swimming (cold). If you want a lesson in pain, continue hiking another five miles. You'll climb the old Dorer Ranch Road, passing mining ruins and abandoned equipment from the Gold Rush era, gaining 2,000 feet in elevation through this dry, dusty country. Correct: This is an old mining trail.

User Groups: Hikers, dogs, and horses. Mountain bikes not advised. No wheelchair facilities.

Permits: Campfire permits are required for overnight use. Parking and access are free.

Maps: For a map, ask the U.S. Forest Service for Tahoe National Forest. For topographic maps, ask the USGS for Dutch Flat and Westville.

Directions: From Auburn, take I-80 east to the Alta exit. Take that exit from Alta to Morton. Turn right on Morton, then turn left on Casa Loma and continue until you see the sign for the Rawhide Mine. Turn right at the sign and drive 0.75 mile past the second railroad crossing to a parking area. The trailhead is 0.1 mile beyond the parking area.

Contact: Nevada City Ranger District, 530/265-4531, www.fs.fed.us/r5.

30 ITALIAN BAR TRAIL
4.5 mi / 3.5 hr   👥5 ⛰8

near the North Fork American River in Tahoe National Forest

Map 6.1, page 213

Miners in the 1850s were like mountain goats, and they knew the most direct route between two points was a straight line. As a result, this route—which miners once used to reach the North Fork American River—is almost straight down going in and straight up coming out, gaining 3,000 feet in elevation over the course of 2.25 miles. It's about as fun as searching for a tiny gold nugget on the beach. As you head down from the trailhead at 5,400 feet, you get little help from switchbacks. The trail ends at the river, and from there, you must scramble and hop from rock to rock along the riverbanks. Eventually you end up at a secluded spot where all seems perfect—until you start the hike back. When you face the 3,000-foot climb out, you will wonder how you ever talked yourself into doing this hike.

User Groups: Hikers, dogs, and horses. Mountain bikes not advised. No wheelchair facilities.

Permits: No permits are required. Parking and access are free.

Maps: For a map, ask the U.S. Forest Service for Tahoe National Forest. For a topographic map, ask the USGS for Westville.

Directions: Take I-80 to Auburn and the exit for Foresthill/Foresthill Road. Take that exit, turn east on Foresthill Road, and drive 16 miles to Foresthill. Continue another 13 miles northeast (the road becomes Foresthill Divide Road) to Humbug Ridge Road (Forest Road 66). Turn left and drive three miles north to the trailhead.

Contact: American River Ranger District, 22830 Foresthill Road, Foresthill, CA 95631, 530/367-2224, ww.fs.fed.us/r5.

31 MUMFORD BAR TRAIL
6.5 mi / 1 day   👥4 ⛰8

near the North Fork American River in Tahoe National Forest

Map 6.1, page 213

You'd have to be part mountain goat and part idiot to want to try this hike. Guess how we know? The trail leads almost straight down to the North Fork American River for more than 3.25 miles, and you know what that means. Right—it's almost straight up coming back. (Guess those gold miners were plenty of both.)

From the trailhead at 5,360 feet, the first mile of trail follows an old four-wheel-drive route that deteriorates and then drops down to the river canyon at 2,640 feet. This stretch of river is designated as "wild and scenic" and is quite pretty, with good canyon views and fishing spots. Consider extending your walk by taking American River Trail (see listing in this chapter) and staying overnight. Otherwise you will have to climb back out of the canyon on the same day, something even most mountain goats or gold miners would choose not to do.

User Groups: Hikers, dogs, and horses. Mountain bikes are not advised. No wheelchair facilities.

Permits: No permits are required. Parking and access are free.

Maps: For a map, ask the U.S. Forest Service for Tahoe National Forest. For topographic maps, ask the USGS for Duncan Peak and Westville.

Directions: Take I-80 to Auburn and the exit for Foresthill/Foresthill Road. Take that exit, turn east on Foresthill Road, and drive 16 miles to Foresthill. Continue another 17 miles northeast (the road becomes Foresthill Divide Road) to the Mumford trailhead, on the left side of the road.

Contact: Tahoe National Forest, Foresthill Ranger District, 22830 Foresthill Road, Foresthill, CA 95631, 530/367-2224, www.fs.fed.us/r5.

32 AMERICAN RIVER TRAIL
15.2 mi / 2 days   👣5 ⛰9

on the North Fork American River east of Foresthill in Tahoe National Forest

Map 6.1, page 213

A 90-minute hike from the Mumford Bar trailhead (see listing in this chapter) gets you down into a steep canyon and alongside the beautiful and remote North Fork American River. There you turn right and start hiking upstream on American River Trail. This is what you came for, the chance to walk along a pristine stretch of river on a steady, easy grade. You will pass old mining sites and abandoned cabins, alternating between dense vegetation and pretty river views. This trail makes a great getaway, and hikers can enjoy exploring and trout fishing. Nothing is perfect, and this hike does have some drawbacks: It crosses two creeks, Tadpole and New York, which are difficult, even dangerous, to ford when running high during the snowmelt in spring and early summer. A mile upriver of Tadpole Creek and then again at New York Creek, the trail runs adjacent to private property. Check your map and stay on the trail in these places. And the hike back out of the canyon to your car is a terrible grunt, going from 2,640 feet along the river up to 5,360 feet. That is a gain of 2,720 feet in just 3.25 miles.

Special Note: The Mumford trailhead is also accessible from Sailor Flat Trail (see listing in this chapter).

User Groups: Hikers, dogs, and horses. Mountain bikes not advised. No wheelchair facilities.

Permits: A campfire permit (free) is required for overnight use. Parking and access are free.

Maps: For a map, ask the U.S. Forest Service for Tahoe National Forest. For a topographic map, ask the USGS for Duncan Peak.

Directions: Take I-80 to Auburn and the exit for Foresthill/Foresthill Road. Take that exit, turn east on Foresthill Road, and drive 16 miles to Foresthill. Continue another 17 miles northeast (the road becomes Foresthill Divide Road) to the Mumford trailhead, on the left side of the road.

Contact: Tahoe National Forest, Foresthill Ranger District, 22830 Foresthill Road, Foresthill, CA 95631, 530/367-2224, www.fs.fed.us/r5.

33 BEACROFT TRAIL
4.5 mi / 1 day   👣5 ⛰9

near the North Fork American River in Tahoe National Forest

Map 6.1, page 213   BEST (

The Beacroft Trail is the "no-option" option to hiking down to the North Fork American River. The trailhead is located four miles beyond the Mumford trailhead, and after having reviewed the steep descent and climb required for that hike, you might want to look elsewhere for an easier route down. That's where Beacroft Trail comes in. Still, it isn't a much of an option, requiring an even more hellacious effort: it drops 3,240 feet in only 2.25 miles. The trip back up will have you howling. How can such a short trail be so steep? Ask the people who built the darn thing; those gold miners apparently had neither an abundance of useful gray matter between their ears nor much gold to carry on the return trip. OK, so you head down the canyon, then what? When you reach the river, turn left on American River Trail, which traces some of the most beautiful, accessible portions of this stream. Even here you face an obstacle. Within the first mile, you must cross New York Creek, a difficult (and sometimes dangerous) ford when full of snowmelt in early summer.

User Groups: Hikers, dogs, and horses. Mountain bikes are not advised. No wheelchair facilities.

Permits: No permits are required. Parking and access are free.

Maps: For a map, ask the U.S. Forest Service for Tahoe National Forest. For a topographic map, ask the USGS for Duncan Peak.

Directions: Take I-80 to Auburn and the exit for Foresthill/Foresthill Road. Take that exit, turn east on Foresthill Road and drive 16 miles to Foresthill. Continue another 19 miles northeast (the road becomes Foresthill Divide Road) to the trailhead, on the left side of the road (one mile past Secret House Campground).

Contact: Tahoe National Forest, Foresthill Ranger District, 22830 Foresthill Road, Foresthill, CA 95631, 530/367-2224, www.fs.fed.us/r5.

34 SAILOR FLAT TRAIL
6.5 mi / 1 day   🏃5 ⛰10

near the North Fork American River in Tahoe National Forest

> Map 6.1, page 213

There are several trailheads heading for Sailor Flat Trail on the Foresthill side of Foresthill Road that provide access to the North Fork American River. But this is the most distant, most remote, and, yes, most difficult. In turn, it is the least traveled. The Sailor Flat trailhead lies at the end of the road, out in the middle of nowhere, at an elevation of 6,400 feet; yet the remains of a long-abandoned gold stamp mill still stand nearby. The hike starts out easily enough—the first 1.5 miles follow an old mining road on which hikers will confront

nothing serious. Don't be fooled though. The trail becomes much steeper, with switchback after switchback leading down into the canyon. When you reach the river at 3,360 feet, you will have dropped 3,040 feet in only 3.25 miles. You can explore farther by turning left (west) on American River Trail, which traces the most beautiful sections of this river, heading downstream past meadows, canyon views, and good spots to fish and pan for gold.

Special Note: With a shuttle vehicle and a partner, you can create a one-way hike covering 15.6 miles. From Sailor Flat trailhead, hike down to American River Trail, turn left, hike along the river to Mumford Bar, make a left turn, and hike out to Foresthill Road (see preceding hikes).

User Groups: Hikers, dogs, and horses. Mountain bikes not advised. No wheelchair facilities.

Permits: No permits are required. Parking and access are free.

Maps: For a map, ask the U.S. Forest Service for Tahoe National Forest. For topographic maps, ask the USGS for Royal Gorge and Duncan Peak.

Directions: Take I-80 to Auburn and the exit for Foresthill/Foresthill Road. Take that exit, turn east on Foresthill Road, and drive 16 miles to Foresthill. Continue another 25 miles northeast (the road becomes Foresthill Divide Road) to Sailor Flat Road. Turn left and drive one mile north to the trailhead.

Contact: Tahoe National Forest, Foresthill Ranger District, 22830 Foresthill Road, Foresthill, CA 95631, 530/367-2224, www.fs.fed.us/r5.

35 STEVENS TRAIL
9.0 mi / 5.0 hr   🏃2 ⛰8

near Colfax

> Map 6.1, page 213

The Stevens Trail is a surprisingly lush and peaceful trail that leaves noisy I-80 in Colfax and drops down into the canyon of the North

Fork American River. The features here are gentle terrain and long-distance canyon and stream views.

After parking, walk 1.3 miles, starting with a gentle climb, and keep a sharp eye off to the left, where a pretty waterfall is hidden just off the trail. From the ridge, continue on a gentle downhill path, descending 1,200 feet over the course of 4.5 miles if you choose to head all the way to the river. The return trip is up but is well graded and not too difficult for most hikers. The biggest problem here is timing. This is no fun on a summer afternoon, with 90-degree temperatures and an afternoon climb out of a canyon. Regardless, this is a great trip for many, especially for those cruising the interstate who desire a quick getaway into a pretty setting where the highway traffic seems like a million miles away.

You can also see the railroad line that was built by Chinese laborers dangling in rope-strung baskets from the cliffs above. In the spring, you will also pass blooming wildflowers and buckeye trees. The trail is well signed, except the section you take to see the waterfall. This trail is registered as a National Historic Trail. It was originally part of a livery trail from the town of Iowa Hill to Colfax (the entire historic route is no longer connected).

User Groups: Hikers, dogs, horses, and mountain bikes. No wheelchair facilities.

Permits: No permits are necessary. Parking and access are free.

Maps: For a topographic map, ask the USGS for Colfax.

Directions: From Sacramento, drive east on I-80 for 45 miles to Colfax and the Colfax/Grass Valley exit. Take that exit and drive a short distance to a stop sign at North Canyon Way (a frontage road). Turn left at the stop sign and drive east 0.7 mile to the trailhead parking area.

Contact: Bureau of Land Management, Mother Lode Field Office, 916/941-3155, www.ca.blm.gov.

36 GREEN VALLEY TRAIL
4.5 mi / 1 day 　　　　🥾5 ⛰8

on the North Fork American River near Sugar Pine Reservoir

Map 6.1, page 213

It's amazing what people will go through to create a space that feels like their own. Hikers can do just that on Green Valley Trail by finding an idyllic spot along the North Fork American River and soaking up the serenity. But the price is steep, and the return trip will put you through more punishment than is typically handed out at Folsom Prison.

The trip starts at a little-known trailhead near Sugar Pine Reservoir (elevation 4,080 feet). From there, Green Valley Trail is steep and often rocky, dropping 2,240 feet in 2.25 miles before reaching the river. We do not advise extending your trip from here. It is possible to continue downriver a short way, or to cross the river (good luck) and hike upstream into Green Valley. However, these sections of the trail are in very poor condition, and the upstream route crosses private property owned by people who don't take kindly to visitors.

User Groups: Hikers, dogs, and horses. Mountain bikes are not advised. No wheelchair facilities.

Permits: No permits are required. Parking and access are free.

Maps: For a map, ask the U.S. Forest Service for Tahoe National Forest. For a topographic map, ask the USGS for Dutch Flat.

Directions: Take I-80 to Auburn and the exit for Foresthill/Foresthill Road. Take that exit, turn east on Foresthill Road, and drive 16 miles to Foresthill. Continue another seven miles (it becomes Foresthill Divide Road) to Forest Road 10. Turn left on Forest Road 10 (Sugar Pine Road) and drive five miles to Sugar Pine Dam. Continue one mile past the dam to Elliot Ranch Road (just past the entrance to Sugar Pine Campground, on the right). Turn north on Elliot Ranch Road and drive three miles to the trailhead.

Contact: Tahoe National Forest, Foresthill

Ranger District, 22830 Foresthill Road, Foresthill, CA 95631, 530/367-2224, www.fs.fed.us/r5.

37 FOREST VIEW TRAIL
1.5 mi / 0.75 hr   🥾1   ⛰9

in Tahoe National Forest east of Foresthill

Map 6.1, page 213

Giant sequoias, the world's largest trees, attract many visitors to this easy, well-maintained interpretive trail that leads through California's northernmost grove of sequoias. It is set at 5,200 feet on Mosquito Ridge Road. The trail meanders through virgin old-growth forest, home to a half dozen truly monster-sized trees. Along the 0.5-mile Big Trees Interpretive Trail are 16 stops marked with numbers that coincide with numbered listings in a brochure that's available at the trailhead, allowing visitors to take an interesting and informative self-guided tour of the fascinating history of these massive trees. Linked with Forest View Trail, the entire loop extends 1.5 miles. Despite the long drive to the trailhead on Mosquito Ridge, the trail gets quite a bit of use. The drive in provides views of an expansive foothill landscape before entering the conifers.
User Groups: Hikers and dogs. No horses or mountain bikes. No wheelchair facilities.
Permits: No permits are required. Parking and access are free.
Maps: Free interpretive brochures are available at the trailhead. For a map, ask the U.S. Forest Service for Tahoe National Forest. For a topographic map, ask the USGS for Greek Store.
Directions: Take I-80 to Auburn and the exit for Foresthill/Foresthill Road. Take that exit, turn east on Foresthill Road, and drive 16 miles to Foresthill and Mosquito Ridge Road. Turn right (east) on Mosquito Ridge Road and drive 23 miles to the trailhead.
Contact: Tahoe National Forest, Foresthill Ranger District, 22830 Foresthill Road, Foresthill, CA 95631, 530/367-2224, www.fs.fed.us/r5.

38 WESTERN STATES TRAIL: MICHIGAN BLUFF TO DEADWOOD
4.0 mi / 2.5 hr   🥾3   ⛰7

in Tahoe National Forest east of Foresthill

Map 6.1, page 213

The attraction here is beautiful Eldorado Canyon, where you can fish for trout and camp along Eldorado Creek. From the trailhead at 3,520 feet, the trail quickly drops about two miles into the canyon. Switchbacks lead to a footbridge over Eldorado Creek. Extend the trip by crossing the bridge and hiking up the other side of the canyon to scenic views of the rugged topography.

Special Note: The Michigan Bluff Trail is a section of the Western States Trail, which spans from Squaw Valley to Auburn.
User Groups: Hikers, dogs, horses, and mountain bikes. No wheelchair facilities.
Permits: No permits are required. Parking and access are free.
Maps: For a map, ask the U.S. Forest Service for Tahoe National Forest. For a topographic map, ask the USGS for Michigan Bluff.
Directions: Take I-80 to Auburn and the exit for Foresthill/Foresthill Road. Take that exit, turn east on Foresthill Road, and drive 16 miles to Foresthill. Continue northeast (it becomes Foresthill Divide Road) and look for the signed turnoff to Michigan Bluff. Turn right on Michigan Bluff Road and drive five miles to Michigan Bluff. The trailhead is located about 0.25 mile east of Michigan Bluff, at the end of the road.
Contact: Tahoe National Forest, Foresthill Ranger District, 22830 Foresthill Road, Foresthill, CA 95631, 530/367-2224, www.fs.fed.us/r5.

39 GROUSE FALLS
1.0 mi / 0.5 hr   🥾1   ⛰10

in Tahoe National Forest near Foresthill

Map 6.1, page 213   **BEST**

Some waterfalls are simply mind-boggling in their beauty, and some provide the centerpiece of a beautiful setting. Grouse Falls is one of the latter. The hike is a 15-minute walk through old-growth forest to a viewing deck. From here you're looking out over a deep and wide canyon with absolutely no sign of human development. The waterfall is about 0.5 mile away across the canyon; it's several hundred feet long, and when it's running full, it can seem like a scene out of Yosemite. The overlook is a wooden platform with benches where you can sit and admire the beauty. You don't see or hear immense Grouse Falls until just before you come out to the overlook, and when you do, it can be a shock to your system.

User Groups: Hikers, dogs, horses, and mountain bikes. No wheelchair facilities.

Permits: No permits are necessary. Parking and access are free.

Maps: For a map, ask the U.S. Forest Service for Tahoe National Forest. For a topographic map, ask the USGS for Michigan Bluff.

Directions: Take I-80 to Auburn and the exit for Foresthill/Foresthill Road. Take that exit, turn east on Foresthill Road, and drive 16 miles to Foresthill and Mosquito Ridge Road. Turn right (east) on Mosquito Ridge Road and drive 19 miles to Peavine Road (Road 33). Turn left on Peavine Road and drive 5.5 miles to the Grouse Falls turnoff, on the left. Turn left and drive 0.5 mile to the trailhead.

Contact: Tahoe National Forest, Foresthill Ranger District, 22830 Foresthill Road, Foresthill, CA 95631, 530/367-2224, www.fs.fed.us/r5.

40 WESTERN STATES TRAIL / MCGUIRE SEGMENT

7.8 mi / 4.0 hr   🚶2 ⛰8

at French Meadows Reservoir in Tahoe National Forest

Map 6.1, page 213

The McGuire Trail has become a favorite side trip for families visiting or camping at French Meadows Reservoir (elevation 5,290 feet). The trail traces the north shore of the lake, poking in and out of timber. It then rises up an easy grade to the top of Red Star Ridge (5,600 feet) and provides good views of the reservoir below. French Meadows is a beautiful and large lake, covering nearly 2,000 acres when full. It is stocked each year with more than 30,000 trout that join a healthy population of resident brown trout and holdovers from stocks of rainbow trout from prior years. Water drawdowns are a common problem in late summer, as they expose many stumps and boulders, creating a navigational hazard for boaters.

User Groups: Hikers, dogs, horses, and mountain bikes. No wheelchair facilities.

Permits: No permits are required. Parking and access are free.

Maps: For a map, ask the U.S. Forest Service for Tahoe National Forest. For a topographic map, ask the USGS for Bunker Hill.

Directions: Take I-80 to Auburn and the exit for Foresthill/Foresthill Road. Take that exit, turn east on Foresthill Road, and drive 16 miles to Foresthill and Mosquito Ridge Road. Turn right (east) on Mosquito Ridge Road and drive 40 miles to the French Meadows Reservoir Dam. Cross the dam, turn left (still Mosquito Ridge Road), and drive 3.5 miles to the trailhead, near McGuire Boat Ramp.

Contact: Tahoe National Forest, Foresthill Ranger District, 22830 Foresthill Road, Foresthill, CA 95631, 530/367-2224, www.fs.fed.us/r5.

41 POWDERHORN TRAIL TO HELL HOLE

13.0 mi one-way / 2 days   🚶5 ⛰9

in the Granite Chief Wilderness east of Hell Hole Reservoir in Tahoe National Forest

Map 6.1, page 213

This is a difficult trek that traverses the Sierra crest, east to west, Tahoe to Hell Hole. The Hell Hole Trail requires hikers to have wilderness skills and, worst of all, to be prepared for a difficult stream crossing and traversing a landslide. Sound fun? Who said anything about fun?

Start at the remote Powderhorn trailhead, set at 6,400 feet on the boundary of the Granite Chief Wilderness. From there, you hike four miles down to Diamond Crossing (fording Powderhorn Creek), where you will meet Hell Hole Trail. Shortly after turning left, you will have to cross Five Lakes Creek, a difficult and sometimes dangerous endeavor, especially during snowmelt. After crossing, you will descend to Little Buckskin Creeks (two more fords, both a lot easier than the first one) and into Steamboat Canyon. Approximately 0.5 mile from Steamboat Canyon, hikers face a slippery landslide that demands caution. The trail then drops toward the Rubicon River and Hell Hole Reservoir.

Do you yearn for a challenging trek in a very remote high-mountain wilderness setting? This is it.

Special Notes: The stream crossings required on this hike can be life threatening during periods of high snowmelt and runoff.

For a day hike or a weekend camping trip, start the trail at the Hell Hole Dam and walk three miles to a hike-in camp set at the head of the lake.

User Groups: Hikers, dogs, and horses. No mountain bikes. No wheelchair facilities.

Permits: A campfire permit (free) is required for overnight use. Parking and access are free.

Maps: For a map, ask the U.S. Forest Service for Tahoe National Forest. For a topographic map, ask the USGS for Wentworth Springs.

Directions: From Truckee, take Highway 89 south and drive to Tahoe City. Turn right on Highway 89 (along Lake Tahoe) and drive four miles to the Kaspian Picnic Area and Blackwood Canyon Road. Turn right (west) on Blackwood Canyon Road and drive 2.3 miles. Cross the creek and continue for another 4.8 miles to Barker Pass and the trailhead.

Contact: Truckee Ranger District, 10811 Stockrest Springs Road, Truckee, CA 96161, 530/587-3558, www.fs.fed.us/r5.

42 GRANITE CHIEF TRAIL TO TINKER KNOB

14.0 mi / 8.0 hr or 2 days 🏃4 ⛰10

in Tahoe National Forest near Squaw Valley

Map 6.1, page 213

Tinker Knob is not an easy summit to attain, but those who reach it always remember it. From the Squaw Valley Fire Station, it's a demanding 3.5-mile hike to the intersection of the Granite Chief Trail and the Pacific Crest Trail. The total gain is 2,000 feet; most of the climb is forested, but there are occasional openings with views of Lake Tahoe and surrounding peaks. When at last you gain the PCT (at 8,200 feet), turn right (north) toward Tinker Knob. Now it's another 3.5 miles, most of it on an easier, winding grade along the top of a ridge, with only one surprising, cruel stretch in which you must drop downhill and then climb up again. The last section of trail is a series of switchbacks up to the Tinker Knob Saddle, then it's a brief 0.25-mile climb to the summit of Tinker Knob, at 8,950 feet. You like views? How about this one—a head-swiveling vista of Anderson Peak, Painted Rock, Silver Peak, the American River Canyon, Donner Lake, and Lake Tahoe. To cut some mileage off your trip, hike this trail as a shuttle trip, leaving one car at the Coldstream trailhead near Donner Memorial State Park. (It's at the horseshoe bend in the railroad tracks at the end of Coldstream Creek access road.) The Coldstream Trail meets the PCT just below the summit of Tinker Knob, so after gaining the summit via the route described above, follow Coldstream Trail four miles down to its trailhead. This makes an 11-mile one-way hike with a shuttle.

User Groups: Hikers, dogs, horses, and mountain bikes. No wheelchair facilities.

Permits: No permits are required. Parking and access are free.

Maps: For a map, ask the U.S. Forest Service for Tahoe National Forest. For topographic maps, ask the USGS for Tahoe City and Granite Chief.

Directions: From Truckee, take Highway 89 south and drive about 8 miles to Squaw Valley Road. Turn right on Squaw Valley Road and drive 2.2 miles to the Squaw Valley Fire Station. The trail begins on its east side. You must leave your car in the large parking lot by the ski lift buildings, not by the fire station. Walk back across the bridge to the trailhead.

Contact: Truckee Ranger District, 10811 Stockrest Springs Road, Truckee, CA 96161, 530/587-3558, www.fs.fed.us/r5.

43 GRANITE CHIEF TRAIL TO EMIGRANT PASS

12.0 mi / 7.0 hr   🥾4 ⛰️9

in Tahoe National Forest near Squaw Valley

Map 6.1, page 213

The Granite Chief Trail begins at the Squaw Valley Fire Station (at 6,200 feet) and climbs, climbs, and climbs some more until it reaches the Pacific Crest Trail 3.5 miles later. This is why many hikers choose to ride the tram at Squaw Valley to reach the PCT, then start hiking around from there. But not you… you like a challenge, right? Well, in either case, see you at the top.

You'll climb 2,000 feet over those 3.5 miles, roughly paralleling Squaw Creek and mostly in the woods. When you reach the PCT, turn left (south) toward Twin Peaks. The view of Lake Tahoe and its cobalt blue waters is stunning. Still ascending, hike for one mile on the PCT to the eastern flank of Granite Chief Peak (elevation 9,086 feet). Finally you begin to descend, and in one more mile you reach an intersection with Western States Trail. Turn left and take a 0.5-mile walk to visit the Watson Monument, a stone marker at Emigrant Pass. You probably won't stay long if you arrive in the afternoon: Although the views are lovely, the wind is usually fierce by midday.

User Groups: Hikers, dogs, horses, and mountain bikes. No wheelchair facilities.

Permits: No permits are required. Parking and access are free.

Maps: For a map, ask the U.S. Forest Service for Tahoe National Forest. For topographic maps, ask the USGS for Tahoe City and Granite Chief.

Directions: From Truckee, take Highway 89 south and drive about 8 miles to Squaw Valley Road. Turn right on Squaw Valley Road and drive 2.2 miles to the Squaw Valley Fire Station. The trail begins on its east side. You must leave your car in the large parking lot by the ski lift buildings, not by the fire station. Walk back across the bridge to the trailhead.

Contact: Truckee Ranger District, 10811 Stockrest Springs Road, Truckee, CA 96161, 530/587-3558, www.fs.fed.us/r5.

44 FIVE LAKES

4.2 mi / 2.0 hr   🥾2 ⛰️9

in the Granite Chief Wilderness near Alpine Meadows

Map 6.1, page 213

Some say that this trek into the Granite Chief Wilderness is too easy, and they may be right. Although the trail has a moderately steep grade, it's mercifully short, which makes it incredibly popular with hikers, especially on weekends. Make your trip in the off-season or during the week, and definitely make this a day trip instead of an overnight in order to minimize impact at the five granite-bound lakes.

The first 0.5 mile is the steepest grade. The next 0.75 mile continues uphill more gradually to the top of a ridge. Switchbacks make it manageable, but there is almost no shade along the route as you climb 1,000 feet. At 1.8 miles, you reach the Granite Chief Wilderness boundary and enter a land of red fir, white fir, and rocks. A signed junction 0.25 mile farther points you to the left toward the lakes, with your trail heading directly downhill to the largest of them. From there, you can follow numerous side trails to the four other lakes, all east of the big one. Most people don't go any farther than the first big lake, where the swimming is excellent. The shallow water is clear and warm. Remember: Minimize your impact in this heavily traveled area. The Five Lakes are set at 7,400 feet.

User Groups: Hikers, dogs, and horses. No mountain bikes. No wheelchair facilities.

Permits: No permits are required for day hiking. Parking and access are free.

Maps: For a map, ask the U.S. Forest Service for Tahoe National Forest. For topographic maps, ask the USGS for Tahoe City and Granite Chief.

Directions: From Truckee, take Highway 89 south and drive about 10 miles to Alpine Meadows Road. Turn right on Alpine Meadows Road and drive two miles to the trailhead, on the right. Park along the road.

Contact: Truckee Ranger District, 10811 Stockrest Springs Road, Truckee, CA 96161, 530/587-3558, www.fs.fed.us/r5.

45 WARD CREEK TRAIL
6.0 mi / 3.0 hr

in Tahoe National Forest near Tahoe City

Map 6.1, page 213

Ward Creek Trail may seem rather tame compared to some of the more famous hikes at Lake Tahoe. There's no stellar waterfall, no drop-dead gorgeous lake views, no towering granite monoliths. But then again, there are no crowds either. For many, the trade-off is a good one. The route passes through fields of mule's ears and forests of sugar pines, with enough open sections to provide wide-open views of the surrounding mountain ridges.

The trail begins as an old dirt road, paralleling Ward Creek for 1.5 miles to a washed-out bridge and a Road Closed sign. Cross the creek on logs and continue hiking, now on a single track. The trail climbs a little higher above Ward Creek, then enters a dense, lovely pine forest. You can go as far as you like (the trail continues to Twin Peaks, 5.3 miles from the trailhead), but for the mileage suggested above, turn around when you are about 0.5 mile into the trees and take an easy stroll home.

User Groups: Hikers, dogs, horses, and mountain bikes. No wheelchair facilities.

Permits: No permits are required. Parking and access are free.

Maps: For a map, ask the U.S. Forest Service for Lake Tahoe Basin Management Unit. For a topographic map, ask the USGS for Tahoe City.

Directions: From Truckee, take Highway 89 south and drive to Tahoe City. Turn right on Highway 89 and drive 2 miles to Pineland Drive (just north of Kilner Park). Turn right on Pineland Drive and go 0.5 mile to Twin Peaks Drive. Turn left and drive 1.7 miles. (Twin Peaks Drive becomes Ward Creek Boulevard.) At 1.7 miles, park in the pullout on the left side of the highway and begin hiking at the gated dirt road, Forest Service Road 15N62. If the gate is open, you can drive inside and park along the dirt road.

Contact: Lake Tahoe Basin Management Unit, 35 College Drive, South Lake Tahoe, CA 96150, 530/543-2600, www.fs.fed.us/r5; Visitors Center (open only in summer), 530/543-2674.

46 ELLIS PEAK TRAIL
6.0 mi / 3.5 hr

in Tahoe National Forest near Tahoe City

Map 6.1, page 213

Some people will spend a week hiking 100 miles to get what is already available in three miles and a few hours at 8,740-foot Ellis Peak. Of the dozen or so landmark peaks that surround Lake Tahoe, Ellis Peak requires one of the shortest hikes, especially compared to renowned Tallac, Freel, and Pyramid. Ellis sits on the threshold of world-class greatness; at the top, it can be difficult to decide which way to face. One side towers over north Lake Tahoe, while the other looks across a false summit and Desolation Wilderness. The Crystal Range and Loon Lake lay below to the southwest, the Granite Chief Wilderness to the northwest. Everywhere you look are miles of spectacular high Sierra grandeur.

This six-mile, round-trip hike has a total elevation gain of roughly 1,500 feet. If there's a catch, you'll find out right off. The trail is hardly graded, but is steep in two spots. In the first mile, you'll climb about 800 feet through forest. As you emerge at a subridge, notice a notch in the cliff on your left—you can peer down through a plummeting drop and see the parking area and your car below. That gives you a sense of how steep the trail is. A nearby clearing blooms with rafts of mule's ears at your feet; off to the right is beautiful Loon Lake in the Crystal Basin. Once you top the first subridge, the trail contours along the ridge, then sails down to a mountain saddle. It then climbs again and gains Knee Ridge. You will cross an OHV road, with oft-mosquito-y Ellis Lake a 0.5-mile side trip to your left. The primary trail is straight ahead.

From the Ellis Lake junction, it's another 0.5-mile climb to the top. You emerge on an old dirt road for a bit to see a false summit directly ahead. Resist the urge to climb it! Instead, stay right and follow the trail as it rings in a half circle, leading up another 0.25-mile to the top of Ellis Peak. After scrambling to the top of that pinnacle, it feels like you are on top of the world. Some of the rocks make perfect chairs; sit and take in the views—the expansive Tahoe blue on one side and an infinity of wilderness on the other—until every frazzled nerve is soothed.

User Groups: Hikers. Dogs, horses permitted, but not advised; only water at Ellis Lake. No mountain bikes (OHV route available 0.5 mile down road on left). No wheelchair facilities.

Permits: No permits are required. Parking and access are free.

Maps: For a map, ask the U.S. Forest Service for Lake Tahoe Basin Management Unit. For a topographic map, ask the USGS for Homewood.

Directions: From Tahoe City, drive south on Highway 89 for 4.3 miles. Look for a sign on the right (west) for Kaspian Campground; just

beyond is Barker Pass Road/Forest Road 3 (unsigned). Turn right and continnue seven miles (paved, watch for road bikes). When the road turns to dirt, drive a short distance to Barker Pass. The signed trailhead is on left; park along the shoulder.

Contact: Lake Tahoe Basin Management Unit, 35 College Drive, South Lake Tahoe, CA 96150, 530/543-2600, www.fs.fed.us/r5; visitors center (summer only), 530/543-2674.

47 STATELINE LOOKOUT
1.0 mi / 0.5 hr 🏃1 ⛰9

off Highway 28 near Crystal Bay

Map 6.1, page 213

For years we avoided this trail because we thought it was just a tourist attraction, located at the lookout tower that straddles the Nevada and California state line. It turns out that *we* were the dumb tourists, because this little trail is great. You can learn all about the cultural history of Lake Tahoe's north shore—which includes stories of timber, railroads, casinos, and resorts—as well as a little about the natural history of the area. After you walk the short self-guided trail, be sure to check out the views of Lake Tahoe from the telescopes located at the lookout (elevation 7,017 feet). Or, hey, forget the telescopes and just look with your own eyes. Either way, the view is unforgettable.

User Groups: Hikers, wheelchairs, and dogs. No horses or mountain bikes.

Permits: No permits are required. Parking and access are free.

Maps: For a map, ask the U.S. Forest Service for Lake Tahoe Basin Management Unit. For a topographic map, ask the USGS for Kings Beach.

Directions: From Truckee, take Highway 89 south and drive to Tahoe City and Highway 28. Turn left on Highway 28 and drive six miles to Reservoir Drive (just east of the old Tahoe Biltmore Casino). Turn left (north) and drive to Lake View Avenue. Turn right and drive through a residential area and continue to Forest Service Road 1601 (at an unmarked iron gate). Turn left on Forest Service Road 1601, park at the gate, and walk 0.5 mile to the lookout. Parking is limited.

Contact: Lake Tahoe Basin Management Unit, 35 College Drive, South Lake Tahoe, CA 96150, 530/543-2600, www.fs.fed.us/r5; Visitors Center (open only in summer), 530/543-2674.

48 BURTON CREEK LOOP
5.0 mi / 2.5 hr   🏃1 ⛰8

off Highway 28 near Tahoe City

Map 6.1, page 213

At more than 2,000 acres, Burton Creek is Lake Tahoe's second-largest state park, so you might wonder why few people have ever heard of it. It's because the park has no visitors center, no campground, no entrance kiosk, and, unfortunately, no trail signs or official map. What really matters is that it has no crowds—a major bonus at Lake Tahoe. A five-mile loop trip is possible in the park, starting near North Tahoe High School and wandering through a mix of fir and pine forest, open meadows, and creekside riparian habitat. Although the trail is not signed, there are numbers painted at most intersections, which help you stay on track. The loop starts 0.25 mile from the trailhead; you can hike it in either direction. Just make sure you remember what the spur trail that leads from the loop back to the trailhead looks like; otherwise you may walk right past it on your return trip. Some advice: If you're visiting this park in summer, stop in at the campground at Tahoe State Recreation Area, across Highway 28 from the turnoff to Burton Creek State Park. Check with the kiosk to see if they have any updated trail information on Burton Creek.

User Groups: Hikers, leashed dogs, horses, and mountain bikes. No wheelchair facilities.

Permits: No permits are required. Parking and access are free.

Maps: For a topographic map, ask the USGS for Tahoe City.

Directions: From Truckee, take Highway 89 south and drive to Tahoe City and Highway 28. Turn left on Highway 28 and drive 2.3 miles to Old Mill Road. Turn left and drive 0.4 mile to Polaris Road. Turn left on Polaris Road and drive 0.5 mile to North Tahoe High School and the dirt road by the school parking lot. Park alongside the dirt road. Be careful not to block the gate.

Contact: Tahoe State Recreation Area, P.O. Box 266, Tahoma, CA 96142, 530/583-3074 or 530/525-3345, fax 530/525-0138.

49 BARKER PASS TO DONNER PASS (PCT)
31.4 mi one-way / 3 days   🏃3 ⛰9

from Barker Pass to Donner Pass

Map 6.1, page 213

The trailhead at Barker Pass (7,650 feet), is one of the best anywhere. It provides direct access to the Granite Chief Wilderness to the north or the Desolation Wilderness to the south. Heading north on the PCT, the trip starts with a climb of 800 feet to enter Granite Chief. Once on the ridge, you're rewarded with 360-degree views of this high-mountain landscape, a mix of volcanic rock and granite ridges, much of it above tree line. Though hikers don't face the long, sustained climbs so common in the southern Sierra, it's enough of a roller-coaster ride to require hikers to be in excellent shape. The trail cuts the flank of Ward Peak, at 8,470 feet, then switchbacks steeply down to Five Lakes and Five Lakes Creek (where there's good camping). The trail then continues up and down canyons all the way to Donner Pass. You can expect to see lots of hikers, because along the way, you'll pass near two ski resorts (Alpine Meadows and Squaw Valley), where hikers can use the ski lifts in the summer to gain easy elevation to the ridgeline, rather than having to grind out long, all-day climbs. Before making the final push to Donner Pass, a descent of more than 1,000 feet, hikers can enjoy breathtaking views of Donner Lake and the miles of surrounding high country.

To continue north on the PCT, see the *Donner Pass to the Yuba River (PCT)* hike in this chapter. If you are walking this trail in reverse, see the *Echo Lakes Resort to Barker Pass (PCT)* hike in this chapter.

User Groups: Hikers, dogs, and horses. No mountain bikes. No wheelchair facilities.

Permits: A backcountry permit is required for traveling through various wilderness and special-use areas that the trail traverses. In addition, a campfire permit is required for the use of portable camp stoves or the building of campfires (where allowed). To make it simple, you can contact the national forest, Bureau of Land Management (BLM), or national park office at your point of entry for a combined permit that is good for traveling through multiple-permit areas during your dates of travel.

Maps: For topographic maps, ask the USGS for Emerald Bay, Rockbound Valley, Homewood, Tahoe City, Granite Chief, and Norden.

Directions: To reach the Barker Pass trailhead: From Truckee, take Highway 89 south and drive to Tahoe City. Turn right on Highway 89 and drive south to Kaspian Picnic Grounds (0.5 north of Tahoe Pines) and Forest Road 15N03. Turn right (west) and drive seven miles to the trailhead.

For the Donner Pass trailhead: From Truckee, drive west on I-80 and exit at Castle Peak Area/Boreal Ridge, just west of the Donner Summit roadside rest area. The sign for the Pacific Crest trailhead is what you're looking for, and it's located on the south side of the highway.

Contact: Truckee Ranger District, 10811 Stockrest Springs Road, Truckee, CA 96161, 530/587-3558, www.fs.fed.us/r5; Lake Tahoe Basin Management Unit, 35 College Drive, South Lake Tahoe, CA 96150, 530/543-2600, www.fs.fed.us/r5; Visitors Center (open only in summer), 530/543-2674.

50 GENERAL CREEK
7.0 mi / 3.5 hr

in Ed Z'berg Sugar Pine Point State Park near Lake Tahoe

Map 6.1, page 213

Marshy Lily Pond is a pretty, serene spot. This trail starts in Sugar Pine Point State Park and follows a flat open stretch of General Creek and then leads gently uphill through the forest to the Lily Pond. Most of the trail is part of a popular cross-country skiing loop in the winter, which means it's on a dirt road. At 2.5 miles from the campground, at the far end of the loop, you'll see the single-track turnoff signed for Lily Pond and Lost Lake. It's a one-mile hike through a rocky, dense forest to the pond, which is indeed covered with lilies. On your return, you can always take the south side of the loop for variety, then turn left on the bridge over General Creek to return to the start of the loop.

There are a couple key factors to enjoying this walk: If you're not staying in the General Creek Campground, the day-use parking area is more than 0.5 mile from campsite No. 149, where the trail begins. To make this walk to the trailhead more pleasant, be sure to take the single-track trail from the parking lot instead of walking along the paved camp road. The trail is somewhat hidden from view, so if you don't see it, ask the attendant in the entrance kiosk where it is. Next, when you finally meet up with the loop, be sure to take the north side of it, which is prettier than the south side, with lots of big sugar pines interspersed with Jeffreys and lodgepoles. The south side is mostly open meadows. This was the site of the 1960 Olympics biathlon.

User Groups: Hikers and mountain bikes. No dogs or horses. No wheelchair facilities.

Permits: No permits are required. A day-use fee of $8 is charged per vehicle.

Maps: A map of Sugar Pine Point State Park is available for a fee at the entrance station. A Lake Tahoe map is available for a fee from

Tom Harrison Maps. For a topographic map, ask the USGS for Homewood.

Directions: From Truckee, take Highway 89 south and drive to Tahoe City. Turn right on Highway 89 and drive south eight miles to the General Creek Campground entrance on the right. Turn right and park in one of the day-use areas by the entrance kiosk, then walk into the campground to site No. 149 and the start of the trail. You can walk into the camp on the park road or take the single-track trail that leads from the parking lot.

Contact: Ed Z'berg Sugar Pine Point State Park, P.O. Box 266, Tahoma, CA 96142, 530/525-7982, www.parks.ca.gov.

51 MEEKS CREEK TRAIL TO RUBICON LAKE

15.0 mi / 1.0-2 days   🏃3 ⛰9

in the Desolation Wilderness

Map 6.1, page 213

This trek into the Desolation Wilderness is a moderate backpacking trip that's loaded with alpine lakes and classic Tahoe scenery. In summer, plan on sharing the trail with lots of other folks. The trip starts as you hike on a closed dirt road (Road 14N42) that leads from the Desolation Wilderness sign near Meeks Bay for 1.3 level miles to a trail sign for Phipps Pass and Tahoe-Yosemite Trail. Bear right here and begin the gradual climb to a chain of alpine lakes. You hike parallel to Meeks Creek on a gently climbing trail, and pass the wilderness boundary at 2.5 miles. You're in forest most of the time, so don't expect a lot of panoramic views, but then again, don't expect any brutal, sunny, exposed ascents. Cross Meeks Creek and continue straight to Lake Genevieve, at 4.5 miles. The lake is shallow but provides swimming. The trail then climbs up to larger Crag Lake, then continues to climb farther to small, lily-covered Shadow Lake. (A right fork beyond Crag Lake leads to small Hidden Lake, less than 0.25 mile off the main trail; it's a good side trip.) From Shadow Lake, it's a

mile farther to Stony Ridge Lake, the largest of this series of lakes, and then yet another mile to Rubicon Lake, 7.5 miles from the trailhead and with a total elevation gain of only 2,000 feet. The main steep stretch is right at the end, between Stony Ridge Lake and Rubicon Lake. Campsites can be found at most all of the lakes, but Rubicon Lake is the preferred site, since it's the most scenic of the group.

User Groups: Hikers, dogs, and horses. No mountain bikes. No wheelchair facilities.

Permits: Permits are required year-round for both day and overnight use. Day hikers may obtain a free permit from a ranger station or may self-issue at most major trailheads. Backpackers camping in Desolation Wilderness are subject to trailhead quotas. There is a $5 reservation fee, plus $5 per person for one night, $10 per person for two or more nights up to 14 days (nonrefundable). Children ages 12 and under are free. Golden Passes do not apply to personal-use permits. For groups, the cost of a single permit will not exceed $100.

Maps: For a map, ask the U.S. Forest Service for Desolation Wilderness or Lake Tahoe Basin Management Unit. A Lake Tahoe or Desolation Wilderness map is also available from Tom Harrison Maps. For topographic maps, ask the USGS for Homewood and Rockbound Valley.

Directions: From Truckee, take Highway 89 south and drive to Tahoe City. Turn right on Highway 89 and drive south for 10 miles to Meeks Bay Resort. Look for a small dirt parking lot across from the resort, on the west side of the highway, and park there. The trailhead is well marked.

Contact: Lake Tahoe Basin Management Unit, 35 College Drive, South Lake Tahoe, CA 96150, 530/543-2600, www.fs.fed.us/r5; Visitors Center (open only in summer), 530/543-2674.

52 RUBICON AND LIGHTHOUSE LOOP
2.0 mi / 1.0 hr　　　🚶1 ⛰️10

in D. L. Bliss State Park on the west shore of Lake Tahoe

Map 6.2, page 214

If you're visiting Lake Tahoe, you should not leave the area without sampling at least a piece of this magnificent pathway. The trail edges along the steep cliffs on the west side of the lake and provides sweeping lake views. An excellent short trip on the Rubicon is this loop, which starts from Calawee Cove Beach, at D. L. Bliss State Park. Although the hike has very little elevation gain, it's not for those who are afraid of heights, because there are 100-foot drop-offs along the trail's edge, leading straight down to Lake Tahoe. Cables are in place in some sections to keep people from falling off the trail. Hike 0.25 mile to a spur trail leading to the old lighthouse (there's no view, but check out the remains of a 1916 lighthouse), then continue beyond it for another 0.5 mile. The lake and mountain views are mind-boggling every step of the way. Bear right at the trail junction and walk to a parking lot, where you can pick up Lighthouse Trail and loop back to Calawee Cove Beach. On the other hand, if you want to see those lake vistas one more time, forget about the loop and just head back the way you came. Not everybody is up for hiking the entire length of the Rubicon Trail (but this loop is a good sample).

User Groups: Hikers only. No dogs, horses, or mountain bikes. No wheelchair facilities.

Permits: No permits are required. A day-use fee of $8 is charged per vehicle.

Maps: A map of D. L. Bliss State Park is available for a fee at the entrance station. A Lake Tahoe map is available for a fee from Tom Harrison Maps. For a topographic map, ask the USGS for Emerald Bay.

Directions: From South Lake Tahoe, take Highway 89 north past Emerald Bay and continue a short distance to the entrance road for D. L. Bliss State Park. Turn right and drive 0.5 mile to the entrance station and continue for 0.7 mile to a fork. Turn right and drive another 0.7 mile to Calawee Cove Beach and the parking lot. The Rubicon Trail begins on the far side of the lot. If this lot is full, you will have to use one of the other day-use parking lots in the park.

Contact: D. L. Bliss State Park, P.O. Box 266, Tahoma, CA 96142, 530/525-7277 or 530/525-3345, www.parks.ca.gov.

53 RUBICON TRAIL
9.0 mi / 5.0 hr　　　🚶2 ⛰️10

in D. L. Bliss State Park on the west shore of Lake Tahoe

Map 6.2, page 214　　　　　　　BEST 🌙

The Rubicon Trail is the premier Lake Tahoe day hike. Accept no substitutes. If you want the best scenery that Lake Tahoe offers, this is the trail to hike. The only problem? Right—it's you and about a zillion other hikers. If you possibly can, walk this trail in the off-season (late September is great), and do it on a weekday. Better yet, do it at dawn or dusk. Then get ready for eye-popping scenery as you gaze out across the surface and deep into the depths of sparkling, clear, 12-mile-wide Lake Tahoe and the rim of mountains that surround it. The trail stays close to the lake edge and has very little elevation change, just some mild ups and downs, holding steady near 6,300 feet. Highlights include Rubicon Point, Emerald Point, Emerald Bay, Fannette Island, Vikingsholm Castle, and Eagle Point. If you stop for a picnic, don't be surprised if several little ground squirrels visit you, hoping for a hand-out. If you prefer, you can start and end your Rubicon hike at Vikingsholm: Leave your car in the Emerald Bay Overlook parking lot, hike down to Vikingsholm, and then head north to the boat-in campground and beyond. But note that finding room in the parking lot in summer is nearly impossible except for those arriving very early in the day. In addition, you'll add on nearly two miles round-trip getting from the parking lot to Vikingsholm, during which there is a 600-foot elevation change.

Note: If you start the hike at Calawee Cove Beach, just after setting out on the Rubicon Trail, be sure to take the left fork, which will keep you on Rubicon Trail.

User Groups: Hikers only. No dogs, horses, or mountain bikes. No wheelchair facilities.

Permits: No permits are required. A day-use fee of $8 is charged per vehicle.

Maps: A map of D. L. Bliss State Park is available for a fee at the entrance station. A Lake Tahoe map is available for a fee from Tom Harrison Maps. For a topographic map, ask the USGS for Emerald Bay.

Directions: From South Lake Tahoe, take Highway 89 north past Emerald Bay and continue a short distance to the entrance road for D. L. Bliss State Park. Turn right and drive 0.5 mile to the entrance station, then continue for 0.7 mile to a fork. Turn right and drive another 0.7 mile to Calawee Cove Beach and the parking lot. The Rubicon Trail begins on the far side of the lot. If this lot is full, you will have to use one of the other day-use parking lots in the park.

Contact: D. L. Bliss State Park, P.O. Box 266, Tahoma, CA 96142, 530/525-7277 or 530/525-3345, www.parks.ca.gov.

54 BALANCING ROCK
1.0 mi / 0.5 hr

in D. L. Bliss State Park on the west shore of Lake Tahoe

Map 6.2, page 214

The Balancing Rock is a big hunk of granite that has been a curiosity at Lake Tahoe for eons. It's a 130-ton rock that sits balanced on a small rock pedestal, like a giant golf ball on an itty-bitty golf tee. The trail's interpretive brochure explains that eventually erosion will wear away the pedestal and cause the Balancing Rock to lose its balance, but Tahoe lovers have been awaiting this event forever, and it

still hasn't happened. In addition to Balancing Rock, the trail shows off many of the plants and trees of the Tahoe area. It's a good learning experience for both kids and adults.

User Groups: Hikers only. No dogs, horses, or mountain bikes. No wheelchair facilities.

Permits: No permits are required. A day-use fee of $8 is charged per vehicle.

Maps: A map of D. L. Bliss State Park is available for a fee at the entrance station. A Lake Tahoe map is available for a fee from Tom Harrison Maps. For a topographic map, ask the USGS for Emerald Bay.

Directions: From South Lake Tahoe, take Highway 89 north past Emerald Bay and continue a short distance to the entrance road for D. L. Bliss State Park. Turn right and drive 0.5 mile to the entrance station, then continue for 0.7 mile to a fork. Turn left and drive 0.25 mile to the Balancing Rock parking lot, on the left.

Contact: D. L. Bliss State Park, P.O. Box 266, Tahoma, CA 96142, 530/525-7277 or 530/525-3345, www.parks.ca.gov.

55 VIKINGSHOLM
2.0 mi / 1.0 hr

in Emerald Bay State Park on the west shore of Lake Tahoe

Map 6.2, page 214

If you can take this walk very early in the morning, and preferably on a weekday, you'll experience the incredible beauty that has made Lake Tahoe the revered vacation destination that it is. If you take this walk at almost any other time, be prepared for a lot of company. Although the destination of this one-mile trail (really a dirt road) is Vikingsholm, a Viking castle built by an heiress in 1929, the beauty lies in the scenery spread out before you as you hike downhill. You'll see spectacular Fannette Island and the deep blue waters of Emerald Bay, and you'll travel through an old-growth cedar and pine forest. You even gain access to some of Lake Tahoe's coveted sandy shoreline.

Although visitors have to pay a buck to tour the inside of the castle, you can hike to it for free and add on a side trip to the base of 150-foot Eagle Falls, situated 0.25 mile from Vikingsholm. For many people, the surprise on this trail is that the return hike has a 500-foot elevation gain. What, you mean we have to breathe hard?

Special Note: Be sure to arrive early. By midmorning on weekends, visitors are forced to park up to two miles away.

User Groups: Hikers only. No dogs, horses, or mountain bikes. No wheelchair facilities.

Permits: No permits are required. A fee of $6 is charged per vehicle. There is a fee to tour the inside of the castle.

Maps: A map of Emerald Bay and D. L. Bliss State Parks is available for a fee at the visitors center at Vikingsholm. A Lake Tahoe map is available for a fee from Tom Harrison Maps. For a topographic map, ask the USGS for Emerald Bay.

Directions: From South Lake Tahoe, take Highway 89 north and drive nine miles to the Emerald Bay Overlook parking lot on the east side of Highway 89. The trail begins from the lake side of the parking lot.

Contact: Emerald Bay State Park, P.O. Box 266, Tahoma, CA 96142, 530/541-3030, visitor center 530/525-3345, www.parks.ca.gov.

56 UPPER EAGLE FALLS AND EAGLE LAKE
2.0 mi / 1.0 hr   👣2 ⛰9

off Highway 89 near South Lake Tahoe

Map 6.2, page 214

This is one of the most popular hikes in the entire Tahoe region, perhaps number two only to the trail to Vikingsholm. A sign by the restroom at the Eagle Falls Picnic Area points hikers to Upper Eagle Falls Trail. Unfortunately this is something of a "designer" path, with natural granite cut into flagstone-like stairs and an elaborate wooden bridge that escorts visitors over the top of the falls.

Still it's a beautiful walk, best taken early in the morning and during the week, when the masses aren't around. The waterfall pours right under the hikers' bridge. (If you want to see the "other" Eagle Falls, the one that drops right along Highway 89, see the listing in this chapter). Immediately after the bridge, the designer aspect of the trail ends as you enter the Desolation Wilderness and climb 400 feet in less than a mile to reach rocky Eagle Lake, surrounded by granite cliffs. People fish and picnic here; some even try to swim in the icy water.

User Groups: Hikers and dogs. No horses or mountain bikes. No wheelchair facilities.

Permits: Day hikers must fill out a free permit at the wilderness trailhead. A $5 parking fee is charged per vehicle.

Maps: For a map, ask the U.S. Forest Service for Desolation Wilderness or Lake Tahoe Basin Management Unit. A Lake Tahoe map is available for a fee from Tom Harrison Maps. For a topographic map, ask the USGS for Emerald Bay.

Directions: From South Lake Tahoe, take Highway 89 north and drive 8.5 miles to the Eagle Falls Picnic Area and trailhead. Turn left into the parking area, or park in the roadside pullout just north of the picnic area on the west side of Highway 89.

Contact: Lake Tahoe Basin Management Unit, 35 College Drive, South Lake Tahoe, CA 96150, 530/543-2600, www.fs.fed.us/r5; Visitors Center (open only in summer), 530/543-2674.

57 VELMA LAKES
10.0 mi / 5.0 hr   👣3 ⛰9

in the Desolation Wilderness

Map 6.2, page 214

The Velma Lakes are classic Desolation: gorgeous, alpine jewels. This route follows the trail to Eagle Falls and Eagle Lake (see listing in this chapter) for the first mile, then climbs through a rugged, glaciated landscape, with only occasional hardy lodgepole pines and twisted junipers providing meager shade. The lack of trees and the abundance of rock mean wide-open views and plenty of granite drama: Welcome to the Sierra high country.

At three miles, you intersect the trail heading southwest (left) to Dicks Lake, but you should head northwest (right) for Velma Lakes. Your trail heads directly to Middle Velma Lake (in one mile), the most popular of the lakes. It has several granite islands and is favored for swimming. You can take a left cutoff just before Middle Velma Lake and head south to Upper Velma Lake in 0.5 mile, or follow a use trail north along a creek to Lower Velma Lake (on your right, also 0.5 mile away).

Note that hikers can also begin the Velma Lakes hike from the trailhead at Bayview Campground, but then they miss out on seeing Eagle Lake and a world-class view of Tahoe. Remember to bring your sunscreen because the rocky trail to the Velma Lakes is exposed and open.

User Groups: Hikers and dogs. No horses or mountain bikes (the Bayview Trail provides access for horses; contact Tahoe Basin National Forest). No wheelchair facilities. To reach Velma Lakes, equestrians must access from another trailhead; Bayview trailhead is the best for this.

Permits: Permits are required year-round for both day and overnight use. Day hikers may obtain a free permit from a ranger station or may self-issue at most major trailheads. Backpackers camping in Desolation Wilderness are subject to trailhead quotas. There is a $5 reservation fee, plus $5 per person for one night, $10 per person for two or more nights up to 14 days (nonrefundable). Children ages 12 and under are free. Golden Passes do not apply to personal-use permits. For groups, the cost of a single permit will not exceed $100. A $7 parking fee is charged per vehicle.

Maps: For a map, ask the U.S. Forest Service for Desolation Wilderness or Lake Tahoe Basin Management Unit. A Lake Tahoe or Desolation Wilderness map is available from Tom Harrison Maps. For topographic maps,

ask the USGS for Emerald Bay and Rockbound Valley.

Directions: From South Lake Tahoe, take Highway 89 north and drive 8.5 miles to the Eagle Falls Picnic Area and trailhead. Turn left into the parking area or park in the roadside pullout just north of the picnic area, on the west side of Highway 89.

Contact: Lake Tahoe Basin Management Unit, 35 College Drive, South Lake Tahoe, CA 96150, 530/543-2600, www.fs.fed.us/r5; Visitors Center (open only in summer), 530/543-2674.

58 CASCADE FALLS

2.0 mi / 1.0 hr   🏃1 ⛰10

off Highway 89 near South Lake Tahoe

Map 6.2, page 214

This trail is the best easy hike at Lake Tahoe. It's short and flat enough for almost anybody to make the trip, including young children, but it still feels like wilderness. The one-mile trail leads to the brink of a stunning 200-foot cascade that drops into the southwest end of Cascade Lake.

From the trailhead at Bayview Campground, take the left fork signed for Cascade Falls. In five minutes, you get tremendous views of Cascade Lake (elevation 6,464 feet) below to your left. Then you start to hear and see the falls. The trail disintegrates as it nears the waterfall's edge, and hikers with children shouldn't get too close. But no matter; the best views are actually farther back on the trail. Upstream of the falls are some lovely pools surrounded by wide shelves of granite. Make sure you visit in spring or early summer, when the waterfall is flowing full and wide, because by August, it loses its drama.

User Groups: Hikers and dogs. No horses or mountain bikes. No wheelchair facilities.

Permits: No permits are required. Parking and access are free.

Maps: For a map, ask the U.S. Forest Service for Lake Tahoe Basin Management Unit. A

Lake Tahoe map is available for a fee from Tom Harrison Maps. For a topographic map, ask the USGS for Emerald Bay.

Directions: From South Lake Tahoe, take Highway 89 north and drive 7.5 miles to the Bayview Campground. Turn left and drive to the far end of the campground to the trailhead parking area. If it's full, park on the shoulder of Highway 89 by the campground entrance.

Contact: Lake Tahoe Basin Management Unit, 35 College Drive, South Lake Tahoe, CA 96150, 530/543-2600, www.fs.fed.us/r5; Visitors Center (open only in summer), 530/543-2674.

59 MOUNT TALLAC (TALLAC TRAILHEAD)

9.0 mi / 6.0 hr   🏃5 ⛰10

in the Desolation Wilderness near Fallen Leaf Lake

Map 6.2, page 214

If you are hiking Mount Tallac for the first time, start instead from the Glen Alpine Trailhead. If you've already done that and you want a steeper challenge, then the Mount Tallac Trailhead is for you. Mount Tallac towers over Lake Tahoe and provides one of the most beautiful lookouts in North America. From the 9,375-foot summit, you look down on Fallen Leaf Lake, Cascade Lake, Emerald Bay, Lake Tahoe, and beyond to Mount Rose on the eastern Tahoe rim. To the west are miles of Desolation Wilderness.

But you pay dearly from this starting point: You climb 2,600 feet over the final three miles, plus another 900-foot climb in the first 1.5 miles. From the trailhead, you make the first butt-kicker climb for 1.7 miles to Floating Island Lake. You get excellent views of Fallen Leaf Lake and Lake Tahoe along the way. Then it's another 0.7 mile to a trail junction just before Cathedral Lake, where a trail from Fallen Leaf Lake joins this trail. Cathedral Lake is a good rest stop before making the final ascent to the top of Mount Tallac, a 2.4-mile butt-kicker of a climb on a rocky trail. It's made somewhat easier by a continuous and inspiring parade of vistas, including long looks at Gilmore Lake, Susie Lake, and Lake Aloha. The trail ends 0.25 mile below the summit, where it meets the other Mount Tallac trail coming from Gilmore Lake. Bear right, and boulder hop your way to the top.

The return trip down is terrible for many, a knee-screaming, toe-jamming affair that will have some questioning the purpose of life.

User Groups: Hikers and dogs. No horses or mountain bikes. No wheelchair facilities.

Permits: Permits are required year-round for both day and overnight use. Day hikers may obtain a free permit from a ranger station or may self-issue at most major trailheads. Backpackers camping in Desolation Wilderness are subject to trailhead quotas. There is a $5 reservation fee, plus $5 per person for one night, $10 per person for two or more nights up to 14 days (nonrefundable). Children ages 12 and under are free. Golden Passes do not apply to personal-use permits. For groups, the cost of a single permit will not exceed $100.

Maps: For a map, ask the U.S. Forest Service for Desolation Wilderness. A Lake Tahoe or Desolation Wilderness map is also available for a fee from Tom Harrison Maps. For a topographic map, ask the USGS for Emerald Bay.

Directions: From South Lake Tahoe, take Highway 89 north and drive 3.8 miles to the signed turnoff for Mount Tallac and Camp Concord (on the left, across the highway from the sign for Baldwin Beach). Drive 0.4 mile to the trailhead spur. Turn left and drive 0.6 mile to the trailhead.

Contact: Lake Tahoe Basin Management Unit, 35 College Drive, South Lake Tahoe, CA 96150, 530/543-2600, www.fs.fed.us/r5; Visitors Center (open only in summer), 530/543-2674.

60 RAINBOW AND LAKE OF THE SKY TRAILS

0.5 mi / 0.5 hr   🚶1 ⛰️8

in Tahoe National Forest near
South Lake Tahoe

Map 6.2, page 214   **BEST** ☾

Several short interpretive walks begin at the Lake Tahoe Visitors Center. The best is the Rainbow Trail and Lake of the Sky Trail. You can hike them both from the same starting point at the visitors center and combine an interesting nature lesson with a walk along Lake Tahoe's shoreline for exceptional scenery and views.

Start with Rainbow Trail, which leads from the visitors center's west side and takes you to Taylor Creek and its Stream Profile Chamber. The creek is where thousands of kokanee salmon come to spawn in the fall, and visitors can view them through the glass walls of the profile chamber. You can also see them the ordinary way, just by peering into the creek as you walk. Then loop back to the visitors center and pick up Lake of the Sky Trail. You'll pass by Taylor Creek Marsh on your way to Tallac Point and Tahoe's shoreline. In summer, people go swimming at this sandy stretch of beach.

User Groups: Hikers and wheelchair users. No dogs, horses, or mountain bikes.

Permits: No permits are required. Parking and access are free.

Maps: For a map, ask the U.S. Forest Service for Lake Tahoe Basin Management Unit. A free forest recreation newspaper is also available. A Lake Tahoe map is available for a fee from Tom Harrison Maps. For a topographic map, ask the USGS for Emerald Bay.

Directions: From South Lake Tahoe, take Highway 89 north and drive three miles to the Lake Tahoe Visitors Center turnoff, on the right. Turn right and drive to the visitors center parking lot, where the trails begin.

Contact: Lake Tahoe Basin Management Unit, 35 College Drive, South Lake Tahoe, CA 96150, 530/543-2600, www.fs.fed.us/ r5; Visitors Center (open only in summer), 530/543-2674.

61 MOUNT TALLAC LOOP (GLEN ALPINE TRAILHEAD)

11.6 mi / 7.5 hr   🚶4 ⛰️10

in the Desolation Wilderness near
Fallen Leaf Lake

Map 6.2, page 214

Your first steps on Mount Tallac are flamed by a craving for one of the greatest 360-degree views in North America. They are also singed and tempered by the challenge of a 3,175-foot climb in 5.8 miles (one-way) to reach the summit. Tallac towers over Lake Tahoe, where the lake and sky seem to merge into a cobalt-blue spectacle. Once at top at 9,735 feet, you can then turn to the west and take in the granite, ice, and lakes of the vast Desolation Wilderness. In all, the scope covers more than 5,000 square miles of Tahoe paradise.

There are two routes up. The preferred route starts at the Glen Alpine Trailhead, located just beyond the head of Fallen Leaf Lake. The trek comes in three stages. The trail starts easy and flat, and in the first mile, becomes a rocky jeep trail to a former historic camp and a few old cabins. On your left, you pass gorgeous Glen Alpine Falls, still flush with runoff from snowmelt. The air is scented with pine duff, and for those who are imprinted by Tahoe, the familiar tang in the air can make you feel like you are home again. Pass a wood sign that marks the entry point for Desolation Wilderness, a threshold moment, and shortly later, before climbing up Glen Alpine Canyon. Most make quick work of the first 1.7 miles to a trail junction, signed for Grass Lake on your left and Gilmore Lake on your right.

The second stage of the hike rises out of the canyon 2.6 miles to Gilmore Lake. It's a steady climb all the way, where trail builders installed enough switchbacks to keep the grade just right; we never went aerobic at any point, just walked right up. Even in early August, it is common to see tons of wildflowers, with lots of lupine, mule's ear, paintbrush, and rafts of corn lilies. Creeks are flush with clear, cold water, and miniature waterfalls. If you stand too long to enjoy them, mosquitoes and biting flies will attack—a small price to pay for beauty in the high country. Gilmore Lake, nestled in a basin at 8,290 feet at the foot of Tallac's backside, is a perfect stop for a rest or snack, with a confluence of trails to meet other hikers. Some will make camp here. It's one of the better lakes in Desolation to fish. At dusk, the trout rise to the surface to feed and sound like little popguns going off.

The last stretch to the top climbs 1,445 feet in 1.6 miles. As you leave Gilmore, the climb is easy and the hillside is buried in greenery and tons of wildflowers. Soon enough though it gets steeper, and most will puff their way above tree line. The last 0.5 mile is the steepest as you approach the cragged rim. In a few steps, you reach the mountain crest and the Tahoe basin is unveiled before you. The trail diminishes in the rock, but you can still make out a faint route that leads to the summit where one of the most eye-popping views in North America is yours. On top, there is a single rock perch that crowns Tallac's summit. Nearby, there are many slabs that seem built for you to take a seat, slow the world down, and take it all in. Pray for a clear day with no haze. Directly below you, the slope plummets 3,000 feet to Fallen Leaf Lake near your starting point, and extends across a sea of pines and aspens to Cascade Lake, Emerald Bay, and Lake Tahoe. The lake is so big and so deep blue, that for many it evokes emotion that can last for years. The eastern horizon is topped by Monument Peak, Freel Peak, and Mount Rose in Nevada. The view to the west into Desolation is equally profound—across distant Aloha Lake to huge snow-packed slopes that reach up to Pyramid Peak, Mount Price, and the rim that crests the Crystal Basin.

User Groups: Hikers and dogs. No horses or mountain bikes. No wheelchair facilities.

Permits: Permits are required year-round for both day and overnight use. Day hikers may obtain a free permit from a ranger station or may self-issue at most major trailheads. Backpackers camping in Desolation Wilderness are subject to trailhead quotas. There is a $5 reservation fee, plus $5 per person for one night, $10 per person for two or more nights up to 14 days (nonrefundable). Children ages 12 and under are free. Golden Passes do not apply to personal-use permits. For groups, the cost of a single permit will not exceed $100.

Maps: For a map, ask the U.S. Forest Service for Desolation Wilderness. A Lake Tahoe or Desolation Wilderness map is also available for a fee from Tom Harrison Maps. For a topographic map, ask the USGS for Echo Lake.

Directions: From South Lake Tahoe, take Highway 89 north and drive 2.9 miles to Fallen Leaf Lake Road. Turn left and drive 4.8 miles on a narrow road past the Fallen Leaf Marina to a fork. Take the left fork on Road 1216, signed for Lily Lake and the Desolation Wilderness. Drive 0.7 mile to the trailhead, at the road's end.

Contact: Lake Tahoe Basin Management Unit, 35 College Drive, South Lake Tahoe, CA 96150, 530/543-2600, www.fs.fed.us/r5; Visitors Center (open only in summer), 530/543-2674.

62 GILMORE LAKE

7.6 mi / 4.0 hr 🚶3 ⛰9

in the Desolation Wilderness near
Fallen Leaf Lake

Map 6.2, page 214

If you only have time to day-hike to one destination near South Lake Tahoe, Gilmore Lake is an excellent choice. Everything about it is a classic Lake Tahoe and Desolation Wilderness trip, a collection of the best the area has to offer. You get to visit a scenic alpine lake, and along the way, you are treated to fields of wildflowers, mountain vistas, forests, and more. Of course, we're not the only ones who like this trail, so all the usual disclaimers apply about timing your trip for the off-season or during the week.

With that said, take off from the Glen Alpine trailhead and hike down the road past the private cabins. The rocky road eventually becomes a rocky trail. This cobblestone-like stretch is by far the worst part of the hike; the rocks make it rough going for hikers' ankles and knees. Bear right at the junction with Grass Lake Trail, 1.5 miles in, where the trail surface improves dramatically. Get ready to do the majority of this trail's climbing, heading for more trail junctions at nearly three miles in, where paths lead off to the left, to Susie and Heather Lakes. Bear right instead for Gilmore Lake, the largest lake in this area between Fallen Leaf Lake and Lake Aloha. You'll reach it at 3.5 miles, with a total 1,700-foot elevation gain. Despite the fact that many people cruise by Gilmore Lake each day on their way to climb Mount Tallac, few take the time to hang out for long by the lake's sapphire-blue waters. The lake, ringed by grassy, flower-filled meadows, manages to stay secluded and pristine.

User Groups: Hikers and dogs. No horses or mountain bikes. No wheelchair facilities.

Permits: Permits are required year-round for both day and overnight use. Day hikers may obtain a free permit from a ranger station or can self-issue at the Glen Alpine trailhead. Backpackers camping in Desolation Wilderness are subject to trailhead quotas. There is a $5 reservation fee, plus $5 per person for one night, $10 per person for two or more nights up to 14 days (nonrefundable). Children ages 12 and under are free. Golden Passes do not apply to personal-use permits. For groups, the cost of a single permit will not exceed $100.

Maps: For a map, ask the U.S. Forest Service for Desolation Wilderness. A Lake Tahoe or Desolation Wilderness map is also available for a fee from Tom Harrison Maps. For a topographic map, ask the USGS for Emerald Bay.

Directions: From South Lake Tahoe, take Highway 89 north and drive 2.9 miles to Fallen Leaf Lake Road. Turn left and drive

4.8 miles on a narrow road past the Fallen Leaf Marina to a fork. Take the left fork on Road 1216, signed for Lily Lake and the Desolation Wilderness. Drive 0.7 mile to the trailhead, at the road's end.

Contact: Lake Tahoe Basin Management Unit, 35 College Drive, South Lake Tahoe, CA 96150, 530/543-2600, www.fs.fed.us/r5; Visitors Center (open only in summer), 530/543-2674.

63 SUSIE AND HEATHER LAKES
10.0 mi / 5.0 hr

in the Desolation Wilderness near
Fallen Leaf Lake

Map 6.2, page 214

Many people believe they must hike for days in the beautiful Desolation Wilderness to see the rugged alpine beauty of the Tahoe wildlands. Not so. This trip, a day hike to Susie and Heather Lakes, is a perfect example.

The trail to Susie and Heather Lakes begins as a rocky road and passes some summer cabins and a waterfall on Glen Alpine Creek. At 1.2 miles, the road ends near an old resort and you'll see a sign for Gilmore, Susie, and Grass Lakes. Start to climb, and shortly, you'll enter the Desolation Wilderness boundary. You can take the short left cutoff to little Grass Lake (adding one mile each way to your trip) or continue straight, which is signed for Susie, Heather, and Aloha Lakes. At four miles, you'll reach the eastern shore of Susie Lake, then hike alongside it and around the lake's southern edge to continue another mile to Heather Lake. The granite-lined lake is deep and wide, and is set in a landscape of classic high Sierra scenery.

User Groups: Hikers, dogs, and horses. No mountain bikes. No wheelchair facilities.

Permits: Permits are required year-round for both day and overnight use. Day hikers may obtain a free permit from a ranger station or may self-issue the Glen Alpine trailhead.

Backpackers camping in Desolation Wilderness are subject to trailhead quotas. There is a $5 reservation fee, plus $5 per person for one night, $10 per person for two or more nights up to 14 days (nonrefundable). Children ages 12 and under are free. Golden Passes do not apply to personal-use permits. For groups, the cost of a single permit will not exceed $100.

Maps: For a map, ask the U.S. Forest Service for Desolation Wilderness. A Lake Tahoe or Desolation Wilderness map is also available for a fee from Tom Harrison Maps. For a topographic map, ask the USGS for Emerald Bay.

Directions: From South Lake Tahoe, take Highway 89 north and drive 2.9 miles to Fallen Leaf Lake Road. Turn left and drive 4.8 miles on a narrow road past the Fallen Leaf Marina to a fork. Take the left fork on Road 1216, signed for Lily Lake and the Desolation Wilderness. Drive 0.7 mile to the trailhead, at the road's end.

Contact: Lake Tahoe Basin Management Unit, 35 College Drive, South Lake Tahoe, CA 96150, 530/543-2600, www.fs.fed.us/r5; Visitors Center (open only in summer), 530/543-2674.

64 FALLEN LEAF LAKE TRAIL
2.0 mi / 1.0 hr

near South Lake Tahoe

Map 6.2, page 214 BEST

Fallen Leaf Lake, at 6,400 feet in elevation, is the second-largest lake in the Tahoe Basin, and some say it's the prettiest. Too bad most of its shorefront lands are privately owned. But luckily, this path allows you access to the part that is public. The short, mostly flat trail leads from the trailhead to the lake and then along its northern edge to the dam, which you can walk across. Much of the trail hugs the lake's shoreline, so you can look out across the blue water and feel that sense of peace that comes from the sight of deep, sapphire waters. You also get excellent views of Glen Alpine Canyon and Mount Tallac. In the fall,

the shoreline of Fallen Leaf Lake is one of the best spots near Tahoe to admire the quaking aspens turning gold. Campers staying at Fallen Leaf Lake Campground can access this trail from their tents.

User Groups: Hikers, dogs, horses, and mountain bikes. No wheelchair facilities.

Permits: No permits are required. Parking and access are free.

Maps: For a map, ask the U.S. Forest Service for Lake Tahoe Basin Management Unit. A Lake Tahoe map is available for a fee from Tom Harrison Maps. For a topographic map, ask the USGS for Emerald Bay.

Directions: From South Lake Tahoe, take Highway 89 north and drive 2.9 miles to Fallen Leaf Lake Road. Turn left and drive 0.8 mile to the Fallen Leaf Lake dirt parking area on the right. It is not signed.

Contact: Lake Tahoe Basin Management Unit, 35 College Drive, South Lake Tahoe, CA 96150, 530/543-2600, www.fs.fed.us/r5; Visitors Center (open only in summer), 530/543-2674.

65 ANGORA LAKES TRAIL
1.0 mi / 0.5 hr

at Angora Lake near South Lake Tahoe in Tahoe National Forest

Map 6.2, page 214 BEST

Upper Angora Lake is a sight to behold. The little lake is a pristine jewel back by a high granite wall. From the parking lot, hike uphill on the signed dirt road, and in 15 minutes, you'll be looking at Lower Angora Lake off to the left, which has a few cabins on its far side. Continue beyond its edge another 0.25 mile and, voilà, you reach the upper lake and Angora Lakes Resort, built in 1917. Although the resort cabins are always rented way in advance, day users can buy a lemonade and sit at a picnic table to watch the action, or take part in it, at the small, picturesque lake. Action? What action? Rowboats can be rented for a few bucks for a romantic cruise about the little lake. In mid-summer, toddlers wade around at the shallow beach area, and plenty of folks just plunk themselves down along the shoreline to stare at the bowl-shaped, glacial cirque lake. It has a high granite wall on its far side, where in early summer a waterfall of snowmelt flows down to the lake. The Angora Lakes are extremely popular with children's day camps and groups, and on some days, the little ones outnumber the old folks.

User Groups: Hikers, dogs, horses, and mountain bikes. No wheelchair facilities.

Permits: No permits are required. Parking is $7.

Maps: For a map, ask the U.S. Forest Service for Lake Tahoe Basin Management Unit. A Lake Tahoe map is available for a fee from Tom Harrison Maps. For a topographic map, ask the USGS for Echo Lake.

Directions: From South Lake Tahoe, take Highway 89 north and drive 2.9 miles to Fallen Leaf Lake Road. Turn left and drive two miles to a fork. Turn left and drive 0.5 mile to Forest Road 12N14. Bear right on Forest Service Road 12N14 and drive 2.3 miles (great views to the right) to the road's end and the trailhead.

Contact: Lake Tahoe Basin Management Unit, 35 College Drive, South Lake Tahoe, CA 96150, 530/543-2600, www.fs.fed.us/r5; Visitors Center, (open only in summer), 530/543-2674.

66 ROCKBOUND PASS AND LAKE DORIS

12.0 mi / 6.0 hr-2 days

in the Desolation Wilderness

Map 6.2, page 214

To make the epic trip to 8,650-foot Rockbound Pass, follow the trail notes for the route to Gertrude and Tyler Lakes (see listing in this chapter) for the first 1.9 miles. Bear left to stay on Rockbound Pass Trail and hike through mixed conifers to get your first glimpse of Rockbound Pass at 2.5 miles, a distant notch

in the mountains to the north. To reach it, you must descend a bit and cross the Jones Fork of Silver Creek, then parallel the stream on its course from Maud Lake. You're traveling in very rocky terrain now. The trail is even blasted out of granite in places. You'll reach the western shores of 7,700-foot Maud Lake at 4.5 miles. Many backpackers make camp here, while day hikers continue the ascent to the pass. It's not much farther; after a steady climb, you gain its wide summit at 5.9 miles. The views of Desolation Wilderness open wide, including views back at Maud Lake and ahead to Lake Doris, but the howling wind often prevents hikers from staying long. If that's the case, descend 0.5 mile to Lake Doris, just to the left of the trail, where you can make camp, or if you're day hiking, just hang out and rest. The total elevation gain on this trip is 1,700 feet, plus a short descent to Lake Doris.

User Groups: Hikers, dogs, and horses. No mountain bikes. No wheelchair facilities.

Permits: Permits are required year-round for both day and overnight use. Day hikers may obtain a free permit from a ranger station or may self-issue at most major trailheads. Backpackers camping in Desolation Wilderness are subject to trailhead quotas. There is a $5 reservation fee, plus $5 per person for one night, $10 per person for two or more nights up to 14 days (nonrefundable). Children ages 12 and under are free. Golden Passes do not apply to personal-use permits. For groups, the cost of a single permit will not exceed $100.

Directions: From Placerville, take Highway 50 east for 40 miles to Kyburz and continue five miles to the signed turnoff for Wrights Lake on the north side of the highway (about 15 miles west of South Lake Tahoe). Turn left (north) on Wrights Lake Road and drive eight miles to Wrights Lake Visitors Center. Continue straight for 0.5 mile to the Rockbound trailhead (on the way to Dark Lake).

Contact: Eldorado National Forest, Pacific Ranger District, 7887 Highway 50, Pollock Pines, CA 95726, 530/644-2349, www.fs.fed.us/r5.

67 GERTRUDE AND TYLER LAKES
9.0 mi / 5.0 hr or 2 days 🥾4 ⛰️9

in the Desolation Wilderness

Map 6.2, page 214

There's a ton of stellar hiking to be accomplished in the Wrights Lake area. The trip to Gertrude and Tyler Lakes stands out. It provides great scenery, a good workout, and a chance to practice your cross-country skills on the way to Tyler Lake. A clearly defined trail leads to pretty Gertrude Lake. But Tyler Lake, higher and lovelier, is found only by those who forge their own way. That makes for a fun little adventure if you desire.

Begin on Rockbound Pass Trail, passing pastoral Beauty Lake 0.5 mile out and continuing on a remarkably easy path until you see a sign for Tyler Lake at 1.9 miles. There, bear right and prepare to work a lot harder for the rest of the hike. One memorable 0.5-mile stretch goes straight uphill and will cause you to question your sanity. Luckily the worst part doesn't last long, and the views of the spectacular peaks of the Crystal Range will distract you. At 3.5 miles you'll reach a hard-to-spot left spur trail (100 yards long) leading to the grave of William Tyler, a rancher who died here in a blizzard in the 1920s. A half mile beyond this cutoff is Gertrude Lake, at 8,000 feet. A nearly invisible right fork just past the grave cutoff is the start of an unmaintained trail to Tyler Lake, which lies 400 feet higher than Gertrude Lake. If you miss the use trail turnoff, watch for occasional rock cairns and keep an eye on your trail map. Tyler Lake lies 0.5 mile southeast of Gertrude Lake.

Of the two lakes, Tyler is more beautiful, set in a granite basin with a few sparse pines on its shores. Because it's slightly difficult to locate, you have an excellent chance at solitude at Tyler Lake, even on summer weekends.

User Groups: Hikers, dogs, and horses. No mountain bikes. No wheelchair facilities.

Permits: Permits are required year-round for both day and overnight use. Day hikers may obtain a free permit from a ranger station or may self-issue at most major trailheads. Backpackers camping in Desolation Wilderness are subject to trailhead quotas. There is a $5 reservation fee, plus $5 per person for one night, $10 per person for two or more nights up to 14 days (nonrefundable). Children ages 12 and under are free. Golden Passes do not apply to personal-use permits. For groups, the cost of a single permit will not exceed $100.

Maps: For a map, ask the U.S. Forest Service for Desolation Wilderness or Eldorado National Forest. A Lake Tahoe or Desolation Wilderness map is also available from Tom Harrison Maps. For topographic maps, ask the USGS for Pyramid Peak and Rockbound Valley.

Directions: From Placerville, take Highway 50 east for 40 miles to Kyburz and continue five miles to the signed turnoff for Wrights Lake (about 15 miles west of South Lake Tahoe). Turn left (north) on Wrights Lake Road and drive eight miles to Wrights Lake Visitors Center. Continue straight past the visitors center for 0.5 mile to the Rockbound trailhead (on the way to Dark Lake).

Contact: Eldorado National Forest, Pacific Ranger District, 7887 Highway 50, Pollock Pines, CA 95726, 530/644-2349, www.fs.fed.us/r5; Lake Tahoe Basin Management Unit, 35 College Drive, South Lake Tahoe, CA 96150, 530/543-2600, www.fs.fed.us/r5; Visitors Center (open only in summer), 530/543-2674.

68 TWIN AND ISLAND LAKES
6.4 mi / 4.0 hr or 2 days 🥾3 ⛰️10

in the Desolation Wilderness

Map 6.2, page 214

Of all the hiking possibilities in the Wrights Lake area, this trip is hands-down the most scenic. It is crowned by the most striking views in the entire Desolation Wilderness and miles of solid granite under your feet as you walk. The trail is extremely well marked, and its moderate grade is suitable for all types of hikers. The first 1.2 miles from the Twin Lakes trailhead have only a gentle climb to the intersection with the trail to Grouse, Hemlock, and Smith Lakes. Bear left for Twin Lakes and climb up over granite until 0.75 mile later you crest a ridge and start to descend. The vistas of jagged Crystal Range peaks to the northeast make an awesome backdrop. At 2.5 miles, you'll reach the dam at Lower Twin Lake. Cross it and continue hiking along the lake's northwest shore to tiny Boomerang Lake, at three miles. The lake is shaped like its name and is shallow enough to provide warm water for swimming. Another 0.25 mile on the trail brings you to the south end of Island Lake, where the vistas of the Crystal Range are the best of the trip, and where most hikers start snapping pics. If you ever wanted to sell somebody on the beauty of the Northern Sierra, this trail would be the place to do it.

The only downer on the trip to Twin and Island Lakes is the sheer number of people who make this journey every day during the summer months. Of course, when you see the lakes, you'll know why they are so darn popular.

User Groups: Hikers, dogs, and horses. No mountain bikes. No wheelchair facilities.

Permits: Permits are required year-round for both day and overnight use. Day hikers may obtain a free permit from a ranger station or may self-issue at most major trailheads. Backpackers camping in Desolation Wilderness are subject to trailhead quotas. There is a $5 reservation fee, plus $5 per person for one night, $10 per person for two or more nights up to 14 days (nonrefundable). Children ages 12 and under are free. Golden Passes do not apply to personal-use permits. For groups, the cost of a single permit will not exceed $100.

Maps: For a map, ask the U.S. Forest Service for Eldorado National Forest or Desolation Wilderness. A Lake Tahoe or Desolation Wilderness map is also available for a fee from Tom Harrison Maps. For a topographic map, ask the USGS for Pyramid Peak.

Directions: From Placerville, take Highway 50 east for 40 miles to Kyburz and continue five miles to the signed turnoff for Wrights Lake (about 15 miles west of South Lake Tahoe). Turn left (north) on Wrights Lake Road and drive eight miles to Wrights Lake Visitors Center. Turn right and continue one mile beyond the campground to the end of the road and the Twin Lakes trailhead.

Contact: Eldorado National Forest, Pacific Ranger District, 7887 Highway 50, Pollock Pines, CA 95726, 530/644-2349, www.fs.fed.us/r5; Lake Tahoe Basin Management Unit, 35 College Drive, South Lake Tahoe, CA 96150, 530/543-2600, www.fs.fed.us/r5; Visitors Center (open only in summer), 530/543-2674.

69 GROUSE, HEMLOCK, AND SMITH LAKES
6.0 mi / 3.0 hr or 2 days   4   10

in the Desolation Wilderness

Map 6.2, page 214

The Crystal Basin area is a magical place on the western edge of the Desolation Wilderness. This is where the high peaks of the Crystal Range overlook the basin and its multitude of lakes. Several excellent day hikes and backpacking trips are possible in this area, most of which begin from popular Wrights Lake Campground. Of those, the trip to Grouse, Hemlock, and Smith Lakes is a favorite, despite the relentless climb required to reach all three lakes. From the parking area, Twin Lakes Trail winds past a meadow and then enters a pine and fir forest interspersed with stretches of hard granite. At a trail junction 1.2 miles out, head right for Grouse, Hemlock, and Smith Lakes. Small and pretty Grouse Lake is a one-mile, heart-pumping climb away, with many fine glances back at Wrights Lake and Icehouse Reservoir as you ascend. Many backpackers camp at Grouse Lake; look for wood posts that indicate designated campsites, and note that camping within 500 feet of Grouse Lake and its tributaries is prohibited. More hardy types and day hikers should head for Hemlock and Smith Lakes, farther uphill. The lakes get progressively prettier as you go, but the ascent gets steeper, too. Tiny Hemlock Lake is only 0.5 mile from Grouse Lake, and it boasts a spectacular rock slide on one shoreline and many scrawny hemlock trees on the other. Smith Lake lies another 0.5 mile beyond, way up high near tree line, at 8,700 feet, and it's a stunner.

User Groups: Hikers, dogs, and horses. No mountain bikes. No wheelchair facilities.

Permits: Permits are required year-round for both day and overnight use. Day hikers may obtain a free permit from a ranger station or may self-issue at most major trailheads. Backpackers camping in Desolation Wilderness are subject to trailhead quotas. There is a $5 reservation fee, plus $5 per person for one night, $10 per person for two or more nights up to 14 days (nonrefundable). Children ages 12 and under are free. Golden Passes do not apply to personal-use permits. For groups, the cost of a single permit will not exceed $100.

Maps: For a map, ask the U.S. Forest Service for Eldorado National Forest or Desolation Wilderness. A Lake Tahoe or Desolation Wilderness map is also available for a fee from Tom Harrison Maps. For a topographic map, ask the USGS for Pyramid Peak.

Directions: From Placerville, take Highway 50 east for 40 miles to Kyburz and continue five miles to the signed turnoff for Wrights Lake (about 15 miles west of South Lake Tahoe). Turn left (north) on Wrights Lake Road and drive eight miles to Wrights Lake Visitors Center. Turn right and continue one mile beyond the campground to the end of the road and the Twin Lakes trailhead.

Contact: Eldorado National Forest, Pacific Ranger District, 7887 Highway 50, Pollock Pines, CA 95726, 530/644-2349, www.fs.fed.us/r5; Lake Tahoe Basin Management Unit, 35 College Drive, South Lake Tahoe, CA 96150, 530/543-2600, www.fs.fed.

us/r5; Visitors Center (open only in summer), 530/543-2674.

🔟 LYONS CREEK TRAIL
9.0 mi / 4.5 hr or 2 days 🥾3 ⛰9

in the Desolation Wilderness

Map 6.2, page 214

This may be the "easiest" hike in the entire Wrights Lake area. That is because is requires "only" a 1,700-foot elevation gain to visit two beautiful lakes. Because this trailhead is a few miles distant from popular Wrights Lake Campground, it gets far fewer visitors than the trails that start right out of camp. The trip's total mileage is long, but the grade is mellow, except for the final 0.5 mile to Lyons Lake.

The trail keeps to the south side of Lyons Creek for four solid miles, passing through woods and meadows, then crosses the stream and reaches a junction 0.1 mile farther on. Lyons Lake is to the left and steeply uphill; Lake Sylvia is 0.5 mile to the right. Take your pick, or better yet, go see both. Lake Sylvia is shadowed by Pyramid Peak and has good campsites along its shoreline. Lyons Lake requires a nasty 450-foot climb in 0.5 mile, but its superior scenery makes it well worth the effort.

If you're fond of walking along coursing waterways, following the gurgle and babble of a creek as you hike, you'll love this hike. Wildflowers proliferate in early summer, and views of Pyramid Peak (just shy of 10,000 feet in elevation) inspire you as you gently ascend.

User Groups: Hikers, dogs, and horses. No mountain bikes. No wheelchair facilities.

Permits: Permits are required year-round for both day and overnight use. Day hikers may obtain a free permit from a ranger station or may self-issue at most major trailheads. Backpackers camping in Desolation Wilderness are subject to trailhead quotas. There is a $5 reservation fee, plus $5 per person for one night, $10 per person for two or more nights up to 14 days (nonrefundable). Children ages 12 and under are free. Golden Passes do not apply to personal-use permits. For groups, the cost of a single permit will not exceed $100.

Maps: For a map, ask the U.S. Forest Service for Eldorado National Forest or Desolation Wilderness. A Lake Tahoe or Desolation Wilderness map is also available for a fee from Tom Harrison Maps. For a topographic map, ask the USGS for Pyramid Peak.

Directions: From Placerville, take Highway 50 east for 40 miles to Kyburz and continue five miles to the signed turnoff for Wrights Lake (about 15 miles west of South Lake Tahoe). Turn left (north) on Wrights Lake Road and drive four miles to the signed spur for the Lyons Creek Trail. Turn right and drive a short distance to the trailhead.

Contact: Eldorado National Forest, Pacific Ranger District, 7887 Highway 50, Pollock Pines, CA 95726, 530/644-2349, www.fs.fed.us/r5; Lake Tahoe Basin Management Unit, 35 College Drive, South Lake Tahoe, CA 96150, 530/543-2600, www.fs.fed.us/r5; Visitors Center (open only in summer), 530/543-2674.

71 HORSETAIL FALLS VISTA
2.0 mi / 1.0 hr   👫1 ⛰9

in Eldorado National Forest near South Lake Tahoe

Map 6.2, page 214

Horsetail Falls is the well-known waterfall that takes your breath away as you're driving west along U.S. 50. Approximately 15,000 people each summer glimpse the falls from their cars, then pull over at the giant parking lot by the trailhead and start hiking to get closer to it. Routed past a gorgeous stretch of Pyramid Creek called the Cascades, the trail stays outside of the wilderness boundary and provides a safe and easy alternative for casual visitors. Although the trail doesn't go all the way to the base of Horsetail Falls, it provides many excellent views of it, as well as of Pyramid Creek's glacier-carved canyon.

The trail has been a source of controversy because the waterfall is located within the Desolation Wilderness boundary on a rough but serviceable route, but the first mile of trail is outside the wilderness boundary and is easily accessible from the highway. That first easy mile has encouraged many inexperienced visitors to try to hike to the falls, resulting in numerous accidents and even deaths in the wilderness area, where the trail dissipates and follows stream banks that are rough and slippery. The Forest Service has carried out the wilderness mandate by not making mechanical alterations to the trail, such as building bridges or blasting an obvious path into the granite. Instead, to decrease the frequent injuries, the 1.5-mile Pyramid Creek Loop Trail was built in 1999. Made specifically for day users who just want to see Horsetail Falls and spectacular, granite-lined Pyramid Creek, the Pyramid Creek Loop takes off from the main trail about 0.5 mile in. This was a sensible solution to a difficult problem. The trail is a winner.

User Groups: Hikers and dogs. No horses or mountain bikes. No wheelchair facilities.

Permits: No permits are required if you stay out of the wilderness boundary. Parking is $3 per vehicle.

Maps: For a map, ask the U.S. Forest Service for Eldorado National Forest. A Lake Tahoe map is available for a fee from Tom Harrison Maps. For a topographic map, ask the USGS for Echo Lake.

Directions: From Placerville, take Highway 50 east to Strawberry (about 20 miles from South Lake Tahoe) and continue about three miles to Twin Bridges and a large pullout on the north side of the highway (.5 mile west of the turnoff for Camp Sacramento). Park in the designated parking lot for the signed trailhead.

Contact: Eldorado National Forest, Pacific Ranger District, 7887 Highway 50, Pollock Pines, CA 95726, 530/644-2349, www.fs.fed.us/r5.

72 RALSTON PEAK
8.0 mi / 5.0 hr   🚶4 ⛰10

in the Desolation Wilderness near South
Lake Tahoe

Map 6.2, page 214

The route to Ralston Peak has a little of everything: dense forest, open manzanita-covered
slopes, meadows, and granite ridges. It also
has lots of one thing: elevation gain. From
trailhead to summit, you ascend from 6,400 to
9,240 feet over the course of four miles.

Begin by walking northward up the paved
road from the east side of the parking area
for 200 yards. Look for the trail leading off
on the left. Climb upward through nonstop
trees and nonstop switchbacks for a mile;
then enter a more open area as you pass the
wilderness boundary sign at 1.5 miles. The
views start to widen. Your lungs request a
lunch break, but they don't get one until 2.5
miles up, when you finally gain the ridge. A
half mile later, the break is over, and you
climb again, this time to another ridge at
3.5 miles, covered in meadow grasses and
wildflowers. Part ways with the main trail
and look for a trail to your right leading
to the top of Ralston Peak, 0.5 mile away.
Scramble up over jumbled rock to gain the
9,235-foot summit, and take in the view of
Lake Tahoe, Fallen Leaf Lake, Carson Pass,
Echo Lakes, and below you (to the north),
Ralston Lake. This is simply a spectacular
lookout. To get it, you may also find that
your butt gets kicked.

User Groups: Hikers and dogs. No horses or
mountain bikes. No wheelchair facilities.

Permits: Permits are required year-round for
both day and overnight use. Day hikers may
obtain a free permit from a ranger station or
may self-issue at most major trailheads. Backpackers camping in Desolation Wilderness are
subject to trailhead quotas. There is a $5 res-
ervation fee, plus $5 per person for one night,
$10 per person for two or more nights up to 14
days (nonrefundable). Children ages 12 and
under are free. Golden Passes do not apply to

personal-use permits. For groups, the cost of
a single permit will not exceed $100.

Maps: For a map, ask the U.S. Forest Service
for Eldorado National Forest or Desolation
Wilderness. A Lake Tahoe or Desolation Wilderness map is also available for a fee from
Tom Harrison Maps. For a topographic map,
ask the USGS for Echo Lake.

Directions: From Placerville, take Highway 50
east to Twin Bridges and continue 1.5 miles
to Camp Sacramento and the turnoff. There
is a parking area off the north side of U.S.
50 and a sign for Ralston Trail to Lake of
the Woods.

From South Lake Tahoe, take Highway
89 south for five miles to Highway 50. Turn
right (west) on U.S. 50 and drive about 14
miles to the turnoff for Camp Sacramento
(if you reach Twin Bridges, you've gone 1.5
miles too far west).

Contact: Eldorado National Forest, Pacific Ranger District, 7887 Highway 50,
Pollock Pines, CA 95726, 530/644-2349,
www.fs.fed.us/r5; Lake Tahoe Basin Management Unit, 35 College Drive, South Lake
Tahoe, CA 96150, 530/543-2600, www.fs.fed.
us/r5; Visitors Center (open only in summer),
530/543-2674.

73 BOAT TAXI TO
   LAKE ALOHA
6.0-12.0 mi / 3.5-6.0 hr   🚶3 ⛰10

in the Desolation Wilderness

Map 6.2, page 214

This is a sensational trip. It starts with a boat
taxi across the two Echo Lakes and before getting dropped off at the trailhead for the Pacific
Crest Trail. Then it's an easy climb to great
views with a series of spur trails to beautiful alpine lakes in Desolation Wilderness, crowned
by Lake Aloha in Desolation Valley.

From the hiker's parking lot, walk 0.25 mile
downhill to the resort and the boat launch
area, at the edge of Echo Lake. The boat
taxi leaves at frequent intervals (or whenever

more than two people show up) from 8 A.M. to 6 P.M. daily all summer. The trip costs $9.50 each way and is well worth it to get you to the border of the Desolation Wilderness. The boat carries hikers two miles to the far end of Upper and Lower Echo Lakes, passing many lovely lakeside cottages.

From the boat taxi drop-off point, gain the main trail (Pacific Crest Trail) and head to your left. The 3.5-mile hike to the eastern edge of Lake Aloha starts with a steady climb up to a ridge. Be sure to stop and turn around to enjoy the stunning lake view. After topping the ridge, the hike is an easy saunter. You'll pass several signed junctions with numerous trails along the way, all of which lead to various lakes in very short distances. Your best bet is to stay on the main path for Lake Aloha, then take some of the cutoffs to neighboring lakes on your way back. When you reach Lake Aloha's shore, hike along its beautiful north side for a distance, admiring the rocky coves and islands of the giant, shallow lake. At one time, Lake Aloha was several small lakes. They were dammed with a unique rock wall to create this huge body of water. The effect is a bit surreal, although beautiful. The lake's elevation is 8,116 feet.

On the trip back, take one or more of the signed trail junctions and visit Lake of the Woods, Lake Lucille, Lake Margery, Tamarack Lake, or Ralston Lake—all less than one mile off Lake Aloha Trail. Tamarack Lake is the best for scenery; Lake of the Woods is the best for fishing.

On the return trip, some bypass the boat taxi and continue on the Pacific Crest Trail back to the parking area. That will add 2.5 miles to your trip. The trail rises well above the lake, eventually passing a series of vacation homes.

User Groups: Hikers and dogs (not advised because sharp rocks can bruise their foot pads). No horses or mountain bikes. No wheelchair facilities.

Permits: Boat taxi (not required) is $10 per hiker one-way, $5 for dogs. Permits are required year-round for both day and overnight use. Day hikers may obtain a free permit from a ranger station or may self-issue at most major trailheads. Backpackers camping in Desolation Wilderness are subject to trailhead quotas. There is a $5 reservation fee, plus $5 per person for one night, $10 per person for two or more nights up to 14 days (nonrefundable). Children ages 12 and under are free. Golden Passes do not apply to personal-use permits. For groups, the cost of a single permit will not exceed $100.

Maps: For a map, ask the U.S. Forest Service for Desolation Wilderness. A Lake Tahoe or Desolation Wilderness map is also available for a fee from Tom Harrison Maps. For a topographic map, ask the USGS for Echo Lake.

Directions: From Placerville, take Highway 50 east toward Tahoe and Echo summit to Sierra at Tahoe Ski Resort and then continue 1.8 miles to Johnson Pass Road and a signed turnoff (brown sign) for Berkeley Camp/Echo Lake (one mile west of Echo Summit). Turn left and drive 0.5 mile to Echo Lakes Road. Turn left and drive one mile to a series of parking lots located 0.25 mile before the road ends at Echo Lakes Resort. Hikers not staying at the resort must park in one of the upper lots or alongside the road, not in the main lower lot by the resort, and walk down to the marina, boat taxi, or trailhead.

From South Lake Tahoe: Take Highway 89 south for five miles to U.S. 50. Turn right (west) on U.S. 50 and drive 5.5 miles to the signed turnoff for Echo Lakes on the right (one mile west of Echo Summit.) Turn right and drive 0.5 mile to Echo Lakes Road. Turn left and drive one mile to a series of parking lots located 0.25 mile before the road ends at Echo Lakes Resort.

Contact: Echo Lakes Chalet, 530/659-7207, www.echochalet.com; Eldorado National Forest, Pacific Ranger District, 7887 Highway 50, Pollock Pines, CA 95726, 530/644-2349, www.fs.fed.us/r5; Lake Tahoe Basin Management Unit, 35 College Drive, South Lake Tahoe, CA 96150, 530/543-2600, www.fs.fed.

us/r5; Visitors Center (open only in summer), 530/543-2674.

74 ECHO LAKES RESORT TO BARKER PASS (PCT)

32.3 mi one-way / 3 days 👣4 ⛰9

from Echo Lake near U.S. 50 south of Lake Tahoe to Forest Road 3 near Barker Pass northwest of Emerald Bay

Map 6.2, page 214

The Desolation Wilderness (and the neighboring Granite Chief Wilderness) are filled with sculpted granite domes and hundreds of gemlike lakes. All is pristine, yet access is also quite easy, making this the most heavily used section of the PCT all summer long. The trip starts at Echo Lake (elevation 7,400 feet), climbs through pines past Upper Echo Lake, and then continues up and north toward Triangle Lake, one of dozens of lakes you pass on your northward route. They come and go—Lake Margery, Lake Aloha, and then Heather, Susie, and Gilmore Lakes, and finally Dicks Lake (at 9,380 feet). There are so many, in fact, that you can plan on a perfect campsite near a lake every night, providing you don't mind the company of other hikers drawn by classic beauty. The views are dramatic as well, across miles and miles of the glacial-carved granite, all of it marvelous high Sierra landscape. As you continue, you'll discover Upper and Middle Velma Lakes, both very pretty and with good fishing. The trail skirts the ridgeline, keeping the higher knobs to the east as it gradually descends toward Richardson Lake, just beyond the Desolation Wilderness boundary—ready now to enter the Granite Chief Wilderness.

To continue north on the PCT, see the *Barker Pass to Donner Pass (PCT)* hike in this chapter. If you are walking this trail in reverse, see the *Carson Pass to Echo Lakes Resort (PCT)* hike in this chapter.

User Groups: Hikers, dogs, and horses. No mountain bikes. No wheelchair facilities.

Permits: A backcountry permit is required for traveling through various wilderness and special-use areas the trail traverses. In addition, a campfire permit is required for the use of portable camp stoves or the building of campfires where allowed. To make it simple, you can contact the national forest, Bureau of Land Management (BLM), or national park office at your point of entry for a combined permit that is good for traveling through multiple-permit areas during your dates of travel.

Maps: For topographic maps, ask the USGS for Echo Lake, Emerald Bay, and Rockbound Valley.

Directions: From Placerville, take Highway 50 east toward Tahoe and Echo summit to Sierra at Tahoe Ski Resort and then continue 1.8 miles to Johnson Pass Road and a signed turnoff (brown sign) for Berkeley Camp/Echo Lakes (one mile west of Echo Summit). Turn left and drive 0.5 mile to Echo Lakes Road. Turn left and drive one mile to a series of parking lots located 0.25 mile before the road ends at Echo Lakes Resort. Hikers not staying at the resort must park in one of the upper lots or alongside the road, not in the main lower lot by the resort, and walk down to the marina, boat taxi, or trailhead.

From South Lake Tahoe: Take Highway 89 south for five miles to U.S. 50. Turn right (west) on U.S. 50 and drive 5.5 miles to the signed turnoff for Echo Lakes on the right (one mile west of Echo Summit.) Turn right and drive 0.5 mile to Echo Lakes Road. Turn left and drive one mile to a series of parking lots located 0.25 mile before the road ends at Echo Lakes Resort.

To reach the Barker Pass trailhead, from Tahoe Pines on Highway 89, head north for 0.5 mile to the Kaspian Picnic Grounds and then bear left (west) for seven miles on Forest Service Road 15N03.

Contact: Echo Lakes Chalet, 530/659-7207, www.echochalet.com; Lake Tahoe Basin Management Unit, 35 College Drive, South Lake Tahoe, CA 96150, 530/543-2600, www.fs.fed.us/r5; Visitors Center (open only in summer), 530/543-2674.

75 DARDANELLES LAKE AND ROUND LAKE

7.6 mi / 4.5 hr   🏃3 ⛰9

near Carson Pass

Map 6.2, page 214

Dardanelles Lake (elevation 7,740 feet) is striking and gorgeous, set in a pocket with a granite backdrop. The route to Dardanelles Lake and Round Lake, along the Tahoe Rim Trail, starts out steep but gets easier as it goes. It enters "Meiss Country," that large and wonderful roadless area south of Lake Tahoe, where the forces that shaped the land were ice (glaciers) and fire (volcanic action). Both have made their presence clearly visible.

From the parking lot, the trail heads south, crosses Highway 89 in about 100 yards, then makes an initial climb through fir and pine forest to Big Meadow. The meadow makes lovely, level walking for 0.25 mile; then it's back into the trees. Follow the trail signs for Round Lake until you complete a steep, short descent at two miles out. At the bottom of the hill, turn sharply right on Meiss Meadow Trail toward Christmas Valley. Walk less than 0.25 mile, then turn left and cross a creek for the final 1.2 miles to Dardanelles Lake. It's good for swimming, fishing, and picnicking. If you time your trip for autumn, you'll be treated to a marvelous color display from the aspens and alders that grow along this trail's many streams.

On your return, retrace your steps to the junction at the bottom of the hill, then hike 0.75 mile in the opposite direction to visit Round Lake. Although not quite as scenic as Dardanelles Lake, Round Lake provides a stark, fascinating contrast to its neighbor: It is surrounded by volcanic rock formations, not granite cliffs.

Note that this trail is open to mountain bikers. On weekdays you might not see a single bike, but on weekends you'll see plenty.

User Groups: Hikers, dogs, horses, and mountain bikes. No wheelchair facilities.

Permits: No permits are required. Parking and access are free.

Maps: For a map, ask the U.S. Forest Service for Lake Tahoe Basin Management Unit. A Lake Tahoe map is available for a fee from Tom Harrison Maps. For a topographic map, ask the USGS for Echo Lake.

Directions: From South Lake Tahoe, take Highway 89 south for five miles to Meyers and the junction with Highway 89, and then continue south on Highway 89 for five more miles to the Big Meadow trailhead parking area on the northwest side of the road. Turn left off the highway, then bear left and park near the restrooms. The trail begins from the south side of the parking lot loop and crosses Highway 89 in about 100 yards.

Contact: Lake Tahoe Basin Management Unit, 35 College Drive, South Lake Tahoe, CA 96150, 530/543-2600, www.fs.fed.us/r5; Visitors Center (open only in summer), 530/543-2674.

76 LAKE MARGARET

4.6 mi / 3.0 hr   🏃1 ⛰9

near Carson Pass and Kirkwood Lake

Map 6.2, page 214   **BEST (**

Can you imagine a hike to an alpine lake with only a 500-foot elevation gain? It might seem too good to be true, but here you are. If you need an easy-trail fix, Lake Margaret should do the trick.

The trail undulates gently, never gaining or losing more than a couple hundred feet. The first stretch is actually downhill. Then the path climbs gently over a small ridge and then descends again over duck-marked granite slabs. You'll cross branches of Caples Creek twice in the first mile. At 1.5 miles, the trail passes by a couple of tiny ponds. At two miles out, after crossing another creek, you'll find yourself in a lovely grove of aspens and knee-high wildflowers. At 2.3 miles, after about an hour of walking and only a minor expenditure of energy, you'll reach the granite shoreline of Lake Margaret. Swimming is excellent. A few tiny islands and many shoreline boulders make fine sunbathing spots. Figure on staying awhile. The lake's elevation is 7,500 feet.

Note that although most of the trails in the Carson Pass area are famous for wildflowers, the proximity of several small streams makes the bloom especially showy on this path. The peak wildflower season is from mid-June to mid-August.

User Groups: Hikers, leashed dogs, horses, and mountain bikes. No wheelchair facilities.

Permits: No permits are required. Parking and access are free.

Maps: For a map, ask the U.S. Forest Service for Eldorado National Forest or Mokelumne Wilderness. For a topographic map, ask the USGS for Caples Lake.

Directions: From South Lake Tahoe, take Highway 89 south for five miles to Meyers and the junction with Highway 89, and then continue south on Highway 89 for 11 miles to Highway 88. Turn west on Highway 88 and drive 14.5 miles to the Lake Margaret sign, on the north side of the road (5.5 miles west of Carson Pass Summit, and 5.5 miles east of Silver Lake.) Turn north and park at the trailhead parking area.

Contact: Eldorado National Forest, Amador Ranger District, 26820 Silver Drive, Pioneer, CA 95666, 209/295-4251, www.fs.fed.us/r5.

77 EMIGRANT LAKE
8.0 mi / 4.0 hr or 2 days

in the Mokelumne Wilderness near
Caples Lake

Map 6.2, page 214

The trailhead at Caples Lake is often jam-packed with backpackers, so do yourself a favor: visit here midweek or in the off-season, or make your trip a day hike instead of an overnight. Why is this trail so popular? It's wonderfully scenic and surprisingly easy.

The trail leads from the spillway at Caples Lake up and along the lake's south side, following an old emigrant route. The first two miles are right along the lake's edge, climbing

gently above the shoreline, always in the shade of big conifers. If you enjoy hiking near water, you'll love this pathway. More climbing alongside Emigrant Creek leads hikers to a stream crossing at 3.5 miles, followed by another crossing. A few switchbacks carry you up to Emigrant Lake, a beautiful cirque lake set at 8,600 feet, with many fine sunbathing rocks. Covered Wagon Peak and Thimble Peak, at 9,500 feet, rise above the scene. The trail's total elevation gain is less than 1,000 feet, making this a surprisingly easy day hike, even with its eight-mile distance. But know before you go: Most of the trail's ascent is packed into the last 1.8 miles, which will leave you breathing hard. Note that no campfires are permitted above 8,000 feet.

User Groups: Hikers, leashed dogs, and horses. No mountain bikes. No wheelchair facilities.

Permits: No day-hiking permits are required. A free wilderness permit is required for overnight stays; it is available from the Amador Ranger Station, the Carson Pass Information Station, or the Eldorado Information Center. Maximum group size for day use is 12. Maximum group size for overnight use is eight. No self-registration is available at the trailhead.

Maps: For a map, ask the U.S. Forest Service for Eldorado National Forest or Desolation Wilderness. For a topographic map, ask the USGS for Caples Lake.

Directions: From South Lake Tahoe, take Highway 89 south for five miles to Meyers and the junction with Highway 89, and then continue south on Highway 89 for 11 miles to Highway 88. Turn west on Highway 88 and drive 14 miles (five miles west of Carson Pass) to the west side of Caples Lake and the trailhead parking area.

Contact: Eldorado National Forest, Amador Ranger District, 26820 Silver Drive, Pioneer, CA 95666, 209/295-4251, www.fs.fed.us/r5.

78 MINKALO TRAIL

7.0 mi / 3.5 hr

near Silver Lake

Map 6.2, page 214

Since Silver Lake has a fair number of rental cabins and private homes on its shore, it appears less wild than nearby Caples Lake. Still, the big blue lake, at 7,300 feet in elevation, is beautiful, and if you want to hike near it, the Minkalo Trail is your best bet. The trail leads to Granite Lake in one mile and to Plasse's Resort, on the south side of the lake, in three miles. Why not hike to both, then buy a pizza or a Power Bar at Plasse's Resort Trading Post to fuel up for the hike back to the Minkalo trailhead?

The trail starts out rocky and stays that way for the first 0.25 mile. Cross a bridge over Squaw Creek to a right fork that leads to Plasse's Resort. Take the left fork first, heading to Granite Lake, which you'll reach in about 20 minutes after a moderate climb. It's a pretty lake and good for swimming. After you've visited, return to the trail junction and hike southward, soon coming close to the edge of Silver Lake and staying in its proximity. You'll have many pretty lake views from here on out, including long looks at Treasure Island, Silver Lake's large island. It takes about an hour to reach the campground at Plasse's, an excellent place for horse lovers (and pizza lovers).

User Groups: Hikers, leashed dogs, horses, and mountain bikes. No wheelchair facilities.

Permits: No permits are required. Parking and access are free.

Maps: For a map, ask the U.S. Forest Service for Eldorado National Forest, or Desolation Wilderness. For a topographic map, ask the USGS for Caples Lake.

Directions: From South Lake Tahoe, take Highway 89 south for five miles to Meyers and the junction with Highway 89, and then continue south on Highway 89 for 11 miles to Highway 88. Turn right (west) on Highway 88 and drive 15.5 miles (10.8 miles west of Carson Pass) to the turnoff for Kit Carson Lodge on the north side of the road. Turn north and drive past Kit Carson Lodge, go left at the first fork, and go right at the second fork, to the parking for Minkalo Trail. (It's a total of 1.4 miles from Highway 88.) Walk back down the road for about 40 yards to find the trailhead.

Contact: Eldorado National Forest, Amador Ranger District, 26820 Silver Drive, Pioneer, CA 95666, 209/295-4251, www.fs.fed.us/r5.

79 OSBORNE HILL

2.6 mi / 1.5 hr

on Highway 4 near Lake Alpine

Map 6.2, page 214

We like the way Lake Alpine looks from close up on Lakeshore Trail, but then again, we like the way Lake Alpine looks from far up on Osborne Hill, also known as Osborne Point. A short, healthy climb brings you to the point, from which you can look down at the lake and beyond into the Carson-Iceberg Wilderness. The trail ends there but connects to Emigrant West Trail if you wish to hike farther. If you're itching for winter to be over so you can go hiking, you'll be happy to know that Highway 4 is always open as far east as Silvertip Campground, but not always farther. Thus if the snow is dwindling, you'll have access to this trailhead often long before you can access the others near Lake Alpine.

User Groups: Hikers, dogs, horses, and mountain bikes. No wheelchair facilities.

Permits: No permits are required. Parking and access are free.

Maps: For a map, ask the U.S. Forest Service for Stanislaus National Forest. For a topographic map, ask the USGS for Tamarack.

Directions: From Angels Camp, take Highway 4 east for 40 miles to Bear Valley. Set your odometer at Bear Valley and drive east on Highway 4 for three miles to the Osborne Ridge trailhead (just east of Silvertip Campground). Take the trail that leads from the south side of the road.

Contact: Stanislaus National Forest, Calaveras Ranger District, P.O. Box 500, Hathaway Pines, CA 95233, 209/795-1381, www.fs.fed.us/r5.

80 LAKESHORE TRAIL AND INSPIRATION POINT
4.0 mi / 2.0 hr ☆☆2 ▲8

on Highway 4 near Lake Alpine

Map 6.2, page 214

It's hard to say which trail is better, Lakeshore Trail or Inspiration Point Trail. To solve the dilemma, hike both of them together. The trip starts with a short walk down a dirt road; then turn right onto a single track. After 10 minutes of hiking through a thick lodgepole pine forest peppered with tiny pinecones, you're at the edge of Lake Alpine, elevation 7,350 feet. Follow the trail to your left, and in another 10 minutes, you reach a left fork for Inspiration Point (Lakeshore Trail continues straight). You'll want to head out and back on both trails; it makes no difference which one you take first.

The Lakeshore Trail is flat and stays within 100 feet of the water's edge, offering many pretty lake vistas. Eventually the trail meets up with Slick Rock, a four-wheel-drive road, but there's no need to go that far. Just walk a mile or so to the dam, and then turn around and head back. The Inspiration Point Trail, on the other hand, is more of a workout: a steep one-mile climb to the summit at Inspiration Point, from which you can see for miles. Pick a clear day, and you'll be pointing out Lake Alpine, Elephant Rock, the Dardanelles, and Spicer Meadow Reservoir.

User Groups: Hikers, dogs, and horses. No mountain bikes. No wheelchair facilities.

Permits: No permits are required. Parking and access are free.

Maps: For a national forest map, ask for Stanislaus National Forest. For a topographic map, ask the USGS for Spicer Meadow Reservoir.

Directions: From Angels Camp, take Highway 4 east for 40 miles to Bear Valley. Set your odometer at Bear Valley and drive east on Highway 4 for 4.3 miles to the Lake Alpine East Shore trailhead turnoff, on the right. Turn right, drive 0.25 mile, and turn right again and drive 0.1 mile past Pine Marten Campground to the signed parking area and the trailhead.

Contact: Stanislaus National Forest, Calaveras Ranger District, P.O. Box 500, Hathaway Pines, CA 95233, 209/795-1381, www.fs.fed.us/r5.

81 DUCK LAKE
3.0 mi / 1.5 hr ☆☆1 ▲8

in the Carson-Iceberg Wilderness off Highway 4 near Lake Alpine

Map 6.2, page 214

The trailhead at Silver Valley Campground is the start of the route to Duck Lake, and it's also one of the busiest trailheads into the Carson-Iceberg Wilderness. The trip to Duck Lake is a perfect easy hike for families or people just in the mood for a stroll, and the more ambitious can continue past the lake on an eight-mile round-trip to Rock Lake. It's only one mile to reach Duck Lake, but once you're there, you'll want to walk the loop trail around its perimeter, adding another mile to your trip. The area is the site of a historic cow camp, where animals have grazed since the late 19th century. You can examine the remains of a couple of early-20th-century cowboy cabins.

User Groups: Hikers, dogs, and horses. No mountain bikes. No wheelchair facilities.

Permits: No day-use permits are required. Parking and access are free.

Maps: For a map, ask the U.S. Forest Service for Stanislaus National Forest or Carson-Iceberg Wilderness. For a topographic map, ask the USGS for Spicer Meadow Reservoir.

Directions: From Angels Camp, take Highway 4 east for 40 miles to Bear Valley. Set your odometer at Bear Valley and drive east

on Highway 4 for 4.3 miles to the Lake Alpine East Shore trailhead turnoff on the right. Turn right and continue straight to Silver Valley Campground and the Silver Valley trailhead.
Contact: Stanislaus National Forest, Calaveras Ranger District, P.O. Box 500, Hathaway Pines, CA 95233, 209/795-1381, www.fs.fed.us/r5.

82 WOODCHUCK BASIN TO WHEELER LAKE

6.4 mi / 3.5 hr 🥾3 ⛰️8

in the Mokelumne Wilderness off Highway 4 near Lake Alpine

Map 6.2, page 214

This trail is located only a mile from the campgrounds at Lake Alpine. So you might think that the Woodchuck Basin trailhead (elevation 7,800 feet) should have a parking lot full of cars. But it rarely does. The trail leads into the Mokelumne Wilderness, and after climbing uphill on it for 1.7 forested miles, you reach a junction where you can go left for Underwood Valley or right for tiny Wheeler Lake. Bear right, pass a Mokelumne Wilderness sign, and in moments, you are heading for a 1.5-mile steep descent to Wheeler Lake. Think it over before you go, because you'll need to regain those 1,000 feet on the way home. But if you're willing to take the plunge, you're treated to a picturesque, tree- and granite-lined lake, where you can pass the afternoon with little fear that you'll be bugged by a busload of other hikers. Dog owners should note that Tuolumne County has a leash law that is strictly enforced.
User Groups: Hikers, leashed dogs, and horses. No mountain bikes. No wheelchair facilities.
Permits: No permits are required. Parking and access are free.
Maps: For a map, ask the U.S. Forest Service for Stanislaus National Forest or Mokelumne Wilderness. For a topographic map, ask the USGS for Spicer Meadow Reservoir.

Directions: From Angels Camp, take Highway 4 east for 40 miles to Bear Valley. Set your odometer at Bear Valley and drive east on Highway 4 for 5.5 miles to the Woodchuck Basin trailhead on the left. Turn left and drive 0.25 mile to the parking area.
Contact: Stanislaus National Forest, Calaveras Ranger District, P.O. Box 500, Hathaway Pines, CA 95233, 209/795-1381, www.fs.fed.us/r5.

83 NORTH GROVE LOOP

1.0 mi / 0.5 hr 🥾1 ⛰️7

in Calaveras Big Trees State Park

Map 6.2, page 214

Even though there are 150 giant sequoias at Calaveras Big Trees State Park, the highlight is actually the one known as The Big Stump. Well, the state park gets a lot of visitors, and this is the most popular walk here, so you can expect other people—lots of 'em—on weekends. The easy trail is routed among the giant sequoias, and the sweet fragrance of the massive trees fills the air. You will never forget that scent. These trees, of course, are known not for their height but for their tremendous diameter: It can take a few dozen people, linking hands, to encircle one. This trip is actually best in winter after fresh snowfall, when your footsteps are the only signs of life, and it feels like you are in a time machine. Near the end of the short loop, you will hike through a walk-through tree, thought the top has broken off.

Now about that stump: Back in the day, a gent wanted to prove how big the trees were to folks on the East Coast, so naturally, he cut the biggest one down, collected the bark and wasted the wood, then took it by railroad to the World's Fair and re-assembled it to prove how big it was. Except everybody thought it was a hoax, and then shortly thereafter, the bark collection was burned in a fire. Surprised the guy didn't shoot a Bigfoot while he was at it? The giant stump has been used for just about everything, including a dance floor. According to projections, if it had been allowed to grow, it would be bigger than the General Sherman Tree in Sequoia National Park, the largest living thing by volume on the planet.

User Groups: Hikers and wheelchairs. No dogs, horses, or mountain bikes.

Permits: No permits are required. A state park entrance fee of $8 is charged each vehicle.

Maps: A brochure and trail map is available for a fee at Calaveras Big Trees State Park. For a topographic map, ask the USGS for Dorrington.

Directions: From Angels Camp, take Highway 4 east for 23 miles to Arnold, and then continue for four miles to the park entrance. The trailhead is adjacent to the park entrance.

Contact: Calaveras Big Trees State Park, P.O. Box 120, Arnold, CA 95223, 209/795-2334, visitor center 209/795-3840, www.parks.ca.gov.

84 SOUTH GROVE LOOP
5.0 mi / 3.0 hr 🏃2 ⛰️8

northeast of Arnold on Highway 4

Map 6.2, page 214

The two largest sequoias in Calaveras Big Trees State Park are found on a spur trail of this hike, and that makes it a must-do for visitors. But so many tourists are content to just walk the little trail at the North Grove, look at the giant stump, and then hit the road. Why rush? As long as you're at the park, take the South Grove Loop. The loop itself is 3.5 miles long, but the highlight is a spur trail that branches off 0.75 mile to the Agassiz Tree and the Palace Hotel Tree, two monster-sized specimens. For a great photograph, have someone take a picture of you standing at the base of one of these trees; you will look like a Lilliputian from *Gulliver's Travels*.

User Groups: Hikers only. No dogs, horses, or mountain bikes. No wheelchair facilities.

Permits: No permits are required. A state park entrance fee of $8 is charged each vehicle.

Maps: A brochure and trail map is available for a fee at Calaveras Big Trees State Park. For a topographic map, ask the USGS for Boards Crossing.

Directions: From Angels Camp, take Highway 4 east for 23 miles to Arnold, and then continue for four miles to the park entrance. Turn right into the park entrance, then drive down the parkway for nine miles to the trailhead, on the right. Note: The road is closed in winter.

Contact: Calaveras Big Trees State Park, P.O. Box 120, Arnold, CA 95223, 209/795-2334; Columbia State Park, 209/532-0150, www.parks.ca.gov.

85 CARSON PASS TO ECHO LAKES RESORT (PCT)
15.8 mi one-way / 1-2 days 🏃4 ⛰️10

from Carson Pass at Highway 88 north to Echo Lake near U.S. 50, just south of Lake Tahoe

Map 6.3, page 215 **BEST (**

When you've hiked on the Pacific Crest Trail for weeks, the first glimpse of Lake Tahoe in the distance can seem like a privileged view into heaven. That view is just a few miles from Ebbetts Pass. You start by hiking over a short mountain rim (nice view to the west of Caples Lake) and then you drop into the headwaters of the Truckee River. As you look northward after making the rim, Lake Tahoe suddenly comes into view. It's like having a divine vision. And finally there is water available from several small creeks as you walk into the Truckee headwaters. At the same time, you will be greeted by a high meadow surrounded by a light forest. All seems right with the world again. With Echo Lakes Resort within one day's hiking time, you will be amazed at how inspired you can get on this section of trail. It's very pretty, weaving through lush canyons and along creeks, eventually reaching beautiful and tiny Showers Lake. Here the trail seems to drop off to never-never land, descending very quickly and steeply in the march toward Tahoe. Contentment reigns. When you reach Little Norway, however, reality sets in. Cars are everywhere. The trail suddenly grinds down amid cabins and vacation property. There's one last hill to climb, and then the PCT drops quickly to the parking lot for Echo Lakes.

Almost nobody hiking the PCT immediately heads north into the Desolation Wilderness from here. Virtually everyone stops for at least a day to get cleaned up, resupplied, and fed by something other than a Power Bar. But after a day, the trail calls again. If you hear it, well, you just have to answer it.

To continue north on the PCT, see the *Echo Lakes Resort to Barker Pass (PCT)* hike in this chapter. If you are walking this trail in reverse, see the *Blue Lakes Road to Carson Pass (PCT)* hike in this chapter.

User Groups: Hikers, dogs, and horses. No mountain bikes. No wheelchair facilities.

Permits: A backcountry permit is required for traveling through various wilderness and special-use areas that the trail traverses. In addition, a campfire permit is required for the use of portable camp stoves or the building of campfires where permitted. To make it simple, you can contact the national forest, Bureau of Land Management (BLM), or national park office at your point of entry for a combined permit that is good for traveling through multiple-permit areas during your dates of travel.

Maps: For national forest maps, ask for Lake Tahoe Basin Management Unit, Tahoe National Forest, Eldorado National Forest, and Stanislaus National Forest. For topographic maps, ask the USGS for Carson Pass, Caples Lake, and Echo Lake.

Directions: To reach the Carson Pass trailhead: From South Lake Tahoe, take Highway 89 south for five miles to Meyers and the junction with Highway 89, and then continue south on Highway 89 for 11 miles to Highway 88.

Turn right (west) on Highway 88 and drive 10 miles to Carson Pass.

For the Echo Lakes Resort trailhead: From South Lake Tahoe, take Highway 89 south for five miles to U.S. 50. Turn right (west) on U.S. 50 and drive 5.5 miles to the signed turnoff for Echo Lakes on the right (one mile west of Echo Summit.) Turn right and drive 0.5 mile to Echo Lakes Road. Turn left and drive one mile to a series of parking lots located 0.25 mile before the road ends at Echo Lakes Resort. Hikers not staying at the resort must park in one of the upper lots or alongside the road, not in the main lower lot by the resort, and walk down to the marina, boat taxi, or trailhead.

Contact: Eldorado National Forest, Amador Ranger District, 26820 Silver Drive, Pioneer, CA 95666, 209/295-4251, www.fs.fed.us/r5; Lake Tahoe Basin Management Unit, 35 College Drive, South Lake Tahoe, CA 96150, 530/543-2600, www.fs.fed.us/r5; Visitors Center (open only in summer), 530/543-2674.

🔳🔳 SHOWERS LAKE
10.0 mi / 6.0 hr 🚶2 ⛰9

near Caples Lake

> **Map 6.3, page 215**

Here's a day hike on the Pacific Crest Trail into the land of Meiss Country, that is, the headwaters for the Upper Truckee River and the home of the endangered Lahontan cutthroat trout.

For the trip to Showers Lake, head uphill from the trailhead on the PCT, climbing through Meiss Pass and then dropping into a huge valley basin. Views along the way include Mount Round Top, Elephant Back, and Red Lake Peak, expanding to include far-off Lake Tahoe, to the north. It's 2.9 miles to a fork with the Tahoe Rim Trail (TRT), just beyond a crossing of Upper Truckee River, which is little more than a stream here. While stopping to pump a canteen's worth of water here, we've had hummingbirds come up and eye us from a foot away.

The right fork leads 2.2 miles to Round Lake, Meiss Country's largest lake and a popular destination, but stay left on the PCT and TRT, and cross the river again on your way to Showers Lake, 2.1 miles farther. The last half mile of trail is a 350-foot descent to Showers Lake, with 9,590-foot Little Round Top poking up above it to the west. The trail leads along the east side of the lake, where campsites can be found. The lake is set at 8,790 feet and is the highest lake in the Upper Truckee River Basin. It's very pretty.

This trip is popular with the horsy set. A separate trail leads to Showers Lake from Schneider Camp, a large horse camp, so weekends bring a fair amount of horse traffic. Also note that the trip begins in Eldorado National Forest, but two-thirds of the trail is within jurisdiction of the Lake Tahoe Basin Management Unit.

Although Meiss Country is not designated wilderness, it might as well be, because there are no roads cutting into it, and all is peaceful and serene. The Pacific Crest Trail and a completed stretch of Tahoe Rim Trail are the main routes through Meiss Country. Note that no bikes are permitted on the PCT, but we've seen plenty of tire tread here.

User Groups: Hikers, leashed dogs, and horses. No mountain bikes. No wheelchair facilities.

Permits: No permits are required. A $3 parking fee is charged per vehicle.

Maps: For a map, ask the U.S. Forest Service for Eldorado National Forest or Mokelumne Wilderness. For topographic maps, ask the USGS for Caples Lake and Carson Pass.

Directions: From South Lake Tahoe, take Highway 89 south for five miles to Meyers and the junction with Highway 89, and then continue south on Highway 89 for 11 miles to Highway 88. Turn west on Highway 88 and drive 10 miles to Carson Pass Summit. The parking area and Meiss trailhead are on the right (north), across the highway from (and slightly west of) the Carson Pass Information Station.

Contact: Eldorado National Forest, Amador Ranger District, 26820 Silver Drive, Pioneer, CA 95666, 209/295-4251 www.fs.fed.us/r5.

87 WINNEMUCCA LAKE FROM WOODS LAKE
3.0 mi / 1.5 hr 　　　 👫 2 ⛺ 10

in the Mokelumne Wilderness near Carson Pass

Map 6.3, page 215 　　　 **BEST ☾**

Woods Lake is a little magical spot where you can drive right up, walk a few feet to the water's edge, and plunk in your fishing line. It's also the trailhead for numerous great hikes into the Mokelumne Wilderness, including this easy trip to deep blue Winnemucca Lake, set at the base of fantastic-looking Mount Round Top (elevation 10,381 feet).

After setting off down the trail, in a mile you will pass by the remains of an arrastra, a device used for crushing gold or silver ore, evidence of this area's mining past. Continue walking through big conifers until you come out to a glacial moraine, where your view of Mount Round Top, a huge old volcanic vent, opens wide. Snowcapped most of summer in most years, imposing Round Top is a stunning sight. So are the early summer wildflowers that bloom in profusion on the open slopes surrounding the path. In 1.5 miles of gentle to moderate climbing, you reach the edge of Winnemucca Lake, right at the foot of Mount Round Top, a gorgeous circle of blue. Although there are several options for hiking farther from here (see listing in this chapter), for many people, this destination is perfect enough.

The peak season for wildflowers is mid-June to mid-August, at its very best in mid-to-late July. If you hiked this trail in years past, you may remember that it once started by crossing a footbridge. That is no longer true.

The land here has been formed by volcanic action, so as you walk, you constantly have to remind yourself that you aren't at Mount

Lassen or Mount Shasta, you're just south of Tahoe in Carson Pass. The beauty attracts a ton of people, often 200 to 300 on summer weekends.

User Groups: Hikers, leashed dogs, and horses. No mountain bikes. No wheelchair facilities.

Permits: A free wilderness permit is required for overnight stays; it is available from the Amador Ranger Station, the Carson Pass Information Station, or the Eldorado Information Center. A parking fee of $3 is charged, good for overnight use.

Maps: For a map, ask the U.S. Forest Service for Mokelumne Wilderness or Eldorado National Forest. For topographic maps, ask the USGS for Caples Lake and Carson Pass.

Directions: From South Lake Tahoe, take Highway 89 south for five miles to Meyers and the junction with Highway 89, and then continue south on 89 for 11 miles to Highway 88. Turn right (west) on Highway 88 and drive 12 miles to the Woods Lake Campground turnoff, on the south side of the road (1.5 miles west of Carson Pass Summit). Turn left and drive one mile to the trailhead parking area (.5 mile before reaching Woods Lake).

Contact: Eldorado National Forest, Amador Ranger District, 26820 Silver Drive, Pioneer, CA 95666, 209/295-4251, www.fs.fed.us/r5.

88 ROUND TOP SUMMIT AND WINNEMUCCA LAKE LOOP

6.6 mi / 4.0 hr 4 ▲10

in the Mokelumne Wilderness near Carson Pass

Map 6.3, page 215

If you want all the scenic beauty of Winnemucca Lake Trail, but you also want a longer walk and a little more solitude, try this loop trip instead. Note that although the loop trail itself is a relatively easy hike, adding on a side trip to the summit of Mount Round Top gives this hike a difficulty rating of a resounding 4.

There is no real trail to Round Top's summit, and the most obvious use trail goes straight uphill at a punishing grade.

The path is the same route as Winnemucca Lake Trail for the first 1.5 miles to Winnemucca's edge, but then you bear right and cross the stream on the west side of the lake. From there, it's one mile uphill to Round Top Lake, steep enough to get you puffing. The gorgeous volcanic scenery makes it all worthwhile. Round Top Lake is set below The Sisters, two peaks that are both over 10,000 feet high. You also have views of Mount Round Top and Fourth of July Peak. It's incredibly dramatic. From the eastern edge of Round Top Lake, you'll see an obvious path heading up the side of Mount Round Top. If you like a little challenge and you're surefooted, go for it. The grade is brutal, but when you reach the top after a final rocky scramble, you have a stunning view of The Dardanelles, Lake Tahoe, Caples Lake, Woods Lake, Round Top Lake, Winnemucca Lake, and Frog Lake. Perhaps most impressive is deep Summit City Canyon, 3,000 feet below the south side of Round Top. At 10,380 feet, Mount Round Top is the highest peak in the Carson Pass area and is the finest place for a bird's-eye view. The summit is more like a knife-thin, rocky ridge, so watch your footing. This is not a place for children or inexperienced hikers.

After your summit visit, return downhill to Round Top Lake to finish out your loop. Follow the lake's outlet creek on Lost Cabin Mine Trail for two miles back to Woods Lake Campground; then wind your way through the camp back to the Woods Lake Picnic Area, where you left your car.

User Groups: Hikers, leashed dogs, and horses. No mountain bikes. No wheelchair facilities.

Permits: A free wilderness permit is required for overnight stays; it is available from the Amador Ranger Station, the Carson Pass Information Station, or the Eldorado Information Center.

Maps: For a map, ask the U.S. Forest Service for Mokelumne Wilderness or Eldorado

National Forest. For topographic maps, ask the USGS for Caples Lake and Carson Pass.

Directions: From South Lake Tahoe, take Highway 89 south for five miles to Meyers and the junction with Highway 89, and then continue south on Highway 89 for 11 miles to Highway 88. Turn right (west) on Highway 88 and drive 12 miles to the Woods Lake Campground turnoff, on the south side of the road (1.5 miles west of Carson Pass Summit). Turn left and drive 1.5 miles to the trailhead parking area, by the picnic area at Woods Lake.

Contact: Eldorado National Forest, Amador Ranger District, 26820 Silver Drive, Pioneer, CA 95666, 209/295-4251, www.fs.fed.us/r5.

89 FOURTH OF JULY LAKE
8.8 mi / 4.5 hr or 2 days 🥾4 ⛰9

in the Mokelumne Wilderness near Caples Lake

Map 6.3, page 215

The biggest problem in a trip to Fourth of July Lake is the high number of people. Carson Pass is a stellar trailhead, and with several lakes and Mount Round Top so close, there can be 200 to 300 hikers on summer weekends. So timing becomes key, along with deciding which way to go. There are so many ways from so many trailheads, including ones at Carson Pass and Upper Blue Lake.

The shortest and most direct route is from Woods Lake trailhead, located 0.5 mile before the Woods Lake Campground and picnic area. This includes a nice stopover at Round Top Lake, two miles in. You pass some old mining cabins before you enter the wilderness boundary. Pass the eastern flank of 9,000-foot Black Butte, an old volcanic vent that is similar in appearance to Mount Round Top a few miles to the east. In less than an hour, you arrive at Round Top Lake, a worthy destination in itself and a good spot for a snack break beneath the sturdy shoulders of the two peaks of The Sisters. It's only two more miles to Fourth of July Lake, but they are steep and downhill, which means

you must climb back out on the way home. This is actually good news: It means you will leave the majority of the crowds behind. Most people give up at Fourth of July Saddle, a rocky overlook that sits 1,000 feet above the lake. In addition to the tough grade, the route is often dusty. At the lake, fishing is good for brook trout, and many campsites can be found near its edge. Late in the summer, a sandy beach gets exposed, perfect for swimmers.

User Groups: Hikers, leashed dogs, and horses. No mountain bikes. No wheelchair facilities.

Permits: A free wilderness permit is required for overnight stays; it is available from the Amador Ranger Station, the Carson Pass Information Station, or the Eldorado Information Center.

Maps: For a map, ask the U.S. Forest Service for Eldorado National Forest or Mokelumne Wilderness. For a topographic map, ask the USGS for Caples Lake.

Directions: From South Lake Tahoe, take Highway 89 south for five miles to Meyers and the junction with Highway 89, and then continue south on Highway 89 for 11 miles to Highway 88. Turn right (west) on Highway 88 and drive 12 miles to the Woods Lake Campground turnoff, on the south side of the road (1.5 miles west of Carson Pass Summit). Turn left and drive one mile to the trailhead (.5 mile before the campground and picnic area).

Contact: Eldorado National Forest, Amador Ranger District, 26820 Silver Drive, Pioneer, CA 95666, 209/295-4251, www.fs.fed.us/r5.

90 FROG LAKE
1.8 mi / 1.0 hr 🥾1 ⛰9

in the Mokelumne Wilderness near Carson Pass

Map 6.3, page 215

Any hiking trip from the Carson Pass trailhead is going to be packed with people. So it is here, with 200-plus people out on weekends. That known, this trail is educational and beautiful. The short walk to Frog Lake is suitable even for small children, and if you're more ambitious, you can continue another 1.5 miles to beautiful Winnemucca Lake. At Frog Lake, you are provided with a fascinating look at Elephant Back (elevation 9,585 feet), which looks exactly like its name. It's a lava dome, a round mass of solid lava. The lake is a beautiful turquoise color, perfect for picnicking, although because the area is rather open and exposed, the wind sometimes blows with ferocity.

Plenty of people take this walk in early summer to see the wildflowers, especially lupine and Indian paintbrush, from mid-June to mid-August (best in late July). A huge patch of wild iris also blooms alongside Frog Lake. It's a sight to behold. There are many other species of wildflowers here. An identification sheet is posted at the billboard near the trailhead and at the visitors center.

At the visitors center, you can learn about Kit Carson, the great explorer for whom this pass was named, and you can learn about the geologic forces that shaped this region, which is called the Round Top Geologic Area. Evidence of both glacial and volcanic action can be seen with every step you take.

User Groups: Hikers, leashed dogs, and horses. No mountain bikes. No wheelchair facilities.

Permits: A free wilderness permit is required for overnight stays between April 1 and November 30; it is available from the Amador Ranger Station, the Carson Pass Information Station, or the Eldorado Information Center. A $3 parking fee is charged per vehicle.

Maps: For a map, ask the U.S. Forest Service for Eldorado National Forest or Mokelumne Wilderness. For a topographic map, ask the USGS for Carson Pass.

Directions: From South Lake Tahoe, take Highway 89 south for five miles to Meyers and the junction with Highway 89, and then continue south on Highway 89 for 11 miles to Highway 88. Turn right (west) on Highway 88 and drive 10 miles to Carson Pass Summit.

The parking area and trailhead are on the left, by the Carson Pass Information Station.

Contact: Eldorado National Forest, Amador Ranger District, 26820 Silver Drive, Pioneer, CA 95666, 209/295-4251, www.fs.fed.us/r5.

91 RAYMOND LAKE
11.0 mi / 1-2 days

in the Mokelumne Wilderness near Blue Lakes

Map 6.3, page 215

Raymond Lake is a popular weekend trip despite the 3,000-foot climb. The pretty campsites at the little lake are used by PCT hikers and weekenders making this a two-day in-and-outer. That is, about five miles in and about five miles out, and that's why it works, especially for couples or young families new to backpacking. The lake is about 10 acres in size and is set at 9,000 feet, with several small campsites sprinkled near the lake. The trail starts near Wet Meadows Reservoir and heads east from the access road on the Pacific Crest Trail. Keep following the PCT for 4.5 miles, then turn right on Raymond Lake Trail. Most of this 4.5-mile stretch is a moderate ascent. The final stretch is only a mile but is a butt-kicker, mostly because you're already getting tired when you begin it. The lake is set below 10,000-foot Raymond Peak, an alpine peak.

User Groups: Hikers, dogs, and horses. No mountain bikes. No wheelchair facilities.

Permits: A free wilderness permit is required for overnight stays; it is available on the wilderness bulletin board at the trailhead, from the ranger station in Markleeville, the Carson Pass Information Station, or the Carson Ranger district in Carson City. Groups are limited to 12, and no campfires are permitted above 8,000 feet.

Maps: For a map, ask the U.S. Forest Service for Humboldt-Toiyabe National Forest, Carson District. For topographic maps, ask the USGS for Pacific Valley and Ebbetts Pass.

Directions: From South Lake Tahoe, take Highway 89 south for five miles to Meyers and the junction with Highway 89, and then continue south on Highway 89 for 11 miles to Highway 88. Turn right (west) on Highway 88 and drive 2.5 miles to the Blue Lakes turnoff, on the south side of the road. Turn south and drive 11 miles to the left turnoff for Tamarack Lake and Wet Meadows. Bear left and drive three miles to the left turnoff for Lower Sunset Lake. Turn left and drive a short distance to the trailhead.

Contact: Humboldt-Toiyabe National Forest, 1200 Franklin Way, Sparks, NV 89431, 775/331-6444, www.fs.fed.us/htnf.

92 GRANITE LAKE
4.0 mi / 2.0 hr   🚶1 ⛰9

in the Mokelumne Wilderness near Blue Lakes

Map 6.3, page 215

Campers at Middle Creek Campground can set out from their tents on this trail to Granite Lake. But everyone else must begin by the dam at Upper Blue Lake and follow a well-signed but meandering route to enter the Mokelumne Wilderness, one mile in. Only one mile beyond the wilderness boundary lies Granite Lake, requiring a total 550-foot climb over well-graded trail. You'll barely notice you're climbing; this is a very easy pathway. A quarter mile past the boundary sign, you'll see a large pond, but don't mistake that for Granite Lake, which is another 20 minutes farther on the trail. The granite basin it's set in and the granite that lines its shores are a dead giveaway that you've made it to the proper destination. Hope you brought your swimsuit for the deep, chilly waters. If you want to hike farther, Grouse Lake is another four miles beyond.

Side note: Don't be concerned if there are lots of cars in the dam parking lot. Most of them belong to anglers, not hikers.

User Groups: Hikers, leashed dogs, and horses. No mountain bikes. No wheelchair facilities.

Permits: A free wilderness permit is required for overnight; it is available from the Amador Ranger Station, the Carson Pass Information Station, or the Eldorado Information Center.

Maps: For a map, ask the U.S. Forest Service for Eldorado National Forest. For a topographic map, ask the USGS for Pacific Valley.

Directions: From South Lake Tahoe, take Highway 89 south for five miles to Meyers and the junction with Highway 89, and then continue south on Highway 89 for 11 miles to Highway 88. Turn right (west) on Highway 88 and drive 2.5 miles to the Blue Lakes turnoff, on the south side of the road. Turn south and drive 12 miles to the fork at Lower Blue Lake. Turn right and drive 1.5 miles to the dam by Upper Blue Lake, shortly past Middle Creek Campground; turn left into the parking area. The Grouse Lake Trail leads to Granite Lake from the west side of the parking area.

Contact: Eldorado National Forest, Amador Ranger District, 26820 Silver Drive, Pioneer, CA 95666, 209/295-4251, www.fs.fed.us/r5.

93 HOT SPRINGS CREEK WATERFALL
3.0 mi / 1.5 hr   🚶1 ⛰8

in Grover Hot Springs State Park near Markleeville

Map 6.3, page 215

Even without a waterfall, this would be a great trail to walk. It leads through the giant Jeffrey pines of Hot Springs Valley, enclosed by rocky cliffs and 10,000-foot peaks. The route starts from just beyond the campgrounds in Grover Hot Springs State Park. From here, you hike on the Burnside Lake and Charity Valley Trails for 0.5 mile, then branch off on a left fork. The trail is well signed for the waterfall. Some people get a bit confused on the trail where you reach a jumbled pile of boulders, but the correct answer is simply to go up and over them. Hot Springs Canyon gradually narrows on its way to the falls, and when you near the creek's edge, you'll see many small trout swimming in its pools. The waterfall is about 50 feet high and is best seen from April to July. Technically it is outside of state parkland and in Toiyabe National Forest, so you'll see backpackers' campfire rings on the cliff above the falls. The trailhead elevation is 5,900 feet, and the waterfalls are set at 6,200 feet; hence, there's a 300-foot climb.

User Groups: Hikers and leashed dogs (not recommended). No horses or mountain bikes. No wheelchair facilities.

Permits: No permits are required. A day-use fee of $8 is charged per vehicle; there is a fee of $5 per person for use of the hot springs pool.

Maps: A map of Grover Hot Springs State Park is available for a fee at the entrance station. For a topographic map, ask the USGS for Markleeville.

Directions: From South Lake Tahoe, take Highway 89 south for five miles to Meyers and the junction with Highway 89, and then continue south on Highway 89 for 11 miles to Highway 88. Turn left on Highway 88/89 and drive 13 miles to Markleeville at Hot Springs Road. Turn right (west) on Hot Springs Road and drive 3.5 miles to the state park entrance. The signed trailhead is 0.25 mile beyond the entrance station and campground turnoffs, at a gated dirt road.

Contact: Grover Hot Springs State Park, P.O. Box 188, Markleeville, CA 96120, 530/694-2248, pool information 530/694-2249, www.parks.ca.gov.

94 BURNSIDE LAKE
8.4 mi / 5.0 hr

in Humboldt-Toiyabe National Forest near Markleeville

Map 6.3, page 215

The Burnside Lake Trail leaves Grover Hot Springs State Park at 5,900 feet in elevation and climbs west to Burnside Lake, at 8,160 feet, a gain of 2,260 feet. The climb is spaced out over four miles, so it's a steady workout to the lake. Along the way, you pass tall and majestic sugar pines and rocky outcrops, with

10,023-foot Hawkins Peak and 9,417-foot Markleeville Peak towering over the scene. The lake is about 10 surface acres and is popular for trout fishing. Although you can start hiking on the trail from Hot Springs Road shortly before the state park entrance, it's best to start from the park's trailhead. Not only does it shave one mile off your trip, but also when you return from your hike, you can take a dip in the 102- to 104-degree hot springs and soothe those aching muscles. Although you may encounter some mountain bikers on the trail at first, they will soon branch off on their way to Charity Valley.

User Groups: Hikers, dogs, horses, and mountain bikes. No wheelchair facilities.

Permits: No permits are required. A day-use fee of $8 is charged per vehicle at Grover Hot Springs State Park. Parking and access are free if you park and begin the trail outside the park entrance.

Maps: For a map, ask the U.S. Forest Service for Humboldt-Toiyabe National Forest, Carson District. A map of Grover Hot Springs State Park is available for $0.25 at the entrance station. For a topographic map, ask the USGS for Markleeville.

Directions: From South Lake Tahoe, take Highway 89 south for five miles to Meyers and the junction with Highway 89, and then continue south on Highway 89 for 11 miles to Highway 88. Turn left on Highway 88/89 and drive 13 miles to Markleeville at Hot Springs Road. Turn right (west) on Hot Springs Road and drive 3.5 miles to the state park entrance. The signed trailhead is 0.25 mile beyond the entrance station and campground turnoffs, at a gated dirt road. Another trailhead is located outside the state park on Hot Springs Road, 0.75 mile before the state park entrance, and is signed for Charity Valley.

Contact: Grover Hot Springs State Park, P.O. Box 188, Markleeville, CA 96120, 530/694-2248 or 530/525-7232, www.parks.ca.gov; Humboldt-Toiyabe National Forest, 1200 Franklin Way, Sparks, NV 89431, 775/331-6444, www.fs.fed.us/htnf.

95 BLUE LAKES ROAD TO CARSON PASS (PCT)
12.0 mi one-way / 1 day 👣4 ⛰9

from Blue Lakes Road north to Carson Pass
and Highway 88

Map 6.3, page 215

Many hikers underestimate the climb over
Elephant Back to reach Carson Pass. After all,
on a map, it doesn't look like much, and from a
distance, as you size it up, it looks easy enough.
Wrong! It's a long, grueling pull. The trip out
of Blue Lakes starts easily, with a dirt road
often in view and adding a bit of early angst
to the affair. As you go, you keep wondering
when the climb will start. Well, eventually it
does, and, alas, it takes a couple of hours—a
long, steady march. After topping the Elephant
Back, the route drops down to Carson Pass at
a rest stop, where you'll likely meet humanity,
but believe it or not, no water! When we hiked
from Yosemite to Tahoe, this was the worst
shock of the trip. Conserve yours if you plan
to go onward, because it takes another hour of
hiking before you'll reach the next trickle.

To continue north on the PCT, see the
Carson Pass to Echo Lakes Resort (PCT) hike
in this chapter. If you are walking this trail
in reverse, see the *Ebbetts Pass to Blue Lakes
Road (PCT)* hike in this chapter.

User Groups: Hikers, dogs, and horses. No
mountain bikes. No wheelchair access.

Permits: A backcountry permit is required
for traveling through various wilderness and
special-use areas that the trail traverses. In
addition, a campfire permit is required for
the use of portable camp stoves or the building of campfires where allowed. To make it
simple, you can contact the national forest,
Bureau of Land Management (BLM), or national park office at your point of entry for a
combined permit that is good for traveling
through multiple-permit areas during your
dates of travel.

Maps: For a map, ask the U.S. Forest Service
for Lake Tahoe Basin Management Unit,
Tahoe National Forest, Eldorado National

Forest, and Stanislaus National Forest. For
topographic maps, ask the USGS for Pacific
Valley and Carson Pass.

Directions: To reach the Blue Lakes Road
trailhead from the Highway 88/89 junction
at Hope Valley, go west on Highway 88 to Blue
Lakes Road and turn left. Stay on Blue Lakes
Road for 11 miles to the trailhead parking,
just before reaching Blue Lakes. For the Carson Pass trailhead from the Highway 88/89
junction at Hope Valley, go west on Highway
88 to Carson Pass.

Contact: Eldorado National Forest, Amador
Ranger District, 26820 Silver Drive, Pioneer,
CA 95666, 209/295-4251, www.fs.fed.us/r5.

96 KINNEY LAKES
5.0 mi / 2.5 hr 👣2 ⛰8

in Humboldt-Toiyabe National Forest near
Ebbetts Pass

Map 6.3, page 215

From the Ebbetts Pass trailhead, Kinney Lakes
is an easy tromp north on the Pacific Crest
Trail (it's quite a bit farther to head south
from Ebbetts Pass to reach Noble Lake; see
the *Noble Lake* listing in this chapter). You pass
little Sherrold Lake on the way to large Upper
Kinney Lake (which is actually a reservoir).

You start hiking at 8,700 feet at the pass, so
even though this trail has an easy to moderate
grade, your lungs are getting a workout. The
trail leads through a landscape of big conifers with little undergrowth, typical of the
high country. When the trees thin out, your
views open wide. Raymond Peak and Reynolds Peak rule the skyline. At 1.6 miles, you
reach a signed junction for Upper and Lower
Kinney Lakes, and you can take your pick as
to which one to visit first. The Pacific Crest
Trail leads directly to the upper lake, while
the lower lake must be visited by following an
eastward fork from the PCT. The upper lake,
though smaller, is the prettier of the two.

User Groups: Hikers, dogs, and horses. No
mountain bikes. No wheelchair facilities.

Permits: Wilderness permits are required for overnight use. No campfires are allowed above 8,000 feet. Parking and access are free.

Maps: For a map, ask the U.S. Forest Service for Humboldt-Toiyabe National Forest, Carson District. For a topographic map, ask the USGS for Ebbetts Pass.

Directions: From Angels Camp, drive east on Highway 4 for about 40 miles to Bear Valley. Set your odometer at Bear Valley, and drive 15 miles farther east on Highway 4 to Ebbetts Pass and the trailhead parking area. The trail is on the north side of the road. If you are coming from Markleeville, drive south on Highway 89/Highway 4 for 15 miles to Ebbetts Pass.

Contact: Humboldt-Toiyabe National Forest, 1200 Franklin Way, Sparks, NV 89431, 775/331-6444, www.fs.fed.us/htnf.

97 EBBETTS PASS TO BLUE LAKES ROAD (PCT)

17.7 mi one-way / 1 day   🥾3 ⛰8

from Highway 4 near Ebbetts Pass north to Blue Lakes Road just south of Carson Pass and Highway 88

Map 6.3, page 215

As you leave Ebbetts Pass heading north, you'll cross a series of fantastic volcanic formations in the Mokelumne Wilderness. The country here may look stark from a distance, but it is loaded with tiny wildflowers. The trail is quite good; a lot of hikers make great time in this area. But the lack of available water can become a concern. Tank up whenever you get the chance, such as at Eagle Creek below Reynold Peak (9,690 feet). The Mokelumne Wilderness is a relative breeze, and you'll find yourself approaching civilization at a series of small lakes in Tahoe National Forest. The trail rises up a stark, wind-blown, sandy ridge, with excellent views of the Blue Lakes, but again, there is no water for several miles until you drop down near Lost Lake. You'll actually cross several roads on this stretch of trail, and maybe even

see a car, a moment of irony for long-distance PCT hikers. But the going is easy; we think this is one of the fastest sections of the PCT in the central Sierra. To continue north on the PCT, see the *Blue Lakes Road to Carson Pass (PCT)* hike in this chapter.

User Groups: Hikers, dogs, and horses. No mountain bikes. No wheelchair facilities.

Permits: A backcountry permit is required for traveling through various wilderness and special-use areas that the trail traverses. In addition, a campfire permit is required for the use of portable camp stoves or the building of campfires (where permitted). To make it simple, you can contact the national forest, Bureau of Land Management (BLM), or national park office at your point of entry for a combined permit good for traveling through multiple-permit areas during your dates of travel.

Maps: For a map, ask the U.S. Forest Service for Lake Tahoe Basin Management Unit, Tahoe National Forest, Eldorado National Forest, and Stanislaus National Forest. For topographic maps, ask the USGS for Ebbetts Pass, Pacific Valley, and Carson Pass.

Directions: To reach the Ebbetts Pass trailhead from Angels Camp, head east on Highway 4 to Ebbetts Pass. To reach the Blue Lakes Road trailhead from the Highway 88/89 interchange at Hope Valley, head west on Highway 88 to Blue Lakes Road and turn left. Stay on Blue Lakes Road to the trailhead parking area, just before reaching Blue Lakes.

Contact: Eldorado National Forest, Amador Ranger District, 26820 Silver Drive, Pioneer, CA 95666, 209/295-4251, www.fs.fed.us/r5.

98 NOBLE LAKE

9.0 mi / 4.5 hr   🥾2 ⛰8

in Humboldt-Toiyabe National Forest near Ebbetts Pass

Map 6.3, page 215

Noble Lake lies just outside of the Carson-Iceberg Wilderness and is reachable by a steady climb on Noble Canyon Trail out of Silver Creek Campground, or by a shorter, gentler route from Ebbetts Pass. The latter is the best choice.

From Ebbetts Pass (elevation 8,700 feet), there's a 1,200-foot climb to the lake at 9,440 feet (which includes some descent as well). The lake is a fine spot for camping or just spending an afternoon. The scenery is classic high Sierra, big conifers, snowcapped peaks, hard granite, and lush meadows. A boulder field above the campsites is loaded with ground squirrels, and if you hike overnight here with a dog, the squirrels will drive your dog crazy. This lake is excellent for swimming but poor for fishing. For camping, group size is limited to 15 people, and a 100-foot setback from the lake is required.

The lake route follows an access trail to the Pacific Crest Trail from the trailhead parking area. After 0.25 mile of climbing, you will join the PCT proper and head south, first climbing and then making a long descent into Noble Canyon. The trail from Silver Creek Campground joins your trail here, and some switchbacks follow. At three miles, you will cross Noble Creek and then climb again to a high meadow. Soon you can see Noble Lake; the main lake is to the right of the trail, but a smaller, unnamed lake is to the left, about 650 feet off the trail. Both have decent campsites and many good rocks to sit on and relax.

User Groups: Hikers, dogs, and horses. No mountain bikes. No wheelchair facilities.

Permits: No day-hiking permits are required. A free wilderness permit is available at the trailhead (self-issue). Parking and access are free.

Maps: For a map, ask the U.S. Forest Service for Humboldt-Toiyabe National Forest, Carson District. For a topographic map, ask the USGS for Ebbetts Pass.

Directions: From Angels Camp at the intersection of Highways 4 and 49, go east on Highway 4 for 40 miles to Bear Valley. Set your odometer at Bear Valley, and drive 15 miles farther east on Highway 4 to Ebbetts Pass and the trailhead parking area (located just east of

Ebbetts Pass; do not park on Highway 4). The trailhead is on the south side of the road.

Contact: Humboldt-Toiyabe National Forest, 1200 Franklin Way, Sparks, NV 89431, 775/331-6444, www.fs.fed.us/htnf.

99 WOLF CREEK TRAIL
9.6 mi / 5.0 hr   🏃2 ⛰️8

in the Carson-Iceberg Wilderness near Markleeville

Map 6.3, page 215

When the temperature heats up around Markleeville, you've got two choices: Head for the mineral springs at Grover Hot Springs State Park (the cool pool, not the hot pool), or take a hike on Wolf Creek Trail in the Carson-Iceberg Wilderness.

If you pick the latter, you're in for a fine time on this easy trail along Wolf Creek, starting at 6,480 feet in elevation. The trail is an old jeep road and is almost entirely shaded, and it meanders upstream and slightly uphill for a total of nine miles one-way. Most people do not hike the entire route, but rather take our suggested trip to Wolf Creek Falls. An ideal day hike is just to stroll along the creek for an hour or two, find a good spot along the stream to hang out for a while, then turn around and stroll back. Energetic types can hike 4.3 miles out to a fork for the steep Bull Canyon Trail to Bull Lake, then bear left and continue 0.5 mile beyond the fork to Wolf Creek Falls. The waterfall is found just off the trail to the left, about 50 yards beyond where the trail passes through a cattle fence. It's quite impressive early in the summer, as it thunders over a cliff of volcanic rock.

User Groups: Hikers, dogs, and horses. No mountain bikes. No wheelchair facilities.

Permits: A free wilderness permit is required for overnight stays; it is available at the trailhead. Parking and access are free.

Maps: For a map, ask the U.S. Forest Service for Humboldt-Toiyabe National Forest, Carson District, and Carson-Iceberg Wilderness.

For a topographic map, ask the USGS for Wolf Creek.

Directions: From South Lake Tahoe, take Highway 89 south for five miles to Meyers and the junction with Highway 89, and then continue south on Highway 89 for 11 miles to Highway 88. Turn left on Highway 88/89 and drive 13 miles to Markleeville. From Markleeville, continue south on Highway 89 for four miles to Monitor Pass Junction and Highway 4. Bear right (south) on Highway 4 and drive 2.5 miles to the signed turnoff for Wolf Creek, on the left. Turn left (south) and drive 4.9 miles to the trailhead, about 100 yards before the end of the road.

Contact: Humboldt-Toiyabe National Forest, 1200 Franklin Way, Sparks, NV 89431, 775/331-6444, www.fs.fed.us/htnf.

100 EAST CARSON RIVER TRAIL

4.0 mi / 2.0 hr   👫2   ⛰8

in the Carson-Iceberg Wilderness near Markleeville

Map 6.3, page 215

The East Carson River Trail can be your salvation in spring when there's still too much snow around Ebbetts Pass. Trailhead elevation is only 6,240 feet at the north side of Wolf Creek Meadows (private property), which means it's snow-free before other nearby areas. Bear left at the trail junction just uphill from the trailhead and the sign noting Carson-Iceberg Wilderness (the right fork is the High Trail northern terminus). An interesting journey is 1.5 miles to Wolf Creek Lake (sometimes dry) and Railroad Canyon, the site of 19th-century logging operations. Although this trail continues onward and eventually meets up with the southern terminus of High Trail (and ends at the junction with Golden Canyon Trail), it is nearly impossible to make a loop trip out of the two trails, especially in early season. The High Trail reaches an elevation of nearly 8,000 feet and is often covered in snow early

in the season. So just hike as far as you like, then head back the way you came.

User Groups: Hikers, dogs, and horses. No mountain bikes. No wheelchair facilities.

Permits: A free wilderness permit is required for overnight stays; it is available at the trailhead. Parking and access are free.

Maps: For a map, ask the U.S. Forest Service for Humboldt-Toiyabe National Forest, Carson District, and Carson-Iceberg Wilderness. For a topographic map, ask the USGS for Wolf Creek.

Directions: From South Lake Tahoe, take Highway 89 south for five miles to Meyers and the junction with Highway 89, and then continue south on Highway 89 for 11 miles to Highway 88. Turn left on Highway 88/89 and drive 13 miles to Markleeville. Continue south on Highway 89/Highway 4 for 7.5 miles to the signed turnoff for Wolf Creek on the left. Turn left (east) and drive 3.5 miles to the left turnoff signed for East Carson River Trail. Turn left and drive one mile to the road junction to Dixon Mine. Turn right and drive 0.25 mile to the trailhead.

Contact: Humboldt-Toiyabe National Forest, 1200 Franklin Way, Sparks, NV 89431, 775/331-6444, www.fs.fed.us/htnf.

101 HEISER LAKE

4.8 mi / 2.5 hr   👫3   ⛰9

in the Carson-Iceberg Wilderness near Ebbetts Pass

Map 6.3, page 215

You know you're in for a good trip when the trailhead is located at a spot as pretty as the Mosquito Lakes, set at an elevation of 8,000 feet on Highway 4. The trail climbs and descends, then climbs and descends some more, mostly heading in a straight-line course due south to the lake. It's one of those trails where you've got to work equally hard traveling in both directions. At a junction with the trail from Bull Run Lake two miles in, bear left and finish out the last 0.5 mile to

Heiser Lake, set at 8,300 feet. The lake is granite bound, with a couple of tiny islands sticking out of its shallow waters. The tiny little lakes are popular with anglers from the nearby campgrounds, but this trail is popular with nature lovers, who set out on the short, moderate, day hike to Heiser Lake for a few hours of peace in the Carson-Iceberg Wilderness.

User Groups: Hikers, dogs, and horses. No mountain bikes. No wheelchair facilities.

Permits: No day-hiking permits are required. Parking and access are free.

Maps: For a map, ask the U.S. Forest Service for Stanislaus National Forest and Carson-Iceberg Wilderness. For topographic maps, ask the USGS for Pacific Valley and Spicer Meadow Reservoir.

Directions: From Angels Camp, take Highway 4 east for 40 miles to Bear Valley. Set your odometer at Bear Valley and drive 10 miles farther east on Highway 4 to the the Mosquito Lakes trailhead and Heiser Lake Trail. Park on the right (south) side of the road, across from the campground; there is only enough space for a few cars.

Contact: Stanislaus National Forest, Calaveras Ranger District, P.O. Box 500, Hathaway Pines, CA 95233, 209/795-1381, www.fs.fed.us/r5.

102 BULL RUN LAKE

7.0 mi / 4.0 hr

in the Carson-Iceberg Wilderness near Ebbetts Pass

Map 6.3, page 215

You might have to share the trail to Bull Run Lake with some horses. After all, their owners like the big parking lot at the trailhead, large enough for horse trailers. Maybe you should pack along a few extra apples or carrots, eh? Although longer than the nearby trail to Heiser Lake, this trip to Bull Run Lake is actually easier, because the trail is well graded, and the only really steep section is in the last 0.5 mile.

The trailhead is set at 7,800 feet. The first 1.3 miles are almost level, traveling slightly downhill through a grassy meadow that is filled with wildflowers in the early summer and turns golden by September. After that, you start to climb, mostly through pine forest and over duck-lined stretches of granite. Watch for a trail junction at 2.2 miles, where you should turn right for Bull Run Lake (straight ahead is Heiser Lake). After a brief flat stretch, prepare for a final mile of climbing, with the last part being the most challenging. The lake is set at 8,300 feet and is a fine reward for your effort, set in a steep-walled granite bowl, with many smooth rock slabs to lie on. Note that the ambitious can add on a trip to Heiser Lake, which is two miles away from the junction. But with a steep up and down, it's better saved for backpackers or day hikers with an early start.

User Groups: Hikers, dogs, and horses. No mountain bikes. No wheelchair facilities.

Permits: No day-hiking permits are required. Parking and access are free.

Maps: For a map, ask the U.S. Forest Service for Stanislaus National Forest or Carson-Iceberg Wilderness. For topographic maps, ask the USGS for Pacific Valley and Spicer Meadow Reservoir.

Directions: From Angels Camp, take Highway 4 east for 40 miles to Bear Valley. Set your odometer at Bear Valley and drive 8.5 miles farther east on Highway 4 to the Stanislaus Meadow turnoff, on the right (Road 8N13). Turn right and drive a short distance to the trailhead parking area.

Contact: Stanislaus National Forest, Calaveras Ranger District, P.O. Box 500, Hathaway Pines, CA 95233, 209/795-1381, www.fs.fed.us/r5.

103 CLARK FORK AND BOULDER LAKE

8.0 mi / 4.0 hr   🏃3 ⛰8

in the Carson-Iceberg Wilderness on Clark Fork Stanislaus River

Map 6.3, page 215

From this trailhead at Iceberg Meadow, you immediately enter the Carson-Iceberg Wilderness at the base of imposing Iceberg Peak. You will hike upstream on the northern edge of the Clark Fork Stanislaus River and enjoy wildflowers and a lovely mixed forest of white firs and Jeffrey pines. At the water's edge, the trees are leafier, including cottonwoods and aspens. The river pools are cold but useful for cooling off on a hot day. At 2.5 miles, you have a choice: Bear right (really straight) and continue along the Clark Fork, or turn left and hike steeply uphill along Boulder Creek. We suggest the left fork, following Boulder Creek for 1.5 miles uphill to tiny Boulder Lake. It's a good workout to a pretty destination. But hey, if you get tired, just cut the trip short and turn around when you reach Boulder Creek. Plenty of fishing holes and picnic spots can be found along the Clark Fork.

User Groups: Hikers, dogs, and horses. No mountain bikes. No wheelchair facilities.

Permits: A free wilderness permit is required for overnight stays and is available from the Summit Ranger Station. Parking and access are free.

Maps: For a map, ask the U.S. Forest Service for Stanislaus National Forest or Carson-Iceberg Wilderness. For a topographic map, ask the USGS for Donnell Lake.

Directions: From Sonora, take Highway 108 east for 46 miles to the left turnoff for Clark Fork Road (about 17 miles east of Strawberry). Turn left and follow Clark Fork Road for about seven miles to its end, at the Clark Fork trailhead at Iceberg Meadow.

Contact: Stanislaus National Forest, Summit Ranger District, 1 Pinecrest Lake Road, Pinecrest, CA 95364, 209/965-3434, www.fs.fed.us/r5.

104 EAGLE MEADOW TO DARDANELLE

4.0 mi one-way / 2.0 hr   🏃2 ⛰8

near Dardanelle

Map 6.3, page 215   **BEST (**

Your first order of business is to convince someone to drop you off at Eagle Meadow and pick you up at Dardanelle Resort. Then you can take this one-way trip, a scenic downhill stroll paralleling Eagle Creek. It's a trip for lovers of sub-alpine meadows, especially in the first mile. After it leaves the meadow, the trail enters a thick and lovely conifer forest, so you get a bit of shade along the path. The route gets a little steep in sections, so make sure your knees are in good enough shape for four miles of downhill before you make the trip.

User Groups: Hikers, leashed dogs, horses, and mountain bikes. No wheelchair facilities.

Permits: No permits are required. Parking and access are free.

Maps: For a map, ask the U.S. Forest Service for Stanislaus National Forest. For topographic maps, ask the USGS for Donnell Lake and Dardanelle.

Directions: From Sonora, take Highway 108 east for 41 miles to the turnoff for Niagara Creek Campground, on the right side of the highway (about 12 miles east of Strawberry). Turn right, then at 0.25 mile, turn right again on Forest Road 5N01 and continue on Forest Road 5N01 for seven miles to Eagle Meadow. This is the start of the one-way shuttle hike; the finish is at Dardanelle Resort on Highway 108, eight miles east of the Niagara Creek turnoff.

Contact: Stanislaus National Forest, Summit Ranger District, 1 Pinecrest Lake Road, Pinecrest, CA 95364, 209/965-3434, www.fs.fed.us/r5.

105 TRAIL OF THE GARGOYLES

3.0 mi / 1.5 hr   👫1 ⛰8

near Strawberry and Pinecrest Lake in Stanislaus National Forest

Map 6.3, page 215   **BEST ⊙**

It's hard to guess what's in store on the Trail of the Gargoyles. The trailhead is nondescript, but that quickly changes. The odd rock formations that line the trail are perched at the edge of a cliff at 7,400 feet in elevation. You walk just inches away from what appears to be the edge of the world, with only thin air between you and the densely forested basin several hundred feet below. It's an easy and nearly flat trail, but if you have kids with you, keep a handhold on them at all times. By the way, the rock formations don't look much like gargoyles except for the fact that they are hanging off the edge of this abrupt abyss. The trailhead is in the middle of the 1.5-mile trail, which means you'll want to walk out and back in both directions. The trail on the north rim is slightly steeper.

User Groups: Hikers and leashed dogs. No horses or mountain bikes. No wheelchair facilities.

Permits: No permits are required. Parking and access are free.

Maps: For a map, ask the U.S. Forest Service for Stanislaus National Forest. For a topographic map, ask the USGS for Pinecrest.

Directions: From Sonora, take Highway 108 east for 32 miles to Strawberry, and then continue east 2.4 miles to Herring Creek Road (Forest Road 4N12). Turn right on Herring Creek Road and drive 6.7 miles to an often-unsigned turnoff on the left. Turn left and drive 0.2 mile to the trailhead.

Contact: Stanislaus National Forest, Summit Ranger District, 1 Pinecrest Lake Road, Pinecrest, CA 95364, 209/965-3434, www.fs.fed.us/r5.

106 COLUMNS OF THE GIANTS

0.5 mi / 0.5 hr   👫1 ⛰8

near Dardanelle

Map 6.3, page 215

This is the central Sierra's answer to Devils Postpile National Monument. Take it from us, it's no cheap imitation. The Columns of the Giants features remaining columns that are 30–40 feet in height and 3–4 feet in diameter. Although many are still standing tall or at least at an angle, others have shattered into thousands of pieces, creating a giant pile of rubble, at times just a jumbled heap of rocks. An interpretive trail sign explains that underneath this rock pile is evidence of the last small ice age in the Sierra, frozen remnants of ice fields that are replenished each year by winter snow and cold. The rock formations at the end of the Columns of the Giants geological trail were formed 150,000 years ago, when a series of volcanic eruptions occurred. The lava flow cooled rapidly, probably during cold weather, and cracked into narrow, hexagonal, basalt columns. This historical information gives you plenty to think about during your very short walk. Make sure you bring your camera.

User Groups: Hikers and leashed dogs. No horses or mountain bikes. No wheelchair facilities.

Permits: No permits are required. Parking and access are free.

Maps: For a map, ask the U.S. Forest Service for Stanislaus National Forest. For a topographic map, ask the USGS for Dardanelle.

Directions: From Sonora, take Highway 108 east for 50 miles to Pigeon Flat Campground (two miles east of Dardanelle) on the south side of the highway. If you're traveling west on Highway 108, the campground is 12.6 miles west of Sonora Pass. Park in the day-use parking lot just outside the camp.

Contact: Stanislaus National Forest, Summit Ranger District, 1 Pinecrest Lake Road, Pinecrest, CA 95364, 209/965-3434, www.fs.fed.us/r5.

107 KENNEDY LAKE

14.8 mi / 2 days   🚶3 ⛺8

in the Emigrant Wilderness near Dardanelle

Map 6.3, page 215

Follow the trail notes to Relief Reservoir (see listing in this chapter), but at 2.6 miles, take the left fork for Kennedy Lake. The trail climbs for another 1.6 miles, then goes flat for the final 3.2 miles to the lake. It's an easy two-day backpack trip, with low mileage and only a 1,200-foot elevation gain. Note that all the campsites are set downstream of the lake rather than along its shoreline.

If the number of cars in the Kennedy Meadows parking lot scares you, take heart. Many of them belong to people day hiking to fish at Relief Reservoir. If you have the time and inclination for a longer trip to Kennedy Lake, you will leave a lot of your fellow hikers behind. Even so, don't expect solitude. You'll likely share the lake with other backpackers, horse packers, and grazing cows.

User Groups: Hikers, leashed dogs, and horses. No mountain bikes. No wheelchair facilities.

Permits: A free wilderness permit is required for overnight stays and is available from the Summit Ranger Station. Parking and access are free.

Maps: For a map, ask the U.S. Forest Service for Stanislaus National Forest or Emigrant Wilderness. For a topographic map, ask the USGS for Sonora Pass.

Directions: From Sonora, take Highway 108 east for 55 miles to the turnoff for Kennedy Meadows (six miles east of Dardanelle) on the south side of the highway. Turn right and drive one mile to the large parking area. If you're traveling west on Highway 108, the Kennedy Meadows turnoff is 9.1 miles west of Sonora Pass.

Contact: Stanislaus National Forest, Summit Ranger District, 1 Pinecrest Lake Road, Pinecrest, CA 95364, 209/965-3434, www.fs.fed.us/r5.

108 RELIEF RESERVOIR

6.0 mi / 3.0 hr   🚶3 ⛰7

on the edge of the Emigrant Wilderness near Dardanelle

Map 6.3, page 215

From the mammoth trailhead and parking lot at Kennedy Meadows, you can hike to Relief Reservoir (elevation 7,200 feet), do a little fishing, then hike back out. The route, called the Huckleberry Trail, leads along the Stanislaus River, enters the Emigrant Wilderness at one mile, then skirts its edge. Quickly you understand why this trip is so popular, the river canyon gets more and more beautiful as you head deeper into it. The trail had to be blasted into the steep and rocky hillside. Pass the left turnoff for roaring Kennedy Creek and Kennedy Lake at 2.6 miles, and then proceed straight for another 0.5 mile to an overlook of the reservoir. It's a steep drop down to the water's edge in the last 0.25 mile, which, of course, must be regained on the return trip.

The only downers are that pack animals have roughed up the trail, and the route is seriously overused. On weekends it seems you must constantly pull off the path to let horses and other hikers go by.

User Groups: Hikers, leashed dogs, and horses. No mountain bikes. No wheelchair facilities.

Permits: No day-use permits are required. Parking and access are free.

Maps: For a map, ask the U.S. Forest Service for Stanislaus National Forest or Emigrant Wilderness. For a topographic map, ask the USGS for Sonora Pass.

Directions: From Sonora, take Highway 108 east for 55 miles to the Kennedy Meadows turnoff (six miles east of Dardanelle) on the south side of the highway. Turn right and go one mile to the well-signed parking area. Day hikers can park 0.5 mile farther down the road, near Kennedy Meadows Resort. If you're traveling west on Highway 108, the Kennedy Meadows turnoff is 9.1 miles west of Sonora Pass.

Contact: Stanislaus National Forest, Summit Ranger District, 1 Pinecrest Lake Road, Pinecrest, CA 95364, 209/965-3434, www.fs.fed.us/r5.

109 SARDINE FALLS
2.0 mi / 1.0 hr

near Sonora Pass

Map 6.3, page 215

An easy hike through a high alpine meadow and culminating at a pretty waterfall is our idea of a fine way to spend an afternoon. The trip to Sardine Falls requires a little route finding, because there is no formal trail. But the going is easy since you can see the falls from the road and there are several overgrown jeep routes to follow.

From parking, head across the northwest side of the meadow. Look for a route that is signed Route Closed to Motorized Vehicles; it's the most direct path. Cross Sardine Creek, which parallels Highway 108, and walk up the right side of larger McKay Creek. After climbing uphill over a rise, you'll hear and then see Sardine Falls, gracefully framed by a few sparse lodgepole pines.

User Groups: Hikers, leashed dogs, and horses. No mountain bikes. No wheelchair facilities.

Permits: No permits are required. Parking and access are free.

Maps: For a map, ask the U.S. Forest Service for Humboldt-Toiyabe National Forest, Bridgeport District. For a topographic map, ask the USGS for Pickel Meadow.

Directions: From the junction of U.S. 395 and Highway 108, take Highway 108 west and drive 12.5 miles (2.5 miles east of Sonora Pass) and park along the road in the gravel pullouts near the overgrown jeep roads on the northwest side of the meadow.

Contact: Humboldt-Toiyabe National Forest, Bridgeport Ranger District, HCR1 Box 1000, Bridgeport, CA 93517, 760/932-7070, www.fs.fed.us/htnf.

110 SONORA PASS TO EBBETTS PASS (PCT)
30.8 mi one-way / 3 days

from Highway 108 at Sonora Pass north to Highway 4 near Ebbetts Pass

Map 6.3, page 215

While this section of the Pacific Crest Trail may not have the glamorous reputation of the stretch of trail in the southern Sierra, it's just as compelling for those of us who have hiked it. From Sonora Pass, you're forced to climb out for a good hour or two. Then you'll rise over Wolf Creek Gap (10,300 feet, the highest, most northern point on the PCT) and make the easy drop down the Carson Canyon. This is the start of the Carson-Iceberg Wilderness, a giant swath of land that is a rare, unpeopled paradise. The Sierra riparian zones here are lined with flowers, seemingly all kinds and all colors, often in luxuriant beds of greenness. The PCT climbs out of Carson Canyon around Boulder Peak, then down and up two more canyons. All the while, you keep crossing creeks filled with natural gardens. You wind your way across and through these areas and eventually climb a ridge, then head down, steeply at times, to Ebbetts Pass. There's no water here. No problem. A short half-hour climb and you can be pumping water, and maybe setting up camp too, at little Sherrold Lake, not far from the edge of the Mokelumne Wilderness.

To continue north on the PCT, see the *Ebbetts Pass to Blue Lakes Road (PCT)* hike in this chapter.

User Groups: Hikers, dogs, and horses. No mountain bikes. No wheelchair facilities.

Permits: A wilderness permit is required for traveling through various wilderness and special-use areas the trail traverses. Contact the Stanislaus National Forest to obtain a permit that is good for the length of your trip.

Maps: For topographic maps, ask the USGS for Pickel Meadow, Disaster Peak, Dardanelles Cone, and Ebbetts Pass.

Directions: From Sonora, take Highway 108

east to Sonora Pass to the parking area and trailhead (south side of parking area).

Contact: Stanislaus National Forest, Summit Ranger District, 1 Pinecrest Lake Road, Pinecrest, CA 95364, 209/965-3434 or 209/532-3671 (for permits), www.fs.fed.us/r5.

111 SECRET AND POORE LAKES

6.5 mi / 3.5 hr 🏃3 ⛰9

near Sonora Pass

Map 6.3, page 215

This hike rates a solid 8, but we nudged it up after discovering one of the most spectacular waterfalls in the Sierra above Poore Lake. This 6.5-mile loop trip begins at a footbridge over West Walker River at Leavitt Meadows Campground. After 0.25 mile, take the left fork for Secret Lake (this is no secret and you won't be alone here, most likely). Climb for nearly two miles through sage and Jeffrey pines, then descend 0.5 mile to Secret Lake. Much larger Poore Lake is visible over your left shoulder. Take a break at Secret Lake, then continue around the right side of the lake, hiking through sparse junipers and pines for 0.5 mile to the left turnoff for Poore Lake. Take the rougher 0.75-mile route to the large lake. If it's quiet, you can swim or fish for a few hours, then retrace your steps to the junction. From there, loop back to the campground on a lower trail that follows closer to the West Walker River through Leavitt Meadow. If

Poore Lake turns out to be less than perfect, you can always hike beyond the return loop junction to little Roosevelt Lake.

Special Notes: No mountain bikes are permitted beyond Poore Lake, so that means Roosevelt Lake is free of them, at least in theory. In addition, there is no bridge available for off-road vehicles, so though this area was once an OHV spot, it is no longer. Finally, a nearby U.S. Marine training facility means it is possible you may see groups dressed in camo outfits running along the road. They do not fire their weapons here and they almost never enter the forest.

User Groups: Hikers, dogs, horses, and mountain bikes. No wheelchair facilities.

Permits: No day-use permits are required. Campfire permits required for overnight use. Parking and access are free.

Maps: For a map, ask the U.S. Forest Service for Humboldt-Toiyabe National Forest, Bridgeport District. For a topographic map, ask the USGS for Pickel Meadow.

Directions: From the junction of U.S. 395 and Highway 108, take Highway 108 west for seven miles to Leavitt Meadows Campground, on the south side of the road. If you are coming from the west, the camp is eight miles east of Sonora Pass. Day hikers may park inside the campground; backpackers must park 0.25 mile west of the camp on Highway 108.

Contact: Humboldt-Toiyabe National Forest, Bridgeport Ranger District, HCR1 Box 1000, Bridgeport, CA 93517, 760/932-7070, www.fs.fed.us/htnf.

SAN FRANCISCO BAY AREA

© TOM STIENST

BEST HIKES

⟨ Beach and Coastal Walks
Coast Trail, **page 304**

⟨ Bird-Watching
Abbotts Lagoon Trail, **page 296**
Audubon Canyon Ranch Trail, **page 319**
Arrowhead Marsh, **page 386**

⟨ Butt-Kickers
Rooster Comb Loop (Long Version), **page 442**

⟨ Hikes with a View
Perimeter Trail, **page 338**

⟨ Kids
Tomales Point Trail, **page 295**
Fitzgerald Marine Reserve, **page 354**
Año Nuevo Trail, **page 416**

⟨ Meadow Hikes
Grass Valley Loop, **page 388**

⟨ Redwoods
Main Trail, **page 330**

⟨ Short Backpack Trips
Coast Trail, **page 304**
Black Mountain, **page 367**

⟨ Summit Hikes
East Peak Mount Tamalpais, **page 323**

⟨ Wheelchair-Accessible Trails
Abbotts Lagoon Trail, **page 296**

⟨ Wildflowers
Chimney Rock Trail, **page 300**
Grass Valley Loop, **page 388**

⟨ Wildlife
Tomales Point Trail, **page 295**
Pescadero Marsh, **page 370**
Año Nuevo Trail, **page 416**

It's ironic that many people who have chosen

to live in the Bay Area are often the ones who complain the most about it. I've even heard some say, "Some day I'm going to get out of here and start having a good time."

Anyone who has ever had these thoughts should consider the view from an airplane encircling the Bay Area at 3,000 feet. What they'd see is that despite strips of roadways and pockets of cities where people are jammed together, most of the region is wild, unsettled, and beautiful. There is no metropolitan area in the world that offers better and more diverse recreation and open space so close to so many people.

The Bay Area has 150 significant parks (including 12 with redwoods), 7,500 miles of hiking and biking trails, 45 lakes, 25 waterfalls, 100 miles of coast, mountains with incredible lookouts, and bays with islands. And in all, there are 1.2 million acres of greenbelt, with hundreds of acres being added each year when land is bought by money earmarked from property taxes. The land has no limit. Enjoy it.

This chapter features over 200 of the best hikes in the Bay Area, high-lighted by Point Reyes National Seashore, Marin Headlands, California state parks, the East Bay Regional Park system, San Francisco Headlands, Midpeninsula Open Space District, Santa Clara and San Mateo county parks, and San Jose Department of Parks. These parks offer trails of all lengths — including long-distance hikes with campgrounds, such as Coast Trail (at Point Reyes), Ohlone Wilderness Trail and East Bay National Skyline Trail (routed through several East Bay parks), and Skyline-to-the-Sea, in the Santa Cruz Mountains.

Note that proximity to a metropolitan area means one thing: The demand is higher. So plan ahead. Scheduling a hike on a Monday, Tuesday, Wednesday, or Thursday will decrease your chances of sharing the trail (and parking areas) with dozens of other people.

People from all over the world come here for good reason, so instead of going far away for a vacation, residents should consider this: Stay and discover the treasures in your own backyard.

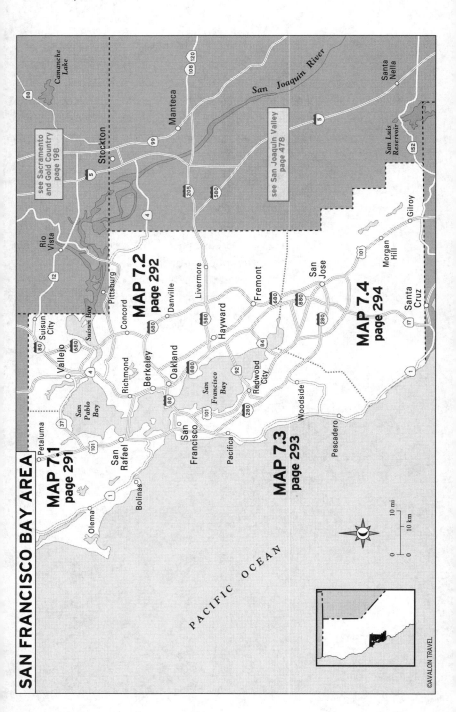

SAN FRANCISCO BAY AREA

MAP 7.1
page 291

MAP 7.2
page 292

MAP 7.3
page 293

MAP 7.4
page 294

see Sacramento and Gold Country page 198

see San Joaquin Valley page 478

PACIFIC OCEAN

10 mi

10 km

©AVALON TRAVEL

Map 7.1

Hikes 1-63

Pages 295-339

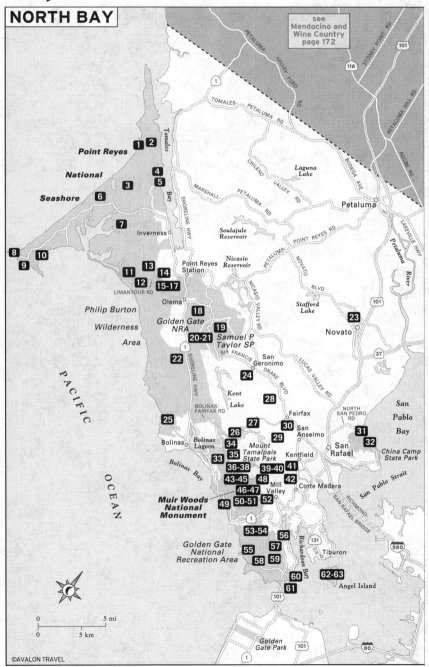

NORTH BAY

see Mendocino and Wine Country page 172

©AVALON TRAVEL

Map 7.2

Hikes 64-113

Pages 340-373

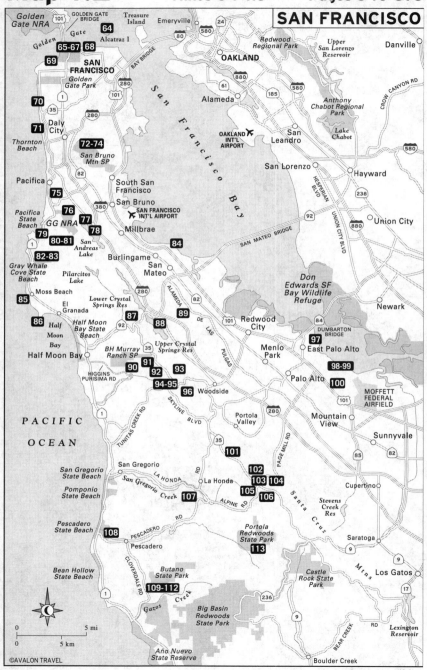

SAN FRANCISCO

©AVALON TRAVEL

Map 7.3

Hikes 114-167   **Pages 373-412**

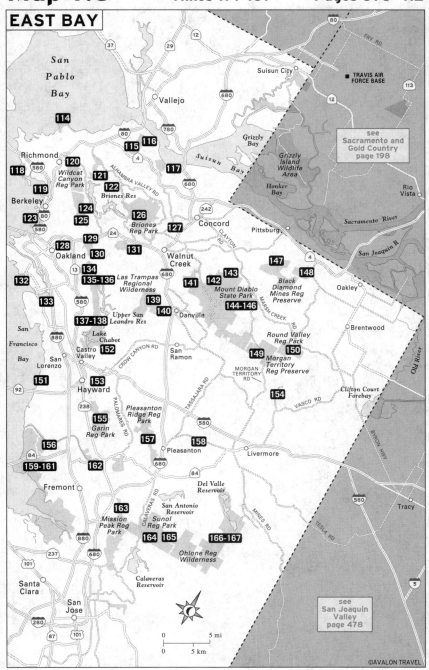

EAST BAY

©AVALON TRAVEL

Map 7.4

Hikes 168-209

Pages 414-445

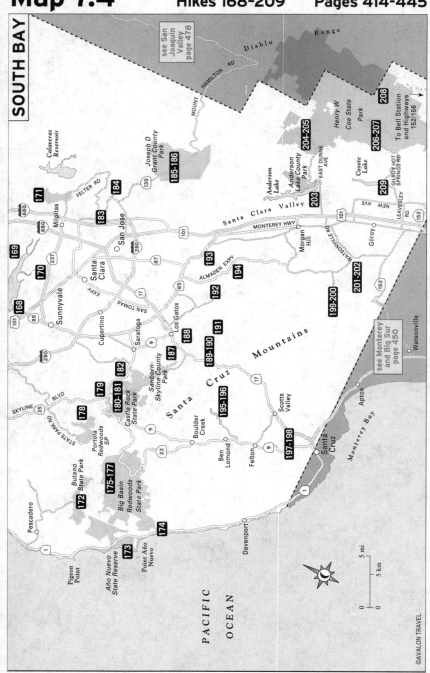

SOUTH BAY

see San Joaquin Valley page 478

Diablo Range

Calaveras Reservoir

MOUNT HAMILTON RD

Joseph D Grant County Park 185-186

Henry W Coe State Park 208

204-205

206-207

To Bell Station and Highways 152/156

FELTER RD

171

Milpitas

680

880

184

130

EAST DUNNE AVE

Anderson Lake County Park

Anderson Lake

203

Coyote Lake

209

GILROY HOT SPRINGS RD

183

San Jose

Santa Clara Valley

MONTEREY HWY

NEW AVE

LEAVESLEY RD

169

170

237

280

101

Morgan Hill

101

WATSONVILLE RD

152

Santa Clara

87

193

Gilroy

168

85

SAN TOMAS EXPY

17

ALMADEN EXPY

194

192

201-202

152

Sunnyvale

Cupertino

Saratoga

9

Los Gatos

188

191

199-200

101

280

85

187

189-190

Mountains

see Monterey and Big Sur page 450

SKYLINE BLVD

35

179

182

Sanborn-Skyline County Park

Cruz

195-196

17

Scotts Valley

Aptos

178

180-181

Santa

Watsonville

STATE PARK RD

Castle Rock State Park

9

Boulder Creek

197-198

Santa Cruz

Monterey Bay

Portola Redwoods SP

172

Butano State Park

175-177

Big Basin Redwoods State Park

23

Ben Lomond

Felton

9

Pescadero

1

174

Davenport

Año Nuevo State Reserve

173

Point Año Nuevo

Pigeon Point

1

PACIFIC OCEAN

5 mi

5 km

0

0

©AVALON TRAVEL

❶ MCCLURES BEACH TRAIL

1.0 mi / 0.5 hr   🏃1   ⛰7

in Point Reyes National Seashore in northwest Marin County

Map 7.1, page 291

McClures Beach is an easy-to-reach spot that is often overlooked in the divine panorama of Point Reyes. It sits in the shadow of nearby Pierce Ranch, with its 500-strong elk herd, and many visitors never drive to the road's end, except perhaps to use the restrooms and telephone there. But an easy 0.5-mile downhill walk will lead you to McClures Beach, where you'll find tidepools to the south and beachfront to the north. The best time to visit is during minus low tides, when the ocean rolls back and unveils acres of beach and a small collection of tidepools to the nearby south. Beachcombing along McClures Beach and Driftwood Beach (to the immediate north) during these low tides also can unveil unusual finds, although park rules prohibit removing any items. One other thing: The sunsets here can be spectacular, especially during fall and early winter, when the skies often look like a scene from *The Ten Commandments*.

Special Note: During periods of big ocean swells, tidepooling at this beach can be dangerous, as incoming tides can cut you off, leaving no way to escape. Consult a tide table, and never turn your back on the waves.

User Groups: Hikers only. No dogs, horses, or mountain bikes. No wheelchair facilities.

Permits: No permits are required. Parking and access are free.

Maps: For a free map, write to Point Reyes National Seashore. For a topographic map, ask the USGS for Tomales.

Directions: From the Golden Gate Bridge, take US 101 north for 7.5 miles to the exit for Sir Francis Drake Boulevard. Turn west and drive about 20 miles west to Olema and Highway 1. Turn right on Highway 1 and drive a short distance to Bear Valley Road. Turn left on Bear Valley Road and drive two miles. Turn left on Sir Francis Drake and drive 5.6 miles to Pierce Point Road. Bear right and drive nine miles to the Pierce Ranch parking area, then turn left and drive 0.5 mile to the parking area and the trailhead.

Contact: Superintendent, Point Reyes National Seashore, Point Reyes, CA 94956; Bear Valley Visitors Center, 415/464-5100, www.nps.gov/pore.

❷ TOMALES POINT TRAIL

6.0 mi / 3.5 hr   🏃2   ⛰10

in Point Reyes National Seashore in northwest Marin County

Map 7.1, page 291   **BEST ◖**

This is the best hike in California for wildlife watching. Imagine meeting up with an elk that stands five feet at the shoulders and has antlers that practically poke holes in the clouds. That is likely to happen on this trail. The elk herd here numbers over 500 and they often wander quite close to the parking area. We have seen as many as 200 elk on a single trip; on another, we counted 13 elk, six deer, three rabbits, and a fox—all within a two-hour span.

This hike starts on the main trail at the north end of the parking lot, just to the left of the ranch. The route has a flat walking surface and easy grades, and is flanked much of the way to the west by the Pacific Ocean and to the east by Tomales Bay—both beautiful sights. About a mile in, you will see elk paths in low brush. The best suggestion is to turn right and trace out one or more of these elk trails. This provides numerous off-trail side trips where you can discover more beautiful views and elk—always a happy surprise.

Most people make this a five-mile round-trip, hiking north to the top of a grade, a great lookout of Dillon Beach and Bodega Bay. The reason most people turn around here is that the trail descends several hundred feet, so if they continue north, it means an additional climb on the way back. It is six miles, but for most, it's an easy six. Note that in summer, wind and fog occasionally envelop the area.

In the evening (and in the fall, when the bulls collect harems), the herd will usually congregate near a watering area set in a valley about three miles from the trailhead, and also in the deep valley that opens up to Tomales Bay. For a bonus, continue hiking the extra 0.5 mile past the elk watering area all the way to Tomales Point.

Special Note: It is a violation of federal law to herd, chase, or otherwise harass elk.

User Groups: Hikers and horses. Nearby Pierce Ranch (a former working ranch) is accessible to wheelchairs, but Tomales Point Trail is not. No dogs or mountain bikes.

Permits: No permits are required. Parking and access are free.

Maps: For a free map, write to Point Reyes National Seashore. For a topographic map, ask the USGS for Tomales.

Directions: From the Golden Gate Bridge, take US 101 north for 7.5 miles to the exit for Sir Francis Drake Boulevard. Turn west and drive about 20 miles west to Olema and Highway 1. Turn right on Highway 1 and drive a short distance to Bear Valley Road. Turn left on Bear Valley Road and drive two miles. Turn left on Sir Francis Drake and drive 5.6 miles to Pierce Point Road. Bear right and drive nine miles to the Pierce Ranch parking area and the trailhead.

Contact: Superintendent, Point Reyes National Seashore, Point Reyes, CA 94956; Bear Valley Visitors Center, 415/464-5100, www.nps.gov/pore.

3 ABBOTTS LAGOON TRAIL
3.2 mi / 1.5 hr

in Point Reyes National Seashore in northwest Marin County

Map 7.1, page 291   **BEST**

Abbotts Lagoon is a gorgeous and easy-to-reach destination. Because it is shielded from view by a hill, many sail past without a clue. Once you make the trip, you'll understand why there are always cars parked at the trailhead on Sundays.

From the trailhead (look for the restrooms), the trail climbs the low ridge and is surfaced with what is known as "soil cement," making it wheelchair accessible about halfway to the ocean bluff. When you pop over the top, just like that, below you lies Abbotts Lagoon, and beyond that, the Pacific Ocean. The lagoon is an ideal place for novice canoeists and kayakers, providing you don't mind the one-mile portage. Birdwatching is often good here, thanks to a rare mix of waterfowl that require freshwater and seabirds migrating along the coast. If you walk past the lagoon (a distance of 1.6 miles from the trailhead), you'll arrive at Point Reyes Beach, where miles and miles of sand dunes and untouched waterfront stretch to the north and south. In spring, this stretch of beach is directly exposed to strong winds out of the northwest.

User Groups: Hikers and mountain bikes (bikers on the first mile only; do not cross the bridge). The first portion of the trail is wheelchair accessible with assistance. No dogs or horses.

Permits: No permits are required. Parking and access are free.

Maps: For a free map, write to Point Reyes National Seashore. For a topographic map, ask the USGS for Drakes Bay.

Directions: From the Golden Gate Bridge, take US 101 north for 7.5 miles to the exit for Sir Francis Drake Boulevard. Turn west and drive about 20 miles west to Olema and Highway 1. Turn right on Highway 1 and drive a short distance to Bear Valley Road. Turn left on Bear Valley Road and drive two miles. Turn left on Sir Francis Drake and drive 5.6 miles to Pierce Point Road. Bear right and drive 3.3 miles to a small parking area with restrooms. The trailhead is on the left side of the road.

Contact: Superintendent, Point Reyes National Seashore, Point Reyes, CA 94956; Bear Valley Visitors Center, 415/464-5100, www.nps.gov/pore.

▲ MARSHALL BEACH TRAIL
2.4 mi / 1.25 hr

in Point Reyes National Seashore in northwest Marin County

Map 7.1, page 291

Marshall Beach is one of the more secluded beaches in Marin County. This pretty spot is set on the waters of Tomales Bay, sheltered from north winds by Inverness Ridge. The trailhead tends to be overlooked, because there are no signs directing hikers to it until you reach the trailhead itself. The hike is 1.2 miles one-way, taking an elliptical route down into a gulch to a protected cove that helps shelter the beach. It's the kind of place where you can just sit and watch the water lap gently at the shore. During the week, you can often have the spot all to yourself. In addition, the beach is overshadowed by nearby Tomales Bay State Park, which you must drive past in order to get here—and many people don't continue driving.

User Groups: Hikers, horses, and mountain bikes. No dogs. No wheelchair facilities.

Permits: No permits are required. Parking and access are free.

Maps: For a free map, write to Point Reyes National Seashore. For a topographic map, ask the USGS for Tomales.

Directions: From the Golden Gate Bridge, take US 101 north for 7.5 miles to the exit for Sir Francis Drake Boulevard. Turn west and drive about 20 miles west to Olema and Highway 1. Turn right on Highway 1 and drive a short distance to Bear Valley Road. Turn left on Bear Valley Road and drive two miles. Turn left on Sir Francis Drake and drive 5.6 miles to Pierce Point Road. Bear right and drive 1.3 miles (just past the entrance road to Tomales Bay State Park, on the right) to Duck Cove/Marshall Beach Road. Turn right and drive 2.6 miles (bear left at the fork) to the parking area for Marshall Beach Trail.

Contact: Superintendent, Point Reyes National Seashore, Point Reyes, CA 94956; Bear Valley Visitors Center, 415/464-5100, www.nps.gov/pore.

▲ JOHNSTONE TRAIL
4.5 mi / 2.5 hr

in Tomales Bay State Park in northwest Marin County

Map 7.1, page 291

Tomales Bay State Park is often lost in the overwhelming shadow of the adjacent Point Reyes National Seashore. In addition, visiting Point Reyes is free, and this park costs $8 per vehicle, so many choose not to make the trip. Yet this is a great park with stellar destinations. The highlights include: Hearts Desire Beach, Indian Beach, Shell Beach, beautiful water views, and the chance to hand-launch kayaks or canoes.

While there are many options, we suggest connecting several trails to create this 4.5-mile loop. Make sure you have a map (some new to the park have missed the turn at the junction of the Johnstone Trail and the Jepson Trail on this recommended route).

From the parking area, start by taking the Johnstone Trail and then hiking south along Tomales Bay. Bring a camera because in the first mile the picnic area provides a beautiful view of the bay, and the side trip to Pebble Beach also provides a gorgeous setting. Continue on the Johnstone Trail, heading west with an easy climb, and then link to the Jepson Trail. Your return on the Jepson Trail features dense forest and vegetation, with old-growth bishop pines with sprawling limbs. The trip ends with a water view. That's it. A stellar trip.

A must-do side trip, a short walk to Indian Beach, is one of the best treasure hunts in the Bay Area. From the parking area, the trail meanders along the pretty shore of Tomales Bay. According to Carlos Porrata, head ranger at the park, this is where visitors have found perfectly crafted arrowheads, ancient bowls, and other Native American artifacts. He reminded that it is illegal, of course, to take any artifact or disturb any archaeological site, and that any finds must be immediately reported.

If you have a car-top boat that can be launched by hand, such as a canoe or kayak, then don't leave it behind. Tomales Bay often provides the best flat-water paddling in the Bay Area. If you paddle north along the western shore, you can often spot many elk in shoreline ravines.

Note: This park was on the state's closure list, but will be kept open and operated, in part, by the Golden Gate National Recreation Area.

User Groups: Hikers only. The park headquarters is wheelchair accessible, but the trail is not. No dogs, horses, or mountain bikes.

Permits: A day-use fee of $8 is charged at the entrance station.

Maps: A brochure and map are available for a fee at the entrance station to Tomales Bay State Park. For a topographic map, ask the USGS for Tomales.

Directions: From the Golden Gate Bridge, take US 101 north for 7.5 miles to the exit for Sir Francis Drake Boulevard. Turn west and drive about 20 miles west to Olema and Highway 1. Turn right on Highway 1 and drive a short distance to Bear Valley Road. Turn left on Bear Valley Road and drive two miles. Turn left on Sir Francis Drake and drive 5.6 miles to Pierce Point Road. Bear right and drive 1.2 miles to the entrance road to Tomales Bay State Park, on the right. Turn right and drive 1.5 miles to the parking area and the trailhead, at Hearts Desire Beach.

Contact: Tomales Bay State Park, Star Route, Inverness, CA 94937, 415/669-1140 or 415/898-4362, fax 415/669-1701; Marin District Headquarters, 415/898-4362, www.parks.ca.gov.

6 SOUTH BEACH TRAIL

0.1-20.0 mi / 0.25 hr-1 day

in Point Reyes National Seashore in northwest Marin County

Map 7.1, page 291

The Point Reyes beach extends for nearly 10 miles, all of it pristine with white, foaming surf that rolls on endlessly. So if you desire miles of untouched beachfront, you've come to the right place. An initial short trail leads from the parking area to South Beach, about three miles north of the Point Reyes Lighthouse. The beach makes a good picnic site and is one of the few places at Point Reyes where you can take a leashed dog. Note that dogs may not be allowed if marine mammals are present. For the best stroll, walk south for about a mile to an expanse of sand dunes. Or walk as far as you'd like and turn around. It is wise to call ahead for weather conditions, as low fog is common, especially during the summer, and strong winds out of the northwest are typical on spring and early-summer afternoons. A word of warning: Do not swim or bodysurf here. This stretch of coast is known for its treacherous undertow, the kind that can trap even the strongest swimmers, pulling people under and pushing them out to sea, despite their attempts to swim back to the beach.

User Groups: Hikers, dogs, and horses. No mountain bikes. No wheelchair facilities.

Permits: No permits are required. Parking and access are free.

Maps: For a free map, write to Point Reyes National Seashore. For a topographic map, ask the USGS for Drakes Bay.

Directions: From the Golden Gate Bridge, take US 101 north for 7.5 miles to the exit for Sir Francis Drake Boulevard. Turn west and drive about 20 miles west to Olema and Highway 1. Turn right on Highway 1 and drive a short distance to Bear Valley Road. Turn left on Bear Valley Road and drive two miles. Turn left on Sir Francis Drake and drive 11.6 miles to the access turnoff for the South

Beach parking lot, on the right. Turn right and drive to the parking lot for South Beach.

Contact: Superintendent, Point Reyes National Seashore, Point Reyes, CA 94956; Bear Valley Visitors Center, 415/464-5100, www.nps.gov/pore.

7 ESTERO TRAIL
7.8 mi / 3.5 hr

in Point Reyes National Seashore in northwest Marin County

Map 7.1, page 291

The Estero Trail is one of the top hikes at Point Reyes, providing glimpses of a variety of settings. The Estero Trail crosses a valley, parallels a bay, ascends a ridge, and leads down to the waterfront, where a perfect, quiet picnic spot awaits. It's an ideal hike for newcomers to Point Reyes National Seashore. After parking, Estero Trail starts by dropping down into a small valley, where you cross a narrow inlet of Home Bay. The surroundings include pretty, low-lying coastal foothills set at the threshold of Drakes Estero, a drop-dead beautiful tidal lagoon. From here, the trail rises gently along the southeastern flank of the Estero. At 2.4 miles in, you will reach a trail junction. Continue straight on Sunset Beach Trail, where it is an easy 1.5-mile glide down to Sunset Beach. This is a great picnic site for a trail lunch, set inside the mouth of the Estero, about a mile from the Pacific Ocean. This makes it a 7.8-mile round-trip. But there is a good option. When you reach the trail junction with Sunset Beach Trail (straight), an option is to instead turn left (south). A 15-minute climb will take you to a short ridge and the junction of Drakes Head Trail. Here you get a sweeping view of Drakes Bay, Estero de Limantour, and more foothills—well worth the effort. All of this is open to mountain bikes. Because it is set in foothill grasslands, visibility is good, so there are no surprises or uncomfortable encounters between hikers and bikers. Those on bikes have plenty of time to slow, stop, and give way to

hikers, which is trail policy. In addition, for those who own a kayak or canoe, Drakes Estero is one of the prettiest settings in the Bay Area for an easy paddle trek; you can explore the four arms of the lagoon or paddle out to the mouth of the estuary and Limantour Spit.

User Groups: Hikers, horses, and mountain bikes. The first two miles are wheelchair accessible, with assistance. No dogs.

Permits: No permits are required. Parking and access are free.

Maps: For a free map, write to Point Reyes National Seashore. For a topographic map, ask the USGS for Drakes Bay.

Directions: From the Golden Gate Bridge, take US 101 north for 7.5 miles to the exit for Sir Francis Drake Boulevard. Turn west and drive about 20 miles west to Olema and Highway 1. Turn right on Highway 1 and drive a short distance to Bear Valley Road. Turn left on Bear Valley Road and drive two miles. Turn left on Sir Francis Drake and drive 7.5 miles to Estero Road, on the left. Turn left and drive one mile to the parking area.

Contact: Superintendent, Point Reyes National Seashore, Point Reyes, CA 94956; Bear Valley Visitors Center, 415/464-5100, www.nps.gov/pore.

8 POINT REYES LIGHTHOUSE
0.8 mi / 0.5 hr

in Point Reyes National Seashore in northwest Marin County

Map 7.1, page 291

In winter, there may be no better place on land from which to watch migrating whales. Year-round, the lookout from Point Reyes Lighthouse can provide the inspiration you may need to set forth on a challenging project (like, say, writing a book). The trail to the lookout is short and paved, and it includes a dramatic descent on a railed stairway. At the lighthouse, a railing at the point provides a perch for stunning ocean views. On the way back, of course, you face a modest climb. Those out of shape will even find it steep, so three rest stops are available for some folks to stop to pant a bit. From Point Reyes, you scan the ocean, searching for what looks like a little puff of smoke on the water's surface: a whale spout. When you find one, zoom in closer. If you are lucky, you might even get a tail salute. The chances are good, because 22,000 gray whales migrate past here every winter on what is called the Great Whale Highway, located just offshore of Point Reyes. On clear weekends, particularly in winter, the place can be crowded. A fence on the edge of the cliff keeps visitors from falling overboard from one of the most dramatic coastal lookouts anywhere. Sunsets here are unforgettable. A shuttle is required (see below) on good-weather Sundays in winter and early spring.

User Groups: Hikers and mountain bikes (bikes are restricted from the stairs and not advised). No dogs or horses.

Permits: No permits are required. Parking and access are free.

Maps: For a free map, write to Point Reyes National Seashore. For a topographic map, ask the USGS for Drakes Bay.

Directions: From the Golden Gate Bridge, take US 101 north for 7.5 miles to the exit for Sir Francis Drake Boulevard. Turn west and drive about 20 miles west to Olema and Highway 1. Turn right on Highway 1 and drive a short distance to Bear Valley Road. Turn left on Bear Valley Road and drive two miles. Turn left on Sir Francis Drake and drive 17.6 miles. The road dead-ends at the parking area for the Point Reyes Lighthouse.

Shuttle bus: On weekends from late December to mid-April when the weather is good, the west end of Sir Francis Drake is closed to vehicle traffic. Shuttle buses transport visitors ($5 per person, youth 16 and under free) to the lighthouse and Chimney Rock areas. Shuttle tickets may be purchased at Drakes Beach (9 A.M.–3 P.M. weekends and holidays, weather permitting). The shuttle buses run approximately every 20 minutes starting at 9:30 A.M. To reach the shuttle pick-up, follow the directions above. On Sir Francis Drake,

look for the sign for a left turn to Visitors Center/Shuttle Bus. Turn left and drive 1.2 miles to the parking lot at the Kenneth Patrick Visitor Center and Drakes Beach.

Contact: Superintendent, Point Reyes National Seashore, Point Reyes, CA 94956; Bear Valley Visitors Center, 415/464-5100, www.nps.gov/pore.

9 CHIMNEY ROCK TRAIL
2.8 mi / 1.25 hr   🥾1 ⛰10

in Point Reyes National Seashore in northwest Marin County

Map 7.1, page 291   **BEST** 🌙

This is one of the most eye-popping easy hikes in California. The trail starts at the south end of the parking lot, next to a park billboard, on a path that is largely sheltered by the towering headlands ridge to your right. In minutes, you will pass through a cypress forest and then emerge for pretty views of Drakes Bay off to your left. The trail then rises along an isthmus, with cliffs on each side—the ocean on the right, and Drakes Bay on the left. The trail curves and rises up to the Chimney Rock Headlands, 0.5 mile in. Be sure to turn and look back for a fantastic 180-degree sweep, with the Pacific now on your left, Drakes Bay on your right. A cutoff trail to the right leads a short distance to a cliff-top overlook of ocean breakers and a secluded beach directly below. Often there are awesome winds that sweep up the cliffs here. The perch is sensational for views, with sightings of whale spouts in winter, the Farallon Islands, and then across the Headlands to the north. Looking back to the east, you can take in the calm waters of Drakes Bay—leading to Drakes Estero, Limantour, and beyond to Inverness Ridge. The main trail continues south to a lookout of a series of rock stacks that emerge from the ocean just beyond land's end. The biggest is Chimney Rock. One of the rock formations has a bridged archway where a surging ocean foams through the center, a cool phenomenon.

In peak spring season, you can count 20 species of wildflowers on the lee side of the headlands on the Chimney Rock Trail, including rafts of Douglas iris and good numbers of checkerbloom. Because of exposure to wind, wildflowers tend to dry out sooner here than at more protected areas, but they are spectacular when you hit it right.

User Groups: Hikers and mountain bikes. The first 0.25 mile of the trail is wheelchair accessible. No dogs or horses.

Permits: No permits are required. Parking and access are free.

Maps: For a free map, write to Point Reyes National Seashore. For a topographic map, ask the USGS for Drakes Bay.

Directions: From the Golden Gate Bridge, take US 101 north for 7.5 miles to the exit for Sir Francis Drake Boulevard. Turn west and drive about 20 miles west to Olema and Highway 1. Turn right on Highway 1 and drive a short distance to Bear Valley Road. Turn left on Bear Valley Road and drive two miles. Turn left on Sir Francis Drake and drive 17.4 miles toward the Point Reyes Lighthouse to a fork with Chimney Rock Road on the left. Turn left and drive one mile to the parking area and trailhead.

Shuttle bus: On weekends from late December to mid-April when the weather is good, the west end of Sir Francis Drake is closed to vehicle traffic. Shuttle buses transport visitors ($5 per person, youth 16 and under free) to the lighthouse and Chimney Rock areas. Shuttle tickets may be purchased at Drakes Beach (9 A.M.–3 P.M. weekends and holidays, weather permitting). The shuttle buses run approximately every 20 minutes starting at 9:30 A.M. To reach the shuttle pick-up, follow the directions above. On Sir Francis Drake, look for the sign for a left turn to Visitors Center/Shuttle Bus. Turn left and drive 1.2 miles to the parking lot at the Kenneth Patrick Visitor Center and Drakes Beach.

Contact: Superintendent, Point Reyes National Seashore, Point Reyes, CA 94956; Bear Valley Visitors Center, 415/464-5100, www.nps.gov/pore.

10 SIR FRANCIS DRAKE TRAIL

1.9 mi / 1.0 hr   👫 1   ⛰ 8

in Point Reyes National Seashore in northwest Marin County

Map 7.1, page 291

This spot is not exactly a secret. In fact, you might as well stand on the Golden Gate Bridge with a megaphone and announce its existence to the world. At the trailhead, for instance, you will discover a large parking lot and visitors center, complete with exhibits, maps, and books (maybe even this one). The trail traces the back of the arcing beaches along Drakes Bay, providing scenic lookouts onto the bay's protected waters. The trail continues to the mouth of Drakes Estero, then returns via an inland loop that includes a short climb up, then down to a waterfront bluff. This is one of the more popular hikes at Point Reyes National Seashore, and why not? It is an easy walk, provides great scenic beauty, and traces three habitats: beach frontage, the mouth of a lagoon, and hillside bluffs.

User Groups: Hikers and mountain bikes. No dogs or horses. No wheelchair facilities.

Permits: No permits are required. Parking and access are free.

Maps: For a free map, write to Point Reyes National Seashore. For a topographic map, ask the USGS for Drakes Bay.

Directions: From the Golden Gate Bridge, take US 101 north for 7.5 miles to the exit for Sir Francis Drake Boulevard. Turn west and drive about 20 miles west to Olema and Highway 1. Turn right on Highway 1 and drive a short distance to Bear Valley Road. Turn left on Bear Valley Road and drive two miles. Turn left on Sir Francis Drake, drive 11.1 miles, and look for the sign indicating a left turn to a visitors center. Turn left and drive 1.2 miles to the parking lot at the Kenneth Patrick Visitors Center and the trailhead.

Contact: Superintendent, Point Reyes National Seashore, Point Reyes, CA 94956; Bear Valley Visitors Center, 415/464-5100, www.nps.gov/pore.

11 SKY TRAIL TO PALOMARIN

15.3 mi one-way/ 2 days 🏃3 ⛰10

in Point Reyes National Seashore in northwest Marin County

Map 7.1, page 291

One of the Bay Area's epic overnight hikes can be transformed and made even greater with a slight change of approach. This trip starts on a Saturday at the Sky Trailhead and parking lot, hiking 7.1 miles to Glen Camp for the night. The next day, complete the route by hiking 8.2 miles out to Palomarin and your shuttle car. While this may not be a more spectacular trek, it splits the weekend into two even days, unlike the famed Coast Trail route, where the first day is a butt-kicker.

On Day 1, hike 7.1 miles to Glen Camp. Don't get disgruntled over the first 15 minutes, where the trail is routed up to the ridge on a service road, with no views. At 1.3 miles, you emerge at Sky Camp at 1,000 feet elevation and the eye-popping views are revealed to the west. The expanse of Drakes Bay below is stunning, along with Arch Rock, Drakes Beach, Chimney Rock, and Point Reyes, from left to right. The views then sparkle for much of the hike, with the route occasionally passing through old-growth bishop pines. Over and over, you emerge for views below of Sculptured Beach, Point Resistance, and Arch Rock. Eventually you top out at Glen Camp, our favorite backcountry camp at Point Reyes. Be sure to bring a light tent—even though the best weather of the year arrives in late summer and early fall, morning fog can be wet.

On Day 2, hike 8.2 miles from Glen Camp to the end of the trail at Palomarin Trailhead and your shuttle car. The day starts by sailing downhill, where you take in pretty views of Wildcat Valley, ocean breakers and Wildcat Beach, and then connecting with the Coast Trail. It is 0.8 mile to the Coast Trail, and then another 1.1 miles to Wildcat Camp.

From Wildcat, as you head south, look for the unsigned cut-off on the right near the wood bridge over Alamere Creek—this is the route to the brink of Alamere Falls (rains revive it in winter and spring). In 2011, the park closed this unofficial trail, though many still figure out a way to get past the closure sign and trek the short distance to the brink of the falls. To get a full front view of Alamere Falls, from Wildcat Beach, hike south one mile on the beach.

From the Alamere Creek bridge, it is 3.6 miles to the end of the trail and the parking lot at Palomarin. In the process, the route contours south in and out of coastal valleys, where you pass Wildcat Lake, Pelican Lake, and Bass Lake, all gorgeous en route to the trail's end. On a fresh, clear April weekend, there may be no better way to celebrate the coronation of spring than this hike.

User Groups: Hikers only. No wheelchair facilities.

Permits: Parking and access are free. Reservations and permit required for camping. Reserve at 415/663-8054; $15 per night for up to six per site. Garbage must be packed out.

Maps: For a free map, write to Point Reyes National Seashore. For a topographic map, ask the USGS for Drakes Bay.

Directions: To Bear Valley Visitor Center: From the Golden Gate Bridge, take US 101 north for 7.5 miles to the exit for Sir Francis Drake Boulevard. Turn west and drive about 20 miles west to Olema and Highway 1. Turn right on Highway 1 and drive a short distance to Bear Valley Road. Turn left and drive 0.7 mile to the Seashore Information sign and access road for Bear Valley Visitors Center. Turn left and go a short distance to the visitors center (campers must pick up permits in person).

To Sky Trailhead: From Bear Valley Visitors Center, exit parking lot to Bear Valley Road. Turn left and drive a short distance to Sir Francis Drake Boulevard. Turn left on Bear Valley Road and drive two miles to Limantour Road. Turn left on Limantour and drive a little over three miles to the Sky parking and trailhead on the left.

Visitor Center to Palomarin: Exit the parking lot to Bear Valley Road, turn right, and go 0.5 mile to Highway 1. Turn right and drive 9.3 miles to Olema-Bolinas Road on the right (the sign is always stolen; if you reach Bolinas Lagoon, turn around and look for the road on left). Turn right and go 1.3 miles to the junction with Horseshoe Hill Road. Turn left (still Olema-Bolinas Road) and go 0.5 mile to Mesa Road. Turn right and go 4.8 miles (pass an antenna farm called The Towers) to the parking area.

Contact: Superintendent, Point Reyes National Seashore, Point Reyes, CA 94956; Bear Valley Visitors Center, 415/464-5100, www.nps.gov/pore.

12 SKY TRAIL
9.6 mi / 4.0 hr
🥾 3 ⛰ 10

in Point Reyes National Seashore in northwest Marin County

Map 7.1, page 291

Hit it right on a clear day and it can feel like you have a foothold in the heavens on the Point Reyes Sky Trail. From the trailhead at the parking area on Limantour Road, you pass around a gate to hike up a service road edged by cypress and, in the spring, occasional patches of forget-me-nots in the shade. The trail climbs, from gentle to moderate, to the south for 0.8 mile to a junction with the Fire Lane Trail (on the right). Ignore that and continue on the service road for another half mile to the Sky Camp. In the process, you will walk along the edge of the burn zone of the 1995 fire. Notice the mix of fresh-sprouted grass, wildflowers, and young pines, and old cypress and pine that the fire missed, and the blackened tree skeletons that still remain. As you near Sky Camp, the views start to open up. When you reach the camp, turn right and climb the obvious short ridge to gain the best perch for Drakes Bay. This 1,000-foot high ridgeline perch towers over Drakes Bay and the Pacific Ocean. Plunging below at your boot tips are miles of foothills reborn

again this spring from the horrific wildfire. Scan from right to left taking in Point Reyes, Chimney Rock, and the curving Limantour Beach to Arch Rock. You can simply turn back for a 2.6-mile romp (mostly downhill on the return) or extend the trek to create a spectacular loop, down to the beach and then back up, for a 9.6-mile round-trip. To continue on to this sensational loop hike, stay on the Sky Trail (more fantastic views) south to Woodward Valley Trail, and then head down to the beach. On the way down, you may experience the unbelievable feeling that you can sense the earth's curve on the distant horizon. Turn right on the Coast Trail, and in less than a mile, turn right on the Laguna Trail/Fire Trail and head back up to the parking area.

User Groups: Hikers only. Bikes, horses permitted to Sky Camp. No wheelchair facilities.

Permits: No permits are required. Parking and access are free. Permits are required to camp at Sky Camp. Reserve at 415/663-8054; $15 per night for up to six per site; 11 campsites with picnic table, fire grills (charcoal only), drinking water, pit toilet. Garbage must be packed out.

Maps: For a free map, write to Point Reyes National Seashore. For a topographic map, ask the USGS for Drakes Bay.

Directions: From the Golden Gate Bridge, take US 101 north for 7.5 miles to the exit for Sir Francis Drake Boulevard. Turn west and drive about 20 miles west to Olema and Highway 1. Turn right and drive a short distance to Bear Valley Road. Turn left and drive 0.7 mile to the Seashore Information sign and access road for Bear Valley Visitor Center. Turn left and head a short distance to the visitors center (campers must pick up permits in person). From Bear Valley Visitors Center, return to Bear Valley Road. Turn left and drive 1.3 miles to Limantour Road (signed Hostel and Limantour Beach). Turn left and drive 3.4 miles to the access road on the left for Sky Trail. Turn left and drive a short distance to the parking area.

Contact: Superintendent, Point Reyes National Seashore, Point Reyes, CA 94956; Bear Valley Visitors Center, 415/464-5100, www.nps.gov/pore.

13 COAST TRAIL
16.1 mi one-way / 2-plus days

🏃3 ⛺10

in Point Reyes National Seashore in northwest Marin County

Map 7.1, page 291	BEST ☾

Of the handful of overnight hiking trips available in the Bay Area, Coast Trail provides the most extended tour into a land of charm. Located north of Bolinas on the remote Marin coast, the trail offers camps at ocean bluffs, a beach with sculpted rocks and tidepools, bluff-top lookouts with a chance to see passing whales, a rare waterfall from an ocean bluff that pours like a fountain to a beach and then runs into the ocean, and coastal freshwater lakes. This continuous backcountry route is 16.1 miles long, enough to allow lingering hikers to spend a weekend at it, and short enough for the ambitious to tackle in a single day. There are only a few catches: You need a hiking partner who will double as a shuttle driver so you can leave a car at each end of the trail. You'll need to come prepared to cook your food using a small backpack stove, not a campfire. Tents are recommended, because the coastal weather is the most unpredictable in the Bay Area—clear, calm, and warm one day, then suddenly foggy, windy, moist, and clammy the next.

The best trailhead for Coast Trail is at the Point Reyes Hostel, from where you will hike north to south, keeping the wind at your back and out of your face. The first camp, Coast Camp, is an easy 2.8 miles, ideal for those heading out on a Friday evening after work. As you hike in, you'll have a panoramic view of the reborn coastal foothills that were burned in the wildfire of October 1995; the campground and trail were untouched. The sound of ocean waves will send you to sleep the first night—or, in some sensitive cases, might keep you awake.

If you try to hike the Coast Trail in two days, you will face a first-day tromp of 10.6 miles, direct to Wildcat Camp. Because of the additional time spent getting camping permits at the Bear Valley Visitors Center and setting up a shuttle car at the trail's end at Palomarin, most hikers get a late start, which means facing a late arrival at Wildcat. One option is to start instead at Sky Trail off Limantour Road and spend the night at Glen Camp (see the listing for *Sky Trail to Palomarin* in this chapter).

The next day you will hike south, getting glimpses along the way of Sculptured Beach, with its magnificent rock stacks and tunnels. There are great cutoff trails along Coast Trail to Sculptured Beach, Kelham Beach (trail repaired), and Arch Rock. The Coast Trail continues south to Wildcat Camp, set on a bluff overlooking the ocean, making day two a hike of 7.8 miles. It's an additional mile to walk south on the beach for a fview of Alamere Falls.

On day three, figure on a 5.5-mile closeout with plenty of sideshows. You will hike past a series of coastal lakes—including nearby Wildcat Lake and little Ocean Lake. After climbing to a short ridge, you will skirt above Pelican Lake and along the northern shore of Bass Lake. The trail then heads up a coastal hill, topping out at 563 feet, and then lateral down a canyon and back to ocean bluffs. Following the trail, you turn left and in a mile arrive at the Palomarin trailhead. You will be ready to reach your shuttle car and head for the barn. If you have a shuttle partner, this is one of the Bay Area's greatest hikes.

User Groups: Hikers and horses. Mountain bikes permitted only from the Laguna trailhead to the Coast Campground and are otherwise prohibited. Partially accessible to wheelchair users who have assistance. No dogs.

Permits: Parking and access are free. Reservations and a permit are required for camping.

Reserve at 415/663-8054; $15 per night for up to six per site. Garbage must be packed out.
Maps: For a free map, write to Point Reyes National Seashore. For a topographic map, ask the USGS for Drakes Bay.
Directions: To Bear Valley Visitors Center: From the Golden Gate Bridge, take US 101 north for 7.5 miles to the exit for Sir Francis Drake Boulevard. Turn west and drive about 20 miles west to Olema and Highway 1. Turn right and drive a short distance to Bear Valley Road. Turn left and drive 0.7 mile to the Seashore Information sign and access road for Bear Valley Visitors Center. Turn left and head a short distance to the visitors center (campers must pick up permits in person).

To Coastal Trail trailhead: After getting a camping permit at Bear Valley Visitors Center, leave the parking lot and take the access road to Bear Valley Road. Turn left and drive to Limantour Road. Turn left and drive six miles, looking for the signed turn on the left for Point Reyes Hostel. Turn left on the access road for the Point Reyes Hostel and continue to where road ends at the parking lot. After parking, hike back to the hostel and look for the trailhead on the left (west, across the road from the hostel).

Visitor Center to Palomarin: Exit the parking lot to Bear Valley Road, turn right and go 0.5 mile to Highway 1. Turn right and drive 9.3 miles to Olema-Bolinas Road on the right (the sign always stolen; if you reach Bolinas Lagoon, turn around and look for the road on left). Turn right and go 1.3 miles to junction with Horseshoe Hill Road. Turn left (still Olema-Bolinas Road) and go 0.5 mile to Mesa Road. Turn right and go 4.8 miles (pass an antenna farm called The Towers) to the parking area.
Contact: Superintendent, Point Reyes National Seashore, Point Reyes, CA 94956; Bear Valley Visitors Center, 415/464-5100, www.nps.gov/pore.

14 LAGUNA LOOP TRAIL
5.5 mi / 2.5 hr 🥾2 ⛰8

in Point Reyes National Seashore in northwest Marin County

Map 7.1, page 291

The Laguna Loop Trail can make for a great Sunday morning walk. You'll get intimate glimpses of foothills that have been reborn since the legendary wildfire of 1995—called "the genesis effect"—as well as sweeping ocean views. The trailhead is just 0.2 mile down the road from the Point Reyes Hostel, adjacent to the park's Environmental Education Center. From there, the trail continues 1.8 miles up to Inverness Ridge, with great views of Drakes Bay along the way. At the ridge, turn right and hike 0.7 mile toward Mount Wittenberg, which at 1,407 feet is the highest point at Point Reyes National Seashore. On the north flank of Mount Wittenberg, hikers should turn right on the Fire Lane Trail, which loops back around for three miles to the Laguna trailhead. This excellent loop hike entails a bit of a climb and offers Pacific lookouts, yet it is short enough to complete in a few hours.
User Groups: Hikers and horses. Mountain bikes are permitted only from the Laguna trailhead to the Coast Campground and are otherwise prohibited. No dogs. No wheelchair facilities.
Permits: No permits are required. Parking and access are free.
Maps: For a free map, write to Point Reyes National Seashore. For a topographic map, ask the USGS for Inverness.
Directions: From the Golden Gate Bridge, take US 101 north for 7.5 miles to the exit for Sir Francis Drake Boulevard. Turn west and drive about 20 miles west to Olema and Highway 1. Turn right and drive a short distance to Bear Valley Road. Turn left at Bear Valley Road and drive two miles to Limantour Road. Turn left and drive six miles. Turn left on the access road for the Point Reyes Hostel and drive 0.2 mile past the hostel to the

parking area and trailhead (on the right side of the road).

Contact: Superintendent, Point Reyes National Seashore, Point Reyes, CA 94956; Bear Valley Visitors Center, 415/464-5100, www.nps.gov/pore.

15 MOUNT WITTENBERG LOOP

4.5 mi / 2.5 hr   🏃3   ⛰9

in Point Reyes National Seashore near Olema in northwest Marin County

Map 7.1, page 291

It is amazing when one little turn off a major trail can lead to a landscape where hiking dreams come true. The Mount Wittenberg Loop is such a trek, one of the best short hikes in the Point Reyes National Seashore. The trail provides a route through deep forest, a climb with a steady grade, and then magnificent lookouts of Drakes Bay to the west and the Olema Valley to the east. The destination is Mount Wittenberg (at 1,407 feet, the highest point in the park), but the best views are from the ridge just west of the rounded summit. After parking at Bear Valley Visitors Center, where there's a huge parking lot, start the trip by taking Bear Valley Trail, located at the south end of the parking area. This is one of the most populated trails in the park, hence comes the trick: Hike on Bear Valley Trail for just 0.2 mile, and then bear right at the cutoff for Sky Trail. From here, it is a 1.4-mile hike with a climb of 1,200 feet at a steady grade, but hikers in decent condition can easily handle it. You'll pass through old-growth forest and lush ravines, with occasional peephole-like lookouts to Olema Valley. It rises to the foot of Mount Wittenberg, and with another 100-foot climb, a cutoff trail takes hikers to the rounded summit. The views are not the greatest from the top, but instead from just nearby on Sky Trail. From here, return to Sky Trail and walk southwest 0.4 mile to Meadow Trail. In the process, there are dramatic views

of Drakes Bay to the west and some hidden meadows to the east. You'll also have a panoramic shot of the coastal foothills, which are recovering from the wildfire of October 1995. From Meadow Trail, you will glide downhill for 1.5 miles back down to Bear Valley Trail. There you turn left, and the trail widens and flattens; then you'll walk out 0.8 mile to the parking lot. There you have it—to paradise and back in just a few hours.

User Groups: Hikers and horses. No dogs or mountain bikes. No wheelchair facilities.

Permits: No permits are required. Parking and access are free.

Maps: For a free map, write to Point Reyes National Seashore. For a topographic map, ask the USGS for Inverness.

Directions: From the Golden Gate Bridge, take US 101 north for 7.5 miles to the exit for Sir Francis Drake Boulevard. Turn west and drive about 20 miles west to Olema and Highway 1. Turn right and drive a short distance to Bear Valley Road. Turn left and drive 0.7 mile to sign for Seashore Information and road on left. Turn left and drive to the parking lot for the Bear Valley Visitors Center. The trailhead is at the south end of the parking lot.

Contact: Superintendent, Point Reyes National Seashore, Point Reyes, CA 94956; Bear Valley Visitors Center, 415/464-5100, www.nps.gov/pore.

16 BEAR VALLEY TRAIL

8.2 mi / 4.0 hr   🏃1   ⛰7

in Point Reyes National Seashore near Olema in northwest Marin County

Map 7.1, page 291

The Bear Valley Trail has all the ingredients needed to earn a 10 rating, but, alas, doesn't quite make it. Starting with a pretty route through forests, it leads past Divide Meadow to Bear Valley, then down along Coast Creek to the beach, Arch Rock, and the Sea Tunnel, where the views are marvelous. So, you ask, why is it rated a 7? The answer is that the trail

San Francisco Bay Area **307**

is actually a park service road made of compressed rock, and it gets a ton of traffic, including bicycles. This is the most heavily used trail in Point Reyes National Seashore. The best element is that it is wheelchair accessible and is, in fact, one of the prettiest wheelchair routes in California. Just put it in power drive, for there's a modest 215-foot climb from park headquarters to Divide Meadow. Wheelchairs and bikes are permitted to Glen Camp Trail, 3.2 miles from park headquarters. After that, you hike down the Coast Creek drainage on a 0.7-mile trek to the beach.

User Groups: Hikers, mountain bikes (first three miles only), and horses (weekdays only). The 1.5-mile trail to Divide Meadow is wheelchair accessible but requires a significant amount of assistance. No dogs.

Permits: No permits are required. Parking and access are free.

Maps: For a free map, write to Point Reyes National Seashore. For a topographic map, ask the USGS for Inverness.

Directions: From the Golden Gate Bridge, take US 101 north for 7.5 miles to the exit for Sir Francis Drake Boulevard. Turn west and drive about 20 miles west to Olema and Highway 1. Turn right and drive a short distance to Bear Valley Road. Turn left and drive 0.7 mile to the sign for Seashore Information and a road on the left. Turn left and drive to the parking lot for the Bear Valley Visitors Center.

Contact: Superintendent, Point Reyes National Seashore, Point Reyes, CA 94956; Bear Valley Visitors Center, 415/464-5100, www.nps.gov/pore.

17 RIFT ZONE TRAIL

5.2 mi one-way / 2.25 hr ₁ ⛰6

in Point Reyes National Seashore near Olema in northwest Marin County

Map 7.1, page 291

The Rift Zone Trail is one of the most fascinating trails at Point Reyes and draws some of the highest interest among visitors. It is one of

the world's classic examples of an earthquake fault line: the San Andreas Fault. Because we like big views, waterfalls and wildflowers, it doesn't quite flip our pancake, but it does provide one of the best lessons you can get from the University of Nature.

From park headquarters, it's a 5.2-mile one-way hike to the Five Brooks trailhead—best completed with a shuttle car. Along the way, the trail traces along Olema Creek, where horizontal movement of 21 feet was recorded during the 1906 earthquake. Much evidence of earthquake activity is visible on this trail, including parallel ridges, but the most obvious sign is the clear difference in vegetation types on each side of the fault. The trail gets heavy use, has no difficult grades, and requires only a few short ups and downs near its southern junction with the Five Brooks trailhead.

User Groups: Hikers and horses. No dogs or mountain bikes. No wheelchair facilities.

Permits: No permits are required. Parking and access are free.

Maps: For a free map, write to Point Reyes National Seashore. For a topographic map, ask the USGS for Inverness.

Directions: From the Golden Gate Bridge, take US 101 north for 7.5 miles to the exit for Sir Francis Drake Boulevard. Turn west and drive about 20 miles west to Olema and Highway 1. Turn right and drive a short distance to Bear Valley Road. Turn left and drive 0.7 mile to the sign for Seashore Information and a road on left. Turn left and drive to the parking lot for the Bear Valley Visitors Center.

Contact: Superintendent, Point Reyes National Seashore, Point Reyes, CA 94956; Bear Valley Visitors Center, 415/464-5100, www.nps.gov/pore.

18 BOLINAS RIDGE

11.1 mi one-way / 4.5 hr   🏃3 ⛰9

in northwest Marin County west of San Rafael

Map 7.1, page 291

What you get here are spectacular lookouts across miles of foothills, as well as an excellent mountain bike route. It is an excellent one-way trip if you arrange to have a shuttle car waiting for you at trail's end. At different points, the surrounding landscape offers a heavily wooded slope and Kent Lake to the east, Olema Valley and Inverness Ridge to the west, and Bolinas Lagoon and the Pacific Ocean to the south. The trail crosses atop Bolinas Ridge, through some of the most remote land in the Golden Gate National Recreation Area. The trailhead near Olema starts with a 700-foot climb in the first 2.5 miles. Many hikers call it quits here, stopping to enjoy the view, then turning around and heading home. If you continue, though, you will discover that the trail keeps climbing to 1,329 feet in the first four miles. From that point on, the hike becomes much easier, with only moderate drops and ascents over the last 6.2 miles to the trail's end, on Bolinas-Fairfax Road. Mountain biking is permitted, but hikers generally need not fear: The trail is not only wide enough for everyone, but has very few hidden turns. Some people (especially bicyclists) prefer to complete this trail in the opposite direction in order to avoid the climb, but done in this direction, you need a rear-view mirror for the best views.

User Groups: Hikers, dogs, horses, and mountain bikes. No wheelchair facilities.

Permits: No permits are required. Parking and access are free.

Maps: For a free map, write to Point Reyes National Seashore. For topographic maps, ask the USGS for Inverness, San Geronimo, and Bolinas.

Directions: From the Golden Gate Bridge, take US 101 north for 7.5 miles to the exit for Sir Francis Drake Boulevard. Turn west and drive 18 miles (3.4 miles past the entrance station to Samuel P. Taylor State Park). The trailhead is on the left side of the road. Park along the road.

Contact: Golden Gate National Recreation Area, Fort Mason, Building 201, San Francisco, CA 94123, 415/561-4700, www.nps.gov/goga.

19 BARNABE PEAK LOOP

6.0 mi / 3.5 hr   🏃3 ⛰9

in Samuel P. Taylor State Park west of San Rafael

Map 7.1, page 291

Even well-known state parks can hide surprises and oft-missed, gemlike destinations. That's how it is at Samuel P. Taylor State Park, where a little-known trailhead, hidden waterfall, and surprise mountaintop lookout—Barnabe Peak, at 1,466 feet—are the rewards for those willing to search out the extra mile (literally).

Instead of parking at headquarters, drive one mile west from the park entrance on Sir Francis Drake Boulevard. Look for the small, paved access road and the sign for the Devil's Gulch Horse Camp, on the right side. Park in the dirt pullout on the road's shoulder on the left, then walk across Sir Francis Drake Boulevard and hike up Devil's Gulch Horse Camp access road for a short distance to a trailhead on your right, overlooking Devil's Gulch Creek. Thus starts a great adventure.

From here, what awaits you is a six-mile loop hike with a 1,300-foot climb to Barnabe Peak (1,466 feet), with spectacular views on clear days of the Marin coast and western foothills. In the process, you will pass a cutoff trail that is routed for 0.5 mile into a canyon to Stairstep Falls.

From the trailhead at Devil's Gulch, take the trail into the canyon and cross the creek on the small bridge. In late December, this is an excellent area to see spawning coho salmon. Take the signed left turn for Bill's Trail (also signed for Barnabe Peak). The hike starts off as a romp; it's an easy climb in forest for about a half hour to the cutoff trail for Stairstep Falls, on the left. After heavy rains, this waterfall is a must-see trip for most. It goes dry in summer, but when fed by storm runoff, it creates a stepped cascade in a deep canyon that runs about 35 to 40 feet. Rangers have cleared most of a wood debris pile so hikers can walk right up to the plunge pool.

If the weather is clear, most will be eager for the climb up to Barnabe Peak. Back at Bill's Trail, the hike gets steeper as you climb out of the canyon. Switchbacks help the grade, and eventually you will top the forest and reach a service road. Here you turn left and reach the lookout in about five minutes. An old lookout tower is positioned here, but there is no access. From the top, you get a sweeping lookout that spans from Mount Tamalpais to Point Reyes. Most will plan a picnic at the base of the old tower.

To return, most take the quickest route possible—after all, you got what you came for. Do that by taking the fire road, a fast two-mile drop back to the bottom.

Samuel P. Taylor State Park is located along Sir Francis Drake Boulevard in western Marin, best known for its stand of redwoods and the lush undergrowth in the canyon along the headwaters of Lagunitas Creek. The park covers 2,700 acres and features excellent hiking, biking, and camping. But most people miss the best of it.

Note: This park was on the state's closure list, but will be kept open and operated, in part, by the Golden Gate National Recreation Area.

User Groups: Hikers, dogs, and mountain bikes (bikes are not permitted on spur trails). No horses.

Permits: Free parking is available along the road. A state park day-use fee of $8 per vehicle is charged at the entrance station.

Maps: A brochure and map are available for a fee at the entrance station to Samuel P. Taylor State Park. For a topographic map, ask the USGS for San Geronimo.

Directions: To park headquarters: From the Golden Gate Bridge, take US 101 north for 7.5 miles to the exit for Sir Francis Drake Boulevard. Take that exit west and drive 14.5 miles to the park entrance, on the left.

To Devil's Gulch trailhead: From park headquarters, drive west for one mile to the dirt pullout, on the left side of the road (across from the paved access road for Devil's Gulch Horse Camp). Park, cross the road, and walk up the access road to the trailhead, on the right.

Contact: Samuel P. Taylor State Park, P.O. Box 251, Lagunitas, CA 94938, 415/488-9897, fax 415/488-4315; Marin District Headquarters, 415/898-4362, www.parks.ca.gov.

20 PIONEER TREE TRAIL
2.0 mi / 1.0 hr   🏃 2   ⛰ 7

in Samuel P. Taylor State Park west of San Rafael

Map 7.1, page 291

If you like big trees and a simple, quiet walk, Pioneer Tree Trail in Samuel P. Taylor State Park will provide it. This loop circles through the park's prize grove of coastal redwoods, the species that produces the tallest trees in the world. The trailhead is at the south side of Lagunitas Creek, at the Redwood Grove Picnic Area, about 0.25 mile from park headquarters. The picnic area features several big redwoods and remnants from the site's past. From there, hike up Wildcat Canyon, then across to the Irving Creek drainage. Follow that creek down near its confluence with Lagunitas Creek. The last 0.5 mile traces the southern edge of the creek back to the picnic area. Surrounded by the scent of redwoods, it's a pleasant hike on a soft dirt trail and includes a 400-foot climb and drop. Bicycles are prohibited on this route from all but the 0.5-mile service road along Lagunitas Creek.

Note: This park was on the state's closure list, but will be kept open and operated, in part, by the Golden Gate National Recreation Area.

User Groups: Hikers only. No dogs, horses, or mountain bikes.

Permits: A state park day-use fee of $8 per vehicle is charged at the entrance station.

Maps: A brochure and map are available for a fee at the entrance station to Samuel P. Taylor State Park. For a topographic map, ask the USGS for San Geronimo.

Directions: From the Golden Gate Bridge, take US 101 north for 7.5 miles to the exit for Sir Francis Drake Boulevard. Take that exit west and drive 14.5 miles to the park entrance, on the left.

Contact: Samuel P. Taylor State Park, P.O. Box 251, Lagunitas, CA 94938, 415/488-9897, fax 415/488-4315; Marin District Headquarters, 415/898-4362, www.parks.ca.gov.

21 KENT DAM TRAIL

1.8 mi / 1.0 hr 🏃1 ⛰6

in northwest Marin County west of San Rafael

Map 7.1, page 291

Most people are astounded the first time they see Kent Lake, for they have no idea such a huge lake is tucked away in a Marin canyon. But here it is, nearly four miles from north to south, with an additional large arm extending east into Big Carson Creek. Start by parking along Sir Francis Drake Boulevard. From here, hike on a ranch road along Lagunitas Creek for about a mile, arriving at the east side of Peters Dam. When the lake fills in late winter, it is a gorgeous sight—emerald water filling a long canyon, bordered on each side by rising slopes filled with conifers.

There is genuine irony here. Most folks in Marin consider themselves environmentally enlightened. Yet by damming the canyon on Lagunitas Creek, the Marin Water District annihilated the runs of steelhead and coho salmon by dewatering the stream and blocking the migratory path to spawning areas. Then, in another illogical stroke, they did not permit boating, not even kayaking or canoeing; in fact, no water contact is permitted. The route was largely reconfigured to reduce downstream

sedimentation into Lagunitas Creek and to protect spawning areas for coho salmon.

User Groups: Hikers, dogs, and mountain bikes. No horses. No wheelchair facilities.

Permits: No permits are required. Groups are limited to 19 people. Parking and access are free.

Maps: This trail is included on a free map of Point Reyes National Seashore (see address below). For topographic maps, ask the USGS for San Geronimo and Bolinas.

Directions: From the Golden Gate Bridge, take US 101 north for 7.5 miles to the exit for Sir Francis Drake Boulevard. Take that exit west and drive about 12 miles, just past Shafter Bridge, which spans Paper Mill/Lagunitas Creek (known by both names). Park here and look for the locked gate at the entrance to the trailhead, on the left side of Lagunitas Creek.

Contact: Sky Oaks Ranger Station, 415/945-1181; Marin Municipal Water District, 220 Nellen Avenue, Corte Madera, CA 94925, 415/945-1195, www.marinwater.org; Superintendent, Point Reyes National Seashore, Point Reyes, CA 94956.

22 OLEMA VALLEY

5.3 mi one-way / 2.25 hr 🏃1 ⛰8

in Point Reyes National Seashore south of Olema in northwest Marin County

Map 7.1, page 291

The phenomenon of two parallel creeks running in opposite directions is the featured attraction of the Olema Valley Trail, which starts at the Five Brooks trailhead (elevation 180 feet) and runs adjacent to the San Andreas Fault rift zone. Two earth plates moving in opposite directions created the fault line and resulted in the strange marvel of Olema Creek and Pine Gulch Creek—the creeks are relatively parallel, but run in opposite directions. From the trailhead, it's 1.3 miles to the headwaters of Pine Gulch Creek. From there, hike southward for four miles along the pretty creek before the trail ends at Highway 1. Most hikers turn back long before that, but with a partner and a shuttle car, it makes a great one-way hike, 5.3 miles in all. Deer are often very plentiful in this area.

User Groups: Hikers, horses, and mountain bikes. No dogs. No wheelchair facilities.

Permits: No permits are required. Parking and access are free.

Maps: For a free map, write to Point Reyes National Seashore. For a topographic map, ask the USGS for Bolinas.

Directions: From the Golden Gate Bridge, take US 101 north for 7.5 miles to the exit for Sir Francis Drake Boulevard. Turn west and drive about 20 miles west to Olema and Highway 1. Turn left on Highway 1 and drive 3.6 miles to the access road for Five Brooks trailhead, located on the west side of the road.

Contact: Superintendent, Point Reyes National Seashore, Point Reyes, CA 94956; Bear Valley Visitors Center, 415/464-5100, www.nps.gov/pore.

23 MOUNT BURDELL

5.8 mi / 3.0 hr

in Olompali State Historic Park in south Novato

Map 7.1, page 291

Your pay-off at Olompali State Historic Park is the view from the upper slopes and summit of 1,558-foot Mount Burdell as it towers over the expanse of San Pablo Bay. Below are the wetlands of Bahia Marsh and the Petaluma River near the Gnoss Field Airport. You can see the Sonoma Mountains to the north and across the bay to the Carquinez Bridge to the east. This 5.8-mile round trip hike to Burdell's summit includes a 1,500-foot climb; it is routed through pretty woodlands and up well-graded switchbacks until emerging in grasslands with a picnic site on top. From the parking area, take the trail that leads uphill; in 1.3 miles, turn left for the signed trail to Mount Burdell. Look for tons of deer and wild turkey.

For those arriving from San Francisco and the Peninsula, this can be like a mission to the moon. After departing the summer cold and fog, you emerge into sunny Marin and arrive at an oak woodland in the foothills of Novato. For those who arriving northbound on US 101, you will have to make a U-turn to access the park (but there's an easy way to do that), and many won't go to the effort. That makes Olompali one of the most overlooked parks in the Bay Area.

Two notes: A reconstructed Miwok village is located a 0.25-mile from the parking area. (Look for the "kitchen rock" with mortars for acorn grinding to leech out the bitter taste.) The Mount Burdell Open Space Preserve neighbors Olompali. Mountain biking and dogs are permitted in the preserve so if you see bikes or dogs, that is where they are coming from.

For a park that gets so hot in the afternoon, it is inconceivable that the entrance gate does not officially open until 10 A.M. It then closes at an equally ludicrous 5 P.M. If you arrive early or late, park outside the gate and save yourself $8; however, this will add 1.5 miles each way to your trip.

Note: This park is on the closure list developed by the California Department of Parks, pending final state budget decisions or the possible transfer of park management to other park agencies or volunteer groups.

User Groups: Hikers. No dogs, horses, and mountain bikes. No wheelchair facilities on Mount Burdell Trail, but they are available near the parking area.

Permits: No permits are required. There is an $8 parking fee.

Maps: A trail map is posted at information billboard near the parking area. For a topographic map, ask the USGS for Burdell.

Directions: From San Francisco, take US 101 north for about 15 miles (past Highway 37 on right) to the exit signed Landfill Access Road. Take that exit, cross over the overpass, then turn left and drive south on US 101 a short distance to the signed turnoff on the right for Olompali State Park.

Note: If you miss the Landfill Access Road on US 101, continue north to San Antonio Road, make a U-turn, and then return south on US 101 for 2.3 miles to the park entrance road on the right.

Contact: Olompali State Historic Park, 415/898-4362 (leave message), www.parks.ca.gov.

BAY RIDGE TRAIL / SAN GERONIMO RIDGE
10.7 mi one-way/ 5 hr

from Samuel P. Taylor State Park in northwest Marin County west of San Rafael

Map 7.1, page 291

This new 10.7-mile stretch of the Bay Area Ridge Trail provides a must-do trip for Marin hikers. The best place to access this trail is from Samuel P. Taylor State Park, located in west Marin on Sir Francis Drake Boulevard, leaving a shuttle car at the end of the trail near Fairfax.

After arriving at Samuel P. Taylor State Park, park at the day-use lot, and then head east on foot, bike, or horseback on the Cross Marin Trail. The route heads west for two miles, following an old railroad grade along the banks of Lagunitas Creek through a pretty redwood-based riparian zone. Eventually you will reach the new Inkwells Bridge, a 170-foot span, that allows visitors to cross the creek and reach the San Geronimo Fire Road set on Marin watershed land. Once across, you can then climb up to the top of the San Geronimo Ridge. This adds another six miles with a climb of 1,400 feet. The payoff is a series of great views: Mount Tamalpais, Barnabe Peak, Kent Lake, Bolinas Ridge, and glimpses of Tomales Bay.

One surprise of this new route is access to one of the only pygmy forests in the Bay Area, located along San Geronimo Ridge. These are miniaturized cypress trees, a natural phenomenon here due to the serpentine rock habitat. Here, with a shuttle, the route can be converted into a great one-way trip. On

San Geronimo Ridge, turn left at the 8-Mile Marker at White Hill Fire Road, and then continue 2.7 miles to the roadside parking area along Sir Francisco Drake Boulevard. Along the way, you'll get more great views of San Francisco Bay as well as the rolling foothills of Loma Alta Preserve and the Big Rock Peak.

Note: This park is on the closure list developed by the California Department of Parks, pending final state budget decisions or the possible transfer of park management to other park agencies or volunteer groups.

User Groups: Hikers, mountain bikes, and horses. No dogs. Limited wheelchair facilities.

Permits: A state park day-use fee of $8 per vehicle is charged at the entrance station.

Maps: A sheet map is available from Bay Ridge Trail Council. For topographic maps, ask the USGS for San Geronimo.

Directions: From the Golden Gate Bridge, take US 101 north for 7.5 miles to the exit for Sir Francis Drake Boulevard. Take that exit and drive west for 14.5 miles to the park entrance, on the left. Park at the day-use area and head east on Cross Marin Trail. For a one-way hike with a shuttle, park an additional car at a dirt pull-out along Sir Francis Drake Boulevard, about one mile west of Fairfax at the trailhead.

Contact: Bay Area Ridge Trail Council, 415/561-2595 or www.ridgetrail.org; Samuel P. Taylor, 415/488-9897 or www.parks.ca.gov.

25 ALAMERE FALLS TRAIL
13.0 mi / 1 day

in Point Reyes National Seashore northwest of Bolinas

Map 7.1, page 291

Alamere Falls tumbles over an ocean bluff, then cascades 40 feet to the beach below and into the Pacific Ocean. It is stunning, beautiful, and constantly changing as the rains come and go. There's one catch: This trip used be

8.4 miles, but a trail closure now makes it 13 miles, though a lot of people break the rules (and we'll get to that).

From the Palomarin Trailhead, follow the southern end of the Coastal Trail as it starts out on a service road that contours along the coastal foothills. At times you'll tower over the ocean and on clear days, the Farallon Islands look close enough to reach with a jump. The trail follows along the ocean for about a mile, then dips down into a ravine to climb out 500 feet to a sub-ridge and trail junction. Stay left on the Coastal Trail for two miles, gently descending past pretty Bass Lake. A mile later, you'll hike along a sub-ridge that overlooks Pelican Lake, a bit bigger than Bass Lake and also gorgeous. This is an excellent area for wildflowers and for sighting deer and birds. After passing Pelican Lake, the route continues north and arrives at a small bridge at Alamere Creek.

The next part of the trip is a continuous point of contention for the park. For eons, visitors have taken an unofficial route from the bridge to the brink of the falls. At the Alamere Creek Bridge, look for a well-worn route on the left along the creek. This was the falls cutoff. In 2011, the park closed this unofficial trail. Previously, hikers took this closed cutoff route and traced it down along the creek past a series of pools to the brink of the falls at the cliff. Of course, this is a violation of National Park rules and you can be issued a ticket.

The new trail hikes another 1.3 miles to Wildcat Camp, drops down to the beach, and then hikes south another mile along the beach to the base of Alamere Falls for the best views and photo ops. This adds another 4.6 miles round-trip. Even with light flows in Alamere Creek, this is one of the Bay Area's most beautiful waterfalls. After toppling over a rocky brink to the beach 40 feet below, the water cuts an ever-changing mosaic in the sand before running into the ocean. At moderate or high flows, it charges over the cliff in a wide sheet of whitewater.

User Groups: Hikers and horses. No dogs or mountain bikes. No wheelchair facilities.
Permits: No permits are required. Parking and access are free.
Maps: For a free map, write to Point Reyes National Seashore. For topographic maps, ask the USGS for Bolinas and Double Point.
Directions: From San Francisco, take US 101 north over the Golden Gate Bridge and continue 9 miles to Exit 450B for Sir Francis Drake Boulevard/San Anselmo. Take that exit (stay in the second lane from the right), continue to Sir Francis Drake, and drive 21 miles to Highway 1. Turn left and drive 9 miles to Olema-Bolinas Road on the right (the sign is always stolen; if you drive reach Bolinas Lagoon, turn around and look for a road on left). Turn right and go 1.3 miles to the junction with Horseshoe Hill Road. Turn left (still Olema-Bolinas Road) and go 0.5 mile to Mesa Road. Turn right and go 4.8 miles (pass an antenna farm called The Towers) to the parking area.

Note: Those familiar with the area can take Highway 1 on the Marin coast past Bolinas Lagoon to an unsigned turn on the left (Olema-Bolinas Road). This saves about 40 minutes.

Contact: Superintendent, Point Reyes National Seashore, Point Reyes, CA 94956; Bear Valley Visitors Center, 415/464-5100, www.nps.gov/pore.

26 ALPINE / KENT LAKE PUMP TRAIL
1.0-8.6 mi / 1.0-4.5 hr

on the northwest slopes of Mount Tamalpais at Alpine Lake Dam

Map 7.1, page 291

On the Kent Lake Pump Trail, you can score a 100 on the Blindfold Test. What's the Blindfold Test? Imagine that someone has blindfolded you and taken you off on an adventure. At some point deep into the trip, they suddenly stop, remove the blindfold, and ask you to answer true or false to these statements: If you really had been blindfolded, you would have no idea of your exact surroundings, and they are beautiful beyond imagination. If the answer is "true," then you have found a spot that passes the test and are on the way to a great adventure.

The trailhead is located adjacent to Alpine Dam. From the start, you get a view of the backside of Alpine Dam. In winter, when the lake fills and overflows at the spillway, the dam becomes a dramatic waterfall. From here you start your trip on a service road, a downhill grade as the route enters the canyon, with Lagunitas Creek on your left. Stay alert for the second cutoff on your left, which leads down to a beautiful, do-it-yourself streamside picnic spot beneath a canopy of Douglas fir and various hardwoods. This is one of the prettiest picnic spots in the Bay Area—and it's where we got the idea for the Blindfold Test.

The Kent Lake Pump Trail continues over the course of another four miles to the headwaters of Kent Lake, with small glimpses urging you forward for a more open look. The trail gradient is generally good, involving a 250-foot descent from Alpine Dam (648 feet) to Kent Lake (403 feet). Few do the entire trip. Throughout this area, you can take a short departure from the trail in the first mile to find an ideal setting for a picnic along Lagunitas Creek. Note that in late March, April, and May, there is often an active osprey nest atop a dead snag near the end of the trail at Kent Lake.

User Groups: Hikers, dogs, horses, and mountain bikes. No wheelchair facilities.

Permits: No permits are required. Groups are limited to 19 people. Parking and access are free.

Maps: A hiking and biking map is available for a fee from the Marin Water District. For a topographic map, ask the USGS for Bolinas.

Directions: From San Francisco, take US 101 north for 7.5 miles to the exit for Sir Francis Drake Boulevard. Take that exit west to Sir Francis Drake and drive six miles to Fairfax

(get in the left lane). As you enter Fairfax, look for a gas station on left and a break in the center median (a very small Fairfax sign is in center median). Turn left at the break in the median (Pacheco, unsigned), then make an immediate right on a frontage road (Broadway, adjacent to Fairfax Theater) and go one block to Bolinas-Fairfax Road. Turn left and drive west eight miles (continuing along Alpine Lake) to the Alpine Dam. Park on the right side of the road (just before the dam) and look for the gated service road/trailhead on the right.

Contact: Sky Oaks Ranger Station, 415/945-1181; Marin Municipal Water District, 220 Nellen Avenue, Corte Madera, CA 94925, 415/945-1195, www.marinwater.org.

27 PINE MOUNTAIN / CARSON FALLS

3.0 mi / 1.5 hr 🥾2 ⛰️9

on the northwest slopes of Mount Tamalpais west of Fairfax

Map 7.1, page 291

Your destination is Carson Falls, a set of small waterfalls that tumble into granite pools. The walk to this quiet, divine spot hidden on the north slopes of Mount Tamalpais is an easy stroll across hilly grasslands (often accompanied by a hawk or two floating about overhead), followed by a short jog down a canyon into the Carson Creek drainage.

The trailhead (at 1,078 feet) is adjacent to one of the better parking areas provided on lands administered by the Marin Water District. After parking, cross Bolinas-Fairfax Road to reach the trailhead, Pine Mountain Road (a water district service road). The road climbs 400 feet over the course of a mile, and merges into a junction with Oat Hill Road on the crest of a hill flanked on both sides by foothill grasslands. Turn left here and in 0.25 mile you'll reach a sign for the Carson Falls turn off on your right. Here you'll leave the fire roads and follow a new trail for 0.5 mile to

Carson Creek and the series of waterfalls. The lowest of the falls is a stunning, high, silver stream that flows over a notch in a boulder and free falls 30 feet into a beautiful pool. Of course, the cascades are best seen after a good rain, but there is usually at least a trickle of water into early summer. A trick: when nearing the waterfalls at the bottom of the valley, hop across the stream and then work your way down on the far side. From here looking up, you get a perfect view of four waterfalls, chutes, and cascades, each pouring into pools through a beautiful rock canyon. The final fall is a 35-foot free fall, silver and powerful. You can peer over its brink and look straight down, and in cool months, adjacent color is often added by nearby bright red toyon berries.

User Groups: Hikers, dogs, horses, and mountain bikes. No wheelchair facilities. Note that mountain bikes are allowed on Pine Mountain and Oat Hill Roads, but not on the hiking trail down to Carson Falls.

Permits: No permits are required. Groups are limited to 19 people. Parking and access are free.

Maps: A hiking and biking map is available for a fee from the Marin Water District. For a topographic map, ask the USGS for Bolinas.

Directions: From San Francisco, take US 101 north for 7.5 miles to the exit for Sir Francis Drake Boulevard. Take that exit west to Sir Francis Drake and drive six miles to Fairfax (get in the left lane). As you enter Fairfax, look for a gas station on the left and a break in the center median (a very small Fairfax sign is in center median). Turn left at the break in the median (Pacheco, unsigned), then make an immediate right on a frontage road (Broadway, adjacent to Fairfax Theater) and go one block to Bolinas-Fairfax Road. Turn left and drive west for 3.8 miles (past the golf course) to the large dirt parking area on the left. The trailhead for Pine Mountain Road and an information billboard are across the road from the parking area.

Note: Once on Sir Francis Drake, as you enter Fairfax, do not continue to the lighted intersection. No left turn to Bolinas-Fairfax Road is possible.

Contact: Sky Oaks Ranger Station, 415/945-1181; Marin Municipal Water District, 220 Nellen Avenue, Corte Madera, CA 94925, 415/945-1195, www.marinwater.org.

28 CARSON FALLS LOOP
7.4 mi / 3.5 hr 🏃3 ⛰10

on the northwest slopes of Mount Tamalpais west of Fairfax

Map 7.1, page 291

How can you take a great hike and make it better? By hiking to Carson Falls, and turning it into a stellar loop hike, sensational from late winter through spring. Start the trip by hiking up Pine Mountain Fire Road for one mile, gaining 300 feet, to the junction with Oat Hill Road. The route up provides sweeping views of surrounding foothills and beyond, including an awesome look at the remote north flank of Mount Tamalpais, and glimpses of Alpine Lake. It's common to see red-tailed hawks hunting and hovering. At the ridge and road junction, turn left at Oat Hill Road and walk 0.25 mile, or about five minutes. At the large sign for Carson Falls, turn right and leave the fire roads behind. Follow the pleasantly switchbacked trail, built in 2008, downhill for 0.5 mile. This fern-lined stretch of single-track deposits you on a narrow, artfully constructed footbridge above Carson Falls. Cross it and work your way down on the far side of the stream to the waterfalls. The best "ah" moment is just below the midway point, where you can look up and see three pool-and-drop waterfalls and a short cascade.

It's only a three-mile trip, out and back, to Carson Falls. This is how you can extend the trip to a great 7.4-mile loop hike: From the falls, continue down the Little Carson Trail to the Kent Pump Road, bear left, and continue 1.4 miles above Kent Lake to Old Vee Road. Turn left and climb 1.2 miles up to Oat Hill Road. Turn left and hike 1.5 miles along the ridge to Pine Mountain Road. Turn right and return one mile downhill to the parking area. Rating: Fantastic.

User Groups: Hikers, dogs, horses, and mountain bikes. No wheelchair facilities. Note that mountain bikes are allowed on Pine Mountain and Oat Hill Roads, but not on the hiking trail down to Carson Falls.

Permits: No permits are required. Groups are limited to 19 people. Parking and access are free.

Maps: A hiking and biking map is available for a fee from the Marin Water District. For a topographic map, ask the USGS for Bolinas.

Directions: From San Francisco, take US 101 north for 7.5 miles to the exit for Sir Francis Drake Boulevard. Take that exit west to Sir Francis Drake and drive six miles to Fairfax (get in the left lane). As you enter Fairfax, look for a gas station on the left and a break in the center median (a very small Fairfax sign is in center median). Turn left at the break in the median (Pacheco, unsigned), then make an immediate right on a frontage road (Broadway, adjacent to Fairfax Theater) and go one block to Bolinas-Fairfax Road. Turn left and drive west for 3.8 miles (past the golf course) to the large dirt parking area on the left. The trailhead for Pine Mountain Road and an information billboard are across the road from the parking area.

Note: Once on Sir Francis Drake, as you enter Fairfax, do not continue to lighted intersection. No left turn to Bolinas-Fairfax Road is possible.

Contact: Sky Oaks Ranger Station, 415/945-1181; Marin Municipal Water District, 220 Nellen Avenue, Corte Madera, CA 94925, 415/945-1195, www.marinwater.org.

29 TWO LAKES TRAIL
5.0 mi / 2.5 hr   👥2   ⛰10

on the northwest slopes of Mount Tamalpais at Lagunitas Lake near San Anselmo

Map 7.1, page 291

This is our favorite hike at Bon Tempe and Lagunitas Lakes. As you clear the rise, Lagunitas Lake first comes into view and the beauty hits you all at once: A pristine little lake, backed by forest and the rising slopes of the northeast face of Mount Tamalpais. This walk is pretty, easy, featuring tons of birds (and maybe a turtle or two), and can be shorted to a really easy 40-minute loop around Lagunitas (easy enough for baby strollers). Note that there is no officially named "Two Lakes Trail," so don't look for a sign. The trailhead lies at an elevation of 740 feet at the Lagunitas Picnic Area, adjacent to Lagunitas Lake, the smallest of Marin County's eight lakes. From here, we suggest hiking past the picnic area up to the earthen dam. You'll pop out with a pretty lake view and a sign warning visitors to watch out for migrating newts. Walk around Lagunitas Lake counterclockwise, eventually linking up with Pilot Knob Trail. Turn left, hike past the parking area, and connect with Bon Tempe Shadyside Trail. This route circles the lake (with one short juncture on the Sky Oaks Trail) and eventually leads all the way back to the parking area. As with any loop that links different trails, a map can be helpful, especially for newcomers. Pick one up at the entrance station.

User Groups: Hikers, leashed dogs. No horses, or mountain bikes. Limited wheelchair facilities.

Permits: A day-use fee of $8 is charged per vehicle. Groups are limited to 19 people.

Maps: A hiking and biking map is available for a fee from the Marin Water District. For a topographic map, ask the USGS for Bolinas.

Directions: From San Francisco, take US 101 north for 7.5 miles to the exit for Sir Francis Drake Boulevard. Take that exit west to Sir Francis Drake and drive six miles to Fairfax (get in the left lane). As you enter Fairfax, look for gas station on left and a break in center median (a very small Fairfax sign is in the center median). Turn left at the break in the median (Pacheco, unsigned), then make an immediate right on a frontage road (Broadway, adjacent to Fairfax Theater) and go one block to Bolinas-Fairfax Road. Turn left and drive 1.5 miles to Sky Oaks Road on left. Turn left and drive 0.5 mile to the entrance station.

Note: Once on Sir Francis Drake, as you enter Fairfax, do not continue to lighted intersection. No left turn to Bolinas-Fairfax Road is possible.

To Lagunitas Lake: From the entrance station, go 0.25 mile to a fork. Bear left and drive 1.25 miles to the parking and picnic area. Park and hike uphill on the service road to dam, lake, and trailhead.

To Bon Tempe Lake: From the entrance station, go 0.25 mile to a fork. Bear right on Bon Tempe Road and drive 0.2 mile to the parking area. Walk a short distance to the dam/spillway for lake access and the nearby trailhead.

Contact: Sky Oaks Ranger Station, 415/945-1181; Marin Municipal Water District, 220 Nellen Avenue, Corte Madera, CA 94925, 415/945-1195, www.marinwater.org.

30 DEER PARK TRAIL / BALD HILL

2.0 mi / 1.25 hr   🏃2   ⛰7

on the northwest slopes of Mount Tamalpais near San Anselmo

Map 7.1, page 291

The trailhead at Deer Park is quite popular, but by taking Deer Park Trail rather than one of the other options, you can find peace in addition to having quite a workout. You get both of these things because the trail climbs about 350 feet in less than a mile. This is one of those situations where you must pay for your pleasure. But pleasure you will get. As the trail rises up the slopes of Bald Hill, views open up

around you, and not just of the surrounding countryside; it is common to see deer in this area, and wildflower blooms are quite good in the spring. If you want even more, you'll have an opportunity to link up with a spiderweb of other trails in the area.

User Groups: Hikers only. No dogs, horses, or mountain bikes. No wheelchair facilities.

Permits: No permits are required. Groups are limited to 19 people. Parking and access are free.

Maps: A hiking and biking map is available for a fee from the Marin Water District. For a topographic map, ask the USGS for San Rafael.

Directions: From San Francisco, take US 101 north for 7.5 miles to the exit for Sir Francis Drake Boulevard. Take that exit west to Sir Francis Drake and drive six miles to Fairfax (get in the left lane). As you enter Fairfax, look for a gas station on the left and a break in the center median (a very small Fairfax sign is in center median). Turn left at the break in the median (Pacheco, unsigned), then make an immediate right on a frontage road (Broadway, adjacent to Fairfax Theater) and go one block to Bolinas-Fairfax Road. Turn left and drive west for 0.5 mile to Porteous Avenue. Turn left on Porteous Avenue and continue to Deer County Park. If you walk behind the school on the left, and completely pass it, the trailhead will be on your left.

Note: Once on Sir Francis Drake, as you enter Fairfax, do not continue to lighted intersection. No left turn to Bolinas-Fairfax Road is possible.

Contact: Marin County Parks, 415/499-6405, www.maringov.org.

31 SHORELINE TRAIL

5.0 mi / 2.5 hr   🏃1   ⛰7

in China Camp State Park east of San Rafael

Map 7.1, page 291

For visitors new to China Camp State Park, the Shoreline Trail is the best introduction you could ask for. From the well-signed trailhead at the parking area, the trail meanders along the shore of San Pablo Bay, bordered by undisturbed hills on one side and waterfront on the other. The first mile provides good lookouts across the bay; the last 0.5 mile crosses a meadow then runs adjacent to tidal areas, marshes, and wetlands—home to many species of waterfowl. The hike doesn't involve serious elevation gains or losses, so you won't face any surprise climbs. A former option for the return trip used to be to take Miwok Fire Trail, but that route is now closed with vegetation growing over it.

Note: This park is on the closure list developed by the California Department of Parks, pending final state budget decisions or the possible transfer of park management to other park agencies or volunteer groups.

User Groups: Hikers, horses, and mountain bikes. No dogs. No wheelchair facilities.

Permits: No permits are required. A state park day-use fee of $5 per vehicle is charged at the entrance station.

Maps: A brochure and map are available for a fee at park headquarters or by contacting the state parks district office. For a topographic map, ask the USGS for San Quentin.

Directions: From US 101 in San Rafael, take the North San Pedro exit and drive east for four miles to the park entrance.

Contact: China Camp State Park, 415/456-0766; California State Parks, Marin District, 7665 Redwood Boulevard, Suite 150, Novato, CA 94945, 415/898-4362, www.parks.ca.gov.

32 PATRICK'S POINT
5.0 mi / 2.5 hr 👫3 ⛰10

in China Camp State Park east of San Rafael

Map 7.1, page 291

A stroke of genius by a state park ranger has created the Bay Area's greatest new lookout. In this case, the strokes of genius were made by a chainsaw. Ranger Patrick Robards, a fire science specialist, ordered a hilltop grove of eucalyptus taken out at China Camp State Park. The result at this spot is a jaw-dropping, five-bridge view of the bay and the region's mountain peaks, as well as a Marin-360 that will have you wishing your neck could full-pivot swivel. So, we named the spot Patrick's Point, and the name has stuck.

This trip starts with the drive on North San Pedro Road from San Rafael out to the Marin shoreline along San Pablo Bay. When you reach a fork to a ranger kiosk, instead stay left on the main road (turning right to the kiosk will take you to the park's campground entrance). Continue on the main road past the sensational picnic areas (on the left, at water's edge) to the turnoff on the right to the ranger station. This is your starting point. From here, it is a 2.5-mile loop with a 500-foot climb to McNear's Ridge and Patrick's Point.

Near the ranger station, with the park map in hand, start at the Shoreline trailhead. Take the Shoreline Trail north (you'll have good views of the San Pablo Bay shore) to the Oak Ridge Trail. Turn left on the Oak Ridge Trail and climb steadily to a junction with the Mc-Near's Fire Trail. Turn right and you pop out on top. Note that on the park map, the lookout is not marked.

What a view: On clear days, you can see the Bay Bridge, the Richmond–San Rafael Bridge, the Carquinez Bridge, the Benicia Bridge, and the tops of the Golden Gate Bridge. We've seen crystal-clear days from this lookout where it seemed you could take a running start and then leap across the bay and land on Point Pinole.

Note: This park is on the closure list developed by the California Department of Parks, pending final state budget decisions or the possible transfer of park management to other park agencies or volunteer groups.

User Groups: Hikers, horses, and mountain bikes. No dogs. No wheelchair facilities.

Permits: No permits are required. A fee of $5 per vehicle is charged at China Camp Village.

Maps: A brochure and map are available for a fee at park headquarters or by contacting the state parks district office. For a topographic map, ask the USGS for San Quentin.

Directions: From San Francisco, take US 101 to San Rafael and the exit for North San Pedro. Take that exit and drive east four miles to park. At the fork (with a kiosk and campground on right), stay left and drive one mile (past the picnic areas on the left) to the ranger station, on the right, and the trailheads.

Contact: China Camp State Park, 415/456-0766; California State Parks, Marin District, 7665 Redwood Boulevard, Suite 150, Novato, CA 94945, 415/898-4362, www.parks.ca.gov.

33 AUDUBON CANYON RANCH TRAIL
0.4 mi / 0.25 hr   👣2 ⛰10

in Martin Griffin Preserve near Bolinas Lagoon

Map 7.1, page 291   BEST (

Here is a little slice of paradise, the premier place on the Pacific Coast to view herons and egrets—those large, graceful seabirds—as they court, mate, nest, and rear their young. From ranch headquarters, the hike is short with a 200-foot climb requiring about 20 minutes to reach the canyon overlook. Benches are provided for rest stops. Scopes installed at the top can be used to peer across the valley and zero in on the giant nests in the redwoods. Birdwatchers might want to repeat this great trip again and again, tracking the mating process of the great birds. The ritual starts when the male offers the female a twig. If the offer is accepted, the two then build a nest together. If rebuffed, the male then seeks another mate. Not much different than humans, actually. May and June are usually the best times to come. In May the eggs start hatching, and by June, there can be as many as 200 hatchlings in the different nests. They eagerly await breakfast, lunch, and dinner, which are provided when their huge parents return from Bolinas Lagoon and vomit the goodies all over the nest. Hey, what's for dessert?

Note: Martin Griffin Preserve was renamed to honor Marty Griffin and recognize his role in protecting the Marin coast. For 40 years, it was known as Bolinas Lagoon Preserve of Audubon Canyon Ranch. The preserve is open only on weekends and holidays, 10 A.M.–4 P.M., mid-March–mid-July.

User Groups: Hikers only. No dogs, horses, or mountain bikes. No wheelchair facilities.

Permits: Entrance to the ranch is free, but donations are requested; a $15 donation from families is suggested.

Maps: A small trail map and brochure are available at ranch headquarters. For a topographic map, ask the USGS for Bolinas.

Directions: From San Francisco, take US 101 north over the Golden Gate Bridge and continue 4 miles to Marin and to Exit 445B for Highway 1/Stinson Beach. Take that exit and continue west for 1 mile to the stoplight at a T Intersection (Tam Junction) for Shoreline Highway/Highway 1. Turn left on Shoreline Highway and drive 11 miles to Stinson Beach. Continue north on Highway 1 for 3.5 miles to the preserve entrance gate on the right.

Contact: Audubon Canyon Ranch, 4900 Highway 1, Stinson Beach, CA 94970, 415/868-9244, www.egret.org.

34 CATARACT FALLS
2.5 mi / 1.5 hr   👣3 ⛰10

on the northwest slopes of Mount Tamalpais at Alpine Lake Dam

Map 7.1, page 291

Cataract Falls is not a single waterfall, but a series of cascades that rushes down a beautifully wooded canyon set in the northwest slopes of Mount Tamalpais. For those who search out the top-rated hikes, there's many a day when this trail is definitely a 10. At times, when the canyon is flush with water, it can rate as one of the best winter day hikes in California. In summer and fall, when the creek is rendered a trickle or even goes dry, it's more like a 7.

The hike requires a climb but is well worth every step. From the trailhead at the south end of Alpine Lake (elevation 644 feet), you face a 750-foot climb over the span of just a mile to reach the centerpiece falls at 1,400 feet. Some hikers take the easier route from the Laurel Dell trailhead, which has a 240-foot drop over 0.4 mile.

The trailhead is a few hundred yards past the west side of the dam at Alpine Lake. This is the best-known fall in the region, and parking along the road is extremely limited, often making for a frustrating encounter on weekends. This will probably increase when word gets out that it's a 10.

The trail starts by contouring along a cove of Alpine Lake. It then rises from the lake, climbing up into a lush canyon where there seems to be one small waterfall after another. These are not big free falls like in Yosemite, but rather small cascades, surrounded by luxuriant riparian beauty. Compared to almost anywhere in the Bay Area environs after such recent heavy rains, the collective beauty can seem nonpareil.

In late winter, especially when the skies have just cleared after heavy rains, the cascades in this canyon can look like something found in Hawaii. This is particularly true when rays of sunlight catch the droplets of water just right, and the refracted light makes them sparkle. From top to bottom, there's one cascade after another, crowned by a silvery chute pouring into a plunge pool. After getting your fill of this sight, return the way you came.

User Groups: Hikers and dogs. No horses or mountain bikes. No wheelchair facilities.

Permits: No permits are required. Groups are limited to 19 people. Parking and access are free.

Maps: A hiking and biking map is available for a fee from the Marin Water District. For a topographic map, ask the USGS for Bolinas.

Directions: From San Francisco, take US 101 north for 7.5 miles to the exit for Sir Francis Drake Boulevard. Take that exit and follow the ramp as it curves around to the west to Sir Francis Drake and continue 6 miles to Fairfax (get in the left lane). Just over a small hill, past a small gas station on the left, look for a break in the center median. Turn left here, and after crossing the oncoming lane, immediately turn right on a frontage road. Continue one block to Bolinas-Fairfax Road. Turn left and drive 8 miles, cross Alpine Dam, and continue a short distance to the trailhead on the left. Park on the road's shoulder; it often fills quickly on Sunday mornings in winter.

Contact: Sky Oaks Ranger Station, 415/945-1181; Marin Municipal Water District, 220 Nellen Avenue, Corte Madera, CA 94925, 415/945-1195, www.marinwater.org; Mount Tamalpais State Park, 801 Panoramic Highway, Mill Valley, CA 94941, 415/388-2070, fax 415/388-2968; California State Parks, Marin District, 415/898-4362, www.parks.ca.gov.

35 LAUREL DELL LOOP
2.5 mi / 1.5 hr

in Mount Tamalpais State Park

Map 7.1, page 291

Cataract Falls is the most adored waterfall on Mount Tamalpais, and the Laura Dell trailhead provides the easiest route there. Instead of the climb from Alpine Lake (see listing in this chapter), here you start high and glide down to the upper set of falls, then return via a gentle loop. The trailhead is at 1,640 feet. Walk down fire road 0.7 mile to the Laurel Dell picnic site, then turn left on Cataract Trail for a 1-mile descent into the steep canyon to see Cataract Falls, a series of tiny waterfalls in a lush setting. When running at full strength, the cascades are a precious sight. At the falls, turn right on the High Marsh Trail, hike onward, and turn right at any of the next three trail intersections to return to the Laurel Dell trailhead. Of the three choices, the second makes the best return loop, as the short cutoff will put you within a few hundred yards of the trailhead. Though you won't get the full flavor of the canyon, as you do with the *Cataract Falls* trail (see listing in this chapter), this does provide a sumptuous taste.

User Groups: Hikers and dogs. No horses or mountain bikes. No wheelchair facilities.

Permits: No permits are required. Parking and access are free.

Maps: A brochure and map of Mount Tamalpais State Park is available for a small fee at the visitors center or by writing to the address below. For topographic maps, ask the USGS for Bolinas and San Rafael.

Directions: From San Francisco, take US 101 north over the Golden Gate Bridge and continue 4 miles to Marin and the exit for Highway 1/Stinson Beach. Take that exit and continue west for 1 mile to the stoplight at T Intersection for Shoreline Highway/Highway 1. Turn left on Shoreline Highway and drive 2.6 miles to the Panoramic Highway. Bear right on Panoramic Highway and drive 5.2 miles to Pantoll (at the four-way junction, continue straight). Bear right on Pantoll Road and go 1.4 miles to Rock Spring and Ridgecrest Boulevard. Turn left and drive 1.4 miles to trailhead. Most folks park along the road.

Contact: Mount Tamalpais State Park, 801 Panoramic Highway, Mill Valley, CA 94941, 415/388-2070, fax 415/388-2968; California State Parks, Marin District, 415/898-4362, www.parks.ca.gov.

36 O'ROURKE'S BENCH / ROCK SPRINGS
0.6 mi / 0.5 hr 🚶1 ⛰10

in Mount Tamalpais State Park

Map 7.1, page 291

Rock Springs is one of Mount Tam's best trailheads. Five trails start at Rock Springs, but our favorite is this short jaunt to O'Rourke's Bench, one of the best lookouts, where hikers can have a picnic while enjoying the awesome view to the west. On one trip, the coast was socked in with low stratus clouds, appearing

from this lookout like a sea of fog dotted with protruding mountaintops resembling islands. On another day, the sunset was heartbreaking. O'Rourke's Bench is quite easy to reach. After parking at Rock Springs, cross Ridgecrest Boulevard and take O'Rourke's Bench Trail for 0.3 mile. After some 10 or 15 minutes, you will come upon a little bench set on a knoll at 2,071 feet. A plaque next to the bench reads: "Give me these hills and the friends I love. I ask no other heaven. To our dad O'Rourke, in joyous celebration of his 76th birthday, Feb. 25th, 1927. From the friends to whom he showed this heaven."

User Groups: Hikers only. No dogs, horses, or mountain bikes. No wheelchair facilities.

Permits: No permits are required. Parking and access are free.

Maps: A hiking and biking map is available for a fee from the Marin Water District. For a topographic map, ask the USGS for San Rafael.

Directions: From San Francisco, take US 101 north over the Golden Gate Bridge and continue 4 miles to Marin and the exit for Highway 1/Stinson Beach. Take that exit and continue west for 1 mile to the stoplight at a T Intersection for Shoreline Highway/Highway 1. Turn left on Shoreline Highway and drive 2.6 miles to the Panoramic Highway. Bear right on Panoramic Highway and drive 4.7 miles to Bootjack on right (at the four-way junction, continue straight). Or continue another 0.5 mile to the Pantoll parking lot on left. Or at Pantoll, bear right on Pantoll Road and go 1.4 miles to Rock Spring parking areas and trailhead (at a T-junction with Ridgecrest Boulevard).

Contact: Mount Tamalpais State Park, 801 Panoramic Highway, Mill Valley, CA 94941, 415/388-2070, fax 415/388-2968; California State Parks, Marin District, 415/898-4362, www.parks.ca.gov.

37 BARTH'S RETREAT
2.0 mi / 1.0 hr 🚶1 ⛰7

in Marin Water District

Map 7.1, page 291

When you link this easy walk with the short hike to O'Rourke's Bench, which also starts from Rock Springs (see *O'Rourke's Bench/ Rock Springs* listing in this chapter), you can feel as if you've seen the world in a two-hour time span. Rarely can the features of the land change more quickly than on the hike to Barth's Retreat on Mount Tamalpais. In just a mile, you cross a serpentine swale, pass a small creek with riparian habitat, go through a forest, and then arrive at an open area called Barth's Retreat (just so you know, O'Rourke's vision of beauty has it all over that of ol' Barth). Barth, by the way, was one Emil Barth, a prolific musician/hiker/trail-builder who constructed a camp here in the early 20th century. This hike provides a quick glimpse of the diversity Mount Tam offers.

User Groups: Hikers only. No dogs, horses, or mountain bikes. No wheelchair facilities.

Permits: No permits are required. Parking and access are free.

Maps: A hiking and biking map is available for a fee from the Marin Water District. For a topographic map, ask the USGS for San Rafael.

Directions: From San Francisco, take US 101 north over the Golden Gate Bridge and continue 4 miles to Marin and the exit for Highway 1/Stinson Beach. Take that exit and continue west for 1 mile to the stoplight at a T Intersection for Shoreline Highway/Highway 1. Turn left on Shoreline Highway and drive 2.6 miles to the Panoramic Highway. Bear right on Panoramic Highway and drive 4.7 miles to Bootjack on the right (at the four-way junction, continue straight). Or continue another 0.5 mile to the Pantoll parking lot on the left. Or at Pantoll, bear right on Pantoll Road and go 1.4 miles to Rock Spring parking areas and trailhead (at a T junction with Ridgecrest Boulevard).

Contact: Mount Tamalpais State Park, 801 Panoramic Highway, Mill Valley, CA 94941, 415/388-2070, fax 415/388-2968; California State Parks, Marin District, 415/898-4362, www.parks.ca.gov.

38 MOUNTAIN THEATER / WEST POINT INN
3.0 mi / 1.5 hr 🚶1 ⛰7

in Marin Water District

Map 7.1, page 291

The round-trip from the Mountain Theater to West Point Inn is a classic Mount Tamalpais walk—pretty, easy, and with a landmark on each end. Mount Tam's masterpiece outdoor amphitheater is actually just a few hundred yards from the parking area; you cross right behind it on Rock Springs Trail en route to West Point Inn. The trail is quiet and tranquil—especially since it's off-limits to bikes—and it weaves in and out of a hardwood forest, descending easily for most of the way. Over the course of 1.5 miles, you drop 295 feet, from a trailhead elevation of 2,080 feet to the trail's end at 1,785 feet. West Point Inn offers great views and a perfect spot for a picnic lunch, and lemonade is often available inside. Here's a secret: Small cabins without electricity can be rented for overnight stays.

User Groups: Hikers only. No dogs, horses, or mountain bikes. No wheelchair facilities.

Permits: No permits are required. Parking and access are free.

Maps: A brochure and map of Mount Tamalpais State Park is available for a small fee at the visitors center or by writing to the address below. For a topographic map, ask the USGS for San Rafael. Much of this trail is on Marin Water District land; contact that agency to obtain a detailed map for a fee.

Directions: From San Francisco, take US 101 north over the Golden Gate Bridge and continue 4 miles to Marin and the exit for Highway 1/Stinson Beach. Take that exit and continue west for 1 mile to the stoplight at a

T Intersection for Shoreline Highway/Highway 1. Turn left on Shoreline Highway and drive 2.6 miles to the Panoramic Highway. Bear right on Panoramic Highway and drive 5.2 miles (at the four-way junction, continue straight) to the Pantoll parking lot. Or, bear right on Pantoll Road and go 1.4 miles to Rock Spring and Ridgecrest Boulevard. Turn right on Ridgecrest and go 0.25 mile to the Mountain Theater Trailhead.

Contact: Mount Tamalpais State Park, 801 Panoramic Highway, Mill Valley, CA 94941, 415/388-2070, fax 415/388-2968; California State Parks, Marin District, 415/898-4362, www.parks.ca.gov; Marin Municipal Water District, 220 Nellen Avenue, Corte Madera, CA 94925, 415/945-1195, www.marinwater.org.

39 EAST PEAK MOUNT TAMALPAIS
0.4 mi / 0.5-1.0 hr 🏃1 ⛰10

in Mount Tamalpais State Park

Map 7.1, page 291   BEST (

Mount Tam is one of those rare spots that projects a feeling of power, and while standing on its highest point, you can sense that power flowing right through you. That is why there is no better place in the Bay Area to watch the sun set than atop the East Peak of Mount Tamalpais. The feelings this experience can inspire might stay with you for many weeks. The hike is very short (after all, a parking lot is set right at the foot of the summit trail) but is quite steep. The trail rises about 330 feet to the top, at an elevation of 2,571 feet. An old lookout station is positioned at the summit, and hikers usually try to find a perch as close as possible to the top.

To the east, the bay resembles the Mediterranean Sea, an azure pool sprinkled with islands. And at night, the lights of the bridges and the surrounding cities can give the Bay Area an almost surreal look. But the true magic happens at sunset, particularly on foggy days.

The peak stands well above the fog line, and when the fiery sun dips into that low stratus to the west, orange light is refracted for hundreds of miles around. Witness this stunning sight even one time, and you will gain a new perspective about what might be possible in this world. Perhaps you'll even set some new horizons for yourself.

If you seek more hiking action, there are two great trailheads nearby. To visit lovely Cataract Falls, take the Laurel Dell Loop (see *Laurel Dell Loop* listing in this chapter). At the foot of the parking area, the Paradise Lookout Fire Road is another good trail on which to extend your hike.

User Groups: Hikers only. Dogs are permitted on the paved trail but not on the mountaintop overlook. No horses or mountain bikes. No wheelchair access on the trail, but good views are available from the wheelchair-accessible parking lot.

Permits: No permits are required. A parking fee of $8 per vehicle is charged.

Maps: A brochure and map of Mount Tamalpais State Park is available for a small fee at the visitors center, located adjacent to the parking area, or by writing to the address below. For a topographic map, ask the USGS for San Rafael.

Directions: From San Francisco, take US 101 north over the Golden Gate Bridge and continue 4 miles to Marin and the exit for Highway 1/Stinson Beach. Take that exit and continue west for 1 mile to the stoplight at a T Intersection for Shoreline Highway/Highway 1. Turn left on Shoreline Highway and drive 2.6 miles to the Panoramic Highway. Bear right on Panoramic Highway and drive 5.2 miles to Pantoll (at the four-way junction, continue straight). Bear right on Pantoll Road and go 1.4 miles to Rock Spring and Ridgecrest Boulevard. Turn right on Ridgecrest and go 3 miles to East Peak and parking. The road dead-ends at the parking area at the base of the summit and trailhead.

Contact: Mount Tamalpais State Park, 801 Panoramic Highway, Mill Valley, CA 94941,

415/388-2070, fax 415/388-2968; California State Parks, Marin District, 415/898-4362, www.parks.ca.gov.

40 INSPIRATION POINT

2.6 mi / 1.0 hr   🥾1 ⛰10

in Mount Tamalpais State Park

Map 7.1, page 291

If you want a similar kind of magic that is found at the Mount Tam summit, yet without all the people, Inspiration Point provides a nearby alternative. To get there, instead of heading up to the East Peak after parking, go the opposite direction and turn right on the fire road, Eldridge Grade. The trail wraps around the northern flank of the East Peak, then makes a hairpin turn to the left around North Knee, set at 2,000 feet. At this point, the bay comes into view to the east, and you start to understand the attraction. But keep on, because Inspiration Peak awaits just down the road. At the hairpin right turn, take the short but steep cutoff trail on the left, and you will quickly reach the top at 2,040 feet—your vantage point for miles and miles of charmed views. All can seem enchanted. Much of this trail is on Marin Water District land.

User Groups: Hikers, dogs, and mountain bikes. No horses. No wheelchair access on the trail, but good views are available from the wheelchair-accessible parking lot.

Permits: No permits are required. A parking fee of $8 per vehicle is charged at the summit parking lot.

Maps: A brochure and map of Mount Tamalpais State Park is available for a small fee at the visitors center, located adjacent to the parking area, or by writing to the address below. For a topographic map, ask the USGS for San Rafael.

Directions: From San Francisco, take US 101 north over the Golden Gate Bridge and continue 4 miles to Marin and the exit for Highway 1/Stinson Beach. Take that exit and continue west for 1 mile to the stoplight at a T

Intersection for Shoreline Highway/Highway 1. Turn left on Shoreline Highway and drive 2.6 miles to the Panoramic Highway. Bear right on Panoramic Highway and drive 5.2 miles to Pantoll (at the four-way junction, continue straight). Bear right on Pantoll Road and go 1.4 miles to Rock Spring and Ridgecrest Boulevard. Turn right on Ridgecrest and go 3 miles to East Peak and parking. The road dead-ends at the parking area at the base of the summit and trailhead.

Contact: Mount Tamalpais State Park, 801 Panoramic Highway, Mill Valley, CA 94941, 415/388-2070, fax 415/388-2968; California State Parks, Marin District, 415/898-4362, www.parks.ca.gov.

41 PHOENIX LAKE TRAIL

2.7 mi / 1.5 hr   🥾1 ⛰7

on the north slope of Mount Tamalpais near Ross

Map 7.1, page 291

Of the eight lakes in Marin County, Phoenix is the least accessible. If you're from out of town, this one just isn't worth the hassle. Not only is the parking situation horrendous, but newcomers can have trouble finding the lake, an intolerable situation considering how beloved it is. If you think you can just drive up on a Sunday, park at the end of the road, and take off on a hike here, you're dreamin'. The little 25-acre jewel set in a pocket just west of the town of Ross is indeed well loved. From Natalie Coffin Greene Park, it's an easy 0.2-mile walk to the lake. Stairs on one side of the small dam take visitors down to a trail at the water's edge. The distance around the entire lake is 2.3 miles. In the winter, the lake is stocked with trout twice a month, and in the spring, bass fishing can be decent. As at all Marin lakes, no one is permitted to make contact with the water.

User Groups: Hikers, leashed dogs, horses, and mountain bikes (restricted from the lake's southern shoreline). No wheelchair facilities.

Permits: No permits are required. Groups are limited to 19 people. Parking and access are free.

Maps: A hiking and biking map is available for a fee from the Marin Water District. For a topographic map, ask the USGS for San Rafael.

Directions: From San Francisco, take US 101 north for 7.5 miles to Sir Francis Drake Boulevard. Take that exit and head west for 2.5 miles to Lagunitas Road. Turn left on Lagunitas Road and drive 1.1 miles into Natalie Coffin Greene Park. The lake is 0.25 mile from the parking area. Parking is extremely limited.

Contact: Sky Oaks Ranger Station, 415/945-1181; Marin Municipal Water District, 220 Nellen Avenue, Corte Madera, CA 94925, 415/945-1195, www.marinwater.org.

42 DAWN FALLS

1.8 mi / 1.0 hr

on the eastern slopes of Mount Tamalpais near Larkspur

Map 7.1, page 291

The Bay Area has many hidden waterfalls, but this one is both easy to reach and a beautiful and energizing sight in winter and spring. Dawn Falls, a 25-foot fountain of water, is best seen in the early morning, when rays of sunlight penetrate the atmosphere—which is how this waterfall got its name. Note, however, that in summer and fall, dry weather reduces the cascade to a trickle, and in drought years, it can go completely dry.

At the trailhead, don't get confused and take Baltimore Canyon Fire Road; that route is far less intimate than Dawn Falls Trail, which probes a dense woodland with model riparian habitat on each side of Larkspur Creek near the falls. This walk starts out easy and stays that way, even with the moderate 300-foot rise to the waterfall. On the way in, many don't expect the waterfall to be much, especially if the creek appears as nothing but a tiny trickle.

The route becomes steeper as you near the waterfall, and is edged by some beautiful trees. When the waterfall comes into view, stop and take it in. This is a favorite and the District has done some fine work rehabilitating this trail, route, and watershed.

User Groups: Hikers, dogs, horses (on the adjacent fire road), and mountain bikes. No wheelchair facilities.

Permits: No permits are required. Groups are limited to 19 people. Parking and access are free.

Maps: A hiking and biking map is available for a fee from the Marin Water District. For a topographic map, ask the USGS for San Rafael.

Directions: From US 101 in Marin, drive north to Corte Madera and the exit for Tamalpais Drive. Take that exit to Tamalpais Drive and head west to Corte Madera Avenue. Turn right and drive about 0.5 mile to Madrone Avenue. Turn left on Madrone Avenue and drive to Valley Way. The trailhead is at the road's end.

Contact: Marin County Parks, Marin Open Space, Civic Center Room 415, San Rafael, CA 94903, 415/499-6387; Ranger Field Office 415/507-2816, www.co.marin.ca.us.

43 BOOTJACK LOOP

6.2 mi / 3.0 hr

in Mount Tamalpais State Park

Map 7.1, page 291

We put together this classic, self-styled Mount Tam loop hike by linking a few favorite trails from a favorite trailhead. In the process, you get glimpses of a dynamic, diverse, and delightful habitat. The trail crosses a meadow, oak woodlands, and some hilly grasslands, then submerges deep into a redwood forest and climbs back out, all in the space of 6.2 miles. It starts with a steady descent, so you face a huff-and-a-puff climb on the return trip, but the redwoods make it worth it.

Start at the Pantoll Ranger Station and

trailhead (elevation 1,500 feet) in Mount Tamalpais State Park. Take the Alpine Trail and
hike north 0.4 mile to Van Wyck Meadow and
the junction with the Bootjack Trail. You will
descend 450 feet in the process. At the trail
junction, turn right on the Bootjack Trail, and
head downhill along a small stream. This leg
leads 1.3 miles into Muir Woods National
Monument and a junction with the Ben Johnson Trail. Turn right on the Ben Johnson Trail
and begin the steep return trip. Over the next
mile, the trail climbs 500 feet, flanked the
entire way by one of the Bay Area's richest
redwood groves, home to many gigantic trees.
To complete the loop, continue up, up, and up
on Ben Johnson Trail (to the Stapelveldt Trail)
for the final 0.9 mile to the Pantoll trailhead,
a total elevation gain of 1,080 feet.

Pantoll is one of our favorite trailheads in
California—with five great hikes selected from
here. While Steep Ravine and the Sunset Trail
are the crown jewels, you can't miss with any
of them.

User Groups: Hikers only. No dogs, horses, or
mountain bikes. No wheelchair facilities.

Permits: No permits are required. A parking
fee of $8 per vehicle is charged.

Maps: A brochure and map of Mount Tamalpais State Park is available for a small fee at
the visitors center or by writing to the address
below. For a topographic map, ask the USGS
for San Rafael.

Directions: From San Francisco, take US
101 north over the Golden Gate Bridge and
continue 4 miles to Marin and the exit for
Highway 1/Stinson Beach. Take that exit and
continue west for 1 mile to the stoplight at a
T Intersection for Shoreline Highway/High-
way 1. Turn left on Shoreline Highway and
drive 2.6 miles to the Panoramic Highway.
Bear right on Panoramic Highway and drive
5.2 miles to Pantoll (at the four-way junction,
continue straight). Turn left at the Pantoll
parking area.

Contact: Mount Tamalpais State Park, 801
Panoramic Highway, Mill Valley, CA 94941,
415/388-2070, fax 415/388-2968; California

State Parks, Marin District, 415/898-4362,
www.parks.ca.gov.

44 MATT DAVIS / COASTAL TRAIL
1.0-3.2 mi one-way / 0.5-1.5 hr

on the western slopes of Mount Tamalpais

Map 7.1, page 291

This downhill glide provides heart-touching
views of the Pacific Ocean. It's a 3.2-mile leg-
stroker from the Pantoll trailhead down to
Stinson Beach. There are many places where
you can stop, spread your arms wide, and feel
as if the entire world is within your grasp.
After parking at Pantoll, elevation 1,500 feet,
cross the road and look for the sign marking
Matt Davis/Coastal Trail. Soon enough, you
will start descending toward the beach, but not
before first entering a lush grove of fir trees.
Here the trail is level for nearly a mile. When
you emerge, the trail begins its steep descent
across open grasslands down to Stinson Beach.
Only thick fog can ruin the day. Many people
just enjoy a mile or two of the expansive sea
views, then return. But it is a great one-way
hike with a partner and a shuttle car waiting at
the trail's end, at the Stinson Beach Firehouse.
Note that the entire Matt Davis Trail is technically nearly double this suggested route, with
the trailhead at Mountain Home.

User Groups: Hikers only. No dogs, horses, or
mountain bikes. No wheelchair facilities.

Permits: No permits are required. A parking
fee of $8 per vehicle is charged.

Maps: A brochure and map of Mount Tamalpais State Park is available for a small fee at
the visitors center or by writing to the address
below. For a topographic map, ask the USGS
for San Rafael.

Directions: From San Francisco, take US
101 north over the Golden Gate Bridge and
continue 4 miles to Marin and the exit for
Highway 1/Stinson Beach. Take that exit and
continue west for 1 mile to the stoplight at a

T Intersection for Shoreline Highway/Highway 1. Turn left on Shoreline Highway and drive 2.6 miles to the Panoramic Highway. Bear right on Panoramic Highway and drive 5.2 miles to Pantoll (at the four-way junction, continue straight). Turn left into the Pantoll parking area.

Contact: Mount Tamalpais State Park, 801 Panoramic Highway, Mill Valley, CA 94941, 415/388-2070, fax 415/388-2968; California State Parks, Marin District, 415/898-4362, www.parks.ca.gov.

45 STEEP RAVINE TRAIL
4.0 mi / 1.5 hr   🏃2 ⛰10

on the western slopes of Mount Tamalpais

Map 7.1, page 291

Just add rain and hiking Steep Ravine Trail is like being baptized by the divine spirit of nature. Those who set foot on it will find a place where they can get their own brand of religion. The trail passes through remarkably beautiful terrain, including cathedral-like redwoods, lush undergrowth, and a pretty stream. Believe it or not, this is one of the few hikes that is best done during a rainstorm. In the canyon, the forest canopy protects you from a direct assault by the raindrops. Everything becomes vibrant with life as it drips with water. From the trailhead at Pantoll, the route descends 1,100 feet over the course of two miles, ending at Highway 1 near Rocky Point. After departing and heading downhill, it doesn't take long before the redwoods surround you. The trail follows Webb Creek, crossing the stream eight times in all. At one point, you have to climb down a ladder adjacent to a small waterfall. The junction with Dipsea Trail is a trail landmark; from this point, it's 0.5 mile to the end. In the most violent rainstorms, this place is a refuge of peace and purity.

User Groups: Hikers only. No dogs, horses, or mountain bikes. No wheelchair facilities.
Permits: No permits are required. A parking fee of $8 per vehicle is charged.

Maps: A brochure and map of Mount Tamalpais State Park is available for a small fee at the visitors center or by writing to the address below. For a topographic map, ask the USGS for San Rafael.

Directions: From San Francisco, take US 101 north over the Golden Gate Bridge and continue 4 miles to Marin and the exit for Highway 1/Stinson Beach. Take that exit and continue west for 1 mile to the stoplight at a T Intersection for Shoreline Highway/Highway 1. Turn left on Shoreline Highway and drive 2.6 miles to the Panoramic Highway. Bear right on Panoramic Highway and drive 5.2 miles to Pantoll (at the four-way junction, continue straight). Turn left into the Pantoll parking area.

Contact: Mount Tamalpais State Park, 801 Panoramic Highway, Mill Valley, CA 94941, 415/388-2070, fax 415/388-2968; California State Parks, Marin District, 415/898-4362, www.parks.ca.gov.

46 PANTOLL / WEST POINT INN
3.8-6.4 mi / 2 hr-2 days   🏃1 ⛰8

in Marin Water District

Map 7.1, page 291

The best cheap overnighter in the Bay Area is a true hideaway called the West Point Inn, set high on the slopes of Mount Tamalpais at 1,785 feet. What you get here is a restored vintage inn, built in 1904, with seven rooms and a full gas-powered kitchen, and five rustic cabins. There is no electricity. Though there is a service road to the inn available for those with disabilities, everyone else must hike two miles. To make it work, visitors must carry in a sleeping bag, food, and a change of clothes, which is no sweat with a backpack. In return you get sensational views, recreation (hiking and biking), and privacy at night.

After parking at Pantoll, the most direct route is to cross the road and take Old Stage Road for 1.9 miles to the inn. For a more scenic trip, instead from Pantoll, take the Alpine Trail 0.4 mile to Bootjack Trail. Turn left and hike 0.3 mile (cross the road and pass Bootjack parking) to the Matt Davis Trail. Turn right and head 2.3 miles to the Nora Trail. Turn left; it's another 0.2 mile to the inn. This makes a 6.4 mile round-trip.

West Point Inn has developed a cult-like following for those who know it. From West Point Inn, mountain bikers can ride the Old Railroad Grade to the East Peak parking lot, a rite of passage for Marin bikers (most start at the summit and ride all the way downhill). Several excellent day hikes are also available, at all levels of difficulty.

User Groups: Hikers, mountain bikes. No dogs, horses. Wheelchair users can get vehicle permit for access.

Permits: Overnight reservations required at 415/646-0702 up to three months in advance (no same-day reservations). Open Tuesday night through Saturday night. Closed Sunday and Monday nights. For day-use visits, no permits are required; $8 parking fee required at Pantoll parking.

Maps: A brochure and map of Mount Tamalpais State Park is available at Pantoll or by writing to the address below. For a topographic map, ask the USGS for San Rafael. Much of this trail is on Marin Water District land; contact that agency to obtain a detailed map for a fee.

Directions: From San Francisco, take US 101 north over the Golden Gate Bridge and continue 4 miles to Marin and the exit for Highway 1/Stinson Beach. Take that exit and continue west for 1 mile to the stoplight at a T Intersection for Shoreline Highway/Highway 1. Turn left on Shoreline Highway and drive 2.6 miles to the Panoramic Highway. Bear right on Panoramic Highway and drive 5.2 miles to Pantoll (at the four-way junction, continue straight). Turn left into the Pantoll parking area.

Contact: West Point Inn, 415/646-0702; Mount Tamalpais State Park, 801 Panoramic Highway, Mill Valley, CA 94941,

415/388-2070, fax 415/388-2968; California State Parks, Marin District, 415/898-4362, www.parks.ca.gov.

▮47▮ PANTOLL / COAST TRAIL
4.0 mi / 1.5 hr 🏃2 ⛰8

on the western slopes of Mount Tamalpais

Map 7.1, page 291

The Coast Trail out of Pantoll is the first new multiuse trail at Mount Tamalpais State Park in 15 years. Within five minutes, by bike or on foot, you will realize that state park rangers turned what was a good idea at headquarters into a stroke of genius in the field.

After parking, face the ocean with the campground on your left and look for the service road to the left that heads west, passing just above the Steep Ravine trailhead. This is how the trip starts. The trailhead is at an elevation of 1,100 feet. From here, the new Coast Trail features a perfect downhill glide, roughly two miles to a foothill ridge (and gate) that overlooks Muir Beach, and less than another mile to Highway 1.

You will hike (or ride) on pavement a short distance to a ranger-service area and then continue as the road turns into a dirt fire road. In another 30 seconds, you emerge at a clearing and with it, get the trail's first great lookout of the ocean and San Francisco. From here, continue straight on the fire road, heading southwest toward Muir Beach. This trail, one of the newest in Marin, is about half the width of a fire road, what mountain bikers would call a double track. It is wide enough to pass on without those surprise "showdown" moments of truth with other trail users, yet narrow enough for an intimate feel.

User Groups: Hikers and mountain bikes. No dogs or horses. No wheelchair facilities.

Permits: No permits are required. A parking fee of $8 per vehicle is charged.

Maps: A brochure and map of Mount Tamalpais State Park is available for a small fee at the visitors center or by writing to the address below. For a topographic map, ask the USGS for San Rafael.

Directions: From San Francisco, take US 101 north over the Golden Gate Bridge and continue 4 miles to Marin and the exit for Highway 1/Stinson Beach. Take that exit and continue west for 1 mile to the stoplight at a T Intersection for Shoreline Highway/Highway 1. Turn left on Shoreline Highway and drive 2.6 miles to the Panoramic Highway. Bear right on Panoramic Highway and drive 5.2 miles to Pantoll (at the four-way junction, continue straight). Turn left into the Pantoll parking area.

Contact: Mount Tamalpais State Park, 801 Panoramic Highway, Mill Valley, CA 94941, 415/388-2070, fax 415/388-2968; California State Parks, Marin District, 415/898-4362, www.parks.ca.gov.

48 MOUNTAIN HOME / TOURIST CLUB

2.4 mi / 1.0 hr 🏃1 ⛰6

in Mount Tamalpais State Park

Map 7.1, page 291

How many hikes end where you can order a cold beer on a hot day? Here's one of the few: a 1.2-mile hike at Mount Tamalpais that ends at a great little inn called the Tourist Club, where you can "slake your thirst," as they say here, with your "favorite elixir." This walk is short and has only one small steep portion. Park at the lot at Mountain Home along Panoramic Highway. From there, take Panoramic Trail 0.4 mile (it parallels Panoramic Highway) to its junction with Redwood Trail, which you then follow for 0.75 mile. The route laterals across the mountain slope before dropping into a pocket where the Tourist Club is perched on a slope. On weekends at this wood-framed building, not only can you get liquid refreshments, you can often drink while listening to German music. There is no other hiking destination like it in California.

User Groups: Hikers only. No dogs, horses, or mountain bikes. No wheelchair facilities.

Permits: No permits are required. Parking and access are free. The Tourist Club is open to the public 1–5 P.M. Saturday–Sunday, except the second weekend of each month (members only).

Maps: A brochure and map of Mount Tamalpais State Park is available for a small fee at the visitors center or by writing to the address below. For a topographic map, ask the USGS for San Rafael.

Directions: From San Francisco, take US 101 north over the Golden Gate Bridge and continue 4 miles to Marin and the exit for Highway 1/Stinson Beach. Take that exit and continue west for 1 mile to the stoplight at a T Intersection for Shoreline Highway/Highway 1. Turn left on Shoreline Highway and drive 2.6 miles to the Panoramic Highway. Bear right on Panoramic Highway and drive 5.2 miles to Pantoll (at the four-way junction, continue straight). Bear right on Pantoll Road and go 1.4 miles to Rock Spring and Ridgecrest Boulevard. Turn right on Ridgecrest and go 0.25 mile to Mountain Theater Trailhead. The trailhead (Panoramic Trail) is on the west side of the road.

Contact: Mount Tamalpais State Park, 801 Panoramic Highway, Mill Valley, CA 94941, 415/388-2070, fax 415/388-2968; California State Parks, Marin District, 415/898-4362, www.parks.ca.gov; Tourist Club, 415/388-9987, www.touristclubsf.org.

49 OWL TRAIL

3.5 mi / 1.5 hr 🏃1 ⛰9

on the Marin coast south of Stinson Beach

Map 7.1, page 291

From start to finish, there's no other coastal walk like this one. It is short, but the hits just keep coming. The trailhead is near the Muir Beach Overlook, which alone is worth the trip for the great views of the southern Marin coast. But don't stop there like so many visitors do.

Typically overlooked is an unsigned trailhead on the north side of the parking area: this is the Owl Trail. From here, the trail is routed through low-lying brush, which makes wearing shorts a prickly proposition. Starting at 440 feet, the trail descends 240 feet in 0.9 mile on its northward course to Slide Ranch. Slide Ranch consists of a hamlet of wood huts and a small farm with goats, sheep, chickens, and even some ducks—all favorites of youngsters. Two-foot-tall great horned owls sometimes roost in the giant cypress trees at Slide Ranch, hence the trail's name, but the owls can be difficult to see in their natural camouflage. From here, the trip down to the beach adds another 15 minutes to your walk; the descent is slippery, and a rope is usually available to aid hikers through the worst spot. Once down, you can explore numerous secret spots amid rocks of all sizes, stacks, and tidepools. On one visit, hundreds of tiny rock crabs were sparring in the shallows.

User Groups: Hikers only. No dogs, horses, or mountain bikes. The Muir Beach Overlook is wheelchair accessible, but Owl Trail is not.

Permits: No permits are required. Parking and access are free.

Maps: A brochure and map are available at the Marin Headlands Visitors Center or by contacting the Golden Gate National Recreation Area, Marin Headlands. For a topographic map, ask the USGS for Point Bonita.

Directions: From San Francisco, take US 101 north over the Golden Gate Bridge and continue 4 miles to Marin and the exit for Highway 1/Stinson Beach. Take that exit and continue west for 1 mile to the stoplight at a T Intersection for Shoreline Highway/Highway 1. Turn left on Shoreline Highway and drive to a signed turn for Muir Beach Overlook. Turn left at the Muir Beach Overlook and drive a short distance to the parking area. The trailhead may at first seem hidden. It is unsigned and located at the north side of the parking area.

Contact: Muir Woods National Monument, Mill Valley, CA 94941, 415/388-2596

(preferred number), www.nps.gov/muwo; Golden Gate National Parks Conservancy, Visitors Center, 415/388-7368.

50 MAIN TRAIL
2.0–3.0 mi / 1.0–1.5 hr 👫1 ⛰8

in Muir Woods National Monument near Mill Valley

Map 7.1, page 291   **BEST ◖**

Tourists from all over the world who visit San Francisco tend to follow the same routine: After they take a picture of the Golden Gate Bridge from Vista Point, they drive to Muir Woods to see a real redwood tree. Many visitors stroll out 0.5 mile or so to take in the grandeur of this redwood forest, then simply return the way they came. As such, the paved and boardwalked Main Trail is one of the most heavily used trails in the Bay Area.

Our suggestion is to create a gorgeous 3-mile loop. From the park entrance, follow the Main Trail to a junction with pretty Fern Creek Trail on the right. Hike Fern Creek Trail until the junction with the Lost Trail on the right. Turn right, then climb about 500 feet up to the junction with Ocean View Trail. Turn right again onto Ocean View Trail and follow the trail down to return to the valley floor.

User Groups: Hikers only. No dogs (except for seeing-eye dogs), horses, or mountain bikes. The first section of the trail is wheelchair accessible.

Permits: An entry fee of $5 per person is charged, free for 15 and under. No permits are required.

Maps: A brochure and map are available for a fee at the visitors center or by contacting Muir Woods National Monument. For a topographic map, ask the USGS for San Rafael.

Directions: From San Francisco, take US 101 north over the Golden Gate Bridge and continue 4 miles to Marin and to Exit 445B for Highway 1/Stinson Beach. Take that exit and continue west for 1 mile to the stoplight at a

T Intersection (Tam Junction) for Shoreline Highway/Highway 1. Turn left on Shoreline Highway and drive 2.6 miles to the Panoramic Highway. Bear right on Panoramic Highway and drive 0.8 mile to a junction with Muir Woods Road. Turn left and go 1.5 miles to the park entrance road (Camp Eastwood Road). Turn right and drive 0.2 mile to the parking lot. Note that a shuttle is available in summer.

Contact: Muir Woods National Monument, Mill Valley, CA 94941, 415/388-2596 (preferred number), www.nps.gov/muwo/; Golden Gate National Parks Conservancy, Visitor Center, 415/388-7368.

51 OCEAN VIEW TRAIL
3.4 mi / 1.5 hr   👣2 ⛰8

in Muir Woods National Monument near Mill Valley

Map 7.1, page 291

Ocean View Trail? Get this: There is no "ocean view." This is still a good hike, if misnamed (some want the name of the trail changed to Panoramic Trail. Various maps and signs list it both ways.) The only sure thing is you aren't going to see the ocean.

Yet this trail is worth knowing. When you arrive at Muir Woods and see tour buses shooting out people like popcorn from a popping machine, you'll be glad you read this. That is because Ocean View Trail provides the best chance of getting away from the crowds. After passing the information stand and starting down the paved path on the valley floor, turn right on Ocean View Trail/Panoramic Highway Trail. In under a minute you will enter a different world, a world of solitude, beautiful redwoods, and, alas, a steep ascent.

From the valley floor, the trail heads up the east side of the canyon on a steady grade, steep enough to get you puffing. It climbs 570 feet in 1.2 miles, rising above the valley to where you can look down into a sea of redwoods. To complete the loop, turn left on Lost Trail,

elevation 750 feet, which descends quite steeply over just 0.4 mile back to the valley floor, at 300 feet. There you turn left on Fern Creek Trail. Turn left onto the main trail to return to headquarters. It's a great escape—a favorite.

User Groups: Hikers only. No dogs (except for seeing-eye dogs), horses, or mountain bikes. The first section of the trail is wheelchair accessible.

Permits: An entry fee of $5 per person is charged. No permits are required.

Maps: A brochure and map are available for a fee at the visitors center or by contacting Muir Woods National Monument. For a topographic map, ask the USGS for San Rafael.

Directions: From San Francisco, take US 101 north over the Golden Gate Bridge and continue 4 miles to Marin and to Exit 445B for Highway 1/Stinson Beach. Take that exit and continue west for 1 mile to the stoplight at a T Intersection (Tam Junction) for Shoreline Highway/Highway 1. Turn left on Shoreline Highway and drive 2.6 miles to the Panoramic Highway. Bear right on Panoramic Highway and drive 0.8 mile to a junction with Muir Woods Road. Turn left and go 1.5 miles to the park entrance road (Camp Eastwood Road). Turn right and drive 0.2 mile to the parking lot.

Contact: Muir Woods National Monument, Mill Valley, CA 94941, 415/388-2596 (preferred number), www.nps.gov/muwo/; Golden Gate National Parks Conservancy, Visitors Center, 415/388-7368.

52 DIPSEA TRAIL
7.5 mi one-way / 3.5 hr   👣3 ⛰10

on Mount Tamalpais from Mill Valley to Stinson Beach

Map 7.1, page 291

In your first steps on the Dipsea Trail, you walk—or run—in the strides of ghosts, shadows, and legends, just as thousands have done over the years. The cross-country Dipsea Trail race is world-renown as the oldest and one of the most beautiful cross-country routes anywhere. The route spans 7.51 miles from Mill Valley to Stinson Beach, crossing the south flank of Mount Tamalpais, up and down from Old Mill Park through Muir Woods and Mount Tamalpais State Park and Steep Ravine en route to the coast. The origin of the name "Dipsea" has been argued about for years, but many figure it comes from the old days when some participants jumped into the ocean to cool off after completing the trek.

Most hikers use a standard route that has mile markers along the way, but since there are no trail signs at many junctions, the trip can turn into guesswork for newcomers. The starting point of the race is the Mill Valley Depot, where you run a short distance down the street to Old Mill Park. Here you head uphill and reach the first of three sets of steps, 688 in all (formerly 671 before they were reworked). The steps are legendary among Dipsea runners. Jack Kirk, who ran the Dipsea for 67 straight years, is credited with the celebrated quote about the steps: "Old Dipsea runners never die. They just reach the 672nd step."

When the trail tops the stairs and reaches pavement, look for the arrows painted on the street to mark the way (at times, the arrows can be faint). They will route you along Sequoia Road, Walsh Drive, and then pair up with someone who knows the way. After crossing Panoramic Highway, you finally get off the pavement and start descending into Muir Woods. Here, the trail signs improve. Cross Redwood Creek on a narrow footbridge, then start a long, steady ascent that is crowned at Cardiac Hill, a 480-foot climb in 0.4 mile (it's not that steep for hikers, but for trail runners, it's like hitting a wall). Once you crest Cardiac Hill, you feel yourself gliding downhill where each leg stroke seems almost effortless. This is where trail runners catch their breath and the first scent of the ocean—and the finish line.

You then plummet down the steps into Steep Ravine and over a wood bridge at Webb Creek. This canyon is stunning, with walls of ferns—including some of the biggest bracken ferns in the Bay Area—and a towering redwood canopy. Webb Creek flows clear and clean over rocks and into pools. When you emerge from Steep Ravine and sail down into the coastal foothills, you can hear the ocean breakers and smell the sea before you catch your first glimpse of water—know then the end is near. A panorama of the ocean, Stinson Beach, and beyond to Duxbury Point comes into view. Most seem to get a second wind and rocket out of the hardwood forest. With a short jog down Highway 1 and a left turn, you arrive at the finish line, and you have completed America's landmark cross-country route. There aren't many rites of passage and this is one of them.

The length of the Dipsea has been argued over time, but Darrell White, who runs the race and is on the Dipsea Board of Directors, walked the route with GPS and a mileage wheel and verified the exact distance at 7.51 miles. In the process, he installed the mileage markers, with classy brass plates embedded in small boulders.

User Groups: Hikers only. No dogs, horses, or mountain bikes. No wheelchair facilities.

Permits: No permits required. Parking and access is free at the primary trailhead, but the trail can be accessed from Muir Woods and Mount Tamalpais State Park, where there are fees. If you start at Mount Tamalpais State Park, a $8 fee is charged per vehicle.

Maps: The Dipsea Trail crosses several jurisdictions. A brochure and map of Mount Tamalpais State Park is available for a small fee at the visitors center or by contacting Mount Tamalpais State Park. For topographic maps, ask the USGS for San Rafael and Bolinas.

Directions: From US 101 in Marin, take the East Blithedale/Tiburon Boulevard exit. Head west on East Blithedale (it becomes Throckmorton Street) into Mill Valley, and follow Throckmorton to Old Mill Park. The trailhead is technically downtown, but for this hike, start at Old Mill Creek and the bridge, which leads to the famed steps.

Contact: Mount Tamalpais State Park, 801 Panoramic Highway, Mill Valley, CA 94941,

415/388-2070, fax 415/388-2968; California State Parks, Marin District, 415/898-4362, www.parks.ca.gov; Muir Woods National Monument, Mill Valley, CA 94941, 415/388-2596 (preferred number), www.nps.gov/muwo/; Golden Gate National Parks Conservancy, Visitors Center, 415/388-7368.

53 TENNESSEE VALLEY
4.2 mi / 2.0 hr

in the Marin Headlands near Sausalito

Map 7.1, page 291

Tennessee Cove is a well-hidden, drop-dead gorgeous cove that extends in a sculpted curve south to Tennessee Point, with many stacks and outcrops in the tidelands to the south that catch the brunt of waves. The hike travels through Tennessee Valley (flat, paved for 0.8 mile, and very popular) and continues at a fork (trail turns to gravel, both forks reconnect in 0.6 mile), then ventures past a small marsh en route to gorgeous Tennessee Cove on the Marin coast. On the way, you are flanked by hills glowing green and peppered with wildflowers. The views of the Pacific Ocean can be gorgeous and the sunsets memorable. This trail has become a favorite for family hiking or biking trips. It is often crowded on weekends, and even on weekday afternoons when the weather is clear.

User Groups: Hikers, horses, and mountain bikes. (Horses and mountain bikes must take the forked fire road.) No dogs. No wheelchair facilities.

Permits: No permits are required. Parking and access are free.

Maps: A brochure and map are available at the Marin Headlands Visitors Center or by contacting the Golden Gate National Recreation Area. For a topographic map, ask the USGS for Point Bonita.

Directions: From San Francisco, take US 101 over the Golden Gate Bridge and go 4 miles (through the Waldo Tunnel and into Marin City) to the exit for Highway 1/Stinson Beach. Take that exit and drive 0.6 mile to Tennessee Valley

Road on the left. Turn left and go two miles to the road's end, parking, and trailheads.

Contact: Golden Gate National Recreation Area, Marin Headlands Visitors Center, Building 948, Fort Barry, Sausalito, CA 94965, 415/331-1540; visitor information, 415/561-4700, www.nps.gov/goga.

54 MIWOK LOOP
3.5 mi / 2.0 hr

in the Marin Headlands near Sausalito

Map 7.1, page 291

When you arrive at the trailhead at Tennessee Valley, you immediately see the usual parade of people on the primary Tennessee Valley Trail. While this is one of the best easy family walks with a pay-off, there are other excellent choices available. This loop trail we created is one of them. The Miwok Loop is a nearly circular hike that traverses the pretty grasslands of the Marin Headlands, connecting a number of trails to provide a decent physical workout. Good views are found throughout, including those from a great 880-foot lookout to the west, at the junction of Ridge Road and Fox Trail. The hike starts at the Miwok Stables (elevation 200 feet), where you head north on Miwok Trail, rising into higher country. The trail turns left, then heads west 0.6 mile, still climbing to the junction of Miwok Trail and Coyote Ridge Road. At this point, to make the loop hike, turn left on Ridge Road, where the trail tops out at 1,000 feet. The next mile offers spectacular views of the ocean, and every step can be special. To return to the Miwok Stables, turn left at the Fox Trail, and hike 1.1 miles; go left again on the paved Tennessee Valley Trail, and hike out the last 0.4 mile to the stables. Trail use is typically high on weekends, and that includes mountain bike traffic on Coyote Ridge Road.

User Groups: Hikers, dogs, horses, and mountain bikes (partial access). No wheelchair facilities.

Permits: No permits are required. Parking and access are free.

Maps: A brochure and map are available at the Marin Headlands Visitors Center or by contacting the Golden Gate National Recreation Area. For a topographic map, ask the USGS for Point Bonita.

Directions: From San Francisco, take US 101 over the Golden Gate Bridge and go 4 miles (through the Waldo Tunnel and into Marin City) to the exit for Highway 1/Stinson Beach. Take that exit and drive 0.6 mile to Tennessee Valley Road on the left. Turn left and go two miles to the road's end, parking, and trailheads.

Contact: Golden Gate National Recreation Area, Marin Headlands Visitors Center, Building 948, Fort Barry, Sausalito, CA 94965, 415/331-1540; visitor information, 415/561-4700, www.nps.gov/goga.

55 OLD SPRINGS / RODEO LAGOON
4.0 mi one-way/ 2.0 hr 🏃2 ⛰9

in the Marin Headlands near Sausalito

Map 7.1, page 291

Here's a great discovery from the Tennessee Valley Trailhead. This route climbs out of Tennessee Valley and then sails down across pretty foothills to gorgeous Rodeo Lagoon and on to the ocean at Rodeo Cove. It works best as a one-way trek, leaving a shuttle car at Rodeo Lagoon.

From the south end of the parking area at Tennessee Valley, take the Old Springs Trailhead. This climbs 400 feet over 1.2 miles to a ridge-top junction. The foothill and valley views are spectacular. Continue straight on the Old Springs Trail for another 0.3 mile to a significant trail junction (with Wolf Ridge Trail). Turn left here on the Miwok Trail and get ready to sail.

From here, the Miwok Trail is a 1.6 downhill glide from ridge to valley floor, ending at a gated parking lot. The surface is a hard-packed service road that eventually merges with Bunker Road at the foot of Rodeo Lagoon.

For the final 0.6 mile, head west along Rodeo Lagoon on your left. There is an excellent picnic area at Fort Cronkhite to your right. The road eventually dead-ends at the gate; here you can walk up to a bluff-top lookout that towers over Rodeo Cove, beach, and lagoon.

User Groups: Hikers, horses, and mountain bikes. No dogs. No wheelchair facilities.

Permits: No permits are required. Parking and access are free.

Maps: A brochure and map are available at the Marin Headlands Visitors Center or by contacting the Golden Gate National Recreation Area. For a topographic map, ask the USGS for Point Bonita.

Directions: From San Francisco, take US 101 over the Golden Gate Bridge and go 4 miles (through the Waldo Tunnel and into Marin City) to the exit for Highway 1/Stinson Beach. Take that exit and drive 0.6 mile to Tennessee Valley Road on the left. Turn left and go two miles to the road's end, parking, and trailheads.

To Rodeo Lagoon: In a shuttle car, take US 101 north over the Golden Gate Bridge to Marin and the exit for Alexander Avenue (located just north of the Golden Gate Bridge). Take that exit and drive 600 yards to a sign for Marin Headlands. Turn left onto unsigned Bunker Road, drive through the tunnel (wait for a green light), and continue on Bunker Road to Rodeo Lagoon. Parking is on the right at the picnic sites.

Contact: Golden Gate National Recreation Area, Marin Headlands Visitors Center, Building 948, Fort Barry, Sausalito, CA 94965, 415/331-1540; visitor information, 415/561-4700, www.nps.gov/goga.

56 BICENTENNIAL BIKE PATH
4.5 mi / 2.0 hr 🏃1 ⛰7

on the San Francisco Bay shoreline from Sausalito to Corte Madera

Map 7.1, page 291

This is a sensational waterfront stroll with easy access. Though popular, and crowded at times, it answers the question: Can folks out for an easy stroll mix well with joggers and bikers? The Bicentennial Bike Path proves this is possible, primarily because it was designed just for that purpose. This paved byway starts in Sausalito and heads north, tracing the shoreline of Richardson Bay into Corte Madera. It is a great nature walk—easy and pleasant. From Sausalito, the route passes beneath the US 101 overpass, then pushes toward Bothin Marsh along the edge of Richardson Bay, crossing two exceptional little bridges that provide passage over tidelands. At low tide, hundreds of tiny sandpipers frequently poke around in the mud; in the nearby sloughs bordered by pickleweed, you can often spot egrets, night herons, and maybe even a pelican. Bikers can continue all the way to Ross but will have to make a few connections on city streets (on an exceptionally well-designed bike trail) to do so.

User Groups: Hikers, dogs, mountain bikes, and wheelchairs. No horses.

Permits: No permits are required. Parking and access are free.

Maps: For a topographic map, ask the USGS for San Francisco North.

Directions: From San Francisco, drive north on US 101 over the Golden Gate Bridge. In Marin, take the Sausalito exit. Follow 2nd Street/Bridgeway through Sausalito to Harbor Drive, then park. The trail starts there.

Contact: Richardson Bay Audubon Center, 376 Greenwood Road, Tiburon, CA 94920, 415/388-2524, www.tiburonaudubon.org/.

57 MORNING SUN TRAIL
0.6–5.2 mi / 0.5–3.0 hr   👥2 ⛰7

in the Marin Headlands near Sausalito

Map 7.1, page 291

This trail didn't get its name by accident: This is one of the best places in the Bay Area to catch a sunrise. After the short but steep climb to the junction with Alta Trail, you will discover this is a magnificent location to watch the sun come up, casting varying hues

of yellow and orange across San Francisco Bay. The trek to the lookout is short enough that it doesn't make the pre-dawn wakeup and drive to the trailhead so bad. There is a good parking area at the trailhead, and from there you climb about 400 feet, peaking out at 800 feet at the Alta Trail junction. From Alta, you can easily extend your trip in either direction, or you can create a pretty 5.2-mile loop by linking Rodeo Valley Trail and Bobcat Trail.

User Groups: Hikers only. No dogs, horses, or mountain bikes. No wheelchair facilities.

Permits: No permits are required. Parking and access are free.

Maps: A brochure and map are available at the Marin Headlands Visitors Center or by contacting the Golden Gate National Recreation Area. For a topographic map, ask the USGS for San Francisco North.

Directions: From San Francisco, drive north on US 101 through the Waldo Tunnel. Take the Spencer Avenue exit, but keep straight on the frontage road on the east side of the freeway. (Do not turn right onto Spencer Avenue.) Drive about 0.5 mile, turn left, and drive under the freeway to the commuter parking area at the trailhead.

Contact: Golden Gate National Recreation Area, Marin Headlands Visitors Center, Building 948, Fort Barry, Sausalito, CA 94965, 415/331-1540; visitor information, 415/561-4700, www.nps.gov/goga.

58 COASTAL TRAIL / FORT CRONKHITE
5.2 mi / 2.5 hr   👥2 ⛰8

in the Marin Headlands at the mouth of San Francisco Bay

Map 7.1, page 291

Fort Cronkhite, perched on an ocean bluff above Rodeo Beach, was the "support community" for the Marin Headlands military fortifications in the 1930s and 1940s. From here, a paved pathway extends north up to Wolf Ridge, climbing to a 960-foot summit at what is known as Hill 88. The land consists primarily of coastal grasslands, so from the summit, you get outstanding views of the Pacific Ocean. The entire route is paved, and you may encounter speeding bikers. Although the round-trip distance is 5.2 miles, you'll surely make the 2.6-mile return hike at least twice as fast as the journey up.

User Groups: Hikers, dogs, horses, and mountain bikes. Fort Cronkhite and the picnic area are partially wheelchair accessible.

Permits: No permits are required. Parking and access are free.

Maps: A brochure and map are available at the Marin Headlands Visitors Center or by contacting the Golden Gate National Recreation Area, Marin Headlands. For a topographic map, ask the USGS for Point Bonita.

Directions: From San Francisco, take US 101 north over the Golden Gate Bridge to Marin and the exit for Alexander Avenue (just north of the bridge). Take that exit west and drive under the highway and curve south to Conzelman Road, signed Marin Headlands Coastal Route. Turn right (west) on Conzelman and drive to Hawk Hill (you will pass a turnoff on the left to a great lookout of the Golden Gate at Battery Spencer), then continue west (the road becomes one-way) toward Point Bonito and Field Road. Turn right on Field Road and drop down into Rodeo Valley (passing the Nike missile site) to Bunker Road (at the foot of Rodeo Lagoon). Turn left on Bunker Road and drive (past Rodeo Lagoon on your left, Fort Cronkhite on your right) to parking at the end of the road for Rodeo Beach.

Contact: Golden Gate National Recreation Area, Marin Headlands Visitors Center, Building 948, Fort Barry, Sausalito, CA 94965, 415/331-1540; visitor information, 415/561-4700, www.nps.gov/goga.

59 COASTAL TRAIL / FORT BARRY

1.4 mi / 0.75 hr

in the Marin Headlands near Rodeo Lagoon

Map 7.1, page 291

Fort Barry was a nerve center for military operations in an era long past. Today it's a place that can calm the nerves of frazzled hikers. After parking and exploring at Fort Barry a bit, take the unpaved road/trail that heads west from the fort. Covering just 0.7 mile, the trail is routed along the south side of Rodeo Lagoon and out to the bluffs overlooking the ocean. This is a great walk, and easy, with good views all around on clear days. The fort, set at the foot of Rodeo Valley, offers a living history lesson.

User Groups: Hikers, dogs, and horses. No mountain bikes. No wheelchair facilities.

Permits: No permits are required. Parking and access are free.

Maps: A brochure and map are available at the Marin Headlands Visitors Center or by contacting the Golden Gate National Recreation Area, Marin Headlands. For a topographic map, ask the USGS for Point Bonita.

Directions: From San Francisco, take US 101 north over the Golden Gate Bridge to Marin and the exit for Alexander Avenue (just north of the bridge). Take that exit west and drive under the highway and curve south to Conzelman Road, signed Marin Headlands Coastal Route. Turn right (west) on Conzelman and drive to Hawk Hill (you will pass a turnoff on the left to a great lookout of the Golden Gate at Battery Spencer), then continue west (the road becomes one-way) toward Point Bonito and Field Road. Turn right on Field Road and drop down into Rodeo Valley (passing the Nike missile site) to Bunker Road (at the foot of Rodeo Lagoon). Turn left on Bunker Road and continue a short distance to Fort Barry. After parking, walk from the visitors center across the street and up the hill to the trailhead.

Contact: Golden Gate National Recreation Area, Marin Headlands Visitors Center,

Building 948, Fort Barry, Sausalito, CA 94965, 415/331-1540 or 415/561-4700 visitor information, www.nps.gov/goga.

Building 948, Fort Barry, Sausalito, CA 94965, 415/331-1540; visitor information, 415/561-4700, www.nps.gov/goga.

60 YELLOW BLUFF TRAIL

1.5 mi / 1.0 hr 🥾1 ⛰️10

in the Marin Headlands at the northern foot of the Golden Gate Bridge

Map 7.1, page 291

This is a little piece of heaven. From your vantage point on Yellow Bluff, San Francisco looks like the Land of Oz. Yellow Bluff is the first major land point along the Marin shore east of the Golden Gate and provides a stunning lookout across San Francisco Bay and the surrounding landmarks. The trail is flat, short, and (best of all) unpublicized, and there are a few picnic tables nearby. From East Fort Baker, walk on the trail that heads east near the shoreline of the bay. You can turn the trip into a triangular loop hike by continuing along the shore, heading toward Sausalito, turning left at the trail junction, and hiking back to Fort Baker. One of the great features of this area is that it is often sunny, even when the Marin Headlands to the west lie buried in fog.

User Groups: Hikers, dogs, and mountain bikes. Fort Baker is wheelchair accessible, but the trail is not. No horses.

Permits: No permits are required. Parking and access are free.

Maps: A brochure and map are available at the East Fort Baker Visitors Center or by contacting the Golden Gate National Recreation Area, Marin Headlands. For a topographic map, ask the USGS for San Francisco North.

Directions: From San Francisco, take US 101 north over the Golden Gate Bridge to Marin and stay to the right at the split. Drive a very short distance, turn left, and drive a few hundred yards to a stop sign. Turn right and drive 0.5 mile to the parking area for Fort Baker.

Contact: Golden Gate National Recreation Area, Marin Headlands Visitors Center,

61 VISTA POINT / EAST FORT BAKER

2.5 mi / 1.5 hr 🥾2 ⛰️9

in the Marin Headlands at the northern foot of the Golden Gate Bridge

Map 7.1, page 291

Vista Point, the famous lookout at the northern end of the Golden Gate Bridge, is like a miniature United Nations, as travelers from around the world stop there to take photos. Little do they know that with a short walk, they can leave the crowds behind and enjoy even more beauty. A paved trail from the parking area loops under the north foot of the bridge, then works its way back and forth, descending to East Fort Baker. There you will find a bay cove; as you look up from the shoreline, the Golden Gate Bridge is even more inspiring. You can stroll along the shore and out to a fishing pier or check out the Bay Area Discovery Museum, which is ideal for families. A nearby large grassy area makes an excellent picnic site, and picnic tables are available near Lime Point, set below the north end of the bridge. You can also extend the trip out to Yellow Bluff for more spectacular views and picnic sites.

User Groups: Hikers, dogs, and mountain bikes. Vista Point is wheelchair accessible, but the trail is not. No horses.

Permits: No permits are required. Parking and access are free.

Maps: A brochure and map are available at the East Fort Baker Visitors Center or by contacting the Golden Gate National Recreation Area. For a topographic map, ask the USGS for San Francisco North.

Directions: From San Francisco, drive north on US 101 over the Golden Gate Bridge, get in the right lane, and take the Vista Point exit.

Contact: Golden Gate National Recreation

Area, Marin Headlands Visitors Center, Building 948, Fort Barry, Sausalito, CA 94965, 415/331-1540; visitor information, 415/561-4700, www.nps.gov/goga.

62 PERIMETER TRAIL
5.0 mi / 2.5 hr   🚶2 ⛰9

in Angel Island State Park in San Francisco Bay

Map 7.1, page 291   **BEST** ☾

A hike around Angel Island on Perimeter Trail provides great views of the bay and a historical tour amid remnants of the island's military past. And it's long enough to provide a decent workout. The trail winds past old barracks and abandoned military buildings, climbs through lush eucalyptus forests and across high bluffs, and looks out over San Francisco Bay and its world-class landmarks. Every turn provides another awesome view.

Most hike the loop counterclockwise. After landing at the ferry dock at Ayala Cove, hike out past the beach, where you'll connect with the Perimeter Road. Bear right and you'll climb easily up through eucalyptus forest. The first highlight is Camp Reynolds, a Civil War–era barracks, with a great view of the Golden Gate Bridge. From here, the road points toward San Francisco, with a fantastic view of the San Francisco waterfront and high-rises as you pass above Point Blunt. The route bears left as you pass along Fort McDowell and the East Garrison. Little known is that a secluded and gorgeous beach is hidden in a cove below the garrison. The route continues in a loop past the North Garrison Immigration State and China Cove with views of the East Bay waterfront and foothills, and then turns again to head back to Ayala Cove.

This is one of the most scenic hikes in the Bay Area. From each lookout, you see San Francisco Bay from a completely new angle. Heavy logging of nonnative eucalyptus has dramatically changed the character of this island and the trail.

User Groups: Hikers and mountain bikes (helmets are required for cyclists 17 years and under). The Perimeter Road is accessible to wheelchairs, but many portions are too steep for use. No dogs (except for seeing-eye dogs) or horses.

Permits: No permits are required. Ferry ticket fees, which include day-use fees, vary according to departure point and season; a fee is charged per bicycle.

Maps: You can purchase a brochure and topographic map for a fee at the park or by mail from the Angel Island Association. For a topographic map, ask the USGS for San Francisco North.

Directions: Ferry service to Angel Island is available from Tiburon, San Francisco, Vallejo, and Oakland/Alameda.

To the Tiburon ferry: Take US 101 in Marin to the exit for Tiburon Boulevard. Head east on Tiburon Boulevard (curving along the bay's shoreline). Park at one of the pay lots in Tiburon, then walk a short distance to the Tiburon Ferry (well signed).

To the San Francisco ferry: Take US 101 to the exit for Marina Boulevard exit (near the southern foot of the Golden Gate Bridge). Take that exit and drive east on Marina Boulevard toward Fisherman's Wharf. Park at a parking garage or pay lot. The ferry departs from Pier 41.

To the Vallejo ferry: Take I-80 to I-780. Take I-780 and drive to Curtola Parkway. Take Curtola Parkway (which becomes Mare Island Way) and continue to 495 Mare Island Way, where free parking is available. The docking area is directly across from the parking lot.

To the Oakland/Alameda ferry: In Oakland drive south on I-980 to the exit for Webster. Take that exit and drive west to the ferry dock at Jack London Square. The ferry goes to San Francisco at Pier 41. Passengers then receive free transfer to the Angel Island ferry. The return trip goes directly to Alameda-Oakland.

Contact: Angel Island State Park, 415/435-1915 or 415/435-5390 (ranger's office); California State Parks, Marin District, 415/898-4362, www.parks.ca.gov; Angel Island Tiburon Ferry, 415/435-2131, www.angelislandferry.com; San Francisco Blue and Gold Fleet, Pier 39 (ticket office), Pier 41 (departures), 415/705-8200, www.blueandgoldfleet.com; Alameda-Oakland ferry, 415/773-1188, www.eastbayferry.com.

63 MOUNT LIVERMORE SUMMIT

4.5 mi / 2.5 hr   🏃3 ⛰10

in Angel Island State Park in San Francisco Bay

Map 7.1, page 291

This is one of the most dramatic urban lookouts in the world. When standing atop Mount Livermore, you will be surrounded by landmarks in every direction. At 788 feet, this is the highest point on Angel Island. The views are superb even at night, when the lights of the Golden Gate Bridge and the city glow with charm. From the Visitor Center, walk to the Perimeter Road and its junction with the Sunset Trail. The Sunset Trail starts by heading west, through a eucalyptus forest, just above the Perimeter Road to your right. The trail then bears left and climbs through a series of graded switchbacks. The trail then turns left to rise up the south flank of the summit. After about two miles, you will reach a trail junction at the foot of the summit ridge. Turn left here and soon you will reach a T-junction with the North Ridge Trail. Turn left again for the final push to the top.

User Groups: Hikers only. No dogs (except for seeing-eye dogs), horses, or mountain bikes (they may not even be walked on this trail). No wheelchair facilities.

Permits: No permits are required. Ferryboat ticket fees, which include day-use fees, vary according to departure point and season; a fee is charged per bicycle.

Maps: You can purchase a brochure and topographic map for a fee at the park or by mail from the Angel Island Association. For a topographic map, ask the USGS for San Francisco North.

Directions: Ferry service to Angel Island is available from Tiburon, San Francisco, Vallejo, and Oakland/Alameda.

To the Tiburon ferry: Take US 101 in Marin to the exit for Tiburon Boulevard. Head east on Tiburon Boulevard (curving along the bay's shoreline). Park at one of the pay lots in Tiburon, then walk a short distance to the Tiburon Ferry (well signed).

To the San Francisco ferry: Take US 101 to the exit for Marina Boulevard exit (near the southern foot of the Golden Gate Bridge). Take that exit and drive east on Marina Boulevard toward Fisherman's Wharf. Park at a parking garage or pay lot. The ferry departs from Pier 41.

To the Vallejo ferry: Take I-80 to I-780. Take I-780 and drive to Curtola Parkway. Take Curtola Parkway (which becomes Mare Island Way) and continue to 495 Mare Island Way, where free parking is available. The docking area is directly across from the parking lot.

To the Oakland/Alameda ferry: In Oakland drive south on I-980 to the exit for Webster. Take that exit and drive west to the ferry dock at Jack London Square. The Alameda-Oakland Ferry goes to San Francisco at Pier 41. Passengers then receive free transfer to the Angel Island ferry. The return trip goes directly to Alameda-Oakland.

Contact: Angel Island State Park, 415/435-1915 or 415/435-5390 (ranger's office); California State Parks, Marin District, 415/898-4362, www.parks.ca.gov; Angel Island Tiburon Ferry, 415/435-2131, www.angelislandferry.com; San Francisco Blue and Gold Fleet, Pier 39 (ticket office), Pier 41 (departures), 415/705-8200, www.blueandgoldfleet.com; Alameda-Oakland, 415/773-1188, www.eastbayferry.com.

64 AGAVE TRAIL
1.5 mi / 1.5 hr 🏃1 ⛰8

on Alcatraz Island

Map 7.2, page 292

The Agave Trail at Alcatraz Island has made accessible one-third of the island that was previously closed to visitors. The catch is you must come in winter, when the trail is open from late September to February; the trail is closed from late winter on into spring and summer to protect nesting birds. The trail—named after the agave plant, which is common here—provides some of the most breathtaking views found on any of the 15,000 miles of Bay Area hiking trails.

Start at the ferry landing on the east side of Alcatraz and follow the trail as it traces the island rim to its southern tip. It's quite wide, with a few benches and cement picnic tables situated for sweeping views of both the East Bay and San Francisco. From its southern end, the trail is routed back to the historic parade ground atop the island, where you will find some sculptural masterpieces, including 110 stone steps. The parade ground is a haven for nesting birds; this area is closed to the public each spring so the birds will not be disturbed. If you visit during low tide, you may discover some relatively little-known tidepools at the island's southwest corner. This part of the island also has abundant bird life, including a population of night herons; in terms of pure cuteness, they're right up there with chipmunks and baby ducks. Birds are thriving in the restored wildlife habitat, especially at the southern end of the island. About 10,000 marine birds live here, mainly gulls, cormorants, and egrets. With about 5,000 visitors a day in summer, that's two birds for every person.

The old cell block is located at the center of the island, with other buildings sprinkled along the eastern shore and on the northern tip. Ranger-led park tours are available, and visitors can rent audiotapes for a self-guided cell-house tour.

User Groups: Hikers only. No dogs, horses, or mountain bikes. No wheelchair facilities.

Permits: No permits are required. Entry tickets include the ferryboat trip to the island and audio tours are available from Alcatraz Cruises for an additional fee. Ferries depart from Pier 31/33 in San Francisco.

Maps: A map is available at the ferry landing for a fee. For a topographic map, ask the USGS for San Francisco North.

Directions: In San Francisco, take I-80/US 101 to the exit for Embarcadero/Harrison Street. Take that exit and drive to Harrison Street. Turn right on Harrison Street and drive five blocks to Embarcadero Street. Turn left on Embarcadero and drive (past the piers) to Bay Street. Continue on Embarcadero Street for two blocks to the Pier 39 garage, on the left. Walk to Pier 31/33, near the junction of Embarcadero and Bay, at Fisherman's Wharf, and look for the prominent sign for Alcatraz Cruises.

Contact: Alcatraz Island, www.nps.gov/alcatraz, reservations at 415/981-7625 or www.alcatrazcruises.com.

65 COASTAL TRAIL
2.5 mi / 1.0 hr 🏃1 ⛰10

in the Presidio on the San Francisco headlands

Map 7.2, page 292

While Vista Point at the north end of the Golden Gate Bridge may be the most popular place from which to take snapshots of the bridge, a lookout on Coastal Trail provides an even more scenic view. This spot is just north of Baker Beach, where San Francisco Bay, the bridge, and the Marin coast form a postcard-perfect scene that fits easily into a 35mm frame.

After parking, hike southwest on Coastal Trail, passing the Fort Scott Overlook, Battery Crosby, and Battery Chamberlain en route to the south end of Baker Beach. The soft dirt pathway is set in cypress, an easy, pretty walk with sensational views. The best strategy for photographers is to make the 30-minute walk in, scanning for photo opportunities along the way, and then capture any ideas on film on the return trip. For more postcard views of the bridge, take a side trip down to mile-long Baker Beach.

But don't forget that this is the big, bad city, so you may occasionally encounter San Francisco's ubiquitous homeless. If this concerns you, hikers can travel in pairs or hike in the morning in order to avoid unwanted encounters.

User Groups: Hikers and wheelchairs. Dogs are not advised. No horses or mountain bikes.

Permits: No permits are required. Parking and access are free.

Maps: For a free map, contact the Presidio. For a topographic map, ask the USGS for San Francisco North.

Directions: From US 101 at the southern end of the Golden Gate Bridge, take the toll plaza parking area exit. Limited parking is available directly east of the toll plaza in a paved area (after parking, you must walk through a short tunnel to reach the trailhead). There is additional unpaved parking 50 yards west of the toll plaza, near the trailhead.

Contact: Presidio Visitors Center, 415/561-4323, www.nps.gov/prsf/index.htm.

66 SHORELINE / COASTAL TRAIL
2.0 mi / 1.0 hr 🥾1 ⛰10

in the Presidio on the San Francisco headlands

Map 7.2, page 292

The Presidio is set on the San Francisco Headlands, covering roughly 1,500 acres, from the southern foot of the Golden Gate Bridge and sprawling inland across coastal headlands and cypress and eucalyptus forests. The Presidio provides a perpetual treasure hunt for visitors: There are 11 miles of hiking trails, 14 miles of bike routes, and a network of roads that provide access to hundreds of historical military buildings. Hikers can find heart-stopping

views of the Bay, as well as great walks and bike rides.

To begin your visit, start at the visitors center and get the small map that details the park's roads, trails, picnic sites, and historical buildings. (Otherwise, newcomers might find themselves in a maze.) From the visitors center, it's an easy walk to the Bay's shoreline, where you'll turn left to head toward Fort Point and the southern foot of the Golden Gate Bridge. The waterfront beauty is breathtaking. Scan across the water to Alcatraz, Angel Island, and Sausalito, and take in the passing ships, fishing boats, windsurfers, and those guys on wakeboards with sails. This is a popular route, of course, also accessed by joggers and walkers heading on the Golden Gate Promenade from Crissy Field and Marina Green to the east. For the more ambitious, this trail can be linked via a slight cutoff trail that climbs a short distance to Battery Lancaster and then links up with the Coastal Trail.

User Groups: Hikers, bikes, and wheelchairs. Dogs are not advised. No horses.

Permits: No permits are required. Parking and access are free.

Maps: For a free map, contact the Presidio. For a topographic map, ask the USGS for San Francisco North.

Directions: From San Francisco, take 19th Avenue north (it will become Park Presidio). Turn left (east) on California Street and drive 13 blocks to Arguello Boulevard. Turn right on Arguello and continue straight through the Presidio gate. Follow Arguello into the park and turn left on Morage Avenue. A large parking area is on the right, and the visitors center is on the left.

Contact: Presidio Visitors Center, 415/561-4323, www.nps.gov/prsf/index.htm.

67 GOLDEN GATE BRIDGE
3.0 mi / 1.25 hr   🥾1 ⛰10

from San Francisco to Marin

Map 7.2, page 292

The top tourist walks in the world include the stroll to Yosemite Falls, the Main Trail in Muir Woods, and this—-the walk over the Golden Gate Bridge and back. And it makes sense: On a warm, clear day, the walk across the bridge feels like a surreal phenomenon. From the center of the bridge, the view is incomparable. Looking eastward, you can see Alcatraz, Angel Island, and the bay framed by the San Francisco waterfront and the East Bay hills. Parking is available at the north end of the bridge (at Vista Point) and at the south end, on each side of the toll plaza. On the San Francisco side, there is also some parking on the west side; you'll then walk through a short tunnel that runs under US 101 and loops up to the pathway entrance. The path on the east side of the bridge is reserved for pedestrians (5 A.M.–6 P.M.), while the west side is for bicyclists (weekends and evenings only). From one end to the other, the bridge is 1.2 miles long (and 220 feet above the water), but most folks walk only halfway out, then return to their cars, for a round-trip of 1.5 miles. Note that mornings are often cold and foggy, and afternoons are often windy.

User Groups: Hikers, wheelchairs, dogs, and mountain bikes (on the west side of the bridge only). No horses.

Permits: No permits are required. Parking and access are free.

Maps: For a free map, contact the Golden Gate National Recreation Area. For a topographic map, ask the USGS for San Francisco North.

Directions: From US 101 at the southern end of the Golden Gate Bridge, take the toll plaza parking area exit. Limited parking is available directly east of the toll plaza. There is additional unpaved parking 50 yards west of the toll plaza; from there you must walk through a short tunnel to reach the foot of the bridge.

Contact: Golden Gate National Recreation Area, Fort Mason, Building 201, San Francisco, CA 94123, 415/561-4700, www.nps.gov/goga.

68 GOLDEN GATE PROMENADE
3.0 mi / 1.25 hr   🥾1 ⛰9

Crissy Field, shore of San Francisco Bay in San Francisco

Map 7.2, page 292

Crissy Field and the adjacent San Francisco shoreline are among the most spectacular waterfronts of any city in America. You get stunning views of the Golden Gate Bridge, the Bay, and Alcatraz, along with access to the beach, restored ponds and marsh wetlands, and coastal sand dunes. On winter days, the weather can be pristine and clear with little wind, often the prettiest of the year. For non-residents, the trip to Crissy Field is a city adventure through San Francisco past many landmarks en route to the waterfront.

From Crissy Field Center at East Beach, walk west over a small bridge to explore the Crissy Field Marsh. Continue west along the waterfront, past the Historic Coast Guard Station to Fort Point Pier, and then on to Fort Point at the foot of the Golden Gate Bridge.

Alternatively, head east from Crissy Field Center to the Saint Francis Yacht Harbor. (Bear left to stay along the waterfront and to see the Wave Organ at the entrance to West Harbor). As you walk, stay right on the Golden Gate Promenade along West Harbor, continue to Marina Green, and then head to East Harbor and Gas House Cove.

Runners can take advantage of the route from the Marina Green to Fort Point and back for 3-miles round-trip.

User Groups: Hikers, wheelchairs, dogs, and mountain bikes. No horses.

Permits: No permits are required. Parking and access are free.

Maps: For a free map, contact the Golden

Gate National Recreation Area. For a topographic map, ask the USGS for San Francisco North.

Directions: BART, Caltrain, and ferries provide public transit options to San Francisco. From the East Bay: Take the Bay Bridge (I-80) west 10.4 miles to Exit 1B for US 101 North/Golden Gate Bridge. Take that exit and merge on US 101 N./Mission Street. Drive 0.4 mile to Van Ness Avenue. Turn left on Van Ness and drive 2 miles to Lombard Street. Turn left on Lombard and go 0.6 mile to Fillmore Street. Turn right on Fillmore and drive 0.5 mile to Marina Boulevard. Turn left on Marina and drive for 0.6 mile; stay right at the fork and go a short distance, continuing onto Mason Street for 0.1 mile to East Beach Street. Turn right and drive a short distance to the parking area for Crissy Field Center.

East Bay residents can take BART to the Powell Street station in San Francisco. Take the cable car at Powell and Market Streets to Fisherman's Wharf. From the wharf, walk west to the Golden Gate Promenade. Return to the BART station before dusk.

From the Peninsula: Take US 101 north to San Francisco, take the exit for US 101 North, and continue as above. Peninsula residents can take Caltrain to the San Francisco station.

From Marin: Take US 101 south over the Golden Gate Bridge and continue to Gorgas Avenue. Make a sharp right on Gorgas and go 0.3 mile to Marshall Street. Turn right and drive a short distance to Mason Street. Turn right on Mason and drive 0.2 mile to East Beach. Turn left and drive a short distance to Crissy Field Center.

Contact: Crissy Field Center, 415/561-7690; Golden Gate National Recreation Area, 415/561-4700, www.nps.gov/goga; public transportation www.511.org.

69 LANDS END TRAIL

2.5 mi / 1.0 hr   🏃1 ⛰10

on the San Francisco headlands at the entrance to San Francisco Bay

Map 7.2, page 292

While the tourists flock to Fisherman's Wharf, the Golden Gate Promenade, and the Golden Gate Bridge, this is a better trip and adventure, with sensational views. One glance from Lands End can take in the mouth of San Francisco Bay and the crashing breakers, with the Golden Gate Bridge and Marin Headlands in the foreground and the Pacific Ocean, Farallon Islands, and Point Reyes in the background. By now you've probably figured out that this is one of San Francisco's greatest lookouts. From the trailhead by the Cliff House Restaurant, meander eastward on a dirt trail set near bluffs topped with cypress trees. You can also tromp down past the ruins of Sutro Baths, then head toward the Golden Gate Bridge atop bluffs, and taking in a series of beautiful views. The path is nearly flat and traces Coastal Trail between Lands End and China Beach on a 2.5-mile round-trip course from the parking area. It is a great destination on Sunday mornings, when hikers take a brisk walk, enjoy the sea breeze on their faces, and then brunch at one of two nearby restaurants: the Cliff House or Louis'. The entire route was once a railroad track out to Sutro Baths. If you time it during a low tide, the alert can spot the top of ships' masts (from old shipwrecks in the rocks) below poking through the sea surface.

User Groups: Hikers, wheelchairs, dogs, and mountain bikes (mountain bikes must be walked through narrow sections of the trail). No horses.

Permits: No permits are required. Parking and access are free.

Maps: For a free map, contact the Golden Gate National Recreation Area. For a topographic map, ask the USGS for San Francisco North.

Directions: From San Francisco, take Geary Boulevard west. As you approach the coast, it becomes Point Lobos Avenue; look for parking near the vicinity of GGNRA trailheads and the Cliff House. Along the Great Highway at Ocean Beach, parking slots go fast on Sundays. Better bets are off Point Lobos Avenue near GGNRA trailheads, Louis' and Cliff House restaurants, and also a few miles south at Fort Funston.

From the Peninsula: Take I-280 north to Exit 47 signed for Highway 1/Pacifica. Take that exit and drive 1.1 miles up the hill to the exit for Skyline Blvd./Highway 35N. Take that exit, merge onto Skyline Blvd. and continue north 4.3 miles to a stop sign (Lake Merced on right, Fort Funston on left). Turn left on Great Highway and drive 3.5 miles north to Cliff House as it merges with Point Lobos Avenue. The road curves to right leading to parking areas.

From the East Bay: Take I-80 west into San Francisco; merge onto US 101 North/Central Freeway (also signed for Golden Gate Bridge). Take the US 101 exit and drive 1.1 miles onto Octavia Boulevard. Turn left onto Fell Street and drive 1.2 miles to Masonic Avenue. Turn right on Masonic and go 0.2 mile to Fulton Street (the third left). Turn left at Fulton and drive 3.6 miles to Great Highway. Turn right and go 0.3 mile to Point Lobos Avenue; continue a short distance to parking and trailheads.

Contact: Golden Gate National Recreation Area, 415/561-4700, www.nps.gov/goga.

70 OCEAN BEACH ESPLANADE

6.0 mi one-way / 3 hr   🥾₁ ⛰₇

in San Francisco along Great Highway

Map 7.2, page 292

Ocean Beach spreads for miles along San Francisco's coastal Great Highway—from the Cliff House on south past Fort Funston to Mussel Rock. This route explores the easiest access to it. Here you can discover a long expanse of sand, a paved jogging trail, and small parks

at Fort Funston and Thornton Beach. The nature of both the trail and the adjacent beach allows visitors to create trips of any length. The beach spans four miles, from Seal Rock (near the Cliff House) south to Fort Funston, from which you can continue to explore south all the way past Center Hole to Mussel Rock, at the north end of Pacifica. The huge swath of sand at Ocean Beach is popular with joggers, especially during low tides, when the hard-packed sand is uncovered. While this is the best area anywhere to find sand dollars during minus low tides, because of park rules, you are not allowed to pick them up unless outside park boundaries.

Warning: Do not swim here. There have been several drownings in this area due to riptides.

User Groups: Hikers, dogs, and horses. Partially wheelchair accessible. No mountain bikes.

Permits: No permits are required. Parking and access are free.

Maps: For a free map, contact the Golden Gate National Recreation Area. For a topographic map, ask the USGS for San Francisco South.

Directions: From San Francisco, take Geary Boulevard west. As you approach the coast, it becomes Point Lobos Avenue. At the Cliff House, the road curves to the left and continues south as it becomes the Great Highway.

From the Peninsula: Take I-280 north to Exit 47 signed for Highway 1/Pacifica. Take that exit and drive 1.1 miles up the hill to the exit for Skyline Blvd./Highway 35N. Take that exit, merge onto Skyline Blvd. and continue north 4.3 miles to a stop sign (Lake Merced on right, Fort Funston on left). Turn left on Great Highway and drive north. Parking is available along the road on the left.

From the East Bay: Take I-80 west into San Francisco and merge onto US 101 North/Central Freeway (also signed for Golden Gate Bridge). Take that exit and drive 1.1 miles onto Octavia Boulevard. Turn left on Fell Street and drive 1.2 miles to Masonic Avenue (just past Central). Turn right on Masonic and go 0.2 mile to Fulton Street (the third left). Turn left at Fulton and drive 3.6 miles to Great Highway. Turn left and look for parking along the right.

Contact: Golden Gate National Recreation Area, 415/561-4700, www.nps.gov/goga.

71 FORT FUNSTON / SUNSET TRAIL

1.5 mi / 0.5 hr 🥾1 ⛰️7

on the San Francisco coast

Map 7.2, page 292

Fort Funston is perched on San Francisco's coastal bluffs, with the Pacific on one side and Lake Merced on the other. This park is one of the most popular places in California to take dogs, and you can count on seeing plenty—up to dozens at a time. It is also the top hang-gliding spot in the Bay Area, and watching those daredevils soar is the main attraction. A viewing deck is adjacent to the parking area, where Sunset Trail begins.

Follow the wide Sunset Trail as it routes north through coastal bluffs and above sand dunes for 0.75 mile to the park's border. This easy loop offers lots of ocean and—hint: what's the name of the trail?—views. This is one of the most heavily used trails in the Bay Area. In fall and winter, the fog clears and the evening sunsets can make your spine tingle.

Down on the beach, you may see thick black sand unique to this part of the coast. It's not an oil spill; rather, the sand is an iron-ore derivative called magnetite. Magnetite lies in the sandstone cliff walls; as the sandstone erodes, it leaves the heavier iron-based magnetite on the beach. (If you bring a strong magnet to the beach, particles will stick to it.) Scan the cliff walls further and you might see a thick, chalky substance about a foot thick. These are veins of volcanic ash from an eruption of Mount Shasta 300 miles north; the ash made its way here via the Sacramento River and San Francisco Bay. (Former Funston ranger Steve Prokop told me he once found a sabertooth tiger tooth here in a vein of volcanic ore.)

No beachcombing or collecting is permitted on Funston's beachfront. Beyond the park boundary, however, it is legal and you can often find sand dollars during low tides. From Center Hole to Mussel Rock, you can often have vast swaths of beach to yourself, especially on weekdays. Rating: Surprise discovery.

Restoration efforts here are ongoing. The Park Service replanted native flowers and plants to protect the bluffs. This has helped a colony of burrowing owls and bank swallows become re-established. You may also see red-tailed hawks.

Hang-gliding: Whether you watch or take part, this is a spectacular scene. Hang gliders launch from a designated area near the bluffs, then ride the updrafts from the cliffs. When the winds are right, you might see gliders flying nearly vertical—an amazing sight—then circle in a series of dipsy-doos. This is the one sport where gravity doesn't always win, especially in the spring, when the north winds come up every afternoon.

Dogs: Fort Funston gets more dogs in a week than many Bay Area parks get people in a month. The National Park Service is reviewing dog policies, including off-leash areas. If you have a dog, check posted rules before venturing out. (Note: Dogs must be on leash in some areas of Ocean Beach to protect the endangered snowy plover.)

User Groups: Hikers, dogs, and horses. Partially wheelchair accessible (on the paved jogging route). No mountain bikes.

Permits: No permits are required. Parking and access are free.

Maps: For a free map, contact the Golden Gate National Recreation Area. For a topographic map, ask the USGS for San Francisco South.

Directions: From San Francisco, drive west on Fell Street to Lincoln Avenue where it ends at the Great Highway. Turn left and drive south on Great Highway to Skyline Boulevard. Turn right (south) and drive a short distance to the secondary parking lot (unpaved at roadside) on the right, or a little less than a mile to the park entrance (also on the right). Both parking lots are accessible only on southbound Skyline Drive. It can be difficult to find a spot on a Sunday after midmorning.

From the Peninsula: Take I-280 north to Highway 1 in Colma. Turn west on Highway 1 and drive 1 mile to Highway 35/Skyline Boulevard. Turn right (north) on Highway 35 and drive about 5 miles to a stop sign at John Muir Drive (adjacent to Lake Merced). Make a U-turn and drive a short way to the main entrance.

Contact: Fort Funston, Golden Gate National Recreation Area, 415/561-4700, www.nps.gov/goga; dog information line 415/561-4728.

72 SUMMIT LOOP TRAIL

3.1 mi / 1.5 hr 2 8

in San Bruno Mountain State and County Park near South San Francisco

Map 7.2, page 292

San Bruno Mountain rises to an elevation of 1,314 feet (it's the big mountain on the north Peninsula near the Cow Palace, west of Monster Park). For unforgettable moments, take the Summit Loop Trail. On clear days, the views are incredible—the best are of South San Francisco Bay and across the East Bay foothills to Mount Diablo. Yet that's only a start. To the north, you can also see across San Francisco, from the downtown skyline to Twin Peaks. Scan to the west and past Sweeney Ridge to the slopes of Montara Mountain. On perfect days, you can even get a glimpse Mount Tamalpais north in Marin.

The signed trailhead for the Summit Loop is located at the south parking lot (not the main parking lot). From that lot, take the 100-yard connector spur that is routed to a three-way junction. Turn left for a short climb, and within a mile, you get sweeping views of South San Francisco Bay. Continue on the trail north (do not turn on the Dairy Ravine Trail) to the cutoff fork on the left for the lookout bench. Bring a friend, a picnic, and a camera. From your perch high atop San Bruno Mountain, you can look down on US 101 in South San Francisco and easily imagine the temporary insanity that grips some drivers in their mission to reach San Francisco International Airport.

When you're ready, return to the main Summit Loop trail. The trail climbs near the antenna-spiked mountaintop for 360-degree views. To complete the trip, head downhill on paved Radio Road, cross the road, and turn left at the signed trail to the right of the gated road. Follow the Summit Loop back to the parking lot. Various routes are also easy to follow with the park map.

Many eucalyptus trees have been cut and blackberries cleared. So far, from a hiker's point of view, it's been an ugly trade.

User Groups: Hikers and horses. No dogs or mountain bikes. No wheelchair facilities.

Permits: No permits are required. An entrance fee of $5 per vehicle is charged (self-registration; bring a $5 bill).

Maps: A brochure and map are available at the entrance kiosk. For a free trail map, contact San Bruno Mountain State and County Park. For a topographic map, ask the USGS for San Francisco South.

Directions: From San Francisco, take US 101 south for 3.3 miles to Exit 429B for Brisbane/Cow Palace. Take that exit, merge onto Bayshore Boulevard and drive 2 miles to Guadalupe Canyon Parkway. Turn west (right) and drive 2.2 miles to the park entrance. Turn right through the entrance kiosk, then continue for 0.2 mile (loop under the road to the south side of Guadalupe Canyon Parkway) to the second parking area, trailhead, and gate for Radio Road.

Contact: San Bruno Mountain State and County Park, 650/589-5707 or 650/573-2592 (park administered by Coyote Point); San Mateo County Department of Parks, 650/363-4020, www.co.sanmateo.ca.us.

73 SADDLE LOOP TRAIL
2.5 mi / 1.25 hr   🥾1 ⛰6

in San Bruno Mountain State and County Park

Map 7.2, page 292

Guadalupe Canyon Parkway splits San Bruno Mountain State and County Park in two, leaving hikers to decide which section to visit on a given day. The north half provides a pair of good loop hikes: Saddle Loop Trail (the featured hike from the parking area/trailhead on the north side) and Bog Trail. Both are easier than Summit Loop (see listing in this chapter), in the park's southern half. From the main parking area, start walking on Old Guadalupe Trail, which junctions with Saddle Loop Trail after about 0.7 mile. From here, take Saddle Trail (right) and loop around the northern boundaries of the park, climbing about 150 feet in the process. The wind can absolutely howl through this area, so pick your hiking days with care. Most of the surrounding terrain is open hillside grassland, so the views of the South Bay are unblocked and, on clear days, are just spectacular.

User Groups: Hikers and horses. No dogs or mountain bikes. No wheelchair facilities.

Permits: No permits are required. An entrance fee of $5 per vehicle is charged (self-registration; bring a $5 bill).

Maps: For a free trail map, contact San Bruno Mountain State and County Park. For a topographic map, ask the USGS for San Francisco South.

Directions: From San Francisco, take US 101 south for 3.3 miles to Exit 429B for Brisbane/Cow Palace. Take that exit and merge onto Bayshore Boulevard. Drive 2 miles to Guadalupe Canyon Parkway. Turn west (right) and drive 2.2 miles to the park entrance. Turn right through the entrance kiosk and park in the main lot.

Contact: San Bruno Mountain State and County Park, 650/589-5707 or 650/573-2592 (park administered by Coyote Point); San Mateo County Department of Parks, 650/363-4020, www.co.sanmateo.ca.us.

74 BOG TRAIL
0.8 mi / 0.5 hr   🥾1 ⛰6

in San Bruno Mountain State and County Park

Map 7.2, page 292

The Bog Trail provides a good introduction to San Bruno Mountain State and County Park, although you need to hike other trails here if you desire a more passionate experience. The trail starts at the trailhead on Guadalupe Canyon Parkway's north side and is routed along the north flank of the mountain, changing only 30 feet in elevation. Open hillsides surround the trail and are quite pretty on clear days in the spring, when the grasslands are green and sprinkled with an explosion of wildflowers. By turning right at the junction with Old Guadalupe Trail, you can make this a short loop hike. (Turn left to continue on the Saddle Loop Trail; see listing in this chapter.) Hikers who make this easy trip quickly get a sense of the importance of the open-space buffer the park provides for the congested north Peninsula.

User Groups: Hikers only. The upper part of the trail is wheelchair accessible. No dogs, horses, or mountain bikes.

Permits: No permits are required. An entrance fee of $5 per vehicle is charged (self-registration; bring a $5 bill).

Maps: For a free trail map, contact San Bruno Mountain State and County Park. For a topographic map, ask the USGS for San Francisco South.

Directions: From San Francisco, take US 101 south for 3.3 miles to Exit 429B for Brisbane/Cow Palace. Take that exit and merge onto Bayshore Boulevard. Drive 2 miles to Guadalupe Canyon Parkway. Turn right and drive 2.2 miles to the park entrance. Continue ahead to parking area and trailhead on the north side of the road.

Contact: San Bruno Mountain State and County Park, 650/589-5707 or 650/573-2592 (park administered by Coyote Point); San Mateo County Department of Parks, 650/363-4020, www.co.sanmateo.ca.us.

75 MILAGRA RIDGE

2.0 mi / 0.75 hr

in Pacifica near Skyline College

Map 7.2, page 292

On Milagra Ridge, you get great ocean views and a great place to fly a kite. The actual hike isn't much, parking near the trailhead is limited, and even long-time local residents overlook this. What you will find is a mile-long paved road/trail that is routed to the top of Milagra Ridge, one of the best places imaginable to fly a kite. Those coastal breezes can almost put a strong kite into orbit; some people even use saltwater fishing rods and reels filled with line, playing the kite as if it were a big fish. Kite flying is allowed only inside the gate on the hill to the left. (Note that hikers must stay on the trail to protect the endangered mission blue butterfly.

The parking area that hikers use to gain access to Milagra Ridge is small and obscure—nobody winds up here by accident. Once you park your car, the hike up to the ridge top is an easy mile and is suitable for wheelchair users with some assistance. The summit was flattened in the 1950s to accommodate a missile site, which has long since been abandoned. Looking westward, visitors are surprised at the sheer dropoff from the ridge down into Pacifica. But in the summer months, this can be one of the foggiest places in the world.

User Groups: Hikers and mountain bikes (bikes allowed on only one mile of paved trail). Wheelchair accessible with assistance. No dogs or horses.

Permits: No permits are required. Parking and access are free.

Maps: For a free map, contact the Golden Gate National Recreation Area. For a topographic map, ask the USGS for San Francisco South.

Directions: From I-280 in San Bruno, take the Westborough exit and then drive west up the hill and across Highway 35/Skyline Boulevard. Drive to College Avenue and turn right (north). Continue a very short distance (there are some residences on the right) to the end of the road and the trailhead. Limited parking is available.

Contact: Golden Gate National Recreation Area, Fort Mason, Building 201, San Francisco, CA 94123, 415/561-4700, www.nps.gov/goga.

76 SWEENEY RIDGE

4.0-5.0 mi / 2.0-3.0 hr

in San Bruno on the Peninsula ridgeline

Map 7.2, page 292

Sweeney Ridge can be an eye-popping getaway to take in the coronation of spring. The drive up to is within easy range of most Bay Area residents and the hits just keep on coming along the way, topped by gorgeous long-distance views.

Sweeney Ridge ridge splits San Bruno to the east and Pacifica to the west. There are four trailheads, but the launch point with the best parking is at Skyline College at Parking Lot #2. From the trailhead to the locked gate, it is an estimated 700-foot climb (with a climb, drop, and climb again on the way in). On the ridge, you get sweeping views to your left of San Andreas Lake, the South Bay, and on the horizon, distant Mount Diablo. To your right, you can scan across the wilderness east flank of Montara Mountain, Pacifica, and the sea. You will pass a graffiti-smeared concrete shell of a building that was once a former Nike radar station, the marker for the Portolá Discovery Site, and then head beyond on the ridge to the Baquiano Trail on your right. On clear days, plan a picnic here, facing out to sea, and take in the view of Pacifica below, and on pristine days, across the ocean to the Farallon Islands. Wildflower blooms are imminent. Sadly, access ends at the locked gate for the Crystal Springs Watershed (instead of allowing you to hike up a service road on the east flank of Montara Mountain). Wildlife includes lots of bush bunnies, decent numbers of small blacktail deer, and if you're lucky, occasional fox or bobcat.

A favorite spot as you approach the gate is South Meadow. Look for a cutoff trail to Cattle Hill on the right (it is unsigned and not on maps). Turn right, and in just five minutes, this small cutoff provides an overlook for what is known as South Meadow—an outstanding wildlife habitat with a stunning view of the ocean.

User Groups: Hikers, dogs, horses, and mountain bikes. No wheelchair facilities.

Permits: No permits are required. Parking and access are free.

Maps: For a free map, contact the Golden Gate National Recreation Area. For a topographic map, ask the USGS for San Francisco South.

Directions: From San Francisco, take I-280 south to Daly City and Exit 47B for Highway 1 south toward Pacifica. Take that exit and drive 1.1 miles up the hill to the exit for Skyline Boulevard/Highway 35. Take the exit for Highway 35 south and drive south on Skyline Blvd. for 3.5 miles (past Sharp Park Drive/Westborough) to College Drive. Turn right on College Drive and go 0.4 mile to College Loop Drive. Turn left and drive a short distance to Parking Lot #2 and the trailhead on south side.

From the Peninsula: Take Highway 280 north to Exit 41 for Skyline Boulevard/Highway 35. Take that exit and drive 2.8 miles north to College Drive. Turn left on College Drive and go 0.4 mile to College Loop Drive. Turn left and drive a short distance to Parking Lot #2 and the trailhead at south side.

Contact: Golden Gate National Recreation Area, 415/561-4700, www.nps.gov/goga; Golden Gate National Parks Conservancy, 415/561-3000, http://parksconservancy.org.

77 SAN ANDREAS TRAIL
6.0 mi / 3.0 hr   🥾1 ⛰️7

in the San Mateo County foothills southwest of San Bruno

Map 7.2, page 292

Of the county trails along the eastern border of Crystal Springs Watershed, this one provides the best views. The San Andreas Trail overlooks Upper San Andreas Lake, winding most of its way through wooded foothills. The only downer is that much of the route runs adjacent to Highway 35/Skyline Boulevard. Regardless, it is worth the trip, because to the west you can see the untouched slopes of Montara Mountain, a game preserve, and that sparkling lake—all off-limits to the public.

The trail starts near the northern end of the lake; a signed trailhead marker is posted on Skyline Boulevard. The route runs about three miles south to the next access point, at Hillcrest Boulevard, and from there, it connects to Sawyer Camp Trail. The view of Montara Mountain to the west is particularly enchanting during the summer, when rolling fog banks crest the ridgeline: a spectacle.

User Groups: Hikers, horses, and mountain bikes. Note that the northern section is paved, but the southern section is not. There are some wheelchair-accessible facilities. No dogs.

Permits: No permits are required. Parking and access are free.

Maps: For a free trail map, contact San Mateo County Division of Parks. For a topographic map, ask the USGS for Montara Mountain.

Directions: To access the north gate: From I-280 in San Bruno, take the Westborough exit and drive west up the hill to the intersection with Highway 35/Skyline Boulevard. Turn left on Highway 35 and drive about 2.5 miles to the trailhead entrance on the right side of the road.

To access the south gate: On I-280, drive to the Millbrae Avenue exit. Take that exit and drive north on Skyline Boulevard, a frontage road on the west side of Highway 280, and continue to the parking area on the left.

Contact: San Mateo County Division of Parks, 455 County Center, 4th Floor, Redwood City, CA 94063-1646, 650/363-4020, www.co.sanmateo.ca.us.

78 SAWYER CAMP RECREATION TRAIL

12.0 mi / 5.0 hr   🥾1 ⛰8

in the San Mateo County foothills south of San Bruno

Map 7.2, page 292

By taking Sawyer Camp Reacreation Trail, hikers get everything that there is on the connecting link to the north (the San Andreas Trail) and more. Alas, not all of the "more" is good. On a positive note, the trail is set away (though parallel) from the road, so you get more peace (at least, that seems the intent). It is routed along a pretty lake and through a forest, so you get more nature. But since this route is paved and hardly a secret, you also get more people. In fact, ever since the biking speed limit was raised to 15 miles per hour, hikers seem to be used as flags in a slalom course. The result is that many hikers have been driven away from this area rather than be put into fight-or-run showdowns with warp-speed bikers.

Although the listed one-way distance is six miles, at any point, you can just turn around and go back, cutting the trip as short as you wish. Or better yet, bring two vehicles, leave one at each of the two trailheads along Highway 35/Skyline Boulevard, and make it a one-way walk. From north to south, the hike includes a drop of 400 feet, so if you plan on a return trip, there will be a little huff-and-puff on the way back. Park benches are provided at viewpoints along the lake, where you can often see trout rising and feeding on summer evenings (but no fishing is permitted). This hike also eventually links up with the Crystal Springs trailhead (see listing in this chapter).

User Groups: Hikers, horses, and mountain bikes. There are some wheelchair-accessible facilities at the south end. No dogs.

Permits: No permits are required. Parking and access are free.

Maps: For a free trail map, contact San Mateo County Division of Parks. For a topographic map, ask the USGS for Montara Mountain.

Directions: From I-280 in San Bruno, take the Westborough exit and drive west up the hill to the intersection with Highway 35/Skyline Boulevard. Turn left on Highway 35 and drive 5.5 miles to the trailhead entrance, on the right.

Contact: San Mateo County Division of Parks, 455 County Center, 4th Floor, Redwood City, CA 94063-1646, 650/363-4020, www.co.sanmateo.ca.us.

79 LINDA MAR / ROCKAWAY POINT TRAIL

2.5 mi / 1.5 hr   🥾1 ⛰7

in Pacifica near Pacifica State Beach/Linda Mar

Map 7.2, page 292

This is a great beach walk with a nice pay-off at the end. After parking at the Pacifica State Beach lot at Linda Mar, head to the beach and walk north. The northern end of this stretch of sand, along the tidal flats, is a great place to throw sticks to a dog. Be aware that the sand dune area provides habitat for the endangered snowy plover and rangers may restrict access for dogs; watch for signs posted at on the west side of the parking lot.

At the north end of the beach, climb up on the dirt trail that traces around Rockaway Point. Here you'll find beautiful views of San Pedro Point, Montara Mountain, and of course, the Pacific Ocean. There are several spots where you can take a perch and enjoy the view and let the beauty flow through you. Then when you feel like it, turn around and follow the same route back to your car.

You could probably hike this route to the end and back in a flash. But sometimes, as you will discover here, taking the time to go slowly sure beats rushing through it as quickly as possible. You just plain won't want to miss anything. In addition, when you first drive up, don't get spooked if the parking lot seems crowded. Why? Because many people often prefer to park and hang out, where they spend time looking down into the mouth of a beer bottle rather than taking this walk and experiencing the full fabric of the place.

User Groups: Hikers and dogs. No horses or mountain bikes. No wheelchair facilities.

Permits: No permits are required. Parking and access are free.

Maps: For a topographic map, ask the USGS for Montara Mountain.

Directions: From San Francisco, head south on I-280 to Daly City. Turn south on Highway 1 and drive about five miles into Pacifica. Drive to the southern end of Pacifica and turn right at the parking lot for Pacifica State Beach/ Linda Mar. The trail starts at the north end of the beach.

Contact: City of Pacifica, Parks Department, 170 Santa Maria Avenue, Pacifica, CA 94044, 650/738-7300, www.cityofpacifica.org.

80 MONTARA MOUNTAIN TRAIL

7.0 mi / 3.0 hr 4 ▲ 10

in San Pedro Valley County Park in Pacifica

Map 7.2, page 292

Here's one of the best day hikes in California. Just 20 minutes south of San Francisco is this sensational trail in San Pedro Valley County Park. Visitors are few, the coastal beauty is divine, and hikers can carve out their own personal slice of heaven. The Montara Mountain Trail is the prize of the park, featuring the best viewing area for wispy Brooks Falls and great lookouts to the Pacific Coast.

After parking, walk about 50 yards along Montara Mountain/Brooks Creek Trail. The trail then splits, with Brooks Creek Trail on the left and Montara Mountain Trail on the right. The two merge again about one mile up Brooks Creek and continue as a common route to the peak. If there have been recent rains, bear left

to see the waterfall; the trail reconnects just past the fall. If it's been dry, stay right on the well-signed Montara Mountain Trail. From here, the next mile climbs several hundred feet.

Brooks Falls is connected in three narrow, silver-tasseled tiers in a gorge of chaparral-covered wilderness canyon. It falls 175 feet in all, from top to bottom, including breaks. And though there never seems to be enough water in this waterfall, it still is a very pretty gorge. One reason Brooks Falls is so little known is that it doesn't flow year-round. As a tributary to San Pedro Creek, Brooks Creek runs only in late winter and spring (best, of course, after several days of rain). Note that a great coastal lookout is available another 10 minutes up the trail on a dramatic rock outcrop.

The hike continues all the way to the North Peak of Montara Mountain (at 1,898 feet), a trip of 3.5 miles one-way, including a final 1.1-mile push on a fire road to reach the summit. On a clear spring day, the views are absolutely stunning in all directions—highlighted by the Pacific Ocean, the Farallon Islands, and miles of the adjacent off-limits Crystal Springs Watershed. If you look downslope to the southeast, you can glimpse of a piece of gorgeous, off-limits Pilarcitos Lake.

This route is the first link in one of the few great one-way hikes (using a shuttle) in the Bay Area. After reaching the top of Montara Mountain, sail down into McNee Ranch State Park above Montara and hike 3.8 miles to Montara State Beach. You descend all the way, with glorious views for the entire route. So with cars parked at each end of the trail, you can hike 7.3 miles one-way from San Pedro Valley County Park, up Montara Mountain, and down to Montara State Beach.

User Groups: Hikers and horses (on designated trails only). Some trails and facilities are wheelchair accessible. No dogs or mountain bikes.

Permits: No permits are required. An entrance fee of $6 per vehicle is charged.

Maps: For a free trail map, contact San Pedro Valley County Park. For a topographic map, ask the USGS for Montara Mountain.

Directions: From San Francisco, take Highway 1 south to Pacifica. Turn east on Linda Mar Boulevard and continue until it dead-ends, at Oddstad Boulevard. Turn right and drive to the park entrance, located about 50 yards on the left. The trailhead is on the southwest side of the parking lot.

Contact: San Pedro Valley County Park, 600 Oddstad Boulevard, Pacifica, CA 94044, 650/355-8289, www.co.sanmateo.ca.us; City of Pacifica, Parks Department, 170 Santa Maria Avenue, Pacifica, CA 94044, 650/738-7300, www.cityofpacifica.org.

81 WEILER RANCH ROAD
1.5 mi / 1.0 hr   🥾1 ⛰️7

in San Pedro Valley County Park in Pacifica

Map 7.2, page 292

This is the best hike for wildlife watching on the San Mateo County coast. It also provides an option for visitors to San Pedro Valley County Park who do not want to take on the climbs up to Brook Falls and Montara Mountain.

From the parking area, head out to Weiler Ranch Road. This is a service road that is routed out through the heart of a valley nestled with meadows that attract wildlife at dawn and dusk. It's common to see deer and rabbits in the meadow, and red-tailed hawks and turkey vultures overhead. If you get real lucky, you might get a glimpse of a bobcat. In fact, we've had these wildlife sightings many times, but it's always best right at dusk. Once you've had your fill, turn around at the end of the meadow and head back.

One tip is to park outside the park entrance, so you have access even when the gate is closed at dawn and dusk. When it comes to seeing wildlife, there's no such thing as a sure thing. The only sure thing is you won't see anything if you don't go.

User Groups: Hikers and horses (on designated trails only). Some trails and facilities are wheelchair accessible. No dogs or mountain bikes.

Permits: No permits are required. An entrance fee of $6 per vehicle is charged.

Maps: A brochure and map are available at entrance kiosk and visitors center. For a free trail map, contact San Pedro Valley County Park. For a topographic map, ask the USGS for Montara Mountain.

Directions: From San Francisco, take Highway 1 south to Pacifica. Turn east on Linda Mar Boulevard and continue until it dead-ends at Oddstad Boulevard. Turn right and drive to the park entrance, located about 50 yards ahead on the left. The trailhead is on the southwest side of the parking lot.

Contact: San Pedro Valley County Park, 600 Oddstad Boulevard, Pacifica, CA 94044, 650/355-8289, www.co.sanmateo.ca.us; City of Pacifica, Parks Department, 170 Santa Maria Avenue, Pacifica, CA 94044, 650/738-7300, www.cityofpacifica.org.

82 SAN PEDRO MOUNTAIN
6.0 mi / 2.5 hr   🥾2 ⛰️7

in McNee Ranch State Park in Montara

Map 7.2, page 292

For people who like dramatic coastal views, this is an ideal trail. It traces the top of coastal bluffs and provides many flawless vistas. To reach them, take special note at the entrance gate and look for the trail that is routed off to the left and up through the hilly grasslands. With those first few steps, it doesn't look like much of a trail. But as you continue, you will rise atop the first crest and then clearly see how it tracks up the spine of the coastal ridgeline. It eventually provides a lookout above Gray Whale Cove. From this viewpoint, you may feel an odd sense of irony: Below is Highway 1, typically filled with a stream of slow-moving cars driven by people who want to get somewhere else; meanwhile, you are in a place of peace and serenity, happy right where you are.

The hike includes a few short climbs across grasslands and can be converted to a loop hike by turning right at the junction with Montara Mountain Trail and returning on a service road to the park entrance.

User Groups: Hikers and dogs. No horses or mountain bikes. No wheelchair facilities.

Permits: No permits are required. Parking and access are free.

Maps: For a topographic map, ask the USGS for Montara Mountain.

Directions: From San Francisco, drive about 17 miles south on Highway 1. Continue through Pacifica, then through Devils Slide, and down to the base of the hill. Look for a small pullout area on the left. The access point is at a yellow gate with a state park property sign. There is room for just a few cars. Do not block the gate. If the pullout area is full, drive south on Highway 1 a short distance and park at the lot on the west side of the highway, at Montara State Beach.

Contact: Half Moon Bay State Parks, 650/726-8820; Half Moon Bay State Ranger, 650/726-8819, www.parks.ca.gov.

83 MONTARA MOUNTAIN / MCNEE RANCH

7.6 mi / 3.75 hr   🥾 4   ⛰️ 9

in McNee Ranch State Park in Montara

Map 7.2, page 292

Of the two major routes to the top Montara Mountain, this is the one with two butt-kicker sections. It is well worth it. On a clear day from the top of Montara Mountain, the Farallon Islands to the northwest appear so close you may think you could reach out and pluck them from the ocean. To the east, it looks as if you could take a giant leap across the bay and land atop Mount Diablo.

Some 10 miles to the north and south, there's nothing but mountain wilderness connecting Sweeney Ridge to an off-limits state game preserve. By now you should be properly motivated for the climb. From the main access gate to the top, it's 3.8 miles, a rise of nearly 2,000 feet that includes two killer "ups."

From the pipe entrance gate, start the trip by hiking straight ahead, on the ranch-style service road. Follow this ranch road up the San Pedro Mountain ridgeline to the Montara Coastal Range. At the first fork, stay to the right on the dirt road as it climbs and turns.

Here's a secret: At the power lines, look for a deer trail that is routed down through the chaparral to the west. This leads to an old concrete military army bunker. Enjoy the history, then head back up to the main road/trail.

After a 20-minute wheezer of an ascent—yes, butt-kicker level—look for a garbage can at a flat spot on the left side of the trail. This garbage can serves as a landmark to a 30-yard cutoff trail to a perch for a dazzling view of Pacifica and northward along the Pacific Coast. After catching your breath, continue on, heading up, up, and up, eventually topping out at the summit. While antennas and transmitters are perched near the top, the actual summit, directly adjacent to the fenced transmitter station, is clean, so you can stand right on the tip-top. All you need for this hike is a clear day, some water, and plenty of inspiration. If you need reason to stay fit, this hike is it.

User Groups: Hikers, dogs, and mountain bikes. No horses. No wheelchair facilities.

Permits: No permits are required. Parking and access are free.

Maps: For a topographic map, ask the USGS for Montara Mountain.

Directions: From San Francisco, drive about 17 miles south on Highway 1. Continue through Pacifica, then through Devils Slide, and down to the base of the hill. Look for a small pullout area on the left. The access point is at a yellow gate with a state park property sign. There is room for just a few cars. Do not block the gate. If the pullout area is full, drive south on Highway 1 a short distance and park at the lot on the west side of the highway, at Montara State Beach.

Contact: Half Moon Bay State Parks, 650/726-8820; Half Moon Bay State Ranger, 650/726-8819, www.parks.ca.gov.

84 BAY TRAIL / COYOTE POINT
1.0-10.0 mi / 0.5-5.0 hr 👣1 ⛰7

in Coyote Point County Park in San Mateo

Map 7.2, page 292

The Bay Trail extends from Coyote Point north for five miles along the shoreline (well, pretty much) of the South Bay to what is called Hotel Row, in Burlingame. The trip starts out well. The first thing you will notice is the dramatic expanse of the South Bay; up close, it is much bigger that most envision, particularly at high tide. There seems to be the highest variety of marine birds during low tides, when mud flats are exposed for miles. Egrets, coots, sandpipers, and other residents of wetlands live here year-round. Avocets arrive every March. They are among the migrants that make regular appearances.

Unfortunately, the trail leaves the waterfront at times, and at this point, most hikers will turn around and head back. Bike riders will keep on, and eventually, the trail returns to the waterfront and arrives at Hotel Row. When the wind is blowing out of the north, the jets will make their approach from the south. That provides a sideshow from the Bay Trail.

A shorter trip is the 0.25-mile walk from the boat ramp out to land's end. The point provides a great lookout of the South Bay, where you can watch boats heading out, as well as good shore-fishing access for rays, sharks, and jacksmelt. From the lookout over the pretty South Bay on a clear day, it looks as if you could get a running start, jump, and glide across the water to the land's edge.

User Groups: Hikers, wheelchairs, and mountain bikes. No dogs or horses.

Permits: No permits are required. An entrance fee of $6 per vehicle is charged.

Maps: For a free trail map, contact Coyote Point County Park. For a topographic map, ask the USGS for San Mateo.

Directions: From San Francisco, take US 101 south to San Mateo and the exit for Poplar Avenue. Take that exit and drive to Humboldt Street (at the first stoplight). Turn right on Humboldt and go to Peninsula Avenue. Turn right and continue over the highway to a frontage road (Bayshore Boulevard). Turn left on the frontage road and drive a short distance to the signed turn and entrance to the park.

From the Peninsula: Take US 101 north to San Mateo and the exit for Dore. Take that exit and make an immediate left turn on the frontage road (Bayshore Boulevard). Continue a short distance to the signed turn and entrance to the park.

Contact: Coyote Point County Park, 1701 Coyote Point Drive, San Mateo, CA 94401, 650/573-2592; San Mateo County Division of Parks, 650/363-4020, www.co.sanmateo.ca.us.

85 FITZGERALD MARINE RESERVE
1.0 mi / 0.5 hr 👣1 ⛰9

in Moss Beach

Map 7.2, page 292 **BEST ☾**

The Fitzgerald Marine Reserve provides the best tidepool hopping in California. The closer you look, the better it gets. When you go tidepool hopping, there is nothing more fascinating than discovering a variety of tiny sea creatures. That's what's so attractive about the Fitzgerald Marine Reserve—a shallow, 30-acre reef that exposes hundreds and hundreds of tidal pockets every time a minus low tide rolls back to the ocean. After parking, it's a short walk down to the tidepools; from here, you walk on exposed rock, watching the wonders of the tidal waters. Be sure to wear boots that grip well, and take care not to crush any fragile sea plants as you walk. In the tidepools, you may see hermit crabs, rock crabs, sea anemones, sculpins, starfish, sea snails, and many other animals and plants in various colors. An option during low tides is to continue walking south on the beach to a beautiful cove at the foot of the Moss Beach Distillery, a popular watering hole. Note: No dogs, no beachcombing, no shell gathering. In other words, okay looky, but no touchy. This is a preserve.

User Groups: Hikers only. No dogs, horses, or mountain bikes. No wheelchair facilities.

Permits: No permits are required. Parking and access are free.

Maps: For a topographic map, ask the USGS for Montara Mountain.

Directions: From San Francisco: Take I-280 to Highway 1 in Daly City and drive through Pacifica, over Devils Slide, and into Moss Beach. Turn right (west) at the signed turnoff at California Street and continue one mile to the parking area.

From the Peninsula: Take Highway 92 into Half Moon Bay and then head north on Highway 1 for seven miles to Moss Beach. Turn left (west) at the signed turnoff at California Street and drive one mile to the parking area.

Contact: Fitzgerald Marine Reserve, P.O. Box 451, Moss Beach, CA 94022, 650/728-3584; San Mateo County Division of Parks, 455 County Center, 4th Floor, Redwood City, CA 94063-1646, 650/363-4020 or 650/340-7598 (group tour reservations), www.co.sanmateo.ca.us.

86 PILLAR POINT
2.5 mi / 1.5 hr   🚶1 ⛰️8

in Princeton at Half Moon Bay

Map 7.2, page 292

When things are right, this easy walk has the prospects of being one of the truly great coastal walks. It includes a secluded beach with inshore kelp beds and sea lions playing peekaboo, and during low tide, you can walk around the corner at Pillar Point and boulder hop in wondrous seclusion.

To start the trip, park at the small lot set just below the radar station, on the western side of Princeton Harbor. Then walk out along the west side of the harbor. The trail here is on hard-packed dirt above two quiet beaches where grebes, cormorants, and pelicans often

cavort. During the evening, the harbor lights are quite pretty here. When you reach the Princeton jetty, turn right and walk along the beach toward Pillar Point; this is where the sea lions frequently play "now-you-see-me, now-you-don't." At low tides, continue around Pillar Point and enjoy the rugged beauty, solitude, and ocean views, taking your time as you hop along from rock to rock. Some people wonder if you can hop your way all the way around the Pillar Point Head and to the beach at the south end of Fitzgerald Marine Reserve. Nope. There's no land bridge across the final piece of water.

Watch your tide book, because the Pillar Point tidal area is underwater most of the time. Also keep an eye out for weather reports, because Pillar Point can be buried in fog for weeks on end in the summer. Also, remember the old giant radar tower atop Pillar Point? Of course. It's gone: replaced by a much smaller sphere-like structure that resembles a giant ball.

User Groups: Hikers, dogs, and horses (not advised). No mountain bikes. No wheelchair facilities.

Permits: No permits are required. Parking and access are free.

Maps: For a topographic map, ask the USGS for Half Moon Bay.

Directions: From the Peninsula, take I-280 to San Mateo and Highway 92. Turn west on Highway 92 and drive to Half Moon Bay. Turn right on Highway 1 and drive five miles to Princeton. Turn left at the traffic signal, drive about 0.5 mile through Princeton Village, and turn left again, going one mile toward the bluffs and radar station. There is limited parking at a small lot on the left side of the road. Follow the trail on the west side of the harbor.

Contact: Pillar Point Harbor, 650/726-5727, www.smharbor.com/pillarpoint.

87 BAY RIDGE TRAIL / CRYSTAL SPRINGS

11.0 mi one-way/ 5.0 hr 🏃3 ⛰10

along Cahill/Fifield ridges in the Woodside foothills

Map 7.2, page 292

The fight that took 70 years to win was resolved with one turn of a key. A locked gate at the Crystal Springs Watershed on the Peninsula was finally cracked open to the public. Access to the 23,000-acre watershed—which we once nicknamed the Forbidden Paradise—is finally possible, though by reservations only, where you join a group. Still, this is something special.

The trip is 11 miles, one-way with a shuttle, from the Quarry Gate near Highway 92 and extending on the Bay Ridge Trail to Sweeney Ridge, and then beyond to Sneath Lane Gate in San Bruno. The trip starts by passing through Quarry Gate. On a service road, climb 640 feet over the course of a mile to Cemetery Gate. This is the hardest part of the trip: a challenging climb on a bike, a steady rhythmic pull for hikers. You will pass through cypress forest and patches of chaparral, with views of Upper Crystal Springs.

Cemetery Gate to Five Points: After topping out at Cahill Ridge, enjoy an easy descent through old-growth cypress and Douglas fir, and farther north, redwoods. Keep an eye out on your left for a giant old-growth Douglas fir called "Big Doug." It's three miles to Five Points, a five-way road junction, and your link north to the Fifield Ridge Route.

Fifield Ridge to Portola Gate: This is the best part of the trip. From Five Points, you are routed up above hidden Pilarcitos Lake to Fifield Ridge, emerging in wilderness for stunning views of the wild east flank of Montara Mountain to your left. As you continue north, you then get sweeping views to your right of the South Bay. In spring, this area is loaded with wildflowers. Deer, bobcat, and fox provide occasional sightings.

Portola Gate to Sneath Lane: First pass a hidden meadow on your left with views of Pacifica and the ocean. Continue to the Bay Discovery Site, with a dramatic scope below of the Peninsula's wildlands, the lakes in the watershed and the South Bay. The end of the trip is a downhill glide to the Sneath Lane Gate and your shuttle car.

As good as this is, it could get far better. For instance, another service road junctions with Fifield Ridge, providing a route up the little-seen eastern flank of Montara Mountain all the way to the 1,898-foot summit. Then the route goes over the top to McNee State Park and San Pedro Valley County Park. Opening that route would provide a sensational one-way hike, starting from the Sneath Lake access. You would climb to Sweeney Ridge, then into the watershed and to the summit of Montara Mountain, and then down the north side to McNee Ranch State Park in Montara.

User Groups: Hiking, biking, and horseback riding permitted, but not at the same time; volunteer trail leader required with all parties. No dogs. Limited wheelchair access from Skylawn trailhead.

Permits: A permit and reservation are required at 650/652-3203 or at www.sfwater.org. Public access is restricted to groups under the supervision of a trained leader on Wednesdays, Saturdays, and Sundays.

Maps: For a free trail map, contact San Francisco Public Utilities Commission. For a topographic map, ask the USGS for San Mateo.

Directions: To Quarry Gate: From the Peninsula, take I-280 to Highway 92. Turn west on Highway 92, drive over Crystal Springs Reservoir and continue 0.5 mile to Quarry Gate on right. Turn right and go short distance to parking and trailhead.

To Sneath Lane Trailhead: To drop off the shuttle car, take I-280 to San Bruno and the exit for Sneath Lane. Take that exit, and drive west on Sneath Lane to the road's end. Leave the car near the access point for Golden Gate National Recreation Area.

Contact: San Francisco Public Utilities Commission, 650/652-3203, www.sfwater.org.

88 CRYSTAL SPRINGS TRAIL
6.4 mi / 3.0 hr

along Crystal Springs Reservoir in the Woodside foothills

Map 7.2, page 292

From the parking area, the Crystal Springs trail runs along the border of San Francisco watershed land, adjacent to Cañada Road. Your destination is 3.2 miles away at the Pulgas Water Temple, where waters from Hetch Hetchy in Yosemite arrive via pipe and thunder into this giant, sunken bathtub-like structure surrounded by Roman pillars and a canopy. It's quite a sight. Beautiful Crystal Springs Reservoir is off to the west for most of the hike, though it occasionally disappears from view behind a hill as you continue south. Deer are commonly seen in this area—a nice bonus. The adjacent road is a famous family bike trip on Cañada Road, which is closed to all vehicles on Bicycle Sundays. Also note that the San Francisco Water Department can restrict access to the Water Temple, so you can't look down into the thing; the pay-off of the trip.

User Groups: Hikers and mountain bikes. No dogs or horses. No wheelchair facilities.

Permits: No permits are required. Parking and access are free.

Maps: For a free trail map, contact San Mateo County Division of Parks. For a topographic map, ask the USGS for San Mateo.

Directions: From I-280 in San Mateo, take the Highway 92 exit and drive west to Cañada Road/Highway 95. Turn south on Cañada Road and drive 0.2 mile to the parking area, on the right.

Contact: San Mateo County Division of Parks, 455 County Center, 4th Floor, Redwood City, CA 94063-1646, 650/363-4020, www.co.sanmateo.ca.us.

89 WATERDOG LAKE TRAIL
4.0 mi / 1.75 hr

in the Belmont foothills

Map 7.2, page 292

Waterdog Lake isn't much more than a mud hole compared to nearby Crystal Springs, San Andreas, and Pilarcitos and Felt Lakes. But since public access is not allowed at any of those lakes, little Waterdog provides a bit of waterfront salvage. Out of the way and often forgotten, the lake was created by damming Belmont Creek in Diablo Canyon. Although not exactly a jewel, it still makes for a recreation site. Parking access is obscure. It takes only 15 minutes to reach the lake, and the trail skirts the northern edge of the shore. Many people stop here, but if you forge on, you will be well compensated. The trail, which is more of a dirt road, rises above the lake and enters John Brooks Memorial Open Space. At the crest of the hill, which is reached after a climb of about 300 feet, there are pretty views of Crystal Springs Reservoir. An option is to extend your trip on Sheep Camp Trail, a dirt road that is linked to a gravel road set adjacent to the San Francisco Fish and Game Refuge.

User Groups: Hikers and mountain bikes. No dogs or horses. No wheelchair facilities.

Permits: No permits are required. Parking and access are free.

Maps: For a trail map, contact the City of Belmont. For a topographic map, ask the USGS for San Mateo.

Directions: From San Mateo take Highway 92 west to the Ralston Avenue exit and turn south (left) at the off-ramp. Drive about two miles and turn right on Lyall Way. Drive to the corner of Lyall Way and Lake Road to find the parking entrance just past Lake Road. Parking is available along the street.

Contact: City of Belmont, Parks, 1225 Ralston Avenue, Belmont, CA 94002, 650/595-7441, www.belmont.gov.

90 HARKINS RIDGE LOOP FROM HALF MOON BAY

6.5 mi / 3.5 hr 🏃3 ⛰9

in Purisima Creek Redwoods Open Space
Preserve near Half Moon Bay

Map 7.2, page 292

What a great trek: a 6.5-mile horseshoe-shaped
loop with a 1,600-foot climb and drop. From
the parking area, take the Harkins Ridge Trail
east through the redwoods. There's one steep
spot, but it's shaded for the most part with
pretty valley views. The route then turns
left and climbs out of the canyon to a ridge,
where a few steep spots on the way up make
for dramatic drops on each side into remote
valleys. At 3 miles, just a short distance from
Skyline (close enough that you might even
hear people at the parking lot), you emerge at
a junction with the North Ridge Trail. Turn
left on the North Ridge Trail for 0.5 mile,
then take another left on Whittemore Gulch
Trail for the easy 2.8 mile downhill glide back
to the trailhead.

This trip can also be started from Skyline
(see listing in this chapter), but the return trip
will be up rather than down.

User Groups: Hikers. No bikes on Purisima
Creek Trail or Harkins Ridge Trail. Bikes
and horses often restricted on Whittemore Gulch
Trail in wet weather. No dogs. No wheelchair
facilities.

Permits: No permits are required. Parking
and access are free.

Maps: For a free map, contact the Midpeninsula Regional Open Space District or pick one
up at the trailhead. For a topographic map,
ask the USGS for Woodside.

Directions: From Half Moon Bay, drive to
the intersection of Highway 92 and Main
Street (lighted intersection). Turn south on
Main Street and drive through town (about
a mile) to Higgins-Purisima Road. Turn left
on Higgins-Purisima and drive 4 miles (becomes curvy) to the staging area for Purisima
Creek Redwoods Open Space Preserve on the
left. If the small parking lot is full (common

on Sunday), park on the road shoulder to the
right.

Contact: Midpeninsula Regional Open Space
District, 330 Distel Circle, Los Altos, CA
94022, 650/691-1200, www.openspace.org.
During nonbusiness hours, a touch-tone phone
menu is available for trail news, conditions,
and events.

91 WHITTEMORE GULCH LOOP FROM SKYLINE

6.5 mi / 3.0 hr 🏃1 ⛰9

in Purisima Creek Redwoods Open Space
Preserve on Skyline Ridge near San Mateo

Map 7.2, page 292

Purisima Creek Redwoods is a magnificent
2,633-acre preserve set on the western slopes
of the Santa Cruz Mountains, from Skyline
Boulevard down to Half Moon Bay. One of
the best ways to explore the area is on this great
loop hike. You can make it a one-way trip by
having a shuttle car waiting at the trail's end
at the Higgins-Purisima parking access.

This trail starts at the Skyline Access on
Skyline Boulevard, elevation 2,000 feet, located at a parking area just south of a small
building (it used to be a store). From the trailhead, descend a short distance to a junction
with the North Ridge Trail. Turn right and
descend a further 0.5 mile to a junction with
the Whittemore Gulch Trail. The trail drops
quickly a first, then more gradually to the rim
of the canyon.

At the canyon rim, a series of switchbacks
takes you down the hill about 1,000 feet into
the redwood canyon. It is well graded (about
10 percent). At the bottom of the forest floor,
turn left on the Harkins Ridge Trail and climb
3.3 miles back to the top.

Timing: On weekday mornings, this place
can be paradise—Purisima can feel like a
vast uninhabited wilderness, complete with
the long-distance coastal views and a hidden
redwood canyon. On Sunday afternoons, however, it's often crowded.

User Groups: Hikers. No bikes on Purisima Creek Trail or Harkins Ridge Trail. Bikes and horses often restricted on Whittemore Gulch Trail in wet weather. No dogs. No wheelchair facilities.

Permits: No permits are required. Parking and access are free.

Maps: For a free map, contact the Midpeninsula Regional Open Space District or pick one up at the trailhead. For a topographic map, ask the USGS for Woodside.

Directions: From San Francisco, drive south on I-280 for about 15 miles to the Highway 92 exit. Turn west on Highway 92 and drive to Highway 35/Skyline Boulevard. Turn south (left) on Highway 35 and drive 4.5 miles to the Purisima Creek Redwoods parking area, on the right (west side) of the road, just past a small building.

Contact: Midpeninsula Regional Open Space District, 330 Distel Circle, Los Altos, CA 94022, 650/691-1200, www.openspace.org. During nonbusiness hours, a touch-tone phone menu is available for trail news, conditions, and events.

92 REDWOOD TRAIL
0.5 mi / 0.5 hr   🏃‍♀️1 ⛰️9

in Purisima Creek Redwoods Open Space Preserve on Skyline Ridge near San Mateo

Map 7.2, page 292

The 0.25-mile-long Redwood Trail allows just about anybody to experience the grandeur of a redwood forest. Anybody? People with baby strollers, wheelchairs, or walkers, as well as those recovering from poor health, will be able to do this trail. It starts at 2,000 feet on Skyline Boulevard and is routed north under a canopy of giant redwoods. At the end, there are picnic tables and restrooms. And the return trip is just as easy. Most people don't really hike the trail, they just kind of mosey along, seeing how it feels to wander freely among ancient trees.

User Groups: Hikers and wheelchairs. No dogs, horses, or mountain bikes.

Permits: No permits are required. Parking and access are free.

Maps: For a free map, contact the Midpeninsula Regional Open Space District or pick one up at the trailhead. For a topographic map, ask the USGS for Woodside.

Directions: From San Francisco, drive south on I-280 for approximately 15 miles to the Highway 92 cutoff. Turn west on Highway 92 and continue to Highway 35/Skyline Boulevard. Turn west on Highway 35 and drive to the Purisima Creek parking area, located on the right at mile marker 16.65.

Contact: Midpeninsula Regional Open Space District, 330 Distel Circle, Los Altos, CA 94022, 650/691-1200, www.openspace.org. During nonbusiness hours, a touch-tone phone menu is available for trail news, conditions, and events.

93 HUDDART PARK LOOP
7.5 mi / 3.5 hr   🏃‍♀️2 ⛰️7

in the Woodside foothills south of San Francisco

Map 7.2, page 292

With two slight changes (and we'll get to that) this hike could be a 9. As it is, the Huddart Park Loop is still a treasure. Huddart Park covers 1,000 acres from the foothills near Woodside on up to Skyline Boulevard. Nestled in a grassy area surrounded by woods, you can picnic, play, or head off into the wild. The best hike is a 7.5-mile loop that provides a tour through deep woods and along hidden creeks. This trek includes a 1,400-foot climb, but because trail makers kept grades at 6 percent, it's a steady, rhythmic pull to the top for hikers or runners, with all junctions signed. The woods extend up the slopes of Kings Mountain and a network of trails are routed through the redwoods, amid patches of hard woods, and along small creeks.

Start the hike at the Zwierlein Picnic Area (set next to a small parking lot near a restroom). Be sure to grab a trail map first, though; there are dozens of loop options at virtually every trail junction. At the trailhead sign, start on the left by hiking 0.2 mile to the Dean Trail, and then continue down into the canyon to the bridge at McGarvey Gulch and the junction with the Crystal Springs Trail. Turn right, and from the start, the trail feels like a tunnel through vegetation. It then quickly drops into redwood forest and crosses two small wood bridges over a pretty creek. From here, the Crystal Springs Trail rises 3.4 miles and 1,400 feet to Skyline. The grade is perfect. From the bridge, it took us an hour and 15 minutes to reach the top (2,000 feet), always in rhythm.

Before reaching Skyline, turn left on Summit Springs Trail (a dirt road) and climb steeply for 0.4 mile to the top of the ridge and the Skyline Trail. Turn left on Skyline Trail and continue another 0.3 mile to the Chinquapin Trail on the left. The Chinquapin Trail is routed in and out of heavily wooded canyons near the headwaters of McGarvey Gulch creek, down all the way. It eventually links to the Dean Trail; turn left to be routed back to the Zwierlein trailhead and parking lot. Add variety to your hike, or make it shorter or longer, by carrying a map.

In 2011, rangers supervised the application of crushed gravel on a good part of the route to stop erosion caused by horses. For many, it looks almost paved. Instead, rangers should clear some trees at Skyline to create what could be a gorgeous sweeping view of the South Bay. (Rangers cleared a wooded hilltop at China Camp State Park in San Rafael to create one of the best lookouts in the Bay Area—see the *Patrick's Point* hike in this chapter).

User Groups: Hikers and horses. Mountain bikes are permitted on paved roads only. Horses restricted when trails are wet. The Chickadee Trail at Huddart Park is wheelchair accessible. No dogs.

Permits: No permits are required. An entrance fee of $6 per vehicle is charged.

Maps: A brochure and map are available in a box at the entrance. For a trail map, contact

Huddart Park. For a topographic map, ask the USGS for Woodside.

Directions: From San Francisco, take I-280 south and drive 20 miles to Woodside and the exit for Highway 84/Woodside Road. Take that exit, turn west (right) on Woodside Road, and drive 2.8 miles to Woodside. Continue 1.7 miles to Kings Mountain Road. Turn right and drive 2.8 miles (curvy) to the park entrance on the right. Take the entrance road to the kiosk, then continue to the parking area at Zwierlein Picnic Area. The trailhead is on the far side of the parking lot (adjacent to a restroom).

Contact: Huddart Park, 1100 Kings Mountain Road, Woodside, CA 94062, 650/851-0326; reservations for group camping and group picnics, 650/363-4021; San Mateo County Division of Parks, 455 County Center, 4th Floor, Redwood City, CA 94063-1646, 650/363-4020. www.openspace.org.

94 TAFONI MONOLITH
3.0 mi / 1.5 hr 👣2 ⛰9

El Corte de Madera Open Space Preserve

Map 7.2, page 292

The Tafoni Monolith is the surprise showstopper at El Corte de Madera Open Space Preserve, set on the San Francisco Peninsula. Most just call it The Tafoni. You emerge from a forest trail to suddenly arrive at a series of 50-foot high Goliaths. These huge sandstone formations are filled with natural carved-out hollows, holes, cuts, and what rangers call "fretwork" and "tree trunks." All of it is the product of erosion over hundreds of years, as wind and rain slowly engraved the soft sandstone into this etched monolith—and it's a stunner.

There's a reason so few have seen this: The parking and trailhead is tricky for newcomers. At El Corte de Madera Open Space Preserve, the trailhead to visit the Tafoni Monolith is located near the CalTrans Skeggs Vista Point, set on the Peninsula's Skyline Ridge above

Woodside. Most park at the vista point and then walk or bike about 50 yards north on the road's shoulder to reach the trailhead, a gated service road.

From here, the Tafoni Trail is routed through a dense second-growth forest (primarily Douglas fir) for 1.2 miles to a junction. Turn right, and in 0.25 mile, look for the signed fork on the right, a hiking path signed Tafoni (bikes are prohibited here; bikers should lock up their bikes and hike out the last piece). This is it: A short descent will lead you to the Tafoni Monolith, and a route circling it provides access to all the strange honeycombs, "petrified tree trunks," and fretwork seemingly etched into rock. It is strange and unforgettable.

In the Bay Area, sandstone formations were originally undersea deposits where sand grains were cemented together. The Tafoni is the softest of the Bay Area sandstone formations and can crumble easily.

Visiting the Tafoni usually whets the appetite for more adventure, whether riding or hiking. This park can certainly provide it. It is a big preserve, covering 2,821 acres and with 36 miles of trails for biking, hiking, and horseback riding. The trails are linked at many junctions, providing a fantastic network to self-style your trip.

In addition to the Tafoni, a must-see is the view from Vista Point off the Manzanita Trail. It's a breathtaking lookout across foothills, canyons, coast, and ocean.

Special Note: The Resolution Trail is the site of a 1953 DC-6 plane crash. The knoll off Fir Trail served as the rescue base. Taking artifacts is illegal. Those breaking this law are subject to a ghost curse.

User Groups: Hiking, mountain bikes, horses. No dogs. No bikes or horses on short spur to Tafoni Monolith. No wheelchairs.

Permits: Parking and access free.

Maps: Obtain a free map at the trailhead or from the Midpeninsula Regional Open Space District. For a topographic map, ask the USGS for Woodside.

Directions: From the Peninsula: Take I-280 to Woodside and Highway 84. Turn east on Highway 84 and go to Skylonda and Highway 35 (Skyline Boulevard). Turn right (north) and go 3.9 miles to CalTrans Skeggs Vista Point, on the right. Park and then walk 50 yards north on road's shoulder to the trailhead, on the west side of road.

From the East Bay: Take Highway 92 west to the junction of Highway 280, and continue straight for three miles to Highway 35/Skyline Boulevard. Turn left (south) and go 8.5 miles to Vista Point, on the left (you must continue straight, then make a U-turn and return to Vista Point). Park and continue as above.

Contact: Midpeninsula Regional Open Space District, 330 Distel Circle, Los Altos, CA 94022, 650/691-1200, www.openspace.org. During nonbusiness hours, a touch-tone phone menu is available for trail news, conditions, and events.

95 ALAMBIQUE TRAIL / SKYLINE TRAILHEAD
4.5 mi / 2.5 hr   🏃2 ⛰7

in Wunderlich County Park near Woodside

Map 7.2, page 292

Comes a time when you don't want to be bugged by anything. Not by traffic, work pressures, or the latest nightmare on the front page. That is when you search out places so quiet that to speak above a whisper seems irreverent. Sure, most everybody loves the excitement of an adventure with sizzle, but sometimes, only harmony will do.

An overlooked trailhead on Skyline Boulevard provides the jump-off point for such a place. It is the Skyline Trailhead at Wunderlich County Park, a short drive north of Sky Londa. Even on Sundays, it's possible that you could not see another soul—despite the thousands of people out biking, hiking, and horseback riding at the half dozen parks and scenic roads in the surrounding foothills.

This trailhead features a 4.5-mile loop

hike that drops into a remote redwood canyon with a creek, then rises back up, looping back through forest to the starting point. The only thing the trail lacks is a series of gorgeous lookouts. You want views? Not here.

The trip starts on the east side of Skyline Boulevard, where a large blue sign for the Bay Ridge Trail marks the trailhead. From Skyline, start the trip on the Alambique Trail (signed). Here you work your way down a canyon for two miles amid a second-growth redwood forest. On foggy mornings, moisture can be so heavy that it can drip from the branches of redwoods and Douglas fir like a sparse rain. Everything smells wet, dense, and old. Our personal preference is a fogbound morning, when the heavy air smothers distant sounds, creating perfect quiet.

It takes only about 40 minutes to reach a canyon bottom, where you cross a feeder stream to Alambique Creek. This watershed is home to many banana slugs and newts, and when the forest is dripping with moisture, they are often on the trail—so be careful not to accidentally squish the little fellers. Though the canyon is cool and moist, it is the kind of place you can sit for awhile and enjoy a trail lunch in complete peace. For the moment, you can let the rest of the world worry about their latest problems. There's always something, right?

Shortly after a creek crossing, you will reach a four-way junction with the Skyline Trail in about 2 miles. To return to the starting point, take the sharpest right on the Skyline Trail and climb back out (with a few short drops) for 2.4 miles to a staging area.

If you want to extend your trip at the junction, instead turn left on the Alambique Trail. This is routed farther down into the park to an additional network of trails. The best offshoots are to The Meadows (turn left on Bear Gulch Trail for 0.3 mile) or to Alambique Flat (to the right for 0.2 mile). Amid the second-growth forest along the lower portion of the Alambique Trail, there is a single awesome redwood giant, called The Methuselah Tree that still

remains. Its trunk is roughly 45 feet around, with massive burls and a burned-out gap.

User Groups: Hikers and horses. No dogs or mountain bikes. No wheelchair facilities.

Permits: No permits are required. Parking and access are free.

Maps: For a trail map, contact Huddart Park. For a topographic map, ask the USGS for Woodside.

Directions: From the Peninsula: Take I-280 to Woodside and Highway 84. Turn east on Highway 84 and go to Sky Londa and Highway 35/Skyline Boulevard. Turn right (north) and go 2.5 miles to the trailhead, on the right (signed Bay Ridge Trail). Limited parking is available on the road's shoulder.

From the East Bay: Take Highway 92 west to the junction of I-280 and continue three miles to Highway 35/Skyline Boulevard. Turn left (south) and go 10 miles to the trailhead, on the left.

Contact: Wunderlich County Park, c/o Huddart Park, 1100 Kings Mountain Road, Woodside, CA 94062, 650/851-1210 or 650/851-0326 (entry kiosk); San Mateo County Division of Parks, 455 County Center, 4th Floor, Redwood City, CA 94063-1646, 650/363-4020, www.co.sanmateo.ce.us.

96 MEADOW LOOP TRAIL
5.5 mi / 3.0 hr

in Wunderlich County Park near Woodside

Map 7.2, page 292

Wunderlich County Park is one of the better spots on the Peninsula for clearing out the brain cobwebs. The network of trails here provides a variety of adventures, from short strolls to all-day treks. Take your pick. The Meadow Loop is the preferred route; it circles much of the park, crossing first through oak woodlands, then rising to open grasslands, and finally passing a redwood forest on the way back.

Make sure you have a trail map, then take this route: Near the park entrance off

Woodside Road, look for the signed trailhead for Alambique Trail and hike for 0.7 mile. At the junction with Meadow Trail, turn right, hike for 0.4 mile, and then turn left on to Meadow Trail and climb up to The Meadows in 1.1 miles. This is a perfect picnic site, with rolling hills, grasslands, and great views. To complete the loop, forge onward, then turn right at Bear Gulch Trail and take it all the way back, including switchbacks, to the park entrance. This hike includes an elevation gain of nearly 1,000 feet, so come prepared for a workout.

User Groups: Hikers and horses. No dogs or mountain bikes. No wheelchair facilities.

Permits: No permits are required. A $6 fee is charged per vehicle.

Maps: For a free map, contact San Mateo County Division of Parks. For a topographic map, ask the USGS for Woodside.

Directions: From San Francisco, take I-280 south and drive 20 miles to the exit for Highway 84/Woodside Road. Take that exit and follow Woodside Road to the park entrance on the right. If the lot is full, there is limited parking along the road.

Contact: Wunderlich Park, c/o Huddart Park, 1100 Kings Mountain Road, Woodside, CA 94062, 650/851-1210 or 650/851-0326 (entry kiosk); San Mateo County Division of Parks, 455 County Center, 4th Floor, Redwood City, CA 94063-1646, 650/363-4020, www.co.sanmateo.ca.us.

97 RAVENSWOOD OPEN SPACE PRESERVE
2.0 mi / 0.75 hr   🥾1 ⛰7

on South San Francisco Bay near Menlo Park

Map 7.2, page 292

This 370-acre parcel of land is rich in marshland habitat and is home to many types of birds. The highlights are two excellent observation decks. From the parking area at the end of Bay Road, backtrack by walking across a bridged slough to the trailhead, on the north side of the road. You will immediately come to a fork in the road. You can turn right and walk 200 feet to an observation deck with great views of the South Bay. If you go left instead, you will find a hard-surface path that heads north and hooks out toward the bay to another wood observation deck. This is the primary destination for most visitors. There always seems to be egrets and herons, but sandpipers and dozens of other species will stop here on their migratory journeys.

User Groups: Hikers, wheelchairs, and mountain bikes. No dogs or horses.

Permits: No permits are required. Parking and access are free.

Maps: For a free map, contact the Midpeninsula Regional Open Space District. For a topographic map, ask the USGS for Mountain View.

Directions: From US 101 in Palo Alto, take the University Avenue exit and drive east to Bay Road. Turn right on Bay Road and drive to the end of the road. The preserve entrance is adjacent to Cooley Landing.

Contact: Midpeninsula Regional Open Space District, 330 Distel Circle, Los Altos, CA 94022, 650/691-1200, www.openspace.org. During nonbusiness hours, a touch-tone phone menu is available for trail news, conditions, and events.

98 BAYLANDS TRAIL
4.0 mi / 1.5 hr   🥾1 ⛰7

on the shore of South San Francisco Bay in Palo Alto

Map 7.2, page 292

A hidden trailhead opens a route to a historic wetland. The farther you go on this trail, the better it gets. The trailhead for the Baylands Trail is located behind the stands enclosure for the Baylands Baseball Park. The trail starts without much fanfare: a simple hard-gravel road with an ugly slough on the left and the Palo Alto Golf Course on the right. If you keep looking ahead, you will often see ground squirrels scurrying about, as well as an occasional jackrabbit popping up at close range. (They can scare the daylights out of you.) The trail then reaches a fork. Bikers should turn left and take the outstanding Baylands Bike Trail that extends to the Dumbarton Bridge, which has a bike lane, and across the bay to San Francisco Bay Wildlife Refuge, Coyote Hills, and Alameda Creek Trail. Hikers are better off turning right. Here the trail softens, and the slough on your left melds into the tidal waters of San Francisquito Creek. The pathway continues along past the golf course, then crosses near the departure runway for the Palo Alto Airport and leads out to Land's End, where the creek pours into South San Francisco Bay. This is a classic salt marsh habitat, with lots of birds and wildlife. The views are pretty, the walk is as flat as it gets, and hikers are always sighting squirrels, rabbits, egrets, coots, and ducks.

User Groups: Hikers, wheelchairs, and mountain bikes. No dogs or horses.

Permits: No permits are required. Parking and access are free.

Maps: For a topographic map, ask the USGS for Mountain View.

Directions: From US 101 in Palo Alto, take the Embarcadero East exit. Take the Embarcadero exit to the second light, across from Ming's Restaurant, to Geng Street. Turn left on Geng Street and drive to the end of the road (a baseball field is on the left). The trailhead is right behind the Baylands Baseball Park grandstand.

Contact: Palo Alto Baylands Nature Center, 650/329-2506, www.city.palo-alto.ca.us.

🟥99 BAYLANDS CATWALK
0.25 mi / 0.5 hr

on the shore of South San Francisco Bay in Palo Alto

Map 7.2, page 292

What the heck is the "Baylands Catwalk," you ask? As you will discover here, it is an old wooden walkway placed across tidal marshland and routed under giant electrical towers and out to the shoreline of South San Francisco Bay. In recent years, the catwalk has been improved, with an observation deck set on the edge of the bay waters. You start at the Baylands Interpretive Center, which houses exhibits explaining the marshland habitat. From there you can make the short walk straight east out to the observation deck, about a 10-minute trip. The marsh supports an abundant population of bird life, especially egrets, coots, and ducks. Migrants can surprise, such as avocets by the dozen in early summer. Occasional dawn and sunset walks are led by naturalists; call the Baylands Interpretive Center for information.

Special Note: The catwalk extends north and south across the marsh for a mile. This was once a great easy walk, but access is now forbidden in order to protect an endangered mouse, and a barbed-wire-edged gate blocks passage.

User Groups: Hikers only. No dogs, horses, or mountain bikes. No wheelchair facilities.

Permits: No permits are required. Parking and access are free.

Maps: A brochure and map are available at the Nature Center. For a topographic map, ask the USGS for Mountain View.

Directions: From US 101 in Palo Alto, take the Embarcadero East exit. Drive toward the bay, bearing left past the airport to a stop sign. Turn left and drive past the yacht harbor until you reach a sharp right turn. Park at the lot on the right (south). The nature preserve is on the left (north). Note: A gate is closed on the access route each evening just after sunset and is opened each day at 8 A.M. year-round; access is still possible by foot or bike.

Contact: Palo Alto Baylands Nature Center, 650/329-2506, www.city.palo-alto.ca.us.

100 CHARLESTON SLOUGH
4.0 mi / 1.5 hr   🏃1 ⛰7

in a South Bay marshland in Palo Alto

Map 7.2, page 292

This trail is actually an old levee road that borders Charleston Slough, providing access to an expanse of wetlands and marsh habitat. It connects to a similar levee road that in turn connects to Shoreline Regional Park, in Mountain View—a great bike route and also good for hikes. From this trailhead, head straight out along the levee next to the slough. Within 10 or 15 minutes, with each step you will gain access to marshland that has been preserved in its natural state. From afar, the surroundings may appear to be nothing more than pickleweed and mud, but look closer, and you will begin to see the huge diversity of birds and wildlife that thrive in this very rich ecosystem. Egrets seem particularly plentiful. Way back in the 1950s, striped bass used to enter the mouth of Charleston Slough here, providing some excellent fishing. Although the stripers are long gone, the serene atmosphere and the variety of birds remain, making this a favorite destination for many people. The trail/road extends out near the shore of the South Bay, near where the slough runs into the South Bay. This is an excellent route for a family bike trip.

User Groups: Hikers and mountain bikes. No dogs or horses. No wheelchair facilities.

Permits: No permits are required. Parking and access are free.

Maps: For a topographic map, ask the USGS for Mountain View.

Directions: From US 101 in south Palo Alto, take the San Antonio exit and turn east toward the bay. After a short distance, turn left on Bayshore Frontage Road and drive about a mile (curving) to Charleston Slough. The parking area is along the right side of the road.

Contact: Shoreline Regional Park, City of Mountain View, 3070 N. Shoreline Boulevard, Mountain View, CA 94043, 650/903-6392, www.mountainview.gov.

101 WINDY HILL LOOP
8.2 mi / 4.0 hr   🏃3 ⛰8

in the Windy Hill Open Space Preserve in the Portola Valley foothills

Map 7.2, page 292

Windy Hill may be known for the north winds that blow through on spring afternoons, but it is even better known among hikers for offering remarkable views on clear days in any season. From the 1,900-foot summit, a grass-covered hilltop west of Portola Valley, hikers can see San Francisco Bay on one side and the Pacific Ocean on the other. If views are all you want, the 0.7-mile Anniversary Trail, which is routed from the parking area to the summit, provides them. If you want more, you can get it by taking an excellent loop hike that drops down into forests and climbs back out to grasslands.

From the main (large) parking lot, take the main trail for 0.4 mile to Hamms Gulch Trail. (Alternatively, you can continue south on the Anniversary Trail to the Hamms Gulch trailhead.) You will drop 1,000 feet in elevation through a remote, pristine, and wooded environment to a junction with the Eagle Trail. Cross a stone bridge and turn right to follow the Eagle Trail to its junction with Alpine Road. Turn left on Alpine Road; the Eagle Trail continues 0.7 mile as it parallels the road before turning right onto a paved road. Feel lost yet? Don't worry; the Razorback Ridge Trail is shortly ahead and is well signed. Razorback Ridge Trail climbs 2.3 miles up an extended series of switchbacks before emerging from the woodlands to junction with the Lost Trail. Turn right on Lost Trail and enjoy the last 2.1 mellow miles to the parking area for great views and a refreshing end to the hike.

User Groups: Hikers, horses, and dogs (allowed on Hamms Gulch Trail, Eagle Trail, and Anniversary Trail; prohibited on others). No mountain bikes (except on the preserve's Spring Ridge Trail). There are wheelchair facilities in the picnic area adjacent to the parking area.

Permits: No permits are required. Parking and access are free.

Maps: A brochure and map are available at the trailhead. For a free trail map and brochure, contact the Midpeninsula Regional Open Space District. For a topographic map, ask the USGS for Mindego Hill.

Directions: From I-280 or US 101 on the Peninsula, drive to Woodside and Highway 84. Take Highway 84 west to Highway 35/Skyline Boulevard. Turn left on Highway 35 and drive 2.3 miles to the second parking area on the left.

Contact: Midpeninsula Regional Open Space District, 330 Distel Circle, Los Altos, CA 94022, 650/691-1200, www.openspace.org. During nonbusiness hours, a touch-tone phone menu is available for trail news, conditions, and events.

102 SAN ANDREAS FAULT TRAIL

0.6 mi / 0.5 hr   🥾1   ⛰7

in Los Trancos Open Space Preserve in the Palo Alto foothills

Map 7.2, page 292

One of the Peninsula's more unique hikes is found here: the San Andreas Fault Trail at Los Trancos Open Space Preserve. This is a self-guided tour of an earthquake trail, and it includes several examples of fault movement. The 13 numbered signposts along the way correspond with numbered explanations in the park brochure. If you don't want a geology lesson, you may be content with the good views of the Peninsula from the 2,000-foot ridgeline. Most hikers connect San Andreas Fault Trail to Lost Creek Loop Trail, a pleasant and easy bonus leg that is routed into secluded spots along a pretty creek. With the Monte Bello Open Space Preserve located on the other side of Page Mill Road, there are nearly 3,000 contiguous acres of public open space here. We've always noticed that the air at Los Trancos Open Space Preserve seems to

have a special scent to it, freshened by leaves and damp woods.

User Groups: Hikers only. The trail is not wheelchair accessible, but the parking lot is and offers a nice view. No dogs, horses, or mountain bikes.

Permits: No permits are required. Parking and access are free.

Maps: A brochure and map are available at the trailhead. For a free trail map, contact the Midpeninsula Regional Open Space District. For a topographic map, ask the USGS for Mindego Hill.

Directions: From I-280 in Palo Alto, turn west on Page Mill Road and drive seven twisty miles to the signed parking area, on the right. The Monte Bello Open Space Preserve is directly across the street, on the left (south).

Contact: Midpeninsula Regional Open Space District, 330 Distel Circle, Los Altos, CA 94022, 650/691-1200, www.openspace.org. During nonbusiness hours, a touch-tone phone menu is available for trail news, conditions, and events.

103 COAL CREEK OPEN SPACE

4.0 mi / 2.0 hr   🥾1   ⛰7

in the Coal Creek Open Space Preserve on the Peninsula's Skyline Ridge

Map 7.2, page 292

Most hikers find this place by accident. What draws them here is the CalTrans Vista Point on Skyline, one of the best lookouts on the Peninsula. Then they see the Clouds Rest Trail adjacent to the parking area. This provides access to a 490-acre parcel of land set just east of Skyline Ridge, with its rolling meadows, open grasslands, and the forested headwaters of two creeks. The park's trails—actually old ranch roads—cover only four miles as they traverse the grasslands past a classic-looking barn and down along a small creek. You can make a quick loop by following Clouds Rest Trail to Meadow Trail and returning back along Alpine Road—or hiking farther north for an out-and-back trip. Plan on enjoying nothing more than a short walk and a picnic. On a clear day, you'll never forget the view. Most Peninsula residents have never heard of the Coal Creek Open Space Preserve—it is one of the lesser-developed parklands in the Bay Area.

User Groups: Hikers, dogs, horses, and mountain bikes. No wheelchair facilities.

Permits: No permits are required. Parking and access are free.

Maps: A brochure and map are available at the trailhead. For a free trail map, contact the Midpeninsula Regional Open Space District. For a topographic map, ask the USGS for Mindego Hill.

Directions: From I-280 in Palo Alto, take the Page Mill Road exit and drive west on a winding two-lane road up the mountain to Skyline Boulevard. Turn right on Skyline Boulevard and drive one mile to the parking area, located on the right at the CalTrans Vista Point.

Contact: Midpeninsula Regional Open Space District, 330 Distel Circle, Los Altos, CA 94022, 650/691-1200, www.openspace.org. During nonbusiness hours, a touch-tone phone menu is available for trail news, conditions, and events.

104 BLACK MOUNTAIN

3.5 mi / 2.0 hr

in the Monte Bello Open Space Preserve in the Palo Alto foothills

Map 7.2, page 292 **BEST (**

The Monte Bello Open Space Preserve encompasses more than 2,700 acres of the most natural and scenic lands on the east-facing slopes of the Peninsula foothills. It includes 2,800-foot Black Mountain, the headwaters of Stevens Creek, and this pretty trail, which is crowned by great views and offers the opportunity to camp at a little-known backpack site.

Though the route to the campground and nearby Black Mountain is short, a map is a

must. From the parking area, start the trip by taking the Stevens Creek Nature Trail for 0.3 mile (ignore the fork) to Canyon Trail. Turn right on Canyon Trail, and go 0.25 mile to the Bella Vista Trail. Turn left and climb a mile to the ridge and the Old Ranch Trail. Turn right on Old Ranch Trail and you will arrive at the Black Mountain Campground (permit only) in about 0.5 mile.

In the process, you will pass the headwaters of Stevens Creek as well as the San Andreas Fault. You'll also get long-distance views of the valley and the ridge above San Jose, and opportunities to see squirrels, hawks, rabbits, and deer. It's about a 500-foot climb from the parking area to the campground.

From the campground, it's a 0.2 mile walk on Monte Bello Road to the summit of Black Mountain (some transmitters mar the perfection). On clear spring days, the views are eye-popping. For campers, bring flashlights with fresh batteries, and be sure to make the walk here in darkness for stargazing, or time the trip for a meteor shower.

From the summit, another bonus is available by continuing on Monte Bello Road for a short distance to a picnic site on the right. It is set adjacent to a sprinkling of rock crags that look like a movie set simulating another planet (great for kids). There are more stellar views of the canyon and foothills below to the east.

User Groups: Hikers, horses, and mountain bikes (restricted from some trails). This trail is not open to wheelchairs, but the parking lot and a short side trail are wheelchair accessible and offer a good view. No dogs.

Permits: No permits are required for day-use. Campers must have reservation and permit for the backpack camp.

Maps: A brochure and map are available at the trailhead. For a free trail map, contact the Midpeninsula Regional Open Space District. For a topographic map, ask the USGS for Mindego Hill.

Directions: From I-280 in Palo Alto, turn west on Page Mill Road and drive seven twisty miles to the signed parking area for Monte Bello Open Space Preserve on the left (south). Los Trancos Open Space Preserve is directly across the street to the right (north).

Contact: Midpeninsula Regional Open Space District, 330 Distel Circle, Los Altos, CA 94022, 650/691-1200, www.openspace.org. During nonbusiness hours, a touch-tone phone menu is available for trail news, conditions, and events.

105 BOREL HILL TRAIL
1.4 mi / 1.0 hr   👣2 🏔8

in the Russian Ridge Open Space Preserve on the Peninsula's Skyline Ridge

Map 7.2, page 292

Borel Hill is one of the great lookouts on the San Francisco Peninsula, topping out at 2,572 feet and surrounded by grasslands so hikers get unobstructed, 360-degree views. Yet the hill is not well known and remains a favorite destination of only a few hikers who visit the Russian Ridge Open Space Preserve. Russian Ridge is that big grassy ridge near the intersection of Alpine Road and Skyline Boulevard above Palo Alto.

From the parking area, hike north on the Bay Area Ridge Trail over the course of 0.7 mile to Borel Hill. The hill is the highest spot around, bordered by grasslands and with no trees. From the summit, with just a turn of the head, you can see Monterey Bay one moment, Mount Diablo and the South Bay the next.

There are several other trails at the preserve. The best is the 2.6-mile (one-way) hike out to Mindego Ridge Trail, which is routed through an oak woodland forest.

User Groups: Hikers, horses, and mountain bikes. A wheelchair-accessible trail starting at the parking area leads to Alpine Pond in the Skyline Ridge Open Space Preserve. No dogs.

Permits: No permits are required. Parking and access are free.

Maps: A brochure and map are available at the trailhead. For a free trail map, contact the Midpeninsula Regional Open Space District. For a topographic map, ask the USGS for Mindego Hill.

Directions: From I-280 in Palo Alto, take the Page Mill Road exit. Turn west on Page Mill and drive up the winding two-lane road to Skyline Boulevard. Cross Skyline Boulevard, drive a short distance, and then turn right into the parking lot, at the northwest corner of the intersection.

Contact: Midpeninsula Regional Open Space District, 330 Distel Circle, Los Altos, CA 94022, 650/691-1200, www.openspace.org. During nonbusiness hours, a touch-tone phone menu is available for trail news, conditions, and events.

106 SKYLINE RIDGE TRAIL
3.0 mi / 1.5 hr   👣1 🏔7

in the Skyline Ridge Open Space Preserve on the Peninsula's Skyline Ridge

Map 7.2, page 292

Many folks can't believe how pretty little Horseshoe Lake is, one of the pay offs at Skyline Ridge. From the parking area on the west side of Skyline Boulevard, Skyline Ridge Trail is routed around Horseshoe Lake, a pretty little farm pond (incredibly, no fishing is permitted). From there, the trail pushes into the interior of the parkland, skirting the flank of the highest mountain in park boundaries (2,493 feet), and then looping back to Skyline Boulevard. You play peekaboo here, heading in and out of woodlands and gaining occasional views of plunging canyons to the west. You can create a loop hike, but that requires going back on a fire road; most people return to the parking area via the same route they walked on the way in. In December, you can parlay an adventure here with a trip to the adjacent choose-and-cut Christmas tree farm.

User Groups: Hikers, horses, and mountain bikes. A wheelchair-accessible trail leads to Horseshoe Lake. No dogs.

Permits: No permits are required. Parking and access are free.

Maps: A brochure and map are available at the trailhead. For a free trail map, contact the Midpeninsula Regional Open Space District. For a topographic map, ask the USGS for Mindego Hill.

Directions: From I-280 in Palo Alto, take the Page Mill Road exit and drive west on a winding two-lane road up the mountain to Skyline Boulevard. Turn left on Skyline Boulevard and drive 0.8 mile to the main entrance and parking area, on the right.

Contact: Midpeninsula Regional Open Space District, 330 Distel Circle, Los Altos, CA 94022, 650/691-1200, www.openspace.org. During nonbusiness hours, a touch-tone phone menu is available for trail news, conditions, and events.

107 RIDGE TRAIL LOOP
2.6 mi / 1.25 hr　　　　🥾2 ⛰8

in Sam McDonald County Park near La Honda

Map 7.2, page 292

This loop trail provides a stellar introduction to the area and makes an excellent hike year-round. It features about a 700-foot climb, a route through deep redwood canyons, and then ridge-top views across coastal foothills. Very enjoyable.

After a quick orientation with the park map (they're self-serve at the ranger station), choose the posted four-mile Ridge Trail Loop. The hike starts on a narrow dirt path that is carved in the side of a steep redwood canyon, heading north. Even on hot Bay Area days, this forest is cool and refreshing, with occasional banana slugs on the trail. The trail contours up and down, then eventually rises into hardwood forest (mainly oaks, bays, and madrones) to a sub-ridge with a partial lookout to the north across miles of pretty foothills.

Here the trail curves left (west) and climbs toward Towne Ridge. You emerge at a crossing

of Pescadero Road (you're now heading south). Here the trail turns from single track to a service road, and you are rewarded with sweeping views of the coastal foothills, into the Pescadero Creek Canyon, and across to Butano Rim. In March, April, and early May, there are also many blooming wildflowers, highlighted by occasional rafts of sprawling forget-me-nots. The trail continues to contour up and down, generally climbing until you reach a horse camp and the Towne Trail, which are set atop foothill grasslands. Turn left on the Towne Trail and you descend into another deep redwood canyon. At a massive water tank, turn right on the Big Tree Loop, which is highlighted by a massive redwood. The Big Tree Loop is routed to a crossing of Pescadero Road and the parking lot.

For a longer trip, this hike can be extended on the Towne Creek Loop. For a short side trip, visit the adjacent Heritage Grove, which is accessible on Alpine Road.

User Groups: Hikers only. No dogs, horses, or mountain bikes. No wheelchair facilities.

Permits: No permits are required. A parking fee of $5 is charged per vehicle.

Maps: A trail map is available for $1 at the ranger station. For a topographic map, ask the USGS for La Honda.

Directions: From I-280 on the Peninsula, take the Woodside/Highway 84 exit. Turn east on Highway 84 and drive up the hill to Skyline Boulevard and Sky Londa, cross straight ahead, and continue another 6.75 miles to La Honda. Continue a short distance past La Honda to La Honda/Pescadero Road. Turn left off La Honda Road onto Pescadero Road and drive 1.1 miles to a Y. Bear right at the Y and drive a short distance (about 0.5 mile) to Sam McDonald County Park, on the right.

Contact: Sam McDonald County Park, Memorial Park Visitors Center, 650/879-0212; San Mateo County Division of Parks, 455 County Center, 4th Floor, Redwood City, CA 94063-1646, 650/363-4020, www.co.sanmateo.ca.us.

108 PESCADERO MARSH
3.0 mi / 1.5 hr 👫1 ⛰8

in Pescadero Marsh south of Pescadero

Map 7.2, page 292 **BEST (**

The centerpiece of a vast wetland lagoon and coastal estuary is Pescadero Marsh Natural Preserve, located just east of Highway 1 along Pescadero Creek, 15 miles south of Half Moon Bay. This is a 600-acre wetlands and lagoon that provides a year-round haven for blue heron, egrets, and owls, as well as a refuge for more than 200 species of shorebirds, waterfowl, and raptors on their migrant routes. The most spectacular is the blue heron, which often grows nearly four feet tall and can have a wingspan of seven feet. A classic experience at any wetlands is watching these huge birds lift off with labored wing beats.

A great easy trip is with a three-mile loop walk through the marsh; it's an easy saunter that gives you a chance to see the most, and at the same time, you can lose yourself in the surrounding wetlands habitat. To make it work, start by taking the North Pond Trail to Audubon Marsh. Then return on the Sequoia Trail, which traces the edge of the marsh and then is routed along Pescadero Creek. This trail is a dirt path that ventures through the heart of the wetlands, providing a good chance to see many birds, as well as occasional deer. We've been coming here for years and have also seen a fox, a skunk, and a badger. An additional bonus is that the parking area, trailhead, and information billboard are greatly improved.

Just across the highway from Pescadero Marsh is the parking lot and access point for Pescadero State Beach. This features an extended beach edged by cliffs, cuts in the bluffs, and sandy coves. It acts as a natural collection point for washed-up driftwood, bottles with notes, and other occasional goodies.

User Groups: Hikers only. No dogs, horses, or mountain bikes. No wheelchair facilities.

Permits: No permits are required. Parking and access are free.

Maps: A map is available from Half Moon Bay State Parks. For a topographic map, ask the USGS for San Gregorio.

Directions: From the Peninsula in San Mateo, take Highway 92 west to Half Moon Bay. Turn south on Highway 1 and drive 17 miles to Pescadero Road. Turn left and drive less than 0.25 mile to the parking area and trailhead on the left.

Contact: Pescadero State Beach, 650/879-2170; Half Moon Bay State Parks, 650/726-8820, www.parks.ca.gov.

109 MILL OX LOOP
5.0 mi / 2.75 hr 👫3 ⛰8

in Butano State Park near Pescadero

Map 7.2, page 292

If you love redwoods and ferns but are also partial to sun and warm afternoons, the Mill Ox Loop at Butano State Park may be the ideal hike for you. Why? Because you get all these things in good doses.

To find the trailhead, enter the park and continue ahead into the redwoods, looking for the signed trailhead on your left. The trail starts by crossing a small creek in a dense redwood forest, then heads up a very steep grade on switchbacks, emerging at the top of the canyon on Butano Fire Road. Some readers emailed that they were stunned at how steep this section is, but the climb is very short and the worst of it is over quickly. At the Butano Fire Road, turn right. You will climb more gradually as you head toward the park's interior. The fire road gets plenty of sun, and plenty of shirts come off en route to 1,138 feet. If you turn and look back to the west, you have views of the Pacific Ocean. When you reach a junction with Jackson Flats Trail, turn right for the return loop. Here the trail descends quite steeply over a bare rock and sandstone facing for 0.25 mile, then drops into Butano Canyon and the surrounding redwood forest. The rest of the hike is beautiful and pleasant, a meandering walk past ferns, trillium, redwoods, and plenty of wild iris. This is one of our favorites.

User Groups: Hikers only. No dogs, horses, or mountain bikes. No wheelchair facilities.

Permits: No permits are required. A state park entrance fee of $10 is charged per vehicle.

Maps: A brochure and map are available at the entrance station. For a topographic map, ask the USGS for Franklin Point.

Directions: In Half Moon Bay, at the junction of Highway 1 and Highway 92, drive south on Highway 1 for 17 miles to the Pescadero Road exit. Turn left on Pescadero Road and drive past the town of Pescadero (for three miles) to Cloverdale Road. Turn right and drive 5.5 miles to the park entrance, on the left. After paying the entrance fee, continue into the park and look for the Mill Ox trailhead, on your left. A small dirt parking area is on the shoulder of the road.

Contact: Butano State Park, 650/879-2040; Half Moon Bay State Parks, 650/726-8820, www.parks.ca.gov.

110 TRAIL CAMP

10.0 mi / 2 days   👣3   ⛺8

in Butano State Park near Pescadero

Map 7.2, page 292

The Bay Area's most hidden, unknown campground is Butano's backpack campground. Seven pretty sites are set in forest just below the west-facing Butano rim at 1,550 feet. The prettiest site is No. 7, set amid towering Douglas firs. It takes a five-mile hike with a 1,500-foot climb to get here.

At the bottom of the canyon near the park entrance, take the Jackson Flats Trail. This is routed east uphill for 2.75 miles to the Canyon Trail. Take the left fork for the Canyon Trail, which rises steeply at times up to the camp.

Just above the Trail Camp, you will find a route that connects to the Butano Fire Road. If you head to the left (northwest), you can find an abandoned air strip. At the end of the old strip, there are great views to the west of the Butano Canyon and beyond to the coast.

The heart of this park is a deep redwood canyon. From here, you can launch off on adventures that explore the slopes up to the horseshoe-shaped mountain rim. On the canyon floor, the place is cool, quiet, and lush. On the canyon rim, peer across a sea of conifers below to glimpses of the Pacific Ocean.

Note: No drinking water is available. You must pump-filter water from a creek located 0.25 mile from camp.

Messing with your mind: Butano is not pronounced "Bew-TAH-no," but rather "Bute-UH-no."

User Groups: Hikers only. No dogs, horses, or mountain bikes. No wheelchair facilities.

Permits: Trail camp fee and permits are required at the entrance station or visitors center (adjacent to entrance station). A state park entrance fee of $10 is charged per vehicle. Register at entrance station; no reservations are accepted.

Maps: A brochure and map are available at the entrance station. For a topographic map, ask the USGS for Franklin Point.

Directions: From Half Moon Bay, at the junction of Highway 1 and Highway 92, drive south on Highway 1 for 17 miles to the Pescadero Road exit. Turn left on Pescadero Road and drive past the town of Pescadero (for three miles) to Cloverdale Road. Turn right and drive 4.5 miles to the park entrance on the left. After paying the entrance fee, continue into the park and look for the Jackson Flats Trailhead.

Contact: Butano State Park, 650/879-2040; Half Moon Bay State Parks, 650/726-8820, www.parks.ca.gov.

111 BUTANO RIM LOOP

11.0 mi / 1–2 days   👣4   ⛺7

in Butano State Park near Pescadero

Map 7.2, page 292

Not many people hike the entire Butano Rim Loop. That is because there is a far better route (see Trail Camp listing in this chapter) to the backpacker's camp for overnight trips, and the

Rim Trail is an exposed service road that is ideal for mountain biking, not hiking. Regardless, we've done it and it has its merits.

Start at the Mill Ox trailhead, at an elevation of 200 feet. Hike up the steep grade, turning right on Butano Fire Road (700 feet). From here, trace the rim of Butano Canyon, and enjoy views of the redwood-filled valley (below) and the Pacific Ocean (behind and off to the west). The trail climbs steadily before reaching 1,713 feet where it crosses an old, abandoned airstrip on the ridgeline. Just past the airstrip, the trail enters forest. A signed cutoff on the right provides a short spur to the Butano Trail Camp (at 1,550 feet). If you were to stay overnight, this would make a first-day total of 5.5 miles.

Our advice is to keep on. This is the halfway point and the rest of the trip is more sheltered. Return by turning right on Olmo Fire Road and hiking out to the Doe Ridge/Goat Hill Trails, which drop back down into the Butano Canyon and the starting point. Much of this second half of the route is a soft dirt trail amid redwoods, and it laterals and descends into the south side of Butano Canyon.

User Groups: Hikers, bikes, horses to Trail Camp. No bikes on single track after Trail Camp (bikes have access to China Grade and other routes). No wheelchair facilities.

Permits: For camping, trail camp permits are required at the entrance station or visitors center (adjacent to entrance station). A state park entrance fee of $10 is charged per vehicle.

Maps: A brochure and map are available at the entrance station. For a free trail map, contact Butano State Park. For a topographic map, ask the USGS for Franklin Point.

Directions: In Half Moon Bay, at the junction of Highway 1 and Highway 92, drive south on Highway 1 for 17 miles to the Pescadero Road exit. Turn left on Pescadero Road and drive past the town of Pescadero (for three miles) to Cloverdale Road. Turn right and drive 5.5 miles to the park entrance, on the left. After paying the entrance fee, continue into the park and look for the Mill Ox trailhead, on

your left. A small dirt parking area is on the shoulder of the road.

Contact: Butano State Park, 650/879-2040; Half Moon Bay State Parks, 650/726-8820, www.parks.ca.gov.

112 AÑO NUEVO LOOKOUT
2.75 mi / 1.5 hr   🥾3 ⛰6

in Butano State Park near Pescadero

Map 7.2, page 292

Do you remember the good ol' days? Back when you could take a seat at a bench here and enjoy a picture-perfect view of Año Nuevo Island, to the south? The view even seemed to be framed on all four sides by conifers. Well, trees grow, and the view is long gone. What remains is a loop trip with a steep ascent followed by a beautiful downhill tromp through redwoods. It still is a decent hike, but not the best at Butano. However, if you desire an aerobic climb to a forested ridge, this is it.

Park at the entrance station and look for the trailhead directly to the right (south). The Año Nuevo Trail to the lookout climbs 730 feet in less than a mile. These days some figure that the bench is positioned here for you to sit and catch your breath. Might as well, eh? From here, it's best to continue on Año Nuevo Trail, then return on Goat Hill Trail, to complete the loop. Although short, this hike provides a good climb and a chance to walk through redwoods on the return descent. Pileated woodpeckers are occasionally seen on this loop.

User Groups: Hikers only. No dogs, horses, or mountain bikes. No wheelchair facilities.

Permits: No permits are required. A day-use fee of $10 is charged per vehicle.

Maps: For a free trail map, contact Butano State Park. For a topographic map, ask the USGS for Franklin Point.

Directions: In Half Moon Bay, at the junction of Highway 1 and Highway 92, drive south on Highway 1 for 17 miles to the Pescadero Road exit. Turn left on Pescadero Road and drive past the town of Pescadero (for three miles) to Cloverdale Road. Turn right and drive 5.5 miles to the park entrance, on the left. Park at the visitors center to the left of the entrance station. The trailhead is on the right near the park entrance kiosk.

Contact: Butano State Park, 650/879-2040; Half Moon Bay State Parks, 650/726-8820, www.parks.ca.gov.

113 SEQUOIA NATURE TRAIL
1.0 mi / 0.5 hr 🚶1 ⛺8

in Portola Redwoods State Park in the Santa Cruz Mountains

Map 7.2, page 292

Portola Redwoods is best known for a pretty second-growth forest, the headwaters of Pescadero Creek, the Shell Tree, a stunning yet hidden old-growth grove, a great mountain bike route, good hikes, and camping. At the minimum, do the easy Sequoia Nature Trail to see the Shell Tree, a giant fallen redwood once scoured by fire. Even on such a short hike, the surrounding forest (much of it redwood and Douglas fir) can provide a sense of remoteness. If you want more of a workout, the Sequoia Nature Trail is linked to the Summit Trail (across from the group camping area), which ventures into remote lands on the eastern border of the park.

The park has many other highlights. The Peters Creek Loop Trail is a 13-mile round-trip hike that enters a pristine grove of old-growth redwoods, with a few trees 30–35 feet around, several over 200 feet tall, and one over 300 feet. The best way to see it is by camping at the Slate Creek Trail Camp, then head out the next day into the forest interior.

Old Haul Road, a former logging road, is now a mountain bike route (10-miles round-trip) with a graded 500-foot climb and a descent that most can handle easily. (This route was previously closed by a bridge washout; rangers and volunteers replaced the bridge and reopened the trail).

Portola Redwoods links to nearby Pescadero Creek County Park, which in turn, borders Heritage Grove (old-growth, with easy access and trails) and San McDonald County Park, and Memorial County Park. Waterfall lovers should visit little Tiptoe Falls (winter and early spring only) to complete their Bay Area list.

Note: This park is on the closure list developed by the California Department of Parks, pending final state budget decisions or the possible transfer of park management to other park agencies or volunteer groups.

User Groups: Hikers only. No dogs, horses, or mountain bikes. No wheelchair facilities.

Permits: No permits are required. A state park entrance fee of $10 is charged per vehicle; pay at the visitors center.

Maps: A map/brochure is available at the visitors center. For a topographic map, ask the USGS for Mindego Hill.

Directions: From San Francisco, take I-280 south and drive 20 miles to Woodside and the exit for Highway 84/Woodside Road. Take that exit, turn west (right) on Woodside Road, and drive 2.8 miles to Woodside. Continue straight on Woodside Road/Highway 84 for 10 miles (at Sky Londa, continue straight on 84) to La Honda and continue a short distance to Pescadero Road. Turn left and drive 1.1 miles to Redwood Triangle and Alpine Road. Turn left on Alpine Road and drive 4 miles (slow, narrow, and twisty) to Portola State Park Road. Turn right and drive 3 miles to the park entrance. Continue 0.5 mile to the Visitor Center.

Contact: Portola Redwoods State Park, 9000 Portola State Park Road, La Honda, CA 94020, 650/948-9098, www.parks.ca.gov.

114 BAY VIEW LOOP
3.0 mi / 1.5 hr 🚶1 ⛺8

in Point Pinole Regional Shoreline

Map 7.3, page 293

On the Bay View Loop, you can walk several miles along the shore of San Pablo Bay, or on a wood bluff overlooking the shore, and take in a beautiful view of water, passing ships and birds. That's because visitors to Point Pinole must park at the entrance station and catch a shuttle bus to the shoreline. There you will find a long, pretty, cobbled beach and beautiful views of San Pablo Bay, Marin, and Mount Tamalpais. An excellent fishing pier is also here.

After parking, the trip starts with a shuttle ride (or with a bike ride) for 1.5 miles to a staging area adjacent to the 1,250-foot fishing pier. This is the launch point for adventuring in this park, whether you're hiking, biking, or fishing. Make sure you head out to the end of the pier to take in the water views and see if anybody has caught a sturgeon or striped bass. Then take the Bay Trail, perched on a bluff above the cobbled beach. Along the way are beautiful glimpses of San Pablo Bay.

To turn this into a three-mile loop, turn back (left) on the Woods Trail. This trail is routed through a small eucalyptus forest, with occasional remnants of the dynamite era, a few small buildings, and pretty dirt roads. The trail eventually returns to the staging area. The park covers 2,147 acres, and this loop trail is a great way to explore it. For an overview of the park, make a complete loop: Take Bayview to the Pier, the Marsh Trail to the Cooks Point, and the Cooks Point west to the junction with Pinole Point Trail (the shuttle trail).

A highlight of Point Pinole Regional Shoreline is a long, undisturbed stretch of shoreline on a cobbled beach along San Pablo Bay. The stone beach is unparalleled, as if this were the final resting place of every stone ever cast in the bay. It is a quiet place, where you can watch passing ships, go for an easy hike, take a dog for a walk, or fish from the pier. Yet the defining landscape feature of the park is the Hayward Fault—marked by the cliffs and Point Pinole itself as it goes out to sea.

You could drive I-80 a thousand times without realizing what's right next door in Pinole: the former site of the nation's largest dynamite factory. In the World War II era, this was the site of the Giant Powder Company—that is, dynamite manufacturers. This was their fourth site in the Bay Area after factories blew up in San Francisco, South San Francisco, and Albany. So no one wanted to be anywhere near the place. The dynamite company built all the present trails and roads, planted eucalyptus trees, and is responsible for the basic layout of the park.

User Groups: Hikers, dogs, horses, and mountain bikes. The trail is partially wheelchair accessible.

Permits: No permits are required. A $3 day-use fee is charged on weekends when the kiosk is attended. The shuttle costs $1 round-trip for people ages 12 through 61; it's free for seniors, and $0.50 for youngsters 6 through 11. There is a $2 dog fee on weekends.

Maps: A brochure and map are available at the trailhead. For a free trail map, phone the East Bay Regional Park District toll-free at 888/327-2757, ext. 5; follow directions, leave your name and address, and ask for the Point Pinole Regional Shoreline brochure. For a topographic map, ask the USGS for Richmond.

Directions: Take I-80 to San Pablo and the exit for Hilltop. Take that exit and drive west on Hilltop to the intersection with San Pablo Avenue. Turn right on San Pablo Avenue and drive north for a short distance to Richmond Parkway. Turn left on Richmond Parkway and drive a few miles to Giant Highway. Turn right and drive a short distance to the park entrance (it's well signed), on the left. Take the shuttle to the bay, the Point Pinole Pier, and trailhead.

Contact: Point Pinole Regional Park, 510/237-6896; East Bay Regional Park District, 2950 Peralta Oaks Court, P.O. Box 5381, Oakland, CA 94605-0381, 888/327-2757, www.ebparks.org.

115 KESTREL LOOP

4.0 mi / 2.0 hr   🏃1 ⛰8

in Crockett Hills Regional Park near Crockett

Map 7.3, page 293

Crockett Hills is one of California's newest parks, spanning 1,300 acres in the Contra Costa foothills. The first pay offs are the ridge-top views: There are five foothill peaks where you get sweeping views of San Pablo Bay, Carquinez Strait, and the Lower Delta, and to the west, a pretty silhouette of Mount Tamalpais. Four new miles of the Bay Ridge Trail were dedicated here, which means that 300 miles of Ridge Trail have been mapped, signed, and dedicated—a major milestone.

The best hike for views and bird-watching is the three-mile Kestrel Loop. For a bonus, take the Big Valley Trail, a suggested cutoff to view a mated pair of golden eagles who often hunt and hover here at mid-morning as the air temperature warms. You'll notice that birds flourish here. A ravine with a small, un-named pond edged by cattails is a sanctuary for redwing blackbirds, many small songbirds, and kestrels, the smallest bird of prey in North America. It turns out that the wildlife habitat here supports all levels of the wildlife food chain.

User Groups: Hikers, mountain bikes, horses, and dogs. No wheelchair facilities.

Permits: No permits are required. Parking and access are free.

Maps: A brochure and map are available at the trailhead. For a free trail map, phone the East Bay Regional Park District toll-free at 888/327-2757, ext. 5; follow directions, leave your name and address, and ask for the Crockett Hills brochure.

Directions: From San Francisco: Take I-80 east to Crockett and the exit for Cummings Skyway. Take that exit south to Crockett Boulevard. Turn left and drive about 0.7 mile to the staging area on the left (well signed).

From the Concord area: Take Highway 4 west to the exit for Cummings Skyway/Vallejo-Crockett. Take that exit to Cummings Skyway and drive about 2.5 miles to Crockett Boulevard. Turn right and drive 0.7 mile to the staging area on the left.

Contact: Crockett Hills, 510/544-3122; East Bay Regional Park District, 2950 Peralta Oaks Court, P.O. Box 5381, Oakland, CA 94605-0381, 888/327-2757, www.ebparks.org.

116 FRANKLIN RIDGE LOOP TRAIL

2.8 mi / 1.75 hr   🏃3 ⛰9

at Carquinez Strait Regional Shoreline near Martinez

Map 7.3, page 293

What you get at Franklin Ridge is a great, easy romp with a number of little side trails to different hilltop lookouts of Carquinez Strait. In just two hours' time, this is an experience that can realign your brain—and there are few places better suited to salvage the day and make a break from a bad case of I-80 tunnel vision. Franklin Ridge is the centerpiece of the Carquinez Straight Regional Shoreline. From I-80, it's about a 10-minute drive to the trailhead, and by then, your personal transformation has already started.

Here's a summary of the adventure: The round-trip hike is 2.8 miles, including a 420-foot climb, with the opportunity to extend the trip on several little cutoffs to additional viewpoints. The trailhead for this adventure is at a parking area called the Carquinez Strait East Staging Area, located on Carquinez Scenic Drive between Hercules and Martinez. You can also launch off from the Negedly Staging Area, but the climb is much steeper.

After parking, you start the trip by heading off on the signed trailhead for the California Riding and Hiking Trail. After just 10 minutes (less than 0.5 mile), you will reach a junction with the Franklin Ridge Loop, a park service road. Here you turn right on the loop trail, generally climbing up Franklin Ridge. By taking the loop counterclockwise, it makes the climb a bit more benign. This loop covers two miles, rising an estimated 620 feet to the highest point on the trip. Although this is mighty short as far as hills go, it still is plenty high enough to provide great views of Carquinez Strait.

Sunsets can be absolutely spectacular here in winter, often with sunlight refracted through distant stratus and a dark silhouette of Mount Tamalpais. Even after sunset, it remains pretty as the lights of the Benicia Bridge and nearby towns take hold.

The loop reconnects with the California Hiking and Riding Trail, from which you make the 10-minute tromp back to the parking area. Some people can rip this loop off in little over an hour, but the views are so good that most spend well over two hours. Late in the day, this water scene features a changing of light and color, almost minute by minute. The boats and bridges add a timeless perspective. A shady bench is perched on the ridge to take it all in.

The park covers 2,795 acres, most of it foothill country, with oaks, short ridges, and ravines. It is wild enough to provide habitat for wildlife; red-tailed hawks and deer are the most common. At dusk, it's possible to see great horned owls, kestrels, and occasionally even golden eagles.

User Groups: Hikers, dogs, horses, and mountain bikes. No wheelchair facilities.

Permits: No permits are required. Parking and access are free.

Maps: A brochure and map are available at the trailhead. For a free trail map, phone the East Bay Regional Park District toll-free at 888/327-2757, ext. 5; follow directions, leave your name and address, and ask for the Carquinez Strait Regional Shoreline brochure. For a topographic map, ask the USGS for Benicia.

Directions: From Berkeley, drive east on I-80 to Hercules and Highway 4. Take Highway 4 east to Martinez and the Alhambra Avenue exit. Take that exit to Alhambra Avenue, turn left, and go two miles to Escobar. Turn left for three blocks to Talbart Street, then turn right and go 0.5 mile (Talbart Street becomes Carquinez Scenic Drive) to the parking area, on the left side of the road.

Contact: Carquinez Strait Regional Shoreline, 925/228-0112; East Bay Regional Park District, 2950 Peralta Oaks Court, P.O. Box 5381, Oakland, CA 94605-0381, 888/327-2757, www.ebparks.org.

117 MARTINEZ SHORELINE
2.2 mi / 1.0 hr 🧍1 △7

at Martinez Regional Shoreline near Martinez

Map 7.3, page 293

The Pickleweed Trail and the Killdeer Trail make a pretty walk along the marshlands and bay frontage of Martinez Waterfront Park. Start hiking from the trailhead near the parking area and walk back on North Court Street to the trailhead at Sand Beach. The hike skirts a pond on the Duck Pond Trail. Follow Killdeer to turn right on Picklweed, crossing Arch Bridge over Alhambra Creek. The trail then runs along the waterfront, past an old schooner hull, to the park's western boundary. The trail is easy and flat, with the bay on one side, marshlands on the other. It is popular for bicycling, jogging, and bird-watching. An option is to walk a short distance from the parking lot to the Martinez Pier, one of the few piers in the Bay Area where striped bass, sturgeon, and steelhead are occasionally caught in the winter.

User Groups: Hikers, horses, and mountain bikes. Dogs are not permitted. The restrooms are wheelchair accessible, but the trail is not.

Permits: No permits are required. Parking and access are free.

Maps: A brochure and map are available at the trailhead. For a free trail map, call the East Bay Regional Park District (888/327-2757, extension 5; follow directions, leave your name and address, and ask for the Martinez Regional Shoreline brochure). For a topographic map, ask the USGS for Benicia.

Directions: From Highway 4 in Martinez, take

the Alhambra Avenue exit. Drive north on Alhambra Avenue for two miles and turn right on Escobar Street. Continue for three blocks to Ferry Street and turn left. Drive across the railroad tracks and bear right onto Joe DiMaggio Drive. Turn left on North Court Street and drive to the parking area, next to the fishing pier.

Contact: Martinez Regional Shoreline, 510/544-3122; East Bay Regional Park District, 2950 Peralta Oaks Court, P.O. Box 5381, Oakland, CA 94605-0381, 888/327-2757, www.ebparks.org.

118 FALSE GUN VISTA POINT
1.0 mi / 0.75 hr 🥾1 ⛰️8

in Miller-Knox Regional Shoreline west of Richmond on the shore of San Francisco Bay

Map 7.3, page 293

A little-known lookout over San Francisco Bay is the highlight of Miller-Knox Regional Shoreline, and getting to it requires only a short hike and climb. This parkland covers 260 acres of hill and shoreline property at Point Richmond, where strong afternoon winds in the summer create excellent conditions for kite flying. Whereas most people just make the short stroll along Keller Beach, this hike is preferred for the view. From the parking area, it leads about 0.5 mile up Old Country Road and Marine View Trail, making a right turn on Crest Trail to reach the False Gun Vista Point. In the process, the trail climbs 300 feet to the lookout, at 322 feet. On clear days, you get picture-perfect views of San Francisco Bay and its many surrounding landmarks.

User Groups: Hikers and dogs. No horses or mountain bikes. No wheelchair facilities.

Permits: No permits are required. Parking and access are free.

Maps: A brochure and map are available at the trailhead. For a free trail map, phone the East Bay Regional Park District toll-free at 888/327-2757, extension 5; follow directions,

leave your name and address, and ask for the Miller-Knox Regional Shoreline brochure. For a topographic map, ask the USGS for San Quentin.

Directions: From Berkeley: Drive north on I-80 to I-580 west. Take I-580 west to Canal Boulevard/Garrard Boulevard. Turn right on Canal Boulevard and drive 0.25 mile to Garrard Boulevard. Turn left and drive through the tunnel (the road becomes Dornan Drive). Continue on Dornan Drive for 0.5 mile to the parking area, on the right.

From Richmond: Drive south on I-80, exit west at Cutting Boulevard, and drive to Garrard Boulevard. Turn left and drive through the tunnel. The road becomes Dornan Drive; follow Dornan Drive 0.5 mile to the parking area, on the right.

Contact: Miller-Knox Regional Shoreline, 888/327-2757, option 3, extension 4544; East Bay Regional Park District, 2950 Peralta Oaks Court, P.O. Box 5381, Oakland, CA 94605-0381, 888/327-2757, www.ebparks.org.

119 POINT ISABEL SHORELINE
1.0 mi / 0.75 hr 🥾1 ⛰️7

at Point Isabel Regional Shoreline near Berkeley

Map 7.3, page 293

Half a million dogs a year visit Point Isabel Shoreline, the ultimate dog park in California, complete with showers, tennis balls, and treats. It's good for people, too. Beautiful bayfront views of San Francisco and the Golden Gate—plus the fact that it's a popular place to walk dogs—attract visitors to this stretch of shore. From the parking area, the trail extends northward along the shore of the bay, then east along Hoffman Channel, where it meets the Bay Trail, and offers great views of Hoffman Marsh. The best time to see birds here is in the fall, when year-round residents are joined by migratory species. It's common to see 100 to 200 dogs at a time here, and just as many tennis points. Point Isabel extends into San Francisco Bay just north of Golden Gate Fields Racetrack, and the 21-acre park provides an easy shoreline walk, rich bird-watching opportunities, and those great views.

User Groups: Hikers and dogs. No horses or mountain bikes. The restrooms and trail are wheelchair accessible.

Permits: No permits are required. Parking and access are free.

Maps: A brochure and map are available at the trailhead. For a free trail map, phone the East Bay Regional Park District toll-free at 888/327-2757, extension 5; follow directions, leave your name and address, and ask for the Point Isabel Regional Shoreline brochure. For a topographic map, ask the USGS for Richmond.

Directions: From I-80 in south Richmond, take the Central Avenue exit and drive west to Isabel Street. Turn right and drive to the parking area, at the end of the road.

Contact: Point Isabel Regional Shoreline, 888/327-2757, option 3, extension 4550; East Bay Regional Park District, 2950 Peralta Oaks Court, P.O. Box 5381, Oakland, CA 94605-0381, 888/327-2757, www.ebparks.org.

120 SAN PABLO RIDGE LOOP
6.2 mi / 3.5 hr 👣3 ⛰9

in Wildcat Canyon Regional Park in the Richmond foothills

Map 7.3, page 293

Newcomers to Wildcat Canyon Regional Park may find it hard to believe how quickly they can get to a remote land with great views. But it is true. Just east of Richmond, San Pablo Ridge rises about 1,000 feet. Start at the parking area and hike up Belgum Trail. Turn right at San Pablo Ridge and climb about 750 feet over the course of 2.5 miles. Once on top, slow down and enjoy the cruise. You will find a series of hilltops to climb for 360-degreee panoramas. To loop around, head back on Mezue Trail, then right again on Wildcat

Creek Trail, and walk back to the parking area. Of all the views of San Francisco, this is certainly one of the best. It takes a short grunt of a hike to get to the top, but you'll find it well worth the grunting. That's because you get great views of San Pablo Reservoir and Briones Reservoir off one side of the ridge, and of San Francisco Bay on the other. These hilltops offer gorgeous views and can also be accessed out of Tilden Regional Park from Inspiration Point on Nimitz Way.

User Groups: Hikers, dogs, horses, and mountain bikes. No wheelchair facilities.

Permits: No permits are required. Parking and access are free.

Maps: A brochure and map are available at the trailhead. For a free trail map, phone the East Bay Regional Park District toll-free at 888/327-2757, extension 5; follow directions, leave your name and address, and ask for the Wildcat Canyon Regional Park brochure. For a topographic map, ask the USGS for Richmond.

Directions: In Richmond, head north on I-80 to the Solano exit. Take that exit, turn left on Amador, and drive three blocks to McBryde Avenue. Turn right on McBryde Avenue and head east. After passing Arlington Boulevard (technically, not Arlington, but McBryde veering off to the right), drive straight (the road becomes Park Avenue) and bear left through a piped gate to the parking area.

Contact: Wildcat Canyon Park Office, 510/544-3092; East Bay Regional Park District, 2950 Peralta Oaks Court, P.O. Box 5381, Oakland, CA 94605-0381, 888/327-2757, www.ebparks.org.

121 LAUREL LOOP TRAIL
0.7 mi / 0.5 hr 👣1 ⛰8

in the Kennedy Grove Regional Recreation Area near the San Pablo Reservoir in El Sobrante

Map 7.3, page 293

Kennedy Grove is set at the base of San Pablo Dam, where visitors will discover a rich grove of eucalyptus adjacent to a large lawn/meadow. This loop hike takes hikers through the eucalyptus and then back, skirting the lawn areas. It is best hiked in a clockwise direction, departing from the trailhead at the gate in the northeast corner of the parking area. This is the kind of park where people toss Frisbees, pass footballs, or play low-key games of softball.

A must-do: A hiking and equestrian trail is located off Laurel Loop Trail; it can extend your adventure and provide sensational views. From the other side of the grove, take the one-mile Seafoam Trail. It ascends a hill through woodlands of bay and oak trees and provides spectacular views of San Pablo Ridge, Wildcat Canyon, San Pablo Reservoir, and San Pablo Bay.

User Groups: Hikers, dogs, and horses. No mountain bikes on the Seafoam Trail. Restrooms and a short walking path at park's main lawn area are wheelchair accessible.

Permits: No permits are required. An entrance fee of $5 per vehicle is charged when the kiosk is attended, $2 for dogs.

Maps: A brochure and map are available at the trailhead. For a free trail map, phone the East Bay Regional Park District toll-free at 888/327-2757, extension 5; follow directions, leave your name and address, and ask for the Kennedy Grove Regional Recreation Area brochure. For a topographic map, ask the USGS for Richmond.

Directions: From Richmond on I-80, take the San Pablo Dam Road exit. Turn east and drive through El Sobrante for 3.5 miles to the park entrance, on the left. Follow the pavement to the northwestern parking lot.

Alternatively, from Orinda on Highway 24, turn north on Camino Pablo and drive north along San Pablo Reservoir to the park entrance, on the right.

Contact: Kennedy Grove Regional Park, 510/223-7840 or 888/327-2757, option 3, extension 4534; East Bay Regional Park District, 2950 Peralta Oaks Court, P.O. Box 5381, Oakland, CA 94605-0381, 888/327-2757, www.ebparks.org.

122 SOBRANTE RIDGE TRAIL
1.6 mi / 1.0 hr 🏃1 ⛰7

in the Sobrante Ridge Regional Preserve near El Sobrante

Map 7.3, page 293

Sobrante Ridge Park covers 277 acres of rolling hills, open ridgeline, and wooded ravines, and this hike accesses the best of it. From the trailhead at Coach Drive, take Sobrante Ridge Trail, which rises in an elliptical half loop to the left. After 0.7 mile, you will come to the junction with Broken Oaks Trail. Turn left here and make the short loop (less than 0.25 mile long), and then retrace your steps on Sobrante Ridge Trail. This walk provides an easy yet intimate look at one of the Bay Area's key parklands, a link to open space on each side of it.

User Groups: Hikers, dogs, horses, and mountain bikes. No wheelchair facilities.

Permits: No permits are required. Parking and access are free.

Maps: A brochure and map are available at the trailhead. For a free trail map, phone the East Bay Regional Park District toll-free at 888/327-2757, extension 5; follow directions, leave your name and address, and ask for the Sobrante Ridge Regional Preserve brochure. For a topographic map, ask the USGS for Briones Valley.

Directions: From I-80 in Richmond, take the San Pablo Dam Road exit. Drive east for three miles and turn left on Castro Ranch Road. Drive about two miles to Conestoga Way, turn left, and proceed to Carriage Drive. Turn left again and drive two blocks to Coach Way. Turn right and proceed to the park entrance and parking area, at the end of the road.

Contact: Sobrante Ridge Regional Preserve, 888/327-2757, option 3, extension 4558, or 510/223-7840 (Kennedy Grove); East Bay Regional Park District, 2950 Peralta Oaks Court, P.O. Box 5381, Oakland, CA 94605-0381, 888/327-2757, www.ebparks.org.

123 BERKELEY PIER

1.2 mi / 0.75 hr 🚶1 ⛰7

near Berkeley on the shore of San Francisco Bay

Map 7.3, page 293

This historic structure extends 3,000 feet into San Francisco Bay amid landmarks that people come from around the world to see. The walk is easy—straight and flat—and while most people can get to the end of the pier in 20 minutes, there is no reason to hurry. The Golden Gate Bridge is a classic sight from the end of the pier, especially during sunsets, when you will discover how the Golden Gate earned its name. Things look different here, especially if you bring a loaf of French bread to nibble on and maybe your favorite elixir to wash it down. Fishing success varies, of course. The best time is early summer when halibut school on the Berkeley flats.

User Groups: Hikers and wheelchairs. No dogs, horses, or mountain bikes.

Permits: No permits are required. Parking and access are free.

Maps: For a topographic map, ask the USGS for Oakland West.

Directions: From the East Bay, take I-80 to Berkeley. Take the exit for University Avenue West/Berkeley Marina (signed) and continue to the stop sign. (If arriving from the south, take the left fork then loop around to the right onto University; turn right and drive over the overpass). Turn left and drive a short distance; the road then turns right. Continue past the bait shop on the right and ahead to the parking area on the left for Berkeley Pier (straight ahead).

Contact: Berkeley Marina Sports Center (bait, tackle, party boats), 510/849-2727; Berkeley City Parks, 510/644-6376, www.ci.berkeley.ca.us/parks.

124 BRIONES CREST LOOP

5.6 mi / 3.25 hr 🚶3 ⛰8

in Briones Regional Park north of Lafayette

Map 7.3, page 293

Briones Regional Park is a 6,255-acre sanctuary of peace set amid several fast-growing communities. With its intricate network of trails, it is one of the best parks for hiking in the East Bay, and this is the best of the lot. There are many trail junctions on the loop, and a map will keep you from making a wrong turn. From the trailhead, take Alhambra Creek Trail and Spengler Trail (turn right) to Old Briones Road Trail. Turn left (you're by the lagoons at this point) and hike a 0.5 mile to Briones Crest Trail. Turn left you will rise to Briones Peak (at 1,483 feet) in less than a mile. It is the highest point in the park and grants a panoramic view of the East Bay's rolling hillsides, quiet and tranquil. The view includes Mount Diablo, the west delta, Suisun Bay, and the Mothball Fleet. To complete the loop, turn left on the Spengler Trail, then right on Diablo View Trail. The latter closes out the hike in 1.1 miles, offering great views of the slopes of Mount Diablo.

User Groups: Hikers, dogs, and horses. Mountain bikes are allowed on all but the last mile of the loop. No wheelchair facilities.

Permits: No permits are required. An entrance fee of $3 per vehicle is charged when the kiosk is attended (there are five entrances at Briones, and only two have kiosks); $2 for dogs.

Maps: A brochure and map are available at the trailhead. For a free trail map, phone the East Bay Regional Park District toll-free at 888/327-2757, extension 5; follow directions, leave your name and address, and ask for the Briones Regional Park brochure. For a topographic map, ask the USGS for Briones Valley.

Directions: From I-680 north of Pleasant Hill, take Highway 4 west for three miles to the Alhambra Avenue exit. Turn south on Alhambra Avenue, drive for 0.5 mile, and bear right onto Alhambra Valley Road. Drive another mile to Reliez Valley Road. Turn left and follow Reliez Valley Road 0.5 mile to the park entrance. Turn right and drive 0.5 mile to the parking area. Look for the trailhead indicating Alhambra Creek Trail.

Contact: Briones Regional Park, 888/327-2757, option 3, extension 4508; East Bay Regional Park District, 2950 Peralta Oaks Court, P.O. Box 5381, Oakland, CA 94605-0381, 888/327-2757, www.ebparks.org.

125 NIMITZ WAY

4.0-10.0 mi / 2.0-5.0 hr

in Tilden Regional Park at Inspiration Point in the Berkeley hills

Map 7.3, page 293

When you start down this trail, you might wonder why it is rated so high. But the farther you go, the better it gets, and then everything explains itself. The views? Sure, the sweeping vistas of the East Bay foothills are great, but hey, the paved trail seems more appropriate for bikes, wheelchairs, and joggers than hikers. And so it is for the first four miles, until suddenly you enter a different universe. After passing a gate, the trail turns to dirt, and just like that, there's no one else around as you climb San Pablo Ridge. The views are stunning in all directions from a series of hilltops along the ridge, with the best views of Briones and San Pablo Reservoirs to the east, and San Francisco Bay and the city's skyline to the west. If you are not ready to commit to the full 10 miles, your goal should be at least 2 miles out to Wildcat Peak (elevation 1,250 feet; just off the trail) before turning around and heading for home. This is one of the best sections of the 31-mile East Bay Skyline National Trail.

User Groups: Hikers, dogs, horses, and mountain bikes. The trail is partially wheelchair accessible.

Permits: No permits are required. Parking and access are free.

Maps: A brochure and map are available at the trailhead. For a free trail map, phone the East Bay Regional Park District toll-free at 888/327-2757, extension 5; follow directions, leave your name and address, and ask for the Tilden Regional Park brochure. For a topographic map, ask the USGS for Briones Valley.

Directions: From Highway 24 in the East Bay, drive to just east of the Caldecott Tunnel and take the Fish Ranch Road exit northwest to Grizzly Peak Boulevard. Turn right, drive up the hill, and turn right again on South Park Drive. Drive one mile to Wildcat Canyon Road, bear right, and drive to the parking area at Inspiration Point, on the left.

Note that South Park Drive is closed each year from November through March to protect migrating newts. To avoid South Park Drive, from Highway 24 drive through the Caldecott Tunnel and exit at Orinda. Turn left on Camino Pablo. Drive north for about two miles, turn left on Wildcat Canyon Road, and continue to Inspiration Point, on the right.

Contact: Tilden Regional Park, 888/327-2757, option 3, extension 4562; East Bay Regional Park District, 2950 Peralta Oaks Court, P.O. Box 5381, Oakland, CA 94605-0381, 888/327-2757, www.ebparks.org.

126 BOTANIC GARDEN LOOP

0.4 mile / 1.0 hr

in Regional Parks Botanic Garden in Tilden Regional Park

Map 7.3, page 293

If you have ever seen a flower, plant, or tree and wondered what the heck it was, you can get the answers on this walk. The Regional Parks District has carved out a 10-acre parcel at Tilden in the Berkeley Hills, creating areas that represent 10 distinctive California landscapes and their respective flora. So what you get is a capsule look at the state's 160,000 square miles over the course of a walk that takes 1–2 hours—and the answer to your question.

This trip is best done counterclockwise from the visitors center. From the visitors center, turnleft and then turn in a right-bending horseshoe—you'll end up in a landscape that resembles the high Sierra. As you walk over a creek on a wood bridge, bear right through some hardwoods, emerging at what looks exactly like a Sierra meadow at 10,000 feet near Bishop Pass—complete with aspens, fir, meadow, and what could be an old miner's cabin. The adventure provides a series of such discoveries. The landscapes captures include Pacific Rain Forest, Southern California Desert, Sea Bluff, Shasta-Klamath, and Valley-Foothills.

The site has 1,500 plant, tree, and wildflower species, including 300 endangered species, including virtually all of the state's oaks, conifers, ceanothus, and manzanita species. One phenomenon of creating a mini-California is that, just like in the great outdoors across the state, there are blooming wildflowers over a seven-month period, depending on landscape. Typical blooms in April, for instance, are Douglas iris, ceanothus, monkeyflower, poppy, and blue dicks. In May and June, mariposa tulips, western azalea, fireweed, and columbines, among many others, are at peak blooms.

User Groups: Hikers only. No dogs, horses, and mountain bikes. The trail is partially wheelchair accessible.

Permits: No permits are required. Parking and access are free.

Maps: A brochure and map are available at the visitors center. For a free trail map, phone the East Bay Regional Park District toll-free at 888/327-2757, extension 5; follow directions, leave your name and address, and ask for the Tilden Regional Park brochure. For a topographic map, ask the USGS for Briones Valley.

Directions: There are multiple ways to reach the Botanic Garden. From Berkeley, take Highway 24 to the exit for Orinda. At the light for Camino Pablo at the end of the ramp, turn north. Drive 2 miles to Wildcat Canyon Road.

Turn left and go 3.7 miles to a junction with South Park Drive. Bear right for 20 yards to a parking lot on the left. Walk across Wildcat Canyon Road to the signed entrance.

Contact: Regional Parks Botanic Garden, 510/544-3169, www.nativeplants.org; East Bay Regional Park District, 2950 Peralta Oaks Court, P.O. Box 5381, Oakland, CA 94605-0381, 888/327-2757, www.ebparks.org.

127 ABRIGO FALLS

2.6 mi / 1.5 hr

in Briones Regional Park north of Orinda

Map 7.3, page 293

Little Abrigo Falls, the Bay Area's smallest waterfall and often one of the most elusive (and for some, most disappointing), can be the missing piece in a hiker's waterfall list. It goes dry in summer and fall, but it is a pretty little chute after heavy rains in winter. Start your hike at the Oak Grove picnic area at the trailhead for Abrigo Valley Trailhead (off of Bear Creek Road, just beyond the Bear Creek Staging Area). Hike 0.9 mile, and just beyond the Maud Whalen campsite, look for the short cut-off to the falls on the right. When it's running strong, you can hear it from the trail at the 30-foot cut-off. This is an easy 2.6-miles round-trip.

You'll hike amid grasslands, oaks, and bays, and along canyons and creeks with riparian habitat. Watch for deer, red-tailed hawks, and golden eagles. Coyotes, foxes, bobcats, and mountain lions are seen occasionally, usually at dusk. A picnic area is available near the trailhead.

User Groups: Hikers, dogs, and horses. No wheelchair facilities.

Permits: No permits are required. An entrance fee of $3 per vehicle is charged when the kiosk is attended (there are five entrances at Briones, and only two have kiosks); there is a $2 fee for dogs.

Maps: A brochure and map are available at the trailhead. For a free trail map, phone the East Bay Regional Park District toll-free at 888/327-2757, extension 5; follow directions, leave your name and address, and ask for the Briones Regional Park brochure. For a topographic map, ask the USGS for Briones Valley.

Directions: Take Highway 24 for 7.5 miles to Orinda and the exit for Camino Pablo North. Take Camino Pablo North for 2.2 miles to Bear Creek Road on right. Turn right on Bear Creek Road and drive to signed turnoff on right for Bear Creek Staging Area (if you reach Alhambra Valley Road, you have gone too far). Turn right and drive past the Bear Creek Staging Area to the Oak Grove Picnic Area and trailhead.

Contact: Briones Regional Park, 888/327-2757, option 3, extension 4508, or 925/370-3020; East Bay Regional Park District, 2950 Peralta Oaks Court, P.O. Box 5381, Oakland, CA 94605-0381, 888/327-2757, www.ebparks.org.

128 LAKE MERRITT LOOP
3.1 mi / 1.0 hr   🥾1 ⛰️7

in Oakland

Map 7.3, page 293

Lake Merritt in Oakland is your classic city lake. It is located minutes from I-580, surrounded by development, and yet here it is, a park with a pretty lake for nonmotorized boating, jogging, and picnics. This is deep in the urban jungle—sirens are common. It is best known as a great lake with afternoon winds that inspire many to learn how to sail in little dinghies. The Aquatic Center provides lessons and rentals. For walks or jogging, the lakeside path is a 3.1 mile-loop. For many, it's an ideal 20–30-minute run. Three permanent picnic tables with lake views are located near the Sailboat House.

User Groups: Hikers and wheelchairs. No dogs, horses, or mountain bikes.

Permits: No permits are required. A day-use fee of $5 per vehicle is charged. Free for walk-ins.

Maps: A brochure and map are sometimes available at the boathouse.

Directions: From Oakland, take I-580 east to the exit for Grand Avenue. Take that exit, turn west on Grand, and drive to Belleview Avenue and the park entrance road. Turn left (a wide left) on Belleview and drive a short distance to the entrance station. Continue 0.25 mile (signed Sailboat House) to Aquatic Center and parking.

Contact: Lake Merritt Boating and Aquatic Center, 510/238-2196, www.oaklandnet.com/parks/facilities/parks.asp.

129 ROUND TOP LOOP TRAIL
1.7 mi / 1.0 hr   🥾1 ⛰️7

in Sibley Volcanic Regional Preserve in the Berkeley hills

Map 7.3, page 293

The remains of the Bay Area's long-extinct volcano, Round Top Peak, as well as other geologic features exposed from past quarry operations, can be explored at the Sibley preserve. Volcanic activity occurred in this area 10 million years ago. Round Top was an in-filling of a great crater and was tilted to the side by strains on the Hayward and Moraga fault systems. Round Top Road, to the right of the visitor center leads uphill to the Round Top Loop Trail. Round Top Loop Trail leads around the peak on the south side by a narrow gauge hiking trail and on the north side by fire road. As you walk along the exposed volcanic rock, you can follow a self-guided tour using a pamphlet at the trailhead. Following the fire road will lead to the Volcanic Trail, which contains markers and spurs referencing major geologic points of interest. Adding the geologic tour on the Volcanic Trail will extend this hike for up to two hours.

User Groups: Hikers and dogs. Partially accessible for wheelchairs, horses, and mountain bikes.

Permits: No permits are required. Parking and access are free.

Maps: A brochure and map are available at the trailhead. For a free trail map, phone the East Bay Regional Park District toll-free at 888/327-2757, extension 5; follow directions, leave your name and address, and ask for the Sibley Volcanic Regional Preserve brochure. For a topographic map, ask the USGS for Briones Valley.

Directions: From Highway 24 in the East Bay, drive to just east of the Caldecott Tunnel and take the Fish Ranch Road exit northwest to Grizzly Peak Boulevard. Turn left and drive to Skyline Boulevard. Then drive straight ahead for another 0.25 mile to the park entrance and parking area, on the left.

From Montclair Village, east of Highway 13 in Oakland, take Snake Road uphill to Skyline Boulevard. Turn left on Skyline Boulevard and drive 0.5 mile to the park entrance, on the right.

Contact: Robert Sibley Volcanic Regional Preserve, 888/327-2757, option 3, extension 4554, or 510/544-3111; East Bay Regional Park District, 2950 Peralta Oaks Court, P.O. Box 5381, Oakland, CA 94605-0381, 888/327-2757, www.ebparks.org.

130 HUCKLEBERRY LOOP PATH
1.7 mi / 1.0 hr　　　🚶2 ⛰7

in the Huckleberry Botanic Regional Preserve in the Oakland hills

Map 7.3, page 293

If you know what you're looking for, this is a trip into an ecological wonderland. If you don't, well, it's still a rewarding, tranquil venture. That is because the Huckleberry Loop is routed through a remarkable variety of rare and beautiful plants. Pick up a brochure at the trailhead and follow the self-guided tour that points out the plants and points of interest specific to this area.

The Huckleberry Path starts at the staging area off of Skyline Boulevard. From the parking area, follow the path to the left fork. At the first junction in 0.5 mile, turn left and descend steeply through a mature bay forest. Follow the lower Huckleberry Path for 0.32 mile and experience the succession of forest, dense ferns, and huckleberries. At the junction with the Skyline National Trail and the Bay Area Ridge Trail, stay right. Continue on the Bay Area Ridge Trail for 0.5 mile until it again junctions with the Huckleberry Path on the right. After a steep stair climb, the Huckleberry Path resumes its loop back to the trailhead in a little over a mile. Along the way, explore the dead-end spur trails that branch off the upper Huckleberry Path on the right. The first trail spur shows off spectacular Pallid Manzanita specimens and provides a great viewpoint. The second spur provides another great view and several plants of interest including the Western Leatherwood.

User Groups: Hikers only on Huckleberry Path; no dogs, horses, or mountain bikes. Horses are allowed on the Skyline National Trail and the Bay Area Ridge Trail. No wheelchair facilities.

Permits: No permits are required. Parking and access are free.

Maps: A brochure and map are available at the trailhead. For a free trail map, phone the East Bay Regional Park District toll-free at 888/327-2757, extension 5; follow directions, leave your name and address, and ask for the Huckleberry Botanic Regional Preserve brochure. For a topographic map, ask the USGS for Oakland East.

Directions: From Highway 24 in the East Bay, drive to just east of the Caldecott Tunnel and take the Fish Ranch Road exit northwest to Grizzly Peak Boulevard. Drive two miles and bear left onto Skyline Boulevard (the roads merge). Drive a short distance past Robert Sibley Volcanic Regional Preserve to the park entrance and parking lot, on the left.

Contact: Huckleberry Botanic Regional Preserve, 888/327-2757, option 3, extension 4532, or 510/544-3111; East Bay Regional Park District, 2950 Peralta Oaks Court, P.O. Box 5381, Oakland, CA 94605-0381, 888/327-2757, www.ebparks.org.

131 LAFAYETTE-MORAGA TRAIL

7.75 mi one-way / 4.0 hr 👥1 ⛰6

Lafayette to Moraga, north of the
San Leandro Reservoir

Map 7.3, page 293

In this recommended route, the Lafayette-Moraga Trail is a 7.75-mile linear park. In other words, the trail is a park that forms a line from Lafayette to Moraga. All of it is paved and it is very popular with bikers and joggers, rather than hikers. On warm weekend mornings in the spring, this trail is a real hit with the locals. The hike starts at the Olympic Staging Area in Lafayette and curls to the left for the first 3.5 miles, eventually heading south along Las Trampas Creek to Bollinger Canyon. It then passes through downtown Moraga to the Valle Vista Staging Area on Canyon Road. For most, this is the end of the trip, as bicycles, dogs, and horses are not allowed to continue. Hikers, however, may keep walking west on land managed by the East Bay Municipal Utility District (EBMUD).

User Groups: Hikers, wheelchairs, dogs, horses, and mountain bikes.

Permits: No permits are required except on EBMUD lands. Parking and access are free.

Maps: A brochure and map are available at the trailhead under the information panel. For a free trail map, phone the East Bay Regional Park District toll-free at 888/327-2757, extension 5; follow directions, leave your name and address, and ask for the Lafayette-Moraga Regional Trail brochure. For topographic maps, ask the USGS for Walnut Creek and Las Trampas Ridge.

Directions: From Highway 24 near Lafayette, take the Pleasant Hill Road exit south. Drive one mile to Olympic Boulevard. Turn right and drive 0.1 mile to the Olympic Staging Area.

Contact: Lafayette-Moraga Linear Park, 888/327-2757, option 3, extension 4517; East Bay Regional Park District, 2950 Peralta Oaks Court, P.O. Box 5381, Oakland, CA 94605-0381, 888/327-2757, www.ebparks.org; East

Bay Municipal Utility District (EBMUD), 510/287-0459 (permits).

132 SHORELINE TRAIL

5.0 mi / 2.25 hr 👥1 ⛰8

at Crown Memorial State Beach on the shore of San Francisco Bay in Alameda

Map 7.3, page 293

The tide book is your bible at Crown Memorial State Beach. This state/regional park beach is set along the shore of San Francisco Bay just south of Crab Cove. High tide is the best time to observe seabirds such as loons, grebes, and ducks. Low tide, however, is the best time to watch shorebirds such as sandpipers poking around the exposed mudflats. Newcomers should start their trip with a tour of the Crab Cove Visitor Center. The trail is a paved bicycle path that follows the bay's shoreline, running 2.5 miles south to an overlook of the Elsie Roemer Bird Sanctuary. The bay views are also quite good. When the wind is down, this is one of the best swimming areas in the bay. When the wind is up, it's excellent for windsurfing.

User Groups: Hikers, wheelchairs, dogs (on the paved trail only, not the beach), and mountain bikes. No horses.

Permits: No permits are required. An entrance fee of $5 per vehicle is charged February through October; there is also a fee for dogs.

Maps: A brochure and map are available at the trailhead. For a free trail map, phone the East Bay Regional Park District toll-free at 888/327-2757, extension 5; follow directions, leave your name and address, and ask for the Crown Memorial State Beach brochure. For a topographic map, ask the USGS for Oakland West.

Directions: From I-580 in the East Bay, take I-980 west into Oakland. Take the 12th Street/Alameda exit. Follow the road under I-880 and turn left onto 5th Street. Drive through the Oakland/Alameda Tube. At the end of the tube, you will be on Webster Street, which dead-ends at Central. Turn left on Central and drive two blocks to 8th Street. Turn right on 8th Street and drive 0.25 mile to the Crown Beach entrance, on the right.

Contact: Crown Memorial State Beach, Crab Cove Visitors Center, 888/327-2757, option 3, extension 4522, or 510/544-3156; East Bay Regional Park District, 2950 Peralta Oaks Court, P.O. Box 5381, Oakland, CA 94605-0381, 888/327-2757, www.ebparks.org.

133 ARROWHEAD MARSH
2.0 mi / 1.0 hr   🚶1 ⛰️8

at Martin Luther King Regional Shoreline on San Leandro Bay near Oakland

Map 7.3, page 293   BEST (

Arrowhead Marsh is one of the best bird-watching areas in the East Bay, with 30 species that are commonly sighted—including several pairs of blue-winged teal. At high tide, this is also a top spot to see rails, which are typically elusive birds that are more often heard than seen. The paved trail skirts the edge of the marsh, which is set along San Leandro Bay. From the parking area, the trail is routed one mile out along the Airport Channel, with the marsh on your left. If you want, extend your walk across a bridge at San Leandro Creek and continue along the shore to Garretson Point, adding 1.4 miles round-trip. This parkland covers 1,220 acres, including some of the bay's most valuable wetlands habitat.

User Groups: Hikers, leashed dogs, wheelchairs, and mountain bikes. No horses.

Permits: No permits are required. Parking and access are free.

Maps: A brochure and map are available at the trailhead. For a free trail map, phone the East Bay Regional Park District toll-free at 888/327-2757, extension 5; follow directions, leave your name and address, and ask for the Martin Luther King Regional Shoreline brochure. For a topographic map, ask the USGS for San Leandro.

Directions: From I-880 in Oakland, take the Hegenberger Road exit and follow it toward the airport and Doolittle Drive. Turn right on Doolittle Drive and proceed to Swan Way. Turn right again and drive a short distance to the park entrance. Turn right on the park entrance road continue to the parking area at the end of the road.

Alternate route: From I-880 in Oakland, take the Hegenberger Road exit and drive 0.5 mile to Pardee Drive. Turn right and drive a few blocks to Swan Way. Turn left and drive one block to Gravel Access Road. Turn right on Gravel Access Road and drive 0.5 mile to the marsh area.

Contact: Martin Luther King Regional Shoreline, 888/327-2757, option 3, extension 4541, or 510/544-3115; East Bay Regional Park District, 2950 Peralta Oaks Court, P.O. Box 5381, Oakland, CA 94605-0381, 888/327-2757, www.ebparks.org.

134 GRAHAM TRAIL LOOP
0.75 mi / 0.5 hr   🚶1 ⛰️6

in the Roberts Regional Recreation Area in the Oakland hills

Map 7.3, page 293

Because the entrance to Roberts Regional Recreation Area lies amid redwood trees, it has proven to be a popular stop for visitors who want to see *Sequoia sempervirens* with a minimum effort. If you want to enter a redwood forest in the East Bay without having to walk far, this is the best bet. From the entrance of the parking area, near the swimming pool, take the short trail that is linked to Graham Trail. Turn right, and you will be routed in a short circle past a restroom to Diablo Vista; then turn right and head back to the parking area. The walk is short and sweet—just right for those who do not wish for a more challenging encounter.

User Groups: Hikers and dogs. No horses or mountain bikes. The restroom is wheelchair accessible, but the trail is not.

Permits: No permits are required. An entrance

fee of $5 per vehicle is charged; $2 for dogs. A fee is charged for access to the swimming pool (wheelchair accessible).

Maps: A brochure and map are available at the trailhead. For a free trail map, phone the East Bay Regional Park District toll-free at 888/327-2757, extension 5; follow directions, leave your name and address, and ask for the Roberts Regional Recreation Area and Redwood Regional Park brochures. For a topographic map, ask the USGS for Oakland East.

Directions: From Highway 24 in the East Bay, drive to Highway 13 in Oakland. Turn south on Highway 13 (follow the signs carefully) and drive three miles to Joaquin Miller Road. Turn left (east) on Joaquin Miller Road and drive one mile to Skyline Boulevard. Turn left on Skyline Boulevard and drive about one mile to the park entrance, on the right.

Contact: Roberts Regional Recreation Area, 888/327-2757, option 3, extension 4555, or 510/544-3156; East Bay Regional Park District, 2950 Peralta Oaks Court, P.O. Box 5381, Oakland, CA 94605-0381, 888/327-2757, www.ebparks.org.

135 STREAM TRAIL LOOP
3.5 mi / 2.0 hr   🏃2 ⛰️8

in Redwood Regional Park in the Oakland hills

Map 7.3, page 293

Newcomers to Redwood Regional Park are often amazed at the beauty of this trail. After all, whoever heard of redwood forests and trout streams in Oakland? But visitors to this park get both of these things here. For the best loop, start from Canyon Meadow and hike 0.28 mile through the Orchard Picnic Area. Turn left onto the Bridle Trail and continue 0.2 mile. Make a right onto Orchard Trail, which is a steep hike to French Trail. Turn right onto French Trail and climb along the western slopes of the redwood canyon for about 1.5 miles, rising to 1,000 feet. With the puffing part behind you (always hike up when you're fresh), turn right on Fern Trail, and you'll meet a junction with Stream Trail in 0.3 mile. The rest of the route back to the park entrance is easy and downhill, tracing along pretty Redwood Creek through the center of the redwood forest. In late winter and spring, a must-see is the fish ladder, located near the parking area. If you're lucky, you can see trout swim upstream from San Leandro Reservoir and jump up the ladder to spawn in these waters (fishing is not permitted).

User Groups: Hikers, wheelchairs, dogs, and horses. No mountain bikes.

Permits: No permits are required. An entrance fee of $5 per vehicle is charged when the kiosk is attended; $2 for dogs.

Maps: A brochure and map are available at the trailhead. For a free trail map, phone the East Bay Regional Park District toll-free at 888/327-2757, extension 5; follow directions, leave your name and address, and ask for the Redwood Regional Park brochure. For a topographic map, ask the USGS for Oakland East.

Directions: From Highway 24 in Oakland, turn south on Highway 13 and drive to Redwood Road. Turn left on Redwood Road and drive two miles past Skyline Boulevard to the park entrance, on the left. Turn left and park at the Canyon Meadow Staging Area, at the end of the road.

Alternate route: From the Bay Bridge, take I-580 to the 35th Avenue exit. Drive east on 35th Avenue, which becomes Redwood Road, and continue past Skyline Boulevard for about two miles to the park entrance, on the left.

Contact: Redwood Regional Park, 888/327-2757, option 3, extension 4553, or 510/544-3127; East Bay Regional Park District, 2950 Peralta Oaks Court, P.O. Box 5381, Oakland, CA 94605-0381, 888/327-2757, www.ebparks.org.

136 EAST RIDGE LOOP
4.0 mi / 2.5 hr 🥾3 ⛰7

in Redwood Regional Park in the Oakland hills

Map 7.3, page 293

This trip is an option to the Stream Trail Loop (see listing in this chapter) for ambitious hikers and mountain bikers; unlike on that trail, bikes are allowed on the East Ridge. From the parking area, turn right on Canyon Trail, climbing up to the East Ridge in 0.36 mile. Turn left onto the East Ridge Trail and make a loop by hiking out on the ridge, climbing much of the way. From atop the East Ridge, at 1,100 feet, you can look down into a canyon that appears to be a sea of redwoods. The view is quite a treat after climbing nearly 900 feet from the trailhead. The payback comes when you turn left and loop down into that canyon, where Redwood Creek awaits under the cool canopy of a lush forest. To do this, turn left again on Prince Trail, and another left on Stream Trail. Follow Stream Trail back to the Canyon Meadow Staging Area.

User Groups: Hikers, dogs, and horses. Mountain bikes and wheelchairs permitted on the paved part of the trail.

Permits: No permits are required. An entrance fee of $4 per vehicle is charged when the kiosk is attended.

Maps: A brochure and map are available at the trailhead. For a free trail map, phone the East Bay Regional Park District toll-free at 888/327-2757, extension 5; follow directions, leave your name and address, and ask for the Redwood Regional Park brochure. For a topographic map, ask the USGS for Oakland East.

Directions: From Highway 24 in Oakland, turn south on Highway 13 and drive to Redwood Road. Turn left on Redwood Road and drive two miles past Skyline Boulevard to the park entrance, on the left. Turn left and park at the Canyon Meadow Staging Area, at the end of the road.

Alternate route: From the Oakland side of the Bay Bridge, take I-580 to the 35th Avenue exit. Drive east on 35th Avenue, which becomes Redwood Road, and continue past Skyline Boulevard for about two miles to the park entrance, on the left.

Contact: Redwood Regional Park, 888/327-2757, option 3, extension 4553, or 510/544-3127; East Bay Regional Park District, 2950 Peralta Oaks Court, P.O. Box 5381, Oakland, CA 94605-0381, 888/327-2757, www.ebparks.org.

137 GRASS VALLEY LOOP
2.8 mi / 1.5 hr 🥾2 ⛰8

in Anthony Chabot Regional Park in the Oakland hills

Map 7.3, page 293   **BEST (**

Grass Valley provides a simple paradise nestled in the East Bay hills. This meadow lines more than a mile of a valley floor that is framed on each side by the crowned rims of foothills. In the spring, the land glows with the various hues of green from wild grasses, along with wild radish, blue-eyed grass, and golden poppies. The scene is quiet and beautiful, and the Grass Valley Trail is one of the quickest routes into tranquility. Start at the Bort Meadow Staging Area (at the MacDonald Trailhead for the East Bay Skyline National Trail) and hike downhill to the Bort Meadow Picnic Area. Turn left onto Grass Valley Trail and head south through Grass Valley, continuing on to Stonebridge, for a distance of 1.5 miles. To get back from Stonebridge, walk north on Brandon Trail, which is routed along the west side of Grass Valley. To crown a perfect day, end the hike with lunch at Bort Meadow.

User Groups: Hikers, dogs, horses, and mountain bikes. No wheelchair facilities.

Permits: No permits are required. Parking and access are free.

Maps: A brochure and map are available at the trailhead. For a free trail map, phone the East Bay Regional Park District toll-free at 888/327-2757, extension 5; follow directions, leave your name and address, and ask for the Anthony Chabot Regional Park brochure.

For a topographic map, ask the USGS for Las Trampas Ridge.

Directions: From I-580 in Oakland, take the 35th Avenue exit and drive east (35th Avenue becomes Redwood Road). Follow Redwood Road past Skyline Boulevard and continue for 4.3 miles to the Bort Meadow Staging Area, on the right.

Contact: Anthony Chabot Regional Park, 888/327-2757, option 3, extension 4502, or 510/690-6676; East Bay Regional Park District, 2950 Peralta Oaks Court, P.O. Box 5381, Oakland, CA 94605-0381, 888/327-2757, www.ebparks.org.

138 BORT MEADOW
5.4 mi / 3.25 hr

in Anthony Chabot Regional Park north of Castro Valley

Map 7.3, page 293

This MacDonald Trail to Bort Meadow has good views of a beautiful valley, and in the spring, there is a diverse array of pretty wildflowers. Start at the Bort Meadow Staging Area(at MacDonald Trailhead for the East Bay Skyline National Trail). Head out north (to the right), where the trail meanders along an old ranch road, climbing only slightly above Bort Meadow and Grass Valley. At the ridge, turn and look south for a great view of Grass Valley—a divine sight in the springtime. From the ridge, the trail/road proceeds north, with valley and hilltop views along the way. Watch closely for the hidden bench on the right side of the trail. You can sit here and look out over the remote foothill country to the east. After enjoying the views, return the way you came. The trail eventually drops steeply and connects to Redwood Regional Park, but most people turn around and return when they reach the drop in the trail.

User Groups: Hikers, dogs, horses, and mountain bikes. No wheelchair facilities.

Permits: No permits are required. Parking and access are free.

Maps: A brochure and map are available at the trailhead. For a free trail map, phone the East Bay Regional Park District toll-free at 888/327-2757, extension 5; follow directions, leave your name and address, and ask for the Anthony Chabot Regional Park brochure. For a topographic map, ask the USGS for Las Trampas Ridge.

Directions: From I-580 in Oakland, take the 35th Avenue exit and drive east (35th Avenue becomes Redwood Road). Follow Redwood Road past Skyline Boulevard and drive 4.3 miles to the Bort Meadow Staging Area, on the right.

Contact: Anthony Chabot Regional Park, 888/327-2757, option 3, extension 4502, or 510/690-6676; East Bay Regional Park District, 2950 Peralta Oaks Court, P.O. Box 5381, Oakland, CA 94605-0381, 888/327-2757, www.ebparks.org.

139 ROCKY RIDGE LOOP
4.4 mi / 2.5 hr

in Las Trampas Regional Wilderness south of Moraga

Map 7.3, page 293

At 3,800 acres, Las Trampas represents a sprawling wilderness amid civilization. With other contiguous regional parklands and watershed lands, it is ringed generally by Castro Valley to the south, Upper San Leandro Reservoir and Crow Canyon to the west, and Danville to the northeast. The primary destination at Las Trampas Regional Wilderness is Rocky Ridge and its 2,024-foot summit. Though the surrounding landscape consists of rolling hills edged by canyons with small creeks, Rocky Ridge is a spectacular sandstone wall with diagonal striations on its west face. On top, you get spectacular views to the east of Mount Diablo and the Livermore Valley; to the west of Crow Canyon plunging at your feet; across the South Bay, from the Bay Bridge and San Francisco down to the San Mateo Bridge and beyond. Spectacular.

Hikers should pick up a brochure and map from the self-serve box at the trailhead. This adventure is best started at the trailhead at the end of Bollinger Road. From the parking area, take the Rocky Ridge View Trail. The first 0.75 mile is a paved service road; it then makes a sharp left to an narrow, unpaved trail for a view of Rocky Ridge. It's a climb of 800 feet in a stretch of about 1.2 miles. At the ridge, there are several options. To complete a 4.4-mile loop, continue south on the Rocky Ridge View Trail and then turn left on the Elderberry Trail. Up on top, you will see there is a true summit, and from here the views of the bay to the west and Mount Diablo to the northeast are spectacular. Elderberry Trail returns to the staging area in 2 miles.

Another option is a side trip to the Wind Caves (these are actually more like sandstone hollows). To get there, follow the Rocky Ridge View Trail (map in hand) to its junction with Sycamore Trail. Turn right on Sycamore Trail and tromp a little more than 0.25-mile down to the caves. This is a fairly steep, though short, descent.

In the afternoon, it's common for winds off the bay to push against the ridge, and then lift almost straight up. Perched atop the ridge, you might be lucky to watch the hawks and falcons at eye-level, floating on the thermals and gliding with scarcely a wingbeat. The cliffs here provide nesting areas for many raptors, including red-tailed hawks, prairie falcons, and the fastest creature on earth—the peregrine falcon (this is where we saw our first peregrine). Golden eagles are also commonly sighted in the region in the winter months. An abundant population of ground squirrels provides a reliable food source, and in turn, the eagles migrate long distances to use the area as a wintering ground.

User Groups: Hikers, dogs, and horses. No mountain bikes (but permitted on the park's service roads). No wheelchair facilities.

Permits: No permits are required. Parking and access are free. A permit is required to access and hike on adjoining EBMUD lands.

Maps: A brochure and map are available at the trailhead. For a free trail map, phone the East Bay Regional Park District toll-free at 888/327-2757, extension 5; follow directions, leave your name and address, and ask for the Las Trampas Regional Wilderness brochure. For a topographic map, ask the USGS for Las Trampas Ridge.

Directions: From San Ramon, take I-680 to the exit for Crow Canyon Road and drive west to Bollinger Canyon Road. Turn north on Bollinger Canyon Road and drive five miles to staging area and trailhead.

Contact: Las Trampas Regional Wilderness, 888/327-2757, option 3, extension 4537, or 510/544-3276; East Bay Regional Park District, 2950 Peralta Oaks Court, P.O. Box 5381, Oakland, CA 94605-0381, 888/327-2757, www.ebparks.org; East Bay Municipal Utility District (EBMUD), 510/287-0459 (permits).

140 IRON HORSE REGIONAL TRAIL

1.0–28.0 mi one-way / 1–3 days

in the San Ramon Valley from San Ramon to Concord

Map 7.3, page 293

The Iron Horse Regional Trail is a focal point of the national Rails to Trails program, which converts abandoned rail lines into hiking trails. The continuous trail runs 28 miles from Dublin north to Concord and Highway 4. (There is another paved mile within the city of Pleasanton, but as of 2012 it is unconnected). The rail route that it follows was established in 1890 and was abandoned officially in 1976. It took only two years to remove all the tracks, but the trail conversion is requiring quite a bit more time. The plan is to extend the Iron Horse Regional Trail into Livermore on the south end, and to Carquinez Strait on the north.

The completed south portion starts at the Dublin-Pleasanton BART and goes north from there to Highway 4. This has become a prominent destination for locals out jogging, biking, and walking. The trail is a 10-foot wide asphalt strip, but the trail corridor ranges from 200 feet to as little as 12 feet in some areas of Walnut Creek. It is often hot and dry out here, with a few drinking fountains sprinkled along the way. Shade trees have been planted, affirmation of the sense of long-range vision. Regardless, most use this trail summer mornings as a cool respite from the blowtorch afternoons.

User Groups: Hikers, wheelchairs, dogs, horses, and mountain bikes.

Permits: No permits are required. Parking and access are free.

Maps: A brochure and map are available at the trailheads. For a free trail map, phone the East Bay Regional Park District toll-free at 888/327-2757, extension 5; follow directions, leave your name and address, and ask for the Iron Horse Regional Trail brochure. For a topographic map, ask the USGS for Las Trampas Ridge.

Directions: South trailhead: Take I-580 east to the Dublin-Pleasanton BART station and park. The trailhead begins on Santa Rita Road.

North trailhead: From I-680 in Walnut Creek, take the Rudgear Road exit. Turn east and park at either the park-and-ride lot (on the east side of the freeway) or the staging area (south side).

Contact: Iron Horse Regional Trail, 888/327-2757, option 3, extension 4517, option 0; East Bay Regional Park District, 2950 Peralta Oaks Court, P.O. Box 5381, Oakland, CA 94605-0381, 888/327-2757, www.ebparks.org.

141 CASTLE ROCK TRAIL

3.9 mi / 2.0 hr

in Diablo Foothills Regional Park on the northwest slopes of Mount Diablo near Walnut Creek

Map 7.3, page 293

The views of Castle Rock, towering Mount Diablo, and access to a shady ravine make a visit to Diablo Foothills Regional Park very special. This unique hike is off the radar for most. While thousands make the long drive to the top of Mount Diablo, this trip can be more memorable, yet it often seems that only locals know about it.

Diablo Foothills encompass more than 1,000 acres and is linked to Shell Ridge Open Space on one side, and Castle Rock Regional Recreation Area and Mount Diablo State Park on the other. There are several staging areas and a network of trails link to the surrounding parks. The busy Walnut Creek/Concord corridor can cause many to overlook the nearby foothills of giant Diablo. Once you depart I-680, the procession to the park moves quickly from highway traffic, past city and suburbia, to rural landscapes and some of Diablo's wildest lands, prettiest trails, and striking geologic formations.

From the Orchard Staging Area, follow Castle Rock Trail south to Stage Road Trail. This pretty, shaded riparian zone runs along Pine Creek and the border of Mount Diablo State Park. To the east are Castle Rock's monolithic sandstone structures, gorgeous when the sun is low in the sky at dawn and dusk. At the junction with Buckeye Ravine Trail, turn right (west) to complete the loop along a short section of the Briones-to-Mount Diablo Regional Trail, with photo-quality views of Castle Rock and the silhouette of Mount Diablo. Buckeye Ravine Trail picks up again to the right and connects with Shell Ridge Loop Trail for pretty, long-distance views on the way back to Castle Rock Trail.

User Groups: Hikers, dogs, horses, and mountain bikes, partially wheelchair accessible.

Permits: No permits are required. Parking and access are free.

Maps: A brochure and map are available at the trailhead. For a free trail map, phone the East Bay Regional Park District toll-free at 888/327-2757, extension 5; follow directions, leave your name and address, and ask for the Diablo Foothills Regional Park brochure. For a topographic map, ask the USGS for Diablo.

Directions: From the Bay Bridge, bear right on I-580 (stay far right) and go 1.5 miles to exit for Highway 24. Take Highway 24 and drive 13.4 miles (through the tunnel) to Walnut Creek and I-680 (stay left). Continue on I-680 for 0.4 mile to exit for Ygnacio Valley Road. At bottom of the ramp, turn right on Ygnacio Valley Road and continue 2.2 miles to Walnut Avenue. Turn right onto Walnut Avenue and go 1.6 miles to a roundabout. Exit the roundabout to the right onto Castle Rock Road. Continue 1.5 miles to the Orchard Staging Area.

Contact: Diablo Foothills Regional Park, 888/327-2757, option 3, extension 4526, or 510/544-3806; East Bay Regional Park District, 2950 Peralta Oaks Court, P.O. Box 5381, Oakland, CA 94605-0381, 888/327-2757, option 3, extension 4526, www.ebparks.org.

142 LITTLE GIANT LOOP
8.1 mi / 4.5 hr   👣4   ⛰10

in Mount Diablo State Park near Danville

Map 7.3, page 293

High on the north flank of Mount Diablo, the world seems simple and clean, with a view that never ends. From Deer Flat and Meridian Ridge, you can peer down Mitchell Canyon, across the Carquinez Strait and lower delta, and across miles of greenbelt to the silhouette of Mount St. Helena, north of Calistoga. At Mount Diablo, the best way to commemorate the annual coronation of spring is from the Mitchell Canyon trailhead.

Our favorite trip here is an 8.1-mile loop, named the Little Giant Loop, and it takes most hikers about four hours to complete. It features an elevation gain of about 1,600 feet, a great picnic site with sensational views, and the option to fork off and create more ambitious trips.

The trip starts at the Mitchell Canyon trailhead (elevation 600 feet), located just outside of Clayton. This provides access to Mount Diablo's prettiest regions in spring.

In the first two miles, the climb is steady, and you can establish a good rhythm as you open the day and gain entry to Mitchell Canyon. You will pass amid grasslands, chaparral, and the first wildflowers of the year. In late March and April, this area features rafts of a purple bloom on a long stalk (linathus), along with dozens of other species. In April and early May, there can also be hummingbirds, butterflies, and ladybugs galore (don't laugh—on one trip we saw maybe 50,000 ladybugs in a 100-yard radius).

Then it gets steep, climbing about 1,000 feet in a mile, but it's graded with switchbacks, making for a strong aerobic rhythm for hikers—but it's butt-kicker level for bikers. You will top out at Deer Flat and reach a fork in the trail. Everybody stops here, turns, and takes in the long-distance views, often enjoying a drink and maybe a trail snack at the picnic table. Deer Flat is primarily grasslands and chaparral, sprinkled with some small pines. The lookout points here tower over Mitchell Canyon and beyond to the valley flatlands to the north.

To complete the loop, turn left at Deer Flat to the Meridian Ridge Fire Road (more great views) and continue to Murchio Gap at a major junction. The best route is to continue straight for a short distance to the Back Trail, turn left and enjoy the saunter downhill into a canyon setting. At the Coulter Pine Trail (single track, no bikes), turn left, which is routed back to the Mitchell Canyon trailhead and parking area.

Mount Diablo is beautiful in the spring. Sometimes we wish the experience could be captured in a bottle, and then taken in little doses when needed for the rest of the year.

User Groups: Hikers and horses. Mountain bikes are allowed on a portion of this route. No dogs. No wheelchair facilities.

Permits: No permits are required. A state park entrance fee of $10 is charged for each vehicle.

Maps: A trail map is available from Mount Diablo State Park (P.O. Box 346, Walnut Creek,

CA 94597; $7.50, including postage). For a topographic map, ask the USGS for Diablo.

Directions: From the Bay Bridge, bear right on I-580 and continue 1.6 miles (stay to the right) to Highway 24. Take Highway 24 east for 13.2 miles to Walnut Creek and I-680. Take I-680 north and go 0.4 mile to the exit for Ygnacio Valley Road. Take that exit, turn right, and drive 10 miles to Clayton and Clayton Avenue. Turn right on Clayton and drive 1 mile to Mitchell Canyon Road. Turn right and drive to the trailhead at the end of the road.

Contact: Mount Diablo State Park, 96 Mitchell Canyon Road, Clayton, CA 94517, 925/837-2525 (recorded info) or 925/837-0904 (ranger at kiosk); weather conditions at summit, 925/838-9225; Mount Diablo Interpretive Association, 925/927-7222, www.mdia.org.

143 DONNER FALLS
6.5 mi / 2.5 hr   👥2 ⛰️10

in Mount Diablo State Park near Danville

Map 7.3, page 293

This hike is a 10? Wait a minute—that's if you hit it perfect. Most of the time, this hike rates a 6–7, but time it right and the world is yours. At Mount Diablo, the Bay Area's grand old mountain rising above the East Bay hills, there is a series of hidden waterfalls that can be as pretty as anything in the East Bay hills after a heavy rain. Reaching them requires a 6.5-mile hike, a good climb, and something of a fortune hunt. In return, you get an experience that shows why the Bay Area is one of the most special places on earth.

The trailhead for Donner Creek Falls is at the end of Regency Drive, which is located off Clayton Road (and becomes Marsh Creek Road) out of Clayton. From here, turn left on an old ranch road and walk alongside a pretty creek set amid rolling hills peppered with oaks. At Cardinet Junction, turn left, and after a short time, cross the creek. Then it's a 600-foot climb in five switchbacks before you reach the signed turnoff for the falls trail.

Rewards feature views to the north of Clayton, Suisun Bay, and the Mothball Fleet, as well as a good chance of seeing rabbits, deer, and hawks.

From here, the trail turns to single track and laterals the left side of a canyon. One by one, the falls start to come in view. The first is a 20-foot cascade across the other side of the canyon. Then, moments later, there's another fall, straight ahead, that's more of a chute. Moving along, two more come into view, including one short but pretty free fall. Continuing straight, the trail will guide you right across two streams, the source of the falls. Most stop to enjoy the treat. If you can time your trip for peak flow, it's a stunner.

When you're ready to head back: The trail loops back to Cardinet Junction, and from there it's an easy (but often muddy in winter) traipse downhill back to the trailhead. It's hard to imagine Diablo any prettier than on this hike.

User Groups: Hikers and horses. No dogs. Mountain bikes permitted on the service road, but not the single-track trail that provides access to the waterfalls. The first half of the trail is designed for wheelchair use.

Permits: No permits are required. Parking and access are free.

Maps: A trail map is available from Mount Diablo State Park (P.O. Box 346, Walnut Creek, CA 94597; $7.50, including postage). For a topographic map, ask the USGS for Diablo.

Directions: From the Bay Bridge, bear right on I-580 and continue 1.6 miles (stay to the right) to Highway 24. Take Highway 24 east for 13.2 miles to Walnut Creek and I-680. Take I-680 north and go 0.4 mile to the exit for Ygnacio Valley Road. Take that exit, turn right, and drive 10 miles to Clayton and Clayton Avenue. Turn right (becomes Marsh Creek Road) and go three miles to Regency Drive. Turn right on Regency Drive and drive 0.5 mile to the end of the road and the trailhead.

Contact: Mount Diablo State Park, 96 Mitchell Canyon Road, Clayton, CA 94517, 925/837-2525 (recording), 925/837-0904 (ranger), or

925/838-9225 (weather conditions at summit); Mount Diablo Interpretive Association, 925/927-7222, www.mdia.org.

144 MOUNT DIABLO DOUBLE SUMMIT

4.0 mi / 2.5 hr   👥3 🔺10

in Mount Diablo State Park near Danville

Map 7.3, page 293

According to Native American legend, at the dawn of time, Tuyshtak was the sacred birthplace of the world. Supernatural beings, the First People, lived here in the Bay Area. Tuyshtak, you see, is the old mountain that towers over the East Bay hills and San Joaquin Delta—today's Mount Diablo. It is still one of the best places anywhere in the spring to visit, explore, and take in the views.

This is a four-mile round-trip hike, but it feels longer and takes 2.5 hours. From the summit parking lot, drive down the hill 0.7 mile past the overflow parking lot and look for the pullout along the east side of the road and the trailhead signed Devil's Elbow/North Peak Trail. The hike starts easy, a downhill romp to Prospector's Gap. You then turn right toward the North Summit and start a rhythmic climb for about a mile, before facing a butt-kicker: a seemingly straight-up section of about 150 yards. Once near the top, hike over to the crag to the east and scramble to the top. This is a sensational picnic site that towers over Brentwood and the Delta.

Note: Mount Diablo is a "dry park." No beer, wine, or alcohol of any kind is permitted.

User Groups: Hikers only. No mountain bikes, dogs or horses. No wheelchair access.

Permits: No permits are required. A state park entrance fee of $10 is charged for each vehicle.

Maps: A trail map is available from Mount Diablo State Park (P.O. Box 346, Walnut Creek, CA 94597; $7.50, including postage). For a topographic map, ask the USGS for Diablo.

Directions: From the Bay Bridge, (bear right on I-580 and continue east 1.6 miles to Highway 24. Take Highway 24 east for 13.2 miles to Walnut Creek and I-680. Take I-680 north and go 0.4 mile to the exit for Ygnacio Valley Road. Take that exit east and drive 0.6 mile to Ygnacio Valley Road. Turn right and go 2.2 miles to Walnut Avenue. Bear right and drive 1.5 miles to Oak Grove Road and one mile to North Gate Road. Turn left and go 1.4 miles to park entrance and kiosk; continue to the upper summit parking lot. After enjoying the views from the lookout station, return down the road 0.7 mile to the Devil's Elbow Trailhead on left (east side).

From Danville on I-680: Take the Diablo Road exit and drive east (after 0.75 mile, bear right to stay on Diablo Road) for three miles to Mount Diablo Scenic Boulevard. Turn left and drive 3.7 miles (the road becomes South Gate Road) to the park entrance station. Continue for 7.3 miles to the summit. After enjoying the views from the lookout station, return down road 0.7 mile to trailhead on left (east side).

Contact: Mount Diablo State Park, 96 Mitchell Canyon Road, Clayton, CA 94517, 925/837-2525 (recorded info) or 925/837-0904 (ranger at kiosk); weather conditions at summit, 925/838-9225; Mount Diablo Interpretive Association, 925/927-7222, www.mdia.org.

145 MARY BOWERMAN TRAIL

1.0 mi / 0.5 hr   👥1 🔺10

in Mount Diablo State Park near Danville

Map 7.3, page 293

With the hills glowing and the skies often clear in late March and April, Mount Diablo can recharge how you feel, and in a sense, provide a restart on life. Yet this easy trip can provide that feeling nearly year-round. Those familiar with the old mountain know this as the former Fire Interpretive Trail, a rim trail that rings the Diablo summit with fantastic views. Mary Bowerman, in case you don't recognize the name, was an esteemed botanist and the author of *The Flowering Plants and Ferns of Mount Diablo.*

From the parking lot at the summit, start your visit by making the short walk to the old lookout station. Head up the stairs to the lookout perch that towers over the San Joaquin Delta and Sacramento Valley. From each side of the lookout, you get a chance to see long distances that encompass a huge landscape. It's well known that the total land area that can be seen from the Diablo is the best in California, and second in the world only to Mount Kilimanjaro in Africa.

The Mary Bowerman Trail is the easiest walk with the best long-distance views in the Bay Area. It starts on the north side of the parking lot at the summit, and most of it (and the views) are accessible to wheelchairs. The trail runs on the shoulder of the summit and takes about a half hour, with the best views looking toward Sacramento and across the Delta. Numbered posts, with a corresponding information sheet, provide information about flora.

Many have never been able to sight Half Dome from the top of Diablo, even with binoculars. That is because you only can see the upper half of the massive granite dome rising above Yosemite Valley's canyon walls (which are far less impressive from a distance). For those who climb Half Dome, a trick is to scan west with binoculars from the Half Dome Summit (or with the naked eye from Dewey Point on the South Yosemite Rim) and you will be amazed at how prominent Mount Diablo appears on the western horizon. Having this reverse perspective makes it far easier to see Half Dome on the next trip up Diablo.

Note: Mount Diablo is a "dry park." No beer, wine, or alcohol of any kind is permitted.

User Groups: Hikers and wheelchairs. No mountain bikes, dogs, or horses.

Permits: No permits are required. A state park entrance fee of $10 is charged for each vehicle.

Maps: A trail map is available from Mount Diablo State Park (P.O. Box 346, Walnut Creek,

CA 94597; $7.50, including postage). For a topographic map, ask the USGS for Diablo.

Directions: From the Bay Bridge, bear right onto I-580 and continue east 1.6 miles to Highway 24. Take Highway 24 east for 13.2 miles to Walnut Creek and I-680. Take I-680 north and drive 0.4 mile to the exit for Ygnacio Valley Road. Take that exit east and drive 0.6 mile to Ygnacio Valley Road. Turn right and go 2.2 miles to Walnut Avenue. Bear right and go 1.5 miles to Oak Grove Road and one mile to North Gate Road. Turn left and go 1.4 miles to park entrance and kiosk. Continue to the upper summit parking lot. After enjoying the views from the lookout station, return down the road 0.7 mile to the Devil's Elbow Trailhead on left (east side).

From Danville on I-680: Take the Diablo Road exit and drive east (after 0.75 mile, bear right to stay on Diablo Road) for three miles to Mount Diablo Scenic Boulevard. Turn left and drive 3.7 miles (the road becomes South Gate Road) to the park entrance station. Continue for 7.3 miles to the summit.

Contact: Mount Diablo State Park, 96 Mitchell Canyon Road, Clayton, CA 94517, 925/837-2525 (recorded info) or 925/837-0904 (ranger at kiosk); weather conditions at summit, 925/838-9225; Mount Diablo Interpretive Association, 925/927-7222, www.mdia.org.

146 SENTINEL ROCK / ROCK CITY
0.5–3.0 mi / 2.0 hr 🏃1 ⛰10

in Mount Diablo State Park near Danville

Map 7.3, page 293

Sentinel Rock at Mount Diablo's Rock City is a stunner. You will be forever imprinted by the sight of this sandstone monolith and the adventures that await. The route up is easy enough that even youngsters can make it; yet Half Dome-like cables will give more adventurous hikers a thrill.

The trailhead is near site 20 at the Live Oak campground; however storm damaged has blocked access in recent years. Instead, park on the paved side road for Lower Rock City, cross the road, and look for the trail located next to the restrooms. (There is a mosaic of unsigned trails in the area, and it can be confusing for first-timers.) Follow Wall Point Road to a spur trail (CCC Trail) south to Sentinel Rock. At the base of Sentinel Rock, on the east side, you'll find a carved staircase that signals the trek to the top (cables are set up for safety). Soak in the views, then return on the spur trail to Wall Point Road and continue following that northwest to other sandstone structures: the Wind Caves, Wall Point, Lower Rock City, and Gibraltar Rock. Below Lower Rock City, Gilbralter Rock is the big attraction. On its back side, it's an easy scramble to the top and you can often see rock climbers rappelling down the face.

Note: Mount Diablo is a "dry park." No beer, wine, or alcohol of any kind is permitted.

User Groups: Hikers. No mountain bikes, dogs, horses or wheelchair access on trail. Some wheelchair facilities at a picnic area.

Permits: No permits are required. A state park entrance fee of $10 is charged for each vehicle.

Maps: A trail map is available from Mount Diablo State Park (P.O. Box 346, Walnut Creek, CA 94597; $7.50, including postage). For a topographic map, ask the USGS for Diablo.

Directions: From the Bay Bridge, bear right on I-580 (stay far right) and go 1.5 miles to exit for Highway 24. Take Highway 24 and go 13.4 miles (through the tunnel) to Walnut Creek (stay right) and I-680. Take the exit to I-680 and drive 7.2 miles to Danville and the exit for Diablo Road. Take Diablo Road east for 2.9 miles (at 0.7 mile, jog right to stay on Diablo Road) to Mount Diablo Scenic Boulevard. Turn left and drive 3.8 miles (becomes South Gate Road) to the kiosk at the park entrance. Continue 0.5 mile to the Lower Rock City parking area.

Contact: Mount Diablo State Park, 96 Mitchell Canyon Road, Clayton, CA 94517,

925/837-2525 (recorded info) or 925/837-0904 (ranger at kiosk); weather conditions at summit, 925/838-9225; Mount Diablo Interpretive Association, 925/927-7222, www.mdia.org.

147 HAZEL-ATLAS MINE
1.0–3.0 mi / 1.5 hr

in Black Diamond Mines Regional Preserve near Antioch

Map 7.3, page 293

Here's a chance to combine a hike through pretty foothill country with an underground tour into the Bay Area's landmark coal and silica mines. Black Diamond Mines spans more than 7,500 acres, with 5,315 acres open to the public and a variety of routes amid 57 miles of trails for hiking (dogs permitted), biking, and horseback riding. The trails include valley walks and climbs to ridges for sweeping foothill views, and a 3.2-mile hike with a moderate climb to a backpack-style primitive campground. Plan your trip for the Hazel-Atlas Mine Tour (noon and 3 P.M. Sat.–Sun. Mar.–Nov.).

After passing the park's entrance kiosk (usually staffed only on weekends), drive straight past the first parking area on the left and continue about one mile to the end of the road. A parking area, picnic area, and several trailheads are located here. From this point, take the signed Hazel-Atlas Mine Trail for a short walk up the hill to the mine entrance on the left. (Remember: Access to the mines is permitted by guided tour only). As you near the mine entrance, on hot days you can feel the rush of cool air emerging from deep below the surface. A few dozen hard hats are provided for public use (mandatory); choose from a wooden box set just inside the mine entrance. In the first 400 feet, you follow a rail line to the underground office of the sand mine boss on the left. Peering through the office door, you see an old desk, a variety of old glass bottles, and other vintage accessories. Outside is the switchback for the rail cars.

The tunnel starts out small, and then opens with a series of cavernous chutes above and below you. Lighted stairways provide access to multiple chambers. Some spurs seem dark, deep, and endless, and are walled off by jail cell—like grates. There are multiple levels, and eventually they lead down into the coal mine chambers.

In the spring, this is one of the best of the 150 parks in the Bay Area for wildflower blooms. Deer, squirrels, fox, hawks, and owl are common sightings.

Stewartville Backpack Camp: This public campground requires a 3.2-mile hike with a moderate climb. There is room for 20 people, with picnic tables and a pit toilet available. There is no drinking water (bring your own) and you must pack out all trash. Reservations required.

User Groups: Hikers, dogs, horses, and mountain bikes. The underground tours are accessible for hikers only. Limited wheelchair facilities.

Permits: No permits are required. A parking fee of $5 per vehicle is charged when the kiosk is attended; $2 per dog. Guided tours of the underground mining museum cost $5 per person; tickets can be purchased at the Sidney Flat Visitor Center. The underground Greathouse Visitor Center is free, but is closed 2011–2012 for renovation. Reservations are required for Stewartville Backpack Camp (510/636-1684, $5 per person per night).

Maps: A brochure and map are available at the trailhead. For a free trail map, phone the East Bay Regional Park District toll-free at 888/327-2757, extension 5; follow directions, leave your name and address, and ask for the Black Diamond Mines Regional Preserve brochure. For a topographic map, ask the USGS for Antioch South.

Directions: From the Bay Bridge, take I-80 northeast for 22 miles to the exit for Highway 4/Martinez. Take that exit and continue east on Highway 4 for 25 miles to Exit 26A for Somersville Road. Take that exit, turn right on Auto Center Road/Somersville Road, and

continue 3 miles to the park entrance Continue straight 0.7 mile to the parking lot and trailhead.

Contact: Black Diamond Mines Regional Preserve, 888/327-2757, option 3, extension 4506; East Bay Regional Park District, 2950 Peralta Oaks Court, P.O. Box 5381, Oakland, CA 94605-0381, 888/327-2757, www.ebparks.org.

148 CONTRA LOMA LOOP
1.6 mi / 1.0 hr

in Contra Loma Regional Park near Antioch

Map 7.3, page 293

Most people go to Contra Loma Regional Park to fish, swim, sunbathe, or picnic at Contra Loma Lake. This short loop trail provides an alternative to those activities, tracing along the northwest shore of the lake, then climbing up and over a short hill and looping back to the starting point. From the parking area, head out on the trail to the Cattail Cove Picnic Area. Just after that, the trail turns right, and you'll follow the shore of the lake, pass a fishing pier, and then start a 10-minute climb up a small hill. To close out the loop, glide down the hill. The trail turns left and a mile later returns to the Cattail Cove Picnic Area. A great, easy romp, this hike is best done in spring.

User Groups: Hikers, wheelchairs, dogs, horses, and mountain bikes.

Permits: No permits are required. A parking fee of $5 per vehicle is charged; $2 for dogs. An additional fee is charged for access to the swim lagoon.

Maps: A brochure and map are available at the trailhead. For a free trail map, phone the East Bay Regional Park District toll-free at 888/327-2757, extension 5; follow directions, leave your name and address, and ask for the Contra Loma Regional Park brochure. For a topographic map, ask the USGS for Antioch South.

Directions: From Highway 4 in Antioch, take the Lone Tree Way exit and drive south to

Golf Course Road. Turn right, drive to Frederickson Lane, bear right, and drive to the gate. Turn right, pass the kiosk, and bear left. Drive to the parking lot by the beach.

Contact: Contra Loma Regional Park, 888/327-2757, option 3, extension 4518, or 510/544-3151; East Bay Regional Park District, 2950 Peralta Oaks Court, P.O. Box 5381, Oakland, CA 94605-0381, 888/327-2757, www.ebparks.org.

149 VOLVON LOOP TRAIL / BOB WALKER RIDGE

5.7 mi / 3.0 hr   👫3 ⛰9

in the Morgan Territory Regional Preserve north of Livermore

Map 7.3, page 293

Morgan Territory Regional Preserve is located within the traditional homeland of the Volvon, one of five historical Indian nations in the Mount Diablo area. This trail, named after the first people to live here, is the preserve's featured hike. You can create an easy 5.7-mile loop, tracing along a ridge as it rises along sandstone hills to a ridgeline with terrific views.

The staging area is set near the ridge at 1,900 feet. Start the trip by heading up the short hill (a 100-foot climb) on the Volvon Trail and then continue over the other side a short distance to the T (about 0.5 mile from the trailhead) at the intersection of the Blue Oak Trail. At the T-intersection, scan across the meadow ahead and to your right and look for the sandstone rocks on the edge of the meadow. You can find a series of bowls in the rock that the Ohlone Indians used for grinding the seeds of acorn into paste and leeching out (with water) the bitter taste.

Then it's on to Bob Walker Ridge. Head back and out north on the Blue Oak Trail and hike 1.3 miles to the Valley View Trail; a Porta-potty is located here and you will pass a few other signed trail junctions. The trail meanders in and out of sub-ridge valleys, green and sprinkled with a few wildflowers in the spring, and is easy all the way. Continue right on the Valley View Trail and continue to Bob Walker Ridge. Here the trail is routed northward on a ranch road to a rounded mountain peak. There are beautiful views of Los Vaqueros Reservoir, as well as below to Round Valley, to the San Joaquin Valley to the east and Mount Diablo to the north.

The Loop Trail circles Bob Walker Ridge in a left-turning horseshoe and then links up again with the Volvon Trail. From here the Volvon Trail runs all the way back to the trailhead. As you near the parking lot, you can take a shortcut by turning right on the Concor Trail and then coasting downhill to the staging area. You can also extend the trip a mile by returning on the Corral Trail/Coyote Trail (hikers only, a good choice on weekends when the bikes are out).

The ridge was named in the 1990s for Bob Walker, a landscape photographer and open-space advocate who helped ensure that Morgan Territory was added to the East Bay Regional Park District. This parkland is most beautiful in the spring, and not just because the hills are greened up; one of the best wildflower displays in the Bay Area occurs here at that time. The one downer: too many cows.

User Groups: The first half of the loop is accessible to hikers, dogs, horses, and mountain bikes. The second half is for hikers and dogs only. No wheelchair facilities.

Permits: No permits are required. Parking and access are free.

Maps: A brochure and map are available at the trailhead. For a free trail map, phone the East Bay Regional Park District toll-free at 888/327-2757, extension 5; follow directions, leave your name and address, and ask for the Morgan Territory Regional Preserve brochure. For a topographic map, ask the USGS for Tassajara.

Directions: From I-580 in Livermore, take the N. Livermore Avenue exit and turn north. Drive to the junction of Morgan Territory Road and turn right. Drive 10.7 miles (narrow, drive slow) to the staging area on the right side of the road.

From I-680 in Concord, take the Clayton Road exit and head east. Clayton Road becomes Marsh Creek Road. Continue to Morgan Territory Road. Turn right and drive 9.4 miles (narrow, drive slow) to the staging area on the left side of the road.

Contact: Morgan Territory Regional Preserve, 888/327-2757, option 3, extension 4546, or 925/757-2620 (c/o Black Diamond); East Bay Regional Park District, 2950 Peralta Oaks Court, P.O. Box 5381, Oakland, CA 94605-0381, 888/327-2757, www.ebparks.org.

150 ROUND VALLEY LOOP
6.0 mi / 3.0 hr 🏃1 ⛰7

Round Valley Regional Preserve in the Mount Diablo Foothills

Map 7.3, page 293

Round Valley Regional Preserve sits in a beautiful pocket below the ridge line that extends from the southeast flank of Mount Diablo, located off Marsh Creek Road. This park is a great backroad discovery and the pay off on this nearly flat hike is seeing the bedrock mortars used for acorn grinding.

The trip starts with a pretty drive into the foothills of Contra Costa County. The park entrance is actually a staging area—a gravel parking lot with chemical toilets. This is the gateway to the 2,024-acre preserve. After parking, begin the trek by crossing a bridge. You then bear right on a service road that runs along Round Valley Creek and continues west to gain entry into Round Valley. The route extends 2.82 miles (as measured by an odometer wheel) to a junction with the Murphy's Meadow Trail. At Murphy's Meadow Trail, look to the left for a nearby grove of oaks. Hidden beneath them is a series of 10 bowl-like mortars in the rock, where Native Americans once met to grind acorns, leech out the bitter taste with water, and turn it into flour.

As you hike amid this riparian-oak woodland habitat, keep a lookout on the valley floor for wildlife, and to the air for raptors. This area is loaded with ground squirrels, and they can pop up and down like a game of pop-goes-the-weasel. Because of the high squirrel population, there are an equally high numbers of raptors that feed on them, with lots of red-tailed hawks, but also golden eagles, prairie falcons, owls, and turkey vultures.

User Groups: Hikers, dogs, horses, and mountain bikes. No wheelchair facilities. Dogs are not permitted in the adjoining Los Vaqueros Watershed to the south.

Permits: No permits are required. Parking and access are free.

Maps: A brochure and map are available at the trailhead. For a free trail map, phone the East Bay Regional Park District toll-free at 888/327-2757, extension 5; follow directions, leave your name and address, and ask for the Round Valley Regional Park brochure. For a topographic map, ask the USGS for Diablo.

Directions: From Walnut Creek: Take I-680 south to the exit for Ygnacio Valley Road. Take that exit, turn east and drive to Clayton Road. Turn right (east) on Clayton Road and go to merge with Marsh Creek Road. Turn right and go 13 miles (1.7 miles past Deer Valley Road) to staging area on right.

Alternate route from Livermore: Take I-580 east to the exit for Vasco Avenue. Take that exit, turn north on Vasco and go 12 miles to Camino Diablo Road. Turn left and go to junction with Marsh Creek Road and continue north 1.5 miles to the staging area on left.

Contact: Round Valley Regional Preserve, 888/327-2757, option 3, extension 4556, or (c/o Black Diamond Preserve) 925/757-2620; East Bay Regional Park District, 2950 Peralta Oaks Court, P.O. Box 5381, Oakland, CA 94605-0381, 888/327-2757, www.ebparks.org.

151 COGSWELL MARSH LOOP

2.8 mi / 1.5 hr   🥾1 ⛰️8

at Hayward Regional Shoreline on South San
Francisco Bay in Hayward

Map 7.3, page 293

Cogswell Marsh is the heart of an 800-acre
marsh wetlands. This is a great place to take
short nature hikes and try to identify many
rare birds. It's always a good choice for viewing shorebirds. As a bonus, peregrine falcons
are typically seen either hovering over the
marsh or perched on power pylons. Hikers
have documented that as many as 200 white
pelicans have been seen here, along with the
occasional merlin. From the parking area,
the trail starts with a 0.37-mile hike across
landfill; then it enters the marshlands, where
a loop trail circles the most vital habitat. To
keep your feet from getting wet, two short
sections are bridged. The loop is best hiked
clockwise, so you face the Bay Bridge and the
San Francisco skyline (an outstanding view) as
you walk along the water's edge of the South
Bay—very pretty. Guided weekend nature
walks are available.

User Groups: Hikers and mountain bikes.
No dogs (south of flood control channel) or
horses. No wheelchair facilities.

Permits: No permits are required. Parking
and access are free.

Maps: A brochure and map are available at
the trailhead. For a free trail map, phone the
East Bay Regional Park District toll-free at
888/327-2757, extension 5; follow directions,
leave your name and address, and ask for the
Hayward Regional Shoreline brochure. For
a topographic map, ask the USGS for San
Leandro.

Directions: From I-880 in Hayward, take
the West Winton Avenue exit and follow the
road west toward the bay to the entrance and
parking area.

Contact: Hayward Regional Shoreline,
888/327-2757, option 3, extension 4531, or
510/783-1066; East Bay Regional Park District, 2950 Peralta Oaks Court, P.O. Box 5381,
Oakland, CA 94605-0381, 888/327-2757,
www.ebparks.org.

152 EAST BAY SKYLINE NATIONAL TRAIL

31.0 mi one-way /
2-4 days   🥾3 ⛰️8

from Lake Chabot Regional Park to Wildcat
Canyon Regional Park

Map 7.3, page 293

A 31-mile trail along the East Bay's skyline
offers a unique opportunity for a long-distance hike that can be chopped into many
short segments over the course of days or even
weeks. The trail spans from the Castro Valley
foothills northward to the ridgeline behind
Richmond, crossing six regional parks for a
view into the area's prettiest and wildest lands.
The East Bay Skyline National Trail can be
hiked from south to north in two days, but it
can also be divided into seven sections from
the different access points at the parking areas.
Bicycles and horses are permitted on 65 percent of the trail, where it is wide enough to
accommodate them.

It is a great trip, whether you do it all in
one weekend or cover a bit at a time over several weeks. No permits are needed, leashed
dogs are allowed in undeveloped areas or as
posted, and access is free. There are no campgrounds directly along the way, but you can
use a shuttle car and come back to do a different section each day. The marked absence
of piped drinking water along much of the
route is another drawback. Water is available
at only four points over the 31 miles, at Lomas
Cantadas, Sibley Preserve, Skyline Gate, and
Bort Meadow. So come prepared with two
full canteens per person, along with a hat and
sunscreen. Following are detailed descriptions
of the trail from south to north.

**Proctor Gate to Bort Meadow, Lake Chabot
and Anthony Chabot Regional Park:** The
Brandon Trail starts adjacent to Willow Park
Public Golf Course and is routed up a ridge.

It then meanders on a ranch road in Anthony Chabot Regional Park. At Stonebridge (don't turn left at the trail junction!), the trail leads into Grass Valley and on to Bort Meadow. Distance: 6.5 miles; climbs 600 feet, then drops 320 feet.

Directions: From I-580 in Oakland, take the 35th Avenue exit and drive east (35th Avenue becomes Redwood Road). Drive on Redwood Road to the Proctor Gate Staging Area, located on the east border of the park, next to Willow Park Public Golf Course.

Bort Meadow to MacDonald Gate, Anthony Chabot Regional Park: If you are hiking the entire East Bay National Skyline Trail, the trail climbs steeply out of Bort Meadow. If you are starting at the parking area, however, no such climb is needed. The trail becomes a service road, from which you can turn and look south for the great view of Grass Valley. Hikers are completely exposed on the ascent; it's hot and dry in the afternoon, so it's best to go early in the morning. Once on top, it's an easy hike, with many wildflowers in spring. It then descends into a canyon, and drops you into MacDonald Staging Area. Continue on MacDonald Trail a very short distance to Big Bear Staging Area (hikers only, no bicycles). You will cross Redwood Road, putting you at the entrance to Redwood Regional Park. Bikers can exit on to Redwood Road, but should use caution. Distance: 2.7 miles; climbs 300 feet, then drops 500 feet.

Directions: From I-580 in Oakland, take the 35th Avenue exit and drive east (35th Avenue becomes Redwood Road). Drive on Redwood Road three miles past Skyline Boulevard to the Bort Meadow Staging Area, on the right.

MacDonald Gate to Skyline Gate, Redwood Regional Park: Hikers have two options here, and the suggested route is to split off at French Trail to hike up the canyon bottom on Stream Trail, enveloped by redwoods. Note that bikes are banned from this section. The alternative, a must-do for bikers, is to take West Ridge Trail for a steep climb to the canyon rim, then drop to the junction at Skyline Gate. Distance:

five miles; French Trail drops 200 feet, then climbs 400 feet; West Ridge Trail climbs 900 feet, then drops 200 feet.

Directions: From I-580 to the west or I-680 to the east, take Highway 24 to Highway 13 and go south. Drive to Redwood Road and turn left. Go straight at the stop sign, then turn right onto Redwood Road at the light. Continue driving east on Redwood Road for 1.7 miles from the intersection of Skyline and turn right into the MacDonald Gate Staging Area.

Skyline Gate through Huckleberry Preserve to Sibley Preserve: This section of trail is a choice hike for nature lovers, who will see an abundance of birdlife and other animals, especially in the early morning and late evening. The trail passes through a deciduous woodland habitat, with a short but quite steep climb after entering Huckleberry Preserve. Distance: three miles; drops 200 feet, then climbs 480 feet.

Directions: From Highway 24 in Oakland, drive east to Highway 13. Go south and drive to Joaquin Miller Road, then head east until you hit Skyline Boulevard. Turn left on Skyline Boulevard and drive to the Skyline Gate Staging Area.

Sibley Preserve to Lomas Cantadas, Tilden Regional Park: A unique section of trail, this part crosses over the Caldecott Tunnel in a relatively unpeopled area. Many hawks are seen here, a nice bonus. Sibley is best known for its volcanic past, and hikers can take a side trip to Round Top Peak (see the *Round Top Loop Trail* listing in this chapter). This area was a volcanic region 10 million years ago, when the Hayward and Moraga fault systems greatly uplifted this land. Bicycles are permitted on the section of the Skyline Trail between Sibley Staging Area (6800 Skyline Blvd.) to Old Tunnel Staging Area. Distance: 3.4 miles; drops 300 feet, then climbs 600 feet.

Directions: From I-580 to the west or I-680 to the east, drive to Highway 24. Continue to just east of the Caldecott Tunnel and take the Fish Ranch Road exit northwest to Grizzly

Peak Boulevard. Turn left and drive to Skyline Boulevard. The park entrance and parking area are on the left.

Lomas Cantadas to Inspiration Point, Tilden Regional Park: This section of trail starts at a major access area off Grizzly Peak Boulevard. Also possible is an adjacent side trip to Vollmer Peak, the highest point on East Bay Skyline National Trail. The trail is then routed north to Inspiration Point at Wildcat Canyon Road, another well-known access point, losing elevation most of the way. Many sweeping views of the East Bay's untouched foothills are found on this hike. Distance: three miles; drops 860 feet.

Directions: From I-580 to the west or I-680 to the east, drive to Highway 24. Continue to just east of the Caldecott Tunnel and take the Fish Ranch Road exit to Grizzly Peak Boulevard. At the stop sign, turn right and drive on Grizzly Peak Boulevard to Lomas Cantadas Road. Turn right, then immediately turn left, following the signs for the Steam Train to the parking area.

Inspiration Point (Tilden Regional Park) to Wildcat Canyon Regional Park: The last stretch starts at the most heavily used section of the entire route, then crosses its most dramatic and unpeopled terrain. From Inspiration Point, the trail is actually paved for four miles—ideal for bicycles and wheelchairs. Beyond that, the trail turns to dirt and traces San Pablo Ridge, with inspiring views in all directions before dropping steeply into Wildcat Canyon Regional Park in the Richmond foothills. Distance: 7.2 miles; drops 800 feet.

Directions: From I-580 to the west or I-680 to the east, drive to Highway 24. Continue to just east of the Caldecott Tunnel and take the Fish Ranch Road exit northwest to Grizzly Peak Boulevard. Turn right, drive up the hill, and turn right on South Park Drive. Drive one mile to Wildcat Canyon Road, bear right, and drive to the parking area at Inspiration Point, on the left.

Alternate Route: To avoid South Park Drive,

which is sometimes closed in the winter due to newt migrations, from Highway 24 go through the Caldecott Tunnel and exit at Orinda. Turn left on Camino Pablo. Drive north for about two miles, then turn left on Wildcat Canyon Road. Follow the road to Inspiration Point on the right.

User Groups: Hikers, dogs, horses, and mountain bikes. Horses and mountain bikes are restricted in some sections. Also see individual trailhead listings.

Permits: No permits are required. Access is free, but a parking fee may be charged at some trailheads.

Maps: For a map of the East Bay Skyline National Trail, contact the East Bay Regional Park District and request the individual regional parks map brochures (the Skyline Trail map brochure is no longer in print).

Directions: See individual trailhead listings for specific directions.

Contact: East Bay Regional Park District, 2950 Peralta Oaks Court, P.O. Box 5381, Oakland, CA 94605-0381, 888/327-2757, www.ebparks.org.

153 DON CASTRO LAKE LOOP

1.7 mi / 1.0 hr 🏃1 ⛰6

in the Don Castro Regional Recreation Area in the Castro Valley foothills

Map 7.3, page 293

Don Castro is a small (23 acres) but pretty lake that attracts swimmers to its lagoon and its clear, warm, blue waters. Hiking is typically an afterthought for visitors, who come primarily to picnic or fish. The trail (actually, it's a road) is routed completely around the lake for an easy walk or jog in a nice setting. From the parking area, circle the lake in a clockwise direction. You will pass a fishing pier and the swimming lagoon. The route continues to the headwaters of the lake at San Lorenzo Creek, crossing the creek. After climbing a short staircase, you will be on top and can hike over the dam and back to the parking area. It's an easy circle.

User Groups: Hikers and dogs. Portions of the trail are paved for bicycle and wheelchair use. No horses.

Permits: No permits are required. An entrance fee of $5 per vehicle is charged when the kiosk is attended; $2 for dogs. A swimming fee is extra.

Maps: A brochure and map are available at the trailhead. For a free trail map, phone the East Bay Regional Park District toll-free at 888/327-2757, extension 5; follow directions, leave your name and address, and ask for the Don Castro Regional Recreation Area brochure. For a topographic map, ask the USGS for Hayward.

Directions: From eastbound I-580 in Castro Valley, take the Center Street exit. Turn right and drive to Kelly Street. Turn left and drive 0.5 mile to Woodroe. Turn left on Woodroe and drive to the park entrance.

From westbound I-580, take the Grove Way exit and drive west on East Castro Valley Boulevard to Grove Way. Turn left and drive to Center Street. Drive 0.5 mile, turn left, and drive to Kelly Street. Make another left on Kelly Street and drive to Woodroe. Turn left and drive to the park entrance.

Contact: Don Castro Regional Recreation Area, 888/327-2757, option 3, extension 4527, or 510/544-3073; East Bay Regional Park District, 2950 Peralta Oaks Court, P.O. Box 5381, Oakland, CA 94605-0381, 888/327-2757, www.ebparks.org.

154 LOS VAQUEROS TRAIL
1–13.0 mi one-way / 0.5 hr–1 day

 1   △ 8

at Los Vaqueros Reservoir near Livermore

Map 7.3, page 293

The Los Vaqueros Trail starts at the marina area and extends halfway around the lake. You get gorgeous views, wildflowers, lots of ground squirrels, and raptor sightings. The trail ranges 1–13 miles and you'll return on the same route. Most people just head out for a mile or two, have a picnic, then return. Golden eagles nest along this route every spring; to protect nesting bald eagles, several trails are often closed in the spring.

Note: In 2012 and 2013, this trail will be rerouted to higher ground to facilitate the raising of the dam and the size of the lake as it doubles.

Los Vaqueros is set in a foothill valley between Livermore and Brentwood, bordered by Morgan Territory and Round Valley regional preserves. In the mid-1990s, the canvas was blank when water officials started flooding the sprawling foothill valley north of Livermore to create Los Vaqueros Reservoir. Nature then took over as the chief artist and with many sweeping brush strokes from heavy winter rains, the picture is now near complete. The watershed lands span 18,500 acres. With the adjoining wildlands, there are roughly 225 square miles of contiguous greenbelt and 55 miles of trails.

User Groups: Hikers only; youth ages 12–17 must not hike alone; those under 12 years old must hike with an adult. No mountain bikes, dogs, or horses. Limited wheelchair facilities. Mountain bikes permitted on ranch-style roads elsewhere in watershed.

Permits: No permits are required. A fee of $6 per car is charged. No alcohol is allowed. Helmets are required for all bike riders. No privately owned boats permitted.

Maps: A brochure and map are available online and at the Interpretive Center (9 A.M.–4 P.M. Fri.–Sun.).

Directions: From San Francisco, take I-80 east over Bay Bridge to the split with I-580. Bear right on I-580 and drive 34 miles to Livermore. Continue east on I-580 to Vasco Road. Take Vasco Road north and drive 4 miles to Los Vaqueros Road. Turn left and drive to South Gate entrance station, then continue to marina.

Contact: Los Vaqueros Marina, 925/371-2628; Los Vaqueros information hotline, 925/688-8225, www.ccwater.com/losvaqueros.

155 HIGH RIDGE LOOP
3.3 mi / 2.0 hr

in Garin Regional Park in the Hayward foothills

Map 7.3, page 293

The hilltops in Garin Regional Park render sweeping views of the East Bay foothills westward to South San Francisco Bay, the number-one attraction at this 3,000-acre parkland. The hills span for miles, and in the fall there are times late in the day when sunbeams will pour through openings between cumulus clouds, creating a divine scene. Of the 20 miles of trails in the park, Ridge Loop Trail is the best way to see the surrounding wildlands, primarily oak grasslands amid rolling foothills.

From the parking area (at 380 feet), follow the Vista Peak Loop Trail 0.25 mile past the picnic areas and Arroyo Flats Group Camp, and through the gate. Then turn left and follow Vista Peak Loop Trail up the hill past the metal corral. In another 0.25 mile, turn right at the intersection and follow the trail in a clockwise direction. You will climb 550 feet in a mile to top out at Vista Peak (934 feet), and shortly after, Garin Peak (948 feet). Take your time and enjoy the views.

User Groups: Hikers, dogs, horses, and mountain bikes. No wheelchair facilities.

Permits: No permits are required. An entrance fee of $5 per vehicle is charged when the kiosk is attended; $2 for dogs.

Maps: A brochure and map are available at the trailhead. For a free trail map, phone the East Bay Regional Park District toll-free at 888/327-2757, extension 5; follow directions, leave your name and address, and ask for the Garin and Dry Creek Pioneer Regional Parks brochure. For a topographic map, ask the USGS for Hayward.

Directions: From Fremont, take Highway 238 (Mission Boulevard) north through Union City to Garin Avenue. Turn right onto Garin Avenue and drive one mile to the park entrance.

Contact: Garin Regional Park, 888/327-2757, option 3, extension 4530, or 510/538-0139; East Bay Regional Park District, 2950 Peralta Oaks Court, P.O. Box 5381, Oakland, CA 94605-0381, 888/327-2757, www.ebparks.org.

156 BAYVIEW TRAIL
3.0 mi / 1.5 hr

in Coyote Hills Regional Park on the shore of the South Bay near Fremont

Map 7.3, page 293

Coyote Hills Regional Park's rich history is visible throughout its 966 acres: four Indian shell middens (heaps of discarded shells from ancient tribes, who ate a lot of shellfish) can be seen. The Bayview Trail is the favorite hike in the park, offering excellent views of the South Bay. This walk circles the park, including a 1.5-mile stretch that borders the bay and a shorter piece that runs adjacent to a marsh. The park is a wildlife sanctuary, with grassy hills and marshes that provide significant habitat for numerous migrating waterfowl. The best way to hike this loop is in a counterclockwise direction from the main parking area. For a short but enjoyable side trip from the main parking area, take the wooden boardwalk out through the north marsh. A must is stopping in at the visitors center and checking out the canoe that rangers made out of tules and then paddled across the bay.

User Groups: Hikers, dogs, horses, and mountain bikes. The trail is paved and is technically wheelchair accessible but is quite steep in some sections.

Permits: No permits are required. An entrance fee of $5 per vehicle is charged when the kiosk is attended; $2 for dogs.

Maps: A brochure and map are available at the trailhead. For a free trail map, phone the East Bay Regional Park District toll-free at 888/327-2757, extension 5; follow directions, leave your name and address, and ask for the Coyote Hills Regional Park brochure. For a topographic map, ask the USGS for Newark.

Directions: From Fremont, drive west on Highway 84 to the Paseo Padre Parkway exit. Turn right on Paseo Padre Parkway and drive to Patterson Ranch Road. Turn left and drive to the parking area.

From I-880 in Fremont, take the Highway 84/Decoto Road exit and drive on Highway 84 to Paseo Padre Parkway. Proceed as above.

From the Peninsula: Turn east on Highway 84, cross the Dumbarton Bridge, and take the Thornton Avenue exit. Turn left (the road becomes Paseo Padre Parkway) and drive north to Patterson Ranch Road. Turn left on Patterson Ranch Road and drive to the parking area.

Contact: Coyote Hills Regional Park, Visitors Center, 8000 Patterson Ranch Road, Fremont, CA 94555, 888/327-2757, option 3, extension 4519, or 510/795-9385; East Bay Regional Park District, 2950 Peralta Oaks Court, P.O. Box 5381, Oakland, CA 94605-0381, 888/327-2757, www.ebparks.org.

157 RIDGELINE TRAIL
7.0 mi / 4.0 hr   🥾3 ⛰️8

in Pleasanton Ridge Regional Park west of Pleasanton

Map 7.3, page 293

People often overlook Pleasanton Ridge Regional Park, not knowing it offers a quiet, natural setting with excellent views from Ridgeline Trail. Development in and around the park has purposely been limited so the surroundings could retain as natural a feel as possible. The plan has succeeded, and the best way to experience it is on this hike. The Ridgeline Trail climbs to elevations of 1,600 feet, with the northern sections giving way to sweeping views featuring miles of rolling foothills and valleys at the threshold of Mount Diablo. From the parking area, elevation 300 feet, start hiking on Oak Tree Trail, which is routed 1.4 miles up to Ridgeline Trail, climbing 750 feet. Turn right and hike two miles along the ridge. You can return on a loop route

by turning left on Thermalito Trail, which is recommended.

User Groups: Hikers, dogs, horses, and mountain bikes. No wheelchair facilities.

Permits: No permits are required. Parking and access are free.

Maps: A brochure and map are available at the trailhead. For a free trail map, phone the East Bay Regional Park District toll-free at 888/327-2757, extension 5; follow directions, leave your name and address, and ask for the Pleasanton Ridge Regional Park brochure. For a topographic map, ask the USGS for Dublin.

Directions: From I-680 in Pleasanton, take the Bernal Road exit west and drive to Foothill Road. Turn left and drive three miles to the parking area and information center on the right.

Contact: Pleasanton Ridge Regional Park, 888/327-2757, option 3, extension 4549, or 925/931-1335; East Bay Regional Park District, 2950 Peralta Oaks Court, P.O. Box 5381, Oakland, CA 94605-0381, 888/327-2757, www.ebparks.org.

158 NORTH ARROYO TRAIL
1.3 mi / 0.75 hr   🥾1 ⛰️6

in the Shadow Cliffs Regional Recreation Area in Pleasanton

Map 7.3, page 293

Though you can't walk all the way around Shadow Cliffs Lake, you can explore a series of smaller ponds in the Arroyo area. There's no place else like it in the East Bay. From the back of the first parking area, you take a trail over the top of a levee and down to the shore of the first pond. Then just follow North Arroyo Trail along the shores of several ponds for about 0.5 mile. For a view of the ponds, make the short climb up the adjacent levee. These ponds are water holes left over from a gravel quarry. Shadow Cliffs Lake, the biggest pond covering some 80 acres, has been stocked with trout and catfish and can be one of the better fishing spots in the East Bay. It is also a good place to swim. The lake often has better clarity than any other lake in the Bay Area.

User Groups: Hikers and dogs. Portions of the trail are accessible to horses and mountain bikes, and wheelchair facilities are available.

Permits: No permits are required. A fee of $6 per vehicle is charged for parking; $2 for dogs.

Maps: A brochure and map are available at the trailhead. For a free trail map, phone the East Bay Regional Park District toll-free at 888/327-2757, extension 5; follow directions, leave your name and address, and ask for the Shadow Cliffs Regional Recreation Area brochure. For a topographic map, ask the USGS for Livermore.

Directions: From I-580 in Pleasanton, take Santa Rita Road south. Drive two miles, turn left on Valley Avenue, and drive about one mile to Stanley Boulevard. Turn left and drive 1.5 miles to the park entrance on the right.

Contact: Shadow Cliffs Regional Recreation Area, 888/327-2757, option 3, extension 4557, or 510/544-3236; East Bay Regional Park District, 2950 Peralta Oaks Court, P.O. Box 5381, Oakland, CA 94605-0381, 888/327-2757, www.ebparks.org.

159 DUMBARTON BRIDGE
4.5 mi / 2.5 hr 👥2 ⛰7

on the Dumbarton Bridge from Fremont to East Palo Alto

Map 7.3, page 293

Let this be a lesson for future bridge designers. When the Dumbarton Bridge was constructed, a biking and hiking path was added along the south side of the roadway, separated from traffic by a cement cordon. That means you can safely hike to the top of the center span for a unique view of the South Bay. The one downer is the car noise; there's just no way to get away from it. This hike is best started from the Fremont side of the bridge, because it is unsafe to leave cars unattended at the western foot of the bridge, in East Palo Alto.

Special Note: The bridge is a link in a unique bicycle trip. Start at Alameda Creek Regional Trail in Niles, head over the Dumbarton Bridge, turn left on the Baylands Trail, and ride through Palo Alto; then go farther south at Charleston Slough on Baylands Trail to Mountain View Baylands.

User Groups: Hikers, wheelchairs, and mountain bikes. No dogs or horses.

Permits: No permits are required. Parking and access are free.

Maps: For a topographic map, ask the USGS for Newark.

Directions: From Redwood City, head east on Highway 84 and cross the Dumbarton Bridge. Take the first exit after the toll plaza, Thornton Avenue. Turn right and drive 0.25 mile to Marshland Road. Turn right and drive four miles to the parking area at the fishing pier.

Contact: Don Edwards San Francisco Bay National Wildlife Refuge, 9500 Thornton Avenue, Newark, CA 94560, 510/792-0222, http://desfbay.fws.gov.

160 TIDELANDS TRAIL
2.5 mi / 1.5 hr 👥1 ⛰7

in the San Francisco Bay National Wildlife Refuge at the eastern foot of the Dumbarton Bridge

Map 7.3, page 293

Bird-watchers from the East Bay make regular trips to San Francisco Bay National Wildlife Refuge. That is because this Refuge provides a resting spot on the Pacific Flyway, where more than 250 species in a given year use this habitat for food, resting space, and nesting sites. It is not unusual to see a half-dozen species of ducks, an egret, a sandpiper, a willet, and herons in just 15 or 20 minutes. The refuge is big, covering 23,000 acres in all, and the Tidelands Trail pours right through it. This is actually a wide dirt pathway on a levee routed amid salt marsh and bay tidewaters. At first arrival, it does not appear very pretty, but it gets better. The views of the South Bay and (on clear days) the surrounding foothills are a panoramic urban backdrop. Don't forget to stop by refuge headquarters before your hike to see the exhibits and pamphlets, which will make your walk more enjoyable. Group nature tours on this trail are offered regularly on weekends.

User Groups: Hikers, dogs, and mountain bikes. There are no wheelchair facilities, but the trail can be navigated by most wheelchair users. No horses.

Permits: No permits are required. Parking and access are free.

Maps: For a free brochure, contact the refuge. For a topographic map, ask the USGS for Newark.

Directions: From San Francisco, drive south on US 101 to the Willow Road–Dumbarton exit. Drive east across the Dumbarton Bridge and take the first exit (Thornton Avenue) after the toll plaza. Turn right and drive 0.25 mile to Marshland Road. Turn right and drive a short distance to the visitors center.

Contact: Don Edwards San Francisco Bay National Wildlife Refuge, 9500 Thornton Avenue, Newark, CA 94560, 510/792-0222, http://desfbay.fws.gov.

walk out to the end of the pier also renders pretty sea views of the South Bay's shoreline. Looking north on a clear day, you can see the city of San Francisco as well as the San Mateo and Bay Bridges.

User Groups: Hikers, wheelchairs, and mountain bikes. No dogs or horses.

Permits: No permits are required. Parking and access are free.

Maps: For a free brochure, contact the refuge. For a topographic map, ask the USGS for Newark.

Directions: From San Francisco, drive south on US 101 to the Willow Road–Dumbarton exit. Drive east across the Dumbarton Bridge and take the first exit (Thornton Avenue) after the toll plaza. Turn right and drive to Marshlands Road. Turn right again and drive past the San Francisco Bay National Wildlife Refuge entrance and visitors center for about three miles, following the signs to Dumbarton Pier (and the entrance to a leg of the San Francisco Bay bicycle trail).

Contact: Don Edwards San Francisco Bay National Wildlife Refuge, 9500 Thornton Avenue, Newark, CA 94560, 510/792-0222, http://desfbay.fws.gov.

161 DUMBARTON PIER
1.0 mi / 0.5 hr 👣1 ⛰6

in South San Francisco Bay in the San Francisco Bay National Wildlife Refuge in Fremont

Map 7.3, page 293

This pier was once the old Dumbarton Bridge. But when the current high-rise span was built in the 1980s, the roadway extending from Fremont was converted to a fishing pier and was made part of the San Francisco Bay National Wildlife Refuge. The pier reaches to the channel of the South Bay, a natural migratory pathway for sharks (in the summer), bat rays (winter), sturgeon (winter), perch (late fall), and jacksmelt (spring). Many seabirds and waterfowl live in this area year-round. The easy

162 ALAMEDA CREEK REGIONAL TRAIL
1–13.6 mi one-way / 0.5–6.0 hr
👣1 ⛰7

on Alameda Creek from Niles to the South Bay

Map 7.3, page 293

An unusual solution to the biker-versus-hiker conflict has been implemented here with the construction of a double trail. Two trails, one on each side of Alameda Creek, are routed from Niles Community Park to the shoreline of the South Bay. The trail on the north bank is designed for horseback riders and hikers. The one on the south bank is paved, perfect for bicyclists and joggers. Markers set at 0.25-mile intervals help joggers keep track of their exact distances. From Niles, the trail goes past Shinn Pond, Alameda Creek Quarries, and Coyote Hills Regional Park. For access to Coyote Hills Regional Park and the San Francisco Bay National Wildlife Refuge, take the trail on the south side of the creek; there is no direct access to either of those areas on the northside trail.

Technically, the Alameda Creek Regional Trail is 11 miles one-way. But you can't end the trip at the end of the trail; the nearest access point is at Coyote Regional Park. That means hiking back two miles to a short cutoff and going another 0.6 mile to the visitor center for a total of 13.6 miles. We recommend it— this is the prettiest part of the trail. Another alternative is to continue on the mud levies to the No Name Trail and get to Coyote Hills Regional Park by that route; that would make it about 14.5 miles.

User Groups: South Trail: Hikers, dogs, and mountain bikes. North Trail: Hikers, dogs, and horses. No wheelchair facilities.

Permits: No permits are required. Parking and access are free.

Maps: A brochure and map are available at the trailhead. For a free trail map, phone the East Bay Regional Park District toll-free at 888/327-2757, extension 5; follow directions, leave your name and address, and ask for the Alameda Creek Regional Trail brochure. For a topographic map, ask the USGS for Niles.

Directions: From I-680 in Fremont, take the Mission Boulevard exit and drive west to Highway 84/Niles Canyon Road. Turn right and make another immediate right on Old Canyon Road. The staging area is on the left.

Contact: Alameda Creek Regional Trail, 510/790-2612 (c/o Quarry Lakes) or 888/327-2757, option 3, extension 4552; East Bay Regional Park District, 2950 Peralta Oaks Court, P.O. Box 5381, Oakland, CA 94605-0381, 888/327-2757, www.ebparks.org.

163 MISSION PEAK TRAIL
7.0 mi / 4.0 hr   🏃4 ⛰8

in the Mission Peak Regional Preserve near Fremont

Map 7.3, page 293

Breathtaking views of the South Bay, wildflowers galore, and a memorable perspective of the Bay Area are the rewards for those who take on the climb to the top of Mission Peak. Among the mainstream public, this is one of the Bay Area's lesser-known peaks, but it's still incredibly popular—even crowded—for those who know and love it. At 2,517 feet, it looms over the Ohlone College campus in Fremont and the South Bay. Yet Mount Hamilton, Mount Diablo, and Mount Umunhum dwarf Mission Peak in size and stature, and for that reason, some overlook it; that equals your gain, others' loss. Hot days don't work here because this tromp to the top features a climb of 2,000 feet in a span of about 3.5 miles (a round-trip of just under 7 miles).

The trailhead is at the end of Stanford Avenue, a short drive from either I-880 or I-680, where you will find a parking area and gated trailhead with a box that contains a free brochure/map from the East Bay Regional Park District. From the parking area, you get a good view up the slopes to the east of the awaiting landscape: rolling grassland foothills cut by a few tree-filled ravines and a barren ridge that promises a great lookout.

Start the trip by taking the Ohlone Wilderness Trail/Hidden Valley Trail, the left fork at the trailhead, well-signed and mapped. The trail is a dirt road, crumbling in spots. As you rise up, the views start quickly of the South Bay, and then beyond across the Santa Clara Valley. Although there is a network of routes that eventually can be linked to the top, the best route is to stay on the Ohlone Wilderness Trail up to the foot of the last summit rise. Here you will reach the Peak Trail. Turn right and climb the last half mile to the summit (ignore the left fork you will pass). The summit is marked by a post. Everybody, and we mean everybody, touches the darn thing. It's like part ceremony, part official procedure.

The views provide a stunning new outlook on a familiar homeland. On clear days, all the prominent peaks in the Bay Area come into view, Tamalpais, Diablo, Hamilton and Umunhum, and to the distant east, you can see the snow-crested Sierra. There must be 100 points of sunlit charm in a 50-mile radius that stand out as landmarks. Other highlights are high numbers of hawks out hovering in rising thermals, and on some weekends, a number of hang gliders joining them. A herd of feral goats used to roam wild in this area, but the last one died a few years ago.

User Groups: Hikers, dogs, and horses. No mountain bikes. No wheelchair facilities.

Permits: No permits are required. Parking is free.

Maps: A brochure and map are available at the trailhead. For a free trail map, phone the East Bay Regional Park District toll-free at 888/327-2757, extension 5; follow directions, leave your name and address, and ask for the Mission Peak Regional Preserve brochure. For a topographic map, ask the USGS for Niles.

Directions: From I-880: Take I-880 to Fremont and the exit for Mission Boulevard. Take that exit to Mission Boulevard, turn east and go 1.5 miles to Stanford Avenue. Turn right and go 0.5 mile to parking. Parking is somewhat limited, which makes most treks best timed for a weekday morning.

From I-680: Take I-680 to Fremont and the exit for Durham Road. Take that exit east and go one mile to Mission Boulevard. Turn right and go 0.75 mile to Stanford Avenue. Turn left and go 0.5 mile to parking.

Contact: Mission Peak Regional Preserve, 888/327-2757, option 3, extension 4545, or 510/544-3247 (c/o Sunol kiosk); East Bay Regional Park District, 2950 Peralta Oaks Court, P.O. Box 5381, Oakland, CA 94605-0381, 888/327-2757, www.ebparks.org.

164 SUNOL LOOP

4.75 mi / 3.5 hr

in the Sunol Regional Wilderness near Sunol

Map 7.3, page 293

There are hidden places around the Bay Area that make you feel as if only you know about them. This is one such place. Sunol Regional Wilderness is a 6,400-acre wilderness. This loop trail leads past many of its most striking spots. They include Little Yosemite, a miniature canyon with a pretty stream (Alameda Creek) with little pool-and-drop waterfalls at high flow in late winter; Cerro Este, at 1,720 feet, one of the higher points in the park; Cave Rocks, a series of natural rock forms; and Indian Joe Creek, a little brook that runs along the start of the trail. This park is a habitat center for the largest number of nesting golden eagles in the world. And in recent years, peregrine falcons have been found nesting on the edges of cliffs.

From the parking area, begin the loop hike by heading north on Indian Joe Creek Trail, then climb one mile to Cave Rocks. Turn right onto Cave Rocks Road/Cerro Este Trail and climb up over the summit and down the other side all the way to Canyon View Trail. Turn right and return to the parking area.

This trip has many options. In winter, a must-do on the Canyon View Trail is to take the short cutoff trail that drops down to Little Yosemite. In the winter, the creek at the bottom of the valley has many tiny pool-and-drop waterfalls.

If Little Yosemite is your destination, park your vehicle instead at the far (eastern) end of the park near the horse corral. Hike on the Camp Ohlone Trail (a ranch road) across the bridge and along Alameda Creek and continue over the short hill to an overlook of Little Yosemite Falls (1.25 miles one-way). From here, it's an easy scramble a short distance down to the center plunge pool. After rains, this waterfall pours through a series of pools-and-drops. Tom Spitz sent in a drop-dead gorgeous photograph where he captured the sensation of turquoise-colored water rushing through the gorge.

User Groups: Hikers, dogs, horses, and mountain bikes. The Indian Joe Creek section of the loop is limited to hikers. Canyon View Trail is limited to hikers on the eastern half, and hikers and horses on the western half. The trail to Little Yosemite is wheelchair accessible.

Permits: No permits are required for day use. A fee of $5 per vehicle is charged; $2 for dogs. A wilderness permit and a camping reservation are required for overnight backpackers.

Maps: A brochure and map are available at the trailhead. For a free trail map, phone the East Bay Regional Park District toll-free at 888/327-2757, extension 5; follow directions, leave your name and address, and ask for the Sunol-Ohlone Regional Wilderness brochure. For a topographic map, ask the USGS for La Costa Valley.

Directions: From San Francisco, take the Bay Bridge east to I-580 and drive 26 miles to I-680. Take the exit for I-680 and drive 8.2 miles to exit for Calaveras Road/Highway 84. Take that exit and go 0.4 mile to a fork; stay left and drive a short distance to Highway 84-Paloma Road. Turn left at 84/Paloma, drive under the freeway, and continue 4.3 miles (becomes Calaveras Road) to Geary Road. Turn left at Geary and drive 2.3 miles to the park entrance and parking.

Contact: Sunol-Ohlone Regional Wilderness, 888/327-2757, option 3, extension 4559, or 510/544-3249; East Bay Regional Park District, 2950 Peralta Oaks Court, P.O. Box 5381, Oakland, CA 94605-0381, 888/327-2757, www.ebparks.org.

165 FLAG ROCK

4.2 mi / 3.0 hr

in the Sunol Regional Wilderness near Sunol

Map 7.3, page 293

This is a great tromp, but with a rough climb for those who are not fit. Flag Hill is a prominent rock outcropping that overlooks the valley floor in Sunol Regional Wilderness. The common route up is on Hayfield Road (2.13 miles one-way, with an 800-foot climb). This trail is actually a ranch-style road, which means you and your hiking buddy can walk side-by-side—a plus. For some, but it can be steep, hot, and hard. Another route, the narrow Flag Hill Trail, is also quite steep (1.38 miles one-way).

But the views are gorgeous. At the top of Flag Hill, golden eagles, prairie falcons, turkey vultures, and red-tailed hawks take turns patrolling the skies along the canyon rim—you are often at eye-level with hawks gliding in the rising thermals. Directly below is Alameda Creek and valley. Always examine the rock outcrops at this park for sea fossils and bedrock mortars. You will find fossilized shells in the rock at the summit that show that this region was once the bottom of an inland sea.

Sunol Regional Wilderness is a big park, spanning 6,858 acres, and yet it is connected to the 9,736-acre Ohlone Wilderness, 4,395-acre Del Valle Regional Park, and the 20,000-acre Alameda Creek/San Antonio/Calaveras watersheds. This massive swath encompasses some of the Bay Area's largest contiguous wildlands, and yet is easily accessed from I-680.

User Groups: Hikers, dogs, horses, and mountain bikes.

Permits: No permits are required for day use. A fee of $5 per vehicle is charged; $2 for dogs. A wilderness permit and a camping reservation are required for overnight backpackers.

Maps: A brochure and map are available at the trailhead. For a free trail map, phone the East Bay Regional Park District toll-free at 888/327-2757, extension 5; follow directions, leave your name and address, and ask for the Sunol-Ohlone Regional Wilderness brochure. For a topographic map, ask the USGS for La Costa Valley. A topographic map/Wilderness Permit is also available for $2 from the Sunol Visitor Center.

Directions: From San Francisco, take the Bay Bridge east to I-580 and drive 26 miles to I-680. Take I-680 and drive 8.2 miles to exit for Calaveras Road/Highway 84. Take that exit and go 0.4 mile to a fork; stay left and drive short distance to Highway 84-Paloma Road. Turn left at Highway 84/Paloma and drive under the freeway. Continue 4.3 miles (becomes Calaveras Road) to Geary Road. Turn left at Geary and drive 2.3 miles to park entrance and parking.

Contact: Sunol-Ohlone Regional Wilderness, 888/327-2757, option 3, extension 4559, or; Sunol Interpretive Center, 510/544/3249; East Bay Regional Park District, 2950 Peralta Oaks Court, P.O. Box 5381, Oakland, CA 94605-0381, 888/327-2757, www.ebparks.org.

166 OHLONE WILDERNESS TRAIL

2.5–28.0 mi one-way / 1–3 days

🏃5 ⛰9

in the Sunol-Ohlone Regional Wilderness from Del Valle Regional Park south of Livermore to Mission Peak in Fremont

Map 7.3, page 293

Hikers can traverse the East Bay's most unspoiled backcountry via the spectacular 28-mile Ohlone Wilderness Trail. The route crosses wildlands from start to finish. Starting south of Livermore at Del Valle Regional Park and cutting west to Fremont, the trail rises through fields of wildflowers, grasslands, and oaks. It also climbs three major summits—Rocky Ridge, Rose Peak (elevation 3,817 feet), and Mission Peak (elevation 2,517 feet)—which makes an ideal three-day backpacking venture; you can set up trail camps at designated wilderness sites.

Trailhead to Del Valle overlook: The trailhead is located on the southwest side of Del Valle Reservoir at the Lichen Bark Picnic Area. Shortly after you start the trek, you will reach a box on the right with a sign-in sheet. After the sign-in, the route starts to climb, easy at first, and then quickly rises more steeply. The trail weaves in a canyon and then up to a subridge. In about 1.25 miles from the trailhead

(quarter mile past the sign-in box), you will reach a clearing where you can turn and get a pretty view of Del Valle Reservoir.

Trailhead to Rocky Ridge: This is an excellent destination for a one-day round-trip hike. From the trailhead, it's 2.4 miles and a 1,700-foot climb to Rocky Ridge (2,426 feet). The trail turns west and cuts up the far side of a deep canyon, and then rises very steeply to crest Rocky Ridge. Here's the catch: 1,600 feet of the climb is in 1.5 miles, one of the steepest sections of trail in the Bay Area. The payoff is a spectacular perch overlooking the Del Valle canyon to the east and beyond to 3,675-foot Cedar Mountain and the southern Diablo Range. Yet you can turn toward Rose Peak and take in a near-equal scope of wild landscape to the west. Wildflower blooms can be among the best in California near Rocky Ridge. An excellent side trip in late winter and early spring from here is to Murietta Falls; see next listed hike.

On to the trail camp: The trail drops 500 feet, then rises up 1,200 feet toward Wauhab Ridge. A short distance after a cow pond, you'll reach the signed Springboard Trail/Murietta Falls. Stewart's Camp, a wilderness-style camp for backpackers is located about 0.5 mile from Murietta Falls. Drinking water and a restroom are available. Reservations required.

Trailhead to Rose Peak: From the trailhead, it's a round-trip of 19.5 miles to Rose Peak (which is why this is a favorite run of ambitious ultra runners). However, it can be a stunning disappointment. After all, at 3,817 feet, Rose Peak is the Bay Area's highest wilderness-style peak. But it is not a conical-shaped summit, so first-timers can get a letdown ("What, this is it?"). But since it is the heart of the Ohlone Wilderness, the 360-degree views from the top provide a fantastic panorama of oak/foothill wildlands, ridges, and canyons.

All the way: To complete the entire 28-mile trek, wilderness camps are set up at the 12- and 16-mile marks. Hiking the trail east to west is the only way to fly. This way you'll face the steepest ascent right at the beginning, when you are still fresh, and end with sweeping views of the South Bay. As you crest the final ridge, Mission Peak, you'll face a moment of truth: You can actually see your car waiting at the parking lot—even though it's still more than a hour away. This last stretch drops 2,100 feet in 3.5 miles, a terrible toe-jammer that will have your knees and thighs screaming for mercy. Weeks later, though, when you replay this adventure in your memory banks, the hike will suddenly seem like "fun."

Most backpackers will cover about 12 miles the first day, followed by two days at about eight miles each. Many even make it a weekend trip, camping 12 miles in on Saturday night, then completing the final 16 miles on Sunday. And it's not unusual for cross-country runners to run the entire route in a single day; an organized race is held here every year.

Note: It is absolutely essential to have your itinerary and water supply timed for the trail camps. This isn't difficult, but those who don't do this may have to be carried out by a camel. You might even encounter a moment of irony as you begin to feel a strange sense of solitude, yet know that just over the final ridge to the west is a pit with 6.8 million people.

User Groups: Hikers, dogs (daytime only, not permitted on overnight trips), and horses. No mountain bikes. No wheelchair facilities.

Permits: A trail permit/map for the Ohlone Wilderness Trail is required; $6 per vehicle at entrance station, $2 trail permit/map per person at park office, or $2.50 by mail at regional park headquarters (see address below); $2 for dogs (no dogs permitted overnight); $5 per person, per night fee for wilderness camping.

Maps: You will receive a trail map when you purchase your permit. For a topographic map, ask the USGS for Mendenhall Springs.

Directions: To reach the east trailhead: Take I-580 east to Livermore, and the exit for North Livermore Avenue. Take that exit, turn right (south) and drive for 3.5 miles (the road goes through town and then becomes Tesla Road) to Mines Road. Turn right on Mines Road and drive 3.5 miles to Del Valle Road. Turn right on Del Valle Road and go three miles to the Del Valle Regional Park entrance. Pay entrance fees and continue ahead to a fork. Turn left at the fork, drive less than a mile to the bridge at Del Valle Reservoir, cross it, then turn right and drive 0.5 mile to the Lichen Bark Picnic Area. Park and walk a short distance to the trailhead for the Ohlone Trail.

To reach the west trailhead: Take I-680 south to Fremont and the exit for Highway 238/Mission Boulevard. Take that exit and turn east (toward the hills) and drive to Stanford Avenue. Turn east on Stanford Avenue and drive to the parking lot and trailhead at the end of the road.

Contact: Del Valle Regional Park, 888/327-2757, option 3, extension 4524; Sunol-Ohlone Regional Wilderness, 510/544-3249; East Bay Regional Park District, 2950 Peralta Oaks Court, P.O. Box 5381, Oakland, CA 94605-0381, 888/327-2757, www.ebparks.org.

167 MURIETTA FALLS TRAIL
12.25 mi / 1 day   🏃5 ⛰8

in the Sunol-Ohlone Regional Wilderness, from Del Valle Regional Park south of Livermore to Mission Peak in Fremont

Map 7.3, page 293

If you want to unplug from the world for a day, one of the best places to do it in winter and spring is at Murietta Falls in the Ohlone Wilderness. Yet this can be a star-crossed adventure. It is the most demanding one-day hike in the Bay Area, a butt-kicker on the way in, a knee-jammer on the way out. And meanwhile, the reward at the end of the rainbow can be dubious.

When the foothills are saturated and the Murietta Canyon has been recharged by a big storm with a heavy spring rain, this is one of the region's most stunning destinations. It is best seen standing below the waterfall, looking up. This waterfall is a 100-foot cataract that tumbles down a rocky gorge, a beautiful mix of short freefalls, horsetails, cascades, and chutes—not a freefall. We've seen it at peak flow and the sharp contrast of white, churning water against the surrounding oak grasslands/foothills is absolutely stunning, enough to make you forget all the problems of the world, and maybe even a few of your own. Except it isn't always churning. In fact, it doesn't churn but a few times a year. If you don't time it after a spring rain, the flows can be reduced to a wisp of a trickle. Typically, the window of hope closes in May.

The trailhead for Murietta Falls is the Ohlone Wilderness Trail out of the southern end of Del Valle Regional Park, located south of Livermore. The trip is a round-trip hike of 12.25 miles with a cumulative elevation gain of 4,000 feet. This is the mother of all Bay Area butt-kickers; the trail must have been configured by a roller-coaster designer. Yet you can add to it by climbing Rose Peak.

You'll know within the first hour if you made a mistake. The hike starts with a 1,700-foot gain to Rocky Ridge (2.4 miles), with a pretty view to the north of Del Valle Reservoir and beyond, and then drops 500 feet in 0.5 mile to the bottom of a canyon. This is just the start. You then climb out of the canyon, gutting it out up 1,200 feet as you rise toward Wauhab Ridge, where you get more pretty long-distance foothill views. You will pass a series of impressive rock outcrops and then reach a little watering hole for cows (mapped as Johnny's Pond). From the pond, continue a short distance to the junction with the Springboard Trail, signed Murietta Falls, signpost 35.

Turn on this trail and walk about 0.25 mile (to a sharp turn in the trail)—then be sharp-eyed for the footpath on your left, along a small creek. Take this path to the brink of the falls. Alas, the view is lousy. No problem. From here, there is a well-worn route that everybody takes that leads down to the plunge pool of the falls. Here you get a picture-perfect view of the gorge and can enjoy a long picnic.

Some choose to extend the trip to two days by camping at a trail site called Stewart's Camp, located about 0.5 mile from the base of the falls. Although this splits the hiking distance into two days, it also means you must carry all your backpacking gear in and out, a heavy price.

Murietta Falls is named after Joaquin Murietta, of course, the legendary outlaw of the 1800s. If you hit it right, when the waterfall is gushing, you might wonder why such a beautiful place was named after a notorious killer. If you hit it wrong, however, you will understand. It is his final curse.

User Groups: Hikers, dogs (daytime only, not permitted on overnight trips), and horses. No mountain bikes. No wheelchair facilities.

Permits: A trail permit/map for the Ohlone Wilderness Trail is required; $6 per vehicle at entrance station, $2 trail permit/map per person at park office, or $2.50 by mail at regional park headquarters (see address below); $2 for dogs (no dogs permitted overnight); $5 per person, per night fee for wilderness camping.

Maps: You will receive a trail map when you purchase your permit. For a topographic map, ask the USGS for Mendenhall Springs.

Directions: To reach the east trailhead: Take I-580 east to Livermore and the exit for North Livermore Avenue. Take that exit, turn right (south) and drive for 3.5 miles (the road goes through town and then becomes Tesla Road) to Mines Road. Turn right on Mines Road and drive 3.5 miles to Del Valle Road. Turn right on Del Valle Road and go three miles to the Del Valle Regional Park entrance. Pay entrance fees and continue ahead to a fork. Turn left at the fork, drive less than a mile to the bridge above Del Valle Reservoir, cross it, then turn right and drive 0.5 mile to the Lichen Bark Picnic Area. Park and walk a short distance to the trailhead for the Ohlone Trail.

Contact: Del Valle Regional Park, 888/327-2757, option 3, extension 4524; East Bay Regional Park District, 2950 Peralta Oaks Court, P.O. Box 5381, Oakland, CA 94605-0381, 888/327-2757, www.ebparks.org.

168 SHORELINE REGIONAL PARK

2.0 mi / 1.0 hr 🏃🏃₁ ⛰₇

along South San Francisco Bay in Mountain View

Map 7.4, page 294

From the small lake at Shoreline Regional Park, the best trail is routed along the east side of the 50-acre lake and then northward on a levee through marshlands. It is quite popular with bird-watchers, who can spot everything from egrets to LBJs (Little Brown Jobs), and there are often quite a few Canada geese and a chance to see burrowing owls. At the start of this trail, you will find that the lake that makes an excellent spot for windsurfing, and there are many good kite-flying areas on the tiny hills. A concession stand near the lake gets a lot of use from the corn-dog-and-Coke crowd. The trail heads north and connects to the levee trail and Charleston Slough. From here, head east to the edge of South San Francisco Bay, with more opportunities for bird-watching. Shoreline Regional Park is an ideal family destination with a wide variety of activities, including pleasant walks and bike rides on wide, crushed-gravel byways. For bikers, the trip can be extended to the Palo Alto Baylands to the north and the Stevens Creek Trail to the south, though some surface roads have to be used as connector links.

User Groups: Hikers, wheelchairs, and mountain bikes. No dogs or horses.

Permits: No permits are required. Parking and access are free.

Maps: A brochure and map are available at the entrance station. For a topographic map, ask the USGS for Mountain View.

Directions: From US 101 in Mountain View, take the exit for Shoreline Boulevard. Turn east (toward the bay) on Shoreline and drive past the Shoreline Amphitheater to the park entrance station.

Contact: Shoreline Regional Park, City of Mountain View, 3070 N. Shoreline Boulevard, Mountain View, CA 94043, 650/903-6392, www.ci.mtnview.ca.us.

169 SOUTH BAY NATURE TRAIL

2.0 mi / 1.0 hr 🏃🏃₁ ⛰₇

in San Francisco Bay National Wildlife Refuge near Alviso

Map 7.4, page 294

This portion of the San Francisco Bay National Wildlife Refuge is set deep in the South Bay marsh near Alviso, where it receives scant attention compared to its big brother to the north at the Dumbarton Bridge.

The trailhead is at the Environmental Education Center. From here, you walk on a dirt path along a wild tidal marshland. As you stroll northward, you will delve into wilder and wilder habitat, and in the process have a chance at seeing a dozen species of birds in a matter of minutes. The endangered harvest salt mouse lives in this habitat. Guided nature walks are held regularly on weekend mornings, and they are well worth attending. The sloughs and quiet waters here also make for a unique opportunity for saltwater canoeing and kayaking.

User Groups: Hikers and mountain bikes. No dogs or horses. No wheelchair facilities.

Permits: No permits are required. Parking and access are free.

Maps: A brochure and map are available at the trailhead. For a topographic map, ask the USGS for Mountain View.

Directions: From US 101 near Sunnyvale, take Highway 237. Drive east on Highway 237 to Zanker Street. Turn left on Zanker Street, make a sharp right turn onto Grand Drive, and drive to the parking area at the Environmental Education Center.

Contact: Environmental Education Center, 408/262-5513; Don Edwards San Francisco Bay National Wildlife Refuge, 510/792-0222 P.O. Box 524, Newark, CA 94560, www.fws.gov/desfbay.

170 SUNNYVALE BAYLANDS

2.0 mi / 1.0 hr 👣1 🏔6

on South San Francisco Bay in Sunnyvale

Map 7.4, page 294

Sunnyvale Baylands County Park really isn't much of a park at all, but rather a wildlife preserve surrounded by a levee that makes a trail for hiking and jogging. It covers 177 acres of South Bay marshland, home to blue herons, great egrets, avocets, black-necked stilts, mallards, pintails, and burrowing owls.

From the parking area adjacent to Highway 237, hike along the levee. You will turn left as it parallels Calabazas Creek. To your left is a seasonal wetlands preserve. The trail continues along the creek, then turns left again and runs alongside Guadalupe Slough. The open-water bird preserve will be just off to your left. One downer is the adjacent proximity of the highway, which is why it does not merit a higher rating, and yet it deserves entry as an urban wildlife area.

On nearly every trip, you will see a jackrabbit or two. In fact, these rabbits have a way of scaring the bejesus out of hikers. They hide in the weeds until you get close, then suddenly pop up and take off at warp speed, shocking you every time.

User Groups: Hikers only. No dogs, horses, or mountain bikes. No wheelchair facilities.

Permits: No permits are required. An entrance fee of $5 per vehicle is charged from May to October (season pass available), with no parking fee from November to April. No fees for walk-in or bike-in traffic.

Maps: For a free map, write to Sunnyvale Baylands County Park. For a topographic map, ask the USGS for Mountain View.

Directions: From Highway 237 in Sunnyvale, take the Caribbean exit. The park is immediately on your right hand side at 999 East Caribbean (well signed, located next to the Twin Creeks softball complex).

Contact: Sunnyvale Baylands County Park, P.O. Box 3707, Sunnyvale, CA 94088, 408/730-7751, www.parkhere.org.

171 MONUMENT PEAK TRAIL

7.5 mi / 4.0 hr 👣3 🏔8

in Ed R. Levin County Park in the Milpitas foothills

Map 7.4, page 294

Monument Peak is overlooked and bypassed by many people, including regular visitors to Ed R. Levin County Park. Yet at 2,594 feet, Monument Peak offers views that nearly rival those from Mount Hamilton, with far-ranging vistas over the Santa Clara Valley. Of the 13 trails in the park, the summit hike is clearly the longest, steepest, and most difficult.

The trailhead is at 300 feet at Sandy Wool Lake, so figure on a 2,300-foot climb over the course of about 3.75 miles. Take the Tularcitos/Agua Caliente Trail for a more gentle climb without having to contend with bikes. It junctions with the Monument Peak Road near the top, where you turn left for the final push to the summit.

Note that there is another route to the top: The Monument Peak Trail is actually a road, and you may run head-on into mountain bikers ripping downhill on it. Most park visitors here do not come for a challenge, but to play golf at Spring Valley, go fishing at Sandy Wool Lake, or just enjoy a picnic.

User Groups: Hikers and horses. Leashed dogs permitted only on Calera Creek Trail and Agua Caliente Trail, a service road. No mountain bikes. No wheelchair facilities.

Permits: No permits are required. A day-use fee of $5 per vehicle is charged. Hikers are encouraged to wait two days after a rain before hiking in order to prevent trail damage.

Maps: For a free trail map, contact Ed R. Levin County Park. For topographic maps, ask the USGS for Milpitas and Calaveras Reservoir.

Directions: Take I-680 to Milpitas and the exit for Calaveras Road East. Take that exit and drive east for two miles to Downing Street. Turn left on Downing Street and drive 0.5 mile to the park entrance (straight ahead). Proceed to the parking area near Sandy Wool Lake.

Contact: Ed R. Levin County Park, 3100 Calaveras Road, Milpitas, CA 95035, 408/262-6980, www.parkhere.org.

172 OHLONE RIDGE TRAIL
1.5 mi / 1.0 hr   👣 1 ⛰ 8

at Costanoa near Año Nuevo State Reserve

Map 7.4, page 294

From Ohlone Ridge, you can face west and take in the scope of the Pacific Ocean, Año Nuevo, and miles of wild coast. Every care, stress, and worry will slip away like the outgoing tide. Ohlone Ridge is the easy must-do loop hike for every visitor to Costanoa, the coastal lodge, camp, and recreation getaway that provides a vacation destination, yet is right in the Bay Area (day use is free).

Costanoa is a located on hillside bluffs overlooking the ocean, just east of Highway 1 near Año Nuevo State Reserve and the San Mateo and Santa Cruz County line. From the lodge headquarters, walk a short distance on the entrance road to the trail on the left. From here, the route passes Whitehouse Creek and rises through a meadow, then climbs into the foothill to a sub-ridge and lookout with a bench. The views of the local coast out toward Año Nuevo are sensational.

If you want more after this taste, or are spending the night here: On the west side of the highway, the Atkinson Bluff Trail extends on the cliff-edge overlooking the beach and is routed in a loop out to Franklin Point and past a secluded beach and tidepools.

What makes Costanoa work as a vacation getaway is the overnight accommodations. They feature 89 canvas bungalows with ocean views, deluxe-style lodge rooms and suites, and campsites for tents and RVs with hookups. Everything is deluxe, including the on-site store and restaurant.

User Groups: Hikers, mountain bikes, and horses. Mountain bike rentals and guided horseback riding trips are available. No dogs. Headquarters is wheelchair accessible.

Permits: No permits are required. Day use and parking are free. Overnight camping and lodging is available.

Maps: A brochure and map are available at the check-in desk. For a topographic map, ask the USGS for Franklin Point.

Directions: From Half Moon Bay, take Highway 1 south and drive 26 miles (nine miles past the turnoff for Pescadero Road) to Rossi Road. Turn left and go 0.5 mile to parking.

Contact: Costanoa, 2001 Rossi Road, Pescadero, CA 94060, 650/879-1100, www.costanoa.com.

173 AÑO NUEVO TRAIL
3.0 mi / 2.0 hr   👣 1 ⛰ 7

in Año Nuevo State Reserve on the San Mateo County coast south of Pescadero

Map 7.4, page 294   **BEST ☾**

Año Nuevo State Reserve is home to the largest breeding colony of northern elephant seals. Yep, this is the place where these giant creatures fight, mate, give birth, sunbathe, and make funny noises. So many people want to watch them that you must make reservations and join a tour group (Dec. 15–Mar. 31).

The rest of the year you are free to hike on your own. But note that the elephant seal population has increased to the point that there are now year-round residents on the beach here. So this has become one of the few sure spottings in the Bay Area.

After parking, start by hiking the well-signed trail through a series of sandy mounds and flats en route to the beach. During the tour-only season, you must be part of a tour group, and you will walk along roped-off trails, winding your way amid the animals. In the offseason, at times rangers will post the beach and nearby routes to it as offlimits.

Elephant seals look like giant slugs, often weighing 2,000–3,000 pounds—even the newborns weigh 75 pounds. The old boars reach nearly 20 feet in length and weigh as much as 5,000 pounds. With a 200mm camera lens, you can get excellent pictures. The best times to visit are in mid-December, when the males battle for harems, and in late January, when hundreds of pups are born. The rest of the year, this is a nice place to enjoy a quiet beach walk, with decent numbers of the giant slothlike mammals available for photos.

User Groups: Hikers only. No dogs, horses, or mountain bikes. No wheelchair facilities.

Permits: A year-round parking fee of $10 is charged per vehicle. From mid-December through March, access to the park is available only by accompanying a ranger on a scheduled walk; $7 per person. To make a reservation, call 800/444-7275.

Maps: A map is available at the entrance station for a fee. For a topographic map, ask the USGS for Franklin Point.

Directions: From I-280 in San Mateo, turn west on Highway 92 and drive to Half Moon Bay and Highway 1. Turn left (south) on Highway 1 and drive about 27 miles to the park entrance on the right (well signed).

Contact: Año Nuevo State Reserve, New Year's Creek Road, Pescadero, CA 94060, 650/879-2025; Half Moon Bay state parks, 650/726-8820, www.parks.ca.gov.

174 MCCRARY RIDGE LOOP
13.6 mi / 7.0 hr   🚶3 ⛰9

at Rancho del Oso on the Santa Cruz County coast south of Año Nuevo

Map 7.4, page 294

The wide dirt road that leads from Rancho del Oso into the Waddell Creek canyon is very popular with mountain bikers who use this out-and-back route to access Berry Creek Falls, 5.8 miles in. Because of the number of bikes on the dirt road, it doesn't always make the best hiking trip, especially on weekends. A better choice is to use it as part of a longer loop, on which you'll spend much of your time on single-track trail (no bikes).

Follow the wide road/trail inland from Highway 1. Where the road is gated near a restroom at 0.2 mile, cut off to the left on the hikers-only alternate trail. Follow this path to Alder Trail Camp, then rejoin the wide dirt road for 1.5 miles to Camp Herbert. Here is the start of your loop (note the McCrary Ridge Trail that cuts off to the right; this is your return route). For now, stay on the wide dirt road all the way to Berry Creek Falls (the last 0.7 mile is a narrow trail for hikers only). Enjoy the refreshing sight and sound of the gorgeous 70-foot falls, then retrace your steps for 0.25 mile to Howard King Trail. This redwood-lined path leads 1.8 miles to Hihn Hammond Road; cross it and pick up McCrary Ridge Trail. Follow it 2.6 miles back to the wide Skyline-to-the-Sea Trail, then cruise through the last three easy miles back to your car.

In the spring, this is a great wildflower walk, with 15–20 species commonly sighted, including a few pockets with rafts of forget-me-nots.

User Groups: Hikers, horses (not permitted past Henry Trail), and mountain bikes (not permitted past Waddell Creek Bridge). No dogs. No wheelchair facilities.

Permits: No permits are required. A parking/access fee of $10 is charged per vehicle. Permits required for overnight use.

Maps: A trail map is available on weekends at the ranger station for a fee. It can be obtained by mail by calling Mountain Parks Foundation, 831/335-3174; credit cards accepted. For a topographic map, ask the USGS for Franklin Point.

Directions: From I-280 in San Mateo, turn west onto Highway 92 and drive to Half Moon Bay. Turn left (south) onto Highway 1 and drive about 35 miles (two miles past Año Nuevo State Reserve) and look for the signs indicating Big Basin Redwoods State Park/Rancho del Oso on the east side of the highway, just past the Santa Cruz County line. Turn and park at Rancho del Oso.

Contact: Rancho del Oso, 831/425-1218; Rancho del Oso Nature Center, 831/427-2288; trail camp reservations, 831/338-8861; equestrian camping, 831/425-1218; Big Basin

Redwoods State Park, 21600 Big Basin Way, Boulder Creek, CA 95006, 831/338-8860; California State Parks, Santa Cruz District, 831/429-2850, www.parks.ca.gov or www.mountainparks.org.

175 REDWOOD LOOP
0.6 mi / 0.5 hr
[icon] 1 [icon] 8

in Big Basin Redwoods State Park in the Santa Cruz Mountains near Boulder Creek

Map 7.4, page 294

Most people come to Big Basin Redwoods State Park to see giant redwoods, and the Redwood Loop is a short, easy path that meanders around many of these giants. The sights include pretty Opal Creek, the Chimney Tree (which has survived many fires), and several other ancient redwoods. The Santa Clara Tree, located across Opal Creek at signpost three, is 17 feet in diameter; the Father-of-the-Forest is about 2,000 years old and stands at signpost eight; and the Mother-of-the-Forest, the tallest tree in the park at 329 feet, is at signpost nine. (If you're wondering why the Mother-of-the-Forest is bigger than the Father-of-the-Forest—when you see the Mother of the Forest, and see the shape of its burned-out hollow at its base, you will understand.) There is no reason to rush and many people take as much as an hour to complete the loop. By using the numbered posts along the way and a trail brochure, you can take a self-guided nature walk. In the nature center, view photos from the early 19th century to see how visitors made the arduous journey here just to see these trees.

User Groups: Hikers only. Wheelchair accessible. No dogs, horses, or mountain bikes.

Permits: No permits are required. A state park entrance fee of $10 per vehicle is charged. For backpack campsites, reservations are required at 831/338-8861.

Maps: Detailed trail maps of Big Basin Redwoods State Park are available for a fee from Mountain Parks Foundation, 525 N. Big Trees Road, Felton, CA 95018, 831/335-3174. For topographic maps, ask the USGS for Castle Rock Ridge and Big Basin.

Directions: From the San Francisco Peninsula, take I-280 south to Sunnyvale/Saratoga Road. Turn south and drive five miles to Saratoga and Highway 9. Turn right at Highway 9 and drive up the hill for about seven miles to Skyline Ridge. Continue over the other side of Highway 9 about seven more miles to Highway 236. Turn right and drive about 10 miles to Big Basin Redwoods State Park. Note: Highway 236 is extremely twisty and not recommended for RVs or trailers.

Alternate route: From San Francisco, take Highway 1 south to Santa Cruz and Highway 9. Turn left on Highway 9 and drive about 12 miles to Boulder Creek and the traffic light for Highway 236. Turn left on Highway 236 and drive 10 miles to park headquarters.

Contact: Big Basin Redwoods State Park, 21600 Big Basin Way, Boulder Creek, CA 95006, 831/338-8860, www.parks.ca.gov; district headquarters, 831/429-2851.

176 BERRY CREEK FALLS
12.0 mi / 6.0 hr
[icon] 3 [icon] 10

in Big Basin Redwoods State Park in the Santa Cruz Mountains near Boulder Creek

Map 7.4, page 294

The prettiest sight in the Bay Area just might be Berry Creek Falls, a 70-foot waterfall framed by a canyon and complete with ferns, redwoods, and the sound of rushing water. Yet we like the view and feel of the canyon just upstream even better: Silver Falls, a beautiful free fall enclosed by a bowl of redwoods, and Golden Falls, a gorgeous series of cascades over gold sandstone. Our favorite spot here is just above the brink of Silver Falls, where you can reach out and touch the water, then take a few steps upstream and admire lower Golden Falls. These three waterfalls, along with the redwood forest, make this the number-one hike in the Bay Area. It is worth repeating many times.

Getting an early start helps to ensure a care-free trip with no pressure to complete the loop by a certain time. Start at park headquarters and take Skyline-to-the-Sea Trail amid the giant redwoods up to the Big Basin rim; then head down the other side, hiking west toward the coast. After topping the rim at 1,200 feet, the hike descends 600 feet over the course of about four miles to Berry Creek Falls (4.7 miles from the trailhead). You round a bend and suddenly, there it is, a divine waterfall. A small bench is perfectly situated for viewing the scene while eating a picnic lunch. At a steady pace, it takes one hour, 50 minutes. So despite the warning sign you will pass, it's a four-hour round-trip if you make it an in-and-outer. The best suggestion is to head beyond, up the canyon.

Go the long way—up the staircase, past the Cascade Falls (Silver Falls and Golden Falls), and return on Sunset Trail. At Silver Falls, it is possible to dunk your head into the streaming water without getting the rest of your body wet—a real thrill. At the brink, the trail is rock steps cut into the canyon, with a woven wire safety rail to keep you from falling off the cliff. Just upstream past the brink, Golden Falls is a beautiful cascade of water over golden sandstone, like a giant water slide. One of the golden cascades looks like a miniature Aztec Temple.

Once you pass Golden Falls, the trail climbs out to a service road near Sunset Camp. Do not miss the right turn off the service road to Sunset Trail. From here, Sunset Trail meanders through the most remote sections of the park, in and out of chaparral and forest, then loops back into redwoods, and leads back to park headquarters. Though you can trim the hiking time down if you double back on the same trail you came in on—why cut the experience short? Not to mention the way back is all uphill.

User Groups: Hikers only. No dogs, horses, or mountain bikes. No wheelchair facilities.

Permits: No permits are required. A state park entrance fee of $10 per vehicle is charged. For backpack campsites, reservations are required at 831/338-8861.

Maps: Detailed trail maps of Big Basin Redwoods State Park are available for a fee from Mountain Parks Foundation, 525 N. Big Trees Road, Felton, CA 95018, 831/335-3174. For topographic maps, ask the USGS for Castle Rock Ridge and Big Basin.

Directions: From the San Francisco Peninsula, take I-280 to Sunnyvale/Saratoga Road. Turn south and drive five miles to Saratoga and Highway 9. Turn right at Highway 9 and drive up the hill for about seven miles to Skyline Ridge. Continue over the other side of Highway 9 about seven more miles to Highway 236. Turn right and drive about 10 miles to Big Basin Redwoods State Park. Note: Highway 236 is extremely twisty and not recommended for RVs or trailers.

From San Francisco, take Highway 1 south to Santa Cruz and Highway 9. Turn left on Highway 9 and drive about 12 miles to Boulder Creek and the traffic light for Highway 236. Turn left on Highway 236 and drive 10 miles to park headquarters.

Contact: Big Basin Redwoods State Park, 21600 Big Basin Way, Boulder Creek, CA 95006, 831/338-8860, www.bigbasin.org, www.parks.ca.gov; Santa Cruz District, 831/429-2850; camping reservations, 800/444-7275; backpack camping reservations, 831/338-8861; tent cabin reservations, 800/874-8368.

177 METEOR TRAIL
5.2 mi / 2.5 hr

in Big Basin Redwoods State Park in the Santa Cruz Mountains near Boulder Creek

Map 7.4, page 294

Under the heavy redwood canopy of Big Basin, most hikers don't worry about whether or not it's foggy on the coast. But with the park's best coastal lookout at trail's end, you don't want fog on this hike. The Meteor Trail starts at the parking area across the lot from park headquarters on the Skyline-to-the-Sea Trail. Walk over the wood bridge at Opal Creek and turn right. If you turn left and see a sign for Berry Creek Falls, you're going in the wrong direction.

For much of the route, you hike along Opal Creek, a pretty stream in the spring, surrounded by redwoods. Two miles out, you will arrive at the intersection with Meteor Trail. This is where you turn left and then climb 400 feet over the space of a mile to the Middle Ridge Fire Road. The Ocean View Summit (1,600 feet) is only a couple hundred yards off, featuring a glimpse to the west of the Waddell Creek watershed and the Pacific Coast. Return by doubling back the way you came. If you visit Big Basin and don't have time for the Berry Creek Falls hike, this is the next best option.

The view from the summit had been eclipsed by trees in recent years but is unbroken once again, thanks to a prescribed burn over a few hundred acres along the summit ridge. Although there are some charred ruins in the foreground, the long-distance view makes for a stellar pay-off. On spring weekends, when the trail to the waterfalls can become very popular, this makes an excellent option.

User Groups: Hikers only. No dogs, horses, or mountain bikes. No wheelchair facilities.

Permits: No permits are required. A state park entrance fee of $10 per vehicle is charged.

Maps: Detailed trail maps of Big Basin Redwoods State Park are available for a fee from Mountain Parks Foundation, 525 N. Big Trees Road, Felton, CA 95018, 831/335-3174. For topographic maps, ask the USGS for Castle Rock Ridge and Big Basin.

Directions: From the San Francisco Peninsula, take I-280 to Sunnyvale/Saratoga Road. Turn south and drive five miles to Saratoga and Highway 9. Turn right at Highway 9 and drive up the hill for about seven miles to Skyline Ridge. Continue over the other side of Highway 9 about seven more miles to Highway 236. Turn right and drive about 10 miles to Big Basin Redwoods State Park.

Note: Highway 236 is extremely twisty and not recommended for RVs or trailers.

From San Francisco, take Highway 1 south to Santa Cruz and Highway 9. Turn left on Highway 9 and drive about 12 miles to Boulder Creek and the traffic light for Highway 236. Turn left on Highway 236 and drive 10 miles to park headquarters.

Contact: Big Basin Redwoods State Park, 21600 Big Basin Way, Boulder Creek, CA 95006, 831/338-8860, www.bigbasin.org, www.parks.ca.gov; Santa Cruz District, 831/429-2850; camping reservations, 800/444-7275; backpack camping reservations, 831/338-8861; tent cabin reservations, 800/874-8368.

178 LONG RIDGE LOOP
4.6 mi / 2.5 hr   📷2 ⛰9

in the Long Ridge Open Space Preserve on Skyline Ridge

Map 7.4, page 294

This is one of the best day hikes on the Peninsula. Long Ridge provides a great escape hatch for a quick launch into the wild outdoors. In just two hours on the trail here, this place has the ability to recharge your senses. Long Ridge is located on Skyline Boulevard, just south of the junction of Page Mill Road.

After parking, get the brochure/trail map from the box near the trailhead and orient yourself. This adventure starts by heading west down into the adjacent valley and past the intersection with the Bay Ridge Trail at 0.4 mile, then reaches the junction with the Long Ridge Trail and Peters Creek Trail (at 0.5 mile). Here you turn right and make a climb through oak woodlands, including one short, steep spot, where the trail horseshoes its way eventually to the south up to Long Ridge Road (at 1.2 miles; a dirt service road). This is a great coastal lookout, one of the best on the Peninsula. Everybody takes at least 5 minutes to enjoy it, and some even have a picnic.

From here, the going is easy to Four

Corners, heading south on Long Ridge, with a slight elevation gain, rewarded by gorgeous views off to the west. On clear days, you get long-distance views of the ocean, and as you continue south, across miles of foothills and forested valleys. The highest point in San Mateo County, 2,600 feet, is just off the trail here, but it is hardly a prominent point in the landscape.

At Four Corners (2.5 miles), you turn left, encounter a series of switchbacks as you descend into a heavily wooded canyon, extremely lush in late winter and spring. The surprise of the trip is just ahead: You will pass a surprise and secret pond (3.0 miles), ringed by tules and quite pretty. To complete the loop hike, continue on the Peters Creek Trail, a rich riparian zone, back to the junction with Long Ridge Trail (4.1 miles). Turn right and hike back to the parking area (4.6 miles).

Trails are routed through a variety of beautiful landscapes, including sheltered canyons, creeks, meadows, and oak woodlands, past a beautiful hidden pond, and up on Long Ridge itself for great open views to the west of the Butano Rim and Pacific Ocean. And you can get this with one 4.6-mile loop trip, including only about a 400-foot climb. There is also a good chance of spotting wild turkey, rabbits, deer, raptors, and songbirds.

User Groups: Hikers, horses, and mountain bikes (restricted from some trails, signed). No dogs. No wheelchair facilities.

Permits: No permits are required. Parking and access are free.

Maps: A brochure and map are available at the trailhead. For a free trail map, contact the Midpeninsula Regional Open Space District. For a topographic map, ask the USGS for Mindego Hill.

Directions: From San Francisco, take I-280 south and drive 20 miles to Woodside and the exit for Highway 84/Woodside Road. Take that exit, turn west (right) on Woodside Road, and drive 2.8 miles to Woodside. Continue straight on Woodside Road/Highway 84 (becomes curvy) to Sky Londa and Highway 35/

Skyline Boulevard. Turn left on Skyline and drive 7.2 miles to Page Mill Road, then continue straight on Skyline for 3.3 miles (a short distance past Portola Heights Road) to pullouts along Skyline for parking. The preserve entrance and trailhead are on the right.

From the South Bay: From Palo Alto at I-280, take Page Mill Road west about 10 miles (becomes curvy, watch out for bikes) to Skyline Boulevard. Turn left and drive 3.3 miles to the preserve entrance on the right.

From Saratoga: Take Big Basin Way/Highway 9 for about 7 miles to Skyline Boulevard. Turn right and drive 3.6 miles to the preserve entrance on the left (parking is also available on the right shoulder).

Contact: Midpeninsula Regional Open Space District, 330 Distel Circle, Los Altos, CA 94022, 650/691-1200, www.openspace.org. During nonbusiness hours, a touch-tone phone menu is available for trail news, conditions, and events.

179 SARATOGA GAP LOOP
8.8 mi / 5.0 hr   🏃2 ⛰8

in the Saratoga Gap and Long Ridge Open Space Preserves on Skyline Ridge in the Santa Cruz Mountains

Map 7.4, page 294

Here's a first-class hike that you can chop short if necessary because of weather or time. With the trail network here linked to five other nearby major parks, you can create a trip of nearly any length, short or long. A favorite is this moderate 8.8-mile round-trip that some call "The Wallace Stegner Special"—one of the late author's favorite treks. The pay offs are a changing panorama of views across foothill woodlands and canyons on the east side of Skyline Ridge, and the Santa Cruz Mountains, a sea of conifers, and the Pacific Ocean on the west side. It's an example of how contiguous parklands can be networked to create a special trek.

After parking, cross Highway 9 to the northeast corner of this junction for the trailhead, signed Saratoga Gap Trail/Bay Area Ridge Trail. This is the starting point: The trail heads north for the first 1.7 miles, adjacent to the road, meandering along Skyline. The landscape is a mix of hardwoods and Douglas fir, with occasional peek-a-boo views to the east. You then enter Upper Stevens Creek County Park and arrive at the junction with Charcoal Road. Continue on the Bay Ridge Trail (it jogs left) for 0.3 mile back to Skyline Boulevard.

At Skyline, cross the road, arriving at Long Ridge Open Space Preserve, and connect to Long Ridge Road/Hickory Oaks Trail. This is routed northwest into the foothills toward Long Ridge. The climb is mostly gentle here, rising over the course of 1.1 miles to a junction with Ward Road.

Continue straight (north) on Long Ridge Road for 1.3 miles, hiking up and down a few hills and with a mostly gentle rise, to arrive at your pay off: a perfectly situated bench on the west-facing ridge for a gorgeous lookout of the Santa Cruz Mountains and Pacific Ocean. To finish the trek, head north for the final 4.4-mile leg.

User Groups: Hikers, horses, and mountain bikes. No dogs. No wheelchair facilities.

Permits: No permits are required. Parking and access are free.

Maps: A brochure and map are available at the trailhead. For a free trail map, contact the Midpeninsula Regional Open Space District. For topographic maps, ask the USGS for Mindego Hill and Cupertino.

Directions: From I-280 near Santa Clara, turn west on Saratoga Avenue and drive to Highway 9. Take Highway 9 up to the ridge to the junction of Highway 9 and Highway 35. At the junction, look for the CalTrans parking area on the left (southeast) corner. Park there. The preserve is on the northeast corner of this junction, across the road from the parking lot.

Contact: Midpeninsula Regional Open Space District, 330 Distel Circle, Los Altos, CA 94022, 650/691-1200, www.openspace.org.

During nonbusiness hours, a touch-tone phone menu is available for trail news, conditions, and events.

180 TRAIL CAMP LOOP
5.3 mi / 2.5 hr

in Castle Rock State Park on Skyline Ridge in the Santa Cruz Mountains

Map 7.4, page 294

Here you can discover a great and easy 5.3-mile walk that takes about 2.5 hours. It is highlighted by a surprise waterfall with a viewing deck, honeycombed sandstone formations, sweeping views of the Santa Cruz Mountains and Monterey Bay to the west, and then a top-of-the-world perch atop Goat Rock.

Begin on Saratoga Gap Trail. In the first few minutes, the trail descends into a lush riparian canyon. Within 0.5 mile, you arrive at the cutoff on your left for the viewing deck. This puts you at the brink of a canyon and adjacent to the waterfall, which is at its fullest after recent rainfall. Back on the main trail, the route breaks out from forest and into the open along a rock facing. On stellar days, those with sharp vision can see the white foam of the breakers on the beaches of Monterey Bay to the west. As you head on, you will pass a series of sandstone formations to your right, where material has eroded over time to create a series of holes and cavities. The most dramatic of these is at Goat Rock, where the trail runs right past its base. At this spot there is a permanent climbing cable, and on weekends, climbers practice technical skills here.

The trail continues to a junction with Ridge Trail, a distance of 2.6 miles from the parking lot. At this junction, turn right and start the loop back to the parking area. The return loop features a gentle climb, primarily amid chaparral and woodlands. Be certain to watch for a cutoff trail on the right to Goat Rock Lookout—don't miss this side trip; walk a short distance to a sweeping, long-distance view across a sea of conifers and beyond to the ocean. Perches atop Goat Rock provide excellent picnic sites for those with trail snacks.

There are 32 miles of hiking trails in 3,600 acres of semi-wilderness land at this park, so extending your adventure can be done quite easily.

Note: This park is on the closure list developed by the California Department of Parks, pending final state budget decisions or the possible transfer of park management to other park agencies or volunteer groups.

User Groups: Hikers and horses. No dogs or mountain bikes. No wheelchair facilities.

Permits: No permits are required, but you must self-register at the park entrance. A day-use fee of $10 per vehicle is charged.

Maps: A brochure and map are available at the trailhead. A trail map of Castle Rock State Park is available for a fee from Mountain Parks Foundation, 525 N. Big Trees Road, Felton, CA 95018, 831/335-3174. For a topographic map, ask the USGS for Castle Rock Ridge.

Directions: From I-280 near Santa Clara, turn west on Saratoga Avenue and drive to Highway 9. Drive west on Highway 9 to the junction with Highway 35 (Skyline Boulevard). Turn left (south) and drive 2.5 miles to the entrance to Castle Rock State Park on the right.

Contact: Castle Rock State Park, 15000 Skyline Boulevard, Los Gatos, CA 95020, 408/867-2952; California State Parks, Santa Cruz District, 831/429-2850; trail camp reservations, 831/338-8861, www.mountainparks.org, www.parks.ca.gov.

181 SKYLINE-TO-THE-SEA TRAIL

34.0 mi one-way / 2.5 days

🏃3 ⛰10

from Castle Rock State Park via Big Basin to Waddell Creek on the Pacific coast

Map 7.4, page 294

This is one of the most worshipped trails in the Bay Area. The workings of this trail started with a vision to create a route that connected Castle Rock State Park on Skyline Ridge to Big Basin and then to Waddell Creek on the coast. The result, much of it built by volunteers, is this 34-mile backpack route, complete with primitive trail camps. It is ideal in many ways, including the fact that the hike is generally downhill, starting at 3,000 feet at Castle Rock and dropping all the way down to sea level. You get fantastic views, redwood forests, waterfalls, and backpack camps. Most hike the trail in three days, camping at Waterman Gap and at Big Basin headquarters, with a shuttle car waiting at the end of the trail at Waddell Creek on Highway 1.

From the trailhead at Castle Rock State Park, head out to the Waterman Gap trail camp (water is available) for a first-day hike of 9.6 miles. In the first two miles, you will cross an open rock facing the leads past the foot of Goat Rock. As the landscape opens up, you get fantastic views of Big Basin and the Pacific Coast to the west. This will help you envision the upcoming route. You then drop down into the headwaters of the San Lorenzo River, pass an old homestead, and through mixed forest.

The logical plan for the second day is to hike from Waterman Gap 9.5 miles to Jay Camp at Big Basin headquarters. Once you cross Highway 9, you will enter the state park. For a few miles the route roughly parallels the park's access road. Then it breaks off, passes an open sandstone face with great westerly views, traces a narrow ridge, and drops down into a lush redwood canyon with a stream. Only Skyline-to-the-Sea hikers typically travel this area, so by seeing this landscape you join a select club. Eventually the trail emerges at the bottom of Big Basin, and you camp relatively near park headquarters. Although this camp is not a backcountry experience, the convenience of restrooms, coin showers, drinking water, and a small store are usually well received.

On the last day, from park headquarters, you face hiking 12.5 miles out to the finish. It starts by heading through giant redwoods, up and over the Big Basin rim, then down a wooded canyon. You will see beautiful 70-foot Berry Creek Falls, a free-fall at high water, and moss-lined water mosaic in low flows. At Berry Creek Falls, be sure to hike up the stairs to the brink of the waterfall, then head up the canyon to see Silver Falls (a gorgeous free-fall, perfect for photographs), and then above that, Golden Falls, where clear water cascades over golden sandstone like a gigantic water slide. After that side-trip adventure, return to the main trail, turn west (right), and cross Waddell Creek.

From Berry Creek Falls to the coast is a breeze, crossing over the stream with a makeshift bridge, then making the sea-level walk to Rancho del Oso and the parking area. It's a shortcut to hike out on the service road and bike path, but in the spring, take the longer, official route that loops around the valley hills (to the north) and down to the parking area to see 20 or 30 species of wildflowers, including occasional rafts of forget-me-nots. Finish up at the coast, and experience a moment of exultation when you arrive at your vehicle.

Note: Castle Rock State Park is on the closure list developed by the California Department of Parks, pending final state budget decisions or the possible transfer of park management to other park agencies or volunteer groups.

User Groups: Hikers and horses. No dogs or mountain bikes. No wheelchair facilities.

Permits: Trail camp reservations are required with a reservation fee, plus a camping fee per night, and a $10 parking fee per extra vehicle at the trailheads. Call 831/338-8861.

Maps: Detailed trail maps of Castle Rock State Park and Big Basin Redwoods State Park are available for a fee from Mountain Parks Foundation, 525 N. Big Trees Road, Felton, CA 95018, 831/335-3174. A free information sheet and a mileage chart between trail camps are available by phoning 831/338-8861, or writing Big Basin Redwoods State Park. For topographic maps, ask the USGS for Castle Rock Ridge and Big Basin.

Directions: To Castle Rock State Park: From

I-280 near Santa Clara, turn west on Saratoga Avenue and drive to Highway 9. Drive west on Highway 9 to the junction with Highway 35 (Skyline Boulevard). Turn south and drive 2.5 miles to the entrance to Castle Rock State Park on the right. Your vehicle must be registered in advance with park rangers.

To Waddell Creek/Rancho del Oso: From I-280 in San Mateo, turn west on Highway 92 and drive to Half Moon Bay. Turn left (south) on Highway 1 and drive about 35 miles, (two miles past Año Nuevo State Reserve) and look for the signs indicating Big Basin Redwoods State Park/Rancho del Oso, just past the Santa Cruz County line. Turn and park at Rancho del Oso. Your vehicle must be registered in advance with park rangers.

Contact: Big Basin Redwoods State Park, 21600 Big Basin Way, Boulder Creek, CA 95006, 831/338-8860; Castle Rock State Park, 15000 Skyline Boulevard, Los Gatos, CA 95020, 408/867-2952; trail camp reservations, 831/338-8861, www.parks.ca.gov, www.mountainparks.org.

182 SUMMIT ROCK LOOP
2.0 mi / 1.0 hr   🥾1 ⛰8

in Sanborn-Skyline County Park on Skyline Ridge in the Santa Cruz Mountains

Map 7.4, page 294

The Santa Clara Valley never looks prettier than it does from Summit Rock. The lookout point is set just east of the Skyline Ridge, towering over the valley below.

The park is so named because it connects Sanborn Creek with the Skyline Ridge, covering some 2,850 acres of mountain terrain in between. Some people get thrown off because this park is technically in Sanborn-Skyline County Park, yet the trailhead is nowhere near the park headquarters, but rather off Sanborn Road where full facilities, a campground, and other trails are available. So ignore the signs for the park when you drive up Highway 9.

From the trailhead across Highway 35 from

Castle Rock State Park, hikers start on the Skyline Trail and head north, adjacent to the road. The Skyline Trail leads right into the Summit Rock Loop, providing easy access to this great lookout. For people who like their views to come even easier, a popular option at the Skyline trailhead is the 0.25-mile hike that leads to Indian Rock.

User Groups: Hikers and horses. No dogs (otherwise permitted on most trails in Sanborn-Skyline; watch for signs at trailheads) or mountain bikes. No wheelchair facilities.

Permits: No permits are required. A day-use fee of $6 is charged per vehicle.

Maps: For a free trail map, contact Sanborn-Skyline County Park. For a topographic map, ask the USGS for Castle Rock Ridge.

Directions: From I-280 near Santa Clara, turn west on Saratoga Avenue and drive to Highway 9. Drive west on Highway 9 to the junction with Highway 35 (Skyline Boulevard). Turn south and drive 2.5 miles to Sanborn-Skyline County Park on the left. The trailhead is located roughly across from Castle Rock State Park on Skyline Boulevard.

Contact: Sanborn-Skyline/Upper Stevens Creek County Park, 16055 Sanborn Road, Saratoga, CA 95070, 408/867-9959; Santa Clara County Parks and Recreation, 408/355-2200, www.parkhere.org.

183 PENITENCIA CREEK
4.0 mi / 1.75 hr

in Penitencia Creek County Park in east San Jose

Map 7.4, page 294

This paved route runs along a creek for a pleasant stroll, jog, or bicycle ride. The Penitencia Creek Trail goes to Noble Avenue, where Noble Avenue connects to Penitencia Creek Road past the Penitencia Creek percolation ponds (run by the City of San Jose). It is a popular destination for trail users, with trailside exercise equipment, picnic benches, a pond, and lawn area.

However, it does not connect to adjacent Alum Rock Park, unless you consider Penitencia Creek Road itself as part of the trail (which it isn't). There are two Penitencia Creek Parks. One belongs to the City of San Jose. The county portion, at Jackson and Mabury, is also referred to as "Penitencia Creek Gardens."

User Groups: Hikers, bikes, leashed dogs and wheelchairs. No horses.

Permits: No permits are required. Parking and access are free.

Maps: For a free trail map, contact Penitencia Creek County Park. For a topographic map, ask the USGS for Calaveras Reservoir.

Directions: From I-680 in San Jose, take the Berryessa Road exit. Drive east on Berryessa Road to Capitol Avenue. Turn right on Capitol Avenue and drive 0.3 mile to Penitencia Creek Road. Turn left and drive 0.5 mile to the parking area on the left.

Contact: Penitencia Creek County Park (Levin County Park), 408/262-6980; Santa Clara County Parks and Recreation, 408/355-2200. www.parkhere.org.

184 EAGLE ROCK LOOP
2.2 mi / 1.0 hr

in Alum Rock City Park in the San Jose foothills

Map 7.4, page 294

Eagle Rock is pretty short as far as mountains go, only 795 feet. But at Alum Rock City Park, it's the best perch in the vicinity for a picnic site and a view of the Santa Clara Valley. In the winter, after rain has cleared the air, it becomes a choice spot. For this hike, park at the lot at the road's end at the eastern end of the park, where you'll find a major trailhead for several routes. Take the one on the left, North Rim Trail, to reach Eagle Rock. The hike climbs 300 feet to a canyon rim overlooking the valley cut by Penitencia Creek, before a short, signed cutoff trail takes you to Eagle Rock. To complete the loop, return to North Rim Trail and walk your way back down the valley floor. Turn left on Creek Trail (more like a road), which is routed along Penitencia Creek to the parking area. Thirteen miles of trails provide access to the park's 700 acres, but this hike is our favorite.

Note: Some unsavory characters are known to occasionally frequent this park. Women are advised to avoid hiking solo.

User Groups: Hikers, horses, and mountain bikes. No dogs. No wheelchair facilities.

Permits: No permits are required. An entrance fee of $10 is charged on weekends and holidays; $6 per vehicle at other times.

Maps: A brochure and map are available at the trailhead. For a free trail map, contact Alum Rock City Park. For a topographic map, ask the USGS for Calaveras Reservoir.

Directions: From I-680 in San Jose, take the Alum Rock Avenue exit. Turn east on Alum Rock Avenue and drive 3.5 miles to the park entrance.

Contact: Alum Rock City Park, 16240 Alum Rock Avenue, San Jose, CA 95127, 408/277-4539 or 408/259-5477, www.sanjoseca.gov.

185 HALLS VALLEY LOOP
5.5 mi / 3.0 hr

in Joseph D. Grant County Park in the Mount Hamilton foothills east of San Jose

Map 7.4, page 294

Grant County Park is the Bay Area's great undiscovered playland and the Halls Valley Loop provides the best introduction to what many call Grant Ranch. From the Grant Lake Parking Area along Mount Hamilton Road (on the left as you drive in from San Jose, not at the headquarters on the right), take the main trail/road routed out past Grant Lake to a junction with the Halls Valley Trail. Bear left at the junction. This route skirts Halls Valley to the left, an open landscape of foothills and grasslands sprinkled with oaks, a quiet and pretty scene. The trail then heads out 2.5 miles, climbing east toward Mount Hamilton until it meets Cañada de Pala Trail.

Turn right, hike up 0.4 mile, and turn right again on Los Huecos Trail to complete the loop. From here, it's a 1.8-mile trip back to the parking area. You will descend steeply on the way back to your car.

There are many great side trips on this route. Here are the best two: 1) After a rain, search out the little creek at the bottom of Halls Valley, then follow it upstream to discover a procession of little waterfalls (this is an off-trail trek); 2) For the ambitious, climb 2.2 miles and 500 feet up the ridge on Pala Seca Trail above Halls Valley to the park's highest point—from Antler Point at 2,999 feet, you can look out over the Santa Clara Valley.

This park covers 9,553 acres in the foothills of Mount Hamilton and can be the perfect setting for hiking and mountain biking. There is plenty of room for both endeavors, with 40 miles of trails, a combination of single track and ranch roads.

User Groups: Hikers, horses, and mountain bikes. No dogs. No wheelchair facilities (wheelchair accessible facilities available at headquarters).

Permits: No permits are required. An entrance fee of $6 per vehicle is charged (pay at the entrance across the street from the trailhead).

Maps: For a free trail map, contact Joseph D. Grant County Park. For a topographic map, ask the USGS for Lick Observatory.

Directions: From I-680 in San Jose, take the Alum Rock Avenue East exit and drive to Mount Hamilton Road. Turn right on Mount Hamilton Road and drive eight miles east to the parking area and trailhead on the left.

Contact: Joseph D. Grant County Park, 18405 Mount Hamilton Road, San Jose, CA 95140, 408/274-6121; trail conditions, Santa Clara County Parks and Recreation, 408/355-2200, www.parkhere.org.

186 HOTEL TRAIL
7.0 mi / 3.25 hr   🚶2 ⛰8

in Joseph D. Grant County Park in the Mount Hamilton foothills east of San Jose

Map 7.4, page 294

The remote landscape around Eagle Lake in Grant County Park provides visitors with precious tranquility as well as good chances of seeing wildlife. Eagle Lake, set in the southernmost reaches of the park's 9,553 acres, is the prime destination of Hotel Trail. After parking at the lot along Mount Hamilton Road, cross the road and look for the trailhead on the south side. Start hiking southeast on the ranch road (Hotel Trail), scanning your surroundings for the wild turkeys that are commonly seen in this area. As you head deeper into the interior, you will be hiking through foothill country; bovines are the most frequently encountered animal (keep your distance from the bulls, of course), but you might see a herd of wild pigs, too. These pigs tend to sprint off when they see or hear people, so don't worry about playing out the fearless-hiker-meets-ferocious-boar scene. The route to Eagle Lake is a direct shot of 3.5 miles, climbing a couple of hundred feet in the process. There are several options for side trips along the way: the best is to turn right on Cañada de Pala Trail and drop down about 0.5 mile to San Felipe Creek, the prettiest stream in the park.

User Groups: Hikers, horses, and mountain bikes. No dogs. No wheelchair facilities.

Permits: No permits are required. An entrance fee of $6 per vehicle is charged.

Maps: For a free trail map, contact Joseph D. Grant County Park. For a topographic map, ask the USGS for Lick Observatory.

Directions: From I-680 in San Jose, take the Alum Rock Avenue East exit and drive to Mount Hamilton Road. Turn right on Mount Hamilton Road and drive eight miles east to the parking area on the left. The Hotel Trail starts on the south side of the road, opposite the parking area.

Contact: Joseph D. Grant County Park, 18405 Mount Hamilton Road, San Jose, CA 95140, 408/274-6121; trail conditions, Santa Clara County Parks and Recreation, 408/355-2200, www.parkhere.org.

187 RIDGE TRAIL
6.0 mi / 2.75 hr   🚶2 ⛰7

in El Sereno Open Space Preserve in the Saratoga foothills

Map 7.4, page 294

El Sereno Open Space is one of the lesser-used parklands in the Bay Area. Why? Not only is it remote, but there's room at the trailhead for only two vehicles to park. From the trailhead at the pullout on Montevina Road, hike on the jeep trail, which traces a ridgeline. Though the trail bobs and weaves, you will generally head east, topping out on a rim and then descending toward Los Gatos for a distance of three miles to the end of the trail. This is where you'll find panoramic views of Lyndon Canyon, Lexington Reservoir, and the South Bay. After taking the time to enjoy the vistas, return via the same route. The preserve covers 1,112 acres and is named for Mount El Sereno, the prominent peak on the adjacent ridge.

User Groups: Hikers, horses, and mountain bikes. No dogs. No wheelchair facilities.

Permits: No permits are required. Parking and access are free.

Maps: A brochure and map are available at the trailhead. For a free trail map, contact the Midpeninsula Regional Open Space District. For a topographic map, ask the USGS for Castle Rock Ridge.

Directions: From the intersection of I-280 and Highway 17 in San Jose, turn south on Highway 17 and drive about eight miles to Los Gatos. Continue south for about three miles to Montevina Road. Turn right and park at the roadside turnout at the end of the road. There is space for only a few cars.

Contact: Midpeninsula Regional Open Space District, 330 Distel Circle, Los Altos, CA

94022, 650/691-1200, www.openspace.org. During nonbusiness hours, a touch-tone phone menu is available for trail news, conditions, and events.

188 PRIEST ROCK TRAIL
6.1 mi / 4.5 hr 🏃3 ⛰7

in the Sierra Azul Open Space Preserve near Lexington Reservoir

Map 7.4, page 294

You get a little bit of hell on this trail to gain entry to a lot of heaven. From the entrance to the Sierra Azul Open Space Preserve, the trail rises in the first mile to 1,762 feet at Priest Rock. There it nearly levels out for about a mile, until you reach the loop junction. Bear to the left at the junction. The trail starts climbing again and climbs another thousand feet or so in the next 1.5 miles to reach the ridgeline at 2,628 feet. Turn right at the ridge and enjoy finally being on top, cruising over the 1.6-mile stretch on the mountain rim. Turn right again at the next ridge junction and take the trail back (three miles to the loop junction), relaxing on the downhill cruise.

The climb is well worth the effort for the long-distance sweeping views of the valley and foothills. Up on top, you will get the sense of a paradox, that landscape this wild could exist so close to so many homes. But they do, and you can explore them on the Sierra Azul Loop, a strenuous hike that climbs, climbs, and climbs as it probes the Sierra Azul Range.

User Groups: Hikers, horses, and mountain bikes. No dogs. No wheelchair facilities.

Permits: No permits are required. No fee.

Maps: A brochure and map are available at the trailhead. For a free trail map, contact the Midpeninsula Regional Open Space District. For a topographic map, ask the USGS for Santa Teresa Hills.

Directions: From Los Gatos, drive south on Highway 17 for about four miles to the Alma Bridge Road exit at Lexington Reservoir. Turn east and drive 1.5 miles across the dam. When

you reach the parking area for county parks (a fee is charged if you park here), continue on Alma Bridge Road to another parking area (free) on the right.

Contact: Midpeninsula Regional Open Space District, 330 Distel Circle, Los Altos, CA 94022, 650/691-1200, www.openspace.org. During nonbusiness hours, a touch-tone phone menu is available for trail news, conditions, and events.

189 ST. JOSEPH'S HILL TRAIL
2.7 mi / 1.75 hr 🏃2 ⛰7

in the St. Joseph's Hill Open Space Preserve near Lexington Reservoir

Map 7.4, page 294

For most people to be willing to hike up, there had better be a pay off waiting at the trail's end. And so there is on this hike, which climbs 600 feet in the space of about 1.5 miles to a perch on top of St. Joseph's Hill, with views of Lexington Reservoir, the Santa Clara Valley, and the adjacent Sierra Azul Range. Start this trip at the parking area and trailhead just east of the Lexington Dam (elevation 645 feet), just opposite the boat launch. Hike north, adjacent to Los Gatos Creek, for about 0.5 mile, to a trail junction for St. Joseph's Hill. At this junction, turn right and begin the climb up St. Joseph's Hill; a loop route is available near the top. From up here, Lexington Reservoir never looked so good.

User Groups: Hikers, dogs, and mountain bikes. No horses. No wheelchair facilities.

Permits: No permits are required. A fee of $5 per vehicle is charged at Lexington Reservoir County Park.

Maps: A brochure and map are available at the trailhead. For a free trail map, contact the Midpeninsula Regional Open Space District. For a topographic map, ask the USGS for Los Gatos.

Directions: From San Jose: Take Highway 17 (to about four miles east of Los Gatos) to the exit for Bear Creek Road. Take that exit, bear right, cross over the freeway, and re-enter Highway 17 and drive a short distance to the exit for Alma Bridge Road. Take that exit and drive east for 1.5 miles (across the Lexington Dam). Parking is available just east of the dam in Lexington Reservoir County Park. The trail starts opposite the boat launching area beyond the dam.

From Santa Cruz: Take Highway 17 (to about four miles east of Los Gatos) to the exit for Alma Bridge Road. Take that exit and drive east for 1.5 miles (across the Lexington Dam). Parking is available just east of the dam in Lexington Reservoir County Park. The trail starts opposite the boat launching area beyond the dam.

Contact: Lexington Reservoir County Park, c/o Vasona Lake County Park, 298 Garden Hill Drive, Los Gatos, CA 95030, 408/356-2729; trail conditions, Santa Clara County Parks and Recreation, 408/355-2200, www.parkhere.org; Midpeninsula Regional Open Space District, 330 Distel Circle, Los Altos, CA 94022, 650/691-1200, www.open-space.org. During nonbusiness hours, a touch-tone phone menu is available for trail news, conditions, and events.

190 LEXINGTON DAM TRAIL
1.0 mi / 0.5 hr   👫1 ⛰6

in Lexington Reservoir County Park in the Saratoga foothills

Map 7.4, page 294

Lexington Reservoir can be one of the prettiest places in Santa Clara County. When the lake is full and spilling in late winter and early spring, some people show up just to stare at all the water. Take it the extra mile for a nice bonus. Park at the lot just east of the dam, then walk across the dam and turn right on the "Pedway." That's as far as many people get, as most come for the view of the lake from the dam. Keep walking, though, and you will be surprised, as the trail drops down along Los Gatos Creek. After 1.5 miles, it links up with Los Gatos Creek Trail. This trail is routed all the way into town and it's also a great bike route.

Great news: Lexington is again open to non-power boating, and with the lake full, the bass fishing can be great in the spring. Often Lexington, as pretty as it can be, can be full of water one year, then drained down to nothing the next. And after a hot summer it can resemble a dust bowl. For more ambitious walks, there are several parklands nearby.

User Groups: Hikers and mountain bikes. No dogs or horses. No wheelchair facilities.

Permits: No permits are required. A day-use fee of $6 per vehicle is charged.

Maps: For a free trail map, contact Lexington Reservoir County Park. For a topographic map, ask the USGS for Los Gatos.

Directions: From San Jose: Take Highway 17 (to about four miles east of Los Gatos) to the exit for Bear Creek Road. Take that exit, bear right, cross over the freeway, and re-enter Highway 17 and drive a short distance to the exit for Alma Bridge Road. Take that exit and drive east for 1.5 miles (across the Lexington Dam). Parking is available just east of the dam in Lexington Reservoir County Park.

From Santa Cruz: Take Highway 17 (to about four miles east of Los Gatos) to the exit for Alma Bridge Road. Take that exit and drive east for 1.5 miles (across the Lexington Dam). Parking is available just east of the dam in Lexington Reservoir County Park.

Contact: Lexington Reservoir (c/o Vasona), 408/356-2729; trail conditions, Santa Clara County Parks and Recreation, 408/355-2200, www.parkhere.org.

191 BALD MOUNTAIN TRAIL
1.0 mi / 0.5 hr 🏃1 ⛰9

in Sierra Azul Open Space Preserve south of Los Gatos

Map 7.4, page 294

The 3,486-foot Mount Umunhum (in an Ohlone language, Umunhum means "resting place of the hummingbird") is the off-limits mountain that crowns the ridge to the west above Santa Clara Valley. Nearby Bald Mountain and Mount El Sobroso both provide hiking access. From Blossom Hill near Los Gatos, the drive rises up from the valley floor, winds its way up through the pretty oak woodlands and foothills, and emerges high in the Sierra Azul Range. The views are sensational across the valley to Mount Hamilton and to the South Bay. On perfect fall days, you can see miles south to the ridge tops above the Hollister valley. This view is a highlight for the 18,000-acre Sierra Azul Open Space Preserve.

The trailhead for Bald Mountain is along Mount Umunhum Road and leads 0.5 mile to 2,387-foot Bald Mountain and sweeping views across Santa Clara Valley.

To reach Mount El Sombroso from the Jaques Ridge parking area, take the 6.2-mile Woods Trail (easy–moderate) across grasslands, in and out of ravines, and topping out at Mount El Sombroso (2,999 feet).

Note: The weird, square building on top of Mount Umunhum looks like a Borg spacecraft out of a Star Trek episode. It's a radar tower that was part of a former Air Force base from the Cold War era. The land is owned by Midpeninsula Regional Open Space District, which will open it for public access when the federal government completes toxic cleanup at the military site.

User Groups: Hikers, horses, and mountain bikes. No dogs. No wheelchair facilities.

Permits: No permits required. Parking and access are free.

Maps: A brochure and map are available at the trailhead. For a free trail map, contact the Midpeninsula Regional Open Space District.

For a topographic map, ask the USGS for Santa Teresa Hills.

Directions: From San Francisco, take US 101 south for 35 miles to Highway 82. Merge right on Highway 82 and drive 16 miles to the exit for Camden Avenue. Take that exit to Camden, turn left, and drive 1.7 miles to Hicks Road. Turn right on Hicks, go 0.2 mile (turn left to stay on Hicks), and drive 6.1 miles (past Guadalupe Reservoir) up the mountain to Mount Umunhum Road. Turn right and Jaques Ridge Parking Area is on your right.

Bald Mountain Trail: From the main parking area, continue up Mount Umunhum Road for 1.6 miles to a closed gate (No. SA08). Park on the shoulder on the right side of the road (space for three cars). The trailhead is just across road (on left side of road).

Woods Trail: The trailhead is located at the Jaques Ridge parking area.

Contact: Midpeninsula Regional Open Space District, 330 Distel Circle, Los Altos, CA 94022, 650/691-1200, www.openspace.org. During nonbusiness hours, a touch-tone phone menu is available for trail news, conditions, and events.

192 MINE HILL TRAIL
2.0-14.5 mi / 1.0-7.0 hr 🏃3 ⛰7

in Almaden Quicksilver County Park in the San Jose foothills

Map 7.4, page 294

Of the dozen trails at Almaden Quicksilver County Park, this is the most unusual. Although Almaden Quicksilver covers 3,977 acres and has two reservoirs (Almaden and Guadalupe), it is the evidence of historical mining operations that makes it fascinating. With a network of trails here, many routes and long trips are possible, but most people cut it short, enjoying a portion.

The Mine Hill Trail starts just inside the park entrance off of Almaden Road (Hacienda entrance). From here, Mine Hill Trail is routed north to a junction (there are several). Turn left (staying on Mine Hill Trail) and you will pass the Day Tunnel (the Day Tunnel is on the Randol Trail about 0.5 mile from Mine Hill Trail) and San Cristobal Tunnel, remnants of the mining days. At that point, most people just return. Some will take the 0.75-mile April Trail Loop, a short cutoff loop off Mine Hill Trail. A bonus is that wildflower blooms are good in this park in the spring.

Almaden was the site of the first quicksilver mine in North America. Mining began in 1845 and continued until 1975. There are still burnt ore dumps along the trail.

Note: Wallace Stegner set part of his novel *Angle of Repose* in the area now contained within Almaden Quicksilver County Park.

User Groups: Hikers, mountain bikes (Hacienda/Wood/Mockingbird entrances only), and horses. Leashed dogs are permitted. No wheelchair trail access.

Permits: No permits are required. Park entrance is free.

Maps: A trail map is also available at the trailhead. For a topographic map, ask the USGS for Santa Teresa Hills.

Directions: Take Highway 82 to the exit for Almaden Expressway. Take that exit and drive south on Almaden Expressway to Almaden Road. Turn right on Almaden Road and drive three miles through New Almaden to the Hacienda park entrance and unpaved staging area on the right (note that there are four major access points to the park).

Contact: Almaden Quicksilver County Park office, (Calero County Park), 23205 McKean Road, San Jose, CA 95120, 408/268-3883; trail conditions, Santa Clara County Parks and Recreation, 408/355-2200, www.parkhere.org.

193 COYOTE PEAK LOOP

3.4 mi / 2.0 hr   🏃2 ⛰7

in Santa Teresa County Park south of San Jose

Map 7.4, page 294

The most notable hike at Santa Teresa County Park is the tromp up to Coyote Peak. This feature destination provides a good loop hike and a lookout to the southern Santa Clara Valley. Start your trip by hiking south on the Hidden Springs Trail, the unsigned trail located across from the parking lot with the call box. Take that trail and climb 2.4 miles to the top, with a short loop cutoff getting you to the summit. To complete the loop, take the Coyote Peak Trail back down, then take Hidden Springs Trail to the Ohlone Trail and finish out the final mile back to the parking area.

This park covers 1,688 acres, but the main attractions are the golf course, driving range, bar, and restaurant. In contrast to the manicured greens of the golf course, this trail provides an insight into the park's most primitive and rugged areas and gives you a good view for your efforts.

User Groups: Hikers, mountain bikers, leashed dogs, and horses. No mountain bikes, except on Ohlone Trail. No wheelchair facilities.

Permits: No permits are required. A $6 park entrance fee is charged per vehicle.

Maps: A brochure and map are available at the trailhead. For a free trail map, contact Santa Teresa County Park. For a topographic map, ask the USGS for Santa Teresa Hills.

Directions: From San Jose on US 101, drive south to Bernal Road (north of Morgan Hill). Take that exit and turn west on Bernal Road and drive 1.25 miles to the park. Park in the main day-use lot.

Contact: Santa Teresa County Park, 408/225-0225 (c/o Hellyer); trail conditions, Santa Clara County Parks and Recreation, 408/355-2200, www.parkhere.org.

194 CALERO LAKE

4.8 mi / 2.0 hr

in Calero County Park southeast of San Jose

Map 7.4, page 294

The pay off for this hike is a sweeping view of Calero Reservoir to the north. Start near the entrance gate and take the Los Cerritos Trail to the right (west). The trail bears right, toward Calero Reservoir, and then runs along the southern shoreline of the reservoir for more than a mile before making a nearly 180-degree looping left turn. If you don't want to climb, turn around and go back at this point. The trail continues and climbs the ridgeline bordering the southern end of the reservoir. As it tops the ridge, it connects to the Pena Trail. To complete the loop, turn left on the Pena Trail and make the descent. A great way to return is to descend the Pena Trail, turn right on the Los Vallecitos Trail, and then turn left on Figueroa Trail. It adds two miles to the trip but is well worth it. This is a very popular horseback trail on weekends, and if you don't watch where you're going, well, you won't be stepping in Shinola.

Note: what was once called the Juan Crespi Trail as part of this hike no longer exists.

User Groups: Hikers and horses. No dogs or mountain bikes. No wheelchair facilities.

Permits: No permits are required. Park entrance is free at this access point for hiking, but a fee is charged at the boat ramp at Calero.

Maps: A brochure and map are available at the trailhead. For a topographic map, ask the USGS for Santa Teresa Hills.

Directions: From San Jose, drive south on US 101 until you reach the Bailey Avenue exit. Turn right onto Bailey Avenue and drive three miles to McKean Road. Turn left on McKean Road for 0.5 mile to the park entrance. Drive to the sign for the park office and park adjacent to the ranger office.

Contact: Calero County Park, 408/268-3883; Santa Clara County Parks and Recreation, 408/355-2200, www.parkhere.org.

195 LOCH LOMOND LOOP

5.0 mi / 3.25 hr

in Loch Lomond Recreation Area in the Santa Cruz Mountains near Ben Lomond

Map 7.4, page 294

Loch Lomond Reservoir is a jewel set in the Santa Cruz Mountains. There is no prettier lake in the greater Bay Area than this, complete with an island and with shores lined by conifers. Of the 12 miles of trails here, the best hike is the Loch Lomond Loop. From the parking area, take the Loch Trail, a level path that extends northward along the lakeshore for 1.5 miles out to Deer Flat. There you turn uphill on Highland Trail, climbing and looping to the east up the ridge on a moderate ascent. It peaks out at a remote weather station where you get a sweeping view of the lake below and the surrounding forested mountains.

To complete the loop, continue southward along the ridgecrest down to the Glen Corrie Picnic Area, or you can take the paved road back to the starting point. A bonus at Loch Lomond is good trout fishing, especially from April through June, and good bass and bluegill fishing in the summer. What a great getaway: great lake, great views, great hike.

Note that the park is closed from mid-September through February, and swimming is not permitted—this is a drinking-water supply lake.

User Groups: Hikers and dogs. No horses or mountain bikes. No wheelchair facilities.

Permits: No permits are required. A day-use fee of $4 per vehicle is charged; $1 for dogs. The Loch Lomond Recreation Area is open only from March 1 through September 15. Rangers are on duty during the winter and will cite trespassers.

Maps: For a free trail map, contact Loch Lomond Recreation Area. For a topographic map, ask the USGS for Felton.

Directions: Coastal route (82 miles): From San Francisco, take I-280 to Daly City and the exit for Highway 1. Bear right at that exit and take Highway 1 to Half Moon Bay and continue south into Santa Cruz and Exit 442 for Ocean Street. Turn left on Ocean Street and drive 0.3 mile to Graham Hill Road. Continue on Graham Hill Road for 5.3 miles to East Zayante Road. Turn right on East Zayante Road and go 2.6 miles to Lompico Road. Turn left and go 1.7 miles to West Drive. Turn left and drive 0.5 mile (it jogs twice on Trinkling Creek Lane) to Sequoia Drive. Turn right on Sequoia and go 0.2 mile (it jogs left); it then becomes Loch Lomond Way. Continue to the entrance station.

Mountain route: From San Francisco, take I-280 south to Cupertino and the exit for Highway 82. Take Highway 82 south to the exit for Sunnyvale-Saratoga Road. Take that exit, turn right (south), and drive into Saratoga to Big Basin Way/Highway 9. Turn right, drive a short distance through town, and continue up the hill (curvy) to Skyline/Highway 35. Drive straight through the intersection and continue (curvy and fun) to Felton and Graham Hill Road. Turn left on Graham Hill Road and after two stoplights reach East Zayante Road. Turn left on East Zayante and continue as above. The trailhead is located adjacent to the boat ramp.

Contact: Loch Lomond Recreation Area, 100 Loch Lomond Way, Felton, CA 95018, 831/420-5320, marina 831/335-7424, www.ci.santa-cruz.ca.us/.

196 BIG TREES NATURE TRAIL

1.0 mi / 0.5 hr 👫1 🔺8

in Loch Lomond Recreation Area in the Santa Cruz Mountains near Ben Lomond

Map 7.4, page 294

This short trail starts at the Glen Corrie Picnic Area and provides an excellent reminder of the power of nature. First, pick up a free trail guide at the park store. As the trail ascends, numbered signs note many natural features and plants of the redwood forest. The only remaining old-growth redwoods in

this watershed are located near the ridgecrest. These massive, 500- to 1,000-year-old trees offer a glimpse into the area's prelogging magnificence. Just around the bend from the giant trees is a highly disturbed area that suffered major storm damage during the 1970s and 1980s from high winds, snowfall, and heavy rainfall. The biggest hit came from a January 1982 storm in which 15 inches of rain fell in a 24-hour period, causing major debris flows (mud slides). As the trail descends through this still-recovering area, you'll notice many trees that had their tops knocked off. The debris flows clogged existing drainage channels and created several massive logjams. Remnants of early-20th-century logging activities can also be seen along this short, fascinating trail.

Note that the park is closed mid-September–February and swimming is not permitted—this is a drinking-water supply lake.

User Groups: Hikers and dogs. No horses or mountain bikes. No wheelchair facilities.

Permits: No permits are required. A day-use fee of $4 per vehicle is charged; there is also a fee for dogs. The Loch Lomond Recreation Area is open only March 1–September 15. Rangers are on duty during the winter and will cite trespassers.

Maps: For a free trail map, contact Loch Lomond Recreation Area. For a topographic map, ask the USGS for Felton.

Directions: Coastal route (82 miles): From San Francisco, take I-280 to Daly City and the exit for Highway 1. Bear right at that exit and take Highway 1 to Half Moon Bay. Continue south into Santa Cruz and Exit 442 for Ocean Street. Turn left on Ocean Street and go 0.3 mile to Graham Hill Road. Continue on Graham Hill Road for 5.3 miles to East Zayante Road. Turn right on East Zayante Road and go 2.6 miles to Lompico Road. Turn left and drive 1.7 miles to West Drive. Turn left and go 0.5 mile (it jogs twice on Trinkling Creek Lane) to Sequoia Drive. Turn right on Sequoia and drive 0.2 mile (it jogs left); it then becomes Loch Lomond Way. Continue to entrance station.

Mountain route: From San Francisco, take I-280 south to Cupertino and the exit for Highway 82. Take Highway 82 south and the exit for Sunnyvale-Saratoga Road. Take that exit, turn right (south), and drive into Saratoga to Big Basin Way/Highway 9. Turn right, drive short distance through town, and continue up the hill (curvy) to Skyline/Highway 35. Continue straight through the intersection and on to Felton and Graham Hill Road (curvy and fun). Turn left on Graham Hill Road and drive pass stoplights to East Zayante Road. Turn left on East Zayante and continue as above.

Contact: Loch Lomond Recreation Area, 100 Loch Lomond Way, Felton, CA 95018, 831/420-5320, www.ci.santa-cruz.ca.us/wt.

197 FALL CREEK LOOP

8.0 mi / 4.5 hr 🏃3 ⛰9

in Henry Cowell Redwoods State Park near Santa Cruz

Map 7.4, page 294

Where in the Santa Cruz area can you find a fast-running, full-flowing stream even in the driest months of summer and fall? Almost nowhere except here, at the Fall Creek Unit of Henry Cowell Redwoods State Park.

This trailhead is located a few miles distant from the main area and campground of Henry Cowell State Park. From the parking lot, take Bennett Creek Trail gently downhill for 0.2 mile, then turn left on Fall Creek Trail. Meander along this fern-laden, creek-side path to the South Fork Trail spur to the limekilns. This is the start of the loop. After checking out the kilns, follow Cape Horn Trail to Lost Empire Trail. The next two miles are a sustained climb with a short level stretch in the middle near Barrel Mill Creek. The high point of the loop is reached at Big Ben Tree, a large virgin redwood situated at a junction of trails. You'll finish out the loop by heading downhill on Big Ben Trail, then turning right on Fall Creek Trail, and finally heading back up Bennett Creek Trail to your car.

Crystal-clear Fall Creek tumbles and cascades through the park year-round. Many visitors just hike a short stretch along the stream, but your best bet is to make a big loop around the park. The park is well known for its campground and steam trains. In addition to its perennial stream and second- and third-growth redwood forest, the park features three 1870s limekilns, an old railroad grade, and other evidence of this area's history as an important lime producer. The lime was used to make mortar to build the brick buildings of San Francisco and San Jose.

Note: This park is on the closure list developed by the California Department of Parks, pending final state budget decisions or the possible transfer of park management to other park agencies or volunteer groups.

User Groups: Hikers and horses. No dogs or mountain bikes. No wheelchair facilities.

Permits: No permits are required. A fee of $10 is charged per vehicle.

Maps: Park maps are available at the visitors center at the main unit of Henry Cowell State Park on Highway 9. For a topographic map, ask the USGS for Felton.

Directions: From San Jose, drive south on Highway 17 for 24 miles to Scotts Valley. Take the Mount Hermon Road exit, turn right and drive toward Felton for 3.5 miles to Graham Hill Road. Turn right on Graham Hill Road and drive 0.1 mile to Highway 9. Continue straight across Highway 9 onto Felton Empire Road and drive 0.6 mile to the Fall Creek trailhead on the right. Note: This is not the primary entrance for Henry Cowell Redwoods.

Contact: Henry Cowell Redwoods State Park, Fall Creek Unit, 101 N. Big Trees Road, Felton, CA 95018, 831/335-4598, Nature Center, 831/335-7077, www.parks.ca.gov, www.mountainparks.org.

198 EAGLE CREEK TRAIL
3.0 mi / 1.5 hr   🏃1 ⛰8

in Henry Cowell Redwoods State Park near
Santa Cruz

Map 7.4, page 294

There are two places you don't want to miss
on a visit to Henry Cowell Redwoods State
Park. The first one is Eagle Creek Trail, the
most direct hiking route to River Trail and
the San Lorenzo River. The other is the park's
observation deck, offering first-class views on
clear days.

The Eagle Creek Trail starts between campsite Nos. 82 and 84, crosses Eagle Creek, and
continues adjacent to the stream as it heads
out toward the San Lorenzo River. As you hike
this portion of the trail, you are surrounded
by redwoods. The trail then crosses Pipeline
Road and junctions with the River Trail.
Many people turn around and head back at
this point. However, a great way to extend
your hike is to head north on the River Trail
alongside the river, adding an extra three miles
to the trip. Another bonus is the observation
deck, the highest point in the park. Trees obscure views of Santa Cruz and Monterey Bay.
It's only a 0.3-mile hike from the campground
via Pine Trail, which starts near campsite No.
49. Right alongside the observation deck are
a few ponderosa pine trees, growing far from
their normal range in the Sierra Nevada. You'll
recognize them by their distinctive jigsaw-
puzzle bark.

Note: This park is on the closure list developed by the California Department of Parks,
pending final state budget decisions or the
possible transfer of park management to other
park agencies or volunteer groups.

User Groups: Hikers and horses. No dogs or
mountain bikes. No wheelchair facilities.

Permits: No permits are required. A day-use
fee of $10 is charged per vehicle.

Maps: Park maps are available at the campground entrance station or at the park visitors
center off Highway 9. For a topographic map,
ask the USGS for Felton.

Directions: From San Jose, drive south on
Highway 17 for 24 miles to Scotts Valley.
Take the Mount Hermon Road exit, turn
right, and drive toward Felton for about one
mile to Lockewood Lane. Turn left on Lockewood Lane and drive one mile to Graham
Hill Road. Turn left on Graham Hill Road
and drive 0.5 mile to the campground entrance
on the right. The trailhead is located between
campsite Nos. 82 and 84.

Contact: Henry Cowell Redwoods State Park,
101 N. Big Trees Road, Felton, CA 95018,
831/335-4598, 831/335-7077 (Nature Center),
or 831/429-2851, www.mountainparks.org or
www.parks.ca.gov.

199 SPRIG LOOP
4.2 mi / 2.5 hr   🏃3 ⛰8

in Mount Madonna County Park in the Santa
Cruz Mountains west of Gilroy

Map 7.4, page 294

This loop hike from the Sprig parking area
at Mount Madonna County Park provides a
close-up look at beautiful Blackhawk Creek
Canyon. This is a shady sanctuary filled with
redwoods, giant ferns, and a carpet of sorrel.
Plan this trip for a cool day, though, because
the first mile has an 800-foot climb. After
that, the rest of the hike is much easier. From
the parking area, follow the dirt road to Blackhawk Trail, where you turn left. Huff and puff
your way uphill until the trail enters the redwoods. The grade lessens soon thereafter. The
loop tops out at a junction of several trails
near Pole Line Road. From that junction, take
Sprig Trail (signed for the campgrounds) and
start heading downhill. After another stint in
the redwoods, you drop into a drier forest of
manzanita, pines, and madrones. Outcrops
of sandstone make an appearance here and
there. Finally you move back into a shady
mixed forest and wind your way back. Those
familiar with the park will remember "Sprig"
was actually "Spring Lake." Per orders from
the feds, the dam was taken out, and Sprig

Lake, a cool little fishing pond popular with youngsters, then disappeared.

User Groups: Hikers, horses, and dogs. No mountain bikes. No wheelchair facilities.

Permits: No permits are required. A day-use fee of $6 is charged per vehicle.

Maps: A free trail map is available at the entrance station. For a topographic map, ask the USGS for Mount Madonna.

Directions: From San Jose, take US 101 south to Gilroy and continue to Highway 152. Turn west on Highway 152 and drive about five miles to Sprig Lake Entrance Road. Turn right (north) and drive to trailhead.

Note: This trailhead is not located at the main entrance to the park.

Contact: Mount Madonna County Park, 7850 Poleline Road, Watsonville, CA 95076, 408/842-2341; Santa Clara County Parks and Recreation, 408/355-2200, www.parkhere.org.

200 BAYVIEW LOOP
2.5 mi / 1.75 hr   🥾1 ⛰8

in Mount Madonna County Park in the Santa Cruz Mountains west of Gilroy

Map 7.4, page 294

Mount Madonna County Park provides great scenic beauty, good hiking, camping, and horseback riding. The park is set around the highest peak in the southern range of the Santa Cruz Mountains. With a network of 18 miles of hiking trails, the best routes are combinations of different trails. So it is with this triangular loop. Start at the park entrance station at Hecker Pass, elevation 1,270 feet. Take Bayview Trail and hike north for 1.1 miles to Redwood Trail. You will find yourself scanning west to Monterey Bay along the way. Turn right on Redwood Trail (it will cross Poleline Road) and head into the forest to Redwood Trail. To complete the loop, take Redwood, Rock Springs, Blackhawk, and Bayview Trails as they join in sequence. Confused? This park is filled with a spiderweb of short

hikes. By linking them, you can customize your adventure. This suggested loop provides a look at some of the park's prettiest settings.

User Groups: Hikers, horses, and dogs. No mountain bikes. No wheelchair facilities.

Permits: No permits are required. A day-use fee of $6 is charged per vehicle.

Maps: A free trail map is available at the park entrance station. For a topographic map, ask the USGS for Mount Madonna.

Directions: From San Jose, take US 101 south to Gilroy and continue to Highway 152. Turn west on Highway 152 and drive about 10 miles to Pole Line Road. Turn right (north) and drive to the entrance station. The trailhead is on the left.

Contact: Mount Madonna County Park, 7850 Poleline Road, Watsonville, CA 95076, 408/842-2341; Santa Clara County Parks and Recreation, 408/355-2200, www.parkhere.org.

201 UVAS PARK WATERFALL LOOP
1.0-4.5 mi / 0.5-2.0 hr   🥾1 ⛰9

in Uvas Canyon County Park near Morgan Hill

Map 7.4, page 294

Uvas Canyon County Park is a little slice of waterfall heaven on the east side of the Santa Cruz Mountains. The best advice is to visit during the rainy season, preferably just after a good downpour when the waterfalls are at peak flows. The one-mile Waterfall Loop Trail parades around Swanson Creek's canyon, crossing wooden footbridges and passing 30-foot Black Rock Falls and several smaller falls. Be sure to walk 0.1 mile past the far end of the loop to see Basin Falls and Upper Falls, both pretty cascades 15 to 25 feet high. When you first see Basin Falls, you may not understand how it was named. If you scramble up to the right side of the falls, you can see how the plunge pool looks just like a big basin-style rock tub.

The entire canyon comes alive with the sound of rushing water, and a myriad of ferns and foliage grow on every inch of ground. It's a happy place where you can hike around in your rain gear and be smiling the whole time. Although the park's creeks flow year-round, only immediately following a good rain can you witness the full watery spectacle.

This trip can also be extended to 4.5 miles for the full show, including a surprise lookout over the south Santa Clara Valley. For the longer version, bear left on the Alec Canyon Trail and climb to the canyon rim for a sweeping view of the South Santa Clara Valley (well worth the short climb). Triple Falls can be reached from a short cutoff trail located just past the lookout, another must-see. To return down into the canyon, take the Contour Trail. It is routed back down to Swanson Creek, where it links up with the Waterfall Loop, and your return to the picnic area.

Always remember this place. It can save a wet winter day.

User Groups: Hikers and dogs. No horses or mountain bikes. No wheelchair facilities.

Permits: No permits are required. A day-use fee of $6 is charged per vehicle.

Maps: A brochure and map are available at the trailhead. For a topographic map, ask the USGS for Loma Prieta.

Directions: From San Jose, drive south on US 101 for five miles to Coyote and Bernal Road. Take the Bernal Road exit west and drive a short distance to Santa Teresa Boulevard. Turn left and drive a short way to Bailey Avenue. Turn right on Bailey Avenue and drive to McKean Road. Turn left on McKean Road and go six miles (passing Calero and Chesbro; the road becomes Uvas Road) to Croy Road. Turn right on Croy Road and drive 4. 5 miles (twisty at times, continue through the private park) to the county park entrance. Bear left at the fork and park up the hill in one of the picnic area parking lots. The trailhead is the gated dirt road at Black Oak Picnic Area.

Contact: Uvas Canyon County Park, 8515 Croy Road, Morgan Hill, CA 95037, 408/779-9232; Santa Clara County Parks and Recreation, 408/355-2200, www.parkhere.org.

202 ALEC CANYON AND CONTOUR LOOP
4.5 mi / 2.5 hr   3 9

in Uvas Canyon County Park near Morgan Hill

Map 7.4, page 294

For hikers looking for more of a workout than the Waterfall Loop in Uvas Park provides, this hike up Alec Canyon Trail will get your heart pumping. It's a good trip for a clear winter day when the views from the trail's overlook at Manzanita Point are at their best. Start hiking on the gated road at Black Oak Picnic Area. You will quickly reach a junction. Bear left, up the hill, heading up and away from the canyon (and away from the Waterfall Loop Trail). You'll get to hike that trail on your way back down. A steep climb up the wide road brings you to Manzanita Point, where you can see far off to the north and east—a dramatic valley view. Continue 0.25 mile beyond the point and take the right cutoff to cascading Triple Falls, the most secluded of all the waterfalls in Uvas Park. Then retrace your steps on Alec Canyon Trail. This time, less than 0.5 mile past Manzanita Point, bear left on Contour Trail. Contour Trail is pure fun, winding like a snake along the hillsides, with minimal elevation change but many curves and twists. Finally it drops back down to Swanson Creek, where you can walk back to the trailhead via the Waterfall Loop.

User Groups: Hikers and dogs. No horses or mountain bikes. No wheelchair facilities.

Permits: No permits are required. A day-use fee of $6 is charged per vehicle.

Maps: A free map of Uvas Canyon County Park is available at the trailhead. For a topographic map, ask the USGS for Loma Prieta.

Directions: From San Jose, drive south on US 101 for five miles to Coyote and Bernal Road. Take the Bernal Road exit west and drive a short distance to Santa Teresa Boulevard. Turn left and drive a short way to Bailey Avenue. Turn right on Bailey Avenue and drive to McKean Road. Turn left on McKean Road and go six miles (passing Calero and Chesbro;

the road becomes Uvas Road) to Croy Road. Turn right on Croy Road and drive 4. 5 miles (twisty at times, continue through the private park) to the county park entrance. Bear left at the fork and park up the hill in one of the picnic area parking lots. The trailhead is the gated dirt road at Black Oak Picnic Area.

Contact: Uvas Canyon County Park, 8515 Croy Road, Morgan Hill, CA 95037, 408/779-9232; Santa Clara County Parks and Recreation, 408/355-2200, www.parkhere.org.

203 DEL COYOTE NATURE TRAIL

1.2 mi / 0.5 hr   🥾1   📐7

along Coyote Creek downstream of Anderson Dam south of San Jose

Map 7.4, page 294

Just east of the highway near Morgan Hill is Coyote-Hellyer County Park with its small, shaded stream. The hike starts at a picnic area and meanders along the stream from there. It is pretty and peaceful, the kind of place you enjoy in the moment, not a trek with a distant pay off. The flowing waters come from nearby Anderson Dam, and steady releases are made well into summer. That is what makes this park so attractive to local residents, who know this is a nice spot for a respite. The Coyote Creek Parkway, primarily a bike trail, extends north to San Jose to Hellyer County Park.

User Groups: Hikers, mountain bikes, leashed dogs, horses. No wheelchair facilities.

Permits: No permits are required. Parking and access is free. A day-use fee of $6 is charged per vehicle if parking at nearby Anderson Lake County Park or Hellyer County Park.

Maps: A brochure and map are available at the trailhead. For a free map, contact Coyote-Hellyer County Park. For a topographic map, ask the USGS for Morgan Hill.

Directions: From San Jose, drive south on US 101 for six miles to Coyote and the Cochran Road exit. Take the Cochran Road exit and drive east (toward the base of Anderson Dam)

to the parking area on the left (Coyote Creek runs downstream of the dam).

Note: There are four main parking/staging areas for the Coyote Creek Trail. The north end is at Hellyer County Park. The south end is at Anderson Lake County Park. In between are two other parking areas: Silvercreek Staging Area at Silver Creek Valley Road and Piercy Road (San Jose); and the Metcalf Staging Area on Monterey Highway, just north of Metcalf Road (San Jose).

To Coyote Creek Parkway (for mountain bikers): From San Jose, drive south on US 101 for six miles to Coyote and the Cochran Road exit. Take the Cochran Road exit west and drive a very short distance to Monterey Road. Turn right at Monterey and drive one mile to Burnett Avenue and the trailhead.

Contact: Coyote-Hellyer County Park, 985 Hellyer Avenue, San Jose, CA 95111, 408/225-0225 (for trail section north of Metcalf Road); Anderson Lake County Park, 19245 Malagerra Avene, Morgan Hill, CA 95037, 408/779-3634 (for trail section south of Metcalf Road); Santa Clara County Parks and Recreation, 408/355-2200, ext. 7, www.parkhere.org.

204 FROG POND LOOP

4.7 mi / 3.0 hr   🥾2   📐6

in Henry W. Coe State Park in the Mount Hamilton Range east of Morgan Hill

Map 7.4, page 294

Henry W. Coe State Park is the Bay Area's backyard wilderness. This wildland is located south of Mount Hamilton and covers 87,000 acres and 134 square miles, the largest state park in Northern California. The best trailheads are not at headquarters, but at Hunting Hollow and Bell Station. From headquarters, the trips are very long and difficult. But this is where a ridgetop drive-to campground is located, with great nightly stargazing, and folks often set out from here. (Fortunately, the Lick Fire of 2004 did not affect this hike.)

From headquarters, the Frog Pond Loop is a

day hike that provides a glimpse of the park's primitive charms, along with a sampling of a few of the ups and downs. Think of it as a test case: If you like this, then load your backpack for an overnighter and launch off on one of the butt-kickers.

Start this trip from park headquarters at Monument Trail, (elevation 2,500 feet), located about 100 yards from the visitors center. The trip starts by hiking 0.5 mile to Hobbs Road, climbing to nearly 3,000 feet. At Hobbs Road, turn left and tromp down for 0.8 mile into Little Fork Coyote Creek (2,400 feet). This stream is very pretty in the spring, and though you must then walk out of the canyon, it is a tranquil and memorable setting. Then make the short 0.25-mile rise from the creek up to Frog Pond. This first leg is about 1.6 miles.

Frog Pond is a pretty little spot, complete with fishing line hanging from tree limbs (this lake is fished often and the catch rates are low). Many people then simply return the way they came. An option is to turn the trip into a loop. This is done by returning to Little Fork Coyote Creek and then turning left onto Flat Frog Trail at a junction on the east side of the road. The route laterals around the ridge that provided the up-and-down huff-and-puff on the way in, extending 2.3 miles with more gradual climbs. It eventually reaches Manzanita Point Road. Cross the road and pick up Corral Trail, which provides a 0.6-mile finish to the trip.

Note: This park is on the closure list developed by the California Department of Parks, pending final state budget decisions or the possible transfer of park management to other park agencies or volunteer groups.

User Groups: Hikers, horses, and mountain bikes. No dogs. No wheelchair facilities. After 0.5 inch of rain or more, bikes are prohibited from single-track trails for 48 hours.

Permits: A state park day-use fee of $8 per vehicle is charged. No permits are required unless you plan to camp in the backcountry.

Maps: A brochure and map are available at the visitors center. For a detailed topographic map, contact Pine Ridge Association, P.O. Box 846, Morgan Hill, CA 95038, 408/779-2728, www.coepark.org. For a topographic map, ask the USGS for Mount Sizer.

Directions: From US 101 in Morgan Hill, take the East Dunne Avenue exit and drive east (over Lake Anderson) for 13 miles (slow and twisty) to the park headquarters and visitors center.

Contact: Henry W. Coe State Park, P.O. Box 846, Morgan Hill, CA 95038, 408/779-2728; Pine Ride Association, 408/779-2728, www.coepark.org or www.parks.ca.gov.

205 MISSISSIPPI LAKE TRAIL

27.0 mi / 3 days   🥾4 ▲6

in Henry W. Coe State Park in the Mount Hamilton Range east of Morgan Hill

Map 7.4, page 294

Mississippi Lake is the marquee destination at Henry W. Coe State Park, yet it is set in the virtual center of the park and reaching it is an endurance test. It is the largest lake and the preeminent destination for many who venture into these vast wildlands. The lake borders the 23,000-acre Orestimba Wilderness to the east; fishing for bass, swimming in cool waters in early summer, and viewing wildflower blooms in spring are exceptional. If you catch it just right, the color of the lake seems almost tourmaline, a beautiful sight in this foothill wildland.

An early start is paramount. From park headquarters, begin this ambitious expedition by hiking out on Corral Trail for 1.9 miles to its junction with Manzanita Point Road. Turn right and hike 1.5 miles, past the group campgrounds, to China Hole Trail on the left. This can seem like a launch point off the edge of the earth—China Hole Trail drops from 2,320 feet elevation to 1,150 feet in the course of 2.6 miles. Switchbacks have improved the trail gradient to about 10 percent.

At China Hole, you'll reach the East Fork

of Coyote Creek, a beautiful trout stream, cool and fresh and full of water in late winter and early spring. Then you'll hike through The Narrows en route to Los Cruzeros, a junction of canyons and streams, in the process adding 1.1 miles to the day. A trail camp is available at Los Cruzeros, one of the park's prettiest spots. Make sure you pump two canteens full of water before leaving Los Cruzeros.

From here, you start to climb, hiking out on Willow Ridge Trail for 1.6 miles with an elevation gain of 1,350 feet to Willow Ridge Road. Turn left on Willow Ridge Road for a series of foothill-like climbs and drops as the trip extends 3.8 miles to the southern edge (and earth dam) at Mississippi Lake. The nearest trail camp, Mississippi Creek Horse Camp, is one mile south of the lake. That makes the trip a one-way excursion of 13.5 miles—a long and challenging day, especially if temperatures are hot.

This is a grueling hike from headquarters, and many unprepared hikers have suffered from dehydration and had to be rescued by park staff. Some hikers will try to shortcut the trip by bringing a mountain bike, but find themselves pushing the bike uphill, then speeding fast on downhill portions. Many can accomplish the hike in two days, but after the workout, you'll most likely want to relax on day two and head back to your car on day three.

Even though Henry W. Coe State Park has been open to the public only since 1981, a few legends have already developed, and the most mysterious involves Mississippi Lake. The lake once had a one-of-a-kind ability to create huge trout. Scientists documented 26-inch wild trout that were only 18 months old. The trout are long gone now, as low water in the feeder creek prevented spawning during the 1988 to 1992 drought; any trout you catch should be released immediately. Still, the legendary huge trout of Mississippi Lake have inspired many to make the trip out, often out of curiosity, to see such a unique habitat. Bass were planted in 1991 and have taken over the lake and provide good fishing.

Note: This park is on the closure list developed by the California Department of Parks, pending final state budget decisions or the possible transfer of park management to other park agencies or volunteer groups.

User Groups: Hikers, horses, and mountain bikes. No dogs. No wheelchair facilities. After 0.5 inch of rain, bikes are prohibited from single-track trails for 48 hours.

Permits: A trail map and camp permit are required. A state park day-use fee of $8 per vehicle is charged.

Maps: A brochure and map are available at park headquarters. For a detailed topographic map, contact Pine Ridge Association, P.O. Box 846, Morgan Hill, CA 95038, 408/779-2728, www.coepark.org. For topographic maps, ask the USGS for Mount Sizer and Mississippi Creek.

Directions: From US 101 in Morgan Hill, take the East Dunne Avenue exit and drive east over Lake Anderson for 13 miles (a twisty road) to the park headquarters and visitors center.

Contact: Henry W. Coe State Park, P.O. Box 846, Morgan Hill, CA 95038, 408/779-2728; Pine Ride Association, 408/779-2728, www.coepark.org or www.parks.ca.gov.

206 COIT LAKE

11.6 mi / 2 days   🥾 4   ⛰ 7

in Henry W. Coe State Park in the Mount Hamilton Range east of Morgan Hill

Map 7.4, page 294

The Hunting Hollow Trailhead near Coyote Lake east of Gilroy is a great launch point for Kelly Lake and Coit Lake. From park headquarters east of Morgan Hill, the canyons and ridges at Henry W. Coe State Park seem to stretch to infinity.

Start by parking at Hunting Hollow, or along the shoulder of the road at the Coyote Creek Gate. From the Coyote Creek Gate, walk a short distance (about 0.1 mile) and look for Grizzly Gulch Trail off to the right. Take Grizzly Gulch Trail. After just five minutes

(0.2 mile) you will reach a fork. Take the left fork to stay on Grizzly Gulch Trail, where you will start a climb through oak woodlands, ridges, and canyons. This extends for 1.2 miles to another fork, with the elevation nearly 1,900 feet. Bear right, staying on Grizzly Gulch Trail, and head out for one mile on the road to a fork with Dexter Trail (2,000 feet). Bear to the left on Dexter Trail, and continue the climb for another 0.6 mile (topping out at 2,400 feet) before finally reaching Wasano Ridge and Wasano Ridge Road. Turn left and hike 0.2 mile on the road to Kelly Lake Trail. Turn right and enjoy the one-mile descent to Kelly Lake. So far you have invested 4.3 miles with a 1,500-foot climb and 300-foot descent.

Note: The edge of the burn zone for the 2007 Lick Fire starts just north of Kelly Lake. The landscape surrounding Coit Lake was burned, but has made a big comeback. Wildflower blooms in the spring have been sensational.

After enjoying pretty Kelly Lake, you are ready to top off the trip by heading 1.5 miles to Coit Lake and the campground that is available there. Most of this is a climb. From below the earth dam at Kelly Lake, take the right fork on Coit Road and climb out 0.8 mile to the junction with Willow Road (2,386 feet). Simply continue straight for 0.3 mile and you will reach the inlet to Coit Lake. A well-worn trail circles the lake. From the Coyote Creek Gate trailhead to Coit Lake with this route will make for a 5.8-mile hike for the day, one-way.

Heading off to Coit Lake (and stopping at Kelly Lake on the way in) is the best introduction to this wildland. But come prepared: The reality for many turns into an endurance test. You go up one canyon, then down the next, over and over. Some people get so worn down, hot, and exhausted that they are practically reduced to nothing more than a little pile of hair lying in the dirt. But it is a good trip for ambitious naturalists, with 400 species of wildflowers documented, as well as deer,

coyote, bobcat, fox, wild turkey, hawks, owls, eagles, and, of course, pigs.

Note that overnight users are required to obtain a camping/wilderness permit. Hikers who choose to enter by the Coyote Creek access point must have a trail map. And if the limited parking along the road's shoulder at the Coyote Creek Gate is full, you must instead park at the Hunting Hollow parking area (along Gilroy Springs Road, the access road you drove in on), which will add two miles to this route.

Note: This park is on the closure list developed by the California Department of Parks, pending final state budget decisions or the possible transfer of park management to other park agencies or volunteer groups.

User Groups: Hikers, horses, and mountain bikes. No dogs. No wheelchair facilities.

Permits: A trail map and camp permit are required. A self-registration area is available at the Hunting Hollow parking area, located just off the trailhead access road. A state park day-use fee of $8 per vehicle is charged. After 0.5 inch of rain or more, bikes are prohibited from single-track trails for 48 hours.

Maps: A brochure and map are available at the trailhead. For a detailed topographic map, contact Pine Ridge Association, P.O. Box 846, Morgan Hill, CA 95038, 408/779-2728, www.coepark.org. For topographic maps, ask the USGS for Gilroy Hot Springs and Mississippi Creek.

Directions: From San Francisco, take US 101 south 75 miles (30 miles south of San Jose) to Gilroy and Exit 357 for Leavesley Road/Highway 152. Take that exit to Leavesley, turn left, and go 1.8 miles to New Avenue. Turn left and drive 0.6 mile to Roop Road. Turn right and go 1.9 miles. Turn left to stay on Roop (well signed) and continue 3.3 miles (becomes Gilroy Hot Springs Road) to Hunting Hollow Parking on right, (9 miles from US 101), or continue 1.8 miles to Coyote Gate.

Contact: Henry W. Coe State Park, P.O. Box 846, Morgan Hill, CA 95038, 408/779-2728; Pine Ride Association, 408/779-2728, www.coepark.org or www.parks.ca.gov.

207 ROOSTER COMB LOOP (LONG VERSION)

60.0 mi / 6 days 🏃5 ⛰7

in Henry W. Coe State Park in the Mount
Hamilton Range southeast of San Jose

Map 7.4, page 294 **BEST (**

Very few do this trip. Be sure to purchase added life insurance before embarking. Not only is it just plain long, but it includes seven climbs that'll have you cussing, and yet explores the park's most remote and arid wildlands where anything over 10 inches of rain a year is considered a flood. So why do it? Because no trail on public land in the Bay Area provides access to more remote spots. A series of short cutoff trips can take you to the park's best fishing spots and little-seen gems: Mississippi Lake, Mustang Pond, Jackrabbit Lake, Paradise Lake, and all the way out to Orestimba Creek—and climb the Rooster Comb, a rock formation that looks something like a miniature stegosaurus-back rim.

But you've got to admit: You could search across California and not find a more remote wildland—and yet here it is within range of the Bay Area and 6.5 million people. There is no metropolitan area in the world with such a remote area, but you have to pay dearly for your pleasures—either that or border insanity. Paradise Lake will seem like a mirage after you've walked 33 miles.

Note: The 2007 Lick Fire burned the northern portion of the route, starting north of Kelly Lake past Coit Lake, Mississippi Lake, and north to Mount Sizer. The fire burned 47,760 acres, most of it within the park's 87,000 acres. The landscape has made a big comeback. Wildflower blooms in the spring have been sensational.

For this 60-mile loop, start at the Coyote Creek entrance gate, or the nearby (two miles) Hunting Hollow parking area. From the gate, it's an 5.8-mile trip to Coit Lake (see listing in this chapter).

From Coit Lake, take Coit Road out 4.2 miles to Pacheco Junction, then continue on Coit Road another 1.8 miles to a major fork. This fork marks the beginning and the end of the Rooster Comb Loop. At this point, you have traveled 15.8 miles.

Turn left at this fork, taking County Line Road, to start the Rooster Comb Loop and a route through the Orestimba Wilderness Zone in a clockwise manner. From the fork, it is 2.7 miles to the short cutoff to Mississippi Lake. Stop, rest up, tank up, fuel up, and get your thoughts straight before heading out. That is because from Mississippi Lake, the trip heads off into a land that seems to have no end. Take County Line Road to a short cut-off, Cahaparral Trail, and then link that to Red Creek Road. Turn right, and it is 6.1 miles to Robinson Creek Trail. Turn left and hike along Robinson Creek, a remote canyon with a sliver of water, for 5.6 miles to Orestimba Creek Road.

Turn right on Orestimba Creek Road and you start your return from the depths of the wilderness (though it won't seem like it). The route heads 3.2 miles to a cutoff trail on the right for Rooster Comb Summit Trail. This is a must-do, if you've come this far, a 1.4-mile hike (2.8 round-trip) up the north flank of the Rooster Comb, topping out at 1,836 feet, a 600-foot climb.

From here you head back, heading south on Orestimba Creek Road, passing short cutoff trails for Paradise Lake, Mustang Pond, and Kingbird Pond, a distance of 8.7 miles back to the fork with Coit Road. This is so far away from anything that it is unbelievable, and it is also typically dry and hot most of the year. We have flown it, driven it with rangers, and hiked it, and the remoteness you will feel at one of the ponds—swimming, fishing, or both—is amazing for a Bay Area destination.

When you reach the junction with Coit Road, you have completed the loop, a distance of 36.9 miles (including the Rooster Comb Summit trail). Turn left and return the final 11.6 miles back to the Coyote Creek entrance station. With this route, in all, you have completed a loop trip of 60.1 miles, not including side-trip cutoff trails to several lakes, which can typically add another 10 miles to the trip.

So there you have it: 60 miles, best done in five or six days, exploring a land that few have seen, and fewer yet have experienced.

Several trail camps are situated along the way, and camping is permitted throughout the wilderness area. If the weather turns hot, physically unprepared hikers can find themselves in real danger. Let me say that again before you head off full of excitement and a limited amount of logic: unprepared hikers can find themselves in real danger. OK? Got it?

To best explore the park, the perfect approach would be to come in on horseback or with a burro carrying your gear and water.

Note: This park is on the closure list developed by the California Department of Parks, pending final state budget decisions or the possible transfer of park management to other park agencies or volunteer groups.

User Groups: Hikers, horses, and mountain bikes. No dogs. No wheelchair facilities. After 0.5 inch of rain, bikes are prohibited from single-track trails for 48 hours.

Permits: A trail map and camp permit are required. A self-registration area is available at the Hunting Hollow parking area, located just off the trailhead access road. A state park day-use fee of $8 per vehicle is charged.

Maps: A brochure and map are available at park headquarters. For a detailed topographic map for a fee, contact Pine Ridge Association, P.O. Box 846, Morgan Hill, CA 95038. For topographic maps, ask the USGS for Gilroy Hot Springs and Mississippi Creek.

Directions: From San Francisco, take US 101 south 75 miles (30 miles south of San Jose) to Gilroy and Exit 357 for Leavesley Road/Highway 152. Take that exit to Leavesley, turn left, and go 1.8 miles to New Avenue. Turn left and drive 0.6 mile to Roop Road. Turn right and go 1.9 miles. Turn left to stay on Roop (well signed) and continue 3.3 miles (becomes Gilroy Hot Springs Road) to Hunting Hollow Parking on right (9 miles from US 101), or continue 1.8 miles to Coyote Gate.

Contact: Henry W. Coe State Park, P.O. Box 846, Morgan Hill, CA 95038, 408/779-2728; Pine Ride Association, 408/779-2728, www.coepark.org or www.parks.ca.gov.

208 ROOSTER COMB LOOP (SHORT VERSION)

27.5 mi / 3 days

in Orestimba Wilderness at Henry W. Coe State Park

Map 7.4, page 294

The oft-closed trailhead at Dowdy Ranch/Bell Station provides access (when open) to the Orestima Wilderness, including fantastic bass fishing at Jackrabbit Lake and a great campsite at the foot of the Rooster Comb. Since Henry W. Coe State Park opened in 1959, at 87,000 acres, this area has been out of reach for almost all that time. It took a 56-mile round-trip with about a 15,000-foot aggregate vertical climb to reach Jackrabbit Lake. You can add a lot of miles if you visit the Rooster Comb and the best small lakes for fishing—Jackrabbit Lake, Mustang Pond, Kingbird Pond, and several others. In the process, you will explore the matrixes of valleys, creeks, and foothill grasslands for wildflowers and wildlife. From park headquarters or Hunting Hollow, the route is so long and grueling that almost nobody tries it. We've been back in this wild country on perfect spring days and the fishing, wildlife, and wildflowers can be spectacular.

This is how it works from the Dowdy Ranch Trailhead:

Hole in the Rock, 1.9 miles: Your destination is a fantastic swimming hole on Pacheco Creek. To get there from the new trailhead, take the main Kaiser-Etna Road (1.9 miles) or the North Fork Trail (2.7 miles). When you reach the creek, walk upstream a few hundred yards to find Hole in the Rock. Another decent swimming hole is located if you head downstream instead.

Kingbird Pond, 7.9 miles: Little Kingbird Pond provides bass fishing and is the first fishing spot out of Bell Station. To reach it, take Kaiser-Etna Road five miles to a four-way junction. Go straight (north) on Orestimba Creek Road for 2.4 miles to the Kingbird Pond Trail. Turn right and go 0.5 mile to the pond. Note: Once you get to Orestimba Corral, about six miles in, the route is pretty flat, with just gentle hills.

Mustang Pond, 11.1 miles: This little lake is only 3.2 miles from Kingbird Pond, but there are several creek crossings on this route. At high water you might get wet, but it's a lot of fun. From Kingbird Pond, head 0.5 mile back to the Orestimba Creek Road. Turn right (so you're going north) and head 2.2 miles to the Mustang Pond Trail on the right. It's 0.5 mile to this pond.

Jackrabbit Lake, 13.9 miles: This lake is about twice the size of Kingbird and Mustang, and provides what is probably the best bass fishing in the park. It is only 2.8 miles from Mustang Pond. To get there, from Mustang Pond continue on the Mustang Pond Trail (it horseshoes) northwest to Orestimba Creek Road. Turn right, heading north again, and go 0.75 mile to a spur junction with Long Ridge Road. Turn right and go 1.2 miles, a bit of a climb, to an unsigned spur junction on the left that we call Jackrabbit Lake Road. Turn left and push out a short climb and drop of 0.4 mile to the lake.

Base of Rooster Comb, 16.5 miles: The Rooster Comb is a large, rocky exposed ridge formation that rises up 500 feet from the valley floor to an elevation of 1,836 feet. Below, Orestimba Creek Flat is a good area to camp. To get here from Jackrabbit Lake, it's a 2.6-mile ride: Backtrack on Jackrabbit Lake Trail to Long Ridge Road. Turn right and return to Orestimba Creek Road. Turn north (right) and go one mile to the base of the Rooster Comb.

Return to park entrance: From the Rooster Comb, it's 11 miles back to the park entrance. This makes for a fantastic 27.5-mile loop, with three lakes and plenty of places to camp.

With April showers and a warm May, the valley flats below Rooster Comb can yield tremendous wildflower blooms: owl clover, California poppy, shooting stars, butter and eggs, and rafts of smooth layia. The layia is found almost only in undeveloped grasslands and is an awesome bloom—kind of like a daisy, yet with yellow petals tipped in white, in spectacular clusters.

Note: This park is on the closure list developed by the California Department of Parks, pending final state budget decisions or the possible transfer of park management to other park agencies or volunteer groups. Even if the park remains open, this remote—and outstanding—trailhead could be closed.

User Groups: Hikers, horses, and mountain bikes. No dogs. No wheelchair facilities.

Permits: A trail map and camp permit are required. A state park day-use fee of $8 per vehicle is charged. After 0.5 inch of rain or more, bikes are prohibited from single-track trails for 48 hours.

Maps: A brochure and map are available at Dowdy Visitors Center. For a detailed topographic map, contact Pine Ridge Association, P.O. Box 846, Morgan Hill, CA 95038, 408/779-2728, www.coepark.org. For topographic maps, contact the Pine Ridge Association.

Directions: From San Jose, drive south on US 101 to Gilroy and Highway 152. Turn east on Highway 152 and drive to Highway 156/Pacheco Pass Highway. Turn east on Highway 156 and drive a little over five miles to Bell Station (look for a restaurant and dirt road on left). Turn left on the dirt road (graded) and go 6.6 miles to the visitors center, parking, and trailhead.

Contact: Henry W. Coe State Park, P.O. Box 846, Morgan Hill, CA 95038, 408/779-2728; Pine Ride Association, 408/779-2728, www.coepark.org or www.parks.ca.gov.

209 HARVEY BEAR / BAY RIDGE TRAIL

6.0 mi / 3.0 hr

in Coyote Lake-Harvey Bear County Park near Coyote Reservoir

Map 7.4, page 294

Coyote Lake–Harvey Bear Ranch County Park, one of California's newest parks, is located in the hills east of Gilroy. The suggested hike is three miles one-way, rolling up and down Coyote Ridge. It provides spectacular views of southern Santa Clara Valley and beyond across the Santa Cruz Mountains. You return the same way you came in—or you could turn it into a 12-mile mountain bike loop. What makes it a perfect fit is that the parkland adjoins Coyote Lake, creating a continuous swath of 4,595 acres of public land.

Start at the new parking area for Harvey Bear (named after the landowner whose family made the park possible). From there, head off on the 4.5-mile trail that is the newest dedicated section of a work-in-progress, the 500-mile Bay Ridge Trail. The landscape consists of rolling hills with oaks and buckeyes and lots of wild turkey, deer, squirrels, red-tailed hawks, and turkey vultures. On summer mornings, it seems spotting wild turkey are a sure thing. You can get in a nice rhythm for easy climbs that average only 200 feet, and then take in the dramatic views of the lower Santa Clara Valley off to the west and gorgeous Coyote Lake backed by a wilderness ridge to the east.

Most will stop here, but you can do better. After climbing a series of hilltops, the Bay Ridge Trail then descends to the north end of Coyote Lake. With a shuttle car, you can turn this into a great one-way trip. Mountain bikers can turn the trip into a 12-mile loop by returning on the paved road along Coyote Lake's west shore and looping back on Gilroy Hot Springs Road.

The routes at Harvey Bear don't require grueling efforts to reach the ridge for top-of-the-world vistas. That is because the old, steep ranch roads were decommissioned, and in their place, a network of double-track and service roads were established with user-friendly grades. A new loop, Rancho La Polka, will open in spring 2012.

User Groups: Hikers, mountain bikes, horses, and dogs on leash. No wheelchair facilities.

Permits: Parking and access $6 per vehicle. No permit required.

Maps: A brochure and map are available at the trailhead.

Directions: Take Highway 101 south to Gilroy and the Leavesley Road exit. Take that exit, turn east and drive two miles to New Avenue. Turn left and go 0.5 mile to Roop Road. Turn right and go three miles (it becomes Gilroy Hot Springs Road) to the park entrance on the left.

Contact: Coyote Lake County Park, 408/842-7800; Santa Clara County Parks and Recreation, 408/355-2200, www.parkhere.org.

MONTEREY
AND BIG SUR

BEST HIKES

It wouldn't be easy to choose the most spectacular

stretch of California coastline, but if pressed, most beach connoisseurs would agree there is no place as visually stunning as the 130 miles of cliffs, rocks, and waves that run from Davenport to San Simeon.

There's nothing not to like here, from the mild climate to the wild landscape. Much of this area is isolated, undeveloped, and difficult to access, with rugged cliffs and few roads. Hiking in this land means wandering along gravel beaches, pausing to watch sunsets over glimmering seas, and walking in the shadows of giant redwoods.

South of Carmel, services are clustered in a few small towns: Big Sur, Lucia, and Gorda. In between is a string of coastal state parks that provide a bounty of hiking trails. The long list of options includes the rock-lined coves of Point Lobos State Reserve; the flower-covered hills of Garrapata State Park; the windswept beaches of Andrew Molera State Park; and the redwood-lined canyons of Julia Pfeiffer Burns State Park, Pfeiffer Big Sur State Park, and Limekiln State Park.

Whereas towns are few and traffic is light on the shore, a different story takes place out at sea. Every winter and spring, like clockwork, thousands of gray whales pass by on their long migrations. Traveling from their summer home in Alaska's Bering Sea to their winter breeding grounds in Baja, then back again a few months later, the whales display occasional flashes of fins or tails and leave hundreds of frothy spouts as their calling cards. Whale-watching is at its best from December to May, on days when the sea is flat and deep blue, with no wind or whitecaps.

Hikers have a chance to witness this great natural spectacle from coastside trails at several Santa Cruz, Monterey, and Big Sur parks, and also while driving scenic Highway 1.

Neighboring this region's coastal splendor is a mountainous area of deeply carved canyons and steep escarpments, where the Santa Cruz Mountains in the north give way to the Santa Lucia Mountains in the south. Here, dense redwood forests thin out, and the forest gradually transitions to drier groves of oaks and pines. Hikers can explore these mountains on the paths of the spectacular Ventana Wilderness and its smaller neighbor, the Silver Peak Wilderness. Trails are easily accessed on the west side of Ventana (off Highway 1) or the east side (off US 101). Although some wilderness destinations, such as Sykes Hot Springs, are notorious for crowds, a hiking trip in the off-season (autumn or winter) can provide solitude on even the most popular trails.

Last but not least, the Monterey and Big Sur region also contains one of California's most unusual national parks, Pinnacles National Monument. Its jagged cliffs, crags, and peaks are not part of any nearby mountain range; instead they are the remains of an ancient volcano that erupted 200 miles to the southeast. Whereas rock climbers flock to the vertical surfaces of the high crags, hikers can choose from a variety of well-built trails that tunnel through caves and ascend over and around the pinnacles. Springtime brings a spectacular display of wildflowers in the park's grasslands, and an opportunity to explore the park before the summer temperatures soar.

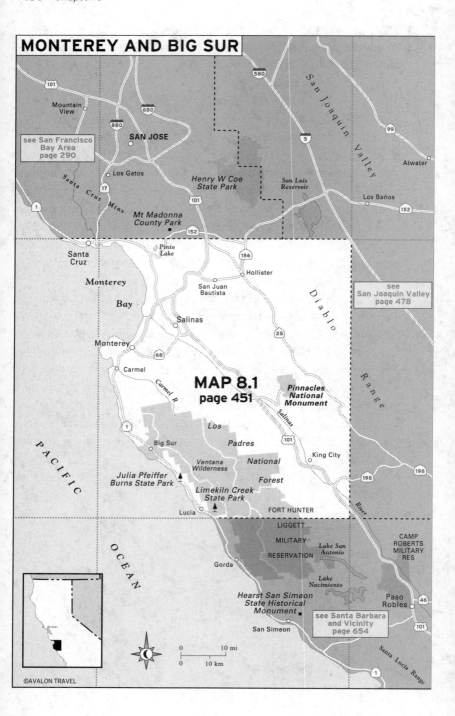

MONTEREY AND BIG SUR

see San Francisco
Bay Area
page 290

SAN JOSE

Mountain View

Los Gatos

Henry W Coe State Park

Mt Madonna County Park

Santa Cruz Mtns

San Joaquin Valley

San Luis Reservoir

Atwater

Los Baños

Santa Cruz

Pinto Lake

see San Joaquin Valley page 478

Monterey Bay

Hollister

San Juan Bautista

Salinas

Monterey

Carmel

Carmel R

**MAP 8.1
page 451**

Pinnacles National Monument

Diablo Range

Big Sur

Los Padres

Ventana Wilderness

National

Forest

King City

Julia Pfeiffer Burns State Park

Limekiln Creek State Park

Lucia

FORT HUNTER

PACIFIC

LIGGETT

MILITARY

RESERVATION

Lake San Antonio

CAMP ROBERTS MILITARY RES

OCEAN

Gorda

Lake Nacimiento

Paso Robles

Hearst San Simeon State Historical Monument

see Santa Barbara and Vicinity page 654

San Simeon

Santa Lucia Range

0   10 mi

0   10 km

©AVALON TRAVEL

Map 8.1

Hikes 1-36
Pages 452-474

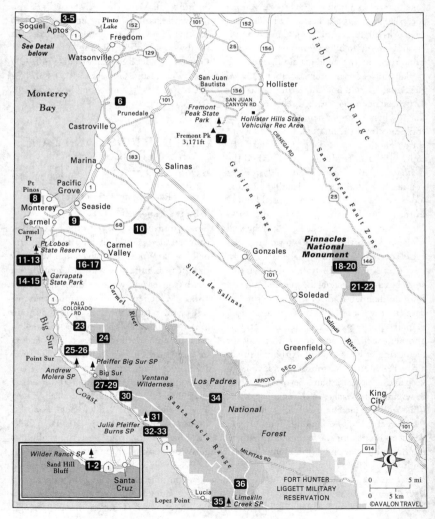

Pinto Lake

Soquel
Aptos **3-5**
Freedom
See Detail below
Watsonville

Monterey Bay

Prunedale **6**
Castroville

San Juan Bautista
Hollister
SAN JUAN CANYON RD
Fremont Peak State Park
Hollister Hills State Vehicular Rec Area
Fremont Pk 3,171ft **7**

Marina
Salinas

Pt Pinos **8**
Pacific Grove
Monterey
Seaside
Carmel **9**
68 **10**

Diablo Range

Gabilan Range

Gonzales

Pinnacles National Monument **18-20**
21-22

Carmel Pt
Pt Lobos State Reserve
11-13
16-17
Carmel Valley
14-15
Garrapata State Park

Sierra de Salinas

Soledad

PALO COLORADO RD
23
24

Big Sur

Point Sur
25-26
Andrew Molera SP
Pfeiffer Big Sur SP
Big Sur
27-29
30

Carmel River

Greenfield

SECO RD
ARROYO

Los Padres

34
Ventana Wilderness

National

King City

Julia Pfeiffer Burns SP
31
32-33

Santa Lucia Range

Forest

MILPITAS RD

Wilder Ranch SP
Sand Hill Bluff
1-2
Santa Cruz

Lucia
Lopez Point **35**
Limekiln Creek SP
36

FORT HUNTER LIGGETT MILITARY RESERVATION

0   5 mi
0   5 km
©AVALON TRAVEL

San Andreas Fault Zone

Salinas River

1 OLD LANDING COVE TRAIL
2.5 mi / 1.5 hr
🥾1 ⛰10

in Wilder Ranch State Park north of Santa Cruz

Map 8.1, page 451   **BEST (**

When you visit Wilder Ranch, you may notice that on some maps and park signs this trail is called Old Cove Landing, while on others it's called Old Landing Cove. Take your pick. The Old Landing Cove Trail is a gem of a coastal hike that offers a look at a seal rookery, some spectacular pocket beaches, and a hidden fern cave. Although the trail is open to both hikers and mountain bikers, everybody seems to mind their manners and get along fine.

The trail leads past brussels sprouts fields to the coast. An odd but interesting fact is that 12 percent of our nation's brussels sprouts production happens right here in this park. The trail leads from the main parking lot toward the ocean, then traces along the coastal blufftops, with farm fields on your right and the dramatic coastline on your left. In short order you reach the trail's namesake, Old Landing Cove, where small schooners loaded lumber in the late 19th century. A little more walking brings you to the bluffs above the seal rookery, where you look down on huge flat rocks covered with wall-to-wall seals. Finally, near post No. 8, a spur trail leads down to a small beach cove. Follow the spur and you will find on the inland side of the cove a shallow cave filled with ferns from floor to ceiling. A quarter mile past the fern-cave beach is another excellent pocket beach, perfect for picnicking or lying around. Although this is a fine destination for most visitors, you can keep hiking along the bluffs beyond this beach to several more beaches in the next few miles. (The trail's name changes from Old Landing Cove Trail to Ohlone Bluff Trail.) If you decide to keep going, be forewarned that you might get an anatomy lesson along the way: Both Three-Mile and Four-Mile Beaches often attract nude sunbathers.

User Groups: Hikers and mountain bikes. No horses or dogs. No wheelchair facilities.

Permits: No permits are required. A $10 day-use fee is charged per vehicle.

Maps: A free map of Wilder Ranch is available at the entrance station or by free download at www.parks.ca.gov. A more detailed map is available from Pease Press (www.peasepress .com). For a topographic map, ask the USGS for Santa Cruz.

Directions: From Santa Cruz, drive north on Highway 1 for four miles. Turn left into the entrance for Wilder Ranch State Park and follow the park road to its end, at the main parking area. Take the signed trail from the southwest side of the parking lot.

Contact: Wilder Ranch State Park, 1401 Old Coast Road, Santa Cruz, CA 95060, 831/423-9703, www.parks.ca.gov or www.santacruz stateparks.org.

2 WILDER RIDGE AND ZANE GREY TRAILS
6.0 mi / 3.0 hr
🥾3 ⛰9

in Wilder Ranch State Park north of Santa Cruz

Map 8.1, page 451

Once you find your way to the hiker/biker tunnel underneath Highway 1 near the farm buildings at Wilder Ranch, you're on your way to a great six-mile hike with just enough of a climb to give you a workout and a spectacular vista of Monterey Bay. Keep in mind that this side of the park is the domain of mountain bikers—hundreds of them on weekends—but the trails are wide, and there's plenty of room for everybody. The Wilder Ridge Trail features a 500-foot climb to a coastal overlook. You reach it by exiting the tunnel and heading straight and then uphill on Wilder Ridge, then bearing right on the Wilder Ridge Loop. At about 2.5 miles out, shortly after Twin Oaks Trail forks right, you come to an obvious grassy overlook at the top of the ridge—about 40 feet off the main trail. Enjoy the wide vista, then continue hiking along the ridgetop on Wilder Ridge Loop. For an interesting loop, take the Zane Grey cutoff on the left (it's single track) and then go left again on the other side of the Wilder Ridge Loop.

User Groups: Hikers, horses, and mountain bikes. No dogs. No wheelchair facilities.

Permits: No permits are required. A $10 day-use fee is charged per vehicle.

Maps: A free map of Wilder Ranch State Park is available at the entrance station or by free download at www.parks.ca.gov. A more detailed map is available from Pease Press (www.peasepress.com). For a topographic map, ask the USGS for Santa Cruz.

Directions: From Santa Cruz, drive north on Highway 1 for four miles. Turn left into the entrance for Wilder Ranch State Park and follow the park road to its end, at the main parking area. Take the trail signed Nature Trail from the southwest side of the parking lot. Walk down the park road to the Wilder Ranch and Cultural Preserve, then through the cultural preserve to the picnic area and chicken coops, to reach the tunnel that leads underneath Highway 1.

Contact: Wilder Ranch State Park, 1401 Old Coast Road, Santa Cruz, CA 95060, 831/423-9703, www.parks.ca.gov or www.santacruz stateparks.org.

₃ MAPLE FALLS
7.0-9.0 mi / 4.5 hr   ₃ ⛰₉

in The Forest of Nisene Marks State Park near Aptos

Map 8.1, page 451

It's either a seven- or nine-mile round-trip hike to Maple Falls, and it all depends on whether the park road is gated at Porter Picnic Area, the main trailhead. In winter and spring, the road is usually closed, which means you need to walk an extra mile in each direction in order to see the falls. Winter and spring are the best seasons to go, of course, because that's when Maple Falls is flowing at its fullest. The trip starts out with an easy walk on Aptos Creek Fire Road, which you'll share with mountain bikers. Follow it 0.25 mile past Porter Picnic

Area, where you turn left on Loma Prieta Grade Trail. The second-growth redwood and Douglas fir forest just keeps getting thicker, greener, and prettier, and the trail turns to sweet single track. Where Loma Prieta Grade splits, stay to the right, heading toward Bridge Creek Historic Site, for the shortest route to the falls. You can take the other side of the Loma Prieta Grade loop on your way back if you still have the energy. When you reach Bridge Creek Historic Site, the site of a former logging camp, the maintained trail ends, and you begin a fun 0.5-mile stream scramble to Maple Falls, following the course of Bridge Creek. The canyon narrows as you travel through a dense green world of ferns, moss, foliage, and water, and at last you reach the back of the canyon, where 30-foot Maple Falls spills over the wall.

User Groups: Hikers only. No dogs or horses. Mountain bikes allowed only on fire roads. No wheelchair facilities.

Permits: No permits are required. An $8 day-use fee is charged per vehicle.

Maps: A free map of The Forest of Nisene Marks is available at the entrance kiosk or by free download at www.parks.ca.gov. A more detailed map is available from Pease Press (www.peasepress.com). For topographic maps, ask the USGS for Laurel, Soquel, and Loma Prieta.

Directions: From Santa Cruz, drive south on Highway 1 for six miles to the Aptos/State Park Drive exit. Bear left at the exit, cross over the highway, then turn right on Soquel Drive and drive 0.5 mile. Turn left on Aptos Creek Road. Stop at the entrance kiosk, then continue up the park road and park at Porter Picnic Area. In the winter months, you must park at George's Picnic Area, a mile before Porter Picnic Area, because the park road is gated off at that point.

Contact: The Forest of Nisene Marks State Park, c/o Sunset State Beach, 201 Sunset Beach Road, Watsonville, CA 95076, 831/763-7063 or 831/429-2850, www.parks.ca.gov or www.santacruzstateparks.org.

4 LOMA PRIETA EARTHQUAKE EPICENTER

4.0 mi / 2.0 hr   🥾2 ⛰8

in The Forest of Nisene Marks State Park near Aptos

Map 8.1, page 451

The destination on this trail is the epicenter of the 1989 Loma Prieta earthquake, but the pleasure of the trip has little to do with its interesting geological history. Instead, the joy is in the scenery, a lush second-growth redwood forest that regenerated after a clear-cut operation at the end of the 19th century. The hike follows Aptos Creek Fire Road, which leads gently uphill (expect plenty of mountain bikers and joggers on the weekends). At 1.5 miles from the Porter Picnic Area, cross a footbridge and descend a bit on the trail until you come to the spot where a large sign once proclaimed the proximity of the earthquake epicenter (the sign was stolen). There's a small bike rack there. Cross the creek and continue up the single-track Aptos Creek Trail for 0.5 mile to the actual epicenter, where you will see surprisingly little evidence of anything earthshaking, but rather a lovely and peaceful redwood forest. Turn around here for a four-mile round-trip (or six miles if you had to start from George's Picnic Area instead of Porter Picnic Area).

It's possible, although quite challenging, to hike Five Finger Falls from the epicenter by following Aptos Creek Trail for 4.5 additional miles. This epic hike has long been a favorite of intrepid waterfall lovers, who revel in the chance to see one of the least visited waterfalls in the Santa Cruz mountains. However, almost every winter, this trail is subject to weather-related damage, including landslides and flood-level waters in Aptos Creek. During the rainy months, plan on getting wet feet as you must walk in the creek where the trail peters out. There is never any guarantee that you will reach your destination when you set out for Five Finger Falls, but nonetheless, this hike remains a beloved challenge for waterfall aficionados.

User Groups: Hikers and mountain bikes. No dogs or horses. No wheelchair facilities.

Permits: No permits are required. An $8 day-use fee is charged per vehicle.

Maps: A free map of the The Forest of Nisene Marks State Park is available at the entrance kiosk or by free download at www.parks.ca.gov. A more detailed map is available from Pease Press (www.peasepress.com). For topographic maps, ask the USGS for Laurel, Soquel, and Loma Prieta.

Directions: From Santa Cruz, drive south on Highway 1 for six miles to the Aptos/State Park Drive exit. Bear left at the exit, cross over the highway, then turn right on Soquel Drive and drive 0.5 mile. Turn left on Aptos Creek Road. Stop at the entrance kiosk, then continue up the park road and park at Porter Picnic Area. In the winter months, you must park at George's Picnic Area, a mile before Porter Picnic Area, because the park road is gated off at that point.

Contact: The Forest of Nisene Marks State Park, c/o Sunset State Beach, 201 Sunset Beach Road, Watsonville, CA 95076, 831/763-7063 or 831/429-2850, www.parks.ca.gov or www.santacruzstateparks.org.

5 WEST RIDGE AND APTOS CREEK LOOP

12.5 mi / 7.0 hr or 2 days   🥾4 ⛰9

in The Forest of Nisene Marks State Park near Aptos

Map 8.1, page 451

The West Ridge and Aptos Creek Loop is the grand tour of the Forest of Nisene Marks State Park, suitable only for hikers in good condition and with a lot of time on their hands. An option is to get reservations for West Ridge Trail Camp and turn this into an overnight trip; the camp is situated conveniently near Sand Point Overlook—a great spot for sunsets. (Backpacking stoves are necessary; no campfires are allowed.) From George's Picnic Area, walk up Aptos

Creek Road for 0.25 mile to the left cutoff for West Ridge Trail, and start climbing uphill along the west ridge of Aptos Canyon. (You can also take Loma Prieta Grade Trail if you prefer. Follow the left side of its loop, then take the connector trail to West Ridge Trail.) Finally you ascend all the way to Hinckley Ridge (at 1,300 feet) and meet up with the fire road that leads to West Ridge Trail Camp and Sand Point Overlook. From the overlook at 1,500 feet, you can see down into the densely forested Bridge Creek drainage and far off across sky-blue Monterey Bay. Finish out the loop with a long downhill walk on Aptos Creek Fire Road, a wide path through dense redwoods and Douglas firs.

User Groups: Hikers and mountain bikes. No dogs or horses. No wheelchair facilities.

Permits: No permits are required. An $8 day-use fee is charged per vehicle. An advance reservation is necessary to stay overnight at West Ridge Trail Camp; call the park for reservations.

Maps: A free map of The Forest of Nisene Marks State Park is available at the entrance kiosk or by free download at www.parks. ca.gov. A more detailed map is available from Pease Press (www.peasepress.com). For topographic maps, ask the USGS for Laurel, Soquel, and Loma Prieta.

Directions: From Santa Cruz, drive south on Highway 1 for six miles to the Aptos/State Park Drive exit. Bear left at the exit, cross over the highway, then turn right on Soquel Drive and drive 0.5 mile. Turn left on Aptos Creek Road. Stop at the entrance kiosk, then continue up the park road and park at George's Picnic Area.

Contact: The Forest of Nisene Marks State Park, c/o Sunset State Beach, 201 Sunset Beach Road, Watsonville, CA 95076, 831/763-7063 or 831/429-2850, www.parks.ca.gov or www.santacruzstateparks.org.

⑥ ELKHORN SLOUGH SOUTH MARSH LOOP

2.5 mi / 1.5 hr 🚶1 ⛰️8

near Moss Landing

Map 8.1, page 451 **BEST (**

Elkhorn Slough is 1,400 acres of marsh and tidal flats, the precious borderline between sea and land that is home to thousands of species of birds, fish, and invertebrates. It's the second-largest salt marsh in California, and in the peak of the migration season, where birds numbering in the thousands can be seen. Hikers with binoculars (and sometimes with just their own eyes) may spot a long list of species that includes peregrine falcons, American white pelicans, and, very rarely, golden eagles. The South Marsh Loop Trail is a 2.5-mile walking tour of this salty, marshy, bird-filled land, crossing footbridges over the slough and staying close to mudflats and the water's edge. Make sure you take all the spurs off the loop, including the short walk to Hummingbird Island, which sits right on the edge of the main channel of the Slough. A highlight in the spring is walking by the rookery, where great blue herons and great egrets raise their offspring.

Special Note: The reserve is open Wednesday through Sunday from 9 A.M. to 5 P.M. Guided tours are available on Saturday and Sunday.

User Groups: Hikers only. No dogs, horses, or mountain bikes. Several boardwalks and overlook areas are wheelchair accessible.

Permits: No permits are required. A $2.50 entrance fee is charged per adult. Children under 16 and anyone in possession of a California fishing or hunting license may enter free.

Maps: A map of Elkhorn Slough is available at the visitors center and online. For a topographic map, ask the USGS for Moss Landing.

Directions: From Highway 1 at Moss Landing, turn east on Dolan Road by the PG&E power station. Drive three miles to Elkhorn Road, turn left (north), and drive two miles to the reserve entrance. The trail begins by the visitors center.

Contact: Elkhorn Slough National Estuarine Research Reserve, 1700 Elkhorn Road, Watsonville, CA 95076, 831/728-2822, www.elkhornslough.org.

7 FREMONT PEAK TRAIL
0.6 mi / 0.5 hr   🏃1 ⛰10

in Fremont Peak State Park near San Juan Bautista

Map 8.1, page 451

Fremont Peak State Park is a small park with a big view. There are only a few choices of hiking trails here, including the 0.6-mile trail to the summit of Fremont Peak (elevation 3,169 feet). But that one little trip packs one heck of a punch. Pick a clear day in winter or spring (summer gets brutally hot, and the visibility worsens) to make the narrow and winding drive from San Juan Bautista, and prepare to witness a panorama of Monterey Bay, Santa Cruz, Salinas, Watsonville, Hollister, and the Santa Lucia Mountains. From the southwest parking area, walk up the gated, paved service road for a few hundred yards, and then cut off to the right on the signed Peak Trail, which winds its way up the mountain. The last 100 yards is very rocky, and the final summit climb is a bit of a scramble. Ignore the close-by radio transmitters, and check out the far-off views.

Another popular activity at the park is stargazing. Fremont Peak Observatory is open to the public on weekends from April to October, and rangers hold astronomy programs here.

User Groups: Hikers only. No dogs, horses, or mountain bikes. No wheelchair facilities.

Permits: No permits are required. A $6 dayuse fee is charged per vehicle.

Maps: A map of Fremont Peak State Park is available at the entrance kiosk. For a topographic map, ask the USGS for San Juan Bautista.

Directions: From Gilroy, drive south on US 101 for 10 miles to the Highway 156 East/San Juan Bautista exit. Turn east on Highway 156 and drive three miles to San Juan Bautista.

Then turn right (south) on the Alameda and then right on San Juan Canyon Road. (It's signed for the state park.) Follow it 11 miles to its end in Fremont Peak State Park. Park in the southwest parking area.

Contact: Fremont Peak State Park, P.O. Box 787, San Juan Bautista, CA 95045, 831/623-4255, www.parks.ca.gov; Fremont Peak Observatory, 831/623-2465, www.fpoa.net.

8 ASILOMAR COAST TRAIL
2.4 mi / 1.5 hr   🏃1 ⛰9

in Pacific Grove

Map 8.1, page 451

Even if you aren't lucky enough to attend a conference at the historic Asilomar Conference Center, you can still walk its adjoining Asilomar Coast Trail, a spectacular 1.2-mile trail along coastal bluffs above rugged, windswept Asilomar Beach. There's plenty to look at and many side trails to explore. You'll see waves crashing against jagged rocks, plentiful tidepools, tiny pocket beaches, wide sandy stretches with big white dunes, and much sea life. Be sure to take the separate boardwalk trail (on the west side of the conference center) that leads across the dunes. Kite flying is also popular along some stretches of Asilomar Beach.

User Groups: Hikers and dogs. No horses or mountain bikes. Portions of the trail are wheelchair accessible.

Permits: No permits are required. Parking and access are free.

Maps: For a topographic map, ask the USGS for Monterey.

Directions: From Salinas on US 101, take the Highway 68/Monterey exit and drive 15 miles into Monterey. Continue into Pacific Grove, where Highway 68 becomes Sunset Drive. Continue to Asilomar State Beach. Park alongside Sunset Drive; the trail begins opposite the conference center.

Contact: Asilomar State Beach, 804 Crocker Avenue, Pacific Grove, CA 93950, 831/646-6440, www.parks.ca.gov.

9 SKYLINE NATURE AND JACKS PEAK TRAILS

1.2 mi / 0.5 hr 1 9

in Jacks Peak County Park near Monterey

Map 8.1, page 451

At 1,068 feet, Jacks Peak is the highest point on the Monterey Peninsula. Hey, it's not the High Sierra, but this summit is still worthy of a hike. The peak and its surrounding park are named after David Jacks, the guy who got his name on Monterey Jack cheese. The Skyline Nature Trail is an easy loop walk around the summit of Jacks Peak, set amid a dense forest of Monterey pines. The Jacks Peak Trail is a smaller loop inside Skyline Nature Trail loop, and you can easily branch off the latter to join the former for a half-hour walk that provides unparalleled views of Carmel Valley, the Monterey Peninsula, Point Lobos, the Santa Lucia Mountains, and the Pacific Ocean. That's on a clear day, of course, which is not every day in Monterey. Even though the view is about the same on both trail loops, make sure you walk a leg of Jacks Peak Trail to the top of Jacks Peak, where you can sit on a bench and pull out a picnic of Jack cheese sandwiches. Don't plan on watching the sun set from here, though; unfortunately the park closes before then.

User Groups: Hikers and dogs. No horses or mountain bikes. No wheelchair facilities.

Permits: No permits are required. A $4 entrance fee is charged per vehicle on weekdays; $5 on weekends and holidays.

Maps: A free map of Jacks Peak County Park is available at the entrance station. For a topographic map, ask the USGS for Seaside.

Directions: From Monterey, take Highway 68 east from Highway 1 for 1.7 miles to Olmsted Road. Turn right on Olmsted Road and drive 1.5 miles to Jacks Peak Drive, then follow Jacks Peak Drive to the park entrance. After passing through the entrance kiosk, turn right and drive to the parking area for Jacks Peak.

Contact: Jacks Peak County Park, 25001 Jacks Peak Park Drive, Monterey, CA 93940, 831/372-8551, www.co.monterey.ca.us/parks.

10 OLLASON PEAK

7.5 mi / 3.5 hr 3 7

in Toro County Park near Monterey

Map 8.1, page 451

Pick a cool day in spring to take this inspiring jaunt to the top of Ollason Peak, elevation 1,800 feet, high up and far away from the madding crowds of popular Toro County Park. Even with a cool breeze, Ollason Trail can be a butt-kicker, with many steep sections over a less-than-smooth route. It leads from the Quail Meadow Group Picnic Area and climbs through wide grasslands and occasional oak groves, most of the time on a wide double-track trail. Increasingly wide views and an excellent variety of grassland wildflowers are your reward for the work. After a long stint heading southwest, the trail suddenly veers east, then resumes its southern course for the final climb to Ollason Peak, four miles from the trailhead. You get lovely views toward Monterey Bay and the Central Valley from the summit, plus a set of rugged-looking peaks to the east. Retrace your steps from there or continue a little farther to Coyote Spring Trail, bearing left for a 7.5-mile loop. If you're making the loop, be sure to watch for the left turnoff on Cougar Ridge from Coyote Spring, which returns you to a connector trail back to Quail Meadow.

User Groups: Hikers and dogs. Mountain bikes and horses allowed on only a portion of the trail. No wheelchair facilities.

Permits: No permits are required. A $6 entrance fee is charged per vehicle on weekdays; $8 on weekends and holidays.

Maps: A free map of Toro County Park is available at the entrance station. For a topographic map, ask the USGS for Spreckels.

Directions: From Monterey, take Highway 68 east from Highway 1 for 13 miles to the Portola Drive exit. Turn right into the Toro County Park entrance road. Drive 0.5 mile past the entrance kiosk to the parking area by Quail Meadow Group Picnic Area.

Contact: Toro County Park, 501 Monterey

Highway, Salinas, CA 93908, 831/484-1108, www.co.monterey.ca.us/parks.

11 SEA LION POINT TRAIL
0.6 mi / 0.5 hr   👣1   ⛰9

in Point Lobos State Reserve near Carmel

Map 8.1, page 451

On summer weekends, the cars are parked in a long line along the road outside Point Lobos State Reserve, one of the crown jewels of the state park system. Even on weekdays, the parking lots are surprisingly full here, but the park's stunning coastal beauty and plentiful wildlife explain why. One of the biggest attractions at the park is Sea Lion Point Trail, a round-trip loop of just over 0.5 mile, part of which is suitable for wheelchairs. Along the way you can look for cute little sea otters floating on their backs in the kelp and chubby harbor seals hauling out on the rocks. When the trail reaches a rocky staircase, wheelchair users can continue around Upper Sea Lion Point, while other visitors can continue down the stairs to Lower Sea Lion Point. Rocks jut upward from the breakers just offshore; these are named Sea Lion Rocks for obvious reasons. Test your hiking partner's literary knowledge with this fact: Robert Louis Stevenson used Point Lobos as the inspiration for his novel *Treasure Island.*

User Groups: Hikers and wheelchairs. No dogs, horses, or mountain bikes. Part of the trail is wheelchair accessible.

Permits: No permits are required. A $10 day-use fee is charged per vehicle.

Maps: A map of Point Lobos State Reserve is available at the entrance station or by free download at www.parks.ca.gov. For a topographic map, ask the USGS for Monterey.

Directions: From Carmel at Rio Road, drive south on Highway 1 for three miles to the entrance to Point Lobos State Reserve, on the right. Turn right and drive through the entrance kiosk, and continue straight to the information station and Sea Lion Point parking area.

Contact: Point Lobos State Reserve, Route 1, Box 62, Carmel, CA 93923, 831/624-4909, www.pointlobos.org.

12 WHALER'S KNOLL AND CYPRESS GROVE
3.0 mi / 2.0 hr   👣2   ⛰10

in Point Lobos State Reserve near Carmel

Map 8.1, page 451

Two excellent trails lead from the north side of the Sea Lion Point parking area near the information station at Point Lobos, and you can connect them to make a stellar three-mile round-trip. Start by hiking on Cypress Grove Trail, which shows off the park's Monterey cypress trees, one of only two remaining native Monterey cypress groves on earth. In addition to getting a look at the marvelous windswept trees, you walk through coastal scrub to rocky cliffs with picture-perfect ocean views. The trail loops around and heads back toward the parking area, but just before you reach it, you can turn left on North Shore Trail and climb a bit to the right turnoff for Whaler's Knoll Trail. Whaler's Knoll Trail makes loose switchbacks uphill to the top of Whaler's Knoll, where you get the best view in the whole park. Luckily there's a bench there, so you can have a seat, catch your breath, and enjoy the scene. The knoll was the spot where early-20th-century whalers would watch for whales, then hang a signal flag when they spotted them. You can continue hiking from there, heading downhill and making a loop along the coast on North Shore Trail.

User Groups: Hikers only. No dogs, horses, or mountain bikes. No wheelchair facilities.

Permits: No permits are required. A $10 day-use fee is charged per vehicle.

Maps: A map of Point Lobos State Reserve is available at the entrance station or by free download at www.parks.ca.gov. For a topographic map, ask the USGS for Monterey.

Directions: From Carmel at Rio Road, drive south on Highway 1 for three miles to the entrance to Point Lobos State Reserve on the right. Turn right and drive through the entrance kiosk and continue straight to the information station and Sea Lion Point parking area.

Contact: Point Lobos State Reserve, Route 1, Box 62, Carmel, CA 93923, 831/624-4909, www.pointlobos.org.

13 POINT LOBOS PERIMETER
6.0 mi / 3.0 hr 🥾2 ⛰10

in Point Lobos State Reserve near Carmel

Map 8.1, page 451   BEST 🏆

The perimeter hike at Point Lobos connects a number of trails to view the best highlights of the park. Make sure you get a park map at the entrance station before hiking so you can scope out the many side-trip options that are possible (and the many shortcuts if you're getting tired). Starting from the Sea Lion Point parking area, make your first destination Sea Lion Point. Then bear left on Sand Hill Trail and connect to South Shore Trail. The latter leads along the quieter, south part of the park, past numerous spectacular beaches and coves, to Bird Island Trail. Make sure you take the short side path to Bird Island Overlook, then maybe walk the stairs down to the sandy beaches at China Cove and Gibson Beach. (China Cove is one of the most beautiful spots on the California coast, in our humble opinion.) From Bird Island Trail, connect with South Plateau Trail, follow it northward, cross the park road to follow Carmelo Meadow Trail, and bear right for a side trip to Granite Point. Don't miss this; it's a rocky outcrop on a short loop trail with great views toward Carmel to the north. Then retrace your steps along Granite Point Trail and finish out your loop by walking along the park's northern shoreline, following Granite Point Trail to Cabin Trail to North Shore Trail. Possible side trips are to Whaler's Cabin Museum, to a lookout of Guillemot Island and its millions of birds (from a spur trail), or to Whaler's Knoll and Cypress

Grove. If you take all of the possible side trips along the route, this hike will take you almost all day—and what a fine day it will be.

User Groups: Hikers only. No dogs, horses, or mountain bikes. No wheelchair facilities.

Permits: No permits are required. A $10 day-use fee is charged per vehicle.

Maps: A map of Point Lobos State Reserve is available at the entrance station or by free download at www.parks.ca.gov. For a topographic map, ask the USGS for Monterey.

Directions: From Carmel at Rio Road, drive south on Highway 1 for three miles to the entrance to Point Lobos State Reserve on the right. Turn right and drive through the entrance kiosk; continue straight to the information station and Sea Lion Point parking area.

Contact: Point Lobos State Reserve, Route 1, Box 62, Carmel, CA 93923, 831/624-4909, www.pointlobos.org.

14 ROCKY RIDGE AND SOBERANES CANYON LOOP
7.0 mi / 3.5 hr 🥾3 ⛰10

in Garrapata State Park south of Carmel

Map 8.1, page 451   BEST 🏆

Garrapata State Park is situated on both sides of Highway 1, with some trails leading to the ocean and others leading up inland canyons and hillsides. Hikers looking for a long, heart-pumping walk will enjoy this loop trip on the inland side of the park, which travels through a remarkable variety of terrain. In spring, the wildflower display along these coastal hills will blow you away. Both the number and variety of species is truly remarkable.

Begin hiking on Soberanes Canyon Trail. What starts out as a ranch road through cactus- and chaparral-covered hillsides quickly becomes single-track trail through an increasingly narrow and wet canyon. The big surprise is a gorgeous stand of redwoods along Soberanes Creek, an extreme contrast to the chaparral and cacti at the start of the trail. The grove is a good turnaround spot for those looking for a short, easy trip. If you continue on, the trail begins a substantial ascent with not nearly enough switchbacks; after the initial easy grade of this trail, this stretch comes as a major surprise for many hikers. The trail then travels north to meet up with Peak Trail heading right, which leads to 1,977-foot Doud Peak, and Rocky Ridge Trail heading left. In case you are wondering why you are so out of breath, you've just climbed 1,850 feet in just under three miles. Unless you are feeling an irresistible urge to bag Doud Peak, turn left and finish out your loop on Rocky Ridge Trail, where on a clear day you can look out over the ocean for miles. The trail then winds back down the hillsides and deposits you back at your car on Highway 1.

User Groups: Hikers only. No dogs, horses, or mountain bikes. No wheelchair facilities.

Permits: No permits are required. Parking and access are free.

Maps: A map of Garrapata State Park is available for free download at www.parks.ca.gov. For a topographic map, ask the USGS for Soberanes Point.

Directions: From Carmel at Rio Road, drive south on Highway 1 for seven miles to mile marker 13 and the dirt pullouts along the highway at Garrapata State Park. It's four miles south of Point Lobos State Park and easy to miss; go slowly and watch for cars parked alongside the road. The Soberanes Canyon Trail begins on the east side of the road.

Contact: Garrapata State Park, c/o Big Sur Station, Highway 1, Big Sur, CA 93920, 831/667-2315 or 831/649-2836, www.parks.ca.gov.

15 SOBERANES POINT TRAIL
2.0 mi / 1.0 hr ⛷️2 ⛰️9

in Garrapata State Park south of Carmel

Map 8.1, page 451

You can access Soberanes Point Trail from three different gates along Highway 1, so if you miss mile marker 13, you can always stop at markers 15 or 16. Wherever you begin, you'll end up on a spectacular and easy set of trails that joins in a series of loops around Soberanes Point, all basically around Whale Peak. If you time your trip at low tide, you'll have access to some excellent tidepools, and even if not, you have views of rocky shoreline bluffs and plenty of birdlife and other animals. Many anglers try their luck rock fishing here at the point, and it's also a popular spot for whale-watching from November to January. Note that if you start from mile marker 13, you can hike a short loop to your right and then a much larger loop to your left. If you start from mile marker 15, you're at the middle of the larger loop, so you can start hiking either right or left. Just wander as you please; the coastline and the perimeter of the point make it impossible to get lost.

User Groups: Hikers only. No dogs, horses, or mountain bikes. No wheelchair facilities.

Permits: A map of Garrapata State Park is available for free download at www.parks.ca.gov. No permits are required. Parking and access are free.

Maps: For a topographic map, ask the USGS for Soberanes Point.

Directions: From Carmel at Rio Road, drive south on Highway 1 for seven miles to mile marker 13 and the dirt pullouts along the highway at Garrapata State Park. It's four miles south of Point Lobos State Park and easy to miss; go slowly and watch for cars parked alongside the road. The Soberanes Point Trail begins on the east side of the road.

Contact: Garrapata State Park, c/o Big Sur Station, Highway 1, Big Sur, CA 93920, 831/667-2315 or 831/649-2836, www.parks.ca.gov.

16 LUPINE, WATERFALL, AND MESA LOOP

3.2 mi / 1.5 hr   🥾2 ⛰️8

in Garland Ranch Regional Park near Carmel

Map 8.1, page 451

Garland Ranch's excellent visitors center is the perfect place to begin your trip to this 4,500-acre park. Take a look inside, get a trail map, and learn a few things about the area's animals, trees, and wildflowers. The center is also the trailhead for this combined loop on Lupine, Waterfall, and Mesa Trails. Although the park's waterfall flows only during the wettest of rainy seasons, the well-maintained trails are good to walk year-round. Begin by heading to the left (southeast) from the visitors center on Lupine Loop, which travels along the open, flat floodplains of the Carmel River. In 0.5 mile, leave the loop and continue straight on the Waterfall Trail, then climb through a more shady area to the rocky cliff where the waterfall sometimes falls. Beyond it, you'll ascend more seriously to the mesa, a large high meadow with views of Carmel Valley and beyond. Continuing farther uphill, 300 feet to the south lies Mesa Pond, which offers year-round fishing for smallmouth bass and bluegill (catch and release only, no fishing license required). Two benches are situated at the pond's eastern edge. Follow Mesa Trail back downhill to the other side of the Lupine Loop and take Lupine Loop back to the visitors center. Expect an excellent wildflower show in the grasslands in springtime.

User Groups: Hikers, dogs, and horses. No mountain bikes. No wheelchair facilities.

Permits: No permits are required. Parking and access are free.

Maps: A free map of Garland Ranch Regional Park is available at the visitors center. For topographic maps, ask the USGS for Mount Carmel and Carmel Valley.

Directions: From Highway 1 at Carmel, turn east on Carmel Valley Road. Drive 8.6 miles on Carmel Valley Road to the Garland Ranch parking area, on the right side of the road. Walk across the river bridge to get to the visitors center and trailheads.

Contact: Garland Ranch Regional Park Visitor Center, 831/659-6065; Monterey Peninsula Regional Park District, 60 Garden Court, #325, Monterey, CA 93940, 831/659-4488 or 831/372-3196, www.mprpd.org.

17 SNIVLEY'S RIDGE TRAIL

5.6 mi / 3.0 hr   🥾3 ⛰️8

in Garland Ranch Regional Park near Carmel

Map 8.1, page 451

If it's winter or spring, a trip to the top of Snivley's Ridge could be just what you need to keep your hiking legs in shape. It's a healthy, 1,600-foot climb up to the ridge, plus a 250-foot climb to get to the ridge's highest point, so be prepared to pant a little. Much of the walk is exposed; be sure to bring water, and pick a cool day to hike the trail. From the visitors center, set out on either side of Lupine Loop (heading left is a little shorter), and continue uphill on Mesa Trail to its junction with Fern Trail. This stretch is moist and shady, so enjoy it while you can. Follow Fern Trail as it steeply ascends, turn left on Sage Trail and then right on Sky Trail, and continue to climb. Well-graded switchbacks make it easier. Many people stop where Sky Trail meets Snivley's Ridge Trail, at a bench with a panoramic view of Carmel Valley, the forested Santa Lucia Mountains, and the ocean. But those determined to go as high as possible should turn right on Snivley's Ridge Trail and walk another 0.75 mile west to the ridge with its spectacular views of Carmel Bay and the Monterey Peninsula. Turn left on the trail that leads to the park's highest point at 2,038 feet. Note that if you want to get to this high point via a slightly longer but less steep route, you can follow Mesa Trail all the way to Sky Trail and bypass the steep Fern Trail.

User Groups: Hikers, dogs, and horses. No mountain bikes. No wheelchair facilities.

Permits: No permits are required. Parking and access are free.

Maps: A free map of Garland Ranch Regional Park is available at the visitors center. For topographic maps, ask the USGS for Mount Carmel and Carmel Valley.

Directions: From Highway 1 at Carmel, turn east on Carmel Valley Road. Drive 8.6 miles on Carmel Valley Road to the Garland Ranch parking area, on the right side of the road. Walk across the river bridge to get to the visitors center and trailheads.

Contact: Garland Ranch Regional Park Visitor Center, 831/659-6065; Monterey Peninsula Regional Park District, 60 Garden Court, #325, Monterey, CA 93940, 831/659-4488 or 831/372-3196, www.mprpd.org.

18 CONDOR GULCH AND HIGH PEAKS LOOP

5.3 mi / 3.0–5.0 hr   👣3 ⛰9

in Pinnacles National Monument near Soledad

Map 8.1, page 451

The Condor Gulch Trail begins across the road from the Bear Gulch Visitors Center, and it's a good 30-minute climb up the hill on a smooth, winding trail to an overlook of High Peaks. Starting early is recommended, especially in warmer temperatures, since this trail is exposed and can get extremely hot in the afternoons. The scent of wild black sage is enticingly aromatic along the route, and your eyes are continually drawn to the colorful lichens growing on equally colorful rocks. The overlook is a piped railing on a high ledge, and it's a good spot to look out over the canyon you just climbed. It's also a good turnaround spot if you don't want to go farther. If you do, continue uphill for 0.7 mile to a junction with High Peaks Trail and turn left. In just over a half mile, you'll reach a split in the trail. One path heads toward the steep and narrow section of the High Peaks Trail; the other toward the Tunnel Trail. Here, people who are afraid of heights should consider taking Tunnel Trail downhill. They can then turn left on the Juniper Canyon Trail to meet up with their fellow hikers at a bench and an overlook area at the junction of Juniper Canyon Trail and High Peaks Trail. This adds about one mile to the total mileage of this hike. Those willing to have an adventure should continue on the High Peaks Trail through narrow passageways and over and under the steep rock formations of the High Peaks.

In many places, the trail is a series of steps and handrails that have been carved into the rock. The near-vertical dropoffs appear daunting, but this trail gives an amazing up-close view of the rock formations in addition to chances of seeing falcons or California condors. After 0.7 mile, you'll reach Scout Peak, where there is a bench, a fine view to the west, and a restroom. Take advantage of any or all of these, then turn left to stay on the High Peaks Trail and head back to Bear Gulch. You'll have to walk down Moses Spring Trail a short distance to get back to your car. There is an option to add about a mile to this hike by visiting the reservoir and Bear Gulch Cave. That detour takes a right turn at the Rim Trail about 1.5 miles below Scout Peak.

User Groups: Hikers only. No dogs, horses, or mountain bikes. No wheelchair facilities.

Permits: No permits are required. There is a $5 per vehicle entrance fee, good for seven days, at Pinnacles National Monument.

Maps: A free map of Pinnacles National Monument is available at the visitors center or by download at www.nps.gov/pinn. For topographic maps, ask the USGS for Bickmore Canyon and North Chalone Peak.

Directions: From King City on US 101, take the First Street exit and head east. First Street turns into Highway G13/Bitterwater Road. Follow it for 15 miles to Highway 25, where you turn left (north). Follow Highway 25 for 14 miles to Highway 146. Turn left on Highway 146 and drive 1.9 miles to Pinnacles Visitors Center, then continue another 3.0 miles to Bear Gulch Nature Center. The trailhead for the Condor Gulch Trail is across the road from Bear Gulch Nature Center.

Alternatively, from Gilroy, drive south on

US 101 for two miles and take the Highway 25 exit. Drive south on Highway 25 for 43 miles to Highway 146. Turn right on Highway 146 and drive 1.9 miles to Pinnacles Visitors Center, then continue another 3.0 miles to Bear Gulch Nature Center. The trailhead for the Condor Gulch Trail is across the road from Bear Gulch Nature Center.

Contact: Pinnacles National Monument, 5000 Highway 146, Paicines, CA 95043, 831/389-4485, www.nps.gov/pinn.

19 BEAR GULCH CAVE
2.2 mi / 1.5 hr

in Pinnacles National Monument near Soledad

Map 8.1, page 451

Pinnacles National Monument is well loved for its craggy volcanic formations, abundant hiking trails, and challenging rock climbing. But what many visitors come to see is the Bear Gulch Cave, a tunnel-like jumble of boulders formed by thousands of years of water erosion. Bear Gulch Cave was closed in 1998 in order to protect its local residents—a colony of Townsend's big-eared bats. In 2004, the Park Service installed a system of gates to protect the roosting bats and allow visitors access to the lower part of the cave for 10 months of the year (mid-July–mid-May). During short periods in October and March when the bats leave their home, the entire cave is open to visitors, and this is the best time to come. (Phone the park before making the long drive to confirm the current status of Bear Gulch Cave; the bats don't conform to an exact timetable.) Be sure to come prepared for this adventure. Bring a flashlight and good walking shoes, and be mentally prepared to wedge through clefts in the rock, duck your head under ledges, and squint in the darkness to locate painted arrows pointing the way through the maze. The adventure is easy enough for children to accomplish, but equally fun for visitors of all ages.

User Groups: Hikers only. No dogs, horses, or mountain bikes. No wheelchair facilities.

Permits: No permits are required. There is a $5 per vehicle entrance fee, good for seven days, at Pinnacles National Monument.

Maps: A free map of Pinnacles National Monument is available at the visitors center or by download at www.nps.gov/pinn. For topographic maps, ask the USGS for Bickmore Canyon and North Chalone Peak.

Directions: From King City on US 101, take the First Street exit and head east. First Street turns into Highway G13/Bitterwater Road. Follow it for 15 miles to Highway 25, where you turn left (north). Follow Highway 25 for 14 miles to Highway 146. Turn left on Highway 146 and drive 1.9 miles to Pinnacles Visitors Center, then continue another 3.0 miles to Bear Gulch Nature Center and the Bear Gulch Cave trailhead.

Alternatively, from Gilroy, drive south on US 101 for two miles and take the Highway 25 exit. Drive south on Highway 25 for 43 miles to Highway 146. Turn right on Highway 146 and drive 1.9 miles to Pinnacles Visitors Center, then continue another 3.0 miles to Bear Gulch Nature Center and the Bear Gulch Cave trailhead.

Contact: Pinnacles National Monument, 5000 Highway 146, Paicines, CA 95043, 831/389-4485, www.nps.gov/pinn.

20 NORTH CHALONE PEAK
8.6 mi / 3.0-5.0 hr

in Pinnacles National Monument near Soledad

Map 8.1, page 451

Sure, the High Peaks at Pinnacles National Monument are high—about 2,700 feet. But if you want to go higher and get a better look around, take this hike to North Chalone Peak. Located in the western area of the park at 3,304 feet in elevation, North Chalone Peak has a decommissioned fire lookout tower on its summit. It's a great place to take in the view and enjoy some peace and quiet. This trail is much less traveled than the popular High Peaks Loop.

Take Moses Spring Trail from the visitors center parking lot, and then climb the stairs up to Bear Gulch Reservoir. Continue over the dam and along the left side of the reservoir until you meet the signed trail for North Chalone Peak. You are likely to see a posse of rock climbers who are busy doing their thing on the cliff faces around the reservoir. As you start along the North Chalone Peak Trail, you are only one mile from the visitors center, but you've left the vast majority of people behind. Enjoy the fascinating volcanic rock formations and spring wildflowers on the next stretch of trail. At 3.5 miles, you'll reach a gate; go through it and close it behind you, then follow the trail until it meets up with a fire road. This road will lead you to a larger second gate; upon passing this gate, the summit is a short distance ahead. The final 0.75 mile is the steepest stretch of the whole trip, but the reward at the top is a fine view of the Salinas River curving through its valley, the Santa Lucia Mountains, and all of Pinnacles. During winter the Santa Lucias may be snow dusted, and on very rare, crystal-clear days, you can see all the way to the Pacific Ocean.

User Groups: Hikers only. No dogs, horses, or mountain bikes. No wheelchair facilities.

Permits: No permits are required. There is a $5 per vehicle entrance fee at Pinnacles National Monument, good for seven days.

Maps: A free map of Pinnacles National Monument is available at the visitors center or by download at www.nps.gov/pinn. For topographic maps, ask the USGS for Bickmore Canyon and North Chalone Peak.

Directions: From King City on US 101, take the First Street exit and head east. First Street turns into Highway G13/Bitterwater Road. Follow it for 15 miles to Highway 25, where you turn left (north). Follow Highway 25 for 14 miles to Highway 146. Turn left on Highway 146 and drive 1.9 miles to Pinnacles Visitors Center, then continue another 3.0 miles to Bear Gulch Nature Center and the trailhead.

Alternatively, from Gilroy, drive south on US 101 for two miles and take the Highway 25 exit. Drive south on Highway 25 for 43 miles to Highway 146. Turn right on Highway 146 and drive 1.9 miles to Pinnacles Visitors Center, then continue another 3.0 miles to Bear Gulch Nature Center and the trailhead.

Contact: Pinnacles National Monument, 5000 Highway 146, Paicines, CA 95043, 831/389-4485, www.nps.gov/pinn.

21 BALCONIES CAVE
2.4 mi / 1.5 hr   🏃 2   ⚠ 10

in Pinnacles National Monument near Soledad

Map 8.1, page 451

Pinnacles National Monument has two famous sets of caves: Bear Gulch Cave, on the east side of the park; and Balconies Cave, on the west. Access to Bear Gulch Cave is often partially restricted in order to protect the resident bats, but Balconies Cave is open almost year-round (except immediately after the heaviest rains when the water can be dangerously high). Got your flashlight and sturdy footwear? Then get ready for tons of fun. Set off on the Balconies Trail, following the often dry west fork of Chalone Creek toward the narrow canyon between Machete Ridge and the Balconies. A mere 0.6 mile brings you to some huge, colorful, lichen-covered volcanic rocks. The sounds of the wind in the gray pines and the scurrying of squirrels keep you company. At the junction with the Balconies Cliffs Trail, turn right to enter the cave. Turn on your flashlight and proceed through a narrow slot-like canyon, squeezing through clefts in the rock, ducking under boulders, and climbing down rocky staircases to the inner portion of the cave. When you emerge back out into the sunlight, follow the trail and be sure to turn left and loop back to the parking area on the Balconies Cliffs Trail, gaining many lovely views of the park's rocky landscape as you climb over the top of the cave.

User Groups: Hikers only. No dogs, horses, or mountain bikes. No wheelchair facilities.

Permits: No permits are required. There is a $5 per vehicle entrance fee at Pinnacles National Monument, good for seven days.

Maps: A free map of Pinnacles National Monument is available at the ranger station or by download at www.nps.gov/pinn. For topographic maps, ask the USGS for Bickmore Canyon and North Chalone Peak.

Directions: From Salinas, drive south on US 101 for 22 miles to Soledad, and take the Soledad/Highway 146 exit. Drive east on Highway 146 for 12 miles. (The road is signed for West Pinnacles.) Highway 146 dead-ends at the Chaparral Ranger Station and trailhead parking lot.

Contact: Pinnacles National Monument, 5000 Highway 146, Paicines, CA 95043, 831/389-4485, www.nps.gov/pinn.

22 JUNIPER CANYON AND HIGH PEAKS LOOP

8.4 mi / 5.0 hr

in Pinnacles National Monument near Soledad

Map 8.1, page 451

Pinnacles National Monument is a hiker's park. The first clue you get is that no road connects the east and west sides of the park, so the only way to get from one side to the other is to walk. And that's just fine, especially since the park's first-rate trail system makes it possible to string together a loop tour around the park on the Juniper Canyon Trail, High Peaks Trail (the part known as the Steep and Narrow Section), Old Pinnacles Trail, and Balconies Trail. If you follow the trails in this order, you get almost all your climbing done in the first half of the trip and then have a fairly easy and flat homestretch.

Begin hiking from the right side of the large parking lot near the Chaparral Ranger Station, following Juniper Canyon Trail from grasslands into the rocky hills. The trail gets steeper as you go, but it's well built and has many switchbacks. Ignore the Tunnel Trail turnoff at 1.2 miles, and keep climbing to the junction

with High Peaks Trail, at 1.8 miles. Here, at a saddle, are fine views to the west and east, as well as a bench and restroom. The High Peaks Trail goes both north and southeast. Turn north (left) and prepare yourself for the most exciting part of the trip: a narrow and exciting stretch of trail with many handrails and footholds carved into the rock. Continue on the High Peaks Trail for 3.3 miles all the way to the junction with the Old Pinnacles Trail, a pleasant route that meanders along the west fork of Chalone Creek. In winter, the creek runs with water, and spring wildflowers are tremendous. In 2.3 miles, you'll go through six unbridged creek crossings and reach a fork for the Balconies Trail. If you've never been to Balconies Cave, take the left fork, which leads you through it. (The right fork climbs above the cave and offers some excellent views.) After ducking your head and bending your knees a lot as you wander through the cave, you'll come out to an easy and flat section of the Balconies Trail, which brings you back to the Chaparral Ranger Station and trailhead parking lot. If you pick a cool day and carry plenty of water, this is a stellar half-day hike at Pinnacles.

User Groups: Hikers only. No dogs, horses, or mountain bikes. No wheelchair facilities.

Permits: No permits are required. There is a $5 per vehicle entrance fee at Pinnacles National Monument, good for seven days.

Maps: A free map of Pinnacles National Monument is available at the ranger station or by download at www.nps.gov/pinn. For topographic maps, ask the USGS for Bickmore Canyon and North Chalone Peak.

Directions: From Salinas, drive south on US 101 for 22 miles to Soledad and take the Soledad/Highway 146 exit. Drive east on Highway 146 for 12 miles. The road is signed for West Pinnacles. Highway 146 dead-ends at the Chaparral Ranger Station and trailhead parking lot.

Contact: Pinnacles National Monument, 5000 Highway 146, Paicines, CA 95043, 831/389-4485, www.nps.gov/pinn.

23 MILL CREEK TRAIL
5.4 mi / 2.5 hr   🥾2 ⛰9

in Mill Creek Redwood Preserve

Map 8.1, page 451

Mill Creek Redwood Preserve is a special place on the Big Sur Coast. In fact, it's so special that you have to obtain a permit in order to hike there. Only eight permits per day are given out for this trail, with a maximum of five people allowed per permit. And that's how it should be, because this redwood grove has the sanctity of a holy cathedral. Although Mill Creek canyon was logged to some extent in the early 20th century, some of the redwoods here are still old-growth, and huge in size. The preserve is home to many special creatures, including a few magnificent owl species: great horned, northern saw-whet, and spotted. The Mill Creek Trail, built in 2006, laterals across Mill Creek's canyon, traveling under a dense canopy of tanoaks, madrones, and redwoods, and crossing over cascading streams on sturdy footbridges. In the wettest months of the year, these small streams produce lovely waterfalls. The trail very gradually gains 250 feet in elevation until it tops out at a high viewpoint that overlooks the Santa Lucia Mountains and the coast. A few wooden benches invite hikers to linger a while over the view, which overlooks the Santa Lucia Mountains and the coast.

User Groups: Hikers only. No dogs, horses, or mountain bikes. No wheelchair facilities.

Permits: A free permit is required to enter the preserve; go to www.mprpd.org to reserve a permit at least 48 hours in advance of your trip. Permits are processed only on weekdays. Parking and access are free.

Maps: For topographic maps, ask the USGS for Mount Carmel and Big Sur.

Directions: From Carmel, drive south on Highway 1 for 12 miles, past Garrapata State Park, to the left (east) turnoff for Palo Colorado Road, about 0.25 mile south of Rocky Point Restaurant. Turn left and drive east 6.8 miles to the trailhead. Park alongside the road.

Contact: Monterey Peninsula Regional Park District, 60 Garden Court #325, Monterey, CA 93940, 831/659-4488 or 831/372-3196, www.mprpd.org.

24 SKINNER RIDGE TRAIL TO DEVIL'S PEAK
7.6 mi / 3.5 hr or 2 days   🥾3 ⛰8

in the Ventana Wilderness near Carmel Valley

Map 8.1, page 451

What's the best thing about this trip? The far-off ocean views in the first mile of the climb? The white marble of giant Pico Blanco to the southwest? The colors of the oak leaves in autumn? The huge old madrone trees that pepper Skinner Ridge? It's hard to decide; you'd better go see for yourself. Pick a cool and clear day to make the trip, preferably in autumn, or arm yourself with a ton of sunscreen and water in summer. The trailhead is at 2,000 feet in an area that was severely burned in the wildfires of 2008, but the trail has been carefully rebuilt and is in better shape now than it was before the fire. It begins with an ascent through chaparral, offering many wide views. Then the trail enters the trees (madrones and oaks) and twists its way to a short, steep ascent to the top of Skinner Ridge, at 3,450 feet and 2.1 miles out. A wide bulldozer line runs up the ridge, left from the huge Marble Cone fire of the 1970s. From the ridge, backpackers usually continue down the other side for 0.75 mile to a trail junction for Turner Creek. Apple Tree Camp is a left turn and one mile away—a good place for an overnight. Day hikers should proceed straight ahead at that junction for the climb to Devil's Peak, elevation 4,158 feet, and one mile farther. That final mile will get you huffing and puffing for sure, but hey, exercise is good for you, right?

User Groups: Hikers, dogs, and horses. No mountain bikes. No wheelchair facilities.

Permits: No day hiking permits are required. A parking fee of $5 per vehicle is charged.

Maps: A Ventana Wilderness or Los Padres National Forest map is available from the U.S.

Forest Service. For topographic maps, ask the USGS for Mount Carmel and Big Sur.

Directions: From Carmel, drive south on Highway 1 for 12 miles, past Garrapata State Park, to the left (east) turnoff for Palo Colorado Road, south of Rocky Point Restaurant. Turn left and drive eight miles to Bottcher's Gap Campground. The Skinner Ridge Trail begins at the edge of the parking lot.

Contact: Big Sur Station, Highway 1, Big Sur, CA 93920, 831/667-2315; Los Padres National Forest, Monterey Ranger District, 406 South Mildred Avenue, King City, CA 93930, 831/385-5434, www.fs.fed.us/r5/lospadres.

25 MOLERA POINT TRAIL
2.5 mi / 1.5 hr   🚶1 ⛰9

in Andrew Molera State Park north of Big Sur

Map 8.1, page 451

Andrew Molera is a low-key state park without all the development and fanfare that often come with state park status. But the park has plenty to offer for hikers and coast lovers. An easy trail leads from the park's main parking lot to Molera Point, where you can look down on spectacular Molera Beach and count the sea lions lying on the rocks. To reach the point, take the trail from the right side of the main parking lot, signed for the campground (not the main trail to the beach, which starts with a bridge crossing). The Molera Point Trail stays on the north side of the Big Sur River and winds past the park's walk-in camp, set in a wide meadow, and historic Cooper Cabin, which was built in 1861 and is the oldest structure on the Big Sur coast. At the river's mouth, the trail forks to the right, heading out to Molera Point. Check out the view from this often windswept promontory; then if the tide is low, go play on the beach at the river's edge before heading back.

User Groups: Hikers and horses. No dogs or mountain bikes. No wheelchair facilities.

Permits: No permits are required. A $10 day-use fee is charged per vehicle.

Maps: A map of Andrew Molera State Park is available at the entrance station or by free download at www.parks.ca.gov. For a topographic map, ask the USGS for Big Sur.

Directions: From Carmel, drive 22 miles south on Highway 1 to Andrew Molera State Park's main entrance, on the west side of the highway. Trails begin at the parking lot. The park is two miles north of Big Sur.

Contact: Andrew Molera State Park, c/o Big Sur Station, Highway 1, Big Sur, CA 93920, 831/667-2315 or 831/649-2836, www.parks.ca.gov.

26 MOLERA STATE PARK LOOP
8.0 mi / 4.0 hr   🚶3 ⛰10

in Andrew Molera State Park north of Big Sur

Map 8.1, page 451

This big loop around the western side of Andrew Molera State Park is easiest in summer, when the footbridge is in place over the Big Sur River. If the bridge isn't there, you must take off your shoes and socks and suffer through a very cold ford over smooth, rounded rocks. But this trail is worth the effort. It offers several miles of lovely ocean vistas, plus a visit to a remote beach. Start by taking the path from the west side of the parking lot and immediately crossing the river. In a few minutes of walking, you'll leave the crowds behind as you turn left (south) on the River Trail, then in less than a mile, turn right on the single-track Hidden Trail. Enjoy a heart-pumping climb through forest and meadows up to the Ridge Trail, where you turn left and hike southward, paralleling the ocean. The Ridge Trail is a wide fire road and rolls gently, still heading generally uphill. In addition to the ocean vistas to the west, you also have fine views inland of Big Sur's rugged peaks, and you pass through a small, surprising grove of redwood trees.

At 3.5 miles, the Ridge Trail meets the Panorama Trail at a bench and overlook point. Turn right and start to switchback steeply downhill toward the ocean, enjoying more wide views all the way. Spring wildflowers are lovely along the open hillsides. As you near the coast, you'll reach a junction with the Spring Trail. Turn left for a few hundred feet to a lovely, driftwood-laden beach. This makes a perfect lunch stop, provided the wind isn't howling. A fascinating log jam at the beach's entrance makes for great photographs. For your return, follow the Bluffs Trail 2.5 miles back to Molera Beach. This is the loveliest stretch of the entire loop, offering long and beautiful looks at Molera Point and beach and Point Sur Light Station. Finally, take the trail from Molera Beach back to the parking lot. Wow, what a perfect Big Sur day.

User Groups: Hikers and horses. No dogs. Mountain bikes are allowed on Ridge Trail and part of Bluffs Trail only. No wheelchair facilities.

Permits: No permits are required. A $10 day-use fee is charged per vehicle.

Maps: A map of Andrew Molera State Park is available at the entrance station or by free download at www.parks.ca.gov. For a topographic map, ask the USGS for Big Sur.

Directions: From Carmel, drive 22 miles south on Highway 1 to Andrew Molera State Park's main entrance, on the west side of the highway. Trails begin at the parking lot. (The park is two miles north of Big Sur.)

Contact: Andrew Molera State Park, c/o Big Sur Station, Highway 1, Big Sur, CA 93920, 831/667-2315 or 831/649-2836, www.parks.ca.gov.

27 PFEIFFER FALLS AND VALLEY VIEW LOOP

1.6 mi / 1.0 hr 🥾2 ⛰️8

in Pfeiffer Big Sur State Park near Big Sur

Map 8.1, page 451

A loop hike to a 60-foot waterfall and an overlook of the Big Sur Valley? Sounds great; let's go. And don't forget, there's a gorgeous redwood forest along the way. You get all of this when you set out on the Pfeiffer Falls Trail from the nature center at Pfeiffer Big Sur State Park and return on the Valley View Trail. After a slightly uphill walk on the Pfeiffer Falls Trail along Pfeiffer Redwood Creek (ignore all the trail junctions and stay along the creek, crossing it a couple of times on bridges), you'll wind up at the foot of tall and narrow Pfeiffer Falls, which stream down a vertical, dark rock face. You can sit for a while at the waterfall's viewing platform, then backtrack along the trail 0.1 mile to its junction with the Valley View Trail. Follow the Valley View Trail as it climbs up and out of the canyon. You'll leave the redwoods almost immediately and hike in an oak forest for 0.5 mile. Look for the brilliant blooms of Douglas iris in the spring. The trail reaches an overlook of the Big Sur Valley and Point Sur. Unfortunately, the sight of Highway 1 somewhat diminishes the beauty of the view. Head back down the Valley View Trail and take the right fork (0.25 mile from the overlook) to finish out your loop. This last downhill stretch is on the steep side, so wear a good pair of boots.

User Groups: Hikers only. No dogs, horses, or mountain bikes. No wheelchair facilities.

Permits: No permits are required. A $10 day-use fee is charged per vehicle.

Maps: A map of Pfeiffer Big Sur State Park is available at the entrance station or by free download at www.parks.ca.gov. For a topographic map, ask the USGS for Big Sur.

Directions: From Carmel, drive 26 miles south on Highway 1 to Pfeiffer Big Sur State Park, on the east side of the highway. It's two miles south of Big Sur. Drive through the entrance kiosk, turn left at the lodge, and then turn right, following the signs to the Pfeiffer Falls trailhead and the nature center. Park just beyond the nature center. The trail is on the left side of the lot, signed as Oak Grove Trail, Valley View Trail, and Pfeiffer Falls Trail. If the small parking lot is full, you may have to park by the lodge and walk to the trailhead.

Contact: Pfeiffer Big Sur State Park, c/o Big Sur Station, Highway 1, Big Sur, CA 93920, 831/667-2315 or 831/649-2836, www.parks.ca.gov.

28 MOUNT MANUEL
9.0 mi / 5.0 hr   🏃4 △9

on the southern edge of the Ventana
Wilderness near Big Sur

Map 8.1, page 451

This trail leads to one of the best vantage points in the Ventana Wilderness, the summit of Mount Manuel, where all of Big Sur, the Santa Lucia Mountains, and the Pacific Ocean are spread out before you. Odd as it seems, the trail starts out by the softball fields and picnic areas at Pfeiffer Big Sur State Park. Over the course of the trail's 4.5-mile length, you'll climb 3,100 feet to Mount Manuel's summit at 3,379 feet in elevation, so make sure you have fresh soles on your boots and plenty of water. Pick a cool day to make the climb, because although the trail starts in the trees, the vast majority of the route is completely exposed, and even more so after the devastating wildfires of 2008. Winter and spring are usually the best seasons to head for the summit, both for the clarity of the view (less chance of fog) and for cool temperatures.

Negotiate your way through a half-mile series of signed state park trails to access the official start of the Mount Manuel Trail. You'll enter Los Padres National Forest and begin a long series of switchbacks over chaparral-covered slopes. As you climb, you gain views of the Big Sur River canyon and the coast. About three miles from the start, the trail enters a forest of tan oaks, bay laurel, and redwoods, then exits it again, returning to the chaparral. Finally you near the summit, or rather, a series of summits. Head for the obvious highest point, where the view of the vast Pacific Ocean and the beauty of the Santa Lucia Mountains will blow you away.

User Groups: Hikers only. No dogs, horses, or mountain bikes. No wheelchair facilities.
Permits: No day hiking permits are required. A $10 day-use fee is charged per vehicle.
Maps: A Ventana Wilderness or Los Padres National Forest map is available from the U.S. Forest Service. For topographic maps, ask the USGS for Pfeiffer Point and Big Sur.

Directions: From Carmel, drive 26 miles south on Highway 1 to Pfeiffer Big Sur State Park, on the east side of the highway. It's two miles south of Big Sur. Drive through the entrance kiosk and continue straight past the campfire center to the parking lot near the picnic areas and softball field. The trailhead is signed for Oak Grove Trail and Mount Manuel.
Contact: Big Sur Station, Highway 1, Big Sur, CA 93920, 831/667-2315 or 831/649-2836, www.parks.ca.gov; Los Padres National Forest, Monterey Ranger District, 406 South Mildred Avenue, King City, CA 93930, 831/385-5434, www.fs.fed.us/r5/lospadres.

29 BUZZARDS ROOST OVERLOOK
4.0 mi / 2.0 hr   🏃3 △9

in Pfeiffer Big Sur State Park near Big Sur

Map 8.1, page 451

Hikers looking for a bit of a challenge in Pfeiffer Big Sur State Park will want to try out this trail to the Buzzards Roost Overlook. Compared to the Pfeiffer Falls Trail, this trail gets surprisingly little traffic, unless there are large groups camping at the nearby group campground. The trail leads along the Big Sur River through a forest of many splendid redwoods, switches back uphill onto slopes filled with oaks and bays, and finally climbs into chaparral country. You get to walk in every kind of Big Sur terrain. High up on Pfeiffer Ridge, there's a 360-degree view of the Pacific Ocean, the Big Sur River gorge, and the Santa Lucia Mountains, providing a fine reward for your effort in climbing here. The trailhead is at 200 feet in elevation, and the overlook is at nearly 1,000 feet.

User Groups: Hikers only. No dogs, horses, or mountain bikes. No wheelchair facilities.
Permits: No permits are required. A $10 day-use fee is charged per vehicle.
Maps: A map of Pfeiffer Big Sur State Park is available at the entrance station or by free download at www.parks.ca.gov. For

topographic maps, ask the USGS for Big Sur and Pfeiffer Point.

Directions: From Carmel, drive 26 miles south on Highway 1 to Pfeiffer Big Sur State Park, on the east side of the highway. It's two miles south of Big Sur. Drive through the entrance kiosk, go past the lodge, and turn right to cross the bridge over the Big Sur River. A parking area is on the left side of the road. The Buzzards Roost trailhead is signed.

Contact: Pfeiffer Big Sur State Park, c/o Big Sur Station, Highway 1, Big Sur, CA 93920, 831/667-2315 or 831/649-2836, www.parks.ca.gov.

30 SYKES HOT SPRINGS
20.0 mi / 2 days   🏃3 ⛰9

in the Ventana Wilderness near Big Sur

Map 8.1, page 451

The trip to Sykes Hot Springs is one that just about every California backpacker takes at one time or another. This is a quintessential Big Sur/Ventana Wilderness trip, with deep swimming holes, three hot springs pools, and plenty of coastal mountain scenery. Although much of the land surrounding the Pine Ridge Trail to the springs was badly burned in 2008 wildfires, the trail has been thoroughly cleared and maintained and this trip remains as popular as ever, so plan your trip for the off-season if possible. Fall and winter are the best times to visit, and if you go on a weekday, you might just get the hot springs all to yourself. The first four miles of Pine Ridge Trail will have you huffing and puffing through shadeless switchbacks, with only occasional breaks as the path travels through small redwood groves. The route eventually levels and gets much easier. At a junction just past the four-mile mark, the left trail leads to Ventana Camp, one mile farther. This camp near Ventana Creek makes a great overnight for people who have gotten a late start; it even has a "wilderness toilet." At 5.4 miles, the trail reaches Terrace Creek Camp, another option for spending the night. At 7.0

miles, you reach the Big Sur River for the first time, and another camp at Barlow Flat. You'll cross the river at 9.7 miles and head for Sykes Camp and the hot springs. Note that after a period of rain, this can be a difficult or even impossible ford, so if you plan to hike in the wet season, check on conditions before setting out. The hot springs are less than a quarter mile from the camp. Depending on current conditions, two or three pools are terraced along the Big Sur River. The largest of the group is 10 feet long and gracefully sheltered by a large boulder. It averages 100 degrees; the other pools are slightly cooler.

User Groups: Hikers, dogs, and horses. No mountain bikes. No wheelchair facilities.

Permits: A free campfire permit is required for overnight stays and is available from Big Sur Station. An $8 parking fee is charged per vehicle.

Maps: A Ventana Wilderness or Los Padres National Forest map is available from the U.S. Forest Service. For topographic maps, ask the USGS for Pfeiffer Point, Partington Ridge, and Ventana Cones.

Directions: From Carmel, drive 30 miles south on Highway 1 to Big Sur Station, on the east side of the highway. It's three miles south of Big Sur. The Pine Ridge Trail begins behind the ranger station at the backpacker's parking lot.

Contact: Big Sur Station, Highway 1, Big Sur, CA 93920, 831/667-2315 or 831/649-2836; Los Padres National Forest, Monterey Ranger District, 406 South Mildred Avenue, King City, CA 93930, 831/385-5434, www.fs.fed.us/r5/lospadres.

31 PARTINGTON POINT AND TANBARK TRAILS
4.0 mi / 2.0 hr   🏃2 ⛰9

in Julia Pfeiffer Burns State Park south of Big Sur

Map 8.1, page 451

If you want to hike at Julia Pfeiffer Burns State Park without the crowds, a combined out-and-back trip on Partington Point and Tanbark

Trails could be just your cup of tea. The two trails are about as different as any trails could be, except that they both start from the same point along Highway 1. The Partington Point Trail is a dirt road that leads westward and steeply downhill to an obvious fork at 0.5 mile. The right fork leads a few hundred feet to a tiny rock-strewn beach at Partington Creek's mouth. The left fork leads into the redwoods, across a wooden footbridge, and through a rock tunnel built in the 1880s by pioneer John Partington. On the tunnel's far side is the remains of a narrow dog-hole port at Partington Cove, where lumber was loaded onto seagoing freighters. Partington Point is home to the park's underwater playground of caves and natural bridges, but unless you're a scuba diver, you won't be able to see them. Instead, you can have a seat on a rock and look for sea otters, sea lions, and pelicans. Also keep your eyes peeled for spouting whales.

When you've seen enough, hike back uphill and cross the highway to the start of Tanbark Trail, which leads along Partington Creek, heading inland. Much of this inland area was burned in the wildfires of 2008, and as of 2011 the trail was in very poor repair, so only hike as far as you feel comfortable. You can walk a short 0.5-mile loop on the trail (a bridge carries you across Partington Creek and then back down the other side), or you can continue farther, climbing steeply uphill for 1.5 miles to a confluence of streams at a redwood-shaded spot known as Swiss Camp. Depending on trail conditions, it is possible to continue beyond Swiss Camp for another half-mile to the trail's end at the upper end of a fire road, which leads to the historic Tin House (yes, it is built of tin), a total of 3.2 miles from the trailhead. From here, you can follow the fire road steeply downhill back down to Highway 1, but this will mean you have to walk a mile alongside the highway to get back to your car.

User Groups: Hikers only. No dogs, horses, or mountain bikes. No wheelchair facilities.

Permits: No permits are required. Parking and access are free.

Maps: A map of Julia Pfeiffer Burns State Park is available at the entrance kiosk (2.2 miles south of this trailhead) or by free download at www.parks.ca.gov. For a topographic map, ask the USGS for Partington Ridge.

Directions: From Carmel, drive 34 miles south on Highway 1 to a dirt pullout along the highway and the trailheads for the Partington Point and Tanbark Trails. The trailheads are 10.5 miles south of Big Sur and 2.2 miles north of the main entrance to Julia Pfeiffer Burns State Park. Partington Point Trail is on the west side of the highway; Tanbark Trail is on the east side.

Contact: Julia Pfeiffer Burns State Park, c/o Big Sur Station, Highway 1, Big Sur, CA 93920, 831/667-2315 or 831/649-2836, www.parks.ca.gov.

32 MCWAY FALLS OVERLOOK
0.5 mi / 0.5 hr   🥾1 ⛰9

in Julia Pfeiffer Burns State Park south of Big Sur

Map 8.1, page 451   BEST (

After Yosemite Falls and Bridalveil Fall, McWay Falls is probably the waterfall that appears most often on family snapshots of California vacations. Although few know its name, its image is unforgettable: an 80-foot waterfall leaping off a rugged ocean bluff and pouring gracefully into the Pacific. The walk to the waterfall's overlook is on a paved trail that leads through a tunnel underneath Highway 1 and comes out to a spectacular overlook of McWay Cove. A bench is placed along the trail, and you can sit there and admire the action—and maybe even catch sight of a passing gray whale. You can continue a few hundred feet beyond the bench, where the trail ends at the ruins of Waterfall House, the home of Lathrop and Helen Hooper Brown in the 1940s. There's not much left of it now, but at one time, it was quite a place.

User Groups: Hikers only. No dogs, horses, or mountain bikes. The McWay Falls Overlook

Trail is wheelchair accessible via a special bridge that bypasses the stairs from the parking lot.

Permits: No permits are required. A $10 day-use fee is charged per vehicle.

Maps: A map of Julia Pfeiffer Burns State Park is available at the entrance kiosk or by free download at www.parks.ca.gov. For a topographic map, ask the USGS for Partington Ridge.

Directions: From Carmel, drive 37 miles south on Highway 1 to Julia Pfeiffer Burns State Park, located on the east side of the highway, 13 miles south of Big Sur. Drive through the entrance kiosk and park near the restrooms. The Overlook Trail starts on a series of wooden stairs across the pavement from the restrooms.

Contact: Julia Pfeiffer Burns State Park, c/o Big Sur Station, Highway 1, Big Sur, CA 93920, 831/667-2315 or 831/649-2836, www.parks.ca.gov.

33 EWOLDSEN LOOP TRAIL
5.3 mi / 2.5 hr   🏃3   ⛰5

in Julia Pfeiffer Burns State Park south of Big Sur

Map 8.1, page 451

The Ewoldsen Trail, previously one of the best day-hiking trails in all of Big Sur, was badly burned in the wildfires of 2008 and has been closed since. It is expected to reopen in 2012, and when it does, many hikers will want to visit here to see what changes have occurred in this fire-scarred redwood forest. The following describes the trail as it was before the 2008 Basin Fire.

The trail begins with an easy saunter along McWay Creek and its spectacular redwood forest, passing within a few yards of the second-largest redwood tree in Monterey County (there's no sign; you have to guess which one it is). Soon the trail splits, with Canyon Trail to the left and Ewoldsen Trail switchbacking uphill. Take the short Canyon Trail spur to its end, 0.25 mile away, and visit McWay Canyon's sweet little waterfall. Then retrace your steps to the junction and head uphill on Ewoldsen Trail, which climbs steadily above the tops of the tall redwood trees below. The next fork, about 1.5 miles in, is the beginning of the loop. Hike the right side first. You'll alternate between dense redwood forest and more sparse oak woodland until at 2.5 miles you'll see a spur trail signed as Overlook. Take it and climb very steeply uphill for 0.25 mile until you come out to a wide, grassy ridgetop with stunning views over McWay Canyon and out to the ocean. After all your time in the forest, this bald, open viewpoint comes as quite a surprise. Pull out your lunch and your camera. After a rest, retrace your steps to the junction, bear right, and take the downhill side of the loop. You're treated to more fine views of the ocean before dropping back into redwood forest. The total elevation gain along the trail is 1,600 feet.

User Groups: Hikers only. No dogs, horses, or mountain bikes. No wheelchair facilities.

Permits: No permits are required. A $10 day-use fee is charged per vehicle.

Maps: A map of Julia Pfeiffer Burns State Park is available at the entrance kiosk or by free download at www.parks.ca.gov. For a topographic map, ask the USGS for Partington Ridge.

Directions: From Carmel, drive 37 miles south on Highway 1 to Julia Pfeiffer Burns State Park, on the east side of the highway. It's 13 miles south of Big Sur. Drive through the entrance kiosk, and park near the restrooms. The Ewoldsen Trail starts near the picnic areas on the inland side of the parking area.

Contact: Julia Pfeiffer Burns State Park, c/o Big Sur Station, Highway 1, Big Sur, CA 93920, 831/667-2315 or 831/649-2836, www.parks.ca.gov.

34 PINE VALLEY
10.6-13.0 mi / 6.0 hr or 2 days

🏃3 ⛰️10

in the Ventana Wilderness near Carmel Valley

Map 8.1, page 451

The Pine Valley hike is a great one-night backpacking trip or long day hike into the Ventana Wilderness and can easily be extended into a 13-mile loop. The hike begins on the northern end of Pine Ridge Trail at China Campground, following an up-and-down course that soon becomes more down than up. At 3.5 miles, you turn right on Carmel River Trail and descend some more to the headwaters of the Carmel River and the beginning of a fir and ponderosa pine forest. Pine Valley Camp is 5.3 miles from the trailhead, set in lush Pine Valley, a spacious high meadow lined with ferns, ponderosa pines, and rocky sandstone formations. A short side trip to Pine Falls is possible from the camp; follow a well-worn route downstream along the river for 0.5 mile to the waterfall. From there, you can retrace your steps to the trailhead for a 10.6-mile round-trip, or make camp at Pine Valley, or take the trail from the upper end of camp, which meets up with Pine Ridge Trail. Turn left on Pine Ridge Trail and hike back to the trailhead to complete a 13-mile loop.

User Groups: Hikers, dogs, and horses. No mountain bikes. No wheelchair facilities.

Permits: A free campfire permit is required for overnight stays and is available from the Monterey Ranger District or Big Sur Station.

Maps: A Ventana Wilderness or Los Padres National Forest map is available from the U.S. Forest Service. For a topographic map, ask the USGS for Chews Ridge.

Directions: From Greenfield on US 101, take the G-16/Monterey County Road exit and drive west for 29 miles. Turn south on Tassajara Road and drive 1.3 miles to Cachagua Road. Turn left and drive nine miles to the trailhead, located just past the turnoff for China Campground. High-clearance vehicles

are recommended. The county sometimes closes the road during bad weather; call the Monterey Ranger District before traveling.

Contact: Los Padres National Forest, Monterey Ranger District, 406 South Mildred Avenue, King City, CA 93930, 831/385-5434, www.fs.fed.us/r5/lospadres.

35 LIMEKILN TRAIL AND LIMEKILN FALLS
1.8 mi / 1.0 hr

🏃2 ⛰️10

in Limekiln State Park south of Big Sur

Map 8.1, page 451

What's Big Sur's best-kept secret? That's easy—the hiking trail at Limekiln State Park. The state park is so far south of Big Sur that it doesn't get inundated by visitors, as does Pfeiffer Big Sur and Julia Pfeiffer Burns State Parks. The Limekiln Trail leads from the inland campground into a gorgeous redwood forest. It follows Limekiln Creek for a half mile to the park's namesake limekilns, which were used to make limestone bricks and cement in the 1880s. The four kilns look like giant smokestacks with mossy, brick bottoms; they're interesting to see and photograph, but in the wet season, they are not the biggest attraction on this trail. What is? A fork off the main trail leads to Limekiln Falls, a spectacular 100-foot waterfall that drops over a limestone face. When the water is running with vigor, you'll probably end up with wet feet as you boulder-hop your way to its base, but it's worth it. This waterfall is a beauty.

User Groups: Hikers only. No dogs, horses, or mountain bikes. No wheelchair facilities.

Permits: No permits are required. A $8 day-use fee is charged per vehicle.

Maps: A map of Limekiln State Park is available at the entrance kiosk or by free download at www.parks.ca.gov. For a topographic map, ask the USGS for Lopez Point.

Directions: From Carmel, drive 52 miles south on Highway 1 to Limekiln State Park, on the east side of the highway. It's 2.5 miles south of Lucia and 14.8 miles south of Julia Pfeiffer Burns State Park. The trailhead is at the far side of the inland campground.

Contact: Limekiln State Park, c/o Big Sur Station, Highway 1, Big Sur, CA 93920, 831/667-2315 or 831/667-2403, www.parks.ca.gov.

36 CONE PEAK LOOKOUT TRAIL

4.8 mi / 2.5 hr 🥾 3 ⛰ 10

in the Ventana Wilderness north of Lucia

Map 8.1, page 451

The 2.4-mile climb to Cone Peak is a classic Ventana Wilderness adventure, and the fun begins with the drive to the trailhead. After leaving Highway 1, first you get wide coastal views and then views of the inland mountain ranges as your car chugs its way uphill. But those are nothing compared to the views you get at the fire lookout on Cone Peak's summit, at 5,155 feet above sea level. This is the second highest mountain in the Santa Lucia Range (after 5,862-foot Junipero Serra Peak, also known as "Pinkolam" and much harder to hike to), but what makes this summit really special is the fact that it is only three miles from the ocean. The average gradient from sea level to the summit is about 30 percent, which creates an extremely dramatic, high-contrast view. The short hike from the trailhead to the summit is a steep climb, and the last mile feels like it goes straight up (total elevation gain is 1,400 feet). Make sure you have plenty of water with you, and in the spring months, bring along a wildflower identification book. These slopes are littered with penstemon, poppies, sticky monkeyflower, paintbrush, and many other colorful blooms. After zig-zagging upward through a mix of low chaparal,

hardwoods, and then conifers (mostly Coulter pines), you reach a trail junction at 1.9 miles. Go east (right) and walk the final half mile to the fire lookout. In this last stretch, the trail is literally cut into the rock. At the top you'll find the historic lookout tower, built in 1923, as well as an eye-popping vista. You can see as far as 100 miles on clear days, and if the fog has burned off, you can look down the west side of Cone Peak for almost a vertical mile to the ocean. Be sure to pack along a good map, so you can name all the peaks and valleys in the 360-degree panorama that surrounds you.

User Groups: Hikers, dogs, and horses. No mountain bikes. No wheelchair facilities.

Permits: No permits are required. Parking and access are free.

Maps: A Ventana Wilderness or Los Padres National Forest map is available from the U.S. Forest Service. For a topographic map, ask the USGS for Cone Peak.

Directions: From Big Sur, drive 27 miles south on Highway 1 to Kirk Creek Campground, on the west side of the highway, and the left turnoff for Nacimiento-Fergusson Road, on the east side of the highway. Turn left and drive 7.2 miles, then turn left on the dirt Coast Ridge Road (sometimes called Cone Peak Road) and drive 5.5 miles to the trailhead on the left (do not follow the road to its end). Park off the road; there is space for about six cars. A high-clearance vehicle is recommended, although not always necessary.

Special Note: Coast Ridge Road/Cone Peak Road is usually closed during the rainy season (Nov.–Mar.).

Contact: Los Padres National Forest, Monterey Ranger District, 406 South Mildred Avenue, King City, CA 93930, 831/385-5434, www.fs.fed.us/r5/lospadres.

SAN JOAQUIN VALLEY

© TERRANCE EMERSON/WWW.123RF.CC

BEST HIKES

Stretching from Stockton, in the north, to

Bakersfield, in the south, the San Joaquin Valley is best known for its agricultural bounty. This "fruit basket of the nation" is part of the larger Central
Valley, a giant basin that reaches all the way north to Chico. Snowmelt from
the western Sierra Nevada Mountains irrigates this immense valley via the
Sacramento and San Joaquin Rivers, which join in the delta before flowing
to the San Francisco Bay and the Pacific Ocean.

The San Joaquin region is bisected by two major freeways – I-5 and
Highway 99. While traveling these corridors, drivers cruise past endless
acres of cotton, orchards, cattle grazing lands, and stick-straight concrete aqueducts that transport water. Most regard this flat, nondescript
landscape as nothing more than an irritation – an obstacle that must be
passed on the way to someplace better. But this land was once much
different from what you see today. Before the Europeans settled here in
the 19th century, the San Joaquin Valley was a vast wetland. Its millions of
acres of marshes, vernal pools, and riparian streams and creeks were the
homeland of immense populations of waterfowl and elk. Native Americans
lived bountifully year-round in this wildlife-rich area.

Enterprising European settlers saw that the San Joaquin Valley could be
useful for growing their nonnative vegetables, and for farming livestock.
They diked and dammed the land to create vast dry patches suitable for
ranching and farming, then built irrigation systems to water the crops. In
relatively short order, populations of native wildlife soon dwindled, having lost their natural habitat. Larger animals, like the tule elk, completely
abandoned the region.

Today, we recognize that this dramatic transformation of the land was
not beneficial to either people or wildlife. Through ongoing conservation
efforts, large stretches of the San Joaquin Valley's agricultural fields are

now purposefully flooded in winter to provide a haven for migrating ducks and geese. Farming and irrigation strategies are being rethought and redesigned. In protected habitat areas, such as wildlife refuges and at Tule Elk State Reserve, tule elk are being reintroduced to their native habitat.

What all this means for hikers is that the few natural areas found in this region should be appreciated for their very existence, and also for their unique look into California's past. The state's largest remaining wetland ecosystem – 160,000 acres of grassland wetlands – is preserved at Los Banos Wildlife Area and the San Luis National Wildlife Refuge complex. Within these protected boundaries, winter visitors can see lakes and ponds that are completely covered by hundreds of thousands of geese and ducks. Smaller regional, county, and privately operated parks provide access to special places like the riparian forest and valley oak woodland at Kaweah Oaks Preserve – a rare, remnant example of what this vast landscape once looked like.

Perhaps the most impressive preservation of "old California" is at Carrizo Plain, which was declared a national monument in 2000. The plains are considered to be California's largest nature preserve, stretching for 50 miles north to south along the San Andreas Fault. Here, hikers have the chance to see the largest remaining example of San Joaquin Valley grassland habitat. Amid the waving grasses live reintroduced pronghorn antelope and tule elk, plus thousands of visiting sandhill cranes in the winter months.

Next time you're driving 70 miles an hour down I-5 or Highway 99, pull off the road, tie up your boot laces, and take a closer look at the landscape of the San Joaquin Valley. You might be surprised at the rare and precious beauty that awaits you.

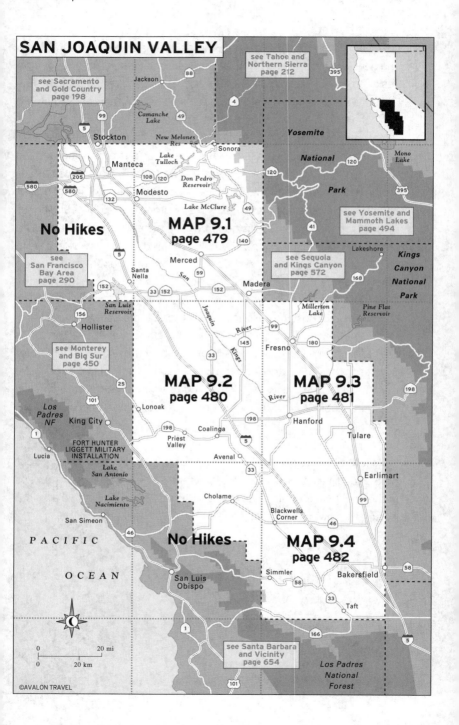

SAN JOAQUIN VALLEY

see Sacramento and Gold Country page 198

see Tahoe and Northern Sierra page 212

Jackson

Stockton

Manteca

Modesto

Merced

Santa Nella

Hollister

King City

Lucia

San Simeon

San Luis Obispo

No Hikes

MAP 9.1 page 479

MAP 9.2 page 480

MAP 9.3 page 481

No Hikes

MAP 9.4 page 482

see San Francisco Bay Area page 290

see Monterey and Big Sur page 450

see Yosemite and Mammoth Lakes page 494

see Sequoia and Kings Canyon page 572

Yosemite

National

Park

Mono Lake

Kings Canyon National Park

Camanche Lake

New Melones Res

Sonora

Lake Tulloch

Don Pedro Reservoir

Lake McClure

Lakeshore

Millerton Lake

Pine Flat Reservoir

Fresno

Madera

Lonoak

Coalinga

Priest Valley

Avenal

Cholame

Blackwells Corner

Hanford

Tulare

Earlimart

Simmler

Bakersfield

Taft

San Luis Reservoir

Los Padres NF

FORT HUNTER LIGGETT MILITARY INSTALLATION

Lake San Antonio

Lake Nacimiento

PACIFIC

OCEAN

see Santa Barbara and Vicinity page 654

Los Padres National Forest

0   20 mi
0   20 km

©AVALON TRAVEL

Map 9.1

Hikes 1-7
Pages 483-486

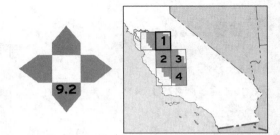

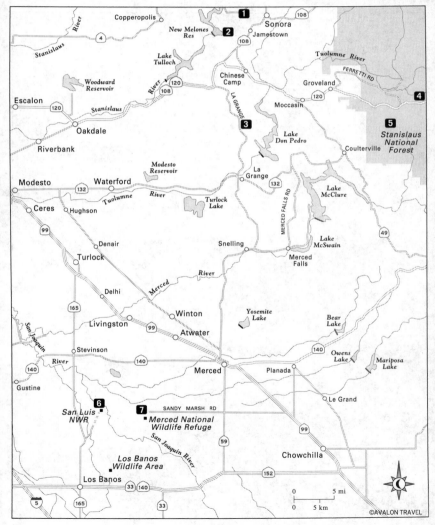

Map 9.2

Hikes 8-9
Pages 487-488

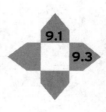

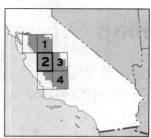

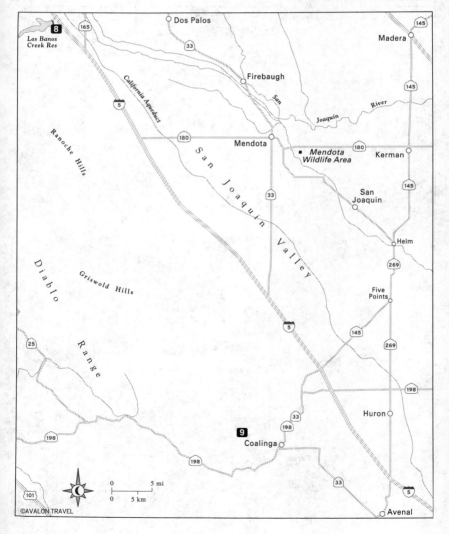

Map 9.3

Hikes 10-11
Pages 488-489

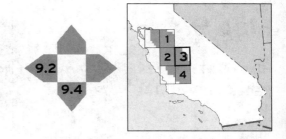

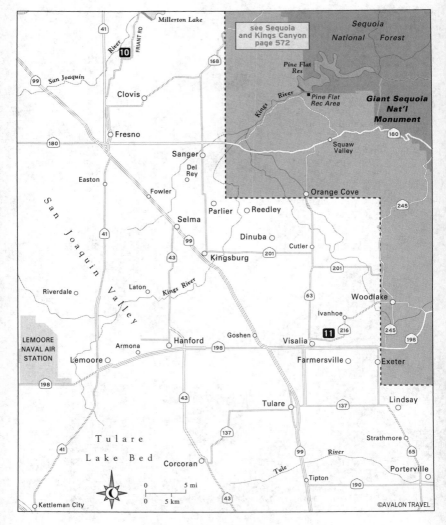

Map 9.4

Hikes 12-13
Pages 489-490

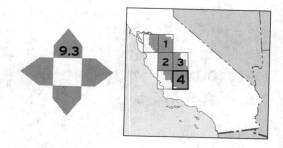

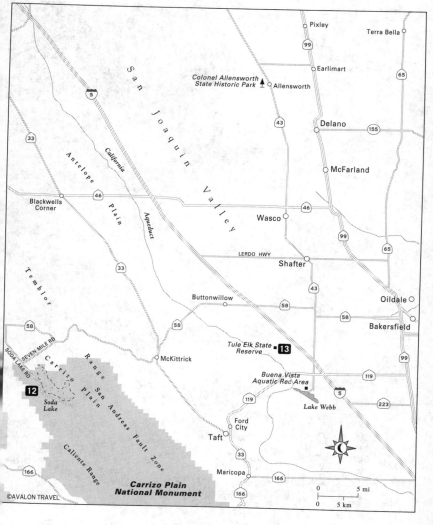

©AVALON TRAVEL

🚻 NATURAL BRIDGES
1.4 mi / 1.0 hr   🚶‍♂️2 🔺8

at New Melones Reservoir near Sonora

Map 9.1, page 479

This short, easy trail leads from Parrotts Ferry Road to Natural Bridges, a unique series of limestone caves with Coyote Creek running through them. This geologic wonder is only a short drive from downtown Sonora, but it's like nothing else around this Gold Rush town. The upper Natural Bridge is 270 feet high, and the clear water underneath it creates a popular locals' swimming hole. Because Coyote Creek is spring-fed, the water is cool year-round. Most swimmers bring inner tubes with them so they can float through the cave. The rocky trail that accesses the upper bridge has a 300-foot elevation gain, but is easily accomplished by children and adults alike. Because it takes thousands of years to create the cave's fragile formations, visitors are asked not to touch them. The oil on human hands can stop the formations from growing. A second bridge lies downstream from the upper bridge, accessible by a rough, unmaintained trail. If you are willing to walk the extra 0.5 mile to the lower bridge, you have a greater chance of solitude.

User Groups: Hikers only. No dogs, horses, or mountain bikes. No wheelchair facilities.

Permits: No permits are required. Parking and access are free.

Maps: A free map is available at the New Melones Visitors Center or by download at www.usbr.gov. For a topographic map, ask the USGS for Sonora.

Directions: From Highway 49 in Sonora, take the turnoff for Parrotts Ferry Road (signed for Columbia State Historic Park). Drive north on Parrotts Ferry Road for about seven miles, crossing the bridge over New Melones Reservoir, to the trailhead on the left side of the road (1.2 miles north of the highway bridge and four miles south of the Hwy. 4 junction).

Contact: New Melones Reservoir Visitors Center, 6850 Studhorse Flat Road, Sonora, CA 95370, 209/536-9543 or 209/536-9094, www.usbr.gov.

🚻 TABLE MOUNTAIN
3.0 mi / 1.5 hr   🚶‍♂️3 🔺8

at New Melones Reservoir near Jamestown

Map 9.1, page 479

Wildflower lovers, this is your trail. The only trick is timing your visit for the exact period when Table Mountain is at its most colorful splendor. Of course, the timing of the bloom varies from year to year, so your best bet is to call the New Melones Visitors Center starting in late February to see how the flowers are coming along. When they say "go time," don't wait too long. Some years the bloom is all over by late April, although Table Mountain's high vistas are there for the taking at any time of year. From the pavement's end at the yellow gate, the trail crosses through a grassy oak woodland dotted with basalt (volcanic) rocks. Straight ahead is Table Mountain, a 2,200-foot-high, 1,200-foot-wide, flat-topped plateau that juts upward from the surrounding lowlands. The plateau was formed by a lava flow about 10 million years ago, when a volcano erupted east of Sonora Pass. Its volcanic soil creates ideal conditions for vernal pools in February and March (look for fairy shrimp in the pools) and a colorful array of grassland wildflowers in April and May, including lupine, Indian paintbrush, blue dicks, and goldfields. Although this trail's distance is short, the last 0.5 mile is slow-going because it requires a modicum of scrambling over rough volcanic rock. Be sure to wear sturdy boots or shoes.

User Groups: Hikers, dogs, horses, and mountain bikes. No wheelchair facilities.

Permits: No permits are required. Parking and access are free.

Maps: A free map is available at the New Melones Visitors Center or by download at www.usbr.gov. For a topographic map, ask the USGS for Sonora.

Directions: From Highway 49 in Sonora, drive south for three miles to Jamestown, then turn right (north) on Rawhide Road. Drive two miles and turn left on Shell Road;

follow Shell Road 1.8 miles (take the left fork) to the pavement's end at a yellow gate across the road. The trail begins to the right of the gate. (You can choose to continue driving past the yellow gate for another mile on a dirt road, but a high-clearance vehicle may be necessary. This will shorten your hike considerably.)

Contact: New Melones Reservoir Visitors Center, 6850 Studhorse Flat Road, Sonora, CA 95370, 209/536-9543 or 209/536-9094, www.usbr.gov.

3 RED HILLS
5 mi / 2.5 hr   🚶2 ⛰7

near Chinese Camp and La Grange

Map 9.1, page 479

Flower aficionados, check your calendar. Is it late March to early May? Then head for the Red Hills Area of Critical Environmental Concern, the very long name for 11 square miles of gray-pine-studded Bureau of Land Management (BLM) land in the Sierra foothills. This is not a place you would ever want to visit in the heat of summer, but in early spring, the rocky landscape comes alive with color from coreopsis, five-spots, bird's-eye gilia, fiddlenecks, goldfields, poppies, and other native wildflowers. The serpentine soil here supports a wide variety of plants, including seven that are rare and/or endangered. Keep an eye out for California verbena, which grows here and nowhere else in the world. It can be found near the stream that parallels Red Hills Road. Numerous loop hikes are possible in the preserve; a good starter hike is to set off on Soaproot Ridge Trail, then bear left and walk Overlook Loop to Verbena Loop. From there you can walk back to your car on Red Hills Road, or cross the road and walk back most of the way on Red Hills Trail, which parallels the road. As you hike, keep scanning the sky for bald eagles, which are fond of this area because of its proximity to huge Don Pedro Reservoir.

User Groups: Hikers, dogs, horses, and mountain bikes. No wheelchair facilities.

Permits: No permits are required. Parking and access are free.

Maps: Free trail maps are available at the trailhead. For a topographic map, ask the USGS for Chinese Camp.

Directions: From Sonora, take Highway 49 south for 15 miles to Chinese Camp. Turn right (south) on Red Hills Road and drive one mile to the trailhead parking on the left.

Or, from Oakdale, drive east on Highway 108/120 for about 20 miles. Turn right on La Grange Road. Drive 1.5 miles and turn left on Red Hills Road. Drive 0.75 mile to the trailhead parking lot on the right side of the road.

Contact: Bureau of Land Management Folsom Resource Area, 63 Natoma Street, Folsom, CA 95630, 916/985-4474, www.blm.gov/ca.

4 RAINBOW POOL AND TUOLUMNE RIVER FALLS
2.5 mi / 1.5 hr   🚶2 ⛰8

in Stanislaus National Forest near Groveland

Map 9.1, page 479

While everybody else is hanging out at Rainbow Pool, a popular swimming hole and waterfall right off Highway 120, you can leave the thronging crowds behind by taking this short but steep hike to the confluence of the South Fork and Middle Fork of the Tuolumne River. Rainbow Pool is located on the south side of Highway 120, but you'll park your car and start hiking on the north side, heading steeply downhill on an old dirt road that parallels the cascading South Fork as it tumbles down a dramatic, rocky gorge. In the springtime, when the powerful Tuolumne is frothing with excess snowmelt, this canyon can really roar with noise. The watery extravaganza reaches a deafening crescendo at the canyon bottom, where the two forks of the river merge. This was once the site of the South Fork Tunnel Camp, one of the major construction sites for the Hetch Hetchy Reservoir system. The old road you are walking on was used to haul men and building materials back and forth to the camp. Where the road ends at a particularly scenic point in the narrow gorge, just retrace your steps back uphill. After a hot, sweaty ascent back to your car, you might just want to walk (or drive) over to Rainbow Pool and take a dip in its ever-popular, refreshing waters.

User Groups: Hikers, dogs, horses, and mountain bikes. No wheelchair facilities.

Permits: No permits are required. Parking and access are free.

Maps: A Stanislaus National Forest map is available from the U.S. Forest Service. For a topographic map, ask the USGS for Jawbone Ridge.

Directions: From Groveland, drive east on Highway 120 for 14 miles to the left turnoff for Cherry Lake Road. Turn left and then left again immediately. Drive about 100 yards and park in the dirt pullout just before the gate across the road. Walk past the gate and then turn right and follow the unsigned dirt road heading downhill.

Contact: Groveland Ranger District, Stanislaus National Forest, 24545 Highway 120, Groveland, CA 95321, 209/962-7825, www.fs.fed.us/r5/stanislaus.

⑤ DIANA FALLS
1.5 mi / 0.5 hr 🥾1 ⛰8

in Stanislaus National Forest near Greeley Hill

Map 9.1, page 479

You could think of it as a neighborhood backyard swimming hole, except there's no neighborhood anywhere nearby. Diana Falls is located not far from the towns of Groveland and Coulterville and within an hour's drive of Yosemite National Park. But it's not on the road to any of those places, so you won't come across it by accident. It's an out-of-the-way waterfall on Bean Creek, near its confluence with the North Fork Merced River. From the trailhead, hike along the west side of the river,

following an old dirt road for 0.5 mile. Here the Merced River is a small, tame stream, with bunches of Indian rhubarb growing along its banks. The dirt road gets narrower as you walk. At a fork in the trail, bear right. You'll leave the river and hike along the Bean Creek canyon. In just a few minutes, or about 250 yards, you'll reach the brink of 20-foot-tall Diana Falls. Several spurs descend the slope to its base. There may be no better place to spend a hot summer afternoon.

User Groups: Hikers, dogs, horses, and mountain bikes. No wheelchair facilities.

Permits: No permits are required. Parking and access are free.

Maps: A Stanislaus National Forest map is available from the U.S. Forest Service. For a topographic map, ask the USGS for Groveland.

Directions: From Groveland, drive east on Highway 120 for seven miles to the right turnoff for Smith Station Road (also signed as County Road J132 to Coulterville). Turn right and drive 5.7 miles, then turn sharply left on Greeley Hill Road. Drive 4.2 miles to the trailhead, just before a one-lane bridge. The trail begins on the right at the gated dirt road signed as "Road Closed."

Contact: Groveland Ranger District, Stanislaus National Forest, 24545 Highway 120, Groveland, CA 95321, 209/962-7825, www.fs.fed.us/r5/stanislaus.

⑥ CHESTER, SOUSA, AND WINTON MARSH TRAILS
4.0 mi / 2.0 hr 🥾1 ⛰8

in the San Luis National Wildlife Refuge north of Los Banos

Map 9.1, page 479   **BEST ☾**

The San Luis National Wildlife Refuge offers two main driving tours: the Tule Elk Auto Tour Loop and the Waterfowl Auto Tour Loop, and both are great opportunities for visitors to see wildlife. But if you want to get out of your car and on to your feet for a while, check out the three short hiking trails located off the 9.7-mile Waterfowl Auto Tour Loop. Walk all three, and you can easily chalk up about four miles of exercise. The trails lead to three different marsh areas, each with its own character.

As you drive the auto route, the first trailhead you reach is for the Chester Marsh Trail. It's open for hiking only from February to September; from October to January, it is part of the refuge's hunting area. It's a one-mile loop, and you can pick up an interpretive brochure at the trailhead. After your walk, get back in your car and continue driving along the Waterfowl Auto Tour Route until you reach the trailhead for the Sousa Marsh. This area consists of an inner and outer loop trail through a canopy of riparian trees. The longest trail (1.2 miles) goes to the Sousa observation platform, with its telescope and benches. The 0.7-mile Winton Marsh Trail, located just beyond the Sousa Marsh parking lot, also leads to an observation platform and several benches situated slightly above the marsh, so you can pull out your binoculars and peer at the feathered fowl below. What will you see? The usual cabal: ducks, geese, moorhens, coots, pheasants, snipe, hawks, owls, egrets, herons, and even some rare types, like the endangered tricolored blackbird. In case you haven't gotten the idea yet, this place is crawling with wildlife. Even while just driving around, we saw a coyote and about a zillion bunnies, in addition to numerous Swainson's hawks.

User Groups: Hikers and dogs. No horses or mountain bikes. No wheelchair facilities.

Permits: No permits are required. Parking and access are free.

Maps: A free map is available by contacting the refuge headquarters. For a topographic map, ask the USGS for Los Banos.

Directions: From Los Banos on Highway 152/33, drive north on Highway 165 (Mercey Springs Road) for 6.4 miles to Wolfsen Road. Bear right and follow Wolfsen Road for 2.5 miles into the National Wildlife Refuge. Follow the signs for the Waterfowl Auto Tour Loop.

Contact: San Luis National Wildlife Refuge, P.O. Box 2176, Los Banos, CA 93635, 209/826-3508, http://sanluis.fws.gov.

7 MEADOWLARK TRAIL
0.25 mi / 0.25 hr 🥾1 ⛰8

in the Merced National Wildlife Refuge southwest of Merced

Map 9.1, page 479

It doesn't seem like a 0.25-mile loop trail could offer much in the way of a pay off, but you may be surprised by the rewards on the diminutive Meadowlark Trail. First off, it's one of only two places in the Merced National Wildlife Refuge where you're allowed to get out of your car and walk. Walking is prohibited in most of the preserve in order to reduce the disturbance to the thousands of geese and cranes that winter here. Driving your car along the Auto Tour Route is okay, though; it turns out that birds aren't bothered much by cars. The Meadowlark Trail gives you a chance to stretch your legs within the wildlife refuge, which serves as a precious island of wildlife habitat in the midst of Merced's vast agricultural fields. A thicket of tules, cattails, and willows in the refuge provides heavy cover for birds—particularly raptors, wintering shorebirds, and waterfowl. Because morning fog is common here in the winter months, bird-watching is often better at midday, when you may see concentrations of snow geese and Ross' geese. Magnificent sandhill cranes also make an appearance in winter. The rest of the year, you're more likely to see a variety of raptors. Barn owls are particularly common—one visitor saw 14 of them while walking this short loop. Great horned owls and a variety of hawks are also frequently sighted.

User Groups: Hikers and dogs. No horses or mountain bikes. No wheelchair facilities.

Permits: No permits are required. Parking and access are free.

Maps: A free map is available by contacting the refuge headquarters. For a topographic map, ask the USGS for Los Banos.

Directions: From Merced, take Highway 59 south for eight miles. Turn west on Sandy Mush Road and drive eight miles to the refuge entrance.

Contact: San Luis National Wildlife Refuge, P.O. Box 2176, Los Banos, CA 93635, 209/826-3508, http://sanluis.fws.gov.

8 PATH OF THE PADRES
5.0 mi / 8.0 hr
🏃2 ⛰️8

on Los Banos Creek, in San Luis Reservoir State Recreation Area

Map 9.2, page 480   BEST ☾

You have to plan way in advance to take this unusual hike at Los Banos Creek Reservoir. That's because the only way to go is in the company of a guide and via boat to the trailhead, and guided trips are offered only on weekends in March and April. The trip has become so popular that it usually sells out as soon as reservations are available, which is February 1 each year. Don't procrastinate on making your call for reservations. Although the hike itself is only five miles, the trip is an all-day affair, so don't forget to bring plenty of water, snacks, and lunch. It begins at 8 A.M. with a boat ride down the long and narrow reservoir, which is set in a steep-walled canyon and is popular for fishing. At the reservoir's far end, everyone gets off the boat and hikes 2.5 miles up the narrow canyon of Los Banos Creek, where old-growth sycamore groves and a cornucopia of spring wildflowers may be seen. Sturdy shoes are a must as the trail is rocky in places. As you walk, your guide will teach you about how the native Yokut Indians used the plants in this area, and you'll see bedrock mortars that they used for pounding acorns and natural medicines. Bird-watchers may thrill to see a peregrine falcon or other cliff-dwelling species. If the conditions are right, the hike may include an optional climb to the top of a knoll that offers panoramic views of the surrounding valleys and the Coast Range. So why is this trail called the Path of the Padres? Because the fathers at Mission San Juan Bautista traveled along the creek in the early 19th century to evangelize the Yokut Indians of the Central Valley. Along the way, they often bathed in the creek, which is why the nearby town is named "Los Banos."

User Groups: Hikers only. No dogs, horses, or mountain bikes. No wheelchair facilities.

Permits: Reservations are required; call to reserve a space starting February 1. A $12 fee is charged for the reservation and guided tour (children must be at least 6 years old). An additional $8 day-use fee is charged per vehicle.

Maps: For a topographic map, ask the USGS for Los Banos Valley.

Directions: From I-5 at the junction with Highway 152 (south of Santa Nella), turn east on Highway 152 and drive 2.5 miles. Turn right (south) on Volta Road and drive one mile. Turn left (east) on Pioneer Road and drive 0.8 mile, then turn right on Canyon Road. Drive south on Canyon Road for five miles to Los Banos Creek Reservoir. (You will cross back to the west side of I-5.) Park near the boat ramp.

Contact: San Luis Reservoir State Recreation Area, Four Rivers Sector, 31426 Gonzaga Road, Gustine, CA 95322, 209/826-1197, www.parks.ca.gov.

9 COALINGA MINERAL SPRINGS NATIONAL RECREATION TRAIL
4.8 mi / 2.5 hr
🏃2 ⛰️8

northwest of Coalinga

Map 9.2, page 480

Most people don't realize that there's a National Recreation Trail out here near Coalinga, the town that was made famous by an earthquake, but it's true. In winter and spring, this is a first-class hike to the summit of Kreyenhagen Peak (elevation 3,558 feet), climbing through chaparral-covered hillsides. The trail begins at the far end of the picnic area and crosses a dry streambed, then begins to ascend.

It's well graded all the way, with the second mile slightly steeper than the first. Plenty of switchbacks ease you through it. Views are good all the way up this 2.4-mile trail, but the impressive vista from the summit ridge includes the Diablo Range, the San Joaquin Valley, and miles of surrounding Bureau of Land Management (BLM) land. That's a pretty wide scope, considering how little effort is required to get here. Have a seat on one of the rock outcrops, pull out your picnic lunch, and enjoy the show.

User Groups: Hikers, dogs, horses, and mountain bikes. No wheelchair facilities.

Permits: No permits are required. A $3 day-use fee is charged per vehicle.

Maps: Free trail maps are available at the trailhead. For a topographic map, ask the USGS for Curry Mountain.

Directions: From Coalinga, drive 20 miles west on Highway 198 to the Coalinga Mineral Springs County Park exit. Turn right (north) and drive four miles to Coalinga Mineral Springs County Park. Park in the main lot and walk to the far end of the park. The trail begins across the creek bed.

Contact: Bureau of Land Management, Hollister Field Office, 20 Hamilton Court, Hollister, CA 95023, 831/630-5000, www.ca.blm.gov/hollister.

10 LEWIS S. EATON TRAIL
1.0-12.0 mi / 0.5-5.5 hr

on the San Joaquin River near Fresno

Map 9.3, page 481

Woodward Park is the kind of city park that has a par course, children's playgrounds, and barbecue areas. But it's also a convenient access point for the San Joaquin River Parkway, also called the Lewis S. Eaton Trail. When completed, the multiuse parkway will cover a 22-mile distance between Highway 99 and Friant Dam in Millerton Lake State Park. Currently six miles are finished, which means you can walk, jog, rollerblade, bike, or cruise

in a wheelchair up to 12 miles round-trip on a paved trail that parallels the river and Friant Road for its entire distance. The good folks at the San Joaquin River Parkway and Conservation Trust are working hard to add to the current trail system; various loops and extensions from the paved trail are in the works. If you want to explore some of them, start with the River Access Trail, which branches off the Lewis S. Eaton Trail on the north side of Woodward Park. The trail meanders down to the riverbanks at the Jensen River Ranch, a small park that is under restoration by the conservancy.

User Groups: Hikers, dogs, horses, mountain bikes, and wheelchairs.

Permits: No permits are required. A $5 fee is charged per vehicle.

Maps: A park map is available at the entrance kiosk. For a topographic map, ask the USGS for Fresno North.

Directions: From Highway 41 heading north in Fresno, take the Friant Road exit. Turn left on Audubon Avenue and then turn right into Woodward Park.

Contact: Woodward Regional Park, 7775 Friant Road, Fresno, CA 93710, 559/621-2900; San Joaquin River Parkway and Conservation Trust, 1550 East Shaw Avenue, Suite 114, Fresno, CA 93710, 559/248-8480, www.riverparkway.org.

11 KAWEAH OAKS PRESERVE
2.0 mi / 1.0 hr

east of Visalia

Map 9.3, page 481

The Kaweah Oaks Preserve is Tulare County's premier private nature preserve, a small remnant of what was once a vast valley oak forest. Groves of majestic oaks still stand, as well as wild grapevines growing as high as 30 feet. Four easy hiking trails take you through a vast alkali meadow, valley oak riparian forests, sycamore woodlands, wild roses, valley elderberries, and swamp habitat. From the parking area, enter through the obvious gateway, which features maps and interpretive signage, and pick up a trail guide. Head west down the old ranch road to the picnic area on the left (less than a quarter mile). Follow the ranch road west or north to hike the self-guided interpretive trails. Because this is a grazing area, leave all cattle gates the way you found them, whether open or closed. As you stroll, listen for sounds of birdlife, and watch for herons, hawks, and owls, as well as the preserve's five species of woodpeckers. In addition to the diverse birdlife, you'll enjoy abundant native flora, including valley oak, California sycamores, cottonwoods, and willows growing near the streams. This is a good walk for late winter, spring, or fall. In the heat of summer, confine your visits to the early morning, when the valley is at its coolest. The preserve closes at dusk, so evening walks are not an option.

User Groups: Hikers only. No dogs, horses, or mountain bikes. No wheelchair facilities.

Permits: No permits are required. Parking and access are free.

Maps: For a topographic map, ask the USGS for Visalia. Trail guides are available at the trailhead for a $3 donation.

Directions: From Tulare on Highway 99, drive north for 10 miles and turn east on Highway 198. Drive 13 miles on Highway 198, passing through Visalia, and take the left turnoff for Road 182. Drive 0.5 mile north on Road 182 to the trailhead parking area on the left.

Contact: Sequoia Riverlands Trust, 427 S. Garden Street, Visalia, CA 93277, 559/738-0211, www.sequoiariverlands.org.

⓬ CARRIZO PLAIN AND PAINTED ROCK
1.5 mi / 1.0 hr   🏃1 ⛰9

in Carrizo Plains National Monument, eastern San Luis Obispo County

Map 9.4, page 482   **BEST (**

Carrizo Plain is one of California's newest national monuments (as of 2001) and is also considered to be one of California's largest grassland ecosystems. It's best known for its abundant wildlife, spring wildflowers, and peace and quiet. Located at the north end of the monument is Soda Lake, a 3,000-acre expanse that comprises one of the largest remaining alkaline wetlands left in California. It is dry for most of the year, but during the wet season, it attracts thousands of migrating birds. In addition to all the birds, tule elk, pronghorn, and coyotes are also found here. In early spring, wildflowers fill the valley and cover the mountains, attracting photographers and visitors from all over the country.

Soda Lake and the surrounding grasslands are spectacular enough, especially when the spring wildflower bloom is on, but if you've driven all the way out here you don't want to miss a visit to Painted Rock. However, you can't just show up and expect to go on your own. You need to obtain a permit in advance or be part of a docent-led tour to hike the easy Painted Rock Interpretive Trail, which leads to the 55-foot-high formation. The interior of this rounded sandstone amphitheater has some of the most significant Native American pictographs in the country. Although many have been vandalized, Painted Rock is still considered a very sacred place by Native Americans. While visiting, please respect the site by not touching the paintings or climbing on the Rock.

User Groups: Hikers only. No dogs, horses, or mountain bikes. No wheelchair facilities.

Permits: While the monument is open year-round, Painted Rock is closed March 1–July 15 to protect nesting birds. You can still sign up for a guided hike to Painted Rock on Saturdays in March, April, and May. The rest of the year, you can visit Painted Rock on your own, but you must obtain a "self-guided tour" permit in advance. Permits and tour reservations can be obtained at www.recreation.gov or by phoning 877/444-6777 ($1.50 fee). Parking and access are free.

Maps: A brochure on Carrizo Plain National Monument is available from the Bureau of Land Management (BLM). For a topographic map, ask the USGS for Painted Rock.

Directions: From San Luis Obispo on US 101, drive north for 10 miles and take the Santa Margarita/Highway 58 exit. Drive east on Highway 58 for 50 miles to the Soda Lake Road turnoff. Turn right (south) and drive 13.5 miles to the Painted Rock Trail and Goodwin Education Center turnoff. Turn right and drive to the visitors center, then turn left and drive two miles to the Painted Rock trailhead.

Contact: Bureau of Land Management, Bakersfield Field Office, 3801 Pegasus Drive, Bakersfield, CA 93308, 661/391-6000; Goodwin Education Center at Carrizo Plain (open Thurs.–Sun. Dec.–May), 805/475-2131, www.blm.gov/ca/st/en/fo/bakersfield.html.

13 TULE ELK STATE RESERVE

0.25 mi / 0.25 hr 🚶1 ⛺8

off I-5 west of Bakersfield

Map 9.4, page 482   **BEST (**

Most people just don't know that there's a herd of magnificent tule elk wandering around a few miles from I-5. If you didn't know, better pull off the highway and get yourself to the Tule Elk State Reserve near Tupman. There aren't a lot of trails to choose from, and you won't do much that resembles true hiking here, but if you've been driving on I-5 long enough, just getting out of the car and stretching your legs is a big deal. The animals are most active in the late summer, when their rutting season begins. Bring binoculars for your best chance at a good view, or take a stroll to the walk-up platform, where you can look through a spotting scope at the elk. Make sure you stop in at the visitors center and check out the interesting displays on the elk and the history of the Central Valley.

User Groups: Hikers and dogs. No horses or mountain bikes. Some facilities are wheelchair accessible.

Permits: No permits are required. An $8 day-use fee is charged per vehicle.

Maps: For a topographic map, ask the USGS for Tupman.

Directions: From the junction of I-5 and Highway 99 north of the Grapevine, drive north on I-5 for 33 miles to the Stockdale Highway exit. Drive west for 1.2 miles and turn left (south) on Morris Road. Drive 1.6 miles on Morris Road and turn left into the Tule Elk State Reserve. The route is well signed.

Contact: Tule Elk State Reserve, 8653 Station Road, Buttonwillow, CA 93206, 661/764-6881, www.parks.ca.gov.

YOSEMITE AND MAMMOTH LAKES

© ANN MARIE BROW

BEST HIKES

Plunging waterfalls, stark granite, alpine lakes,

pristine meadows, giant sequoias, and raging rivers – you'll find them all in the Yosemite and Mammoth Lakes region, which encompasses not only world-famous Yosemite National Park but also the popular recreation areas of Mammoth Lakes and the Eastern Sierra.

The centerpiece of this region, of course, is Yosemite National Park, a must-see on every hiker's itinerary. From Yosemite Valley's famous waterfalls – three of which are among the tallest in the world – to the towering granite domes and glistening meadows of Tioga Pass, Yosemite is a place that can only be described in superlatives. Hikers can choose from short-and-easy jaunts to world-class destinations such as Vernal Fall and Sentinel Dome, or exhaustive treks to the summits of Half Dome or Clouds Rest – but there's also a wealth of moderate trails in between the two extremes. One thing is certain: Every trail in Yosemite leads to a destination that is completely worth the effort to reach it.

As scenic as the national park itself are the resort areas just to the east, particularly Mammoth Lakes and June Lake on the U.S. 395 corridor, as well as the surrounding wilderness areas – Hoover, Ansel Adams, and John Muir. Best known for skiing and snowboarding in winter, the resort towns of the Eastern Sierra are ideal base camps for hiking trips in the warmer seasons.

The alpine lakes of this region are a major draw for day hikers and backpackers alike, but equally as compelling are the Eastern Sierra's alpine meadows, fir and pine forests, and sagebrush-covered plains. This is a region known for its unusual diversity – including volcanic craters, hot springs, lava flows, and the strange beauty of Mono Lake, an ancient and majestic body of water covering 60 square miles. An easy, popular hiking trail provides access to its lakeshore.

More uncommon geologic features are found nearby at Devils Postpile National Monument. This 800-acre national park preserves the Devils Postpile – a "pile" of 60-foot-high basalt columns that are remnants of an ancient lava flow – plus breathtaking 101-foot Rainbow Falls. Hikers can spend a day walking to these and other destinations within the monument, or they can hike beyond park borders into the glacially carved backcountry of the Ansel Adams Wilderness.

Key to enjoying your experience in the Yosemite and Mammoth Lakes region is planning your visit for the least crowded months of the year. Summer weekends are the busiest time and are best avoided, especially in the national park. After school starts in September, the crowds lessen substantially. Autumn is a fine time for hiking in and around Yosemite, even though most of the Valley's famous waterfalls (except for dependable Bridalveil) have run dry by midsummer. This lack of falling water is more than made up for by the show of fall colors on the Valley floor and the chance for solitude in this too-well-loved park. Another option, especially for waterfall aficionados, is to show up before school lets out in June. Although the high country is snowed in and inaccessible at this time, Yosemite Valley is in its full watery splendor in April and May.

Likewise, if there is a perfect time to visit the Eastern Sierra, it's in the transition between summer and winter. Autumn transforms the scenic canyons and pristine lakeshores into a wave of blazing color. Aspens, willows, and cottonwoods turn showy hues of orange, yellow, and red. The trees generally begin their color change early in September; peak viewing time is usually late September and early October.

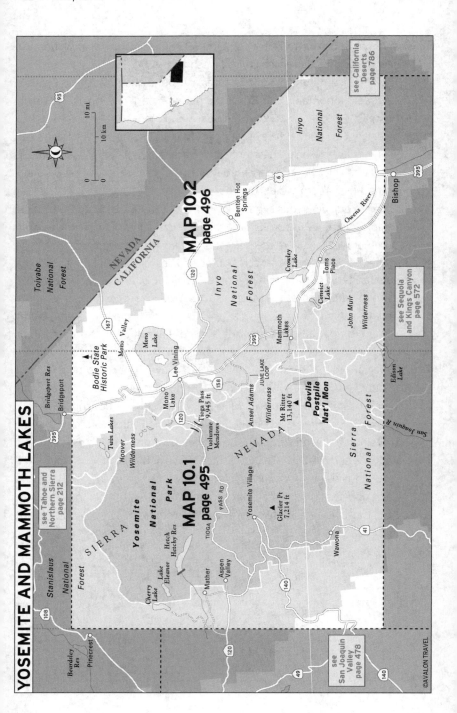

YOSEMITE AND MAMMOTH LAKES

MAP 10.2
page 496

MAP 10.1
page 495

see Tahoe and
Northern Sierra
page 212

see California
Deserts
page 786

see Sequoia
and Kings Canyon
page 572

see
San Joaquin Valley
page 478

©AVALON TRAVEL

Map 10.1

Hikes 1-94
Pages 497-561

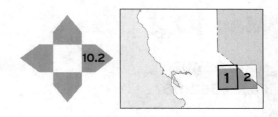

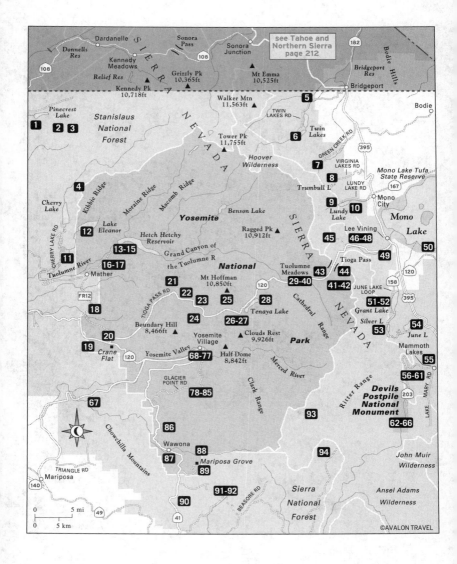

©AVALON TRAVEL

Map 10.2

Hikes 95-102
Pages 562-567

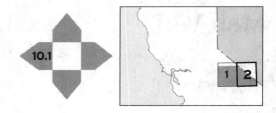

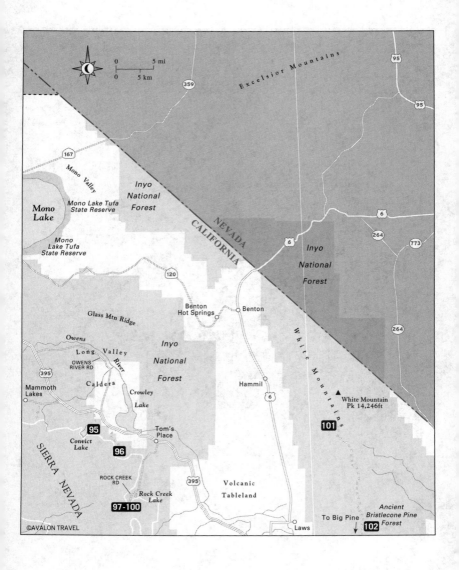

■ PINECREST LAKE NATIONAL RECREATION TRAIL

4.0 mi / 2.0 hr

on Pinecrest Lake near Strawberry in Stanislaus National Forest

Map 10.1, page 495   BEST ◖

Pinecrest Lake is a tremendously popular family vacation resort just off Highway 108, the kind of place that people go year after year for a week of boating, camping, and fishing. The trail that circles its shoreline is a lot like the lake itself—it's pretty, it's popular, and it's no place to go if you like solitude. However, the four-mile loop makes a pleasant early morning walk or run if you're up and at it before the crowds get out of bed. In the afternoons, you can hike to the east side of the lake and follow a spur trail along the South Fork Stanislaus River to some excellent swimming holes, called Cleo's Bath. Keep in mind that this trail is by no means a wilderness experience. The south side of the loop is littered with vacation homes, and pay telephones are located at a few points alongside the trail.

User Groups: Hikers and dogs. No horses or mountain bikes. No wheelchair facilities except at the fishing ramp and day-use area.

Permits: No permits are required. Parking and access are free.

Maps: An Emigrant Wilderness map is available from Tom Harrison Maps or Stanislaus National Forest. For a topographic map, ask the USGS for Pinecrest.

Directions: From Sonora, drive east on Highway 108 for 31 miles to the Pinecrest turnoff. Turn right on Pinecrest Lake Road and continue for another mile to the day-use parking area, on the south side of the lake. Park as close to the end of the road as possible.

Contact: Stanislaus National Forest, Summit Ranger District, 1 Pinecrest Lake Road, Pinecrest, CA 95364, 209/965-3434, www.fs.fed.us/r5/stanislaus.

■ CAMP AND BEAR LAKES

8.0 mi / 4.0 hr

in the Emigrant Wilderness near Pinecrest Lake

Map 10.1, page 495

The Crabtree trailhead, at elevation 7,180 feet, is the trailhead of choice for most casual hikers and backpackers entering the Emigrant Wilderness. It's easy to reach and allows access to many excellent destinations with a relatively short walk. From Crabtree, it's a moderate 2.5-mile hike to Camp Lake, which is just inside the Emigrant Wilderness boundary. Despite its name, camping is not allowed at Camp Lake, so while day users may choose to linger along its shores, backpackers must continue another 1.5 miles to Bear Lake, accessible via a one-mile left spur trail. Both lakes offer stellar granite-country scenery, good (but icy) swimming, decent rainbow trout fishing, and the chance of seeing plenty of wildflowers along the route in summer. You, too, can be wowed by the wandering daisies and blue lupine. You'll face only one sustained hill climb along the route; most of the trail gently undulates. Watch for beaver evidence at Bear Lake.

User Groups: Hikers, dogs, and horses. No mountain bikes. No wheelchair facilities.

Permits: A free wilderness permit is required for overnight stays and is available from the Summit Ranger Station. Parking and access are free.

Maps: An Emigrant Wilderness map is available from Tom Harrison Maps or Stanislaus National Forest. For a topographic map, ask the USGS for Pinecrest.

Directions: From Sonora, drive east on Highway 108 for 31 miles to the Pinecrest turnoff. Turn right on Pinecrest Lake Road and continue 0.5 mile to the right fork for Dodge Ridge Ski Area. Bear right and drive 2.9 miles, then turn right at the sign for Aspen Meadow and Gianelli trailhead. Drive 0.5 mile, turn left, and drive four miles to the turnoff for the Crabtree trailhead (follow the signs). Turn right and drive 0.25 mile.

Contact: Stanislaus National Forest, Summit Ranger District, 1 Pinecrest Lake Road, Pinecrest, CA 95364, 209/965-3434, www.fs.fed.us/r5/stanislaus.

❸ BURST ROCK/POWELL LAKE

4.0 mi / 2.5 hr

in the Emigrant Wilderness near Pinecrest Lake

Map 10.1, page 495

Both Burst Rock and Powell Lake are supreme day-hike destinations, but they present a problem for first-time visitors: Neither one is located right along the trail and neither one is signed. This results in a lot of people wandering around asking, "So which rock is Burst Rock?"

The short answer is, it doesn't matter all that much. After hiking gently but steadily uphill for one mile, you'll reach an interpretive sign that details the difficulties of pioneers who tried to use this route, called the West Walker–Sonora Emigrant Trail, to cross the Sierra in the 1850s. From the wilderness boundary sign, cut off to your left for about 50 yards, and you'll witness an incredible vista and dropoff to the valley below—and who knows, you might even be standing on Burst Rock. After feeling suitably humbled, retrace your steps and continue another mile until you reach an unsigned fork. Go left for less than 0.25 mile to Powell Lake, a favorite spot of young anglers. If you miss the fork, shortly you'll catch sight of the lake, off to your left, and you'll know to go back and find it. The peninsula of rocks that juts out into the water is the perfect place to launch into a swan dive.

User Groups: Hikers, dogs, and horses. No mountain bikes. No wheelchair facilities.

Permits: A free wilderness permit is required for overnight stays and is available from the Summit Ranger Station. Parking and access are free.

Maps: An Emigrant Wilderness map is available from Tom Harrison Maps or Stanislaus National Forest. For a topographic map, ask the USGS for Pinecrest.

Directions: From Sonora, drive east on Highway 108 for 31 miles to the Pinecrest turnoff. Turn right on Pinecrest Lake Road and continue for 0.5 mile to the right fork for Dodge Ridge Ski Area. Bear right, drive 2.9 miles, and turn right at the sign for Aspen Meadow and Gianelli trailhead. Drive 0.5 mile, turn left, and drive 8.3 miles to the trailhead parking area. The route is well signed.

Contact: Stanislaus National Forest, Summit Ranger District, 1 Pinecrest Lake Road, Pinecrest, CA 95364, 209/965-3434, www.fs.fed.us/r5/stanislaus.

❹ KIBBIE LAKE

8.4 mi / 1-2 days

in northwest Yosemite National Park

Map 10.1, page 495

This day hike or easy backpacking trip starts near Cherry Lake in Stanislaus National Forest and heads into the Hetch Hetchy region of Yosemite. The hike is easy enough that it makes a rewarding weekend trip for beginning backpackers, who can easily carry a pack over the 4.2-mile distance. From the trailhead, you hike the Kibbie Ridge Trail 1.2 miles to the Kibbie Lake Trail, then go right and head for the lake in another 3.0 miles. Near this main junction you leave Stanislaus National Forest and enter Yosemite National Park, so dogs are not allowed past this point. Much of the route travels through a fire-scarred lodgepole pine forest that is rapidly regenerating. Once you near the lake, the burned areas are left behind and the forest is pristine. The trail deposits you at the southern tip of the granite-bound lake, elevation 6,513 feet. Although quite large (more than 100 surface acres), Kibbie Lake is fairly shallow and supports a good population of rainbow trout. The long and narrow body of water has high rocky cliffs on some of its shoreline, so not all of it is easily accessible. On summer weekends, the lake gets visited fairly heavily, but on weekdays, you are likely to be the only soul around.

Special Note: Check your calendar before you go. The gate at Cherry Lake is closed every year one week before deer season, which is usually sometime in September, and doesn't reopen until spring. Most years, the road is open from May 1 to September 15.

User Groups: Hikers and horses. No dogs or mountain bikes. No wheelchair facilities.

Permits: There is a $20 entrance fee per vehicle at Yosemite National Park, good for seven days. Free wilderness permits are required for overnight stays. They are available on a first-come, first-served basis up to one day in advance at the Yosemite Wilderness kiosk near your chosen trailhead, or further in advance by mail, phone, or online for a $5 reservation fee per person.

Maps: A Hetch Hetchy map is available from Tom Harrison Maps. For topographic maps, ask the USGS for Kibbie Lake and Hetch Hetchy Reservoir.

Directions: From Groveland, drive east on Highway 120 for 14 miles toward Yosemite National Park. Turn left on Cherry Lake Road and drive 24 miles to Cherry Lake's dam, then cross it. On the far side of the dam, bear right and drive 0.4 mile, then turn left on Road 1N45Y and follow it for 4.5 miles to its end at the Kibbie Ridge trailhead.

Contact: Yosemite National Park, P.O. Box 577, Yosemite, CA 95389, 209/372-0200 or 209/372-0740 (permit reservations), www.nps.gov/yose or www.nps.gov/yose/wilderness (permit reservations).

most hikers do less than that; they just take off from Buckeye Campground (7,000 feet), maybe pack along their fishing rods, and walk a couple of miles each way up and down the stream. Brook trout are planted close to the campground all summer. It's rare to hike far in the Eastern Sierra without having to climb, but that's what you get here at the base of Buckeye Canyon. If you don't like to fish, there's plenty of other stuff to do, like admire the wildflowers in the meadows or gape at the impressive walls of glacial summits and ridges that surround you. A popular hot spring is found in Buckeye Creek less than a mile from the campground, but be forewarned: You might get an anatomy lesson there. Occasional Buckeye Creek bathers have been spotted wearing only birthday suits.

User Groups: Hikers, dogs, and horses. No mountain bikes. No wheelchair facilities.

Permits: No day-hiking permits are required. Parking and access are free.

Maps: A Hoover Wilderness map is available from Tom Harrison Maps or the U.S. Forest Service. For a topographic map, ask the USGS for Twin Lakes.

Directions: From Bridgeport on U.S. 395, drive west on Twin Lakes Road for seven miles to the Buckeye Road turnoff. Turn right on Buckeye Road and drive 3.5 miles to the Buckeye Campground and trailhead. (Buckeye Road turns to dirt at Doc and Al's Resort.)

Contact: Humboldt-Toiyabe National Forest, Bridgeport Ranger District, HCR1 Box 1000, Bridgeport, CA 93517, 760/932-7070, www.fs.fed.us/r4/htnf.

5 BUCKEYE CREEK TRAIL
5.0 mi / 2.5 hr   🥾1 ⛰️8

in Humboldt-Toiyabe National Forest west of Bridgeport and Highway 395

Map 10.1, page 495

You can hike up to eight miles one-way along Buckeye Creek to the Hoover Wilderness boundary at the Buckeye Roughs. But

6 BARNEY LAKE TRAIL
7.8 mi / 5.0 hr   🥾2 ⛰️8

in the Hoover Wilderness west of Bridgeport

Map 10.1, page 495

Some call it Barney Lake Trail and others call it Robinson Creek Trail. Whatever you call it, you should know that this is the busiest trail into the Hoover Wilderness. Why?

It's downright easy, gaining only 1,000 feet along its four-mile length. The remedy for the crowds? Start hiking very early in the day, before the hundreds of campers in the Twin Lakes area have risen from their sleeping bags. You must park outside Mono Village Campground and then walk due east through it to reach the trailhead, which is signed for Barney Lake. (The attendant in the camp entrance kiosk can point you to the trailhead.) The trail roughly parallels Robinson Creek, first in a pine forest and then skirting big meadows highlighted by vast stands of aspen trees. While in the wide open meadows, you are rewarded with impressive views of the jagged Sawtooth Range. The path passes a Hoover Wilderness sign at 2.6 miles, then climbs a bit more steeply and reaches the lake at 3.9 miles. If you get there before everyone else, you are one lucky hiker. Ambitious day hikers and backpackers can continue another 3.5 miles to larger Peeler Lake. Because of the amount of aspens seen along this trail, it's a real treat to hike here from late September to mid-October when the color show happens.

User Groups: Hikers, dogs, and horses. No mountain bikes. No wheelchair facilities.

Permits: A free wilderness permit is required for overnight stays and is available from the Bridgeport Ranger Station. Quotas are in effect from the end of June to mid-September; permits are available in advance by mail for this period for a $3 fee per person.

Maps: A Hoover Wilderness map is available from Tom Harrison Maps or the U.S. Forest Service. For a topographic map, ask the USGS for Twin Lakes.

Directions: From Bridgeport on U.S. 395, drive west on Twin Lakes Road for 13.2 miles to the signed parking area, on the west end of the lakes, near Mono Village Campground.

Contact: Humboldt-Toiyabe National Forest, Bridgeport Ranger District, HCR1 Box 1000, Bridgeport, CA 93517, 760/932-7070, www.fs.fed.us/r4/htnf.

7 GREEN, EAST, AND WEST LAKES
8.6-11.6 mi / 5.0 hr   🥾3 ⛰9

in the Hoover Wilderness west of Bridgeport

Map 10.1, page 495

Three beautiful lakes—Green, East, and West—are situated right around 9,000 feet in elevation in the spectacular Hoover Wilderness. They offer fair trout fishing and are accessible via Green Creek Trail (sometimes called Green Lake Trail). It's only 4.6 miles round-trip to Green Lake, but you can go two miles farther for an 8.6-mile round-trip that includes East Lake as well. Or, you can take a 1.5-mile spur off the main trail for a much steeper (but well worth it) jaunt to stark, rockbound West Lake. Some people make a short backpacking trip out of it and see all three lakes. If you do, note that Green Lake is the only one of the three that is just below 9,000 feet in elevation, which means it is the only one where campfires are permitted. (You must use the established campfire rings.) At the other, higher lakes, only backpacking stoves are allowed. The fishing is generally better at East and West Lakes than at Green Lake, although it's nothing to write home about. The high mountain scenery, on the other hand, will knock your socks off.

The Green Creek Trail climbs, of course—but not so much that you'll be worn out when you reach Green Lake; just enough to provide you with expansive valley views most of the way. The path closely parallels the tumbling cascades of the west fork of Green Creek, and the July wildflower show is outstanding here. (The autumn aspen show is also noteworthy.) The turnoff for West Lake is on the right at 2.2 miles. This trail makes a memorably steep 1,000-foot ascent over 1.5 miles, climbing high above Green Lake. After the easy grade of the first two miles of trail, this last stretch can really take you by surprise. For solitude lovers, West Lake is your best bet. The main trail reaches the shore of Green Lake 200 yards past the West Lake turnoff. East Lake can be reached by heading left off the main trail and gaining another 500 feet in elevation over two miles. All three lakes are sparkling, rock-bound gems, so you can't go wrong here no matter which one you choose to visit.

User Groups: Hikers, dogs, and horses. No mountain bikes. No wheelchair facilities.

Permits: A free wilderness permit is required for overnight stays and is available from the Bridgeport Ranger Station. Quotas are in effect from the end of June to mid-September; permits are available in advance by mail for this period for a $3 fee per person.

Maps: A Hoover Wilderness map is available from Tom Harrison Maps or the U.S. Forest Service. For a topographic map, ask the USGS for Twin Lakes.

Directions: From Bridgeport, drive south on U.S. 395 for 4.5 miles to Green Creek Road (dirt). Turn west and drive 8.2 miles to the signed trailhead parking area, shortly before Green Creek Campground.

Contact: Humboldt-Toiyabe National Forest, Bridgeport Ranger District, HCR1 Box 1000, Bridgeport, CA 93517, 760/932-7070, www.fs.fed.us/r4/htnf.

8 VIRGINIA LAKES TRAIL
6.2-10.2 mi / 3.0 hr-2 days

🥾3 ⛰9

in the Hoover Wilderness south of Bridgeport

Map 10.1, page 495

Virginia Lakes form the gateway to a beautiful high-mountain basin that contains eight small alpine lakes within a two-mile radius. The trailhead is at the Big Virginia Lake day-use area, set at 9,500 feet between mountain peaks that jut 12,000 feet into the sky. From here, you hike west past Blue Lake to Cooney Lake and on to Frog Lakes (a very easy 1.4 miles), then start climbing seriously, continuing 1.8 more miles to 11,100-foot Summit Pass (sometimes called Burro Pass). The landscape here is windswept, barren, and beautiful—a mix of rock, occasional whitebark pines, and

high alpine wildflowers. Many hikers take a look at the scene from the pass, then retreat to one of the aforementioned lakes to spend the afternoon, making a 6.2-mile day. If you continue beyond the pass, you curve downhill through dozens of switchbacks for 1.4 miles, then climb gently 0.5 mile west to Summit Lake (at 10,203 feet), on the northeast boundary of Yosemite National Park. Summit Lake is set between Camiaca Peak (11,739 feet) to the north and Excelsior Mountain (12,446 feet) to the south. This is the logical place for backpackers to make camp, and for day-trippers to turn around for a 10.2-mile day. If you want to take a longer trip into even wilder country, you can do so from this point. The trail skirts Summit Lake's north side, then enters Yosemite National Park in Virginia Canyon, one of the least-visited areas of the park. Another option is to take the fork right before Summit Lake that leads east (right) to the double Hoover Lakes, connecting with the Green Creek Trail. Some backpackers and day hikers make a one-way hike of about 11 miles out of this trip by arranging to have a shuttle car waiting for them at the Green Creek trailhead (see listing in this chapter).

User Groups: Hikers, dogs, and horses. No dogs on trail in the Yosemite National Park portion. No mountain bikes. No wheelchair facilities.

Permits: A free wilderness permit is required for overnight stays and is available from the Bridgeport Ranger Station. Quotas are in effect from the end of June to mid-September; permits are available in advance by mail for this period for a $3 fee per person.

Maps: A Hoover Wilderness map is available from Tom Harrison Maps or the U.S. Forest Service. For a topographic map, ask the USGS for Dunderberg Peak.

Directions: From Bridgeport, drive 13.5 miles south on U.S. 395 (or from Lee Vining, drive 12 miles north on U.S. 395) to Conway Summit. Turn west on Virginia Lakes Road and drive 6.5 miles to the trailhead, at the Big Virginia Lake day-use area.

Contact: Humboldt-Toiyabe National Forest, Bridgeport Ranger District, HCR 1, Box 1000, Bridgeport, CA 93517, 760/932-7070, www.fs.fed.us/r4/htnf.

9 LUNDY CANYON TRAIL
4.4-10.0 mi / 2.0 hr-2 days

🏃3 ⛰️9

north of Lee Vining in the Hoover Wilderness

Map 10.1, page 495	BEST (

The Lundy Canyon Trail is the back door into the 20 Lakes Basin, a well-traveled area of the Hoover Wilderness that is most commonly accessed from Saddlebag Lake off Highway 120. The trailhead lies about two miles past Lundy Lake, a long, narrow pool set at 7,800 feet. From here, the trail rises along Mill Creek, passing several beaver ponds, a dilapidated trapper's cabin, and two small but boisterous waterfalls (Lower and Upper Lundy Falls, also called Mill Creek Falls) as it heads into the Hoover Wilderness. Most visitors hike to the first or second falls, enjoying the gorgeous Eastern Sierra scenery with a relatively mellow walk, then hike back out. Those who continue find that the trail, which climbed gently but steadily for the first 2.2 miles, suddenly reaches what appears to be the back of the canyon. But look straight up the canyon wall to your left—that's where the path continues, although it isn't much of a path. An unmaintained, marginally switchbacked route leads 0.8 mile upward through a frighteningly steep wall of shale, and the difficulty rating for this trail changes abruptly from a 3 to a 4 (and maybe a 5 on the way back downhill). Use great caution here; one slip and you could take a nasty fall. You don't want to be carrying a pack that is too heavy or unbalanced on this stretch.

When you finally make it to the top of the canyon wall, you come out to a beautiful high mountain meadow and a junction near the austere shores of Lake Helen, elevation 10,100 feet (3.3 miles from your start). By going right, you can follow the trail to Shamrock and Steelhead Lakes. Shamrock is 0.3 mile farther and dotted with many islands; Steelhead is another 0.5 mile beyond and is framed by 12,242-foot North Peak, towering above. The opposite trail goes left to Odell Lake (3.6 miles from your start). From Odell Lake, you could continue on to Hummingbird Lake, then to the north shore of Saddlebag Lake. If you can arrange a car shuttle at Saddlebag Lake, you can extend your trip into a one-way hike of seven miles, and that would save you the harrowing trip back down that shale-covered slope.

Note that one of the best times to visit here is in October, when Lundy Canyon's stands of quaking aspen turn bright gold and seem to dance in the breeze. This is one of the best places to admire fall colors in the Eastern Sierra. July is another first-rate time to visit; the canyon's wildflower displays are remarkable.

User Groups: Hikers, horses, and dogs. No mountain bikes. No wheelchair facilities.

Permits: A free wilderness permit is required for overnight stays and is available from the Mono Basin Scenic Area Visitors Center. There are no quotas on this trail, so advance reservations are not required.

Maps: A Hoover Wilderness map is available from Tom Harrison Maps or the U.S. Forest Service. For topographic maps, ask the USGS for Lundy and Dunderberg Peak.

Directions: From Lee Vining, drive north on U.S. 395 for seven miles to Lundy Lake Road. Turn west on Lundy Lake Road and drive five miles to Lundy Lake. Continue beyond the lake and Lundy Lake Resort, driving two miles farther on a dirt road that ends at the trailhead.

Contact: Inyo National Forest, Mono Basin Scenic Area Visitors Center, P.O. Box 429, Lee Vining, CA 93541, 760/647-3044, www.fs.usda.gov/inyo.

🔟 LAKE CANYON AND MAY LUNDY MINE

7.0 mi / 3.5 hr or 2 days 🥾3 ⛰9

north of Lee Vining in the Hoover Wilderness

Map 10.1, page 495

The Lundy Lake area is blessed with two first-rate day-hiking trails that lead into two separate and distinct canyons: Lundy Canyon (see listing in this chapter) and Lake Canyon. Both paths offer so many rewards that when you drive up to Lundy Lake, it's hard to decide which one to take. History buffs and fishing-minded hikers would do well to take this trip from Lundy's dam into Lake Canyon, where they can see the remains of the May Lundy Mine. The mine was worked continuously for two decades starting in 1878, producing a total of about $2 million in gold. As a result, the surrounding community of Lundy grew to support 500 people, despite severe winters and deadly avalanches. Besides mining, a primary activity here was the operation of three sawmills along Lundy Creek, used to supply timber to the nearby bustling gold rush town of Bodie.

The hike to the May Lundy Mine is a fairly steep 3.5 miles one-way, climbing above Lundy Lake on the old mine road that was built in 1881. You can see the trail plain as day from the trailhead on the east side of Lundy Lake. The road/trail passes Blue Lake and Crystal Lake, where mining relics can be found. (Crystal Lake is 0.3 mile off the trail via a left fork.) Continue on the main trail, and you'll see the mine remains—old railcar tracks, tailings, and a closed-off mine shaft. Just beyond is Oneida Lake, whose waters were used to run the stamp mill for the mine. Even without the fascinating traces of history, this is an extraordinarily beautiful place. You'll want to linger awhile at sparkling Oneida Lake. Both the scenery and the fishing are quite rewarding.

User Groups: Hikers, horses, and dogs. No mountain bikes. No wheelchair facilities.

Permits: A free wilderness permit is required for overnight stays and is available from the Mono Basin Scenic Area Visitors Center.

There are no quotas on this trail, so advance reservations are not required.

Maps: A Mono Lake map is available from Tom Harrison Maps. An Inyo National Forest map is available from the U.S. Forest Service. For a topographic map, ask the USGS for Lundy.

Directions: From Lee Vining, drive north on U.S. 395 for seven miles to Lundy Lake Road. Turn west on Lundy Lake Road and drive five miles to Lundy Lake's dam, on the east side of the lake. Turn left and drive 0.25 mile to a locked gate and trailhead.

Contact: Inyo National Forest, Mono Basin Scenic Area Visitors Center, P.O. Box 429, Lee Vining, CA 93541, 760/647-3044, www.fs.usda.gov/inyo.

11 PRESTON FLAT TRAIL

8.8 mi / 4.0 hr or 2 days 🥾2 ⛰8

in Stanislaus National Forest

Map 10.1, page 495

Although some day hikers choose to suffer through the nearly intolerable grade of the Poopenaut Valley Trail to reach the swimming holes and fishing spots on the Tuolumne River's free-flowing stretch west of Hetch Hetchy Dam, a much more pleasant approach is on the Preston Flat Trail. The trailhead is off Cherry Lake Road in Stanislaus National Forest, outside Yosemite's border. The path travels 4.4 miles up the north side of the Tuolumne River Canyon on a gently undulating grade. Shortly before the trail's end is a rock chimney and a few other remains of an old cabin that was built here by a homesteader named Preston. A few hundred yards farther is a photogenic vista of Preston Falls, a cascade formed where the Tuolumne River drops 15 feet over a granite ledge into a wide, clear pool. The cataract is just a half-mile downstream of Yosemite's boundary line. If you want to stay overnight, you can. Several good campsites are found along the trail, which sticks closely to the river for most of its length.

Compared to the Poopenaut Valley Trail, the Preston Flat Trail is by far the better choice for hikers who wish to reach the river. Hike it in early spring, when the raging Tuolumne River provides the most exciting viewing. Those who wish to fish or swim should wait to visit until late spring or early summer, when the river quiets down. Wintertime is another nice time to visit here; the elevation is low enough that the trail is always snow-free.

User Groups: Hikers, horses, dogs, and mountain bikes. No wheelchair facilities.

Permits: A free campfire permit is required for overnight stays and is available from the Groveland Ranger Station. Parking and access are free.

Maps: A Stanislaus National Forest map is available from the U.S. Forest Service. For a topographic map, ask the USGS for Cherry Lake South.

Directions: From Groveland drive east on Highway 120 for 14 miles toward Yosemite. Turn left on Cherry Lake Road and drive 8.5 miles to Early Intake, where you cross a bridge over the Tuolumne River. Turn right on the far side of the bridge and drive 0.8 mile to the trailhead parking area at the end of the road, just beyond Kirkwood Powerhouse.

Contact: Stanislaus National Forest, Groveland Ranger District, 24545 Highway 120, Groveland, CA 95321, 209/962-7825, www.fs.fed.us/r5/stanislaus.

12 LAKE ELEANOR
3.0 mi / 1.5 hr

in northwest Yosemite National Park

Map 10.1, page 495

Lake Eleanor is a second, less famous reservoir in the Hetch Hetchy region of Yosemite. Originally a naturally shallow glacial lake, Lake Eleanor was "improved" by the city of San Francisco by damming Eleanor Creek in 1928, five years before O'Shaughnessy Dam at Hetch Hetchy was completed. The dam raised the lake's water level 40 feet. Today it is the second largest lake in Yosemite after Hetch Hetchy. Its waters are not used by San Francisco as a drinking supply but rather to generate power. Set at an elevation of 4,657 feet, Lake Eleanor is popular with hikers who tote along a fishing rod while traversing the trail around the three-mile-long lake's edge. The access road to Lake Eleanor ends at a gate 0.25 mile before the lake, so start your hike there, then take a mellow walk along the lake's south and west shores. Much of Lake Eleanor's western side is dotted with picturesque islands. A backcountry ranger station is located near the lake's dam and is usually staffed in the summer months.

It takes more than an hour's drive from Highway 120 to access Lake Eleanor, so people who come here to hike or fish often plan on spending the night. A first-come, first-served campground is located at nearby Cherry Lake, and several backpacking campsites are located on the northwest edge of Lake Eleanor (a wilderness permit is required). Note that the road to Lake Eleanor is open only May 1 to September 15 each year (the road is usually closed beyond Cherry Lake's dam).

User Groups: Hikers and horses. No dogs or mountain bikes. No wheelchair facilities.

Permits: No permits are required for day hiking. Parking and access are free (the trailhead is outside Yosemite National Park).

Maps: A Hetch Hetchy map is available from Tom Harrison Maps. For a topographic map, ask the USGS for Lake Eleanor.

Directions: From Groveland, drive east on Highway 120 for 14 miles toward Yosemite National Park. Turn left on Cherry Lake Road and drive 24 miles to Cherry Lake's dam, then across it. On the far side of the dam, bear right and drive 0.4 mile, then turn right on the dirt road that is signed for Lake Eleanor. Follow this road four miles to its end, at the gated Yosemite National Park boundary, 0.25 mile south of the lake.

Contact: Yosemite National Park, P.O. Box 577, Yosemite, CA 95389, 209/372-0200, www.nps.gov/yose.

13 WAPAMA FALL
4.8 mi / 2.5 hr

in northwest Yosemite National Park

Map 10.1, page 495

The trail to this spectacular early-season waterfall starts by crossing the giant O'Shaughnessy Dam, where you may pause to curse (or admire, depending on your sensibilities) the San Francisco politicians who in 1908 believed that flooding Hetch Hetchy Valley was a good idea. In terms of geology and natural features, Hetch Hetchy is a near twin to Yosemite Valley, although somewhat smaller in scale. The valley today is filled by an immense, 400-foot-deep reservoir that supplies water and power to the city of San Francisco and environs. After walking across its impressive dam and passing through a dimly lit, 500-foot-long tunnel, the trail opens out to a mixed forest along the edge of the deep blue lake. Wildflower displays are often excellent in late spring. In 1.5 miles you reach Tueeulala Fall, a delicate wisp of a freefall that only runs during peak snowmelt, and is often dry by late May. Less than a mile farther you reach powerful Wapama Fall on Falls Creek, a Bridalveil-like plume of whitewater that makes a dramatic plunge into the reservoir. Depending on how early in the year you visit, you may get soaking wet standing on the sturdy steel bridges that cross over Wapama Fall's coursing flow. In early spring, Wapama Falls sometimes flows so furiously that the park rangers have to close this trail. In late spring and early summer, the temperature can get hot out at Hetch Hetchy, so this spray of water can be very refreshing. If this is your first trip to this part of Yosemite, be sure to stop and read the interpretive plaques at the dam that explain about the building of Hetch Hetchy Reservoir and its service to the city of San Francisco. Whatever else you may think about it, it's a fascinating story.

User Groups: Hikers only. No dogs, horses, or mountain bikes. No wheelchair facilities.

Permits: No permits are required. There is a $20 entrance fee per vehicle at Yosemite National Park, good for seven days.

Maps: A Hetch Hetchy map is available from Tom Harrison Maps. For topographic maps, ask the USGS for Lake Eleanor and Hetch Hetchy Reservoir.

Directions: From Groveland, drive east on Highway 120 for 22.5 miles to the Evergreen Road turnoff signed for Hetch Hetchy Reservoir on the left, a mile west of the Big Oak Flat entrance to Yosemite. Drive north on Evergreen Road for 7.4 miles and turn right on Hetch Hetchy Road. Drive 9.0 miles to the dam and trailhead.

Contact: Yosemite National Park, P.O. Box 577, Yosemite, CA 95389, 209/372-0200 or 209/372-0740 (permit reservations), www.nps.gov/yose or www.nps.gov/yose/wilderness (permit reservations).

14 RANCHERIA FALLS
13.0 mi / 1 or 2 days

in northwest Yosemite National Park

Map 10.1, page 495

It's spring and you are hungering for a Yosemite backpacking trip, but Tuolumne Meadows is knee-deep in melting snow. This is a good time to hike the northern edge of Hetch Hetchy Reservoir (elevation 3,796 feet), admiring three stunning waterfalls along the way: Tueeulala, Wapama, and Rancheria. This easy backpacking trip (or long day hike, if you prefer) travels along the length of the reservoir to its far eastern edge, where the bears are some of the boldest in all of Yosemite. (Bear canisters are required for backpackers.) Whereas Tueeulala and Wapama Falls are both freefalling cataracts, Rancheria Falls is a series of rolling cascades pouring over polished granite.

To make the trip, follow the trail notes for Wapama Falls (see listing in this chapter), then continue onward, following the trail as it contours along the reservoir's edge. Much of the time you are high above the water, which allows fine views of Kolana Rock and its neighboring granite formations across the reservoir. The trail follows a gentle grade with many small ups and downs, gaining only 1,300 feet along its entire length. This trip is manageable even for beginning backpackers. Shoreline trout fishing in the reservoir can be good in spring and fall. And remember: Swimming in Hetch Hetchy is not allowed.

User Groups: Hikers and horses. No dogs or mountain bikes. No wheelchair facilities.

Permits: There is a $20 entrance fee per vehicle at Yosemite National Park, good for seven days. Free wilderness permits are required for overnight stays. They are available on a first-come, first-served basis up to one day in advance at the Yosemite Wilderness kiosk near your chosen trailhead, or farther in advance by mail, phone, or online for a $5 reservation fee per person.

Maps: A Hetch Hetchy map is available from Tom Harrison Maps. For topographic maps, ask the USGS for Lake Eleanor and Hetch Hetchy Reservoir.

Directions: From Groveland, drive east on Highway 120 for 22.5 miles to the Evergreen Road turnoff signed for Hetch Hetchy Reservoir on the left, a mile west of the Big Oak Flat entrance to Yosemite. Drive north on Evergreen Road for 7.4 miles and turn right on Hetch Hetchy Road. Drive 9.0 miles to the dam and trailhead.

Contact: Yosemite National Park, P.O. Box 577, Yosemite, CA 95389, 209/372-0200 or 209/372-0740 (permit reservations), www.nps.gov/yose or www.nps.gov/yose/wilderness (permit reservations).

15 LAUREL LAKE
14.6 mi / 1 or 2 days

in northwest Yosemite National Park

Map 10.1, page 495

The Hetch Hetchy region of Yosemite is ideal for late-spring backpacking trips, with far fewer crowds than Yosemite Valley and far less snow than Tuolumne Meadows. And Laurel Lake is an ideal weekend destination in the region—just far enough to make you feel like you've gotten away, but close enough for a two-day trip (or even a one-day trip, if you're an ambitious day hiker). The trip begins at Hetch Hetchy Reservoir, and after an initial one-mile stretch along the lakeshore, you turn left and head up, up, and up on the Beehive Trail. The trail follows an old roadbed through a series of switchbacks, climbing 1,200 feet over 1.8 miles to the canyon rim and a junction with the Miguel Meadow Trail. Turn right and your trail meanders on a much easier grade through pine and incense-cedar forest. In another 2.4 miles, turn right and stroll for a mile to perennially soggy Beehive Meadow (water is found at a spring here, and a few campsites are available). From Beehive, take either of two trails to the lake (most people opt for the shorter trail on the left; both are signed). Beautiful Laurel Lake is surrounded by aspen groves, firs, and lodgepole pines, and its waters are a fair bet for rainbow trout fishing.

Those who want to add on another night or two to this trip can set out for even more scenic Lake Vernon the next day (4.5 miles distant). Whereas Laurel Lake is forested, Lake Vernon is surrounded by rock. From Lake Vernon, you can make a long loop back via Tiltill Valley, or if you are short on time, retrace your steps.

User Groups: Hikers and horses. No dogs or mountain bikes. No wheelchair facilities.

Permits: There is a $20 entrance fee per vehicle at Yosemite National Park, good for seven days. Free wilderness permits are required for overnight stays. They are available on a first-come, first-served basis up to one day in advance at the Yosemite Wilderness kiosk near your chosen trailhead, or farther in advance by mail, phone, or online for a $5 reservation fee per person.

Maps: A Hetch Hetchy map is available from Tom Harrison Maps. For topographic maps, ask the USGS for Lake Eleanor and Hetch Hetchy Reservoir.

Directions: From Groveland, drive east on Highway 120 for 22.5 miles to the Evergreen Road turnoff signed for Hetch Hetchy

Reservoir (on the left), a mile west of the Big Oak Flat entrance to Yosemite. Drive north on Evergreen Road for 7.4 miles and turn right on Hetch Hetchy Road. Drive 16 miles to the dam and trailhead.

Contact: Yosemite National Park, P.O. Box 577, Yosemite, CA 95389, 209/372-0200 or 209/372-0740 (permit reservations), www.nps.gov/yose or www.nps.gov/yose/wilderness (permit reservations).

16 LOOKOUT POINT
2.6 mi / 1.2 hr

in northwest Yosemite National Park

Map 10.1, page 495

Check your calendar. Is it springtime? Are most of the high-country trails in Yosemite National Park still snowed in? Then it's time to take the easy jaunt to Lookout Point, where you can admire Hetch Hetchy Reservoir and its waterfalls from an unusual perspective, and count the plentiful wildflowers along the trail as you walk. The Lookout Point Trail begins by the Mather Ranger Station, on Hetch Hetchy Road. Begin hiking at the trail sign for Cottonwood and Smith Meadows and Hetch Hetchy (it's not signed for Lookout Point). Turn left at the first junction, then follow the trail as it roughly parallels Hetch Hetchy Road for 0.5 mile. You turn away from the road with a brief uphill stretch, then you enter a level, forested area that was severely burned in the wildfires of 1996. This is where the flowers bloom profusely in springtime. Look for a trail junction at one mile out, and bear left for Lookout Point, 0.3 mile away. The path gets rather faint in places, but rock cairns mark the way. Just head for the highest point you see atop a granite knob dotted with a few pines. You'll know you're at Lookout Point when you can see the west end of Hetch Hetchy Reservoir (including its immense dam) and two of Hetch Hetchy's beautiful waterfalls: Wapama and Tueeulala. If you visit much later than May or June, you may see only Wapama,

the most robust of Hetch Hetchy's waterfalls. Tueeulala dries up early in the year. Although the vista is not perfect from Lookout Point—it would be better if it were 500 feet higher or if there weren't so many trees—this is still a fine spot to spread out a picnic. You probably won't have any company, either.

User Groups: Hikers and horses. No dogs or mountain bikes. No wheelchair facilities.

Permits: No permits are required. There is a $20 entrance fee per vehicle at Yosemite National Park, good for seven days.

Maps: A Hetch Hetchy map is available from Tom Harrison Maps. For a topographic map, ask the USGS for Lake Eleanor.

Directions: From Groveland, drive east on Highway 120 for 22.5 miles to the Evergreen Road turnoff (on the left), signed for Hetch Hetchy Reservoir (it's a mile west of the Big Oak Flat entrance to Yosemite). Drive north on Evergreen Road for 7.4 miles, then turn right on Hetch Hetchy Road. Drive 1.6 miles to the entrance kiosk by the Mather Ranger Station; the trail begins 100 yards past the entrance kiosk, just beyond the ranger station, on the right.

Contact: Yosemite National Park, P.O. Box 577, Yosemite, CA 95389, 209/372-0200, www.nps.gov/yose.

17 SMITH PEAK
15.0 mi / 1 or 2 days

in northwest Yosemite National Park

Map 10.1, page 495

If summit vistas strike your fancy, and it's too early in the summer for bagging some of Yosemite's highest peaks, head for the top of Smith Peak, elevation 7,751 feet. The route begins by the Mather Ranger Station. Follow the Lookout Point Trail for 1.2 miles, then turn right on the trail signed for Smith Meadow. You'll travel through a fire-scarred forest, then climb up a ridge to meet up with Cottonwood Creek at Lower Cottonwood Meadow, shortly followed by Upper Cottonwood Meadow.

Smith Meadow lies another two miles farther, and just beyond it you'll find a junction of trails. The path on the right is another popular route to Smith Peak leading from White Wolf Campground off Tioga Road. Campsites are found a short distance to the west at this junction. Get a good night's rest before bagging Smith Peak the next morning. (You've hiked six miles thus far; it's only 1.5 more to the summit.) The peak, like the nearby meadows, was named after a 1920s sheep rancher. It is covered with pockmarked granite boulders and offers a panoramic view of the Hetch Hetchy Reservoir and the Grand Canyon of the Tuolumne River, situated 4,000 dramatic feet below you. To the east, Yosemite's high country peaks are prominent, among them distinctive Mount Conness, Matterhorn Peak, and Mount Hoffman. Total elevation gain on this trip is 2,900 feet.

User Groups: Hikers only. No dogs, horses, or mountain bikes. No wheelchair facilities.

Permits: There is a $20 entrance fee per vehicle at Yosemite National Park, good for seven days. Free wilderness permits are required for overnight stays. They are available on a first-come, first-served basis up to one day in advance at the Yosemite Wilderness kiosk near your chosen trailhead, or farther in advance by mail, phone, or online for a $5 reservation fee per person.

Maps: A Hetch Hetchy map is available from Tom Harrison Maps. For topographic maps, ask the USGS for Hetch Hetchy Reservoir.

Directions: From Groveland, drive east on Highway 120 for 22.5 miles to the Evergreen Road turnoff (on the left), signed for Hetch Hetchy Reservoir (it's a mile west of the Big Oak Flat entrance to Yosemite). Drive north on Evergreen Road for 7.4 miles, then turn right on Hetch Hetchy Road. Drive 1.6 miles to the entrance kiosk by the Mather Ranger Station; the trail begins 100 yards past the entrance kiosk, just beyond the ranger station, on the right.

Contact: Yosemite National Park, P.O. Box 577, Yosemite, CA 95389, 209/372-0200

or 209/372-0740 (permit reservations), www.nps.gov/yose or www.nps.gov/yose/wilderness (permit reservations).

18 CARLON FALLS
3.8 mi / 2.5 hr

on the border of Stanislaus National Forest and northwest Yosemite National Park

Map 10.1, page 495

Carlon Falls is a pretty cascade on the South Fork Tuolumne River in the far western region of Yosemite. It is so far west that the trailhead is actually in Stanislaus National Forest, outside the park border. You hike about 100 feet and then you enter Yosemite National Park. This means there is no park entrance fee, no waiting in line at the entrance kiosk, and no crowds. The trailhead is across the river from Carlon Day-Use Area, a popular picnicking and fishing spot on the Tuolumne River. Follow the trail along the river's northern bank to reach the falls in just under two miles. The path is completely shaded, mostly level (except for one brief steep climb that skirts a landslide area), and fairly easy to follow, although it does require clambering over a few fallen trees. The waterfall drops in two tiers over wide granite ledges, and the riverbanks surrounding it are covered with big conifers and dense foliage. A bonus is that unlike most Yosemite waterfalls, Carlon Falls runs year-round. The waterfall's namesakes are Dan and Donna Carlon, who operated the popular Carl Inn from 1916 to 1930 near what is now the Carlon Day-Use Area. This trail is popular with swimmers and anglers in summer, but mostly deserted the rest of the year.

User Groups: Hikers only. No dogs, horses, or mountain bikes. No wheelchair facilities.

Permits: No permits are required. Parking and access are free.

Maps: For a topographic map, ask the USGS for Ackerson Mountain.

Directions: From Groveland, drive east on Highway 120 for 22.5 miles to the Evergreen

Road turnoff, signed for Hetch Hetchy Reservoir, one mile west of the Big Oak Flat entrance to Yosemite. Follow Evergreen Road north for one mile to the far side of the bridge just past Carlon Day-Use Area. Park on the right at the closed-off dirt road on the north side of the bridge, signed only as No Camping. There is room for about five cars. Begin hiking on the closed road, heading upstream. The road narrows to single track after about 100 yards.

Contact: Yosemite National Park, P.O. Box 577, Yosemite, CA 95389, 209/372-0200, www.nps.gov/yose.

19 MERCED GROVE
3.0 mi / 1.5 hr

in western Yosemite National Park

Map 10.1, page 495

There are three giant sequoia groves in Yosemite National Park—Merced, Tuolumne, and Mariposa. Because the Merced Grove is the smallest of the three groves and requires the longest walk to reach it, it is the least visited. Generally it only gets traffic from people who enter Yosemite at the Big Oak Flat entrance and drive by it on their way to Yosemite Valley. The hiking is on a closed-off dirt road that is ideal for snowshoeing in winter. The trail cuts a level course through a mixed conifer forest for the first 0.5 mile. Bear left at the only junction and head downhill through a canopy of white firs, incense cedars, ponderosa pines, and sugar pines. You reach the small sequoia grove at 1.5 miles; the first group of six trees will take your breath away. Continue another 100 yards past these beauties; the two largest sequoias of the Merced Grove are directly across from a handsome old log cabin. It was originally built as a retreat for the park superintendent but is no longer used. Retrace your steps from the cabin, hiking uphill for your return.

User Groups: Hikers only. No dogs, horses, or mountain bikes. No wheelchair facilities.

Permits: No permits are required. There is a $20 entrance fee per vehicle at Yosemite National Park, good for seven days.

Maps: A Yosemite National Park map is available from Tom Harrison Maps. For a topographic map, ask the USGS for Ackerson Mountain.

Directions: From Merced, drive 70 miles northeast on Highway 140 to Yosemite National Park. Follow the signs toward Yosemite Valley, entering through the Arch Rock entrance station. Continue 4.5 miles to the left turnoff for Highway 120, looping back out of the valley on Big Oak Flat Road. Continue straight on Big Oak Flat Road for 13.5 miles (past the Tioga Pass Road turnoff) to the Merced Grove parking area, on the left. If you enter Yosemite at the Big Oak Flat entrance station on Highway 120, drive 4.3 miles southeast to reach the trailhead, on your right.

Contact: Yosemite National Park, P.O. Box 577, Yosemite, CA 95389, 209/372-0200, www.nps.gov/yose.

20 TUOLUMNE GROVE
2.5 mi / 1.5 hr

in western Yosemite National Park

Map 10.1, page 495

Up until 1993 you could drive right in to the Tuolumne Grove of Giant Sequoias, but now the road is closed off and visitors have to hike in. The grove is found on the old Big Oak Flat Road, a paved, six-mile historic road/trail that is open to bikes and hikers (although bikes are a rarity here). This is a popular destination, so arrive early in the morning to have the best chance at solitude. Leave your car at the parking lot near Crane Flat and hike downhill into the big trees. It's one mile to the first sequoias. The Tuolumne Grove's claim to fame is that it has one of the two remaining walk-through trees in Yosemite; this one is called the Dead Giant. It's a tall stump that was tunneled in 1878. Go ahead, walk through it—everybody does. At a small picnic area, a half-mile trail loops around the forest. Make sure you save some energy for the trip back uphill to the parking lot; the moderate grade ascends 550 feet. The old paved road continues downhill beyond the grove all the way to Hodgdon Meadow Campground. Some people hike the entire six-mile distance, then have someone pick them up at Hodgdon Meadow.

User Groups: Hikers and mountain bikes. No dogs or horses. No wheelchair facilities.

Permits: No permits are required. There is a $20 entrance fee per vehicle at Yosemite National Park, good for seven days.

Maps: A Yosemite National Park map is available from Tom Harrison Maps. For a topographic map, ask the USGS for Ackerson Mountain.

Directions: From Merced, drive 70 miles northeast on Highway 140 to Yosemite National Park. Follow the signs toward Yosemite Valley, entering through the Arch Rock entrance station. Continue 4.5 miles to the left turnoff for Highway 120, looping back out of the valley on Big Oak Flat Road. In 9.3 miles at Crane Flat, turn right on Tioga Pass Road, then drive 0.5 mile to the Tuolumne Grove parking lot, on the left, near Crane Flat. If you enter Yosemite at the Big Oak Flat entrance station on Highway 120, drive 7.7 miles southeast to the Crane Flat/Highway 120 East turnoff. Turn left and drive 0.5 mile to the Tuolumne Grove trailhead.

Contact: Yosemite National Park, P.O. Box 577, Yosemite, CA 95389, 209/372-0200, www.nps.gov/yose.

21 HARDEN LAKE
5.6 mi / 3.0 hr

off Tioga Pass Road in Yosemite National Park

Map 10.1, page 495

Harden Lake itself isn't a scene stealer—by late summer, it's not much more than a large pond, framed by a few stands of aspen trees on its northeast shore. But many people come here for another reason, and that's to see the wildflowers that bloom in a region known informally as Harden's Gardens, about a quarter-mile beyond the lake. July is the most dependable month for the wildflower bloom. Plus there are other rewards, including fine views of the Grand Canyon of the Tuolumne River just a half-mile north of the lake. Also, because of the small size of Harden Lake, it is dependably warm for swimming by mid-summer. The hike is simple enough. The trail follows White Wolf's gravel service road (a stretch of the original Tioga Road) past the campground entrance and across the Tuolumne River. Follow the obvious signs that point you through a few junctions to a blossom-filled marshy area. A few more steps and you're at the lake. If you haven't yet gotten your fill of the flower show, proceed a short distance farther and feast your eyes on Harden's Gardens.

User Groups: Hikers only. No dogs, horses, or mountain bikes. No wheelchair facilities.

Permits: No permits are required. There is a $20 entrance fee per vehicle at Yosemite National Park, good for seven days.

Maps: A Yosemite National Park map is available from Tom Harrison Maps. For a topographic map, ask the USGS for Tamarack Flat.

Directions: From Merced, drive 70 miles northeast on Highway 140 to Yosemite National Park. Follow the signs to Yosemite Valley, entering through the Arch Rock entrance station. Continue 4.5 miles to the left turnoff for Highway 120, looping back out of the valley on Big Oak Flat Road. In 9.3 miles at Crane Flat, turn right on Tioga Pass Road and drive 14 miles to the left turnoff for White Wolf. Turn left and drive one mile to the lodge and trailhead.

Contact: Yosemite National Park, P.O. Box 577, Yosemite, CA 95389, 209/372-0200, www.nps.gov/yose.

22 LUKENS LAKE

1.5-4.6 mi / 1.0-2.0 hr   🏃1 ⛰️8

off Tioga Pass Road in Yosemite National Park

Map 10.1, page 495

The Lukens Lake Trail is the perfect introductory lake hike for families in Yosemite National Park. A six-year-old could make the trip easily. A bonus is that the trailhead is on the western end of Tioga Road, so it's quickly reached from points in Yosemite Valley. The trail is 0.75 mile long and leads from Tioga Road up to a saddle, then drops down to a meadow on the lake's eastern edge. The path winds through a dense red fir forest, filled with mammoth trees, then skirts alongside a corn lily–filled meadow to the southern edge of the shallow, spring-fed lake (the trail used to travel on the lake's north side, but it was rerouted in 2009). If you time it right—usually late July—you may see a spectacular wildflower show featuring thousands of pink shooting stars. Swimming in Lukens Lake is highly recommended; by midsummer, this is one of the warmest lakes in the park. If you want to take a longer trail to Lukens Lake, you can start from the trailhead at White Wolf Lodge and make a 4.6-mile round-trip.

User Groups: Hikers only. No dogs, horses, or mountain bikes. No wheelchair facilities.

Permits: No permits are required. There is a $20 entrance fee per vehicle at Yosemite National Park, good for seven days.

Maps: A Yosemite National Park map is available from Tom Harrison Maps. For a topographic map, ask the USGS for Tamarack Flat.

Directions: From Merced, drive 70 miles northeast on Highway 140 to Yosemite National Park. Follow the signs to Yosemite Valley, entering through the Arch Rock entrance station. Continue 4.5 miles to the left turn-off for Highway 120, looping back out of the valley on Big Oak Flat Road. In 9.3 miles at Crane Flat, turn right on Tioga Pass Road and drive 16.2 miles to the Lukens Lake trailhead parking area, on the south side of the road. The trail begins across the road.

Contact: Yosemite National Park, P.O. Box 577, Yosemite, CA 95389, 209/372-0200, www.nps.gov/yose.

23 TEN LAKES / GRANT LAKES

12.8 mi / 1 or 2 days   🏃3 ⛰️10

off Tioga Pass Road in Yosemite National Park

Map 10.1, page 495

The Ten Lakes area is incredibly popular with backpackers, so get your wilderness permit early. Or get an early-morning start and make this trip as a day hike; just be prepared for some serious climbing and long miles. From the Ten Lakes trailhead at Tioga Pass Road (elevation 7,500 feet), the path climbs steadily for the first four miles. There's only one brutally steep stretch, which comes between miles four and five, after a pretty stroll around Half Moon Meadow. A series of tight switchbacks pulls you through a nasty 800-foot elevation gain to the top of a ridge and the Ten Lakes/Grant Lakes junction. From there, you make a choice. Turn right to reach Grant Lakes and head mostly downhill for a mile; or, to reach Ten Lakes, continue straight, soon heading steeply downhill for 1.4 miles. The Grant Lakes offer a little more solitude (good for day hikers), while the two larger of the Ten Lakes have the best campsites, with many trees along their shorelines offering protection from the wind. All of the lakes are sparkling, rockbound beauties. Whether you go to Ten Lakes or Grant Lakes, don't miss taking a side trip to the rocky overlook above the Ten Lakes Basin. It's only 0.5 mile from the Ten Lakes/Grant Lakes junction (continue straight for Ten Lakes, then take the unsigned trail to the left of the main trail and head for the highest point). Four of the Ten Lakes are visible from this promontory, as well as a section of the Grand Canyon of the Tuolumne.

User Groups: Hikers only. No dogs, horses, or mountain bikes. No wheelchair facilities.

Permits: There is a $20 entrance fee per vehicle at Yosemite National Park, good for seven days. Free wilderness permits are required for overnight stays. They are available on a first-come, first-served basis up to one day in advance at the Yosemite Wilderness kiosk near your chosen trailhead or farther in advance by mail, phone, or online for a $5 reservation fee per person.

Maps: A Yosemite National Park map is available from Tom Harrison Maps. For topographic maps, ask the USGS for Yosemite Falls and Ten Lakes.

Directions: From Merced, drive 70 miles northeast on Highway 140 to Yosemite National Park. Follow the signs toward Yosemite Valley, entering through the Arch Rock entrance station. Continue 4.5 miles to the left turnoff for Highway 120, looping back out of the valley on Big Oak Flat Road. In 9.3 miles at Crane Flat, turn right on Tioga Pass Road and drive 19.4 miles to the Yosemite Creek and Ten Lakes trailhead parking area, which is on the south side of the road. The trail begins on the north side of the road.

Contact: Yosemite National Park, P.O. Box 577, Yosemite, CA 95389, 209/372-0200 or 209/372-0740 (permit reservations), www.nps.gov/yose or www.nps.gov/yose/wilderness (permit reservations).

24 NORTH DOME
9.0 mi / 5.0 hr

off Tioga Pass Road in Yosemite National Park

Map 10.1, page 495

There are those who say that climbing Half Dome is a bit of a disappointment, and not just because of the crowds. When you reach the top and check out the commanding view, the panorama of granite is not quite as awesome as you might expect, and that's because you can't see Half Dome—you're standing on it.

That's a dilemma that's easy to fix. If Half Dome is an absolute necessity in your view of Yosemite, climb North Dome instead, which offers a heart-stopping view of that big piece of granite. The route is not for the faint of heart, but when you are way up high looking down at Tenaya Canyon and across at Half Dome and Clouds Rest—well, you'll know why you came. The preferred route to North Dome begins at the Porcupine Creek trailhead on Tioga Pass Road, and has only a 1,500-foot gain to the summit. A dirt access road quickly brings you to a proper trail, signed as Porcupine Creek. Continue straight at two possible junctions near the 2.5-mile mark, heading due south for North Dome. After the third mile, your views begin to open up, providing fine vistas of North Dome and Half Dome and increasing your anticipation. At the trail junction at 4.5 miles, take the left spur for the final hike to North Dome's summit. Surprise—it's a downhill grade to reach it. Hope you brought a full supply of film or memory cards with you; the view from the top is sublime. Half Dome, just across the canyon, appears close enough to touch. Clouds Rest is a dramatic sight to the northeast. To the southwest, you can see cars crawling along the Yosemite Valley floor. On your return trip, consider taking the unsigned spur trail two miles from North Dome, at an obvious saddle. The spur leads a steep 0.25 mile to Indian Rock, the only natural arch on land in Yosemite. It's great fun to climb around on.

User Groups: Hikers only. No dogs, horses, or mountain bikes. No wheelchair facilities.

Permits: There is a $20 entrance fee per vehicle at Yosemite National Park, good for seven days. Free wilderness permits are required for overnight stays. They are available on a first-come, first-served basis up to one day in advance at the Yosemite Wilderness kiosk near your chosen trailhead or farther in advance by mail, phone, or online for a $5 reservation fee per person.

Maps: A Half Dome or Yosemite National Park map is available from Tom Harrison Maps. For a topographic map, ask the USGS for Yosemite Falls.

Directions: From Merced, drive 70 miles northeast on Highway 140 to Yosemite

National Park. Follow the signs toward Yosemite Valley, entering through the Arch Rock entrance station. Continue 4.5 miles to the left turnoff for Highway 120, looping back out of the valley on Big Oak Flat Road. In 9.3 miles at Crane Flat, turn right on Tioga Pass Road and drive 24.5 miles to the Porcupine Creek trailhead parking area, on the right, a mile past Porcupine Flat Campground.

Contact: Yosemite National Park, P.O. Box 577, Yosemite, CA 95389, 209/372-0200 or 209/372-0740 (permit reservations), www.nps.gov/yose or www.nps.gov/yose/wilderness (permit reservations).

25 MAY LAKE AND MOUNT HOFFMAN
2.4–6.0 mi / 2.0–4.0 hr

off Tioga Pass Road in Yosemite National Park

Map 10.1, page 495   BEST (

Here's a hike that you can take the kids on—well, the first part, anyway. It's an easy 1.2 miles to May Lake, tucked in below 10,850-foot Mount Hoffman. The trail to the lake has a total elevation gain of only 400 feet, and better yet, it's downhill all the way home. Attaining the summit of Mount Hoffman, on the other hand, requires a challenging ascent, and is best left to more seasoned hikers. (Leave the kids at home if you are going to continue from the shores of May Lake to the top of Mount Hoffman.) The trail to both destinations begins at the Snow Flat trailhead (two miles off Tioga Pass Road), passes through a lodgepole pine forest, climbs up a granite-lined slope, then drops down to May Lake's southern shore. A High Sierra Camp is located here. Wandering along the scenic, granite-ringed shoreline is a pleasant way to spend the afternoon.

To turn this easy walk into a moderate butt-kicker, follow the obvious use trail to the west, which leads around to the north side of May Lake. From the northwest shore, a fairly distinct use trail leads to Hoffman's

summit. This is not an official park trail, and it requires scrambling skills and sure footing, especially as you near the top. It also requires good lungs and legs: You have to gain another 1,500 feet in about two miles. So why do it? The view from Mount Hoffman's ridgeline is first-class, with Half Dome, Clouds Rest, Tenaya Lake, and May Lake all in sight. Mount Hoffman is the exact geographical center of Yosemite National Park. The peak has two main summits; the one with the weather station on top is the highest. Explore the entire ridgeline, and visit both summits if you have the time; the view is surprisingly different.

User Groups: Hikers and horses. No dogs or mountain bikes. No wheelchair facilities.

Permits: No permits are required. There is a $20 entrance fee per vehicle at Yosemite National Park, good for seven days.

Maps: A Tuolumne Meadows or Yosemite National Park map is available from Tom Harrison Maps. For a topographic map, ask the USGS for Tenaya Lake.

Directions: From Merced, drive 70 miles northeast on Highway 140 to Yosemite National Park. Follow the signs toward Yosemite Valley, entering through the Arch Rock entrance station. Continue 4.5 miles to the left turnoff for Highway 120, looping back out of the valley on Big Oak Flat Road. In 9.3 miles at Crane Flat, turn right on Tioga Pass Road and drive 26.6 miles to the May Lake Road turnoff, on the left (near road marker T-21). Drive two miles to the trailhead parking lot.

Contact: Yosemite National Park, P.O. Box 577, Yosemite, CA 95389, 209/372-0200, www.nps.gov/yose.

26 CLOUDS REST
14.0 mi / 8.0 hr   🏃3 ⛰10

off Tioga Pass Road in Yosemite National Park

Map 10.1, page 495   BEST (

Hiking to Clouds Rest is a trip that's as epic as climbing Half Dome, but with far fewer people elbowing you along the way. With a 2,300-foot climb and 14 miles to cover, it's not for those who are out of shape. The trail ascends steadily for the first four miles, descends steeply for 0.5 mile, then climbs again more moderately. Keep the faith—the first 2.5 miles from the trailhead are the toughest. The final summit ascent is a little dicey because of the terrifying dropoffs, but as with other Yosemite peaks, watch your footing on the granite slabs, and you'll be fine. Overall, the route is much safer than climbing Half Dome, because the final ascent is far more gradual, and there are no cables to maneuver. The view from the top of Clouds Rest—of Tenaya Canyon, Half Dome, Yosemite Valley, Tenaya Lake, the Clark Range, and various peaks and ridges—will knock your socks off (hope you brought along an extra pair). Note that if this long hike has made you hot and sweaty, you can stop at the Sunrise Lakes for a swim on the way back—the first lake is only 0.25 mile from the Clouds Rest/Sunrise Trail junction.

User Groups: Hikers only. No dogs, horses, or mountain bikes. No wheelchair facilities.

Permits: No permits are required. There is a $20 entrance fee per vehicle at Yosemite National Park, good for seven days.

Maps: A Tuolumne Meadows or Yosemite National Park map is available from Tom Harrison Maps. For a topographic map, ask the USGS for Tenaya Lake.

Directions: From Merced, drive 70 miles northeast on Highway 140 to Yosemite National Park. Follow the signs toward Yosemite Valley, entering through the Arch Rock entrance station. Continue 4.5 miles to the left turnoff for Highway 120, looping back out of the valley on Big Oak Flat Road. In 9.3 miles at Crane Flat, turn right on Tioga Pass Road and drive 30.3 miles to the Sunrise Lakes trailhead, on the south side of the highway just west of Tenaya Lake.

Contact: Yosemite National Park, P.O. Box 577, Yosemite, CA 95389, 209/372-0200, www.nps.gov/yose.

27 SUNRISE LAKES

7.5 mi / 4.5 hr or 2 days

off Tioga Pass Road in Yosemite National Park

Map 10.1, page 495

With all the people hiking to Clouds Rest, combined with all the people hiking to the Sunrise Lakes, the Sunrise trailhead can look like a mall parking lot on a Saturday. But don't be scared off; the hike to Sunrise Lakes is a great day hike or easy backpacking trip, especially during the week or off-season, with only a 1,000-foot elevation gain and a ton of stellar scenery, including great views of Clouds Rest at your back as you hike the final stretch to the lakes. You follow the trail as it climbs steeply above the edge of Tenaya Canyon. At 2.5 miles, turn left at the sign for the Sunrise High Sierra Camp. In about 10 minutes of easy walking, Lower Sunrise Lake shows up on the right, and the other lakes are shortly after it, on the left. The upper lake is the largest and by far the most popular; lots of folks like to swim and picnic there on warm summer days. Backpackers can pick a site here or continue onward for two more miles to the backpackers' camp or the High Sierra Camp, depending on where they've made their plans.

User Groups: Hikers only. No dogs, horses, or mountain bikes. No wheelchair facilities.

Permits: There is a $20 entrance fee per vehicle at Yosemite National Park, good for seven days. Free wilderness permits are required for overnight stays. They are available on a first-come, first-served basis up to one day in advance at the Yosemite Wilderness kiosk near your chosen trailhead or farther in advance by mail, phone, or online for a $5 reservation fee per person.

Maps: A Tuolumne Meadows or Yosemite National Park map is available from Tom Harrison Maps. For a topographic map, ask the USGS for Tenaya Lake.

Directions: From Merced, drive 70 miles northeast on Highway 140 to Yosemite National Park. Follow the signs toward Yosemite Valley, entering through the Arch Rock entrance station. Continue 4.5 miles to the left turnoff for Highway 120, looping back out of the valley on Big Oak Flat Road. In 9.3 miles at Crane Flat, turn right on Tioga Pass Road and drive 30.3 miles to the Sunrise Lakes trailhead, on the south side of the highway just west of Tenaya Lake.

Contact: Yosemite National Park, P.O. Box 577, Yosemite, CA 95389, 209/372-0200 or 209/372-0740 (permit reservations), www.nps.gov/yose or www.nps.gov/yose/wilderness (permit reservations).

28 TENAYA LAKE
2.0 mi / 1.0 hr   🚶1 ⛰9

off Tioga Pass Road in Yosemite National Park

Map 10.1, page 495

Lots of people drive east down Tioga Pass Road in a big rush to get to Tuolumne Meadows, but when they see giant Tenaya Lake right along the road, they stop short in their tire tracks. Luckily the 150-acre, sapphire-blue lake has a parking lot and picnic area at its east end, where you can leave your car and take a stroll down to the lake's edge. Although most people stop at the white-sand beach and picnic tables to watch the rock climbers on nearby Polly Dome, you can leave the crowds behind by strolling to the south side of the beach. Look for the trail there; it leads along the back side of Tenaya Lake, far from the road on the north side. When you get to the lake's west end, where the trail continues but the water views end, just turn around and walk back. It's a perfect, easy hike alongside one of the most beautiful lakes in Yosemite.

User Groups: Hikers only. No dogs, horses, or mountain bikes. No wheelchair facilities.

Permits: No permits are required. There is a $20 entrance fee per vehicle at Yosemite National Park, good for seven days.

Maps: A Tuolumne Meadows or Yosemite National Park map is available from Tom Harrison Maps. For a topographic map, ask the USGS for Tenaya Lake.

Directions: From Merced, drive 70 miles northeast on Highway 140 to Yosemite National Park. Follow the signs toward Yosemite Valley, entering through the Arch Rock entrance station. Continue 4.5 miles to the left turnoff for Highway 120, looping back out of the valley on Big Oak Flat Road. In 9.3 miles at Crane Flat, turn right on Tioga Pass Road and drive 31.7 miles to the eastern Tenaya Lake Picnic Area (another Tenaya Lake picnic area lies 0.5 mile west). The trail leads from the parking lot.

Contact: Yosemite National Park, P.O. Box 577, Yosemite, CA 95389, 209/372-0200, www.nps.gov/yose.

29 CATHEDRAL LAKES
7.4 mi / 4.0 hr or 2 days   🚶3 ⛰10

near Tuolumne Meadows in Yosemite National Park

Map 10.1, page 495

The Cathedral Lakes are a tremendously popular easy backpacking destination in Yosemite, but it's such a short hike to reach them that they also make a great day trip. Located on a 0.5-mile spur off John Muir Trail, the lakes are within a classic glacial cirque, tucked in below 10,840-foot Cathedral Peak. It's as scenic a spot as you'll find anywhere in Yosemite. Campsites are found close to the lakes, but you will need to secure your wilderness permit way in advance in order to spend the night. From the trail's start at Tioga Pass Road, you hike 3.2 miles on the John Muir Trail, with a 1,000-foot elevation gain. Much of the trail is shaded by lodgepole pines, but when the path breaks out of the trees, views of surrounding peaks (especially distinctive Cathedral Peak, which looks remarkably different from every angle) keep you oohing and ahhing the whole way. At 3.2 miles, turn right on the Cathedral Lake spur to reach the lower, larger lake in 0.5 mile. You'll follow the lake's inlet stream through a gorgeous meadow to the water's edge—then start snapping photographs like crazy. Many hikers stop here and go no farther, but it's a pity not to see Upper Cathedral Lake as well. To reach the upper lake, retrace your steps to John Muir Trail and continue another 0.5 mile. Fishing is often better in the upper lake, and the scenery is even more sublime.

User Groups: Hikers and horses. No dogs or mountain bikes. No wheelchair facilities.

Permits: There is a $20 entrance fee per vehicle at Yosemite National Park, good for seven days. Free wilderness permits are required for overnight stays. They are available on a first-come, first-served basis up to one day in advance at the Yosemite Wilderness kiosk near your chosen trailhead or farther in advance by mail, phone, or online for a $5 reservation fee per person.

Maps: A Tuolumne Meadows or Yosemite National Park map is available from Tom Harrison Maps. For a topographic map, ask the USGS for Tenaya Lake.

Directions: From Merced, drive 70 miles northeast on Highway 140 to Yosemite National Park. Follow the signs toward Yosemite Valley, entering through the Arch Rock entrance station. Continue 4.5 miles to the left turnoff for Highway 120, looping back out of the valley on Big Oak Flat Road. In 9.3 miles at Crane Flat, turn right on Tioga Pass Road and drive 37.4 miles to the Cathedral Lakes trailhead, on the right, by Tuolumne Meadows. Park your car in the pullouts on either side of Tioga Pass Road near the trailhead; there is no formal parking lot.

Contact: Yosemite National Park, P.O. Box 577, Yosemite, CA 95389, 209/372-0200 or 209/372-0740 (permit reservations), www.nps.gov/yose or www.nps.gov/yose/wilderness (permit reservations).

30 VOGELSANG LOOP

19.0 mi / 3 or 4 days

near Tuolumne Meadows in Yosemite National Park

Map 10.1, page 495

Although this loop is popular with hikers staying at the Vogelsang High Sierra Camp, backpackers who plan early can get a wilderness permit for their own self-designed trip. The traditional route is to head out on the western side of the loop along Rafferty Creek, then take a short spur and spend the night at Vogelsang Lake, which is without question the most visually dramatic spot seen on this trip. It's flanked by Fletcher Peak, a steep and rugged wall of glacier-carved granite. Few trees can grow in this sparse, high-alpine environment. The next day, you rejoin the loop and continue eastward to Evelyn Lake, another favorite camping spot. When it's time to return, you hike down to Lyell Fork, a 2,000-foot descent that takes a few hours, then meet up with John Muir Trail and follow it north through lush green and gorgeous Lyell Canyon, back to the trailhead at Tuolumne Meadows. The trailhead is at 8,600 feet—plenty high to start—and for the most part, the trail undulates along, never gaining or losing more than 2,000 feet.

User Groups: Hikers and horses. No dogs or mountain bikes. No wheelchair facilities.

Permits: There is a $20 entrance fee per vehicle at Yosemite National Park, good for seven days. Free wilderness permits are required for overnight stays. They are available on a first-come, first-served basis up to one day in advance at the Yosemite Wilderness kiosk near your chosen trailhead or farther in advance by mail, phone, or online for a $5 reservation fee per person.

Maps: A Tuolumne Meadows or Yosemite National Park map is available from Tom Harrison Maps. For a topographic map, ask the USGS for Vogelsang Peak.

Directions: From Merced, drive 70 miles northeast on Highway 140 to Yosemite National Park. Follow the signs toward Yosemite Valley, entering through the Arch Rock entrance station. Continue 4.5 miles to the left turnoff for Highway 120, looping back out of the valley on Big Oak Flat Road. In 9.3 miles at Crane Flat, turn right on Tioga Pass Road and drive 39.5 miles to the Tuolumne Lodge and Wilderness Permits turnoff, on the right. Turn right and drive 0.4 mile toward Tuolumne Lodge. Park in the lot on the left signed for Dog Lake and John Muir Trail. The trail begins across the road from the parking lot. Additional parking is available in the Wilderness Permit parking lot, at the turnoff from Tioga Pass Road.

Contact: Yosemite National Park, P.O. Box 577, Yosemite, CA 95389, 209/372-0200 or 209/372-0740 (permit reservations), www.nps.gov/yose or www.nps.gov/yose/wilderness (permit reservations).

31 LOWER GAYLOR LAKE
8.0 mi / 4.0 hr 🥾2 ⛰9

near Tioga Pass in Yosemite National Park

Map 10.1, page 495

This mellow, pretty hike starts on John Muir Trail near Tuolumne Lodge, then heads east along the south side of the Dana Fork of the Tuolumne River. After two miles, the trail crosses the river and Tioga Pass Road, and heads uphill through a dense lodgepole pine forest to Lower Gaylor Lake, elevation 10,049 feet. The shallow lake is a deep turquoise color and is surrounded by a grassy alpine meadow. From its edge, you gain wide vistas of the peaks in the Tuolumne Meadows area. This is classic high-country beauty at its finest. Note that if you wish to get to the Middle and Upper Gaylor Lakes from the lower lake, you have to go cross-country. An easier way is to drive to the Tioga Pass trailhead and follow the trail notes in this chapter for the *Middle and Upper Gaylor Lakes* hike. Elevation at this trailhead is 9,250 feet; the total gain is about 800 feet to Lower Gaylor Lake, a gentle climb the whole way.

User Groups: Hikers only. No dogs, horses, or mountain bikes. No wheelchair facilities.

Permits: No permits are required. There is a $20 entrance fee per vehicle at Yosemite National Park, good for seven days.

Maps: A Tuolumne Meadows or Yosemite National Park map is available from Tom Harrison Maps. For topographic maps, ask the USGS for Vogelsang Peak and Tioga Pass.

Directions: From Merced, drive 70 miles northeast on Highway 140 to Yosemite National Park. Follow the signs toward Yosemite Valley, entering through the Arch Rock entrance station. Continue 4.5 miles to the left turnoff for Highway 120, looping back out of the valley on Big Oak Flat Road. In 9.3 miles at Crane Flat, turn right on Tioga Pass Road and drive 39.5 miles to the Tuolumne Lodge and Wilderness Permits turnoff, on the right. Turn right and drive 0.4 mile toward Tuolumne Lodge, then park in the lot on the left signed for Dog Lake and John Muir Trail. The trail begins across the road from the parking lot. Additional parking is available in the Wilderness Permit parking lot, at the turnoff from Tioga Pass Road.

Contact: Yosemite National Park, P.O. Box 577, Yosemite, CA 95389, 209/372-0200, www.nps.gov/yose.

32 ELIZABETH LAKE
4.5 mi / 2.5 hr 🥾2 ⛰8

near Tuolumne Meadows in Yosemite National Park

Map 10.1, page 495

Starting at the trailhead elevation of 8,600 feet, you have a mere 850-foot elevation gain over 2.25 miles to get to lovely Elizabeth Lake, set in a basin at the foot of distinctive Unicorn Peak. It's a day hike that is attainable for almost anybody, and you can bet that every camper at Tuolumne Meadows Campground makes the trip at some point during their vacation. For noncampers, the trailhead is a bit tricky to find—it's tucked into the back of Tuolumne Meadows Campground, across from the group camp restrooms. Once you locate it, be prepared to climb steeply for the first mile, then breathe easier when the trail levels out. Fortunately the route is mostly shaded by a dense grove of lodgepole pines. Upon reaching its shore, you'll see that

Elizabeth Lake is a gorgeous body of alpine water. Some visitors swim or fish here; others try to climb Unicorn Peak (10,900 feet); most are happy to sit near the lake's edge and admire the views of the sculpted peak and its neighbors in the Cathedral Range.

User Groups: Hikers only. No dogs, horses, or mountain bikes. No wheelchair facilities.

Permits: No permits are required. There is a $20 entrance fee per vehicle at Yosemite National Park, good for seven days.

Maps: A Tuolumne Meadows or Yosemite National Park map is available from Tom Harrison Maps. For a topographic map, ask the USGS for Vogelsang Peak.

Directions: From Merced, drive 70 miles northeast on Highway 140 to Yosemite National Park. Follow the signs toward Yosemite Valley, entering through the Arch Rock entrance station. Continue 4.5 miles to the left turnoff for Highway 120, looping back out of the valley on Big Oak Flat Road. In 9.3 miles at Crane Flat, turn right on Tioga Pass Road and drive 39 miles to the Tuolumne Meadows Campground. Turn right and follow the signs through the main camp to the group camp. The trail begins across from the group camp restrooms, near group site No. B49.

Contact: Yosemite National Park, P.O. Box 577, Yosemite, CA 95389, 209/372-0200, www.nps.gov/yose.

33 LYELL CANYON
6.0 mi / 3.0 hr

near Tuolumne Meadows in
Yosemite National Park

Map 10.1, page 495

This hike is one of the easiest in the Yosemite high country, and since it starts out beautiful and stays that way, you can hike it as long or as short as you like. The total trail length is eight miles one-way, paralleling the Lyell Fork of the Tuolumne River on the Pacific Crest Trail/John Muir Trail. But most people just head out for two or three miles, carrying

their fishing rods, and then turn back. To reach the Lyell Fork, you must first cross the Dana Fork on a footbridge less than 0.5 mile from the parking lot. Then after 0.5 mile, you cross the Lyell Fork on a second footbridge, and head left along the river's south side. A third bridge takes you across Rafferty Creek and into Lyell Canyon. If you like looking at gorgeous meadows and a meandering river, this is your hike. Small trout are plentiful. A bonus is that backpacking sites are located three to four miles out on the trail, so if you get a wilderness permit, you can linger for a few days in paradise.

User Groups: Hikers and horses. No dogs or mountain bikes. No wheelchair facilities.

Permits: No permits are required. There is a $20 entrance fee per vehicle at Yosemite National Park, good for seven days.

Maps: A Tuolumne Meadows or Yosemite National Park map is available from Tom Harrison Maps. For a topographic map, ask the USGS for Vogelsang Peak.

Directions: From Merced, drive 70 miles northeast on Highway 140 to Yosemite National Park. Follow the signs toward Yosemite Valley, entering through the Arch Rock entrance station. Continue 4.5 miles to the left turnoff for Highway 120, looping back out of the valley on Big Oak Flat Road. In 9.3 miles at Crane Flat, turn right on Tioga Pass Road and drive 39.5 miles to the Tuolumne Lodge and Wilderness Permits turnoff, on the right. Turn right and drive 0.4 mile toward Tuolumne Lodge; park in the lot on the left signed for Dog Lake and John Muir Trail. The John Muir Trail begins across the road from the parking lot. Additional parking is available in the Wilderness Permit parking lot, at the turnoff from Tioga Pass Road.

Contact: Yosemite National Park, P.O. Box 577, Yosemite, CA 95389, 209/372-0200, www.nps.gov/yose.

34 YOUNG LAKES LOOP

14.6 mi / 1 or 2 days   👣3 ⛰10

near Tuolumne Meadows in
Yosemite National Park

Map 10.1, page 495

Starting from the Lembert Dome parking lot at 8,600 feet in elevation, the Young Lakes Loop is a classic Yosemite trip that works equally well as a short backpacking trip or a long day hike. The destination is a series of lakes set in a deep and wide glacial cirque—the kind of awesome scenery that sticks in your mind months later, when you're sitting at a desk somewhere staring at your computer screen. The trip starts with a walk down the wide dirt road that leads to Soda Spring. Pick up the trail near Parson's Lodge that leads to Glen Aulin, and follow it through lodgepole pines for 1.8 miles until you see the right turn-off for Young Lakes. Follow Young Lakes Trail for 3.5 more miles, climbing steadily. At 5.5 miles out, you'll see the return leg of your loop leading off to the right (signed for Dog Lake). You'll continue straight for another 1.5 miles to Lower Young Lake and a stunning view of Ragged Peak, Mount Conness, and White Mountain. Two more lakes are accessible within a mile to the east. If you have the energy, don't miss the third, upper lake, the most visually stunning of them all, perched in a high meadow at 10,218 feet in elevation. When you're ready to head home, retrace your steps to the junction, and take the eastern (left) fork, returning via Dog Lake and Lembert Dome. Be forewarned: If you loop back this way, it won't be an all-downhill cruise, but the scenery makes the additional climbing worthwhile. If you're exhausted from your trip to the lakes, skip the loop and return the way you came—it's downhill all the way.

User Groups: Hikers and horses. No dogs or mountain bikes. No wheelchair facilities.

Permits: There is a $20 entrance fee per vehicle at Yosemite National Park, good for seven days. Free wilderness permits are required for overnight stays. They are available on a first-come, first-served basis up to one day in advance at the Yosemite Wilderness kiosk near your chosen trailhead or farther in advance by mail, phone, or online for a $5 reservation fee per person.

Maps: A Yosemite National Park map is available from Tom Harrison Maps. For topographic maps, ask the USGS for Tioga Pass and Falls Ridge.

Directions: From Merced, drive 70 miles northeast on Highway 140 to Yosemite National Park. Follow the signs toward Yosemite Valley, entering through the Arch Rock entrance station. Continue 4.5 miles to the left turnoff for Highway 120, looping back out of the valley on Big Oak Flat Road. In 9.3 miles at Crane Flat, turn right on Tioga Pass Road and drive 39 miles to the Lembert Dome/Soda Spring/Dog Lake/Glen Aulin trailhead parking, on the left. Begin hiking on the western edge of the parking lot, where there is a gated dirt road signed for Soda Spring.

Contact: Yosemite National Park, P.O. Box 577, Yosemite, CA 95389, 209/372-0200 or 209/372-0740 (permit reservations), www.nps.gov/yose or www.nps.gov/yose/wilderness (permit reservations).

35 WATERWHEEL FALLS

16.0 mi / 1 or 2 days   👣3 ⛰10

near Tuolumne Meadows in
Yosemite National Park

Map 10.1, page 495   **BEST(**

This hike could be called the Epic Waterfall Trip. If you hike the entire route, you'll see so many waterfalls and so much water along the way that you'll have enough memories to get you through a 10-year drought. Arrange for a wilderness permit in advance, or reserve a stay at the Glen Aulin High Sierra Camp, so that you can divide the 16 miles over two or more days. If you're in good enough shape, you can do the trip in one day, because the trail is nearly level for the first four miles (a 400-foot elevation loss), then descends more steeply over the next four miles (a 1,500-foot elevation loss). Unfortunately, all the climbing must be done on the way home, so you must reserve your energy and have plenty of food and water (or at least a purifying device so you can filter water from the river).

Follow the trail notes for Glen Aulin and Tuolumne Falls (see listing in this chapter) for the first four miles of trail; then continue downstream past Glen Aulin Camp, alternating between stretches of stunning flower- and aspen-lined meadows and stark granite slabs. Waterwheel Falls is only three miles from the camp, and two other major cascades, California and LeConte, are along the way. To see all three falls, make sure you take each spur trail you see that leads to the river; none of the waterfalls is apparent from the main trail. Other hikers will stop you on the trail to ask if you know where the waterfalls are. Whereas all three falls are long whitewater cascades, Waterwheel is considered Yosemite's most unusual-looking waterfall because it has sections of churning water that dip into deep holes in the granite, then shoot out with such velocity that they double back on themselves. When the river level is high, they actually appear to circle around like waterwheels.

User Groups: Hikers and horses. No dogs or mountain bikes. No wheelchair facilities.

Permits: There is a $20 entrance fee per vehicle at Yosemite National Park, good for seven days. Free wilderness permits are required for overnight stays. They are available on a first-come, first-served basis up to one day in advance at the Yosemite Wilderness kiosk near your chosen trailhead or farther in advance by mail, phone, or online for a $5 reservation fee per person.

Maps: A Tuolumne Meadows or Yosemite National Park map is available from Tom Harrison Maps. For topographic maps, ask the USGS for Tioga Pass and Falls Ridge.

Directions: From Merced, drive 70 miles northeast on Highway 140 to Yosemite National Park. Follow the signs toward Yosemite Valley, entering through the Arch Rock entrance station. Continue 4.5 miles to the left turnoff for Highway 120, looping back out of the valley on Big Oak Flat Road. In 9.3 miles at Crane Flat, turn right on Tioga Pass Road and drive 39 miles to the Lembert Dome/Soda Spring/Dog Lake/Glen Aulin trailhead parking, on the left. Begin hiking on the western edge of the parking lot, where there is a gated dirt road signed for Soda Spring.

Contact: Yosemite National Park, P.O. Box 577, Yosemite, CA 95389, 209/372-0200 or 209/372-0740 (permit reservations), www.nps.gov/yose or www.nps.gov/yose/wilderness (permit reservations).

36 GLEN AULIN AND TUOLUMNE FALLS
9.0 mi / 5.0 hr 👣2 ⛰9

near Tuolumne Meadows in Yosemite National Park

Map 10.1, page 495   BEST ☾

Those who aren't up for the Epic Waterfall Trip to Waterwheel Falls (see listing in this chapter) can take this trip instead and maybe even sneak in a good meal at the Glen Aulin High Sierra Camp. To stay in the camp, you must reserve a spot far in advance, but you can often purchase a hot meal just by showing up. Tuolumne Falls drop right by the High Sierra Camp, and reaching the waterfall requires only a 4.5-mile walk with a 400-foot elevation loss. The return climb is easy, with most of the ascent being in the first mile as you head up and over the various cascades of Tuolumne Falls on granite stairs. Follow the dirt road from the Lembert Dome parking lot toward Soda Spring. When you near Parson's Lodge, veer right on the signed trail to Glen Aulin. You'll walk through lodgepole pine forest, then move closer to the Tuolumne River and get incredible views of Cathedral and Unicorn Peaks, as well as Fairview Dome. After three miles, you'll cross the Tuolumne on a footbridge, and in another 0.25 mile, you'll reach the first stunning drop of Tuolumne Falls, a 100-foot, churning freefall. Keep descending past more cascades to the base of the falls, where another footbridge leads back across the river and to Glen Aulin. Pick a spot downstream beside a river pool or near the bridge at the base of the waterfall, have a seat, and ponder the exquisite beauty of this place.

User Groups: Hikers and horses. No dogs or mountain bikes. No wheelchair facilities.

Permits: No permits are required. There is a $20 entrance fee per vehicle at Yosemite National Park, good for seven days.

Maps: A Tuolumne Meadows or Yosemite National Park map is available from Tom Harrison Maps. For topographic maps, ask the USGS for Tioga Pass and Falls Ridge.

Directions: From Merced, drive 70 miles northeast on Highway 140 to Yosemite National Park. Follow the signs toward Yosemite Valley, entering through the Arch Rock entrance station. Continue 4.5 miles to the left turnoff for Highway 120, looping back out of the valley on Big Oak Flat Road. In 9.3 miles at Crane Flat, turn right on Tioga Pass Road and drive 39 miles to the Lembert Dome/Soda Spring/Dog Lake/Glen Aulin trailhead parking, on the left. Begin hiking on the western edge of the parking lot, where there is a gated dirt road signed for Soda Spring.

Contact: Yosemite National Park, P.O. Box 577, Yosemite, CA 95389, 209/372-0200, www.nps.gov/yose.

37 LEMBERT DOME
2.8 mi / 1.5 hr   ☆3 ⛰10

near Tuolumne Meadows in
Yosemite National Park

Map 10.1, page 495

Lembert Dome is a *roche moutonnée* (a French geologic term that means it looks something like a sheep). We never see the resemblance, but we did feel like a couple of mountain goats when we climbed Lembert Dome, elevation 9,450 feet. From the parking area at the base, you can see rock climbers practicing

their stuff on the steep side of the dome, but luckily the hiker's trail heads around to the more-sloped back side. You can walk right up the granite—no ropes necessary. The Dog Lake and Lembert Dome Trail winds its way steeply around to the dome's north side (see listing in this chapter); from there, pick any route along the granite that looks manageable. When you reach the top of the dome, you know that you've accomplished something. The view from its highest point—of Tuolumne Meadows and surrounding peaks and domes—is more than worth the effort.

User Groups: Hikers only. No dogs, horses, or mountain bikes. No wheelchair facilities.

Permits: No permits are required. There is a $20 entrance fee per vehicle at Yosemite National Park, good for seven days.

Maps: A Tuolumne Meadows or Yosemite National Park map is available from Tom Harrison Maps. For a topographic map, ask the USGS for Tioga Pass.

Directions: From Merced, drive 70 miles northeast on Highway 140 to Yosemite National Park. Follow the signs toward Yosemite Valley, entering through the Arch Rock entrance station. Continue 4.5 miles to the left turnoff for Highway 120, looping back out of the valley on Big Oak Flat Road. In 9.3 miles at Crane Flat, turn right on Tioga Pass Road and drive 39 miles to the Lembert Dome/Soda Spring/Dog Lake/Glen Aulin trailhead parking, on the left. Begin hiking on the trail near the restrooms.

Contact: Yosemite National Park, P.O. Box 577, Yosemite, CA 95389, 209/372-0200, www.nps.gov/yose.

38 DOG LAKE
3.4 mi / 2.0 hr   ☆2 ⛰8

near Tuolumne Meadows in
Yosemite National Park

Map 10.1, page 495

Dog Lake is an easy-to-reach destination from Tuolumne Meadows, a perfect place for a family to spend an afternoon in the high country. The hike begins near the base of Lembert Dome, then heads through a gorgeous meadow that offers views of snowy Cathedral and Unicorn Peaks. The trail traverses a granite slab, then splits off from the path to Lembert Dome and starts to climb quite steeply through a lodgepole pine and fir forest. When you reach an intersection with Young Lakes Trail, you're only 0.25 mile from Dog Lake. The lake is a delight, although with its grassy shoreline, it is often plagued with mosquitoes (don't forget the bug spray). Set at 9,170 feet in elevation, it is wide, shallow, and deep blue. The colorful peaks to the east are Mount Dana and Mount Gibbs. You can hike around Dog Lake's perimeter if you please, take a swim in late summer, or just sit by the peaceful shoreline and relax.

User Groups: Hikers and horses. No dogs or mountain bikes. No wheelchair facilities.

Permits: No permits are required. There is a $20 entrance fee per vehicle at Yosemite National Park, good for seven days.

Maps: A Tuolumne Meadows or Yosemite National Park map is available from Tom Harrison Maps. For a topographic map, ask the USGS for Tioga Pass.

Directions: From Merced, drive 70 miles northeast on Highway 140 to Yosemite National Park. Follow the signs toward Yosemite Valley, entering through the Arch Rock entrance station. Continue 4.5 miles to the left turnoff for Highway 120, looping back out of the valley on Big Oak Flat Road. In 9.3 miles at Crane Flat, turn right on Tioga Pass Road and drive 39 miles to the Lembert Dome/Soda Spring/Dog Lake/Glen Aulin trailhead parking, on the left. Begin hiking on the trail near the restrooms.

Contact: Yosemite National Park, P.O. Box 577, Yosemite, CA 95389, 209/372-0200, www.nps.gov/yose.

39 TUOLUMNE MEADOWS TO SONORA PASS (PCT)

77.0 mi one-way / 8 days 🏃5 ⛰10

from Tuolumne Meadows on Highway 120 north to Sonora Pass on Highway 108

Map 10.1, page 495

This is a spectacular week-plus backpack trip that follows a section of the Pacific Crest Trail (PCT). The beauty of this region's deep canyons, glacial-cut peaks, verdant meadows, and abundant wildlife make it a hiker's paradise.

From Tuolumne Meadows, the trail starts out deceptively easy as it follows the Tuolumne River toward the Grand Canyon of the Tuolumne River. It heads gently downhill to Glen Aulin, where you get a great view of Tuolumne Falls. When you cross the bridge at the base of the falls and head up-canyon, you'll leave the day hikers behind. In the next three days, you'll go up one canyon and down the next, one after another, with breathtaking views and long, demanding climbs. Highlights include Matterhorn Canyon (many deer, trout, and views), Benson Lake (the largest white-sand beach in the Sierra Nevada), Dorothy Lake (panoramic views to the north), and many pristine, high-country meadows. The incredible clouds of mosquitoes at the Wilmer Lake area during early summer can be a major annoyance.

When you leave Yosemite and enter Humboldt-Toiyabe National Forest, the landscape changes quickly from glacial-cut granite to volcanic rock. The trail drops past several pretty lakes and into a river drainage, and at points can be difficult to follow. In a few areas, you may be surprised to meet up with grazing cows, especially from midsummer onward. You'll make a long, slow, climb up toward Leavitt Pass, set just below 10,800-foot Leavitt Peak. This landscape is entirely above tree line, in gray, stark country. At Leavitt Pass, the wind whistles by at high speed almost year-round. The final drop down to Sonora Pass is a one-hour descent that seems to wind all over the mountain. When you reach Highway 108, cross the road and walk about 100 yards west to a large day-use parking area. That's where your car shuttle should be waiting for you.

User Groups: Hikers and horses. No dogs or mountain bikes. No wheelchair facilities.

Permits: A wilderness permit is required for traveling through various wilderness and special-use areas the trail traverses. Contact either the Wilderness Office of the National Park Service or the Stanislaus National Forest for a permit that is good for the length of your trip. There is a $20 entrance fee per vehicle at Yosemite National Park, good for seven days.

Maps: For topographic maps, ask the USGS for Pickel Meadow, Tower Peak, Piute Mountain, Matterhorn Peak, Dunderberg Peak, Vogelsang Peak, Tioga Pass, Falls Ridge, Buckeye Ridge, and Sonora Pass.

Directions: From Merced, drive 70 miles northeast on Highway 140 to Yosemite National Park. Follow the signs toward Yosemite Valley, entering through the Arch Rock entrance station. Continue 4.5 miles to the left turnoff for Highway 120, looping back out of the valley on Big Oak Flat Road. In 9.3 miles at Crane Flat, turn right on Tioga Pass Road and drive 39 miles to the Lembert Dome/Soda Spring/Dog Lake/Glen Aulin trailhead parking, on the left. Begin hiking on the western edge of the parking lot, where there is a gated dirt road signed for Soda Spring.

Contact: Yosemite National Park, P.O. Box 577, Yosemite, CA 95389, 209/372-0200, www.nps.gov/yose; Stanislaus National Forest, Calaveras Ranger Station, P.O. Box 500, Hathaway Pines, CA 95233, 209/795-1381, www.fs.fed.us/r5/stanislaus.

40 TUOLUMNE MEADOWS TO YOSEMITE VALLEY (JMT)

22.0 mi one-way / 2 days 🏃5 ⛺10

near Tuolumne Meadows in
Yosemite National Park

Map 10.1, page 495

The first glimpses of Yosemite Valley will seem like a privileged view into heaven after having hiked the entire John Muir Trail (JMT) from Mount Whitney. For hikers making only this 22-mile section, the rewards can seem just as profound. The trip starts at Tuolumne Meadows, where backpackers can buy a good cheap breakfast, obtain wilderness permits, and camp in a special area set aside for JMT hikers. When you take your first steps away from Tuolumne Meadows, resist the urge to rush to the finish line in order to close out a historic expedition. Instead, relax and enjoy the downhill glide, always remembering that you are in sacred land. Compared to the rest of the JMT, this leg will come with far less strain, starting with a 3.1-mile tromp past Cathedral Lakes and requiring a 0.5-mile walk on a signed cutoff trail. If you can time it right, this area can make a great layover camp, with deep, emerald-green water and Cathedral Peak in the background. Beyond Cathedral Lakes, the trail makes a relatively short 500-foot climb over Cathedral Pass, skirts Tresidder Peak, and then descends through pristine Long Meadow. After passing Sunrise Trail Camp, a decent layover, the trail picks up little Sunrise Creek and follows it all the way down to Little Yosemite Valley, a popular trail camp. From Cathedral Lakes, it's 14.5 miles to the junction of Half Dome Trail, and another 2.2 miles to Little Yosemite.

For JMT hikers, making the climb to the top of Half Dome is a must, even though it often means putting up with a parade of people and even delays waiting for the line to move at the climbing cable. The Half Dome climb starts with a steep hike for the first mile, followed by steep switchbacks across granite on good trail to the foot of Half Dome's back wall. Here you'll find climbing cables to aid your final 300-foot ascent, and as you go, you'll discover breathtaking views of Tenaya Canyon. This is considered one of the world's glamour hikes, and while it turns hiking into an act of faith, we have seen eight-year-olds and 70-year-olds make the cable climb. By the way, if you take on Half Dome, be certain to have two canteens of water per person.

Adding the Half Dome side trip to the rest of the JMT leg will add a round-trip of 5.2 miles to your hike. Because of its proximity to Half Dome, the Little Yosemite Valley Trail Camp is often crowded. From here, though, it's an easy five-mile hike downhill to Yosemite Valley. Again, try not to speed through to the end, even though it's an easy tromp downhill all the way. The magic is in the moment.

From Little Yosemite, the JMT is routed along the Merced River. In a mile, you'll reach Liberty Cap, and shortly later, Nevada Fall. Then down, down you go, with the trail often turning to giant granite steps, down past Emerald Pool and then to Vernal Fall, another spectacular waterfall. Since Vernal Fall is just 1.7 miles from the end of the trail, you'll start meeting lots of day hikers coming from the other direction, many gasping for breath as they make the uphill climb out of Yosemite Valley. Many will ask how far you've hiked; some may even want to take your photograph. It may feel a bit inane, but, hey, enjoy it. After all, you just finished John Muir Trail, the greatest hiking trail in the world.

User Groups: Hikers and horses. No dogs or mountain bikes. No wheelchair facilities.

Permits: A wilderness permit is required for traveling through various wilderness and special-use areas that the trail traverses. Contact the Wilderness Office of the National Park Service for a permit that is good for the length of your trip. There is a $20 entrance fee per vehicle at Yosemite National Park, good for seven days.

Maps: A John Muir Trail Map Pack is available from Tom Harrison Maps. For topographic maps, ask the USGS for Vogelsang Peak, Half Dome, Yosemite Falls, and Tenaya Peak.

Directions: From Merced, drive 70 miles northeast on Highway 140 to Yosemite National Park. Follow the signs toward Yosemite Valley, entering through the Arch Rock entrance station. Continue 4.5 miles to the left turnoff for Highway 120, looping back out of the valley on Big Oak Flat Road. In 9.3 miles at Crane Flat, turn right on Tioga Pass Road and drive 39.5 miles to the Tuolumne Lodge and Wilderness Permits turnoff, on the right. Turn right and drive 0.4 mile toward Tuolumne Lodge; park in the lot on the left signed for Dog Lake and John Muir Trail. The John Muir Trail begins across the road from the parking lot. Additional parking is available in the Wilderness Permit parking lot, at the turnoff from Tioga Road.

Contact: Yosemite National Park, P.O. Box 577, Yosemite, CA 95389, 209/372-0200 or 209/372-0740 (permit reservations), www.nps.gov/yose or www.nps.gov/yose/wilderness (permit reservations).

41 MONO PASS
8.4 mi / 4.5 hr 🥾2 ⛰9

near Tioga Pass in Yosemite National Park

Map 10.1, page 495

With an elevation gain of only 900 feet spread out over four miles, you'll hardly even notice you're climbing on the route to Mono Pass. That's if you're acclimated, of course, because you start out at 9,700 feet, where the air is mighty thin. The Mono Pass Trail begins in a mix of lodgepole pines and grassy meadows, then crosses the Dana Fork of the Tuolumne River, which is an easy boulder-hop by midsummer. (Earlier in the season you may need to find a log to cross.) The trail soon meets up with Parker Pass Creek and parallels it for most of the trip. As you proceed, you'll gain great views of Mount Gibbs, Mount Dana, and the Kuna Crest. At a trail junction at 2.0 miles, bear left and start to climb more noticeably. When you reach the Mono Pass sign at 3.8 miles, take the right spur trail (unsigned). It leads 0.3 mile to a cluster of four 19th-century mining cabins, which have been beautifully restored. It's fascinating to explore the small cabins and surrounding mine ruins and consider the hard life of those who lived and worked here. Then, heading back to the main trail, continue another 0.5 mile beyond the sign marking Mono Pass for the best views of the trip. From a granite promontory above a water-filled tarn, you can see far down Bloody Canyon to Mono Lake and the surrounding desert.

User Groups: Hikers and horses. No dogs or mountain bikes. No wheelchair facilities.

Permits: No permits are required. There is a $20 entrance fee per vehicle at Yosemite National Park, good for seven days.

Maps: A Yosemite High Country map is available from Tom Harrison Maps. For a topographic map, ask the USGS for Tioga Pass.

Directions: From Merced, drive 70 miles northeast on Highway 140 to Yosemite National Park. Follow the signs toward Yosemite Valley, entering through the Arch Rock entrance station. Continue 4.5 miles to the left turnoff for Highway 120, looping back out of the valley on Big Oak Flat Road. In 9.3 miles at Crane Flat, turn right on Tioga Pass Road and drive 44.5 miles to the Mono Pass trailhead on the right, 1.5 miles west of Tioga Pass.

Contact: Yosemite National Park, P.O. Box 577, Yosemite, CA 95389, 209/372-0200, www.nps.gov/yose.

42 SPILLWAY AND HELEN LAKES

9.0 mi / 5.0 hr   🚶3 ⛰9

near Tioga Pass in Yosemite National Park

Map 10.1, page 495

Another option on the Mono Pass Trail (see trail notes for previous hike) is to take the right fork at 2.0 miles and head for Spillway Lake, a wide, shallow lake that is only 1.6 miles from this junction, and then large Helen Lake, which is reached by some easy cross-country travel. It seems like a completely different trip than the aforementioned hike to Mono Pass. The highlights here are two high alpine lakes that epitomize the beauty of the Yosemite high country. Backpackers rarely travel to these lakes, so day hikers are likely to have more solitude here. The views of the Kuna Crest

and the high alpine meadow surrounding the upper reaches of Parker Pass Creek will take your breath away. A maintained trail travels to Spillway Lake, and from its southeast edge you simply follow Helen Lake's outlet creek uphill to the shores of Helen Lake. Helen Lake is set at 11,000 feet in elevation, and it's as lovely as any high mountain lake can be. Total elevation gain to see both lakes is only 1,300 feet.

User Groups: Hikers only. No dogs, horses, or mountain bikes. No wheelchair facilities.

Permits: No permits are required. There is a $20 entrance fee per vehicle at Yosemite National Park, good for seven days.

Maps: A Yosemite High Country map is available from Tom Harrison Maps. For a topographic map, ask the USGS for Tioga Pass.

Directions: From Merced, drive 70 miles northeast on Highway 140 to Yosemite National Park. Follow the signs toward Yosemite Valley, entering through the Arch Rock entrance station. Continue 4.5 miles to the left turnoff for Highway 120, looping back out of the valley on Big Oak Flat Road. In 9.3 miles at Crane Flat, turn right on Tioga Pass Road and drive 44.5 miles to the Mono Pass trailhead on the right, 1.5 miles west of Tioga Pass.

Contact: Yosemite National Park, P.O. Box 577, Yosemite, CA 95389, 209/372-0200, www.nps.gov/yose.

43 MIDDLE AND UPPER GAYLOR LAKES

4.0 mi / 2.5 hr   🚶3 ⛰9

near Tioga Pass in Yosemite National Park

Map 10.1, page 495

Middle and Upper Gaylor Lakes are deservedly popular destinations, because of the short distance required to reach them and their great opportunities for trout fishing. Oh yeah, and then there is the amazing high-alpine scenery. Starting near Tioga Pass (at nearly 10,000 feet), the trail climbs a steep ridge and then drops down to Middle Gaylor Lake. Although it's only one mile of ascent, it's a high-elevation butt-kicker that causes many to beg for mercy. From the middle lake, you can follow the creek gently uphill to the east for another mile to reach smaller Upper Gaylor Lake. Be sure to take the trail around its north side and uphill for a few hundred yards to the site of the Great Sierra Mine and the remains of an old stone cabin. The Great Sierra Mine turned out to be not so great—no silver ore was ever refined, and the mine was eventually abandoned. The hauntingly beautiful glacial scenery is what remains. Total elevation gain on the hike to Upper Gaylor Lake is about 1,000 feet, and it's worth every step. If you want to see more of this sublime lake basin, the twin Granite Lakes lie about 0.75 mile northwest of Middle Gaylor Lake. Although there is no formal trail, it's an easy cross-country ramble to see the Granite Lakes as well, which are tucked in below a massive granite cirque.

User Groups: Hikers only. No dogs, horses, or mountain bikes. No wheelchair facilities.

Permits: No permits are required. There is a $20 entrance fee per vehicle at Yosemite National Park, good for seven days.

Maps: A Yosemite High Country map is available from Tom Harrison Maps. For a topographic map, ask the USGS for Tioga Pass.

Directions: From Merced, drive miles northeast on Highway 140 to Yosemite National Park. Follow the signs toward Yosemite Valley, entering through the Arch Rock entrance station. Continue 4.5 miles to the left turnoff for Highway 120, looping back out of the valley on Big Oak Flat Road. In 9.3 miles at Crane Flat, turn right on Tioga Pass Road and drive 46 miles to the parking lot just west of the Tioga Pass entrance station, on the north side of Tioga Pass Road.

Contact: Yosemite National Park, P.O. Box 577, Yosemite, CA 95389, 209/372-0200, www.nps.gov/yose.

44 MOUNT DANA
6.0 mi / 4.0 hr 🥾4 ⛰9

near Tioga Pass in Yosemite National Park

Map 10.1, page 495　　BEST (

Mount Dana is a grueling hike. Yet many hikers make the trip every summer, perhaps as some sort of rite of passage to affirm that the long winter has truly ended in the high country. The path to the 13,053-foot summit requires a 3,100-foot elevation gain condensed into a mere three miles. To make matters more difficult, there is no maintained trail, only a series of informal "use" trails created by generations of hearty Yosemite hikers who have traveled the route. To join their ranks, leave your car at the Gaylor Lakes trailhead by the Tioga Pass entrance station, then cross the road and hike southeast on the unsigned but obvious trail that begins just a few feet from the park entrance kiosk. The path starts with a pleasant ramble through Dana Meadows, then enters a dense lodgepole pine forest. Soon the grade becomes more intense, but this first stretch of climbing is highlighted by a spectacular wildflower show that usually peaks in late July. Lupine, larkspur, Indian paintbrush, senecia—they're all here, in all their glory. The climbing gets tougher on the second mile of the hike, but stick with it and soon you've climbed above 11,000 feet, and now you're above tree line. The path keeps ascending to the 11,600-foot mark, where a giant trail cairn marks a large, rock-covered plateau. This is a good place to rest and do a check on your physical and mental state. Although the summit may look close from here, you still have a long, hard way to go. Two fairly obvious paths head uphill from this point; if you're feeling comfortable with the altitude, pick either one and continue onward, zigzagging your way up the shale-covered slope. In the final mile you must gain 1,500 feet, and to say it is slow going would be a major understatement. There's no shade, often a fierce wind, plenty of loose rock underfoot, and the breathtakingly thin air of high altitude. With what may seem like your last breath, you finally reach the summit, where you are witness to one of the finest views in the Sierra. Your field of vision encompasses Mono Lake, Ellery and Saddlebag Lakes, Glacier Canyon, Tuolumne Meadows, Lembert Dome, and an untold wealth of high peaks. Bring a map and identify all you can survey, or forget the map and just take in the majesty of it all.

A few tips for making the ascent safely: First, wait until mid-July or later to make the trip, as Mount Dana can be snow-covered long into the summer. Second, get an early start in the morning so you have no chance of encountering afternoon thunderstorms. Third, carry (and drink) as much water as you can. Fourth, wear good sunglasses and sun protection at this high elevation. And lastly, pace yourself to give your body a chance to adjust to the 13,000-foot altitude.

User Groups: Hikers only. No dogs, horses, or mountain bikes. No wheelchair facilities.

Permits: No permits are required. There is a $20 entrance fee per vehicle at Yosemite National Park, good for seven days.

Maps: A Yosemite High Country map is available from Tom Harrison Maps. For a topographic map, ask the USGS for Tioga Pass.

Directions: From Merced, drive miles northeast on Highway 140 to Yosemite National Park. Follow the signs toward Yosemite Valley, entering through the Arch Rock entrance station. Continue 4.5 miles to the left turnoff for Highway 120, looping back out of the valley on Big Oak Flat Road. In 9.3 miles at Crane Flat, turn right on Tioga Pass Road and drive 46 miles to the parking lot just west of the Tioga Pass entrance station, on the north side of Tioga Pass Road. The trail begins on the south side of Tioga Pass Road; begin hiking on the unsigned trail across from the park entrance kiosk.

Contact: Yosemite National Park, P.O. Box 577, Yosemite, CA 95389, 209/372-0200, www.nps.gov/yose.

45 BENNETTVILLE

2.6 mi / 2.0 hr　🏃2　⛰10

in Inyo National Forest just east of Tioga Pass

Map 10.1, page 495

This first-class high-country hike is suitable for even the most novice hikers, and is sure to spark your imagination. The remote high-country region of Bennettville was the site of a 19th-century silver mining community. Although the town thrived only from 1882 to 1884, it was the primary reason for the construction of the Tioga Pass Road from the west. The original road, called the Great Sierra Wagon Road, was built by the Great Sierra Consolidated Silver Company in anticipation of the riches they would make from the mines at Bennettville and nearby. Ultimately, no valuable minerals were ever extracted, and the company went broke in record time. A mostly level trail leads to the two buildings that remain from Bennettville's heyday: the assay office and barn/bunkhouse. An open mine tunnel lined with railcar tracks can also be seen, as well as some rusting mining equipment. Much of the machinery and supplies for this mine was hauled here from the May Lundy Mine over Dore Pass. Men and animals carried several tons of equipment on their backs and on sleds, sometimes through driving snowstorms in the middle of winter at this 10,000-foot elevation.

You can extend this hike by following the trail alongside Mine Creek 0.5 mile uphill from the mine buildings to small Shell Lake, followed by three more shallow lakes in the next mile or so: Mine, Fantail, and finally Spuller. More mine sites can be seen along the way. The high-country landscape here is a mix of open meadows, delicate high-alpine wildflowers, and wind-sculpted whitebark pines. The scenery is as good as you'll find anywhere, and you'll want to return to this area again and again.

User Groups: Hikers, horses, dogs, and mountain bikes. No wheelchair facilities.

Permits: No permits are required. Parking and access are free.

Maps: A Yosemite High Country map is available from Tom Harrison Maps. An Inyo National Forest map is available from the U.S. Forest Service. For a topographic map, ask the USGS for Tioga Pass.

Directions: From Merced, drive 70 miles northeast on Highway 140 to Yosemite National Park. Follow the signs toward Yosemite Valley, entering through the Arch Rock entrance station. Continue 4.5 miles to the left turnoff for Highway 120, looping back out of the valley on Big Oak Flat Road. In 9.3 miles at Crane Flat, turn right on Tioga Pass Road and drive 48 miles (you'll exit the park) to the Saddlebag Lake turnoff, on the left, two miles east of Tioga Pass. Turn left, and then left again immediately, to enter Junction Campground. The trail begins at the campground entrance.

Contact: Inyo National Forest, Mono Basin Scenic Area Visitors Center, P.O. Box 429, Lee Vining, CA 93541, 760/647-3044, www.fs.usda.gov/inyo.

46 GARDISKY LAKE

2.0 mi / 2.0 hr   🏃3 ⛰️8

in Inyo National Forest just east of Tioga Pass

Map 10.1, page 495

How can a two-mile round-trip hike be rated a 3 for difficulty? It can because it goes straight up, gaining 700 feet in just one mile, with not nearly enough switchbacks. Although the trail distance is short, the trailhead is set at 9,800 feet, which means you need to be well acclimated to pant your way through that steep of a grade. The trip offers many rewards, though, including many fewer people than at nearby Saddlebag Lake and a stellar high-alpine setting. Once you huff and puff your way to the ridgetop, you have a nearly level 0.25-mile stroll through a fragile alpine meadow to reach the lake, a shallow body of water, surrounded by high-alpine meadows. That 11,513-foot mountain you see as you climb (ahead and to your right) is Tioga Peak; from the southwest edge of Gardisky Lake it's a short but steep tromp to its windy summit (this will

add a couple extra miles and 1,000 feet of extra elevation gain to your day). White Mountain and Mount Conness are also prominent, both over 12,000 feet.

User Groups: Hikers, horses, dogs, and mountain bikes. No wheelchair facilities.

Permits: No permits are required. Parking and access are free.

Maps: A Yosemite High Country map is available from Tom Harrison Maps. An Inyo National Forest map is available from the U.S. Forest Service. For a topographic map, ask the USGS for Tioga Pass.

Directions: From Merced, drive 70 miles northeast on Highway 140 to Yosemite National Park. Follow the signs toward Yosemite Valley, entering through the Arch Rock entrance station. Continue 4.5 miles to the left turnoff for Highway 120, looping back out of the valley on Big Oak Flat Road. In 9.3 miles at Crane Flat, turn right on Tioga Pass Road and drive 48 miles (you'll exit the park) to the Saddlebag Lake turnoff, on the left, two miles east of Tioga Pass. Turn left and go 1.3 miles to the trailhead parking area, on the west side of the road before you reach Saddlebag Lake. The trail begins across the road.

Contact: Inyo National Forest, Mono Basin Scenic Area Visitors Center, P.O. Box 429, Lee Vining, CA 93541, 760/647-3044, www.fs.usda.gov/inyo.

47 SLATE CREEK TRAIL TO GREEN TREBLE LAKE

4.5 mi / 2.0 hr   🏃2 ⛰️9

in Inyo National Forest just east of Tioga Pass

Map 10.1, page 495

One of the most beautiful and serene campgrounds in the High Sierra, Sawmill Walk-In Camp is accessed by a quarter-mile walk from its parking area. A wide trail continues through and past the campsites into Hall Research Natural Area, a specially protected region of Inyo National Forest that is open to day hikers only (no backpacking). The trail leads one mile to Timberline Station, an old research station built in 1929. From here you can cross Slate Creek and hike another mile to Green Treble Lake at the headwaters of Slate Creek. Where two forks of the creek join, about 0.5 mile beyond Timberline Station, follow the south fork (left) another 0.5 mile to Green Treble Lake. This is a remarkably level hike at 10,000-plus feet in elevation—pristine high country that is only accessible a few months each year. You know you are in a special place when you are here.

User Groups: Hikers, horses, dogs, and mountain bikes. No wheelchair facilities.

Permits: No permits are required. Parking and access are free.

Maps: A Yosemite High Country map is available from Tom Harrison Maps. An Inyo National Forest map is available from the U.S. Forest Service. For a topographic map, ask the USGS for Tioga Pass.

Directions: From Merced, drive 70 miles northeast on Highway 140 to Yosemite National Park. Follow the signs toward Yosemite Valley, entering through the Arch Rock entrance station. Continue 4.5 miles to the left turnoff for Highway 120, looping back out of the valley on Big Oak Flat Road. In 9.3 miles at Crane Flat, turn right on Tioga Pass Road and drive 48 miles (you'll exit the park) to the Saddlebag Lake turnoff, on the left, two miles east of Tioga Pass. Turn left and drive 1.5 miles north on Saddlebag Lake Road to Sawmill Campground's parking area on the left.

Contact: Inyo National Forest, Mono Basin Scenic Area Visitors Center, P.O. Box 429, Lee Vining, CA 93541, 760/647-3044, www.fs.usda.gov/inyo.

48 SADDLEBAG LAKE LOOP
3.6-8.4 mi / 2.0-4.0 hr 🏃2 ⛰9

in Inyo National Forest just east of Tioga Pass

Map 10.1, page 495

Starting from the resort buildings at the south end of 10,087-foot Saddlebag Lake, you can design a wonderfully scenic hiking trip into the 20 Lakes Basin of any length that suits your time and energy. A benefit of hiking here is that you can cut off some miles by taking the boat taxi across the lake, rather than hiking along its lakeshore. A one-way ride on the boat taxi will cut 1.5 miles off your mileage; a round-trip cuts off three miles. Unfortunately, this high-country region is so beautiful, so easy to access, and so close to Yosemite that on summer weekends, it can be as crowded as the most popular trails in the park. A great time to hike here is a few weeks after Labor Day, when the vacation crowds have dispersed.

To hike alongside Saddlebag Lake instead of riding in the boat taxi, follow the trail on either the lake's east or west side. The east side trail is more scenic; the west side trail is shorter. If you just want to make a short 3.6-mile loop, hike out on one trail and back on the other, but be sure to take the short left spur at Saddlebag's northwest edge to Greenstone Lake, which is backed by photogenic North Peak. If you want to hike farther, you can continue past Greenstone Lake to Wasco Lake and then on to deep, stark Steelhead Lake (three miles out if you start on the west side trail). Several more lakes lie beyond, including Shamrock, Helen, and Odell. If you hike the entire loop and visit all six lakes that lie immediately beyond Saddlebag, you'll have an 8.4-mile day (or a 5.4-mile day, if you take the boat taxi round-trip). No matter how far you go, you'll be awed by the incredible high-country scenery—a blend of blue sky, granite, water, and hardy whitebark pines.

User Groups: Hikers and dogs. No horses or mountain bikes. No wheelchair facilities.

Permits: No permits are required. Parking and access are free.

Maps: A Yosemite High Country map is available from Tom Harrison Maps. An Inyo National Forest map is available from the U.S. Forest Service. For a topographic map, ask the USGS for Tioga Pass.

Directions: From Merced, drive 70 miles northeast on Highway 140 to Yosemite

National Park. Follow the signs toward Yosemite Valley, entering through the Arch Rock entrance station. Continue 4.5 miles to the left turnoff for Highway 120, looping back out of the valley on Big Oak Flat Road. In 9.3 miles at Crane Flat, turn right on Tioga Pass Road and drive 48 miles (you'll exit the park) to the Saddlebag Lake turnoff, on the left, two miles east of Tioga Pass. Turn left and drive another 2.7 miles to the trailhead parking area.

Contact: Inyo National Forest, Mono Basin Scenic Area Visitors Center, P.O. Box 429, Lee Vining, CA 93541, 760/647-3044, www.fs.usda.gov/inyo.

49 GIBBS LAKE

5.4 mi / 2.5 hr or 2 days

west of Lee Vining on the northern boundary of the Ansel Adams Wilderness

Map 10.1, page 495

The 2.7-mile hike from Upper Horse Meadow to Gibbs Lake is a great day hike that sees surprisingly few people. Since the trailhead isn't located at a lake or some other attractive setting, nobody gets here by accident. The trail starts at Upper Horse Meadow (elevation 8,000 feet), and climbs up Gibbs Canyon to Gibbs Lake, at 9,530 feet. That's about a 1,500-foot climb, but unfortunately the first stretch goes straight uphill on an old dirt road with nary a switchback. Once you get through that grunt of an ascent, the rest of the route is on a much mellower grade as it travels alongside Gibbs Creek. The trail ends at Gibbs Lake, a lovely glacial cirque that is backed by bare granite and fronted by conifers. Are you feeling ambitious? If you study the lake's back wall for a few minutes, it will soon become obvious that there is another, higher lake in this drainage. If you are sure-footed and have plenty of energy, you can pick out your route and go take a look at that lake. Although Gibbs Lake is pretty, the higher Kidney Lake (10,388 feet) is a stunner. It will take you about 40 minutes

of challenging cross-country scrambling to get from Gibbs to Kidney; you'll gain almost 900 feet in less than a mile. Just pick your route carefully and go slow. Kidney Lake is indeed kidney-shaped, and it is flanked by the Dana Plateau on one side and Mount Gibbs (12,773 feet) on the other.

Special Note: While not required, high-clearance vehicles are a good idea on Forest Road 1N16.

User Groups: Hikers, horses, and dogs. No mountain bikes beyond the wilderness boundary. No wheelchair facilities.

Permits: A free wilderness permit is required for overnight stays and is available from the Mono Basin Scenic Area Visitors Center. Quotas are in effect from May 1 to November 1; for this period, permits are available in advance for a $5 reservation fee per person.

Maps: Mono Lake and Mammoth High Country maps are available from Tom Harrison Maps. An Inyo National Forest or Ansel Adams Wilderness map is available from the U.S. Forest Service. For a topographic map, ask the USGS for Lee Vining.

Directions: From Lee Vining, drive 1.3 miles south on U.S. 395 and turn west on unsigned Forest Road 1N16 (look for the sign indicating Horse Meadow). Drive 3.4 miles past Upper Horse Meadow to the trailhead at the end of the road. A high-clearance vehicle is recommended.

Contact: Inyo National Forest, Mono Basin Scenic Area Visitors Center, P.O. Box 429, Lee Vining, CA 93541, 760/647-3044, www.fs.usda.gov/inyo.

50 MONO LAKE SOUTH TUFA TRAIL

1.0 mi / 0.5 hr

at the southern end of Mono Lake in Mono Lake Tufa State Reserve

Map 10.1, page 495 **BEST (**

The strange and remarkable tufa towers at Mono Lake create one of the most extraordinary landscapes in California. The terrain resembles a moonscape, but a strangely beautiful one. The area is extremely popular with photographers, especially at sunset. This short loop trail is the best way to get a good look at the tufa formations, which are formed when calcium-rich underwater springs are released from the lake bottom and then combine with Mono Lake's saline water, forming calcium carbonate. The trail leads through sagebrush plains to the southern shore of the lake, where the tufas rest like old, untouched earth castles. Some of them poke out of the lake surface; others are high and dry on land. Mono Lake itself is vast (covering 60 square miles) and is estimated to be more than 700,000 years old, making it one of the oldest lakes in North America. The lake's basin has become one of the world's most prolific stopover points for gulls, grebes, plovers, and phalaropes during their annual southbound flights. That's because the alkaline properties of the water create prime habitat for brine shrimp (an ideal food for these birds), and the lake's two large islands provide isolation from predators. Eighty-five percent of the California gull population was born at Mono Lake.

User Groups: Hikers, horses, dogs, and wheelchairs. No mountain bikes.

Permits: No permits are required. A $3 entrance fee is charged per adult. Youth ages 17 and under are free.

Maps: A Mono Lake map is available from Tom Harrison Maps. For topographic maps, ask the USGS for Lee Vining and Mono Mills.

Directions: From Lee Vining, drive five miles south on U.S. 395 and turn east on Highway 120 (signed for Mono Lake South Tufa). Drive 4.7 miles, then turn left and drive one mile on a dirt road to the parking area.

Contact: Mono Lake Tufa State Reserve, 760/647-6331, www.parks.ca.gov; Inyo National Forest, Mono Basin Scenic Area Visitors Center, P.O. Box 429, Lee Vining, CA 93541, 760/647-3044, www.fs.usda.gov/inyo.

51 BLOODY CANYON TRAIL
8.2 mi / 5.0 hr   🏃4 ⛰9

southwest of Lee Vining at the northeastern boundary of the Ansel Adams Wilderness

Map 10.1, page 495

Lower Sardine Lake is a jewel cradled in a high glacial cirque at 9,888 feet, the kind of lake that makes the Ansel Adams Wilderness one of the most treasured places in the world. Beyond the first easy mile, this hike is tough and steep. Much of the trail is a historic Native American trading route, used by the Indians of the Mono Basin to visit the Indians of the Yosemite high country. The first mile to Walker Lake is an easy downhill cruise, dropping 600 feet in elevation. Walker Lake is a popular destination for anglers and has a small private resort on its eastern shore. From the aspen-lined western edge of the lake, you head up Bloody Canyon, climbing nearly 2,000 feet in about three miles. The hike parallels Walker Creek, requiring two stream crossings on the way up to Lower Sardine Lake. For anyone who is either out of shape or not acclimated to the altitude, the climb can be rough going. As you near Lower Sardine Lake, the sight of a beautiful waterfall (the lake's outlet stream) will help to spur you on. When you reach the lake at elevation 9,888 feet, you'll find it is surrounded by rocky cliffs on three sides and provides great views of the Mono Basin to the east. Backpackers can continue hiking up and over Mono Pass and into Yosemite National Park's backcountry, but to do so, they face still more of a climb. Remember that if you are entering the national park, dogs are not allowed.

User Groups: Hikers, horses, and dogs. No mountain bikes beyond the wilderness boundary. No wheelchair facilities.

Permits: A free wilderness permit is required for overnight stays and is available from the Mono Basin Scenic Area Visitors Center. Quotas are in effect from May 1 to November 1; for this period, permits are available in advance for a $5 reservation fee per person.

Maps: Yosemite High Country and Mammoth High Country maps are available from Tom Harrison Maps. An Inyo National Forest or Ansel Adams Wilderness map is available from the U.S. Forest Service. For topographic maps, ask the USGS for Mount Dana and Koip Peak.

Directions: From Lee Vining, drive five miles south on U.S. 395 to the north end of the June Lake Loop (Highway 158). Turn right and drive 1.3 miles on Highway 158, then turn right on a dirt road signed for Parker and Walker Lakes. Drive 0.5 mile to a junction, turn right, then drive 0.3 mile and turn right again, following the signs for Walker Lake. Drive 0.5 mile and turn left on Forest Road 1S23. Drive 2.7 miles to the Walker Lake trailhead.

Contact: Inyo National Forest, Mono Basin Scenic Area Visitors Center, P.O. Box 429, Lee Vining, CA 93541, 760/647-3044, www.fs.usda.gov/inyo.

52 PARKER LAKE TRAIL
3.8 mi / 2.0 hr   🏃2 ⛰️8

in the Ansel Adams Wilderness
west of Grant Lake

Map 10.1, page 495   **BEST (**

This short trail has a whole lot going for it. The beauty of Parker Lake and towering Parker Peak just might knock your boots off—or at least your socks. Although the nearby June Lake Loop gets a lot of vacation traffic, this trailhead is obscure enough that most visitors pass it by. And get this: The 1.9-mile-long trail has an elevation gain of only a little more than 300 feet. Beginning at an elevation of 8,000 feet above Parker Creek, the trail follows the creek upstream on a fairly mellow grade before arriving at Parker Lake, at 8,318 feet. As you ascend, the landscape transitions from sagebrush plains into a mixed forest alongside Parker Creek, complete with quaking aspens and mammoth-sized Jeffrey pines. Look behind you once in a while, and you'll catch great views of Mono Lake. In short order, you will suddenly emerge from the forest onto the lake's shore. Parker Lake is a deep blue beauty backed by 12,861-foot Parker Peak—a great place to have a picnic or just sit and enjoy the scenery. The only downer on this trip is that many of the largest aspen trees have had their trunks carved with initials by idiots. Let's hope they didn't know any better. Please teach your children never, ever to carve into trees.

User Groups: Hikers, dogs, and horses. No mountain bikes. No wheelchair facilities.

Permits: A free wilderness permit is required for overnight stays and is available from the Mono Basin Scenic Area Visitors Center. Quotas are in effect from May 1 to November 1; for this period, permits are available in advance for a $5 reservation fee per person.

Maps: A Mammoth High Country map is available from Tom Harrison Maps. An Inyo National Forest or Ansel Adams Wilderness map is available from the U.S. Forest Service. For topographic maps, ask the USGS for Mount Dana and Koip Peak.

Directions: From Lee Vining, drive five miles south on U.S. 395 to the north end of the June Lake Loop (Highway 158). Turn right and drive 1.3 miles on Highway 158, then turn right on a dirt road signed for Parker and Walker Lakes. Drive 2.4 miles to the Parker Lake trailhead, at the end of the road.

Contact: Inyo National Forest, Mono Basin Scenic Area Visitors Center, P.O. Box 429, Lee Vining, CA 93541, 760/647-3044, www.fs.usda.gov/inyo.

53 RUSH CREEK TRAIL
19.2 mi / 3 days   🏃4 ⛰️10

on the eastern boundary of the Ansel Adams Wilderness west of June Lake

Map 10.1, page 495

Some places will never change, and people are drawn to them because they provide a sense of permanence that can't be found anywhere else. That is how it is at the Rush Creek headwaters.

Created from drops of melting snow near the Sierra crest (at 10,500 feet), this stream runs downhill for miles, rolling into the forest like a swirling, emerald-green fountain. Even a short visit requires a long drive to the trailhead, followed by a demanding backpacking trek. In the process, hikers contend with a 10-mile climb out, ice-cold stream crossings, and the possibility of afternoon thunderstorms, in which lightning bolts and thunderclaps rattle off the canyon rims.

The trailhead lies near the pack station at Silver Lake (elevation 7,215 feet). After departing Silver Lake, follow the trail as it climbs above the June Lake Loop and soon starts to parallel Lower Rush Creek. You'll cross over an old tramway system that was used for the hydroelectric projects found in this watershed. Near the dam at Agnew Lake, you reach a trail junction, 2.2 miles from your start. The left fork heads up to Agnew Pass, but continue straight and in one more mile you arrive at beautiful Gem Lake (9,058 feet) and then Waugh Lake (9,442 feet), at the seven-mile point. Many visitors never venture farther than these lakes, simply stopping to camp, swim, or fish. But upstream of Waugh Lake is where you find the Rush Creek headwaters, along with the flawless symmetry of the untouched high country. Getting there requires a total climb of 3,300 feet over the course of 9.6 miles, but it is one of the prettiest streams anywhere and is well worth the effort.

Note that because this trail begins near the Silver Lake pack station, it is heavily used by horses. On some days, the amount of horse "evidence" on this trail can be a real downer, especially in the first few miles.

User Groups: Hikers, dogs, and horses. No mountain bikes. No wheelchair facilities.

Permits: A free wilderness permit is required for overnight stays and is available from the Mono Basin Scenic Area Visitors Center. Quotas are in effect from May 1 to November 1; for this period, permits are available in advance for a $5 reservation fee per person.

Maps: A Mammoth High Country map is available from Tom Harrison Maps. An Inyo National Forest or Ansel Adams Wilderness map is available from the U.S. Forest Service. For topographic maps, ask the USGS for June Lake and Koip Peak.

Directions: From Lee Vining, drive about 11 miles south on U.S. 395 to June Lake Junction. Turn right on Highway 158/June Lake Road and drive 7.2 miles to the Rush Creek trailhead, between Silver Lake Resort and the pack station.

Contact: Inyo National Forest, Mono Basin Scenic Area Visitors Center, P.O. Box 429, Lee Vining, CA 93541, 760/647-3044, www.fs.usda.gov/inyo.

54 YOST LAKE
4.8-9.4 mi / 2.5 hr-1 day

in Inyo National Forest near June Lake

Map 10.1, page 495

Yost Lake is a small glacial lake hidden at 9,000 feet on the June Mountain slopes. Many people visit the June Lake area for years without even knowing Yost exists. But it is up here, tucked away and accessible only to those willing to hike. From the trailhead (7,800 feet) at June Lake, Yost Meadows Trail rises very steeply in the first mile, climbing 800 feet—a real butt-kicker for many. That discourages many from going farther—after all, it is 4.7 miles to the lake. But after that first grunt of a climb, the trail gets much easier, contouring across the mountain slopes. It rises gradually to the headwaters of Yost Creek and then drops into the small basin that guards the lake.

A shorter option is to begin at the Yost Creek/Fern Lake trailhead, making it a much shorter, 4.8-mile round-trip. It is just as pretty, but it has a more difficult grade and can be slippery for those not wearing heavy, firm-gripping hiking boots. The trailhead is located three miles west of the town of June Lake, on the west (left) side of June Lake Road, past the ski resort.

User Groups: Hikers, dogs, horses, and mountain bikes. No wheelchair facilities.

Permits: No permits are required. Parking and access are free.

Maps: A Mammoth High Country map is available from Tom Harrison Maps. An Inyo National Forest or Ansel Adams Wilderness map is available from the U.S. Forest Service. For topographic maps, ask the USGS for June Lake and Mammoth Mountain.

Directions: From Lee Vining, drive about 11 miles south on U.S. 395 to June Lake Junction. Go right on Highway 158/June Lake Road and drive two miles to the town of June Lake. The trailhead is on the west (left), across the road from the fire station.

Contact: Inyo National Forest, Mono Basin Scenic Area Visitors Center, P.O. Box 429, Lee Vining, CA 93541, 760/647-3044, www.fs.usda.gov/inyo.

55 INYO CRATERS
0.5 mi / 0.5 hr

in Inyo National Forest north of Mammoth Lakes

Map 10.1, page 495

A geologic phenomenon, the Inyo Craters make a great destination for an easy day hike in the Mammoth Lakes area. They are part of a chain of craters and other volcanic formations that reaches from Mammoth Lake to Mono Lake. The craters—evidence of Mammoth's fiery past—are the remains of a volcanic explosion of steam that occurred a mere 600 years ago. At that time, the mountain was a smoldering volcano. Magma pushed up into the water table, heated the water, and kaboom! The result was a phreatic blast that created these craters. The hike to see them is a short, gentle climb, but the elevation sucks the air out of many visitors who have just arrived in Mammoth. The trail leads through a lovely open forest of red fir and Jeffrey pine. In each of the two Inyo Craters a small pond fills with melted snow

each spring, and at least some water remains throughout the summer.

User Groups: Hikers, horses, and dogs. No mountain bikes. No wheelchair facilities.

Permits: No permits are required. Parking and access are free.

Maps: A Mammoth High Country map is available from Tom Harrison Maps. An Inyo National Forest map is available from the U.S. Forest Service. For a topographic map, ask the USGS for Mammoth Mountain.

Directions: From the Mammoth Lakes junction on U.S. 395, turn west on Highway 203 and drive four miles through the town of Mammoth Lakes to the junction of Minaret Road/Highway 203 and Lake Mary Road. Turn right on Minaret Road and drive one mile. At the sign for Mammoth Lakes Scenic Loop, turn right and drive 2.7 miles. Turn left at the sign for Inyo Craters (the road turns to dirt) and drive 1.3 more miles to the Inyo Craters parking lot.

Contact: Inyo National Forest, Mammoth Lakes Welcome Center, P.O. Box 148, Mammoth Lakes, CA 93546, 760/924-5500, www.fs.usda.gov/inyo.

56 BARRETT AND TJ LAKES
1.0 mi / 0.5 hr

at Lake George in Mammoth Lakes

Map 10.1, page 495

Campers at Lake George and Mammoth Lakes visitors who just want a short and easy day hike, will be pleased to find that this no-sweat trail provides access to hidden Barrett and TJ Lakes. The trail starts on the northeast shore of Lake George (which in itself is a gorgeous spot), follows the lakeshore for about 100 yards, then climbs alongside a small stream to little Barrett Lake. The tiny lake is framed by Red Mountain in the background. Hey, this was so easy, you might as well continue another 0.25 mile to TJ Lake, the more scenic of the two lakes. The distinctive granite fin of Crystal Crag (10,377 feet) towers above TJ

Lake's basin, adding drama to the scene. In addition to the pretty but popular lakes, this trail shows off some lovely mountain meadows, gilded with colorful penstemen, shooting stars, and paintbrush in midsummer.

User Groups: Hikers and horses. No mountain bikes. No wheelchair facilities.

Permits: No permits are required. Parking and access are free.

Maps: A Mammoth High Country map is available from Tom Harrison Maps. An Inyo National Forest map is available from the U.S. Forest Service. For a topographic map, ask the USGS for Crystal Crag.

Directions: From the Mammoth Lakes junction on U.S. 395, turn west on Highway 203 and drive four miles through the town of Mammoth Lakes to the junction of Minaret Road/Highway 203 and Lake Mary Road. Continue straight on Lake Mary Road and drive four miles to a junction for Lake George. Turn left here, drive 0.3 mile, then turn right and drive another 0.4 mile to Lake George. The trailhead is located near the campground.

Contact: Inyo National Forest, Mammoth Lakes Welcome Center, P.O. Box 148, Mammoth Lakes, CA 93546, 760/924-5500, www.fs.usda.gov/inyo.

57 CRYSTAL LAKE
3.8 mi / 2.0 hr

at Lake George in Mammoth Lakes

Map 10.1, page 495

If you think Lake George is gorgeous, wait until you see Crystal Lake, located southwest of Lake George in a bowl scoured by glaciers and tucked into a hollow below 10,377-foot Crystal Crag. The trail to reach it has a 700-foot elevation gain and is pleasantly shaded by a hearty hemlock, pine, and fir forest. The path begins near the cabins at Woods Lodge but rises quickly above them. Many hikers huff and puff as they climb this ridge, but the view of the Mammoth Lakes Basin makes it

all worthwhile. This high ridge gives you a bird's-eye look at the basin's four major lakes: George, Mary, Mamie, and Twin. At a junction at one mile, go left and descend to Crystal Lake. The lake is a true jewel, highlighted by permanent snowfields that line its granite backdrop. You aren't likely to find much solitude here, since the lake is so easy to reach, but the scenery more than makes up for it.

If you want to turn this into a longer hike, you can take the other trail at the fork and head for Mammoth Crest, at 10,400 feet, two miles farther. The trail gains another 700 feet as it leaves the forest and enters a stark, volcanic landscape peppered with whitebark pines. The expansive view from the high point on the crest includes the Mammoth Lakes Basin, the San Joaquin River, the Minarets and the Ritter Range, and Mammoth Mountain. If this hike hasn't taken your breath away, the vista will.

User Groups: Hikers, horses, and dogs. Mountain bikes are not advised. No wheelchair facilities.

Permits: No permits are required. Parking and access are free.

Maps: A Mammoth High Country map is available from Tom Harrison Maps. An Inyo National Forest map is available from the U.S. Forest Service. For a topographic map, ask the USGS for Crystal Crag.

Directions: From the Mammoth Lakes junction on U.S. 395, turn west on Highway 203 and drive four miles through the town of Mammoth Lakes to the junction of Minaret Road/Highway 203 and Lake Mary Road. Continue straight on Lake Mary Road and drive four miles to a junction for Lake George. Turn left, drive 0.3 mile, then turn right and drive another 0.4 mile to Lake George. The trailhead is on the right, near some cabins.

Contact: Inyo National Forest, Mammoth Lakes Welcome Center, P.O. Box 148, Mammoth Lakes, CA 93546, 760/924-5500, www.fs.usda.gov/inyo.

58 EMERALD LAKE AND SKY MEADOWS

4.0 mi / 2.0 hr

at Lake Mary in Mammoth Lakes

Map 10.1, page 495

This is one of the Eastern Sierra's premier wild-flower trails, and it's easy enough for children to hike. The trail starts just south of Lake Mary, at the end of the Coldwater Campground road. The hike is short and direct, climbing straight to Emerald Lake on an easy grade. Picnickers are often found seated among the rocks by the water's edge, although by midsummer, the tiny lake dwindles to something that more closely resembles a pond. No matter, the lake is not the star of the show here—the flowers are. The trail skirts the east shore of Emerald Lake and continues along its inlet stream. Three brief climbs lead you past Gentian Meadow to the southeast edge of Sky Meadows, which is filled with wildflowers throughout the summer. Beyond the meadows, permanent snow fields decorate the granite cliffs of Mammoth Crest. Among the wide variety of flower species to be seen and admired, one standout is the tall orange tiger lilies, a flower that is showy enough to be in a florist's shop.

User Groups: Hikers, dogs, and horses. No mountain bikes allowed past the wilderness boundary. No wheelchair facilities.

Permits: No day permits are required. Parking and access are free.

Maps: A Mammoth High Country map is available from Tom Harrison Maps. An Inyo National Forest map is available from the U.S. Forest Service. For a topographic map, ask the USGS for Crystal Crag.

Directions: From the Mammoth Lakes junction on U.S. 395, turn west on Highway 203 and drive four miles through the town of Mammoth Lakes to the junction of Minaret Road/Highway 203 and Lake Mary Road. Continue straight on Lake Mary Road and drive 3.5 miles to a fork just before Lake Mary; turn left and drive 0.6 mile to the Coldwater Campground turnoff, on the left. Turn left

and drive 0.5 mile through the camp to the trailhead, at the first parking lot.

Contact: Inyo National Forest, Mammoth Lakes Welcome Center, P.O. Box 148, Mammoth Lakes, CA 93546, 760/924-5500, www.fs.usda.gov/inyo.

59 DUCK LAKE

10.0 mi / 6.0 hr or 2 days

in the John Muir Wilderness near Mammoth Lakes

Map 10.1, page 495

How far you hike on Duck Pass Trail is up to you, but if it were up to us, we'd hike at least as far as five miles to Duck Lake, elevation 10,450 feet. Sure, lots of people stop at the other lakes this trail passes along the way—Arrowhead Lake at 1.3 miles out, Skelton Lake at two miles, or Barney Lake at three miles—and these make fine destinations. But you might as well see them all and then keep climbing through Duck Pass to much larger Duck Lake, at five miles. The pass is a 1,600-foot climb from the trailhead at Coldwater Campground. Just beyond the pass, the trail drops 300 feet to reach Duck Lake, one of the largest natural lakes in the Eastern Sierra. Most of the climbing is in the stretch from Barney Lake to the pass, as the trail switchbacks up a talus-covered slope. Day hikers can make their way from Duck Lake on a faint path to Pika Lake, which is visible in the distance about a half-mile away. Backpackers can continue on to Purple Lake (at 7.5 miles) and Lake Virginia (at nine miles). The only downer on this trail is the presence of horses and pack mules, which can make the trail quite dusty by late summer. There are usually tons of people on the trail, too, but with this kind of scenery, everybody is in a good mood.

User Groups: Hikers, dogs, and horses. No mountain bikes allowed past the wilderness boundary. No wheelchair facilities.

Permits: A free wilderness permit is required for overnight stays and is available from the

Mammoth Lakes Welcome Center. Quotas are in effect from May 1 to November 1; for this period, permits are available in advance for a $5 reservation fee per person.

Maps: A Mammoth High Country map is available from Tom Harrison Maps. An Inyo National Forest or John Muir Wilderness map is available from the U.S. Forest Service. For a topographic map, ask the USGS for Crystal Crag.

Directions: From the Mammoth Lakes junction on U.S. 395, turn west on Highway 203 and drive four miles, through the town of Mammoth Lakes, to the junction of Minaret Road/Highway 203 and Lake Mary Road. Continue straight on Lake Mary Road and drive 3.5 miles to a fork just before Lake Mary; turn left and drive 0.6 mile to the Coldwater Campground turnoff, on the left. Turn left and drive 0.8 mile through the camp to the Duck Pass trailhead at the farthest parking lot.

Contact: Inyo National Forest, Mammoth Lakes Welcome Center, P.O. Box 148, Mammoth Lakes, CA 93546, 760/924-5500, www.fs.usda.gov/inyo.

60 VALENTINE LAKE TRAIL
11.2 mi / 6.0 hr or 2 days 🏃3 ⛰9

in the John Muir Wilderness
south of Mammoth Lakes

Map 10.1, page 495

The Mammoth Lakes area is one of the Eastern Sierra's star attractions, yet nearby Valentine Lake is perhaps overlooked because the trailhead (at 7,600 feet) is not found at one of the lakes in the Mammoth Lakes Basin. Or perhaps it's because the climb required to get there is so steep. Regardless of the reason, a morning's hike—rising some 1,900 feet over 5.6 miles, but with most of the climb compressed into two miles—gets you to the lake, which sits at 9,698 feet.

Some say the lake is shaped like a teardrop, but we think it looks more like a drop of sweat. The hike starts out with a very steep climb

(including 0.5 mile of sandy switchbacks in a dry pine forest) and doesn't level out for the first two miles. You'll pass a side trail to the Sherwin Lakes at 2.9 miles (a fine destination for those who have had enough, or those who just want to catch fish). Continue uphill, much more gently now, finally meeting up with Valentine Lake's outlet stream. Valentine Lake has rocky cliffs ringing its edges, making it difficult to explore its shoreline. Pick a spot and toss in a line; the lake has plentiful brook trout.

User Groups: Hikers, dogs, and horses. No mountain bikes. No wheelchair facilities.

Permits: A free wilderness permit is required for overnight stays and is available from the Mammoth Lakes Welcome Center. Quotas are in effect from May 1 to November 1; for this period, permits are available in advance for a $5 reservation fee per person.

Maps: A Mammoth High Country map is available from Tom Harrison Maps. An Inyo National Forest or John Muir Wilderness map is available from the U.S. Forest Service. For a topographic map, ask the USGS for Crystal Crag.

Directions: From the Mammoth Lakes junction on U.S. 395, turn west on Highway 203 and drive 2.6 miles to Old Mammoth Road. Turn left and drive 0.8 mile to Sherwin Creek Road. Turn left and drive 2.9 miles to the signed trailhead on the right for Valentine Lake (past the Sherwin Creek Campground and YMCA camp).

Contact: Inyo National Forest, Mammoth Lakes Welcome Center, P.O. Box 148, Mammoth Lakes, CA 93546, 760/924-5500, www.fs.usda.gov/inyo.

61 RED CONES LOOP
6.7 mi / 4.0 hr 🏃3 ⛰7

at Horseshoe Lake in Mammoth Lakes

Map 10.1, page 495

Horseshoe Lake, elevation 8,900 feet, lies at the end of the Mammoth Lakes road and has an excellent trailhead that makes for a great day hike. Don't be put off by the dead trees and the barren look of the place. A relatively small area by the lake has been affected by carbon-dioxide gas venting up through the soil—the result of seismic activity. You get away from this strange-looking forest quickly. Set out from the northwest side of the lake, ascend the slope, and take the left fork for McLeod Lake. In just under two miles, you'll reach the start of the loop. Go right to reach Crater Meadow, a beautiful little spot set just below Red Cones, and then circle around to Upper Crater Meadow. Either meadow is a fine destination for a picnic lunch in peace. The contrast is striking: Just a short distance below, there are typically many people at Twin Lakes, Lake Mary, Lake Mamie, and Lake George, yet you are separated from them by Mammoth Pass. You will be surprised at how relatively few people take this loop hike, and glad that you made the choice to do so.

User Groups: Hikers, dogs, and horses. No mountain bikes. No wheelchair facilities.

Permits: No permits are required. Parking and access are free.

Maps: A Mammoth High Country map is available from Tom Harrison Maps. An Inyo National Forest map is available from the U.S. Forest Service. For a topographic map, ask the USGS for Crystal Crag.

Directions: From the Mammoth Lakes junction on U.S. 395, turn west on Highway 203 and drive four miles through the town of Mammoth Lakes to the junction of Minaret Road/Highway 203 and Lake Mary Road. Continue straight on Lake Mary Road and drive 4.8 miles to the road's end, at Horseshoe Lake. The trailhead is on the northwest side of the lake, signed for Mammoth Pass.

Contact: Inyo National Forest, Mammoth Lakes Welcome Center, P.O. Box 148, Mammoth Lakes, CA 93546, 760/924-5500, www.fs.usda.gov/inyo.

62 DEVILS POSTPILE AND RAINBOW FALLS

2.0-5.0 mi / 1.0-2.0 hr 🥾2 ⛰️10

in Devils Postpile National Monument west of Mammoth Lakes

Map 10.1, page 495   **BEST (**

The first time you lay eyes on 101-foot Rainbow Falls, the tall, wide, and forceful waterfall comes as an awesome surprise. Most first-time visitors see it before or after a trip to the Devils Postpile, a fascinating collection of volcanic rock columns and rubble left from a lava flow nearly 100,000 years ago. It's like nothing you've seen anywhere else. You can hike to Rainbow Falls two ways, either from the ranger station at Devils Postpile National Monument or from the Rainbow Falls trailhead, near Reds Meadow Resort. Either way, this is one of the best short hikes in California.

Your best bet is to start at the ranger station, then pass by the Devils Postpile lava columns in only 0.5 mile. Stop and gape at this geologic wonder, and perhaps take the short but steep side trip to the top of the columns, then continue downhill to Rainbow Falls, at 2.5 miles. (If you start at the trailhead by Reds Meadow, your trip to Rainbow Falls is only one mile, but you'll miss out on the Postpile.)

In order to see the rainbow that gives the waterfall its name, you must show up in late morning or at midday. The rainbow is the result of a prism effect from sun's rays refracting through the falling water. Two overlook areas across from the waterfall's brink give you an excellent view, but you can hike down a series of stairs to the falls' base for an even better vantage point. If you're inspired, you can travel another 0.5 mile on the trail to find a smaller waterfall on the San Joaquin River, called Lower Falls.

User Groups: Hikers and horses. No mountain bikes. Dogs must be leashed in the national monument. No wheelchair facilities.

Permits: Each person entering the Devils Postpile/Reds Meadow area must purchase an access pass. (See *Access Note,* below.) The fee is $7 per adult and $4 for children ages 3 to 16. Children ages 2 and under are free. Passes may be purchased at the Mammoth Mountain Adventure Center at Mammoth Ski Area.

Maps: A Devils Postpile map is available from Tom Harrison Maps. An Inyo National Forest map is available from the U.S. Forest Service. For a topographic map, ask the USGS for Mammoth Mountain.

Directions: From the Mammoth Lakes junction on U.S. 395, turn west on Highway 203 and drive four miles through the town of Mammoth Lakes to Minaret Road (still Highway 203). Turn right and drive 4.5 miles to the shuttle bus terminal (adjacent to the Mammoth Mountain Ski Area). Purchase an access pass and board a shuttle bus here. Disembark at the Devils Postpile Ranger Station or Rainbow Falls trailhead, which is just before Reds Meadow Resort.

Access Note: Visitors arriving between 7 A.M. and 7 P.M. are required to ride a shuttle bus (free with purchase of an access pass) from Mammoth Mountain Ski Area. If you are camping in the Devils Postpile area, or if you arrive before 7 A.M., you are permitted to drive your own car instead of taking the shuttle, but you must pay an entrance fee of $10 per vehicle.

Contact: Inyo National Forest, Mammoth Lakes Welcome Center, P.O. Box 148, Mammoth Lakes, CA 93546, 760/924-5500, www.fs.usda.gov/inyo; Devils Postpile National Monument, P.O. Box 3999, Mammoth Lakes, CA 93546, 760/934-2289 (summer only), www.nps.gov/depo.

63 MINARET LAKE
16.0 mi / 2 days

in the Ansel Adams Wilderness
west of Mammoth Lakes

Map 10.1, page 495

Minaret Lake is a real prize, set just below the awesome glacial-carved Ritter Range, at 9,793 feet. Reaching it requires an eight-mile hike with a 2,400-foot elevation gain, and every step is completely worth it. From the trailhead at Devils Postpile Ranger Station, you hike south to access a bridge across the San Joaquin River, then head northward two miles on John Muir Trail. (You can also start from Upper Soda Spring Campground and hike south on the Pacific Crest Trail, then turn north on the John Muir Trail. The distance is about the same.) After passing tiny Johnston Lake, you reach the junction with Minaret Lake Trail. Turn left and follow Minaret Creek. The trail rises with the creek and in the last mile climbs steeply above tree line before skirting the Minaret Lake outlet and tracing the line of the north shore. The granite peaks that form the lake's backdrop are Clyde and Ken Minaret. Good campsites are found near Minaret Lake's rocky shore. If you want to do some exploring, Cecile Lake (at 10,239 feet) can be reached via a cross-country route to the northwest of the lake.

User Groups: Hikers, dogs, and horses. Dogs must be leashed in national monument. No mountain bikes. No wheelchair facilities.

Permits: Each person entering the Devils Postpile/Reds Meadow area must purchase an access pass. (See *Access Note,* below.) The fee is $7 per adult and $4 for children ages 3–16. Children ages 2 and under are free. Passes may be purchased at the Mammoth Mountain Adventure Center at Mammoth Ski Area.

A free wilderness permit is required for overnight stays and is available from the Mammoth Lakes Welcome Center. Quotas are in effect from May 1 to November 1; for this period, permits are available in advance for a $5 reservation fee per person.

Maps: A Devils Postpile map is available from Tom Harrison Maps. An Inyo National Forest or Ansel Adams Wilderness map is available from the U.S. Forest Service. For topographic maps, ask the USGS for Mammoth Mountain and Mount Ritter.

Directions: From the Mammoth Lakes junction on U.S. 395, turn west on Highway 203 and drive four miles through the town of Mammoth Lakes to Minaret Road (still Highway 203). Turn right and drive 4.5 miles to the shuttle bus terminal (adjacent to the Mammoth Mountain Ski Area). Purchase an access pass and board a shuttle bus here. Disembark at the Devils Postpile Ranger Station.

Access Note: Visitors arriving between 7 A.M. and 7 P.M. are required to ride a shuttle bus (free with purchase of an access pass) from Mammoth Mountain Ski Area. If you are camping in the Devils Postpile area, or if you arrive before 7 A.M., you are permitted to drive your own car instead of taking the shuttle, but you must pay an entrance fee of $10 per vehicle.

Contact: Inyo National Forest, Mammoth Lakes Welcome Center, P.O. Box 148, Mammoth Lakes, CA 93546, 760/924-5500, www.fs.usda.gov/inyo; Devils Postpile National Monument, P.O. Box 3999, Mammoth Lakes, CA 93546, 760/934-2289 (summer only), www.nps.gov/depo.

64 FERN LAKE LOOP

10.0-16.0 mi / 1-2 days

in the Ansel Adams Wilderness
west of Mammoth Lakes

Map 10.1, page 495

Fern Lake can be the destination on an ambitious day hike from Devils Postpile, or the start of a great 15-mile backpacking loop. Either way, this is an excellent hike that has become very popular. Starting from the ranger station at Devils Postpile, you head south to access the bridge across the San Joaquin River, then follow the King Creek Trail. About two miles in, you face a crossing of King Creek that can be tricky early in the summer. Exercise some caution. Then climb through the pine forest to reach a junction, at 4.9 miles. Follow the spur to Fern Lake, elevation 8,800 feet, where many good campsites are found. The lake is set in a small rock bowl at tree line, below Iron Mountain, in the Minarets.

Day hikers will often while away a few hours here and then retrace their steps for a 10-mile round-trip.

Those continuing onward will find the trail pokes in and out of sparse forest for the next two miles to Becks Cabin. From here, a one-mile side trip leads to Superior Lake (7.5 miles from your start, and at 9,400 feet), another excellent spot for an overnight. A faint path leads 0.7 mile from Superior Lake to the two Beck Lakes (at 9,800 feet), which are surrounded by high granite ridges. A visit to Beck Lakes—set in a glacial-formed pocket below the Minarets and amid celestial mountain scenery—is highly recommended. When you return to the loop at Becks Cabin, you have a 4.8-mile descent to reach John Muir Trail, where you turn right and head back to the bridge and the ranger station.

User Groups: Hikers, dogs, and horses. Dogs must be leashed in national monument. No mountain bikes. No wheelchair facilities.

Permits: Each person entering the Devils Postpile/Reds Meadow area must purchase an access pass. (See *Access Note,* below.) The fee is $7 per adult and $4 for children ages 3 to 16. Children ages 2 and under are free. Passes may be purchased at the Mammoth Mountain Adventure Center at Mammoth Ski Area.

A free wilderness permit is required for overnight stays and is available from the Mammoth Lakes Welcome Center. Quotas are in effect from May 1 to November 1; for this period, permits are available in advance for a $5 reservation fee per person.

Maps: A Devils Postpile map is available from Tom Harrison Maps. An Inyo National Forest or Ansel Adams Wilderness map is available from the U.S. Forest Service. For topographic maps, ask the USGS for Mammoth Mountain and Mount Ritter.

Directions: From the Mammoth Lakes junction on U.S. 395, turn west on Highway 203 and drive four miles through the town of Mammoth Lakes to Minaret Road (still Highway 203). Turn right and drive 4.5 miles to the shuttle bus terminal (adjacent to the

Mammoth Mountain Ski Area). Purchase an access pass and board a shuttle bus here. Disembark at the Devils Postpile Ranger Station.

Access Note: Visitors arriving between 7 A.M. and 7 P.M. are required to ride a shuttle bus (free with purchase of an access pass) from Mammoth Mountain Ski Area. If you are camping in the Devils Postpile area, or if you arrive before 7 A.M., you are permitted to drive your own car instead of taking the shuttle, but you must pay an entrance fee of $10 per vehicle.

Contact: Inyo National Forest, Mammoth Lakes Welcome Center, P.O. Box 148, Mammoth Lakes, CA 93546, 760/924-5500, www.fs.usda.gov/inyo; Devils Postpile National Monument, P.O. Box 3999, Mammoth Lakes, CA 93546, 760/934-2289 (summer only), www.nps.gov/depo.

65 SHADOW LAKE
7.6 mi / 4.0 hr or 2 days

**in the Ansel Adams Wilderness
west of Mammoth Lakes**

Map 10.1, page 495

Shadow Lake is one of the most popular destinations in the Devils Postpile region simply because of its sheer beauty. The only unpleasant part of this hike is making your way through the busy trailhead parking lots at Agnew Meadows. Once that's accomplished and you're on the trail, all is bliss, as long as you're in good condition and ready for a sustained climb. (Campers at Agnew Meadows can cut a half mile off this trip each way by starting from the trail at camp, not from the trailhead parking lot.) The route starts out quite mellow as it wanders through the wildflowers at Agnew Meadows. It then follows the River Trail along the middle fork of the San Joaquin River. Just beyond shallow Olaine Lake (at two miles) lies a junction, where you go left for Shadow Lake. Cross a bridge and prepare to climb. A long series of steep,

shadeless switchbacks ensues as you climb alongside a narrow creek gorge. Fortunately the view looking down the San Joaquin River Canyon becomes ever more grand as you rise upward. At last you reach the waterfall on Shadow Lake's outlet stream and then climb the final stretch to the lake. Its backdrop is like something you've seen on a million Sierra postcards, with the Minarets and Mounts Ritter and Banner towering above the lake. Day hikers have the best deal here; they can just pick a spot along the 8,737-foot lakeshore and drink in the view. Camping is not permitted at Shadow Lake, so backpackers must continue on to smaller Rosalie Lake (much more climbing over the next two miles). Ediza Lake is also a popular overnight option, 2.5 miles from Shadow Lake.

User Groups: Hikers, dogs, and horses. No mountain bikes. No wheelchair facilities.

Permits: Each person entering the Devils Postpile/Reds Meadow area must purchase an access pass. (See *Access Note*, below.) The fee is $7 per adult and $4 for children ages 3–16. Children ages 2 and under are free. Passes may be purchased at the Mammoth Mountain Adventure Center at Mammoth Ski Area.

A free wilderness permit is required for overnight stays and is available from the Mammoth Lakes Welcome Center. Quotas are in effect from May 1 to November 1; for this period, permits are available in advance for a $5 reservation fee per person.

Maps: A Devils Postpile map is available from Tom Harrison Maps. An Inyo National Forest or Ansel Adams Wilderness map is available from the U.S. Forest Service. For topographic maps, ask the USGS for Crystal Crag and Cattle Mountain.

Directions: From the Mammoth Lakes junction on U.S. 395, turn west on Highway 203 and drive four miles through the town of Mammoth Lakes to Minaret Road (still Highway 203). Turn right and drive 4.5 miles to the shuttle bus terminal (adjacent to the Mammoth Mountain Ski Area). Purchase an access pass and board a shuttle bus here.

Disembark at the Agnew Meadows Campground. Walk through the trailhead parking lots to the Shadow Lake trailhead.

Access Note: Visitors arriving between 7 A.M. and 7 P.M. are required to ride a shuttle bus (free with purchase of an access pass) from Mammoth Mountain Ski Area. If you are camping in the Devils Postpile area, or if you arrive before 7 A.M., you are permitted to drive your own car instead of taking the shuttle, but you must pay an entrance fee of $10 per vehicle.

Contact: Inyo National Forest, Mammoth Lakes Welcome Center, P.O. Box 148, Mammoth Lakes, CA 93546, 760/924-5500, www.fs.usda.gov/inyo; Devils Postpile National Monument, P.O. Box 3999, Mammoth Lakes, CA 93546, 760/934-2289 (summer only), www.nps.gov/depo.

66 AGNEW MEADOWS TO TUOLUMNE MEADOWS (JMT/PCT)

28.0 mi one-way / 3 days 🏃5 ⛰10

from the Agnew Meadows trailhead north to the trailhead parking area at Tuolumne Meadows on Highway 120

Map 10.1, page 495

This section of the JMT/PCT features breathtaking views of the Minarets, many glacial-cut lakes, and the wondrous descent into Yosemite. The PCT starts here by leaving Reds Meadow, an excellent place to arrange a food drop and a chance to eat your first cheeseburger in weeks. The trail heads out into the most beautiful section of Inyo National Forest and the Ansel Adams Wilderness. All in a row, the PCT passes Rosalie, Shadow, Garnet, and Thousand Island Lakes. If they look like Ansel Adams' pictures in real life, it's because they are. The background setting of Banner and Ritter Peaks is among the most spectacular anywhere. From Thousand Island Lake, the PCT makes a fair climb over Island Pass (10,200 feet), then drops down into the headwaters of Rush

Creek, where emerald green flows swirl over boulders, pouring like a wilderness fountain. From here, it's a decent, steady ascent back above tree line to Donohue Pass (11,056 feet), the southern wilderness border of Yosemite National Park. It was here, while munching a trail lunch, that we saw a huge landslide on the westward canyon wall. A massive amount of rock material fell in just a few seconds—an unforgettable show of natural forces. The trail becomes quite blocky at Donohue Pass, and you rock hop your way down to the headwaters of Lyell Fork, a pretzel-like stream that meanders through the meadows. It pours all the way to Tuolumne Meadows, and following it, the trail is nearly flat for more than four miles. At Tuolumne Meadows you can resupply—and get another cheeseburger.

To continue north on the JMT, see the *Tuolumne Meadows to Yosemite Valley (JMT)* hike in this chapter. If you are walking this trail in reverse, see the *Lake Thomas Edison to Agnew Meadows (JMT/PCT)* hike in the *Sequoia and Kings Canyon* chapter.

User Groups: Hikers and horses. No dogs or mountain bikes. No wheelchair facilities.

Permits: A wilderness permit is required for traveling through various wilderness and special-use areas the trail traverses. Contact either the Inyo National Forest or Yosemite National Park for a permit that is good for the length of your trip.

Maps: A John Muir Trail Map Pack is available from Tom Harrison Maps. An Inyo National Forest map is available from the U.S. Forest Service. For topographic maps, ask the USGS for Vogelsang Peak, Mount Ritter, Koip Peak, and Mammoth Mountain.

Directions: From Lee Vining, drive 26 miles south on Highway 395 to Mammoth Junction. Turn west on Highway 203/Minaret Summit Road to the town of Mammoth Lakes and drive 14 miles to the Agnew Meadows Campground and the trailhead parking area.

Contact: Yosemite National Park, P.O. Box 577, Yosemite, CA 95389, 209/372-0200, www.nps.gov/yose; Inyo National Forest,

Mono Basin Scenic Area Visitors Center, P.O. Box 429, Lee Vining, CA 93541, 760/647-3044, www.fs.usda.gov/inyo.

67 HITE COVE TRAIL
9.0 mi / 5.0 hr 👣2 ⛰10

on the South Fork Merced River
in Sierra National Forest

Map 10.1, page 495   **BEST ❰**

Considered by many to be the premier Sierra spring wildflower trail, Hite Cove Trail offers hikers a look at 60 flower varieties, including goldfields, lupine, poppies, brodaiea, monkeyflower, shooting stars, fiesta flowers, fairy lanterns, baby blue eyes, and Indian pinks. To see them, visit from late February to early May, before the show is over. Conveniently, this is usually the only time of the year when the trail is open, because the first 0.75 mile of trail is on private property, and access is restricted during fire season.

You start hiking on a paved driveway, but the asphalt only lasts for a few yards, then the trail transitions to a narrow single track that hugs the side of the steep canyon wall, high above the South Fork Merced River. Even if you aren't terribly interested in wildflowers, the river and canyon views are tremendous. About one mile out is an obvious rock outcrop, a few feet off the trail, where you can sit and enjoy the rushing river below. Another 0.5 mile farther, the trail drops down right alongside the river, and where the current mellows out, there are many tempting swimming holes. Those wishing to turn this hike into an overnight trip can camp at Hite Cove, the site of the 1879 Hite Cove Hotel. A campfire permit is required for overnight stays. From there, you can continue hiking to Devils Gulch, 2.5 miles farther. To do so, however, requires crossing the South Fork Merced River at Hite Cove, a difficult feat early in the year.

Special Note: Call the Bass Lake Ranger Station or visit the Sierra National Forest website to make sure this trail is open before

planning your trip. Access to the trail is restricted during fire season.

User Groups: Hikers, dogs, and horses. No mountain bikes. No wheelchair facilities.

Permits: No permits are required. Parking and access are free.

Maps: A Sierra National Forest map is available from the U.S. Forest Service. For a topographic map, ask the USGS for El Portal.

Directions: From Mariposa, drive 22 miles east on Highway 140 to Savage's Trading Post. The parking area is on the north side of the road, but the trail begins on the south side, near Savage's Trading Post.

Contact: Sierra National Forest, Bass Lake Ranger Station, 57003 Road 225, North Fork, CA 93643, 559/877-2218, www.fs.fed.us/r5/sierra.

68 UPPER YOSEMITE FALL
7.4 mi / 5.0 hr 👣4 ⛰10

in Yosemite Valley

Map 10.1, page 495   **BEST ❰**

At 2,425 feet, Yosemite Falls is the highest waterfall in North America. That's why hundreds of park visitors hike this strenuous trail every day in the spring and summer. There's no feeling quite like standing at the waterfall's brink and realizing you've conquered a landmark of this magnitude.

Still, if you tucker out on this demanding climb to Upper Yosemite Fall, just remember that you always have a fallback position: you can hike only 1.2 miles one-way to the Columbia Point overlook, which is reached via more than 100 switchbacks and a total gain of 1,200 feet, then call it a day. The view of Yosemite Valley from Columbia Point is a stunner, and plenty of people who planned on hiking to Upper Yosemite Fall turn around here and still leave satisfied.

Those who push on are also rewarded. After a level section and then a short, surprising descent, you get your first full-impact view of horsetail-shaped Upper Yosemite Fall. In the spring and early summer months, this view will blow you away. The trail then switchbacks upward, more steeply now, through a canyon to the west of the fall, which allows passage to the top of the north rim of Yosemite Valley. At this point, you've gained 2,700 feet and hiked 3.5 miles; it's only another 0.2 mile to the brink of Upper Yosemite Fall. (Make sure you take the spur trail signed as Overlook.) From the metal fence above the fall's lip, you gain an incredible perspective on the waterfall's drop and the valley floor far below.

If this trip hasn't provided you with enough exertion, continue another 0.75 mile, crossing the bridge above the falls, to Yosemite Point at 6,936 feet in elevation, where you get a stunning view of the south rim of the Valley, Half Dome, and North Dome, and a look at the top of Lost Arrow Spire, a single shaft of granite jutting into the sky.

User Groups: Hikers only. No dogs, horses, or mountain bikes. No wheelchair facilities.

Permits: No permits are required. There is a $20 entrance fee per vehicle at Yosemite National Park, good for seven days.

Maps: A Half Dome or Yosemite National Park map is available from Tom Harrison Maps. For a topographic map, ask the USGS for Yosemite Falls.

Directions: From Merced, drive 70 miles northeast on Highway 140 to Yosemite National Park. Follow the signs toward Yosemite Valley, entering through the Arch Rock entrance station. Continue on Highway 140/El Portal Road, which becomes Southside Drive, for 10.5 miles. Just beyond the Yosemite Chapel, bear left at the fork and head toward Yosemite Village and the visitors center, then turn left and drive west on Northside Drive 0.75 mile to the Yosemite Lodge parking lot. Park in the lot (do not park in the spaces marked Permit Parking Only), then walk to Camp 4, which is across Northside Drive and 0.25 mile west of Yosemite Lodge. You may not park in the Camp 4 lot unless you are camping there. If you are riding the free Yosemite Valley shuttle bus, disembark at Camp 4 or Yosemite Lodge.

Contact: Yosemite National Park, P.O. Box 577, Yosemite, CA 95389, 209/372-0200, www.nps.gov/yose.

69 EAGLE PEAK
13.5 mi / 1 or 2 days   🥾4   ⛰️10

in Yosemite Valley

Map 10.1, page 495

If you seek more of a challenge than the day hike to Upper Yosemite Fall, the trail to Eagle Peak delivers the stunning destinations of the shorter trip (Columbia Point and Upper Yosemite Fall) plus an additional three miles one-way to a lookout atop of the highest rock of the Three Brothers formation. Here, the vista is sublime. All of Yosemite Valley comes into view from the top of Eagle Peak, including an interesting perspective on North Dome, Clouds Rest, and Half Dome. On rare, extremely clear days you can also see the mountains and foothills of the Coast Range, 100 miles to the west.

Follow the trail notes for the hike to Upper Yosemite Fall (see listing in this chapter), then after taking the spur trail to the fall's brink, backtrack 0.25 mile to the trail junction for Eagle Peak Trail. Follow Eagle Peak Trail northwest for 1.5 miles, enjoying plentiful shade from Jeffrey pines and white firs, then hike south for one mile through Eagle Peak Meadows (prepare to get your feet wet here unless it is very late in summer). At a trail junction with El Capitan Trail, bear left for a 0.6-mile ascent to your final destination—the summit of Eagle Peak, elevation 7,779 feet. After completing this trip, you'll never view the Three Brothers from the valley floor the same way again.

User Groups: Hikers only. No dogs, horses, or mountain bikes. No wheelchair facilities.

Permits: There is a $20 entrance fee per vehicle at Yosemite National Park, good for seven days. Free wilderness permits are required for overnight stays. They are available on a first-come, first-served basis up to one day in advance at the Yosemite Wilderness kiosk near your chosen trailhead or farther in advance by mail, phone, or online for a $5 reservation fee per person.

Maps: A Half Dome or Yosemite National Park map is available from Tom Harrison Maps. For a topographic map, ask the USGS for Yosemite Falls.

Directions: From Merced, drive 70 miles northeast on Highway 140 to Yosemite National Park. Follow the signs toward Yosemite Valley and enter through the Arch Rock entrance station. Continue on Highway 140/El Portal Road, which becomes Southside Drive, for 10.5 miles. Just beyond the Yosemite Chapel, bear left at the fork and head toward Yosemite Village and the visitors center, then turn left and drive west on Northside Drive 0.75 mile to the Yosemite Lodge parking lot. Park in the lot (do not park in the spaces marked Permit Parking Only), then walk to Camp 4, which is across Northside Drive and 0.25 mile west of Yosemite Lodge. You may not park in the Camp 4 lot unless you are camping there. If you are riding the free Yosemite Valley shuttle bus, disembark at Camp 4 or Yosemite Lodge.

Contact: Yosemite National Park, P.O. Box 577, Yosemite, CA 95389, 209/372-0200 or 209/372-0740 (permit reservations), www.nps.gov/yose or www.nps.gov/yose/wilderness (permit reservations).

70 LOWER YOSEMITE FALL
1.1 mi / 0.5 hr   🏃1 ⛰9

in Yosemite Valley

Map 10.1, page 495   **BEST (**

It's so short you can hardly call it a hike, and the route is perpetually crawling with people. Still, the trail to Lower Yosemite Fall is an absolute must for visitors to Yosemite Valley. When the falls are roaring with snowmelt in the spring and early summer, they never disappoint even the most seasoned hiker.

The Lower Yosemite Fall Trail received a major facelift in 2004. The old parking lot was removed, the trail was extended so that it now makes a pleasant loop, and new, modern restrooms and facilities were added. The only problem is that now that the parking lot is gone, many visitors can't figure out where to leave their car and start the hike. Your best bet is to ride the shuttle bus from other points in the Valley, which deposits you at the "new" Yosemite Fall Trailhead, which is an attractive log structure positioned alongside Northside Drive. You can also park your car alongside the road near the shuttle bus stop, but good luck finding a space in the summer months. Either way, once you get started, the trail is simple enough to follow. Within about 10 minutes of walking, you are standing at the footbridge below the falls, and in the spring you can get soaking wet from the incredible mist and spray. By late summer, on the other hand, the fall often dries up completely. Be sure to walk the entire loop instead of just heading out-and-back to the falls; there is much to see along the way. And most important of all: if you really want to see the waterfall at its most magnificent, plan your trip for sometime between April and June, during peak snowmelt. Seasoned waterfall lovers should also plan to visit on full moon nights in spring, when if conditions are just right, they will be treated to the appearance of a "moonbow" surrounding the lower fall.

User Groups: Hikers and wheelchairs. No dogs, horses, or mountain bikes.

Permits: No permits are required. There is a $20 entrance fee per vehicle at Yosemite National Park, good for seven days.

Maps: A Half Dome or Yosemite National Park map is available from Tom Harrison Maps. For a topographic map, ask the USGS for Half Dome.

Directions: From Merced, drive 70 miles northeast on Highway 140 to Yosemite National Park. Follow the signs to Yosemite Valley, entering through the Arch Rock entrance station. Continue on Highway 140/El Portal Road, which becomes Southside Drive, for 10.5 miles. Just beyond the Yosemite Chapel, bear left at the fork and head toward Yosemite Village and the visitors center, then turn left and drive west on Northside Drive 0.75 mile to the Yosemite Lodge parking lot. Park in the lot (do not park in the spaces marked Permit Parking Only). The trail begins across Northside Drive from Yosemite Lodge. You can also park on either side of Northside Drive near the Lower Yosemite Fall bus shuttle stop and walk from there.

Contact: Yosemite National Park, P.O. Box 577, Yosemite, CA 95389, 209/372-0200, www.nps.gov/yose.

🟦 71 MIST TRAIL TO VERNAL FALL

3.0 mi / 2.0 hr

in Yosemite Valley

Map 10.1, page 495

This is a hike that every visitor to the Valley should take, even if it's the only trail they walk all year. Despite how crowded the trail inevitably is, this is a world-class hike to one of the most photographed waterfalls in the world. Make your trip more enjoyable by starting as early in the morning as possible, before the hordes are out in full force.

Start by taking the free Yosemite shuttle bus to the trailhead at Happy Isles. (Or you can add on an extra mile each way by hiking from the day-use parking area in Curry Village to Happy Isles.) The partially paved route is a moderate 500-foot climb to the Vernal Fall footbridge, then a very steep tromp up the seemingly endless granite staircase to the top of the fall. Although many people hike only to the footbridge, 0.8 mile from Happy Isles, it's definitely worth the extra effort to push on another 0.5 mile to reach the top of Vernal Fall.

Doing so means ascending another 500 feet on the Mist Trail's famous granite stairway, which frames the edge of Vernal Fall. You will come so close to the plunging spray that you may feel as if you are part of it. Sometimes you are—during peak snowmelt in spring, hikers are frequently drenched in spray and mist. Remember to bring a rain poncho if you don't like getting wet.

When you reach the 317-foot-high fall's brink, you can stand at the railing and watch the dizzying flow of rushing whitewater as it tumbles downward. This is a trip you have to do at least once in your life.

Warning: Do not cross or wade the Merced River at the top of Vernal Falls, and do not under any circumstances climb over the railing, especially during peak flows. Fatalities do occur here; don't be one of them.

User Groups: Hikers only. No dogs, horses, or mountain bikes. No wheelchair facilities.

Permits: No permits are required. There is a $20 entrance fee per vehicle at Yosemite National Park, good for seven days.

Maps: A Half Dome or Yosemite National Park map is available from Tom Harrison Maps. For a topographic map, ask the USGS for Half Dome.

Directions: From Merced, drive 70 miles northeast on Highway 140 to Yosemite National Park. Follow the signs toward Yosemite Valley, entering through the Arch Rock entrance station. Continue on Highway 140/El Portal Road, which becomes Southside Drive, for 11.6 miles to the day-use parking lot at Curry Village. Then ride the free Yosemite Valley shuttle bus to Happy Isles. In winter, when the shuttle does not run, you must hike from the day-use parking lot in Curry Village, adding two miles to your round-trip. The Mist Trail may be closed in winter; call to check on weather conditions.

Contact: Yosemite National Park, P.O. Box 577, Yosemite, CA 95389, 209/372-0200, www.nps.gov/yose.

🟦 72 MIST TRAIL AND JOHN MUIR LOOP TO NEVADA FALL

6.8 mi / 4.0 hr

in Yosemite Valley

Map 10.1, page 495   **BEST (**

You can hike either the John Muir Trail or Mist Trail to reach Yosemite's classic Nevada

Fall, but the best choice is to make a loop out of it by hiking up on the Mist Trail, then down partway or all the way on the John Muir Trail. Both trails join above and below Nevada Fall, so you have some options. By hiking uphill rather than downhill on the Mist Trail's treacherous granite staircase, you can look around at the gorgeous scenery every time you stop to catch your breath. The John Muir Trail is somewhat less scenic, especially in its lower reaches, so save it for the way back downhill.

Start at Happy Isles and follow the signed trail to the footbridge over the Merced River, below Vernal Fall. After crossing the bridge, stay close along the river's edge on the Mist Trail for 1.2 miles to the top of Vernal Fall. If it's springtime, make sure you bring your rain gear for this stretch, or you will be drenched in spray. After a brief rest at the waterfall overlook, continue along the river's edge, passing a gorgeous stretch of stream known as the Emerald Pool, still following the Mist Trail. In 0.5 mile, the path crosses the river again, then climbs another mile to the brink of Nevada Fall. Total elevation gain to the top of the 594-foot falls is 2,600 feet, a healthy ascent. But when you get to walk this close to two world-class waterfalls, who's complaining? For your return trip, cross the footbridge above Nevada Fall and follow John Muir Trail to loop back. As you descend, check out the great view of Nevada Fall with Liberty Cap in the background. This is one of the most memorable scenes in Yosemite Valley.

Note that you can cut back over to the Mist Trail at Clark Point, just above Vernal Fall, if you so desire. That way, you get a second chance to see Vernal Fall and hike the Mist Trail's granite staircase. But let your knees decide—plenty of hikers don't want to face those stairs a second time, especially in the downhill direction.

User Groups: Hikers only. No dogs or mountain bikes. Horses are allowed only on John Muir Trail. No wheelchair facilities.

Permits: No permits are required. There is a $20 entrance fee per vehicle at Yosemite National Park, good for seven days.

Maps: A Half Dome or Yosemite National Park map is available from Tom Harrison Maps. For a topographic map, ask the USGS for Half Dome.

Directions: From Merced, drive 70 miles northeast on Highway 140 to Yosemite National Park. Follow the signs toward Yosemite Valley, entering through the Arch Rock entrance station. Continue on Highway 140/El Portal Road, which becomes Southside Drive, for 11.6 miles to the day-use parking lot at Curry Village. Then ride the free Yosemite Valley shuttle bus to Happy Isles, stop No. 16. In winter, when the shuttle does not run, you must hike from the day-use parking lot in Curry Village, adding two miles to your round-trip. Trails may be closed in winter; call to check on weather conditions.

Contact: Yosemite National Park, P.O. Box 577, Yosemite, CA 95389, 209/372-0200, www.nps.gov/yose.

73 MIRROR LAKE LOOP
4.6 mi / 2.0 hr   🏃1 ⛰️7

in Yosemite Valley

Map 10.1, page 495

Thousands of Yosemite visitors walk to Mirror Lake every day in summer, but the vast majority of them miss the best part of this hike. The first thing you need to know: Mirror Lake is not really a lake; it's a large, shallow pool in Tenaya Creek. The pool is undergoing the process of sedimentation (filling with sand and gravel from Tenaya Creek), so every year it shrinks a little more. Many visitors walk up and down this canyon, shake their heads, and ask each other "Where's Mirror Lake?" If you know what you are looking for, the shallow pool is interesting to see, especially when its still waters produce a lovely reflective image of the granite domes above. But if you leave

Mirror Lake behind and head back a mile or more into Tenaya Canyon, you will get the most out of this hike, and perhaps find the kind of quiet nature experience that most visitors seek in Yosemite.

Start by riding the free shuttle from Curry Village parking lot to Mirror Lake Junction. (Or walk there, if you wish, adding 1.5 miles round-trip to your hike.) From the bus stop, walk 0.5 mile on pavement to Mirror Lake and check out the interpretive signs at its edges. Then follow the foot trail up Tenaya Creek for 1.5 miles, passing the left turnoff for Snow Creek Trail. When you reach a footbridge across Tenaya Creek, cross it and loop back on the other side. Views of Half Dome, Mount Watkins, and neighboring granite walls are spectacular, and the forested creek canyon presents an intimate amphitheater in which to view them. Find a boulder somewhere, have a seat, and take in the show. This loop trail is nearly level the whole way, and once you go beyond Mirror Lake and into the lower Tenaya Creek Canyon, you are likely to find a little solitude.

User Groups: Hikers only. No dogs, horses, or mountain bikes. No wheelchair facilities.

Permits: No permits are required. There is a $20 entrance fee per vehicle at Yosemite National Park, good for seven days.

Maps: A Half Dome or Yosemite National Park map is available from Tom Harrison Maps. For a topographic map, ask the USGS for Half Dome.

Directions: From Merced, drive 70 miles northeast on Highway 140 to Yosemite National Park. Follow the signs toward Yosemite Valley, entering through the Arch Rock entrance station. Continue on Highway 140/El Portal Road, which becomes Southside Drive, for 11.6 miles to the day-use parking lot at Curry Village. Then ride the free Yosemite Valley shuttle bus to Mirror Lake Junction.

Contact: Yosemite National Park, P.O. Box 577, Yosemite, CA 95389, 209/372-0200, www.nps.gov/yose.

74 HALF DOME
17.0 mi / 1 or 2 days   🥾5   ⛰9

in Yosemite Valley

Map 10.1, page 495   **BEST (**

No argument about it, Half Dome is one of those once-in-your-life-you-gotta-do-it hikes. Just be sure you know what you're in for before you set out on this epic trail.

The season is fairly short: if the weather cooperates, the Half Dome cables are usually in place from the weekend before Memorial Day in May through Columbus Day in early October. If the cables aren't up and signs state that Half Dome is closed to hikers, *turn around*. You're in for 17 miles round-trip and a 4,800-foot elevation gain—a demanding hike by any standards. You'll have an unbelievable amount of company. During the summer about 400 people a day make the trek to Half Dome's summit.

The vast majority of people make the trek as a day hike, and that's why a permit system was put in place to manage traffic and help keep hikers safe on the Half Dome Trail. Now backpackers *and* day-hikers need a permit to hike Half Dome, and getting your hands on one for the day you want is a little like trying to score Rolling Stones tickets. Permits are available up to four months in advance through the National Recreation Reservation Service (www.recreation.gov, 518/885-3639 or 877/444-6777 from outside the U.S. and Canada) for a service fee of $1.50 per permit. Up to four permits are available per web session or phone call, and permits for the peak summer months sell out quickly. Permits are not available in the park, so the only way to get one is in advance through the reservation service. The good news is that even though permits may be sold out for the day you want to hike, you can keep calling back (or checking the website) right up until midnight before your chosen day. Last-minute cancellations often become available.

Got your permit? Okay, now check the contents of your backpack. All day hikers should be sure to bring a load of water and food with them. You'll be handing it out to others who are not so well prepared, as well as gulping it down yourself. To begin the trip, follow either the John Muir Trail or the Mist Trail from Happy Isles to the top of Nevada Fall (the Mist Trail is 0.6 mile shorter), then go left and enter Little Yosemite Valley, where backpackers make camp. At 6.2 miles the John Muir Trail splits off from the Half Dome Trail and you head left for Half Dome. Just under two miles later you approach Half Dome's shoulder, which is a massive hump that is informally called Sub Dome. This is where a ranger is usually stationed to check to make sure that you have a permit (people without permits will not be allowed beyond the base of Sub Dome). A granite stairway, consisting of about 600 steps, leads you up the dauntingly steep face of Sub Dome. Then the trail descends a bit, and you reach the steel cables that run 200 yards up the back of Half Dome. Here, many people start praying a lot and wishing there weren't so many other hikers on the cables at the same time. Do some soul-searching before you begin the cable ascent; turning around is not an option once you're halfway up. Pick up a pair of old work gloves from the pile at the base of the cable route; you'll need them to protect your hands as you pull yourself up the cables. It takes both hands and feet to haul yourself up 440 feet of nearly vertical granite. Unless you somehow managed to get here before the rest of the Half Dome hopefuls, the going will be slow as you wait for the masses ahead to make the ascent. When you reach the top, the views are so incredible that you forget all about your tired arms and feet. There's plenty of room for everyone on top of Half Dome; its vast, mostly flat surface covers about 13 acres.

To make the trip easier, you can choose to split the hike into two days by camping at Little Yosemite Valley, 4.7 miles in (a wilderness permit is required, and these are much harder to obtain than Half Dome day-hiking permits). This lets you save the final ascent for the next day. Don't plan on sleeping much,

though. Little Yosemite Valley is one zoo of a backpacking camp.

Special Note: The permit system currently in place for Half Dome day-hiking permits is likely to change in 2012 or 2013. To best plan your visit, please check the Yosemite website (www.nps.gov/yose) for the most up-to-date information on Half Dome permits.

User Groups: Hikers only. No dogs, horses, or mountain bikes. No wheelchair facilities.

Permits: There is a $20 entrance fee per vehicle at Yosemite National Park, good for seven days. Free wilderness permits are required for overnight stays. They are available on a first-come, first-served basis up to one day in advance at the Yosemite Wilderness kiosk near your chosen trailhead or farther in advance by mail, phone, or online for a $5 reservation fee per person.

Maps: A Half Dome or Yosemite National Park map is available from Tom Harrison Maps. For a topographic map, ask the USGS for Half Dome.

Directions: From Merced, drive 70 miles northeast on Highway 140 to Yosemite National Park. Follow the signs toward Yosemite Valley, entering through the Arch Rock entrance station. Continue on Highway 140/El Portal Road, which becomes Southside Drive, for 11.6 miles to the day-use parking lot at Curry Village. Then ride the free Yosemite Valley shuttle bus to Happy Isles.

Contact: Yosemite National Park, P.O. Box 577, Yosemite, CA 95389, 209/372-0200 or 209/372-0740 (permit reservations), www.nps.gov/yose or www.nps.gov/yose/wilderness (permit reservations).

75 INSPIRATION AND STANFORD POINTS

7.6 mi / 4.0 hr 🥾3 ⛰️9

in Yosemite Valley near the Wawona Tunnel

Map 10.1, page 495

Many consider the view from Inspiration Point at the entrance to the Wawona Tunnel to be one of the finest scenes in Yosemite—a wide panorama of Yosemite Valley, El Capitan, Half Dome, and Bridalveil Fall. If you like this view, you might want to see more of it by taking this hike from the trailhead at the vista point parking lot. The Pohono Trail leads uphill on a moderately steep grade until at 1.3 miles it reaches the "old" Inspiration Point. This is where the road to Yosemite Valley went through in the days before the Wawona Tunnel, and the view is now largely obscured by trees. Keep climbing, however, because with another 1,000 feet of elevation gain, you will cross Meadow Brook and reach the left cutoff trail for Stanford Point. You're 3.8 miles from the trailhead and you've climbed 2,200 feet, but your reward is an eagle's-eye view of the valley floor, 3,000 feet below, and a vista to the east of Half Dome and all its granite cousins. This stretch of the Pohono Trail is a dependable workout and the trail is never crowded with hikers.

User Groups: Hikers only. No dogs, horses, or mountain bikes. No wheelchair facilities.

Permits: No permits are required. There is a $20 entrance fee per vehicle at Yosemite National Park, good for seven days.

Maps: A Yosemite National Park map is available from Tom Harrison Maps. For a topographic map, ask the USGS for El Capitan.

Directions: From Merced, drive 70 miles northeast on Highway 140 to Yosemite National Park. Follow the signs to Yosemite Valley, entering through the Arch Rock entrance station. Continue 6.3 miles on Highway 140/El Portal Road, which becomes Southside Drive, and turn right at the fork for Highway 41/Wawona/Fresno. Continue 1.5 miles to the parking lots on either side of the road just before you enter the Wawona Tunnel. The trailhead is at the parking lot on the left (south) side of the road.

Contact: Yosemite National Park, P.O. Box 577, Yosemite, CA 95389, 209/372-0200, www.nps.gov/yose.

76 BRIDALVEIL FALL
0.5 mi / 0.5 hr

in Yosemite Valley

Map 10.1, page 495   BEST (

Bridalveil Fall is right up there with Lower Yosemite Fall as a must-do walk for visitors (including nonhikers) to Yosemite Valley. Like that other famous waterfall walk, the path to Bridalveil Fall is paved with people. But the best thing about this waterfall is that unlike other falls in Yosemite Valley, Bridalveil runs year-round. It never dries up and disappoints visitors. The walk to its overlook is short and nearly level; the trail delivers you to a small viewing area about 70 yards from the fall. You can look straight up and see Bridalveil Creek plunging 620 feet off the edge of the south canyon wall. In high wind the fall billows and sways; if you are lucky you might see rainbows dancing in its mist. Another bonus is that your position at the Bridalveil overlook is such that if you do an about-face, you have an excellent view of Ribbon Fall flowing off the northern Yosemite Valley rim. Ribbon Fall is the highest single drop in the park at 1,612 feet, but it only flows in the earliest months of spring.

User Groups: Hikers and wheelchairs. No dogs, horses, or mountain bikes.

Permits: No permits are required. There is a $20 entrance fee per vehicle at Yosemite National Park, good for seven days.

Maps: A Yosemite National Park map is available from Tom Harrison Maps. For a topographic map, ask the USGS for El Capitan.

Directions: From Merced, drive 70 miles northeast on Highway 140 to Yosemite National Park. Follow the signs toward Yosemite Valley, entering through the Arch Rock entrance station. Continue for 6.3 miles on Highway 140/El Portal Road, which becomes Southside Drive, and turn right at the fork for Highway 41/Wawona/Fresno. Turn left almost immediately into the Bridalveil Fall parking lot. The trail begins at the far end of the parking lot. If you are driving into Yosemite Valley on Highway 41 from the south, watch for the

Bridalveil Fall turnoff on your right about one mile after you exit the Wawona Tunnel.

Contact: Yosemite National Park, P.O. Box 577, Yosemite, CA 95389, 209/372-0200, www.nps.gov/yose.

77 FOUR-MILE TRAIL
9.6 mi / 6.0 hr 🏃3 ⛺8

in Yosemite Valley

Map 10.1, page 495

Many years ago, we hiked this trail on our first-ever visit to Yosemite and were shocked when we got to the top and found a giant parking lot and refreshment stand located there. What, you mean we could have driven to the high point on this trail? It's true, but your arrival at dramatic Glacier Point is somehow made all the more meaningful if you get there the hard way, which means hiking Four-Mile Trail all the way up from the valley floor, gaining 3,220 feet in 4.8 miles (not 4.0 miles, as the name implies). The trail is partially shaded and makes for a terrific day hike with an early morning start. Then you can have a leisurely brunch or lunch from your bird's-eye perch on Glacier Point. Don't like what you brought in your daypack? No problem. A snack shop sells hot dogs and the like all summer. From Glacier Point, you have unobstructed views of just about every major landmark in Yosemite Valley—most notably Half Dome, Basket Dome, Yosemite Falls, Vernal and Nevada Falls, and the valley floor far, far below you.

User Groups: Hikers only. No dogs, horses, or mountain bikes. No wheelchair facilities.

Permits: No permits are required. There is a $20 entrance fee per vehicle at Yosemite National Park, good for seven days.

Maps: A Half Dome or Yosemite National Park map is available from Tom Harrison Maps. For a topographic map, ask the USGS for Half Dome.

Directions: From Merced, drive 70 miles northeast on Highway 140 to Yosemite National Park. Follow the signs to Yosemite

Valley, entering through the Arch Rock entrance station. Continue on Highway 140/El Portal Road, which becomes Southside Drive, for 9.5 miles. The trailhead is located next to mile marker V18 on the right side of Southside Drive. Park in the pullouts along the road.

Contact: Yosemite National Park, P.O. Box 577, Yosemite, CA 95389, 209/372-0200, www.nps.gov/yose.

78 MCGURK MEADOW AND DEWEY POINT
2.0-7.0 mi / 1.0-4.0 hr 🏃2 ⛺8

off Glacier Point Road in Yosemite National Park

Map 10.1, page 495   **BEST(**

Some trails seem to capture the essence of Yosemite, and the McGurk Meadow Trail is one of those. The trailhead is the first one you reach as you wind along Glacier Point Road to spectacular Glacier Point. It's worth a stop to take the short walk through a fir and pine forest to pristine McGurk Meadow, a mile-long meadow crossed by a footbridge over a small feeder creek. A quarter-mile before the meadow the trail passes an old pioneer cabin, still standing in half-decent repair.

You can turn around at the meadow for a short and easy trip, or you can follow the trail until it connects to the Pohono Trail, which traverses Yosemite's south rim. An ideal destination is Dewey Point, a spectacular promontory with an unforgettable view of Yosemite Valley, located just off the Pohono Trail. That option turns this hike into a seven-mile round-trip.

User Groups: Hikers only. No dogs, horses, or mountain bikes. No wheelchair facilities.

Permits: No permits are required. There is a $20 entrance fee per vehicle at Yosemite National Park, good for seven days.

Maps: A Yosemite National Park map is available from Tom Harrison Maps. For a topographic map, ask the USGS for El Capitan.

Directions: From Merced, drive 70 miles

northeast on Highway 140 to Yosemite National Park. Follow the signs toward Yosemite Valley, entering through the Arch Rock entrance station. Continue 6.3 miles on Highway 140/El Portal Road, which becomes Southside Drive, and turn right at the fork for Highway 41/Wawona/Fresno. Continue for 9.2 miles, turn left on Glacier Point Road, and drive 7.5 miles to the McGurk Meadow trailhead, on the left. Park in the pullout about 75 yards farther up the road.

Contact: Yosemite National Park, P.O. Box 577, Yosemite, CA 95389, 209/372-0200, www.nps.gov/yose.

79 BRIDALVEIL CREEK

3.2 mi / 1.5 hr

off Glacier Point Road in Yosemite National Park

> **Map 10.1, page 495**

Perhaps the best time to take this hike to Bridalveil Creek is immediately after visiting Bridalveil Fall. After a short walk from Glacier Point Road through a forested area, you wind up at the edge of Bridalveil Creek, a babbling brook that seems far too tame to produce the giant waterfall downstream. To make the trip, follow Ostrander Lake Trail from Glacier Point Road for 1.4 miles. This stretch is almost completely level and is framed by colorful bunches of lupine in midsummer. When the trail splits, take the right fork toward Bridalveil Creek. The stream is so tame here that there is no bridge to cross—it's an easy rock hop by midsummer, although it can be a dangerous crossing in late spring. Pick a spot along its banks, and spend some time counting the wildflowers or the small, darting trout. If you are camping at Bridalveil Creek Campground or just heading up the road to visit Glacier Point, this easy walk is a pleasant leg-stretcher that will take you away from the crowds that throng so many of Yosemite's famous destinations.

User Groups: Hikers only. No dogs, horses, or mountain bikes. No wheelchair facilities.

Permits: No permits are required. There is a $20 entrance fee per vehicle at Yosemite National Park, good for seven days.

Maps: A Yosemite National Park map is available from Tom Harrison Maps. For a topographic map, ask the USGS for Half Dome.

Directions: From Merced, drive 70 miles northeast on Highway 140 to Yosemite National Park. Follow the signs toward Yosemite Valley, entering through the Arch Rock entrance station. Continue for 6.3 miles on Highway 140/El Portal Road, which becomes Southside Drive, and turn right at the fork for Highway 41/Wawona/Fresno. Continue for 9.2 miles, turn left on Glacier Point Road, and drive another 8.9 miles to the Ostrander Lake trailhead, on the right.

Contact: Yosemite National Park, P.O. Box 577, Yosemite, CA 95389, 209/372-0200, www.nps.gov/yose.

80 OSTRANDER LAKE

12.5 mi / 1 or 2 days

off Glacier Point Road in Yosemite National Park

> **Map 10.1, page 495**

While many people take short day hikes from Glacier Point Road, a longer 12.5-mile trip to Ostrander Lake may better suit your taste. The trail is surprisingly easy, considering the long miles, and the first half is quite level. You can hike out and back in a day, or get a wilderness permit and camp near the lake's shores. The wide blue lake, set at 8,580 feet, is a popular destination for cross-country skiers in the winter, as is evidenced by the stone Ostrander Ski Hut and the ski markers tacked high up on trees along the route. Although the trail (really an old road) begins in a regenerated forest fire area, it traverses a typical high-country landscape of firs, pines, and, as you ascend, granite. You have to gain 1,600 feet along the way, most of it in the final three miles to the lake. The culmination of the climb occurs at nearly six miles out, as you reach the trail's highest point, a saddle on top of 8,700-foot Horizon Ridge. Here you are rewarded with excellent views of Half Dome, North Dome, Basket Dome, and Liberty Cap. This is a fine place to catch your breath. From here, the lake is less than 0.5 mile farther. On summer days, bring your swimsuit and a book, and plan to spend a few hours on Ostrander's sand- and boulder-lined shoreline.

User Groups: Hikers only. No dogs, horses, or mountain bikes. No wheelchair facilities.

Permits: There is a $20 entrance fee per vehicle at Yosemite National Park, good for seven days. Free wilderness permits are required for overnight stays. They are available on a first-come, first-served basis up to one day in advance at the Yosemite Wilderness kiosk near your chosen trailhead or farther in advance by mail, phone, or online for a $5 reservation fee per person.

Maps: A Yosemite National Park map is available from Tom Harrison Maps. For topographic maps, ask the USGS for Half Dome and Mariposa Grove.

Directions: From Merced, drive 70 miles northeast on Highway 140 to Yosemite National Park. Follow the signs toward Yosemite Valley, entering through the Arch Rock entrance station. Continue for 6.3 miles on Highway 140/El Portal Road, which becomes Southside Drive, and turn right at the fork for Highway 41/Wawona/Fresno. Continue for 9.2 miles, turn left on Glacier Point Road, and drive 8.9 miles to the Ostrander Lake trailhead, on the right.

Contact: Yosemite National Park, P.O. Box 577, Yosemite, CA 95389, 209/372-0200 or 209/372-0740 (permit reservations), www.nps.gov/yose or www.nps.gov/yose/wilderness (permit reservations).

81 SENTINEL DOME
2.2 mi / 1.0 hr

off Glacier Point Road in Yosemite National Park

Map 10.1, page 495

It's hard to believe you can get so much for so little, but on Sentinel Dome Trail, you can. The granite dome is located about a mile before Glacier Point on Glacier Point Road, and its elevation is 1,000 feet higher than the point's. Views from the dome's summit extend a full 360 degrees. A short and nearly level walk leads you to the base of the dome, and a 100-yard climb up its smooth granite backside brings you to its summit. There you are greeted by stunning vistas in all directions, including an unusual perspective on Upper and Lower Yosemite Falls. This is one of the best places in Yosemite to watch the sun set. To make a longer excursion, you can easily combine this hike with the hike to Taft Point and the Fissures (see listing in this chapter), which starts from the same trailhead but heads in the opposite direction.

User Groups: Hikers only. No dogs, horses, or mountain bikes. No wheelchair facilities.

Permits: No permits are required. There is a $20 entrance fee per vehicle at Yosemite National Park, good for seven days.

Maps: A Half Dome or Yosemite National Park map is available from Tom Harrison Maps. For a topographic map, ask the USGS for Half Dome.

Directions: From Merced, drive 70 miles northeast on Highway 140 to Yosemite National Park. Follow the signs to Yosemite Valley, entering through the Arch Rock entrance station. Continue 6.3 miles on Highway 140/El Portal Road, which becomes Southside Drive, and turn right at the fork for Highway 41/Wawona/Fresno. Continue for 9.2 miles, turn left on Glacier Point Road, and drive 13.2 miles to the Taft Point/Sentinel Dome trailhead parking lot, on the left side of the road.

Contact: Yosemite National Park, P.O. Box 577, Yosemite, CA 95389, 209/372-0200, www.nps.gov/yose.

82 TAFT POINT AND THE FISSURES
2.2 mi / 1.0 hr   🥾1 ⛰8

off Glacier Point Road in
Yosemite National Park

Map 10.1, page 495

It's not so much the sweeping vista from Taft
Point that you remember (although certainly
you could say that the views of Yosemite's
north rim and the valley floor are stunning).
What you remember is the incredible sense of
awe that you feel, perhaps mixed with a little
fear and a lot of respect, as you peer down
into the fissures in Taft Point's granite—huge
cracks in the rock that plunge hundreds of feet
down toward the valley. One of the fissures
has a couple of large boulders captured in its
jaws; they're stuck there, waiting for the next
big earthquake or ice age to set them free. Be
sure to walk to the metal railing along the
edge of Taft Point's cliff, where you can hold
on tight and peer down at the valley far, far
below. If you have kids with you or anyone
who is afraid of heights, be sure to keep a tight
handhold on them.

User Groups: Hikers only. No dogs, horses, or
mountain bikes. No wheelchair facilities.

Permits: No permits are required. There is a
$20 entrance fee per vehicle at Yosemite Na-
tional Park, good for seven days.

Maps: A Half Dome or Yosemite National
Park map is available from Tom Harrison
Maps. For a topographic map, ask the USGS
for Half Dome.

Directions: From Merced, drive 70 miles
northeast on Highway 140 to Yosemite National Park. Follow the signs to Yosemite Valley, entering through the Arch Rock entrance
station. Continue for 6.3 miles on Highway
140/El Portal Road, which becomes Southside
Drive, and turn right at the fork for Highway
41/Wawona/Fresno. Continue for 9.2 miles,
turn left on Glacier Point Road, and drive 13.2
miles to the Taft Point/Sentinel Dome trailhead parking lot, on the left side of the road.

Contact: Yosemite National Park, P.O. Box
577, Yosemite, CA 95389, 209/372-0200,
www.nps.gov/yose.

83 POHONO TRAIL
13.0 mi one-way / 7.0 hr   🥾3 ⛰10

off Glacier Point Road in
Yosemite National Park

Map 10.1, page 495

If you can arrange a shuttle trip, Pohono
Trail from Glacier Point downhill to its end
at Wawona Tunnel is worth every step of its
13 miles. The two ends of the trail have the
best drive-to viewpoints in all of Yosemite, and
in between, you are treated to dozens of other
scenic spots (including Sentinel Dome, at 1.5
miles, and Taft Point, at 3.8 miles), as well as
four bird's-eye lookouts over the valley floor:
Inspiration, Stanford, Dewey, and Crocker
Points. Starting at Glacier Point and ending
at Wawona Tunnel, you'll cover a 2,800-foot
descent, but there are some "ups" along the
way, too—like at the very beginning (from
Glacier Point to Sentinel Dome), and between
Bridalveil Creek and Dewey Point. The trail
stays on or near Yosemite Valley's southern
rim the entire way except for one major detour
into the woods to access the bridge crossing of
Bridalveil Creek. Remember to bring along a
good map, because many of the trail's best of-
ferings are just off the main path. If you don't
take the short spur routes to reach them, you'll
miss out on some spectacular scenery.

The view of Yosemite Falls from Pohono
Trail in front of Sentinel Dome is the best in
all of Yosemite. For the best overall vista along
the trail, it's a toss-up between Glacier Point,
Taft Point, and Dewey Point.

User Groups: Hikers only. No dogs, horses, or
mountain bikes. No wheelchair facilities.

Permits: There is a $20 entrance fee per ve-
hicle at Yosemite National Park, good for seven
days. Free wilderness permits are required for
overnight stays. They are available on a first-
come, first-served basis up to one day in advance at the Yosemite Wilderness kiosk near

your chosen trailhead, or farther in advance by mail, phone, or online for a $5 reservation fee per person.

Maps: A Yosemite National Park map is available from Tom Harrison Maps. For topographic maps, ask the USGS for Half Dome and El Capitan.

Directions: From Merced, drive 70 miles northeast on Highway 140 to Yosemite National Park. Follow the signs to Yosemite Valley, entering through the Arch Rock entrance station. Continue for 6.3 miles on Highway 140/El Portal Road, which becomes Southside Drive, and turn right at the fork for Highway 41/Wawona/Fresno. Continue for 9.2 miles, turn left on Glacier Point Road, and drive 15.7 miles to Glacier Point. Park and walk toward the main viewing area across from the café and gift shop. Look for the Pohono Trail sign about 150 feet southeast of the café building, on your right.

Contact: Yosemite National Park, P.O. Box 577, Yosemite, CA 95389, 209/372-0200 or 209/372-0740 (permit reservations), www.nps.gov/yose or www.nps.gov/yose/wilderness (permit reservations).

84 PANORAMA TRAIL
8.5 mi one-way / 5.0 hr 3 ⚠10

off Glacier Point Road in
Yosemite National Park

Map 10.1, page 495   **BEST (**

The Panorama Trail follows a spectacular route from Glacier Point to Yosemite Valley, heading downhill most of the way, but you must have a shuttle car waiting at the end or it's one heck of a long climb back up. A great option is to take the Yosemite Lodge tour bus for one leg of the trip; call 209/372-1240 to reserve a seat (fee required).

The aptly named Panorama Trail begins at Glacier Point, elevation 7,214 feet. You switchback downhill, accompanied by ever-changing perspectives on Half Dome, Basket Dome, North Dome, Liberty Cap, and, in the distance, Vernal and Nevada Falls. You will gape a lot. After passing Illilouette Fall and ascending a bit for the first time on the trip, continue eastward to the Panorama Trail's end near the top of Nevada Fall. Turn right to reach the top of the fall and have a rest at the overlook, then continue downhill on the Mist Trail on the north side of the river. After a view-filled descent along the north side of Nevada Fall, you'll cross the river in 1.4 miles and walk alongside lovely Emerald Pool on your way to the top of Vernal Fall. Enjoy the show here, then tromp down the granite staircase on the busy trail back to Happy Isles. From there you can take the free valley shuttle bus back to your car, parked somewhere in Yosemite Valley.

Note that the route has a 3,200-foot elevation loss over its course, but there is also a 760-foot climb after you cross Illilouette Creek. Also be forewarned that while the starting miles of the trip are quite tranquil, the final two miles by Vernal Fall are usually a parade of people.

User Groups: Hikers only. No dogs, horses, or mountain bikes. No wheelchair facilities.

Permits: No permits are required. There is a $20 entrance fee per vehicle at Yosemite National Park, good for seven days.

Maps: A Half Dome or Yosemite National Park map is available from Tom Harrison Maps. For a topographic map, ask the USGS for Half Dome.

Directions: From Merced, drive 70 miles northeast on Highway 140 to Yosemite National Park. Follow the signs to Yosemite Valley, entering through the Arch Rock entrance station. Continue for 6.3 miles on Highway 140/El Portal Road, which becomes Southside Drive, and turn right at the fork for Highway 41/Wawona/Fresno. Continue for 9.2 miles, turn left on Glacier Point Road, and drive 15.7 miles to Glacier Point. Park and walk toward the main viewing area, across from the café and gift shop. Look for the Panorama Trail sign about 150 feet southeast of the café building, on your right.

Contact: Yosemite National Park, P.O. Box 577, Yosemite, CA 95389, 209/372-0200, www.nps.gov/yose; Yosemite Lodge Tour Buses, 209/372-1240.

85 ILLILOUETTE FALL
4.0 mi / 2.5 hr   👫2 ⛰10

off Glacier Point Road in
Yosemite National Park

Map 10.1, page 495

Those who can't afford the time or make the car shuttle arrangements necessary to hike the entire Panorama Trail should at least take this incredible out-and-back trip on the top portion of the route. Glacier Point is your starting point, and the bridge above Illilouette Fall becomes your destination, but what happens in between is sheer magic. Some say that hiking Panorama Trail is like staring at a life-size Yosemite postcard, but we say it's more like being in the postcard. As you walk, you feel as if you've become one with the magnificent panorama of Half Dome, Basket Dome, North Dome, Liberty Cap, and far-off Vernal and Nevada Falls. The trail is downhill all the way to Illilouette Fall in two miles, which means you have a 1,200-foot elevation gain on the return trip. The path is extremely well graded, so even children can make the climb. After viewing the waterfall from a trailside overlook, walk another 0.25 mile and stand on the bridge that is perched just above the 370-foot drop. For obvious reasons, don't think about swimming here.

User Groups: Hikers only. No dogs, horses, or mountain bikes. No wheelchair facilities.

Permits: No permits are required. There is a $20 entrance fee per vehicle at Yosemite National Park, good for seven days.

Maps: A Half Dome or Yosemite National Park map is available from Tom Harrison Maps. For a topographic map, ask the USGS for Half Dome.

Directions: From Merced, drive 70 miles northeast on Highway 140 to Yosemite National Park. Follow the signs to Yosemite Valley, entering through the Arch Rock entrance station. Continue for 6.3 miles on Highway 140/El Portal Road, which becomes Southside Drive, and turn right at the fork for Highway 41/Wawona/Fresno. Continue for 9.2 miles, turn left on Glacier Point Road, and drive 15.7 miles to Glacier Point. Park and walk toward the main viewing area, across from the café and gift shop. Look for the Panorama Trail sign on your right, about 150 feet southeast of the café building.

Contact: Yosemite National Park, P.O. Box 577, Yosemite, CA 95389, 209/372-0200, www.nps.gov/yose.

86 ALDER CREEK FALLS
8.2 mi / 5.0 hr   👫3 ⛰9

off Highway 41 near Wawona
in Yosemite National Park

Map 10.1, page 495

Maybe the best thing about Alder Creek Falls is that with all the world-famous waterfalls in Yosemite, this one just plain gets overlooked. Or maybe the best thing is the fun hike to reach it, starting with the challenge of locating the hidden trailhead along Highway 41. After you accomplish this feat, you begin with a one-mile beeline hike straight uphill through the forest, which will surely get your heart pumping. At the top of the ridge and a trail junction, turn left and hike through the trees for two more miles, still heading uphill but now more gently. Three miles from the trailhead, the route suddenly goes level as it joins an old railroad grade, and then it's a one-mile easy stroll to the spot where Alder Creek takes the plunge off a granite lip. The waterfall is about 250 feet tall, and the best view of it is from the trail, about 100 yards away from it. If you choose to keep hiking beyond the falls, you'll find many fine picnic spots among meadows filled with wildflowers.

User Groups: Hikers and horses. No dogs or mountain bikes. No wheelchair facilities.

Permits: There is a $20 entrance fee per vehicle at Yosemite National Park, good for seven days. Free wilderness permits are required for overnight stays. They are available on a first-come, first-served basis up to one day in advance at the Yosemite Wilderness kiosk near your chosen trailhead, or farther in advance by mail, phone, or online for a $5 reservation fee per person.

Maps: A Yosemite National Park map is available from Tom Harrison Maps. For a topographic map, ask the USGS for Wawona.

Directions: From Merced, drive 55 miles northeast on Highway 140 to Yosemite National Park. Follow the signs to Yosemite Valley, entering through the Arch Rock entrance station. Continue for 6.3 miles on Highway 140/El Portal Road, which becomes Southside Drive, and turn right at the fork for Highway 41/Wawona/Fresno. Drive south on Highway 41 for 21 miles to a hairpin turn in the road (if you are coming from the south, it is exactly 4.2 miles north of Chilnualna Falls Road in Wawona). Park in the large dirt pullout on the west side of the road; the trailhead is on the east side of Highway 41. There is no marker except for a Yosemite Wilderness sign.

Contact: Yosemite National Park, P.O. Box 577, Yosemite, CA 95389, 209/372-0200 or 209/372-0740 (permit reservations), www.nps.gov/yose or www.nps.gov/yose/wilderness (permit reservations).

87 WAWONA MEADOW LOOP
3.2 mi / 1.25 hr   🏃1 ⛰7

off Highway 41 near Wawona
in Yosemite National Park

Map 10.1, page 495

Sometimes you just want to take a stroll in the park, and the Wawona Meadow Loop is exactly that. Many hikers ignore this trail because of its proximity to the Wawona Golf Course, but they are missing out on an easy, pleasant meander. On this level trail (a former stage road), you can see terrific wildflowers in

early summer and enjoy the good company of butterflies as you take a lazy stroll. From the signed trailhead across the road from the Wawona Hotel, hike to your left on the dirt road, following the split rail fence. At the end of the meadow the old road crosses the stream and returns to the hotel on the north side of the golf course. If you wish, you can even bring your dog or ride your bike on this trail. If you're staying at the Wawona Hotel, you can hike from there, crossing the Wawona Road on your way out and back.

User Groups: Hikers, dogs, and mountain bikes. No horses. No wheelchair facilities.

Permits: No permits are required. There is a $20 entrance fee per vehicle at Yosemite National Park, good for seven days.

Maps: A Yosemite National Park map is available from Tom Harrison Maps. For a topographic map, ask the USGS for Wawona.

Directions: From Merced, drive 70 miles northeast on Highway 140 to Yosemite National Park. Follow the signs toward Yosemite Valley, entering through the Arch Rock entrance station. Continue for 6.3 miles on Highway 140/El Portal Road, which becomes Southside Drive, and turn right at the fork for Highway 41/Wawona/Fresno. Drive 27 miles to the trailhead, which is just south of the golf course and across the road from the Wawona Hotel.

Contact: Yosemite National Park, P.O. Box 577, Yosemite, CA 95389, 209/372-0200, www.nps.gov/yose.

88 CHILNUALNA FALL
8.2 mi / 5.0 hr   🏃3 ⛰9

off Highway 41 near Wawona
in Yosemite National Park

Map 10.1, page 495

Are you ready to climb? It's good to be mentally prepared for this hike, which includes a steady four-mile uphill, gaining 2,400 feet to reach the top of Chilnualna Falls. Pick a nice, cool day because this trail is in the lower-elevation part of Yosemite. Your nose will be continually assaulted with the intoxicating smell of bear clover, which together with manzanita and oaks makes up the majority of the vegetation along the route. Halfway up you get a great view of Wawona Dome (elevation 6,897 feet) from a granite overlook. This is a great place to take a break and stretch your hamstrings. Shortly thereafter you glimpse a section of Chilnualna Falls high up on a cliff wall, still far ahead. The trail leads above the brink of the fall's lower drop to a series of higher cascades. Keep hiking until you reach the uppermost cascade, which consists of five pool-and-drop tiers just 100 yards off the granite-lined trail. You'll want to spread out a picnic here before you begin the long descent back to the trailhead.

User Groups: Hikers and horses. No dogs or mountain bikes. No wheelchair facilities.

Permits: There is a $20 entrance fee per vehicle at Yosemite National Park, good for seven days. Free wilderness permits are required for overnight stays. They are available on a first-come, first-served basis up to one day in advance at the Yosemite Wilderness kiosk near your chosen trailhead, or farther in advance by mail, phone, or online for a $5 reservation fee per person.

Maps: A Yosemite National Park map is available from Tom Harrison Maps. For topographic maps, ask the USGS for Wawona and Mariposa Grove.

Directions: From Merced, drive 55 miles northeast on Highway 140 to Yosemite National Park. Follow the signs to Yosemite Valley, entering through the Arch Rock entrance station. Continue for 6.3 miles on Highway 140/El Portal Road, which becomes Southside Drive, and turn right at the fork for Highway 41/Wawona/Fresno. Drive south on Highway 41 for 25 miles to Wawona, and turn left on Chilnualna Falls Road. Drive 1.7 miles east and park in the lot on the right side of the road. Walk back to Chilnualna Falls Road and pick up the single-track trail across the pavement.

Contact: Yosemite National Park, P.O. Box 577, Yosemite, CA 95389, 209/372-0200 or 209/372-0740 (permit reservations), www.nps.gov/yose or www.nps.gov/yose/wilderness (permit reservations).

89 MARIPOSA GROVE
2.0-6.4 mi / 1.0-3.0 hr

off Highway 41 near Wawona
in Yosemite National Park

Map 10.1, page 495

The Mariposa Grove is the largest of the three groves of giant sequoias in Yosemite National Park. That's why in summer the parking lot fills up and people wait in line in their cars to see the hundreds of big trees here (and on the busiest days, you will be required to ride a shuttle bus to the trailhead). The star tree in the Mariposa Grove is the Grizzly Giant, with a circumference of more than 100 feet. At approximately 2,700 years old, it's one of the oldest known giant sequoias. If you want to see only the most famous trees in the grove, including the Grizzly Giant, take the well-signed two-mile hike through the lower grove and turn around at the signs pointing to the upper grove. If you hike the entire lower and upper grove, you will cover 6.4 miles of trail. One surprise to first-time visitors is the motorized open-air trams that run through the grove, which are ideal for people who don't want to hike. Some visitors choose to ride the tram to the top of the grove, then hike back downhill for a one-way trip of about three miles. For the best chance of avoiding the summer crowds, time your visit for early in the morning or just before sunset.

User Groups: Hikers only. No dogs, horses, or mountain bikes. No wheelchair facilities.

Permits: No permits are required. There is a $20 entrance fee per vehicle at Yosemite National Park, good for seven days.

Maps: A brochure and trail map are available at the trailhead. A Yosemite National Park map is available from Tom Harrison Maps.

For a topographic map, ask the USGS for Mariposa Grove.

Directions: From Merced, drive 70 miles northeast on Highway 140 to Yosemite National Park. Follow the signs toward Yosemite Valley, entering through the Arch Rock entrance station. Continue for 6.3 miles on Highway 140/El Portal Road, which becomes Southside Drive, and turn right at the fork for Highway 41/Wawona/Fresno. Drive 32 miles to the well-signed Mariposa Grove access road by Yosemite's south entrance. Turn east and drive two miles to the parking lot. During the busy summer months, park your car at the Wawona Store and ride the free shuttle bus into the Mariposa Grove. During the winter, the two-mile-long road into the grove is usually closed due to snow and ice, but you can still walk or snowshoe in.

If you enter the park on Highway 41 from the south, the Mariposa Grove is on the right, just after you drive through the park entrance station.

Contact: Yosemite National Park, P.O. Box 577, Yosemite, CA 95389, 209/372-0200, www.nps.gov/yose.

90 LEWIS CREEK TRAIL
4.0 mi / 2.0 hr 🏃1 ⛰8

off Highway 41 north of Oakhurst

Map 10.1, page 495

Three separate trailheads access Lewis Creek Trail, but unless you want to hike its entire 3.7-mile one-way distance, the best place to start is at the trail's midpoint, just off Highway 41. From this roadside trailhead, you can take a 10-minute walk south to Corlieu Falls and/or walk 1.8 miles north to see Red Rock Falls. Neither waterfall is a showstopper, although both are pretty. Instead, the highlight of the trip is the hike itself, a gorgeous walk along flower-lined Lewis Creek, following the route of the historic Madera Sugar Pine lumber flume. Sugar Pine Lumber Company used the flume (an artificial river in a huge

wooden trough) to float lumber over 50 miles to the town of Madera. You'll pass many anglers along the hike; Lewis Creek is stocked with catchable trout. Fishing is best below Corlieu Falls. In addition, the white western azaleas along the stream bloom in profusion in early summer, shaded by a thick canopy of dogwoods, oaks, ponderosa pines, and incense cedars.

User Groups: Hikers and dogs. No horses or mountain bikes. No wheelchair facilities.

Permits: No permits are required. Parking and access are free.

Maps: A Sierra National Forest map is available from the U.S. Forest Service. For a topographic map, ask the USGS for Ahwahnee.

Directions: From Oakhurst, drive north on Highway 41 for eight miles to the signed trailhead for Lewis Creek Trail, on the east side of the highway. The trailhead is four miles south of Westfall Picnic Area.

Contact: Sierra National Forest, Bass Lake Ranger Station, 57003 Road 225, North Fork, CA 93643, 559/877-2218, www.fs.fed.us/r5/sierra.

91 SHADOW OF THE GIANTS
1.2 mi / 0.5 hr 🏃1 ⛰9

off Highway 41 south of Yosemite National Park and north of Oakhurst in Sierra National Forest

Map 10.1, page 495   BEST (

Shadow of the Giants is a National Recreation Trail that is located within the Nelder Grove of Giant Sequoias. For the sheer numbers of sequoias and the blissful peace and quiet, it beats the heck out of the sequoia groves a few miles north, in Yosemite National Park. On a Saturday afternoon in June, it's not impossible to walk the one-mile interpretive trail all by yourself. The self-guided signs along the trail are interesting and informative, and the babble of Nelder Creek is a perfect accompaniment to the huge, majestic trees. In addition to the sequoias, the forest is filled with western azaleas, dogwoods, incense cedars, wild rose, sugar pines, and white firs. What's the best thing we learned on the trail? The bark of mature sequoias is so soft that squirrels use it to line their nests. The trail makes an easy loop and is set at 5,000 feet in elevation. The best sequoias are at the far end of the loop, so make sure you walk all the way.

User Groups: Hikers and dogs. No horses or mountain bikes. No wheelchair facilities.

Permits: No permits are required. Parking and access are free.

Maps: A Sierra National Forest map is available from the U.S. Forest Service. For a topographic map, ask the USGS for Bass Lake.

Directions: From Oakhurst, drive north on Highway 41 for five miles to Sky Ranch Road/Road 632. Turn east on Sky Ranch Road and drive six miles to the turnoff for Nelder Grove. Turn left, drive 1.5 miles, and take the left fork, signed for Shadow of the Giants. Drive 0.5 mile to the trailhead.

Contact: Sierra National Forest, Bass Lake Ranger Station, 57003 Road 225, North Fork, CA 93643, 559/877-2218, www.fs.fed.us/r5/sierra.

92 FRESNO DOME
2.0 mi / 1.0 hr

off Highway 41 south of Yosemite National Park and north of Oakhurst

Map 10.1, page 495

It's best to plan one hour of time for this trip, but you might want to leave room for more, because once you reach the top of Fresno Dome, you won't want to leave. The trailhead elevation is 8,000 feet, and the trail is beautiful right from the start. It traverses a verdant meadow filled with corn lilies, quaking aspens, and lavender shooting stars. The first 0.5 mile is completely flat; in the second 0.5 mile, you climb up the sloped back side of Fresno Dome. After a moderate ascent (manageable by almost anybody), you're rewarded with 360-degree views, mostly of conifer-filled valleys. You can

just make out a corner of Bass Lake, the town of Oakhurst, and the far-off snowy peaks of the John Muir Wilderness. From up on top of Fresno Dome, it all looks like heaven.

User Groups: Hikers and dogs. No horses or mountain bikes. No wheelchair facilities.

Permits: No permits are required. Parking and access are free.

Maps: A Sierra National Forest map is available from the U.S. Forest Service. For a topographic map, ask the USGS for Bass Lake.

Directions: From Oakhurst, drive north on Highway 41 for five miles to Sky Ranch Road/Road 632. Turn east on Sky Ranch Road, drive approximately 12 miles, and bear left at the sign for Fresno Dome Campground. Drive 4.8 miles to the trailhead (two miles past the camp).

Contact: Sierra National Forest, Bass Lake Ranger Station, 57003 Road 225, North Fork, CA 93643, 559/877-2218, www.fs.fed.us/r5/sierra.

93 THE NICHE AND CORA LAKES
8.6 mi / 4.0 hr-2 days

in the Ansel Adams Wilderness southeast of Yosemite National Park

Map 10.1, page 495

Reaching the trailhead for The Niche and Cora Lakes requires a long drive on the Sierra Vista National Scenic Byway, the showpiece road of the North Fork area. If you have the time for it, it's a great trip. The best approach is to drive out and spend the night at Granite Creek Campground or nearby Clover Meadow Campground, then start hiking the next day. The trip starts with a 3.1-mile gentle ascent through red firs and lodgepole pines to The Niche (at 8,000 feet), where you enter the Ansel Adams Wilderness boundary. Bear left and follow the signs to Cora Lakes, at 4.3 miles. Only one of the Cora Lakes is of substantial size; that's the lower lake, the first one you come to, on the left. The lake is partly forested and has dependable trout fishing. Because the total ascent to Cora Lakes is only 1,200 feet, you may have some energy left to burn. Backpackers should consider adding on a jaunt to Joe Crane Lake, another four miles to the north. The lake has a long and lovely sandy beach, good fishing, and even better swimming than at Cora Lakes.

User Groups: Hikers, dogs, and horses. No mountain bikes. No wheelchair facilities.

Permits: A free wilderness permit is required for overnight stays and is available from the Bass Lake Ranger Station. Quotas are in effect year-round; permits can be reserved in advance for a $5 reservation fee per person.

Maps: A Sierra National Forest or Ansel Adams Wilderness map is available from the U.S. Forest Service. For a topographic map, ask the USGS for Timber Knob.

Directions: From the town of North Fork south of Bass Lake, drive southeast on Road 225 to Minarets Road. Turn left (north) on Minarets Road/Road 81 and follow it for approximately 50 winding miles to the Clover Meadow Ranger Station/Granite Creek turnoff, on the right. Drive 4.5 miles to the Isberg trailhead, just beyond Granite Creek Campground.

Contact: Sierra National Forest, Bass Lake Ranger Station, 57003 Road 225, North Fork, CA 93643, 559/877-2218, www.fs.fed.us/r5/sierra.

94 JACKASS LAKES
7.2 mi / 4.0 hr or 2 days

in the Ansel Adams Wilderness southeast of Yosemite National Park

Map 10.1, page 495

Campers in the Clover Meadow and Upper Chiquito campground areas have this pleasant day hike to look forward to. The trailhead is an easy reach (right off of Beasore Road), and in about two hours of hiking, you can be cooling your toes in the crystal-blue waters of Lower Jackass Lake. The trail climbs

immediately from the road, then enters the Ansel Adams Wilderness boundary in one mile. This first mile can be hot and steep, but it's over with quickly. At the boundary, the grade mellows out, and you reach a junction just before the lakes, at 3.4 miles. The right fork goes to Lower Jackass Lake (the largest of three choices) in 0.2 mile, and the left fork goes to the tiny upper lake. A third lake lies in the basin above the upper lake. Many people just bear right at the junction and visit Lower Jackass Lake, which at 8,600 feet is backed by granite cliffs and offers good swimming and fishing prospects. No, this isn't the most beautiful lake in the Sierra, but if you just want to visit a pretty spot without a whole lot of effort, this trip fits the bill.

User Groups: Hikers, dogs, and horses. No mountain bikes. No wheelchair facilities.

Permits: A free wilderness permit is required for overnight stays and is available from the Bass Lake Ranger Station. Quotas are in effect year-round; permits can be reserved in advance for a $5 reservation fee per person.

Maps: A Sierra National Forest or Ansel Adams Wilderness map is available from the U.S. Forest Service. For a topographic map, ask the USGS for Timber Knob.

Directions: From Oakhurst, drive north on Highway 41 for four miles, then turn right on Road 222 toward Bass Lake. In four miles, bear left on Road 274. Drive two miles and turn left on Beasore Road (gravel). Drive 29 miles to a turnoff for the Norris Trailhead. Bear left and drive two miles to the trailhead parking area.

Contact: Sierra National Forest, Bass Lake Ranger Station, 57003 Road 225, North Fork, CA 93643, 559/877-2218, www.fs.fed.us/r5/sierra.

95 CONVICT CANYON TO LAKE DOROTHY

15.0 mi / 2 days   🏃3   ⛰10

in the John Muir Wilderness south of Mammoth Lakes

Map 10.2, page 496   **BEST (**

Framed by a back wall of bare granite peaks, Convict Lake is a mountain shrine, and the trail that leads from here into the backcountry wilderness makes hikers feel as if they're ascending into heaven. But this is no easy trip. Not only is there a 2,700-foot climb, but a tricky and sometimes dangerous stream crossing is involved. The trail starts near Convict Lake (at 7,621 feet), skirts along the lake's north shore, and then leads up through a canyon alongside Convict Creek. At 2.8 miles, you have to ford the creek, which usually requires getting wet and can be dangerous in the early summer because of high snowmelt. The trail meets the creek in the middle of a small waterfall. Many attempts to bridge this crossing have failed, as the bridge always gets washed out by high flows in early summer.

If you can get past that crossing, you follow the trail up to a series of large, untouched lakes: Mildred Lake at 4.9 miles, Lake Dorothy at 6.2 miles (10,275 feet), Lake Genevieve at 7.2 miles (10,000 feet), and beyond them, Bighorn, Edith, and Cloverleaf Lakes. Take your pick. Lake Dorothy is by far the largest of the lot. You can spend days exploring this high-mountain paradise.

Special Note: The crossing of Convict Creek is considered to be one of the most treacherous in the Sierra Nevada. This trail should only be hiked late in the season, when the stream flow has dropped. Check with the Mammoth Lakes Welcome Center for current conditions before planning a trip.

User Groups: Hikers, dogs, and horses. No mountain bikes. No wheelchair facilities.

Permits: A free wilderness permit is required for overnight stays and is available from the Mammoth Lakes Welcome Center. Quotas are in effect from May 1 to November 1; for this period, permits are available in advance for a $5 reservation fee per person.

Maps: A Mammoth High Country map is available from Tom Harrison Maps. An Inyo National Forest or John Muir Wilderness map is available from the U.S. Forest Service. For a topographic map, ask the USGS for Bloody Mountain.

Directions: From U.S. 395 at the Mammoth Lakes junction, drive south for six miles to Convict Lake Road. Turn west and drive 1.8 miles to a spur road on the right as you near the lake. Turn right and drive 0.25 mile to the parking area for the trailhead.

Contact: Inyo National Forest, Mammoth Lakes Welcome Center, P.O. Box 148, Mammoth Lakes, CA 93546, 760/924-5500, www.fs.usda.gov/inyo.

96 MCGEE CREEK TO STEELHEAD LAKE

11.4 mi / 6.0 hr or 2 days   🏃3   ⛰9

in the John Muir Wilderness

Map 10.2, page 496   **BEST (**

Unlike many trails leading into the John Muir Wilderness, the McGee Creek Trail has the benefit of starting out with a mostly level stretch. It follows the remains of an old mining road, giving your legs and lungs the opportunity to warm up before you start to climb. In the first two miles, you pass plains of sage and rabbit brush, heading toward a colorful and dramatic mountain backdrop: Mount Baldwin on the right, Mount Crocker on the left, and Red and White Mountain straight ahead—all at over 12,000 feet in elevation. To your left, along McGee Creek, grows a lush garden of aspens and cottonwoods. Pass Horsetail Falls on the right at two miles out. Soon the trail enters a lodgepole pine forest and the climb steepens, and at 4.5 miles, you reach a junction with Steelhead Lake Trail heading left (east). Switchbacks carry you to a short spur to tiny Grass Lake, then to much larger Steelhead Lake (10,350 feet). The total climb is 2,300 feet over 5.7 miles, but most of the work is in the last 1.2 miles.

User Groups: Hikers, dogs, and horses. No mountain bikes. No wheelchair facilities.

Permits: A free wilderness permit is required for overnight stays and is available from the Bishop/White Mountain Ranger Station. Quotas are in effect from May 1 to November 1; for this period, permits are available in advance for a $5 reservation fee per person.

Maps: A Mammoth High Country map is available from Tom Harrison Maps. An Inyo National Forest or John Muir Wilderness map is available from the U.S. Forest Service. For a topographic map, ask the USGS for Convict Lake.

Directions: From U.S. 395 at the Mammoth Lakes junction, drive south eight miles to the McGee Creek Road turnoff on the right (30 miles north of Bishop). Drive three miles southwest on McGee Creek Road (past the pack station) to the trailhead.

Contact: Inyo National Forest, White Mountain Ranger District, 798 N. Main Street, Bishop, CA 93514, 760/873-2500, www.fs.usda.gov/inyo.

🟦97 MONO PASS

7.4 mi / 4.0 hr   👥4 ⛰10

in the John Muir Wilderness

Map 10.2, page 496

Since wilderness permits are hard to come by for this trail, your best bet is a day hike up to scenic, austere Mono Pass, where William Brewer and his party crossed the Sierra in 1864. Trailhead elevation is 10,300 feet, and the pass is at 12,600 feet, so get ready to climb in thin air (gasp). Also, expect it to be cold and windy at the pass, no matter how warm it is at the trailhead. Start your trip by following the trail alongside Rock Creek, with a wall of mammoth mountain peaks surrounding you. A half mile in, leave most of the crowds behind as you bear right for Mono Pass, switchbacking uphill. As you climb, you gain a view of

Little Lakes Valley below, as well as continual eyefuls of classic Sierra scenery—clear blue sky, jagged mountain backdrops, and plenty of rock. Pass the side trail to Ruby Lake at two miles out (save this 0.25-mile spur for your return trip). Continue on the rocky, treeless trail until at last you reach the summit, where you get a full panoramic view, which is probably hardly different from when Brewer saw it more than a century ago. That peak just to the east of you is Mount Starr, elevation 12,835 feet. To the south, the 13,000-foot-plus peaks reign: Mount Abbot and Mount Mills. Mono Rock and the Mono Recesses lie to the west, and the blue lakes of the Pioneer Basin are to the north.

User Groups: Hikers, dogs, and horses. No mountain bikes. No wheelchair facilities.

Permits: No permits are required. Parking and access are free.

Maps: A Mono Divide High Country map is available from Tom Harrison Maps. A John Muir Wilderness map is available from the U.S. Forest Service. For topographic maps, ask the USGS for Mount Morgan and Mount Abbot.

Directions: From U.S. 395 at the Mammoth Lakes junction, drive south 15 miles to Tom's Place and the Rock Creek Road turnoff, on the right (24 miles north of Bishop). Follow Rock Creek Road southwest for 10.5 miles to its end, at the Mosquito Flat parking area.

Contact: Inyo National Forest, White Mountain Ranger District, 798 N. Main Street, Bishop, CA 93514, 760/873-2500, www.fs.usda.gov/inyo.

🟦98 LITTLE LAKES VALLEY

3.0-9.0 mi / 2.0-5.0 hr   👥2 ⛰10

in the John Muir Wilderness

Map 10.2, page 496

If the mileage shown above reflects some indecision, that's because the Little Lakes Valley makes it hard to decide which lake to visit or how far to hike. It's best to decide as you go, depending on how busy the trail is and how your energy is holding up. The Little Lakes Valley is a spectacularly beautiful, glacially carved area that is littered with lakes both large and small, and is surrounded by 13,000-foot peaks. What makes it even more special is that its trailhead is at 10,300 feet, so your car does most of the climbing, instead of your feet. For this reason, the trail is extremely popular, especially with beginning backpackers, day hikers, and dog walkers.

The trail leads past Mack Lake and shallow Marsh Lake to Heart Lake, 1.5 miles in. Box Lake is 0.25 mile farther, and then another 0.25 mile farther is the still larger Long Lake, both popular destinations right along the trail. Those with more stamina can continue to Chickenfoot Lake, at 3.0 miles out, or the Gem Lakes, at 3.5 miles. Most people consider the Gem Lakes to be the most gorgeous of the lot, but frankly, it's pretty hard to choose. Those who are willing and able continue upward through 11,100-foot Morgan Pass and descend a couple hundred feet to Upper and Lower Morgan Lakes, at 4 and 4.5 miles out, respectively. There are enough hiking options along this one trail to keep most lake-lovers busy for a week.

User Groups: Hikers, dogs, and horses. No mountain bikes. No wheelchair facilities.

Permits: A free wilderness permit is required for overnight stays and is available from the Bishop/White Mountain Ranger Station. Quotas are in effect from May 1 to November 1; for this period, permits are available in advance for a $5 reservation fee per person.

Maps: A Mono Divide High Country map is available from Tom Harrison Maps. A John Muir Wilderness map is available from the U.S. Forest Service. For topographic maps, ask the USGS for Mount Morgan and Mount Abbot.

Directions: From U.S. 395 at the Mammoth Lakes junction, drive south 15 miles to Tom's Place and the Rock Creek Road turnoff, on the right (24 miles north of Bishop). Follow Rock Creek Road southwest for 10.5 miles to its end, at the Mosquito Flat parking area.

Contact: Inyo National Forest, White Mountain Ranger District, 798 N. Main Street, Bishop, CA 93514, 760/873-2500, www.fs.usda.gov/inyo.

99 TAMARACK LAKES
9.4 mi / 6.0 hr or 2 days 3 ▲10

in the John Muir Wilderness

Map 10.2, page 496

This fantastic Eastern Sierra hike offers a great deal of variety in terrain, a couple of gorgeous lakes with good fishing prospects, and the chance of seeing bighorn sheep. Perhaps best of all, this trail sees a lot less foot traffic than the other pathways in the popular Rock Creek area. The trailhead elevation at Rock Creek Lake is 9,700 feet, so the first stretch of this trail can be a bit breathtaking as you climb steadily for a mile on a brushy slope. Soon the trail levels out and follows an old dirt road for awhile, which connects to a mountain-biking route in Sand Canyon. The terrain you are walking through is dry and sandy, with only a few pines to create some sparse shade, and it gives little indication of the dramatic high-country scenery that lies ahead. You'll pass a turnoff for Francis Lake on the right (0.7 mile distant), and shortly thereafter, Kenneth Lake on the left (0.1 mile distant). Kenneth Lake is really just a muddy pond, which usually dries up by late summer, but its surrounding meadow is filled with blooming gentian in late summer. Stay on the path to Tamarack Lakes, and you'll find that the climbing you will face will result in a dramatic change of landscape. The trail ascends over a series of glacial moraines, and you soon find yourself in a high-alpine area, where bighorn sheep are sometimes seen grazing on the fragile grasses. You'll pass the left turnoff for Dorothy Lake (there are good camping spots here, but fishing is usually poor), but stay right, and in another mile, you will begin to follow the outlet stream from the Tamarack Lakes. Now the real work begins, as you must gain

800 more feet to climb into the high basin where the Tamarack Lakes lie. The trail ends at a small tarn just before the largest Tamarack Lake. Just beyond the big Tamarack Lake is Buck Lake, which most people assume is just another of the Tamarack Lakes. The lakes are set in a steeply sloped rocky bowl and have that barren, austere look that is common to lakes above 11,000 feet. You won't find much in the way of flat, soft spots to put your tent, but the scenery more than makes up for it. The largest Tamarack Lake has good fishing for golden trout. The total elevation gain on this hike is 2,000 feet, and it is worth every bit of it.

User Groups: Hikers, dogs, and horses. No mountain bikes. No wheelchair facilities.

Permits: A free wilderness permit is required for overnight stays and is available from the Bishop/White Mountain Ranger Station. Quotas are in effect from May 1 to November 1; for this period, permits are available in advance for a $5 reservation fee per person.

Maps: A Mono Divide High Country map is available from Tom Harrison Maps. A John Muir Wilderness map is available from the U.S. Forest Service. For a topographic map, ask the USGS for Mount Morgan.

Directions: From U.S. 395 at the Mammoth Lakes junction, drive south 15 miles to Tom's Place and the Rock Creek Road turnoff, on the right (24 miles north of Bishop). Follow Rock Creek Road southwest for 8.5 miles to the left turnoff for Rock Creek Lakes campground. Turn left and drive 0.4 mile to the trailhead.

Contact: Inyo National Forest, White Mountain Ranger District, 798 N. Main Street, Bishop, CA 93514, 760/873-2500, www.fs.usda.gov/inyo.

100 RUBY LAKE

4.5 mi / 2.5 hr

in the John Muir Wilderness

Map 10.2, page 496

For both day hikers and backpackers, the Little Lakes Valley is the premier destination from the Rock Creek Canyon trailhead. The only problem is the crowds, especially on the weekends, which can turn a supposedly peaceful wilderness experience into a large group encounter. A visit to Ruby Lake is a possible solution, because it's off the main trail that leads into the Little Lakes Valley, situated instead on the right fork that leads to Mono Pass. Since most trail users on this fork are backpackers heading to Mono Pass and the Pioneer Basin beyond, few take the time to stop at Ruby Lake, 0.25 mile off the main trail. From the trailhead, hike 0.5 mile, and bear right at the junction for Mono Pass. Grunt it out through the switchbacks as you enjoy a series of stunning vistas of the Little Lakes Valley. You'll reach the Ruby Lake spur trail at two miles out, on the left. A 0.25-mile walk brings you to cliffbound Ruby Lake, which is much larger than you'd expect and perfectly ringed by granite. The fishing is not great, but the picnicking is highly recommended. The lake's elevation is 11,121 feet.

User Groups: Hikers, dogs, and horses. No mountain bikes. No wheelchair facilities.

Permits: No permits are required. Parking and access are free.

Maps: A Mono Divide High Country map is available from Tom Harrison Maps. A John Muir Wilderness map is available from the U.S. Forest Service. For topographic maps, ask the USGS for Mount Abbot and Mount Morgan.

Directions: From U.S. 395 at the Mammoth Lakes junction, drive south 15 miles to Tom's Place and the Rock Creek Road turnoff, on the right (24 miles north of Bishop). Follow Rock Creek Road southwest for 10.5 miles to its end, at the Mosquito Flat parking area.

Contact: Inyo National Forest, White Mountain Ranger District, 798 N. Main Street, Bishop, CA 93514, 760/873-2500, www.fs.usda.gov/inyo.

101 WHITE MOUNTAIN PEAK TRAIL

14.4 mi / 8.0 hr   🥾5   ⛰10

in Inyo National Forest northeast of Bishop

Map 10.2, page 496   BEST (

White Mountain Peak is the third-tallest peak in California, only 259 feet lower than the highest, Mount Whitney (Mount Williamson is second in line), yet it is little known to hikers outside of the area. In contrast to Whitney, this 14,246-foot summit is not reached by a narrow foot trail, but instead via an old Navy-built road that climbs 2,600 feet in 7.2 miles. The trail starts at a locked gate at 11,630 feet in elevation and then leads past Mount Barcroft (13,040 feet) on a long grind. The road/trail is completely above tree line, so it's exposed and often windswept. Sunscreen alone won't suffice here; wear a hat to give yourself a break from the sun. If you aren't acclimated, the high altitude will make the trip very difficult. The summit constitutes an impressive granite massif with grand views. To the east, you can see 200 miles into Nevada; to the west, the Owens Valley and Volcanic Tableland, plus a wide panorama of the Sierra Nevada. Some hikers choose to pack along their headlamps and do all or part of the trip by moonlight. The road/trail is simple to navigate, so this is easily accomplished. Forget turning this into a backpack trip: The area is so exposed that you won't find a suitable place to camp. Also, if you are planning an early summer visit, call the White Mountain Ranger Station to be sure the dirt road to the trailhead is open. The road is frequently snowed in at the higher elevations until mid-June or later.

User Groups: Hikers only. Dogs, horses, and mountain bikes permitted, but not advised due to extremely high altitudes. No wheelchair facilities.

Permits: No permits are required. Parking and access are free.

Maps: An Inyo National Forest map is available from the U.S. Forest Service. For a topographic map, ask the USGS for White Mountain Peak.

Directions: From U.S. 395 at Big Pine, take Highway 168 east for 13 miles to White Mountain Road. Turn left on White Mountain Road and drive north for 10.5 miles to Schulman Grove. Continue on White Mountain Road (it becomes unpaved just past the Schulman Grove turnoff) for 16 miles to the locked gate and trailhead, at the road's end.

Contact: Inyo National Forest, White Mountain Ranger Station, 798 N. Main Street, Bishop, CA 93514, 760/873-2500, www.fs.usda.gov/inyo.

102 METHUSELAH TRAIL

4.2 mi / 2.5 hr   🥾2   ⛰8

in Inyo National Forest northeast of Bishop

Map 10.2, page 496   BEST (

The Methuselah Tree is the prize of the Ancient Bristlecone Pine Forest. Here for more than 4,000 years, it's the oldest documented living tree in the world. But forest rangers won't tell you which one it is, out of fear that some dimwit will cut it down. So you have to be satisfied just knowing you have walked among the ancients, rather than actually seeing the grandfather of all trees. No matter; each one of the thousands of trees here will impress you with its beautifully sculpted form. Amateur photographers have a field day along this trail. The path starts at the patio of the Schulman Grove Visitors Center (elevation 10,000 feet) and follows a meandering route through a forest of ancient and younger bristlecone pines, plus a few limber pines and pinyon pines. The first half of the loop drops 800 feet, which of course must be regained on your return, but the climb is nicely spread out. Still, if you're not acclimated, the high elevation will leave you huffing and puffing. Plan on bringing a picnic with you (you're a long way from the nearest convenience store), and make sure you spend some time at the excellent visitors center, which is open daily. If you want to hike a bit more, try the one-mile Discovery Trail loop (more bristlecone pines) or the one-mile

Bristlecone Cabin Trail, which leads to an old Mexican mine site. If you're accustomed to modern conveniences, it's worth noting that cell phone service is limited in the area and water is not available at the trailhead or visitors center. Make sure your vehicle is well stocked for the trip.

User Groups: Hikers and leashed dogs. No horses or mountain bikes. No wheelchair facilities.

Permits: No permits are required. There is a $3 fee per person with a maximum of $6 per vehicle.

Maps: Brochures and trail maps are available at the trailhead. An Inyo National Forest map is available from the U.S. Forest Service. For a topographic map, ask the USGS for Westgard Pass.

Directions: From U.S. 395 at Big Pine, take Highway 168 east for 13 miles to White Mountain Road. Turn left on White Mountain Road and drive north for 10.5 miles to Schulman Grove, on the right.

Contact: Inyo National Forest, White Mountain Ranger Station, 798 N. Main Street, Bishop, CA 93514, 760/873-2500, www.fs.usda.gov/inyo.

SEQUOIA AND KINGS CANYON

© LANDIS BENNE

BEST HIKES

Located on the western slope of the Sierra

Nevada, Sequoia and Kings Canyon National Parks are famous for their giant sequoia groves, tall mountains, deep canyons, roaring rivers, and spectacular hiking trails with views of the jagged peaks of the Great Western Divide. Often referred to as "Yosemite without the masses," these two side-by-side national parks offer classic Sierra scenery without the infamous overcrowding that plagues that great park to the north. Kings Canyon and Sequoia have been managed jointly by the National Park Service since 1943.

The parks abound with superlatives. The highest peak in the contiguous United States — Mount Whitney, at 14,496 feet — is located in Sequoia National Park, although most people hike to it from the east side, in Inyo National Forest. Several other park summits top out at more than 14,000 feet. The largest living tree in the world, the Sherman Tree, is found in Sequoia National Park. At 275 feet tall and with a 103-foot circumference at the ground, the massive tree is still growing; every year it adds enough wood to make another 60-foot-tall tree. The second- and third-largest trees in the world, named Washington and General Grant, respectively, are also found in Sequoia and Kings Canyon. No nature experience is quite as awe-inspiring or as humbling as hiking through a grove of these giant trees.

Three powerful rivers course through the boundaries of Sequoia and Kings Canyon: the Kings, Kern, and Kaweah. The canyon of the Kings River is carved to a depth of 8,000 feet below the summit of neighboring Spanish Mountain, making Kings Canyon deeper than the Grand Canyon or any other canyon in North America. Hikers who make the long drive on Highway 180 alongside this dramatic river eventually find themselves at

Roads End, where civilization ends and the wilderness begins. To continue through the Sierra from here, your only choice is to walk. Trail options range from easy strolls along the riverbanks to long, steep treks into the Monarch Wilderness.

A less-visited area of the parks, but a mecca for hikers, is the Mineral King region. A glacier-carved bowl surrounded by massive peaks, Mineral King Valley is crowned by the distinct, pointed pinnacle known as Sawtooth Peak. Reaching the 7,800-foot valley requires a circuitous 25-mile drive from the foothills of Three Rivers. Once the drive is accomplished, hikers can choose from a wide variety of day-hiking and backpacking trails, many of which lead to 10,000-foot-plus alpine lakes.

In December 2000 a new park was tacked on to the borders of Sequoia and Kings Canyon: Giant Sequoia National Monument. Administered by the U.S. Forest Service, not the National Park Service, the national monument contains two noncontiguous land areas, both designated to increase protection for the last remaining giant sequoia groves in the world.

The recreation options don't stop at the national park and monument borders. Hikers can walk through much-less-visited giant sequoia groves in national forest and state forest lands near Dinkey Lakes (McKinley Grove) and Springville (Mountain Home State Forest). Visitors seeking the polished granite landscape of the national parks without the accompanying crowds can find it along the trails of the Kaiser Wilderness area, near Huntington Lake. And far across the Sierra Nevada, on the U.S. 395 corridor in the Eastern Sierra, hikers can access one trailhead after another at the end of almost every road leading west off the highway. From Bishop to Big Pine to Independence to Lone Pine, each westward-bound road is a gateway to a world of hiking opportunities.

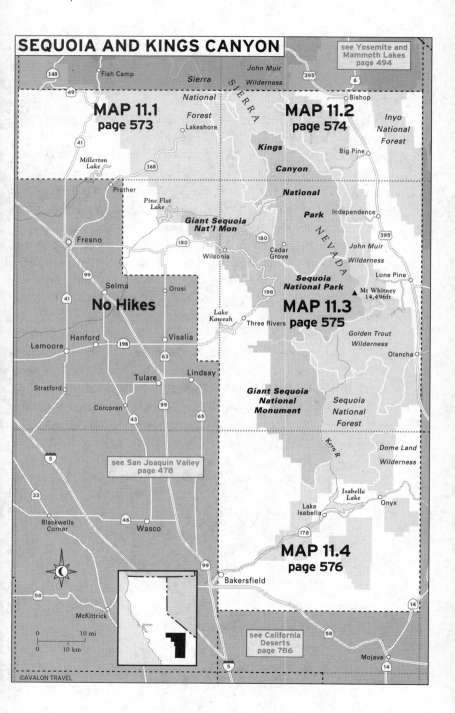

SEQUOIA AND KINGS CANYON

see Yosemite and Mammoth Lakes page 494

Fish Camp

Sierra

National

Forest

Lakeshore

MAP 11.1
page 573

John Muir Wilderness

Bishop

MAP 11.2
page 574

Inyo

National

Forest

Big Pine

Kings

Canyon

Millerton Lake

Prather

Pine Flat Lake

National   *Park*

Independence

Fresno

Giant Sequoia Nat'l Mon

Wilsonia

Cedar Grove

John Muir

Wilderness

Lone Pine

Selma

Orosi

No Hikes

Sequoia National Park

▲ Mt Whitney 14,496ft

Lake Kaweah

Three Rivers

MAP 11.3
page 575

Hanford

Visalia

Golden Trout

Wilderness

Lemoore

Stratford

Tulare

Lindsay

Olancha

Corcoran

Giant Sequoia National Monument

Sequoia National Forest

see San Joaquin Valley page 478

Blackwells Corner

Wasco

Dome Land Wilderness

Isabella Lake

Lake Isabella

Onyx

MAP 11.4
page 576

Bakersfield

McKittrick

0   10 mi

0   10 km

see California Deserts page 786

Mojave

©AVALON TRAVEL

Map 11.1

Hikes 1-10
Pages 577-581

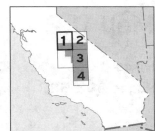

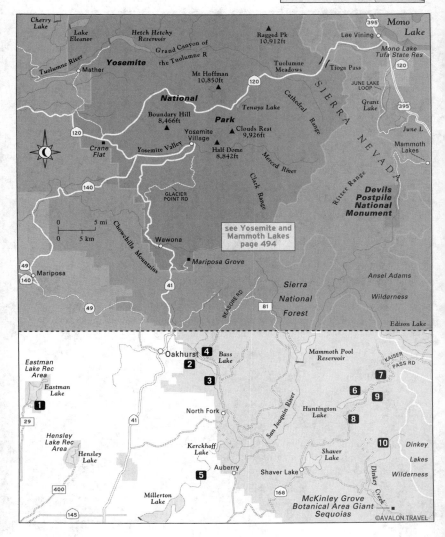

Map 11.2

Hikes 11-20
Pages 582-588

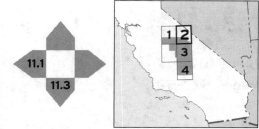

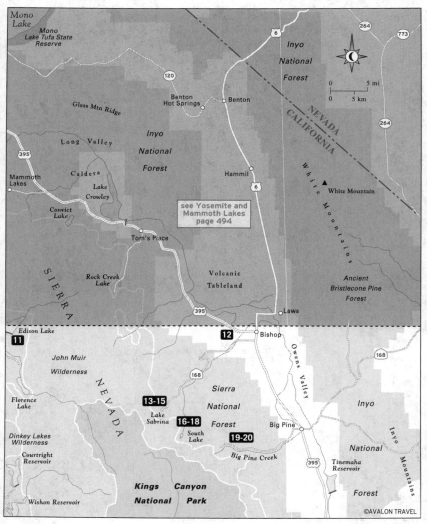

©AVALON TRAVEL

Map 11.3

Hikes 21-105
Pages 589-641

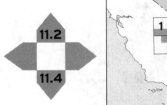

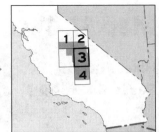

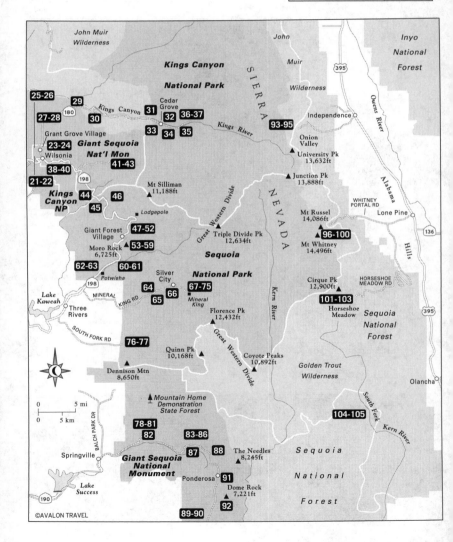

©AVALON TRAVEL

Map 11.4

Hikes 106-119
Pages 642-649

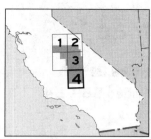

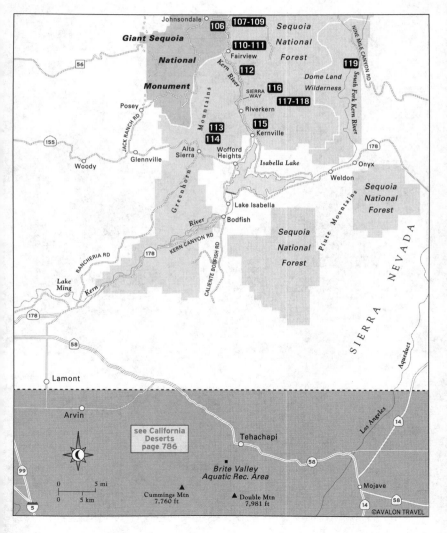

1 LAKEVIEW TRAIL
4.2 mi one-way / 2.0 hr

on the southeast shore of
Eastman Lake east of Chowchilla

Map 11.1, page 573

Let's get one thing straight: You don't want to hike here at midday in July. Got it? Good. But if it's spring and the wildflowers are in bloom, you'd be wise to head out here to Eastman Lake, then hike the Lakeview Trail that leads along its south and east sides. Sure, a reservoir is a reservoir, but when the water level is high, the grasslands are green, and the flowers are blooming, this reservoir can seem like a little slice of paradise in the Central Valley. The Lakeview Trail leads a total of 4.2 miles one-way from the trailhead at the group campground to Raymond Bridge. Hike as little or as much of it as you please, watching for birds and identifying the wildflowers as you go. Bald eagle sightings are not uncommon; in the spring of 2007, part of this trail was temporarily closed to protect a family of bald eagles nesting along the lakeshore. You probably won't have a lot of company on this trail; after all, most people come to Eastman Lake to fish, not hike. In addition to its trophy bass fishery, the lake also boasts populations of crappie, bluegill, and catfish. They even stock rainbow trout here in the winter when the temperature cools down.

User Groups: Hikers, dogs, horses, and mountain bikes. No wheelchair facilities.

Permits: No permits are required. A $5 day-use fee is charged.

Maps: A free map of Eastman Lake is available at the visitors center. For a topographic map, ask the USGS for Raymond.

Directions: From Merced, drive south on Highway 99 for 20 miles to Chowchilla. Take the Avenue 26 exit and head east for 17 miles. Turn north on County Road 29 and drive eight miles to the lake entrance. Turn right and drive to the parking area by Cordorniz Group Campground.

Contact: U.S. Army Corps of Engineers, Eastman Lake, P.O. Box 67, Raymond, CA 93653, 559/689-3255.

2 WAY OF THE MONO
0.5 mi / 0.5 hr

on the northwest end of
Bass Lake near Oakhurst

Map 11.1, page 573

The Way of the Mono is an educational trail that teaches about the Mono Indians, who were the first people to live in the Bass Lake area. They inhabited the area for more than 1,000 years. The interpretive displays along the trail point out grinding holes in the rocks, where the Mono people pounded acorns into meal, and describe different methods they used to live through the area's seasonal changes. In addition to a cultural history lesson, the trail also offers beautiful vistas of Bass Lake and its surroundings. Check out the view from the large granite outcrop of Bass Lake and surrounding peaks. This great loop hike takes only about 20 minutes to walk, but leaves you with a much greater understanding of the Bass Lake area.

User Groups: Hikers and dogs. No horses or mountain bikes. No wheelchair facilities.

Permits: No permits are required. Parking and access are free at the trailhead; parking in the day-use area is $3.

Maps: A Sierra National Forest map is available from the U.S. Forest Service. For a topographic map, ask the USGS for Bass Lake.

Directions: From Oakhurst, drive north on Highway 41 for four miles and then turn right on Road 222. Drive four miles and bear right to stay on Road 222. The signed trailhead parking area is across from Little Denver Church Day Use Area, between the Forks Resort and the California Land Management Office.

Contact: Sierra National Forest, Bass Lake Ranger District, 57003 Road 225, North Fork, CA 93643, 559/877-2218, www.fs.fed.us/r5/sierra.

❸ GOAT MOUNTAIN FIRE LOOKOUT
8.0 mi / 4.0 hr   🏃3   ⛰8

on the south end of Bass Lake near Oakhurst

Map 11.1, page 573

The route to Goat Mountain Fire Lookout can be hiked from trailheads at either Forks Campground or Spring Cove Campground. This is a must-do hike for the legions of campers who spend their summer vacations at Bass Lake. Both trails intersect in about two miles, then join and form one path for the last two miles to the lookout. No matter how you do it, the grade is memorably steep, but also rewarding. As you climb up the trail, you have nearly nonstop views of Bass Lake and the forested valleys surrounding it. You'll also be breathing hard. If you can talk someone into driving a second car to the other trailhead and campground, you can turn this into a pleasant semi-loop trip by hiking up one trail and down the other. Note that this trail has become increasingly popular with mountain bikers in the last few years. If you don't like sharing the trail with them, plan your hike for a weekday, when you're more likely to be out here by yourself. The fire lookout is perched at 4,675 feet in elevation, set on top of a 20-foot steel tower, and offers a 360-degree view.

User Groups: Hikers, dogs, horses, and mountain bikes. No wheelchair facilities.

Permits: No permits are required. Parking and access are free in the campgrounds, but $3 if you park in the day-use area.

Maps: A Sierra National Forest map is available from the U.S. Forest Service. For a topographic map, ask the USGS for Bass Lake.

Directions: From Oakhurst, drive north on Highway 41 for four miles and turn right on Road 222. Drive four miles and bear right to stay on Road 222. Continue along the western shore of Bass Lake for about five miles to Spring Cove Campground. The Spring Cove Trail begins on the east side of the campground entrance. If there is no parking there, you can park at Rocky Point Picnic Area ($3

fee). You can also hike to Goat Mountain Fire Lookout from Forks Campground, three miles north on Road 222.

Contact: Sierra National Forest, Bass Lake Ranger District, 57003 Road 225, North Fork, CA 93643, 559/877-2218, www.fs.fed.us/r5/sierra.

❹ WILLOW CREEK
4.8 mi / 2.5 hr   🏃2   ⛰8

on the northeast end of
Bass Lake near Oakhurst

Map 11.1, page 573

Most people hike Willow Creek Trail with one of two things in mind: fishing or swimming. You can't blame them, since the moderately steep trail runs alongside Willow Creek and offers myriad quiet pools and fast, granite-lined cascades. The Forest Service requests that visitors don't swim upstream of Angel Falls, a wide cascade that looks like angel wings, because the creek is used as a domestic water supply. Downstream swimming is allowed, but be wary of the slippery granite. At 2.4 miles from the trailhead, be sure to take the left spur for Devils Slide, at a junction where the main trail continues to its end (0.4 mile farther) at McLeod Flat Road. Devils Slide is a remarkable granite water slide, with large rounded indentations in the rock. A chain-link fence keeps hikers off the dangerously slick granite. From Devils Slide, head back to the main trail and retrace your steps downhill. Expect to see some great views of bright-blue Bass Lake on the return trip.

User Groups: Hikers and dogs. No horses or mountain bikes. No wheelchair facilities.

Permits: No permits are required. Parking and access are free.

Maps: A Sierra National Forest map is available from the U.S. Forest Service. For a topographic map, ask the USGS for Bass Lake.

Directions: From Oakhurst, drive north on Highway 41 for four miles and turn right on Road 222. Drive four miles and bear left on

Road 274. Drive one mile to the trailhead parking area, on the left side of the road, on the west side of the highway bridge over Willow Creek. Alternatively, you can park near Falls Beach Picnic Area on Road 222 by Bass Lake's dam and access the trail via a connector route alongside Willow Creek.

Contact: Sierra National Forest, Bass Lake Ranger District, 57003 Road 225, North Fork, CA 93643, 559/877-2218, www.fs.fed.us/r5/sierra.

5 SQUAW LEAP LOOP
7.8 mi / 4.0 hr   2   8

near Millerton Lake

Map 11.1, page 573

The Squaw Leap area, managed by the Bureau of Land Management, straddles the San Joaquin River upstream of Millerton Lake State Park. This pretty foothill country is best visited in winter or spring, primarily due to the cooler temperatures but also for a chance to see wildflowers. The well-built Six-Mile Loop Trail, which is actually 7.8 miles as described here, rolls through chaparral country. Ceanothus and manzanita line the hillsides; gray pines and blue oaks dot the landscape. The trail begins with a one-mile stretch that leads you down to the river and the start of the loop. A surprisingly well-built footbridge takes you across the river canyon, where you have fine views of whitewater cascades, both upstream and down. On the far side of the bridge, go left on River Trail for 0.7 mile, then bear right on Ridge Trail. At mileage marker No. 3, you have a fine view of the river canyon; this is the best place to stop for a snack. Ridge Trail brings you right back downhill to the bridge you crossed earlier; cross it again and head back to your car to finish out the trip.

User Groups: Hikers, dogs, horses, and mountain bikes. No wheelchair facilities.

Permits: No permits are required. Parking and access are free.

Maps: For a topographic map, ask the USGS for Millerton Lake East.

Directions: From Fresno, drive 37 miles east on Highway 168 and turn left on Auberry Road. Drive through Auberry and turn left on Powerhouse Road. Drive 1.9 miles and turn left on Smalley Road at the sign for Squaw Leap Management Area. Park by the campground and signed trailhead.

Contact: Bureau of Land Management, Bakersfield Field Office, 3801 Pegasus Drive, Bakersfield, CA 93308, 661/391-6000, www.ca.blm.gov/bakersfield.

6 KAISER PEAK
10.6 mi / 6.0 hr or 2 days   4   9

in the Kaiser Wilderness north of Huntington Lake near Lakeshore

Map 11.1, page 573

While many visitors to Huntington Lake take the short strolls to Rancheria Falls or the Indian Pools on Big Creek, far fewer attempt the ascent of Kaiser Peak. Why? Because it's a butt-kicking, 5.3-mile climb to the top, gaining 3,000 feet of elevation on the way to the 10,320-foot peak. Luckily, you get many excellent views of Huntington Lake on the way up, and at the halfway point, you can scramble up for a view and a rest on huge College Rock. Then it's up, up, and up some more, for what seems like an eternity. Finally, you gain the rocky summit, and at last you know why you came. You're wowed by incredible 360-degree views, which take in Mammoth Pool Reservoir, Huntington Lake, Shaver Lake, Mount Ritter, and Mount Goddard. Wow. Backpackers looking for more mileage can turn the hike into a 14-mile loop trip.

User Groups: Hikers, dogs, and horses. No mountain bikes. No wheelchair facilities.

Permits: A free wilderness permit is required for overnight stays and is available from the High Sierra/Prather Ranger Station. Quotas are in effect year-round; permits are available in advance for a $5 reservation fee per person.

Maps: A Sierra National Forest or Kaiser Wilderness map is available from the U.S. Forest Service. For a topographic map, ask the USGS for Kaiser Peak.

Directions: From Fresno, drive northeast on Highway 168 through Clovis for 70 miles to Huntington Lake, turn left on Huntington Lake Road, and drive one mile. Look for the large sign for the horse stables and pack station, and turn right. Follow the pack station road (Deer Creek Road) for 0.5 mile to the hikers' parking area. The trailhead is signed Kaiser Loop Trail.

Contact: Sierra National Forest, High Sierra Ranger District, P.O. Box 559, Prather, CA 93651, 559/855-5360, www.fs.fed.us/r5/sierra.

7 TWIN LAKES AND GEORGE LAKE
8.0-9.8 mi / 6.0-7.0 hr or 2 days   🚶3 ⛰9

in the Kaiser Wilderness north of Huntington Lake near Lakeshore

Map 11.1, page 573

Trails into the Kaiser Wilderness always seem to come with a climb, and the route to Twin Lakes and George Lake is no exception. But if you're willing to work your heart and lungs, your reward is a spectacular day hike or backpacking trip to three scenic alpine lakes. Along the way, you must ascend to Kaiser Ridge and cross over it through Potter Pass. You're witness to wildflower-filled meadows, dense conifer forests, and a classic Sierra view from the pass. You can easily make out the jagged outline of the Minarets. It's a great spot to stop and catch your breath. Then it's downhill from the pass to the granite-lined Twin Lakes, at three miles out. Many people make this their destination, then turn around for a six-mile round-trip. If you do, make sure you visit the second Twin Lake, which is much prettier than the first. For those continuing onward, it's uphill again to George Lake, 1.3

miles from Upper Twin Lake. The final push is definitely worth it. Trailhead elevation is 8,200 feet, Twin Lakes are at 8,800 feet, and George Lake is at 9,300 feet. Another good route to these lakes is from the trailhead near Sample Meadow Campground, farther north on Kaiser Pass Road. If you're willing to drive farther, this trail has less of a climb.

User Groups: Hikers, dogs, and horses. No mountain bikes. No wheelchair facilities.

Permits: A free wilderness permit is required for overnight stays and is available from the High Sierra/Prather Ranger Station. Quotas are in effect year-round; permits are available in advance for a $5 reservation fee per person.

Maps: A Sierra National Forest or Kaiser Wilderness map is available from the U.S. Forest Service. For a topographic map, ask the USGS for Kaiser Peak.

Directions: From Fresno, drive northeast on Highway 168 through Clovis for 70 miles to Huntington Lake; turn right on Kaiser Pass Road and drive 4.8 miles to a large parking area on the south side of the road. The trail begins across the road from the parking area. Look for a trail sign for Trail 24E03, Twin Lakes and Potter Pass. Park on the south side of the road; the trail begins on the north side of the road.

Contact: Sierra National Forest, High Sierra Ranger District, P.O. Box 559, Prather, CA 93651, 559/855-5360, www.fs.fed.us/r5/sierra.

8 INDIAN POOLS
1.5 mi / 1.0 hr   🚶1 ⛰8

off Highway 168 near Huntington Lake

Map 11.1, page 573

When campers at Huntington Lake's many campgrounds are looking for a place to cool off in the afternoon, Indian Pools is where they go. The hike is really a walk, suitable for all ages and abilities. You can stop almost anywhere you like along Big Creek, pick a pool, and wade in. The trailhead is a bit tricky to find; it's all the way at the far end of the Sierra Summit Ski Area parking lot, near some mobile homes and trailers. Ignore the wide dirt road and instead look for the single-track trail signed for Indian Pools. It's a smooth, dirt path that quickly meets up with Big Creek. Flowers bloom in profusion along the stream and the rocky areas of the trail. The official path ends 0.7 mile east of the trailhead, at a huge, clear pool that is big enough to jump into and swim across. A use trail continues farther upstream, marked by trail cairns. If you follow it, you can reach quieter, more private pools.

User Groups: Hikers and dogs. No horses or mountain bikes. No wheelchair facilities.

Permits: No permits are required. Parking and access are free.

Maps: A Sierra National Forest map is available from the U.S. Forest Service. For a topographic map, ask the USGS for Huntington Lake.

Directions: From Fresno, drive northeast on Highway 168 through Clovis for 70 miles, past Shaver Lake. One mile before reaching Huntington Lake, turn right at the signed Sierra Summit Ski Area. Drive 0.5 mile to the far end of the ski area parking lot and look for the signed trailhead for Indian Pools. Occasionally the Sierra Summit parking lot is closed, and you must park on Highway 168 and walk the short distance into the ski area.

Contact: Sierra National Forest, High Sierra Ranger District, P.O. Box 559, Prather, CA 93651, 559/855-5360, www.fs.fed.us/r5/sierra.

9 RANCHERIA FALLS
2.0 mi / 1.0 hr   👣1 ⛰9

off Highway 168 near Huntington Lake

Map 11.1, page 573

At 7,760 feet in elevation in Sierra National Forest, the air is clean and fresh, butterflies flutter amid the wildflowers, and a 150-foot waterfall sparkles in the sunlight. Wanna go?

It's an easy trip, with the trailhead located close to popular Huntington Lake. The hike to Rancheria Falls is a well-graded one mile on a National Recreation Trail, suitable for hikers of all levels. The route leads through a fir forest with an understory of wildflowers and gooseberry, and it delivers you at Rancheria Falls' base, where you watch the creek tumble over a 50-foot-wide rock ledge. On weekends the destination can be a little crowded, but you can pick a boulder downstream from the falls and call it your own. Then have a seat and watch the watery spectacle unfold.

User Groups: Hikers, dogs, horses, and mountain bikes. No wheelchair facilities.

Permits: No permits are required. Parking and access are free.

Maps: A Sierra National Forest map is available from the U.S. Forest Service. For a topographic map, ask the USGS for Huntington Lake.

Directions: From Fresno, drive northeast on Highway 168 through Clovis for 70 miles, past Shaver Lake. A half mile before reaching Huntington Lake, take the right turnoff signed for Rancheria Falls (Road 8S31). Follow the dirt road for 1.3 miles to the signed trailhead, at a sharp curve in the road. Park off the road.

Contact: Sierra National Forest, High Sierra Ranger District, P.O. Box 559, Prather, CA 93651, 559/855-5360, www.fs.fed.us/r5/sierra.

10 DINKEY LAKES
7.0 mi / 4.0 hr or 2 days   👣2 ⛰9

in Dinkey Lakes Wilderness off Highway 168 near Shaver Lake

Map 11.1, page 573

We've never met anybody who doesn't love the Dinkey Lakes. What's not to love? The small wilderness area has dozens of lakes, and most are so easily accessible that you can see them in a day hike rather than packing along all your gear for an overnight stay. The trip begins with a stream crossing over Dinkey Creek, where you are immediately awed by the incredible array of colors in the rock streambed. Walk on level trail through a flower-filled forest, recross the creek, and start to climb. At 1.3 miles, you reach the junction for the start of the loop. Go right and meet Mystery Lake at 1.6 miles, Swede Lake at 2.3 miles, South Lake at 3.2 miles, and finally First Dinkey Lake at 3.8 miles. First Dinkey Lake is the most beautiful of them all. After taking in the scenery, continue on the loop, now heading westward back to the parking lot. One caveat: Don't expect much solitude. The easy hiking here makes this area extremely popular. Note that the loop described here works as either a day hike or backpacking trip, but if you choose to backpack, you can explore much farther, taking the spurs off the end of the main loop, between South Lake and First Dinkey Lake, to Second Dinkey Lake, Island Lake, Rock Lake, and so on.

User Groups: Hikers, dogs, and horses. No mountain bikes. No wheelchair facilities.

Permits: A wilderness permit is required for overnight stays and is available from the High Sierra/Prather Ranger Station. Quotas are in effect year-round; permits are available in advance for a $5 reservation fee per person.

Maps: A Dinkey Lakes Wilderness map is available from Tom Harrison Maps or the U.S. Forest Service. For topographic maps, ask the USGS for Huntington Lake and Dogtooth Peak.

Directions: From Fresno, drive northeast on Highway 168 through Clovis for 50 miles to the town of Shaver Lake. Turn right on Dinkey Creek Road and drive nine miles. Turn left on Rock Creek Road/9S09, drive 6 miles, turn right on 9S10, and drive 4.7 miles. Turn right at the sign for Dinkey Lakes, on Road 9S62, and drive 2.2 miles to the trailhead. These last two miles are very rough road. Stay left at the fork to bypass the four-wheel-drive area and go straight to the trailhead.

Contact: Sierra National Forest, High Sierra Ranger District, P.O. Box 559, Prather, CA 93651, 559/855-5360, www.fs.fed.us/r5/sierra.

🟦11 LAKE THOMAS EDISON TO AGNEW MEADOWS (JMT / PCT)

38.0 mi one-way / 3 days 👥4 ⛰10

from Lake Thomas Edison
north to Agnew Meadows

Map 11.2, page 574

The world is not perfect, but the scene from Silver Pass comes close. At 10,900 feet, you scan a bare, high-granite landscape sprinkled with alpine lakes. Just north of the pass are five small lakes: Chief, Papoose, Warrior, Squaw, and Lake of the Lone Indian. This is the highlight on this 38-mile section of the Pacific Crest Trail. The trip starts at Mono Creek, with a good resupply point at Edison Lake (7,650 feet), just two miles away. From the Mono Creek junction, you head north toward Silver Pass, climbing along Silver Pass Creek much of the way. Before you get to Silver Pass, there's a stream crossing that can be dangerous in high-runoff conditions. Top Silver Pass at 10,900 feet, and enjoy a five-mile descent and then a quick ascent to Tully Hole (9,250 feet). Climbing north, you pass Deer Creek, Purple Lake, and Lake Virginia. You head up to Red Cones and then make a steady descent toward Devils Postpile National Monument. A good resupply point is at nearby Reds Meadows Pack Station.

To continue north on the John Muir Trail/Pacific Crest Trail (JMT/PCT), see the *Agnew Meadows to Tuolumne Meadows (JMT/PCT)* hike in the *Yosemite and Mammoth Lakes* chapter. If you are walking this trail in reverse, see the *Whitney Portal to Lake Thomas Edison (JMT/PCT)* hike in this chapter.

Special Note: For food drop information, call the Vermillion Valley Resort. It is open only in summer and fall.

User Groups: Hikers, dogs, and horses. No mountain bikes. No wheelchair facilities.

Permits: A wilderness permit is required for traveling through various wilderness and special-use areas the trail traverses. Contact the Inyo National Forest or Sierra National Forest at the addresses below.

Maps: A John Muir Trail Map Pack is available from Tom Harrison Maps. For topographic maps, ask the USGS for Mammoth Mountain, Crystal Crag, Bloody Mountain, Graveyard Peak, Mount Ritter, and Coip Peak.

Directions: From Fresno, drive northeast on Highway 168 for about 68 miles to the Lakeshore Resort Area, at Huntington Lake. Turn northeast onto Kaiser Pass Road/Forest Service 4S01. Kaiser Pass Road becomes Edison Lake Road at Mono Hot Springs. Drive another five miles north, past the Vermillion Resort and Campground, and beyond to the parking area for backcountry hikers. The trail begins near the west end of the lake.

Contact: Inyo National Forest, Mammoth Ranger Station, P.O. Box 148, Mammoth Lakes, CA 93546, 760/924-5500 or 760/873-2400 (permits), www.fs.usda.gov/inyo; Sierra National Forest, High Sierra Ranger District, P.O. Box 559, Prather, CA 93651, 559/855-5360, www.fs.fed.us/r5/sierra; Vermillion Valley Resort, 559/855-6558 (food drop).

12 HONEYMOON LAKE
12.0 mi / 1-2 days

in the John Muir Wilderness

Map 11.2, page 574

Since the trailhead elevation in Pine Creek Canyon is only 7,400 feet, the best destinations must be gained with a climb. That includes Honeymoon Lake, six miles and a 3,000-foot ascent away. Luckily, you pass Upper and Lower Pine Lake along the route, and there's enough spectacular scenery to keep you motivated as you huff and puff. The route begins by the pack station in the trees along Pine Creek, then joins a mining road that leads to the Brownstone Mine. (Don't be put off by the mining activity at this trailhead. You soon leave it behind as you enter the John Muir Wilderness.) As you switchback up and out of the trees, you gain views of the Owens River Valley and the desertlike White Mountains. Above the mine, the road becomes a trail and

also becomes extremely rocky as it ascends more switchbacks to meet first Lower and then Upper Pine Lake, at 4.7 and 5.7 miles. The upper lake is at 10,400 feet and is reached by following the trail along the lower lake's northwest shore. A quarter mile beyond the upper lake, you reach a trail junction and take the right fork toward Italy Pass, heading west to Honeymoon Lake (in 0.1 mile). Many campsites are found near the granite-bound lake, set at 10,400 feet.

User Groups: Hikers, dogs, and horses. No mountain bikes. No wheelchair facilities.

Permits: A free wilderness permit is required year-round for overnight stays and is available from the Bishop/White Mountain Ranger Station. Quotas are in effect from May 1 to November 1; permits are available in advance for a $5 reservation fee per person.

Maps: A John Muir Wilderness map is available from the U.S. Forest Service. A map of the Mono Divide High County is available from Tom Harrison Maps. For topographic maps, ask the USGS for Bishop and Tungsten Hills.

Directions: From Bishop, drive north on U.S. 395 for seven miles and turn left (west) on Pine Creek Road. Drive 9.5 miles to the trailhead parking area, near the pack station, on the left side of the road.

Contact: Inyo National Forest, White Mountain Ranger Station, 798 North Main Street, Bishop, CA 93514, 760/873-2500, www.fs.usda.gov/inyo.

13 BLUE LAKE
6.0 mi / 3.0 hr or 2 days

in the John Muir Wilderness

Map 11.2, page 574   **BEST (**

The Sabrina Basin Trail leads to a series of gorgeous alpine lakes set below lofty, 13,000-foot granite peaks. Of these, one of the easiest to reach is scenic Blue Lake, a popular spot for photographers, trout anglers, and cold-water swimmers. If you catch the light just right, you can take pictures of Blue Lake with towering Mount Thompson and the Thompson Ridge mirrored on its surface. It's a 1,250-foot climb to the lake (at 10,400 feet), but it is spread out gradually over three miles. Nonetheless, be prepared for the thin air here, which can make the climb seem pretty strenuous if you're not acclimated. Start by hiking along the shore of Lake Sabrina, then switchback your way uphill to Blue Lake. The trail is very rocky in places; wear good boots. If you get inspired to see more of this high-alpine scenery, you can bear left from Blue Lake to Donkey Lake and the Baboon Lakes (1.5 miles farther), or bear right and hike eastward to the Emerald Lakes and Dingleberry Lake (1.8 miles farther). Any of these are likely to have fewer visitors than Blue Lake.

User Groups: Hikers, dogs, and horses. No mountain bikes. No wheelchair facilities.

Permits: A free wilderness permit is required year-round for overnight stays and is available from the Bishop/White Mountain Ranger Station. Quotas are in effect from May 1 to November 1; permits are available in advance for a $5 reservation fee per person.

Maps: A John Muir Wilderness map is available from the U.S. Forest Service. A Bishop Pass map is available from Tom Harrison Maps. For topographic maps, ask the USGS for Mount Thompson and Mount Darwin.

Directions: From Bishop on U.S. 395, turn west on Line Street/Highway 168 and drive 18.5 miles to Lake Sabrina. Day-use parking is located near the end of the road, just before the boat launch area. Backpackers' parking is located at a turnout near the road to North Lake, 0.5 mile before the end of the road.

Contact: Inyo National Forest, White Mountain Ranger Station, 798 North Main Street, Bishop, CA 93514, 760/873-2500, www.fs.usda.gov/inyo.

⬛14 LAMARCK LAKES

6.0 mi / 3.0 hr or 2 days   🥾3   ⛰9

in the John Muir Wilderness

Map 11.2, page 574

The only downer on the Lamarck Lakes Trail is that from the trailhead parking area, you have to walk 0.5 mile down the road to get to the actual trailhead, which is located in North Lake Campground. No problem, though; the scenery is so lovely around here you won't mind the extra walk. Once you access the trailhead, the path heads through the aspens and crosses Bishop Creek on a footbridge. You'll climb gently for one mile through a lodgepole pine forest, gaining only 600 feet to the left fork for Grass Lake, a small and shallow lake in a wide meadow. Grass Lake is worth a brief glance, but it doesn't hold a candle to the Lamarck Lakes. Back on the main trail, the climb begins in earnest, but it's less than a mile more to the short right spur to Lower Lamarck Lake. The lower lake is quite scenic, set in a rock-lined granite basin. Look for Mount Emerson, Mount Lamarck, and the red-colored Piute Crags in the background. Many people make this their destination for the day, but if you want to see more, cross the lake's outlet creek and continue 0.5 mile farther to the Upper Lamarck Lake, which is nearly double in size. There isn't much in the way of a formal trail to Upper Lamarck; you just make your way by following the course of the outlet creek. Those looking for an adventure can make their way from the Lower Lamarck Lake to the Wonder Lakes, set in the basin northwest of Lower Lamarck. Trailhead elevation for this hike is 9,300 feet, the lower lake is at 10,662 feet, and the upper lake is at 10,918 feet.

User Groups: Hikers, dogs, and horses. No mountain bikes. No wheelchair facilities.

Permits: A free wilderness permit is required year-round for overnight stays and is available from the Bishop/White Mountain Ranger Station. Quotas are in effect from May 1 to November 1; permits are available in advance for a $5 reservation fee per person.

Maps: A John Muir Wilderness map is available from the U.S. Forest Service. A Bishop Pass map is available from Tom Harrison Maps. For topographic maps, ask the USGS for Mount Thompson and Mount Darwin.

Directions: From Bishop on U.S. 395, turn west on Line Street/Highway 168 and drive 18 miles toward Lake Sabrina. Just before reaching the lake, turn right at the turnoff for North Lake. Drive 1.5 miles and turn right to park in the hiker parking lot by North Lake, near the pack station. Then walk 0.5 mile down the road to the trailhead, at the edge of North Lake Campground.

Contact: Inyo National Forest, White Mountain Ranger Station, 798 North Main Street, Bishop, CA 93514, 760/873-2500, www.fs.usda.gov/inyo.

15 LOCH LEVEN LAKE
5.0 mi / 3.0 hr   3   9

in the John Muir Wilderness
Map 11.2, page 574

If you're in the mood for a shorter hike in the Bishop Creek and North Lake area, Loch Leven Lake could fit the bill. After walking 0.5 mile from the trailhead parking area to North Lake Campground's trailhead, take the trail marked for Piute Pass. A steep climb in the first mile will leave you panting. Luckily, the route is shaded by lodgepole pines. After you leave the forest, the grade lessens. You traverse a series of switchbacks that take you to the top of a high ridge, where Loch Leven Lake is nestled at 10,740 feet. As you curve your way up the ridge, be sure to stop occasionally and look back at the incredible valley below and the reddish-colored Piute Crags towering above. You'll say "wow" a bunch of times.

Loch Leven Lake is set right alongside the trail in a rocky glacial bowl. It is very long and narrow, with little accessible shoreline. A steep talus slope, usually snow covered, frames its back side. There are a few campsites on the far side of the lake in the whitebark pines.

Ambitious hikers can continue another 1.2 miles to Piute Lake, with little additional elevation gain. A bonus on this trip: In autumn, the quaking aspens along the lower reaches of the route can take your breath away. Total elevation gain to Loch Leven Lake is 1,400 feet.

User Groups: Hikers, dogs, and horses. No mountain bikes. No wheelchair facilities.

Permits: No permits are required. Parking and access are free.

Maps: A John Muir Wilderness map is available from the U.S. Forest Service. A Bishop Pass map is available from Tom Harrison Maps. For topographic maps, ask the USGS for Mount Thompson and Mount Darwin.

Directions: From Bishop on U.S. 395, turn west on Line Street/Highway 168 and drive 18 miles toward Lake Sabrina. Just before reaching the lake, turn right at the turnoff for North Lake. Drive 1.5 miles and turn right to park in the hiker parking lot by North Lake, near the pack station. Walk 0.5 mile down the road to the trailhead, at the edge of North Lake Campground.

Contact: Inyo National Forest, White Mountain Ranger Station, 798 North Main Street, Bishop, CA 93514, 760/873-2500, www.fs.usda.gov/inyo.

16 TYEE LAKES
7.0 mi / 4.0 hr or 2 days   3   9

in the John Muir Wilderness
Map 11.2, page 574   BEST

There's so much excellent hiking in the South Fork Bishop Creek Canyon, it's hard to choose where to go. Since so many backpackers opt for Bishop Pass Trail and its many lakes (see listing in this chapter), day hikers might do well to choose this trail to the Tyee Lakes instead. Just make sure that you are in the mood for hiking up, because you'll do plenty of that, with a total 2,000-foot elevation gain to the highest lakes. From the bridge over Bishop Creek, your climb begins immediately as you tromp up a hillside covered with sagebrush and aspens, gradually making your way through a few dozen switchbacks. You get great views of the Bishop Creek Canyon as you climb, which is an especially beautiful sight when the aspens are putting on their autumn color show. Finally you enter a lodgepole pine forest, and after two miles of climbing, the grade eases up. You reach one of the smaller, lower Tyee Lakes at 2.3 miles. Another 0.5 mile of climbing brings you to the next small lake (called Tyee Lake number two). These first two lakes are small and pondlike, edged with grass, and not worth much more than a second glance. But keep pushing onward, and in another 0.5 mile, you reach one of the larger Tyee Lakes (number three). The fourth and fifth lakes are only 0.25 mile farther and are separated by a small boulder field. The fifth lake is very small, but the fourth lake (elevation 11,015 feet) is large and beautiful. Backpackers usually set up their tent at the third lake and then day hike to the fourth and fifth lakes. Named for a brand of salmon eggs, the Tyee Lakes offer dependably good trout fishing and the chance to enjoy plenty of classic high Sierra scenery. Backpackers looking to make a semi-loop can arrange to have a car waiting at Lake Sabrina in Bishop Creek Canyon, then continue from the Tyee Lakes to George Lake and then Lake Sabrina.

User Groups: Hikers, dogs, and horses. No mountain bikes. No wheelchair facilities.

Permits: A free wilderness permit is required year-round for overnight stays and is available from the Bishop/White Mountain Ranger Station. Quotas are in effect from May 1 to November 1; permits are available in advance for a $5 reservation fee per person.

Maps: A John Muir Wilderness map is available from the U.S. Forest Service. A Bishop Pass map is available from Tom Harrison Maps. For a topographic map, ask the USGS for Mount Thompson.

Directions: From Bishop on U.S. 395, turn west on Line Street/Highway 168 and drive 14 miles to the junction for South Lake. Go left and drive 4.5 miles on South Lake Road to the footbridge that crosses Bishop Creek. It is on the right, just before Willow Campground, and it is signed as Tyee Lakes and George Lake trailhead. Park alongside the road.

Contact: Inyo National Forest, White Mountain Ranger Station, 798 North Main Street, Bishop, CA 93514, 760/873-2500, www.fs.usda.gov/inyo.

17 GREEN AND BROWN LAKES

6.6 mi / 3.0 hr 🏃3 ⛰9

in the John Muir Wilderness

Map 11.2, page 574

Brown Lake and Green Lake are two excellent day-hiking destinations from the South Lake trailhead in Bishop Creek's South Fork Canyon. With only a 1,500-foot climb, you can visit both lakes, maybe do a little fishing for rainbow trout, and be home in time for supper. Access the trail from the pack station trailhead, and follow a stock trail as it climbs along Bishop Creek through a conifer forest and joins the main Green Lake Trail at one mile. Bear left and level out to an alpine meadow at two miles, where you have a spectacular view of Mount Tom behind you. Soon you'll meet Brown Lake's outlet stream and the little lake itself (really a pond), at 2.5 miles and 10,750 feet. Pay a brief visit, then continue another 0.5 mile to much larger and prettier Green Lake, at 11,050 feet, surrounded by wildflowers and ancient-looking whitebark pines. Both lakes host an abundance of rainbow trout, who might just invite themselves to dinner.

User Groups: Hikers, dogs, and horses. No mountain bikes. No wheelchair facilities.

Permits: No permits are required. Parking and access are free.

Maps: A John Muir Wilderness map is available from the U.S. Forest Service. A Bishop Pass map is available from Tom Harrison Maps. For a topographic map, ask the USGS for Mount Thompson.

Directions: From Bishop on U.S. 395, turn west on Line Street/Highway 168 and drive 14 miles to the junction for South Lake. Go left and drive six miles on South Lake Road to Parchers Resort and pack station, on the left side of the road, just beyond Willow Campground.

Contact: Inyo National Forest, White Mountain Ranger Station, 798 North Main Street, Bishop, CA 93514, 760/873-2500, www.fs.usda.gov/inyo.

18 RUWAU AND CHOCOLATE LAKES LOOP
6.6 mi / 3.5 hr or 2 days 🏃3 ⛰10

in the John Muir Wilderness

Map 11.2, page 574

Lakes, lakes, lakes everywhere. That's how it is on Bishop Pass Trail, where in the space of only five miles you can access Long Lake, Spearhead Lake, Saddlerock Lake, Bishop Lake, and so on. But if you prefer a loop trip to an out-and-back hike, Bishop Pass Trail provides another lake-filled option: a two-mile hike to Long Lake, then a circular route to Ruwau Lake, the Chocolate Lakes, and Bull Lake. It's the kind of trip that fills your mind with precious memories of blue-sky Sierra scenery and gemlike, rock-lined lakes. Still, the trip is not for everyone; some of the trail is an indistinct route with steep, rocky sections that are not an official trail. Bring a good map with you.

The trail begins on the south side of the parking lot, and you head uphill along the eastern shore of South Lake. The views begin almost immediately, particularly of South Lake, Mount Thompson, and Mount Goode. Take the left fork at 0.75 mile, heading for Long Lake and Bishop Pass. Continue straight, ignoring all turnoffs as you hike up around the spectacular western shore of Long Lake, popular with anglers and backpackers. At 2.5 miles (before you reach the lake's far end), instead of continuing straight to Saddlerock

Lake and Bishop Pass, take the left fork for Ruwau Lake, a steep but short 0.5 mile away. Skirt the edge of Ruwau Lake for about 75 yards, then look for a use trail leading uphill to your left. Make a steep uphill climb for 0.5 mile to the ridgetop, where you'll look down and see the Chocolate Lakes, set below Chocolate Peak. Make the steep descent to the lakes, picking your way along the rocky slope. Once you're there, the hard part is over. You'll find an easy-to-follow trail at the Chocolate Lakes, and then you'll walk downhill for 0.5 mile to Bull Lake, which is big, round, and beautiful. From Bull Lake, you keep on hiking, and in less than 0.25 mile, you rejoin Bishop Pass Trail. Turn right and walk just under two miles back to the parking lot. Wow, what a day.

User Groups: Hikers, dogs, and horses. No mountain bikes. No wheelchair facilities.

Permits: A free wilderness permit is required year-round for overnight stays and is available from the Bishop/White Mountain Ranger Station. Quotas are in effect from May 1 to November 1; permits are available in advance for a $5 reservation fee per person.

Maps: A John Muir Wilderness map is available from the U.S. Forest Service. A Bishop Pass map is available from Tom Harrison Maps. For a topographic map, ask the USGS for Mount Thompson.

Directions: From Bishop on U.S. 395, turn west on Line Street/Highway 168 and drive 14 miles to the junction for South Lake. Go left and drive 7.5 miles on South Lake Road to the end of the road and the trailhead parking area. This parking is for day-use only. If you are backpacking, you must park 1.5 miles from the trailhead, east of Parchers Resort.

Contact: Inyo National Forest, White Mountain Ranger Station, 798 North Main Street, Bishop, CA 93514, 760/873-2500, www.fs.usda.gov/inyo.

19 FIRST AND SECOND FALLS
3.0 mi / 1.5 hr 🚶2 ⛰9

in the John Muir Wilderness

Map 11.2, page 574

If you're camping or fishing in Big Pine Canyon, or maybe just wandering around exploring the area, there's a great walk to take starting from the end of the road near Glacier Lodge. Since it's just a day hike, you can park in the parking area right by the lodge and save yourself the long walk from the backpackers' parking lot.

Head west from the trailhead on the wide road, passing some private cabins, and in seconds you cross a bridge over First Falls, a noisy, 200-foot-long whitewater cascade. Bear right onto a narrower trail and start switchbacking uphill, paralleling the cascade. As you climb, you get awesome views into Big Pine Canyon's South Fork. At the top of the falls, cross another bridge over the creek and take a hard left onto a dirt road, staying along the creek. Now it's a flat stroll into the north fork of Big Pine Canyon. Your goal is Second Falls, a larger, more impressive cascade than First Falls; it's less than a mile away and clearly visible from the trail. Since the route is set along the canyon bottom, you get many interesting vistas along the way, from the tall surrounding canyon walls to occasional lodgepole pines and many mountain wildflowers. When the trail starts to climb out of the canyon, take the left spur cutoff to head closer to the waterfall, or just pick a big rock to sit on and admire the scenery.

User Groups: Hikers, dogs, and horses. No mountain bikes. No wheelchair facilities.

Permits: No permits are required. Parking and access are free.

Maps: A John Muir Wilderness map is available from the U.S. Forest Service. A Palisades map is available from Tom Harrison Maps. For a topographic map, ask the USGS for Coyote Flat.

Directions: From Bishop, drive 15 miles south on U.S. 395 to Big Pine. Turn right (west) on Crocker Street, which becomes Glacier Lodge Road, and drive 10.5 miles to Glacier Lodge and the Big Pine Canyon trailhead, at the end of the road. Day hikers may park in the day-use area near the lodge, but backpackers must park 0.5 mile east, on Glacier Lodge Road, in the backpackers' parking lot.

Contact: Inyo National Forest, White Mountain Ranger Station, 798 North Main Street, Bishop, CA 93514, 760/873-2500, www.fs.usda.gov/inyo.

20 FIRST AND SECOND LAKES
9.6 mi / 6.0 hr or 2 days 🚶3 ⛰9

in the John Muir Wilderness

Map 11.2, page 574

The trail to First and Second Lakes in Big Pine Canyon follows the same route as the trail to First and Second Falls, above, but then continues onward, climbing up and over Second Falls on the well-graded trail to Cienaga Mirth, at three miles out. Off to the left of the trail you'll see a magnificent stone cabin (now sometimes used as a backcountry ranger residence) built by movie star Lon Chaney. Wildflowers are excellent at the swampy, spring-fed mirth. You reach First Lake at 4.5 miles, and Second Lake is just a few hundred yards farther. By Second Lake, you've climbed to over 10,000 feet, and the lake water is a stunning glacial blue-green. Those who wish to see more lakes can continue on a loop past Second Lake to Third, Fourth, Fifth, and Black Lakes, making a long, 14-mile day. Fifth Lake, just off the loop by a third of a mile, is the most scenic. You'll see hardy mountaineer-types with climbing equipment turning left beyond Third Lake. They're hiking a full nine miles one-way to the edge of Palisade Glacier, the southernmost glacier in the Sierra. Considering it has a 5,000-foot elevation gain, the route to the glacier is not for everybody.

User Groups: Hikers, dogs, and horses. No mountain bikes. No wheelchair facilities.

Permits: A free wilderness permit is required year-round for overnight stays and is available from the Bishop/White Mountain Ranger Station. Quotas are in effect from May 1 to November 1; permits are available in advance for a $5 reservation fee per person.

Maps: A John Muir Wilderness map is available from the U.S. Forest Service. A Palisades map is available from Tom Harrison Maps. For topographic maps, ask the USGS for Coyote Flat and Split Mountain.

Directions: From Bishop, drive 15 miles south on U.S. 395 to Big Pine. Turn right (west) on Crocker Street, which becomes Glacier Lodge Road, and drive 10.5 miles to Glacier Lodge and the Big Pine Canyon trailhead, at the end of the road. Day hikers may park in the day-use area near the lodge, but backpackers must park 0.5 mile east, on Glacier Lodge Road, in the backpackers' parking lot.

Contact: Inyo National Forest, White Mountain Ranger Station, 798 North Main Street, Bishop, CA 93514, 760/873-2500, www.fs.usda.gov/inyo.

21 BIG STUMP TRAIL
1.0 mi / 0.5 hr 🏃1 ⛰8

in the Grant Grove area of
Kings Canyon National Park

Map 11.3, page 575

Normally it would be hard for us to get excited about a trail called the Big Stump Trail. In fact, this sort of thing could be quite depressing. But Big Stump Trail, at the entrance to Kings Canyon National Park, is a pleasant nature walk and provides an excellent history lesson as well. The size of the mammoth trees—oops, make that stumps—just blows you away. Most of the big trees were cut for timber in the 1880s, and you'll see the remains of logging activities. Be sure to pick up an interpretive brochure at the Kings Canyon Visitors Center or at the trailhead. The trail is a short loop that circles a meadow. A few mature sequoias still thrive along the route,

including one in the first 50 feet from the parking lot. The path's highlights include the Burnt Monarch, a shell of a giant sequoia that has been ravaged by fire but still stands, and the Mark Twain Stump. The latter belonged to a 26-foot-wide tree that took two men 13 days to cut down.

User Groups: Hikers only. No dogs, horses, or mountain bikes. No wheelchair facilities.

Permits: No permits are required. There is a $20 entrance fee per vehicle at Sequoia and Kings Canyon National Parks, good for seven days.

Maps: A Sequoia and Kings Canyon map is available from Tom Harrison Maps. For a topographic map, ask the USGS for Hume.

Directions: From Fresno, drive east on Highway 180 for 55 miles to the Big Stump Entrance at Kings Canyon National Park. The trail begins 0.5 mile past the entrance station, at the Big Stump Picnic Area.

Contact: Sequoia and Kings Canyon National Parks, 47050 General Highway, Three Rivers, CA 93271-9651, 559/565-3341 or 559/565-4307, www.nps.gov/seki.

22 SUNSET TRAIL
5.0 mi / 2.5 hr 🏃2 ⛰8

in the Grant Grove area of
Kings Canyon National Park

Map 11.3, page 575

The Sunset Trail leaves Sunset Campground (elevation 6,590 feet) and heads gently downhill for 2.25 miles to Ella Falls, a pretty 40-foot cascade on Sequoia Creek. At 1.5 miles down the trail, you reach a junction with South Boundary Trail and can take a short side trip to the left to Viola Falls, which isn't much of a waterfall but is a memorably scenic spot on granite-sculpted Sequoia Creek. Most people just mosey down the trail, enjoying the big pines and firs and the flowering western azaleas, and maybe stealing a kiss on one of the wooden footbridges. If you like, you can follow the trail for its entire 2.5-mile length to

Sequoia Lake. Although the lake is privately owned, hikers are allowed to walk along its edge. While you're enjoying the lake, don't forget that the return trip is all uphill with a 1,300-foot elevation gain, so save some water and energy.

User Groups: Hikers only. No dogs, horses, or mountain bikes. No wheelchair facilities.

Permits: No permits are required. There is a $20 entrance fee per vehicle at Sequoia and Kings Canyon National Parks, good for seven days.

Maps: A Sequoia and Kings Canyon map is available from Tom Harrison Maps. For topographic maps, ask the USGS for Hume and General Grant Grove.

Directions: From Fresno, drive east on Highway 180 for 55 miles to the Big Stump Entrance at Kings Canyon National Park. Continue 1.5 miles and turn left, following signs for Kings Canyon. Drive 1.5 miles to Grant Grove Village, and park in the large parking lot near the visitors center. Cross the road and walk on the paved trail toward Sunset Campground's amphitheater. Continue heading left through the camp to site No. 118, where the trail begins.

Contact: Sequoia and Kings Canyon National Parks, 47050 General Highway, Three Rivers, CA 93271-9651, 559/565-3341 or 559/565-4307, www.nps.gov/seki.

23 MANZANITA AND AZALEA TRAILS
3.3 mi / 2.0 hr 🥾2 ⛰7

in the Grant Grove area of
Kings Canyon National Park

Map 11.3, page 575

This hike is a good exercise route for vacationers staying in Grant Grove Village or in the nearby campgrounds. It climbs 800 feet, which gives your heart and lungs a workout, and it's pretty every step of the way. From the edge of the dirt service road by the tent cabins, Manzanita Trail climbs a dry slope uphill to

Park Ridge. Near the top, you'll parallel the dirt road that leads to the Park Ridge Fire Lookout. Then Manzanita Trail meets up with Azalea Trail, and you'll descend on a much shadier, moister slope. The azaleas bloom bright white with prolific, showy blossoms in June and July. Azalea Trail ends at Wilsonia, a private community within the national park, so just retrace your steps to return back to your car.

User Groups: Hikers only. No dogs, horses, or mountain bikes. No wheelchair facilities.

Permits: No permits are required. There is a $20 entrance fee per vehicle at Sequoia and Kings Canyon National Parks, good for seven days.

Maps: A Sequoia and Kings Canyon map is available from Tom Harrison Maps. For a topographic map, ask the USGS for Hume.

Directions: From Fresno, drive east on Highway 180 for 55 miles to the Big Stump Entrance at Kings Canyon National Park. Continue 1.5 miles and turn left, following signs for Kings Canyon. Drive 1.5 miles to Grant Grove Village and park in the large parking lot near the visitors center. Walk on the service road near the tent cabins to reach the start of the Manzanita Trail.

Contact: Sequoia and Kings Canyon National Parks, 47050 General Highway, Three Rivers, CA 93271-9651, 559/565-3341 or 559/565-4307, www.nps.gov/seki.

24 PANORAMIC POINT AND PARK RIDGE LOOKOUT
4.7 mi / 3.0 hr 🥾2 ⛰9

in the Grant Grove area of
Kings Canyon National Park

Map 11.3, page 575

Start your trip by taking the 300-yard paved walk from the parking area to Panoramic Point, which delivers what its name implies. An interpretive display names the many peaks and valleys you can see, including the big pointy one, which is Mount Goddard at

13,560 feet. From Panoramic Point, take the dirt Park Ridge Trail that leads to the right along the ridge. Your views continue as you contour along the ridgeline, climbing gently uphill. The trail intersects a dirt road, which you follow for about 50 yards; then bear left onto the trail again. You'll intersect this dirt road once more about 100 yards before the Park Ridge Fire Lookout. Follow the road to the lookout tower, and check out the nifty outdoor shower at its base. If someone is stationed in the tower and gives you permission to come up, do so and sign the visitors register. (The lookout person rarely gets visitors on cloudy days, but he or she gets a good number of them when it's sunny, and you can see for miles around.) The lookout is operated by volunteers during the fire season, which is usually May to October. For your return trip, you can walk down the trail back to Panoramic Point or take the shorter fire road, which also leads back to the parking lot. Views are far better along the trail than on the fire road.

User Groups: Hikers only. No dogs, horses, or mountain bikes. No wheelchair facilities.

Permits: No permits are required. There is a $20 entrance fee per vehicle at Sequoia and Kings Canyon National Parks, good for seven days.

Maps: A Sequoia and Kings Canyon map is available from Tom Harrison Maps. For a topographic map, ask the USGS for Hume.

Directions: From Fresno, drive east on Highway 180 for 55 miles to the Big Stump Entrance at Kings Canyon National Park. Continue 1.5 miles and turn left, following signs for Kings Canyon. Drive 1.5 miles to Grant Grove Village and turn right by the visitors center and store. Follow the road past the cabins, and just before the John Muir Lodge, turn right on the road signed for Panoramic Point. It's 2.3 miles from the visitors center to Panoramic Point.

Contact: Sequoia and Kings Canyon National Parks, 47050 General Highway, Three Rivers, CA 93271-9651, 559/565-3341 or 559/565-4307, www.nps.gov/seki.

25 GENERAL GRANT TREE TRAIL
0.6 mi / 0.5 hr ♨₁ ⛰₈

in the Grant Grove area of
Kings Canyon National Park

Map 11.3, page 575   **BEST (**

This paved loop through a giant sequoia grove allows visitors a look at the General Grant Tree, the second-largest tree in the world. Estimated to be 1,800 to 2,000 years old, the General Grant is 267 feet tall and 107 feet in circumference at its base. Every year since 1926, the City of Sanger has held a Christmas celebration around its base, and so the tree is known as "the Nation's Christmas Tree." Its neighbors include the Fallen Monarch, a hollow downed tree that is so wide, it was once used as a park employee camp. Also nearby is a group of big sequoias named after various U.S. states. It may seem a little campy, but there are many excellent photo opportunities in the grove. A bonus: Most, but not all, of this trail is accessible to wheelchair users.

User Groups: Hikers. No dogs, horses, or mountain bikes. Partial wheelchair accessibility.

Permits: No permits are required. There is a $20 entrance fee per vehicle at Sequoia and Kings Canyon National Parks, good for seven days.

Maps: A Sequoia and Kings Canyon map is available from Tom Harrison Maps. For topographic maps, ask the USGS for Hume and General Grant Grove.

Directions: From Fresno, drive east on Highway 180 for 55 miles to the Big Stump Entrance at Kings Canyon National Park. Continue 1.5 miles and turn left, following signs for Kings Canyon. Drive one mile, passing Grant Grove Village, to the left turnoff for General Grant Tree. Turn left and follow the access road for 0.75 mile to the parking lot.

Contact: Sequoia and Kings Canyon National Parks, 47050 General Highway, Three Rivers, CA 93271-9651, 559/565-3341 or 559/565-4307, www.nps.gov/seki.

26 NORTH GROVE AND DEAD GIANT LOOP

3.0 mi / 1.5 hr 🏃2 ⛰7

in the Grant Grove area of
Kings Canyon National Park

Map 11.3, page 575

For people who want a little more hiking than what the General Grant Tree Trail (see listing in this chapter) provides, the combined North Grove and Dead Giant Loop Trails are the answer. The walk begins at the oversized vehicle parking at the General Grant Tree parking lot. Past the gate, follow an old dirt road that leads downhill through a mixed forest of sequoia, sugar pine, white fir, and dogwood. Don't expect to see dense groves of sequoias here; the big trees are few and far between. However, the forest is pleasant, quiet, and shady.

Stay to the right at the first junction to follow the posted North Grove Loop Trail. At the bottom of the hill, you'll pass an obscure junction with an old wagon road that was used to take logged sequoias to the mill. Continue to a more obvious junction at one mile out. Turn right and walk 0.25 mile downhill to Lion Meadow. Turn right on a single-track trail and circle around the meadow, heading for the Dead Giant. This sequoia, like some others in the park, is a nearly hollow, dead tree that somehow keeps standing. From the Dead Giant, it's a short tromp to the Sequoia Lake Overlook, a tranquil high point where you can have a snack and enjoy the view of the large, private lake in Sequoia National Forest. From the overlook, backtrack a few yards and turn right to finish out the loop, returning uphill on the wide dirt road. There is a 400-foot gain on the return.

User Groups: Hikers only. No dogs, horses, or mountain bikes. No wheelchair facilities.

Permits: No permits are required. There is a $20 entrance fee per vehicle at Sequoia and Kings Canyon National Parks, good for seven days.

Maps: A Sequoia and Kings Canyon map is available from Tom Harrison Maps. For topographic maps, ask the USGS for Hume and General Grant Grove.

Directions: From Fresno, drive east on Highway 180 for 55 miles to the Big Stump Entrance at Kings Canyon National Park. Continue 1.5 miles and turn left, following signs for Kings Canyon. Drive two miles, passing Grant Grove Village, to the left turnoff for General Grant Tree. Turn left and follow the access road for one mile to the parking lot. The North Grove Loop starts from the far end of the lower parking lot.

Contact: Sequoia and Kings Canyon National Parks, 47050 General Highway, Three Rivers, CA 93271-9651, 559/565-3341 or 559/565-4307, www.nps.gov/seki.

27 CHICAGO STUMP TRAIL

0.5 mi / 0.5 hr 🏃1 ⛰7

in Giant Sequoia National Monument
north of the Grant Grove area of
Kings Canyon National Park

Map 11.3, page 575

Before the loggers extracted their toll, the Converse Basin once sheltered one of the largest and finest groves of giant sequoias in the world. Where the giants once stood, second-growth sequoias have now taken hold. This short and easy stroll takes you through a regenerated mixed forest to the Chicago Stump, a massive stump that belonged to one of the largest trees in the area. The General Noble tree was cut down in 1893, and the lower portion of the tree was reassembled and exhibited at the Chicago World's Fair. The stump that remains is at least 10 feet high and over 25 feet wide. In addition to its historical interest, this easy trail provides a pleasant, peaceful change from the hustle and bustle of the neighboring national parks.

User Groups: Hikers, horses, and dogs. No mountain bikes. No wheelchair facilities.

Permits: No permits are required. There is a $20 entrance fee per vehicle at Sequoia and Kings Canyon National Parks, good for seven days.

Maps: A Sequoia National Forest map is available from the U.S. Forest Service. A map of Sequoia and Kings Canyon is available from Tom Harrison Maps. For a topographic map, ask the USGS for Hume.

Directions: From Fresno, drive east on Highway 180 for 55 miles to the Big Stump Entrance at Kings Canyon National Park. Continue 1.5 miles and turn left, following signs for Kings Canyon. Drive approximately 4.5 miles, passing Grant Grove Village, and turn left at the sign for Forest Road 13S03. Drive two miles, turn right on Road 13S65, and continue 0.1 mile to the Chicago Stump trailhead.

Contact: Giant Sequoia National Monument/Sequoia National Forest, Hume Lake Ranger District, 35860 East Kings Canyon Road, Dunlap, CA 93621, 559/338-2251, www.fs.fed.us/r5/sequoia.

28 BOOLE TREE LOOP

2.5 mi / 1.0 hr   🏃2 ⛰9

in Giant Sequoia National Monument north of the Grant Grove area of Kings Canyon National Park

Map 11.3, page 575

The drive in to the Boole Tree trailhead is worth the trip by itself, as you pass through a beautiful, ghostly meadow filled with giant sequoia stumps. The sight of them is so otherworldly that it may stay engrained in your memory for a long time. The Boole Tree hike is a loop, and it's a good idea to take the right side of the loop first, making the ascent more gradual. You climb 500 feet to the top of a ridge, then descend the other side, reaching the Boole Tree in one mile. (It's just off the main loop, accessible via a short, obvious spur.) At 269 feet tall and with a diameter of 35 feet, the Boole Tree is the largest tree in any of the national forests, and it's one of the largest trees in the world. It is one of a very few giant sequoias left standing in the Converse Basin grove, as the rest were clear-cut in the

late 1800s. Although some people go see the Boole Tree and then turn around, it's better to finish out the loop. You'll be rewarded with a stellar view of Spanish Mountain and the Kings River Canyon.

User Groups: Hikers, horses, and dogs. No mountain bikes. No wheelchair facilities.

Permits: No permits are required. There is a $20 entrance fee per vehicle at Sequoia and Kings Canyon National Parks, good for seven days.

Maps: A Sequoia National Forest map is available from the U.S. Forest Service. A map of Sequoia and Kings Canyon is available from Tom Harrison Maps. For a topographic map, ask the USGS for Hume.

Directions: From Fresno, drive east on Highway 180 for 55 miles to the Big Stump Entrance at Kings Canyon National Park. Continue 1.5 miles and turn left, following signs for Kings Canyon. Drive approximately six miles, passing Grant Grove Village. Turn left at the sign for Forest Road 13S55, Boole Tree, Converse Basin, and Stump Meadow. Drive 2.6 miles, and park in the wide parking pullout.

Contact: Giant Sequoia National Monument/Sequoia National Forest, Hume Lake Ranger District, 35860 Kings Canyon Road, Dunlap, CA 93621, 559/338-2251, www.fs.fed.us/r5/sequoia.

29 YUCCA POINT

4.0 mi / 2.25 hr   🏃3 ⛰8

in Giant Sequoia National Monument west of the Cedar Grove area of Kings Canyon National Park

Map 11.3, page 575

The Yucca Point Trail is an upside-down hike—the kind where you go down on the way in (so easy) and up on the way back (not so easy). The path descends from Highway 180 to the Kings River, dropping 1,200 feet along the way. As long as you don't climb uphill at high noon, the hike back is not as bad as it looks from the top. The trail is well graded; the only hardship is that the terrain is all chaparral, so there's almost no shade, just the occasional tall yucca plant. The path is mostly used by anglers heading down to the wild trout section of the Kings River, but hikers like the excellent views it provides and the access to the river's cool, emerald green pools.

User Groups: Hikers only. No dogs, horses, or mountain bikes. No wheelchair facilities.

Permits: No permits are required. There is a $20 entrance fee per vehicle for access to this section of Sequoia National Forest, payable at any of the entrance stations to Kings Canyon and Sequoia National Parks. The fee is good for seven days in both the national forest and the national parks.

Maps: A Sequoia National Forest map is available from the U.S. Forest Service. A map of Sequoia and Kings Canyon is available from Tom Harrison Maps. For a topographic map, ask the USGS for Wren Peak.

Directions: From Fresno, drive east on Highway 180 for 55 miles to the Big Stump Entrance at Kings Canyon National Park. Continue 1.5 miles and turn left, following signs for Kings Canyon. Drive another 16 miles on Highway 180, past Grant Grove and Kings Canyon Lodge, to the Yucca Point trailhead, on the left. Park in the pullouts alongside Highway 180.

Contact: Giant Sequoia National Monument/ Sequoia National Forest, Hume Lake Ranger District, 35860 Kings Canyon Road, Dunlap, CA 93621, 559/338-2251, www.fs.fed.us/r5/ sequoia.

🔟 WINDY CLIFFS
3.0 mi / 1.5 hr

in Giant Sequoia National Monument
west of the Cedar Grove area of
Kings Canyon National Park

Map 11.3, page 575

The Forest Service concessionaire charges a fee for tours of Boyden Cave, one of many limestone caverns in the vicinity of Kings Canyon

and Sequoia National Parks, and the parking lot is always busy with carloads and busloads of people waiting to take the tour. The cave is fascinating and worth a visit, but if you're low on cash, you can take this stellar hike instead and get million-dollar views of Kings Canyon for free. From the cave gift shop, walk up the paved path and take the left fork near the entrance to the cave (you'll need to go under the rope that borders the trail to the cave). The trail has a metal bar across it, but the Forest Service says it's perfectly legal to hike it; they just don't want to encourage casual visitors because the trail is unmaintained with very steep drop-offs. Once on the trail, in no time you'll climb a little higher and see a sweeping panorama of Highway 180 and the fast-flowing Kings River below. In one mile, Boulder Creek cascades down the hillside. The path ends when it reaches creekside at 1.5 miles. (A faint path continues, but it's badly overgrown.) Note that poison oak is prolific along this trail, so it might be a good idea to wear long pants and long sleeves.

User Groups: Hikers only. No dogs, horses, or mountain bikes. No wheelchair facilities.

Permits: No permits are required. There is a $20 per vehicle entrance fee for access to this section of Sequoia National Forest, payable at any of the entrance stations to Kings Canyon and Sequoia National Parks. The fee is good for seven days in both the national forest and the national parks.

Maps: A Sequoia National Forest map is available from the U.S. Forest Service. A map of Sequoia and Kings Canyon is available from Tom Harrison Maps. For a topographic map, ask the USGS for Wren Peak.

Directions: From Fresno, drive east on Highway 180 for 55 miles to the Big Stump Entrance at Kings Canyon National Park. Continue 1.5 miles and turn left, following signs for Kings Canyon. Drive 22 miles on Highway 180, passing Grant Grove and Kings Canyon Lodge, to the parking area for Boyden Cave, on the right side of the road.

Contact: Giant Sequoia National Monument/

Sequoia National Forest, Hume Lake Ranger District, 35860 Kings Canyon Road, Dunlap, CA 93621, 559/338-2251, www.fs.fed.us/r5/sequoia.

31 LEWIS CREEK TRAIL
11.6 mi / 6.0 hr or 2 days 🥾4 ⛰9

off Highway 180 in the Cedar Grove area of Kings Canyon National Park

Map 11.3, page 575

Up, up, and up. If you're willing to climb 3,200 feet over the course of 5.5 miles, your reward is pristine Frypan Meadow, at 7,800 feet in elevation. In early summer, the meadow is green and littered with wildflowers, creating a glorious vision after the hot, sunny climb. But there's no way to see it without first putting in some effort on the Lewis Creek Trail. The good news is that if the first mile or so proves to be too demanding, or too hot if you don't start first thing in the morning, you can always take the right fork at 1.6 miles and head back downhill on Hotel Creek Trail, making a seven-mile loop out of the trip. If you push onward on Lewis Creek Trail, you cross lovely Comb Creek (at 3.2 miles), then Lewis Creek one mile farther. Many day hikers make the Lewis Creek crossing their destination; its pools make fine swimming holes. Backpackers continue another 1.5 miles to Frypan Meadow. If you have your wilderness permit, campsites are available there.

User Groups: Hikers and horses. No dogs or mountain bikes. No wheelchair facilities.

Permits: There is a $20 entrance fee per vehicle at Sequoia and Kings Canyon National Parks, good for seven days. Wilderness permits are required for overnight stays. They are available on a first-come, first-served basis at the wilderness permit station at Roads End or the Kings Canyon Visitor Center. For advanced wilderness permits or information on trail conditions, go to www.nps.gov/seki. Trailhead quotas are in effect from May to September.

Maps: A Sequoia and Kings Canyon map is available from Tom Harrison Maps. For a topographic map, ask the USGS for Cedar Grove.

Directions: From Fresno, drive east on Highway 180 for 55 miles to the Big Stump Entrance at Kings Canyon National Park. Continue 1.5 miles and turn left, following signs for Kings Canyon and Cedar Grove. Drive 31 miles on Highway 180 to the Lewis Creek Trail parking area, on the north side of the road, before you reach Cedar Grove Village.

Contact: Sequoia and Kings Canyon National Parks, 47050 General Highway, Three Rivers, CA 93271-9651, 559/565-3341 or 559/565-4307, www.nps.gov/seki.

32 HOTEL CREEK TRAIL TO CEDAR GROVE OVERLOOK
5.0 mi / 2.5 hr 🥾3 ⛰9

off Highway 180 in the Cedar Grove area of Kings Canyon National Park

Map 11.3, page 575

The destination on this trip is a stunning overlook of Kings Canyon, the deepest canyon in the continental United States with a plunge of 8,200 feet at its deepest point. In truth, the canyon vistas are continual for most of the hike, so if you don't make it to the overlook, you'll still get an eyeful. The Hotel Creek Trail consists of dozens of switchbacks over open, sunny slopes, climbing 1,200 feet over two miles to a trail junction with Overlook Trail. Turn left to head to the overlook, which peers down on Cedar Grove and the length of Kings Canyon. Some of the best views are of Monarch Divide's high peaks to the north. We hope you came with picnic supplies. For a five-mile round-trip, retrace your steps back to Cedar Grove. If you want to walk farther, you can continue from the overlook junction for another 1.5 miles and turn left, hiking downhill on Lewis Creek Trail and making a seven-mile loop out of the trip. This stretch of Lewis Creek Trail is lined with sweet-smelling ceanothus. Unfortunately, the final 1.2 miles of the loop parallels a park road. Along the way, the trail overlooks a level area next to the South Fork Kings River where wildlife can often be spotted among the meadows and shrubs.

User Groups: Hikers and horses. No dogs or mountain bikes. No wheelchair facilities.

Permits: No permits are required. There is a $20 entrance fee per vehicle at Sequoia and Kings Canyon National Parks, good for seven days.

Maps: A Sequoia and Kings Canyon map is available from Tom Harrison Maps. For a topographic map, ask the USGS for Cedar Grove.

Directions: From Fresno, drive east on Highway 180 for 55 miles to the Big Stump Entrance at Kings Canyon National Park. Continue 1.5 miles and turn left, following signs for Kings Canyon and Cedar Grove. Drive 31.5 miles on Highway 180 to Cedar Grove Village. Turn left at the sign for the visitors center and Cedar Grove Lodge. Continue on the main road past the lodge for 0.25 mile and turn right. The Hotel Creek trailhead is on the left after a few hundred feet.

Contact: Sequoia and Kings Canyon National Parks, 47050 General Highway, Three Rivers, CA 93271-9651, 559/565-3341 or 559/565-4307, www.nps.gov/seki.

🔢 DON CECIL TRAIL TO LOOKOUT PEAK

12.0 mi / 7.0 hr   👣5   ⛰10

off Highway 180 in the Cedar Grove area of Kings Canyon National Park

Map 11.3, page 575   **BEST** (

Lookout Peak, at 8,531 feet in elevation, is a summit worth ascending, even though it's an all-day trip with a 3,900-foot elevation gain. From the top, you get an unforgettable Sierra view, with Cedar Grove far below you and peaks and ridges all around. In addition, just a few hundred yards from the summit is

Summit Meadow, filled with summer wildflowers. The key is to carry plenty of water and plan on an early-morning start to beat the heat. You can filter water from Sheep Creek, one mile in. Luckily, there's a decent amount of shade in the first few miles. Even though this trailhead is located right by the Cedar Grove campgrounds, few people hike all the way to the peak, so you have a chance at peace and quiet along the trail. The only downer on this hike is that when you near the summit, you see that other people have driven their cars on an alternate route to Lookout Peak (from the Big Meadows area of Giant Sequoia National Monument), and they are gaining the summit after only a 0.25-mile hike. Hey, at least you earned it.

User Groups: Hikers and horses. No dogs or mountain bikes. No wheelchair facilities.

Permits: No permits are required. There is a $20 entrance fee per vehicle at Sequoia and Kings Canyon National Parks, good for seven days.

Maps: A Sequoia and Kings Canyon map is available from Tom Harrison Maps. For a topographic map, ask the USGS for Cedar Grove.

Directions: From Fresno, drive east on Highway 180 for 55 miles to the Big Stump Entrance at Kings Canyon National Park. Continue 1.5 miles and turn left, following signs for Kings Canyon and Cedar Grove. Drive 31.5 miles on Highway 180 and take the right fork for Cedar Grove. The Don Cecil trailhead is on the right side of the road, just beyond the turnoff for Cedar Grove Village and the visitors center. If you reach Canyon View and Moraine Campgrounds, you've gone too far.

Contact: Sequoia and Kings Canyon National Parks, 47050 General Highway, Three Rivers, CA 93271-9651, 559/565-3341 or 559/565-4307, www.nps.gov/seki.

34 ROARING RIVER FALLS

0.4 mi / 0.25 hr   🥾1 ⛰8

off Highway 180 in the Cedar Grove area of
Kings Canyon National Park

Map 11.3, page 575   **BEST (**

It's an easy stroll to Roaring River Falls, a
pretty waterfall that drops through a narrow
gorge into the South Fork Kings River. It's the
only waterfall in Sequoia and Kings Canyon
National Parks that is partially accessible via
wheelchair. (The trail is paved and accessible
for most of its length, but one section may be
too steep for some wheelchair users.) If hikers
want a longer walk, they can continue downstream on the River Trail to Zumwalt Meadow
in 1.6 miles or Road's End in 2.7 miles. What's
extraordinary about the waterfall is not the
cascade itself, but the giant rocky pool into
which it falls; it's at least 50 feet wide. From
where the paved trail ends, at the edge of the
pool, the waterfall is perfectly framed by two
big conifers. Many beautiful photos have been
snapped here.

User Groups: Hikers and wheelchairs. No
dogs, horses, or mountain bikes.

Permits: No permits are required. There
is a $20 entrance fee per vehicle at Sequoia
and Kings Canyon National Parks, good for
seven days.

Maps: A Sequoia and Kings Canyon map is
available from Tom Harrison Maps. For a
topographic map, ask the USGS for Sphinx.

Directions: From Fresno, drive east on
Highway 180 for 55 miles to the Big Stump
Entrance at Kings Canyon National Park.
Continue 1.5 miles and turn left, following
signs for Kings Canyon and Cedar Grove.
Continue 35 miles on Highway 180 to the
sign for Roaring River Falls and the River
Trail, three miles past Cedar Grove Vil-
lage. The trailhead is on the right side of
the road.

Contact: Sequoia and Kings Canyon National
Parks, 47050 General Highway, Three Rivers,
CA 93271-9651, 559/565-3341 or 559/565-
4307, www.nps.gov/seki.

35 ZUMWALT MEADOW LOOP

2.0 mi / 1.0 hr   🥾1 ⛰9

off Highway 180 in the Cedar Grove area of
Kings Canyon National Park

Map 11.3, page 575   **BEST (**

What's the prettiest easy hike in Kings Canyon National Park? The Zumwalt Meadow
Loop Trail wins hands down. A scenic two-
mile walk along the South Fork Kings River,
the Zumwalt Meadow Loop is a delight for
hikers of all abilities. Many people bring their
fishing rods along to try their luck in the river,
but for most, the hiking is better than the
fishing. From the parking area, walk downstream along the river to an old suspension
footbridge, cross it, and walk back upstream.
The loop begins at an obvious fork, and you
can hike it in either direction. The south side
traverses a boulder field of jumbled rocks that
have tumbled down from the Grand Sentinel
(elevation 8,504 feet). The north side cuts
through a thick, waist-high fern forest and
follows a wooden walkway over a marsh. Views
of 8,717-foot North Dome are awe inspiring.
Trees, meadow, rock, stream, river, canyon
walls—Zumwalt Meadow Trail has it all.

User Groups: Hikers only. No dogs, horses, or
mountain bikes. No wheelchair facilities.

Permits: No permits are required. There is a $20
entrance fee per vehicle at Sequoia and Kings
Canyon National Parks, good for seven days.

Maps: A Sequoia and Kings Canyon map is
available from Tom Harrison Maps. For a topographic map, ask the USGS for Cedar Grove.

Directions: From Fresno, drive east on
Highway 180 for 55 miles to the Big Stump
Entrance at Kings Canyon National Park.
Continue 1.5 miles and turn left, following
signs for Kings Canyon and Cedar Grove.
Continue 36 miles on Highway 180 to the
parking area for Zumwalt Meadow, on the
right side of the road.

Contact: Sequoia and Kings Canyon National
Parks, 47050 General Highway, Three Rivers,
CA 93271-9651, 559/565-3341 or 559/565-
4307, www.nps.gov/seki.

🗿 MIST FALLS

9.2 mi / 5.0 hr

off Highway 180 in the Cedar Grove area of
Kings Canyon National Park

Map 11.3, page 575

The Mist Falls Trail is probably the most well-used pathway in Kings Canyon National Park, with good reason. It's a stellar 4.6-mile walk to an impressive cascade on the South Fork Kings River, with only a 650-foot gain in elevation along the way. Many backpackers use this trail to access Paradise Valley and points beyond, while most day hikers turn around at Mist Falls. The first two miles are a flat walk up the Kings River Valley, with canyon walls towering above you on both sides. You spend a lot of time craning your neck, looking up at the high canyon rims, from which springtime waterfalls cascade down. You're in a dry, open forest much of the time.

At two miles, you'll reach a trail junction. Bear left, then start to climb over granite. The farther you go, the more expansive the views become; make sure you keep turning around so you can take in the whole panorama. At four miles, the river starts to look more waterfall-like, with crashing pools and rocky granite slides becoming increasingly vertical. A quarter mile later you reach Mist Falls, which fans out over a 45-foot wide granite ledge and crashes into a boulder-lined pool. It creates a tremendous spray and mist in early summer, and mellows out as the season goes on. Take a look at the falls, then walk back down the trail 0.2 mile to the obvious, immense slab of granite you just passed. This is a favorite spot to have lunch, with its wide-open view of 10,007-foot Avalanche Peak. Look carefully and you can pick out the stone face of The Sphinx.

There are two ways to beat the crowds on this path. First, start early in the morning. Second, hike part of the route on an alternate trail on the river's south side. This trail travels from the Road's End parking lot to the Bailey Bridge at the trail intersection mentioned above. If you get an early start, save this alternate route for the return trip. By then, the day hikers will be out in full force.

User Groups: Hikers and horses. No dogs or mountain bikes. No wheelchair facilities.

Permits: No permits are required. There is a $20 entrance fee per vehicle at Sequoia and Kings Canyon National Parks, good for seven days.

Maps: A Sequoia and Kings Canyon map is available from Tom Harrison Maps. For a topographic map, ask the USGS for Sphinx.

Directions: From Fresno, drive east on Highway 180 for 55 miles to the Big Stump Entrance at Kings Canyon National Park. Continue 1.5 miles and turn left, following signs for Kings Canyon and Cedar Grove. Continue 38 miles on Highway 180 to Road's End, six miles past Cedar Grove Village. The trailhead is at the east end of the parking lot, near the wilderness ranger station.

Contact: Sequoia and Kings Canyon National Parks, 47050 General Highway, Three Rivers, CA 93271-9651, 559/565-3341 or 559/565-4307, www.nps.gov/seki.

🗿 COPPER CREEK TRAIL

21.0 mi / 3-4 days

off Highway 180 in the Cedar Grove area of
Kings Canyon National Park

Map 11.3, page 575

The Copper Creek trailhead is at 5,000 feet, and Granite Lake is at 9,972 feet, so it's not hard to do the math. If you're up for a backpacking trip with a 5,000-foot elevation gain over 10 miles, the Granite Lake Basin is your ticket to happiness. But keep in mind that the route can be hot and dry as it switchbacks up manzanita-covered slopes; this trail is considered one of the most strenuous in the Cedar Grove area. Your first night's camp is at Lower Tent Meadow, four miles in and at 7,800 feet. After that, things start to get really good. With Mount Hutchings looming over your left shoulder, the second day's six miles will go easier, bringing you to rocky, jewel-like Granite Lake in only a few hours. You must have a backpacking stove for camping by the lake or anywhere above 10,000 feet.

User Groups: Hikers and horses. No dogs or mountain bikes. No wheelchair facilities.

Permits: There is a $20 entrance fee per vehicle at Sequoia and Kings Canyon National Parks, good for seven days. Wilderness permits are required for overnight stays. They are available on a first-come, first-served basis at the wilderness permit station at Roads End or the Kings Canyon Visitor Center. For advanced wilderness permits or information on trail conditions, go to www.nps.gov/seki. Trailhead quotas are in effect from May to September.

Maps: A Sequoia and Kings Canyon map is available from Tom Harrison Maps. For a topographic map, ask the USGS for Sphinx.

Directions: From Fresno, drive east on Highway 180 for 55 miles to the Big Stump Entrance at Kings Canyon National Park. Continue 1.5 miles and turn left, following signs for Kings Canyon and Cedar Grove. Continue 38 miles on Highway 180 to Road's End, six miles past Cedar Grove Village. The trail begins at the long-term parking area.

Contact: Sequoia and Kings Canyon National Parks, 47050 General Highway, Three Rivers, CA 93271-9651, 559/565-3341 or 559/565-4307, www.nps.gov/seki.

38 REDWOOD CANYON
4.0 mi / 2.0 hr ??2 ??10

southeast of the Grant Grove area of
Kings Canyon National Park

Map 11.3, page 575   BEST (

Several loop trips are possible in the Redwood Mountain area of Kings Canyon National Park, but one of the prettiest and simplest trips is just an out-and-back walk on Redwood Canyon Trail, paralleling Redwood Creek. The beauty begins before you even start walking; on the last mile of the drive to the trailhead,

the dirt access road winds through giant sequoias that are so close, you can reach out your car window and touch them. The trail leads downhill from the parking area, and in just over 0.3 mile, you reach a junction and follow Redwood Creek Trail to the right. You'll find that this sequoia grove is far denser than many. Because they are situated by Redwood Creek, the sequoias grow amid a thriving background of dogwoods, firs, ceanothus, and mountain misery. Though the standing sequoias are impressive, some of the fallen ones are really amazing, because you get a close-up look at their immense size. Make sure you hike the full two miles to the stream crossing of Redwood Creek. Some of the best tree specimens are found there, near the junction with Sugar Bowl Loop Trail. The return trip is all uphill but easier than you'd expect.

User Groups: Hikers only. No dogs, horses, or mountain bikes. No wheelchair facilities.

Permits: No permits are required. There is a $20 entrance fee per vehicle at Sequoia and Kings Canyon National Parks, good for seven days.

Maps: A Sequoia and Kings Canyon map is available from Tom Harrison Maps. For a topographic map, ask the USGS for General Grant Grove.

Directions: From Fresno, drive east on Highway 180 for 55 miles to the Big Stump Entrance at Kings Canyon National Park. Continue 1.5 miles and turn right on the Generals Highway, heading for Sequoia National Park. Drive approximately three miles on the Generals Highway to Quail Flat, signed for Hume Lake to the left, and turn right on the dirt road to Redwood Saddle. Drive 1.5 miles and park in the parking lot. Take the trail signed for the Hart Tree and Redwood Canyon.

Contact: Sequoia and Kings Canyon National Parks, 47050 General Highway, Three Rivers, CA 93271-9651, 559/565-3341 or 559/565-4307, www.nps.gov/seki.

39 REDWOOD MOUNTAIN LOOP

10.0 mi / 5.0 hr 3 🏔10

southeast of the Grant Grove area of
Kings Canyon National Park

Map 11.3, page 575

If you have most of a day to hike in the Redwood Mountain area of Kings Canyon National Park, you're in luck. This is one of the
best day hikes in all of Kings Canyon. The
Redwood Mountain Loop combines the best
highlights of the area into one long trail, on
which you'll wander in near solitude among
the giant sequoias. If the paved, crowded trails
to the General Grant Tree and the General
Sherman Tree turn you off, this trail will turn
you on. Start by hiking on the signed Burnt
Grove/Sugar Bowl Loop Trail, which leads uphill from the parking lot. It's one mile to Burnt
Grove and 2.5 miles to Sugar Bowl Grove;
both are very dense stands of sequoias. Beyond
the groves you descend for two miles to intersect with Redwood Canyon Trail. Head downhill and cross Redwood Creek, then proceed to
the Fallen Goliath, a mammoth downed tree.
One mile farther, you reach the Hart Tree, the
largest tree in this area and a real show-stop-
per. In the final three miles, you get to walk
through the Tunnel Log, a hollowed sequoia,
and pass by pretty Hart Meadow. Note that
if you tire out halfway through this loop, you
can always follow the Redwood Canyon Trail
uphill back to the start, cutting three miles off
your round-trip.

User Groups: Hikers only. No dogs, horses, or
mountain bikes. No wheelchair facilities.

Permits: No permits are required. There is a $20
entrance fee per vehicle at Sequoia and Kings
Canyon National Parks, good for seven days.

Maps: A Sequoia and Kings Canyon map is
available from Tom Harrison Maps. For a
topographic map, ask the USGS for General
Grant Grove.

Directions: From Fresno, drive east on
Highway 180 for 55 miles to the Big Stump
Entrance at Kings Canyon National Park.
Continue 1.5 miles and turn right on the Gen-
erals Highway, heading for Sequoia National
Park. Drive approximately three miles on the
Generals Highway to Quail Flat, signed for
Hume Lake to the left, and turn right on the
dirt road to Redwood Saddle. Drive 1.5 miles
and park in the parking lot. Take the trail
signed as Burnt Grove/Sugar Bowl Loop.

Contact: Sequoia and Kings Canyon National
Parks, 47050 General Highway, Three Rivers,
CA 93271-9651, 559/565-3341 or 559/565-
4307, www.nps.gov/seki.

40 BUENA VISTA PEAK

2.0 mi / 1.0 hr 1 🏔9

southeast of the Grant Grove area of
Kings Canyon National Park

Map 11.3, page 575

Forget driving to the Kings Canyon Overlook,
because just across the road is a trailhead with
an easy walk and even better views, plus a
chance at a private picnic spot. Buena Vista
Peak is not a summit but a rocky dome, peaking at 7,603 feet, and it is one of the highest
points west of Generals Highway. It offers
far-reaching views of what looks like a million conifers at your feet and the hazy foothills to the southwest. But the best vistas are
to the east of the snowcapped peaks of the
John Muir and Monarch Wildernesses. An
easy half-hour walk takes you up the back
side of the dome, passing through pine and fir
forest, manzanita, and sage, and walking by
some interesting rock formations. Don't miss
the giant boulder sculptures in the trail's first
0.25 mile. At the top of Buena Vista Peak, you
can wander all around the spacious granite
summit, enjoying different perspectives on
the vista, before heading back to the parking
lot. It's downhill all the way.

User Groups: Hikers only. No dogs, horses, or
mountain bikes. No wheelchair facilities.

Permits: No permits are required. There is a $20
entrance fee per vehicle at Sequoia and Kings
Canyon National Parks, good for seven days.

Maps: A Sequoia and Kings Canyon map is available from Tom Harrison Maps. For a topographic map, ask the USGS for General Grant Grove.

Directions: From Fresno, drive east on Highway 180 for 55 miles to the Big Stump Entrance at Kings Canyon National Park. Continue 1.5 miles and turn right on the Generals Highway, heading for Sequoia National Park. Drive approximately five miles on the Generals Highway to the Buena Vista trailhead on the right, just across the road and slightly beyond the large pullout for the Kings Canyon Overlook, on the left.

Contact: Sequoia and Kings Canyon National Parks, 47050 General Highway, Three Rivers, CA 93271-9651, 559/565-3341 or 559/565-4307, www.nps.gov/seki.

41 WEAVER LAKE

6.2 mi / 3.0 hr or 2 days

in the Jennie Lakes Wilderness

Map 11.3, page 575

Tucked into a corner just outside the border of Kings Canyon and Sequoia National Parks, the Jennie Lakes Wilderness is a 10,500-acre wilderness area that is often overlooked by park visitors. It offers much of the same scenery as the national parks, with beautiful lakes, meadows, forests, and streams, but without all the fanfare and crowds. Weaver Lake is the easiest-to-reach destination in the wilderness, and it makes a perfect family backpacking trip or an equally nice day hike. The trail is well signed and passes through a mix of fir forest and meadows. At 1.7 miles, take the left fork for Weaver Lake, climbing uphill to the lake's basin. You'll spy the shelflike slabs of Shell Mountain peeking out above the trees. At just over three miles and at 8,700 feet in elevation, shallow but pretty Weaver Lake is set at the base of Shell Mountain's high, rounded ridge. You can try your luck fishing, or just find a lakeside seat and gaze at the view. On warm days, the brave go swimming.

Note that the road to Big Meadows is usually the last road to open in the area after snowmelt. If you're planning an early season trip, call to check on road and trail conditions.

User Groups: Hikers, dogs, and horses. No mountain bikes. No wheelchair facilities.

Permits: A free campfire permit is required for overnight stays and is available from the Hume Lake Ranger Station. There is a $20 entrance fee per vehicle at Sequoia and Kings Canyon National Parks, good for seven days in both the national forest and the national parks.

Maps: A Jennie Lakes Wilderness map is available from the U.S. Forest Service. A map of Sequoia and Kings Canyon is available from Tom Harrison Maps. For a topographic map, ask the USGS for Muir Grove.

Directions: From Fresno, drive east on Highway 180 for 55 miles to the Big Stump Entrance at Kings Canyon National Park. Continue 1.5 miles and turn right on the Generals Highway, heading for Sequoia National Park. Drive seven miles and turn left on Forest Road 14S11, at the sign for Big Meadows and Horse Corral. Drive three miles to the Big Meadows trailhead.

Contact: Giant Sequoia National Monument/Sequoia National Forest, Hume Lake Ranger District, 35860 Kings Canyon Road, Dunlap, CA 93621, 559/338-2251, www.fs.fed.us/r5/sequoia.

42 JENNIE ELLIS LAKE

12.0 mi / 6.0 hr or 2 days

in the Jennie Lakes Wilderness

Map 11.3, page 575

This trail into the Jennie Lakes Wilderness offers more of a challenge than the route to Weaver Lake, climbing 1,500 feet over six miles with some short, steep pitches. The rewards are also greater, because Jennie Ellis Lake is a beauty and receives fewer visitors than Weaver Lake. The trail is the same as the Weaver Lake Trail for 1.7 miles, but at the fork, you bear right for Jennie Ellis Lake. The trail climbs and dips through fir, pine, and manzanita forest, then crosses Poop Out Pass at 4.7 miles, the highest point on this trip. At nearly six miles, you reach the outlet stream for Jennie Ellis Lake. Follow the short spur trail to the lake, set at 9,000 feet. With a white granite backdrop and some sparse trees, the shoreline looks austere and barren, but beautiful just the same. Campsites are found around the lake, and catching fish for dinner is a fair possibility. If you only came for the day, find a comfortable spot to sit and admire the scenery before you head back.

Note that there is a somewhat shorter trail to reach Jennie Ellis Lake from Stony Creek Campground (10 miles round-trip instead of 12), but shorter doesn't necessarily mean easier. The shorter trail requires a 2,500-foot climb over the first 3.5 miles to Poop Out Pass, with several noticeably steep pitches along the way. At the pass, the two trails join and are one and the same on the final stretch to the lake.

User Groups: Hikers, dogs, and horses. No mountain bikes. No wheelchair facilities.

Permits: A free campfire permit is required for overnight stays and is available from the Hume Lake Ranger Station. There is a $20 entrance fee per vehicle at Sequoia and Kings Canyon National Parks, good for seven days in both the national forest and the national parks.

Maps: A Jennie Lakes Wilderness map is available from the U.S. Forest Service. A map of Sequoia and Kings Canyon is available from Tom Harrison Maps. For a topographic map, ask the USGS for Muir Grove.

Directions: From Fresno, drive east on Highway 180 for 55 miles to the Big Stump Entrance at Kings Canyon National Park. Continue 1.5 miles and turn right on the Generals Highway, heading for Sequoia National Park. Drive seven miles and turn left on Forest Road 14S11, at the sign for Big Meadows and Horse Corral. Drive three miles to the Big Meadows trailhead.

Contact: Giant Sequoia National Monument/ Sequoia National Forest, Hume Lake Ranger District, 35860 Kings Canyon Road, Dunlap, CA 93621, 559/338-2251, www.fs.fed.us/r5/ sequoia.

43 MITCHELL PEAK

5.2 mi / 3.0 hr   🥾4 ⛰9

in the Jennie Lakes Wilderness

Map 11.3, page 575

If you have the legs for a 2,000-foot climb over 2.6 miles, you can stand atop the summit of Mitchell Peak, the highest point in the Jennie Lakes Wilderness, at 10,365 feet in elevation. The peak used to have a fire lookout tower on top of it, but the Forest Service stopped using it and burned it down. What remains is the fabulous view, one of the best in this area. It's a one-mile climb from the trailhead to Marvin Pass and the boundary of the Jennie Lakes Wilderness. Bear left (east) and climb some more. At 1.6 miles, you reach the next junction, signed for Mitchell Peak. Head left (north), and in one more mile, you'll make the brief climb to Mitchell's summit, which straddles the border of Kings Canyon National Park. From your rocky perch, you can look out on the Great Western Divide and the Silliman Crest. It's an exemplary spot to catch your breath.

User Groups: Hikers, dogs, and horses. No mountain bikes. No wheelchair facilities.

Permits: A free campfire permit is required for overnight stays and is available from the Hume Lake Ranger Station. There is a $20 entrance fee per vehicle at Sequoia and Kings Canyon National Parks, good for seven days in both the national forest and the national parks.

Maps: A Jennie Lakes Wilderness map is available from the U.S. Forest Service. A map of Sequoia and Kings Canyon is available from Tom Harrison Maps. For a topographic map, ask the USGS for Muir Grove.

Directions: From Fresno, drive east on Highway 180 for 55 miles to the Big Stump Entrance at Kings Canyon National Park. Continue 1.5 miles and turn right on the Generals Highway, heading for Sequoia National Park. Drive seven miles and turn left on Forest Road 14S11, at the sign for Big Meadow and Horse Corral. Drive four miles to the Big Meadow Campground and continue six more miles to Horse Corral Meadow. Turn right on Forest Road 13S12 and drive 2.8 miles to the Marvin Pass trailhead.

Contact: Giant Sequoia National Monument/ Sequoia National Forest, Hume Lake Ranger District, 35860 Kings Canyon Road, Dunlap, CA 93621, 559/338-2251, www.fs.fed.us/r5/ sequoia.

44 BIG BALDY

4.6 mi / 2.5 hr

southeast of the Grant Grove area of
Kings Canyon National Park

Map 11.3, page 575

The trip to Big Baldy comes with a million views and a little workout besides. Views? We're talking Redwood Canyon, Redwood Mountain, Buena Vista Peak, Little Baldy, Buck Rock, and the Great Western Divide. A little workout? You've got to climb 1,000 feet, but it's nicely spread out over two miles. The trail alternates between thick forest cover and open granite areas as it winds along the rim of Redwood Canyon. In the forested stretches, we were amazed at how many birds were singing in the tall firs and cedars. The trail's initial vistas are to the west, but they keep changing and getting more interesting all the way to Big Baldy's 8,209-foot summit, where your view opens up to 360 degrees. Here you get your first wide-open views of the high Sierra peaks and the Great Western Divide to the east. This trail is so fun and rewarding, with so little suffering involved, that you may feel like you're getting away with something. A bonus: Because the first mile of trail faces to the west, this is a great area for watching the sunset. Big Baldy Trail is also ideal for snow-shoeing in the winter.

User Groups: Hikers only. No dogs, horses, or mountain bikes. No wheelchair facilities.

Permits: No permits are required. There is a $20 entrance fee per vehicle at Sequoia and Kings Canyon National Parks, good for seven days.

Maps: A Sequoia and Kings Canyon map is available from Tom Harrison Maps. For a topographic map, ask the USGS for Muir Grove.

Directions: From Fresno, drive east on Highway 180 for 55 miles to the Big Stump Entrance at Kings Canyon National Park. Continue 1.5 miles and turn right on the Generals Highway, heading for Sequoia National Park. Drive approximately 6.5 miles on the Generals Highway to the Big Baldy trailhead, on the right, shortly before the turnoff for Big Meadows, on the left.

Contact: Sequoia and Kings Canyon National Parks, 47050 General Highway, Three Rivers, CA 93271-9651, 559/565-3341 or 559/565-4307, www.nps.gov/seki.

45 MUIR GROVE

4.0 mi / 2.0 hr

northwest of the Lodgepole area of
Sequoia National Park

Map 11.3, page 575

Few people hike this trail unless they are staying at Dorst Campground, so you have a lot better chance of seeing giant sequoias in solitude in the Muir Grove than at many places in the park. After crossing a wooden footbridge, the trail enters a mixed forest of red fir, white fir, sugar pines, and incense cedars. In early summer, you can count the many varieties of wildflowers along the trail, especially where you cross tiny streams. The trail heads west and curves around a deeply carved canyon at one mile out. Just off the trail to your right is a bare granite slab with an inspiring westward view. The trail undulates, never climbing or dropping much, making this an easy and pleasant stroll. At 1.9 miles, you reach the Muir Grove, a small, pristine grove of huge sequoias. The first one you come to on your left is a doozy. The grove is made even more enchanting by the thick undergrowth of blue and purple lupine blooming amid the trees in early summer.

User Groups: Hikers only. No dogs, horses, or mountain bikes. No wheelchair facilities.

Permits: No permits are required. There is a $20 entrance fee per vehicle at Sequoia and Kings Canyon National Parks, good for seven days.

Maps: A Sequoia and Kings Canyon map is available from Tom Harrison Maps. For a topographic map, ask the USGS for Muir Grove.

Directions: From Fresno, drive east on Highway 180 for 55 miles to the Big Stump Entrance at Kings Canyon National Park. Continue 1.5 miles and turn right on the Generals Highway, heading for Sequoia National Park. Drive approximately 17 miles on the Generals Highway to the right turnoff for Dorst Campground. Turn right and drive through the campground to the amphitheater parking lot. Park there; the trail begins at a footbridge between the amphitheater parking lot and the group campground.

Contact: Sequoia and Kings Canyon National Parks, 47050 General Highway, Three Rivers, CA 93271-9651, 559/565-3341 or 559/565-4307, www.nps.gov/seki.

46 LITTLE BALDY
3.5 mi / 2.0 hr

northwest of the Lodgepole area of Sequoia National Park

Map 11.3, page 575

Little Baldy, Big Baldy, Buena Vista Peak.... Along this stretch of the Generals Highway, there are so many peak trails that offer far-reaching views, it's hard to choose where to start. Start here, on the Little Baldy Trail. It's a little more challenging than the Buena Vista Peak Trail, but it's shorter than Big Baldy Trail, and it offers eye-popping drama for remarkably little effort. Some claim that Little Baldy's view of the Silliman Crest, the Great Western Divide, Castle Rocks, Moro Rock, the Kaweah River Canyon, and the San Joaquin foothills is the best panorama in the park.

To see for yourself, set out from the trailhead, climbing through long, tree-shaded switchbacks, heading first north, then south. Check out the unusual view of Big Baldy off to your left (far across the highway) as you climb. After 1.2 miles, the trail leaves the forest and its many wildflowers, and your views start to open up. Hike along Little Baldy's ridgeline and make the final steep summit ascent. The trail gets a little hard to discern as you near Little Baldy's wide, bare summit, but just wander around until you find the highest spot with the best view. Take a seat—you'll want to stay a while.

Special Note: Be sure to pick a clear day for this hike. In summer, your best bet is to hike the trail early in the morning, before the Central Valley haze rises to the mountains.

User Groups: Hikers only. No dogs, horses, or mountain bikes. No wheelchair facilities.

Permits: No permits are required. There is a $20 entrance fee per vehicle at Sequoia and Kings Canyon National Parks, good for seven days.

Maps: A Sequoia and Kings Canyon map is available from Tom Harrison Maps. For topographic maps, ask the USGS for Muir Grove and Giant Forest.

Directions: From Fresno, drive east on Highway 180 for 55 miles to the Big Stump Entrance at Kings Canyon National Park. Continue 1.5 miles and turn right on the Generals Highway, heading for Sequoia National Park. Drive approximately 18 miles on the Generals Highway to the Little Baldy trailhead, on the left, a mile beyond the turnoff for Dorst Campground.

Contact: Sequoia and Kings Canyon National Parks, 47050 General Highway, Three Rivers, CA 93271-9651, 559/565-3341 or 559/565-4307, www.nps.gov/seki.

47 THE LAKES TRAIL
13.0 mi / 2-3 days

off the Generals Highway in the Wolverton area of Sequoia National Park

Map 11.3, page 575

The Wolverton trailhead is at 7,200 feet, which gives you a boost at the start for this trip into the high country. The Lakes Trail is the most popular backpacking trip in Sequoia National Park, and it's easy to see why. Wide-open views and dramatic granite walls are standard fare as you hike. Part of the route is on a loop, with one side of the loop traveling to the Watchtower—a 1,600-foot-tall granite cliff that offers incredible vistas of Tokopah Valley and beyond. The trailside scenery begins in red fir forest, then enters polished granite country, and culminates in a rocky basin with three gemlike lakes—Heather, Emerald, and Pear—as well as many sparkling creeks. The total climb to Pear Lake is a mere 2,300 feet, spread out over 6.5 miles. Backpackers take note: You may camp only at Emerald and Pear Lakes, and no campfires are allowed.

Special Note: The Watchtower Trail usually isn't open until midsummer. When it is closed, you must take the alternate Hump Trail, which is not as scenic. If you're planning a trip for early in the year, check with the park to be sure Watchtower Trail is open.

User Groups: Hikers only. No dogs, horses, or mountain bikes. No wheelchair facilities.

Permits: There is a $20 entrance fee per vehicle at Sequoia and Kings Canyon National Parks, good for seven days. Wilderness permits are required for overnight stays. They are available on a first-come, first-served basis at the Lodgepole Visitors Center. For advanced wilderness permits or information on trail conditions, go to www.nps.gov/seki. Trailhead quotas are in effect from May to September.

Maps: A Sequoia and Kings Canyon map is available from Tom Harrison Maps. For a topographic map, ask the USGS for Lodgepole.

Directions: From Fresno, drive east on Highway 180 for 55 miles to the Big Stump Entrance at Kings Canyon National Park. Continue 1.5 miles and turn right on the Generals Highway, heading for Sequoia National Park. Drive approximately 27 miles on the Generals Highway, past the Lodgepole Village turnoff, to the Wolverton turnoff, on the left (east) side of the road. Turn left and drive to the parking area and trailhead.

Contact: Sequoia and Kings Canyon National Parks, 47050 General Highway, Three Rivers, CA 93271-9651, 559/565-3341 or 559/565-4307, www.nps.gov/seki.

48 HEATHER LAKE AND THE WATCHTOWER
9.0 mi / 5.0 hr   3   10

off the Generals Highway in the Wolverton area of Sequoia National Park

Map 11.3, page 575

There's no reason that day hikers should be denied the incredible joys of hiking Lakes Trail from the Wolverton area of Sequoia National Park. You don't have to carry a backpack, get a wilderness permit, or have two or more free days to hike the first part of Lakes Trail, which ascends to the top of the 1,600-foot Watchtower (a big chunk of granite) and then continues to rocky Heather Lake. If you're hiking in spring or early summer, call the park first to make sure Watchtower Trail is open. Otherwise you'll have to take the alternate Hump Trail, which is steeper and nowhere near as scenic. The route to the Watchtower is a ledge trail, blasted into hard granite, which creeps along the high rim of Tokopah Valley. Your view is 1,500 feet straight down. You can even see tiny people walking on the path to Tokopah Falls. It's incredible, although perhaps not a good idea for people who are afraid of heights. Walking up to the Watchtower is plenty exciting, but it's even more so when you reach the other side, where you can look back and see what you were walking on. Just 0.75 mile farther and you're at Heather Lake, which is designated for day use only, so it has no campsites. It has a steep granite backdrop and a few rocky ledges to sit on. Too many people here when you arrive? No big deal. It's only another 0.5 mile to even prettier Emerald Lake, and the trail is nearly level. After a rest, you get to head back and hike the Watchtower route all over again.

User Groups: Hikers only. No dogs, horses, or mountain bikes. No wheelchair facilities.

Permits: No permits are required. There is a $20 entrance fee per vehicle at Sequoia and Kings Canyon National Parks, good for seven days.

Maps: A Sequoia and Kings Canyon map is available from Tom Harrison Maps. For a topographic map, ask the USGS for Lodgepole.

Directions: From Fresno, drive east on Highway 180 for 55 miles to the Big Stump Entrance at Kings Canyon National Park. Continue 1.5 miles and turn right on the Generals Highway, heading for Sequoia National Park. Drive approximately 27 miles on the Generals Highway, past the Lodgepole Village turnoff, to the Wolverton turnoff on the left (east) side of the road. Turn left and drive to the parking area and trailhead.

Contact: Sequoia and Kings Canyon National Parks, 47050 General Highway, Three Rivers, CA 93271-9651, 559/565-3341 or 559/565-4307, www.nps.gov/seki.

49 ALTA PEAK
13.0 mi / 1-2 days 🥾5 ⛺10

off the Generals Highway in the Wolverton area of Sequoia National Park

Map 11.3, page 575   BEST ◖

You say you like heights? You like vistas? Here's your trail, a 4,000-foot climb to the top of Alta Peak, an 11,204-foot summit in the Alta Country. Alta Peak and Mount Whitney are the only major summits in Sequoia National Park that have established trails, but both of them are still butt-kickers to reach. The trail to Alta Peak and Alta Meadow starts out the same as the Lakes Trail (from the Wolverton parking area), then it heads south (right) to Panther Gap, at 1.8 miles. After climbing through the forest to Panther Gap (at 8,450 feet), you get your first set of eye-popping views—of the Middle Fork Kaweah River and the Great Western Divide. Continue on the Alta Trail to Mehrten Meadow (at 3.9 miles), a popular camping spot, then reach a junction where you can go left for Alta Peak or right to Alta Meadow. You'll want to take both spurs

if you have the time and energy. If you're exhausted, just walk to Alta Meadow, with its flower-filled grasses and exquisite mountain views, a flat one mile away. Alta Peak is two miles away via the left fork, with a 2,000-foot climb. These two miles are considered one of the toughest stretches of trail in Sequoia National Park due to the brutal grade and the 10,000-plus foot elevation here above tree line. The summit is at 11,204 feet, and, of course, it offers a complete panorama. Even Mount Whitney and the Coast Range are visible on a clear day.

User Groups: Hikers only. No dogs, horses, or mountain bikes. No wheelchair facilities.

Permits: There is a $20 entrance fee per vehicle at Sequoia and Kings Canyon National Parks, good for seven days. Wilderness permits are required for overnight stays. They are available on a first-come, first-served basis at the Lodgepole Visitors Center. For advanced wilderness permits or information on trail conditions, go to www.nps.gov/seki. Trailhead quotas are in effect from May to September.

Maps: A Sequoia and Kings Canyon map is available from Tom Harrison Maps. For a topographic map, ask the USGS for Lodgepole.

Directions: From Fresno, drive east on Highway 180 for 55 miles to the Big Stump Entrance at Kings Canyon National Park. Continue 1.5 miles and turn right on the Generals Highway, heading for Sequoia National Park. Drive approximately 27 miles on the Generals Highway, past the Lodgepole Village turnoff, to the Wolverton turnoff, on the left (east) side of the road. Turn left and drive to the parking area and trailhead.

Contact: Sequoia and Kings Canyon National Parks, 47050 General Highway, Three Rivers, CA 93271-9651, 559/565-3341 or 559/565-4307, www.nps.gov/seki.

50 PANTHER GAP LOOP
6.0 mi / 3.5 hr 🥾3 ⛰8

off the Generals Highway in the Wolverton
area of Sequoia National Park

Map 11.3, page 575

If you're not up for the marathon trip to Alta
Peak, you can still get a taste of the high country on this loop from the Wolverton trailhead.
Start hiking on the Lakes Trail from the east
end of the Wolverton parking lot, and at 1.8
miles, bear right on the Alta Trail to parallel
Wolverton Creek, following it to Panther Gap.
Here, at 8,450 feet, you get an inspiring vista
of the Middle Fork Kaweah River and the
Great Western Divide. Check out 9,081-foot
Castle Rocks, an obvious landmark. From the
gap, turn right (west) and follow the Alta Trail
to Panther Peak and Panther Meadow, then on
to Red Fir Meadow. Finally, at 4.6 miles, bear
right and complete the loop by descending to
Long Meadow and then edging along its east
side to return to the parking lot. By the way,
don't get any smart ideas about hiking this
loop in the opposite direction—it's a much
steeper climb.

User Groups: Hikers and horses. No dogs or
mountain bikes. No wheelchair facilities.

Permits: No permits are required. There is a
$20 entrance fee per vehicle at Sequoia and
Kings Canyon National Parks, good for seven
days.

Maps: A Sequoia and Kings Canyon map is
available from Tom Harrison Maps. For a topographic map, ask the USGS for Lodgepole.

Directions: From Fresno, drive east on
Highway 180 for 55 miles to the Big Stump
Entrance at Kings Canyon National Park.
Continue 1.5 miles and turn right on the Gen-
erals Highway, heading for Sequoia National
Park. Drive approximately 27 miles on the
Generals Highway, past the Lodgepole Village
turnoff, to the Wolverton turnoff, on the left
(east) side of the road. Turn left and drive to
the parking area and trailhead.

Contact: Sequoia and Kings Canyon National
Parks, 47050 General Highway, Three Rivers,

CA 93271-9651, 559/565-3341 or 559/565-
4307, www.nps.gov/seki.

51 TOKOPAH FALLS
3.6 mi / 2.0 hr 🥾1 ⛰10

off the Generals Highway in the Giant Forest
area of Sequoia National Park

Map 11.3, page 575

This is unquestionably the best waterfall day
hike in Sequoia and Kings Canyon National
Parks, leading to 1,200-foot-high Tokopah
Falls. It's also a perfect family hike, easy on the
feet and even easier on the eyes. The scenery is
spectacular the whole way, from the up-close
looks at wildflowers and granite boulders to
the more distant views of the Watchtower, a
1,600-foot glacially carved cliff on the south
side of Tokopah Valley. Then there's the valley
itself, with Tokopah Falls pouring down the
smooth back curve of its U shape. Because
the trail begins by the three huge Lodgepole
Campgrounds, it sees a lot of foot traffic.
Your best bet is to start early in the morning.
Another unusual feature of the trail? Hikers see more yellow-bellied marmots on the
Tokopah Falls route than anywhere else in
the two parks. We saw at least 40 of the cute
little blond guys sunning themselves on rocks.
If you're lucky, one of them will whistle at you
as you walk by.

User Groups: Hikers and horses. No dogs or
mountain bikes. No wheelchair facilities.

Permits: No permits are required. There is a
$20 entrance fee per vehicle at Sequoia and
Kings Canyon National Parks, good for seven
days.

Maps: A Sequoia and Kings Canyon map is
available from Tom Harrison Maps. For a topographic map, ask the USGS for Lodgepole.

Directions: From Fresno, drive east on
Highway 180 for 55 miles to the Big Stump
Entrance at Kings Canyon National Park.
Continue 1.5 miles and turn right on the
Generals Highway, heading for Sequoia Na-
tional Park. Drive approximately 25 miles

on the Generals Highway to the Lodgepole Campground turnoff, then drive 0.75 mile to the Log Bridge area of Lodgepole Camp. Park in the large lot just before the bridge over the Marble Fork Kaweah River, and walk 150 yards to the trailhead, which is just after you cross the bridge.

Contact: Sequoia and Kings Canyon National Parks, 47050 General Highway, Three Rivers, CA 93271-9651, 559/565-3341 or 559/565-4307, www.nps.gov/seki.

52 TWIN LAKES
13.6 mi / 1-2 days 🥾3 ⛰9

off the Generals Highway in the Giant Forest area of Sequoia National Park

Map 11.3, page 575

From the Lodgepole Campground trailhead (at 6,740 feet), the Twin Lakes are a 2,800-foot elevation gain and 6.8 miles away, making this a moderate backpacking trip or a long, strenuous day hike. It's a classic Sequoia National Park trip; one that is heavily traveled each summer. The terrain is an interesting mix of dense conifer forests, glacial moraine, and open meadows. From the trailhead, you climb past Wolverton's Rock to Cahoon Meadow at three miles, 0.5 mile beyond a crossing of Silliman Creek. You then continue to Cahoon Gap at 4.2 miles, cross over Clover Creek at five miles (campsites are found along the creek), bear right at the J. O. Pass Trail junction at 5.5 miles, and reach the Twin Lakes at 6.8 miles. The trail leads you directly to the larger Twin Lake; the smaller one is reached by following a spur. Both are shallow and have forested banks; some hikers try their luck fishing in the larger lake. Backpackers spending the night at Twin Lakes can hike farther the next day—over rocky Silliman Pass (at 10,100 feet) to the less-visited Ranger Lakes, three miles farther. Note that campfires are not allowed at Twin Lakes.

User Groups: Hikers and horses. No dogs or mountain bikes. No wheelchair facilities.

Permits: There is a $20 entrance fee per vehicle at Sequoia and Kings Canyon National Parks, good for seven days. Wilderness permits are required for overnight stays. They are available on a first-come, first-served basis at the Lodgepole Visitors Center. For advanced wilderness permits or information on trail conditions, go to www.nps.gov/seki. Trailhead quotas are in effect from May to September.

Maps: A Sequoia and Kings Canyon map is available from Tom Harrison Maps. For a topographic map, ask the USGS for Lodgepole.

Directions: From Fresno, drive east on Highway 180 for 55 miles to the Big Stump Entrance at Kings Canyon National Park. Continue 1.5 miles and turn right on the Generals Highway, heading for Sequoia National Park. Drive approximately 25 miles on the Generals Highway to the Lodgepole Campground turnoff, and then drive 0.75 mile to the Log Bridge area of Lodgepole Camp. The Twin Lakes trailhead is just beyond the Tokopah Falls trailhead and the bridge over the Marble Fork Kaweah River.

Contact: Sequoia and Kings Canyon National Parks, 47050 General Highway, Three Rivers, CA 93271-9651, 559/565-3341 or 559/565-4307, www.nps.gov/seki.

53 CONGRESS TRAIL LOOP
2.9 mi / 1.5 hr 🥾1 ⛰9

off the Generals Highway in the Giant Forest area of Sequoia National Park

Map 11.3, page 575   BEST (

The Congress Trail, a two-mile loop that starts (and ends) at the General Sherman Tree, is a much-traveled route through the Giant Forest's prize grove of sequoias. The General Sherman sees the greatest number of visitors, because it is recognized as the largest living thing in the world (not by height, but by volume). After you leave its side and start on the Congress Trail, the crowds lessen substantially. You'll pass by many huge trees with placards displaying their very patriotic names, like the House and Senate clusters, the McKinley Tree, the Lincoln Tree, and… well, you get the idea. Every single giant sequoia is worth stopping to gape at. We rate the Congress Trail as the best level, easy trail for sequoia viewing in the park. Plus, the farther you walk, the more solitude you get. Make sure you pick up an interpretive brochure at the trailhead or at the Lodgepole Visitors Center.

The parking area for the Sherman Tree and the Congress Trail is 0.4 mile from the Sherman Tree for a total mileage of 2.9 miles—two miles for the loop plus the out-and-back to the parking area. (You can't park on the Generals Highway by the Sherman Tree as you could prior to 2005. This parking area is now reserved for the Giant Forest shuttle bus and wheelchair users only).

User Groups: Hikers only. No dogs, horses, or mountain bikes. Wheelchair users can access this trail; in some areas they may need assistance.

Permits: No permits are required. There is a $20 entrance fee per vehicle at Sequoia and Kings Canyon National Parks, good for seven days.

Maps: A Sequoia and Kings Canyon map is available from Tom Harrison Maps. For a topographic map, ask the USGS for Giant Forest.

Directions: From Fresno, drive east on Highway 180 for 55 miles to the Big Stump Entrance at Kings Canyon National Park. Continue 1.5 miles and turn right on the Generals Highway, heading for Sequoia National Park. Drive approximately 27 miles on the Generals Highway, past Lodgepole Village, to the Wolverton turnoff on the left (east) side of the road. Turn left and drive to the General Sherman Tree parking area. (If you are riding the free Giant Forest shuttle bus, you can disembark right at the Sherman Tree. For details see www.sequoiashuttle.com.)

Contact: Sequoia and Kings Canyon National Parks, 47050 General Highway, Three Rivers, CA 93271-9651, 559/565-3341 or 559/565-4307, www.nps.gov/seki.

54 HAZELWOOD AND HUCKLEBERRY LOOP
4.5 mi / 2.0 hr   👣2 ⛰️8

off the Generals Highway in the Giant Forest area of Sequoia National Park

Map 11.3, page 575

This hike combines two loop trails in the Giant Forest area for an easy but excellent day hike, passing by many giant sequoias and peaceful grassy meadows. A bonus: These trails are generally less crowded than the other day hikes in the Giant Forest area.

From the Generals Highway, pick up the Hazelwood Nature Trail and take the right side of the loop to join Alta Trail and Huckleberry Meadow Trail Loop. Take Alta Trail for 0.25 mile and bear right on Huckleberry Meadow Trail, climbing a bit for 1 mile to the site of Squatter's Cabin, one of the oldest structures in Sequoia National Park, dating back to the 1880s. To stay on the loop, turn left by the cabin (don't take the trail signed for The Dead Giant). The trail skirts the edge of Huckleberry Meadow and heads north to Circle Meadow, where giant sequoias line the meadow's edges. There are several junctions, but stay on Huckleberry Meadow Trail. A half mile farther is a short spur trail on the left heading to the Washington Tree. Follow the spur to see the second-largest tree in the world (after General Sherman)—it's 30 feet in diameter and 246.1 feet tall. The trip finishes out on Alta Trail, where you return to Hazelwood Nature Trail and walk the opposite side of its short loop back to the Generals Highway.

User Groups: Hikers only. No dogs, horses, or mountain bikes. No wheelchair facilities.

Permits: No permits are required. There is a $20 entrance fee per vehicle at Sequoia and Kings Canyon National Parks, good for seven days.

Maps: A Sequoia and Kings Canyon map is available from Tom Harrison Maps. For topographic maps, ask the USGS for Giant Forest and Lodgepole.

Directions: From Fresno, drive east on Highway 180 for 55 miles to the Big Stump

Entrance at Kings Canyon National Park. Continue 1.5 miles and turn right on the Generals Highway, heading for Sequoia National Park. Drive approximately 30 miles on the Generals Highway, past Lodgepole and Wolverton, to the Giant Forest area of Sequoia National Park. The Hazelwood trailhead is on the south side of the highway, 0.25 mile before you reach the Giant Forest Museum.

Contact: Sequoia and Kings Canyon National Parks, 47050 General Highway, Three Rivers, CA 93271-9651, 559/565-3341 or 559/565-4307, www.nps.gov/seki.

55 HIGH SIERRA TRAIL TO HAMILTON LAKE

30.0 mi / 3 days

off the Generals Highway in the Giant Forest area of Sequoia National Park

Map 11.3, page 575

This is a classic, easy-to-moderate, three-day backpacking trip in the High Sierra, with a two-night stay at Bearpaw Meadow Camp, a shady campground that clings to the edge of a granite gorge. The route follows High Sierra Trail from Crescent Meadow to Eagle View, then continues for 10 nearly level miles along the north rim of the Middle Fork Kaweah River Canyon. It's views, views, views all the way.

After a good night's sleep at Bearpaw Meadow, elevation 7,700 feet (reservations for a wilderness permit are definitely necessary in the summer months), you start out on an eight-mile round-trip day hike to Upper and Lower Hamilton Lake (at 8,300 feet), set in a glacially carved basin at the base of the peaks of the Great Western Divide. On the final day, you hike 11 miles back to Crescent Meadow, once again witnessing 180-degree views from the sunny High Sierra Trail. By the time it's all over and you're back home, your mind is completely blown by all the high-country beauty, and you've shot about a million pictures, none of which can compare to the experience of actually being there.

User Groups: Hikers only. No dogs, horses, or mountain bikes. No wheelchair facilities.

Permits: There is a $20 entrance fee per vehicle at Sequoia and Kings Canyon National Parks, good for seven days. Wilderness permits are required for overnight stays. They are available on a first-come, first-served basis at the Lodgepole Visitors Center. For advanced wilderness permits or information on trail conditions, go to www.nps.gov/seki. Trailhead quotas are in effect from May to September.

Maps: A Sequoia and Kings Canyon map is available from Tom Harrison Maps. For topographic maps, ask the USGS for Giant Forest and Lodgepole.

Directions: From Fresno, drive east on Highway 180 for 55 miles to the Big Stump Entrance at Kings Canyon National Park. Continue 1.5 miles and turn right on the Generals Highway, heading for Sequoia National Park. Drive approximately 30 miles on the Generals Highway, past Lodgepole and Wolverton, to the Giant Forest area of Sequoia National Park. Just beyond the museum, turn left on Crescent Meadow Road and drive 3.5 miles to the Crescent Meadow parking area.

Contact: Sequoia and Kings Canyon National Parks, 47050 General Highway, Three Rivers, CA 93271-9651, 559/565-3341 or 559/565-4307, www.nps.gov/seki.

56 HIGH SIERRA TRAIL AND EAGLE VIEW

1.5 mi / 1.0 hr

off the Generals Highway in the Giant Forest area of Sequoia National Park

Map 11.3, page 575

Are you ready to be wowed? From the lower parking lot at Crescent Meadow, follow the trail that leads to the southern edge of Crescent Meadow, and at 0.1 mile, take the right fork that leads up the ridge on High Sierra Trail toward Eagle View. The High Sierra Trail is a popular trans-Sierra route that eventually leads to Mount Whitney, the highest peak in the contiguous United States. On this trip you won't go quite that far, but you will get a taste of the visual delights of this extraordinary trail. In less than 0.5 mile, you'll gain the ridge and start getting wondrous, edge-of-the-world views. Numerous wildflowers line the path, which hugs the edge of this high ridge. At 0.7 mile, you'll reach Eagle View, an unsigned but obvious lookout from which you get a fascinating look at Moro Rock to your right, Castle Rocks straight ahead, and dozens of peaks and ridges of the Western Divide far across the canyon. The vistas are so fine and the trail is so good that you might just want to keep walking all the way to Mount Whitney.

User Groups: Hikers only. No dogs, horses, or mountain bikes. No wheelchair facilities.

Permits: No permits are required. There is a $20 entrance fee per vehicle at Sequoia and Kings Canyon National Parks, good for seven days.

Maps: A Sequoia and Kings Canyon map is available from Tom Harrison Maps. For topographic maps, ask the USGS for Giant Forest and Lodgepole.

Directions: From Fresno, drive east on Highway 180 for 55 miles to the Big Stump Entrance at Kings Canyon National Park. Continue 1.5 miles and turn right on the Generals Highway, heading for Sequoia National Park. Drive approximately 30 miles on the Generals Highway, past Lodgepole and Wolverton, to the Giant Forest area of Sequoia National Park. Just beyond the museum, turn left on Crescent Meadow Road and drive 3.5 miles to the Crescent Meadow parking area.

Contact: Sequoia and Kings Canyon National Parks, 47050 General Highway, Three Rivers, CA 93271-9651, 559/565-3341 or 559/565-4307, www.nps.gov/seki.

57 CRESCENT MEADOW AND THARP'S LOG

1.6 mi / 1.0 hr 🥾1 ⛰️8

off the Generals Highway in the Giant Forest area of Sequoia National Park

Map 11.3, page 575

Crescent Meadow is more than 1.5 miles long and is surrounded by giant sequoias. John Muir called it "the gem of the Sierras." We don't know how Muir would feel about the pavement that lines the trail around this precious meadow, but we hope he'd like this loop hike anyhow. Follow the pavement for 200 yards from the eastern side of the parking lot, and just like that, you're at the southern edge of beautiful Crescent Meadow. Take the right fork and head for Log Meadow and Tharp's Log. Log Meadow is as large and beautiful as Crescent Meadow, and Tharp's Log was the homestead of Hale Tharp, the first white man to enter this forest. He grazed cattle and horses here, and built a modest home inside a fallen, fire-hollowed sequoia. You can look inside Tharp's Log and see his bed, fireplace, dining room table, and the door and windows he fashioned into the log. (Children find this incredibly thrilling.) From Tharp's Log, continue your loop back to Crescent Meadow and around its west side, where you return to the north edge of the parking lot.

User Groups: Hikers and wheelchairs (with assistance). No dogs, horses, or mountain bikes.

Permits: No permits are required. There is a $20 entrance fee per vehicle at Sequoia and Kings Canyon National Parks, good for seven days.

Maps: A Sequoia and Kings Canyon map is available from Tom Harrison Maps. For topographic maps, ask the USGS for Giant Forest and Lodgepole.

Directions: From Fresno, drive east on Highway 180 for 55 miles to the Big Stump Entrance at Kings Canyon National Park. Continue 1.5 miles and turn right on the Generals Highway, heading for Sequoia

National Park. Drive approximately 30 miles on the Generals Highway, past Lodgepole and Wolverton, to the Giant Forest area of Sequoia National Park. Just beyond the museum, turn left on Crescent Meadow Road and drive 3.5 miles to the Crescent Meadow parking area.

Contact: Sequoia and Kings Canyon National Parks, 47050 General Highway, Three Rivers, CA 93271-9651, 559/565-3341 or 559/565-4307, www.nps.gov/seki.

58 MORO ROCK
0.6 mi / 0.5 hr
🚶 2   ⛰ 10

off the Generals Highway in the Giant Forest area of Sequoia National Park

Map 11.3, page 575   **BEST ☾**

Just about everybody has heard of Moro Rock, the prominent, pointy granite dome with the top-of-the-world sunset vistas, and if you're visiting the Giant Forest area of Sequoia National Park, well, you just have to hike to the top of it. When you climb those 380 stairs to the dome's summit and check out the view, you realize that unlike many famous attractions, Moro Rock is not overrated. It's as great as everybody says, and maybe even better. If you start your trip from the Moro Rock parking area, it's only 0.3 mile to the top, climbing switchbacks, ramps, and granite stairs the whole way. Railings line the rock-blasted trail to keep you from dropping off the 6,725-foot granite dome. What's the view like? Well, on a clear day, you can see all the way to the Coast Range, 100 miles away. In closer focus is the Middle Fork Kaweah River, the Great Western Divide, Castle Rocks (at 9,180 feet), Triple Divide Peak (at 12,634 feet), Mount Stewart (at 12,205 feet)... and on and on. In a word, it's awesome. And even better, you don't get this view just from the top of Moro Rock—you get it all the way up, at every turn in the trail.

If you want the absolute best visibility, show up early in the morning, before the afternoon haze from the Central Valley obscures the view. On the other hand, that same haze creates amazingly colorful sunsets, so early evening is another fine time to be on top of Moro Rock.

User Groups: Hikers only. No dogs, horses, or mountain bikes. No wheelchair facilities.

Permits: No permits are required. There is a $20 entrance fee per vehicle at Sequoia and Kings Canyon National Parks, good for seven days.

Maps: A Sequoia and Kings Canyon map is available from Tom Harrison Maps. For a topographic map, ask the USGS for Giant Forest.

Directions: From Fresno, drive east on Highway 180 for 55 miles to the Big Stump Entrance at Kings Canyon National Park. Continue 1.5 miles and turn right on the Generals Highway, heading for Sequoia National Park. Drive approximately 30 miles on the Generals Highway, past Lodgepole and Wolverton, to the Giant Forest area of Sequoia National Park. Just beyond the museum, turn left on Crescent Meadow Road, drive 1.5 miles, and take the right fork to the Moro Rock parking area.

Contact: Sequoia and Kings Canyon National Parks, 47050 General Highway, Three Rivers, CA 93271-9651, 559/565-3341 or 559/565-4307, www.nps.gov/seki.

59 SUNSET ROCK
2.0 mi / 1.0 hr
🚶 1   ⛰ 9

off the Generals Highway in the Giant Forest area of Sequoia National Park

Map 11.3, page 575

The trail to Sunset Rock is a first-rate easy hike, perfect at sunset or any time. It gets much less traffic than you might expect, considering its proximity to Giant Forest. Leave your car in the lot across from the Giant Forest museum (make sure you stop in before or after your trip), then pick up the trail on the west side of the lot. The level path leads through a mixed forest (with a handful of giant sequoias) and crosses Little Deer Creek on its way to Sunset Rock. The rock is a gargantuan, flat piece of granite—about the size of a football field—set at 6,412 feet in elevation. Standing on it, you get a terrific overlook of Little Baldy to your right and a sea of conifers below, in the Marble Fork Kaweah River Canyon.

User Groups: Hikers only. No dogs, horses, or mountain bikes. No wheelchair facilities.

Permits: No permits are required. There is a $20 entrance fee per vehicle at Sequoia and Kings Canyon National Parks, good for seven days.

Maps: A Sequoia and Kings Canyon map is available from Tom Harrison Maps. For a topographic map, ask the USGS for Giant Forest.

Directions: From Fresno, drive east on Highway 180 for 55 miles to the Big Stump Entrance at Kings Canyon National Park. Continue 1.5 miles and turn right on the Generals Highway, heading for Sequoia National Park. Drive approximately 30 miles on the Generals Highway, past Lodgepole and Wolverton, to the Giant Forest area of Sequoia National Park. Park in the lot across from the Giant Forest museum, then pick up the signed trail on the west side of the lot.

Contact: Sequoia and Kings Canyon National Parks, 47050 General Highway, Three Rivers, CA 93271-9651, 559/565-3341 or 559/565-4307, www.nps.gov/seki.

60 PARADISE CREEK TRAIL
1.2 mi / 0.75 hr   🏃1 ⛰8

off Highway 198 in the Foothills region of Sequoia National Park

Map 11.3, page 575   **BEST (**

From Buckeye Flat Campground, Paradise Creek Trail meanders through oaks and buckeyes, and crosses a long, picturesque footbridge over the Middle Fork Kaweah River. An inviting, Olympic-sized pool is on the right side of the bridge, where campers often go swimming on summer afternoons. Save the pool for after

your hike; for now, take the signed Paradise Creek Trail, at the far side of the bridge. You'll briefly visit the creek and then leave it, climbing into oak and grassland terrain. There are some high views of Moro Rock and Hanging Rock, but most of the beauty is right at your feet, in the springtime flowers that grow in the grasses and in the leafy blue oaks that shade them. The maintained trail ends when it reaches Paradise Creek again, although a faint route continues along its banks.

User Groups: Hikers only. No dogs, horses, or mountain bikes. No wheelchair facilities.

Permits: No permits are required. There is a $20 entrance fee per vehicle at Sequoia and Kings Canyon National Parks, good for seven days.

Maps: A Sequoia and Kings Canyon map is available from Tom Harrison Maps. For a topographic map, ask the USGS for Giant Forest.

Directions: From Visalia, drive east on Highway 198 for 47 miles to the turnoff, on the right, for Buckeye Flat Campground, across from Hospital Rock. Turn right and drive 0.6 mile to the campground. Park in any of the dirt pullouts outside of the camp entrance; no day-use parking is allowed in the camp. You can also park at Hospital Rock and walk to the campground. The trailhead is near campsite No. 28.

Contact: Sequoia and Kings Canyon National Parks, 47050 General Highway, Three Rivers, CA 93271-9651, 559/565-3341 or 559/565-3135, www.nps.gov/seki.

61 MIDDLE FORK TRAIL TO PANTHER CREEK
6.0 mi / 3.0 hr   🏃2 ⛰8

off Highway 198 in the Foothills region of Sequoia National Park

Map 11.3, page 575

You want to be alone? You don't want to see anybody else on the trail? Just sign up for this trip any time between June and September, when the foothills have warmed up to their summer extremes. Don't be fooled by this path's name: The Middle Fork Trail is no streamside meander. Rather, it's a shadeless, exposed trail that leads high along the canyon of the Middle Fork Kaweah River—always at least 250 feet above it. In summer, it's hot as Hades, but this trail is perfect in winter and spring. Whereas most other trails in Sequoia and Kings Canyon are still snowed under, you can take an early-season day hike or backpacking trip along Middle Fork Trail. The main destination is Panther Creek (at three miles), where the trail leads across the brink of Panther Creek's 100-foot dive into the Kaweah River. But you can hike farther if you wish. Although Middle Fork Trail is set in grasslands and chaparral, it offers some stunning views of the area's geology, including Moro Rock, Castle Rocks, and the Great Western Divide. We hiked this trail in August, and despite the fact that we were wilting from the heat, the expansive views kept our spirits up.

User Groups: Hikers only. No dogs, horses, or mountain bikes. No wheelchair facilities.

Permits: No permits are required. There is a $20 entrance fee per vehicle at Sequoia and Kings Canyon National Parks, good for seven days.

Maps: A Sequoia and Kings Canyon map is available from Tom Harrison Maps. For a topographic map, ask the USGS for Giant Forest.

Directions: From Visalia, drive east on Highway 198 for 47 miles to the turnoff, on the right, for Buckeye Flat Campground, across from Hospital Rock. Turn right and drive 0.5 mile to a left fork just before the campground. Bear left on the dirt road and drive 1.3 miles to the trailhead and parking area. In the winter, you must park at Hospital Rock and walk in to the trailhead, adding 3.6 miles to your round-trip.

Contact: Sequoia and Kings Canyon National Parks, 47050 General Highway, Three Rivers, CA 93271-9651, 559/565-3341 or 559/565-3135, www.nps.gov/seki.

62 POTWISHA TO HOSPITAL ROCK

5.0 mi / 2.5 hr 👣2 ⛰8

off Highway 198 in the Foothills region of Sequoia National Park

Map 11.3, page 575

First, some advice: Don't hike this trail on a hot day. If it's summertime and you want to see the Monache Indian historical sites at Potwisha and Hospital Rock, drive to each of them and see them separately. In winter or spring, however, it's far more fun to take this five-mile hike through chaparral and oak woodlands, especially in March, when the wildflowers bloom. In the first 100 yards from the trailhead, you'll see Native American grinding holes and pictographs that look roughly like people and animals. You'll also pass many tempting pools in the Middle Fork Kaweah, which are frequented by swimmers and bathers in the summer. The trail climbs a gradual 2.5 miles from Potwisha to Hospital Rock, crossing the highway after the first mile. When you reach Hospital Rock, which is just a few feet off the road to Buckeye Flat Campground, you see a huge display of pictographs on its side. Across the campground road are more grinding holes in the boulders, and near them, a short paved path leads to deep pools and sandy beaches on the Middle Fork. Another path leads from the camp road to the underside of Hospital Rock, where there's a large, cavelike shelter. This is where a Native American medicine man healed the sick and injured, resulting in a white man naming this place Hospital Rock.

User Groups: Hikers only. No dogs, horses, or mountain bikes. No wheelchair facilities.

Permits: No permits are required. There is a $20 entrance fee per vehicle at Sequoia and Kings Canyon National Parks, good for seven days.

Maps: A Sequoia and Kings Canyon map is available from Tom Harrison Maps. For a topographic map, ask the USGS for Giant Forest.

Directions: From Visalia, drive east on Highway 198 for 44 miles to the turnoff, on the left, for Potwisha Campground, 3.8 miles east of the Ash Mountain entrance station to Sequoia National Park. Don't turn left into Potwisha campground; instead, turn right on the paved road opposite the campground. Drive past the RV dumping station to the signed trailhead and parking area.

Contact: Sequoia and Kings Canyon National Parks, 47050 General Highway, Three Rivers, CA 93271-9651, 559/565-3341 or 559/565-3135, www.nps.gov/seki.

63 MARBLE FALLS
7.0 mi / 4.0 hr

off Highway 198 in the Foothills region of Sequoia National Park

Map 11.3, page 575

This is the waterfall to see in Sequoia National Park in late winter and spring. March and April are particularly good months to visit because of high flows in the Marble Fork Kaweah River and blooming wildflowers in the grasslands and chaparral that line the trail. From its rather banal start as a dirt road, this trail just keeps getting better as it follows the Marble Fork Kaweah River. There are no trail junctions to worry about; at 3.5 miles, the path simply dead-ends near the lower cascades of Marble Falls. Although much of the falls are hidden in the narrow, rocky river gorge, tucked out of sight, what is visible is an impressive billowing cascade of whitewater. Be very careful on the slippery granite near the river's edges; the current and the cold water are even more dangerous than they look. Aside from the waterfalls and the wildflowers, the other highlights on this trail are the colorful outcroppings of marble, particularly in the last mile as you near the falls. Remember, though, that in summer this area of the park can bake like an oven. If you make the trip to the falls from late May to September, get an early morning start.

User Groups: Hikers only. No dogs, horses, or mountain bikes. No wheelchair facilities.

Permits: No permits are required. There is a $20 entrance fee per vehicle at Sequoia and Kings Canyon National Parks, good for seven days.

Maps: A Sequoia and Kings Canyon map is available from Tom Harrison Maps. For a topographic map, ask the USGS for Giant Forest.

Directions: From Visalia, drive east on Highway 198 for 44 miles to the turnoff, on the left, for Potwisha Campground, 3.8 miles east of the Ash Mountain entrance station to Sequoia National Park. The trail begins across from campsite No. 15 in Potwisha Campground; park in the trailhead parking area in the camp.

Contact: Sequoia and Kings Canyon National Parks, 47050 General Highway, Three Rivers, CA 93271-9651, 559/565-3341 or 559/565-3135, www.nps.gov/seki.

64 PARADISE RIDGE
3.2 mi / 1.5 hr

off Highway 198 in the Mineral King region of Sequoia National Park

Map 11.3, page 575

OK, you've just driven the 20 twisting miles into Mineral King from Three Rivers. You're tired, dusty, and itching to get out of the car and move your legs. What's the first trail you can reach in Mineral King? The Paradise Ridge Trail, and it climbs right away, getting you huffing and puffing and clearing out the road dust from your lungs. After the initial steepness of the trail, the grade becomes easier as it moves into switchbacks ascending the hill. Although much of this forest has been burned in recent years, the giant sequoia trees are thriving, some in clusters as large as 10 or more. At your feet are tons of ferns. As you climb, the views just keep improving—you see the East Fork Kaweah River Canyon below you, and far off, the Great Western

Divide. You can hike all the way to the top of the ridge at three miles, but the views aren't any better there than they are on the way up. Most people just cruise uphill a way, and turn around when they've had enough. Besides the big trees and the big views, our favorite thing about this trail was that we saw more bears than people.

User Groups: Hikers and horses. No dogs or mountain bikes. No wheelchair facilities.

Permits: No permits are required. There is a $20 entrance fee per vehicle at Sequoia and Kings Canyon National Parks, good for seven days.

Maps: A Mineral King map is available from Tom Harrison Maps. For a topographic map, ask the USGS for Silver City.

Directions: From Visalia, drive east on Highway 198 for 38 miles to Mineral King Road, 2.5 miles east of Three Rivers. If you reach the Ash Mountain entrance station, you've gone too far. Turn right on Mineral King Road and drive 20 miles to the Hockett Trail parking area, on the right, 0.25 mile past Atwell Mill Camp. Park there and walk back west on Mineral King Road about 0.3 mile to the trailhead for Paradise Ridge, on the north side of the road.

Contact: Sequoia and Kings Canyon National Parks, 47050 General Highway, Three Rivers, CA 93271-9651, 559/565-3341 or 559/565-3135, www.nps.gov/seki.

65 HOCKETT TRAIL TO EAST FORK BRIDGE
4.0 mi / 2.0 hr 🏃1 ⛰️8

off Highway 198 in the Mineral King region of Sequoia National Park

Map 11.3, page 575

The Hockett Trail makes a fine day-hiking path in Mineral King. It's suitable for all kinds of hikers. Families with small children can just walk a mile downhill to the footbridge over the East Fork Kaweah River, where there is a small waterfall and many sculptured granite pools, and then turn around and head back. People looking for a longer trip can continue another mile to the East Fork Grove of sequoias and Deer Creek. Although some of this forest has been burned in recent years, most of the big conifers were spared, and the area is still quite beautiful. The trail starts in an area of sequoia stumps, near where the Atwell Mill cut lumber in the 1880s. Live sequoias still flourish farther down the path, near the river's edge; apparently they were spared because of their distance from the mill. The trail is well graded, and even the uphill return is only a moderate climb.

User Groups: Hikers and horses. No dogs or mountain bikes. No wheelchair facilities.

Permits: No permits are required. There is a $20 entrance fee per vehicle at Sequoia and Kings Canyon National Parks, good for seven days.

Maps: A Mineral King map is available from Tom Harrison Maps. For a topographic map, ask the USGS for Mineral King.

Directions: From Visalia, drive east on Highway 198 for 38 miles to Mineral King Road, 2.5 miles east of Three Rivers. If you reach the Ash Mountain entrance station, you've gone too far. Turn right on Mineral King Road and drive 20 miles to the Hockett Trail parking area, on the right, 0.25 mile past Atwell Mill Camp. Park there and walk into the campground to campsite No. 16, where the trail begins.

Contact: Sequoia and Kings Canyon National Parks, 47050 General Highway, Three Rivers, CA 93271-9651, 559/565-3341 or 559/565-3135, www.nps.gov/seki.

66 COLD SPRINGS NATURE TRAIL
2.0 mi / 1.0 hr 🥾1 ⛰8

off Highway 198 in the Mineral King region of Sequoia National Park

Map 11.3, page 575

You may not expect much from a campground nature trail, but Cold Springs Nature Trail is guaranteed to exceed your expectations. Not only is it lined with wildflowers along the East Fork Kaweah River and informative signposts that teach you to identify junipers, red and white firs, cottonwoods, and aspens, but the views of the Sawtooth Ridge are glorious. The loop is less than 0.5 mile, but from the far end of it, the trail continues along the East Fork Kaweah River, heading another mile into Mineral King Valley. Walk to the loop's far end, and then continue at least another 0.25 mile along the trail. It just gets prettier as it goes. You're in for a real treat if you take this walk right before sunset, when the valley's surrounding mountain peaks turn every imaginable shade of pink, orange, and coral, reflecting the sun setting in the west. The vistas are so beautiful that they can practically make you weep.

User Groups: Hikers and horses. No dogs or mountain bikes. No wheelchair facilities.

Permits: No permits are required. There is a $20 entrance fee per vehicle at Sequoia and Kings Canyon National Parks, good for seven days.

Maps: A Mineral King map is available from Tom Harrison Maps. For a topographic map, ask the USGS for Mineral King.

Directions: From Visalia, drive east on Highway 198 for 38 miles to Mineral King Road, 2.5 miles east of Three Rivers. If you reach the Ash Mountain entrance station, you've gone too far. Turn right on Mineral King Road and drive 23.5 miles to Cold Springs Campground on the right. The trail begins near site six. If you aren't staying in the camp, you can park by the Mineral King Ranger Station and walk into the campground.

Contact: Sequoia and Kings Canyon National Parks, 47050 General Highway, Three Rivers, CA 93271-9651, 559/565-3341 or 559/565-3135, www.nps.gov/seki.

67 FAREWELL GAP TRAIL TO ASPEN FLAT
2.0 mi / 1.0 hr 🥾1 ⛰9

off Highway 198 in the Mineral King region of Sequoia National Park

Map 11.3, page 575 **BEST (**

If ever there was a perfect family hike, this would have to be it. Actually, if ever there was a perfect hike for every two-legged person on the planet, this would have to be it. The glacial-cut Mineral King Valley—a peaceful paradise of meadows, streams, and 100-year-old cabins—has to be one of the most scenic places in the West, and possibly in the world. An easy stroll along the canyon floor leads you past waterfalls and along the headwaters of the East Fork Kaweah River, in the awesome shelter of thousand-foot cliffs. After walking to the trailhead near the horse corral, you follow Farewell Gap Trail (an old dirt road) for a mile, then cross Crystal Creek and take the right fork off the main trail. This brings you closer to the river, where you follow a narrow use trail to Aspen Flat (a lovely grove of trees), or to Soda Springs, situated right along the river's edge. There you can see mineral springs bubbling up from the ground, turning the earth around them a bright orange color. Bring a fishing rod on this trail if you like, but be absolutely certain to bring your camera.

User Groups: Hikers and horses. No dogs or mountain bikes. No wheelchair facilities.

Permits: No permits are required. There is a $20 entrance fee per vehicle at Sequoia and Kings Canyon National Parks, good for seven days.

Maps: A Mineral King map is available from Tom Harrison Maps. For a topographic map, ask the USGS for Mineral King.

Directions: From Visalia, drive east on Highway 198 for 38 miles to Mineral King Road,

2.5 miles east of Three Rivers. If you reach the Ash Mountain entrance station, you've gone too far. Turn right on Mineral King Road and drive 25 miles to the end of the road and the Eagle/Mosquito trailhead. Take the right fork at the end of the road to reach the parking area. Walk back out of the parking lot and follow the road to the horse corral; the Farewell Gap Trail begins just beyond it.

Contact: Sequoia and Kings Canyon National Parks, 47050 General Highway, Three Rivers, CA 93271-9651, 559/565-3341 or 559/565-3135, www.nps.gov/seki.

68 MOSQUITO LAKES
8.0 mi / 4.0 hr or 2 days

off Highway 198 in the Mineral King region of Sequoia National Park

Map 11.3, page 575

Ah, paradise. You know you're in it as soon as you park your car at the end of Mineral King Road. The Eagle/Mosquito trailhead is at 7,830 feet, and you set out from the parking lot near one of Mineral King's adorable cabins, left from the early 20th century and privately owned. Feel jealous? Keep walking; you'll get over it. In minutes you cross a footbridge over Spring Creek's cascade, called Tufa Falls because of the calcium carbonate in Spring Creek's water. Don't expect to see much of a waterfall—most of it is hidden by brush. At one mile, you reach the junction for Eagle Lake, the Mosquito Lakes, and White Chief Trails. Take the right fork, climbing steadily. At two miles, you reach the Mosquito Lakes junction and go right, leaving Eagle Lake Trail for another day. Climb up and then down the other side of Miner's Ridge, at 9,300 feet. The final descent covers 0.5 mile; you reach Mosquito Lake number one at 9,040 feet and 3.6 miles. It's considered to be the easiest lake to reach in Mineral King, with a mostly shaded trail and only a 1,500-foot gain on the way in, plus a 250-foot gain on the way out. Still, if you've visited any of the other spectacular

Mineral King lakes, this lake will look a little disappointing. It's small, shallow, and greenish. But fear not: This is the first of several Mosquito Lakes, all of which are linked by Mosquito Creek. Hikers with excess energy can follow the stream uphill to four more lakes. There is no maintained trail to the upper lakes, but if you follow the use trail near the stream, the going is easier. The use trail begins on the west side of the stream at the first lake, navigates around the rocky slope behind the lake, and then crosses the stream above it. The climb from lake number one to lake number two is steep, with a 600-foot elevation gain in 0.5 mile, but it's worth it. Lake number two is the usual destination for day hikers; it's a blue, deep, granite-bound beauty and makes for an eight-mile round-trip. Backpackers will find the first campsites at Mosquito Lake number two (no camping is allowed at the first lake). Mosquito Lake number five is five miles from the Eagle/Mosquito trailhead.

User Groups: Hikers and horses. No dogs or mountain bikes. No wheelchair facilities.

Permits: There is a $20 entrance fee per vehicle at Sequoia and Kings Canyon National Parks, good for seven days. Wilderness permits are required for overnight stays. They are available on a first-come, first-served basis at the Mineral King Ranger Station. For advanced wilderness permits or information on trail conditions, go to www.nps.gov/seki. Trailhead quotas are in effect from May to September.

Maps: A Mineral King map is available from Tom Harrison Maps. For a topographic map, ask the USGS for Mineral King.

Directions: From Visalia, drive east on Highway 198 for 38 miles to Mineral King Road, 2.5 miles east of Three Rivers. If you reach the Ash Mountain entrance station, you've gone too far. Turn right on Mineral King Road and drive 25 miles to the end of the road and the Eagle/Mosquito trailhead. Take the right fork at the end of the road to reach the parking area. The trail begins at the far end of the parking lot.

Contact: Sequoia and Kings Canyon National Parks, 47050 General Highway, Three Rivers,

CA 93271-9651, 559/565-3341 or 559/565-3135, www.nps.gov/seki.

69 EAGLE LAKE TRAIL
6.8 mi / 4.0 hr   👣3 ⛰10

off Highway 198 in the Mineral King region of Sequoia National Park

Map 11.3, page 575

Eagle Lake has always been the glamour destination in Mineral King; the trail to hike if you can hike only one trail in the area. Why? The blue-green lake is drop-dead gorgeous, that's why, and the trail to reach it is challenging but manageable for most day hikers, with a 2,200-foot elevation gain spread out over 3.4 miles. Nonetheless, hikers who made the trek to Eagle Lake in the summer of 2003 were heartily disappointed when they arrived. The lake's historic dam had sprung a leak, and the water had dropped to a sadly diminished level. However, the Park Service got to work on fixing the dam, and soon the lake was restored to its formerly gorgeous self. The Eagle Lake Trail follows the same route as the Mosquito Lakes Trail (see listing in this chapter) until the two-mile point, near the Eagle Sink Holes. These geological oddities are small craters in the ground where Eagle Creek suddenly disappears underground. At the trail junction by the sink holes, go left for Eagle Lake. Enjoy the brief flat stretch here, because shortly, you'll gain another 1,000 feet over 1.4 miles. Much of the climb is in an exposed, rocky area—a large boulder field that gets baked by the sun on warm days. Well-graded switchbacks and beautiful scenery make it easier. Soon you arrive at Eagle Lake's dam, at 10,000 feet. The big lake is surrounded by glacially carved rock and has a few rocky islands. Brook trout swim in its clear waters. The trail continues along the lake's west side to many good picnicking spots and photo opportunities. Campsites are found near the lake; no camping is allowed between the trail and the lake.

User Groups: Hikers and horses. No dogs or mountain bikes. No wheelchair facilities.

Permits: There is a $20 entrance fee per vehicle at Sequoia and Kings Canyon National Parks, good for seven days. Wilderness permits are required for overnight stays. They are available on a first-come, first-served basis at the Mineral King Ranger Station. For advanced wilderness permits or information on trail conditions, go to www.nps.gov/seki. Trailhead quotas are in effect from May to September.

Maps: A Mineral King map is available from Tom Harrison Maps. For a topographic map, ask the USGS for Mineral King.

Directions: From Visalia, drive east on Highway 198 for 38 miles to Mineral King Road, 2.5 miles east of Three Rivers. If you reach the Ash Mountain entrance station, you've gone too far. Turn right on Mineral King Road and drive 25 miles to the end of the road and the Eagle/Mosquito trailhead. Take the right fork at the end of the road to reach the parking area. The trail begins at the far end of the parking lot.

Contact: Sequoia and Kings Canyon National Parks, 47050 General Highway, Three Rivers, CA 93271-9651, 559/565-3341 or 559/565-3135, www.nps.gov/seki.

70 FRANKLIN LAKES
10.8 mi / 6.0 hr or 2 days 👣3 ⛰10

off Highway 198 in the Mineral King region of Sequoia National Park

Map 11.3, page 575

Maybe the best thing about hiking to Franklin Lakes is the waterfalls you get to pass along the way—especially our favorite cascades, on Franklin Creek. Or maybe it's the prolific wildflowers along the trail, or the spectacular views over Mineral King Valley that you gain as you climb. Maybe it's the big lake itself, set below Tulare and Florence Peaks, or the fact that the trail to reach it is so well graded, with a 2,500-foot elevation gain spread out over 5.4 miles. What the heck—this trail is about as close to hiking perfection as you get.

The first two miles are nearly flat; the route winds along the bottom of Mineral King's canyon, following Farewell Gap Trail alongside the East Fork Kaweah River. You'll pass Tufa Falls, across the canyon, at 0.25 mile and Crystal Creek's cascades, on your side of the canyon, at one mile. The trail leaves the valley floor and starts to climb moderately, reaching the bottom of Franklin Creek's cascades at 1.7 miles. After crossing Franklin Creek, you continue south along Farewell Canyon, negotiating some switchbacks as you gain elevation. The views get better and better. One mile farther, Franklin Lakes Trail forks left off Farewell Gap Trail and starts climbing in earnest up the Franklin Creek Valley. At nearly 10,000 feet, the trail crosses Franklin Creek again, then parallels the creek for another mile to the largest Franklin Lake. Note that when you see the lake's dam straight ahead and an obvious campsite about 150 yards below it to the right of the trail, you should cut off the main trail. Walk to the camp and follow its use trail to the dam and the lake. The main trail switchbacks up and above the lake but doesn't go directly to its shoreline. Franklin Lake is a dramatic sight, surrounded by steep, snow-covered slopes and a few pines and junipers. Rainbow Mountain is on its northeast side; Tulare Peak is to the southwest.

User Groups: Hikers and horses. No dogs or mountain bikes. No wheelchair facilities.

Permits: There is a $20 entrance fee per vehicle at Sequoia and Kings Canyon National Parks, good for seven days. Wilderness permits are required for overnight stays. They are available on a first-come, first-served basis at the Mineral King Ranger Station. For advanced wilderness permits or information on trail conditions, go to www.nps.gov/seki. Trailhead quotas are in effect from May to September.

Maps: A Mineral King map is available from Tom Harrison Maps. For a topographic map, ask the USGS for Mineral King.

Directions: From Visalia, drive east on Highway 198 for 38 miles to Mineral King Road, 2.5 miles east of Three Rivers. If you reach the Ash Mountain entrance station, you've gone too far. Turn right on Mineral King Road and drive 25 miles to the end of the road and the Eagle/Mosquito trailhead. Take the right fork at the end of the road to reach the parking area. Walk back out of the parking lot, and follow the road to the horse corral; Farewell Gap Trail begins just beyond it.

Contact: Sequoia and Kings Canyon National Parks, 47050 General Highway, Three Rivers, CA 93271-9651, 559/565-3341 or 559/565-3135, www.nps.gov/seki.

71 WHITE CHIEF MINE TRAIL
5.8 mi / 3.0 hr 🥾3 ⛰10

off Highway 198 in the Mineral King region of Sequoia National Park

Map 11.3, page 575

If you're one of those liberated hikers who doesn't need to have an alpine lake in your itinerary to be happy, the trail to White Chief Bowl is a scenic route with much to offer, including an exploration of the White Chief Mine tunnel. Until the Park Service purchased it in 1998, the mine was private property within the national park and off-limits to hikers.

The first mile of the trail is the same as the route to Eagle and Mosquito Lakes, but you'll leave most everyone behind when you continue straight at the one-mile junction, while they bear right for Eagle Lake and the Mosquito Lakes. The White Chief Trail continues with a hefty grade—this second mile is the toughest part of the whole trip—until it tops out at the edge of a gorgeous meadow. Just after you cross a seasonal stream (often a dry ravine by late summer), look for the ruins of Crabtree Cabin, to the right of the trail. The cabin ruins are what is left of the oldest remaining structure in Mineral King. It was built by the discoverer of the White Chief Mine in the 1870s. Next comes White Chief Meadows, surrounded by high granite walls and filled with dozens of downed trees, evidence of harsh winter avalanches.

Beyond the meadow, the trail ascends slightly until it nears a waterfall on White Chief Creek. Shortly before the falls, the trail crosses the creek and heads uphill. Look for the opening to White Chief Mine in a layer of white rock just above the trail. Scramble off the trail a few yards to reach it. The mine tunnel is tall enough to walk into and dead-ends in about 150 feet. Beyond the mine the trail continues to Upper White Chief Bowl, passing dozens of limestone caverns along the way. Although tempting, these caverns should only be explored by those who are experienced and well equipped.

User Groups: Hikers and horses. No dogs or mountain bikes. No wheelchair facilities.

Permits: No permits are required. There is a $20 entrance fee per vehicle at Sequoia and Kings Canyon National Parks, good for seven days.

Maps: A Mineral King map is available from Tom Harrison Maps. For a topographic map, ask the USGS for Mineral King.

Directions: From Visalia, drive east on Highway 198 for 38 miles to Mineral King Road, 2.5 miles east of Three Rivers. If you reach the Ash Mountain entrance station, you've gone too far. Turn right on Mineral King Road and drive 25 miles to the end of the road and the Eagle/Mosquito trailhead. Take the right fork at the end of the road to reach the parking area. The trail begins from the far end of the parking lot.

Contact: Sequoia and Kings Canyon National Parks, 47050 General Highway, Three Rivers, CA 93271-9651, 559/565-3341 or 559/565-3135, www.nps.gov/seki.

72 TIMBER GAP TRAIL
4.0 mi / 2.0 hr   🥾3 ⛰️8

off Highway 198 in the Mineral King region of Sequoia National Park

Map 11.3, page 575

On this short but steep trail, you'll stand witness to the mining history of Mineral King. The trail climbs abruptly from the Sawtooth trailhead on an old mining path along Monarch Creek, and forks in 0.25 mile. Take the left fork for Timber Gap, which climbs through a dense fir forest and then opens out to switchbacks in a wide and treeless slope—the result of continual winter avalanches. The exposed slope is home to many mountain wildflowers. The climb ends in two miles at Timber Gap, elevation 9,450 feet, a forested pass. The stumps you see among the red firs remain from early miners who cut down the trees to fuel their fires and support their mining tunnels. A faint path heads east from the pass and leads to the remains of the Empire Mine and its buildings in just over one mile.

User Groups: Hikers and horses. No dogs or mountain bikes. No wheelchair facilities.

Permits: No permits are required. There is a $20 entrance fee per vehicle at Sequoia and Kings Canyon National Parks, good for seven days.

Maps: A Mineral King map is available from Tom Harrison Maps. For a topographic map, ask the USGS for Mineral King.

Directions: From Visalia, drive east on Highway 198 for 38 miles to Mineral King Road, 2.5 miles east of Three Rivers. If you reach the Ash Mountain entrance station, you've gone too far. Turn right on Mineral King Road and drive 24.5 miles to the Sawtooth parking area, 0.5 mile before the end of the road.

Contact: Sequoia and Kings Canyon National Parks, 47050 General Highway, Three Rivers, CA 93271-9651, 559/565-3341 or 559/565-3135, www.nps.gov/seki.

73 MONARCH LAKES
8.4 mi / 5.0 hr or 2 days   🥾3 ⛰️10

off Highway 198 in the Mineral King region of Sequoia National Park

Map 11.3, page 575

The Monarch Lakes Trail leads from the Sawtooth trailhead at 8,000 feet in elevation and climbs 2,500 feet to the rocky, gemlike Monarch Lakes. The first lake is good, but the second lake is simply awesome, and the scenery along the trail is unforgettable. Walk 0.25 mile from the trailhead and take the right fork for Monarch and Crystal Lakes. After one steep mile, you'll reach Groundhog Meadow, named for the adorable yellow-bellied marmots that inhabit the area. (We like their blond coats and shrill whistles.) Beyond the meadow, the trail starts seriously switchbacking in and out of red fir forest, making a gut-thumping climb to the Crystal Lake trail junction. The trail forks sharply right for Crystal Lake, but you head left for one more mile—a relatively smooth mile, with the easiest grade of the whole route—to Lower Monarch Lake. (This section crosses an incredible talus slope.) Snow can often be found near the lake even in late summer, and the vista is dramatic, with Sawtooth Peak dominating the skyline. If you have a wilderness permit, you can find a campsite near the lake.

While the main trail continues north to Sawtooth Pass, a use trail leads southeast from the lower lake for 0.5 mile to Upper Monarch Lake. Basically you head directly up the cliff that forms the back wall of the lower lake. It's worth the climb. The upper lake is wide, deep blue, and dramatic, set at the base of barren, pointy Monarch Peak. The view from the upper lake's basin, looking back down at the lower lake and various Mineral King peaks, is breathtaking. A big surprise is that the upper lake has been dammed, like many of the high lakes in Mineral King, and is operated by Southern California Edison. Note: If you're backpacking and want to take a first-rate side trip, the trail to Sawtooth Pass is a 1.3-mile, 1,200-foot climb that's not easy, but Sawtooth Pass offers one of the best views in the Southern Sierra.

User Groups: Hikers and horses. No dogs or mountain bikes. No wheelchair facilities.

Permits: There is a $20 entrance fee per vehicle at Sequoia and Kings Canyon National Parks, good for seven days. Wilderness permits are required for overnight stays. They are available on a first-come, first-served basis at the Mineral King Ranger Station. For advanced wilderness permits or information on trail conditions, go to www.nps.gov/seki. Trailhead quotas are in effect from May to September.

Maps: A Mineral King map is available from Tom Harrison Maps. For a topographic map, ask the USGS for Mineral King.

Directions: From Visalia, drive east on Highway 198 for 38 miles to Mineral King Road, 2.5 miles east of Three Rivers. If you reach the Ash Mountain entrance station, you've gone too far. Turn right on Mineral King Road and drive 24.5 miles to the Sawtooth parking area, 0.5 mile before the end of the road.

Contact: Sequoia and Kings Canyon National Parks, 47050 General Highway, Three Rivers, CA 93271-9651, 559/565-3341 or 559/565-3135, www.nps.gov/seki.

7.4 CRYSTAL LAKE TRAIL
9.8 mi / 6.0 hr or 2 days 🏃4 ⛰10

off Highway 198 in the Mineral King region of Sequoia National Park

Map 11.3, page 575

The long and arduous path to Crystal Lake follows the same route as the trail to Monarch Lakes (see listing in this chapter) for the first 3.2 miles. In Chihuahua Bowl, a sharp right-hand turn puts you on the trail to Crystal Lake. In 0.5 mile, the trail leads past the ruins of the Chihuahua Mine (on the right), one of Mineral King's last hopes for silver riches. Like the other mines in the area, it never produced ore to equal the miners' dreams. The trail climbs abruptly over a rocky slope to a ridge of reddish foxtail pines, where your vista opens wide. Far off you can see the Farewell Gap peaks, and down below you see the Cobalt Lakes and Crystal Creek, pouring down to the Mineral King Valley and the East Fork Kaweah River. The trail continues, following more switchbacks, to upper Crystal Creek and Crystal Lake, which has been dammed. Off to the left (north), Mineral Peak stands out at 11,500 feet, and to the right (south), Rainbow Mountain shows off its colorful rock. Views are spectacular in every direction. If you scramble 0.25 mile off-trail toward Mineral Peak, you will reach Little Crystal Lake, where you have a near guarantee of solitude and a vista you won't forget.

User Groups: Hikers and horses. No dogs or mountain bikes. No wheelchair facilities.

Permits: There is a $20 entrance fee per vehicle at Sequoia and Kings Canyon National Parks, good for seven days. Wilderness permits are required for overnight stays. They are available on a first-come, first-served basis at the Mineral King Ranger Station. For advanced wilderness permits or information on trail conditions, go to www.nps.gov/seki. Trailhead quotas are in effect from May to September.

Maps: A Mineral King map is available from Tom Harrison Maps. For a topographic map, ask the USGS for Mineral King.

Directions: From Visalia, drive east on Highway 198 for 38 miles to Mineral King Road, 2.5 miles east of Three Rivers. If you reach the Ash Mountain entrance station, you've gone too far. Turn right on Mineral King Road and drive 24.5 miles to the Sawtooth parking area, 0.5 mile before the end of the road.

Contact: Sequoia and Kings Canyon National Parks, 47050 General Highway, Three Rivers, CA 93271-9651, 559/565-3341 or 559/565-3135, www.nps.gov/seki.

75 BLACK WOLF FALLS
0.5 mi / 0.5 hr 👫1 ⛰8

off Highway 198 in the Mineral King region of Sequoia National Park

Map 11.3, page 575

This hike is really just a stroll, and the destination is readily apparent from the Sawtooth trailhead: Black Wolf Falls, tumbling down the canyon wall in Mineral King Valley. But aside from the chance to get close to a pretty waterfall, the hike is interesting because of its historical significance. Black Wolf's name is actually an alteration of its original moniker, which was Black Wall Falls, named for the Black Wall copper mine that was located at the waterfall's base. Back in the 1870s, when miners believed that Mineral King was rich in more than just scenery, they mined the base of Monarch Creek with a modicum of success. Today you can walk right up to the falls and see the mine tunnel on its right side (it looks like a cave, but don't go inside; it's unstable). In summer, rangers lead group hikes to the waterfall and talk about Mineral King's mining history. Although the route to Black Wolf Falls isn't an official trail, the path is well used and clearly visible. If you can find its beginning across the road from the No Parking Any Time sign, the rest of the hike is easy.

User Groups: Hikers only. No dogs, horses, or mountain bikes. No wheelchair facilities.

Permits: No permits are required. There is a $20 entrance fee per vehicle at Sequoia and Kings Canyon National Parks, good for seven days.

Maps: A Mineral King map is available from Tom Harrison Maps. For a topographic map, ask the USGS for Mineral King.

Directions: From Visalia, drive east on Highway 198 for 38 miles to Mineral King Road, 2.5 miles east of Three Rivers. If you reach the Ash Mountain entrance station, you've gone too far. Turn right on Mineral King Road and drive 24.5 miles to the Sawtooth parking area, 0.5 mile before the end of the road. Walk up the road toward Black Wolf Falls, then look for a use trail across the road from the No Parking Any Time sign, just beyond where Monarch Creek flows under the road.

Contact: Sequoia and Kings Canyon National Parks, 47050 General Highway, Three Rivers, CA 93271-9651, 559/565-3341 or 559/565-3135, www.nps.gov/seki.

76 LADYBUG TRAIL

3.8 mi / 2.0 hr   👫2 ⛰8

off Highway 198 in the South Fork region of Sequoia National Park

Map 11.3, page 575   BEST (

The South Fork area is the forgotten region of Sequoia National Park. Accessible only by a 13-mile dead-end road out of Three Rivers, South Fork is the place to go when you just want to get away from it all. Solitude in a national park? You can find it here (mostly because it takes about 40 minutes just to drive from Highway 198 in Three Rivers to the trailhead). The elevation is low (only 3,600 feet), so the area is accessible year-round, and there may be no finer winter walk than a hike on Ladybug Trail out of South Fork. The trail leaves the far end of South Fork Campground and heads through an oak and bay forest along the South Fork Kaweah River. At 1.7 miles, you reach Ladybug Camp, a primitive camping area along the river's edge, in the shade of pines and firs. A short scramble downstream of the camp gives you a look at Ladybug Falls, a 25-foot waterfall set in a rocky grotto. If you continue upstream, the trail leads another few hundred yards and then switchbacks uphill, heading for Whiskey Log Camp. A use trail leaves the main trail and continues a short distance upriver, where there are many beautiful rocky pools. And in case you haven't guessed, the trail, camp, and falls are named for the millions of ladybugs that winter near the river, then take flight in the spring to head back to the Central Valley to feed.

User Groups: Hikers and horses. No dogs or mountain bikes. No wheelchair facilities.

Permits: No permits are required. There is a $20 entrance fee per vehicle at Sequoia and Kings Canyon National Parks, good for seven days.

Maps: A Sequoia and Kings Canyon map is available from Tom Harrison Maps. For a topographic map, ask the USGS for Dennison Peak.

Directions: From Visalia, drive east on Highway 198 for 35 miles to one mile west of Three Rivers. Turn right on South Fork Drive and drive 12.8 miles to South Fork Campground. (Nine miles out, the road turns to dirt.) Park at the Ladybug trailhead parking area.

Contact: Sequoia and Kings Canyon National Parks, 47050 General Highway, Three Rivers, CA 93271-9651, 559/565-3341 or 559/565-3135, www.nps.gov/seki.

77 GARFIELD-HOCKETT TRAIL

5.8 mi / 3.0 hr   👫3 ⛰9

off Highway 198 in the South Fork region of Sequoia National Park

Map 11.3, page 575

The trip to the magnificent Garfield Grove is only 2.9 miles from South Fork Campground, and if you don't mind a steep climb and possibly sharing the trail with horse packers, you should be sure to take this hike. The trail climbs immediately and keeps climbing, but fortunately, it is shaded by oaks most of the way. The ascent rewards you with a continual view of distant Homer's Nose, a granite landmark that, although prominent, looks little like anybody's nose. In just under three miles of nonstop climbing, you reach the first of many sequoias in the Garfield Grove, reported to be one of the largest groves in the national parks. By the time you reach it, you've gained 2,000 feet in elevation, so pick a big tree to lean against, pull out a snack, and take a breather.

User Groups: Hikers and horses. No dogs or mountain bikes. No wheelchair facilities.

Permits: No permits are required. There is a $20 entrance fee per vehicle at Sequoia and Kings Canyon National Parks, good for seven days.

Maps: A Sequoia and Kings Canyon map is available from Tom Harrison Maps. For topographic maps, ask the USGS for Dennison Peak.

Directions: From Visalia, drive east on Highway 198 for 35 miles to one mile west of Three

Rivers. Turn right on South Fork Drive and drive 12.8 miles to South Fork Campground. (Nine miles out, the road turns to dirt.) Park at the trailhead at the far end of the campground loop, just before the parking lot for the Ladybug Trailhead.

Contact: Sequoia and Kings Canyon National Parks, 47050 General Highway, Three Rivers, CA 93271-9651, 559/565-3341 or 559/565-3135, www.nps.gov/seki.

78 BALCH PARK NATURE TRAIL
1.0 mi / 0.5 hr   🏃1 ⛰️7

in Mountain Home Demonstration State Forest off Highway 190 near Springville

Map 11.3, page 575

Balch Park is the small county-run park within the borders of Mountain Home Demonstration State Forest, and its easy, one-mile nature trail is a great place to take your kids for the afternoon. The trail begins next to the main entrance to Balch Park Camp, across from the museum, and your first stop is a visit to the Hollow Log, which was used as a dwelling by various pioneers, Indians, and prospectors. You also get to see the Lady Alice Tree, which was incorrectly billed in the early 20th century as the largest tree in the world. Nonetheless, it's no slacker in the size department. Continuing along the route, you'll see and learn all about dogwoods, bracken ferns, manzanita, and gooseberry. When you're finished hiking the nature trail, you can cross the road and throw a line into one of Balch Park's two small fishing ponds, which are stocked weekly.

User Groups: Hikers, dogs, and horses. No mountain bikes. No wheelchair facilities.

Permits: No permits are required. Parking and access are free.

Maps: A free brochure and map of Mountain Home Demonstration State Forest, which includes Balch Park, are available from park headquarters. For a topographic map, ask the USGS for Camp Wishon.

Directions: From Porterville, drive east on Highway 190 for 18 miles to Springville. At Springville, turn left (north) on Balch Park Road/Road 239, drive 3.5 miles, and turn right on Bear Creek Road/Road 220. Drive 14 miles to Mountain Home Demonstration State Forest Headquarters, pick up a free park map, and then continue 1.5 miles farther to the entrance to Balch Park and the nature trail.

Contact: Balch Park, 559/539-3896; Mountain Home Demonstration State Forest, P.O. Box 517, Springville, CA 93265, 559/539-2321 (summer) or 559/539-2855 (winter).

79 ADAM AND EVE LOOP TRAIL
2.0 mi / 1.0 hr   🏃2 ⛰️9

in Mountain Home Demonstration State Forest off Highway 190 near Springville

Map 11.3, page 575

On the Adam and Eve Loop Trail you can see the Adam Tree standing tall and proud, but its companion, the Eve Tree, is no longer thriving. It (she?) was axed during the infamous sequoia logging years, and it's strangely touching to see the gaping slash in her side. Begin your trip by taking the left side of the loop, heading uphill to the Adam Tree, the second-largest tree in this state forest, at 240 feet tall and 27 feet in diameter. The Eve Tree is shortly after. The big draw on the trail is visiting the "Indian bathtubs" at Tub Flat, halfway around the loop; these are basins, formed in solid granite, that were probably used by Native Americans. No one is sure whether they are natural or handmade. The basins are much larger than the traditional Indian grinding holes that are found elsewhere in the Sierra; they are truly large enough to take a bath in.

User Groups: Hikers, dogs, and horses. No mountain bikes. No wheelchair facilities.

Permits: No permits are required. Parking and access are free.

Maps: A free brochure and map of Mountain Home Demonstration State Forest are available from park headquarters. For a topographic map, ask the USGS for Camp Wishon.

Directions: From Porterville, drive east on Highway 190 for 18 miles to Springville. At Springville, turn left (north) on Balch Park Road/Road 239 and drive 3.5 miles; then turn right on Bear Creek Road/Road 220. Drive 14 miles to Mountain Home Demonstration State Forest Headquarters, pick up a free park map, and then continue one mile farther, turning right at the sign for Hidden Falls Recreation Area. Drive three miles to just past the pack station and before Shake Camp Campground, to the trailhead for Adam and Eve Loop Trail, on the left.

Contact: Mountain Home Demonstration State Forest, P.O. Box 517, Springville, CA 93265, 559/539-2321 (summer) or 559/539-2855 (winter).

80 REDWOOD CROSSING
4.0 mi / 2.0 hr 　　🥾1 ⛰9

in Mountain Home Demonstration
State Forest off Highway 190 near Springville

Map 11.3, page 575

An excellent easy hike for campers and day visitors at Mountain Home Demonstration State Forest is on Long Meadow Trail, from Shake Camp Campground to Redwood Crossing, on the Tule River. The trail starts by the public corral (elevation 6,800 feet) and leads through logged sequoia stumps to a thick mixed forest on the slopes high above the Wishon Fork Tule River. When the trail reaches clearings in the trees, the views of the Great Western Divide are excellent. At two miles out, you reach Redwood Crossing, a boulder-lined stretch of the river. Those willing to ford can cross to the other side and head into the Golden Trout Wilderness, but day hikers should pull out a picnic at the river's edge and make an afternoon of it. Backpackers heading for the wilderness need to secure a wilderness permit from the Tule River Ranger District office.

User Groups: Hikers, dogs, and horses. No mountain bikes. No wheelchair facilities.

Permits: No permits are required. Parking and access are free.

Maps: A free brochure and map of Mountain Home Demonstration State Forest are available from park headquarters. For a topographic map, ask the USGS for Camp Wishon.

Directions: From Porterville, drive east on Highway 190 for 18 miles to Springville. At Springville, turn left (north) on Balch Park Road/Road 239, drive 3.5 miles, and turn right on Bear Creek Road/Road 220. Drive 14 miles to Mountain Home Demonstration State Forest Headquarters, pick up a free park map, and then continue one mile farther. Turn right at the sign for Hidden Falls Recreation Area. Drive 3.5 miles to Shake Camp Campground. The Long Meadow trailhead is located by the public corral.

Contact: Mountain Home Demonstration State Forest, P.O. Box 517, Springville, CA 93265, 559/539-2321 (summer) or 559/539-2855 (winter); Tule River Ranger District, 32588 Highway 190, Springville, CA 93265, 559/539-2607, www.fs.fed.us/r5/sequoia.

81 MOSES GULCH TRAIL
4.0 mi / 2.0 hr 　　🥾2 ⛰9

in Mountain Home Demonstration
State Forest off Highway 190 near Springville

Map 11.3, page 575

For a less-crowded alternate to the popular Redwood Crossing (see listing in this chapter), you can take the other trail from the public corral at Shake Flat Campground and wind your way through stands of beautiful virgin sequoias to the Wishon Fork Tule River at Moses Gulch Campground. The Moses Gulch Trail crosses park roads twice—the only downer—but it's an easy walk for families, and it's peaceful besides. Once you reach the river (at two miles), you have the option of hiking alongside it to the north or south, adding some distance to your trip. The northern stretch leads to Hidden Falls Campground (the home of many small falls and pools), and the southern stretch crosses pretty Galena and Silver Creeks, leading past a mining cabin and an old copper mine.

User Groups: Hikers, dogs, and horses. No mountain bikes. No wheelchair facilities.

Permits: No permits are required. Parking and access are free.

Maps: A free brochure and map of Mountain Home Demonstration State Forest are available from park headquarters. For a topographic map, ask the USGS for Camp Wishon.

Directions: From Porterville, drive east on Highway 190 for 18 miles to Springville. At Springville, turn left (north) on Balch Park Road/Road 239, drive 3.5 miles, and then turn right on Bear Creek Road/Road 220. Drive 14 miles to Mountain Home Demonstration State Forest Headquarters and pick up a free park map, then continue one mile farther and turn right at the sign for Hidden Falls Recreation Area. Drive 3.5 miles to Shake Camp Campground. The Moses Gulch trailhead is by the public corral.

Contact: Mountain Home Demonstration State Forest, P.O. Box 517, Springville, CA 93265, 559/539-2321 (summer) or 559/539-2855 (winter).

82 DOYLE TRAIL
6.0 mi / 3.0 hr

in Giant Sequoia National Monument near Springville

Map 11.3, page 575

The Doyle Trail is a great alternative to the heat of the Springville and Porterville Valleys. It's in the transition zone between foothills and conifers, with plenty of shade from tall manzanita, oaks, madrones, and pines. Squirrels and lizards are your primary companions on the trail, which laterals along the slopes above the Wishon fork of the Tule River. From the gated trailhead, hike up the paved road and bear left to bypass Doyle Springs, a community of private cabins. Follow the trail that is signed Trail to Upstream Fishing.

The route climbs gently through the forest for 2.5 miles and then suddenly descends to the same level as the river, where there are some primitive campsites available. Then the trail rises again, climbing for another 0.5 mile to a clearing on the right, where there is an outcrop of jagged green rock alongside the river. Leave the trail and cross over the rock, where you'll find a few picture-perfect swimming holes and small waterfalls.

User Groups: Hikers, dogs, horses, and mountain bikes. No wheelchair facilities.

Permits: No permits are required. Parking and access are free.

Maps: A Sequoia National Forest map is available from the U.S. Forest Service. For a topographic map, ask the USGS for Camp Wishon.

Directions: From Porterville, drive east on Highway 190 for 18 miles to Springville. From Springville, continue east on Highway 190 for 7.5 miles to Wishon Drive/Road 208, a left fork. Turn left and drive four miles on Wishon Drive, then take the left fork, which is signed for day-use parking (above the campground). Drive 0.25 mile and park off the road, near the gate.

Contact: Giant Sequoia National Monument/Sequoia National Forest, Tule River Ranger District, 32588 Highway 190, Springville, CA 93265, 559/539-2607, www.fs.fed.us/r5/sequoia.

83 JORDAN PEAK LOOKOUT
1.8 mi / 1.0 hr

in Giant Sequoia National Monument near Quaking Aspen

Map 11.3, page 575

You'll see some logging activity out here by Jordan Peak, but if you can put up with it, you can climb a mere 600 feet over less than a mile to reach the summit of this 9,100-foot mountain. Few summits are so easily attained (it's a well-graded and well-maintained trail), and this one is not lacking in dramatic vistas.

You can see the Wishon Fork Canyon of the Tule River, Camp Nelson, the Sequoia Crest, Slate Mountain, Maggie Mountain, and Moses Mountain close up, and the Tehachapis and the Coast Range far, far away. The peak is covered with microwave equipment, but it doesn't mar the stupendous view. Head west from the trailhead on Jordan Lookout Trail, switchbacking up until you reach the cat-walked stairs to the lookout, which was built in 1934. All the materials to construct the lookout were hauled in by mules.

User Groups: Hikers, dogs, horses, and mountain bikes. No wheelchair facilities.

Permits: No permits are required. Parking and access are free.

Maps: A Sequoia National Forest map is available from the U.S. Forest Service. For a topographic map, ask the USGS for Sentinel Peak.

Directions: From Porterville, drive 45 miles east on Highway 190 to Forest Service Road 21S50, near Quaking Aspen Campground. Turn left on Road 21S50 and drive five miles. Bear left and continue on Road 21S50 for 2.8 miles, bearing left on Road 20S71, signed for Jordan Peak Lookout, and following it one mile to its end, at the trailhead.

Contact: Giant Sequoia National Monument/ Sequoia National Forest, Tule River Ranger District, 32588 Highway 190, Springville, CA 93265, 559/539-2607, www.fs.fed.us/r5/ sequoia.

Little Kern River. The route crosses the creek several times. Shade lovers will thrill at the conifer forests that line the route, interspersed by large and grassy meadows, and anglers can bring along their gear to try their luck with the golden trout in the river. There are many possible campsites along the Little Kern, where the elevation is 6,200 feet.

User Groups: Hikers, dogs, and horses. No mountain bikes. No wheelchair facilities.

Permits: A free wilderness permit is required for overnight stays and is available from the Springville or Kernville Ranger Stations at the addresses below. Parking and access are free.

Maps: A Golden Trout Wilderness map is available from the U.S. Forest Service or Tom Harrison Maps. For a topographic map, ask the USGS for Sentinel Peak.

Directions: From Porterville, drive 45 miles east on Highway 190 to Forest Service Road 21S50 near Quaking Aspen Campground. Turn left on Road 21S50 and drive five miles; bear left and continue on Road 21S50 for 1.5 miles to the Clicks Creek trailhead, at Log Cabin Meadow.

Contact: Sequoia National Forest, Tule River Ranger District, 32588 Highway 190, Springville, CA 93265, 559/539-2607, www.fs.fed.us/ r5/sequoia; Sequoia National Forest, Kern River Ranger District, 105 Whitney Road, P.O. Box 9, Kernville, CA 93238, 760/376-3781, www.fs.fed.us/r5/sequoia.

84 CLICKS CREEK TRAIL
14.0 mi / 2 days   🥾3 ⛰9

in the Golden Trout Wilderness near Quaking Aspen

Map 11.3, page 575

If you like peace and quiet on your backpacking trips, Clicks Creek Trail, in the Golden Trout Wilderness, may suit you just fine. The trail leads northeast from Log Cabin Meadow (elevation 7,800 feet), heading steadily downhill along Clicks Creek to the

85 JOHN JORDAN / HOSSACK MEADOW TRAIL
5.0-6.0 mi / 2.5-3.0 hr   🥾2 ⛰8

in Giant Sequoia National Monument near Quaking Aspen

Map 11.3, page 575

Your route on the John Jordan Trail begins with a crossing of McIntyre Creek, then traverses a level mile to an old fence, gate, and McIntyre Rock—a huge pile of granite boulders with an excellent view. Climb on top of the rock's well-graded, cracking-granite back side and peer over its startlingly steep front side. Surprise! It's straight down, about 600 feet. The trail heads downhill through a red fir forest to Nelson Creek, the site of some logging work. Although you can walk another 0.5 mile to the trail's end (at Hossack Meadow), most people turn around at the sight of logged trees, making for a five-mile round-trip with a 1,000-foot elevation gain on the return. So who was John Jordan, anyway? He was a trailblazer in the 1870s who unfortunately was most famous for drowning in the Kern River on his way back to the Central Valley to tell everybody he had completed this trail, a proposed toll road.

User Groups: Hikers, dogs, horses, and mountain bikes. No wheelchair facilities.

Permits: No permits are required. Parking and access are free.

Maps: A Sequoia National Forest map is available from the U.S. Forest Service. For a topographic map, ask the USGS for Sentinel Peak.

Directions: From Porterville, drive 45 miles east on Highway 190 to Forest Service Road 21S50, near Quaking Aspen Campground. Turn left on Road 21S50 and drive 6.6 miles, then bear left on Road 20S81. Follow Road 20S81 for 1.4 miles to the signed trailhead.

Contact: Giant Sequoia National Monument/Sequoia National Forest, Tule River Ranger District, 32588 Highway 190, Springville, CA 93265, 559/539-2607, www.fs.fed.us/r5/sequoia.

more than 1,000 years old. Among them is a tree named for former President George Bush Sr., who visited the grove in 1992. The trail is a pleasant downhill stroll along Freeman Creek, reaching the first sequoias in about one mile, after crossing the creek. In between the big trees are large meadow areas (many of which bloom with spring and summer wildflowers) and forests of red firs. Many campsites are found along the creek. The path finally ends at Lloyd Meadows, three miles from the trailhead, but most people don't travel that far, since it requires too much climbing on the way back. Two miles out and back is just about perfect.

User Groups: Hikers, dogs, horses, and mountain bikes. No wheelchair facilities.

Permits: No permits are required. Parking and access are free.

Maps: A Sequoia National Forest map is available from the U.S. Forest Service. For topographic maps, ask the USGS for Sentinel Peak.

Directions: From Porterville, drive 45 miles east on Highway 190 to Forest Service Road 21S50, near Quaking Aspen Campground. Turn left on Road 21S50 and drive 0.5 mile, then turn right at the sign for the Freeman Creek Grove.

Contact: Giant Sequoia National Monument/Sequoia National Forest, Tule River Ranger District, 32588 Highway 190, Springville, CA 93265, 559/539-2607, www.fs.fed.us/r5/sequoia.

86 FREEMAN CREEK TRAIL
4.0 mi / 2.0 hr   🏃2 ⛺8

in Giant Sequoia National Monument near Quaking Aspen

Map 11.3, page 575

The easternmost grove of sequoias in the world is your destination on Freeman Creek Trail. Compared to most sequoia groves in the Sierra, the trees of the 1,700-acre Freeman Creek Grove are mere adolescents—probably not

87 SUMMIT TRAIL TO SLATE MOUNTAIN
8.0 mi / 4.0 hr   🏃3 ⛺9

in Giant Sequoia National Monument near Quaking Aspen

Map 11.3, page 575

If you're staying at Quaking Aspen Campground, you can set out on Summit National Recreation Trail from outside your tent door, but if you're not, drive to the trailhead just south of the camp off Road 21S78. Few people hike all 12 miles of the trail, but many take this four-mile jaunt to the summit of 9,302-foot Slate Mountain, the highest peak in the area. The first two miles of trail are easy, climbing gently through meadows and forest (some logging activity can be seen); then the route climbs more steeply, ascending first the east side and then the north side of Slate Mountain. Views of the granite spires of The Needles and Olancha Peak can be seen. At 3.8 miles you reach a junction with Bear Creek Trail, and from there, it's a short scramble to your left to the top of Slate Mountain, which is a big pile of rocks with a tremendous 360-degree view. There's no trail, but a couple well-worn routes are visible.

User Groups: Hikers, dogs, horses, and mountain bikes. No wheelchair facilities.

Permits: No permits are required. Parking and access are free.

Maps: A Sequoia National Forest map is available from the U.S. Forest Service. For a topographic map, ask the USGS for Sentinel Peak.

Directions: From Porterville, drive 46 miles east on Highway 190 to Forest Service Road 21S78, which is 0.5 mile south of Quaking Aspen Campground. Turn right on Road 21S78 and drive 0.5 mile to the Summit trailhead.

Contact: Giant Sequoia National Monument/Sequoia National Forest, Tule River Ranger District, 32588 Highway 190, Springville, CA 93265, 559/539-2607, www.fs.fed.us/r5/sequoia.

88 NEEDLES LOOKOUT
5.0 mi / 2.5 hr 🏃2 ⛰10

in Giant Sequoia National Monument near Quaking Aspen

Map 11.3, page 575   **BEST ☾**

Here it is, the perfect easy day hike in Giant Sequoia National Monument. It's just long enough and undulating enough for beginning and intermediate hikers, without being too demanding, and it's full of visual rewards. The trail starts with a placard bearing a great old black-and-white photo that shows what the fire lookout on top of The Needles looked like early in the 20th century. Five minutes down the trail, you leave the forest and come out to two wooden benches, good places to stare out at the magnificent view of the Kern River Basin before you. If you look ahead, you get a glimpse of the fire lookout, perched in what looks like a precarious fashion on top of The Needles' tall granite spires. As you continue along the trail, you lose your view of the lookout. The trail goes up, then down, then up again, through firs, ponderosa, sugar pines, granite, and sand. The only steep section is the final set of switchbacks up The Needles; they lead to a series of stairs and catwalks that ascend to the lookout tower. When you reach the first catwalk, the rest is a cakewalk. A sign tells you if the tower is open and you may come up and visit. If it's closed, just climb up on any boulder to admire the view—it's just as fine from the base of the tower as it is from above. You look out over Lloyd Meadow and the western half of the Golden Trout Wilderness. This is a perfect place to take someone who needs to get inspired.

User Groups: Hikers, dogs, horses, and mountain bikes. No wheelchair facilities.

Permits: No permits are required. Parking and access are free.

Maps: A Sequoia National Forest map is available from the U.S. Forest Service. For topographic maps, ask the USGS for Sentinel Peak and Durrwood Creek.

Directions: From Porterville, drive 46 miles east on Highway 190 to Forest Service Road 21S05, which is 0.5 mile south of Quaking Aspen Campground. Turn left (east) on Road 21S05 and drive 2.8 miles to the trailhead.

Contact: Giant Sequoia National Monument/Sequoia National Forest, Tule River Ranger District, 32588 Highway 190, Springville, CA 93265, 559/539-2607, www.fs.fed.us/r5/sequoia.

89 TRAIL OF 100 GIANTS
0.5 mi / 0.5 hr   🏃1 ⛰10

in Giant Sequoia National Monument near Johnsondale

Map 11.3, page 575   **BEST ⬤**

The Trail of 100 Giants is as good as many of the giant sequoia trails in Sequoia and Kings Canyon National Parks. Trailhead elevation is 6,400 feet, and the trail is an easy and nearly flat loop that is paved and suitable for wheelchairs and baby strollers. Located within the Long Meadow Giant Sequoia Grove, the second-most southern grove where sequoias are found, the big trees on the Trail of 100 Giants are situated amid a mixed forest of cedars and pines. A dozen interpretive signs along the path unlock the secrets of this forest. As you walk in from the parking lot across the road, the first sequoia tree on your right is a doozy—probably the best one on the loop. Of all the sequoia groves we've seen and admired, the Trail of 100 Giants grove stands out because it has an unusual amount of twins—two sequoias growing tightly side by side in order to share resources. In fact, this grove even has one twin that rangers call a "sequedar," a sequoia and a cedar that have grown together. If you're staying at Redwood Meadow Campground, you have your own entrance to this loop, so you don't have to drive down the road to the main trailhead and parking lot.

User Groups: Hikers, wheelchairs, dogs, and horses. No mountain bikes.

Permits: No permits are required. A $5 parking fee is charged per vehicle.

Maps: A Sequoia National Forest map is available from the U.S. Forest Service. For a topographic map, ask the USGS for Johnsondale.

Directions: From Kernville on the north end of Isabella Lake, drive north on Sierra Way/Road 99 for 27 miles to Johnsondale R-Ranch. Continue west (the road becomes Road 50) for 5.5 miles, turn right on the Western Divide Highway, and drive 2.4 miles to the trailhead parking area, on the right, just before Redwood Meadow Campground. Cross the road to begin the trail.

Contact: Giant Sequoia National Monument/ Sequoia National Forest, Tule River Ranger District, 32588 Highway 190, Springville, CA 93265, 559/539-2607, www.fs.fed.us/r5/ sequoia.

90 MULE PEAK LOOKOUT
1.2 mi / 1.0 hr   🏃1 ⛰9

in Giant Sequoia National Monument near Johnsondale

Map 11.3, page 575

While rock climbers come to Mule Peak to do their daring work, hikers can take a not-so-daring walk up the back side of Mule Peak; it's attainable for all ages and levels of hikers. The area around the peak has been logged, but much of the forest has grown back. The trail follows a series of easy switchbacks up the hillside, gaining 600 feet to the summit of Mule Peak (elevation 8,142 feet). A lookout tower is positioned there, built in 1936 and still in operation by Sequoia National Forest. The summit view includes Onion Meadow Peak, Table Mountain, the Tule River Valley, and the Tule River Indian Reservation to the west.

User Groups: Hikers, dogs, horses, and mountain bikes. No wheelchair facilities.

Permits: No permits are required. Parking and access are free.

Maps: A Sequoia National Forest map is available from the U.S. Forest Service. For a topographic map, ask the USGS for Sentinel Peak.

Directions: From Kernville on the north end of Isabella Lake, drive north on Sierra Way/Road 99 for 27 miles to Johnsondale R-Ranch. Continue west (the road becomes Road 50), then in 5.5 miles, turn right on the Western Divide Highway. Drive five miles to the left turnoff signed for Mule Peak/Road 22S03. Turn left and follow Road 22S03 for five miles to the Mule Peak trailhead.

Contact: Giant Sequoia National Monument/ Sequoia National Forest, Tule River Ranger District, 32588 Highway 190, Springville, CA 93265, 559/539-2607, www.fs.fed.us/r5/ sequoia.

91 DOME ROCK
0.25 mi / 0.5 hr   👥1 ⛰9

in Giant Sequoia National Monument near Quaking Aspen

Map 11.3, page 575

Dome Rock wins the prize for "Granite Dome with the Most Pedestrian Name." But never mind. It also wins the prize for "Shortest Walk to an Incredible View." Trailhead elevation is 7,200 feet, and the trail is really just a route leading from the left side of the parking lot. Signs at the parking lot warn you not to drop or throw anything off the top of the dome, because there are rock climbers down below on the dome's steep side. It's a mere five-minute walk to the top of Dome Rock—a huge cap of bare granite—where the views are incredible of Slate Mountain, Isabella Lake, and The Needles. If you look very carefully, you can just make out the fire lookout tower on top of The Needles. You'll want to hang around here for a while to ooh and aah. If your scrambling skills are good, consider checking out another stunning destination just a few miles from here. Jump back in your car and drive back to the Western Divide Highway, then head south for four miles to an unmarked pullout on the east side of the road, 0.25 mile south of the Crawford Road turnoff. Start hiking on the dirt road that begins at the turnout; bear right where it forks. The path draws near to Nobe Young Creek, and soon you will hear a noisy waterfall. Take one of several spur trails on your left leading down to the base of the 125-foot fall, which drops over three granite ledges. The entire hike is only one mile round-trip, but because there is no formal trail, it's not for novices. Wear good boots and use caution on the steep and slippery slope.

User Groups: Hikers, dogs, horses, and mountain bikes. No wheelchair facilities.

Permits: No permits are required. Parking and access are free.

Maps: A Sequoia National Forest map is available from the U.S. Forest Service. For a topographic map ask the USGS for Sentinel Peak.

Directions: From Kernville on the north end of Isabella Lake, drive north on Sierra Way/ Road 99 for 27 miles to Johnsondale R-Ranch. Continue west (the road becomes Road 50) for 5.5 miles, and turn right on the Western Divide Highway. Drive 12 miles to the Dome Rock/Road 21S69 turnoff, on the right, across from Peppermint Work Center. Turn right and follow the dirt road for a few hundred yards; where it forks, bear left and continue to the trailhead, 0.5 mile from the Western Divide Highway. If you're traveling from the north, the turnoff is two miles south of Ponderosa Lodge.

Contact: Giant Sequoia National Monument/ Sequoia National Forest, Tule River Ranger District, 32588 Highway 190, Springville, CA 93265, 559/539-2607, www.fs.fed.us/r5/ sequoia.

92 ALDER CREEK TRAIL
1.8 mi / 1.0 hr   👥1 ⛰8

in Giant Sequoia National Monument near Johnsondale

Map 11.3, page 575   **BEST ☾**

The granite slabs and pools on Alder Creek have gotten so popular with hikers, swimmers, and picnickers that the Forest Service has installed No Parking Any Time signs all over the road near the trailhead. But as long as you park where you're supposed to (off the road, in the day-use parking area), you can still pay a visit to the tons-of-fun pools and slides along Alder Creek. To reach them, walk up the gated dirt road (Road 22S83) and turn right on the single-track trail. The path descends to the confluence of Alder Creek and Dry Meadow

Creek, where there is a long length of swimming holes and rocky slides that pour into them. Make sure you wear denim or some other heavy material on your backside so you can while away many happy hours pretending you are a river otter. It's exhilarating, but please use caution as you slip and slide. Slick granite can be very unforgiving.

User Groups: Hikers and dogs. No horses or mountain bikes. No wheelchair facilities.

Permits: No permits are required. Parking and access are free.

Maps: A Sequoia National Forest map is available from the U.S. Forest Service. For a topographic map, ask the USGS for Sentinel Peak.

Directions: From Kernville on the north end of Lake Isabella, drive north on Sierra Way/Road 99 for 27 miles to 0.5 mile north of Johnsondale R-Ranch. Turn right on Road 22S82 and drive 5.7 miles to the day-use parking area, on the right side of the road. Walk across Road 22S82 to the gated dirt road and the trailhead.

Contact: Giant Sequoia National Monument/Sequoia National Forest, Tule River Ranger District, 32588 Highway 190, Springville, CA 93265, 559/539-2607, www.fs.fed.us/r5/sequoia.

93 KEARSARGE PASS
10.0 mi / 6.0 hr or 2 days 🥾3 ⛰10

in the John Muir Wilderness
in Inyo National Forest

Map 11.3, page 575

The trailhead elevation for Kearsarge Pass Trail is 9,200 feet, and the elevation at Kearsarge Pass is 11,823 feet. Five miles and a good amount of climbing lie in between, but the route is well graded, and the scenery is spectacular. The trail, which was once an Indian trading route, leads to the backcountry of Kings Canyon National Park, but most day hikers just make the trip to the pass. Along the way, you are witness to several sparkling lakes and whitewater cascades, and a wealth of high-country wildflowers. Not surprisingly, this is a very popular trail. Remember to bring sunglasses, sunscreen, and a jacket for the summit, which is windy and exposed.

The trail climbs gradually from the trailhead, often nearing Independence Creek then veering away again as it winds through a multitude of switchbacks. You pass Little Pothole Lake at 1.5 miles, Gilbert Lake at 2.2 miles, and Flower Lake at 2.6 miles. Continue climbing high above tree line to Kearsarge Pass. You'll get a long-distance view of Heart Lake and pass the left spur trail leading to Big Pothole Lake along the way. Finally, just when you think you can climb no farther, you reach the pass, at five miles. A sign announces your arrival in Kings Canyon Park, and extraordinary Sierra views surround you. You'll gaze at Bullfrog and Kearsarge Lakes, University Peak, and Mount Gould.

Note that if you decide to turn this into an overnight trip, food storage regulations are in effect. Bear-resistant canisters are required for all backpackers, and no wood fires are permitted. Good camping and fishing is located 3.5 miles beyond the pass, at Charlotte Lake, but a one-night stay limit is in effect.

User Groups: Hikers, dogs, and horses. Dogs are allowed to Kearsarge Pass, but not beyond it. No mountain bikes. No wheelchair facilities.

Permits: A free wilderness permit is required year-round for overnight stays and is available from the Eastern Sierra Interagency Visitor Center, 1.5 miles south of Lone Pine. Quotas are in effect from May 1 to November 1; permits are available in advance for a $5 reservation fee per person.

Maps: A John Muir Wilderness map is available from the U.S. Forest Service. A Kearsarge Pass map is available from Tom Harrison Maps. For a topographic map, ask the USGS for Kearsarge Peak.

Directions: From Lone Pine, drive 15 miles north on U.S. 395 to Independence. Turn west on Market Street, which becomes Onion

Valley Road. Drive 14 miles to the end of the road and the trailhead parking area.

Contact: Inyo National Forest, Mount Whitney Ranger Station, P.O. Box 8, Lone Pine, CA 93545, 760/876-6200, www.fs.usda.gov/inyo; Eastern Sierra Interagency Visitor Center, 760/876-6222.

94 FLOWER AND MATLOCK LAKES
6.4 mi / 3.5 hr   🥾2 ⛰️8

in the John Muir Wilderness
in Inyo National Forest

Map 11.3, page 575

If you don't have the time or the energy for Kearsarge Pass (see listing in this chapter), the route to Flower Lake and Matlock Lake is a good second choice. Although it doesn't offer the astounding views that the pass has, it is still a stellar trip into dramatic granite country. Both lakes are deep blue waterways that draw in all the color of the Sierra sky. The trail climbs gradually from the trailhead, switchbacking along Independence Creek. You pass Little Pothole Lake at 1.5 miles and Gilbert Lake at 2.2 miles, reaching a junction for Matlock Lake at 2.5 miles. Continue straight for 0.1 mile to Flower Lake, then retrace your steps to the junction and head south for 0.7 mile to larger Matlock Lake. Pull out your camera and a picnic, and while away some time before returning to the trailhead.

User Groups: Hikers, dogs, and horses. No mountain bikes. No wheelchair facilities.

Permits: No day-hiking permits are required. Parking and access are free.

Maps: A John Muir Wilderness map is available from the U.S. Forest Service. A Kearsarge Pass map is available from Tom Harrison Maps. For a topographic map, ask the USGS for Kearsarge Peak.

Directions: From Lone Pine, drive 15 miles north on U.S. 395 to Independence. Turn west on Market Street, which becomes Onion Valley Road. Drive 14 miles to the end of the road and the trailhead parking area.

Contact: Inyo National Forest, Mount Whitney Ranger Station, P.O. Box 8, Lone Pine, CA 93545, 760/876-6200, www.fs.usda.gov/inyo; Eastern Sierra Interagency Visitor Center, 760/876-6222.

95 ROBINSON LAKE
3.0 mi / 2.0 hr   🥾4 ⛰️9

in the John Muir Wilderness
in Inyo National Forest

Map 11.3, page 575

The Robinson Lake Trail is best described as relentlessly steep but mercifully short. The hike is challenging in places due to the grade, loose surface, and relative obscurity of the trail, but the destination is superlative. In addition to beautiful Robinson Lake (at 10,500 feet), you get a close and personal view of 11,744-foot Independence Peak and an excellent wildflower display along Robinson Creek. Start at the trailhead by campsite No. 7 in Onion Valley Campground. Watch out for the overgrown vegetation that can sometimes hide the trail. Just climb, catch your breath, and climb some more. After a fairly punishing ascent, you'll reach the small, shallow lake in less than an hour. Campsites and picnicking sites are found in the sand on the lake's east side, or in the pine forest on the northwest side. Equally as pretty as the lake are the views from its shores of the valley below. Plan your trip for July to September; the trail is usually free of snow by midsummer. But whenever you go, watch your footing carefully. This trail is not maintained very often.

User Groups: Hikers, dogs, and horses. No mountain bikes. No wheelchair facilities.

Permits: No day-hiking permits are required. Parking and access are free.

Maps: A John Muir Wilderness map is available from the U.S. Forest Service. A Kearsarge Pass map is available from Tom Harrison Maps. For a topographic map, ask the USGS for Kearsarge Peak.

Directions: From Lone Pine, drive 15 miles north on U.S. 395 to Independence. Turn west on Market Street, which becomes Onion Valley Road. Drive 14 miles to the end of the road and the hikers' parking area. Walk into Onion Valley Campground to find the trailhead, by site No. 7.

Contact: Inyo National Forest, Mount Whitney Ranger Station, P.O. Box 8, Lone Pine, CA 93545, 760/876-6200, www.fs.usda.gov/inyo; Eastern Sierra Interagency Visitor Center, 760/876-6222.

96 MOUNT WHITNEY TRAIL
22.0 mi / 15.0 hr or 2-3 days

🏃5 ⛰10

in the John Muir Wilderness

Map 11.3, page 575　　　　**BEST (**

Mount Whitney, at 14,505 feet in elevation, is the highest peak in the contiguous United States and is also probably the most frequently climbed. It has become so well traveled that not only are quotas enforced for backpackers, but even day hikers must obtain a wilderness permit to hike the trail. And, yes, many people do hike the entire 22-mile round-trip trail in one single day, ascending and descending more than a vertical mile along the way (6,131 feet in all), but it means a predawn start and a grueling march. Many people who try this suffer from a variety of ailments, including dehydration, hypoglycemia, and even altitude sickness, and never make it to the top. Others make it but realize they would have had a lot more fun if they had divided the trip into two or even three days. So here's the smart way to hike Mount Whitney: Get your wilderness permit way in advance (see the permit information below), and plan your trip for a weekday, not a weekend. If possible, wait to make the climb until September or early October, when the crowds have thinned considerably; August sees the highest trail usage. Spend a couple days at high elevation before you set out on the Mount Whitney Trail, and come prepared with sunglasses, sunscreen, good boots, and warm clothes for the summit. And since all solid human waste must be packed out (not buried, as is permitted in other areas of the Sierra), it's a good idea to obtain a free "human waste pack-out kit" from the Eastern Sierra Interagency Visitor Center before leaving on your trip. Consider this: In the summer of 2010, visitors to Mount Whitney packed out more than 6,800 pounds of human waste. For more information on the Mount Whitney Trail, see the trail notes for the *Whitney Portal to Lake Thomas Edison (JMT/PCT)* hike in this chapter.

User Groups: Hikers only. No dogs, horses, or mountain bikes. (Dogs are allowed on the first 6.2 miles of trail, but not beyond.) No wheelchair facilities.

Permits: A wilderness permit is required year-round for both day hikers and backpackers and is available from the Eastern Sierra Interagency Visitor Center, 1.5 mile south of Lone Pine. Quotas are in effect from May 1 to November 1 for both day hikers and backpackers. Permit application forms are entered into a lottery during the month of February for all dates in the following season's quota period. Print out a permit application form online, or phone 760/873-2483 to have one mailed or faxed to you. All applications must be submitted by mail, with a February postmark, to be entered into the lottery. There is a $15 reservation fee per person. Bear canisters are required for overnight stays and no wood fires are permitted.

Special note: The reservation system for Mount Whitney hiking permits is expected to change significantly in 2012. Please contact the Eastern Sierra Interagency Visitor Center (760/876-6222) for the most updated information. The visitor center is located 1.5 miles south of Lone Pine at the junction of U.S. 396 and Hwy. 136.

Maps: A Mount Whitney Zone map is available from Tom Harrison Maps. For topographic maps, ask the USGS for Mount Whitney and Mount Langley.

Directions: From Lone Pine on U.S. 395, drive west on Whitney Portal Road for 13 miles to the end of the road and the trailhead.

Contact: Inyo National Forest, Mount Whitney

Ranger Station, P.O. Box 8, Lone Pine, CA 93545, 760/876-6200, www.fs.usda.gov/inyo; Eastern Sierra Interagency Visitor Center, 760/876-6222.

97 WHITNEY PORTAL NATIONAL RECREATION TRAIL
4.0 mi one-way / 2.0 hr 🥾1 ⛰9

in Inyo National Forest near Whitney Portal

Map 11.3, page 575

Don't confuse this trail with the Mount Whitney Trail, because except for their nearby trailheads, they have zero in common. Although if you try to hike the Whitney Portal National Recreation Trail in both directions, instead of as a one-way downhill hike, you may find it feels darn near as demanding as the Mount Whitney Trail, which climbs nearly 6,000 feet to the top of Mount Whitney. (Okay, maybe not quite that demanding.) The recreation trail begins at Whitney Portal (elevation 8,360 feet) and heads downhill through conifers and granite to Lone Pine Campground (elevation 5,640). The best thing about the route is that no matter how crowded it is at Whitney Portal, this trail gets surprisingly few hikers, especially after the first 0.5 mile, which skirts Whitney Portal Campground. You get to leave the multitudes behind as you walk downhill along Lone Pine Creek, among the good company of granite formations and big pines. Vistas are excellent along the way, including Mount Whitney to the west and the Alabama Hills and White Mountains to the east.

User Groups: Hikers, dogs, and horses. No mountain bikes. No wheelchair facilities.

Permits: No permits are required. Parking and access are free.

Maps: A Mount Whitney High Country map is available from Tom Harrison Maps. For a topographic map, ask the USGS for Mount Langley.

Directions: From Lone Pine on U.S. 395, drive west on Whitney Portal Road for 13 miles to the end of the road and the trailhead, located across from the fishing pond. You will need to leave a shuttle car or arrange a pickup at Lone Pine Campground, four miles downhill on Whitney Portal Road.

Contact: Inyo National Forest, Mount Whitney Ranger Station, P.O. Box 8, Lone Pine, CA 93545, 760/876-6200, www.fs.usda.gov/inyo; Eastern Sierra Interagency Visitor Center, 760/876-6222.

98 MEYSAN LAKE
11.0 mi / 6.0 hr or 2 days 🥾5 ⛰9

in the John Muir Wilderness near Mount Whitney

Map 11.3, page 575

The Meysan Lake Trail is less popular than the neighboring trail to the top of Mount Whitney, but still, you should get your wilderness permit in advance or plan on day hiking. Better yet, plan your trip for late September and during the week. The trail to Meysan Lake is long, steep, hot, and dry—let's just say it's grueling—but it leads to a beautiful alpine lake basin and provides spectacular views of granite walls. It also gives climbers access to climbing routes on Mount Mallory and Lone Pine Peak. The trail is parallel to Meysan Creek and is not well maintained, which makes it even more demanding. You reach a left fork for Grass Lake at 4.5 miles, where the first water is available. The right fork continues to Camp Lake and its beautiful meadow (at five miles). The elevation here is 11,200 feet. The trail from Camp Lake to Meysan Lake is rather sketchy. Head to the right of Camp Lake, cross the inlet stream, and watch for rock cairns marking the way up the steep, rocky slope. Meysan Lake is often still frozen as late as June, even though the trail can be as hot as an oven. The trailhead elevation is 7,900 feet; Meysan Lake is at 11,460 feet.

User Groups: Hikers and dogs. No horses or mountain bikes. No wheelchair facilities.

Permits: A free wilderness permit is required year-round for overnight stays and is available from the Eastern Sierra Interagency Visitor Center, 1.5 miles south of Lone Pine. Quotas are in effect from May 1 to November 1; permits are available in advance for a $5 reservation fee per person.

Maps: A John Muir Wilderness map is available from the U.S. Forest Service. A Mount Whitney Zone map is available from Tom Harrison Maps. For topographic maps, ask the USGS for Mount Whitney and Mount Langley.

Directions: From Lone Pine on U.S. 395, drive west on Whitney Portal Road for 12 miles to Whitney Portal Campground and the Meysan Lake trailhead. Park on the side of Whitney Portal Road by the camp and walk through the camp to reach the trailhead.

Contact: Inyo National Forest, Mount Whitney Ranger Station, P.O. Box 8, Lone Pine, CA 93545, 760/876-6200, www.fs.usda.gov/inyo; Eastern Sierra Interagency Visitor Center, 760/876-6222.

99 LONE PINE LAKE
5.8 mi / 3.0 hr   🥾2 ⛰8

in the John Muir Wilderness near Whitney Portal

Map 11.3, page 575

The route to the top of Mount Whitney is so popular and so overcrowded that it has permits and quotas and regulations up the wazoo, but guess what? Sweet little Lone Pine Lake is just outside of the regulated Mount Whitney Zone, so you can hike to it anytime without dealing with any bureaucracy. However, you will have to deal with extremely limited parking at the trailhead during the summer months, so plan your trip for September or later if at all possible. Hiking to Lone Pine Lake is a fun trip for people who have always daydreamed of climbing Mount Whitney, because it follows the first three miles of the summit trail. While other people are trudging along carrying heavy backpacks, you're stepping lightly, with only a sandwich and a bottle of water in your day pack. The trail leads through Jeffrey pines and manzanita to the John Muir Wilderness border at one mile, then switchbacks uphill and opens up to views of the Alabama Hills far below. You'll cross Lone Pine Creek at 2.8 miles, then bear left at a junction to leave the main Mount Whitney Trail and head a few hundred yards to Lone Pine Lake. It's a sweet spot, and although privacy is rare, you have a greater chance of it after Labor Day and on a weekday. Who knows, you might just get so inspired that next time you'll come back and hike all the way to the summit.

User Groups: Hikers and dogs. No horses or mountain bikes. No wheelchair facilities.

Permits: No day-hiking permits are required. Parking and access are free.

Maps: A John Muir Wilderness map is available from the U.S. Forest Service. A Mount Whitney Zone map is available from Tom Harrison Maps. For topographic maps, ask the USGS for Mount Whitney and Mount Langley.

Directions: From Lone Pine on U.S. 395, drive west on Whitney Portal Road for 13 miles to the end of the road and the Mount Whitney trailhead.

Contact: Inyo National Forest, Mount Whitney Ranger Station, P.O. Box 8, Lone Pine, CA 93545, 760/876-6200, www.fs.usda.gov/inyo; Eastern Sierra Interagency Visitor Center, 760/876-6222.

100 WHITNEY PORTAL TO LAKE THOMAS EDISON (JMT / PCT)
112.0 mi one-way / 11 days 🥾5 ⛰10

from the trailhead parking area at Whitney Portal north to the trailhead parking area at Lake Thomas Edison

Map 11.3, page 575   **BEST (**

You have a foothold in the sky with every step on the John Muir Trail (JMT). This part of the trail is shared with the Pacific Crest Trail (PCT) and starts at practically the tip-top of North America—Mount Whitney—and takes you northward across a land of 12,000-foot passes and Ansel Adams–style panoramas.

From the trailhead at Whitney Portal, the hike climbs more than 6,100 feet over the course of 11 miles to reach Whitney's summit at 14,505 feet. That includes an ascent over 100 switchbacks, which are often snow covered even late in summer, to reach Trail Crest (13,560 feet). Here you turn right and take Summit Trail. In the final stretch to the top, the ridge is cut by huge notch windows in the rock; you look through, and the bottom drops out more than 10,000 feet to the town of Lone Pine below, at an elevation of 3,800 feet. Finally you make it to the top and notice how the surrounding giant blocks of rock look as if they were sculpted with a giant hammer and chisel. From here, the entire Western Divide is visible, and to the north, rows of mountain peaks are lined up for miles to the horizon. Be sure to sign your name in the register, kept in a lightning-proof metal box. You may feel a bit dizzy from the altitude, but you'll know you're someplace very special.

The journey farther north is just as captivating. The route drops into Sequoia National Park, then climbs above timberline for almost a day's worth of hiking as it nears Forester Pass (13,180 feet). It's not only the highest point on the PCT; it's the most dangerous section of trail on the entire route as well. The trail is narrow and steep, cut into a high vertical slab of rock, and is typically icy, with an iced-over snowfield near the top that's particularly treacherous. An ice ax is an absolute must. If you slip here, and you could fall thousands of feet.

Once through Forester, the trail heads onward into the John Muir Wilderness along Bubbs Creek, with great wildflowers at nearby Vidette Meadow. Then it's up and over Kearsarge Pass (10,710 feet), and after a short drop, you're back climbing again, this time

over Glen Pass (11,978 feet)—a spectacular, boulder-strewn ridge with great views to the north looking into Kings Canyon National Park. Just two miles from Glen Pass is Rae Lakes, a fantasy spot for camping (one-night limit), with pristine meadows, shoreline campsites, and lots of eager brook trout.

The JMT then heads through Kings Canyon National Park by following sparkling streams much of the way, finally climbing up and over Pinchot Pass (12,130 feet), then back down along the upper Kings River for a long, steady ascent over Mather Pass (12,100 feet). The wonders continue as you hike along Palisade Lakes, then down into LeConte Canyon, followed by an endless climb up to Muir Pass (11,965 feet). In early summer, snowfields are common here, and this can be difficult and trying, especially if your boots keep postholing through the snow. The country near Muir Pass is extremely stark—nothing but sculpted granite, ice, and a few small turquoise lakes—crowned by the stone Muir Hut at the pass, where hikers can duck in and hide for safety from sudden afternoon thunderstorms and lightning bolts.

The views astound many visitors as the trail drops into Evolution Valley. It's like a trip back to the beginning of time, where all is pure and primary, yet incredibly lush and beautiful. You finally leave Kings Canyon National Park, following the headwaters of the San Joaquin River into Sierra National Forest. After bottoming out at 7,890 feet, the trail rises steeply in switchback after switchback as it enters the John Muir Wilderness. Finally you top Selden Pass (10,900 feet), take in an incredible view (where the rows of surrounding mountaintops look like the Great Pyramids), then make the easy one-mile descent to Marie Lakes, a pretty campsite with excellent trout fishing near the lake's outlet.

The final push on this section of the JMT is climbing up Bear Mountain, then down a terrible, toe-jamming stretch to Mono Creek. Here you make a left turn and continue for two more miles until you come to Edison

Lake, an excellent place to have a food stash waiting. (To continue north on the JMT/PCT, see the *Lake Thomas Edison to Agnew Meadows* hike in this chapter.)

Special Note: Crossing Mono Creek at the North Fork can be dangerous during high-runoff conditions.

User Groups: Hikers and horses. No dogs or mountain bikes. No wheelchair facilities.

Permits: A wilderness permit is required for traveling through various wilderness and special-use areas the trail traverses. Contact the Eastern Sierra Interagency Visitor Center for more information.

Maps: A John Muir Trail Map Pack is available from Tom Harrison Maps. For topographic maps, ask the USGS for Mount Whitney, Mount Williamson, Kearsarge Peak, Mount Clarence King, Mount Pinchot, North Palisade, Mount Goddard, Mount Darwin, Mount Henry, Ward Mountain, Florence Lake, and Graveyard Peak.

Directions: To reach the Mount Whitney trailhead from Lone Pine and U.S. 395, head west on Whitney Portal Road for approximately 13 miles to Whitney Portal and the trailhead for the Mount Whitney Trail. To reach the Lake Thomas Edison trailhead from the town of Shaver Lake, drive north on Highway 168 for approximately 21 miles to the town of Lakeshore. Turn northeast onto Kaiser Pass Road/Forest Service 4S01. Kaiser Pass Road becomes Edison Lake Road at Mono Hot Springs. Drive another five miles north past town to the Vermillion Campground and parking area for backcountry hikers. The PCT begins near the east end of the lake.

Contact: Inyo National Forest, Mount Whitney Ranger Station, P.O. Box 8, Lone Pine, CA 93545, 760/876-6200 or 760/873-2400, www.fs.usda.gov/inyo; Sierra National Forest, High Sierra Ranger District, P.O. Box 559, Prather, CA 93651, 559/855-5360, www.fs.fed.us/r5/sierra; Sequoia National Forest, Sequoia National Forest, Kern River Ranger District, 105 Whitney Road, P.O. Box 9, Kernville, CA 93238, 760/376-3781, www.fs.fed.us/r5/

sequoia; Eastern Sierra Interagency Visitor Center, 760/876-6222.

101 COTTONWOOD LAKES
**10.0-12.5 mi /
6.0 hr or 2 days**

in the John Muir Wilderness south of Mount Whitney

> **Map 11.3, page 575**

The trailhead elevation is just over 10,000 feet here at Horseshoe Meadow, which makes this a wildly popular trailhead for climbing deeper into the backcountry. With the trailhead situated so high, you get a jump on the ascent; your four wheels do the work, instead of your two feet. An unusual feature of this hike is that it passes through two wilderness areas—first a small portion of the Golden Trout Wilderness and then the John Muir Wilderness. Cottonwood Creek accompanies you for much of the trip. The trail starts out in a sandy pine forest with a mellow grade. At 3.7 miles you reach a junction. Most hikers go left; the trail forms a loop around Cottonwood Lakes numbers one, two, and three. If you just want to see the closest lake and head back without making a loop, Cottonwood Lake number one is to the left, 1.5 miles from the junction. Your round-trip will be an even 10 miles. If you complete the whole loop, passing all three lakes, you'll travel 11.5 miles. But the most beautiful lakes by far are numbers four and five, worth an extra 0.5 mile of hiking beyond the far end of the loop. Total elevation gain is only 1,000 feet. Once at the lakes, remember two points: 1) Because the Cottonwood Lakes are home to golden trout, special fishing regulations are in effect, so get updated on the latest rules. 2) No wood fires are allowed, so bring your backpacking stove.

User Groups: Hikers, dogs, and horses. No mountain bikes. No wheelchair facilities.

Permits: A free wilderness permit is required year-round for overnight stays and is available from the Eastern Sierra Interagency Visitor

Center, 1.5 miles south of Lone Pine. Quotas are in effect from May 1 to November 1; permits are available in advance for a $5 reservation fee per person. Bear canisters are required.

Maps: A John Muir Wilderness map is available from the U.S. Forest Service. A Mount Whitney High Country map is available from Tom Harrison Maps. For a topographic map, ask the USGS for Cirque Peak.

Directions: From Lone Pine on U.S. 395, drive west on Whitney Portal Road for 3.3 miles and turn left (south) on Horseshoe Meadow Road. Continue 19.5 miles and bear right for the Cottonwood Lakes trailhead parking area, near the end of Horseshoe Meadow Road.

Contact: Inyo National Forest, Mount Whitney Ranger Station, P.O. Box 8, Lone Pine, CA 93545, 760/876-6200, www.fs.usda.gov/inyo; Eastern Sierra Interagency Visitor Center, 760/876-6222.

102 COTTONWOOD PASS
8.0 mi / 5.0 hr or 2 days 🏃2 ⛰9

in the Golden Trout Wilderness

Map 11.3, page 575

The Cottonwood Pass Trail provides access to the Pacific Crest Trail and the Kern Plateau, a land of stark, sub-alpine meadows. You're entering the Golden Trout Wilderness, home of California's state fish and located at the very south end of the Sierra Nevada. This is where the steep, nearly perpendicular mountains start to mellow out into more gentle terrain—mostly in the form of rolling high-country hills and meadows. Start from wide Horseshoe Meadow and climb gently through forest for the first two miles of trail. Shortly, the switchbacks begin and the ascent becomes serious. After an 1,100-foot climb, you reach the pass (at four miles), where you can gaze out at the Great Western Divide, Big Whitney Meadows, and the Inyo Mountains. Bring a jacket with you for the windy, 11,250-foot summit. Ambitious hikers can continue beyond the pass and

take the right fork for Chicken Spring Lake, one mile away on the Pacific Crest Trail (no campfires allowed).

User Groups: Hikers, dogs, and horses. No mountain bikes. No wheelchair facilities.

Permits: A free wilderness permit is required year-round for overnight stays and is available from the Eastern Sierra Interagency Visitor Center, 1.5 miles south of Lone Pine. Quotas are in effect from May 1 to November 1; permits are available in advance for a $5 reservation fee per person.

Maps: A Golden Trout Wilderness map is available from the U.S. Forest Service or Tom Harrison Maps. For a topographic map, ask the USGS for Cirque Peak.

Directions: From Lone Pine on U.S. 395, drive west on Whitney Portal Road for 3.3 miles and turn left (south) on Horseshoe Meadow Road. Continue 19.5 miles to the Horseshoe Meadow trailhead, on the left, at the end of Horseshoe Meadow Road.

Contact: Inyo National Forest, Mount Whitney Ranger Station, P.O. Box 8, Lone Pine, CA 93545, 760/876-6200, www.fs.usda.gov/inyo; Eastern Sierra Interagency Visitor Center, 760/876-6222.

103 TRAIL PASS
5.0 mi / 3.0 hr 🏃1 ⛰7

in the Golden Trout Wilderness

Map 11.3, page 575

Trail Pass may not be as spectacular as the other trails at Horseshoe Meadow, but it has two things going for it—far fewer people and an easier grade. It's only five miles round-trip from the trailhead to the pass, with a mere 500-foot elevation gain, unheard of in these parts. The main folks using the trail are backpackers accessing the Pacific Crest Trail and Golden Trout Wilderness, so a lot of the time, you can have this gently rolling, high-country terrain all to yourself. Follow the trail from the parking area to a junction 0.25 mile in, and bear left. In another 0.5 mile, the trail forks, and you bear right for Trail Pass. You'll hike past Horseshoe Meadow and Round Valley, where you'll have the company of many pack-horses. Views of Mount Langley and Cirque Peak are sure to inspire you. The pass is situated at 10,500 feet, just below Trail Peak (at 11,600 feet).

User Groups: Hikers, dogs, and horses. No mountain bikes. No wheelchair facilities.

Permits: No day-hiking permits are required. Parking and access are free. A free wilderness permit is required year-round for overnight stays and is available from the Eastern Sierra Interagency Visitor Center, 1.5 miles south of Lone Pine.

Maps: A Golden Trout Wilderness map is available from the U.S. Forest Service or Tom Harrison Maps. For a topographic map, ask the USGS for Cirque Peak.

Directions: From Lone Pine on U.S. 395, drive west on Whitney Portal Road for 3.3 miles and turn left (south) on Horseshoe Meadow Road. Continue 19.5 miles to the Horseshoe Meadow trailhead, on the right, at the end of Horseshoe Meadow Road.

Contact: Inyo National Forest, Mount Whitney Ranger Station, P.O. Box 8, Lone Pine, CA 93545, 760/876-6200, www.fs.usda.gov/inyo; Eastern Sierra Interagency Visitor Center, 760/876-6222.

▇▇ CASA VIEJA MEADOW
4.0 mi / 2.0 hr   🏃2 ⛰9

in the Golden Trout Wilderness

Map 11.3, page 575   **BEST (**

The Blackrock Mountain trailhead, at 8,800 feet, is the jump-off point for a variety of backpacking trips into the Golden Trout Wilderness. But day hikers can also sample the delights of this large, waterway-filled land, the home of California's state fish, the golden trout. From the end of Blackrock Road, walk for less than 0.25 mile to the wilderness boundary, then head gently downhill through a red fir forest to the western edge of Casa Vieja Meadow. There you'll find a snow survey cabin and a wide expanse of grass and wildflowers. Hope your day pack is full of picnic supplies. At the far end of the meadow, you must ford Ninemile Creek to continue hiking farther, so make this your turnaround point. Some people try their luck fishing here. You'll have a gradual 800-foot elevation gain on your return trip.

User Groups: Hikers, dogs, and horses. No mountain bikes. No wheelchair facilities.

Permits: No permits are required. Parking and access are free.

Maps: A Golden Trout Wilderness map is available from the U.S. Forest Service or Tom Harrison Maps. For a topographic map, ask the USGS for Casa Vieja Meadows.

Directions: From Kernville on the north end of Isabella Lake, drive north on Sierra Way/Road 99 for 22 miles to the turnoff for Sherman Pass Road/22S05. Turn right and drive approximately 35 miles on Sherman Pass Road to the Blackrock Information Station; continue straight on Road 21S03/Blackrock Road. Follow Road 21S03 north for eight miles to the end of the road and the Blackrock Mountain trailhead.

Contact: Sequoia National Forest, Kern River Ranger District, 105 Whitney Road, P.O. Box 9, Kernville, CA 93238, 760/376-3781, www.fs.fed.us/r5/sequoia; Inyo National Forest, Mount Whitney Ranger Station, P.O. Box 8, Lone Pine, CA 93545, 760/876-6200, www.fs.usda.gov/inyo.

▇▇ JORDAN HOT SPRINGS
12.0 mi / 7.0 hr or 2 days   🏃4 ⛰9

in the Golden Trout Wilderness

Map 11.3, page 575

You can do it in a day if you're ambitious, or you can take a more leisurely two-day trip to Jordan Hot Springs. But however you do it, it's critical to remember that almost all the work is on the way home. The trail is a descent (sometimes knee-jarring) to the grounds of an old hot springs resort, which was closed when this area became part of the Golden Trout Wilderness. The original buildings still stand, and the hot springs are still hot, which is the reason that this is one of the most popular trips in the wilderness. From the trailhead, take Blackrock Trail for two miles to Casa Vieja Meadow (see listing in this chapter), then cross Ninemile Creek and turn left (west) on Jordan Hot Springs Trail. Hike another three miles downhill along Ninemile Creek, crossing it a few more times. Once you reach the old resort, have a good soak and pull your energy together, because you've got a 2,600-foot gain on the return trip.

User Groups: Hikers, dogs, and horses. No mountain bikes. No wheelchair facilities.

Permits: A free wilderness permit is required year-round for overnight stays and is available from the Kern River Ranger Station. Parking and access are free.

Maps: A Golden Trout Wilderness map is available from the U.S. Forest Service or Tom Harrison Maps. For a topographic map, ask the USGS for Casa Vieja Meadows.

Directions: From Kernville on the north end of Isabella Lake, drive north on Sierra Way/Road 99 for 22 miles to the right turnoff for Sherman Pass Road/22S05. Turn right and drive approximately 35 miles on Sherman Pass Road to the Blackrock Information Station; continue straight on Road 21S03/Blackrock Road. Follow Road 21S03 north for eight miles to the end of the road and the Blackrock Mountain trailhead.

Contact: Sequoia National Forest, Kern River Ranger District, 105 Whitney Road, P.O. Box 9, Kernville, CA 93238, 760/376-3781, www.fs.fed.us/r5/sequoia.

106 NORTH FORK KERN RIVER TRAIL

10.4 mi / 5.0 hr or 2 days

in Sequoia National Forest north of Kernville

Map 11.4, page 576

Sometimes you just want to walk alongside a beautiful river, and if that's what you're in the mood for, the Wild and Scenic North Fork Kern is a first-rate choice. From the giant parking lot, walk across the hikers' bridge (separate from but next to the highway bridge) to reach the far side of the river, and then descend on stairs to reach the trail. The North Fork Kern River Trail winds along gently, heading deep into the dramatic Kern Canyon, sometimes under the shade of digger pines, live oaks, and incense cedars, and sometimes out in the bright sunshine. Spring wildflowers are stunning, especially in March and April. Spring river rafters are also entertaining to watch. Most people who walk this trail bring a fishing rod with them, and if you do, make sure you're up-to-date on the special fishing regulations. They're in effect for the first four miles of river, which is a wild trout area. Backpackers will find many campsites along the trail, including some that are under the cavelike canopy of big boulders. This easy, mellow trail offers something for everyone. Note that if you venture out here at the height of spring runoff, parts of the trail may be submerged.

User Groups: Hikers and dogs. No mountain bikes or horses. No wheelchair facilities.

Permits: A free campfire permit is required for overnight stays and is available from the Springville or Kernville Ranger Stations at the addresses below. Parking and access are free.

Maps: A Sequoia National Forest map is available from the U.S. Forest Service. For a topographic map, ask the USGS for Fairview.

Directions: From Kernville on the north end of Lake Isabella, drive north on Sierra Way/Road 99 for 22 miles to the Johnsondale highway bridge over the Kern River. Turn right and park in the large paved parking lot by the signboard at the bridge.

Contact: Sequoia National Forest, Kern River Ranger District, 105 Whitney Road, P.O. Box 9, Kernville, CA 93238, 760/376-3781, www.fs.fed.us/r5/sequoia; Tule River Ranger District, 32588 Highway 190, Springville, CA 93265, 559/539-2607, www.fs.fed.us/r5/sequoia.

107 SHERMAN PEAK TRAIL
4.0 mi / 2.0 hr 🥾1 ⛰9

in Sequoia National Forest near Sherman Pass

Map 11.4, page 576

From the Sherman Pass Vista along the highway, you can look to the north to Mount Whitney and the Great Western Divide. After crossing the highway and hiking Sherman Peak Trail to the top of Sherman Peak (at 9,909 feet), you can pivot around and have a panoramic look at an even bigger chunk of the world. The trail is mostly forested with red firs and pines, and is gradual enough for children to climb. If you read the interpretive display at the vista, you'll be able to identify the myriad mountains you're looking at from the peak, including Split Rock and Dome Rock. It's only a 700-foot climb to the summit, mostly through a series of easy switchbacks. At one time, a fire lookout tower was positioned up here, but modern technology made it obsolete and it was taken down.

User Groups: Hikers, dogs, horses, and mountain bikes. No wheelchair facilities.

Permits: No permits are required. Parking and access are free.

Maps: A Sequoia National Forest map is available from the U.S. Forest Service. For topographic maps, ask the USGS for Durrwood Creek and Sirretta Peak.

Directions: From Kernville on the north end of Lake Isabella, drive north on Sierra Way/Road 99 for 22 miles to the right turnoff for Sherman Pass Road/22S05. Turn right and drive approximately 15 miles on Sherman Pass Road to the Sherman Pass Vista. The trailhead is across the road.

Contact: Sequoia National Forest, Kern River Ranger District, 105 Whitney Road, P.O. Box 9, Kernville, CA 93238, 760/376-3781, www.fs.fed.us/r5/sequoia.

108 BALD MOUNTAIN LOOKOUT
0.25 mi / 0.25 hr 🥾1 ⛰9

in Sequoia National Forest on the north edge of the Dome Land Wilderness

Map 11.4, page 576

This short hike to the summit of 9,430-foot Bald Mountain is the easiest possible introduction to the Dome Land Wilderness. It's a brief stroll to the lookout, which is perched on the very northern edge of the wilderness. This region is famous for its many granite domes and monolithic rocks, the happy hunting ground of rock climbers from all over Southern California. Of the many big hunks of rock, Church Dome is perhaps the most outstanding, and it can be seen from here directly to the south. White Dome and Black Mountain are also visible (east of Church Dome), as well as a sweeping vista of the Kern Plateau, the Whitney Range, and the Great Western Divide. Bald Mountain Lookout has the distinction of being the highest fire lookout tower in the southern Sierra Nevada.

User Groups: Hikers, dogs, horses, and mountain bikes. No wheelchair facilities.

Permits: No permits are required. Parking and access are free.

Maps: A Sequoia National Forest or Dome Land Wilderness map is available from the U.S. Forest Service. For a topographic map, ask the USGS for Crag Peak.

Directions: From Kernville on the north end of Lake Isabella, drive north on Sierra Way/Road 99 for 22 miles to the right turnoff for Sherman Pass Road/22S05. Turn right and drive approximately 25 miles on Sherman Pass Road to Forest Service Road 22S77, signed for Bald Mountain Lookout. Turn east (right) on Road 22S77 and follow it for one mile to its end.

Contact: Sequoia National Forest, Kern River Ranger District, 105 Whitney Road, P.O. Box 9, Kernville, CA 93238, 760/376-3781, www.fs.fed.us/r5/sequoia.

109 JACKASS CREEK NATIONAL RECREATION TRAIL
5.0 mi / 2.5 hr   🚶2 ⛰9

in Sequoia National Forest near the South Sierra Wilderness

Map 11.4, page 576

The Jackass Creek Trail is way out there on the Kern Plateau, at a trailhead elevation of 8,000 feet. The trail climbs 5.5 miles to Jackass Peak (elevation 9,245 feet) on the border of the South Sierra Wilderness. Most people don't bother traveling that far; instead, they follow the trail along Jackass Creek for a couple of miles through red fir forest to the western edge of Jackass Meadow. In addition to the beautiful meadow, the trail offers a look at many handsome old-growth aspens. The trail is an old dirt road, wide enough for holding hands with your hiking partner. Unfortunately, it's also wide enough for motorcycles, which are allowed here. Our recommendation? Hike this trail in late September or early October for the best show of autumn colors, and for the best chance at having the trail to yourself. If you drive all the way out here and see a parking lot full of motorcycle trailers, try hiking the nearby Hooker Meadow Trail instead (the trailhead is at the end of Road 21S29, just east of Fish Creek Campground). The machines aren't allowed there, and this trail also leads to an outstanding grove of quaking aspens.

User Groups: Hikers, dogs, horses, and mountain bikes. No wheelchair facilities.

Permits: No permits are required. Parking and access are free.

Maps: A Sequoia National Forest map is available from the U.S. Forest Service. For a topographic map, ask the USGS for Crag Peak.

Directions: From Kernville on the north end

of Lake Isabella, drive north on Sierra Way/Road 99 for 22 miles to the right turnoff for Sherman Pass Road/22S05. Turn right and drive approximately 35 miles on Sherman Pass Road to the four-way intersection with Road 21S03, near Blackrock Information Station. Turn right to continue on Road 22S05, and drive five miles to Fish Creek Campground and Road 21S01, where the trail begins.

Contact: Sequoia National Forest, Kern River Ranger District, 105 Whitney Road, P.O. Box 9, Kernville, CA 93238, 760/376-3781, www.fs.fed.us/r5/sequoia.

110 WHISKEY FLAT TRAIL
5.0 mi / 2.5 hr   🚶2 ⛰8

in Sequoia National Forest near Fairview

Map 11.4, page 576

The Whiskey Flat Trail is a 14.5-mile trail that parallels the Kern River from Fairview Lodge all the way south to Burlando Road in Kernville. Primarily used by anglers working the Kern River, it's also a good springtime stroll for river lovers. If you walk out and back for a few miles on the northern end of the trail by Fairview, you can end the day with a meal at Fairview Lodge's restaurant, where you can brag about the fish you did or didn't catch, like everybody else there. The Whiskey Flat Trail can be somewhat difficult to follow, especially in springtime, when the numerous creeks you must cross are running full. Early in the year, the creeks can sometimes be impassable. The path begins on a suspension bridge, which is reminiscent of Huck Finn and his friends. You can hike as far as you please; a good distance is 2.5 miles out, or about an hour's walk each way. The terrain is grasslands and chaparral, with occasional digger pines, which means no shade but plenty of spring wildflowers. Although the route is basically level, there are numerous steep stretches where you climb in and out of stream drainages running into the Kern. The trailhead elevation is 2,800 feet.

User Groups: Hikers, dogs, horses, and mountain bikes. No wheelchair facilities.

Permits: No permits are required. Parking and access are free.

Maps: A Sequoia National Forest map is available from the U.S. Forest Service. For a topographic map, ask the USGS for Fairview.

Directions: From Kernville on the north end of Lake Isabella, drive north on Sierra Way/Road 99 for 17 miles to Fairview and the Fairview Lodge, on the left side of the road. A large parking area and a trailhead for the Whiskey Flat Trail are to the right of the lodge.

Contact: Sequoia National Forest, Kern River Ranger District, 105 Whitney Road, P.O. Box 9, Kernville, CA 93238, 760/376-3781, www.fs.fed.us/r5/sequoia.

111 PACKSADDLE CAVE TRAIL
4.6 mi / 2.3 hr   👣2 ⛰️8

in Sequoia National Forest near Fairview

Map 11.4, page 576

Everybody enjoys the trip to Packsaddle Cave, even though the cave was long ago vandalized of its jewel-like stalactites and stalagmites. Nonetheless, the appeal of visiting the limestone cave keeps this trail well used and fairly well maintained. From the parking lot on Sierra Way, cross the highway and hike uphill on the path, huffing and puffing through some steep pitches. This is not a trail for summertime, because there is little shade among the manzanita, sagebrush, and deer brush, and the total climb is about 1,200 feet. At 1.8 miles, you cross Packsaddle Creek and see several campsites near it. Continue a short distance farther; the cave is off to the left, 0.25 mile before this trail's junction with Rincon Trail. Don't forget your flashlight so you can take a peek inside.

User Groups: Hikers, dogs, horses, and mountain bikes. No wheelchair facilities.

Permits: No permits are required. Parking and access are free.

Maps: A Sequoia National Forest map is available from the U.S. Forest Service. For a topographic map, ask the USGS for Fairview.

Directions: From Kernville on the north end of Lake Isabella, drive north on Sierra Way/Road 99 for 18 miles to the Packsaddle Cave trailhead, on the right, 0.25 mile beyond Fairview Campground. The parking area is across the road.

Contact: Sequoia National Forest, Kern River Ranger District, 105 Whitney Road, P.O. Box 9, Kernville, CA 93238, 760/376-3781, www.fs.fed.us/r5/sequoia.

112 RINCON TRAIL
4.0 mi / 2.0 hr

in Sequoia National Forest near Fairview

Map 11.4, page 576

Let's say right away that this Rincon has absolutely nothing in common with the other Rincon, the classic surfing break on the Ventura coast. For one, there's no water here, and two, there's no cool ocean breeze. That means you should plan your hike for winter or spring, before the Kern Valley heats up. The trail leads first east and then steadily north along the Rincon Fault, heading for Forks of the Kern. It undulates, following the drainages of Salmon and other creeks. The destination on this trail is the long-distance view of Salmon Creek Falls, about two miles in, and the good fishing and camping prospects on the way along Salmon Creek. The trail crosses Salmon Creek on a bridge 1.7 miles in, but the waterfall view is about 0.25 mile farther. You might want to bring your binoculars to get a good look. If you wish to hike farther on Rincon Trail, it intersects the route to Packsaddle Cave in another two miles, then crosses Sherman Pass Road in another 2.5 miles, and keeps going straight north all the way to Forks of the Kern. The total one-way trail length is a whopping 19.5 miles. Be forewarned that the Rincon Trail is popular with motorcycle enthusiasts, so your peaceful nature experience may be shattered by their noise.

User Groups: Hikers, dogs, and mountain bikes. No horses. No wheelchair facilities.

Permits: No permits are required. Parking and access are free.

Maps: A Sequoia National Forest map is available from the U.S. Forest Service. For a topographic map, ask the USGS for Kernville.

Directions: From Kernville on the north end of Isabella Lake, drive north on Sierra Way/Road 99 for 13 miles to the Rincon trailhead, on the right, across from the Ant Canyon dispersed camping area.

Contact: Sequoia National Forest, Kern River Ranger District, 105 Whitney Road, P.O. Box 9, Kernville, CA 93238, 760/376-3781, www.fs.fed.us/r5/sequoia.

113 SUNDAY PEAK TRAIL
3.4 mi / 2.0 hr   🏃2 ⛰9

in Sequoia National Forest near Wofford Heights

Map 11.4, page 576

From the Sunday Peak trailhead, at 7,200 feet in the Greenhorn Mountains, it's a 1,000-foot climb to the top of Sunday Peak, an excellent day hike for families. The grade is moderate and shaded by big conifers, and the destination is perfect on a day when the heat is sweltering down near Isabella Lake. From the top, you can look down at the Kern River Valley and feel sorry for all those people sweating it out down there. The peak's fire lookout tower was abandoned and then destroyed by the Forest Service in the 1950s when it was determined that nearby Tobias Peak was a better spot to have a lookout. However, the wide-angle views of the Kern Valley, Kern Plateau, and far-off high Sierra peaks are still here for the taking. There are many good picnicking spots on the summit.

User Groups: Hikers, dogs, horses, and mountain bikes. No wheelchair facilities.

Permits: No permits are required. Parking and access are free.

Maps: A Sequoia National Forest map is

available from the U.S. Forest Service. For a topographic map, ask the USGS for Posey.

Directions: From Wofford Heights on the west side of Isabella Lake, turn west on Highway 155 and drive eight miles to Greenhorn Summit. Turn right on Road 24S15/Forest Highway 90, signed for Portuguese Pass, and drive 6.5 miles north to the parking area for Sunday Peak Trail, near the Girl Scout Camp.

Contact: Sequoia National Forest, Kern River Ranger District, 105 Whitney Road, P.O. Box 9, Kernville, CA 93238, 760/376-3781, www.fs.fed.us/r5/sequoia.

114 UNAL TRAIL
3.0 mi / 1.5 hr   🏃1 ⛰8

in Sequoia National Forest near Wofford Heights

Map 11.4, page 576   **BEST ☾**

This is a first-rate trail for families or for anybody who wants a good leg-stretching walk or run around a beautiful mountain. The Unal Trail is a three-mile loop that climbs gently for two miles to Unal Peak, and then descends in one mile of switchbacks back to the trailhead. (After the first 100 yards, where the trail forks, be sure you take the left fork and hike the trail clockwise.) The trail passes a Native American cultural site on the return of the loop, the homestead of the Tubatulabal Indians. With only a 700-foot climb and an excellent grade, even mountain bikers can manage this trail, although few bother with it. You'll likely see some deer on the hillsides, and the view from the top of Unal Peak makes the whole world seem peaceful and serene. Although most of the trail is lined with conifers, the top of the loop is a little exposed and catches a strong breeze.

User Groups: Hikers, dogs, horses, and mountain bikes. No wheelchair facilities.

Permits: No permits are required. Parking and access are free.

Maps: A Sequoia National Forest map is available from the U.S. Forest Service. For a topographic map, ask the USGS for Posey.

Directions: From Wofford Heights on the west side of Lake Isabella, turn west on Highway 155 and drive eight miles to Greenhorn Summit. Turn left at the sign for Shirley Ski Meadows and drive 100 yards to the Greenhorn Fire Station and Unal trailhead, on the right side of the road.

Contact: Sequoia National Forest, Kern River Ranger District, 105 Whitney Road, P.O. Box 9, Kernville, CA 93238, 760/376-3781, www.fs.fed.us/r5/sequoia.

115 CANNELL MEADOW NATIONAL RECREATION TRAIL

24.0 mi / 3 days   👫4 ⛰8

in Sequoia National Forest north of Kernville

Map 11.4, page 576

The Cannell Meadow National Recreation Trail is the first trailhead you reach out of Kernville, and if it's summertime, you should start at the other end of this 12-mile trail. That's because the Kernville end is at 2,800 feet, set in rocky chaparral and digger pine country, and, baby, it's hot out here. Still, if you can time your trip for late winter or spring, hiking this end of Cannell Trail is a great adventure, watching the terrain and environment change as the elevation rises. The shadeless trail climbs right away, through sage and occasional live oaks, affording views of the Kern River Valley. The trail gets more and more steep as you near conifer country at Pine Flat, but then you also get some blessed shade. It crosses Cannell Creek twice and reaches the Cannell Meadow Forest Service Cabin, a log cabin that was built in 1904. Cannell Meadow is a beautiful spot on the western edge of the Kern Plateau, edged by Jeffrey and lodgepole pines. Elevation is 7,500 feet, which means a total climb of 4,700 feet. Spread it out over a few days.

User Groups: Hikers, dogs, horses, and mountain bikes. No wheelchair facilities.

Permits: A free campfire permit is required for overnight stays and is available from the Kernville Ranger Station. Parking and access are free.

Maps: A Sequoia National Forest map is available from the U.S. Forest Service. For a topographic map, ask the USGS for Kernville.

Directions: From Kernville on the north end of Isabella Lake, drive north on Sierra Way/Road 99 for 1.4 miles to the Cannell Meadow trailhead, on the right. Parking is available near the horse corrals.

Contact: Sequoia National Forest, Kern River Ranger District, 105 Whitney Road, P.O. Box 9, Kernville, CA 93238, 760/376-3781, www.fs.fed.us/r5/sequoia.

116 SALMON CREEK FALLS

8.0 mi / 4.0 hr or 2 days   👫2 ⛰9

in Sequoia National Forest near Big Meadow

Map 11.4, page 576

The eight-mile round-trip to the brink of Salmon Creek Falls is a stellar walk through lodgepole pines and white fir, with a chance for fishing, skinny-dipping, and admiring a lot of beautiful scenery at 7,600 feet in elevation. Since there are campsites located along the trail, it's easy enough to turn the trip into an overnight excursion, but the trail also makes a good long day hike. The trail is downhill all the way, dropping 600 feet over 0.5 mile, and follows granite-lined Salmon Creek. After skirting the edge of Horse Meadow, you simply follow the creek's meander. Trails run on both sides of the stream for the first two miles, so you can walk either side, but then they join as one. The path comes to an end above Salmon Creek Falls, where you can swim, fish, and camp, but don't expect to gaze out at the big waterfall. There's no way to get a good look at it from here, since you're perched on top of it.

User Groups: Hikers, dogs, horses, and mountain bikes. No wheelchair facilities.

Permits: A free campfire permit is required for overnight stays and is available from the Springville or Kernville Ranger Stations at the addresses below. Parking and access are free.

Maps: A Sequoia National Forest map is available from the U.S. Forest Service. For topographic maps, ask the USGS for Sirretta Peak and Fairview.

Directions: From Kernville on the north end of Isabella Lake, drive north on Sierra Way/Road 99 for 22 miles to the right turnoff for Sherman Pass Road/22S05. Turn right and drive 6.1 miles on Sherman Pass Road, then turn right on Road 22S12, signed for Horse Meadow Campground. Drive 6.3 miles on Road 22S12 until you reach a fork. Stay straight. At eight miles, bear left. At 9.3 miles, turn right at the Horse Meadow Campground sign (Road 23S10). You'll reach the camp at 10.7 miles, but take the right turnoff just before the camp to reach the trailhead.

Contact: Sequoia National Forest, Kern River Ranger District, 105 Whitney Road, P.O. Box 9, Kernville, CA 93238, 760/376-3781, www.fs.fed.us/r5/sequoia; Tule River Ranger District, 32588 Highway 190, Springville, CA 93265, 559/539-2607, www.fs.fed.us/r5/sequoia.

117 SIRRETTA PEAK
8.0 mi / 5.0 hr   🏃4 ⛰10

near the Dome Land Wilderness

Map 11.4, page 576

Hey, what's that big meadow down there? It's Big Meadow, of course, that huge expanse of green you see from the top of Sirretta Peak. From Sirretta's summit, you get an eyeful of it, as well as long, lingering glances at the many granite domes of the Dome Land Wilderness Area, Sirretta and Deadwood Meadows, and the peaks of the High Sierra. The route to the peak starts at Big Meadow's northern edge, then travels north on Cannell Trail for 0.5 mile. Bear right (northeast) at the fork with Sirretta Peak Trail and climb 2.5 miles to a spur trail that leads to the summit. There are many switchbacks and plenty of fine views along the way. Take the left spur (it's obvious) for 0.5 mile to the rocky summit, and congratulate

yourself on your fine mountaineering skills. The trail has an elevation gain of 1,200 feet, and if you decide to make the final summit climb, you'll add on another 700 feet. Sirretta Peak is just shy of 10,000 feet in elevation.

User Groups: Hikers and dogs. No horses or mountain bikes. No wheelchair facilities.

Permits: No day-hiking permits are required. Parking and access are free.

Maps: A Sequoia National Forest map is available from the U.S. Forest Service. For a topographic map, ask the USGS for Sirretta Peak.

Directions: From Kernville on the north end of Isabella Lake, drive north on Sierra Way/Road 99 for 22 miles to the right turnoff for Sherman Pass Road/22S05. Turn right and drive 6.1 miles on Sherman Pass Road. Turn right on Road 22S12, signed for Horse Meadow Campground, and drive 6.3 miles on Road 22S12 until you reach a fork. Stay straight. At eight miles, bear left, staying on Road 22S12. Continue four more miles, passing the Horse Meadow Campground turnoff, to Road 23S07, at the northern edge of Big Meadow. Turn left on Road 23S07 and drive 0.5 mile to the Cannell trailhead.

Contact: Sequoia National Forest, Kern River Ranger District, 105 Whitney Road, P.O. Box 9, Kernville, CA 93238, 760/376-3781, www.fs.fed.us/r5/sequoia.

118 MANTER MEADOW LOOP
10.0 mi / 6.0 hr   🏃2 ⛰9

in the Dome Land Wilderness

Map 11.4, page 576   **BEST**

For people who love meadows, granite, and solitude, this loop trip is just about perfect. From the South Manter trailhead at 7,800 feet, the trail goes uphill for four miles to Manter Meadow, so bring your wildflower identification book and a map to identify surrounding peaks and domes. Along the way, several side trails branch off the main trail, leading to some of the granite domes of the Dome Land Wilderness, including spectacular Taylor Dome and Church Dome. A two-mile loop trail encircles the entire perimeter of the meadow, which you can add on to your trip if you wish. At the meadow's western edge, South Manter Trail meets North Manter Trail, and you follow the latter back to Forest Service Road 23S07 (the road you drove in on). Then it's a 1.5-mile walk on the dirt road back to your car. If you want to avoid the road, hike South Manter Trail both ways, and take the loop walk around the meadow. The mileage is about equal to the other trip.

User Groups: Hikers, dogs, and horses. No mountain bikes. No wheelchair facilities.

Permits: No permits are required. Parking and access are free.

Maps: A Sequoia National Forest or Dome Land Wilderness map is available from the U.S. Forest Service. For a topographic map, ask the USGS for Sirretta Peak.

Directions: From Kernville on the north end of Isabella Lake, drive north on Sierra Way/Road 99 for 22 miles to the right turnoff for Sherman Pass Road/22S05. Turn right and drive 6.1 miles on Sherman Pass Road. Turn right on Road 22S12, signed for Horse Meadow Campground, and drive 6.3 miles on Road 22S12 until you reach a fork. Stay straight. At eight miles, bear left, staying on Road 22S12. Continue four more miles, passing the Horse Meadow Campground turnoff, to Road 23S07 at the northern edge of Big Meadow. Turn left on Road 23S07 and drive three miles to the southeast edge of Big Meadow and the South Manter trailhead.

Contact: Sequoia National Forest, Kern River Ranger District, 105 Whitney Road, P.O. Box 9, Kernville, CA 93238, 760/376-3781, www.fs.fed.us/r5/sequoia.

119 ROCKHOUSE BASIN

8.6 mi / 4.0 hr

on the eastern side of the
Dome Land Wilderness

Map 11.4, page 576

You're driving along in no-man's-land on Highway 178 between U.S. 395 and Lake Isabella, staring at thousands of those odd-looking piñon pines. This is the transition zone between the Mojave Desert to the east and the Sierra Nevada to the west, and it doesn't look quite like either one of them. Want to see this strange land up close? This hike to Rockhouse Basin can take you there, and since it requires a long drive on dirt roads to reach the trailhead, you're likely to be free of the Eastern Sierra's hiking masses. The trail heads downhill through a burned area, losing about 1,500 feet in elevation on its way to the Kern River and Rockhouse Basin. A half mile from the trailhead, turn right and head north to Rockhouse Basin, where the noise of cicadas serenades you almost as loudly as the river. Explore the rocks and cool off in the river. It can be as hot as Hades out here, so plan your trip for early in the year, when you can hike along the Kern River in relative comfort.

User Groups: Hikers, dogs, and horses. No mountain bikes. No wheelchair facilities.

Permits: No permits are required. Parking and access are free.

Maps: A Sequoia National Forest or Dome Land Wilderness map is available from the U.S. Forest Service. For a topographic map, ask the USGS for Rockhouse Basin.

Directions: From the junction of Highway 14 and Highway 178 north of Mojave, drive west on Highway 178 for 18 miles to the right turnoff for Chimney Peak National Backcountry Byway, or Canebrake Road. Turn right and drive approximately nine miles. Turn left (west) on Long Valley Loop Road and drive 13 miles to the gate at the start of Rockhouse Basin Trail.

Contact: Bureau of Land Management, Ridgecrest Field Office, 300 South Richmond Road, Ridgecrest, CA 93555, 760/384-5400, www.ca.blm.gov/ridgecrest; Sequoia National Forest, Kern River Ranger District, 105 Whitney Road, P.O. Box 9, Kernville, CA 93238, 760/376-3781, www.fs.fed.us/r5/sequoia.

SANTA BARBARA AND VICINITY

© SABRINA YOU

BEST HIKES

The Santa Barbara region, which extends 200

miles from the artsy town of Cambria and terraced vineyards of Paso Robles to the white sands of Ventura, encompasses what many consider to be Southern California's finest stretch of coast. The Santa Barbara County shoreline, curving upcoast from Carpinteria to Point Conception, has a southern, not western, exposure, which results in exceptionally mild weather. To the south, Ventura County's coast offers 40 miles of fine sandy beaches.

Hikers can explore this meeting of land and sea on a wealth of trails in state-protected lands: San Simeon State Beach, Morro Bay State Park, Montaña de Oro State Park, Gaviota State Park, McGrath State Beach, and Point Mugu State Park. Trails wind along the tops of oceanside bluffs, across coastal grasslands gilded with wildflowers in the spring, and on top of boardwalks spanning coastal dunes and wetlands.

Lest you think the Santa Barbara region is all sun and sand, note that it also contains more than a million acres of national forest land in the Santa Barbara and Ojai backcountry – the southern section of Los Padres National Forest. This landscape is a conglomeration of pine-clad high mountain peaks, river-cut canyons, and chaparral-covered hillsides. The Santa Ynez Mountains, a centerpiece of southern Los Padres National Forest, are part of the unique Transverse Range, a system of mountains that defies the rules of California geography: They run from east to west, rather than north to south.

Not surprisingly, these mountains provide myriad hiking opportunities, although most trails are little known except by Santa Barbara locals.

Hikers wishing to explore the remote backcountry can choose from five wilderness areas: San Rafael, Dick Smith, Matilija, Chumash, and Sespe. Those seeking easily accessible day-use areas will find Los Padres National Forest trails just beyond the town limits in Santa Barbara, Montecito, and Ojai. Paths lead to waterfalls, high overlooks of mountains and ocean, and sculpted sandstone formations, and many destinations can be visited with only a small investment of mileage and time.

Perhaps the most remarkable stretch of land in the Santa Barbara region is a parcel surrounded entirely by water – the five rugged and remote islands of Channel Islands National Park. The islands are often referred to as "the Galapagos of California" because of the amount and diversity of endemic animals and plant life. More than 100 species of plants and animals are found on the Channel Islands and nowhere else.

Although reaching the islands requires more effort than simply driving your car (boat concessionaires are located in Santa Barbara and Ventura), hikers who make the trip are rewarded with a chance to see coastal California in a nearly primitive state. Wildlife – particularly seals, sea lions, and seabirds – are remarkably plentiful. Depending on which island you visit, you can take an easy stroll past 10-foot-tall blooming coreopsis or a demanding trek to see a ghost forest of caliche formations – calcium-carbonate sand castings of dead plants. Catch a glimpse of the endemic island scrub jay or the island gray fox. Visit a stand of Torrey pines – the only existing grove outside of Torrey Pines State Reserve, in San Diego. One trip to the Channel Islands, and you'll be convinced: This place is California like you've never seen it before.

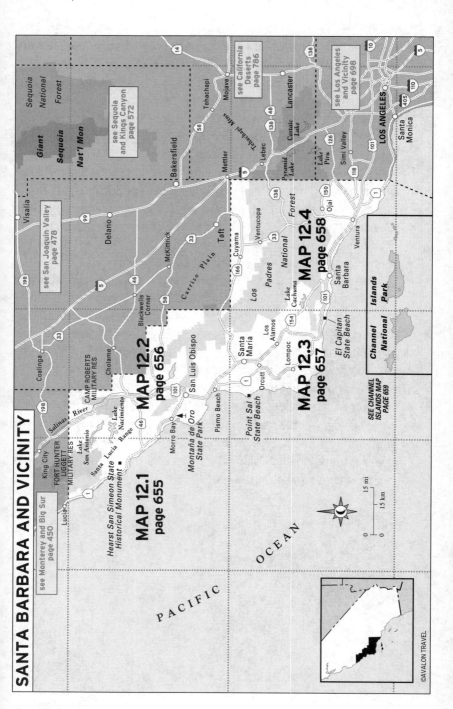

SANTA BARBARA AND VICINITY

see Monterey and Big Sur
page 450

see San Joaquin Valley
page 478

see Sequoia
and Kings Canyon
page 572

see California
Deserts
page 786

see Los Angeles
and Vicinity
page 698

Sequoia National Forest

Giant Sequoia Nat'l Mon

Visalia

Bakersfield

Delano

McKittrick

Taft

Cuyama

Ventucopa

Tehachapi

Mojave

Lancaster

Castaic Lake

Pyramid Lake

Lake Piru

Simi Valley

LOS ANGELES

Santa Monica

Los Padres National Forest

Lake Cachuma

Santa Barbara

Ojai

Ventura

Coalinga

Blackwells Corner

Cholame

CAMP ROBERTS MILITARY RES

King City

Lucia

FORT HUNTER LIGGETT MILITARY RES

Salinas River

Lake San Antonio

Lake Nacimiento

Santa Lucia Range

Hearst San Simeon State Historical Monument

Morro Bay

Montaña de Oro State Park

Pismo Beach

San Luis Obispo

Santa Maria

Los Alamos

Lompoc

Orcutt

Point Sal State Beach

El Capitan State Beach

MAP 12.1
page 655

MAP 12.2
page 656

MAP 12.3
page 657

MAP 12.4
page 658

Channel Islands National Park

SEE CHANNEL ISLANDS MAP PAGE 659

Carrizo Plain

Tehachapi Mtns

Mettler

Lebec

PACIFIC OCEAN

0   15 mi
0   15 km

©AVALON TRAVEL

Map 12.1

Hikes 1-3
Pages 660-661

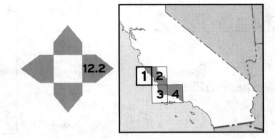

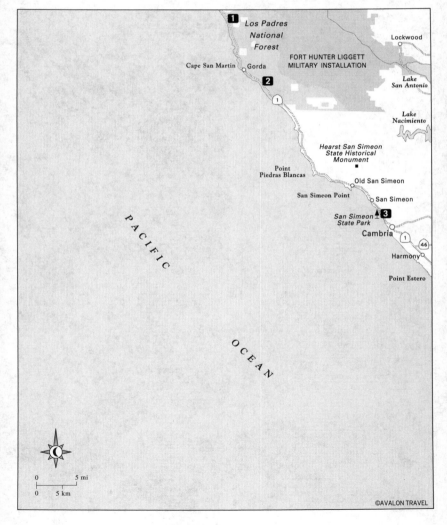

Los Padres
National
Forest

Lockwood

Cape San Martin — Gorda

FORT HUNTER LIGGETT
MILITARY INSTALLATION

Lake
San Antonio

Lake
Nacimiento

Hearst San Simeon
State Historical
Monument

Point
Piedras Blancas

Old San Simeon

San Simeon Point — San Simeon

San Simeon
State Park

Cambria

Harmony

Point Estero

PACIFIC

OCEAN

0   5 mi
0   5 km

©AVALON TRAVEL

Map 12.2

Hikes 4-16
Pages 662-669

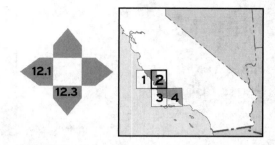

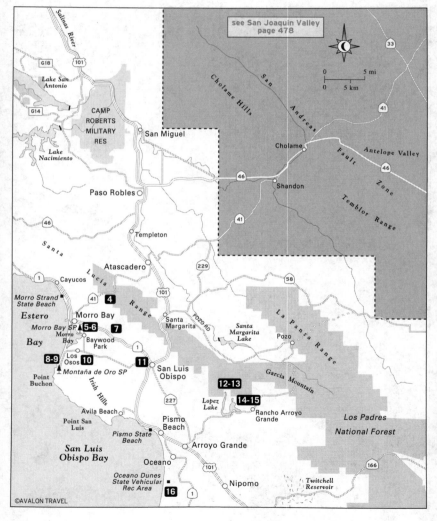

see San Joaquin Valley page 478

©AVALON TRAVEL

Map 12.3

Hikes 17-21
Pages 670-672

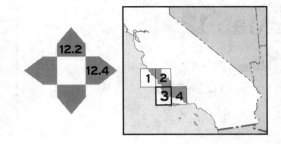

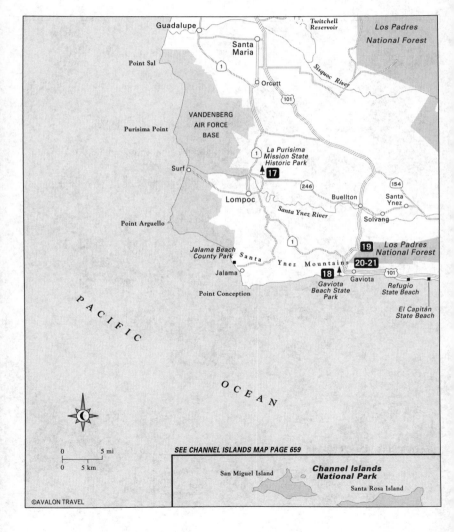

Map 12.4

Hikes 22-47
Pages 672-688

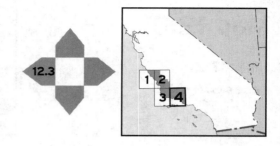

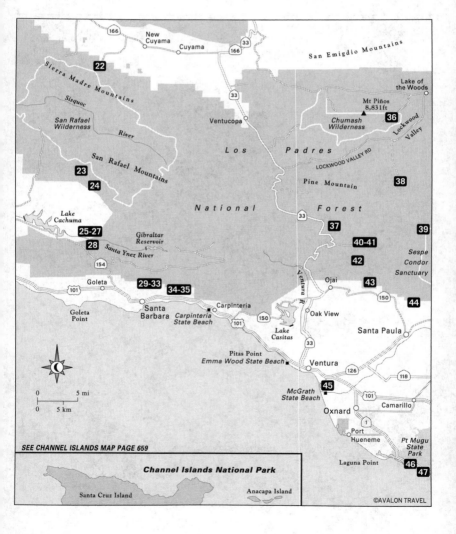

SEE CHANNEL ISLANDS MAP PAGE 659

Channel Islands National Park

Santa Cruz Island   Anacapa Island

©AVALON TRAVEL

Channel Islands Detail   Hikes 48-52   Pages 689-693

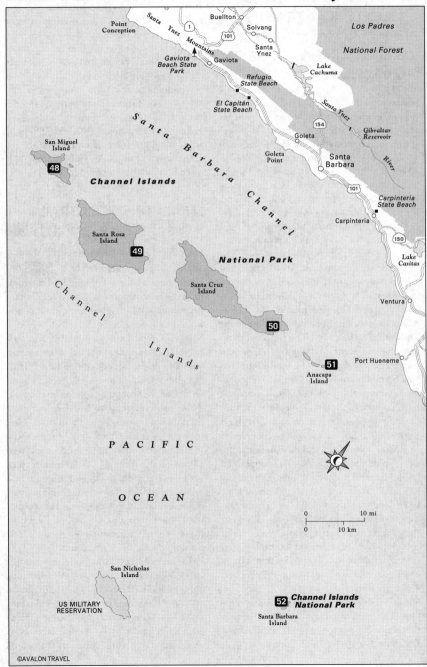

©AVALON TRAVEL

1 KIRK CREEK / VICENTE FLAT TRAIL
10.0 mi / 6.0 hr or 2 days 🥾3 ⛰9

in the Ventana Wilderness south of Lucia

Map 12.1, page 655

What you see at the trailhead is not exactly what you get on this popular backpacking trail. You see chaparral and no shade, but you get chaparral and no shade only part of the time; the rest of the time, you're hiking in shady redwood groves or along lush ravines. The Kirk Creek Trail (also called Vicente Flat Trail) is full of surprises. The absence of trees in some sections is actually a positive, because it allows for wide-reaching views over the big, blue Pacific. Your destination is Vicente Flat Camp, reached after five miles, with a 1,800-foot elevation gain, mostly on a well-graded trail. The trail leads steadily northeast, passing occasional odd-looking rocks and meandering in and out of dense groves of redwoods, madrones, oaks, and bay laurel. Pass small Espinoza Camp at 3.2 miles, which is seldom used because of the superiority of Vicente Flat Camp, a larger camp with a nearby stream and a beautiful setting in a lovely redwood grove. The final 0.5 mile of trail is a descent to Stone Ridge Trail junction, where you bear left for Vicente Flat Camp. You have a choice of sites in the shade or the sun; Hare Creek provides a water source. If you'd like to walk this beautiful trail but don't want to go to so much effort, make arrangements for a car shuttle, then start at the Coast Ridge Road trailhead and hike downhill almost all the way (7.5 miles) to this trailhead on Highway 1.

User Groups: Hikers, dogs, and horses. No mountain bikes. No wheelchair facilities.

Permits: A free campfire permit is required for overnight stays from May to December; permits are available from the Monterey Ranger District or the Big Sur Station. Parking and access are free.

Maps: A Los Padres National Forest or Ventana Wilderness map is available from the U.S. Forest Service. For topographic maps, ask the USGS for Lopez Point and Cone Peak.

Directions: Drive 55 miles south from Carmel on Highway 1 to Kirk Creek Campground, on the west side of the highway. (It's four miles south of Lucia and six miles north of Gorda.) The trailhead is on the east side of the highway; you must park alongside Highway 1 in the pullout and not in the campground.

Contact: Los Padres National Forest, Monterey Ranger District, 406 South Mildred Avenue, King City, CA 93930, 831/385-5434, www.fs.fed.us/r5/lospadres; Big Sur Station, Highway 1, Big Sur, CA 93920, 831/667-2315 or 831/649-2836.

2 SALMON CREEK TRAIL
4.2 mi / 2.0 hr or 2 days 🥾3 ⛰9

in the Silver Peak Wilderness south of Gorda

Map 12.1, page 655

While heading for a day hike or short backpacking trip on Salmon Creek Trail, many people walk right by and miss seeing spectacular Salmon Creek Falls, which is just off Salmon Creek Trail and a 0.25-mile walk from Highway 1. Don't be one of them; start your trip at the signed Salmon Creek Trail, but after walking a few hundred feet, cut off on any of the spur trails to your left and pay a visit to the impressive 100-foot waterfall, surrounded by cabin-sized boulders. Then return to Salmon Creek Trail, say good-bye to the creekside shade and dampness, and start a steep climb to the ridge, where you can look back down at the highway and marvel at how far you've gone, and how fast. From there, it's still more climbing, gaining a total of 800 feet, until you start to see Douglas firs, a sure sign that you're nearing misnamed Spruce Creek Camp, at 1,325 feet. At Spruce Creek Trail fork, two miles from your start, stay straight (left). The final 0.1 mile is downhill along Spruce Creek, a beautiful stream with myriad pools and cascades. The camp here is blissfully shaded by Douglas firs, and there are many good spots to stick your feet (or other body parts) into the stream. If you want to spend the night but somebody already has this spot (which happens often due to its proximity to the highway), you can continue another mile to Estrella Camp. If you want to explore more of this beautiful area, follow the right fork instead of the left fork at 2.0 miles out, and you'll climb higher up over a ridge to a beautiful meadow known as Dutra Flats.

User Groups: Hikers, dogs, and horses. No mountain bikes. No wheelchair facilities.

Permits: A free campfire permit is required for overnight stays from May to December; permits are available from the Monterey Ranger District or the Big Sur Station. Parking and access are free.

Maps: A Los Padres National Forest or Ventana Wilderness map is available from the U.S. Forest Service. For a topographic map, ask the USGS for Villa Creek.

Directions: From Big Sur, drive 33 miles south on Highway 1 to Gorda; continue 7.6 miles south of Gorda to the trailhead for Salmon Creek Trail, on the east side of the highway at a hairpin turn. Park in the large parking pullout along the road. The Salmon Creek Trail leads from the south end of the guardrail.

Contact: Los Padres National Forest, Monterey Ranger District, 406 South Mildred Avenue, King City, CA 93930, 831/385-5434, www.fs.fed.us/r5/lospadres; Big Sur Station, Highway 1, Big Sur, CA 93920, 831/667-2315 or 831/649-2836.

⊠ LEFFINGWELL LANDING AND MOONSTONE BEACH
4.0 mi / 2.0 hr 🏃2 △8

near Cambria

Map 12.1, page 655

What's the best time to make the trip to Cambria? That's easy—in the spring, when the rolling hills along Highway 46 on the drive to the coast are lush and green. Of course, any time of year is a good time to walk the trail that leads from Leffingwell Landing along the bluffs above Moonstone

Beach. Although Moonstone Beach Drive parallels the trail all the way, the road isn't much of a bother, because the vistas out to sea hold all of your attention. The parking lot at Leffingwell Landing is in the middle of this trail, which means you can walk out and back in both directions. To the south you may have a wet creek crossing at Leffingwell Creek, but you can go around it via the golf course. The bluff trail's southern terminus is at the intersection of Moonstone Beach Drive and Weymouth Street, but you can descend to the beach there and keep walking. If you head in the other direction, about 0.25 mile north of Leffingwell Landing the trail again descends on a wooden staircase to the beach, and you continue your walk there. In addition to the coastal vistas from the bluffs, there are many colorful patches of ice plant and cypress trees, as well as several benches and overlooks (accessible via short spurs off the main trail)—places where you can find a spot to call your own. We watched a winter squall come in from one of these overlooks; it was sudden, dramatic, and beautiful. Right below Leffingwell Landing are fine tidepools to be explored. Keep on the lookout for passing whales in the winter.

User Groups: Hikers and dogs. No horses or mountain bikes. No wheelchair facilities.

Permits: No permits are required. Parking and access are free.

Maps: A park map is available by free download at www.parks.ca.gov. For a topographic map, ask the USGS for Cambria.

Directions: From north of Templeton on US 101, take the Highway 46 West/Cambria/Hearst Castle exit. Drive west on Highway 46 for 22 miles to Highway 1; continue three miles north on Highway 1, past Cambria, to Moonstone Beach Drive. Turn left on Moonstone Beach Drive and park at Leffingwell Landing.

Contact: San Simeon State Beach, San Simeon District, 750 Hearst Castle Road, San Simeon, CA 93452, 805/927-2020 or 805/927-2068, www.parks.ca.gov.

4 CERRO ALTO SUMMIT
7.0 mi / 3.5 hr   🏃3 ⛰9

off Highway 41, east of Morro Bay

Map 12.2, page 656

We hope you like to climb, because that's what you do on Cerro Alto Trail to the summit of Cerro Alto, elevation 2,620 feet. The 1,600-foot ascent is divided over 3.5 miles of mostly steep terrain, but the reward for your exertion is one of the finest views of the Central Coast—a panoramic vista of the Pacific Ocean, Whale Rock Reservoir, Morro Bay, Piedras Blancas Lighthouse, and the Santa Lucia Mountains. In recent years, the trails to Cerro Alto have become extremely popular with mountain bikers. If you don't like sharing the trail with bikes, visit on a weekday. From the trailhead at the far end of the Cerro Alto Campground road, you follow a pleasant trail alongside Morro Creek in a bay and live oak forest, then (too soon) leave the shady stream behind and head for chaparral country. After 0.75 mile, bear left, and shortly thereafter bear right. After a series of switchbacks and some rocky sections of trail, you reach the road to the peak, at 1.7 miles. Turn left and circle the peak as you climb another 0.25 mile to the summit. The view is divine even before you get to the top, for one simple reason: Located on West Cuesta Ridge, Cerro Alto is one of the highest points in this coastal region.

Note that if you want to semi-loop back from the summit, you can take a shorter trail on the way back. Retrace your steps downhill for 1.2 miles, then turn left and prepare for an incredibly steep descent of only one mile back to the campground. Your knees may not be very happy with you when this is over.

User Groups: Hikers, dogs, horses, and mountain bikes. No wheelchair facilities.

Permits: No permits are required. A national forest Adventure Pass is required for each vehicle; fees are $5 for one day or $30 for a year. Interagency access passes are also accepted. If you don't have a pass, you can pay $5 at the trailhead parking lot.

Maps: A Los Padres National Forest map is available from the U.S. Forest Service. For a topographic map, ask the USGS for Atascadero.

Directions: From Atascadero on US 101, take the Highway 41 West/Morro Bay exit. Drive eight miles west on Highway 41 to Cerro Alto Campground, on the left. (Or, from Morro Bay on Highway 1, exit on Highway 41 and drive eight miles east to Cerro Alto Campground, on the right.) Turn in to the campground entrance and follow the road all the way to its end, at the hikers' parking lot near the camp host's residence. Start hiking on the signed Cerro Alto Trail from there.

Contact: Los Padres National Forest, Santa Lucia Ranger District, 1616 North Carlotti Drive, Santa Maria, CA 93454, 805/925-9538, www.fs.fed.us/r5/lospadres.

5 BLACK HILL
0.5 mi / 0.5 hr   🏃1 ⛰8

in Morro Bay State Park near Morro Bay

Map 12.2, page 656

The Black Hill Trail in Morro Bay State Park is no wilderness trek, but it does provide a wonderful view with an amazingly short walk—one that thousands of Central Coast visitors take every summer. Black Hill is an ancient 661-foot volcanic peak, the most accessible of the "Nine Sisters" or nine *morros* in the San Luis Obispo/Morro Bay area. The short trail offers a big payoff; Black Hill's summit overlooks Morro Bay and its estuary, Estero Point, Cayucos, Chorro Valley, and the nearby *morros* of Cerro Cabrillo and Hollister Peak. From the parking lot at the end of Black Hill Road, it's just a quarter-mile walk to the rocky summit. Black Hill got its name from a tar seep on the hill's north side. The only tricky part is finding the trailhead, which is at the top of a maze of roads at the Morro Bay Golf Course. If you want to take a longer walk to reach Black Hill, you can start at a separate trailhead on Park View Road and hike for about a mile to reach the top. And if you are visiting Morro Bay State Park between February and June, don't miss a short side-trip to the park's Heron Rookery Natural Preserve, across State Park Road from the golf course and just north of the natural history museum. Here you can walk near a grove of eucalyptus and cypress trees where double-breasted cormorants, great egrets, and great blue herons nest in the trees.

User Groups: Hikers and horses. No dogs or mountain bikes. No wheelchair facilities.

Permits: No permits are required. Parking and access are free.

Maps: A map of Morro Bay State Park is available at the natural history museum on State Park Road, or by free download at www.parks.ca.gov. For a topographic map, ask the USGS for Morro Bay South.

Directions: From San Luis Obispo, take Highway 1 north to the Los Osos/Baywood Park exit. Turn left, drive one mile and turn right on State Park Road. Drive a short distance and then turn right on Park View Road and follow it up the hill to the golf course. Turn right on Black Hill Road and follow it to its end.

Contact: Morro Bay State Park, State Park Road, Morro Bay, CA 93442, 805/772-7434; San Luis Obispo Coast State Parks, 805/927-2065, www.parks.ca.gov or www.slostateparks.com.

⑥ CERRO CABRILLO

3.0 mi / 1.5 hr

in Morro Bay State Park near Morro Bay

Map 12.2, page 656

You hardly realize you're in a state park when you reach the trailhead for Cerro Cabrillo, which is just a small dirt parking lot alongside a busy road. Where's the entrance kiosk? What about the state park entrance fee? Where are all the campgrounds and restrooms? None of that applies here at Morro Bay State Park's Cerro Cabrillo Trail, which is a quiet refuge from the hustle and bustle of Morro

Bay tourism. Cerro Cabrillo, also known as Cabrillo Peak, is one of nine *morros*—small volcanic peaks that lie in a loose chain along the central coast. (Morro Rock is another of these and is the most famous of the group.) Although no trail goes to the top of Cerro Cabrillo, you can hike on the peak's lower reaches on Quarry Trail and Park Ridge Trail. Both are accessible from two small parking areas off South Bay Boulevard; if you miss the first one, just take the second. The Park Ridge Trail goes straight up, then veers left and joins Quarry Trail. The Cerro Cabrillo area contains a variety of native plants and grasslands, including these spring bloomers: bird's eye gilia, brodiea, and mariposa lilies. On the sunniest slopes, coastal sage scrub grows, including black sage and bush monkeyflower. Translation? No shade. That makes the views of Morro Bay and Morro Rock are first class, but it also means you'd better carry water.

User Groups: Hikers, horses, and mountain bikes. No dogs. No wheelchair facilities.

Permits: No permits are required. Parking and access are free.

Maps: A map of Morro Bay State Park is available at the natural history museum on State Park Road, or by free download at www.parks.ca.gov. For a topographic map, ask the USGS for Morro Bay South.

Directions: From San Luis Obispo, take Highway 1 northwest for 11 miles to Morro Bay. Take the Morro Bay State Park exit and continue on South Bay Boulevard. In 0.75 mile, continue straight ahead over the bridge and drive another 0.5 mile to the Cerro Cabrillo dirt parking lot, on the left side of the road. The first parking lot is for the Quarry Trail; another parking lot shortly following it is for the Park Ridge Trail. Park at either; the two trails join.

Contact: Morro Bay State Park, State Park Road, Morro Bay, CA 93442, 805/772-7434; San Luis Obispo Coast State Parks, 805/927-2065, www.parks.ca.gov or www.slostateparks.com.

7 EAGLE ROCK
2.2 mi / 1.0 hr   🚶2 ⛰8

in El Chorro Regional Park in San Luis Obispo

Map 12.2, page 656

El Chorro Regional Park is better known for its popular off-leash dog park and golf course than it is for its hiking trails, but the park's Eagle Rock Trail is a little gem that deserves some recognition. The well-maintained trail starts from the gate just past the dog park. Be sure to pick up an interpretive brochure at the trailhead, which will help you spot Native American grinding holes, pack rat nests, and other interesting features along the path. Follow Dairy Creek Trail, a paved road, for about 100 yards to the start of the Eagle Rock Trail. The path climbs up into the coastal hills, gaining just enough elevation to bring you to Eagle Rock Vista, where you can enjoy big views of Moro Rock and the coastline. The trail eventually loops back downhill on the paved Dairy Creek Trail, traveling past coast live oaks and spring wildflowers. Most of the time you're likely to have this trail all to yourself, and that's just fine, because there's nothing to distract you from the fine vistas. And one more thing; don't be surprised if you hear the occasional sound of gunfire in the distance. It's coming from nearby Camp San Luis Obispo, a military base.

User Groups: Hikers, dogs, horses, and mountain bikes. No wheelchair facilities.

Permits: No permits are required. A $3 entrance fee is charged per vehicle.

Maps: Free brochures and trail maps are available at the park entrance station and trailhead. For a topographic map, ask the USGS for San Luis Obispo.

Directions: From San Luis Obispo, drive six miles north on Highway 1 to El Chorro Regional Park (across from Cuesta College). Turn right and drive past the baseball fields to the end of the day-use area, by the dog park. Park your car and walk through the gate for about 100 yards to the trail's start.

Contact: El Chorro Regional Park, c/o San Luis Obispo County Parks, 1087 Santa Rosa Street, San Luis Obispo, CA 93408, 805/781-5930, www.slocountyparks.org.

8 MONTAÑA DE ORO BLUFFS TRAIL
3.0 mi / 1.5 hr   🚶1 ⛰10

in Montaña de Oro State Park west of San Luis Obispo

Map 12.2, page 656   **BEST (**

How can a park this good be free of charge? We can't figure it out, but we're glad it is. The Bluffs Trail at Montaña de Oro State Park is one of the finest coast walks in Central and Southern California, blissfully free of the blight of human development and loaded with classic oceanside beauty. The flat trail winds along the top of Montaña de Oro's shale and sediment bluffs, with nonstop views of rocky offshore outcrops, colorful rock cliffs and arches, and the big blue Pacific. Wooden railings keep hikers from leaning too far over the edge of the constantly eroding bluffs. In addition to all the coastal vistas, the grasses alongside the trail explode in a display of orange poppies and other wildflowers in February, March, and April. The trail ends at a barbed-wire fence and PG&E property lined with huge cacti to keep people out. Just follow the tiny loop and retrace your steps on the trail. A good side trip is to explore the beach right across from the visitors center turnoff, near where you left your car.

User Groups: Hikers and mountain bikes. No dogs or horses. No wheelchair facilities.

Permits: No permits are required. Parking and access are free.

Maps: A map of Montaña de Oro State Park is available at the park entrance, the visitors center, or by free download at www.parks.ca.gov. For a topographic map, ask the USGS for Morro Bay South.

Directions: From US 101 in San Luis Obispo, take the Los Osos exit and head west on Los Osos Valley Road. Drive 12 miles on Los Osos

Valley Road to the Montaña de Oro entrance. Continue 2.5 miles to the small parking area on the right side of the road, 100 yards beyond the left turnoff for the visitors center. The signed Bluffs Trail begins there.

Contact: Montaña de Oro State Park, 3550 Pecho Valley Road, Los Osos, CA 93402, 805/528-0513; Morro Bay State Park, 805/772-7434; San Luis Obispo Coast State Parks, 805/927-2065, www.parks.ca.gov or www.slostateparks.com.

9 VALENCIA AND OATS PEAKS

7.0 mi / 3.5 hr   🏃4 ▲9

in Montaña de Oro State Park west of San Luis Obispo

> **Map 12.2, page 656**

With a cool ocean breeze keeping you comfortable, this seven-mile round-trip hike to two coastal peaks is a spectacular day trip. If you forget to carry water and/or hike in the heat of high noon, it can be a nightmare, so get prepared. The Valencia Peak Trail begins in Montaña de Oro State Park. The wide route heads briefly south and then turns inland for a gradual ascent through grasslands and wildflowers, chaparral, and scrub. There are several junctions; all are well marked.

In two miles and with an elevation gain of 1,100 feet, you arrive at the top of Valencia Peak, elevation 1,347 feet. On a clear day you can see all the way from Point Sal, in the south, to Piedras Blancas, in the north. You won't even need a map to pick out Rocky Butte, Morro Rock (that's an easy one), and the Morro Bay estuary. From there, you must descend for a mile, losing nearly 500 feet, to join a road that connects to Oats Peak Trail, then hike upward once again on Oats Peak Trail. Sorry, but there's no other way to do it from the top of Valencia Peak.

Oats Peak is more easily gained (in 1.2 miles), and a survey marker tells you when you reach its summit, at 1,373 feet. From there, you can

walk along the ridge for a while to enjoy more of the spectacular views of the ocean, Morro Rock, and the inland mountains, or you can head back downhill. Keep to Oats Peak Trail for your descent. If you take Oats Peak Trail all the way back, you'll have a 10-minute walk on the park road to get back to your car. One more thing to think about: If you can possibly visit between February and April, you get a good chance at crystal-clear vistas and the best chance of seeing Montaña de Oro's signature wildflower display. These hills are "mountains of gold" in season; hence the park's name.

User Groups: Hikers and horses. No dogs or mountain bikes. No wheelchair facilities.

Permits: No permits are required. Parking and access are free.

Maps: A map of Montaña de Oro State Park is available at the park entrance, the visitors center, or by free download at www.parks.ca.gov. For a topographic map, ask the USGS for Morro Bay South.

Directions: From US 101 in San Luis Obispo, take the Los Osos exit and head west on Los Osos Valley Road. Drive 12 miles on Los Osos Valley Road to the Montaña de Oro entrance. Continue 2.5 miles to the small parking area on the right side of the road, 100 yards beyond the left turnoff for the visitors center. The Valencia Peak Trail begins on the left side of the road.

Contact: Montaña de Oro State Park, 3550 Pecho Valley Road, Los Osos, CA 93402, 805/528-0513; Morro Bay State Park, 805/772-7434; San Luis Obispo Coast State Parks, 805/927-2065, www.parks.ca.gov or www.slostateparks.com.

10 LOS OSOS OAKS RESERVE

2.0 mi / 1.0 hr   🏃1 ▲8

west of San Luis Obispo in Los Osos

> **Map 12.2, page 656**

It's hard to believe that a bunch of old oak trees right alongside a busy road could make for such great walking, but they do. The hike is an odd mix of elements, since you hear road noise much of the time, but the forest still seems peaceful. The venerable old oaks in Los Osos Oaks Reserve are as old as 800 years, and they can be visited by wandering on any of three short, flat trails. It's easy to walk a brief stretch on all of them. The Chumash Loop, Oak View Trail, and Los Osos Creek Trail all lead from the parking lot and split off from each other. Oak View is just a short out-and-back trip through the trees and provides the best look at the reserve's highlights; Chumash Loop is a little longer and loops around the reserve. The Los Osos Creek Trail is the least impressive of the three, showing off the fewest fine tree specimens and following a marshy stretch of creek. The oak forest is a mix of very large, old trees with moss hanging from their branches, and tiny, dwarfed ones. Some of the oaks' trunks and branches are so twisted, gnarled, and wrinkled that they look like a tangled web of elephants' trunks. If you're into photography, this is the kind of place that is best captured in black and white. And, if the coast is foggy, this hike is ideal, because all the beauty of the forest is close enough to touch.

User Groups: Hikers only. No dogs, horses, or mountain bikes. No wheelchair facilities.

Permits: No permits are required. Parking and access are free.

Maps: For a topographic map, ask the USGS for Morro Bay South.

Directions: From US 101 in San Luis Obispo, take the Los Osos exit and head west on Los Osos Valley Road. Drive 8.5 miles on Los Osos Valley Road to the Los Osos Oaks Reserve, on the left side of the road, which is marked by a small sign. The reserve is exactly one mile east of 10th Street, in Los Osos, and just west of the bear statue on the road. There is a small parking area by the trailhead, just off Los Osos Valley Road.

Contact: Los Osos Oaks Reserve, c/o Morro Bay State Park, State Park Road, Morro Bay, CA 93442, 805/772-7434; San Luis Obispo Coast State Parks, 805/927-2065, www.parks.ca.gov, www.slostateparks.com.

11 BISHOP PEAK
4.4 mi / 2.0 hr

in Bishop Peak Natural Reserve in San Luis Obispo

Map 12.2, page 656

People have been hiking to Bishop Peak for centuries, but it wasn't until 1998 that this trail from the end of Patricia Drive was completed through a joint effort by government agencies and volunteers. Constructed by the Sierra Club, California Conservation Corps, and California Department of Forestry, this well-built pathway allows easy neighborhood access to one of the most prominent of the nine San Luis Obispo-area *morros*. It's the kind of trail that local people flock to for an early morning or after-work walk, often in the company of their canine companions (leashes are required). The trail leads from the west side of Patricia Drive and travels uphill, gaining a total of 1,200 feet in elevation. Go left at the first junction, heading around a cattle pond. You'll soon leave the open grasslands behind and enter a dense oak and bay laurel forest, where several short spur trails lead to rock-climbing sites. At a signed junction, head left to follow the summit trail to Bishop Peak. The last mile is a dramatic climb through well-graded switchbacks to the peak's rocky summit at elevation 1,559 feet. Once on top, enjoy the fine vista of all of San Luis Obispo, but watch your footing. It's easy to get inspired by the views and be tempted to climb to the top of the highest rock, but this has resulted in a few tragic accidents. Note that if you don't have the time or energy to bag Bishop Peak, you can always hike the Felsman Loop instead, which travels along the peak's lower slopes. Access the Felsman Loop by turning right at this trail's first junction instead of left.

User Groups: Hikers and dogs. No horses or mountain bikes. No wheelchair facilities.

Permits: No permits are required. Parking and access are free.

Maps: A map of Bishop Peak Natural Reserve is available for free download at www.slocity.org.

For a topographic map, ask the USGS for San Luis Obispo.

Directions: From San Luis Obispo, head west on Foothill Boulevard. Turn right on Patricia Drive and drive about one mile. Continue past the stop sign at Highland Drive for 0.25 mile to the trailhead on the left, just past Patricia Court. Park on the left (west) side of Patricia Drive, away from the private driveways.

Contact: City of San Luis Obispo Parks and Recreation, 990 Palm Street, San Luis Obispo, CA 93401, 805/781-7300, www.slocity.org.

12 BIG FALLS
3.0 mi / 1.5 hr

in the Santa Lucia Wilderness near Arroyo Grande

Map 12.2, page 656   **BEST**

The journey to Big Falls in the Santa Lucia Wilderness is a wacky, water-filled adventure. Even as late as June, the drive to the trailhead can require dozens of crossings of Lopez Creek. In some places, the stream simply becomes the road. In comparison to the drive, the hike is surprisingly easy and fast. You walk through a fern- and flower-filled sycamore and oak forest to the first waterfall, only 0.5 mile in. This is not actually Big Falls; it's a smaller waterfall, although plenty of people mistake it for Big Falls. This waterfall is only about 30 feet high, with many small trout swimming in its lower pool and a much deeper pool just above its lip. Sunbathers enjoy the rocky pools upstream. You can continue hiking beyond this cataract to the real Big Falls, another mile farther. Spring wildflowers are excellent along the route. The terrain gets drier and rockier as you climb up out of the canyon to Big Falls, and you'll find different types of flowers and foliage on this upper part of the trail. Big Falls is about 80 feet tall, but it's only impressive early in the year. By June it has much less flow than the smaller waterfall downstream. If you want to hike more, the trail continues beyond Big

Falls for another mile, making an exposed and steep ascent to Hi Mountain Road.

User Groups: Hikers, dogs, and horses. No mountain bikes. No wheelchair facilities.

Permits: No day-use permits are required. Parking and access are free.

Maps: A Los Padres National Forest map is available from the U.S. Forest Service. For a topographic map, ask the USGS for Tar Spring Ridge.

Directions: From San Luis Obispo, drive 15 miles south on US 101 to Arroyo Grande and the Highway 227/Lopez Lake exit. Head east on Highway 227 and turn right on Lopez Drive, following the signs toward Lopez Lake for 10.3 miles. Turn right on Hi Mountain Road (before Lopez Lake's entrance station). Drive 0.8 mile, turn left on Upper Lopez Canyon Road, and drive 6.3 miles, passing a Scout Camp, and turn right. In 0.1 mile, the pavement ends. Continue for 3.5 miles on the dirt road, crossing Lopez Creek numerous times in the wet season, to the Big Falls trailhead. The trail leads from the right side of the road. Note: Four-wheel-drive vehicles are recommended.

Contact: Los Padres National Forest, Santa Lucia Ranger District, 1616 North Carlotti Drive, Santa Maria, CA 93454, 805/925-9538, www.fs.fed.us/r5/lospadres.

13 LITTLE FALLS
1.0 mi / 0.5 hr

in the Santa Lucia Wilderness near Arroyo Grande

Map 12.2, page 656   **BEST**

Little Falls is just as pretty as its neighbor Big Falls (see listing in this chapter), and getting to it requires the same wet and rugged drive, but a lot less of it. If your car isn't up to the 3.5 miles of rocky road and stream crossings that it takes to get to Big Falls, maybe you can convince it to go only 1.6 miles to Little Falls. If even that's too much, you can always park where the pavement ends and walk to Little

Falls, adding 3.2 miles round-trip to the mileage shown above. It's still a fairly easy hike, offering plenty of lovely scenery. You hike from the trailhead along Little Falls Creek—a cool, shady stream that is teeming with small trout and lined with oaks, sycamores, bays, and maples. Maidenhair and giant woodwardia ferns line its rocky pools. After only 15 minutes of hiking (less than 0.5 mile), you'll see a spur trail heading off to the left, which you can follow upstream for a few hundred feet to Little Falls, a 50-foot limestone waterfall. The main trail continues beyond this spur to many fine, water-carved pools, perfect for wading into. The trail eventually climbs out of the canyon to Hi Mountain Road.

User Groups: Hikers, dogs, and horses. No mountain bikes. No wheelchair facilities.

Permits: No day-use permits are required. Parking and access are free.

Maps: A Los Padres National Forest map is available from the U.S. Forest Service. For a topographic map, ask the USGS for Tar Spring Ridge.

Directions: From San Luis Obispo, drive 15 miles south on US 101 to Arroyo Grande and the Highway 227/Lopez Lake exit. Head east on Highway 227; turn right on Lopez Drive, following the signs toward Lopez Lake for 10.3 miles. Turn right on Hi Mountain Road (before Lopez Lake's entrance station). Drive 0.8 mile and turn left on Upper Lopez Canyon Road. Drive 6.3 miles, passing a Scout Camp, and then turn right. The pavement ends 0.1 mile farther on. Continue for 1.6 miles on the dirt road, crossing Lopez Creek numerous times in the wet season, to the Little Falls trailhead (the sign can be hard to spot; check your odometer carefully). The trail leads from the right side of the road. Note: Four-wheel-drive vehicles are recommended.

Contact: Los Padres National Forest, Santa Lucia Ranger District, 1616 North Carlotti Drive, Santa Maria, CA 93454, 805/925-9538, www.fs.fed.us/r5/lospadres.

14 DUNA VISTA LOOP AND ENCINAL TRAILS

2.2–7.2 mi / 1.0–3.0 hr 🏃2 ⛰9

at Lopez Lake east of Arroyo Grande

Map 12.2, page 656

Most people on the Central Coast know that Lopez Lake is completely set up for water recreation—boating, waterskiing, windsurfing, fishing, you name it—but not everyone knows that the park is also great for hiking, especially in springtime. The best path in the park, Duna Vista Loop, is accessible via either a long hike or a short hike and a boat ride. The latter option works great for people who want to go hiking while their loved ones go fishing; they can be dropped off and picked up later. If you're going by boat, there are two ways to access the Duna Vista Loop Trail. From the Encinal Boat Camp dock on the Lopez arm of the lake, follow the Encinal Trail about 0.6 mile to the Duna Vista Loop Trail junction. Or, from the Wittenburg arm at Miller Cove, follow the Duna Vista Loop Trail up to the Encinal Trail junction. You can start from either trailhead, or arrange a shuttle pickup with a friend so that you can start at one end and finish at the other. California fushias bloom along the trail, mixed in among the sage and chaparral. After a 600-foot-climb, you're rewarded with views of the Santa Lucia Wilderness, the Pacific Ocean, and Pismo Dunes. If you can't arrange a boat ride, you can start your trip from the Duna Vista Loop Trailhead on the far side of the park. Start walking from the end of Lopez Drive along the Wittenburg arm. You will pass through Camp French (a Scout Camp), and then skirt along the Wittenburg arm on the opposite side of the lake from where you started. The trail will start to cimb and then loop back on itself at Millers Cove. Keep in mind that this changes a 2.2-mile round-trip into a 7.2-mile round-trip.

User Groups: Hikers, horses, dogs, and mountain bikes. No wheelchair facilities.

Permits: No permits are required. A $9 day-use fee is charged per vehicle.

Maps: A map of Lopez Lake Recreation Area is available at the ranger station. For a topographic map, ask the USGS for Tar Spring Ridge.

Directions: From San Luis Obispo, drive 15 miles south on US 101 to Arroyo Grande and the Highway 227/Lopez Lake exit. Head east on Highway 227 and turn right on Lopez Drive, following the signs to Lopez Lake for 10.4 miles. To reach the Duna Vista Loop Trail, you can take a boat ride up the Wittenburg or Lopez arms of the lake, or add four miles to your trip by hiking from the Wittenburg trailhead. To reach the latter, drive 1.5 miles past the park entrance station to the parking area near where the park road is gated off.

Contact: Lopez Lake Recreation Area, 6800 Lopez Drive, Arroyo Grande, CA 93420, 805/788-2381, www.slocountyparks.org.

15 BLACKBERRY SPRINGS AND HIGH RIDGE LOOP
2.0 mi / 1.0 hr   🏃2 ⛰9

at Lopez Lake east of Arroyo Grande

Map 12.2, page 656

Great views of the grassy hills and blue water of Lopez Lake are yours for the taking on High Ridge Trail. Start from the Blackberry Springs trailhead at Squirrel Campground. As you hike uphill through a foliage-rich creek canyon, watch for fruit-covered blackberry bushes in early summer. Many other plants along the trail are also edible and were used by the Chumash. The trail steepens as it climbs to connect with High Ridge Trail at 0.75 mile, where you turn left and wander along a firebreak, which offers wide-open views. It's hot and sunny up here, so that may dictate how far you wander, but the trail travels 2.2 miles before it drops down to the Wittenburg arm of the lake. You might as well just head out for 0.5 mile or so, enjoy the views of the Santa Lucia Wilderness and the coast, and then turn around and head back. Another

option is to turn right instead of left on the High Ridge Trail, walk 0.5 mile, and connect with the Turkey Ridge Trail. Take the Turkey Ridge Trail back to the parking lot by Squirrel Campground for a nice two-mile loop trip.

User Groups: Hikers and dogs. No horses or mountain bikes. No wheelchair facilities.

Permits: No permits are required. A $9 day-use fee is charged per vehicle.

Maps: A map of Lopez Lake Recreation Area is available at the ranger station. For a topographic map, ask the USGS for Tar Spring Ridge.

Directions: From San Luis Obispo, drive 15 miles south on US 101 to Arroyo Grande and the Highway 227/Lopez Lake exit. Head east on Highway 227 and turn right on Lopez Drive, following the signs to Lopez Lake for 10.4 miles. Continue past the entrance station to Squirrel Campground and the trailhead for the Blackberry Springs Trail.

Contact: Lopez Lake Recreation Area, 6800 Lopez Drive, Arroyo Grande, CA 93420, 805/788-2381, www.slocountyparks.org.

16 OSO FLACO LAKE
3.0 mi / 1.5 hr   🏃1 ⛰9

southwest of Arroyo Grande

Map 12.2, page 656

Oso Flaco Lake and its environs were the site of an extensive dune restoration and native plant revegetation project in the 1980s. The result is an 800-acre natural area that is the perfect place to view coastal wildflowers and wildlife. The trail to Oso Flaco Lake starts out on a gravel causeway for 0.3 mile, then cuts off to the left on a wooden boardwalk and footbridge that bisects the small lake, one of the few remaining freshwater dune lakes. Immediately you are in the good company of shorebirds and waterfowl, including ducks that play hide-and-seek in the islands of reeds. The boardwalk extends beyond the lake's border and over a series of sand dunes. It serves the dual purpose of making the trail suitable for wheelchairs and protecting the dunes' fragile plant life, which includes several threatened species. (Wheelchair users note: After heavy rains, the boardwalk may be partially submerged under a few inches of water. Call the park to check on trail conditions before planning a visit in winter or spring.) Where the boardwalk ends, you can continue walking on the dunes or head to the beach on your right. By the way, what does Oso Flaco mean? Skinny bear. But it's been a long time since they've seen one of those around here.

User Groups: Hikers and wheelchairs. No dogs, horses, or mountain bikes.

Permits: No permits are required. A $5 day-use fee is charged per vehicle.

Maps: For a topographic map, ask the USGS for Oceano.

Directions: From Santa Maria on US 101, take the Highway 166/Guadalupe exit, drive nine miles west, and then turn north on Highway 1 at Guadalupe. Drive 3.6 miles to Oso Flaco Lake Road, turn left, and drive three miles to the trailhead, at the end of the road.

Contact: Oceano Dunes State Vehicular Recreation Area, 928 Pacific Boulevard, Oceano, CA 93445, 805/473-7230 or 805/473-7223, www.parks.ca.gov.

17 LAS ZANJAS AND EL CAMINO LOOP

2.5 mi / 1.25 hr   🚶1 🏔8

at La Purisima Mission north of Lompoc

Map 12.3, page 657

If you came to La Purisima Mission seeking heavenly sanctuary but instead found a bunch of screaming school kids, you can still find your heaven in the hills surrounding the mission. There's a surprising number of good hiking trails here, considering this is a state historic park and not a recreation park. The best place to start is on a level loop trail around the mission. Set out on Las Zanjas Trail (also spelled Las Zonas on some signs), a wide ranch road that leads behind the mission buildings.

If you like, take the short cutoff on the right to the large cross on the hill (the trail is signed as Vista de la Cruz). A steep climb gives you wide views of the mission area and the Pacific Coast. Then continue on Las Zanjas to the park boundary, where you can loop back on El Camino Real, an old paved park road. Along the way, you'll be accompanied by cool ocean breezes, blooming buckeye trees and bush monkeyflower, and green grasslands in springtime. Be sure to take a tour of the mission before or after your hike.

User Groups: Hikers, dogs, horses, and mountain bikes. No wheelchair facilities.

Permits: No permits are required. A $6 day-use fee is charged per vehicle.

Maps: A map of La Purisima Mission State Historic Park is available at the entrance station or visitors center. For a topographic map, ask the USGS for Los Alamos.

Directions: From Buellton on US 101, take the Solvang/Lompoc/Highway 246 exit, drive west 13.2 miles, and turn right on Purisima Road. The park entrance is one mile down the road, on the right. The trailhead is at the far end of the parking lot, near the visitors center.

Contact: La Purisima Mission State Historic Park, 2295 Purisima Road, Lompoc, CA 93436, 805/733-3713, www.lapurisimamission.org.

18 GAVIOTA OVERLOOK

3.0 mi / 1.5 hr   🚶2 🏔8

in Gaviota State Park near Gaviota

Map 12.3, page 657

If you don't mind a little climbing to get a great coastal view, Gaviota Overlook Trail will suit you just fine. The trail (really a ranch road) is completely out in the open as it climbs from US 101 to the top of the ridge above Gaviota Beach, but as long as the weather is cool, it's an easy ascent. There are two main trail forks; bear left at both. Since this is coastal grasslands territory, wildflowers are prolific in springtime, but things get kind of arid-looking by late summer.

No matter; the view from the top is priceless—miles of open ocean on the one side (including the Channel Islands), and miles of grasslands and chaparral on the other side. Hey, where are all the condominiums? Just kidding. The trail ends at some microwave towers below the highest point on the ridge, but the views are just fine from where you are. The only catch on this trail is that the trailhead is darn near impossible to find, so follow directions precisely.

User Groups: Hikers, horses, and mountain bikes. No dogs. No wheelchair facilities.

Permits: No permits are required. Parking and access are free.

Maps: A map of Gaviota State Park is available for free download at www.parks.ca.gov. For topographic maps, ask the USGS for Solvang and Gaviota.

Directions: Drive south from Buellton on US 101 for 10 miles to just north of Gaviota Pass, to the blue sign that reads Rest Area 1 Mile, Tourist Information. Immediately beyond it you'll drive over a concrete bridge and must quickly turn right into the very small parking area just beyond the bridge. It's easy to miss. If you reach the rest area, you've gone past it. (Coming from Santa Barbara and points south on US 101, you must exit at Highway 1/Lompoc, then get back on the freeway heading south.)

Contact: Gaviota State Park, c/o Refugio State Beach, 10 Refugio Beach Road, Goleta, CA 93117, 805/968-1033 or 805/899-1400, www.parks.ca.gov.

19 NOJOQUI FALLS
0.5 mi / 0.5 hr

🥾1 ⛰️8

Nojoqui Falls County Park near Gaviota

Map 12.3, page 657

A favorite spot of Santa Barbarans cruising upcoast on US 101, Nojoqui Falls County Park has plenty of picnic areas, sports fields, and the like, but only one hiking trail. It's a great, short stroll from the parking area to impressive Nojoqui Falls, which drops 80 feet over a sandstone cliff that is almost completely covered with delicate Venus maidenhair ferns. The hike is good no matter how much or how little the falls are flowing—it's an easy walk through a cooling canopy of oaks and laurels, with Nojoqui Creek babbling alongside the trail. Check out the interesting rocks along the route. They're made of shale, while the waterfall cliff is made of sandstone. You'll see the difference. There's a stair-stepped rock perch right by the waterfall's pool, where you can sit in the shade of big-leaf maples and admire the scene. By the way, how do you pronounce the name of this waterfall and park? It's "no-HO-wee." Not "no-HO-kee" or, heaven forbid, "no-JOKE-ee."

User Groups: Hikers and dogs. No horses or mountain bikes. No wheelchair facilities.

Permits: No permits are required. Parking and access are free.

Maps: For a topographic map, ask the USGS for Solvang.

Directions: From Santa Barbara, drive 40 miles north on US 101 to the signed turnoff for Nojoqui Park, north of Gaviota State Beach. Drive one mile on the Old Coast Highway and turn east on Alisal Road. Drive 0.8 mile to the park entrance on your right. Drive 0.25 mile down the park access road to the parking lot and trailhead. The trail starts from the far end of the parking lot loop.

Contact: Nojoqui Falls County Park, 805/688-4217; Santa Barbara County Parks and Recreation, 300 Goodwin Road, Santa Maria, CA 93455, 805/934-6123 or 805/568-2461, www.sbparks.com.

20 GAVIOTA HOT SPRINGS
1.0 mi / 0.5 hr

🥾2 ⛰️6

in Gaviota State Park near Gaviota

Map 12.3, page 657

Gaviota State Park got smart and started charging a few bucks for people to park at this trailhead, since hot springs always draw a crowd. Still, if you show up first thing in the morning or anytime during the week, you can most likely soak all by yourself in one of the two small pools here. They're not very big or very deep or very hot either, but, hey—whaddya want for a couple bucks? The pools are a quick-to-reach destination, requiring a short but steep climb from the trailhead, mostly on a fire road. The smell of sulfur and the sway of the palm tree above the upper pool will lull you into believing you're at your own private spa. The upper pool is also the hotter of the two, nearly at bathtub temperature. If you look closely, you can see little bubbles coming up from the ground under the pool—geology in action. If you want to hike more, you can combine this trip with the trek to Gaviota Peak (see listing in this chapter).

User Groups: Hikers, horses, and mountain bikes. No dogs. No wheelchair facilities.

Permits: No permits are required. A $10 day-use fee is charged per vehicle.

Maps: A map of Gaviota State Park is available for free download at www.parks.ca.gov. For a topographic map, ask the USGS for Gaviota.

Directions: From Santa Barbara, drive north on US 101 for 35 miles, pass through the tunnel at Gaviota Pass, and take the first exit after the tunnel, which is signed as Highway 1/Lompoc/Vandenburg Air Force Base. At the stop sign, turn right and head south on the frontage road that parallels the freeway. (Don't bear left on Highway 1.) The frontage road ends in 0.25 mile at the trailhead parking area.

Contact: Gaviota State Park, c/o Refugio State Beach, 10 Refugio Beach Road, Goleta, CA 93117, 805/968-1033 or 805/899-1400, www.parks.ca.gov.

instead of taking the short spur trail to Gaviota Hot Springs, head left on Gaviota Peak Trail and begin your assault on Gaviota Hill—oops, that's Gaviota Peak, elevation 2,450 feet. The climb isn't too bad (2,000 feet in 3.2 miles), but geez, it can get hot here without much shade. The trail is a dirt road (plus a few single-track sections) that climbs a series of knolls on its way to Gaviota Peak. Technically the peak is actually in Los Padres National Forest, not in the state park. Once you're there, you'll find the views are downright awesome. What can you see? Point Conception, the Pacific, the Channel Islands, Lompoc Valley, and Gaviota Pass at your feet. Hope you picked a day when the fog wasn't visiting.

User Groups: Hikers, horses, and mountain bikes. No dogs. No wheelchair facilities.

Permits: No permits are required. A $10 day-use fee is charged per vehicle.

Maps: A map of Gaviota State Park is available for free download at www.parks.ca.gov. For a topographic map, ask the USGS for Gaviota.

Directions: Drive north from Santa Barbara on US 101 for 35 miles, pass through the tunnel at Gaviota Pass, and take the first exit after the tunnel, which is signed as Highway 1/Lompoc/Vandenburg Air Force Base. Turn right at the stop sign and head south on the frontage road that parallels the freeway. (Don't bear left on to Highway 1.) The frontage road ends in 0.25 mile at the trailhead parking area.

Contact: Gaviota State Park, c/o Refugio State Beach, 10 Refugio Beach Road, Goleta, CA 93117, 805/968-1033 or 805/899-1400, www.parks.ca.gov.

21 GAVIOTA PEAK
6.4 mi / 3.5 hr

in Gaviota State Park near Gaviota

Map 12.3, page 657

The best hike for a good workout in Gaviota State Park is the trail to Gaviota Peak. Start from the Gaviota Hot Springs trailhead, but

22 MCPHERSON PEAK TRAIL
10.0 mi / 2 days

in San Rafael Wilderness

Map 12.4, page 658

McPherson Peak, elevation 5,747 feet, is just on the edge of the spectacular San Rafael Wilderness, a land of condors and steep canyons.

Although the trail is steep and can be hot in summer, it gives hikers outstanding views of the wilderness and the desertlike lands of Cuyama to the northeast. From Aliso Park Campground, you start hiking on the dirt road that is signed for Hog Pen Spring Campground, quickly saying good-bye to the shady canyon. Reach the camp in 1.5 miles (there's a spring nearby if you need water); then pick up a trail that continues climbing, now more steeply, to Sierra Madre Road, on the wilderness boundary. Turn right on the dirt road and hike another 2.5 miles through chaparral to McPherson Peak, passing McPherson Camp along the way. The camp has a spring and is an excellent place to spend the night. You can watch the sunset from McPherson Peak and then crawl into your sleeping bag and watch the stars.

User Groups: Hikers, dogs, horses, and mountain bikes (mountain bikes may not go past the wilderness boundary). No wheelchair facilities.

Permits: A free California campfire permit is required for building a fire or using a backpacking stove; permits are available at the Santa Maria Ranger Station. Parking and access are free if you park outside the campground.

Maps: A Los Padres National Forest map is available from the U.S. Forest Service. For a topographic map, ask the USGS for Peak Mountain.

Directions: From Santa Maria on US 101, take Highway 166 east for 48 miles to just west of New Cuyama. Turn right (south) on Aliso Canyon Road and follow it for six miles to Aliso Park Campground. Park outside the campground. The dirt road can be very rough; high-clearance vehicles are recommended. If you are coming from Ventura or Ojai, take Highway 33 north to Highway 166, then go west past New Cuyama.

Contact: Los Padres National Forest, Santa Lucia Ranger District, 1616 North Carlotti Drive, Santa Maria, CA 93454, 805/925-9538, www.fs.fed.us/r5/lospadres.

23 UPPER MANZANA CREEK TRAIL
14.0 mi / 1-2 days 🏃3 ⛰8

in San Rafael Wilderness

Map 12.4, page 658

From Nira Campground, a major entry point into the San Rafael Wilderness, you can hike east or west along Manzana Creek. Hikers and backpackers can take Upper Manzana Creek Trail to the east and stop at any one of several excellent campsites, including Manzana (six miles out) and Manzana Narrows (seven miles out). Both are set near inviting swimming holes. The trail climbs gently from the campground, sometimes switchbacking away from the creek but always returning. A modicum of shade is provided by blue oaks and gray pines, mixed in among the low-lying chaparral and manzanita. Note that the creek gets low and is less attractive by midsummer, but that winter hiking can be dangerous if the water level is too high. March through May is the best time to visit.

User Groups: Hikers, dogs, and horses. No mountain bikes. No wheelchair facilities.

Permits: A free California campfire permit is required for building a fire or using a backpacking stove; permits are available at the Santa Maria Ranger Station. A national forest Adventure Pass is required for each vehicle; fees are $5 for one day or $30 for a year. Interagency access passes are also accepted.

Maps: A Los Padres National Forest map is available from the U.S. Forest Service. For a topographic map, ask the USGS for Bald Mountain.

Directions: From Santa Barbara on US 101, take Highway 154 north and drive 23 miles, past Lake Cachuma, to Armour Ranch Road. Turn right and drive 1.5 miles to Happy Canyon Road (not suitable for trailers). Turn right and drive 14 miles to Cachuma Saddle and a junction with Figueroa Mountain Road; then continue straight on Sunset Valley Road and follow it for 5.6 miles to its end at Nira Campground. Park in the hikers' parking lot.

Contact: Los Padres National Forest, Santa Lucia Ranger District, 1616 North Carlotti Drive, Santa Maria, CA 93454, 805/925-9538, www.fs.fed.us/r5/lospadres.

24 PIÑO ALTO TRAIL
0.5 mi / 0.5 hr   🏃1 ⛰8

on Figueroa Mountain in Los Padres National Forest

Map 12.4, page 658   **BEST (**

Figueroa Mountain is one of the most popular wildflower-viewing spots in all of the Central Coast, with a spectacular springtime bloom cloaking its slopes from February through April. But a trip to the mountain is a great escape at any time of year, and a good way to appreciate the uniqueness of this area is to hike the short Piño Alto Interpretive Trail. Whether or not the flower show is happening, the high views will knock your socks off. From one point on the trail, the Santa Ynez Valley is visible for some 20 miles from the northwest to the southeast. You can see Cuyama, Lake Cachuma, the Santa Ynez Mountains, and sometimes even the Channel Islands far off to sea. The trail is located at 4,600 feet in elevation, situated among ponderosa and Jeffrey pines and big cone spruce. Conifers? In Santa Barbara? That's right. The paved trail surface makes it suitable for wheelchairs. If you want wider vistas, make sure that you drive 0.5 mile uphill from the trailhead parking lot to the Figueroa lookout tower site. From there you can survey all the mountains of the San Rafael Wilderness. Note that if you like what you see on Figueroa Mountain, many longer day hikes are possible on the nearby Davy Brown/Fir Canyon Trail, starting at either Davy Brown Campground or at the trailhead on Figueroa Mountain Road.

User Groups: Hikers, wheelchairs, and dogs. No horses or mountain bikes.

Permits: No permits are required. A national forest Adventure Pass is required for each vehicle; fees are $5 for one day or $30 for a year. Interagency access passes are also accepted.

Maps: A Los Padres National Forest map is available from the U.S. Forest Service. For a topographic map, ask the USGS for Figueroa Mountain.

Directions: From Santa Barbara, drive north on US 101, through Buellton, for 45 miles to the Highway 154 East turnoff. Turn east onto Highway 154 and drive three miles to Los Olivos, then turn north (left) on Figueroa Mountain Road. Drive 13 miles to the fork for Figueroa Mountain Lookout Road (dirt). Bear left and drive two miles to the Piño Alto Picnic Area.

Contact: Los Padres National Forest, Santa Lucia Ranger District, 1616 North Carlotti Drive, Santa Maria, CA 93454, 805/925-9538, www.fs.fed.us/r5/lospadres.

25 SNYDER TRAIL
12.0 mi / 7.0 hr   🏃3 ⛰9

near the Santa Ynez Recreation Area

Map 12.4, page 658

While Snyder Trail may start out looking like a plain old fire road at its lower end at Paradise Road, by the time it climbs six miles to East Camino Cielo, it becomes a lovely single-track trail that is bordered by more wildflowers than you can count and has more wide-reaching vistas than you can imagine. Don't bother twisting your neck to catch the views on your way up, because on your return trip downhill, they will be laid out in front of you. The nice thing about the trail is that you start gaining vistas fairly quickly, so if you're tiring of the climb, you can simply find a knoll somewhere, have a seat, and pull out your sandwiches. If you decide to go all the way up, just before the top is a popular side trip to the ruins of *Knapp's Castle* (see listing in this chapter). Take the gated dirt road on the left, 5.5 miles up. If you hike the Snyder Trail's entire length, you'll be tired by the end of the day, but you'll have a whole storehouse of fine memories. One caveat: This trail is also popular with mountain bikers, usually heading in the downhill direction. Watch out for them.

User Groups: Hikers, dogs, horses, and mountain bikes. No wheelchair facilities.

Permits: No permits are required. A national forest Adventure Pass is required for each vehicle; fees are $5 for one day or $30 for a year. Interagency access passes are also accepted.

Maps: A Los Padres National Forest map is available from the U.S. Forest Service. For a topographic map, ask the USGS for San Marcos Pass.

Directions: From US 101 in Santa Barbara, take the Highway 154/State Street exit and drive north for 11.5 miles. Turn right on Paradise Road and drive 4.2 miles to the trailhead for the Snyder Trail, which is at a locked gate on the right side of the road 0.25 mile west of the Los Prietos Ranger Station.

Contact: Los Padres National Forest, Santa Barbara Ranger District, 3505 Paradise Road, Santa Barbara, CA 93105, 805/967-3481, www.fs.fed.us/r5/lospadres.

26 ALISO CANYON LOOP TRAIL

3.5 mi / 2.0 hr   👣3 ⛰8

in the Santa Ynez Recreation Area

Map 12.4, page 658

From the east end of Sage Hill Campground, you can set off on Aliso Canyon Trail and choose between a one-mile interpretive walk or a 3.5-mile loop trail. The former is the first mile of the latter and follows Aliso Creek. Be sure to bring along a trail brochure so you can learn all about how the Chumash Indians lived in this area and what plants they used and ate. In the spring, a wildflower-identification book also may be a good idea, as the variety of flowers along this short route is surprising. At the end of the interpretive trail, you can either turn around and hike back or continue on the longer loop trip. To do so, walk back a few feet to a trail junction and ascend for 0.5 mile to a meadow on a grassy plateau. From there, you climb rather steeply to the top of the ridge that divides Aliso and Oso Canyons, where there

are excellent views of the Santa Ynez Canyon and distant mountains. At the ridge top, turn right (often there is no trail sign), following the ridge's backbone. You'll loop around and soon head back downhill. Note that after winter rains, the sloping trails beyond the interpretive trail are often badly eroded. If you're walking the entire loop, wear some good boots.

User Groups: Hikers, dogs, horses, and mountain bikes. No wheelchair facilities.

Permits: No permits are required. A national forest Adventure Pass is required for each vehicle; fees are $5 for one day or $30 for a year. Interagency access passes are also accepted.

Maps: A Los Padres National Forest map is available from the U.S. Forest Service. For a topographic map, ask the USGS for San Marcos Pass.

Directions: From US 101 in Santa Barbara, take the Highway 154/State Street exit and drive north for about 11.5 miles. Turn right on Paradise Road and drive 4.5 miles to the ranger station. Turn left at the ranger station and drive one mile to Sage Hill Campground. Proceed to the day-use area at the east end of the camp and the trailhead for the Aliso Canyon Trail.

Contact: Los Padres National Forest, Santa Barbara Ranger District, 3505 Paradise Road, Santa Barbara, CA 93105, 805/967-3481, www.fs.fed.us/r5/lospadres.

27 SANTA CRUZ TRAIL

4.0 mi / 2.0 hr   👣1 ⛰8

in the Santa Ynez Recreation Area

Map 12.4, page 658

The Santa Cruz Trail is one of the most popular in the Santa Ynez Recreation Area, and it's no wonder. The hiking is easy and the swimming holes along Oso Creek are plentiful. Cooling off in the water is the number-one reason that people pay a visit to the Santa Ynez Recreation Area in summertime. The destination on this trip is Nineteen Oaks Camp, a popular picnicking spot near the base of Little Pine Mountain. The trail follows an unattractive dirt road out of

Upper Oso Campground, but it becomes lovely single-track trail as it continues into the shady canyon. The sandstone-carved creek pools are lovely to see even when the water level is low, and as you climb a bit, you get views of Little Pine Mountain. A spur trail on the right, at 1.9 miles, leads a few hundred yards to Nineteen Oaks Camp, with shady oaks and a few campsites and picnic tables. Most day hikers end their trip there before the trail begins its hot, exposed switchbacks to the top of Little Pine Mountain, elevation 4,506 feet. Be forewarned: You may see off-road motorcyclists at the trailhead, but don't let them scare you off. They'll be exiting your trail in the first mile.

User Groups: Hikers, dogs, horses, and mountain bikes. No wheelchair facilities.

Permits: No permits are required. A national forest Adventure Pass is required for each vehicle; fees are $5 for one day or $30 for a year. Interagency access passes are also accepted.

Maps: A Los Padres National Forest map is available from the U.S. Forest Service. For a topographic map, ask the USGS for San Marcos Pass.

Directions: From US 101 in Santa Barbara, take the Highway 154/State Street exit and drive north for 11.5 miles. Turn right on Paradise Road and drive 5.5 miles, past the ranger station, to the left turnoff for Upper Oso Campground. Turn left and drive one mile to the campground.

Contact: Los Padres National Forest, Santa Barbara Ranger District, 3505 Paradise Road, Santa Barbara, CA 93105, 805/967-3481, www.fs.fed.us/r5/lospadres.

28 KNAPP'S CASTLE

0.8 mi / 0.5 hr

north of Santa Barbara

Map 12.4, page 658

Some hikes are just right for all kinds of hikers, no matter what their abilities or tastes, and the trail to Knapp's Castle is one of those. The tricky part is that Knapp's Castle, or

technically just the scattering of chimneys, stonework, and archways that are the remains of Knapp's Castle, is on a chunk of private property within Los Padres National Forest, and it's only by the good graces of the landowner that the public is allowed to hike there. In 2005, the property was sold to a new owner, who since 2010 has been doing some minor construction work to preserve what is left of the "castle" ruins. As of 2011, the owner still allows hikers to visit the land, and if we all mind our manners, hopefully this beautiful spot with its impressive view of the Santa Ynez Mountains will remain open to the public for many years to come. So who was the Knapp of Knapp's Castle? George Owen Knapp was the former chairman of the board of Union Carbide, and in 1916 he built a five-bedroom sandstone mansion on this site. His mountain lodge hosted many of Knapp's rich and important friends, who were treated to after-dinner concerts by the resident organist playing the lodge's massive pipe organ. Although the building burned down in a canyon fire in 1940, its foundation still stands, and the site offers a fine spot to sit and look out over the Santa Ynez River Canyon and distant mountains. You can even see far-off Lake Cachuma. The trail to reach Knapp's Castle is a well-graded dirt road. You hike past the gate signed as Private Property Ahead, pass through another gate, stay on the dirt road, and reach the castle remains and its amazing vista in less than 0.5 mile of walking.

Special Note: Because Knapp's Castle is on private property, its accessibility to the public is subject to change at any time. Call the Santa Barbara Ranger District office for an update before visiting.

User Groups: Hikers and dogs. No horses or mountain bikes. No wheelchair facilities.

Permits: No permits are required. Parking and access are free.

Maps: A Los Padres National Forest map is available from the U.S. Forest Service. For a topographic map, ask the USGS for San Marcos Pass.

Directions: From US 101 in Santa Barbara, take the Highway 154/State Street exit and drive north for eight miles. Turn right on East Camino Cielo and drive 2.9 miles to the parking pullout on the right, across from a locked gate and dirt road on the left. The gate is signed Private Property Ahead.

Contact: Los Padres National Forest, Santa Barbara Ranger District, 3505 Paradise Road, Santa Barbara, CA 93105, 805/967-3481, www.fs.fed.us/r5/lospadres.

29 SEVEN FALLS
3.0 mi / 1.5 hr

north of Santa Barbara

Map 12.4, page 658

Seven Falls is a perfect springtime day trip in Santa Barbara, best visited between February and April. It has a little bit of everything: waterfalls, swimming holes, vistas, wildflowers, and a good trail. The trail has a lot of unsigned junctions, however, so remember to stay left at all of them until after you cross Mission Creek for the second time. From the end of Tunnel Road, start hiking on the gated continuation of the road, passing a water tank and heading uphill on pavement for 0.75 mile. After a few minutes of climbing, you'll be able to see all the way out to the ocean. Cross a bridge over Mission Creek and continue hiking straight ahead on the road, which turns to dirt. In a few hundred feet you come to a junction; a sign on your left directs you to Jesusita Trail. Follow it to the left and bear left again as the path cuts down on single-track to Mission Creek, where you'll find many good swimming holes. Cross the creek, but instead of following the continuation of the Jesusita Trail, head to your right, upstream, on a use trail. (Remember, this is the only right turn on the route.) After 0.25 mile of combined hiking and scrambling, you'll reach the first of the sandstone-carved cascades of Seven Falls. These falls flow with force only immediately after a period of rain, but the sandstone pools

and canyon walls are pretty to look at even when the creek is nearly dry.

User Groups: Hikers, dogs, horses, and mountain bikes. No wheelchair facilities.

Permits: No permits are required. Parking and access are free.

Maps: A Los Padres National Forest map is available from the U.S. Forest Service. For a topographic map, ask the USGS for Santa Barbara.

Directions: From US 101 in Santa Barbara, take the Mission Street exit and follow it east for just over a mile, crossing State Street. When Mission Street ends, turn left on Laguna Street and drive past the Santa Barbara Mission, turning right on Los Olivos, directly in front of the mission. Passing the mission, bear left on Mission Canyon Road for 0.8 mile. Turn right on Foothill Boulevard. In 0.1 mile, turn left onto the continuation of Mission Canyon Road. Then bear left on Tunnel Road and follow it for 1.1 miles until it ends. Park alongside the road, on the right.

Contact: Los Padres National Forest, Santa Barbara Ranger District, 3505 Paradise Road, Santa Barbara, CA 93105, 805/967-3481, www.fs.fed.us/r5/lospadres.

30 INSPIRATION POINT
5.0 mi / 2.5 hr

north of Santa Barbara

Map 12.4, page 658

The trail to Inspiration Point is sure to get you inspired if only because it's a great path for year-round exercise in Santa Barbara. Follow the Tunnel Road Trail to Jesusita Trail, as if you were going to Seven Falls (see listing in this chapter), but after crossing Mission Creek, keep following the main Jesusita Trail instead. Get ready for a switchbacking climb up to Inspiration Point, which is only one mile away. The tan-colored rock outcrops you see everywhere are coldwater sandstone; often you'll see hang gliders taking off from some of the highest rocks and gliding, seemingly effortlessly, overhead. When you reach Inspiration Point at 1,750 feet, you are rewarded with sweeping views of the Pacific Coast, Santa Barbara and Goleta, and the Channel Islands.

User Groups: Hikers, dogs, horses, and mountain bikes. No wheelchair facilities.

Permits: No permits are required. Parking and access are free.

Maps: A Los Padres National Forest map is available from the U.S. Forest Service. For a topographic map, ask the USGS for Santa Barbara.

Directions: From US 101 in Santa Barbara, take the Mission Street exit and follow it east for just over a mile, crossing State Street. When Mission Street ends, turn left on Laguna Street and drive past the Santa Barbara Mission, turning right on Los Olivos, directly in front of the mission. Passing the mission, bear left on Mission Canyon Road for 0.8 mile. Turn right on Foothill Boulevard. In 0.1 mile, turn left onto the continuation of Mission Canyon Road. Then bear left on Tunnel Road and follow it for 1.1 miles until it ends. Park alongside the road, on the right.

Contact: Los Padres National Forest, Santa Barbara Ranger District, 3505 Paradise Road, Santa Barbara, CA 93105, 805/967-3481, www.fs.fed.us/r5/lospadres.

31 RATTLESNAKE CANYON
5.0 mi / 2.5 hr ⛷️3 🏕️8

north of Santa Barbara

Map 12.4, page 658

Rattlesnake Canyon Trail is probably the most popular canyon trail in Santa Barbara and also one of the prettiest, despite its menacing name. The lower reaches of the trail can look like a parade, especially on weekends, but the higher you go, the fewer folks you see. The path is especially popular with people walking their dogs. Rattlesnake Canyon is a lush riparian environment around a year-round creek; a place where the plant life is so lavish that you may think you're in Mendocino or

the northern coast. The trail starts out as a wide dirt path (an old carriage road) but soon narrows to single track. It crosses rocky Rattlesnake Creek many times, tunneling through a forest of oak, bay, and sycamore trees on the lower stretch of the trail. In the spring and summer months, the wildflowers here are as good as you'll find anywhere in Santa Barbara. As you climb out of the canyon, you'll gain increasingly broad views of the Pacific Coast and Channel Islands. Watch for hang gliders soaring overhead. At an intersection with a connector trail to Tunnel Trail at 1.7 miles, bear right to finish the steep climb to Gibraltar Road. Suddenly your surroundings aren't quite so lush anymore, but the coastal views—well, on a clear day, they don't get much better than this.

User Groups: Hikers, dogs, and horses. No mountain bikes. No wheelchair facilities.

Permits: No permits are required. Parking and access are free.

Maps: A Los Padres National Forest map is available from the U.S. Forest Service. For a topographic map, ask the USGS for Santa Barbara.

Directions: From US 101 in Santa Barbara, take the Mission Street exit and follow it east for just over a mile, crossing State Street. When Mission Street ends, turn left on Laguna Street and drive past the Santa Barbara Mission, turning right on Los Olivos, directly in front of the mission. Passing the mission, bear left on Mission Canyon Road for 0.8 mile. Turn right on Foothill Boulevard. In 0.1 mile, turn left onto the continuation of Mission Canyon Road. Drive 0.4 mile and turn right on Las Conoas Road. Drive 1.2 miles and park on the right side of the road, across from the sign for Skofield Park and Rattlesnake Canyon Wilderness Area.

Contact: Los Padres National Forest, Santa Barbara Ranger District, 3505 Paradise Road, Santa Barbara, CA 93105, 805/967-3481, www.fs.fed.us/r5/lospadres.

32 MONTECITO OVERLOOK

3.0 mi / 1.5 hr

in Montecito

Map 12.4, page 658

The east fork of Cold Springs is a perfect introductory hike to the Santa Barbara front country. For people who think the mountains in Santa Barbara are all chaparral-covered slopes, this trail is an eye-opener to the lush beauty of the mountain canyons. The climb to Montecito Overlook is a good aerobic workout but not a killer and affords great views of the Santa Barbara coast and Channel Islands. Many people don't go all the way to the overlook; they just hike through the shady forest to a bench that overlooks the confluence of the east and middle forks of Cold Springs Creek and find themselves a cool pool to soak their feet. From the roadside pullout, follow the path through the alders alongside Cold Springs Creek, staying on the creek's right (east) side. After the first mile, you leave the creek and begin to switchback uphill to the overlook— really just a flat semi-clearing where the trail intersects a dirt road. Pick any spot amid the invading brush where the views are clear and wide. The best spot is a few hundred feet down the road to your right. Hikers looking for more trail to cover can continue another two miles to Montecito Peak, elevation 3,214 feet. The climb is steep and hot (no shade), but for many it's worth it. In addition to the views of the Santa Barbara coast, you can see all the way to the Santa Monica Mountains.

User Groups: Hikers, dogs, horses, and mountain bikes. No wheelchair facilities.

Permits: No permits are required. Parking and access are free.

Maps: A Los Padres National Forest map is available from the U.S. Forest Service. For a topographic map, ask the USGS for Santa Barbara.

Directions: From Santa Barbara, drive south on US 101 for four miles and exit on Hot Springs Road. Turn left on Hot Springs Road and drive 2.5 miles to Mountain Drive. Turn left and continue 1.2 miles to the Cold Springs trailhead. Park off the road, near the sharp curve where the creek runs across the road. The trail is marked by a rusty Forest Service sign.

Contact: Los Padres National Forest, Santa Barbara Ranger District, 3505 Paradise Road, Santa Barbara, CA 93105, 805/967-3481, www.fs.fed.us/r5/lospadres.

33 WEST FORK COLD SPRINGS

4.0 mi / 2.0 hr

in Montecito

Map 12.4, page 658

The West Fork Cold Springs Trail covers some diverse terrain, showing off the wide variety of landscapes that the Santa Barbara region has to offer. The trail begins by branching off the East Fork Trail and used to travel all the way uphill to Gibraltar Road, but it is now impassable in its upper sections. Still, there is much to see along the way. Start hiking on East Fork Cold Springs Trail from the rusty Forest Service sign near Mountain Drive. After a 0.5-mile stretch through a shady forest canopy alongside the creek, you'll reach a bench that overlooks the confluence of the east and middle forks of Cold Springs Creek. Cross the creek here and watch carefully for the West Fork trail sign. Soon you leave the dense, shady, fern-laden area surrounding Cold Springs Creek and climb out of the canyon into a drier and more exposed landscape. In the rainy season, look for spectacular Tangerine Falls up ahead, in the Middle Fork Canyon; the waterfall is clearly visible, although distant, from the West Fork Trail. (A use trail cuts off from the main trail to reach it, but it requires good scrambling abilities and a near-immunity to poison oak.) Whether you remain on the West Fork Trail until it becomes impassable or take the cutoff for Tangerine Falls, you'll climb high enough to gain great views of the valley below and the Montecito coast. On your return trip, exercise some caution—the West Fork Trail is not as well used as the East Fork Trail, and it's steep and eroded in places, especially when wet. But that's a small price to pay for beauty along this trail and the relative solitude available here, compared to the more popular East Fork Trail.

User Groups: Hikers, dogs, horses, and mountain bikes. No wheelchair facilities.

Permits: No permits are required. Parking and access are free.

Maps: A Los Padres National Forest map is available from the U.S. Forest Service. For a topographic map, ask the USGS for Santa Barbara.

Directions: From Santa Barbara, drive south on US 101 for four miles and exit on Hot Springs Road. Turn left on Hot Springs Road and drive 2.5 miles to Mountain Drive. Turn left and continue 1.2 miles to the Cold Springs trailhead. Park off the road, near the sharp curve where the creek crosses the road.

Contact: Los Padres National Forest, Santa Barbara Ranger District, 3505 Paradise Road, Santa Barbara, CA 93105, 805/967-3481, www.fs.fed.us/r5/lospadres.

34 SAN YSIDRO TRAIL
8.0 mi / 4.5 hr   🏃3 ⛰9

in Montecito

Map 12.4, page 658

If you like running water, San Ysidro Canyon is your chance at seeing some, even long after the last rain. Other streams in the Santa Barbara area are often nearly dry by May, but San Ysidro keeps on flowing year-round. The trail up its canyon offers many possible destinations and stopping points; few hike all the way to its terminus, at East Camino Cielo—it's four miles one-way with a 3,000-foot elevation gain. The rewards are great no matter how far you go, beginning with swimming holes and waterfalls in the first two miles of trail, mostly under the shade of oaks and sycamores. After a rocky section, you climb out of the

canyon into chaparral country, entering into a series of steep, exposed switchbacks. Most people give up somewhere along this stretch, but those who continue come out near Cold Spring Saddle on East Camino Cielo, elevation 3,480 feet. From there, you'll feel on top of the world.

User Groups: Hikers, dogs, horses, and mountain bikes. No wheelchair facilities.

Permits: No permits are required. Parking and access are free.

Maps: A Los Padres National Forest map is available from the U.S. Forest Service. For a topographic map, ask the USGS for Carpinteria.

Directions: From US 101 in Montecito, take the San Ysidro Road exit and head east for one mile to East Valley Road/Highway 192. Turn right on East Valley Road/Highway 192 and travel 0.9 mile. Turn left on Park Lane and drive 0.4 mile; then bear left on East Mountain Drive and drive 0.25 mile to the end of the road. Park alongside the road and walk to the trailhead, on the right.

Contact: Los Padres National Forest, Santa Barbara Ranger District, 3505 Paradise Road, Santa Barbara, CA 93105, 805/967-3481, www.fs.fed.us/r5/lospadres.

35 MCMENEMY TRAIL
2.5 mi / 1.0 hr   🏃2 ⛰8

in Montecito

Map 12.4, page 658

If you only have time for a short hike, this lovely trip in San Ysidro Canyon includes a stint on McMenemy Trail, an old favorite of many Santa Barbara hikers. It has just enough of a climb to make you feel that you did your workout for the day but enough pretty views to make you forget that hiking is actually exercise. Begin your trip on the San Ysidro Trail (see listing in this chapter), but bear left at the sign for McMenemy Trail, 0.5 mile in. Unfortunately, this part of the trail is routed through a construction site on private property near the

San Ysidro Ranch and has looked unsightly for the last few years. Until the situation improves, just endure it, because soon, a series of switchbacks brings you to the Colonel's stone bench—Colonel McMenemy, that is—where you have a fine view down into Montecito and out to the coast. It's a good place to catch your breath, read a book, or have a picnic. A horse hitch is available, just in case you brought Mr. Ed along. If you want to keep hiking, you can make a five-mile loop by continuing on the McMenemy Trail to the Saddle Rock Trail. Turn right, then right again on the Edison Catwalk to return to the San Ysidro Trail.

User Groups: Hikers, dogs, horses, and mountain bikes. No wheelchair facilities.

Permits: No permits are required. Parking and access are free.

Maps: A Los Padres National Forest map is available from the U.S. Forest Service. For a topographic map, ask the USGS for Carpinteria.

Directions: From US 101 in Montecito, take the San Ysidro Road exit and head east for one mile to East Valley Road/Highway 192. Turn right on East Valley Road/Highway 192 and travel 0.9 mile. Turn left on Park Lane and drive 0.4 mile; then bear left on East Mountain Drive and drive 0.25 mile to the end of the road. Park alongside the road and walk to the trailhead, on the right.

Contact: Los Padres National Forest, Santa Barbara Ranger District, 3505 Paradise Road, Santa Barbara, CA 93105, 805/967-3481, www.fs.fed.us/r5/lospadres.

36 VINCENT TUMAMAIT TRAIL

8.6 mi / 4.0 hr   🏃3   ⛰9

in the Chumash Wilderness west of Frazier Park

Map 12.4, page 658

A day hike in the Chumash Wilderness means the possibility of seeing a magnificent condor fly overhead, as well as a visit to Mount Pinos (8,831 feet), the highest point in Los Padres National Forest. This is conifer country, with the peak covered in snow a good part of the year, to the great delight of Southern California cross-country skiers. The Vincent Tumamait Trail begins on the summit of Mount Pinos and runs five miles to Mount Abel, elevation 8,286 feet (also called Mount Cerro Noroeste). If you wish, you can leave a car at Mount Abel and take a one-way shuttle trip between the two impressive peaks. The closest you can park to the summit of Mount Pinos is 1.8 miles away at the Chula Vista parking area; the summit road has been closed for several years to protect sacred Chumash Indian sites. Instead, you hike 1.8 miles to the summit, gaining only about 600 feet, check out the far-reaching views, then set off on Vincent Tumamait Trail. Head out two miles, downhill at first and then up Sawmill Mountain to the North Fork Trail junction. Bear left at the junction and walk 0.5 mile to primitive Sheep Camp, a sweet spot in the shade of fir and pine trees, where you can open up your day pack and have lunch. After a rest, you'll be all fueled up for the uphill return trip to the summit, and then the final 1.8-mile descent to your car. As you hike, keep scanning the skies for those giant condors, many of which nest in the nearby condor sanctuary. So who was Vincent Tumamait? He was a Chumash elder and a beloved storyteller who lived from 1919 to 1992.

User Groups: Hikers, dogs, and horses. No mountain bikes. No wheelchair facilities.

Permits: No permits are required. Parking and access are free.

Maps: A Los Padres National Forest map is available from the U.S. Forest Service. For a topographic map, ask the USGS for Sawmill Mountain.

Directions: From I-5 near Lebec, take the Frazier Park/Mount Pinos exit and turn west. Drive 12 miles on Frazier Mountain Park Road, which will become Cuddy Valley Road. At 12 miles, bear left on Mount Pinos Highway and drive 10 miles to the Chula

Vista parking lot (Mount Pinos Recreation Area). Begin hiking on the dirt road to Mount Pinos Summit (the gated dirt road on the west side).

Contact: Los Padres National Forest, Mount Pinos Ranger District, 34580 Lockwood Valley Road, Frazier Park, CA 93225, 661/245-3731, www.fs.fed.us/r5/lospadres.

37 POTRERO JOHN
3.2 mi or 5.4 mi / 1.5 hr or 3.0 hr
🏃1 ⛰8

in the Sespe Wilderness north of Ojai

Map 12.4, page 658

There's nothing nicer than a trail that follows a stream, especially in a place as notoriously dry as Ojai. The Potrero John Trail follows Potrero John Creek to Potrero John Camp, set at 4,140 feet in elevation. The creek has water most of the year but frequently dries up in the summer, so visit here in winter or spring if possible. From the roadside trailhead, the trail starts out with a brief steep pitch, but it quickly levels off. The trail travels along the bottom of a narrow canyon, with conifers growing precariously on the steep canyon walls. It follows the canyon floor for 1.5 miles, then crosses the creek on a bridge and enters primitive Potrero Camp, which consists of a rock-lined fire pit and rusty metal barbecue, plus some stone and log benches. You have a fair chance of having this spot all to yourself because the maintained trail ends just beyond the camp. In the wet season, though, intrepid visitors keep on hiking, because they want to see Potrero John Falls, which is 1.2 miles farther upstream. Depending on how much it has rained in the weeks before your visit, the going can be very difficult or very easy, and your feet can get completely soaked or not wet at all. There's no real trail, but just stay along the creek and you'll get there eventually. Plan at least an hour to traverse the 1.2 miles from the campground to the falls—maybe double that if the water is high and the rocks

slippery. When you reach the waterfall, you'll know why you went to the effort: Potrero John's 70-foot-high drop is a stunner. This sparkling freefall is one of the best waterfalls in Los Padres National Forest.

User Groups: Hikers, dogs, and horses. No mountain bikes. No wheelchair facilities.

Permits: No day-hiking permits are required. Parking and access are free.

Maps: A Los Padres National Forest map is available from the U.S. Forest Service. A map of the Sespe Wilderness is available from Tom Harrison Maps. For a topographic map, ask the USGS for Lion Canyon.

Directions: From Ojai, drive north on Highway 33 for 21 miles to where Potrero John Creek crosses the highway. The trailhead is signed on the right (north) side of the road.

Contact: Los Padres National Forest, Ojai Ranger District, 1190 East Ojai Avenue, Ojai, CA 93023, 805/646-4348, www.fs.fed.us/r5/lospadres.

38 CEDAR CREEK AND THE FISHBOWLS
11.8 mi / 6.0 hr or 2 days
🏃3 ⛰9

in the Sespe Wilderness northeast of Ojai

Map 12.4, page 658   **BEST ☾**

Despite the length of this trail and the fact that the area has been badly burned by wildfires in recent years, the Fishbowls along Piru Creek remain a popular spot, mostly because there is little that is finer in life than a creek with good swimming holes. That and the fact that the trail has a moderate elevation gain, so even with the nearly 12-mile round-trip, it is a manageable day hike for most people. The Cedar Creek Trail starts at the trailhead a mile from Thorn Meadows Campground (elevation 5,050 feet) and follows the south fork of Piru Creek much of the way. What starts out as a wide dirt road eventually narrows to a single-track trail. At 3.5 miles, bear right on the Fishbowls Trail, hike along a ridgeline that offers big views of the partly burned forest below, then descend to Fishbowls Camp. Walk upstream from the camp for about 300 yards to reach the Fishbowls, a series of rounded sandstone pools on Piru Creek.

User Groups: Hikers, dogs, and horses. No mountain bikes. No wheelchair facilities.

Permits: A free California campfire permit is required for building a fire or using a backpacking stove; permits are available at any Southern California Forest Service ranger station. Parking and access are free.

Maps: A Los Padres National Forest map is available from the U.S. Forest Service. A map of the Sespe Wilderness is available from Tom Harrison Maps. For a topographic map, ask the USGS for Lockwood Valley.

Directions: From Ojai, drive 40 miles north on Highway 33 and turn right on Lockwood Valley Road. Drive approximately 15 miles and turn right on Mutau Road. Drive 7.5 miles and turn right on Thorn Meadows Road. Drive 0.5 mile to the Cedar Creek trailhead. Or, from I-5, take the Frazier Mountain Road exit. Drive six miles and turn left on Lockwood Valley Road. Drive approximately 10 miles and turn right on Mutau Road. Drive 7.5 miles and turn right on Thorn Meadows Road. Drive 0.5 mile to the Cedar Creek trailhead, one mile north of Thorn Meadows Campground.

Contact: Los Padres National Forest, Mount Pinos Ranger District, 34580 Lockwood Valley Road, Frazier Park, CA 93225, 661/245-3731, www.fs.fed.us/r5/lospadres.

39 SESPE HOT SPRINGS
16.0 mi / 8.0 hr or 2 days 🥾3 ⛰9

in the Sespe Wilderness northeast of Ojai

Map 12.4, page 658

Sespe Hot Springs have the hottest natural mineral water in Southern California, reaching temperatures as hot as 210°F. This year-round spring heats several pools downstream on Sespe Creek to a temperature warm enough for bathing. While this sounds like an ideal year-round

destination, don't even think about making a summer trip. The air temperature here is often close to 100°F, and there is no vegetation around the springs. In fact, it looks something like the surface of the moon. Still, in fall, winter, or spring, the hot springs are a wonderful spot. Hike in 1.5 miles on the main wilderness trail to a fork where Little Mutau Creek Trail goes left and Johnson Ridge Trail goes right. Bear right and follow Johnson Ridge Trail, which years ago was open to motorcycle use but is now part of the Sespe Wilderness. It drops steeply to Sespe Creek over the next 6.2 miles, with almost no shade along the route. You'll lose 2,500 feet along the way. A final left spur leads you a half mile to the hot springs; you'll probably smell the sulphur before you see the pools. You've now hiked about eight miles, so if you head back out you'll have a 16-mile day. To spend the night, you must hike another mile south from the springs to Sespe Camp. The nearest water is another half mile away in Sespe Creek; carry plenty with you as a backup.

User Groups: Hikers, dogs, and horses. No mountain bikes. No wheelchair facilities.

Permits: A free California campfire permit is required for building a fire or using a backpacking stove; permits are available at any Southern California Forest Service ranger station. Parking and access are free.

Maps: A Los Padres National Forest map is available from the U.S. Forest Service. A map of the Sespe Wilderness is available from Tom Harrison Maps. For a topographic map, ask the USGS for Lockwood Valley.

Directions: From Ojai, drive 40 miles north on Highway 33 and turn right on Lockwood Valley Road. Drive approximately 15 miles and turn right on Mutau Road. Follow Mutau Road to its end (about 10 miles), at the Mutau Flat trailhead.

Or, from I-5, take the Frazier Mountain Road exit. Drive six miles and turn left on Lockwood Valley Road. Drive approximately 10 miles and turn right on Mutau Road. Follow Mutau Road to its end (about 10 miles), at the Mutau Flat trailhead.

Contact: Los Padres National Forest, Mount Pinos Ranger District, 34580 Lockwood Valley Road, Frazier Park, CA 93225, 661/245-3731, www.fs.fed.us/r5/lospadres.

40 PIEDRA BLANCA
4.0 mi / 2.0 hr　　🥾2 ⛰9

in the Rose Valley Recreation Area
north of Ojai

Map 12.4, page 658

Sandstone lovers, this is your spot. Piedra Blanca is a series of huge, rounded sandstone boulders that are somewhat otherworldly looking. If rocks can look sensual, these are. They're set in the Rose Valley Recreation Area, just a short stretch away from Sespe Creek, in what looks a lot like the desert—plenty of sand, desert scrub, and rocks. Start from the Piedra Blanca Trailhead. In the first 0.5 mile you will cross Lion Creek and two branches of the Sespe River. At the junction, turn left and follow the signs. The rocks of Piedra Blanca are clearly visible, so it's easy to see where you're going. Although the trail continues down the back side of the boulders and beyond, most people just climb to the top of the rocks, then spend some time wandering around and exploring. As you might guess, this is a first-class spot for watching sunsets.

User Groups: Hikers, dogs, and horses. No mountain bikes. No wheelchair facilities.

Permits: No permits are required. A national forest Adventure Pass is required for each vehicle; fees are $5 for one day or $30 for a year. Interagency access passes are also accepted.

Maps: A Los Padres National Forest map is available from the U.S. Forest Service. For a topographic map, ask the USGS for Lion Canyon.

Directions: From Ojai, drive north on Highway 33 for 15 miles to Sespe Road/Rose Valley Road and the sign for Rose Valley Recreation Area. Turn right and drive 6.5 miles to the Piedra Blanca Trailhead.

Contact: Los Padres National Forest, Ojai Ranger District, 1190 East Ojai Avenue, Ojai, CA 93023, 805/646-4348, www.fs.fed.us/r5/lospadres.

41 SESPE RIVER TRAIL TO BEAR CREEK CAMP
9.0 mi / 1-2 days　　🥾3 ⛰9

in the Sespe Wilderness north of Ojai

Map 12.4, page 658

The Sespe River Trail is an easy way to access the Sespe Wilderness, on a mostly level trail that follows the river. A typical destination on this trail is Bear Creek Camp, at 4.5 miles out, but you could hike as much as 27 miles one way to the Dough Flat trailhead outside of Fillmore. Start your trip at the Piedra Blanca Trailhead. In the first half mile, you will cross Lion Creek and two branches of the Sespe River. At a junction, turn right and follow the riverbed, hiking downstream on another old road, which was once a four-wheel-drive route to the Sespe Hot Springs. If you're lucky, you'll visit when the creek level is high enough so that there are plenty of deep pools accessible for swimming. In good years, almost every bend in the river offers a tempting pool, but by late summer, the stream can drop to a trickle. Dispersed camping spots are plentiful along this trail. By the way, this is called the Sespe River Trail, but on maps, the "river" is called "creek." Generally it looks much more like the latter than the former.

User Groups: Hikers, dogs, and horses. No mountain bikes. No wheelchair facilities.

Permits: A free California campfire permit is required for building a fire or using a backpacking stove; permits are available at any California Forest Service ranger station. A national forest Adventure Pass is required for each vehicle; fees are $5 for one day or $30 for a year. Interagency access passes are also accepted.

Maps: A Los Padres National Forest map is available from the U.S. Forest Service. A map of the Sespe Wilderness is available from Tom

Harrison Maps. For a topographic map, ask the USGS for Lion Canyon.

Directions: From Ojai, drive north on Highway 33 for 15 miles to Sespe Road/Rose Valley Road and the sign for Rose Valley Recreation Area. Turn right and drive 6.5 miles to the Piedra Blanca Trailhead.

Contact: Los Padres National Forest, Ojai Ranger District, 1190 East Ojai Avenue, Ojai, CA 93023, 805/646-4348, www.fs.fed.us/r5/lospadres.

42 ROSE VALLEY FALLS
0.8 mi / 0.5 hr   👫1 ⛰9

in the Rose Valley Recreation Area north of Ojai

Map 12.4, page 658

The trip to Rose Valley Falls is an easy walk in the woods to the base of a stunning and unusual sandstone waterfall. If you're making the drive to Rose Valley Recreation Area to camp, fish, or hike, a side trip to Rose Valley Falls is just about mandatory. Start hiking on the signed trail in Rose Valley Campground. The path is bordered on both sides by oaks and fragrant bays, and it parallels Rose Creek. Cross the creek a few times, and as you walk into the canyon, keep looking ahead (up high) for your first glimpse of the 300-foot waterfall. If it has rained lately, you'll see it for sure. In 15 minutes you reach the base of the waterfall, which is glaringly different in appearance from the falls you were just looking at. That's because this is the bottom tier of huge Rose Valley Falls, and you were seeing the upper tier. The lower tier is layered with limestone and sandstone slabs and oozing with wet moss. You can't resist touching it. Some daredevils attempt to climb up and over this lower tier to see more of the upper part of the waterfall, but this should only be attempted by experts with proper climbing equipment.

User Groups: Hikers, dogs, horses, and mountain bikes. No wheelchair facilities.

Permits: No permits are required. A national

forest Adventure Pass is required for each vehicle; fees are $5 for one day or $30 for a year. Interagency access passes are also accepted.

Maps: A Los Padres National Forest map is available from the U.S. Forest Service. For a topographic map, ask the USGS for Lion Canyon.

Directions: From Ojai, drive north on Highway 33 for 15 miles to Sespe Road/Rose Valley Road and the sign for Rose Valley Recreation Area. Turn right, drive three miles, then turn right again on Chief Peak Road, at the sign for Rose Valley Camp. Drive 0.6 mile to the campground. The trail leads from the far end of the camp.

Contact: Los Padres National Forest, Ojai Ranger District, 1190 East Ojai Avenue, Ojai, CA 93023, 805/646-4348, www.fs.fed.us/r5/lospadres.

43 NORDHOFF PEAK
13.8 mi / 7.0 hr   👫4 ⛰9

east of Ojai

Map 12.4, page 658

The hike to Nordhoff Peak is a rite of passage for Ojai hikers. After all, journalist Charles Nordhoff was the guy who made Ojai famous. In the late 19th century, he wrote various magazine articles about Ojai Valley's many charms, which encouraged people to move here, carrying with them the dream of a new life. Nordhoff's summit is at 4,425 feet—high enough to get an occasional few inches of snow—and a hike to the top is a fine way to spend an early spring day in Ojai. That's if you're up to the challenge of the 6.9-mile, 3,300-foot climb, of course. Forget hiking in the heat of summer; much of the trail is on dusty, open fire roads, with no shade. From the Gridley trailhead, hike up to Gridley Fire Road and turn right, passing by seemingly endless avocado groves. Continuing straight ahead, you'll enter a shadier canyon and pass the primitive camp at Gridley Spring. This is almost the halfway point (2.7 miles); take a breather. Prepare yourself for the next three miles—the steepest on the trip—then begin switchbacking your way up to Nordhoff Fire Road, where you turn left and hike one more mile to the peak. If you think that after all this climbing you ought to get some good views, you won't be disappointed. The last mile of trail offers excellent vistas, and when you reach the old Nordhoff Fire Lookout Tower, you can see all the way to the Pacific Ocean and Channel Islands, Ojai Valley and Lake Casitas closer in, and miles of Los Padres National Forest and its wilderness areas.

User Groups: Hikers, dogs, horses, and mountain bikes. No wheelchair facilities.

Permits: No permits are required. Parking and access are free.

Maps: A Los Padres National Forest map is available from the U.S. Forest Service. For a topographic map, ask the USGS for Ojai.

Directions: From Ojai at the intersection of Highways 150 and 33, drive east on Highway 150 for two miles and turn left on Gridley Road, 0.25 mile past the ranger station. Drive 1.5 miles north on Gridley Road until it dead-ends. The trailhead is on the north side of the road.

Contact: Los Padres National Forest, Ojai Ranger District, 1190 East Ojai Avenue, Ojai, CA 93023, 805/646-4348, www.fs.fed.us/r5/lospadres.

44 SANTA PAULA CANYON TO BIG CONE CAMP

6.8 mi / 3.5 hr or 2 days   2   ▲8

east of Ojai in Los Padres National Forest

Map 12.4, page 658   **BEST (**

What starts out rather pedestrian soon gets much more interesting on the Santa Paula Canyon Trail. The first 1.3 miles of the route are mostly on pavement, meandering around the grounds of Thomas Aquinas College and a private ranch and oil-drilling operation. If you haven't hiked here in a few years, you'll be surprised to find that the old trail, which used

to begin at the edge of this private property, was completely washed out in the floods of 2005, and then washed out again in another flood in 2009. But you can still hike in Santa Paula Canyon by following the posted signs up the riverbed. The new route is similar to the direction of the former trail. The forest is green and dense here and the spring wildflowers are sublime, but the canyon's main attractions are a narrow gorge and beautiful waterfalls that cascade into deep pools of water. Not surprisingly, this trail receives heavy use on weekends, so we highly recommend that you hike it on a weekday. Also, be very careful when hiking here due to the many steep dropoffs and high cliffs. At 3.4 miles, the route passes Big Cone Camp, which has a few campsites set in a shady grove of big-cone Douglas firs. The trail leads a short distance from the camp steeply down to the main and east forks of Santa Paula Creek, where waterfalls and swimming holes await. Since this camp is heavily used, if you want to spend the night in peace, consider traveling less than a mile farther up the trail to Cross Camp. Just beyond the camp, the stream enters a canyon highlighted by a waterfall called the Punchbowl. The only disappointment in this lovely canyon is that many of its rocks and boulders have been defiled with ugly graffiti. The Forest Service has made efforts to remove the taggings, but those who can't appreciate this wilderness keep coming back and doing it again.

User Groups: Hikers and dogs. No horses or mountain bikes. No wheelchair facilities.

Permits: A free California campfire permit is required for building a fire or using a backpacking stove; permits are available at the Ojai Ranger Station. Parking and access are free.

Maps: A Los Padres National Forest map is available from the U.S. Forest Service. For a topographic map, ask the USGS for Santa Paula Peak.

Directions: From Ojai at the junction of Highways 33 and 150, drive east on Highway 150 for 11.5 miles to Thomas Aquinas College on the left (look for iron gates and stone buildings). Drive 100 yards farther to the parking pullout on the right side of the road, just beyond the highway bridge over Santa Paula Creek. Park there and walk back across the bridge to the paved road on the right side of the college.

Contact: Los Padres National Forest, Ojai Ranger District, 1190 East Ojai Avenue, Ojai, CA 93023, 805/646-4348, www.fs.fed.us/r5/lospadres.

45 MCGRATH STATE BEACH NATURE TRAIL

0.5 mi / 0.5 hr   🏃1 ⛰️7

in McGrath State Beach in Oxnard

Map 12.4, page 658   **BEST (**

There's a great little nature trail at McGrath State Beach that offers a far different hike from a walk along the sandy public beach. The trail runs along the Santa Clara Estuary, which is designated as a natural preserve. It's the place where the Santa Clara River joins the Pacific Ocean. In that meeting place, freshwater and saltwater plants and animals intermingle, which means you have the chance to see migrating birds, resident shorebirds, and fish swimming in the estuary. The problem is that this meeting place is in constant flux, especially during the stormy months of winter. Some years this trail gets completely washed out, or buried in driftwood, or overgrown. As a general rule, you can count on more of the trail existing in the summer months. The path starts out in a shaded willow thicket, a secluded and peaceful change from the hustle and bustle of the beach campground. Watch for the endangered California least tern or Belding's savannah sparrow. When you reach the beach, you can continue hiking along the shoreline, or turn around and head back.

User Groups: Hikers only. No dogs, horses, or mountain bikes. A short stretch of this trail is wheelchair-accessible.

Permits: No permits are required. A $10 day-use fee is charged per vehicle.

Maps: For a topographic map, ask the USGS for Ventura.

Directions: From US 101 in Ventura, take the Seaward Avenue exit to Harbor Boulevard. Turn south on Harbor Boulevard and drive four miles to the park entrance. The nature trail begins at the day-use parking lot, a quick right turn after the entrance kiosk. (If you are traveling north on US 101, you must take the Victoria Avenue exit to reach Harbor Boulevard.)

Contact: McGrath State Beach, 901 S. San Pedro, Ventura, CA 93001, 805/654-4744, www.parks.ca.gov.

46 LA JOLLA VALLEY LOOP

5.5 mi / 3.0 hr or 2 days   🏃2 ⛰️9

in Point Mugu State Park south of Oxnard

Map 12.4, page 658

We rate Point Mugu State Park as the best of all the parks in the Santa Monica Mountains, partly because of its more remote northern location, partly because of its proximity to the ocean, and partly because of its fine hiking trails. One of the best of the latter is this loop trip starting in La Jolla Canyon, which can be an excellent day hike or an easy two-day backpacking trip with an overnight at La Jolla Valley walk-in camp. Follow the La Jolla Canyon Trail from the Ray Miller trailhead (that's the wide dirt trail on the left, not the single-track trail on the right) gently uphill. You hike through an open valley that is continually freshened by ocean breezes blowing up the canyon. Pass a small seasonal waterfall that is bracketed on both sides by canyon walls covered in bright yellow coreopsis, then climb into a rocky area, where hidden among the chaparral are rock caves that were once used by Native Americans. Go right at the first fork 1.2 miles in (going left will be the return of your loop), and left at a second fork signed for La Jolla Valley walk-in camp. Situated in a high meadow of native grasses, the camp is 0.4 mile beyond a cattail-bordered pond. From the camp, bear left on the dirt road that runs just north of it, which soon narrows to double track. Continue on La Jolla Valley Loop Trail and circle around, through more native grasses, back to La Jolla Canyon Trail. Turn right on La Jolla Canyon Trail to head down the canyon to your car. This trip is outstanding in winter or spring, when the hillside grasses are green and the wildflowers bloom. If you like, you can make this loop longer by detouring around Mugu Peak on Chumash Trail and Mugu Peak Trail, which will add 1.5 more miles to your round-trip.

User Groups: Hikers and horses. No dogs or mountain bikes. No wheelchair facilities.

Permits: No day-hiking permits are necessary. Backpacking campsites are available on a first-come, first-served basis; backpackers must register at Thornhill-Broome Campground ($7 fee per person per night). An $8 day-use fee is charged per vehicle at the Ray Miller trailhead.

Maps: A trail map is available from any park ranger station, or by free download at www.parks.ca.gov. A map of Point Mugu State Park is available from Tom Harrison Maps. For a topographic map, ask the USGS for Point Mugu.

Directions: From US 101 in Agoura Hills, exit at Kanan Road and drive 12.5 miles to Highway 1/Pacific Coast Highway on the Malibu coast. Turn west (right) and drive 14.8 miles to the La Jolla Canyon trailhead parking area on the right, one mile west of Big Sycamore Canyon Campground.

Alternatively, from Highway 1/Pacific Coast Highway in Malibu, drive west on Highway 1 for 22 miles to the La Jolla Canyon trailhead parking area, on the right.

Contact: Point Mugu State Park, 9000 Pacific Coast Highway, Malibu, CA 90265, 805/488-5223 or 805/488-1827; California State Parks, Angeles District, 1925 Las Virgenes Road, Calabasas, CA 91302, 818/880-0363, www.parks.ca.gov.

47 BIG SYCAMORE CANYON LOOP

9.2 mi / 5.5 hr   🥾 2   ⛰ 9

in Point Mugu State Park south of Oxnard

Map 12.4, page 658

If you don't mind hiking on fire roads and maybe sharing the trail with mountain bikers and horses, this loop trip in Point Mugu State Park offers a shady stroll in a sycamore-lined canyon, followed by miles and miles of unforgettable coastal views. Start from the gate at the far end of the campground and follow the Big Sycamore Canyon Trail as it climbs very gently uphill, paralleling the creek. The sycamore trees here are large and old, and from October to February, you may spot monarch butterflies that cluster among them for the winter. You'll cross Big Sycamore Creek a half dozen times before the 2.9-mile mark, where you'll turn left on the Wood Canyon Vista Trail (also signed as the Backbone Trail). This trail gently ascends about 750 feet over its 1.8-mile distance, topping out at Overlook Fire Road. Turn left here for a long, rambling walk back to the trailhead. Overlook Fire Road divides Point Mugu's two canyons, Big Sycamore and La Jolla, and is a ridge-top route that offers nonstop views of the coastline to the west and the canyons on either side of you. On a clear day, it's glorious.

Note: When you near the end of the trail, you can take the single-track Scenic Trail to return to the trailhead. It shaves off a little distance, and it's more interesting than the final stretch of the fire road.

User Groups: Hikers and mountain bikes. No dogs or horses. No wheelchair facilities.

Permits: No permits are required. A $12 day-use fee is charged per vehicle.

Maps: A trail map is available from any park ranger station, or by free download at www.parks.ca.gov. A map of Point Mugu State Park is available from Tom Harrison Maps. For a topographic map, ask the USGS for Point Mugu.

Directions: From US 101 in Agoura Hills, exit at Kanan Road and drive 12.5 miles to

Highway 1/Pacific Coast Highway on the Malibu coast. Turn west (right) and drive 13.8 miles to Big Sycamore Canyon Campground at Point Mugu State Park. Park to the left of the entrance kiosk in the day-use lot, then walk to the far end of the campground to access the trailhead.

Alternatively, from Highway 1 in Malibu, drive west on Highway 1 for 21 miles to Sycamore Canyon Campground, on the right.

Contact: Point Mugu State Park, 9000 Pacific Coast Highway, Malibu, CA 90265, 805/488-5223 or 805/488-1827; California State Parks, Angeles District, 1925 Las Virgenes Road, Calabasas, CA 91302, 818/880-0363, www.parks.ca.gov.

48 CALICHE FOREST AND POINT BENNETT
15.0 mi / 2 days

on San Miguel Island in Channel Islands National Park

Channel Islands Detail Map, page 659

After finding out there's an easy way and a hard way to do something, some people immediately choose the hard way. If you're in that camp, you'll choose San Miguel Island as the Channel Island you want to visit, instead of Anacapa, Santa Cruz, or any of the other islands. San Miguel Island is 58 miles from Ventura Harbor and getting there requires a 3.5–4-hour boat ride. Given that, once you finally get to San Miguel, you'll probably want to stay for a couple days. To add to the challenge, strong winds and fog are nearly constant on the island, so you must plan accordingly for both hiking and camping. Of course, if you're willing, your reward is having a spectacular island practically all to yourself. No more than 30 campers are allowed on San Miguel Island at one time, and only rarely will that many people show up at once.

From Cuyler Harbor, where a skiff drops you off, you hike eastward along the beach for 0.5 mile, then follow the path another 0.5 mile over a large sand dune, then up Nidever Canyon. It's a steep stretch, especially if you're carrying a lot of camping gear. When you reach the ridge at the top, you can take a short spur to see a stone monument to Juan Rodriguez Cabrillo, who claimed this island for the Spaniards in 1542, and who may or may not be buried here—nobody's sure. The trail continues to the campground, and then to the remains of the Lester Ranch. The Lester family lived on the island for 12 years and grazed sheep here.

Outside of the Cuyler Harbor/Lester Ranch area, you may hike only in the company of a ranger, in order to protect the island's fragile resources. If you do so, you'll find that the most noticeable wildlife on and around San Miguel Island are pinnipeds—seals and sea lions. Up to five different species and more than 30,000 individuals can be seen at certain times of the year at Point Bennett, a 14-mile round-trip hike from the campground. If you take this hike, plan for a long day and bring lots of water with you. An interesting feature along the way is the Caliche Forest, where the calcium-carbonate sand castings of dead plant roots and trunks stand like frozen statues. They're a bit like the tufa spires at Mono Lake. Seeing the Caliche Forest requires only a seven-mile round-trip.

Special Note: For those who do not wish to camp, the boat concessionaires offer occasional single-day trips to San Miguel Island. Such trips typically include a guided day hike to the Caliche Forest with a naturalist or ranger.

User Groups: Hikers only. No dogs, horses, or mountain bikes. No wheelchair facilities.

Permits: A camping permit is required (877/444-6777 or www.recreation.gov). The camping fee is $15 per night. A fee is charged for boat transportation to the island. As of 2011, the fare is $140 per adult for an overnight camping trip or $100 per adult for a day trip.

Maps: A free map of Channel Islands National Park is available by download at www.nps.gov/chis. A more detailed map is available for a fee from Trails Illustrated. For topographic maps, ask the USGS for San Miguel Island East and San Miguel Island West.

Directions: Island Packers provides boat transportation to San Miguel Island from Ventura Harbor. Truth Aquatics provides boat transportation to San Miguel Island from Santa Barbara Harbor. Reservations are required and should be obtained before you get your camping permit.

Contact: Channel Islands National Park, 1901 Spinnaker Drive, Ventura, CA 93001, 805/658-5700 or 805/658-5730, www.nps.gov/chis. Camping permits: 877/444-6777 or www.recreation.gov. Boat trips: Island Packers, 805/642-7688 or 805/642-1393, www.island-packers.com and Truth Aquatics, 805/963-3564, www.truthaquatics.com.

49 TORREY PINES TRAIL
5.0 mi / 2.5 hr   🥾2 ⛰8

on Santa Rosa Island in Channel Islands National Park

Channel Islands Detail Map, page 659

One of the many charms of Santa Rosa Island is that you can fly there in about 20 minutes in a small plane instead of taking a three-hour boat ride from Ventura or Santa Barbara harbors, both of which are about 40 miles away. The National Park Service has allowed one airplane concessionaire, Channel Islands Aviation, permission to take passengers to the island (in addition to the two boat concessionaires). For people prone to seasickness, this makes Santa Rosa Island the Channel Island of choice. Another of the island's charms is its stand of Torrey pines—yes, the same conifers you see at Torrey Pines State Reserve, in San Diego. These are the only two places in the world where those slow-growing, windswept pines are found, and no one knows why. To see them from the boat pier or the landing strip, follow the main dirt road to the southeast, paralleling the shore. Near the far (southeast) end of the landing strip on the inland side,

you'll see a gate and a road that leads uphill to Water Canyon Campground. Pass this gate and continue to the next junction of roads, where you can choose to hike up above the Torrey pines or down below. You can make a loop and circle around the grove if you like, or just take the lower road to stay along the coast and avoid any further climbing. The higher you go, of course, the more outstanding the coastal views.

Another great hiking option for visitors to Santa Rosa Island is the Cherry Canyon Trail, which leads to scenic views of Bechers Bay, the private Vail Vickers Ranch, and a large sandy stretch known as Skunk Point.

User Groups: Hikers only. No dogs, horses, or mountain bikes. No wheelchair facilities.

Permits: If you choose to stay overnight, you must get a camping permit (877/444-6777 or www.recreation.gov). The camping fee is $15 per night. A fee is charged for transportation to the island. As of 2011, the boat fare is approximately $78 per adult for a day trip or $108 per adult for an overnight camping trip. Air travel is $160 per adult for a day trip or $300 per adult for an overnight trip.

Maps: A free map of Channel Islands National Park is available by download at www.nps.gov/chis. A more detailed map is available from Trails Illustrated. For topographic maps, ask the USGS for Santa Rosa Island North and East.

Directions: Island Packers provides boat transportation to Santa Rosa Island from Ventura Harbor; reservations are required. Truth Aquatics provides boat transportation to Santa Rosa Island from Santa Barbara Harbor. Channel Islands Aviation provides air transportation to Santa Rosa Island from Camarillo Airport.

Contact: Channel Islands National Park, 1901 Spinnaker Drive, Ventura, CA 93001, 805/658-5700 or 805/658-5730, www.nps.gov/chis. Camping permits: 877/444-6777 or www.recreation.gov. Boat trips: Island Packers, 805/642-7688 or 805/642-1393, www.islandpackers.com and Truth Aquatics,

805/963-3564, www.truthaquatics.com. Air transport: Channel Islands Aviation, 805/987-1301, www.flycia.com.

50 POTATO HARBOR TRAIL

5.0 mi / 2.5 hr 🏃3 ⛰8

on east Santa Cruz Island in Channel Islands National Park

Channel Islands Detail Map, page 659

Only the eastern quarter of huge Santa Cruz Island belongs to the National Park Service; the other 76 percent of the island is managed by The Nature Conservancy. Although it's possible to hike on The Nature Conservancy's land (call the boat concessionaires listed below for information), you may do so only with a special permit and in the company of a guide. If you prefer to wander on your own or if you want to camp overnight on the island, you need to visit the eastern, national park side of Santa Cruz Island. The boat ride is short enough (it takes a little over an hour to cover about 20 miles) to make this a day trip, or if you prefer a longer stay, the National Park Service runs a campground in Scorpion Canyon, plus a backcountry camp called Del Norte, 10 miles to the west. You'll have the luxury of water faucets at Scorpion but not at Del Norte.

The trail to Potato Harbor begins at Scorpion campground, which is 0.5 mile beyond Scorpion Anchorage, where the boat drops you off. Head back into the upper end of the campground (passing the ranch and the first set of campsites) until you see a road veering off to the right, climbing above the canyon. Like almost all of the trails on eastern Santa Cruz Island, this trail is a wide dirt road, best hiked before the end of summer, when it can be dry and dusty. The road climbs steeply for 0.5 mile, then goes mostly flat, continuing along the bluff tops almost straight west, paralleling the mainland coast. Far ahead you can see a long series of hills and canyons that eventually fade out of view in the haze, and

it's easy to assume that these belong to one of the neighboring Channel Islands. Wrong. They are more of the immense bulk of this island—the largest in the chain, at 96 square miles. At two miles out, the trail curves to the southwest, following the line of a fence at the bluff's edge. Look for a spur trail that leads to the edge, and follow it to the obvious view of Potato Harbor—a potato-shaped cove lined with rugged cliffs and filled with deep, clear water.

If you're camping on the island and have more time than the day-trippers, make sure you take the seven-mile round-trip hike to Smuggler's Cove and its lovely cobble beach. A stand of eucalyptus provides a shady picnic area at the edge of the sand.

User Groups: Hikers only. No dogs, horses, or mountain bikes. No wheelchair facilities.

Permits: If you choose to stay overnight, you must get a camping permit (877/444-6777 or www.recreation.go). The camping fee is $15 per night. A fee is charged for boat transportation to the island. As of 2011, the fare is $56 per adult for a day trip, or $75 per adult for an overnight trip.

Maps: A free map of Channel Islands National Park is available by download at www.nps.gov/chis. A more detailed map is available from Trails Illustrated. For topographic maps, ask the USGS for Santa Cruz Island C and D.

Directions: Island Packers provides boat transportation to Santa Cruz Island from Ventura Harbor; reservations are required. Truth Aquatics provides boat transportation to Santa Cruz Island from Santa Barbara Harbor.

Contact: Channel Islands National Park, 1901 Spinnaker Drive, Ventura, CA 93001, 805/658-5700 or 805/658-5730, www.nps.gov/chis. Camping permits: 877/444-6777 or www.recreation.gov. Boat trips: Island Packers, 805/642-7688 or 805/642-1393, www.island-packers.com and Truth Aquatics, 805/963-3564, www.truthaquatics.com.

51 EAST ANACAPA ISLAND LOOP TRAIL

2.0 mi / 1.0 hr   🏃2 ⛰10

on Anacapa Island in Channel Islands
National Park

Channel Islands Detail Map, page 659

Of all the Channel Islands to choose from,
why do more people go to Anacapa Island
than any other? Because it's easy. At only 12
miles from Port Hueneme, it's the closest
island to the mainland. The boat ride takes
less than an hour. As you cruise, you're likely
to be entertained by dolphins, sea lions, and
sometimes even flying fish. The island is
actually three tiny islets; the boat drops
you off on the easternmost of the three. If
you're feeling the slightest bit seasick, you'll
quickly get over it when the boat pulls away
and your first task is to climb up the 154
metal steps that cling to the island's cliffs.
You'll get plenty of fresh air as you make
your way to the island's visitors center,
pick up some interpretive information, and
set out on this trail, which tours this entire 0.3-square-mile islet. The trail's main
highlights are two overlooks at Inspiration
Point and Cathedral Cove, where you can
look down on seals and sea lions on the rocks
below. From Inspiration Point, you can also
gaze at the other two Anacapa islets and huge
Santa Cruz Island beyond them. Bring your
binoculars: There are millions of opportunities for bird-watching, particularly when
thousands of western gulls nest in spring and
summer. Where you can see over the edge
of the rocky cliffs, you'll spot some of the
island's 130 sea caves, which attract hordes
of kayakers all summer long.

Spring wildflowers are superb on Anacapa,
including the giant coreopsis, which blooms so
brilliantly that its yellow glow can sometimes
be seen from the mainland. The bloom period
varies from year to year, but generally occurs
from late February to mid-April. The beaches
on East Anacapa are not accessible because
the sea cliffs are hundreds of feet high, but
on calm days, you can swim at the landing
cove. Bring your snorkeling gear so you can
look eye-to-eye with the garibaldis and giant
sea kelp. The landing area is inside a 37-acre
marine reserve that has been a no-hunting
area since 1980. With all the species living
protected around the kelp forests and reefs, it
makes for a divers' wonderland.

Even though the island is small and its one
hiking trail is short, this rates as one of the
greatest day trips possible in California. Don't
miss it. After a day spent on Anacapa, you may
go home feeling like a different person.

User Groups: Hikers only. No dogs, horses, or
mountain bikes. No wheelchair facilities.

Permits: If you choose to stay overnight, you
must get a camping permit (see phone number
below). The camping reservation fee is $15 per
night. A fee is charged for boat transportation to the island. Call the concessionaires
at the numbers below for rates and departure
information. As of 2011, the fare is $56 per
adult for a day trip, or $75 per adult for an
overnight trip.

Maps: A free map of Channel Islands National
Park is available by download at www.nps.gov/
chis. A more detailed map is available from
Trails Illustrated. For a topographic map, ask
the USGS for Anacapa Island.

Directions: Island Packers provides boat
transportation to Anacapa Island from Ven-
tura Harbor and Oxnard (Channel Island
Harbor); reservations are required. Truth
Aquatics occasionally provides boat transpor-
tation to Anacapa Island from Santa Barbara
Harbor, although the boat trip is shorter from
Ventura.

Contact: Channel Islands National Park,
1901 Spinnaker Drive, Ventura, CA 93001,
805/658-5700 or 805/658-5730, www.nps.gov/
chis; camping permits: 877/444-6777 or
www.recreation.gov; maps: Trails Illustrated, 800/962-1643; boat trips: Island Packers,
805/642-7688 or 805/642-1393, www.island-
packers.com; Truth Aquatics, 805/963-3564,
www.truthaquatics.com.

52 SIGNAL PEAK LOOP TRAIL
2.5 mi / 1.5 hr 🥾2 ⛰9

on Santa Barbara Island in Channel Islands National Park

Channel Islands Detail Map, page 659

Santa Barbara Island is the loneliest island in Channel Islands National Park. Located about 50 miles south of Ventura, it is geographically isolated from the other four islands that make up the national park, being closer in latitude to San Pedro than to Santa Barbara or Ventura. (Yet it's much farther out to sea than developed Catalina Island, which is its closest neighbor.) Getting to Santa Barbara Island requires a 2.5–3-hour boat ride from Ventura, and the boat concessionaire runs only about a dozen trips to the island each year—much less frequently than to the other islands. And Santa Barbara Island is tiny; at only one square mile, it's the smallest of the Channel Islands. Similar to Anacapa Island in both its size and barren landscape, Santa Barbara Island has 5.5 miles of hiking trails, all of which are worth exploring. One of the best is Signal Peak Trail, which makes a loop over much of the south half of the island, from the landing cove to Signal Peak, which at 634 feet is the highest point on the island. A great feature of this trail is its fine views of Sutil Island, an even smaller island that lies 0.25 mile southwest of Santa Barbara Island. (Sutil Island is an important seabird rookery; bird-watching is first rate all over Santa Barbara Island.) The trail begins by heading inland from the landing cove. Take the left fork 0.5 mile out to head south, and curve around the southern end of the island to Signal Peak, on the southwest edge. From the peak, you loop back through the center of the island over gently rolling grasslands.

If you're wondering what season to visit Santa Barbara Island, keep this in mind: As on Anacapa Island, the giant coreopsis produces its huge yellow flowers here from late March to May.

User Groups: Hikers only. No dogs, horses, or mountain bikes. No wheelchair facilities.

Permits: If you choose to stay overnight, you must get a camping permit (877/444-6777 or www.recreation.gov). The camping reservation fee is $15 per night. A fee is charged for boat transportation to the island. Call the boat concessionaire at the number below for rates and departure information As of 2011, the fare is approximately $78 per adult for a day trip or $108 per adult for an overnight trip.

Maps: A free map of Channel Islands National Park is available by download at www.nps.gov/chis. A more detailed map is available from Trails Illustrated. For a topographic map, ask the USGS for Santa Barbara Island.

Directions: Island Packers provides boat transportation to Santa Barbara Island from Ventura Harbor; reservations are required.

Contact: Channel Islands National Park, 1901 Spinnaker Drive, Ventura, CA 93001, 805/658-5700 or 805/658-5730, www.nps.gov/chis. Camping permits: 877/444-6777 or www.recreation.gov. Boat trips: Island Packers, 805/642-7688 or 805/642-1393, www.islandpackers.com.

LOS ANGELES AND VICINITY

© KLOTZ/123RF.C

BEST HIKES

Islands, mountains, beaches, lakes, deserts – the

Los Angeles region offers all this diversity and more. The region is so large, and so varied, it's impossible to describe it without dividing it into smaller pieces.

Two large national forests hold most of the high-country land in the region – Angeles and San Bernardino. The 700,000-acre Angeles National Forest contains the San Gabriel Mountains, which form a high, impenetrable shield that prevents Los Angeles' smog from dissipating. The mountains, which geologists claim are the most fractured and unstable in California (rock slides are an everyday occurrence), sustain a network of more than 500 miles of hiking trails. So close to the freeways, high-rises, and smog of Los Angeles, these high mountains and their clean, sweet air are a hiker's paradise. Sick of the freeway rat race? Head for the trails that grace the slopes of Mount Williamson or Mount Baden-Powell. You can hike all day and be back in L.A. in time for dinner.

A few miles to the east, the San Bernardino Mountains, in San Bernardino National Forest, are one of the highest mountain ranges in California, with peaks that rise to more than 11,000 feet in elevation. The San Bernardinos also contain Southern California's three major recreation lakes: Big Bear, Arrowhead, and Silverwood, plus smaller lakes Gregory and Green Valley. Big Falls, the highest year-round waterfall in Southern California, is located near Big Bear Lake and the San Gorgonio Wilderness. A wealth of hiking trails are found in and around these popular recreation areas.

Yet another mountain range is found in San Bernardino National Forest: the San Jacintos, topped by Mount San Jacinto, which towers over the low desert at Palm Springs. The San Jacintos rise abruptly from the desert floor, completely separated from the other high-elevation ranges of Southern California by low passes and valleys. John Muir called the view from the summit of Mount San Jacinto "one of the most sublime spectacles seen anywhere on Earth." Most recreationists access the San Jacinto range from the resort town of Idyllwild. Destinations like 7,528-foot Suicide Rock and 8,828-foot Tahquitz Peak attract hikers and rock climbers from all over Southern California.

Combined together, these three mountain ranges – San Gabriels, San Bernardinos, and San Jacintos – contain Southern California's great triumvirate of hikeable peaks: Mount San Gorgonio at 11,501 feet, Mount San Jacinto at 10,834 feet, and Mount Baldy at 10,068 feet. Every Los Angeles area hiker worth his or her salt will bag all three summits at some point in his or her career.

One more mountain range is found in the Los Angeles region: the Santa Monica Mountains, a gentler stretch of sloping peaks along the coast. Much of the public land here is part of the Santa Monica Mountains National Recreation Area, but another portion is divided into several state parks: Topanga, Malibu Creek, Leo Carrillo, and Will Rogers. Several smaller parks are managed by the Santa Monica Mountains Conservancy. The trails in the Santa Monica Mountains crisscross chaparral- and sage-covered hillsides, oak woodlands, and native grasslands. Rocky sandstone outcrops poke up here and there, adding variety to the landscape.

If your hiking sensibilities run more toward sunset walks along the coast, hop on a ferry and pay a visit to Catalina Island. Or head to Laguna Beach, where the seaside white sands give way to view-filled coastal hills at Crystal Cove State Park and Laguna Coast Wilderness Park. For wide views of the Malibu coast, check out the trails at Charmlee Wilderness Park. Or, for a true L.A. experience, head for Griffith Park and climb to the top of Mount Hollywood. Who knows, you might just see a movie star on the trail.

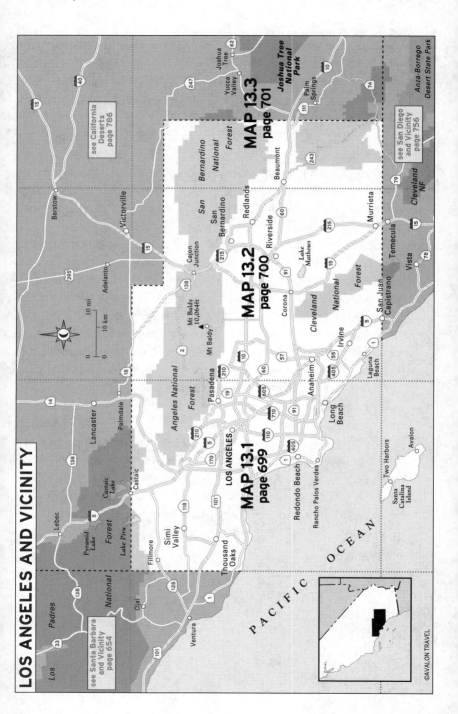

LOS ANGELES AND VICINITY

see Santa Barbara and Vicinity page 654

see California Deserts page 786

see San Diego and Vicinity page 756

MAP 13.3 page 701

MAP 13.2 page 700

MAP 13.1 page 699

Joshua Tree National Park

Anza-Borrego Desert State Park

Cleveland NF

San Bernardino National Forest

Angeles National Forest

Los Padres National Forest

Cleveland National Forest

PACIFIC OCEAN

Mt Baldy 10,064ft

Lake Mathews

0   10 mi
0   10 km

©AVALON TRAVEL

Map 13.1

Hikes 1-33
Pages 702-723

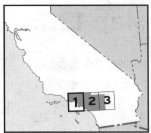

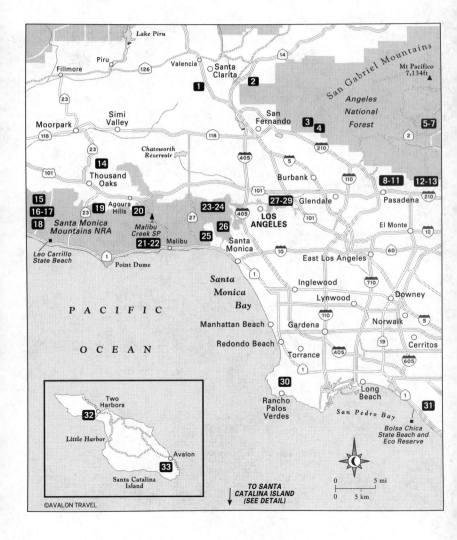

Map 13.2

Hikes 34-56
Pages 724-740

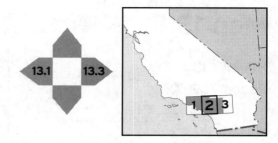

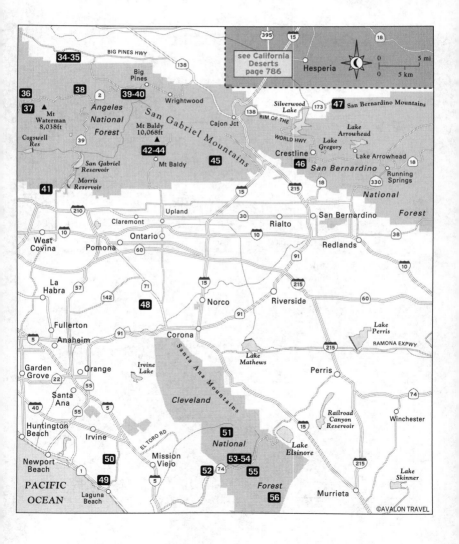

©AVALON TRAVEL

Map 13.3

Hikes 57-72
Pages 741-751

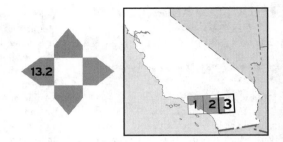

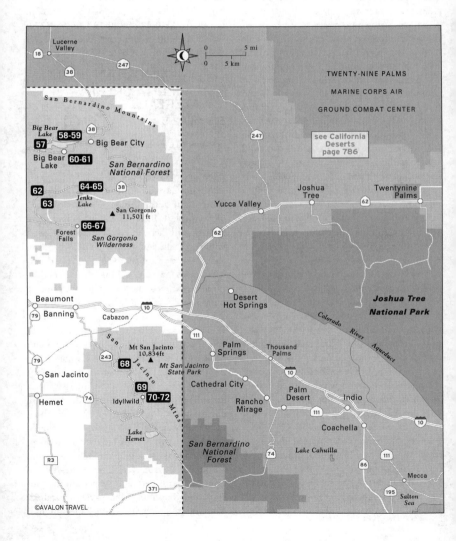

1 TOWSLEY AND WILEY CANYONS

5.0 mi / 2.5 hr   🏃‍♀️3 ⛰️8

in Ed Davis Park in Towsley Canyon south of Valencia

Map 13.1, page 699

Little Ed Davis Park in Towsley Canyon is a part of the larger Santa Clarita Woodlands Park, which is a part of the giant Santa Monica Mountains Conservancy parcel of lands. If you visit the park any time except during the sweltering heat of summer, you can walk a five-mile loop and pay a visit to all of Towsley Canyon's major plant communities—grasslands, sage and scrub, riparian, oak woodlands, and just about everything except old-growth redwood forest—in one short trip. How can a park this close to I-5 be this wild looking? We can't figure it out, but it is. Start the trip by following the park entrance road through the first and second parking lots, heading past the ranger station and picnic area. The road quickly turns to gravel and becomes more trail-like. Only a mile from your car the canyon walls squeeze in as you enter a remarkable section of Death Valley–style sandstone narrows. If there is water running in Towsley Canyon's stream, you'll get your feet wet here. Too soon, the narrows come to an end, and you begin a surprisingly steep climb to one of the park's highest points. As you ascend, watch for tar seeps coming up from the ground right alongside the trail. At the top of the climb, you gain big views of the sprawling Santa Clara Valley, which is enough to make you glad you're up here instead of down there. The loop continues downhill through Wiley Canyon, which is much greener and more lush than Towsley Canyon.

User Groups: Hikers, dogs, horses, and mountain bikes. No wheelchair facilities.

Permits: No permits are required. Parking is free if you park outside the entrance gate; $5 if you park inside.

Maps: A trail map is available at the ranger station and nature center, or can be downloaded at www.lamountains.com. For topographic maps, ask the USGS for Newhall and Oat Mountain.

Directions: From the San Fernando Valley, drive north on I-5 to Santa Clarita (five miles north of the I-5 and Highway 14 junction). Take the Calgrove exit, turn left (west), drive 0.4 mile, and turn right into the park entrance. You can park outside the gate for free, or inside the gate for a $5 fee.

Contact: Santa Monica Mountains Conservancy, 5750 Ramirez Canyon Road, Malibu, CA 90265, 310/589-3200 or 310/858-7272, www.lamountains.com; contact the rangers at Towsley Canyon, 661/255-2974.

2 PLACERITA CREEK WATERFALL

5.5 mi / 2.5 hr   🏃‍♀️2 ⛰️8

in Placerita Canyon County Park southeast of Valencia

Map 13.1, page 699

Placerita Canyon County Park is just far enough out of the Los Angeles Basin to feel like someplace different, and its trails are easy enough for hikers of almost any ability. Start your trip at the park nature center, where you should pay a visit to all the live and taxidermied animals and learn a thing or two about the flora and fauna of the area. Then start hiking on the Canyon Trail, which leads from the southeast side of the parking lot and crosses Placerita Creek. Hike through Placerita Canyon, often under the shade of sycamores and oaks, to Walker Ranch Group Campground. At its far side, look for a trail on the right signed as the Waterfall Trail, and get ready for the best part of the trip. (Make sure you don't take the Los Piñetos Trail, which is just before the Waterfall Trail and doesn't go to the falls.) The canyon begins to narrow, and you twist and curve your way through it, crossing and recrossing the creek a few times. In the final 100 yards before the waterfall, the trail ends, and you simply hike up the streambed. Although the waterfall is only 25 feet high, it forms a lovely little grotto—a perfect place for a snack before heading back.

User Groups: Hikers and dogs. No horses or mountain bikes. No wheelchair facilities.

Permits: No permits are required. Parking and access are free.

Maps: Free maps of Placerita Canyon County Park are available at the park nature center. For topographic maps, ask the USGS for San Fernando and Mint Canyon.

Directions: From the San Fernando Valley, drive north on I-5 to Highway 14. Follow Highway 14 northeast for four miles to Newhall; exit on Placerita Canyon Road. Turn right (east) and drive 1.5 miles to the park entrance, on the right. Park in the nature center parking lot.

Contact: Placerita Canyon County Park, 19152 Placerita Canyon Road, Newhall, CA 91321, 661/259-7721, www.placerita.org.

◼3 TRAIL CANYON
4.0 mi / 2.0 hr

in Angeles National Forest near Sunland

Map 13.1, page 699

Trail Canyon is located on the western side of the San Gabriel Mountains in an area that was nearly obliterated in the Station Fire of 2009. At this book's press time, the U.S. Forest Service has closed the trail and the access road to the trailhead, but officials say they expect to have it reopened by the summer of 2012. Many L.A. hikers eagerly await the chance to get back into Trail Canyon and witness its regeneration after a few years of being left in peace to heal. Those who have visited the canyon before the fire will notice that most of the 1930s-era cabins located near the trailhead burned to the ground. Sadly, only a handful still stand. Nonetheless, Gold Creek still flows through the canyon, and once the trail is reopened, Trail Canyon Falls, a 40-foot-high waterfall, will still make a fine destination for a day-hike, especially during the spring months. Getting to the falls during the wet

season has always been a bit of an adventure, with several stream crossings along the way, and that will certainly not change. After about a mile of wet walking, the trail climbs out of the canyon and rises high above the creek. At 2.0 miles out, a sharp left curve suddenly reveals the waterfall a short distance ahead. The trail leads to the top of the falls, where the creek spills over a smooth granite precipice. The path used to continue from the waterfall for another 2.2 miles to Tom Lucas Trail Camp, set at the edge of Big Cienaga Meadow, but the camp was burned in the fire and will probably not be rebuilt.

User Groups: Hikers, dogs, horses, and mountain bikes. No wheelchair facilities.

Permits: No permits are required. A national forest Adventure Pass is required for each vehicle; fees are $5 for one day or $30 for a year. Interagency access passes are also accepted.

Maps: An Angeles National Forest map is available from the U.S. Forest Service. A map of the Angeles Front Country is available from Tom Harrison Maps. For a topographic map, ask the USGS for Sunland.

Directions: From I-210 in Sunland, take the Sunland Boulevard exit. Cross Sunland Boulevard and head east on Foothill Boulevard for 0.75 mile. Turn left (north) on Oro Vista Avenue. In 0.8 mile, Oro Vista Avenue turns into Big Tujunga Canyon Road. Drive four miles on Big Tujunga Canyon Road to a sign for Trail Canyon on the left. Bear left on a dirt road (Road 3N29), drive 0.25 mile to a fork, then bear right and drive 0.25 mile to a large parking lot. The trailhead is on the left side of the lot.

Contact: Angeles National Forest, Los Angeles River Ranger District, 12371 N. Little Tujunga Canyon Road, San Fernando, CA 91342, 818/899-1900, www.fs.fed.us/r5/angeles.

4 MOUNT LUKENS
7.5 mi / 4.0 hr   👣4 ⛰7

in Angeles National Forest near Sunland

Map 13.1, page 699

Mount Lukens, always a favorite butt-kicker hike for fit L.A. hikers, was badly burned in the Station Fire of 2009. At this book's press time, the U.S. Forest Service has closed the trail to access the summit and the trailhead at Wildwood Picnic Area, but officials say they expect to have them reopened by the summer of 2012. When it does reopen, it will be fascinating to observe the processes of fire ecology on 5,074-foot Lukens' slopes. (The big-cone Douglas fir that once graced the upper slopes were badly burned in the fire, and it will be interesting to see how many of them remain.)

Although there are several ways to hike here, the Stone Canyon Trail has always been a popular route to the summit, which is also known as Sister Elsie Peak. That's despite the fact that the trail gains 3,300 feet in less than four miles. The trail starts out fairly mellow but once it starts to climb, there is no rest for the weary. The Stone Canyon Trail leads for 3.4 seemingly relentless miles to a fire road. Turn left (east) to walk the final quarter-mile to the top. The summit view is rewarding: the Verdugo Mountains are spread out before you, with downtown L.A. beyond. On clear days, the Pacific Ocean and Catalina Island round out the scene. When the trail reopens, keep these pointers in mind: This area is mostly without shade and can really bake in summer, so confine your hiking to the cooler months. However, one factor can stop you in your tracks in the winter. The Stone Canyon Trail requires a crossing of Big Tujunga Creek in the first 100 yards, and after big rains, the stream can be impassable. Most of the year, it's a fairly easy boulder-hop.

User Groups: Hikers, dogs, horses, and mountain bikes. No wheelchair facilities.

Permits: No permits are required. A national forest Adventure Pass is required for each vehicle; fees are $5 for one day or $30 for a year. Interagency access passes are also accepted.

Maps: An Angeles National Forest map is available from the U.S. Forest Service. A map of the Angeles Front Country is available from Tom Harrison Maps. For a topographic map, ask the USGS for Sunland.

Directions: From I-210 in Sunland, take the Sunland Boulevard exit. Cross Sunland Boulevard and head east on Foothill Boulevard for 0.75 mile. Turn left (north) on Oro Vista Avenue. In 0.8 mile, Oro Vista Avenue turns into Big Tujunga Canyon Road. Drive 5.5 miles on Big Tujunga Canyon Road to Doske Road. Turn right on Doske Road and park at Wildwood Picnic Area. This lot is usually closed from November to March; if so you must park in pullouts alongside the road. The trail begins at the far eastern end of the picnic area parking lot.

Contact: Angeles National Forest, Los Angeles River Ranger District, 12371 N. Little Tujunga Canyon Road, San Fernando, CA 91342, 818/899-1900, www.fs.fed.us/r5/angeles.

5 MOUNT HILLYER
6.0 mi / 3.0 hr   👣3 ⛰8

in Angeles National Forest near the Chilao Visitors Center

Map 13.1, page 699

What, you say you have never heard of Mount Hillyer? Well, it doesn't have the clout or the elevation of Mount Baden-Powell or Mount Baldy, but it is one of the nicest places to seek out a little solitude in a wooded, rocky wonderland. The route to Mount Hillyer is a 1,100-foot climb spread out over three miles, following a short stretch of the 14-mile Silver Moccasin National Recreation Trail. The trail starts in chaparral and occasional gray pines, interspersed with many tall, blooming yucca plants in the spring. After a moderate one-mile climb, you near the edge of Horse Flats Campground and turn left to pick up the Mount Hillyer Trail. The path climbs through a steep, rocky area and delivers you to Hillyer's summit, which some hikers describe as "just a bump on a hill." On our first trip here, we walked right past the summit without even noticing it. It's the pile of boulders just off the trail to your left. If you find yourself hiking downhill for a while, heading toward looming Mount Pacifico, you've missed the summit. Views of the surrounding mountains are only fair from the summit, but the air is clean and sweet, and the crowds are nonexistent. Mount Hillyer is surrounded by beautiful stands of Jeffrey pines and incense cedars. The sound of the wind in the pines is divine.

User Groups: Hikers, dogs, horses, and mountain bikes. No wheelchair facilities.

Permits: No permits are required. A national forest Adventure Pass is required for each vehicle; fees are $5 for one day or $30 for a year. Interagency access passes are also accepted.

Maps: An Angeles National Forest map is available from the U.S. Forest Service. A map of the Angeles Front Country is available from Tom Harrison Maps. For a topographic map, ask the USGS for Chilao Flat.

Directions: From I-210 in La Cañada, take Highway 2/Angeles Crest Highway northeast for 26.5 miles to the Chilao Visitors Center turnoff on the left (not the turnoff for Chilao Campgrounds). Drive 0.7 mile on the Chilao Visitors Center road to a small parking pullout where the Silver Moccasin Trail crosses the road. Park here and follow the trail that is signed for Horse Flats Campground.

Contact: Angeles National Forest, Los Angeles River Ranger District, 12371 N. Little Tujunga Canyon Road, San Fernando, CA 91342, 818/899-1900, www.fs.fed.us/r5/angeles.

6 DEVIL'S CANYON TRAIL
7.0 mi / 4.0 hr or 2 days 4 ▲8

in the San Gabriel Wilderness near Chilao

Map 13.1, page 699

The area surrounding the Devil's Canyon Trail was badly burned in 2009 wildfires, but the Forest Service expects to have this trail reopened by summer 2012.

This is an upside-down hike—down on the way in and up, up, up on the way out. Trailhead elevation is 5,200 feet, and it is a trail of extremes. There's chaparral on some slopes and tall pines and big-cone Douglas fir on others. There's sun, then shade. It's dry for the first two miles, and then you reach a tributary creek and follow its meander. The trip down to Devil's Canyon is usually pretty quick—about an hour and a half for most people. Along the edge of Devil's Creek you'll find plenty of flat spots for a picnic, and a few primitive campsites may still remain. Some intrepid hikers choose to continue down the canyon beyond the trail's end, but prolific poison oak and slippery rocks will stop most sane people from doing so. Remember to save plenty of energy and water for the 3.5-mile trip from the canyon back to the trailhead, which has a 2,000-foot elevation gain. It's easy to convince yourself that the miles on the way up are twice as long as they were on the trip down.

User Groups: Hikers and horses. No dogs or mountain bikes. No wheelchair facilities.

Permits: No permits are required for day hiking. A free campfire permit is required for hikers using a backpacking stove (no campfires permitted). A national forest Adventure Pass is required for each vehicle; fees are $5 for one day or $30 for a year. Interagency access passes are also accepted.

Maps: An Angeles National Forest map is available from the U.S. Forest Service. A map of the Angeles High Country is available from Tom Harrison Maps. For topographic maps, ask the USGS for Chilao Flat and Waterman Mountain.

Directions: From I-210 in La Cañada, take Highway 2/Angeles Crest Highway northeast for 25.5 miles to the Chilao Campground turnoff on the left, then continue past it for 0.75 mile to a parking lot on the left side of the highway. (It is 0.25 mile west of the Chilao Visitors Center turnoff.) The signed Devil's Canyon trailhead is located across the road.

Contact: Angeles National Forest, Los Angeles River Ranger District, 12371 N. Little Tujunga

Canyon Road, San Fernando, CA 91342, 818/899-1900, www.fs.fed.us/r5/angeles.

⑦ GABRIELINO NATIONAL RECREATION TRAIL TO BEAR CANYON

8.0 mi / 4.0 hr or 2 days 🏃3 ⛰8

in Angeles National Forest near La Cañada

| Map 13.1, page 699 | BEST (|

The area surrounding Switzer Picnic Area, Switzer Falls, and Bear Canyon was badly burned in 2009 wildfires, but the Forest Service expects to have this trail reopened by summer 2012. Soon after the fire, the water slides, mini cascades, and pools of spectacular Arroyo Seco and Bear Canyon were silted in by runoff from the burned slopes, but in a few years, these will likely run clear again.

Gabrielino National Recreation Trail is still your ticket to visiting this area. Begin hiking from the Switzer Picnic Area, heading downstream on the smooth dirt trail. A few creek crossings and one mile of trail should bring you to the site of the old Commodore Switzer Trail Camp. Cross the stream once more and head uphill, still on the Gabrielino National Recreation Trail. The trail passes 50-foot Switzer Falls, affording a decent view of it from across the canyon. A stone foundation is the remains of the Switzer Chapel, where visitors at Switzer's Camp, a popular trail resort in the early 20th century, attended Sunday services above the falls. A few steps farther brings you to a junction where the Gabrielino National Recreation Trail heads right and uphill, and the Bear Canyon Trail heads left and downhill. Enjoy the lofty view of Arroyo Seco Canyon from this point, then bear left and descend steeply for 0.25 mile, being cautious of the steep dropoffs. At the canyon bottom, take a quick detour to the left to see the lower cascades of Switzer Falls, then retrace your steps to this junction and follow the Bear Canyon Trail downstream. The canyon becomes increasingly wild here and you may have this special place all to yourself. One mile from the junction below Switzer Falls you reach a fork in the creek. Head upstream for another 1.2 miles to Bear Canyon Trail Camp. (This last stretch of trail was in poor repair; the path crosses and recrosses the creek dozens of times and can be difficult to discern.) Once the area recovers, the camp will again be a fine spot to spend an hour or an overnight.

User Groups: Hikers, dogs, horses, and mountain bikes. No wheelchair facilities.

Permits: No permits are required for day hiking. A free campfire permit is required for hikers using a backpacking stove (no campfires permitted). A national forest Adventure Pass is required for each vehicle; fees are $5 for one day or $30 for a year. Interagency access passes are also accepted.

Maps: An Angeles National Forest map is available from the U.S. Forest Service. A map of the Mount Wilson area is available from Tom Harrison Maps. For topographic maps, ask the USGS for Condor Peak and Pasadena.

Directions: From I-210 in La Cañada, take Highway 2/Angeles Crest Highway northeast for 9.8 miles to Switzer Picnic Area. It is on the south side of the road, 0.5 mile past Clear Creek Information Station. Turn right, drive down the access road 0.3 mile, and park in the main lot.

Contact: Angeles National Forest, Los Angeles River Ranger District, 12371 N. Little Tujunga Canyon Road, San Fernando, CA 91342, 818/899-1900, www.fs.fed.us/r5/angeles.

⑧ MILLARD FALLS

1.0 mi / 0.5 hr 🏃2 ⛰9

in Angeles National Forest near Pasadena

| Map 13.1, page 699 |

If you want to guarantee your kids (or adult friends) a good time, take them to Millard Campground for the short hike and scramble to Millard Falls. In springtime, make sure you're dressed to get wet, because you may have to spend more time in the stream than on a dry trail, especially if it has rained lately. There is no official trail to the falls; it's just a well-used route that follows the stream, making an easy adventure that is suitable for hikers of all abilities. The only minus is the abundance of carvings found on the smooth-barked alder trees; the carvings desecrate almost every tree, as high as human hands can reach. (Take this opportunity to teach your children never, ever to carve anything on trees.) The route to the falls is a 0.5-mile walk up the stream canyon, partly in the creek and partly on trail. Start walking at the edge of the campground just beyond the camp host's site, where the trail leads to the right and passes a couple of cabins. Simply head upstream, rock hopping where necessary, until the canyon walls come together at 60-foot Millard Falls. The stream splits in two at the fall's lip, forced to detour around two boulders that are stuck in the waterfall's notch. The two streams rejoin about two-thirds of the way down, creating a tremendous rush of water in springtime. Trailhead elevation is 1,900 feet.

User Groups: Hikers and dogs. No horses or mountain bikes. No wheelchair facilities.

Permits: No permits are required. A national forest Adventure Pass is required for each vehicle; fees are $5 for one day or $30 for a year. Interagency access passes are also accepted.

Maps: An Angeles National Forest map is available from the U.S. Forest Service. Maps of the Angeles Front Country and High Country are available from Tom Harrison Maps. For a topographic map, ask the USGS for Pasadena.

Directions: From I-210 in Pasadena, exit on Lake Avenue and drive north for 3.5 miles to Loma Alta Drive. Turn west (left) on Loma Alta Drive and drive one mile to Chaney Trail at the flashing yellow light. Turn right and drive 1.5 miles on Chaney Trail, keeping left at the fork, to Millard Campground. Park in the parking lot and follow the fire road on the right (as you drove in) that leads into the campground.

Contact: Angeles National Forest, Los Angeles River Ranger District, 12371 N. Little Tujunga Canyon Road, San Fernando, CA 91342, 818/899-1900, www.fs.fed.us/r5/angeles.

⑨ EATON CANYON
3.0 mi / 1.5 hr

in Eaton Canyon Natural Area

Map 13.1, page 699

Eaton Canyon Natural Area is the kind of place where elementary school groups come in the spring. The buses unload their cargoes of children, who then set off (on what may be their first real hike) through Eaton Canyon's wash. And what a fine introduction to the outdoors—a hike along Eaton Canyon in the good company of cactus, chaparral plants, willows, oaks, and occasionally bunnies, lizards, and red-tailed hawks. The park trails connect to other trails in Angeles National Forest, including one of L.A.'s favorite hiking destinations, Eaton Canyon Falls. Start at Eaton Canyon's nature center, where you can pick up a free map of the area, then walk to the far north end of the parking lot and take the dirt road straight past the picnic shelter. Cross the wash and hike along the wide canyon trail, with the wash on your left. The stream attracts a large variety of wildlife, especially birds that sing all day in this canyon. Just before a bridge where your trail intersects with the Mount Wilson Toll Road, cut down to the wash and pass under the bridge. From there, hike upstream, crossing the creek several times as the canyon narrows on its way to Eaton Canyon Falls. Sadly, the waterfall's cliffs are often found desecrated by graffiti, but the falls remain a well-loved destination in Eaton Canyon.

One odd side note: If you hear the sound of gunfire at the trailhead, don't panic—the local police have a shooting range nearby. As you walk into the canyon, you'll quickly get away from the noise.

User Groups: Hikers, dogs, and horses. No mountain bikes. No wheelchair facilities.

Permits: No permits are required. Parking and access are free.

Maps: A free map of Eaton Canyon Natural Area is available at the nature center. For topographic maps, ask the USGS for Pasadena and Mount Wilson.

Directions: Heading east from I-210 in Pasadena, take the Sierra Madre Boulevard/Altadena Drive exit and go north on Altadena Drive for 1.6 miles. Turn right into the entrance for Eaton Canyon Natural Area, which is one block north of New York Drive. If you are heading west on I-210, take the San Gabriel Boulevard/San Marino exit. Turn right (north) at the second light, which is Altadena Drive, and drive 1.5 miles to the park entrance.

Contact: Eaton Canyon Natural Area, 1750 N. Altadena Drive, Pasadena, CA 91107, 626/398-5420, www.ecnca.org.

🔟 BIG SANTA ANITA CANYON LOOP

8.9 mi / 5.0 hr   2 ⛰️ 9

in Angeles National Forest near Arcadia

Map 13.1, page 699

Big Santa Anita Canyon is probably the top easy day-hike destination in all of the Los Angeles River District of Angeles National Forest. The shady, overgrown, magical gulch is just a handful of miles from the Pasadena freeway. Its easy-to-moderate trails provide a short, simple, and sweet escape from urban life. The problem is that the access road to the trailhead at Chantry Flat is subject to washouts and landslides almost every winter, so the trails here are often inaccessible for more months of the year than they are accessible. Check for current status of the Chantry Flat Road before making the drive. The other problem is that when the road is open and the weather is good, this place is incredibly popular. The parking lots sometimes fill up by 8 A.M. on sunny weekend days, so get an early start.

Assuming you can get in, start hiking on the Gabrielino National Recreation Trail downhill. It's paved for the first 0.7 mile heading down into the canyon. When you reach the bottom, cross the Roberts Footbridge and head to the right on the dirt pathway. Day hikers can't help but covet the adorable summer cabins in the canyon, which are privately owned on land leased from the Forest Service. The artificial waterfalls you see are small check dams, designed (poorly) to keep the creek from flooding. Walking under the shade of oaks and alders, and along Big Santa Anita Creek for one mile upstream, leads you to 60-foot-high Sturtevant Falls. Where the Gabrielino Trail forks left and heads uphill, continue straight along the creek, admiring ferns and vines as you walk another 0.25 mile to the waterfall. It drops 60 feet over a granite cliff into a perfectly shaped rock bowl. After a visit, retrace your steps to the junction and follow the Gabrielino Trail uphill. Take the lower trail (the upper trail is safer for horses), which clings to the steep hillsides as it climbs above Sturtevant Falls to Cascade Picnic Area, a shady spot alongside the fern-lined creek. Take a break here before continuing uphill for another mile to Spruce Grove Trail Camp. A quarter-mile beyond the camp, you'll bear left on the Mount Zion Trail to begin the return leg of the loop. The trail drops very steeply down to Hoegee's Camp, where you connect with the Lower Winter Creek Trail, which travels 1.5 back to the Roberts Footbridge and the start of your loop. It's a quick 0.6-mile hike back uphill on the paved road to your car.

User Groups: Hikers, dogs, horses, and mountain bikes. No wheelchair facilities.

Permits: No permits are required. A national forest Adventure Pass is required for each vehicle; fees are $5 for one day or $30 for a year. Interagency access passes are also accepted.

Maps: An Angeles National Forest map is available from the U.S. Forest Service. A map of the Mount Wilson area is available from Tom Harrison Maps. For a topographic map, ask the USGS for Mount Wilson.

Directions: From I-210 in Pasadena, drive seven miles east to Arcadia. Exit on Santa Anita Avenue and drive six miles north to the road's end, at Chantry Flat. The trail begins across the road from the first parking area.

Contact: Angeles National Forest, Los Angeles River Ranger District, 12371 N. Little Tujunga Canyon Road, San Fernando, CA 91342, 818/899-1900, www.fs.fed.us/r5/angeles.

11 FIRST WATER TRAIL TO HERMIT FALLS

3.0 mi / 1.5 hr   🏃2 ⛰9

in Angeles National Forest near Arcadia

Map 13.1, page 699

You say you flat out refuse to hike on pavement? Then the trip on the Gabrielino Trail to Sturtevant Falls might not be right for you, but don't bypass beautiful Big Santa Anita Canyon because of it. An alternate trail drops down into the canyon, but this one is on gorgeous singletrack trail all the way, lined with tall oaks and alders, huge chain ferns, slender sword ferns, and a half dozen other fern varieties. You begin at the same trailhead, and the first few hundred yards of the walk are the same, but then you bear off the Gabrielino Trail at the sign for the First Water Trail and Hermit Falls (on your right). The trail switchbacks gently down into the canyon and then heads south (downstream) along the north fork of Big Santa Anita Creek. The near-constant shade of the canyon, combined with the presence of a year-round stream, makes it possible for every inch of ground to spring forth plant life. As on the Gabrielino Trail, you pass many artificial waterfalls (made by check dams on Santa Anita Creek) that are surprisingly beautiful. The First Water Trail crosses the creek a few times, which can be a little tricky early in the year, and follows the stream on its downstream course. The trail ends at the last cabin in the canyon, just above Hermit Falls. Pick a granite boulder, have a seat, and watch the water flow by. In the winter months, this is a very peaceful spot, perfect for nature-lovers, but in the late spring and summer, Hermit Falls has become a raucous hangout spot, complete with coolers of beer. As you can imagine, the cabin owners aren't very happy about that.

User Groups: Hikers, dogs, horses, and mountain bikes. No wheelchair facilities.

Permits: No permits are required. A national forest Adventure Pass is required for each vehicle; fees are $5 for one day or $30 for a year. Interagency access passes are also accepted.

Maps: An Angeles National Forest map is available from the U.S. Forest Service. A map of the Mount Wilson area is available from Tom Harrison Maps. For a topographic map, ask the USGS for Mount Wilson.

Directions: From I-210 in Pasadena, drive seven miles east to Arcadia. Exit on Santa Anita Avenue and drive six miles north to the road's end, at Chantry Flat. The trail begins across the road from the first parking area.

Contact: Angeles National Forest, Los Angeles River Ranger District, 12371 N. Little Tujunga Canyon Road, San Fernando, CA 91342, 818/899-1900, www.fs.fed.us/r5/angeles.

12 MONROVIA CANYON FALLS

1.4-3.4 mi / 1.0-2.0 hr   🏃1 ⛰9

in Monrovia Canyon Park

Map 13.1, page 699

Everything about Monrovia Canyon Park is a great experience, including the hike to the park's showpiece: Monrovia Canyon Falls. Three different trailheads allow you to select the distance you wish to hike: Starting at the Bill Cull trailhead by the entrance station, the hike is 3.4 miles round-trip. Starting at the middle parking lot makes a 2.0-mile round-trip. Starting from the trailhead behind the nature center is the easiest, shortest round-trip of 1.4 miles—perfect for families with small children. No matter how you do it, you'll hike through a lush and lovely stream canyon, passing several check dams along the creek. The dense woodland is crowded with oaks, alders, and ferns, creating cool and pleasant shade. When you reach the base of the 40-foot waterfall, you'll find many big rocks that are perfectly situated for gazing in admiration.

Special Note: Check your calendar before you go. Monrovia Canyon Park is closed on Tuesdays. The rest of the week, the park is open only from 8 A.M. to 5 P.M.

User Groups: Hikers and dogs. No horses or mountain bikes. No wheelchair facilities.

Permits: No permits are required. A $5 day-use fee is charged per vehicle.

Maps: A free park map is available at the nature center or entrance station. For a topographic map, ask the USGS for Azusa.

Directions: From I-210 in Monrovia, take the Myrtle Avenue exit and drive north for one mile through Old Town Monrovia to Foothill Boulevard. Turn right and drive 0.2 mile to Canyon Boulevard. Turn left and drive 1.6 miles to the park (bear right where the road forks). Drive past the entrance kiosk for 0.5 mile and park near the picnic area and nature center, for the shortest hike to the falls.

Contact: Monrovia Canyon Park, 1200 N. Canyon Boulevard, Monrovia, CA 91016, 626/256-8282, www.ci.monrovia.ca.us.

13 BEN OVERTURFF TRAIL
6.4 mi / 3.0 hr   🏃3 ⛰7

in Monrovia Canyon Park

Map 13.1, page 699

Ben Overturff was the man who made Monrovia Canyon a popular recreation area in the early 20th century. He ran Deer Park Lodge, a wilderness getaway for city dwellers, from 1910 to 1945. This trail to the site of Deer Park Lodge was reconstructed in the 1990s and named in his honor. From the lower parking lot by the entrance station, walk up the park road about 50 yards to the right turnoff for the Trask Boy Scout Camp. Turn right and ascend 1.25 miles along this mostly paved

access road. You'll pass the massive, 157-foot-high Sawpit Dam, which was built for flood control in 1927. It's the only interesting sight on this rather unpleasant stint of pavement. Sawpit Canyon Road soon turns to dirt and continues its monotonous climb. At 1.3 miles, you leave the dull fire road behind and join the single-track Ben Overturff Trail. Follow the trail as it winds its way up Sawpit and Sycamore Canyons, mostly in the shade of a bay laurel and oak forest. One memorable stretch skirts across a narrow, backbone ridge separating the two canyons. At 2.5 miles from the start, you reach the Twin Springs Junction and bear left. A few minutes later is a second junction, where you bear left again and soon reach the Deer Park Lodge site, comprised of a few crumbling foundations, rusted pipes and mattress springs, and bits and pieces of stone walls and steps. This is the turnaround point for this hike; if you want to loop back instead of retracing your steps, connect to Sawpit Canyon Road at either of the two junctions you passed, then follow the road back down to the trailhead.

Special Note: Check your calendar before you go. Although the entire park is closed on Tuesdays, the Ben Overturff Trail is closed on Tuesdays and Wednesdays. Otherwise, the park is open from 8 A.M. to 5 P.M.

User Groups: Hikers and dogs. Horses, mountain bikes, and wheelchairs can use only the fire road portion of the trail.

Permits: No permits are required. A $5 day-use fee is charged per vehicle.

Maps: A free brochure and trail map of the Ben Overturff Trail is available at the nature center. For a topographic map, ask the USGS for Azusa.

Directions: From I-210 in Monrovia, take the Myrtle Avenue exit and drive north for one mile through Old Town Monrovia to Foothill Boulevard. Turn right and drive 0.2 mile to Canyon Boulevard. Turn left and drive 1.6 miles to the park (bear right where the road forks). Park at the first available parking lot just before the entrance station.

Contact: Monrovia Canyon Park, 1200 N. Canyon Boulevard, Monrovia, CA 91016, 626/256-8282, www.ci.monrovia.ca.us.

14 WILDWOOD PARK LOOP
4.0 mi / 2.0 hr   👫2 ⚠8

in Wildwood Park in Thousand Oaks

Map 13.1, page 699

Wildwood Park is one of the best-kept park secrets in Los Angeles, known mostly to the school kids who come here for outdoor field trips in the spring. From the Arboles trailhead in Thousand Oaks, you can hike downhill into Wildwood Canyon and then stroll along its year-round stream, which produces a stunningly beautiful waterfall when the stream flow is strong. Numerous trails cross and interconnect throughout the park, so you can put together a different loop trip or out-and-back hike every time you visit.

For first timers, a good tour is to hike due west on the Mesa Trail for 0.5 mile to the North Tepee Trail and turn left, dropping down into the canyon. Once there, walk to your right, and then bear left at the next fork, which puts you right at the base of the 70-foot waterfall. Hey, isn't Los Angeles supposed to be a semi-arid desert? Yes, but it's full of surprises. (It's also full of rules; don't even think about swimming here.) From the falls, you can continue walking downstream and then pick up the Lizard Rock Trail to loop back to the Mesa Trail. The presence of year-round water makes this canyon a haven for wildlife; look for mule deer, rabbits, coyotes, and numerous songbirds and raptors. Interpretive signs teach you to identify various plants and trees along the stream.

User Groups: Hikers, dogs, horses, and mountain bikes. No wheelchair facilities.

Permits: No permits are required. Parking and access are free.

Maps: Park maps are available at the park visitors center. For a topographic map, ask the USGS for Thousand Oaks.

Directions: From US 101 in Thousand Oaks,

take the Lynn Road exit and head north. Drive 2.5 miles to Avenida de los Arboles, then turn left. Drive 0.9 mile and make a U-turn into the Arboles parking lot, on the left side of the road.

Contact: Conejo Recreation and Park District, 403 W. Hillcrest Drive, Thousand Oaks, CA 91360, 805/381-2741 or 805/495-6471, www.crpd.org.

15 SATWIWA LOOP TRAIL AND WATERFALL
3.0 mi / 1.5 hr   👫2 ⚠9

in Santa Monica Mountains National Recreation Area near Newbury Park

Map 13.1, page 699

You know the hike will be good when at the trailhead parking lot, you're greeted by two friendly roadrunners and a half dozen bunnies. That's how it is here at Rancho Sierra Vista/ Satwiwa, a part of Santa Monica Mountains National Recreation Area, just a couple miles off US 101. The park's proximity to millions of L.A. commuters makes it a perfect place to show up after work and hike or jog on Satwiwa Loop Trail, and in the rainy season, you can take a side trip to see the waterfall just inside the border of Point Mugu State Park. From the parking lot, walk up the paved Sycamore Canyon Trail for a few hundred yards, then bear left on the Satwiwa Loop Trail by the Satwiwa Native American Indian Culture Center. Be sure to take a peek at the dome-shaped stick dwelling, known to the Chumash as an "ap", which was reconstructed to show traditional Native American life. Follow the Satwiwa Loop for just under a mile, passing a small pond, a windmill, and grassy hillsides, then connect to the Old Boney Trail, on the south side of the loop. The Old Boney Trail leads downhill, and where the Upper Sycamore Canyon Trail comes in sharply from the right, stay left on the Old Boney Trail and cross the creek (an easy rockhop even in winter and spring). Walk about 100 yards and then make one final left. In about 50 yards of easy stream scrambling, you're at Sycamore Canyon Falls. The waterfall is a pretty, multitiered cascade over sandstone, with a surprising amount of foliage growing around it (including some nasty poison oak). Even when the fall is only a trickle, the big-leaf maples and woodwardia ferns are a delight to visit.

User Groups: Hikers and dogs. (Dogs are not allowed past the border of Point Mugu State Park or at the waterfall, only on the Satwiwa Loop.) No horses or mountain bikes. No wheelchair facilities.

Permits: No permits are required. Parking and access are free.

Maps: Free trail maps are available at the trailhead or by download at www.nps.gov/samo. A map of Point Mugu State Park is available from Tom Harrison Maps. For a topographic map, ask the USGS for Newbury Park.

Directions: From US 101 in Thousand Oaks, exit at Lynn Road and head south for 5.5 miles. Turn left at Via Goleta and drive 0.75 mile to the last parking area. Walk up the trail leading toward the Satwiwa Native American Cultural Center.

Contact: Santa Monica Mountains National Recreation Area, 401 W. Hillcrest Drive, Thousand Oaks, CA 91360, 805/370-2300, www.nps.gov/samo.

🔢 GROTTO TRAIL

3.4 mi / 2.0 hr   🥾2 ⛰️8

in Santa Monica Mountains National Recreation Area at Circle X Ranch

Map 13.1, page 699

If you don't mind hiking downhill to your destination and then uphill on your return, the Grotto Trail is a fine route for a little excursion in the Santa Monica Mountains. The trail roughly follows the west fork of the Arroyo Sequit on its downhill course to The Grotto, an area of jumbled volcanic boulders, many that are bigger than your average Volkswagen. Hidden among the giant rocks are small caves, pools, and waterfalls. After a brief walk

downhill from the Circle X Ranch Ranger Station parking lot, you access the Grotto by following the Grotto Trail from the ranch's group campground. The 1.3-mile trail makes a moderate descent on a pleasant grade. The 500-foot elevation loss must be gained back on the return trip, but fortunately there is a good amount of shade along the route. Only 0.3 mile beyond the campground you meet up with the Canyon View Trail coming in from the left. A few footsteps farther, you cross over the brink of 35-foot-high Botsford Falls, named by the legions of Boy Scouts who frequented the Circle X Campground. After a stint through a lovely grassland meadow, the trail moves close to the water again. Keep traveling gently downhill on this charming pathway and soon you emerge just above the sycamore-shaded Grotto. When the water is high, the trail disappears and you must boulder hop. Just keep heading downstream as far as it is safe to travel, then stand back and listen to the water roar. The Grotto's boulders are tempting to climb on and explore, but park rangers request that hikers tread gently and carefully to protect the many sensitive plant species that grow in the crevasses. Portions of the Grotto's rocks are completely closed off to protect these plants. And although dogs are allowed on this trail, they aren't allowed at the waterfall.

User Groups: Hikers and dogs (trail only). No horses or mountain bikes. No wheelchair facilities.

Permits: No permits are required. Parking and access are free.

Maps: Maps are available by free download at www.nps.gov/samo. A map of Point Mugu State Park, which includes Circle X Ranch, is available from Tom Harrison Maps. For a topographic map, ask the USGS for Triunfo Pass.

Directions: From Highway 1/Pacific Coast Highway in Malibu, drive northwest for 10 miles to Yerba Buena Road, 1.5 miles past Leo Carrillo State Park. Turn right and drive 5.3 miles up Yerba Buena Road to the entrance to Circle X Ranch on the right. Park by the ranger station, then follow the trail to the group campground. The Grotto Trail begins at the group camp.

Contact: Santa Monica Mountains National Recreation Area, 401 W. Hillcrest Drive, Thousand Oaks, CA 91360, 805/370-2300, www.nps.gov/samo. Or contact Circle X Ranger Station at 310/457-6408.

17 MISHE MOKWA AND SANDSTONE PEAK LOOP
6.0 mi / 3.0 hr   🥾3 ⛰9

in Santa Monica Mountains National Recreation Area near Circle X Ranch

Map 13.1, page 699

A great six-mile loop in the Santa Monica Mountains begins a short distance from Circle X Ranch, on Yerba Buena Road. See all those wild-looking volcanic outcrops on the hillsides? That's where you're going. You can hike the loop in either direction, but most people start on the Mishe Mokwa Trail. From the trailhead, hike uphill for 0.25 mile and take the right fork to access Mishe Mokwa's single track. It's 1.9 gentle miles on trail bordered by chaparral and spring wildflowers to a stream crossing and Split Rock, a big boulder with a cleft in the middle. It's an unspoken requirement to walk through the cleft. A picnic area at Split Rock is set among the oaks and sycamores, ideally situated for catching some shade. From there, continue on the well-signed loop, now in more exposed terrain. At 3.2 miles from the start, turn left to join the Backbone Trail, a wide road. A half mile farther, be sure to take the short right spur to Inspiration Point for inspiring views of the coast, and shortly beyond that, take the next right spur to 3,111-foot Sandstone Peak, the highest point in the Santa Monica Mountains. Despite its name, the peak is not made of sandstone; it's volcanic rock. The views are outstanding. On the clearest days, you can pick out six of the Channel Islands, plus far inland, the high peaks of the San Gabriel Mountains. Sandstone Peak actually has another name, Mount Allen, so when you climb to the top and see the Mount Allen plaque, don't think you're in the wrong place.

User Groups: Hikers and dogs. No horses or mountain bikes. No wheelchair facilities.

Permits: No permits are required. Parking and access are free.

Maps: Maps are available by free download at www.nps.gov/samo. A map of Point Mugu State Park, which includes Sandstone Peak, is available from Tom Harrison Maps. For a topographic map, ask the USGS for Triunfo Pass.

Directions: From Highway 1/Pacific Coast Highway in Malibu, drive northwest for 10 miles to Yerba Buena Road, 1.5 miles past Leo Carrillo State Park. Turn right and drive 6.5 miles up Yerba Buena Road to the Mishe Mokwa trailhead on the left (not the Backbone trailhead, which is 0.7 mile before the Mishe Mokwa trailhead).

Contact: Santa Monica Mountains National Recreation Area, 401 W. Hillcrest Drive, Thousand Oaks, CA 91360, 805/370-2300, www.nps.gov/samo.

18 NICHOLAS FLAT TRAIL
7.0 mi / 3.5 hr   🥾3 ⛰9

in Leo Carrillo State Park near Malibu

Map 13.1, page 699

Most Southern California state beaches are long stretches of sand with big campgrounds and lots of happy beachgoers, but few have any hiking trails worth writing home about. Leo Carrillo State Park is the exception to the rule, with a couple excellent trails that are far more than just a stroll along the sand. The Nicholas Flat Trail is the park's best path, a fairly steep trail that climbs from the coast to a pond at Nicholas Flat, where redwing blackbirds and other songbirds are easily seen. Start hiking from the Willow Creek/Nicholas Flat trailhead, and at the first junction, take either path. The

Nicholas Flat Trail on the left is shorter but steeper; Willow Creek is longer, gentler, and more scenic. Both trails connect in less than a mile, where a spur trail heads off to a spot signed as Ocean Vista. This is a fine viewpoint and an excellent spot to look for passing whales in winter. From the spur trail, backtrack a few feet and then continue uphill on the Nicholas Flat Trail. The climb gets steeper from here, and you'll gain 1,200 feet more as you climb along an extended ridgeline, but you are rewarded with many more spectacular vistas along the way (just turn around and take a look), plus in spring, a bonanza of wildflowers—mariposa lilies, poppies, golden yarrow, and popcorn flower among them. At 2.7 miles from the start, after the trail has attained its highest point, you reach a junction of trails, shortly followed by another junction. Follow the signs and you'll come out at the artificial pond at Nicholas Flat after a total 3.5 miles of hiking. Originally used for cattle ranching, the huge pond is mostly tule-lined except for its southwest edge. Sit still for a moment and you'll notice that the pond is a very birdy place. Red-winged blackbirds, starlings, mallards, coots, and myriad other species can be seen by those willing to wait and watch. A small, lightweight pair of binoculars would come in handy here.

If the best spots around the pond are already taken, you can follow a half-mile loop around the grasslands at Nicholas Flat and pick another spot for a rest and a picnic lunch. When it's time to start heading back, the best part of the trip is about to start. Not only is the route entirely downhill except for a brief initial climb, but you can look forward to nearly nonstop ocean views all the way. When you're finished hiking this trail, make sure to check out the beach across the road (take the pedestrian tunnel under the highway), where you'll find a sea-carved tunnel and many small caves and pocket beaches.

User Groups: Hikers only. No horses, dogs, or mountain bikes. Wheelchair users have access to the park's "sand wheelchairs" to explore the beach area.

Permits: No permits are required. A $12 day-use fee is charged per vehicle.

Maps: A map of Leo Carrillo State Park is available at the park entrance station or visitor center, or by free download at www.parks.ca.gov. A map of Point Mugu State Park, which includes Leo Carrillo State Park, is available from Tom Harrison Maps. For a topographic map, ask the USGS for Triunfo Pass.

Directions: From US 101 in Agoura Hills, exit at Kanan Road and drive 12.5 miles to Highway 1/Pacific Coast Highway on the Malibu coast. Turn west (right) and drive eight miles to Leo Carrillo State Park. Turn right into the park entrance and park in the day-use lot (fee charged), or park for free on Pacific Coast Highway just outside the park entrance. The Nicholas Flat Trail begins by the entrance kiosk on the inland side of the highway.

Contact: Leo Carrillo State Park, 35000 W. Pacific Coast Highway, Malibu, CA 90265, 805/488-5223, 805/488-1827, or 818/880-0363, www.parks.ca.gov.

19 MEADOW TRAIL AND OCEAN OVERLOOK LOOP

3.0 mi / 1.5 hr

in Charmlee Wilderness Park near Zuma Beach

Map 13.1, page 699

Maybe you need to change your perspective. If you've been hiking around in the lower canyons of the Santa Monica Mountains, it might be time to get up high and wander around where the wind blows and the vistas are wide. Charmlee Wilderness Park is the place to do it, located four miles up the hill from Zuma Beach. It's high enough so that you don't have to climb anywhere to gain a view; the vistas begin right at the trailhead. The park's hiking trails are all fire roads, but that's okay. You can hold hands with your hiking partner while you walk, or carry on a serious discussion about the coastal weather. Walk through the park's picnic area and follow Old Ranch Road for 0.25

mile to the old ranch foundation, surrounded by a meadow filled with wildflower blooms in spring. Here, at a T-junction, go left, and walk 0.5 mile to the old ranch reservoir. From the reservoir, you can loop back by heading left or right; all trails eventually connect back with the Old Ranch Road. From several points, you have vistas in almost every direction, not just to the coast but also up and down the Boney Mountain Ridge of the Santa Monica Mountains. On clear days, you can pick out a few of the Channel Islands.

If you want to participate in something special, sign up for one of Charmlee's naturalist-led full-moon hikes. Call the park for dates and to make reservations.

User Groups: Hikers, dogs, horses, and mountain bikes. No wheelchair facilities.

Permits: No permits are required. A $4 day-use fee is charged per vehicle.

Maps: A map of the Santa Monica Mountains is available from Tom Harrison Maps. For topographic maps, ask the USGS for Triunfo and Point Dume.

Directions: From Highway 1 in Zuma Beach, drive north on Encinal Canyon Road for four miles to the park entrance on the left. Turn left and drive 0.4 mile to the parking area near the park office and restrooms.

Contact: Charmlee Wilderness Park, 2577 Encinal Canyon Road, Malibu, CA 90265, 310/457-7247 or 310/317-1364, www.ci.malibu.ca.us.

20 ROCK POOL AND CENTURY LAKE
4.4 mi / 2.0 hr

in Malibu Creek State Park

Map 13.1, page 699

The first time you lay eyes on the Rock Pool at Malibu Creek State Park or cross the wide bridge over Malibu Creek or visit pretty blue Century Lake, you may have to ask yourself the question: Where am I? Suddenly it's hard to believe you're in Los Angeles, and just a few miles off the freeway—but you are. Start hiking from the large main parking area on the flat fire road, called Crags Road, that heads for the visitors center. Continue past the visitors center on a wide bridge, and take the left spur to the Rock Pool, a startlingly beautiful pool in Malibu Creek that is dammed by huge volcanic boulders. Although the pool can nearly dry up in late summer, during the rainy season and shortly thereafter, it is quite dramatic. Retrace your steps to Crags Road (you'll probably pass some rock climbers practicing their craft on an outcrop along the spur trail), turn left, and continue your park tour by visiting Century Lake, which was dammed in 1901; it's now silting up and slowly becoming a marsh. Walk another 0.5 mile along Crags Road to the old set of the *M*A*S*H* television series, where you'll find a few remaining props from the show. From there, retrace your steps through the park to the trailhead.

User Groups: Hikers, horses, and mountain bikes. No dogs. No wheelchair facilities.

Permits: No permits are required. A $12 day-use fee is charged per vehicle.

Maps: A map of Malibu Creek State Park is available at the park entrance station or by free download at www.parks.ca.gov, or from Tom Harrison Maps. For a topographic map, ask the USGS for Point Dume.

Directions: From Agoura Hills on US 101, take the Las Virgenes exit and drive 3.5 miles south to the entrance to Malibu Creek State Park, on the right. Continue past the entrance kiosk to the day-use parking area.

From Malibu on Highway 1, drive north on Malibu Canyon Road/Las Virgenes Road for six miles to the park entrance, on the left.

Contact: Malibu Creek State Park, 1925 Los Virgenes Road, Calabasas, CA 91302, 818/880-0367 or 818/880-0363, www.parks.ca.gov.

21 ESCONDIDO FALLS

4.2 mi / 2.0 hr   🏃2 ⛰9

in Escondido Canyon near Malibu

Map 13.1, page 699

The first mile of this trail is a bit odd. That's because of an access problem; you have to park in the lot at the start of Winding Way and then walk up the paved road for a mile, past some gargantuan Malibu homes, to the actual beginning of the Escondido Canyon Trail. It's weird, but worth it. Try not to gawk too much at all the affluence. When you reach the trail sign for the Santa Monica Mountains Conservancy lands, veer off to the left, heading into the canyon. You'll walk upstream, crossing the creek numerous times. The nearly level path tunnels through the shade of sycamore trees and opens out to grassy flats; it's a lovely sylvan setting all the way. About 0.5 mile from the start of the "real" trail, you'll glimpse a big waterfall up ahead, and in 0.5 mile more, you're at its base. This is the lower tier of the huge limestone waterfall. The adventurous can follow the side trail that leads up and over this 50-foot tier, and climb up to a higher, larger tier. Getting there requires some careful rock scrambling, so be cautious. The upper tier is 150 feet tall, with a deep pool at its base that is perfect for wading.

User Groups: Hikers, dogs, horses, and mountain bikes. No wheelchair facilities.

Permits: No permits are required. Parking and access are free.

Maps: A free map of the Santa Monica Mountains Conservancy lands is available at www.lamountains.com. A map of Malibu Creek State Park, which includes Escondido Canyon, is available from Tom Harrison Maps. For a topographic map, ask the USGS for Point Dume.

Directions: From Malibu, drive west on Highway 1 for 5.5 miles to Winding Way East, on the right, and the large sign for Winding Way Trail. If you reach Kanan Dume Road, you've gone 1.5 miles too far. Turn right, then left immediately into the well-signed parking lot.

Contact: Santa Monica Mountains Conservancy, 5750 Ramirez Canyon Road, Malibu, CA 90265, 310/589-3200, www.lamountains.com.

22 SOLSTICE CANYON TRAIL AND RISING SUN LOOP

2.8 mi / 1.2 hr   🏃2 ⛰8

in Santa Monica Mountains National Recreation Area near Malibu

Map 13.1, page 699

Solstice Canyon has long been a favorite hiking spot for Malibu-area locals, because it's easy to reach and dependably serene. This easy loop travels along the Solstice Canyon Trail to the Roberts Ranch site and returns via the winding Rising Sun Trail. Although the first mile on the Solstice Canyon Trail is on pavement, it parallels Solstice Creek and is a pleasant stroll.

Hike past the restrooms at the parking lot, then turn right at the T junction and head up the canyon, enjoying an array of wildflowers in spring. This area was burned in the 2007 Corral Canyon fire which destroyed the old stone Keller House which once stood here, one of the oldest homes in Malibu. Continue to the ruins of Tropical Terrace, at the Roberts Ranch. This once-beautiful home burned down in a fire in 1982 (and of course, many more fires have burned through here since), but its stone terraces and foundation remain. If you walk around to the far side of the foundation, you'll discover a 30-foot waterfall that drops on Solstice Creek. Enjoy its sweet music and maybe a sandwich from your pack. Then hike to the end of the Solstice Canyon Trail and pick up the Rising Sun Trail, which undulates over the hillsides for 1.7 miles. From there you can take the left side of the TRW Loop Trail back to the parking lot.

User Groups: Hikers, dogs, and horses. Mountain bikes are allowed only on the Solstice Canyon Trail. No wheelchair facilities.

Permits: No permits are required. Parking and access are free.

Maps: A free trail map is available at the parking area or by download at www.nps.gov/samo. A map of Malibu Creek State Park, which includes Solstice Canyon, is available from Tom Harrison Maps. For a topographic map, ask the USGS for Malibu Beach.

Directions: From Malibu, drive west on Highway 1 for 3.5 miles and turn right on Corral Canyon Road. Drive 0.2 mile to the park entrance, on the left. Turn left and drive 0.3 mile to the parking area. Start hiking on the paved road.

Contact: Santa Monica Mountains National Recreation Area, 401 W. Hillcrest Drive, Thousand Oaks, CA 91360, 805/370-2300, www.nps.gov/samo.

23 EAGLE ROCK LOOP
4.5 mi / 2.5 hr

at Trippet Ranch in Topanga State Park

Map 13.1, page 699

Topanga State Park's most notable feature is sandstone Eagle Rock, and a loop hike from Trippet Ranch takes you to see it. One half of this loop travels on Musch Trail, a hikers-only path, while the other half travels on fire roads. If you are a single-track lover, or if you don't like sharing the trail with bikes, simply take Musch Trail out and back to Eagle Rock. From the trailhead, the Musch Trail travels through a mix of oak and bay forest, grassy meadows, and chapparal. In one mile you reach Musch Camp, a pleasant hike-in camp that is surrounded by meadows. A restroom and horse corral are located here. From the camp, the trail gets even better—flower-filled grasslands and oak groves await. Look for mariposa lilies, blue-eyed grass, and owl's clover in bloom in springtime. Two miles from the start you reach Eagle Junction, where your trail meets up with a passel of fire roads. Take a hard left on Eagle Rock Fire Road, and climb steeply for 0.5 mile to Eagle Rock. After just a few minutes of walking, you come around a curve and get your first big-impact view of it. The

rock is so large and prominent that it may remind you of the big granite domes of the Sierra, but Eagle Rock is made of sandstone. Your trail runs right alongside the rock; leave the trail so you can explore its many caves, hollows, nooks, and crannies. Perhaps best of all are the views of the Santa Ynez Canyon below and the ocean beyond. When you've had enough, retrace your steps to the Eagle Junction, then choose between a return trip on the Musch Trail (making this a five-mile round-trip) or a loop back on the fire road. To make the loop, bear left on Eagle Springs Fire Road for a 4.5-mile round-trip.

User Groups: Hikers, horses, and mountain bikes. No dogs. No wheelchair facilities.

Permits: No permits are required. A $10 day-use fee is charged per vehicle.

Maps: A map of Topanga State Park is available at the Trippet Ranch ranger station or by free download at www.parks.ca.gov, or from Tom Harrison Maps. For a topographic map, ask the USGS for Topanga.

Directions: From Santa Monica, drive north on Highway 1 and turn right on Topanga Canyon Boulevard. Drive 4.7 miles to Entrada Road, then turn right and drive one mile to the park entrance at Trippet Ranch. The trailhead is at the far side of the parking lot.

Contact: Topanga State Park, 20825 Entrada Road, Topanga, CA 90290, 310/455-2465, www.parks.ca.gov.

24 SANTA YNEZ CANYON
2.4 mi / 1.2 hr

in Topanga State Park in Pacific Palisades

Map 13.1, page 699

Topanga State Park is a park with nebulous borders, a patchwork of wilderness interspersed between continually growing housing developments. The park's Santa Ynez Canyon Trail, for instance, begins in a residential neighborhood where you park your car right along the street. The surprising thing is that once you walk about 50 yards on the trail, you feel as if you've gotten away from it all, especially the sights and sounds of urban living. The canyon bottom makes for level walking and is pleasantly shaded by oaks, willows, and sycamores. Five-foot-tall tiger lilies grow alongside the trail.

At 0.5 mile in, cross the creek (don't take the spur trail up its right side), and you'll shortly reach a trail junction, where you should head right. The left fork continues for several miles, all the way to Trippet Ranch and the main section of Topanga State Park. A short walk and stream scramble brings you to the base of Santa Ynez Canyon's 15-foot limestone waterfall, a lovely spot that unfortunately has been defiled by graffiti. Even so, it's worth a look, and the canyon walk is pleasant whether or not the stream is flowing strong.

User Groups: Hikers only. No dogs, horses, or mountain bikes. No wheelchair facilities.

Permits: No permits are required. Parking and access are free.

Maps: A map of Topanga State Park is available at the Trippet Ranch ranger station or by free download at www.parks.ca.gov, or from Tom Harrison Maps. For a topographic map, ask the USGS for Topanga.

Directions: From Santa Monica, drive north on Highway 1 and turn right on Sunset Boulevard in Pacific Palisades. Drive 0.5 mile and turn left on Palisades Drive. Drive 2.4 miles, and then turn left onto Vereda de la Montura. The trailhead is at the intersection of Camino de Yatasto (a private road) and Vereda de la Montura. Park alongside the road.

Contact: Topanga State Park, 20825 Entrada Road, Topanga, CA 90290, 310/455-2465, www.parks.ca.gov.

25 TEMESCAL CANYON AND RIDGE LOOP

3.8 mi / 2.0 hr

in Temescal Gateway Park in Pacific Palisades

Map 13.1, page 699

Here's an urban-edge hike—smack in the middle of Pacific Palisades—that will make you forget all about the proximity of the urban edge. Sure, it can be crowded here, but deservedly so. For its scenic beauty alone, this loop hike is one of the best treks in the Santa Monica Mountains. The signed trail leads from beyond the camp store, heading up and around the park's youth camp. In about 100 feet you'll come to a junction and the start of your loop: the Temescal Canyon Trail on the right and the Temescal Ridge Trail on the left. Go right on the Temescal Canyon Trail and climb very gradually uphill. In 0.5 mile, at a boardwalk over the wide wash of Temescal Creek, you pass a Topanga State Park boundary sign. The trail then climbs again, now more earnestly. The path is lined with small rounded pebbles embedded in conglomerate rock. Bunnies and lizards scurry by as you parallel the stream, hiking underneath a canopy of big-leaf maples and sycamores. At 1.1 miles, you cross a footbridge over a small, seasonal waterfall, then you'll cross over to the west side of the canyon to ascend to an intersection with the Temescal Ridge Trail. Follow the Temescal Ridge Trail as it ascends for another 0.25 mile and then levels out, offering stupendous views of the coast and Santa Monica Bay. In spring, this high ridge is lined with wildflowers—mariposa lilies, purple nightshade, California poppies, and monkeyflower, to name a few. A few steps farther and you're at Skull Rock, a somewhat spooky-looking sandstone formation, with what looks like eyeholes and a large forehead. After a thorough examination of the rock and its neighboring sandstone outcrops, return to the junction and finish out the loop by heading downhill on the Temescal Ridge Trail, with fine views of the coast entertaining you as you walk.

User Groups: Hikers only. No dogs, horses, or mountain bikes. No wheelchair facilities.

Permits: No permits are required. A $7 day-use fee is charged per vehicle. Annual passes are available.

Maps: A free trail map is available at the Temescal Gateway Park kiosk. A map of the Topanga State Park, which includes Temescal

Gateway Park, is available from Tom Harrison Maps. For a topographic map, ask the USGS for Topanga.

Directions: From Santa Monica, drive north on Highway 1 to Temescal Canyon Road in Pacific Palisades. Turn right and drive one mile to Sunset Boulevard, then cross it to enter Temescal Gateway Park. Continue up the park road for 0.5 mile to the parking lot just before the camp store.

Contact: Temescal Gateway Park, 15601 Sunset Boulevard, Pacific Palisades, CA 90272, 310/454-1395, www.lamountains.com.

26 INSPIRATION POINT TRAIL

3.8 mi / 2.0 hr

in Will Rogers State Historic Park

Map 13.1, page 699

Most folks come to Will Rogers State Historic Park to visit the home of the late "cowboy philosopher" and humorist Will Rogers. His humble abode was a gigantic 31-room ranch/mansion. But even if you never heard of the guy and have no interest in cowboy decorating style, this short hike to Inspiration Point and beyond makes a visit to the park worthwhile. Finding the trailhead is a bit tricky; it's behind the Rogers' mansion, at the far edge of the grassy lawn. Cross a tiny footbridge, and you'll see the trailhead sign. The wide dirt road is dually signed as Rogers Road Trail and Inspiration Point Trail. A very easy climb of 0.9 mile brings you to a junction of trails and the Inspiration Point turnoff on your left. Go left and walk 100 yards to the summit of Inspiration Point, where the view includes the Pacific Ocean, the rugged Santa Monica Mountains, and downtown Los Angeles to the southeast. Considering the visual expanse, it's hard to believe you're at only 750 feet in elevation. On the clearest of days, you can see all the way to Catalina Island, 20-plus miles away. There's a horse-hitching post on the summit (this being a cowboy's park, of course), and a few picnic

tables and benches. After enjoying the vista, head back down to the junction, then go left at the sign that marks the the Backbone Trail and the entrance to Topanga State Park. Continue uphill on the Backbone Trail, climbing for another 0.9 mile. The trail crosses over a bridge that spans Chicken Ridge, a remarkably narrow sandstone ridge that gives much deeper meaning to the moniker "Backbone Trail." A high overlook with an even more commanding view than Inspiration Point is situated just above the bridged section of trail. Make this your turnaround for the hike and enjoy more views as you make your way back downhill.

User Groups: Hikers and horses. No dogs or mountain bikes. No wheelchair facilities.

Permits: No permits are required. A $12 dayuse fee is charged per vehicle.

Maps: A map of Will Rogers State Historic Park is available at the park entrance station or by free download at www.parks.ca.gov. For a topographic map, ask the USGS for Topanga.

Directions: From Highway 1/Pacific Coast Highway in Pacific Palisades, turn north on Temescal Canyon Road. Drive one mile to Sunset Boulevard. Turn right and drive 1.4 miles to Will Rogers State Park Road, then turn left and drive one mile to the park entrance. The trail begins behind, and just east of, the Rogers' ranch house, near the nature center and horse arena.

Contact: Will Rogers State Historic Park, 1501 Will Rogers State Park Road, Pacific Palisades, CA 90272, 310/454-8212 or 818/880-0363, www.parks.ca.gov.

27 RUNYON CANYON

3.4 mi / 1.5 hr

in Runyon Canyon Park near Hollywood

Map 13.1, page 699

Runyon Canyon Park is Hollywood's favorite neighborhood escape, where the young and hip socialize while getting a little nature time and staying in shape. The park isn't exactly wilderness, but it's a good example of how necessary city parks are for the people who live and work near them. It's a great place to take your dog for a walk, too; there are always tons of pooches here. Once you find street parking around the Fuller Avenue entrance—not an easy task on weekends—enter the park and take the main trail to the right. Walking this loop counterclockwise provides a steep climb in the beginning, then a longer, gradual descent. The trail ascends about 0.5 mile to the first overlook, dubbed Inspiration Point (like so many other high points in the Los Angeles area). The point offers good views of Hollywood, but it gets even better. The dirt trail narrows and ascends steeply up some steps to Cloud's Rest, the second and main overlook. Here you can catch your breath and sit on an oversized bench so high your feet won't touch the ground. This is a great spot to take in views near and far. The people-watching here is almost as good as the view, which takes in the famous Hollywood sign, Griffith Observatory, and, on exceptionally clear days, the distant ocean and even Catalina Island.

After quenching your visual appetite, continue on the trail, which now heads downhill. Almost immediately there's a turnoff to the right, which will lead to a third overlook in about 0.75 mile, at Mulholland Drive. Or, finish the loop by skipping the third overlook and continuing on the main trail downhill.

User Groups: Hikers and dogs. No horses or mountain bikes. No wheelchair facilities.

Permits: No permits are required. Parking and access are free.

Maps: A map of Runyon Canyon Park is available at www.runyon-canyon.com. For a topographic map, ask the USGS for Beverly Hills.

Directions: From US 101 in Hollywood, exit at Highland Avenue and head south 0.5 mile to Franklin Avenue. Turn right (west) on Franklin. Drive 0.6 mile and turn right (north) on Fuller Avenue. Runyon Canyon Park is in 0.25 mile at the end of Fuller Avenue. Street parking fills up quickly on weekends; beware of permit parking zones on surrounding streets.

Contact: Runyon Canyon Park, 2001 N. Fuller Avenue, Los Angeles, CA 90046, 323/913-7390 or 323/666-5046, www.laparks.org.

28 HASTAIN TRAIL

2.3 mi / 1.5 hr

in Franklin Canyon Recreation near Beverly Hills

Map 13.1, page 699

Despite being just a few miles from Hollywood and Studio City, Franklin Canyon always seems remarkably peaceful. Once in the canyon, you can't even hear the ever-present hum of the L.A. freeways. A hike on the park's Hastain Trail is a moderate climb on a fire road to an overlook with views of Franklin Canyon, its reservoir, west Los Angeles, and all the way out to the ocean on clear days. The fire road ascends along chaparral-covered slopes. Along the way, you'll enjoy a quintessential L.A. view. If you know what you are looking for, you can pick out the Beverly Hills estate of your favorite celebrity. Beyond the mansions are the Wilshire high-rises, and farther beyond is the serene Pacific Ocean. After nearly a mile, you'll depart the fire road and veer right on a single-track trail that descends to the Doheny ranch house and grassy picnic area below. The ranch served as a weekend retreat for Edward Doheny, who discovered oil in Los Angeles in 1892. Walk back to your car on a trail that parallels the park road. As you hike, be sure to obey all posted trail signs; this trail borders private property and some sections are closed off. Before or after your hike, be sure to stop in at the park's Sooky Goldman Nature Center, where you can learn all about the natural history of the Santa Monica Mountains.

User Groups: Hikers, dogs, and horses. No mountain bikes. No wheelchair facilities.

Permits: No permits are required. Parking and access are free.

Maps: A trail map is available at the Sooky Goldman Nature Center or can be downloaded at www.lamountains.com. For a topographic map, ask the USGS for Beverly Hills.

Directions: From US 101 in Studio City, take the Coldwater Canyon exit and drive south for 2.3 miles to the intersection of Mulholland Drive and Franklin Canyon Drive. Turn right on Franklin Canyon Drive. Drive 1.5 miles to the fork with Lake Drive, and bear left on Lake Drive. Just beyond the park entrance, look for a parking area and trailhead at a fire road, on the left.

Contact: Santa Monica Mountains Conservancy, 5750 Ramirez Canyon Road, Malibu, CA 90265, 310/589-3200 or 310/858-7272, www.lamountains.com.

29 MOUNT HOLLYWOOD
3.0 mi / 1.5 hr   🏃2 ⛰8

in Griffith Park

Map 13.1, page 699

About 800 acres of Los Angeles' beloved Griffith Park, including the area around Mount Hollywood, burned in a devastating wildfire in 2007. Since that time, Mother Nature has done what she does best, which is to heal and regrow the landscape. Only a few years' time has mitigated the fire's initially devastating effects. As before the wildfire, no trail in the park is more popular than this one to the top of Mount Hollywood. People hike to this summit simply because the view from the top is unforgettable. Out-of-towners need to be told that this is not the peak that bears the famous "HOLLYWOOD" sign (that's Mount Lee), although you can see that sign from this peak.

Start hiking across the street from the famous Griffith Observatory, which was spared in the fire. The road/trail meanders on a gentle grade over sage- and chaparral-covered slopes, offering worthwhile city views at every curve. The wide fire road is simple and straightforward, with no junctions to negotiate until you near the top, where a half-mile loop circles the summit. You'll reach a four-way junction just below, and north of, the summit. Turn left to walk the final few steps to the top. As flat as a pancake and about half the size of a football field, the summit of Mount Hollywood tops out at 1,625 feet in elevation. Check out the view that stretches from downtown all the way out to the ocean. The San Gabriel Mountains loom large in the background, and on the clearest days it is possible to pick out Southern California's big three peaks, far off to the east: Mount Baldy, Mount San Gorgonio, and Mount San Jacinto.

User Groups: Hikers, dogs, and horses. No mountain bikes. No wheelchair facilities.

Permits: No permits are required. Parking and access are free.

Maps: A free map is available at the park ranger station. For a topographic map, ask the USGS for Hollywood.

Directions: From US 101 in Hollywood, take the Sunset Boulevard exit and drive east three blocks to Western Avenue. Turn left and go north on Western Avenue for 0.4 mile; the road veers right and becomes Los Feliz Boulevard. Turn left immediately on Fern Dell Drive and drive two miles (it becomes Western Canyon Road) to West Observatory Road. Turn right and drive 0.3 mile; park near the observatory. The trail begins across from the observatory at the Charlie Turner Trailhead.

Alternatively, from I-5 in Los Feliz, exit at Los Feliz Boulevard and head west. Drive 2.4 miles and turn right (north) on Fern Dell Drive. Continue as above.

Contact: Griffith Park Ranger Station, 4730 Crystal Springs Drive, Los Angeles, CA 90027, 323/913-4688 or 323/913-7390, www.laparks.org.

30 BURMA ROAD TO PEACOCK FLAT
2.0 mi / 1.0 hr   🏃2 ⛰9

in Portuguese Bend Reserve on the Palos Verdes Peninsula

Map 13.1, page 699

Hiking on the Palos Verdes Peninsula isn't particularly user-friendly. The Peninsula is laced with trails, but most are unmarked and many can only be accessed if you are a resident of one of the Peninsula's exclusive gated communities. But this trail is open to everybody, and it could easily rate as one of the most scenic in Los Angeles County. The trail is part of the 400-acre Portuguese Bend Reserve, the largest of 10 reserves that comprise the Palos Verdes Nature Preserve. It's an easy walk along a fire road to Peacock Flat in Rancho Palos Verdes. The hike starts where Crenshaw Boulevard ends at its southernmost point. A dirt road begins here, and most people call it Burma Road or Burma Trail, although some still call it Crenshaw Extension. That name remains from the days before the 1956 Portuguese Bend landslide put an end to the developers' dreams to extend the road and build houses all over this area. Mother Nature always bats last. The hike is simple enough: Just follow the dirt road gently downhill as you enjoy nonstop cerulean blue Catalina Channel views. If you want to get off the wide road, several narrower trails intersect with it, including Peacock Flat Trail and Ailor Trail, and they all eventually rejoin with the road, so there is no chance of getting lost. In about a mile you'll come to a meadow called Peacock Flats, named for the showy-feathered fowl that once roamed the area. Climb the pine-dotted knoll on your left, known as Eagle's Roost, and marvel at the beauty of the Pacific. This makes a good turnaround spot for a two-mile round-trip, or if you prefer, you can continue wandering farther southward. Either way, you'll have a bit of an ascent to get back to the trailhead, so make sure you bring some water with you, especially on warm days.

User Groups: Hikers, dogs, and horses. No mountain bikes. No wheelchair facilities.

Permits: No permits are required. Parking and access are free.

Maps: Trail maps are available for free download at www.pvplc.org.

Directions: From I-110 in Wilmington, exit at Highway 1/Pacific Coast Highway, heading west. Drive three miles to Crenshaw Boulevard and turn left (south). Drive four miles south on Crenshaw Boulevard until it ends in Rancho

Palos Verdes (the nearest cross street is Burrell Lane). Park alongside the street or at Del Cerro Park and walk south along Crenshaw until it turns into a dirt road/trail.

Contact: Palos Verdes Peninsula Land Conservancy, 916 Silver Spur Road #207, Rolling Hills Estates, CA 90274, 301/541-7613, www.pvplc.org.

31 BOLSA CHICA ECOLOGICAL RESERVE

1.5 mi / 0.75 hr 　　　　🥾1 ⛰8

in Huntington Beach

Map 13.1, page 699

What a dichotomy. From the footbridge over the water at Bolsa Chica Ecological Reserve, you can see mussels, minnows, egrets, cordgrass, pickleweed, and huge flocks of shorebirds swirling in unison over the sparkling waters. But just a few hundred yards away, the state beach is lined with RVs, the oil-drilling grasshoppers are doing their monotonous job, and the traffic is crawling past on Highway 1. Where would you rather be? Right. The 1.5-mile loop trail at Bolsa Chica Ecological Reserve reminds us of what our coastline is supposed to look like and who depends on it the most—the birds on the Pacific Flyway. The 530-acre reserve is a migratory rest stop, and the birds are plentiful and fascinating to watch. The trail runs along the top of a levee, providing a vantage point that's just a few feet above the water's edge. What birds will you see? Brown pelicans, widgeons, pie-billed grebes, mergansers, pintails, and terns. If you're lucky, you may even spot a few endangered species, like the Belding's savannah sparrow (an unusual bird because it can drink seawater) or the California least tern. Consider this: For years, private developers have been trying to pave over this place and build pricey homes and condominiums, but so far, the birds are winning. We're rooting for them.

If you want to hike with a trained naturalist, show up on the first Saturday of any month at

9 A.M. Bring a jacket and binoculars and plan on getting a well-rounded education on bird identification, ecology, and endangered species.

User Groups: Hikers only. No dogs, horses, or mountain bikes. No wheelchair facilities.

Permits: No permits are required. Parking and access are free.

Maps: For a topographic map, ask the USGS for Seal Beach.

Directions: From I-405 in Seal Beach, exit at Seal Beach Boulevard and drive west to Highway 1. Turn south on Highway 1 and drive 4.5 miles to the Bolsa Chica Ecological Reserve entrance on the inland side of the highway, across from Bolsa Chica State Beach.

Contact: Amigos de Bolsa Chica, 16531 Bolsa Chica Road No. 312, Huntington Beach, CA 92649, 714/840-1575, www.amigosdebolsachica.org.

32 TWO HARBORS TO EMERALD BAY
9.0 mi / 5.0 hr

on Catalina Island

Map 13.1, page 699

If you want to take a hiking trip to Catalina Island, but you don't want your trip to be complicated or crowded with people, follow this one key instruction: Take the ferry to Two Harbors, not to Avalon. This applies whether you are going for the day or staying overnight. From the ferry drop point at Two Harbors pier, you can pick up your hiking permit and begin hiking right away on the West End Road, a dirt road that is nearly level and sticks close to the shoreline for its entire route. Head west—getting eyefuls of rocky outcrops, steep headlands, beckoning coves, and the beautiful blue Pacific—until at 1.25 miles you reach Cherry Valley and Cherry Cove. The area is named for the native Catalina cherry tree that grows there, which displays beautiful white flowers in the spring. Continue hiking on the flat dirt road, passing Howland Landing at almost four miles out. Stay far away from the plentiful No

Trespassing signs there. Remain on the road until you see an obvious cutoff trail on your right leading to beautiful Emerald Bay, at 4.5 miles. Have a picnic on the gorgeous white-sand beach and ponder how lucky we are to have this fabulous island so close to Los Angeles.

Although this excursion makes a fine day trip getaway from the mainland, your best bet is to spend the night in Two Harbors (either camping or in more luxurious accommodations), then continue hiking and exploring the next day. If you're on a day trip, you'll have to be back in Two Harbors in time for the boat home.

User Groups: Hikers only. No dogs, horses, or mountain bikes. No wheelchair facilities.

Permits: A free Santa Catalina Island hiking permit is required and may be obtained on the day of your hike from Two Harbors Visitors Center, or in advance at www.catalinaconservancy.org. Fees are charged for the ferry from the mainland to Two Harbors.

Maps: A trail map of Catalina Island is provided when you pick up your hiking permit. For a topographic map, ask the USGS for Santa Catalina West.

Directions: Catalina Express provides ferry transportation to Two Harbors from San Pedro. As of 2011, fares are approximately $70 per adult round-trip.

Contact: Two Harbors Visitor Services, P.O. Box 5044, Two Harbors, CA 90704, 310/510-0303, www.catalina.com; Santa Catalina Island Conservancy, 310/510-2595, www.catalinaconservancy.org; boat trips: Catalina Express, 310/519-1212 or 800/481-3470, www.catalinaexpress.com.

33 EMPIRE LANDING ROAD TRAIL
8.3 mi one-way / 4.0 hr

on Catalina Island

Map 13.1, page 699

This spectacular one-way hiking trip on Catalina Island requires a bare minimum of planning in exchange for tremendous rewards. First, you have to arrange to take the ferry from the mainland to Avalon, Catalina's "big city." When you arrive, you must pick up your free hiking permit in town and take the shuttle bus from Avalon to Airport in the Sky. That's where your hike on the Empire Landing Road finally begins. Along its 8.3-mile length, you'll travel along the north side of the island on a curvy, up-and-down road that passes by a marble quarry, numerous coves and beaches, and fascinating rock formations. If you're lucky, you'll see an island fox, a huge bison, or maybe even a wild turkey.

When the trail ends at Two Harbors, you have three choices: Take the bus shuttle back to Avalon, camp or stay at the various lodgings in Two Harbors, or take the ferry from Two Harbors back to the mainland. For the latter two possibilities, you must plan in advance. If you want to take the ferry back to the mainland, you need to alert the ferry company that you're going in to Avalon but leaving from Two Harbors. There is no extra fee for this service, but you have to make sure you finish your hike in time to catch the last boat. One more thing to consider: When is the best time of year to visit Catalina? Unquestionably, it's spring or fall, when the weather is good and the summer crowds are nonexistent.

User Groups: Hikers only. No dogs, horses, or mountain bikes. No wheelchair facilities.

Permits: A free Santa Catalina Island hiking permit is required and may be obtained on the day of your hike from the Santa Catalina Island Conservancy, the Catalina Island Interpretive Center, or at the Catalina Airport, or in advance at www.catalinaconservancy.org. Fees are charged for the ferry from the mainland to Avalon, and for the shuttle bus from Avalon to the airport.

Maps: A trail map of Catalina Island is provided when you pick up your hiking permit. For a topographic map, ask the USGS for Santa Catalina.

Directions: Several companies, including Catalina Express and Catalina Flyer, provide ferry transportation to Avalon from San Pedro, Long Beach, Dana Point, and Newport Beach. As of 2011, fares are approximately $70 per adult round-trip. Transportation is also provided by through Island Express Helicopter Service.

Contact: Santa Catalina Island Conservancy, 310/510-2595, www.catalinaconservancy.org; Two Harbors Visitor Services, 310/510-0303 (lodging and campgrounds), www.catalina.com (general information, permits); boat trips: Catalina Express, 310/519-1212 or 800/481-3470, www.catalinaexpress.com; Catalina Flyer, 949/673-5245, catalinainfo.com; air transport: Island Express, 800/228-2566; inter-island shuttle service: 310/510-0143.

34 DEVIL'S PUNCHBOWL LOOP

1.0 mi / 0.5 hr　　　🥾 2　⛰ 9

in the Devil's Punchbowl Natural Area south of Pearblossom

Map 13.2, page 700

The Devil's Punchbowl is visual proof that you're in earthquake country, where faulting and erosion have made bizarre shapes out of ancient sedimentary rocks. They thrust and jut upward, creating vertical walls as high as 300 feet, and they look as if they're about to topple inward on each other. From the viewpoint behind the visitors center, you look down into the land of the devil: the Punchbowl, a giant abyss that is the working of the San Andreas Fault and the result of centuries of stream carving. Juniper, piñon pine, and manzanita manage to eke out a meager living amidst all the sandstone. The park's easy, one-mile loop trail offers fine views into the depths of the Punchbowl. It switchbacks gently downhill to the canyon bottom and then climbs back up, passing by some of the taller rock slabs in the park. Here's a great tip: Park rangers hold full-moon hikes here once a month in the summer. Note: If you find this type of geological action fascinating, you might want to hike the park's longer trail to the dramatic Devil's Chair, a breathtaking overlook above the Punchbowl. Make sure you stop in at the nature center here at Devil's Punchbowl, where you can see its excellent display of wild birds.

User Groups: Hikers, dogs, and horses. No mountain bikes. No wheelchair facilities.

Permits: No permits are required. Parking and access are free.

Maps: Free trail maps are available at the nature center. For a topographic map, ask the USGS for Valyermo.

Directions: From Highway 14 near Palmdale, take the Highway 138 exit east for 16 miles to Pearblossom. Turn right on County Road N-6 (Longview Road) and drive south for 7.5 miles to the Devil's Punchbowl entrance. (The road makes several turns and changes names all the way, but all junctions are signed for the park.) From the park entrance, continue another 0.25 mile to the parking lot by the nature center. The trail begins behind the park nature center.

Contact: Devil's Punchbowl Natural Area, 28000 Devil's Punchbowl Road, Pearblossom, CA 93553, 661/944-2743, www.devils-punchbowl.com.

35 BURKHARDT TRAIL TO THE DEVIL'S CHAIR

7.0 mi / 3.5 hr   👫 3   ⛰ 9

in the Devil's Punchbowl Natural Area south of Pearblossom

Map 13.2, page 700

This is one of the most interesting and enjoyable hikes in the entire Los Angeles area, although, for a lot of people, it's a long drive to get here. It's worth it even if you may not think so in the first 20 minutes or so of hiking, where the trail leaves the Devil's Punchbowl parking lot and quickly joins a boring dirt road set in rather barren terrain. Finally, after 0.9 mile of steady climbing on this uninspiring road/trail, you reach a sign

for the Devil's Chair Trail, a left turnoff. Follow it and immediately you are in the pines and walking on a smoothly graded, pleasant trail. You'll cross Punchbowl Creek and enter an easy grade as you lateral across the slopes above the Devil's Punchbowl. The trail undulates gently up and down, crossing one small ravine after another. As you gradually gain elevation, you also gain views of the white rocks of the Devil's Punchbowl and the desert beyond. Two different rocky promontories, just off the trail, provide particularly imposing viewpoints.

At a junction with a trail coming in from South Fork Campground, head left and begin the final leg of your journey. Surprisingly, the final jaunt to the Devil's Chair is downhill. To be exact, it's 10 short switchbacks downhill. The last 50 yards of the path, which follow a narrow backbone ridge to the Chair itself, are so prone to erosion that the trail is encased in a tunnel of fencing. Have a seat on the Devil's Chair and enjoy this surreal scene for a while, then retrace your steps and head back up those switchbacks.

User Groups: Hikers, dogs, horses, and mountain bikes. No wheelchair facilities.

Permits: No permits are required. Parking and access are free.

Maps: Free trail maps are available at the nature center. For a topographic map, ask the USGS for Valyermo.

Directions: From Highway 14 near Palmdale, take the Highway 138 exit east for 16 miles to Pearblossom. Turn right on County Road N-6 (Longview Road) and drive south for 7.5 miles to the Devil's Punchbowl entrance. (The road makes several turns and changes names all the way, but all junctions are signed for the park.) From the park entrance, continue another 0.25 mile to the parking lot by the nature center. The Burkhardt Trail begins on the south side of the parking lot.

Contact: Devil's Punchbowl Natural Area, 28000 Devil's Punchbowl Road, Pearblossom, CA 93553, 661/944-2743, www.devils-punchbowl.com.

36 COOPER CANYON FALLS
3.6 mi / 2.0 hr

in Angeles National Forest near
Mount Waterman

Map 13.2, page 700

After the snow has melted, here's a first-rate reason to make the 34-mile drive to the high country of the Angeles Crest Highway: a visit to Cooper Canyon Falls. The waterfall is set in a beautiful, 6,000-foot-elevation forest, a dependably cool place on any hot day in L.A. Start your hike north of Buckhorn Campground, at the trailhead parking lot for Burkhart Trail. The hike is a mostly downhill trip through a dense forest of big firs, cedars, and pines. There's almost no undergrowth in these woods—just conifers and big rocks. It feels as if you're in the southern Sierra Nevada, but, no, this is the San Gabriels. The Burkhart Trail laterals along the canyon slopes, high above Buckhorn Creek, then makes a left turn into Cooper Canyon and traces a long switchback downhill. At 1.75 miles from the camp, you'll reach a junction with the Pacific Crest Trail. Turn right, toward Burkhart Saddle and Eagle's Roost. It's only 300 feet to the waterfall, which drops just below the trail's edge. Some hikers choose to scramble down the steep cliff to its base, where you can stand on an island of boulders and enjoy the falls' noisy, 35-foot drop. Be sure to get here early in the year, when the stream flow is still strong. Trailhead elevation is 6,300 feet.

User Groups: Hikers, dogs, and horses. Mountain bikes are allowed on the Burkhart Trail but not on the Pacific Crest Trail. No wheelchair facilities.

Permits: No permits are required. A national forest Adventure Pass is required for each vehicle; fees are $5 for one day or $30 for a year. Interagency access passes are also accepted.

Maps: An Angeles National Forest map is available from the U.S. Forest Service. Maps of the Angeles Front Country and High Country are available from Tom Harrison Maps. For a topographic map, ask the USGS for Waterman Mountain.

Directions: From I-210 in La Cañada, take Highway 2/Angeles Crest Highway northeast for 35 miles to Buckhorn Campground, on the left. It's 1.2 miles past the Mount Waterman ski lift, and just beyond Cloudburst Summit. As of 2011, a new trailhead parking lot is being constructed just north of Buckhorn Campground; follow the signs and park there.

Contact: Angeles National Forest, Los Angeles River Ranger District, 12371 N. Little Tujunga Canyon Road, San Fernando, CA 91342, 818/899-1900, www.fs.fed.us/r5/angeles.

37 MOUNT WATERMAN
5.6 mi / 3.0 hr

in Angeles National Forest at Mount Waterman

Map 13.2, page 700

The peak of Mount Waterman (at 8,038 feet) is a fine destination for a moderate day hike in the San Gabriel Mountains, and the view from the summit is one you won't soon forget. The only problem that awaits is figuring out which peak is really the peak, because the top of Mount Waterman is so wide that there are three summits. From the trailhead (elevation 6,700 feet), you simply head uphill on remarkably smooth, well-graded single track. The ascent is partially shaded by a mixed pine, cedar, and fir forest. At one mile out, you'll reach a saddle where your views open wide, taking in the Mojave Desert and the San Gabriel Wilderness. Climb some more, through long switchbacks, to a junction at 2.1 miles, then turn right for the summit. It's an easy 0.6 mile to the peak. Keep your eyes peeled for Nelson bighorn sheep, which are sometimes seen in the area. Also check out the huge sugar pine cones that are found alongside the trail. When you reach the flat top of Mount Waterman, the trail heads east and then south to the highest of Waterman's summits, atop a jumble of boulders. This spot provides the best possible view, looking out over the magnificent San Gabriel Mountains. On the clearest days, you can see all the way to 10,834-foot

Mount San Jacinto, standing sentinel above Palm Springs. Total elevation gain along this trail is 1,300 feet.

User Groups: Hikers, dogs, horses, and mountain bikes. No wheelchair facilities.

Permits: No permits are required. A national forest Adventure Pass is required for each vehicle; fees are $5 for one day or $30 for a year. Interagency access passes are also accepted.

Maps: An Angeles National Forest map is available from the U.S. Forest Service. Maps of the Angeles Front Country and High Country are available from Tom Harrison Maps. For a topographic map, ask the USGS for Waterman Mountain.

Directions: From I-210 in La Cañada, take Highway 2/Angeles Crest Highway northeast for 34 miles to the signed trailhead for the Mount Waterman Trail on the right (south) side of the road, east of the Mount Waterman ski lift operation and west of Buckhorn Campground. Park in the pullout across the road from the trailhead sign.

Contact: Angeles National Forest, Los Angeles River Ranger District, 12371 N. Little Tujunga Canyon Road, San Fernando, CA 91342, 818/899-1900, www.fs.fed.us/r5/angeles.

38 MOUNT WILLIAMSON
5.0 mi / 3.0 hr   🏃3 ⛰10

in Angeles National Forest near Islip Saddle

Map 13.2, page 700

This summit trail feels a bit rougher and more remote than those to many other peaks in the San Gabriel Mountains, and it's famous for its steep dropoffs. But the trail's total elevation gain is only 1,600 feet, and the visual rewards are tremendous. Mount Williamson is on the north side of the Angeles Crest Highway, which means that although you are hiking in a mountain environment, you're on the desert side of the mountain. The forest on this slope is more sparse (the upper slopes are dotted with wind-sculpted Jeffrey pines), the trail is more exposed, and many of the best vistas are of the western Mojave Desert, to the north. Even if you're not in the mood to climb to the 8,214-foot summit, you can hike to a saddle at 1.9 miles out, where the Pacific Crest Trail drops down to the west. Views to the south are excellent here, with a big chunk of the San Gabriel Mountains spread out before you. From the saddle, take the summit trail on your right, heading 0.6 mile farther north on a remarkably steep grade. (A few switchbacks would be convenient here, but there are none.) Although the views have been excellent all along, nothing prepares you for the scene on top of Mount Williamson's narrow ridgeline, which offers dizzying views on both sides. The San Gabriels are on your left, and on the clearest days you can see far beyond them to the L.A. basin and beyond to the Pacific Ocean. A vast sweep of Mojave Desert is on your right, 5,000 feet below. Don't turn around at the first pointy summit you reach; follow the backbone trail a bit farther to a second and flatter summit, which is 30 feet higher. The view from here is even more extraordinary— you can look directly down into the Devil's Punchbowl and the San Andreas Fault. All in all, it's an extraordinary place.

User Groups: Hikers, dogs, and horses. No mountain bikes. No wheelchair facilities.

Permits: No permits are required. A national forest Adventure Pass is required for each vehicle; fees are $5 for one day or $30 for a year. Interagency access passes are also accepted.

Maps: An Angeles National Forest map is available from the U.S. Forest Service. Maps of the Angeles Front Country and High Country are available from Tom Harrison Maps. For a topographic map, ask the USGS for Crystal Lake.

Directions: From I-210 in La Cañada, take Highway 2/Angeles Crest Highway northeast and drive 42 miles to Islip Saddle (one mile east of the tunnels). Park in the large parking lot on the north side of the road; the trail begins by the restrooms. (If you are coming from Highway 138 near Phelan or Piñon Hills, take Highway 2/Angeles Crest Highway west for 25 miles to Islip Saddle, 16 miles west of Big Pine.)

Contact: Angeles National Forest, Los Angeles River Ranger District, 12371 N. Little Tujunga Canyon Road, San Fernando, CA 91342, 818/899-1900, www.fs.fed.us/r5/angeles.

39 VINCENT GAP TO MOUNT BADEN-POWELL
8.0 mi / 4.0 hr 🏃4 ⛰10

in Angeles National Forest near Big Pines

Map 13.2, page 700

Like the climb to the summit of Mount Baldy, the climb to the summit of Mount Baden-Powell is something of a requirement for Southern California hikers. Luckily, this requirement is a little easier to attain, because the Pacific Crest Trail heading up to Mount Baden-Powell is a mere eight-mile round-trip with a 2,800-foot elevation gain. The summit of Baden-Powell is at 9,399 feet and is directly across the East Fork San Gabriel River Basin from, and slightly northwest of, Mount Baldy. As you might guess, the views from the summit are extraordinary. The summit area is also a botanist's delight, as 2,000-year-old limber pines can be found growing there. From the southwest edge of Vincent Gap, the Pacific Crest Trail leads through open forest—first oak, sugar pine, and Jeffrey pine, and as you climb, mostly lodgepole pine and occasional limber pines. The trail is extremely well maintained, with 42 switchbacks following a moderate grade all the way up. A quarter mile from the top, you leave the Pacific Crest Trail and follow the summit trail south (left). Once on top, you can see more than a vertical mile below you to the East Fork San Gabriel River Basin. Mount Baldy is of course prominent, as is the Mojave Desert, Catalina Island, Mount San Jacinto, and Mount San Gorgonio. In case you haven't heard, the British Lord Baden-Powell, for whom this peak is named, founded the Boy Scouts organization. The Scouts have placed a monument to him at the summit.

User Groups: Hikers, dogs, and horses. No mountain bikes. No wheelchair facilities.

Permits: No permits are required. A national forest Adventure Pass is required for each vehicle; fees are $5 for one day or $30 for a year. Interagency access passes are also accepted.

Maps: An Angeles National Forest map is available from the U.S. Forest Service. An Angeles High Country map is available from Tom Harrison Maps. For topographic maps, ask the USGS for Crystal Lake and Mount San Antonio.

Directions: From I-210 in La Cañada, take Highway 2/Angeles Crest Highway northeast and drive 53 miles to Vincent Gap. Follow the Pacific Crest Trail uphill from the parking lot. If you are coming from Highway 138 near Phelan or Piñon Hills, take Highway 2/Angeles Crest Highway west for 15 miles to Vincent Gap, which is 5.5 miles west of Big Pines.

Contact: Angeles National Forest, Santa Clara/Mojave Rivers Ranger District, 30800 Bouquet Canyon Road, Saugus, CA 91390, 661/296-9710, www.fs.fed.us/r5/angeles; Big Pines Visitors Center, 760/249-3504.

40 BIG HORN MINE
4.0 mi / 2.0 hr 🏃2 ⛰9

in Angeles National Forest near Big Pines

Map 13.2, page 700

If you want to get a good look at a piece of California history, take this easy walk to the Big Horn Mine, probably the most impressive of all Southern California mine sites. The mine was founded in 1894 by Civil War veteran Charles Tom Vincent, and although it was said to have produced as much as $50,000 in gold during its good years, neither Vincent nor anybody else ever got rich. An abundance of mine ruins remain at the site, and the trail itself is the mine's old wagon road. Follow the gated road from Vincent Gap and after only a mile, you'll pass a water-filled shaft and some debris left from the cabins that housed the miners. Soon you round a bend and see the large stamp mill building perched precariously on a hillside. Years ago hikers were able to explore this ramshackle building and walk through the mine tunnels, but now everything is gated off in the interest of safety. (Rumors abound that the Forest Service intends to destroy these ruins completely, but as of summer 2011, they are still intact. For updates, check with the Big Pines Visitor Center, 760/249-3504). Choose a spot nearby and pull out your lunch. From this perch at about 7,000 feet in elevation, you'll enjoy fine views across the gorge of the East Fork San Gabriel River to Mount Baldy and its sibling peaks. On your way to or from the mine site, be sure to take the half-mile side trail that leads to the remains of Vincent's cabin. The turnoff is at the Sheep Mountain Wilderness sign, just 150 yards from the trailhead.

User Groups: Hikers, dogs, and horses. No mountain bikes. No wheelchair facilities.

Permits: A free Sheep Mountain Wilderness permit is required; they are available at the trailhead. A national forest Adventure Pass is required for each vehicle; fees are $5 for one day or $30 for a year. Interagency access passes are also accepted.

Maps: An Angeles National Forest map is available from the U.S. Forest Service. An Angeles High Country map is available from Tom Harrison Maps. For topographic maps, ask the USGS for Crystal Lake and Mount San Antonio.

Directions: From I-210 in La Cañada, take Highway 2/Angeles Crest Highway northeast and drive 53 miles to Vincent Gap. Park on the south side of the highway and start hiking on the gated road (not the nearby trails). If you are coming from Highway 138 near Phelan or Piñon Hills, take Highway 2/Angeles Crest Highway west for 15 miles to Vincent Gap, which is 5.5 miles west of Big Pines.

Contact: Angeles National Forest, Santa Clara/Mojave Rivers Ranger District, 30800 Bouquet Canyon Road, Saugus, CA 91390, 661/296-9710, www.fs.fed.us/r5/angeles; Big Pines Visitors Center, 760/249-3504.

41 FISH CANYON FALLS
3.2 mi / 1.5 hr

in Angeles National Forest near Duarte

Map 13.2, page 700

Fish Canyon Falls is one of the loveliest waterfalls set in one of the most beautiful canyons in the San Gabriel Mountains, and yet for years, access to the falls has been a problem. Many decades ago, you could hike right to it on an easy trail through Fish Canyon, but access to the trailhead was blocked by the expansion of a private rock quarry owned by the Azusa Rock Company (a.k.a. Vulcan Materials). For most of the 1980s and 1990s, hikers had no access at all to Fish Canyon. Then, in 1998, a three-mile-long bypass trail was created to solve the problem, but unfortunately, the trail was steep, loose, narrow, riddled with poison oak, and didn't have nearly enough switchbacks. Still, from 1998 until 2008, many hikers endured this trail and the total 9.4 mile round-trip for the chance to see the prized 90-foot-high falls.

Today, thankfully, access to the falls is easy once again, at least on certain days of the year. Azusa Rock Company has arranged a bus shuttle system on "open access days" which takes hikers through the quarry's private property and deposits them at the old trailhead to Fish Canyon, located on adjacent Angeles National Forest land. (To find out which days are "open access days," check the calendar at www.azusarock.com.) Gates open at 7 A.M. and free shuttles run throughout the morning to the trailhead, with the last trip at noon. Once the shuttle drops you off at the back of the quarry, you cross a bridge over Fish Creek and are walking in lovely Fish Canyon. Waterfall lovers, rejoice. This makes the hike to the waterfall only 3.2 miles round-trip on a beautifully maintained, gently graded trail. The Fish Canyon Trail meanders gently uphill for 1.6 miles, sticking closely to Fish Creek and passing by the ruins of old cabins from the early 1900s. The path tops out at a high box canyon, where the waterfall is found. If the water flow is high, Fish Canyon Falls is a stunner, dropping 90 feet in four stair-stepped tiers.

If you want to hike to the falls when the bus shuttle is not running, you can still take the three-mile-long bypass trail to get around the quarry, but remember that this turns an easy hike into a very difficult hike. The bypass trail begins near the quarry entrance, then ascends steeply for 1.4 miles to Van Tassel Ridge. Here you join a dirt road and continue the unpleasant ascent for another 0.5 mile. As if that wasn't punishment enough, next the path abruptly plummets down the other side (don't forget your hiking poles) on a trail bordered by a bumper crop of poison oak. The brutal up-and-down to the ridge must be accomplished in both directions of this trip, and that makes up the majority of the total 3,000-foot elevation gain. At 3.2 miles from the start, the trail joins the old, pleasant Fish Canyon Trail in the canyon bottom, and suddenly your hike is transformed from misery to nirvana.

User Groups: Hikers and dogs. No horses or mountain bikes. No wheelchair facilities.

Permits: No permits are required. Parking and access are free.

Maps: A Fish Canyon trail guide, with a topographical map, is available from the city of Duarte (and is also usually available from a signboard near the trail's start).

Directions: From the junction of I-210 and I-605 near Duarte, follow I-605 north to its end, then turn right (east) on Huntington Drive. Drive 0.6 mile and turn left on Encanto Parkway and drive 1.4 miles northeast to the parking area just before the quarry entrance. To find out when the free shuttle bus is available through the quarry, check the Fish Canyon public access calendar at www.azusarock.com.

Contact: City of Duarte Parks and Recreation Department, 1600 Huntington Drive, Duarte, CA 91010, 626/357-7931, www.accessduarte.com.

42 SAN ANTONIO FALLS

1.5 mi / 1.0 hr   🥾1 △9

on Mount Baldy

Map 13.2, page 700

Mount Baldy is that big mountain that you can see from almost everywhere in the Los Angeles Basin (on a clear day), and if you hike the trail to San Antonio Falls, you'll be able to see almost everywhere in the Los Angeles Basin. Trailhead elevation is 6,160 feet, a fine elevation to start at if you like clean, fresh, mountain air. For the best waterfall show, you've got to time your trip carefully for the first warm days after winter, sometimes as early as March, when the snow melts off the mountain and pours into 80-foot San Antonio Falls. By early summer, the waterfall show is over. The hike to the falls is easy, following the Mount Baldy ski lift maintenance road, which is paved and has only a slight uphill grade. At 0.7 mile, you round a sharp curve and see the falls, gracefully dropping in three tiers. If you wish, you can follow a well-worn path through loose gravel and talus to the waterfall's base, but be careful on the unstable slope. One of the best parts of this trip comes on your return walk to the trailhead. You're witness to lofty views of the far-away San Gabriel Basin as you stroll back down the road.

User Groups: Hikers, dogs, horses, and mountain bikes. No wheelchair facilities.

Permits: No permits are required. A national forest Adventure Pass is required for each vehicle; fees are $5 for one day or $30 for a year. Interagency access passes are also accepted.

Maps: An Angeles National Forest map is available from the U.S. Forest Service. A Mount Baldy map is available from Tom Harrison Maps. For a topographic map, ask the USGS for Mount San Antonio.

Directions: From I-210 in Upland, take the Mountain Avenue/Mount Baldy exit and drive north for 4.3 miles (Mountain Avenue becomes Shinn Road). At a T-junction with Mount Baldy Road, turn right and drive nine miles to San Antonio Falls Road on the left, 0.3 mile past Manker Flats Campground. Park in the dirt pullouts by Falls Road and begin walking on the gated, paved road.

Contact: Angeles National Forest, San Gabriel River Ranger District, 110 N. Wabash Avenue, Glendora, CA 91741, 626/335-1251, www.fs.fed.us/r5/angeles; Mount Baldy Visitors Center, 909/982-2829.

43 MOUNT BALDY
13.6 mi / 8.0 hr
🤸5 ⛰10

in Angeles National Forest near Upland

Map 13.2, page 700   **BEST (**

You just can't call yourself a Southern California hiker until you've climbed to the top of Mount Baldy (elevation 10,064 feet), the highest peak in the San Gabriel Mountains. The shortest and easiest route (which is neither short nor easy, with a 13.6-mile round-trip and a 3,500-foot elevation gain) starts from San Antonio Falls Road. Follow the trail to San Antonio Falls (see listing in this chapter), but from the waterfall, continue uphill on the road for another 3.5 miles to Mount Baldy Notch. Go left and follow another fire road 1.4 miles, mostly in the shade of stately conifers, to the upper end of the ski lift. At the top of the upper lift, you access the infamous Devil's Backbone, a steep and jagged ridge. Some hikers find this section of trail, with its sheer dropoffs on both sides into the Lytle Creek Canyon and San Antonio Canyon, to be quite hair-raising. Soon you'll pass the south side of Mount Harwood at 9,552 feet (really just a high bump on Baldy's ridge), and then reach a wind-blown saddle between Harwood and Baldy. A few gnarled, wind-sculpted limber pines eke out a living in this barren terrain. From the saddle, it's only a short tromp to the top, but this is the steepest stretch of the entire day. When you finally reach Baldy's rock-strewn summit, what can you see? If it's a clear day, it's the best vista in the San Gabriel Mountains. Just about everything comes into view—desert, city, ocean, the peaks of the San Bernardino Mountains, even a few high summits of the southern Sierra and Death Valley,

130 miles distant. The earlier in the season you take this hike, the better your chance for good visibility. But there's a caveat: unless you are an experienced mountaineer, don't think about making the trip until the Devil's Backbone is free of snow and ice, which is usually in late May. The Devil's Backbone stretch is extremely treacherous in icy conditions.

If you want to cut seven miles and 1,300 feet of elevation gain off your round-trip, you can ride the Mount Baldy ski lift up to Baldy Notch, rather than hiking 3.5 miles up (and then down) San Antonio Falls Road. The ski lift operates only on weekends and holidays during the hiking season, however. By the way, in case you were wondering, Mount Baldy's formal name is Mount San Antonio. "Baldy" has just been its nickname for as long as anybody can remember.

User Groups: Hikers and dogs. No horses or mountain bikes. No wheelchair facilities.

Permits: A free campfire permit is required for hikers using a camp stove (no open fires permitted). A national forest Adventure Pass is required for each vehicle; fees are $5 for one day or $30 for a year. Interagency access passes are also accepted.

Maps: An Angeles National Forest map is available from the U.S. Forest Service. A Mount Baldy map is available from Tom Harrison Maps. For topographic maps, ask the USGS for Mount San Antonio and Telegraph Peak.

Directions: From I-210 in Upland, take the Mountain Avenue/Mount Baldy exit and drive north for 4.3 miles (Mountain Avenue becomes Shinn Road). At a T-junction with Mount Baldy Road, turn right and drive nine miles to San Antonio Falls Road on the left, 0.3 mile past Manker Flats Campround. Park in the dirt pullouts by Falls Road and begin walking on the gated, paved road.

Contact: Angeles National Forest, San Gabriel River Ranger District, 110 N. Wabash Avenue, Glendora, CA 91741, 626/335-1251, www.fs.fed.us/r5/angeles; Mount Baldy Visitors Center, 909/982-2829.

44 ICEHOUSE SADDLE

7.2 mi / 4.0 hr   🥾 3 ⛰ 9

in the Cucamonga Wilderness

Map 13.2, page 700

When it's wintertime in Southern California and you get the itch to throw a few snowballs, where do you go? Icehouse Canyon on Mount Baldy, of course. But Icehouse Canyon is good in the summer too, especially if you want a hiking escape far from the smog of the Inland Empire. You can go for as long or as short as you like in the canyon—it's a great place to just set out from your car, climb until you're tired, then turn around and head back. The canyon got its name in the 1850s, when 100-pound blocks of ice were carved from its frigid stream canyon and carried by mule-drawn wagon to satisfy the thirst of the growing city of Los Angeles.

Many people don't hike very far in the canyon before picking a spot to sit and relax by the cold, clear water, but if you're looking for a destination, Icehouse Saddle at 7,580 feet is a good one, perfect for picnicking, with lovely views to the east and west. The saddle is also the site of a major trail junction, where routes lead in four directions, including the famous Three Ts Trail that travels to Timber Mountain, Telegraph Peak, and Thunder Mountain. The Icehouse Canyon Trail begins by passing a few summer cabins, some still in use and others in ruins. The trail sticks close to the stunningly clear stream that runs all the way through the canyon. The surrounding forest is a lovely mix of oak, big-cone Douglas fir, pine, fir, and cedar. At one mile in, you reach a junction with the Chapman Trail. Both the Chapman and Icehouse Canyon Trails lead to Icehouse Saddle, but the Icehouse Canyon Trail stays along the creek and gets to Icehouse Saddle sooner via a steeper grade. Stay on your trail and at 1.8 miles, you reach a Cucamonga Wilderness boundary sign, where you must fill out a free permit if you have not already done so at the Mount Baldy Visitors Center in town. From here, you have another 1.8 miles to go, with a total 2,600-foot elevation gain from the trailhead. It's an aerobic ascent for sure. You'll pass trickling Columbine Spring at 2.8 miles, then a second junction with the Chapman Trail at 3.0 miles. If you like, you can make a semi-loop back from Icehouse Saddle by following the Chapman Trail, which will make this an 8.8-mile round-trip. Along the way, the trail camp at Cedar Flats (also called Cedar Glen) offers another fine rest stop.

User Groups: Hikers, dogs, and horses. No mountain bikes. No wheelchair facilities.

Permits: A free wilderness permit is required for both day hiking and backpacking in the Cucamonga Wilderness and is available from the Mount Baldy Visitors Center or at the self-serve permit kiosk along the trail at the Cucamonga Wilderness boundary. A national forest Adventure Pass is required for each vehicle; fees are $5 for one day or $30 for a year. Interagency access passes are also accepted.

Maps: An Angeles National Forest map is available from the U.S. Forest Service. A Mount Baldy map is available from Tom Harrison Maps. For topographic maps, ask the USGS for Cucamonga Peak and Telegraph Peak.

Directions: From I-210 in Upland, take the Mountain Avenue/Mount Baldy exit and drive north for 4.3 miles (Mountain Avenue becomes Shinn Road). At a T-junction with Mount Baldy Road, turn right and drive 6.4 miles, then bear right on Ice House Canyon Road. Drive 100 yards to the parking lot at the end of the road.

Contact: Angeles National Forest, San Gabriel River Ranger District, 110 N. Wabash Avenue, Glendora, CA 91741, 626/335-1251, www.fs.fed.us/r5/angeles; Mount Baldy Visitors Center, 909/982-2829.

45 ETIWANDA FALLS

3.0 mi / 1.5 hr   2 ▲8

in North Etiwanda Preserve in Rancho
Cucamonga

Map 13.1, page 699

There's a waterfall in Rancho Cucamonga?
Why, as a matter of fact, there is. Way out there
in the inner Inland Empire, where it is more
often hot and dry than wet and watery, lies
beautiful Etiwanda Falls, the prize of North
Etiwanda Preserve. Not only that, but the
preserve is also home to several endangered,
threatened, and sensitive species, including the
coastal California gnatcatcher, Southwestern
willow flycatcher, least Bell's vireo, San Bernardino kangaroo rat, rufous-crowned sparrow,
and San Diego horned lizard.

From the preserve trailhead, getting to the
falls is easy. Simply hike north, following the
main fire road and enjoying fine views of the
high peaks above Rancho Cucamonga. At
0.3 mile from the start, you'll reach a fork
with a sign pointing right for the picnic area
and left for the trail. Don't go left or right;
instead, head straight, hiking around a large
metal gate and staying on the fire road. From
here it is another 1.2 miles to the falls, heading gently-to-moderately uphill on the rocky
fire road. Ignore all the side roads and just
keep heading straight. In the last half-mile
you'll hike past a second metal gate, this one
painted bright yellow. There is no mistaking
the roar of the 40-foot cascade; the falls drop
over bright-orange-colored rocks in a glorious
rush of noisy whitewater.

User Groups: Hikers, dogs, horses, and mountain bikes. No wheelchair facilities.

Permits: No permits are required. Parking
and access are free.

Maps: A trail map is available at the trailhead
or by free download at www.specialdistricts
.org/2/nep.

Directions: From the junction of I-210 and
I-15, take I-15 south and exit at Baseline
Road. Drive 0.5 mile west on Baseline Road,
then turn right (north) on Etiwanda Avenue.
Drive 2.2 miles north on Etiwanda Avenue
to its junction with Wilson Avenue. Bear left
(west) on Wilson Avenue for about 100 yards
to where it reconnects with Etiwanda Avenue,
then turn right and continue on Etiwanda for
one more mile until it deadends at the parking
lot of North Etiwanda Preserve.

Contact: San Bernardino County Special
Districts Department, 157 West 5th Street,
San Bernardino, CA 92415, 909/387-5940,
www.specialdistricts.org/2/nep.

46 SEELEY CREEK TRAIL

2.0 mi / 1.0 hr   2 ▲9

in San Bernardino National Forest near
Crestline

Map 13.2, page 700

To reach the start of the Seeley Creek Trail,
you have to drive through a town called Valley
of Enchantment, and that should tell you just
about all you need to know about the area and
the trail. It's beautiful up here—no, let's say
it's enchanting—and although the elevation
is only 4,000 feet, the conifers grow so big
you'll think you're in the southern Sierra. The
Seeley Creek Trail is a short and easy walk to
a destination called Heart Rock, which during periods of rain or after snowmelt becomes
Heart Rock Falls. Heart Rock is a smooth
giant boulder in which nature has carved a
perfect, heart-shaped bowl, about three feet
deep and five feet wide. When Seeley Creek
is running strong, a 25-foot waterfall spills
into the heart's crown, then flows out the
bottom and free falls downward. The stream
flows year-round, and Heart Rock is always
fascinating to see, but it's most compelling
when the waterfall is flowing strong. The trail
begins in a rather pedestrian fashion, along a
road opposite the buildings of Seeley Camp, a
Los Angeles Parks and Recreation camp. But
once you walk beyond the camp boundary,
the enchantment begins.

User Groups: Hikers, dogs, horses, and mountain bikes. No wheelchair facilities.

Permits: No permits are required. A national forest Adventure Pass is required for each vehicle; fees are $5 for one day or $30 for a year. Interagency access passes are also accepted.

Maps: A San Bernardino National Forest map is available from the U.S. Forest Service. For a topographic map, ask the USGS for San Bernardino North.

Directions: From I-10 near San Bernardino, take I-215 north five miles to Highway 30 east. Drive two miles east on Highway 30 and exit on Highway 18/Waterman Avenue. Drive north on Highway 18 for about 20 miles to the junction of Highways 18 and 138. Turn north on Highway 138 and drive 2.5 miles to the sign for Camp Seeley, just past the town of Valley of Enchantment. Turn left at the camp sign on Road 2N03 and take the left fork in the road (don't park in the camp parking lot). Cross the creek, which usually flows over the road, and look for the double-track trail on the right, near a sewer pipeline sign. Park alongside the road. You will be directly across the creek from the main parking lot for Camp Seeley, near the playground area.

Contact: San Bernardino National Forest, Arrowhead Ranger Station, P.O. Box 350, 28104 Highway 18, Skyforest, CA 92385, 909/382-2782, www.fs.fed.us/r5/sanbernardino.

47 DEEP CREEK HOT SPRINGS

4.0 mi / 2.0 hr

in San Bernardino National Forest near Hesperia

Map 13.2, page 700

This trail is not the highlight of this trip, but its destination is. Deep Creek's hot springs are well known, well loved, and heavily visited. Although there are a few ways to hike to them, this route is the most popular simply because it's the shortest. It's called the Goat Trail for a reason—this is a no-nonsense path that leads straight down from the trailhead to the creek, and straight up on the return. The total elevation change is only 700 feet, but on a hot day, it's, well… hot. Summer temperatures can easily exceed 100°F, so most sane people visit on cool days in winter and spring. The hot springs consist of three pools alongside the creek; the hottest one is the farthest from the stream's edge. Note that the Goat Trail ends on the north side of Deep Creek, and you must ford the creek to reach the hot springs, then hike a short distance downstream. When Deep Creek is running high, this ford can be difficult, so check with the Arrowhead Ranger Station before planning an early spring visit. And keep in mind that although the hot springs are located on public Forest Service land, the trailhead is not, so you have to pay a fee to park and start your hike here. If you want to access the hot springs without paying a fee, you can start your hike on the Bradford Ridge Path, which begins where Highway 173 crosses Kinley Creek. Since these hot springs are quite popular, several rules are in effect: no camping, no nudity, and no glass containers.

User Groups: Hikers and dogs. No horses or mountain bikes. No wheelchair facilities.

Permits: No permits are required. A fee is charged by Bowen Ranch for crossing over their private land.

Maps: A San Bernardino National Forest map is available from the U.S. Forest Service. For a topographic map, ask the USGS for Lake Arrowhead.

Directions: From Cajon Pass at I-15, drive north for six miles and take the Hesperia exit. Drive east through the town of Hesperia on Main Street and turn left (east) on Rock Springs Road. Follow Rock Springs Road to its end. Turn left on Kiowa Road and drive 0.5 mile, then turn right on Roundup Way. Follow Roundup Way for 4.4 miles (it turns to dirt), then turn right on Bowen Ranch Road (dirt). Drive 2.5 miles to a fork, bear right, and drive 3.3 miles farther on Bowen Ranch Road. Stop and register at the ranch house (a fee is charged), then continue to the road's end and the parking area and trailhead.

Contact: San Bernardino National Forest,

Arrowhead Ranger Station, P.O. Box 350, 28104 Highway 18, Skyforest, CA 92385, 909/382-2782, www.fs.fed.us/r5/sanbernardino.

48 TELEGRAPH CANYON AND SOUTH RIDGE LOOP

4.0 mi / 2.0 hr   🚶2 ⛰8

in Chino Hills State Park near Riverside

Map 13.2, page 700

If you don't mind sharing your walk with equestrians and mountain bikers, this loop trail in Chino Hills State Park may be just what you need to revive yourself from a day of office work, freeways, and rush-hour traffic. Start walking on the wide Telegraph Canyon Trail from near park headquarters, following a seasonal creek. You'll head out for about two miles, climbing fairly steeply in the second mile, and then loop back on the South Ridge Trail. If you're in the mood for some single-track hiking, take the right fork one mile out on the Hills for Everyone Trail, turning left when it ends at Four Corners and returning to park headquarters on the Telegraph Canyon Trail. This makes a loop of five miles instead of four, but the grade is gentler, and since the Hills for Everyone Trail is open to hikers only, it is blissfully free of bikes and horses. The park is mostly grasslands and oaks, with a few wet canyon ravines providing homes for sycamore groves and wildlife. Native California walnut trees also grow here. Remember that the best time to visit the park is in winter or spring; if you come in summer, make it as early in the morning as possible. In addition to the heat, summer brings with it the infamous Inland Empire smog.

User Groups: Hikers, horses, and mountain bikes. No dogs. No wheelchair facilities.

Permits: No permits are required. An $8 day-use fee is charged per vehicle.

Maps: A map of Chino Hills State Park is available at the entrance kiosk or by free download at www.parks.ca.gov. For topographic maps, ask the USGS for Yorba Linda and Prado Dam.

Directions: From the junction of Highway 71 and Highway 91 near Corona, drive north on Highway 71 to Soquel Canyon Parkway. Turn left on Soquel Canyon Parkway and drive one mile to Elinvar Avenue. Turn left and drive to the end of Elinvar Avenue, at its intersection with Sapphire Road. Turn left on Sapphire Road and then right immediately at the Chino Hills State Park sign. Continue down the park road for three miles to park headquarters and turn into the parking area. The Telegraph Canyon Trail begins just below park headquarters.

Contact: Chino Hills State Park, 4721 Sapphire Road, Riverside, CA 92504, 951/780-6222, www.parks.ca.gov or www.chinohillsstatepark.org.

49 EL MORO CANYON AND RIDGE LOOP

5.2 mi / 2.5 hr   🚶2 ⛰9

in Crystal Cove State Park near Laguna Beach

Map 13.2, page 700

El Moro Canyon is on the inland side of Crystal Cove State Park, and when you see how much foliage thrives here, you'll have a hard time believing that on average, only 12 inches of rain falls each year (although during the winter of 2010–2011, the park received a whopping 48 inches!). Although El Moro Creek flows only in the wet season, its edges are lined with oaks, sycamores, and willows, and it attracts tons of birds, small mammals, and butterflies. We managed to identify the anise swallowtail butterfly (yellow and black) and the red admiral butterfly (brown, red, and black) on one trip. Unlike the other trails on the inland side of the park, the El Moro Canyon Trail is on a gentle grade, which makes it a fine route to take into the park's backcountry. The trail begins on a dirt road by the park entrance kiosk. At 1.6 miles out, turn right on the East Cut Across Trail and make a switchbacking climb up to Moro Ridge. The ascent will get your heart pumping. After a mile, turn right on the Moro Ridge Trail and follow it as it rolls along the ridge top, offering many fine ocean views. Be sure to take the short spur trail off the Moro Ridge Trail to Emerald Vista, a scenic spot for a lunch break before heading back downhill. Then backtrack to the Moro Ridge Trail and finish out your loop by turning right on the BFI Trail (don't ask us what it stands for because we can't print it). It's pretty hard to get lost in this park; every major junction is marked with a "you are here" trail map.

User Groups: Hikers, horses, and mountain bikes. No dogs. No wheelchair facilities.

Permits: No permits are required. A $15 day-use fee is charged per vehicle.

Maps: A trail map of Crystal Cove State Park is available at the visitors center or by free download at www.parks.ca.gov. For a topographic map, ask the USGS for Laguna Beach.

Directions: From Corona del Mar, drive south on Highway 1 for three miles to the entrance to Crystal Cove State Park, on the inland side of the highway. Park near the ranger station; the El Moro Canyon Trail begins down the park road by the entrance kiosk.

Contact: Crystal Cove State Park, 8471 Pacific Coast Highway, Laguna Beach, CA 92651, 949/494-3539 or 949/492-0802, www.parks.ca.gov or www.crystalcove-statepark.com.

50 BOMMER RIDGE AND BOAT CANYON

9.6 mi / 5.0 hr

in Laguna Coast Wilderness Park near Laguna Beach

Map 13.2, page 700

If you are a nature lover living in or visiting Southern California, Orange County is probably not the first place you think about when it comes to hiking. Shopping, maybe. Beach-going, definitely. But if you haven't visited Orange County's Laguna Coast Wilderness Park, you're in for a pleasant surprise. In a county

largely given over to development, this 6,500-acre park contains one of the few remaining parcels of coastal sage scrub habitat. You'll smell its wonderful scent almost everywhere you walk. It also holds the only natural lakes in Orange County.

This view-filled hike starts with a climb up Willow Canyon to the Bommer Ridge Trail. The ridge offers expansive vistas of neighboring sage-covered canyons and the wide blue Pacific. Connect to the Boat Canyon Trail and head out for more views, now of Emerald Bay, Irvine Cove, and the beaches around Laguna. You'll have to backtrack to find your way back to your car, but who wouldn't want to see this scenery all over again? On the final stretch, you can opt to take the Laguna Laurel Canyon Trail instead of the Willow Trail. Many interesting rock outcrops can be seen along this stretch, plus wildflowers and plentiful birds. If you're not up for this long hike but would still like to explore Laguna Coast Wilderness Park, a 3.5-mile docent-led hike through Laurel Canyon is offered every Saturday morning at 9 A.M. Or just wander on your own; this is one park where it doesn't matter much where you go. It's all good. If you'd like to learn more about Laguna Coast Wilderness Park and its many trails, stop in at the James and Rosemary Nix Nature Center at the Little Sycamore Canyon Staging Area on Laguna Canyon Road. The center is open daily 9 A.M.–4 P.M.

User Groups: Hikers, horses, and mountain bikes. No dogs. No wheelchair facilities.

Permits: No permits are required. A $3 day-use fee is charged per vehicle.

Maps: A trail map is available at the parking area. For a topographic map, ask the USGS for Laguna Beach.

Directions: From I-405 in Irvine, exit south on Laguna Canyon Road. The main park entrance is located 0.3 mile south of the El Toro Road intersection. Or, from Laguna Beach, drive 3.1 miles north on Laguna Canyon Road to the park entrance on the left.

Contact: Laguna Coast Wilderness Park, 18751 Laguna Canyon Road, Laguna Beach, CA 92651,

949/923-2235, www.ocparks.com/lagunacoast or www.lagunacanyon.org.

51 HOLY JIM FALLS

2.5 mi / 1.5 hr   👣2   ⛰9

in Trabuco Canyon in Cleveland National Forest

Map 13.2, page 700

It seems that everybody in Orange County knows about and likes to visit Holy Jim Falls. The waterfall and its canyon were named for a beekeeper who lived here in the 1890s—James T. Smith, better known as Cussin' Jim. Apparently he had a temper and a colorful way with language. But conservative map makers who plotted Trabuco Canyon in the early 20th century found Smith's nickname in bad taste, so they changed it to Holy Jim, and it remains. Whether it's because of the interesting history of the area or the beauty that it still exhibits today, the trail to Holy Jim Falls is well known and frequently walked, especially in springtime. The 2.5-mile stroll is in the cool shade along Holy Jim Creek. Start by walking down the dirt road, past some leased cabins, to the signed trailhead. There the trail turns to single track. You're surrounded by a lush canyon filled with oaks, vine maples, wildflowers, and even a few bracken ferns. The trail crosses the creek several times and gently gains some elevation as it heads upstream. Where the trail steepens noticeably as you pass a large, old oak tree on your left, cross the creek one final time. Instead of following the main trail as it switchbacks uphill, you'll head to the right, continuing along the stream. An easy 300-yard stream scramble brings you to the waterfall's base, and if there isn't a scout troop there eating lunch (as there was on our trip), you'll be able to listen to the sweet music of the falls.

User Groups: Hikers, dogs, horses, and mountain bikes. No wheelchair facilities.

Permits: No permits are required. A national forest Adventure Pass is required for each vehicle; fees are $5 for one day or $30 for a year. Interagency access passes are also accepted.

Maps: A Cleveland National Forest map is available from the U.S. Forest Service. For a topographic map, ask the USGS for Santiago Peak.

Directions: From Laguna Hills (north of San Juan Capistrano) on I-5, exit on El Toro Road and drive east for six miles. Turn right on Live Oak Canyon Road and drive about four miles (two miles past the entrance to O'Neill Regional Park). Turn left on Trabuco Canyon Road, which is an often unsigned, rocky, dirt road just past the paved Rose Canyon Road turnoff. The road is usually suitable for passenger cars. Go five miles on the dirt road to the well-signed parking area for the Holy Jim Trail. The trail leads from the left side of the parking lot.

Contact: Cleveland National Forest, Trabuco Ranger District, 1147 E. Sixth Street, Corona, CA 92879, 909/736-1811, www.fs.fed.us/r5/cleveland.

52 BELL CANYON AND EAST RIDGE LOOP

5.2 mi / 2.5 hr   👣2   ⛰8

in Ronald W. Caspers Wilderness Park

Map 13.2, page 700

Caspers is Orange County's largest public parkland, covering a whopping 8,000 acres in the western Santa Ana Mountains. The park received a bad rap in 1986 when two children were attacked by a mountain lion. While some people may be scared off by this terrible piece of history, many locals consider Caspers to be the best park in Orange County. Even the drive to reach it is a pleasure—a winding cruise inland from the coast, past ranches, nurseries, and long stretches of open space. The 5.2-mile Bell Canyon and East Ridge Loop is a great introduction to the park's myriad charms. Start on the East Ridge Trail across from Live Oak Campground. The initial steep climb will get your heart pumping, but in spring, you are rewarded with a colorful display of wildflowers. At any time of year you'll gain panoramic views of Bell Canyon below and the surrounding peaks and ridges of Cleveland National Forest. On clear days the town of San Juan Capistrano comes into view, as well as the coast beyond, and sometimes even San Clemente Island. After two miles on the East Ridge Trail, turn left on the Sun Rise Trail and hike 0.6 mile through grasslands and coastal sage scrub to connect to the Bell Canyon Trail (via a short stint on the Cougar Pass Trail). A left turn on the Bell Canyon Trail will lead you through the canyon's lush, leafy canopy of oaks and sycamores. You'll cross Bell Creek a few times, then pass through a gate that leads into the Old Corral Picnic Area. Here you'll find the park's often-photographed old windmill, a reminder of this fertile valley's cattle ranching days in the 1940s. The Bell Canyon Trail continues past the park's equestrian campground and then winds its way back to your starting point at Live Oak Campground.

User Groups: Hikers and horses. No dogs or mountain bikes. No wheelchair facilities.

Permits: No permits are required. A $3 day-use fee is charged per vehicle.

Maps: Free trail maps are available at the trailhead, or you can download one at www.ocparks.com/caspers. For a topographic map, ask the USGS for Canada Gobernadora.

Directions: From I-5 at San Juan Capistrano, take the Ortega Highway (Highway 74) exit and drive northeast for 7.6 miles. The park entrance is on the left. Park near Live Oak Campground; the trail begins there.

Contact: Ronald W. Caspers Wilderness Park, 33401 Ortega Highway, San Juan Capistrano, CA 92675, 949/923-2210, www.ocparks.com.

53 SAN JUAN LOOP TRAIL

2.0 mi / 1.0 hr   👫2 ⛰8

in Cleveland National Forest
near Lake Elsinore

Map 13.2, page 700

The San Juan Loop Trail is an easy and informative walk that serves as a good introduction to the Santa Ana Mountains. The only factor you must consider: Don't try to hike here in summer, when these mountains can feel hotter than the desert. The trailhead features a rather negative sign, which explains in doomsday-style the dangers of mountain lions, rattlesnakes, poison oak, and rugged terrain. If the sign doesn't convince you to get back in the car and go to Disneyland instead, start hiking on the loop trail, which parallels the road for its first 0.5 mile. You'll forget about the car noise as you start examining all the plant life along the trail, which includes deep red monkeyflowers, purple nightshade, and tall, spiky yuccas with their silky, milk-white flowers. Lizards dart here and there among the foliage. The terrain is dry and exposed, but thriving nonetheless. A half mile out, you'll pass a railing and overlook above a small seasonal waterfall on San Juan Creek, which has many clear, granite-lined pools. In another 0.5 mile, you'll pass the turnoff for the Chiquito Basin Trail (it's highly recommended for those seeking a longer trip), and then you'll pass through a lovely grove of ancient oaks. The loop trail finishes out by bringing you back to the opposite side of the parking lot.

User Groups: Hikers, dogs, horses, and mountain bikes. No wheelchair facilities.

Permits: No permits are required. A national forest Adventure Pass is required for each vehicle; fees are $5 for one day or $30 for a year. Interagency access passes are also accepted.

Maps: A Cleveland National Forest map is available from the U.S. Forest Service. For a topographic map, ask the USGS for Sitton Peak.

Directions: From I-5 at San Juan Capistrano, take the Ortega Highway/Highway 74 exit and drive north. In 21 miles, you'll reach the Ortega Oaks store on the right, 0.75 mile past Upper San Juan Campground. The trailhead is across the road from the store; turn left and park in the large parking lot. Start the loop trail on the right (north) side of the parking lot.

Contact: Cleveland National Forest, Trabuco Ranger District, 1147 E. Sixth Street, Corona, CA 92879, 909/736-1811, www.fs.fed.us/r5/cleveland.

54 BEAR CANYON LOOP TRAIL

6.7 mi / 3.5 hr 🥾2 ⛰️8

in the San Mateo Canyon Wilderness near Lake Elsinore

Map 13.2, page 700

Is it winter or spring? Is the weather cool and clear? If you've answered yes to both, this is a fine time to take a hike on the Bear Canyon Trail—either a little out-and-back trip for as far as you like, or the full 6.7-mile loop, which circles a junction called Four Corners. First, stock up on some chocolate from the candy store at the trailhead (this is why it must be a cool day; otherwise, carrying chocolate is out of the question). Set off on the trail adjacent to the store, heading into the San Mateo Canyon Wilderness and climbing gently through chaparral-covered slopes. In spring, many yuccas bloom along this stretch. Take the right fork one mile in, and in another mile, you'll reach the start of the loop; take the right branch to start. The trail has a mere 700-foot elevation gain, and in places, it offers expansive views of the San Juan Canyon. Pigeon Springs is a popular resting point, where you can find some shade among the oaks. Four Corners is 0.5 mile beyond Pigeon Springs, and there, you'll turn sharply left to loop back. If you're looking for more of a workout, you can always turn right at Four Corners to head for 3,280-foot Sitton Peak. On the clearest days, you can see up to 50 miles distant from the summit. It looks like you could take a big leap and land on Catalina Island. Sitton Peak is a 9.5-mile round-trip.

User Groups: Hikers, dogs, and horses. No mountain bikes. No wheelchair facilities.

Permits: No permits are required. A national forest Adventure Pass is required for each vehicle; fees are $5 for one day or $30 for a year. Interagency access passes are also accepted.

Maps: A Cleveland National Forest map is available from the U.S. Forest Service. For a topographic map, ask the USGS for Sitton Peak.

Directions: From I-5 at San Juan Capistrano, take the Ortega Highway/Highway 74 exit and drive north. In 21 miles, you'll reach the Ortega Oaks store on the right, 0.75 mile past Upper San Juan Campground. The parking area is across the road from the store; turn left and park in the large parking lot. Cross the road to begin hiking on the Bear Canyon Trail, to the right of the store.

Contact: Cleveland National Forest, Trabuco Ranger District, 1147 E. Sixth Street, Corona, CA 92879, 909/736-1811, www.fs.fed.us/r5/cleveland.

55 TENAJA FALLS

1.5 mi / 1.0 hr 🥾2 ⛰️9

in the San Mateo Canyon Wilderness near Murrieta

Map 13.2, page 700

The only hard part about getting to Tenaja Falls is the long drive to the unmarked trailhead. But if you follow the driving directions exactly, even that shouldn't be a problem. Once you've parked, head for the fence that blocks vehicles from the road into the San Mateo Canyon Wilderness. Cross the creek on a concrete apron, or if the water is too deep, follow a use trail upstream and cross the creek where it's narrower. Just be sure to join up with the main road again; following the streamside use trails is a needlessly difficult way to the falls. (Guess how we know.) On the wide canyon road, you'll hike northward, rising out of the canyon alongside sage- and chaparral-covered hillsides. In a few minutes, you'll round a curve and be treated to a partial view of the waterfall ahead. What a sight—Tenaja Falls is huge compared to other waterfalls in Orange County, dropping 150 feet in five tiers. It's magnificent when flowing full, which is only after a period of rain, usually between December and March. Keep walking toward the waterfall; the trail deposits you at its lip. When the water is low enough, you can cross over the top of the falls to the other side of the creek, but be extremely cautious on the slippery granite if you choose to do so. Note that you can also hike to Tenaja Falls from the Tenaja trailhead (you'll pass it on your way in), but it's a much longer, 5.4-mile one-way trek.

User Groups: Hikers, dogs, and horses. No mountain bikes. No wheelchair facilities.

Permits: No permits are required. A national forest Adventure Pass is required for each vehicle; fees are $5 for one day or $30 for a year. Interagency access passes are also accepted.

Maps: A Cleveland National Forest map is available from the U.S. Forest Service. For a topographic map, ask the USGS for Sitton Peak.

Directions: From Lake Elsinore, drive south on I-15 for about 12 miles to the Clinton Keith Road exit in Murrieta. Drive south on Clinton Keith Road, which becomes Tenaja Road, for 4.5 miles. At a signed intersection with Tenaja Road, turn right and drive 4.3 miles west. Turn right on Cleveland Forest Road and drive one mile to the Tenaja trailhead. Stay straight, passing by the trailhead, and reset your odometer. Continue 4.4 miles on Road 7S04 to a hairpin turn and a parking pullout on the left.

Contact: Cleveland National Forest, Trabuco Ranger District, 1147 E. Sixth Street, Corona, CA 92879, 909/736-1811, www.fs.fed.us/r5/cleveland.

56 SANTA ROSA PLATEAU ECOLOGICAL RESERVE

4.5 mi / 2.5 hr   🥾2 ⛰️8

in the Santa Rosa Plateau Ecological Reserve

Map 13.2, page 700

Those volcanic-looking rocky mesas you see as you drive through the foothills along Clinton Keith Road are home to some of Southern California's last vernal pools. These are seasonal ponds that give life to endangered plants and wildflowers and provide a resting place for wintering birds. Whereas these pools are more common in the San Joaquin Valley, in Southern California they have all but vanished, which is one reason for the establishment of the Santa Rosa Plateau Ecological Reserve. Another reason is the existence of the rare Engelmann oak, a semi-deciduous species of oak that only loses its leaves during times of drought. Several fine groves of Engelmann oaks are found within the reserve's border.

If you're visiting in late winter or early spring and you just want to see the vernal pools, you can do so with a one-mile walk on the Vernal Pool Trail from a trailhead located two miles west of the reserve visitors center, on Clinton Keith Road. If you're here at any other time of the year, your best bet is to start your trip at the visitors center. If you can, show up on weekday afternoons or on Saturday morning and go on one of the ranger-led interpretive hikes (call ahead for an exact schedule). If you'd rather hike on your own, start out on the left side of the Granite Loop Trail. Connect to the Vista Grande Trail and head uphill to its junction with Monument Road. You'll pass some lovely Engelmann oaks along the way. Turn right on Monument Road, then take the left spur to the top of Monument Hill (elevation 2,046 feet), the highest point in the reserve. The views of the chaparral- and cactus-covered hills and rolling grasslands are lovely. If you arrive early in the morning before the frequent afternoon haze moves in, you'll be able to pick out classic Southern California landmarks: Mounts San Gorgonio, San Jacinto, and Palomar;

Cuyamaca Peak and Mount Woodson, in San Diego; the high summits of the San Gabriel Mountains; and yes, even the Pacific Ocean. Retrace your steps to head back, or make a semi-loop by turning left on the Tenaja Truck Trail, then right on Waterline Road.

User Groups: Hikers, horses, and mountain bikes. (Horses and mountain bikes allowed only on signed multiuse trails.) No dogs. No wheelchair facilities.

Permits: No permits are required. A $2 day-use fee is charged per adult; $1 for children 12 and under.

Maps: A trail map is available at the visitors center and at all four trailheads in the reserve. For a topographic map, ask the USGS for Wildomar.

Directions: From Lake Elsinore, drive south on I-15 for about 12 miles to the Clinton Keith Road exit in Murrieta. Drive west on Clinton Keith Road for four miles (past Aveneda La Cresta) to the visitors center entrance, on the left. Park near the visitors center.

Contact: Santa Rosa Plateau Ecological Reserve, 39400 Clinton Keith Road, Murrieta, CA 92562, 909/677-6951, www.rivcoparks.org.

57 GRAY'S PEAK
7.0 mi / 3.5 hr

in San Bernardino National Forest
near Big Bear Lake

Map 13.3, page 701

Check your calendar before you set off on this peak hike; this trail is closed from November 1 to April 1 to protect bald eagles that nest in the area. But the rest of the year, if you want to get up high and get a good look at Big Bear Lake, this trail will fit the bill. A bonus is that it is easy enough (only a 1,200-foot elevation gain) that most older children can make the trip comfortably. A negative, for some, is that this is also a popular mountain-biking trail, but the riders we saw were all very courteous to hikers. The trail starts out by heading roughly west, then joins with a dirt road. There are only two junctions

to worry about. Turn right at the first junction, walk about 200 yards, and then turn left to access the "official" Gray's Peak Trail. From there it is 2.75 miles to the top, with a little scrambling required in the last 0.25 mile. The summit is located at 7,920 feet, and offers inspiring views of the lake through a filter of lodgepole pines. The sound of the wind in the pines will accompany you for much of this hike. Like so many places in Big Bear, the boulder outcrops along this trail and on the summit are fascinating, and will tempt you to climb on top.

User Groups: Hikers, dogs, horses, and mountain bikes. No wheelchair facilities.

Permits: No permits are required. A national forest Adventure Pass is required for each vehicle; fees are $5 for one day or $30 for a year. Interagency access passes are also accepted.

Maps: A San Bernardino National Forest map is available from the U.S. Forest Service. For a topographic map, ask the USGS for Fawnskin.

Directions: From the town of Big Bear Lake on Highway 18, take the Stanfield cutoff to the north shore of the lake, where it junctions with Highway 38. Turn left and drive 3.5 miles on Highway 38 to the Gray's Peak trailhead, on the right side of the road 0.6 mile west of the town of Fawnskin. If the parking area at the trailhead is full, you can park across the highway at Grout Bay Picnic Area.

Contact: San Bernardino National Forest, Big Bear Discovery Center, P.O. Box 66, 41397 North Shore Drive, Fawnskin, CA 92333, 909/866-3437 or 909/382-2790, www.fs.fed.us/r5/sanbernardino.

58 COUGAR CREST TRAIL TO BERTHA PEAK
6.0 mi / 3.0 hr

in San Bernardino National Forest
near Big Bear Lake

Map 13.3, page 701

Put on your hiking boots and prepare to climb. That's what you have to do on the Cougar Crest

Trail—gain 1,300 feet over three miles to reach Bertha Peak, elevation 8,201 feet. You can see the peak, capped with electronic relay equipment, from the trailhead parking lot. Views of the Big Bear area are spectacular along the route, and the trail is well built, making this an excellent day hike—or running path if you're a jogger. The first mile is on dirt roads in a forest of piñon and Jeffrey pines, but soon the path narrows to single track. The more you climb upward, the more you see; turn around every now and then to check out the lake and mountain views. Finally, at two miles, you reach the Pacific Crest Trail (PCT), where the grade eases considerably. Turn right and follow the PCT for 0.5 mile to a dirt road, then turn right again and climb steeply to reach Bertha's summit. Look for old, gnarled juniper trees along the route. The view from the peak includes Big Bear Lake, of course, plus Mount San Gorgonio and other high peaks and ridges, and green Holcomb Valley below you.

User Groups: Hikers, dogs, and horses. No mountain bikes. No wheelchair facilities.

Permits: No permits are required. A national forest Adventure Pass is required for each vehicle; fees are $5 for one day or $30 for a year. Interagency access passes are also accepted.

Maps: A San Bernardino National Forest map is available from the U.S. Forest Service. For a topographic map, ask the USGS for Fawnskin.

Directions: From the town of Big Bear Lake on Highway 18, take the Stanfield cutoff to the north shore of the lake, where it junctions with Highway 38. Turn left and drive 1.3 miles on Highway 38 (.5 mile past the Big Bear Ranger Station) to the Cougar Crest trailhead, on the right side of the road. If you are traveling from Fawnskin, the trailhead is 2.4 miles east of Fawnskin on Highway 38, on the left side of the road.

Contact: San Bernardino National Forest, Big Bear Discovery Center, P.O. Box 66, 41397 North Shore Drive, Fawnskin, CA 92333, 909/866-3437 or 909/382-2790, www.fs.fed.us/r5/sanbernardino.

59 WOODLAND TRAIL
1.5 mi / 0.75 hr

in San Bernardino National Forest
near Big Bear Lake

Map 13.3, page 701

If you're spending the weekend or the week in Big Bear, you'd be well advised to pay a visit to the Big Bear Discovery Center, in Fawnskin. You can get all the information you want about hiking, fishing, and exploring around the Big Bear area from the nice people there. Then take this terrific short walk on the Woodland Trail, which starts near the visitors center. You can pick up an interpretive brochure and learn all about serviceberry, yerba santa, Jeffrey and ponderosa pines, indigo bush, and piñon pines. A bonus is that on the return leg of the loop, you get great views of the lake, but you're far enough away that you don't get hit by the wind that often blows on the north side. From high points on the trail, your vista expands all the way across the lake to Big Bear City.

User Groups: Hikers, dogs, and mountain bikes. No horses. No wheelchair facilities.

Permits: No permits are required. A national forest Adventure Pass is required for each vehicle; fees are $5 for one day or $30 for a year. Interagency access passes are also accepted.

Maps: A San Bernardino National Forest map is available from the U.S. Forest Service. For a topographic map, ask the USGS for Fawnskin.

Directions: From the town of Big Bear Lake on Highway 18, take the Stanfield cutoff to the north shore of the lake, where it junctions with Highway 38. Turn left on Highway 38 and drive 0.5 mile to the Woodland trailhead, on the right side of the road. It's directly across the highway from the East Boat Ramp, or one mile east of the Big Bear Discovery Center.

Contact: San Bernardino National Forest, Big Bear Discovery Center, P.O. Box 66, 41397 North Shore Drive, Fawnskin, CA 92333, 909/866-3437 or 909/382-2790, www.fs.fed.us/r5/sanbernardino.

60 CHAMPION LODGEPOLE PINE

1.0 mi / 0.5 hr   🏃1 ⛰8

in San Bernardino National Forest
near Big Bear Lake

Map 13.3, page 701

Let's see now. The biggest giant sequoia tree is the General Sherman Tree, in Sequoia National Park. But which is the biggest lodgepole pine tree, and where do you find it? We're delighted you asked. It's the Champion Lodgepole, located only a few miles from Big Bear Lake. The big tree is growing in a grove of world champions, the largest lodgepole pines around. What's strange is that these big guys are growing at 7,500 feet in elevation, when usually in Southern California, lodgepole pines won't grow at less than 8,000 feet. The Champion is about 400 years old, stands 112 feet tall, and has a circumference of 20 feet. After a long but enjoyable drive on a dirt road to the trailhead, you'll find the trail to the big tree is flat and easy. It follows a small stream to a junction. Turn right and walk the last few yards to the Champion, which is surrounded by a fence and situated at the edge of a pretty meadow.

User Groups: Hikers, dogs, horses, and mountain bikes. No wheelchair facilities.

Permits: No permits are required. A national forest Adventure Pass is required for each vehicle; fees are $5 for one day or $30 for a year. Interagency access passes are also accepted.

Maps: A San Bernardino National Forest map is available from the U.S. Forest Service. For a topographic map, ask the USGS for Big Bear Lake.

Directions: From the dam on the west end of Big Bear Lake, drive 3.5 miles east on Highway 18/Big Bear Boulevard to Mill Creek Road. Turn right (south) on Mill Creek Road/Forest Service Road 2N10 and follow it for five miles, through several junctions. (The road turns to dirt.) At Forest Service Road 2N11, turn right and drive one mile to the parking area. The route is well signed for the Champion Lodgepole Pine.

Contact: San Bernardino National Forest, Big Bear Discovery Center, P.O. Box 66, 41397 North Shore Drive, Fawnskin, CA 92333, 909/866-3437 or 909/382-2790, www.fs.fed.us/r5/sanbernardino.

61 CASTLE ROCK TRAIL

2.0 mi / 1.0 hr   🏃3 ⛰9

in San Bernardino National Forest
near Big Bear Lake

Map 13.3, page 701

There are a couple tricky elements about this trail: There's no real parking area, just a pullout along the highway, and although the path to Castle Rock has a mere 700-foot elevation gain, it's compressed into one mile and climbs steeply right from the trailhead. The trail is smooth sand, surrounded by manzanita, big ponderosa pines, and a ton of rocks. It's located by the area of Big Bear Lake called Boulder Bay, a perfectly descriptive name. As you climb, you gain tremendous views of the lake, but you'll miss them completely unless you turn around. In about 20 minutes you'll reach a rocky overlook, which is where many people stop and pull up a granite boulder to sit on. The main trail becomes a spiderweb of trails, as people have chosen all different routes around the rocks. If you continue upward, you'll reach a saddle and then start to descend slightly. Castle Rock, which is easily distinguishable by its shape, is just to the east, off the trail as you head downhill. If you tire out before the saddle, just pick any boulder that's easy to climb and get on top to enjoy the lovely views of the lake. On one trip in late March we were treated to a lovely shower of snow flurries. Isn't Big Bear the greatest? Trailhead elevation is 6,700 feet.

User Groups: Hikers, dogs, and mountain bikes. No horses. No wheelchair facilities.

Permits: No permits are required. A national forest Adventure Pass is required for each vehicle; fees are $5 for one day or $30 for a year. Interagency access passes are also accepted.

Maps: A San Bernardino National Forest map is available from the U.S. Forest Service. For a topographic map, ask the USGS for Big Bear Lake.

Directions: From the dam on the west end of Big Bear Lake, drive one mile east on Highway 18/Big Bear Boulevard to the signed Castle Rock trailhead, on the right (it's by the Big Bear City Limit sign). Park in the turnout on the lake side of Highway 18, about 50 yards farther east, and then walk across the road to the trailhead.

Contact: San Bernardino National Forest, Big Bear Discovery Center, P.O. Box 66, 41397 North Shore Drive, Fawnskin, CA 92333, 909/866-3437 or 909/382-2790, www.fs.fed.us/r5/sanbernardino.

62 PONDEROSA VISTA NATURE TRAIL

1.0 mi / 0.5 hr

in San Bernardino National Forest
near Angelus Oaks

Map 13.3, page 701   **BEST (**

The Ponderosa Vista Nature Trail wins hands down for the trail with the most corny interpretive plaques. When you visit, you'll see what we mean. But aside from the overdone prose, everything else on this trail is first-rate, making for a great introduction to the flora and fauna of San Bernardino National Forest. You can choose between the short loop (0.3 mile) and the long loop (0.6 mile), but why not hike both? You can learn about assorted birds of the forest, such as acorn woodpeckers, redbreasted sapsuckers, and yellow-rumped warblers, as well as various trees—ponderosa pine is the most common conifer in the area, but incense cedars, black oaks, white firs, and piñon pines also grow. The highlight of the trail is an overlook point with a view across the Santa Ana River Canyon. An old photograph at the overlook shows what the canyon used to look like and explains about the building of the Rim of the World Highway in 1935. That was the same year that black bears were introduced to the area. No wonder—with

the new highway, they could just get into their RVs and drive in.

User Groups: Hikers, dogs, horses, and mountain bikes. No wheelchair facilities.

Permits: No permits are required. A national forest Adventure Pass is required for each vehicle; fees are $5 for one day or $30 for a year. Interagency access passes are also accepted.

Maps: A San Bernardino National Forest map is available from the U.S. Forest Service. For a topographic map, ask the USGS for Big Bear Lake.

Directions: From I-10 at Redlands, take the Highway 38 exit and drive northeast for 25 miles to the trailhead for the Ponderosa Vista Nature Trail, on the left side of the road. If you reach the Jenks Lake turnoff, you've passed it. Park in the parking lot by the trailhead.

Contact: San Bernardino National Forest, Mill Creek Ranger Station, 34701 Mill Creek Road, Mentone, CA 92359, 909/382-2882, www.fs.fed.us/r5/sanbernardino.

63 WHISPERING PINES TRAIL

0.5 mi / 0.5 hr

in San Bernardino National Forest
near Angelus Oaks

Map 13.3, page 701

Right across the road from the Ponderosa Vista Trail is the Whispering Pines Trail, another short, easy interpretive trail that is both fun and informative. Time to play *Trivial Pursuit:* This trail appeared on what television show, filmed in 1969, about a blind girl and a furry dog? If you guessed *Lassie,* you win. In the show, the girl walked this trail and read the braille interpretive displays. Anyway, this nature trail has less of a grade than the one across the highway, although it's not quite as scenic. You will see numerous pines with an incredible amount of holes drilled in them—the work of industrious acorn woodpeckers. A minus is the sound of nearby Highway 38, but the pluses are the sound of the wind in the pines and lots of squirrels and jays.

User Groups: Hikers, dogs, horses, and mountain bikes. No wheelchair facilities.

Permits: No permits are required. A national forest Adventure Pass is required for each vehicle; fees are $5 for one day or $30 for a year. Interagency access passes are also accepted.

Maps: A San Bernardino National Forest map is available from the U.S. Forest Service. For a topographic map, ask the USGS for Big Bear Lake.

Directions: From I-10 at Redlands, take the Highway 38 exit and drive northeast for 25 miles to the trailhead for the Whispering Pines Trail, on the right side of the road. If you reach the Jenks Lake turnoff, you've passed it. Park in the well-signed parking lot by the trailhead.

Contact: San Bernardino National Forest, Mill Creek Ranger Station, 34701 Mill Creek Road, Mentone, CA 92359, 909/382-2882, www.fs.fed.us/r5/sanbernardino.

64 JENKS LAKE

1.0 mi / 0.5 hr

in San Bernardino National Forest
near Angelus Oaks

Map 13.3, page 701

If you can get to Jenks Lake on a weekday when nobody is around, you'll find it's a magical little spot of bright blue water, with Mount San Gorgonio looming in the background. Even in April, the peak can be crested with snow and the wind can whip off the surface of the small lake, creating little whitecaps. If you visit Jenks Lake on a Saturday in July, however, it's another story. The place is likely to be packed with picnicking families, kids from nearby summer camps, and people fishing for largemouth bass, bluegill, and rainbow trout in the stocked lake. (No swimming is allowed, though.) No matter when you arrive, you should take the short walk around the perimeter of the lake, then head off on the nature trail that leads behind the picnic area. The south shore of the lake is the quieter side.

After looping around the lake, walk to the back side of the picnic area, where you're likely to be surprised by the view from the trail—the canyon drops off vertically, with sheer cliffs that fall hundreds of feet. Yes, this is the Rim of the World, just like the highway of the same name. Fortunately a railing is in place to keep you from leaning too far over the edge. Note that hikers looking for a longer adventure can set off from either the South Fork or Forsee Creek trailheads (near Jenks Lake) and head into the San Gorgonio Wilderness. If you don't have a permit, you can always walk just to the wilderness boundary and turn around.

User Groups: Hikers and dogs. No horses or mountain bikes. Some wheelchair facilities available.

Permits: No permits are required. A $5 day-use fee is charged per vehicle (the national forest Adventure Pass does not apply here).

Maps: A San Bernardino National Forest map is available from the U.S. Forest Service. For a topographic map, ask the USGS for Big Bear Lake.

Directions: From I-10 at Redlands, take the Highway 38 exit and drive northeast for 27 miles to the Jenks Lake turnoff on the right. Turn right and follow Jenks Lake Road west for two miles to the parking area for the lake. Note that Jenks Lake Road continues and reconnects to Highway 38 a few miles to the east.

Contact: San Bernardino National Forest, Mill Creek Ranger Station, 34701 Mill Creek Road, Mentone, CA 92359, 909/382-2882, www.fs.fed.us/r5/sanbernardino.

65 ASPEN GROVE TRAIL

5.0 mi / 2.5 hr

in the San Gorgonio Wilderness
near Angelus Oaks

Map 13.3, page 701

From the Aspen Grove trailhead, a short walk down a dirt road leads you into a cool and shady grove of aspen trees along Fish Creek, one of only two remaining in San Bernardino National Forest. For decades this small grove was threatened by nonnative beavers, which were introduced to the area by the California Department of Fish and Game in the 1940s. After the beavers chewed down a whole bunch of the aspens, the smart folks at Fish and Game decided it would be best to remove them. You may still see evidence of their presence in the form of chewed stumps, but the beavers are gone. If you're accustomed to the aspen trees of the eastern Sierra, you'll notice that these have smaller leaves—an adaptation to the dry climate. One tip: Don't show up in winter or early spring, when the aspens have no leaves at all. Autumn is the best time to see them, when they are bright gold in color. If you want to do more than hike down the hill and wander among the aspens, you must have a wilderness permit. Once you cross Fish Creek, you're in the San Gorgonio Wilderness. The trail to the right leads to a few more aspens and then peters out. Follow the trail to your left (uphill), heading away from the creek. A pretty walk of less than two miles through a mixed conifer forest will deliver you to two meadows—first, tiny Monkey Flower Flat, and then, after crossing Fish Creek again, Lower Fish Creek Meadow. It's a fine place to lay out a picnic and count the wildflowers. A side note: The drive to and from the Aspen Grove trailhead is awesome, with wide views at every turn in the road, but if it hasn't been graded recently, it may be impassible for low-clearance, two-wheel-drive vehicles. It is also subject to winter closures.

User Groups: Hikers, dogs, and horses. No mountain bikes. No wheelchair facilities.

Permits: A free wilderness permit is required for both day hiking and backpacking and is available in advance from the Mill Creek Ranger Station. Permits can also be obtained in person at the Mill Creek Ranger Station or Barton Flats Visitors Center on Highway 38. A national forest Adventure Pass is required for each vehicle; fees are $5 for one day or $30 for a year. Interagency access passes are also accepted.

Maps: A San Bernardino National Forest or San Gorgonio Wilderness map is available from the U.S. Forest Service. A San Gorgonio Wilderness map is available from Tom Harrison Maps. For a topographic map, ask the USGS for Moonridge.

Directions: From I-10 at Redlands, take the Highway 38 exit and drive northeast for 32 miles to Forest Service Road 1N02, signed for Heart Bar Campground, Coon Creek, and Fish Creek. Turn right (south) and drive 1.25 miles to Road 1N05, then bear right. Drive 1.5 miles to the Aspen Grove trailhead, on the right. This last stretch of dirt road can sometimes be difficult for low-clearance, two-wheel-drive vehicles, depending on recent weather.

Contact: San Bernardino National Forest, Mill Creek Ranger Station, 34701 Mill Creek Road, Mentone, CA 92359, 909/382-2882, www.fs.fed.us/r5/sanbernardino.

66 BIG FALLS

0.6 mi / 0.5 hr

in Big Falls Recreation Area near Forest Falls

Map 13.3, page 701

Quick—what's the largest year-round waterfall in Southern California? Big Falls, of course. At 500 feet tall, Big Falls delivers on its name, but unfortunately it's difficult to see the waterfall's full height. That's okay, though, because the Big Falls Recreation Area is still a great destination, and the short hike to the overlook of Big Falls is a fun and easy walk. The elevation at the trailhead is just over 6,000 feet, which means the air is cool and clear. Begin hiking at the lower parking lot, below the picnic area, and set off on an unsigned path heading downstream along Mill Creek Wash. When you pass a private cabin alongside the wash, look for a good place to cross Mill Creek by rock hopping, and then do so. On the far side of the stream, pick up the trail leading uphill on the right side of Falls Creek, which is a feeder stream to Mill Creek. Hike past a small cascade on the bottom of Falls Creek, and head uphill for about five minutes to the overlook area for Big Falls. What you see is the top 40 to 50 feet of a very Yosemite-like free fall, and then some cascading water below. The huge middle part of the fall is hidden in the rocky canyon. Darn. So where can you get a better view of Big Falls? Actually, the best view is from your car window, as you drive past the last few houses along Valley of the Falls Road, shortly before entering the Big Falls Recreation Area. Along this stretch, you can see the full-length vista of Big Falls that usually appears on postcards. Another good spot is at the turnaround loop just before you enter the main parking lot for the falls.

User Groups: Hikers, dogs, horses, and mountain bikes. No wheelchair facilities.

Permits: No permits are required. A national forest Adventure Pass is required for each vehicle; fees are $5 for one day or $30 for a year. Interagency access passes are also accepted.

Maps: A San Bernardino National Forest is available from the U.S. Forest Service. For a topographic map, ask the USGS for Forest Falls.

Directions: From I-10 at Redlands, take the Highway 38 exit and drive northeast for approximately 14 miles to the intersection with Valley of the Falls Road. Bear right and continue for 4.5 miles to the Big Falls Recreation Area, past the town of Forest Falls. Park in the first parking lot on the left.

Contact: San Bernardino National Forest, Mill Creek Ranger Station, 34701 Mill Creek Road, Mentone, CA 92359, 909/382-2882, www.fs.fed.us/r5/sanbernardino.

67 VIVIAN CREEK TRAIL TO MOUNT SAN GORGONIO

16.0 mi / 1-2 days 🥾5 ⛺10

in the San Gorgonio Wilderness
near Forest Falls

Map 13.3, page 701 BEST (

There are lots of ways to reach the summit of Mount San Gorgonio, the tallest mountain in Southern California, but the shortest way is on the Vivian Creek Trail. That's the good news. The bad news is that it's also the steepest way. The summit of San Gorgonio is at 11,502 feet, and the Vivian Creek trailhead is at 6,100 feet, so you can see what you're in for. Luckily, there are several camps along the way: Vivian Creek Camp at 1.2 miles, Halfway Camp at 2.5 miles, and High Creek Camp at 4.8 miles. It's an eight-mile one-way trip to the summit, and although some people hike the round-trip in a day, it's much better to take two or more days so you can enjoy yourself and not have to rush back before dark. Here's one more precautionary tale: This is the busiest trail in the wilderness. Often it is impossible to get a day-hiking or backpacking permit at the last minute, so in summertime, make a permit reservation far in advance.

The trail leaves the upper end of Big Falls Picnic Area and crosses Mill Creek Wash (be careful at this crossing; Mill Creek is subject to flash floods). On the far side, the path starts on a steep mile-long climb to the hanging valley of Vivian Creek, where Vivian Creek Falls sometimes fall. Vivian Creek Camp is located just past here on the east side of the trail. (No camping is allowed on the west side of the trail.) Vivian Creek Camp is a convenient place to camp if you've gotten a late afternoon start. The trail continues along Vivian Creek, crossing it numerous times under the shade of a mixed conifer forest, to Halfway Camp. A few more switchbacks and you cross High Creek, arriving at High Creek Camp, at 9,000 feet. High Creek Camp is famous for being a cold and windy place to spend the night, so remember to bring your ear plugs. At this elevation, only lodgepole pines grow, and as you gain another 2,000 feet in elevation, even these stalwarts give way to granite. At the base of San Gorgonio's summit, you meet up with the trail from Dollar Lake Saddle. Turn right, then left at the next junction, and climb to the 11,502-foot summit of Old Greyback, as it's called. Are you exhausted? Join the party. So is everybody else who makes it this far, but what an accomplishment. Hope you brought a good map so you can identify all the major landmarks of Southern California.

User Groups: Hikers, dogs, and horses. No mountain bikes. No wheelchair facilities.

Permits: A free wilderness permit is required for both day hiking and backpacking and is available in advance from the Mill Creek Ranger Station. Permits can also be obtained in person at the Mill Creek Ranger Station or Barton Flats Visitors Center on Highway 38. A national forest Adventure Pass is required for each vehicle; fees are $5 for one day or $30 for a year. Interagency access passes are also accepted.

Maps: A San Bernardino National Forest or San Gorgonio Wilderness map is available from the U.S. Forest Service. A San Gorgonio Wilderness map is available from Tom Harrison Maps. For topographic maps, ask the USGS for Forest Falls and San Gorgonio.

Directions: From I-10 at Redlands, take the Highway 38 exit and drive northeast for about 14 miles to the intersection with Valley of the Falls Road. Bear right and continue for 4.5 miles to the Big Falls Recreation Area, past the town of Forest Falls. Drive to the parking area at the end of the road and walk uphill through the picnic area on the dirt road. Cross Mill Creek Wash at the trail sign.

Contact: San Bernardino National Forest, Mill Creek Ranger Station, 34701 Mill Creek Road, Mentone, CA 92359, 909/382-2882, www.fs.fed.us/r5/sanbernardino.

68 BLACK MOUNTAIN LOOKOUT

8.0 mi / 4.0 hr

in San Bernardino National Forest near Idyllwild

Map 13.3, page 701

The summit of Black Mountain is at 7,772 feet and this trailhead is at 5,100 feet, so you have nearly 2,700 feet of climbing to do over only four miles. Along the way, you'll pass through several ecosystems, starting in chaparral and oaks and ending up in pine and fir forest. In April and early May, the wildflowers along the route can be exceptional. From near the start, your views open up to include mighty Mount San Gorgonio, various peaks in the San Gabriel Mountains, and Banning Pass. The Black Mountain Trail departs the highway and climbs steadily for 3.6 miles, then meets up with the fire road to the lookout. Turn right at the only junction and you are there. The 360-degree summit view takes in some of Southern California's most beautiful country, including most of the big peaks of the San Gabriel, San Jacinto, and San Bernardino Mountains. This is no L.A. city view. It may discourage you somewhat to see that so many others have come in from the opposite direction by driving to within a half-mile of the top; this is a popular trip for folks who are camped at nearby Boulder Basin and Black Mountain Campgrounds. Just remember: You earned this summit. And if you don't want to see anybody else, try hiking this trail in winter, when the road is closed and the only way to get to Black Mountain is on foot. This is also the season when visibility is at its best.

User Groups: Hikers, horses, dogs, and mountain bikes. No wheelchair facilities.

Permits: A national forest Adventure Pass is required for each vehicle; fees are $5 for one day or $30 for a year. Interagency access passes are also accepted.

Maps: A San Bernardino National Forest map is available from the U.S. Forest Service. A San Jacinto Wilderness map is available from Tom Harrison Maps. For a topographic map, ask the USGS for San Jacinto Peak.

Directions: From Idyllwild, drive northwest on Highway 243 for about 10 miles to the Black Mountain trailhead on the right (east) side of the highway. The trailhead is 1.3 miles south of the Vista Grande Ranger Station.

Contact: San Bernardino National Forest, San Jacinto Ranger District, P.O. Box 518, 54270 Pinecrest, Idyllwild, CA 92549, 909/382-2921, www.fs.fed.us/r5/sanbernardino.

69 SEVEN PINES TRAIL

7.4 mi / 4.0 hr   👫 3   ⛰ 9

in the San Jacinto Wilderness near Idyllwild

Map 13.3, page 701

The best thing about the Seven Pines Trail is that you can just wander as far as you please and have a good time. The mileage above reflects hiking 3.7 miles, with a 2,300-foot elevation gain, to the junction with the Deer Springs Trail, but even a mile or two on this path is enjoyable. The first mile climbs steeply through beautiful conifers and many granite boulders and then joins the beginning of the north fork of the San Jacinto River. Where the path crosses the stream, you enter a gorgeous forest of pines and incense cedars. Hanging out right here might suit you just fine, but if you want more exercise, continue uphill to Deer Springs Junction, which is also the headwaters for the north fork. You'll cross the stream twice more on your way. Trailhead elevation is 6,320 feet.

User Groups: Hikers, horses, and dogs. No mountain bikes. No wheelchair facilities.

Permits: A free wilderness permit is required for day hiking or backpacking and is available in person or in advance by mail from the San Jacinto Ranger District. A national forest Adventure Pass is required for each vehicle; fees are $5 for one day or $30 for a year. Interagency access passes are also accepted.

Maps: A San Bernardino National Forest or San Jacinto Wilderness map is available from the U.S. Forest Service. A San Jacinto Wilderness map is available from Tom Harrison Maps. For a topographic map, ask the USGS for San Jacinto Peak.

Directions: From Idyllwild, drive northwest on Highway 243 for 5.5 miles to the right turnoff for Stone Creek, Fern Basin, Marion Mountain, and Dark Canyon Campgrounds. Turn right and drive 0.2 mile, then bear left, following the signs for Dark Canyon Campground. Continue through the campground and up the hill to reach the Seven Pines trailhead.

Contact: San Bernardino National Forest, San Jacinto Ranger District, P.O. Box 518, 54270

Pinecrest, Idyllwild, CA 92549, 909/382-2921, www.fs.fed.us/r5/sanbernardino.

70 DEER SPRINGS TRAIL TO SUICIDE ROCK

7.0 mi / 4.0 hr   👫 3   ⛰ 10

in the San Jacinto Wilderness near Idyllwild

Map 13.3, page 701

If you're wondering how to spend a morning or an afternoon in Idyllwild, the hike to Suicide Rock will turn your visit into a trip you'll never forget. Pick up a wilderness permit and head for the trailhead, but be sure to pack some snacks and water for a little celebration at the top. Most of the work is in the first 2.4 miles to Suicide Junction, as you climb up through manzanita, ceanothus, and oaks, heading into the higher country of cedars and pines. At the junction, bear right and leave the Deer Springs Trail for the last mile to Suicide Rock, which contours on an easier grade. From the three-mile point onward, your views of Lily Rock and Tahquitz Peak are outstanding, and once you're on Suicide Rock, at 7,528 feet in elevation, you are directly across from Lily Rock's Yosemite-like chunk of white granite. You can watch clouds drift between you and the neighboring peaks, right at eye level. The view below is of the Idyllwild area—there's little in sight besides a few houses and water tanks tucked in among a vast sea of conifers.

User Groups: Hikers, dogs, and horses. No mountain bikes. No wheelchair facilities.

Permits: A free wilderness permit is required for both day hiking and backpacking and is available in person or in advance by mail from the San Jacinto Ranger District.

Maps: A San Bernardino National Forest or San Jacinto Wilderness map is available from the U.S. Forest Service. A San Jacinto Wilderness map is available from Tom Harrison Maps. For topographic maps, ask the USGS for San Jacinto Peak and Idyllwild.

Directions: From Idyllwild, drive northwest on Highway 243 for one mile to the Deer Springs trailhead on the right side of the road (across the highway from the Idyllwild County Park visitors center parking area).

Contact: San Bernardino National Forest, San Jacinto Ranger District, P.O. Box 518, 54270 Pinecrest, Idyllwild, CA 92549, 909/382-2921, www.fs.fed.us/r5/sanbernardino.

7.1 ERNIE MAXWELL SCENIC TRAIL

5.2 mi / 2.5 hr

🚶2 ⛰️8

in San Bernardino National Forest near Idyllwild

Map 13.3, page 701

The Ernie Maxwell Scenic Trail is the perfect route for hikers who aren't up to the climbing that is de rigueur for most trails in the Idyllwild area. With only a 600-foot elevation change on an undulating trail, even families with small children could manage this path, which leads through a lovely conifer forest. Keep in mind, however, that since you're not climbing, you will not get the spectacular views that are granted on most other trails in the area; this is a walk that is built for enjoying the close up, rather than the far off. The trail leads downhill from the start, contouring through a forest of Jeffrey, ponderosa, and coulter pines, with scattered firs and incense cedars among them. You can practice your tree identification. The trail's end is a bit of a disappointment; it simply reaches a dirt road where you turn around and hike back. Along the way, you'll see some good views of Suicide Rock and Tahquitz Peak.

User Groups: Hikers, dogs, horses, and mountain bikes. No wheelchair facilities.

Permits: No permits are required. A national forest Adventure Pass is required for each vehicle; fees are $5 for one day or $30 for a year. Interagency access passes are also accepted.

Maps: A San Bernardino National Forest is available from the U.S. Forest Service. For a topographic map, ask the USGS for Idyllwild.

Directions: From Idyllwild on Highway 243, turn east on North Circle Drive in downtown, which becomes South Circle Drive, and then becomes Fern Valley Road. Follow Fern Valley Road to Humber Park. You will drive a total of 3.5 miles from downtown. The trailhead is on the right, at the lower end of the parking lot.

Contact: San Bernardino National Forest, San Jacinto Ranger District, P.O. Box 518, 54270 Pinecrest, Idyllwild, CA 92549, 909/382-2921, www.fs.fed.us/r5/sanbernardino.

7.2 DEVILS SLIDE TRAIL TO TAHQUITZ PEAK

8.4 mi / 4.0 hr

🚶3 ⛰️10

in the San Jacinto Wilderness near Idyllwild

Map 13.3, page 701   **BEST (**

The Devils Slide Trail is the premier hiking trail in the Idyllwild area, with 8,828-foot Tahquitz Peak as the favored destination, especially for hikers from out of town. The best solution to the crowds? Plan a trip before Memorial Day, after Labor Day, or any time during the week. We've hiked the trail in mid-May and saw almost nobody, but then again, it snowed on our trip.

The trail leads from Idyllwild's Humber Park on a steady but manageable uphill climb through the forest to Saddle Junction, 2.5 miles up. Once you reach the junction, head right for Tahquitz Peak. The next mile is loaded with far-reaching views of the desert below and the San Jacinto Mountains, seen from an increasingly open lodgepole pine forest. At the next junction, head right again, soon saying good-bye to the trees and hello to a stark landscape of granite. The summit is only 0.5 mile away. Tahquitz Peak has the only operating fire lookout you can hike to in the San Jacinto Ranger District, and it's sometimes staffed by volunteers. (Two other lookouts in the district are accessible by road, but not by trail.) From the lookout, which was constructed in 1938, you're offered a panoramic view of both the San Jacinto and Santa Rosa Mountains.

Special Note: If you want to hike to Tahquitz

Peak via an alternate trail that sees fewer people, take the South Ridge Trail instead of the Devils Slide Trail. (You still need to pick up a free wilderness permit at the Idyllwild Ranger Station.) It's a 7.2-mile round-trip via the South Ridge Trail from the vicinity of Saunders Meadow Road. Be sure to hike early in the day in the summer months—this trail is even more exposed than the Devils Slide Trail.

User Groups: Hikers, dogs, and horses. No mountain bikes. No wheelchair facilities.

Permits: A free wilderness permit is required for both day hiking and backpacking and is available in person or in advance by mail from the San Jacinto Ranger District. A national forest Adventure Pass is required for each vehicle; fees are $5 for one day or $30 for a year. Interagency access passes are also accepted.

Maps: A San Bernardino National Forest or San Jacinto Wilderness map is available from the U.S. Forest Service. A San Jacinto Wilderness map is available from Tom Harrison Maps. For topographic maps, ask the USGS for Idyllwild and San Jacinto Peak.

Directions: From Idyllwild on Highway 243, turn east on North Circle Drive in downtown, which becomes South Circle Drive, and then becomes Fern Valley Road. Follow Fern Valley Road to Humber Park. You will drive a total of 3.5 miles from downtown. The trailhead is on the right, at the upper end of the parking lot.

Contact: San Bernardino National Forest, San Jacinto Ranger District, P.O. Box 518, 54270 Pinecrest, Idyllwild, CA 92549, 909/382-2921, www.fs.fed.us/r5/sanbernardino.

SAN DIEGO
AND VICINITY

© STEVEN HEAP/123

BEST HIKES

❰ Beach and Coastal Walks
Razor Point and Beach Trail Loop, **page 765**
Bayside Trail, **page 768**
Cabrillo Tidepools, **page 769**

❰ Bird-Watching
Silverwood Wildlife Sanctuary, **page 777**

❰ Fall Colors
Boucher Trail and Scott's Cabin Loop, **page 770**

❰ Kids
Cabrillo Tidepools, **page 769**

❰ Self-Guided Nature Walks
Inaja Memorial Trail, **page 772**

❰ Swimming Holes
Green Valley Falls, **page 778**

San Diego is a sun-drenched region with 76 miles

of beaches and two distinct mountain ranges (the Palomar and Laguna-Cuyamaca Mountains). In few other places of the world can you walk on the beach and hike to a 6,500-foot mountain peak all in the same day. Blessed with a nearly perfect year-round climate and stunning natural beauty, San Diego is an ideal place for hikers to lace up their boots.

If your idea of San Diego isn't climbing mountains or wandering through conifer forests, but rather traipsing alongside the ocean, head for the coastside parks of Torrey Pines State Reserve or Cabrillo National Monument. In addition to providing wide vistas of San Diego's spectacular coastline, both parks offer a close-up look at the meeting place of sand and sea. Explore the wildlife-rich tidepools at Cabrillo or hike through Torrey Pines' sandstone badlands to the beach. A few miles to the north, bird-watchers flock to San Elijo Lagoon, where the oceanside saltwater and freshwater marshes attract a variety of native and migratory species.

Just to the west of San Diego proper lie the Laguna and Cuyamaca Mountains. The Cuyamacas are mostly contained within Cuyamaca Rancho State Park. The parklands have undergone extensive regeneration after a series of wildfires in the early 21st century, and its mixed forests of ponderosa and Jeffrey pine, fir, incense cedar, and live and black oak are making a steady comeback. With elevations ranging from 4,000 to 6,500 feet, the landscape of the Cuyamaca Mountains is a world vastly different from neighboring Anza-Borrego Desert.

Alongside the Cuyamacas are the Lagunas, which are managed as part of Cleveland National Forest. With a dramatic setting that overlooks the desert thousands of feet below, the Lagunas are easily explored on foot. Hikers can visit a series of waterfalls on Cottonwood Creek or ascend to the summit of 5,900-foot Garnet Peak.

Situated to the north of the Laguna-Cuyamaca range is the smaller Palomar range, which is well known for its Sierra-like landscape. The entire range extends only 25 miles along the northern border of San Diego County, but what it lacks in size it makes up for in beauty. Its 6,000-foot elevation gives rise to dense stands of fir, cedar, spruce, and black oak. Most of the land in the Palomar Mountains is part of Palomar Mountain State Park or Cleveland National Forest. The mountains' most notable feature is the Palomar Observatory, home of the 200-inch Hale telescope, which for many years was the world's largest. You can drive to the observatory site, but it's far more rewarding to hike the trail to it.

Adding up the sum of all these parts begs the question: For hikers who want it all, does San Diego have it all? The answer: Unquestionably, yes.

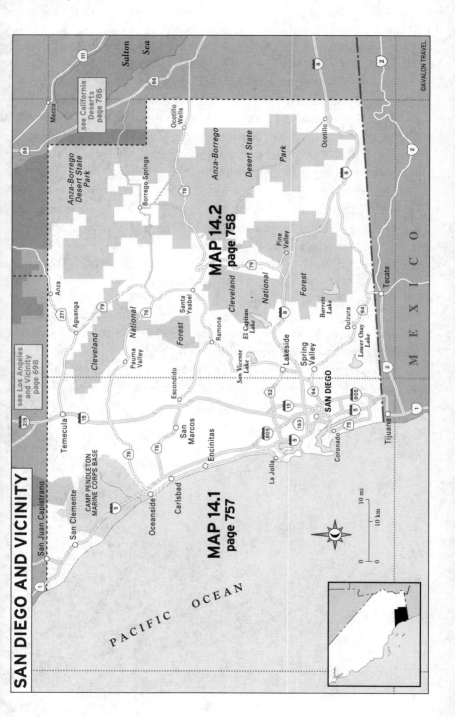

SAN DIEGO AND VICINITY

©AVALON TRAVEL

Salton Sea

see California Deserts page 786

see Los Angeles and Vicinity page 698

Anza-Borrego Desert State Park

Borrego Springs

Ocotillo Wells

Anza-Borrego Desert State Park

Ocotillo

MAP 14.2 page 758

Mecca

Anza

Aguanga

Cleveland National Forest

Pauma Valley

Santa Ysabel

Ramona

El Capitan Lake

Pine Valley

Cleveland National Forest

Tecate

Barrett Lake

Dulzura

Lower Otay Lake

San Vicente Lake

Lakeside

Spring Valley

M E X I C O

Temecula

CAMP PENDLETON MARINE CORPS BASE

Escondido

San Marcos

Encinitas

SAN DIEGO

Coronado

Tijuana

MAP 14.1 page 757

San Juan Capistrano

San Clemente

Oceanside

Carlsbad

La Jolla

PACIFIC OCEAN

10 mi

10 km

0

0

Map 14.1

Hikes 1-19
Pages 759-769

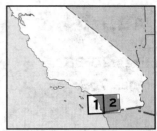

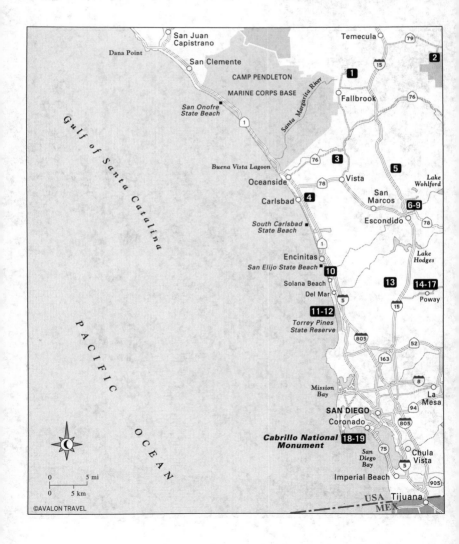

Map 14.2

Hikes 20-38
Pages 769-781

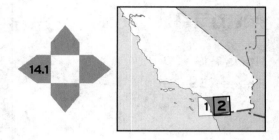

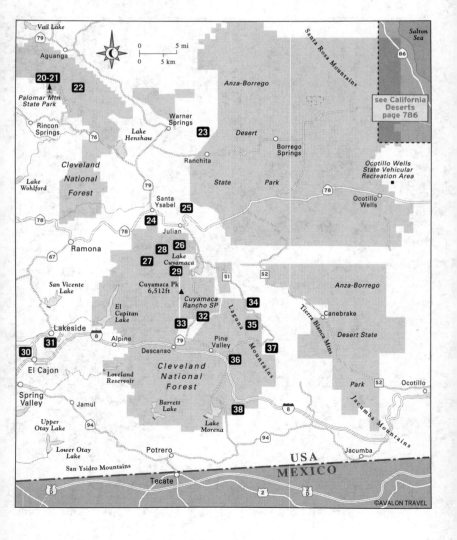

1 SANTA MARGARITA RIVER TRAIL

5.6 mi / 3.0 hr 🥾2 ⛰️8

in Fallbrook

Map 14.1, page 757

A few miles north of downtown Fallbrook lies the Santa Margarita River, one of the last free-flowing rivers in Southern California. The river forms a native riparian habitat attracting many kinds of wildlife, particularly birds. There are six miles of marked trail, but the most popular walk is a 2.8-mile one-way hike from the Sandia Creek Drive trailhead. It has only a 400-foot elevation gain, so it is suitable for walkers and joggers, as well as people looking for a longer outing. An equestrian trail runs parallel to the hiking trail. There are several places where you can cross the river, but you'll have to get your feet wet; there are no bridges. First-time visitors here are amazed by the beauty of the Santa Margarita River Canyon, with its moss-covered rock outcrops, side canyons that branch off the main river, and dense forest canopy. It's like nothing you'll find anywhere else in San Diego County.

User Groups: Hikers, dogs, horses, and mountain bikes. No wheelchair facilities.

Permits: No permits are required. Parking and access are free.

Maps: For topographic maps, ask the USGS for Temecula and Fallbrook.

Directions: From I-15 south of Temecula, take the Mission Road (S13) exit west and drive to De Luz Road in Fallbrook. Turn north on De Luz Road and drive about a mile, then turn right on Sandia Creek Drive. Drive 0.5 mile to the parking lot on the right, just before the road crosses the river at Rock Mountain Drive.

Contact: Fallbrook Land Conservancy, P.O. Box 2701, Fallbrook, CA 92028, 760/728-0889, www.sdlcc.org/flc.

2 DRIPPING SPRINGS TRAIL

13.6 mi / 2 days 🥾3 ⛰️8

in the Aqua Tibia Wilderness

Map 14.1, page 757

At the very northern edge of San Diego County lies the Aqua Tibia Wilderness, a land of extreme summer heat, exposed slopes, no available water sources, and thick chaparral-chamise, ceanothus, manzanita, and ribbonwood. The place appears suitable for only the most steadfast of hikers. Or so it seems. Actually, if you hike the Dripping Springs Trail in early spring, when the temperature is just right, the Aqua Tibia is a pastoral place with blooming shrubs and wildflowers, crystal-clear vistas, and flitting butterflies and bees. Trailhead elevation at Dripping Springs Campground is 1,600 feet, and the peak of Aqua Tibia Mountain is at 4,547 feet. The trail leaves the campground, crosses the rocky wash of Arroyo Seco Creek, and starts to climb. In the first three miles of trail, you get views of Vail Lake to the north and the big mountains of Southern California—San Jacinto, San Gorgonio, and San Antonio (Baldy). Another mile passes, and you can see Santiago Peak and the white dome of Palomar Observatory to the south, plus fine views of the Pacific Ocean, the Santa Rosa Plateau, and the rest of the Santa Ana Mountains. The chaparral gets taller as you go, and the trail gets steeper and narrower. When you finally near the peak of Aqua Tibia Mountain, you've climbed out of the chaparral and into oak woodland with a few scattered pines, which means—yes!—shade. Remember, hike this on a cool day in early spring, and you're in heaven. Hike it in summer, and you're in Temecula's version of hell.

User Groups: Hikers, dogs, and horses. No mountain bikes. No wheelchair facilities.

Permits: A free wilderness permit is required for overnight stays and can be obtained at the Dripping Springs station near the campground or from the Palomar Ranger District. Day users should sign the register at the trailhead. A $5 parking fee is charged unless you have a national forest Adventure Pass or interagency access pass.

Maps: A Cleveland National Forest map is available from the U.S. Forest Service. For a topographic map, ask the USGS for Vail Lake.

Directions: From I-15 in Temecula, take the Highway 79 east exit. Drive 11 miles east on Highway 79 to Dripping Springs Campground, on the right. Free parking is available outside the camp entrance. The trail begins at the south end of the campground.

Contact: Cleveland National Forest, Palomar Ranger District, 1634 Black Canyon Road, Ramona, CA 92065, 760/788-0250, www.fs.fed.us/r5/cleveland.

3 GUAJOME LAKE TRAIL
3.0 mi / 1.5 hrs   🚶2 ⛰7

in Guajome Regional Park near Oceanside

Map 14.1, page 757

Guajome Regional Park is home to one of the richest riparian areas of any of San Diego County's parks. The big draw is a spring-fed lake and marsh, which have enticed nearly 200 species of birds to pass some time in the park. The waterways are also the happy home of many frogs, which you will hear but probably not see. In fact, *Guajome* means home of the frog. The park's main hiking trail leads from the parking lot and skirts the edge of midsized Guajome Lake, then continues up to the park's wedding gazebo and alongside Guajome Marsh. It's a popular trip for dog-walkers and families. An out-and-back trip will cover about three miles, and along the way you might see a few red-winged blackbirds, a white-faced ibis, or even the rare least Bell's vireo. Bring your binoculars. Fishing for bullheads, crappie, catfish, and sunfish is also popular at Guajome Lake. If you want to hike farther, additional trails lead into the grassland and chaparral interior areas of the park.

User Groups: Hikers, dogs, horses, and mountain bikes. No wheelchair facilities.

Permits: No permits are required. A $3 day-use fee is charged per vehicle.

Maps: A free trail map is available for download at www.sdparks.org. For a topographic map, ask the USGS for San Luis Rey.

Directions: From I-5 in Oceanside, take the Highway 76 exit, and drive east for seven miles to Guajome Lake Road. Turn right (south) into the park entrance.

Contact: Guajome Regional Park, 3000 Guajome Lake Road, Oceanside, CA 92057, 760/724-4489, www.sdparks.org.

4 BATIQUITOS LAGOON
3.2 mi / 1.5 hr   🚶1 ⛰7

near Carlsbad

Map 14.1, page 757

The trail around Batiquitos Lagoon is more of a walk than a hike, and it is never free from the nearby roar of the freeway, but nonetheless, the lagoon is one of San Diego's special places. Surrounded by I-5, a golf course, ritzy homes, and a big hotel, the lagoon is a small island of nature amid a sea of development and artifice. It's a wonderful place to study the peaceful movements of birds and small animals, who go about their daily lives ignoring the surrounding chaos of human activity. This is also a great place to walk your dog after work (just be sure to keep him or her on a leash so the wildlife is not disturbed). From the end of Gabbiano Lane, walk toward the nature center, then pick up the trail that skirts along the edge of the lagoon, heading from west to east. The path runs for 1.6 miles one-way; most people just stroll as far as they please and then turn back. Four other small parking lots off Batiquitos Drive provide additional access points. While you walk, you'll have a near-guarantee of spotting herons, egrets, mudhens, mallards, teal, and other common water birds, as well as bunnies and lizards galore. Many rare birds can also be seen, including the elegant tern, marbled godwit, snowy plover, and yellow warbler.

User Groups: Hikers and dogs. No horses or mountain bikes. No wheelchair facilities.

Permits: No permits are required. Parking and access are free.

Maps: For a topographic map, ask the USGS for San Luis Rey.

Directions: From I-5 in Carlsbad, take the Poinsettia Lane exit and head east. Turn right on Batiquitos Drive, then bear right on Gabbiano Lane and drive to its end. Park in the small lot (there is space for about six cars) or alongside the road.

Contact: Batiquitos Lagoon, 7380 Gabbiano Lane, Carlsbad, CA 92013, 760/931-0800, www.batiquitosfoundation.org.

5 HELLHOLE CANYON
4.8 mi / 2.0 hr   🏃3 ⛰7

Hellhole Canyon Preserve near Valley Center

Map 14.1, page 757

Hellhole Canyon Preserve seems a bit misnamed. We didn't think there was anything hellish about it, except maybe the heat on a summer afternoon. The preserve takes up 1,712 acres on the west flank of Rodriguez Mountain and is bounded by Indian reservations to the north and west. Although much of the preserve was badly burned in the wildfires of 2003 and 2007, it has reopened with many improvements, including interpretive signs explaining fire ecology. Because of the fire-adapted foliage that blankets this preserve—primarily chaparral and sage scrub plants such as redberry, manzanita, lilac, and monkey flower—the land has recovered quickly. Still, count on almost no shade anywhere in the preserve. From the trailhead staging area, the only choice is to head steeply downhill into the canyon on Hell Creek Trail. One mile down the trail you'll reach Hell Creek, which runs with vigor in the wet season and maintains a small trickle in the summer. Beyond the creek, the trail follows the route of the old Escondido flume. You walk alongside the rock-lined bed of this 15-mile-long canal, which was built

in 1895 to transport water from the San Luis Rey River to Lake Wohlford. At 1.4 miles you reach a fork, where you can head left or right to walk a pleasant two-mile loop through rolling grasslands and chaparral, then head back up the trail the way you came. And on a hot day, that uphill return will be memorable. Ambitious hikers have the choice of continuing on a steep ascent to the summit of Rodriguez Mountain, where they will be treated to a view of the distant Pacific Ocean.

User Groups: Hikers and horses. No dogs or mountain bikes. No wheelchair facilities.

Permits: No permits are required. Parking and access are free.

Maps: A free trail map is available for download at www.sdparks.org. For an interesting hike, download a free interpretive brochure (www.hellholecanyon.org) that describes the plants seen in this preserve. For a topographic map, ask the USGS for Rodriguez Mountain.

Directions: From I-15 south of Temecula, take Highway 76 east for 15 miles and turn right (south) on Road S6/Valley Center Road. Drive five miles and turn left on North Lake Wohlford Road. Drive two miles and turn left on Paradise Mountain Road. Drive 3.3 miles to a T-intersection, where you turn right on Los Hermanos Ranch Road and then immediately left on Kiavo Road. Drive 0.5 mile on Kiavo Road to Santee Lane and the preserve entrance.

From Escondido and points south, take East Valley Parkway to North Lake Wohlford Road. Turn right and follow North Lake Wohlford Road for six miles to Paradise Mountain Road. Turn right on Paradise Mountain Road and follow it for 3.5 miles to Kiavo Road. Take Kiavo Road one block to Santee Lane and turn left into the preserve entrance.

Contact: Hellhole Canyon Preserve, 19324 Santee Lane, Valley Center, CA 92082, 760/742-1631, www.sdparks.org.

6 JACK CREEK NATURE TRAIL

1.0 mi / 0.5 hr 🚶2 ⛰8

in Dixon Lake Recreation Area near Escondido

Map 14.1, page 757

If you are exceptionally lucky, it will be a rainy year in San Diego, and you will be able to see the waterfall flow along Jack Creek at Dixon Lake Recreation Area. We've only seen it trickle, but we've seen pictures of the 20-foot falls at flood, and it's quite beautiful. Nonetheless, a stroll on the 0.5-mile Jack Creek Nature Trail is good in any season, although best in winter and spring, when the hills are green and the flowers in bloom. The trail begins just inside the park entrance at the primitive road gate, and travels past a picnic area and along Jack Creek to the lake's edge. You can pick up an interpretive brochure at the park ranger station, or you can just march off boldly without one. Be on the alert: Many cute bunnies are likely to cross your path. (They are western cottontails, to be precise.) If the creek is flowing strong, be sure to take the right spur to the waterfall's base; otherwise, just head straight for the lake. At the water's edge, the trail connects to the Sage Trail leading into Daley Ranch, which is useful if you're in the mood to hike more. Many people choose instead to plunk a line in the water and see if they can catch a largemouth bass, rainbow trout, or catfish. If you do so, be sure to purchase a Dixon Lake fishing permit (a California fishing license is not required here).

User Groups: Hikers only. No dogs, horses, or mountain bikes. No wheelchair facilities.

Permits: No permits are required. A $5 day-use fee is charged per vehicle on weekends and holidays only.

Maps: For a topographic map, ask the USGS for Valley Center.

Directions: From Escondido, drive north on I-15 and take the El Norte Parkway exit. Drive 3.1 miles east on El Norte Parkway, turn left (north) on La Honda Drive, and drive 1.3 miles to the Dixon Lake entrance, on the right. Turn right, then park at the Jack Creek Picnic Area.

Contact: Dixon Lake Ranger Station, 1700 N. La Honda Drive, Escondido, CA 92027, 760/839-4680, www.ci.escondido.ca.us.

7 CHAPARRAL INTERPRETIVE TRAIL

0.6 mi / 0.5 hr 🚶1 ⛰7

in Dixon Lake Recreation Area near Escondido

Map 14.1, page 757

Short and sweet, the Chaparral Interpretive Trail lies on the boundary between Dixon Lake Recreation Area and 3,161-acre Daley Ranch Preserve. The trail is a great place to get an education on San Diego's natural ecology. It travels through four distinct Southern California plant communities—mixed chaparral, oak woodlands, coastal sage scrub, and a mature riparian area. Interpretive signs along the way identify the foliage you see, including Engelmann and coast live oaks, toyon, various sages, and blue-eyed grass. It is not uncommon for hikers to catch sight of a coyote or a bobcat along this trail, especially when hiking early in the morning. In addition to being an easy stroll, much of this trail is under a canopy of shade, making it pleasant for visitors of all ages and most hiking capabilities.

User Groups: Hikers only. No dogs, horses, or mountain bikes. No wheelchair facilities.

Permits: No permits are required. A $5 day-use fee is charged per vehicle on weekends and holidays only.

Maps: For a topographic map, ask the USGS for Valley Center.

Directions: From Escondido, drive north on I-15 and take the El Norte Parkway exit. Drive 3.1 miles east on El Norte Parkway, turn left (north) on La Honda Drive, and drive 1.3 miles to the Dixon Lake entrance on the right. Turn right, then park at the Jack Creek Picnic Area.

Contact: Dixon Lake Ranger Station, 1700

N. La Honda Drive, Escondido, CA 92027, 760/839-4680, www.ci.escondido.ca.us.

8 BERNARDO MOUNTAIN
7.2 mi / 3.5 hr   🏃2 ⛰8

by Lake Hodges near Escondido

Map 14.1, page 757

If you're spending the day anywhere near Lake Hodges, make sure you save a few hours to take this nice hike up to the summit of Bernardo Mountain. The mountain rises 900 feet above Lake Hodges and offers great views of the lake, the nearby Laguna Mountains, much of northern San Diego County, and on clear days, the Pacific Ocean and Mexico. The trail was opened to the public in 2002 as part of the partially completed Coast-to-Crest Trail, which will someday span 55 miles from the ocean at Del Mar to the San Dieguito River's source on Volcan Mountain. This section of the trail has quickly become well known to Escondido-area hikers and mountain bikers. The route begins with a less-than-promising start on a concrete path that parallels the I-15 freeway. In about 0.5 mile, the concrete turns sharply right and crosses under the freeway, and soon things start to get a whole lot better. At 1.5 miles you'll cross lovely Felicita Creek, a year-round stream that is lined with oaks and sycamores and provides an excellent place for spotting birds. In another mile you will have circled around to Bernardo Mountain's north slope, which is covered in tall chaparral. Keep heading uphill, switchbacking your way up the slope on a remarkably mellow grade, until you top out at the summit at 3.6 miles. This is a good spot to say a few words of thanks to The Nature Conservancy, The Trust for Public Land, the San Dieguito River Valley Conservancy, and the city of Escondido for purchasing this land and making it available for public use.

User Groups: Hikers, dogs, horses, or mountain bikes. No wheelchair facilities.

Permits: No permits are required. Parking and access are free.

Maps: For a topographic map, ask the USGS for Valley Center.

Directions: From San Diego, drive north on I-15 to south Escondido and take the Via Rancho Parkway exit east for about 100 yards. Turn right (south) at the first light on Sunset Drive. Follow Sunset Drive 0.2 mile to its end and the trailhead.

Contact: San Dieguito River Park, 18372 Sycamore Creek Road, Escondido, CA 92025, 858/674-2270, www.sdrp.org.

9 RANCH HOUSE, BOULDER, AND EAST RIDGE LOOP
4.8 mi / 2.5 hr   🏃3 ⛰8

at Daley Ranch Preserve near Escondido

Map 14.1, page 757

Since its opening in the late 1990s, Daley Ranch has become a favorite park of locals in the Escondido area. This 3,161-acre park contains a biologically unique landscape consisting of lush oak forests, coastal sage scrub, and native grasslands. The park also has great historical significance, being rich in Native American history as well as the home of English immigrant Robert Daley, who settled here in 1869. The Daley family farmed, raised horses, built a dairy, and later vacationed in this area until late in the 20th century, when the land was purchased by the city of Escondido. Although many visitors ride a free, wheelchair-accessible shuttle bus that runs every Sunday to the park's redwood-constructed Ranch House, it's far better to hike there via a meandering loop that heads out on the Ranch House Trail and the Boulder Loop Trail, then returns on the East Ridge and Creek Crossing Trails. Along the way, you'll enjoy fine views of Escondido, pass by two small ponds, and get a look at the Daleys' impressive homestead. Pick up a park map at the trailhead; all junctions are well signed. If you'd rather not hike on your own, the park offers a wide range of naturalist-led hikes most Saturdays and Sundays.

User Groups: Hikers, dogs, horses, and mountain bikes. No wheelchair facilities except the bus to the ranch house.

Permits: No permits are required. Parking and access are free.

Maps: Free park maps are available at the trailhead. For a topographic map, ask the USGS for Valley Center.

Directions: From Escondido, drive north on I-15 and take the El Norte Parkway exit. Drive 3.1 miles east on El Norte Parkway, and turn left (north) on La Honda Drive. Drive one mile on La Honda Drive and park in the dirt lot on the left.

Contact: Daley Ranch Preserve, 3024 La Honda Drive, Escondido, CA 92027, 760/839-4680, www.ci.escondido.ca.us.

🔟 SAN ELIJO LAGOON
5.0 mi / 2.5 hr   🏃2 ⛰️8

in Solana Beach

Map 14.1, page 757

San Elijo Lagoon Ecological Reserve is bordered by the housing developments and shopping centers of Encinitas, Solana Beach, and Rancho Santa Fe, but the lagoon's multitudes of resident and migratory birds don't seem to mind. When you first see it, you may find it hard to imagine enjoying a nature experience so close to the freeways and roads. Suspend your disbelief for a while and pay a visit to the lagoon, which is a mixture of freshwater from inland creeks and saltwater from the ocean. The south side is a little wilder than the Manchester Avenue side, and the trails are longer, so it's the preferred side for hiking. A gated fire road leads down to the lagoon from the north end of North Rios Avenue, and you can hike either right or left. Birds are abundant, especially great egrets, stilts, gulls, and godwits. Great blue herons occasionally make an appearance, and as you wander inland, you'll see many songbirds among the chaparral.

If you want to educate yourself about what you are seeing, an intelligent series of interpretive signs is displayed on the Nature Center Trail, a one-mile loop located on the north side of the lagoon (off Manchester Avenue, in Cardiff). The signs explain about saltwater and freshwater marshes, coastal sage scrub, and the wildlife living in these communities.

User Groups: Hikers and dogs. The one-mile Nature Center Trail is wheelchair accessible. No horses or mountain bikes.

Permits: No permits are required. Parking and access are free.

Maps: A free trail map is available for download at www.sdparks.org. For a topographic map, ask the USGS for Encinitas.

Directions: From I-5 in Solana Beach, take the Lomas Santa Fe Drive exit and drive west to North Rios Avenue. Turn right and go 0.8 mile to the end of the road and the trailhead. Park alongside the road.

Contact: San Elijo Lagoon Ecological Reserve, 2710 Manchester Ave., Cardiff, CA 92007, 760/634-3026, www.sdparks.org or San Elijo Lagoon Conservancy, 760/436-3944, www.sanelijo.org.

1️⃣1️⃣ GUY FLEMING LOOP TRAIL
0.75 mi / 0.5 hr   🏃1 ⛰️9

in Torrey Pines State Reserve near Del Mar

Map 14.1, page 757

Torrey Pines is one of the greatest hiking destinations in San Diego, with several short but sweet trails and enough spectacular scenery to keep you coming back for more. The Guy Fleming Loop Trail is the easiest of the trails in the park, with almost no elevation change, so it's suitable for all levels of hikers. The path has great views of the Pacific Ocean, La Jolla, Del Mar, and Los Peñasquitos Marsh. If you hike the right side of the loop first, you come to the North Overlook, where you can check out the vistas, as well as San Diego's rare tree, the Torrey pine. The trail then loops around to the South Overlook, where you can sometimes see San Clemente and Catalina Islands. People frequently hold weddings at the South Overlook. If they're smart, they plan them for spring, when the wildflowers bloom along the trail.

User Groups: Hikers only. No dogs, horses, or mountain bikes. No wheelchair facilities.

Permits: No permits are required. A $10 day-use fee is charged per vehicle.

Maps: A free map of Torrey Pines State Reserve is available at the park visitors center. For a topographic map, ask the USGS for Del Mar.

Directions: From I-5 in Del Mar, take the Carmel Valley Road exit and drive west 1.5 miles. Turn south on Camino del Mar and drive 0.7 mile to the reserve entrance. Turn right, drive up the hill 0.7 mile, and park at the first parking area on the right, signed for the Guy Fleming Trail. If this lot is full, you can park farther up the hill, at the visitors center, and walk back down the road.

Contact: Torrey Pines State Reserve, 4477 Pacific Highway, San Diego, CA 92110, 858/755-2063, www.parks.ca.gov.

12 RAZOR POINT AND BEACH TRAIL LOOP

2.5 mi / 1.5 hr   🥾2 ⛰9

in Torrey Pines State Reserve near Del Mar

Map 14.1, page 757   BEST (

If you can get a parking spot in the lot by the visitors center at Torrey Pines State Reserve (it's not easy on weekend afternoons), you can start hiking right away on the Razor Point Trail, cutting over to the Beach Trail from Razor Point and heading to the beach. The Razor Point Trail provides dramatic views of the reserve's eroded coastal badlands, which would look like something straight out of the desert if not for the ocean beyond. There's a spiderweb of paths, only some of which are signed, but it's fine to just wander around at random and visit as many of the overlooks as

possible. Windswept Torrey pines grace the bluffs, and wildflowers bloom in the sandy soil in springtime. When you're in the mood, head south from Razor Point (paralleling the ocean) until you hook up with the Beach Trail, and turn right, squeezing through the narrow, steep sandstone entrance to the beach. It's great fun. A return uphill on the Beach Trail makes an excellent loop.

User Groups: Hikers only. No dogs, horses, or mountain bikes. No wheelchair facilities.

Permits: No permits are required. A $10 day-use fee is charged per vehicle.

Maps: A free map of Torrey Pines State Reserve is available at the park visitors center. For a topographic map, ask the USGS for Del Mar.

Directions: From I-5 in Del Mar, take the Carmel Valley Road exit and drive west for 1.5 miles. Turn south on Camino del Mar and drive 0.7 mile to the reserve entrance. Turn right, drive up the hill one mile, and park by the reserve office and visitors center. The trailhead is across the park road from the visitors center.

Contact: Torrey Pines State Reserve, 4477 Pacific Highway, San Diego, CA 92110, 858/755-2063, www.parks.ca.gov.

13 LOS PEÑASQUITOS CANYON

6.5 mi / 3.0 hr   🥾1 ⛰8

in Los Peñasquitos Canyon Preserve near Poway

Map 14.1, page 757

If it is winter or spring and your thoughts are turning to love, there may be no better spot in San Diego for a first date than Los Peñasquitos Canyon Preserve. The trail that runs from one end of the canyon to the other is wide and level, perfectly built for good conversation and maybe some hand-holding. When the cascades along the creek are flowing, you can find a big volcanic boulder to sit on and watch the reflections of the sky in the water. If not, there are numerous places where you could lay out a picnic blanket under a spreading oak or sycamore tree. Early in the year, the wildflowers bloom and the grasses become verdant. Can this much beauty be found so close to a large urban area? You bet. Although you can hike the trail starting from either end, the eastern trailhead near Poway is preferred, because that end of the path is more shaded. As you wander, keep watching for mileage marker 3, because soon after it, you will see a hitching post and bike rack on the right, where you can head off the main trail and scramble down to the cascades on Los Peñasquitos Creek. Even when the stream is reduced to a trickle, the car-sized boulders in the creek are fascinating to see; they are remnants of a volcanic island chain formed underwater 140 million years ago.

User Groups: Hikers, dogs, horses, and mountain bikes. No wheelchair facilities.

Permits: No permits are required. A $3 day-use fee is charged per vehicle.

Maps: A free trail map is available for download at www.sdparks.org. For a topographic map, ask the USGS for Poway.

Directions: From Escondido, drive south on I-15 for 16 miles to the Mercy Road exit. Turn right (west) on Mercy Road and follow it for one mile, crossing Black Mountain Road, to the trailhead parking area.

Contact: Los Peñasquitos Canyon Preserve, 12020 Black Mountain Road, San Diego, CA 92123, 858/484-7504, www.sdparks.org.

14 BLUE SKY ECOLOGICAL RESERVE

4.0 mi / 2.0 hr

in the Blue Sky Ecological Reserve near Poway

Map 14.1, page 757

The 470-acre Blue Sky Ecological Reserve provides habitat for several rare and threatened animal and plant species, including harried San Diego humans who desperately need a place to stop and smell the flowers. The reserve is the home of the San Diego horned lizard and a lovely grove of Engelmann oaks. It's a great place to hike on hot days in San Diego because so much of the reserve is shaded by a dense tree canopy, and there are numerous pools in the creek where water is found year-round. From the trailhead, hike along the wide, flat fire road, ignoring the first two turnoffs. Deer, bunnies, and birds of many kinds are commonly seen. Poison oak is prevalent, too, but stay on the main trails and you can easily avoid it. At the third junction, turn right to pay a visit to Lake Poway, a short ascent away. The lake is a fine place to catch catfish and trout or to rent a rowboat and row your hiking partner around the lake. You can also hike the perimeter of the lake, which will add some climbing and descending to your basically level route. Retrace your steps to the main trail, and head back to the trailhead for a four-mile round-trip. If you want to see more, continue on the main trail to the left fork for Lake Ramona. By taking the fork, you'll face a fairly steep climb up to Lake Ramona's dam, but the reward is a lovely view all the way to the Pacific Ocean.

If you enjoy hiking with a naturalist, show up at the Blue Sky Ecological Reserve on Saturday or Sunday at 9 A.M.; free guided hikes are offered every weekend. The trips are usually only one mile in length—just right for families.

User Groups: Hikers, dogs, and horses. No mountain bikes. No wheelchair facilities.

Permits: No permits are required. Parking and access are free.

Maps: For a topographic map, ask the USGS for Escondido.

Directions: From I-15 near Poway, drive north to the Rancho Bernardo Road exit. Drive east for 3.5 miles on Rancho Bernardo Road; the reserve is on the left, at the junction of Rancho Bernardo Road and Espola Road.

Contact: Blue Sky Ecological Reserve, 858/668-4781; City of Poway, 13325 Civic Center Drive, Poway, CA 92074, 858/668-4400, www.ci.poway.ca.us.

15 MOUNT WOODSON
3.6 mi / 2.0 hr   🚶3 ⛰8

near Poway

Map 14.1, page 757

Mount Woodson is the neighborhood summit to climb for the thousands of people who live in the Poway, Scripps Ranch, and Rancho Bernardo areas. The light-colored, rocky mountain—a favorite playground of rock climbers from all over San Diego—is always there in the background, looming over the suburbs below. If you've never seen Mount Woodson except from the bottom looking up, maybe it's time to lace up your hiking boots. The trail has a 1,500-foot elevation gain to reach the 2,894-foot peak, so you'll get in your workout for the day, but you won't be so wiped out that you can't enjoy the vistas or the fascinating rock formations you'll see along the trail. Hike on the path south of the fire station, and then follow the paved Mount Woodson Road. You'll reach the top at 1.8 miles, where a ton of electronic equipment is in place. Wander around a bit on the ridge until you find the best spot to look out over the wide blue Pacific, pick out the summits of Mount Baldy and Palomar Mountain, and then congratulate yourself for having bagged Mount Woodson's peak. If you are looking for more of a challenge on the way to Woodson's summit, you can take a longer trail (6.4 miles round-trip) that starts at Lake Poway. This alternate trail is the preferred route for people who can't stand hiking on pavement. The path is steep and narrow in places, and has a 2,000-foot elevation gain to the summit. It begins on the east side of Lake Poway, so from the lake's main parking lots you must walk about a half mile around the lake (counterclockwise) to access it.

User Groups: Hikers only. No dogs, horses, or mountain bikes. No wheelchair facilities.

Permits: No permits are required. Parking and access are free.

Maps: For a topographic map, ask the USGS for San Pasqual.

Directions: From Poway, drive east on Poway Road for 3.5 miles and turn north on Highway 67. Drive three miles to the Ramona CDF Fire Station, on the left. The trail begins by the fire station.

Contact: Lake Poway Recreation Area, 14644 Lake Poway Road, Poway, CA 92064, 858/668-4770, www.ci.poway.ca.us.

16 GOODAN RANCH SYCAMORE CANYON PRESERVE
3.1–5.0 mi / 1.5–2.5 hr   🚶2 ⛰8

in Sycamore Canyon Preserve near Poway

Map 14.1, page 757

Are you looking for a good spot to watch the sun set, but you don't feel like braving the traffic to the beach? A trip to the adjoining Goodan Ranch Sycamore Canyon Preserve could be just the ticket. The terrain is coastal sage scrub, chaparral, and oak woodland (no surprises here), but the path leads into beautiful canyons and offers wide vistas of San Diego County. The preserve's trails are well maintained and well signed, with trail maps posted at major intersections. From the parking lot, take the winding single-track trail on the left through the chaparral, heading down through Martha's Grove (a group of ancient oak trees), then out into the open grasslands. Turn right on the fire road and then right again to loop back for a 3.1-mile round-trip. If you want to hike longer, continue downhill on the Martha's Grove Trail and add on a two-mile loop around the southern half of Goodan Ranch, which is dotted with historic buildings dating back to the 1930s and year-round streams. This will give you a five-mile loop hike. Note that the preserve is also popular with mountain bikers, but the ones we met were extremely courteous to hikers.

User Groups: Hikers, dogs, horses, and mountain bikes. No wheelchair facilities.

Permits: No permits are required. Parking and access are free.

Maps: A free trail map is available for download at www.sdparks.org. For a topographic map, ask the USGS for San Vicente Reservoir.

Directions: From Poway drive east on Poway Road to Garden Road. Turn right, drive one mile on Garden Road, and turn right on Sycamore Canyon Road. Drive 2.5 miles to the road's end at the Goodan Staging Area.

Contact: Goodan Ranch Sycamore Canyon Preserve, 16281 Sycamore Canyon Road, Poway, CA 92061, 858/513-4737, www.sdparks.org.

17 IRON MOUNTAIN
6.4 mi / 3.5 hr 🚶3 ⛰8

near Poway

Map 14.1, page 757

A well-maintained trail leads to the summit of 2,696-foot Iron Mountain, where the view of northern San Diego County is inspiring. The hike is challenging enough to make you feel like you got a workout, but short enough that it can be accomplished after work on the long days of summer, assuming the day is not too hot. If you are wondering about the name "Iron Mountain," its meaning is revealed about one mile up the trail, where a side trail goes very steeply uphill to the remains of an old iron ore mine. A half mile past this side trail is the right turnoff for the summit, which lies 1.6 miles farther. A hiker's register can usually be found on top, where most visitors are inclined to scribble a few wise words. Many comments revolve around the pointy summit's commanding view, which extends all the way to the shimmering Pacific. There are likely to be plenty of other users on this trail, including mountain bikers, hardcore joggers, and equestrians, but everybody is usually friendly. Note that this is one of two possible routes to Iron Mountain. The other route starts just a short distance north of this one at the end of Ellie Lane (just off Highway 67), and is much more challenging. Both trails offer the same reward, but the route described here is easier by far, with an elevation gain of only 1,150 feet.

User Groups: Hikers, dogs, horses, and mountain bikes. No wheelchair facilities.

Permits: No permits are required. Parking and access are free.

Maps: For a topographic map, ask the USGS for San Vicente Reservoir.

Directions: From Poway, drive east on Poway Road for 3.5 miles to its junction with Highway 67. The trailhead is at this junction, on the east side of Highway 67 at a small gravel parking area. Park there or alongside the road.

Contact: City of Poway, 13325 Civic Center Drive, Poway, CA 92074, 858/668-4400, www.ci.poway.ca.us.

18 BAYSIDE TRAIL
2.0 mi / 1.5 hr 🚶2 ⛰10

in Cabrillo National Monument

Map 14.1, page 757   BEST ☾

While everybody else at Cabrillo National Monument is visiting the old Point Loma Lighthouse, having their picture taken by the statue of Juan Rodríguez Cabrillo, or checking out the wonderful view of San Diego from the visitors center, you can sneak off for a hike on the Bayside Trail and find a surprising amount of solitude. Gorgeous coastal vistas will accompany that solitude, as well as an interesting lesson in native coastal vegetation. This coastal Mediterranean habitat is one of the eight most sensitive in the world.

Take the paved sidewalk trail from the parking lot to the lighthouse, where you can peer inside at the period furniture and imagine what life was like for the lighthouse keeper and his family in the 1890s. Then check out the Lighthouses of Point Loma exhibit in the Assistant Keeper's Quarters next door and the great views from the overlooks on the lighthouse's far side. After this short tour, pick up the paved road on the east side of the lighthouse, signed as the Bayside Trail. Take the left fork, which is gravel, and wind gently downhill around Point Loma, occasionally tearing your eyes away from the view so you can read the interpretive signs. If you do, you'll learn all about coastal sage scrub, local and migrating birds, and fire ecology. On every step of the trail, the whole of San Diego Bay and the Pacific Ocean are yours to survey. You'll see huge navy ships sailing out to sea, flocks of gulls following the fishing boats back into harbor, plus sailboats and jet skiers galore. The trail ends 300 feet below the statue of Cabrillo, where a sign says Trail Ends—Return by the Same Route. Darn.

User Groups: Hikers only. No dogs, horses, or mountain bikes. No wheelchair facilities.

Permits: No permits are required. A $5 entrance fee is charged per vehicle, which is good for seven days.

Maps: A free brochure and trail map of Cabrillo National Monument are available at the entrance station or visitors center. For a topographic map, ask the USGS for Point Loma.

Directions: From I-5 South or I-8 West in San Diego, take the Rosecrans Street exit and drive south. Staying on Rosecrans Street, you will turn right on Cañon Street and then left on Catalina Boulevard. The road ends at Cabrillo National Monument. The trail begins by the old lighthouse.

Contact: Cabrillo National Monument, 1800 Cabrillo Memorial Drive, San Diego, CA 92106, 619/557-5450, www.nps.gov/cabr.

19 CABRILLO TIDEPOOLS
1.0 mi / 0.5 hr 👫1 ⛰10

in Cabrillo National Monument

Map 14.1, page 757 **BEST**

We love tidepools, and the ones at Cabrillo National Monument are some of the best in Southern California. You might want to stop in at the Cabrillo National Monument visitors center before you head straight for the tidepools. A film on tidepool life plays continually in the auditorium and the Cabrillo Store sells brochures and books on how to explore the pools and identify the various creatures that live there. Even more important, you should check your tide table before you visit (or phone

the park), or else your hike may be very, very short. A fenced trail leads along the bluff tops for a few hundred feet, but then you descend to the rocky beach and walk a long stretch. (You have to stop below the coast guard station, as that area is closed to the public for restoration.) What will you see? Most likely, you'll get a peek at mussels, crabs, sea hares, barnacles, starfish, anemones, snails, and limpets. If you're lucky, you might see an octopus, an abalone, or a sea urchin. Is it wintertime? Why, we believe a passing gray whale just waved her flipper at you. Gray whales may be seen returning to their breeding grounds in Baja California from late December though early March.

User Groups: Hikers and dogs. No horses or mountain bikes. No wheelchair facilities.

Permits: No permits are required, unless you are traveling in a group of 10 people or more. A $5 entrance fee is charged per vehicle, which is good for seven days.

Maps: A free brochure and trail map of Cabrillo National Monument are available at the entrance station or visitors center. For a topographic map, ask the USGS for Point Loma.

Directions: From I-5 South or I-8 West in San Diego, take the Rosecrans Street exit and drive south. Staying on Rosecrans Street, turn right on Cañon Street, left on Catalina Boulevard, and continue to the monument entrance. After paying the entrance fee, take the right fork (immediately following the entrance station) that is signed as Tidepools Parking Area. Continue down the hill to the parking area.

Contact: Cabrillo National Monument, 1800 Cabrillo Memorial Drive, San Diego, CA 92106, 619/557-5450, www.nps.gov/cabr.

20 WEIR AND LOWER DOANE VALLEY LOOP
3.0 mi / 1.5 hr 👫2 ⛰9

in Palomar Mountain State Park

Map 14.2, page 758

If you've never visited before, Palomar Mountain State Park is like a shock to your system—a good shock. At 5,500 feet in elevation, the air is cool, the conifers are big, and suburban sprawl seems far, far away. We kept shaking our heads in disbelief at the Sierra Nevada–like feel of the place. A good introduction to the park is this loop hike on three trails: the Doane Valley Nature Trail, the Weir Trail, and the Lower Doane Valley Trail. From the parking area at Doane Pond (which is always busy with children learning to fish), head away from Doane Pond on the trail that crosses the park road. Start your walk on the Doane Valley Nature Trail and veer left onto the Weir Trail, following pretty Doane Creek under the shade of big pines, firs, and cedars. Cross the creek about one mile out (shortly after the left fork for the Baptist Trail), then follow the Lower Doane Valley Trail as it loops back around a meadow. You'll probably see deer and mountain quail and hear many birdcalls. You'll certainly see the evidence of resident woodpeckers in the big old trees. When the trail nears Doane Valley Campground, cross the creek again and make a sharp switchback to the right, on the Doane Valley Nature Trail. The nature trail will close out your trip, bringing you back to the trailhead in 0.75 mile. As you pass the giant conifers and grassy meadows along the way, you will ask yourself again and again, "Is this really San Diego?"

User Groups: Hikers only. No dogs, horses, or mountain bikes. No wheelchair facilities.

Permits: No permits are required. An $8 day-use fee is charged per vehicle.

Maps: A map of Palomar Mountain State Park is available at the entrance station or park headquarters, or by free download at www.parks.ca.gov. For topographic maps, ask the USGS for Boucher Hill and Palomar Observatory.

Directions: From I-15 north of Escondido, drive east on Highway 76 for 21 miles. Turn left (north) on Road S6/South Grade Road and drive 6.5 miles to the junction with Road S7. Turn left on Road S7 and drive three miles into the park. Pay your fee at the entrance

station, then continue on the park road, turn right, and drive to the parking area by Doane Pond and the school camp.

Contact: Palomar Mountain State Park, P.O. Box 175, Palomar Mountain, CA 92060, 760/742-3462 or 760/767-5311, www.parks.ca.gov.

21 BOUCHER TRAIL AND SCOTT'S CABIN LOOP
4.0 mi / 2.0 hr   👫 2 ⛰ 9

in Palomar Mountain State Park

| Map 14.2, page 758 | BEST (|

You may be wowed by the view of Pauma Valley from Boucher Lookout (at elevation 5,438 feet), but start walking on the Boucher Trail, and you'll be wowed even more. The trail descends from the fire lookout, passing a burn area. It crosses Nate Harrison Grade Road and heads for Cedar Grove Campground. The camp is well named; the cedars are huge and memorable here. Bear right at the fork by the campground, walk a brief stretch on the camp road, and then cross the park road to pick up the Scott's Cabin Trail, which leads to the cabin site of an 1880s homesteader. Only the base of the cabin remains—it's a rather sad-looking pile of sticks and logs. From the site, take the right fork to head back to park headquarters and Silvercrest Picnic Area. Walk to your right on the park road for a few hundred yards until you can pick up the Boucher Trail once more and walk back to the lookout. Here the Boucher Trail is the narrow trail that runs between the legs of the driving loop to the lookout. What? You say you forgot your troubles along the way? That's what happens here at Palomar Mountain.

User Groups: Hikers only. No dogs, horses, or mountain bikes. No wheelchair facilities.

Permits: No permits are required. An $8 day-use fee is charged per vehicle.

Maps: A map of Palomar State Park is available at the entrance station or park headquarters, or by free download at www.parks.ca.gov. For topographic maps, ask the USGS for Boucher Hill and Palomar Observatory.

Directions: From I-15 north of Escondido, drive east on Highway 76 for 21 miles. Turn left (north) on Road S6 (South Grade Road) and drive 6.5 miles to the junction with Road S7. Turn left on Road S7 and drive three miles into the park. Pay your fee at the entrance station, then continue on the park road and bear left at the sign for Boucher Lookout. Park at the lookout and begin hiking on Boucher Trail.

Contact: Palomar Mountain State Park, P.O. Box 175, Palomar Mountain, CA 92060, 760/742-3462 or 760/767-5311, www.parks.ca.gov.

22 OBSERVATORY TRAIL
4.4 mi / 2.5 hr 🏃3 ⛺9

in Cleveland National Forest on Palomar Mountain

Map 14.2, page 758

The hike to reach Palomar Observatory is far better than the drive to reach it. Even if you have absolutely no interest in astronomy, the National Recreation Trail to the observatory is just plain fun to walk. From Observatory Campground, the trail is an aerobic uphill climb, but on a well-graded, well-maintained trail with only a 600-foot elevation gain. The shade is dense from oaks and pines, and you'll find many giant-sized pine cones along the trail. At 0.5 mile, you reach an overlook platform with a lovely view of Mendenhall Valley, and then you head back into the forest to climb some more. The last stretch of trail brings you out to the observatory parking lot, where you turn right, walk through the lot and past the museum, and head straight for what looks like a big white golf ball—the 200-inch Hale telescope. Be sure to walk up the couple flights of stairs to the telescope viewing area and learn all about how the amazing gadget works. More than 100 billion galaxies like ours are within spotting range of the giant telescope. Every clear night of the year, the scope is scanning the skies in an attempt to unveil the mysteries of the universe. The astronomy museum in the neighboring building is also worth a look.

User Groups: Hikers, dogs, horses, and mountain bikes. No wheelchair facilities.

Permits: No permits are required. A $5 parking fee is charged unless you have a national forest Adventure Pass or interagency access pass.

Maps: A Cleveland National Forest map is available from the U.S. Forest Service. For a topographic map, ask the USGS for Palomar Observatory.

Directions: From I-15 north of Escondido, drive east on Highway 76 for 21 miles. Turn left (north) on Road S6 (South Grade Road) and drive 6.5 miles to the junction with Road S7, and then continue north on Road S6 for three more miles to Observatory Campground, on the right. Drive through the camp to the signed parking area for the amphitheater and trailhead.

Contact: Cleveland National Forest, Palomar Ranger District, 1634 Black Canyon Road, Ramona, CA 92065, 760/788-0250, www.fs.fed.us/r5/cleveland.

23 HOT SPRINGS MOUNTAIN
5.6 mi / 3.0 hr 🏃3 ⛺9

on the Los Coyotes Indian Reservation near Warner Springs

Map 14.1, page 757

Most people drive all the way out to Warner Springs and hike to the summit of Hot Springs Mountain at 6,533 feet so they can say they've climbed the highest mountain in San Diego County (even though it's a mere 20 feet taller than Cuyamaca Peak in Rancho Cuyamaca State Park). But if it's April or early May, another great reason to hike here is to see the wildflower display, which is surprisingly diverse and colorful. The entrance gate at the Los Coyotes Indian Reservation is only attended on weekends and Monday holidays, so if you plan to visit on a weekday, write or call ahead for permission to visit.

Once you've gotten your permit and map, access the trailhead and get ready to hike. The trail's first mile is the toughest, with a 550-foot gain on an old jeep trail. At the top, you meet up with a better dirt road that runs up the south slope of Hot Springs Mountain. Turn right (west) on this road and ascend 1.5 miles along the ridgeline, passing by small meadows peppered with spring flowers interspersed among groves of Coulter pines and oaks. Technically, Hot Springs Mountain has two summits, east and west, and on the latter you'll find an abandoned fire lookout tower that has been closed since the mid-1970s. Continue past it on a rough use trail to the eastern summit and the mountain's highest point, where a concrete slab sits on top of a rock outcrop. The summit vista gives a fascinating perspective on the immense size of the Salton Sea, the surrounding desert, the Henshaw Valley, and the Pacific Ocean. Be sure to locate the summit register and add your signature with a few pithy comments. The total elevation gain for this hike is 1,300 feet. Warning: Four-wheel-drive vehicles are permitted on this road/trail, so it is possible you may be passed by a few gas guzzlers.

User Groups: Hikers, dogs, horses, and mountain bikes. No wheelchair facilities.

Permits: An access permit is required and is available at the entrance gate. The entrance fee is $9 per vehicle. The entrance gate is attended 8 A.M.–4 P.M. on weekends and Monday holidays.

Maps: A trail map is provided when you pay the entrance fee. For a topographic map, ask the USGS for Hot Springs Mountain.

Directions: From Santa Ysabel at the junction of Highways 78 and 79, take Highway 79 north for 12 miles toward Warner Springs. Turn east (right) on Camino San Ignacio (about two miles before Warner Springs Resort). Continue for about six miles to the reservation entrance gate. You will be given a map to the trailhead when you pay your entrance fee.

Contact: Los Coyotes Band of Indians, P.O. Box 189, Warner Springs, CA 92086, 760/782-0711 or 760/782-2790, www.kumeyaay.info.

24 INAJA MEMORIAL TRAIL
0.5 mi / 0.5 hr 　　　🥾1 ⛰7

in Cleveland National Forest near Santa Ysabel

Map 14.2, page 758 　　　BEST (

At 3,200 feet in elevation, you can look down a long way into the steep canyon of the San Diego River. And that's what you do here on the Inaja Memorial National Recreation Trail, a short but interesting path that begins at the Inaja Picnic Area. The path undulates along the canyon edge, sometimes following stairs and sometimes on a gently graded trail, passing through a brushy landscape of rocks and chaparral. If you pick up an interpretive brochure at the trailhead, you can learn all about the plants that thrive in this area—live oak, scrub oak, wild lilac, toyon, manzanita, and chamise—and the geology of its granitic rocks. Yours for the taking are wide views of both the Santa Ysabel Valley and Volcan Mountain near Julian. The picnic area and trail have an interesting history: They were named to honor the 11 firefighters who lost their lives in the 60,000-acre Inaja forest fire of 1956.

User Groups: Hikers and dogs. No horses or mountain bikes. No wheelchair facilities except at the picnic area.

Permits: No permits are required. A $5 parking fee is charged unless you have a national forest Adventure Pass or interagency access pass.

Maps: A Cleveland National Forest map is available from the U.S. Forest Service. For a topographic map, ask the USGS for Santa Ysabel.

Directions: From Julian, drive northwest on Highway 78/79 for six miles (to one mile south of Santa Ysabel). Inaja Picnic Area and the trailhead are on the south (left) side of the road.

Contact: Cleveland National Forest, Palomar Ranger District, 1634 Black Canyon Road, Ramona, CA 92065, 760/788-0250, www.fs.fed.us/r5/cleveland.

25 FIVE OAKS TRAIL AND VOLCAN MOUNTAIN

3.2-5.4 mi / 1.5-2.5 hr 🥾2 ⛰️8

in Volcan Mountain Wilderness Preserve near Julian

Map 14.2, page 758

Volcan Mountain Wilderness Preserve is a San Diego County parkland that is open to hiking, mountain biking, and equestrians (sorry, no dogs). The first-rate Five Oaks Trail was built in 2003 for hikers only. It provides a route along the lower slopes of Volcan Mountain that bypasses most of the alternate multi-use trail, a steep and unattractive fire road. To access it, follow the fire road for the first 0.4 mile, and then cut off on to Five Oaks Trail (watch for the stone steps on the right). Once on the trail, you are dwarfed by dense groves of tree-sized manzanitas. On warm days, you may feel a huge debt of gratitude for their shade. Farther along the trail, black oaks provide a cool canopy, plus a splash of rich color in the autumn. Where the foliage opens up, you'll gain glimpses of Palomar Mountain and the Anza-Borrego Desert. After 1.2 miles on the Five Oaks Trail, you reach a stone bench on a ridge with a view to the south, overlooking the Julian area.

If hiking this trail has whetted your appetite for a trip to the summit of Volcan Mountain, it's only another 1.1 mile up the fire road. The view from the top is a wide panorama from the desert to the coast. If you'd like to hike to the summit with a knowledgeable guide, free ranger-led hikes are offered on weekends once a month from April to November (call 760/765-4098).

User Groups: Hikers only. No dogs. Horses and mountain bikes are allowed on fire roads, but not Five Oaks Trail. No wheelchair facilities.

Permits: No permits are required. Parking and access are free.

Maps: A free map is available at the trailhead or by free download at www.sdparks.org. For a topographic map, ask the USGS for Julian.

Directions: From Julian, drive north on Farmer Road for 2.2 miles. Turn right on Wynola Road, drive 100 yards, then turn left on the continuation of Farmer Road. Drive 200 yards and park on the right side of Farmer Road by the Volcan Mountain Preserve sign.

Contact: Volcan Mountain Wilderness Preserve, 1209 Farmer Road, Julian, CA 92036, 760/765-4098, www.sdparks.org.

26 DESERT VIEW AND CANYON OAK LOOP

3.5 mi / 2.0 hr 🥾2 ⛰️8

in William Heise County Park near Julian

Map 14.2, page 758

William Heise County Park, a favorite of San Diego hikers, is located near Julian at 4,000 feet in elevation. The park was badly burned in the wildfires of 2003 and 2007, but its oak forests are rapidly regenerating and smaller shrubs and grasses are green and lush again. The Desert View and Canyon Oak Loop provides hikers with a great opportunity to view the process of fire ecology close up. From the trailhead, start hiking through the oaks. You'll leave the Nature Trail to join the Canyon Oak Trail in 0.25 mile. Bear left on the loop, then bear left on the Desert View Trail. The route is steep, but in 0.1 mile, you reach an overlook with an expansive view of the Cuyamaca and Laguna Mountains. The trail continues upward for another 0.75 mile to a spur trail leading to a higher overlook—Glen's View. Since the fire, the vista here is better than it has been for years. You'll spy the Anza-Borrego Desert, the Salton Sea, and even the Pacific Ocean. A makeshift scope on top of a stone monument at Glen's View helps you identify all of San Diego County's best features. We hope you picked a clear day.

User Groups: Hikers only. No dogs, horses, or mountain bikes. No wheelchair facilities.

Permits: No permits are required. A $3 day-use fee is charged per vehicle.

Maps: A free trail map is available at the entrance station or by free download at www.sdparks.org. For a topographic map, ask the USGS for Julian.

Directions: From Julian, drive two miles west on Highway 78/79 and turn left (south) on Pine Hills Road. Drive two miles, turn left on Frisius Drive, and drive two more miles. Frisius Drive turns into Heise Park Road and enters the park. From the park entrance kiosk, continue straight on the park road and drive to near its end. Trail parking is located above campsite No. 64 or next to campsite No. 77. The trailhead is located near campsite No. 87 at the top of the campground.

Contact: William Heise County Park, 4945 Heise Park Road, Julian, CA, 760/765-0650, www.sdparks.org.

27 CEDAR CREEK FALLS
4.4 mi / 2.5 hr 🥾 2 ⛰ 9

in Cleveland National Forest near Julian

Map 14.1, page 757

Since it's a fantastic waterfall and swimming hole that's a relatively short hike from the car, Cedar Creek Falls is no secret among San Diego hikers. Word gets around fast about these kinds of great destinations. Additionally, it's easy to find: the trailhead is well signed and is a major access point for the California Riding and Hiking Trail. The only hard part is the long drive in on a dirt road (about eight miles), but it's doable for passenger cars (except immediately after the most extreme storms). Begin by hiking downhill and to the right on the wide fire road, enjoying views of the far-off San Diego River Canyon, as well as colorful spring wildflowers on the slopes alongside the road. At 1.4 miles, look for a left fork off the main trail. It may be unsigned, but it's the first and only left turnoff you'll see. Follow it

southeast, heading up and over a small saddle. When you come down the other side, you'll see two possible trail options. The left fork takes you to the top of the falls; the right fork continues down to the valley, where you turn left and head upstream to Cedar Creek Falls. It's worth taking the left fork so you can see what the waterfall looks like from above—it's like a gorgeous infinity pool with a dizzying 100-foot dropoff—but then you'll need to backtrack to this junction and take the opposite fork to access the 50-foot-wide pool at the waterfall's base. (It's too dangerous to scramble down the waterfall's cliff to the base; follow the trail instead.)

Note that if you'd like to visit this waterfall without the long drive on a dirt road, it can be accessed via another trailhead in the town of Ramona, off Thornbush Road (take San Vicente Road to Ramona Oaks Road to Cathedral Way to Thornbush Road). The trail from Ramona to Cedar Creek Falls is about five miles round-trip.

User Groups: Hikers, dogs, horses, and mountain bikes. No wheelchair facilities.

Permits: No permits are required. A national forest Adventure Pass is required for each vehicle; fees are $5 for one day or $30 for a year. Interagency access passes are also accepted.

Maps: A Cleveland National Forest map is available from the U.S. Forest Service. For a topographic map, ask the USGS for Santa Ysabel.

Directions: From Julian, drive two miles west on Highway 78/79, then turn left (south) on Pine Hills Road. In 1.5 miles, bear right on Eagle Peak Road. In 1.4 miles, bear right again, staying on Eagle Peak Road. Continue 8.2 miles on this partly paved, partly dirt road to the signed trailhead just beyond mile marker 9, at a four-way junction of roads. (The road gets a bit rough after the first four miles, but it's usually suitable for passenger cars.)

Contact: Cleveland National Forest, Palomar Ranger District, 1634 Black Canyon Road, Ramona, CA 92065, 760/788-0250, www.fs.fed.us/r5/cleveland.

28 THREE SISTERS FALLS
4.0 mi / 2.0 hr   🏃3 ⛰9

in Cleveland National Forest near Julian

Map 14.1, page 757

Three Sisters Falls is a must-see for serious San Diego waterfall lovers, but the trip is not for everybody. The drive to the trailhead is fairly arduous (several miles of bumpy driving on dirt road) and the hike, although fairly short, is mercilessly steep and follows an unmaintained route, not a real trail. It's mostly downhill on the way in and mostly uphill on the way back, so save some energy for your return trip.

Start at the signboard for the Cedar Creek Trail, an old ranch road. Follow it for 0.7 mile, heading slightly uphill to a saddle where you can see and hear the falls in springtime, and then switchback down to the left for 0.4 mile until you meet up with tiny Sheep Camp Creek. Cross Sheep Camp Creek and pick up the good trail on its far side, heading right. You'll ascend slightly for 0.3 mile to a second low saddle, where once again you should be able to spot the Three Sisters in the canyon below. This visual incentive is critical, because you're about to face some remarkably steep downhill scrambling, which might be more accurately called "bouldering." Wear your best-gripping boots and bring hiking poles if you have them; the footing is loose and/or nonexistent in places. After descending a rugged 500 feet, you'll finally reach Boulder Creek. Hike, rockhop, or wade upstream for a few hundred yards to get to the base of the falls. Depending on Boulder Creek's flow, there may be several possible routes, but whatever you do, stay off the slick rock as much as possible. If you have to choose between stepping on these rocks and wading through poison oak, choose the poison oak. Really. So what's the payoff? A triple set of waterfalls on Boulder Creek, the Three Sisters creates an impressive display of white water on smooth granite. The middle fall is the tallest at about 50 feet, and the large pool at the bottom will tempt you to swim.

User Groups: Hikers, dogs, horses, and mountain bikes. No wheelchair facilities.
Permits: No permits are required. A national forest Adventure Pass is required for each vehicle; fees are $5 for one day or $30 for a year. Interagency access passes are also accepted.
Maps: A Cleveland National Forest map is available from the U.S. Forest Service. For a topographic map, ask the USGS for Cedar Creek.
Directions: From Julian, drive two miles west on Highway 78/79, then turn left (south) on Pine Hills Road. In 1.5 miles, bear right on Eagle Peak Road. In 1.4 miles, bear left (south) on Boulder Creek Road and drive 8.4 miles to a hairpin turn and junction with another dirt road. A Forest Service signboard for Cedar Creek Trail is located there. Park alongside the road and take the trail from the signboard.

From I-8 in downtown San Diego, take Highway 79 north (Descanso exit) for 1.3 miles. Turn left on Riverside Drive and drive 0.6 mile to "downtown" Descanso and its intersection of roads. Follow Oak Grove Drive 1.6 miles to Boulder Creek Road, on the right. Turn north on Boulder Creek Road and drive 13 miles on this part-paved, part-dirt road to a hairpin turn and junction with dirt Cedar Creek Road. Park alongside the road and take the trail from the signboard.
Contact: Cleveland National Forest, Palomar Ranger District, 1634 Black Canyon Road, Ramona, CA 92065, 760/788-0250, www.fs.fed.us/r5/cleveland.

29 CUYAMACA PEAK TRAIL
6.0 mi / 3.0 hr   🏃2 ⛰9

in Cuyamaca Rancho State Park near Julian

Map 14.1, page 757

A 6,512-foot summit in San Diego? Yes, it's true. Cuyamaca Peak is the undisputed king of the peaks in Cuyamaca Rancho State Park, and it's just shy of being the tallest summit in the county. (Hot Springs Mountain near Warner Springs is a bit taller at 6,533 feet.)

The main trail to the summit is the paved Lookout Fire Road that is closed to vehicle traffic. Normally we avoid paved trails like the plague, but this one is so pleasantly graded (1,650 feet of climbing spread out over 2.8 miles) and delivers such a fantastic 360-degree view at the top that it's worth making an exception. If you like, you can bypass some of the pavement by starting your trip on the Azalea Glen Trail from Paso Picacho Campground, then connecting to Azalea Glen Road, Conejos Trail, and finally the paved summit road. (This will add another mile to your trip.) What do you see when you attain the summit of Cuyamaca? Just about everything that surrounds San Diego: the ocean (see if you can pick out Catalina Island on the clearest days), Mexico, Mount San Jacinto, Mount San Gorgonio, Palomar Observatory, Anza-Borrego Desert, and the Salton Sea. So what does Cuayamaca mean? Roughly, it's "place beyond the rain."

User Groups: Hikers only. Leashed dogs are permitted on Lookout Fire Road. No horses or mountain bikes. No wheelchair facilities.

Permits: No permits are required. An $8 day-use fee is charged per vehicle.

Maps: A map of Cuyamaca Rancho State Park is available at the entrance kiosk or by free download at www.parks.ca.gov. A more detailed map is available from Tom Harrison Maps. For a topographic map, ask the USGS for Cuyamaca.

Directions: From San Diego, drive east on I-8 for 40 miles to the Highway 79 exit. Drive north on Highway 79 for 11 miles and turn left into Paso Picacho Campground. Park at the day-use parking lot.

Contact: Cuyamaca Rancho State Park, 12551 Highway 79, Descanso, CA 91916, 760/765-0755, www.cuyamacasp.org or www.parks. ca.gov.

30 COWLES MOUNTAIN
3.0 mi / 1.5 hr

in Mission Trails Regional Park

Map 14.2, page 758

Mission Trails Regional Park is a playland for outdoor lovers; the visitors center alone provides enough entertainment to fill an entire afternoon. It's a huge, architecturally unique building with state-of-the-art displays, and it's better designed than many museums. If you only have time to hike one trail in the park, you might as well go for the summit of Cowles Mountain, a 1,591-foot peak with a 360-degree view of the city. They say Cowles Mountain is the highest point in San Diego, but they mean the city, not the county. Pick a cool day, because the trail is sunny and exposed, ascending through chaparral and sage scrub, and with a 951-foot elevation gain to the summit. When you reach the top and look out at the city below, consider the temporary state of all you survey compared to the rock you're standing on, which is nearly 150 million years old. If you feel like hiking some more, you can continue another 1.5 miles from Cowles Mountain Summit to Pyles Peak Summit. If you want to take a somewhat mellower grade to Cowles Mountain, you can start at the trailhead at Mesa Road. From there, it's 2.2 miles to the top.

User Groups: Hikers and dogs. No mountain bikes or horses. No wheelchair facilities.

Permits: No permits are required. Parking and access are free.

Maps: A free map of Mission Trails Regional Park is available at the visitors center. For a topographic map, ask the USGS for La Mesa.

Directions: From I-15 south of Poway, take Highway 52 east and exit at Mast Boulevard. Turn left on Mast Boulevard and then right on West Hills Parkway. Turn right on Mission Gorge Road, drive two miles, and then turn left on Golfcrest Drive. Follow Golfcrest Drive to its intersection with Navajo Road, where the trailhead for Cowles Mountain trailhead is located, on the left. If you wish to go to the park visitors center first, continue past

Golfcrest Drive on Mission Gorge Road and turn right at the park entrance.

Contact: Mission Trails Regional Park, 1 Father Junipero Serra Trail, San Diego, CA 92119, 619/668-3281, www.mtrp.org.

31 SILVERWOOD WILDLIFE SANCTUARY

1.5 mi / 1.0 hr   👫1 ⛰8

in the Silverwood Wildlife Sanctuary near Lakeside

Map 14.2, page 758   **BEST (**

The Silverwood Wildlife Sanctuary, a favorite spot of San Diego bird-watchers, is open to hikers on Sundays only (9 A.M.–4 P.M.). If it's your first visit, stop in at the Frank Gander Nature Education Center before stepping out on the trails. Exhibits focus on the process of fire ecology and how birds and animals adapt to fire. Silverwood was badly burned in the Cedar Fire of 2003, but there has been so much regrowth among the chaparral and oaks here that many visitors don't even notice the signs of the burn. Late winter and spring are the best times to visit; wildflowers are profuse and many birds, from bluebirds to wrens, make their nests here. Binoculars are a must; more than 160 bird species have been sighted in the sanctuary, including Costas hummingbirds, various woodpeckers, flycatchers, towhees, and an abundance of songbirds. If you are new to birding, show up at 10 A.M. or 1:30 P.M. on Sunday for a free guided hike (Oct.–June). The Audubon Society naturalists who lead the walks are incredibly knowledgeable, and they tailor the walk to the ability of the people who attend. This is a wonderful, educational trip for bird-watchers and non-bird-watchers alike.

User Groups: Hikers only. No dogs, horses, or mountain bikes. No wheelchair facilities.

Permits: Hikers must sign in at the trailhead register. Parking and access are free, but donations are gratefully accepted.

Maps: Maps are available at the trailhead register. For a topographic map, ask the USGS for San Vicente Reservoir.

Directions: From I-8 in San Diego, drive east to Highway 67 near El Cajon. Drive north on Highway 67 to Lakeside, where you turn right on Mapleview Street. Drive a short distance, turn left on Ashwood Street (which becomes Wildcat Canyon Road), and drive 4.8 miles to 13003 Wildcat Canyon Road.

Contact: Silverwood Wildlife Sanctuary, 13003 Wildcat Canyon Road, Lakeside, CA 92040, 619/443-2998, www.sandiegoaudubon.org.

32 STONEWALL PEAK TRAIL

4.0 mi / 2.0 hr   👫2 ⛰10

in Cuyamaca Rancho State Park

Map 14.2, page 758

The Cedar Fire of 2003 obliterated more than 90 percent of Cuyamaca Rancho State Park, but the landscape has recovered remarkably. Although it will be decades until the dense forests of Cuyamaca Rancho return to their previous splendor, the lower growing plants and shrubs are dense and green, and spring wildflower displays are excellent. If you are a new visitor to the park, a great trail for first-timers is the Stonewall Peak Trail across from Paso Picacho Campground. Although slightly dwarfed by neighboring Cuyamaca Peak, Stonewall Peak is no slouch in the summit department: its peak towers at 5,730 feet in elevation. Stonewall Peak overlooks the site of the turn-of-the-century Stonewall Mine, as well as a large chunk of the Cuyamaca Mountains and Anza-Borrego Desert. The trail has only an 850-foot elevation gain and is remarkably well graded. A series of multiple switchbacks whisk you to the summit on a well-graded path. The final 50 yards of trail are cut into an exposed stone ridge; granite stairs and a handrail keep you from going over the edge. The summit view is nothing short of grand, taking in all of the park, Lake Cuyamaca, and the desert far to the east. Squint hard and you can see the Palomar Observatory, Mount San Gorgonio, Mount San Jacinto, and the Salton Sea.

User Groups: Hikers only. No dogs, horses, or mountain bikes. No wheelchair facilities.

Permits: No permits are required. An $8 day-use fee is charged per vehicle.

Maps: A map of Cuyamaca Rancho State Park is available at the entrance kiosk or by free download at www.parks.ca.gov. A more detailed map is available from Tom Harrison Maps. For a topographic map, ask the USGS for Cuyamaca.

Directions: From San Diego, drive east on I-8 for 40 miles to the Highway 79 exit. Drive north on Highway 79 for 11 miles and turn left into Paso Picacho Campground. Park at the day-use parking lot. The trail begins across the highway from the campground.

Contact: Cuyamaca Rancho State Park, 12551 Highway 79, Descanso, CA 91916, 760/765-0755, www.cuyamaca.us or www.parks.ca.gov.

33 GREEN VALLEY FALLS
0.5–3.0 mi / 0.5–1.5 hr   👣1   ⛰9

in Cuyamaca Rancho State Park

Map 14.2, page 758   **BEST**

The Green Valley area in the southern region of Cuyamaca Rancho State Park is a lush, cool oasis for park visitors. A trip to Green Valley Falls is an easy walk with a good payoff on a warm day. From the picnic area parking lot at Green Valley Campground, follow the wide fire road along the Sweetwater River to the cutoff for the falls, then hike downhill to your left. By summer, the river's cascades aren't terribly dramatic, but there are still many cool pools where you can soak your toes, as well as wide granite ledges where you can lay out a towel and lounge around on the rocks. If you feel like logging a few more miles, you can continue past the falls cutoff to the fire road's junction with South Boundary Fire Road. Turn right and loop back via South Boundary and Arroyo Seco Fire Roads, making a three-mile round-trip.

User Groups: Hikers, horses, and mountain bikes (on the fire road only). No dogs. No wheelchair facilities.

Permits: No permits are required. An $8 day-use fee is charged per vehicle.

Maps: A map of Cuyamaca Rancho State Park is available at the entrance kiosk or by free download at www.parks.ca.gov. A more detailed map is available from Tom Harrison Maps. For a topographic map, ask the USGS for Cuyamaca.

Directions: From San Diego, drive east on I-8 for 40 miles to the Highway 79 exit. Drive north on Highway 79 for seven miles and turn left (west) at the sign for Green Valley Campground. Follow the signs to the picnic area. One sign points either straight ahead or to the left for the picnic area; continue straight to reach the trailhead.

Contact: Cuyamaca Rancho State Park, 12551 Highway 79, Descanso, CA 91916, 760/765-0755, www.cuyamaca.us or www.parks.ca.gov.

34 GARNET PEAK
4.4 mi / 2.5 hr   👣2   ⛰10

in the Laguna Mountain Recreation Area

Map 14.2, page 758

The route to Garnet Peak begins on the Pacific Crest Trail (PCT) at the Penny Pines trailhead, where you can see the list of names of the good people who have donated funds to California's national forests for reforestation. Garnet Peak's magnificent summit view and the relative ease of this trail has made this a favorite of San Diego hikers. Follow the well-graded PCT to the north (left). The trail has pleasantly little elevation gain, and it hugs the Laguna Mountain rim, offering nearly continual views of Storm Canyon and the Anza-Borrego Desert. You won't see any trail signs directing you to the peak. Ignore the first two right turnoffs at 1.5 miles out (they lead to expansive overlooks, but they won't take you to the summit). Instead, turn right at the third right turnoff, signed for the Garnet Peak Trail. The trail makes a rocky ascent, but in less than a mile, you reach the jagged, 5,900-foot summit. There you're rewarded with mind-boggling views of the Anza-Borrego Desert, Palomar Observatory, Mount San Jacinto and Mount San Gorgonio, the Laguna and Cuyamaca Mountains, and on and on. On a crisp January day, we were able to spot snow-covered Mount Baldy, 90 miles to the northwest, as well. Most remarkable is that the desert floor is 5,000 feet below you, and it appears to be straight down. This summit vista can boggle your mind. Total elevation gain on the trail? A mere 500 feet. Judging by the popularity of this trail on the weekends, it might just be too easy.

User Groups: Hikers and dogs. No horses or mountain bikes. No wheelchair facilities.

Permits: No permits are required. A national forest Adventure Pass is required for each vehicle; fees are $5 for one day or $30 for a year. Interagency access passes are also accepted.

Maps: A Cleveland National Forest map is available from the U.S. Forest Service. A map of the Laguna Mountain Recreation Area is available from the Descanso Ranger District or the Laguna Mountain Visitors Center. For a topographic map, ask the USGS for Monument Peak.

Directions: From Julian, drive south on Highway 79 to the left fork for Road S1/Sunrise Scenic Byway. Bear left and drive south for about 12 miles to the Penny Pines Plantation, between mile markers 27.5 and 27.0. Park along the road.

Contact: Cleveland National Forest, Descanso Ranger District, 3348 Alpine Boulevard, Alpine, CA 91901, 619/445-6235, www.fs.fed.us/r5/cleveland.

35 LIGHTNING RIDGE TRAIL
1.5 mi / 1.0 hr 🏃1 ⛰8

in the Laguna Mountain Recreation Area

Map 14.2, page 758

The Lightning Ridge Trail is one of the show-and-tell trails of the Laguna Mountain Recreation Area, where you can get up high and get a clear view of how beautiful and unusual this tall, cool mountain on the edge of the desert really is.

The trail is easy enough for almost any hiker to accomplish, with only 250 feet of elevation gain. It begins at a small stone monument at Laguna Campground's amphitheater parking lot and follows the edge of a meadow, making several long, sweeping switchbacks uphill through pines and oaks. Kick a few pine cones as you walk. The trail tops out at a water tank at the top of the ridge. The cement tank is uninspiring, but the view is sweet: Laguna Meadow lies directly below, a beautiful, green expanse in spring. If you time your trip for after a good season of rain, you may see a rare sight: Little Laguna Lake, in the middle of the meadow. This is the secret vanishing lake of the Laguna Mountains.

What's the best time to hike this trail? Unquestionably it's winter or spring—by Memorial Day, the meadow grasses are often dry and brown. If you're lucky, you can walk this trail on a clear winter day, when it's covered with a few inches of snow.

User Groups: Hikers and dogs. No horses or mountain bikes. No wheelchair facilities.

Permits: No permits are required. A $5 fee is charged for parking inside Laguna Campground. If you have a national forest Adventure Pass or interagency access pass, you can park outside the campground for free.

Maps: A Cleveland National Forest map is available from the U.S. Forest Service. A map of the Laguna Mountain Recreation Area is available from the Descanso Ranger District or the Laguna Mountain Visitors Center. For a topographic map, ask the USGS for Monument Peak.

Directions: From Julian, drive south on Highway 79 to the left fork for Road S1/Sunrise Scenic Byway. Bear left and drive south for approximately 13 miles to Laguna Campground, on the right, between mile markers 26.5 and 26.0. Turn right on the camp road, and drive 0.75 mile to the amphitheater parking lot. Park there and then look for the small stone monument just beyond the restrooms, on the northeast side of the parking lot. The trail begins there.

Contact: Cleveland National Forest, Descanso Ranger District, 3348 Alpine

Boulevard, Alpine, CA 91901, 619/445-6235, www.fs.fed.us/r5/cleveland.

36 COTTONWOOD CREEK FALLS

2.0 mi / 1.0 hr   🏃🏃2 ⛰️9

in the Laguna Mountain Recreation Area

Map 14.2, page 758

If you don't have the time for the day hike to spectacular Kitchen Creek Falls, this shorter trip to nearby Cottonwood Creek Falls is a close second choice for scenic beauty. With only a one-mile downhill walk, you'll quickly be exploring the many small waterfalls and big pools along Cottonwood Creek, or happily counting the bright pink flowers on the streamside cacti. The trail is unsigned at its start, and it usually appears overgrown with brush, but after about 100 yards, the path widens, and the downhill grade becomes less steep. When you reach the canyon bottom, which takes about 15 minutes, turn sharply left and walk alongside Cottonwood Creek, heading upstream. In just a few minutes, you'll reach the first of several cascades, each about 12 feet high. Hike as far as you like, pick your favorite waterfall or pool, and have a seat alongside it.

User Groups: Hikers and dogs. No horses or mountain bikes. No wheelchair facilities.

Permits: No permits are required. A national forest Adventure Pass is required for each vehicle; fees are $5 for one day or $30 for a year. Interagency access passes are also accepted.

Maps: A Cleveland National Forest map is available from the U.S. Forest Service. A map of the Laguna Mountain Recreation Area is available from the Descanso Ranger District or the Laguna Mountain Visitors Center. For a topographic map, ask the USGS for Mount Laguna.

Directions: From San Diego, drive east on I-8 for 47 miles to the Highway S1/Sunrise Scenic Byway turnoff. Drive north on Highway S1 for about two miles to the large pullout, on the west side of the road (it has an obvious, graffiti-covered rock wall), between mile markers 15.0 and 15.5. Cross the road on foot and locate the unmarked trail at the north end of the guardrail.

Contact: Cleveland National Forest, Descanso Ranger District, 3348 Alpine Boulevard, Alpine, CA 91901, 619/445-6235, www.fs.fed.us/r5/cleveland.

37 DESERT VIEW NATURE TRAIL

1.2-3.0 mi / 1.0-2.0 hr   🏃🏃1 ⛰️9

in the Laguna Mountain Recreation Area

Map 14.2, page 758

Wow, what a view. If you've never before stood on a conifer-covered mountain and looked down on the vastness of the desert, your first time is something you'll always remember. That's what you get on the Desert View Nature Trail, near the summit of Laguna Mountain. Start hiking from Burnt Rancheria Campground, heading east to meet the Pacific Crest Trail (PCT). Turn north (left) on the PCT, hiking along the mountain rim. The trail hugs the rim, which is perched on the edge of the Anza-Borrego Desert, providing fine views of the desert floor 4,000 feet below you. On a clear day you can see all the way to Salton Sea shimmering in the distance, and to the odd-looking smokestacks of Plaster City. The trail continues north to Desert View Picnic Area and returns via a loop through a shady forest of pines and oaks. When you reach a clearing 0.5 mile out, you'll find a water fountain with a plaque commemorating the great outdoors. Take the spur trail here, heading east and uphill for a short distance, for the best view of the day. If you hike the nature trail loop only, you'll have a 1.2-mile round-trip, but most people get so captivated by the views that they wind up walking a bit farther on the PCT to the north. It's so compelling, it's hard to stop.

User Groups: Hikers and dogs. No horses or mountain bikes. No wheelchair facilities.

Permits: No permits are required. A national forest Adventure Pass is required for each vehicle; fees are $5 for one day or $30 for a year. Interagency access passes are also accepted.

Maps: A Cleveland National Forest map is available from the U.S. Forest Service. A map of the Laguna Mountain Recreation Area is available from the Descanso Ranger District or the Laguna Mountain Visitors Center. For a topographic map, ask the USGS for Mount Laguna.

Directions: From San Diego, drive east on I-8 for 47 miles to the Highway S1/Sunrise Scenic Byway turnoff. Drive north on Highway S1 for about 10 miles to Burnt Rancheria Campground, on the right, between mile markers 22.5 and 23.0 (near the town of Mount Laguna). Park by the amphitheater at Burnt Rancheria Campground, where the trail begins.

Contact: Cleveland National Forest, Descanso Ranger District, 3348 Alpine Boulevard, Alpine, CA 91901, 619/445-6235, www.fs.fed.us/r5/cleveland.

38 KITCHEN CREEK FALLS
4.5 mi / 2.5 hr 🥾3 ⛰10

in Cleveland National Forest near Pine Valley

Map 14.2, page 758

Kitchen Creek Falls is the most beautiful waterfall in San Diego, a visually stunning 150-foot drop that is hidden just a few hundred yards off the Pacific Crest Trail (PCT). Thousands of PCT hikers go right past it without even knowing it's there, although they may shake their heads and wonder where all those day hikers are heading. The hike to reach the general vicinity of the falls is quite easy, since it follows the well-graded PCT from Boulder Oaks, which crosses underneath I-8 and then climbs uphill. The total gain is only about 500 feet. The tricky part comes in finding the unmarked cutoff for Kitchen Creek Falls and then scrambling your way down steep slopes to reach its base. Here's how you do it: After 45–50 minutes of hiking, start looking carefully to your left for a narrow spur trail. You'll reach it at exactly two miles up, which for most people is about an hour of trail time. Turn left on the spur and hike a short distance to see if you're looking down on Kitchen Creek—a fairly flat stream with many good-looking pools. If you are, you're also right above the waterfall, and to reach it, you must cut down the hillside on one of many use trails, heading downstream. (Keep the creek on your right; don't cross it.) Use great caution in getting to the waterfall's base—stay on the dirt trails, and stay off the polished granite, even when it's dry. Get yourself safely to a spot where you can look up and admire the gorgeous falls, which are a series of tiered cascades that twist and turn over rounded ledges in the bedrock. Plan on staying awhile.

User Groups: Hikers and dogs. No horses or mountain bikes. No wheelchair facilities.

Permits: No permits are required. A national forest Adventure Pass is required for each vehicle; fees are $5 for one day or $30 for a year. Interagency access passes are also accepted.

Maps: A Cleveland National Forest map is available from the U.S. Forest Service. For a topographic map, ask the USGS for Live Oak Springs.

Directions: From San Diego, drive east on I-8 for 50 miles to the Buckman Springs Road turnoff. Drive south on the frontage road (old Highway 8) for 2.3 miles to the Boulder Oaks Campground. Stay on the frontage road; do not turn onto Buckman Springs Road. Park at the campground, at the signed trailhead for the PCT.

Contact: Cleveland National Forest, Descanso Ranger District, 3348 Alpine Boulevard, Alpine, CA 91901, 619/445-6235, www.fs.fed.us/r5/cleveland.

CALIFORNIA DESERTS

© SABRINA YOUN

BEST HIKES

The landscape of the California Deserts is

dramatically different from anywhere else in the United States – and in fact, from most of the world. This vast region of desert beauty comprises everything from soaring sand dunes and mountain ranges to below-sea-level salt flats.

Death Valley is home to the lowest point in elevation in the Western hemisphere: Badwater, at 282 feet below sea level. In stark contrast, it's also home to Telescope Peak, elevation 11,043 feet, which is snow-covered six months of the year. With a little effort, hikers can set foot in both places in the same day. In between these extremes are a wide range of ecological communities, from desert scrub to piñon and juniper woodlands. More than 900 plant species and 50 mammal species live in Death Valley. Hikers can choose from an amazing diversity of trails that lead to destinations such as 700-foot-high sand dunes, colorful badlands, towering rock walls, volcanic craters, old mining ruins, and even a waterfall in the desert.

Joshua Tree is best known for its wide desert plains covered with strange-looking Joshua trees, amazing rock formations and boulder piles, rugged mountains, and gold-mining ruins. The park is situated where the high Mojave Desert meets the low Colorado Desert, producing a wide variety of desert flora. Much of the park is higher than 4,000 feet in elevation. The most comfortable weather usually occurs from October to May; summer temperatures frequently soar past 100 degrees. Hiking trails in Joshua Tree are plentiful and varied; destinations include gold-mine stamp mills, old homesteads, mountain summits, and fan palm oases.

Only 50 miles to the north, Mojave National Preserve is where the Mojave, Great Basin, and Sonoran Deserts join. As a result of this convergence, the Mojave contains a wide diversity of plant and animal life, as well as interesting geological features. Hiking trails lead to the summit of Cima

Dome, a granite batholith covered with a dense forest of Joshua trees, and through the volcanic rock cliffs of Hole-in-the-Wall. The 500-foot-tall Kelso Dunes, second highest in California, are another of the preserve's attractions. No official trails lead to the top of the dunes because of the constantly swirling desert sands; hikers simply pick a route and start climbing.

The desert's most famous city, Palm Springs, was originally the home of the Agua Caliente band of the Cahuilla Indians, who still own major portions of the town's land. Not unlike today's Palm Springs visitors, the Agua Caliente worshipped the pure water flowing down the desert canyons, the natural hot springs, and the wind-sheltering curve of the San Jacinto Mountains. Hikers should pay a visit to the Agua Caliente Indian Canyons for a real taste of the Palm Springs desert. You won't find manicured golf courses or trendy nightclubs in the Indian Canyons, but you will find lush stands of palms, mesquite, and creosote, as well as the magical silence of the desert.

Farther south, Anza-Borrego Desert State Park encompasses 600,000 acres of palm groves, year-round creeks, slot canyons, and badlands. It is California's largest state park and more than three times the size of Zion National Park. Desert flora runs the gamut from the expected, like barrel cactus and mesquite, to the rare: stands of jumping cholla cactus and aptly named elephant trees. Majestic and endangered bighorn sheep are commonly seen. Hiking trails lead to leafy fan palm groves, cholla cactus gardens, and old homesteading sites. Hikers who show up in spring are treated to an array of desert wildflowers, including the distinctive flaming-red plumes of ocotillos.

Come armed with a big hat and a plentiful supply of water, and you can help yourself to an abundance of options for desert hiking.

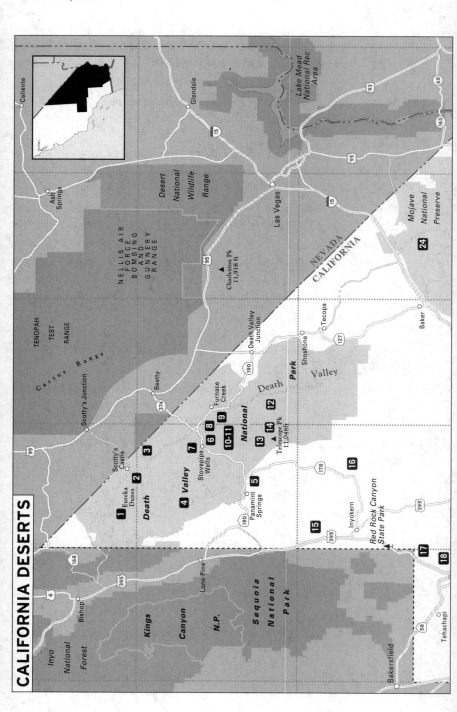

CALIFORNIA DESERTS

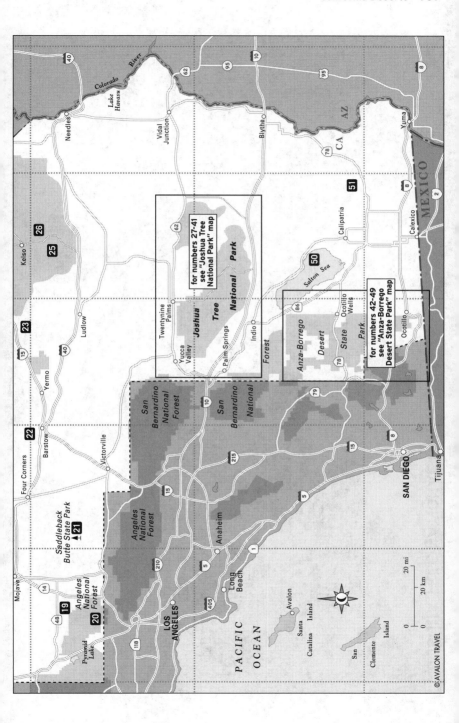

for numbers 27-41
see "Joshua Tree
National Park" map

for numbers 42-49
see "Anza-Borrego
Desert State Park" map

©AVALON TRAVEL

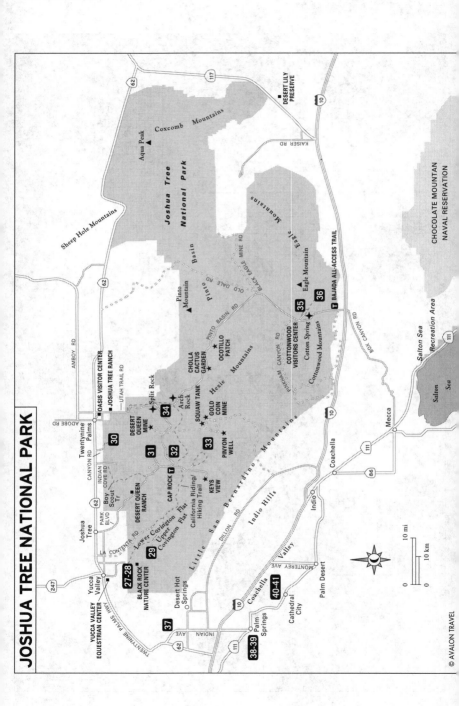

JOSHUA TREE NATIONAL PARK

© AVALON TRAVEL

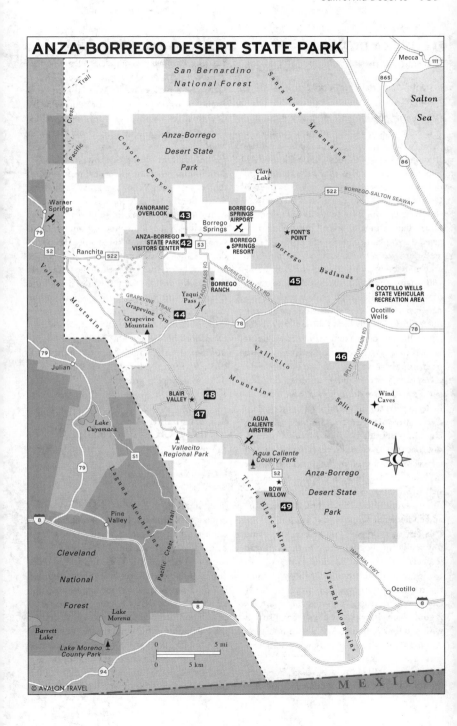

1 EUREKA DUNES

2.0 mi / 1.0 hr

in Death Valley National Park north of Scotty's Castle

Map page 786

It takes a heck of a lot of time and patience to drive to Eureka Dunes, but as soon as you see those giant icons of the desert, you'll know why you came. Eureka Dunes are the tallest sand dunes in California, and among the tallest in North America. They rise nearly 700 feet from their base, creating a sandy, miniature mountain range that is home to several rare and endangered desert plants. Simply put, Eureka Dunes are a must-see in Death Valley. Hike to the top and snap a few pictures, and you'll go home with many weird and wonderful photographs of wind patterns on sand or your hiking partner traversing swirling dune ridge tops. From the trailhead, simply head for the clearly visible dunes. Because of the continually shifting desert sand, there is no marked trail, so make your own path. Your best bet is to climb to the top of the tallest dune you can find, then trace a ridgeline path from dune to dune. It's a strange, wonderful feeling to walk on the silky-soft sand crystals. And as you might expect, climbing the dunes is a slow proposition—take two steps forward, slide one step back, then repeat the process. Just take your time and enjoy the uniqueness of the experience. Also, be extremely careful not to step on any of the fragile dune vegetation—the Eureka Dunes are home to three different rare and endangered plants.

A few tips: Prepare yourself mentally and physically for the long drive to the trailhead (especially the bumpy 44-mile section on dirt roads), and you'll be far more likely to enjoy the trip. Make sure your car tires are sturdy and in excellent shape, and that your spare tire is good to go. Take plenty of water and snacks with you for a long day. And most important: Attempt this adventure only when temperatures are cool in Death Valley.

User Groups: Hikers only. No dogs, horses, or mountain bikes. No wheelchair facilities.

Permits: No permits are required. There is a $20 entrance fee per vehicle at Death Valley National Park, good for seven days.

Maps: Free park maps are available at park entrance stations and visitor centers or by download at www.nps.gov/deva. A more detailed map is available from Tom Harrison Maps. For a topographic map, ask the USGS for Last Chance Range Southwest.

Directions: From the Furnace Creek Visitors Center in Death Valley National Park, drive north on Highway 190 for 17 miles, then bear right on Scotty's Castle Road. In 32 miles you will pass the Grapevine entrance station. Continue northwest for three miles (keep left; don't bear right for Scotty's Castle) to the dirt road on the right signed for Eureka Dunes. (If you reach Ubehebe Crater, you've passed the dirt road.) Turn right and drive 44 miles to the Eureka Dunes parking area. A high-clearance vehicle is recommended; call to check on road conditions before heading out.

Contact: Death Valley National Park, P.O. Box 579, Death Valley, CA 92328, 760/786-3200, www.nps.gov/deva.

2 UBEHEBE AND LITTLE HEBE CRATER TRAIL

1.0 mi / 0.5 hr

in Death Valley National Park near Scotty's Castle

Map page 786

A walk along the rim of a not-so-ancient volcano is what you get on Little Hebe Crater Trail. The trail leads along Ubehebe Crater's southwest rim to Little Hebe and several older craters. Ubehebe Crater is 500 feet deep and 0.5 mile across, and was formed by volcanic activity that occurred between 300 and 1,000 years ago. Little Hebe and the other craters are much smaller but similar in appearance—mostly black and ash colored, with eroded walls that reveal a colorful blend of orange and rust from the minerals in the rock. At 0.5 mile from the trailhead, you reach a junction where you can continue straight ahead to Little Hebe Crater or just loop all the way around Ubehebe's rim. Take your pick—from the high rim of Ubehebe, it's easy to see where you're going, as well as down into the valley below, and far off to the Last Chance Range. Note that the trail surface is a mix of loose gravel and cinders, so it's a good idea to bring hiking boots or high-top shoes. A side note: Most visitors to Ubehebe Crater don't even bother with this trail. Instead, they just get out of their cars, make a beeline run for the bottom of the huge crater, and then moan and groan when they realize they have to make the steep climb back up. Go figure.

User Groups: Hikers only. No dogs, horses, or mountain bikes. No wheelchair facilities.

Permits: No permits are required. There is a $20 entrance fee per vehicle at Death Valley National Park, good for seven days.

Maps: Free park maps are available at park entrance stations and visitor centers or by download at www.nps.gov/deva. A more detailed map is available from Tom Harrison Maps. For a topographic map, ask the USGS for Ubehebe Crater.

Directions: From the Furnace Creek Visitors Center in Death Valley National Park, drive north on Highway 190 for 17 miles, then bear right on Scotty's Castle Road. In 32 miles you will pass the Grapevine entrance station. Continue northwest for five miles to the left turnoff to Ubehebe Crater.

Contact: Death Valley National Park, P.O. Box 579, Death Valley, CA 92328, 760/786-3200, www.nps.gov/deva.

☑ FALL CANYON
5.6 mi / 3.0 hr 🥾3 ⛰9

in Death Valley National Park near Scotty's Castle

Map page 786

Most park visitors take the one-way drive through Titus Canyon to see a desert canyon with giant alluvial fans and towering rock walls. But if you want to witness a similarly imposing desert scene on foot, take a hike in Titus Canyon's next-door neighbor, Fall Canyon. There is no formal trail, but the canyon walls keep you funneled in the right direction. From the parking area, hike to your left (north) on the unsigned trail. In 0.5 mile, you'll reach a wash, but its walls quickly narrow, then later widen again, then repeat the process. A gravel surface makes the walking a bit strenuous. Scan the walls' colorful surfaces as you walk, and you'll notice tiny arch formations and miniature caves and alcoves. At 2.8 miles, you are faced with a 20-foot dry fall, and this is where most hikers turn back. If you are experienced at rock scrambling, however, you can locate and follow a use trail on the canyon's south side to bypass the fall. After doing so, you'll enter a 0.5-mile-long, polished narrows area, which many consider to be as beautiful as the narrows in Death Valley's Mosaic Canyon.

User Groups: Hikers only. No dogs, horses, or mountain bikes. No wheelchair facilities.

Permits: No permits are required. There is a $20 entrance fee per vehicle at Death Valley National Park, good for seven days.

Maps: Free park maps are available at park entrance stations and visitor centers or by download at www.nps.gov/deva. A more detailed map is available from Tom Harrison Maps. For a topographic map, ask the USGS for Ubehebe Crater.

Directions: From the Furnace Creek Visitors Center in Death Valley National Park, drive north on Highway 190 for 17 miles, then bear right on Scotty's Castle Road. In 14 miles, turn right at the sign for Titus Canyon. Drive 2.7 miles to the parking area, just before Titus Canyon Road becomes a one-way road. Begin hiking to the left of Titus Canyon on a narrow, unsigned trail heading north.

Contact: Death Valley National Park, P.O. Box 579, Death Valley, CA 92328, 760/786-3200, www.nps.gov/deva.

4 UBEHEBE PEAK

6.0 mi / 3.0 hr   🏃4 ⛰9

in Death Valley National Park

Map page 786	BEST (

Are you prepared for a long drive and then a difficult hike? If you are, the rewards on this trip are great. The climb to Ubehebe Peak would be strenuous enough if you just accounted for the steep grade, but add in the fact that this is Death Valley, and the hike becomes a butt-kicker. The long drive on dirt roads to the trailhead is enough to keep the majority of visitors away. If you decide to make the trip, be sure your car has high clearance, your tires are sturdy and in excellent shape, and your spare tire and jack are at the ready. Once you get to the trailhead, the rewards are great. Ubehebe Peak offers tremendous views of both the snowy Sierra Nevada and the desertlike Last Chance Range, as well as Racetrack and Saline Valleys. The trail is a narrow miners' route that switchbacks up and up and up, and you can be darn sure that you won't come across any shade on the way. There is no trail for the final 0.5 mile to the summit; most hikers content themselves with the view from the saddle below. (If you stop there, you won't miss out. The view is incredible, especially of the Grandstand rock formation far below, and the salt flats of the Saline Valley to the west.) Experienced climbers can make the final summit scramble. Total elevation gain is 1,900 feet; the summit is at 5,678 feet in elevation. Note: Before or after your trip, be sure to explore around the Racetrack area, where you can see the tracks of rocks that have slid along the surface of the mudflats, pushed by strong winds. To see them, drive about two miles south of this trailhead to the pullout and interpretive sign for the sliding rocks, then walk about a half mile out on the playa. Many a fine photograph has been shot of these fascinating rock tracks.

User Groups: Hikers only. No dogs, horses, or mountain bikes. No wheelchair facilities.

Permits: No permits are required. There is a $20 entrance fee per vehicle at Death Valley National Park, good for seven days.

Maps: Free park maps are available at park entrance stations and visitor centers or by download at www.nps.gov/deva. A more detailed map is available from Tom Harrison Maps. For a topographic map, ask the USGS for Ubehebe Peak.

Directions: From the Furnace Creek Visitors Center in Death Valley National Park, drive north on Highway 190 for 17 miles, then bear right on Scotty's Castle Road. In 32 miles, you will pass the Grapevine entrance station, then continue northwest for 5.8 miles (keep left; don't bear right for Scotty's Castle). Turn right on the dirt road signed for Racetrack. Drive 20 miles on Racetrack Road. Bear right at Teakettle Junction and drive 5.9 miles to a pullout on the right side of the road, across from the large rock formation called the Grandstand. High-clearance vehicles are necessary on Racetrack Road.

Contact: Death Valley National Park, P.O. Box 579, Death Valley, CA 92328, 760/786-3200, www.nps.gov/deva.

5 DARWIN FALLS

2.2 mi / 1.0 hr   🏃1 ⛰8

in Death Valley National Park near Panamint Springs

Map page 786

Darwin Falls is a must-do desert hike. A waterfall in the desert is a rare and precious thing, a miracle of life in a harsh world. The trip is easy enough for young children, and although the temperatures in this area can be extreme in the summer, an early-morning start makes the short hike manageable almost year-round. Of course, be sure to carry water with you. Follow the trail into the canyon, and you'll soon see a trickle of water on the ground that grows wider and more substantial the farther you walk. You simply follow the stream, crossing it a few times, for about a mile. The canyon walls narrow, and the vegetation becomes much more lush. Just beyond a small stream-gauging station, you come to the waterfall—a 30-foot cascade tucked into a box canyon. A large cottonwood tree grows at its lip. In the spring, more than 80 species of resident and migrating birds have been sighted in this canyon. Although it may be tempting to cool off your feet in the water, park rangers request that people refrain from bathing or swimming in order to protect this rare environment that supports so many native species.

User Groups: Hikers only. No dogs, horses, or mountain bikes. No wheelchair facilities.

Permits: No permits are required. Parking and access are free.

Maps: Free park maps are available at park entrance stations and visitor centers or by download at www.nps.gov/deva. A more detailed map is available from Tom Harrison Maps. For a topographic map, ask the USGS for Panamint Springs.

Directions: From Lone Pine on U.S. 395, drive east on Highway 136 for 18 miles, and then continue straight on Highway 190 for 30 miles. The right (south) turnoff for Darwin Falls is exactly one mile before you reach the Panamint Springs Resort. Look for a small Darwin Falls sign and a dirt road. Turn right and drive 2.5 miles on the dirt road to a fork in the road; bear right and park at the signed trailhead. Alternatively, you can exit U.S. 395 at Olancha and Highway 190 and drive east on Highway 190 for 44 miles.

Contact: Death Valley National Park, P.O. Box 579, Death Valley, CA 92328, 760/786-3200, www.nps.gov/deva.

6 MOSAIC CANYON
1.0 mi / 0.5 hr

in Death Valley National Park near Stovepipe Wells

Map page 786   **BEST**

The Mosaic Canyon hike is one of the scenic highlights of Death Valley, and it's accessible to all levels of hikers. The trail shows off plenty of colorful slickrock and polished marble as it winds its way up a narrow, high-walled canyon, which was formed by a fault zone. A rock formation called mosaic breccia—multicolored rock fragments that appear to be cemented together—is embedded in the canyon walls. The best mosaics are visible in the first 0.25 mile, making this trip rewarding even for those who don't like to hike more than a short distance.

From the trailhead, the route enters the canyon almost immediately, and the smooth marble walls close in around you. At various points, the fissure you're walking through opens wider into "rooms" bordered by marble walls, then narrows again. After 0.3 mile, the canyon walls open out to a wide alluvial fan that is not quite as interesting as the narrows area. Many people turn around here, but if you like, you can continue walking another 1.5 miles. The path ends at a dry waterfall that is too high to be scaled.

User Groups: Hikers only. No dogs, horses, or mountain bikes. No wheelchair facilities.

Permits: No permits are required. There is a $20 entrance fee per vehicle at Death Valley National Park, good for seven days.

Maps: Free park maps are available at park entrance stations and visitor centers or by download at www.nps.gov/deva. A more detailed map is available from Tom Harrison Maps. For a topographic map, ask the USGS for Stovepipe Wells.

Directions: From Lone Pine on U.S. 395, drive east on Highway 136 for 18 miles. Continue east on Highway 190 for approximately 60 miles to 0.25 mile west of Stovepipe Wells Village. Look for the Mosaic Canyon turnoff, on the right. If you reach Stovepipe Wells Village, you missed the turnoff. Turn right and drive 2.2 miles to the trailhead parking lot. The last two miles are rough dirt road but are usually passable by passenger cars.

Contact: Death Valley National Park, P.O. Box 579, Death Valley, CA 92328, 760/786-3200, www.nps.gov/deva.

◪ MESQUITE FLAT SAND DUNES
3.0 mi / 1.0 hr   🥾1 ⛰8

in Death Valley National Park near
Stovepipe Wells

Map page 786

Nothing makes a better introduction to Death Valley than a visit to the 80-foot-high Mesquite Flat sand dunes, near Stovepipe Wells. No, these aren't the giant sand dunes that Death Valley is famous for; those are the Eureka Dunes. But if you've just driven into the park, this hike will convince your senses that you're really in Death Valley, a place like no place else. There is no marked trail because of the continually shifting desert sands, so you just make a beeline from the roadside parking area to the dunes. How far you wander is completely up to you. Early in the morning or right about sunset are the best times to visit because of the incredible show of color and light in the ghostlike dunes. Full-moon nights are also popular, and it's easy to imagine why. They'll have you dreaming of Arabian nights.

Note: The walk from the highway to the dunes is so short that many visitors underestimate how hot and dry this trip can be. Not only should you carry plenty of water, but avoid visiting during the hottest part of the day. There have been more than a few fatalities here, which could have easily been avoided by more careful planning.

User Groups: Hikers only. No dogs, horses, or mountain bikes. No wheelchair facilities.

Permits: No permits are required. There is a $20 entrance fee per vehicle at Death Valley National Park, good for seven days.

Maps: Free park maps are available at park entrance stations or by contacting Death Valley National Park. A more detailed map is available from Tom Harrison Maps. For a topographic map, ask the USGS for Stovepipe Wells.

Directions: From Lone Pine on U.S. 395, drive east on Highway 136 for 18 miles. Continue east on Highway 190 for approximately 62 miles, past Stovepipe Wells Village, to the Mesquite Sand Dunes parking lot on the north side of Highway 190 (2.4 miles east of Stovepipe Wells).

Contact: Death Valley National Park, P.O. Box 579, Death Valley, CA 92328, 760/786-3200, www.nps.gov/deva.

◪ SALT CREEK INTERPRETIVE TRAIL
1.0 mi / 0.5 hr   🥾1 ⛰8

in Death Valley National Park

Map page 786   **BEST ☾**

Salt Creek is exactly what its name implies—a stream of saline water—and it's home to the Salt Creek pupfish, a species that lives nowhere else. The fish underwent an incredible evolutionary change in order to live in this saline creek, which was once a part of a much larger freshwater lake. The biological alteration would be roughly the same as if humans decided to drink gasoline instead of water. In the spring (usually late February and March), you can look down into Salt Creek and spot the minnow-sized pupfish swimming about. The plants along the stream are typical of California coastal wetlands—salt grass and pickleweed. Birds congregate by the stream, including great blue herons. Because the trail is on a wooden boardwalk, it is accessible to all hikers, including wheelchair users.

User Groups: Hikers and wheelchairs. No dogs, horses, or mountain bikes.

Permits: No permits are required. There is a $20 entrance fee per vehicle at Death Valley National Park, good for seven days.

Maps: Interpretive trail brochures are available at park visitors centers or at the trailhead. Free park maps are available at park entrance stations and visitor centers or by download at www.nps.gov/deva. A more detailed map is available from Tom Harrison Maps. For a topographic map, ask the USGS for Beatty Junction.

Directions: From the Furnace Creek Visitors Center in Death Valley National Park, drive

12 miles north on Highway 190 to the turnoff for Salt Creek. Turn left and drive one mile to the Salt Creek parking area.

Contact: Death Valley National Park, P.O. Box 579, Death Valley, CA 92328, 760/786-3200, www.nps.gov/deva.

9 HARMONY BORAX WORKS AND BORAX FLATS
1.0 mi / 0.5 hr 　　 🏃1 ⛰8

in Death Valley National Park

Map page 786

A stroll on Harmony Borax Works Interpretive Trail, combined with a longer excursion on neighboring Borax Flats, makes an easy and interesting walk through Death Valley's history. Borax was first discovered in Death Valley in 1881, but transporting it proved difficult, because the nearest railroad was 165 miles away, in Mojave, over fierce, rugged terrain. Enterprising miners figured out the solution: Build specially designed wagons that could carry huge, extra-heavy loads pulled by teams of 20 mules. The rest, as they say, is history. The paved loop leads past examples of the 20-mule team wagons, as well as equipment used for refining borax. At the west end of the loop, you can leave the pavement and walk out to the site where Chinese laborers gathered the stuff from the salt flats. The flats are easy to walk on, with a crusty, hard surface. Eventually the trail dissipates in the mud, so when your curiosity is satisfied, just turn around and head back.

User Groups: Hikers only. No dogs, horses, or mountain bikes. No wheelchair facilities.

Permits: No permits are required. There is a $20 entrance fee per vehicle at Death Valley National Park, good for seven days.

Maps: Free park maps are available at park entrance stations and visitor centers or by download at www.nps.gov/deva. A more detailed map is available from Tom Harrison Maps. For a topographic map, ask the USGS for Furnace Creek.

Directions: From the Furnace Creek Visitors Center in Death Valley National Park, drive north on Highway 190 for 1.3 miles to the left turnoff for Harmony Borax Works and Mustard Canyon. Turn left, then stay to the left to reach the trailhead parking area.

Contact: Death Valley National Park, P.O. Box 579, Death Valley, CA 92328, 760/786-3200, www.nps.gov/deva.

10 GOLDEN CANYON INTERPRETIVE TRAIL
2.0 mi / 1.0 hr 　　 🏃1 ⛰9

in Death Valley National Park

Map page 786

The Golden Canyon Interpretive Trail is a perfect path for first-timers in Death Valley National Park. Because the trail is so short, most people continue beyond the end of the self-guided stretch, heading deeper into Golden Canyon to Red Cathedral, 0.3 mile from the last numbered trail marker. The interpretive trail follows the path of an old road through a flat alluvial fan exhibiting a colorful array of volcanic rocks, sand, and gravel. Imagine every shade of gold you can think of—from yellow to orange to apricot. That's what you'll see here in the cliffs, which are composed of the layered remains of ancient lake beds. They're especially gorgeous near sunrise and sunset. At the final interpretive post, you can turn around and head back, or take the left fork of the trail and continue to Red Cathedral, the huge red cliff that looms in the background. Its lovely hue is caused by the weathering of rocks containing a large quantity of iron. A surprise is that by the time you reach Red Cathedral, you've gained some 300 feet in elevation—enough to provide some wide views looking back the way you came.

Note: This may be an easy walk, but it's in Death Valley, so more than a few fatalities have occurred here from people who tried to hike during the hottest part of the day in spring or fall, or worse yet, any time in the summer. Always carry plenty of water with you and avoid hiking at this low elevation when the temperature is high.

User Groups: Hikers only. No dogs, horses, or mountain bikes. No wheelchair facilities.

Permits: No permits are required. There is a $20 entrance fee per vehicle at Death Valley National Park, good for seven days.

Maps: Interpretive trail brochures are available at park visitors centers or at the trailhead. Free park maps are available at park entrance stations and visitor centers or by download at www.nps.gov/deva. A more detailed map is available from Tom Harrison Maps. For a topographic map, ask the USGS for Furnace Creek.

Directions: From the Furnace Creek Visitors Center in Death Valley National Park, drive southeast on Highway 190 for 1.2 miles to the right turnoff for Badwater. Bear right and drive south for two miles to the Golden Canyon parking area, on the east side of the road.

Contact: Death Valley National Park, P.O. Box 579, Death Valley, CA 92328, 760/786-3200, www.nps.gov/deva.

11 GOWER GULCH LOOP
5.5 mi / 3.0 hr 🥾3 ⚠9

in Death Valley National Park

Map page 786

This hike is an extension of Golden Canyon Interpretive Trail (see listing in this chapter) for slightly more experienced hikers. When you reach the last interpretive trail marker on Golden Canyon Trail, take the right fork for Gower Gulch Loop. The path is signed with small hiker symbols; watch for them as you continue your trek into the colorful badlands—deeply creased, eroded, and barren hillsides. Hike across the shoulder of Manly Beacon, a yellow sandstone hill with lovely views. At the base of Manly Beacon's south slope, you reach a junction. Turn right to loop back through Gower Gulch (the left fork leads to Zabriskie Point, a popular drive-

to overlook). On your return, remember to stay in the wide main wash and keep heading downhill; this will keep you from making a wrong turn in the canyons of Gower Gulch. You'll notice white outcroppings in the rock, the raison d'être for the old borax mines still found in the area. Also look for mine adits (horizontal shafts); several are bored into the canyon walls. Eventually the canyon narrows, and the trail leads around the side of a 40-foot dry fall. The final mile of the loop parallels the highway, heading back to the mouth of Golden Canyon and its parking area.

One thing to keep in mind: Be sure to carry enough water for the few hours you'll be out on the trail. The total elevation gain is only 800 feet, but it's pretty darn hot out here.

User Groups: Hikers only. No dogs, horses, or mountain bikes. No wheelchair facilities.

Permits: No permits are required. There is a $20 entrance fee per vehicle at Death Valley National Park, good for seven days.

Maps: Free park maps are available at park entrance stations and visitor centers or by download at www.nps.gov/deva. A more detailed map is available from Tom Harrison Maps. For a topographic map, ask the USGS for Furnace Creek.

Directions: From the Furnace Creek Visitors Center in Death Valley National Park, drive southeast on Highway 190 for 1.2 miles to the turnoff for Badwater. Turn right and drive south for two miles to the Golden Canyon parking area, on the east side of the road.

Contact: Death Valley National Park, P.O. Box 579, Death Valley, CA 92328, 760/786-3200, www.nps.gov/deva.

12 NATURAL BRIDGE CANYON
1.2 mi / 1.0 hr 🥾2 ⚠9

in Death Valley National Park

Map page 786

Natural Bridge Canyon is a good spot to take a short walk and get a good taste of what Death

Valley is all about. Because the canyon has an abrupt slope, the hike is not as easy as you might expect. The loose gravel surface of its floor makes walking a workout. Still, you should at least go as far as the natural bridge the canyon is named for, which is only 0.3 mile in, or about 15 minutes from your car. The "bridge" is an imposing overhang about 40 feet high and 25 feet wide. It was formed by repeated flash flooding over thousands of years. Take a walk underneath it, then head up the canyon a little farther and watch other visitors walk underneath it. All the while, you can't help but ponder the amazing geologic action that has created Death Valley. If you want to head farther back into the canyon, you'll find more interesting features, such as dry waterfalls and "wax drippings," which are formed when water drips down the canyon walls and forms a type of mud. The canyon walls come together at a 15-foot dry fall 0.6 mile in, so that's your turnaround point.

User Groups: Hikers only. No dogs, horses, or mountain bikes. No wheelchair facilities.

Permits: No permits are required. There is a $20 entrance fee per vehicle at Death Valley National Park, good for seven days.

Maps: Free park maps are available at park entrance stations and visitor centers or by download at www.nps.gov/deva. A more detailed map is available from Tom Harrison Maps. For a topographic map, ask the USGS for Furnace Creek.

Directions: From the Furnace Creek Visitors Center in Death Valley National Park, drive southeast on Highway 190 for 1.2 miles to the right turnoff for Badwater. Bear right and drive south for 13.2 miles to the left turnoff for Natural Bridge Canyon. Turn left and drive 1.7 miles to the trailhead.

Contact: Death Valley National Park, P.O. Box 579, Death Valley, CA 92328, 760/786-3200, www.nps.gov/deva.

13 WILDROSE PEAK TRAIL
8.4 mi / 5.0 hr   3   10

in Death Valley National Park

Map page 786   **BEST**

If it's boiling in Death Valley, you can always make the long drive out to Wildrose Canyon and begin your hike at a trailhead elevation of 6,800 feet. Get this: You'll even find trees here. Whew, what a relief—at least until you start climbing in earnest, heading for 9,064-foot Wildrose Peak. The hike begins at the 10 charcoal kilns (they look strangely like beehives) that were built in the 1870s to make charcoal for the local mines. Walk to the north end of the kilns to find the signed trail, then start climbing through scattered piñon pines and junipers. You can see far off to the Sierra, even Mount Whitney, and then as you climb higher, you can look down at Death Valley and Panamint Valley. Well-graded switchbacks make the 2,200-foot climb manageable, and the panoramic views make the energy expenditure completely worth it. If you tire out, at least try to hike the first 2.5 miles of trail, where you'll get a good dose of vistas from a saddle below the summit. The last mile to the summit is the steepest.

Special Note: This trail can be snowed in any time between November and May. Check with the park before making the long drive.

User Groups: Hikers and horses. No dogs or mountain bikes. No wheelchair facilities.

Permits: No permits are required. There is a $20 entrance fee per vehicle at Death Valley National Park, good for seven days.

Maps: Free park maps are available at park entrance stations and visitor centers or by download at www.nps.gov/deva. A more detailed map is available from Tom Harrison Maps. For a topographic map, ask the USGS for Wildrose Peak.

Directions: From Stovepipe Wells, drive west on Highway 190 for eight miles to Emigrant Canyon Road, then turn left (south). Drive 21 miles to a junction with Wildrose Canyon Road. Turn left (east) and drive seven miles to the parking area on the right, across from the Charcoal Kilns.

Note: Trailers and vehicles longer than 25 feet are prohibited on Emigrant Canyon Road; travelers with these types of vehicles should access Wildrose Canyon via Panamint Valley Road (18 miles farther west on Highway 190 than Emigrant Canyon Road).

Contact: Death Valley National Park, P.O. Box 579, Death Valley, CA 92328, 760/786-3200, www.nps.gov/deva.

14 TELESCOPE PEAK TRAIL
14.0 mi / 9.0 hr   🏃4 ⛰10

in Death Valley National Park

Map page 786

The chief highlight of the long hike to the summit of Telescope Peak is this: When you get there, you can pivot around and in one long, sweeping glance take in Mount Whitney to the west and Badwater to the east. For the uninitiated, that means you're seeing the highest point in the contiguous United States and the lowest point in the Western Hemisphere from the same spot (one is ahead of you, one to your back). The other big deal about the hike is that the trailhead is at 8,000 feet, so you don't have to worry about passing out from the valley's heat. The peak (at 11,049 feet) is the highest in Death Valley National Park, and the trail to reach it is well graded and well maintained. Nonetheless, the 3,000-foot climb and the long mileage take their toll, so don't try this hike unless you're in good shape. In addition to passing piñon pines and junipers, you'll also see some ancient bristlecone pine trees once you climb above 10,000 feet. To supplement the vistas of Mount Whitney and Badwater, you are also witness to Death Valley and Panamint Valley, as well as the White Mountains to the north. It's beyond spectacular. But the climb is one heck of a workout, so be prepared.

Special Note: This trail can be snowed in any time between November and May. Check with the park before making the long drive.

User Groups: Hikers only. No dogs, horses, or mountain bikes. No wheelchair facilities.

Permits: No permits are required. There is a $20 entrance fee per vehicle at Death Valley National Park, good for seven days.

Maps: Free park maps are available at park entrance stations and visitor centers or by download at www.nps.gov/deva. A more detailed map is available from Tom Harrison Maps. For a topographic map, ask the USGS for Telescope Peak.

Directions: From Stovepipe Wells, drive west on Highway 190 for eight miles to Emigrant Canyon Road, then turn left (south). Drive 21 miles to a junction with Wildrose Canyon Road. Turn left (east) and drive nine miles to the end of Wildrose Canyon Road at Mahogany Flat Campground. The road gets very rough and steep for the last two miles after the charcoal kilns. High-clearance vehicles are recommended.

Note: Trailers and vehicles longer than 25 feet are prohibited on Emigrant Canyon Road; travelers with these types of vehicles should access this trailhead via Panamint Valley Road (18 miles farther west on Highway 190 than Emigrant Canyon Road).

Contact: Death Valley National Park, P.O. Box 579, Death Valley, CA 92328, 760/786-3200, www.nps.gov/deva.

15 FOSSIL FALLS
1.0 mi / 0.5 hr   🏃1 ⛰8

off U.S. 395 north of the Highway 178 and Highway 14 junction

Map page 786

Now don't get your hopes up and think you're going to find a waterfall way out here in the desert east of U.S. 395. There's no water to be found anywhere at Fossil Falls, but there's an excellent hike to an ancient lava field where you'll find polished and sculptured rock formations. The trail is well maintained, flat, and easy enough for children, although you don't want to hike it at high noon on a hot day. The falls look more like a giant pit or crevice in the ground, carved with beautiful water-sculpted lava formations, which were polished in the last ice age. Fossil Falls is not just appealing to geology buffs; there's something here for history buffs as well: This area was used by Native Americans for at least 10,000 years. There are petroglyphs and rock rings adjacent to the trail. Look and enjoy, but remember that these artifacts are protected by federal law—don't touch or take them.

User Groups: Hikers and dogs. No horses or mountain bikes. No wheelchair facilities.

Permits: No permits are required. Parking and access are free.

Maps: For a topographic map, ask the USGS for Little Lake.

Directions: From the junction of Highway 14 and U.S. 395 near Inyokern, drive north on U.S. 395 for 20 miles to just north of Little Lake, and turn east on Cinder Road. Drive 0.6 mile, bear right at the fork, and drive another 0.6 mile to the Fossil Falls trailhead.

Contact: Bureau of Land Management, Ridgecrest Field Office, 300 S. Richmond Road, Ridgecrest, CA 93555, 760/384-5400, www.ca.blm.gov/ridgecrest.

16 TRONA PINNACLES
0.5 mi / 0.5 hr

east of Ridgecrest and south of Trona

Map page 786

If the Trona Pinnacles were miniaturized, they'd look like oblong-shaped lumps of modeling clay ready to be turned on a potter's wheel. They're actually tufa spires made of calcium carbonate, and the Trona Pinnacles National Natural Landmark features more than 500 of them, some as high as 140 feet. Like the tufa spires at Mono Lake, the Trona Pinnacles were formed underwater from calcium-rich springs in the days when giant Searles Lake still had water in it—probably 50,000 years ago. Now the lake bed is dry, so the tufa spires jut upward from a flat, dry plain. Yes, they're weird looking, but in a good way. If you're the kind of person who likes the weird-looking tufa formations at Mono Lake (we are), you'll enjoy this area. A 0.5-mile loop trail leads through the pinnacles, but most people just wander around at random, gazing at the strange, giant tufa spires. Wear sturdy hiking shoes—the tufa is quite sharp.

User Groups: Hikers and dogs. No horses or mountain bikes. No wheelchair facilities.

Permits: No permits are required. Parking and access are free.

Maps: A free brochure on the Trona Pinnacles is available from the Bureau of Land Management. For a topographic map, ask the USGS for Searles Lake.

Directions: From Ridgecrest, drive east on Highway 178 for 20 miles to the junction with Trona-Red Mountain Road. Continue on Highway 178 for 7.7 more miles to the signed right turnoff for the trailhead. (High-clearance vehicles are recommended.)

Contact: Bureau of Land Management, Ridgecrest Field Office, 300 S. Richmond Road, Ridgecrest, CA 93555, 760/384-5400, www.ca.blm.gov/ridgecrest.

17 DESERT TORTOISE DISCOVERY LOOP
2.0 mi / 1.0 hr

in Desert Tortoise Natural Area off Highway 14 near California City

Map page 786   **BEST (**

The Desert Tortoise Natural Area features an easy interpretive trail that teaches visitors all about *Gopherus agassizii,* better known as the desert tortoise, California's state reptile. Don't get your heart set on seeing one, though, as the creatures are rather shy. You have to look for them, and you have to get lucky. At the preserve, you can also learn all about other desert reptiles and desert plants. A few short interpretive trails are worth strolling, but the two-mile Discovery Trail offers the best chance of seeing tortoises. Look for their burrows underneath creosote bushes, and keep your fingers crossed that one decides to pop his or her head out. Spring (usually from early March to late May) is the best time for tortoise sightings, when the wildflowers are in bloom. The tortoises like to eat them. The best tortoise fact we learned on our trip? During a sudden rainstorm, a tortoise may emerge from its burrow and drink enough water to last a full year.

User Groups: Hikers, horses, and wheelchairs. No dogs or mountain bikes.

Permits: No permits are required. Parking and access are free.

Maps: A free map to the Desert Tortoise Natural Area is available at the trailhead. For topographic maps, ask the USGS for California City North and Galileo Hill.

Directions: From Mojave, at the junction of Highways 58 and 14, drive northeast on Highway 14 for 4.5 miles to California City Boulevard. Drive east on California City Boulevard for nine miles to 20 Mule Team Parkway. Go east on the parkway and continue driving 1.3 miles to Randsburg-Mojave Road. Turn left (northeast) on Randsburg-Mojave Road and drive four miles to the signed parking area.

Contact: Bureau of Land Management, Ridgecrest Field Office, 300 S. Richmond Road, Ridgecrest, CA 93555, 760/384-5400, www.ca.blm.gov/ridgecrest.

18 RED CLIFFS
2.0 mi / 1.0 hr   🥾2 ⛰️8

in Red Rock Canyon State Park off Highway 14 north of Mojave

Map page 786

Red Cliffs Natural Preserve is a hikers-only section of Red Rock Canyon State Park, where you can walk along and view close up the reddish columns of 300-foot desert cliffs. The color is caused by iron oxide, or rust, but the myriad creases and folds in the cliffs have been formed by a combination of fire and water—volcanic action and the course of streams and rivers. You hike on old jeep tracks, not a formal trail, passing occasional Joshua trees as you go and gaining views of El Paso Mountains. It's hard to believe that this wildernesslike desert is so close to urban Los Angeles, because when you're out here, you feel like you're really far away. At the preserve boundary 0.75 mile from the trailhead, you can continue on the old jeep road into the Scenic Cliffs Preserve or turn around and retrace your steps. The Scenic Cliffs area is closed each year from February 1 to July 1, the nesting season for various birds of prey. If you really want to be wowed, take this hike at sunset, spend the night in the state park campground, and see the stars as you've never seen them before.

User Groups: Hikers, dogs, and horses. No mountain bikes. No wheelchair facilities.

Permits: No permits are required. A $6 day-use fee is charged per vehicle.

Maps: For a topographic map, ask the USGS for Cantil.

Directions: From Mojave, at the junction of Highways 58 and 14, drive northeast on Highway 14 for about 20 miles to the Red Cliffs parking area, on the right (east) side of the road.

Contact: Red Rock Canyon State Park, 661/320-4001; Mojave Desert Information Center, 43779 15th Street W., Lancaster, CA 93534, 661/942-0662, www.parks.ca.gov.

19 ANTELOPE VALLEY POPPY RESERVE LOOP
2.0 mi / 1.0 hr   🥾2 ⛰️9

west of Lancaster and Highway 14

Map page 787   **BEST (**

Our first trip to the Antelope Valley California Poppy Reserve was a wee bit disappointing. We showed up in late March, expecting to see the hillsides completely covered in bright orange flowers, but only a few straggler poppies were left, dry and shriveled from the desert wind. It was our own darn fault for poor planning. If you want to see the magic poppy show at Antelope Valley, you simply must time your trip perfectly. The best way to do so is to call the recorded wildflower update phone line (661/724-1180) or monitor the park website starting in late February; you'll find out exactly when the bloom is expected to be at its best. It can be anywhere from late February to May, and it's different every year. There are several possible loop trips in the park, but the best one for poppy-watching is the North and South Poppy Loop, a combined two-mile loop that leads from the west side of the Jane S. Pinheiro Interpretive Center. Wheelchairs can access a short section of this trail. On either leg of the loop, be sure to take the cutoff trail that leads to the Tehachapi Vista Point, where you can get up high and take a look around.

User Groups: Hikers and wheelchairs. No dogs, horses, or mountain bikes.

Permits: No permits are required. An $8 day-use fee is charged per vehicle.

Maps: For a topographic map, ask the USGS for Del Sur.

Directions: From Lancaster on Highway 14, take the Avenue I exit and turn west on Avenue I, which becomes Lancaster Road. Drive 14 miles to the entrance to the Antelope Valley California Poppy Reserve, on the right. The trail begins by the interpretive center.

Contact: Antelope Valley California Poppy Reserve, 15101 W. Lancaster Road, Lancaster, CA 93536, 661/724-1180, www.parks.ca.gov; Mojave Desert Information Center, 661/942-0662.

20 VASQUEZ ROCKS
3.0 mi / 1.5 hr   🏃2   ⛰️8

in Agua Dulce

Map page 787

In case you're wondering whether there is any "country" left near the city of Los Angeles, the park office at Vasquez Rocks Natural Area should convince you. It's a barn, complete with hay and horses. After stopping by and picking up a trail map, take a walk on the Foot Trail and get a close-up look at the bizarre tilted

rock slabs that have made this place famous. (The park has been used in various TV and movie productions.) The largest rock slabs are nearly 150 feet high, and they are tilted as much as 50 degrees, jutting out at various angles toward the sky. The geologic wonders are a result of continuing earth movement along the Elkhorn Fault, which has compressed, folded, and tilted the underlying sandstone rock layers. If you think about it too much, you won't want to stand still in one place for too long. From the parking area, begin hiking on the Foot Trail through the colorful sandstone slabs, then loop back on the Pacific Crest Trail (a dirt road), which returns to the other side of the parking area.

User Groups: Hikers, dogs, horses, and mountain bikes. No wheelchair facilities.

Permits: No permits are required. Parking and access are free.

Maps: Free trail maps are available at the park office. For a topographic map, ask the USGS for Agua Dulce.

Directions: From the junction of I-5 and Highway 14, drive northeast on Highway 14 for 15 miles to Agua Dulce. Take the Vasquez Rocks/Escondido Canyon exit and drive north on Escondido Canyon Road for 2.2 miles to the park entrance. Continue down the dirt road to the large parking lot and picnic area, and begin hiking on the Foot Trail.

Contact: Vasquez Rocks Natural Area, 10700 W. Escondido Canyon Road, Agua Dulce, CA 91390, 661-268-0840, http://parks.co.la.ca.us.

21 SADDLEBACK BUTTE PEAK TRAIL
3.2 mi / 2.0 hr   🏃3   ⛰️9

east of Lancaster and Highway 14

Map page 787

Saddleback Butte State Park is a 3,000-acre Joshua tree woodland, but if those funny-looking trees aren't enough to inspire you to make the trip, this hike to the summit of Saddleback

Butte should do it. After a 1,000-foot climb to the 3,651-foot summit, you're rewarded with sweeping vistas of Antelope Valley, the San Gabriel Mountains, the Tehachapi Mountains, and the Mojave Desert. Make sure you've picked a cool day, then start hiking from the park campground through sand and plentiful Joshua trees, heading directly for the clearly visible peak. The first stretch of trail is nearly flat. At one mile out, a trail leads off to the left to Little Butte; ignore it, and continue straight for granite Saddleback Butte. The last 0.5 mile of trail is remarkably steep and rocky. A saddle near the summit provides excellent views. Keep going to the very top, where you can fully survey the strange surrounding landscape—the meeting place of the western Mojave Desert and the high San Gabriel Mountains.

User Groups: Hikers only. No dogs, horses, or mountain bikes. No wheelchair facilities.

Permits: No permits are required. A $6 day-use fee is charged per vehicle.

Maps: For a topographic map, ask the USGS for Hi Vista.

Directions: From Lancaster on Highway 14, take the 20th Street exit. Drive north on 20th Street for less than 0.5 mile, then turn right (east) on Avenue J. Drive 19 miles on Avenue J to 170th Street East. Turn right, drive one mile, and turn left on Avenue K, at the sign for the state park campground.

Contact: Saddleback Butte State Park, 17102 E. Avenue J, Lancaster, CA 93535, 661/727-9899 or 661/942-0662, www.parks.ca.gov.

22 OWL CANYON / RAINBOW BASIN

4.0 mi / 2.0 hr

northwest of Barstow

Map page 787

You just never know what kind of good stuff you'll find when you travel around the state, and that's certainly true when you reach the Rainbow Basin area north of Barstow. From the Bureau of Land Management's (BLM's) Owl Canyon Campground, you can take a four-mile round-trip hike into some colorful desert country. The well-named Rainbow Basin is made from a cornucopia of colorful sediments—deposits that were formed in lake beds 20 million years ago. The most colorful areas can be seen by taking an auto tour around the basin, but before or after you do so, you should take this hike in Owl Canyon.

The trail begins at Owl Canyon Campground in an ordinary-looking dirt-and-gravel wash. Within minutes, the canyon walls get narrower and rockier, and various colorful sediments begin to show themselves in the rock. There's so much to look at and photograph, and so many boulders and obstacles to climb over and around, that you won't be moving very fast. At 0.6 mile, look for a cave entrance on your right. If you have a flashlight, you can tunnel through it and enter a small side canyon. If you keep traveling in the main canyon, you can hike a total of two miles out. The trail ends near the base of Velvet Peak (a granite ridge), in a colorful rock bowl.

User Groups: Hikers and dogs. No horses or mountain bikes. No wheelchair facilities.

Permits: No permits are required. Parking and access are free.

Maps: For a topographic map, ask the USGS for Mud Hills.

Directions: From I-15 at Barstow, take the Barstow Road exit and drive north 0.8 mile. Turn left on Main Street, drive 0.2 mile, then turn right on First Avenue. Drive one mile, and you will cross over two bridges; just after the second bridge is Irwin Road. Turn left on Irwin Road and drive 5.6 miles. Turn left on Fossil Beds Road (a gravel road), and drive 2.9 miles to the access road for Owl Canyon Campground. Turn right, drive 0.3 mile, then turn right again and drive 1.6 miles to the family campground (go past the group camp). The trail begins by campsite No. 11.

Contact: Bureau of Land Management, Barstow District Office, 2601 Barstow Road, Barstow, CA 92311, 760/252-6000, www.ca.blm.gov/barstow.

23 AFTON CANYON
3.0 mi / 1.5 hr   🏃2   ⛰6

east of Barstow

Map page 787

They call Afton Canyon "the Grand Canyon of the Mojave," and although its proportions may be smaller than the other Grand Canyon, Afton is no slacker in terms of desert drama. Sheer walls of pink and red rock rise straight up, 300 feet above the Mojave River, where a thin strip of water flows almost year-round. From the campground, follow the trail east along the river, amid a surprising amount of foliage. Saltcedar trees thrive along the stream, as well as planted cottonwoods and willows, creating a protective habitat for birds and other wildlife. As you travel farther, the canyon gets more interesting. Its walls tower above you, beautifully carved and sculpted by the Mojave River in the days when it was a much bigger waterway—probably 50,000 years ago. Hike as far as you like into the canyon, then turn around and head back. A good side trip is a visit to Pyramid Canyon, one of Afton's side canyons. Start from the campground and cross the river under the first set of railroad trestles, then head south into Pyramid Canyon. The walls slowly narrow until it becomes a classic slot canyon. In the first 0.25 mile, you can see why they call it Pyramid Canyon.

User Groups: Hikers, dogs, horses, and mountain bikes. No wheelchair facilities.

Permits: No permits are required. Parking and access are free.

Maps: For topographic maps, ask the USGS for Cave Mountain and Dunn.

Directions: From Barstow, drive 36 miles east on I-15 and take the Afton Road exit. Drive 3.5 miles southwest to Afton Campground (the dirt road is well graded). Park near the railroad trestles.

Contact: Bureau of Land Management, Barstow District Office, 2601 Barstow Road, Barstow, CA 92311, 760/252-6000, www.ca.blm.gov/barstow.

24 TEUTONIA PEAK
4.0 mi / 2.0 hr   🏃3   ⛰9

in the Mojave National Preserve east of Barstow

Map page 786

Teutonia Peak on Cima Dome is the perfect summit for geometry enthusiasts. Cima Dome's claim to distinction is its nearly symmetrical dome, a weathered geological feature that once was much higher than it is now. Though not perfectly symmetrical (the apex is off-center), the dome presents an apparent bulge on the horizon when viewed from a distance. It rises 1,500 feet above the surrounding landscape, covers almost 70 square miles, and spreads some 10 miles in diameter. In fact, the dome is so massive that when you're on top of it, you can't see it.

Nonetheless, you'll definitely know you're on top of it. The peak is at 5,755 feet and offers head-swiveling desert vistas. A two-mile trail ascends moderately to its summit. The first mile of trail is level and pleasant, leading through cacti, pinyon pines, and Joshua trees, the Mojave Desert's signature plant. The tree yucca, or Joshua tree, raises it arms to the heavens, calling to mind the Biblical prophet-warrior Joshua, for whom it was named by Mormon pioneers. The Cima Dome yucca tree forests, on the south face of the New York Mountains to the southeast, are the densest Joshua trees in the Southwest, where it is endemic. Some of these trees grow as tall as 25 feet and are 200-years old or more. (They're a different, bushier subspecies from the kind found in Joshua Tree National Park.)

As you walk, you can clearly see your destination, Teutonia Peak, as well as the rugged-looking New York Mountains in the distance. At 1.5 miles, the final ascent begins. At 1.9 miles, you reach a saddle just shy of Teutonia's summit, where panoramic desert views are revealed. Scramble the last short stretch to reach the summit and catch your breath, enjoying the far-reaching vistas. In winter, you might not stay very long, because the wind can howl up here. As you look around, chew on this: The flatlands below are all a part of massive Cima Dome.

User Groups: Hikers, dogs, and horses. No mountain bikes. No wheelchair facilities.

Permits: No permits are required. Parking and access are free.

Maps: A map of Mojave National Preserve is available at the park visitors center or by download at www.nps.gov/moja. A more detailed map is available from Tom Harrison Maps. For a topographic map, ask the USGS for Cima Dome.

Directions: From Baker, take I-15 east for approximately 25 miles to Cima Road. Turn right (south) on Cima Road and drive 12 miles to the trailhead, on the right side of the road.

Contact: Mojave National Preserve, 2701 Barstow Road, Barstow, CA 92311, 760/252-6100 or 760/252-6108, www.nps.gov/moja.

25 KELSO DUNES
3.0 mi / 1.5 hr

in the Mojave National Preserve
southeast of Barstow

Map page 787

What's the most popular place in Mojave National Preserve to watch the sun set? Unquestionably it's the Kelso Dunes, which rank second in both height and range of all the California dunes. The Kelso Dunes cover 45 square miles, reaching a height of about 650 feet. (Eureka Dunes in Death Valley are the highest at about 700 feet; the Algodones Dunes in the Imperial Valley cover the largest area, 270 square miles.) In a wet spring, desert wildflowers bloom on and around the dunes, adding brighter colors to the gold and pink sand.

Be sure to read the interesting interpretive signs at the Kelso Dunes trailhead, then walk a short distance toward the closest dunes, which are plainly visible. Constantly moving sand makes a formal trail impossible. If you climb high enough in the sand, you are rewarded

with views of the surrounding desert, including the Granite and Providence Mountains. Many people don't bother to climb to the top, though. They just plop themselves down and make sand angels or roll around on the dunes' silky surface. Another popular activity is trying to cause small sand avalanches that sometimes produce harmonic booming sounds. For this to occur, the sand must be extremely dry. Some desert lovers swear by the healing power of these vibrating noises.

User Groups: Hikers and dogs. No horses or mountain bikes. No wheelchair facilities.

Permits: No permits are required. Parking and access are free.

Maps: A map of Mojave National Preserve is available at the park visitors center or by download at www.nps.gov/moja. A more detailed map is available from Tom Harrison Maps. For a topographic map, ask the USGS for Kelso Dunes.

Directions: From Barstow, take I-15 east for approximately 60 miles to Baker, then turn south on Kelbaker Road and drive 42 miles, past Kelso, to the signed road on the right for Kelso Dunes. Turn right (west) and drive three miles to the dunes parking area.

If you are coming from the south on I-40, take the Kelso/Amboy exit and drive 14 miles north on Kelbaker Road to the signed road on the left for Kelso Dunes.

Contact: Mojave National Preserve, 2701 Barstow Road, Barstow, CA 92311, 760/252-6100 or 760/252-6108, www.nps.gov/moja.

26 CRYSTAL SPRINGS TRAIL
1.6 mi / 1.0 hr

in the Providence Mountains State
Recreation Area southeast of Barstow

Map page 787

The big draw at the Providence Mountains State Recreation Area is touring Mitchell Caverns on a guided walk, so a lot of people miss out on the excellent do-it-yourself hiking trails in the area. The Crystal Springs Trail is the best of those, leading from the visitors center uphill to a rocky overlook in the Providence Mountains. The trailhead elevation is 4,300 feet. The trail is moderately steep—it gains 700 feet over its brief length—and feels surprisingly remote compared to the parking lot full of people waiting to tour the caverns. You hike upward through Crystal Canyon, where lucky hikers sometimes see bighorn sheep. Rocky outcrops shoot up from both sides of the trail. You'll witness a remarkable variety of high-desert foliage: piñon pines, junipers, and prickly plants galore—chollas, barrel cactus, catclaw, cliff rose, and the like. As you climb, keep turning around to check out the increasingly widening vistas. The trail ends near Crystal Springs, where you get a fine view of the surrounding desert and mountains. Then just turn around and head back downhill.

A good side trip is to add a jaunt in the opposite direction from the visitors center. Follow the Niña Mora Overlook Trail from the park campground for 0.25 mile to an overlook of the Marble Mountains and Clipper Valley. And, of course, if you've driven all the way out here, you should sign up for a tour of Mitchell Caverns. The limestone caverns and their stalagmites, stalactites, and helictites are fascinating to see. Tours are held at 1:30 P.M. on weekdays and 10 A.M., 1:30 P.M., and 3 P.M.on weekends and holidays from September through May. In summer, tours are offered at 1:30 P.M. daily.

User Groups: Hikers only. No dogs, horses, or mountain bikes. No wheelchair facilities.

Permits: No permits are required. A $6 fee is charged per adult for a cavern tour ($3 for children ages 6–16; children 5 and under are free but not recommended on the tour).

Maps: For a topographic map, ask the USGS for Fountain Peak.

Directions: From Barstow, take I-40 east for 100 miles to the exit for Essex Road, Mitchell Caverns, and Providence Mountains State Recreation Area near the town of Essex. Turn north on Essex Road and drive 15.5 miles to the Providence Mountains visitors center.

Contact: Providence Mountains State Recreation Area, P.O. Box 1, Essex, CA 92332, 760/928-2586, www.parks.ca.gov.

⅏ HIGH VIEW NATURE TRAIL
1.3 mi / 1.0 hr   🏃2 ⛰8

in Joshua Tree National Park near Yucca Valley

Map page 788

You're unlikely to have much company on this trail. This lack of popularity, along with its fine vistas and easy grade, is one of its best selling points. The trail is a loop that begins and ends at a parking area near Black Rock Canyon Campground. If you pick up an interpretive brochure at the Black Rock Canyon Nature Center (you'll pass it as you drive in), you can get a brief education on desert plants and animals as you walk. The trail undulates along, climbing a total of only 350 feet, until it reaches a high point with a lovely view of 11,502-foot Mount San Gorgonio and a less-inspiring view of the sprawling desert towns of Yucca Valley and Joshua Tree. A bench marks the spot, and there's a trail register where you can record your comments. The loop back downhill is longer and flatter than the way up. This trail is perfect for a clear winter morning's hike. Note that the loop can also be accessed from the campground and nature center via a 0.5-mile spur trail that begins just west of the nature center.

User Groups: Hikers only. No dogs, horses, or mountain bikes. No wheelchair facilities.

Permits: No permits are required. Parking and access are free in the Black Rock Canyon area of Joshua Tree National Park.

Maps: Free park maps are available at park entrance stations and visitor centers or by download at www.nps.gov/jotr. A more detailed map is available from Tom Harrison Maps or Trails Illustrated. For a topographic map, ask the USGS for Yucca Valley South.

Directions: From Banning, drive east on I-10 for 16 miles to the Highway 62 exit. Turn north on Highway 62 and drive 24 miles to the town of Yucca Valley. Turn right on Joshua Lane (signed for Black Rock Canyon) and drive five miles to the entrance to Black Rock Canyon Campground. Just before the entrance, turn right on a dirt road signed for South Park Parking Area and follow it to its end at the trailhead. The parking area is just outside of the national park boundary, but the trail is inside the park.

Contact: Joshua Tree National Park, 74485 National Park Drive, Twentynine Palms, CA 92277, 760/367-5500, www.nps.gov/jotr.

28 WARREN PEAK

6.0 mi / 3.0 hr

in Joshua Tree National Park near Yucca Valley

Map page 788

If you seek a less tame adventure than you get on many short trails in Joshua Tree National Park, the trip to Warren Peak might suit you well. Located in the far northwest corner of the park, the trail and its 5,103-foot summit destination feel surprisingly remote. The peak provides a terrific view of Southern California's tallest mountains, which are crowned with a mantle of snow in winter and early spring. The trail out of Black Rock Canyon Campground starts in a desert wash, with plenty of Joshua trees, piñon pines, and cholla cacti keeping you company. Keep your eyes on the trail signs, which funnel you into the correct forks in the canyon. (There are several critical turns to make.) The sandy wash narrows to a walled canyon, then broadens again. As you climb gently but steadily, you'll see junipers, oaks, and piñon pines replacing some of the lower desert flora. At about two miles out, you'll spy Warren Peak's pointy fractured rock ahead and to the right. The trail gets a bit hard to discern in places, but watch for trail ducks, and keep your eye on Warren Peak. The last 0.25 mile to the summit is steep and requires some scrambling but is easily accomplished.

If it's not too windy, you'll want to stay on top of the pointy, conical peak for a while, and not just so you can read the summit register. Views of Mount San Gorgonio, Mount San Jacinto, San Gorgonio Pass, and the Mojave Desert will make your heart pound. To the southwest are Palm Springs and the Morongo and Coachella Valleys.

User Groups: Hikers only. No dogs, horses, or mountain bikes. No wheelchair facilities.

Permits: No permits are required. Parking and access are free in the Black Rock Canyon area of Joshua Tree National Park.

Maps: Free park maps are available at park entrance stations and visitor centers or by download at www.nps.gov/jotr. A more detailed map is available from Tom Harrison Maps or Trails Illustrated. For a topographic map, ask the USGS for Yucca Valley South.

Directions: From Banning, drive east on I-10 for 16 miles to the Highway 62 exit. Turn north on Highway 62 and drive 24 miles to the town of Yucca Valley. Turn right on Joshua Lane (signed for Black Rock Canyon) and drive five miles to the Black Rock Canyon Nature Center. Park and then walk uphill to the Black Rock Canyon trailhead, at the upper end of the campground.

Contact: Joshua Tree National Park, 74485 National Park Drive, Twentynine Palms, CA 92277, 760/367-5500, www.nps.gov/jotr.

29 EUREKA PEAK

10.8 mi / 6.0 hr

in Joshua Tree National Park near Yucca Valley

Map page 788

The total elevation gain on this trip is only 1,500 feet to reach the summit of Eureka Peak (at 5,518 feet), but it feels more difficult than that. The problem is sand and rocks—lots of them—and the fact that the trail is hard to discern in places. However, if you're willing to put in some effort, your reward is a commanding view of the western edge of Joshua Tree National Park, as well as Mount San Jacinto and Mount San Gorgonio. Sand and snow—you see it all from here. Begin hiking on the California Riding and Hiking Trail, which you'll follow for two miles until you come to a major wash. This is where things start to get tricky; keep looking for trail markers signed as EP (for Eureka Peak) to keep you on track. Take the right fork in the wash, leaving the California Riding and Hiking Trail. In another 0.5 mile, take the next right fork into another wash. Hike through this wash for 1.7 miles to its end. A trail marker directs you to your left, heading up and over a ridge. At the top, turn right (south), hike up to a saddle, and then continue on to the south side of Eureka Peak, where there's a short path to the summit. When you get to the top, what's the only downer? You find that plenty of people have driven their cars up to the peak via a dirt road from Covington Flat. No fair. An option is to follow this road back downhill for one mile to the California Riding and Hiking Trail, turn left, and follow the trail back to your starting point. It makes a good loop trip and only adds one mile to your total distance.

User Groups: Hikers only. No dogs, horses, or mountain bikes. No wheelchair facilities.

Permits: No permits are required. Parking and access are free in the Black Rock Canyon area of Joshua Tree National Park.

Maps: Free park maps are available at park entrance stations and visitor centers or by download at www.nps.gov/jotr. A more detailed map is available from Tom Harrison Maps or Trails Illustrated. For topographic maps, ask the USGS for Yucca Valley South and Joshua Tree South.

Directions: From Banning, drive east on I-10 for 16 miles to the Highway 62 exit. Turn north on Highway 62 and drive 24 miles to the town of Yucca Valley. Turn right on Joshua Lane (signed for Black Rock Canyon) and drive five miles to the Black Rock Canyon Nature Center. Park at the nature center and then walk uphill to the California Riding and Hiking Trail trailhead, on the left (east) side of the campground entrance.

Contact: Joshua Tree National Park, 74485 National Park Drive, Twentynine Palms, CA 92277, 760/367-5500, www.nps.gov/jotr.

30 FORTYNINE PALMS OASIS
3.0 mi / 1.5 hr 🥾2 ⛰️8

in Joshua Tree National Park near Twentynine Palms

Map page 788

The biggest surprise on the Fortynine Palms Oasis Trail is not the large and lovely grove of palm trees at the trail's end. It's that there are no Joshua trees to be found anywhere along the trail. What? No Joshua trees in this part of Joshua Tree National Park? It's true—the elevation is a bit too low for them here. Taking their place are the namesake 49 palms, of course, and lovely spring wildflowers, including some orchids growing near the pools in the oasis. Try to hike here in March or April, when you may get lucky and catch the red barrel cacti in bloom. Winter is another lovely season here.

The trail is an old Native American pathway, and it's well maintained and easy to follow. It winds around, climbs up and over a small ridge, and then curves around to the palm grove. First you'll see a cluster of 10 palms, and then a larger grouping a short distance away. Although you can see and hear Highway 62 and its sprawling suburban towns as you hike, once you reach the palm grove, all traces of civilization are left behind. Have a seat on a boulder to listen and watch for birds. Orioles, finches, and hummingbirds congregate here for both the trickling spring water and the palm fruits. This is a lush, green, vibrant spot, and it is critically important as a watering hole for bighorn sheep and coyotes. The only downer: Some of the beautiful palm trunks have been carved with people's initials.

User Groups: Hikers only. No dogs, horses, or mountain bikes. No wheelchair facilities.

Permits: No permits are required. Parking and access are free in this area of Joshua Tree National Park.

Maps: Free park maps are available at park entrance stations and visitor centers or by download at www.nps.gov/jotr. A more detailed map is available from Tom Harrison Maps or Trails Illustrated. For a topographic map, ask the USGS for Queen Mountain.

Directions: From Banning, drive east on I-10 for 16 miles to the Highway 62 exit. Turn north on Highway 62 and drive 29 miles to the town of Joshua Tree. Continue east on Highway 62 for 10 miles to just west of the town of Twentynine Palms. Turn right (south) on Canyon Road, located by the High Desert Animal Hospital. Drive 1.7 miles on Canyon Road; bear left where the road forks. The pavement ends at the Fortynine Palms Oasis trailhead.

Contact: Joshua Tree National Park, 74485 National Park Drive, Twentynine Palms, CA 92277, 760/367-5500, www.nps.gov/jotr.

31 BARKER DAM LOOP
1.5 mi / 1.0 hr   🏃1   ⛰8

in Joshua Tree National Park near Twentynine Palms

Map page 788

There's a lake in the desert (well, in wet years, anyway), and it's hidden in a magical place called the Wonderland of Rocks. You can't water-ski or fish there, but you can enjoy bird-watching and photograph the reflections of odd-shaped boulders in the water's surface. The lake was last seen in 1998, before a series of dry years hit Southern California, but with a few good winter rains, it will be back. When it exists, the lake is formed by Barker Dam, built at the beginning of the 20th century to improve upon a natural boulder dam that captured rain runoff in this basin. Even if the lake is only a mirage when you visit, this short loop is still a great walk, as it also leads past many of the unique granite boulders of the Wonderland of Rocks. Rock climbers can often be seen strutting their stuff here. The trail loops back past some petroglyphs (take

the short spur trail) and Indian grinding holes. If the petroglyphs seem remarkably visible and clear to you, it's because years ago a movie crew painted over them to make them more visible to the camera. For this tragic reason, the park calls these paintings the "Disney petroglyphs."

User Groups: Hikers only. No dogs, horses, or mountain bikes. No wheelchair facilities.

Permits: No permits are required. There is a $15 entrance fee per vehicle at Joshua Tree National Park, good for seven days.

Maps: Free park maps are available at park entrance stations and visitor centers or by download at www.nps.gov/jotr. A more detailed map is available from Tom Harrison Maps or Trails Illustrated. For a topographic map, ask the USGS for Indian Cove.

Directions: From Banning, drive east on I-10 for 16 miles to the Highway 62 exit. Turn north on Highway 62 and drive 29 miles to the town of Joshua Tree. Turn right on Park Boulevard and drive 14 miles to Hidden Valley Campground, on the left. Follow the signs for Barker Dam.

Contact: Joshua Tree National Park, 74485 National Park Drive, Twentynine Palms, CA 92277, 760/367-5500, www.nps.gov/jotr.

32 RYAN MOUNTAIN TRAIL
3.0 mi / 2.0 hr   🏃2   ⛰10

in Joshua Tree National Park near Twentynine Palms

Map page 788   **BEST (**

If you hike only one trail in Joshua Tree National Park, this should be the one. Ryan Mountain (at 5,470 feet) provides what many insist is the best view in the park. You can see the Queen Valley, Wonderland of Rocks, Lost Horse Valley, Pleasant Valley, and the far-off mountains, San Gorgonio and San Jacinto. It's a complete panorama. The route travels through boulders and Joshua trees—no surprises here—on a well-maintained and easy-to-follow trail. The ascent is a bit steep—a 1,000-foot elevation gain over only 1.5 miles—but it's over with quickly, so just sweat it out. Be sure to sign the summit register and then have a seat on one of the rocks of Ryan Mountain to enjoy the view. The peak's boulders are estimated to be several hundred million years old, which gives you something to think about while you admire the vista.

User Groups: Hikers only. No dogs, horses, or mountain bikes. No wheelchair facilities.

Permits: No permits are required. There is a $15 entrance fee per vehicle at Joshua Tree National Park, good for seven days.

Maps: Free park maps are available at park entrance stations and visitor centers or by download at www.nps.gov/jotr. A more detailed map is available from Tom Harrison Maps or Trails Illustrated. For a topographic map, ask the USGS for Keys View.

Directions: From Banning, drive east on I-10 for 16 miles to the Highway 62 exit. Turn north on Highway 62 and drive 45 miles to Twentynine Palms and the park visitors center. Turn right on Utah Trail Road and drive eight miles to a Y junction. Bear right and continue for nine miles, past Sheep Pass Campground to the trailhead parking area, on the south side of the road. You can also reach the trailhead via Park Boulevard out of the town of Joshua Tree, turning left at Cap Rock Junction and continuing 2.5 miles to the trailhead.

Contact: Joshua Tree National Park, 74485 National Park Drive, Twentynine Palms, CA 92277, 760/367-5500, www.nps.gov/jotr.

33 LOST HORSE MINE
4.2 mi / 2.0 hr   👥2 ⛰8

in Joshua Tree National Park near Twentynine Palms

Map page 788

You get the full desert experience on the Lost Horse Mine Trail, including spectacular mountain and valley vistas, high-desert flora, and a visit to an old gold mine. The trail (really an old road) leads uphill for 1.8 miles

to Lost Horse Mine. The mine produced a gold profit at the turn of the century—9,000 ounces of gold—and is the best preserved of all the mines in the national park. Still standing are the mine's stamp mill, old building foundations, and a few open mine shafts. Continue from the mine another 0.3 mile up the old road, climbing more steeply up the ridge to wide overlooks of the Queen Valley, Lost Horse Valley, Pleasant Valley, and the eastern stretch of the national park. The summit here is 5,278 feet; turn around and retrace your steps before the trail begins to descend.

User Groups: Hikers only. No dogs, horses, or mountain bikes. No wheelchair facilities.

Permits: No permits are required. There is a $15 entrance fee per vehicle at Joshua Tree National Park, good for seven days.

Maps: Free park maps are available at park entrance stations and visitor centers or by download at www.nps.gov/jotr. A more detailed map is available from Tom Harrison Maps or Trails Illustrated. For a topographic map, ask the USGS for Keys View.

Directions: From Banning, drive east on I-10 for 16 miles to the Highway 62 exit. Turn north on Highway 62 and drive 29 miles to the town of Joshua Tree and Park Boulevard. Turn right on Park Boulevard and drive 15.8 miles to Cap Rock junction. Bear right and drive 2.4 miles to the dirt road on the left that is signed for Lost Horse Mine. Turn left and follow the dirt road to the trailhead parking area.

Contact: Joshua Tree National Park, 74485 National Park Drive, Twentynine Palms, CA 92277, 760/367-5500, www.nps.gov/jotr.

34 SKULL ROCK NATURE TRAIL
1.7 mi / 1.0 hr   👥1 ⛰7

in Joshua Tree National Park near Twentynine Palms

Map page 788

Joshua Tree National Park is arguably more famous for its rock formations than it is for Joshua trees. If you want a close look at some of the park's weird and wonderful hunks of quartz monzonite, the Skull Rock Trail will provide it. The official trail is only 0.25 mile long, but if you're okay with doing a little cross-country hiking, you can easily turn it into a 1.7-mile loop. The trail provides a quick education: Interpretive signs point out paper-bag bush, turbinella oak, cholla cactus, and other desert flora. The path runs between the Skull Rock parking area and Loop E in Jumbo Rocks Campground, so you can start at either place. It winds among giant, rounded rock formations and passes by its namesake, Skull Rock. The big boulder looks loosely like what its name implies. A spiderweb of paths leads around Skull Rock; this is where everyone abandons the formal trail and starts climbing around on the smooth, rounded rock surfaces. To complete the longer loop, you must cross the park road twice, navigate an unmaintained stretch on the north side of the road, and walk a 0.5-mile stretch of the Jumbo Rocks Campground entrance road. It sounds complicated, but it's quite doable.

User Groups: Hikers only. No dogs, horses, or mountain bikes. No wheelchair facilities.

Permits: No permits are required. There is a $15 entrance fee per vehicle at Joshua Tree National Park, good for seven days.

Maps: Free park maps are available at park entrance stations and visitor centers or by download at www.nps.gov/jotr. A more detailed map is available from Tom Harrison Maps or Trails Illustrated. For a topographic map, ask the USGS for Malapai Hill.

Directions: From Banning, drive east on I-10 for 16 miles to the Highway 62 exit. Turn north on Highway 62 and drive 45 miles to Twentynine Palms and the park visitors center. Turn right on Utah Trail Road and drive eight miles to a Y junction. Bear right and continue four miles to the trailhead parking area alongside the road shortly before the entrance to Jumbo Rocks Campground. Begin hiking on the left (south) side of the road. If you are camping at Jumbo Rocks, you can start hiking from the entrance to Loop E.

Contact: Joshua Tree National Park, 74485 National Park Drive, Twentynine Palms, CA 92277, 760/367-5500, www.nps.gov/jotr.

35 MASTODON PEAK

3.0 mi / 1.5 hr

in Joshua Tree National Park near Cottonwood Spring

Map page 788   BEST (

Note: Due to a flash flood in September 2011, the access road to Cottonwood Campground and this hike's trailhead is closed. The National Park Sevice hopes to have access to this trail restored by late 2012, but please call ahead before making the long drive.

The Mastodon Peak Trail begins at Cottonwood Spring Oasis, a little slice of watery paradise for birds and wildlife. After a short paved section, the trail sets off in the desert sand, and after 0.5 mile, you take the left fork for Mastodon Peak. Shortly you'll pass another trail junction with the path to Cottonwood Spring Campground; stay right. The route has almost no elevation change along its route to the base of the peak. It's a pleasant, easy stroll among tall ocotillos, yucca, and smaller cacti. At the Mastodon's base, you must choose whether or not to scramble to the top; the going is steep but short. Although it's a nice trip just to hike to the peak's base and try to imagine the Mastodon's profile, it's recommended you go for the summit. The easiest route is around the back of the Mastodon, on its east side. In a few minutes you are at the top, admiring the surprisingly wide view: Not only do you see a great expanse of Joshua Tree's desert and the Eagle Mountains, but also snowcapped Mount San Jacinto and the miragelike Salton Sea shimmering in the distance some 30 miles away.

If you want to add some history to your hike, retrace your steps to the junction with the trail to Cottonwood Spring Camp. Turn right there and hike past the Mastodon Gold Mine and the Winona Mill Site. The mine was worked in the 1920s with a modicum of success. From the mill site, you don't need to backtrack to the main trail; the path loops back to the Cottonwood Spring parking area.

User Groups: Hikers only. No dogs, horses, or mountain bikes. No wheelchair facilities.

Permits: No permits are required. There is a $15 entrance fee per vehicle at Joshua Tree National Park, good for seven days.

Maps: Free park maps are available at park entrance stations and visitor centers or by download at www.nps.gov/jotr. A more detailed map is available from Tom Harrison Maps or Trails Illustrated. For a topographic map, ask the USGS for Cottonwood Spring.

Directions: From Indio, drive east on I-10 for approximately 25 miles. Turn north on Cottonwood Spring Road and drive seven miles to Cottonwood Spring visitors center. Turn right and drive another mile, passing the campground entrance, to the day-use parking area at Cottonwood Spring Oasis.

Contact: Joshua Tree National Park, 74485 National Park Drive, Twentynine Palms, CA 92277, 760/367-5500, www.nps.gov/jotr.

🔢36 LOST PALMS OASIS
7.5 mi / 3.5 hr

in Joshua Tree National Park near
Cottonwood Spring

Map page 788	BEST (

Note: Due to a flash flood in September 2011, the access road to Cottonwood Campground and this hike's trailhead is closed. The National Park Sevice hopes to have access to this trail restored by late 2012, but please call ahead before making the long drive.

If the weather is cool and accommodating and you're in the mood for a longer hike in southern Joshua Tree National Park, the Lost Palms Oasis Trail comes highly recommended. Many consider Lost Palms Oasis to be the best palm grove in Joshua Tree, and the hike to reach it has little elevation change. The trail begins at Cottonwood Spring Oasis and for the first 0.5 mile follows the same path as the Mastodon Peak Trail. Stay straight at the junction with the trail to Mastodon Peak; continue straight through a series of washes and low ridges covered with various low-elevation desert cacti. There is no indication of the huge palm oasis until you are almost on top of it, at slightly more than three miles out. The main trail brings you to an overlook point above the palms, and a steep use trail descends 0.25 mile into the grove. Make the rugged 200-foot descent to the canyon bottom; the remoteness of the area and the lush atmosphere of the leafy palm grove make it worth the effort. The Lost Palms Oasis grove contains more than 100 palms in its main canyon. In the upper end of the canyon is a side canyon with more palms, although these are more difficult to reach.

User Groups: Hikers only. No dogs, horses, or mountain bikes. No wheelchair facilities.

Permits: No permits are required. There is a $15 entrance fee per vehicle at Joshua Tree National Park, good for seven days.

Maps: Free park maps are available at park entrance stations and visitor centers or by download at www.nps.gov/jotr. A more detailed map is available from Tom Harrison Maps or Trails Illustrated. For a topographic map, ask the USGS for Cottonwood Spring.

Directions: From Indio, drive east on I-10 for approximately 25 miles. Turn north on Cottonwood Spring Road and drive seven miles to Cottonwood Spring visitors center. Turn right and drive a mile, past the campground entrance, to the day-use parking area at Cottonwood Spring Oasis.

Contact: Joshua Tree National Park, 74485 National Park Drive, Twentynine Palms, CA 92277, 760/367-5500, www.nps.gov/jotr.

37 BIG MORONGO CANYON LOOP

1.5 mi / 1.0 hr 🥾1 ⛰️8

in the Big Morongo Canyon Preserve
north of Palm Springs

Map page 788

Big Morongo Canyon Preserve is a bird-watcher's place, plain and simple. In fact, if you're not carrying binoculars and a field book when you visit, you'll feel like a real outsider. Fortunately, you don't have to know anything about birds to have a good time. We examined the interpretive exhibit at the trailhead kiosk, and within a few minutes of hiking, we were able to spot and identify a pair of western tanagers. (And usually we can't tell a blue jay from a blue grouse.) The best bird-watching seasons are spring and fall, so time your trip for those times if possible. Although a fire burned through this preserve in June 2005, consuming much of the willows and riparian plants, the vegetation is quickly returning.

Start this loop from the kiosk by bearing left to connect to the Desert Willow Trail, an exposed pathway through a desert wash, then in 0.4 mile turn left again on the Yucca Ridge Trail. As you climb Yucca Ridge, you'll gain panoramic views of Big Morongo Canyon and the San Jacinto and San Gorgonio Mountains. Note the gneiss and schist rock formations along the trail; they are some of the oldest rocks in California—one to two billion years old. In 0.7 mile, connect to the Mesquite Trail and enjoy a streamside walk alongside Fremont cottonwoods and red willows that are regenerating after the 2005 fire. You may smell the distinct scent of sulfur from underground springs. Finally you'll join the Marsh Trail for the final stint back to the trailhead, following a boardwalk made of recycled plastic milk containers. If you haven't added a few species to your bird list by this point in the hike, you will now. More than 1,400 pairs of birds per square kilometer nest here annually, making the Marsh Trail a bird-watcher's paradise.

User Groups: Hikers only. No dogs, horses, or mountain bikes. Wheelchair users can follow the fully accessible Marsh Trail.

Permits: No permits are required. Parking and access are free.

Maps: For a topographic map, ask the USGS for Morongo Valley.

Directions: From Banning, drive east on I-10 for 16 miles to the Highway 62 exit. Turn north on Highway 62 and drive 11 miles to Morongo Valley. Look for a sign on the right for the Big Morongo Canyon Preserve (at East Drive); turn right and drive 200 yards to the preserve entrance, on the left. Trails begin at the kiosk/information center.

Contact: Big Morongo Canyon Preserve, P.O. Box 780, Morongo Valley, CA 92256, 760/363-7190, www.bigmorongo.org.

38 AERIAL TRAMWAY TO DESERT VIEW TRAIL

2.0 mi / 1.0 hr 🥾1 ⛰️10

in Mount San Jacinto State Park and Wilderness

Map page 788

The first time you ride the Palm Springs Aerial Tramway, you realize that human beings are capable of creating miracles. In just a few minutes (which you spend gaping out the big windows at the view), you are whooshed from the desert floor, at 2,643 feet in elevation, to the Mount San Jacinto State Park and Wilderness, at 8,516 feet. From cacti to clouds, from palms to pines, and in our case, from desert heat to snow flurries. There are dozens of possible hikes from the top of the tramway, but the easiest of them all is on the Desert View Trail. Since the trail is in the state park but not in the state wilderness, you don't even need a permit—just get off the tram and start hiking. Where else for so little effort can you get expansive views of the desert and high mountain country? Not too many places.

To reach the Desert View Trail, follow the park's nature trail to the left from the back of the tram station; it joins Desert View. The vistas are awesome every step of the way, especially looking out over Palm Springs and the Indian Canyons. As you walk, be on the lookout for Cooper's hawks and yellow-rumped warblers.

Here's an insider's tip for planning your trip: The best deal on the Palm Springs Aerial Tramway is to buy the Ride and Dine Ticket (available after 3 p.m.). For a moderate additional charge, you get a huge buffet dinner to go with your tram ride and day of exploring on the mountain. It's an incredible experience to spend the afternoon hiking, have dinner in the huge dining room as the sun goes down, and then ride the tram back downhill in the darkness.

User Groups: Hikers only. No dogs, horses, or mountain bikes. No wheelchair facilities.

Permits: No permits are required. The Palm Springs Aerial Tramway charges $23.25 per adult, $16.25 per child ages 3–12, and $21.25 for seniors ages 60 and older for a round-trip ticket to Mountain Station. Contact the Palm Springs Aerial Tramway for information about schedules, fees, and special programs.

Maps: A trail map of Mount San Jacinto State Park and Wilderness is available at the offices listed below. For a topographic map, ask the USGS for San Jacinto Peak.

Directions: From Banning, drive 12 miles east on I-10 and take the Highway 111/Palm Springs exit. Drive nine miles south on Highway 111 to Tramway Road, then turn right and drive 3.5 miles to the tramway parking area. Walk to the tram station, buy your ticket, and ride the tram to its end at Mountain Station. Walk out the back side of Mountain Station, follow the paved path downhill, and walk to your left for the Desert View Trail.

Contact: Mount San Jacinto State Park and Wilderness, P.O. Box 308, 25905 Highway 243, Idyllwild, CA 92549, 951/659-2607, www.parks.ca.gov; Palm Springs Aerial Tramway, 888/515-8726, www.pstramway.com.

39 AERIAL TRAMWAY TO SAN JACINTO PEAK
11.6 mi / 6.6 hr 🏃3 ⛰10

in Mount San Jacinto State Park and Wilderness

Map page 788 BEST (

You could hike to 10,834-foot San Jacinto Peak the hard way, upward from Idyllwild on one of several possible trails, but then you'd miss out on the many delights of the Palm Springs Aerial Tramway and hiking through Long and Round Valleys. So take the tram instead, get your wilderness permit at the ranger station, and begin hiking on the Round Valley Trail. It switchbacks gently uphill through the pines and firs, most of the time following a creek laden with corn lilies, to reach beautiful Round Valley, at 9,100 feet. At the west end of Round Valley, you reach a Y in the trail, near the seasonal ranger station. Take the left fork heading toward Wellmans Divide, with a short, steep ascent just before you reach it. The views to the north and east are inspiring, including jagged Tahquitz Peak and Red Tahquitz—a bit of foreshadowing of things to come.

At the divide, turn right on the Deer Springs Trail. You have 2.6 miles to go, and the views stay with you the whole way. Climb northward on the granite slopes of Miller Peak, make a sharp left switchback, and head southwest to the spur trail for San Jacinto Peak, on the right. Once you're on the spur, it's only a few hundred yards to the peak, where the views are truly breathtaking. You can see just about all of Southern California, even into Mexico and Nevada, and out to the Pacific Ocean. John Muir said that the vista from San Jacinto was "one of the most sublime spectacles seen anywhere on Earth," and he was a guy who saw a lot of vistas. Total elevation gain is 2,300 feet.

User Groups: Hikers only. No dogs, horses, or mountain bikes. No wheelchair facilities.

Permits: A free wilderness permit is required for day hiking or backpacking in the San

Jacinto Wilderness and is available from the ranger station at Mountain Station. Backpackers should obtain a permit in advance by mail from Mount San Jacinto State Park and Wilderness. No permits are required. The Palm Springs Aerial Tramway charges $23.25 per adult, $16.25 per child ages 3–12, and $21.25 for seniors ages 60 and older for a round-trip ticket to Mountain Station. Contact the Palm Springs Aerial Tramway for information about schedules, fees, and special programs.

Maps: A trail map of Mount San Jacinto State Park and Wilderness is available at the offices listed below. A map of the San Jacinto Wilderness is available from Tom Harrison Maps. For a topographic map, ask the USGS for San Jacinto Peak.

Directions: From Banning, drive 12 miles east on I-10 and take the Highway 111/Palm Springs exit. Drive nine miles south on Highway 111 to Tramway Road, then turn right and drive 3.5 miles to the tramway parking area. Walk to the tram station, buy your ticket, and ride the tram to its end, at Mountain Station. Walk out the back side of Mountain Station, follow the paved path downhill, and head right (west) for a few hundred yards to the ranger station. Get a day-hiking permit and continue hiking on the well-signed trail heading for Round Valley.

Contact: Mount San Jacinto State Park and Wilderness, P.O. Box 308, 25905 Highway 243, Idyllwild, CA 92549, 951/659-2607, www.parks.ca.gov; Palm Springs Aerial Tramway, 888/515-8726, www.pstramway.com.

40 MURRAY CANYON TRAIL
4.0 mi / 2.0 hr 🚶2 ⛰9

on the Agua Caliente Indian Reservation in Palm Springs

Map page 788

If you think Palm Springs is all tennis courts, golf courses, and beauty parlors, you haven't been to the Indian Canyons off South Palm Canyon Drive. The Indian Canyons—Palm, Andreas, and Murray—are what's left of the old Palm Springs. They're wide-open stretches of desert, with red rock, fan palms, sulfur streams, barrel cactus, bighorn sheep, and broad vistas of surprising color and beauty. The Murray Canyon Trail is an excellent exploration of this area, beginning at the picnic grounds between Murray and Andreas Canyons. The trail is well-packed sand and is clearly marked along the way. After an initial wide-open desert stretch, you enter Murray Canyon, which narrows and twists and turns, so you never see where you're going until you come around the next bend. The stream you've been following begins to exhibit a stronger flow, and the streamside reeds, grasses, palm trees, and wild grapes intensify their growth accordingly. If you're a fan of red rock, you'll love the 100-foot-tall slanted rock outcrops and cliffs. After passing a left fork for the Coffman Trail, climb up and over a small waterfall in Murray Canyon, staying on the left side of the stream. In another 0.25 mile, you'll reach a larger set of falls. These falls block any possible further progress but provide many good pools for swimming and granite shelves for picnicking. Birders, keep on the alert for a possible sighting of the endangered Least Bells Vireo, which nests in this canyon.

One thing to keep in mind when you visit Murray Canyon, or any of the Indian Canyons: Make sure you check what time the park gates are closing for the day, and then make sure you finish your hike so your car is out of the parking lot by closing time. Show up 15 minutes late, and you can have a real problem on your hands. (Guess how we know.)

User Groups: Hikers and horses. No dogs or mountain bikes. No wheelchair facilities.

Permits: No permits are required. A $9 day-use fee is charged per adult, $7 for seniors 62 and older, and $5 for children ages 6–12.

Maps: A brochure and trail map are available at the entrance kiosk. For topographic maps, ask the USGS for Palm Springs and Cathedral City.

Directions: From Palm Springs, drive south

through the center of town on Highway 111/ Palm Canyon Drive and take the right fork signed for South Palm Canyon Drive. Drive 2.8 miles, bearing right at the sign for Palm Canyon/Andreas Canyon. Stop at the entrance toll gate, drive about 200 yards, and turn right for Murray Canyon. Drive past the Andreas Canyon trailhead and continue to Murray Canyon Picnic Area, a mile from the entrance kiosk.

Contact: Indian Canyons Visitor Center, 760/323-6018, www.indian-canyons.com.

41 TAHQUITZ CANYON
2.0 mi / 1.0 hr 🏃1 ⛰10

on the Agua Caliente Indian Reservation in Palm Springs

Map page 788   **BEST ❰**

Just about everything in Palm Springs has a legend behind it, and Tahquitz Canyon (pronounced TAW-kits) is no exception. Named for an Agua Caliente Indian shaman who abused his powers and was banished from his tribe, Tahquitz Canyon is a spectacular outdoor museum of desert flora and fauna. Yet the curse of Tahquitz remains so powerful that even today, some local tribe members refuse to venture into the evil shaman's rock-studded canyon.

Not so for the thousands of Palm Springs visitors who have hiked here since Tahquitz Canyon's public reopening in 1999. After years of abuse by raucous, partying crowds in the 1960s and 1970s, the canyon was closed to public access for more than two decades. The Agua Caliente Indians, owners of this land, went to great pains to clean out all the garbage, graffiti, and debris and to restore this desert canyon to its native state. Now visitors can join hike on their own or join a ranger-guided walk along this easy trail through the canyon to the base of its 60-foot waterfall. Movie buffs will recognize the showering falls as the entrance to the land of Shangri-La in Frank Capra's 1937 film *Lost Horizon*. Tahquitz's other treasures include plentiful bird life, Indian rock art,

and lush stands of desert lavender, mesquite, and creosote. Don't miss a trip to this unique place; it is sure to be the highlight of your visit to Palm Springs.

User Groups: Hikers only. No dogs, horses, or mountain bikes. No wheelchair facilities.

Permits: Entrance fees are $12.50 per adult and $6 for children 12 and under. Reservations are recommended for guided hikes, which are held October–May (8 A.M., 10 A.M., noon, and 2 P.M.). You may hike on your own 7:30 A.M.–3:30 P.M.

Maps: For topographic maps, ask the USGS for Palm Springs and Cathedral City.

Directions: From Palm Springs, drive south through the center of town on Highway 111/ Palm Canyon Drive and turn right on Mesquite Avenue. Drive 0.5 mile to the Tahquitz Canyon visitors center.

Contact: Tahquitz Canyon Visitors Center, 500 W. Mesquite Avenue, Palm Springs, CA 92256, 760/416-7044, www.tahquitzcanyon.com.

42 MAIDENHAIR FALLS
5.0 mi / 3.0 hr 🏃3 ⛰9

in Anza-Borrego Desert State Park near Hellhole Canyon

Map page 789

If you have taken the hike to Borrego Palm Canyon Falls and found that it suited your taste for desert adventure, this trip to Maidenhair Falls is a more challenging path to a slightly bigger and more dramatic desert waterfall. Stop in at the park visitors center before you begin, and pick up a handout with trail directions. Also remember to be prepared for a longer excursion in the desert (bring tons of extra water, and cover your head with a light-colored hat). Your destination is a 20-foot waterfall with a walled backdrop of maidenhair ferns and mosses. The route to reach it travels from Highway S22 south of the visitors center into the mouth of Hellhole Canyon. Begin on the California Riding and Hiking Trail for the first 200 yards and turn right. You'll pass a few fan palms, myriad cacti, some odd-shaped rocks, and Native American grinding holes along the route. Cottonwoods grow in places along the stream. Maidenhair Falls is a bit tricky to find, tucked into a narrow canyon corner, but with luck, there will be enough water running in the stream to clue you in to its location.

User Groups: Hikers only. No dogs, horses, or mountain bikes. No wheelchair facilities.

Permits: No permits are required. Parking and access are free.

Maps: Maps and brochures are available at the park visitor center, or by free download at www.parks.ca.gov. An Anza-Borrego Desert State Park map is also available from Tom Harrison Maps or Wilderness Press. For a topographic map, ask the USGS for Tubb Canyon.

Directions: From Julian, drive east on Highway 78 for approximately 19 miles to Highway S3/Yaqui Pass Road. Turn left (north) on Highway S3/Yaqui Pass Road and drive for 12 miles to Borrego Springs. Turn left on Highway S22/Palm Canyon Drive and drive one mile to the signed junction just before the park visitors center. Turn left and drive 0.75 mile to the large parking lot on the west side of the road.

Contact: Anza-Borrego Desert State Park, 200 Palm Canyon Drive, Borrego Springs, CA 92004, 760/767-5311; visitors center, 760/767-4205, www.parks.ca.gov.

43 BORREGO PALM CANYON
3.0 mi / 1.5 hr   🏃2 ⛺9

in Anza-Borrego Desert State Park near Borrego Springs

Map page 789   **BEST (**

The hike to Borrego Palm Canyon Falls is only 1.5 miles in length, but it feels like a trip from the desert to the tropics. You start out in a sandy, rocky, open plain, sweating it out with the cacti and ocotillo, and you end up in a shady oasis of fan palms, dipping your feet in the pool of a boulder-choked waterfall. If you haven't visited this special place in recent years, you may be surprised at how much has changed. A series of severe rainstorms and flash floods in the canyon in the years between 2003 and 2010 have wiped out a large number of palms and left their trunks scattered all over the canyon floor, wedged under large boulders, and stacked on top of one another. These floods created walls of water that were reported to be higher than 10 feet. On a sunny, calm day, it's hard to imagine the destruction that raging water in the desert can cause, but the evidence is all around you. The trip begins on the Borrego Palm Canyon Trail from the state park campground; make sure you top off your water bottles before you start walking. If you pick up an interpretive brochure at the park visitors center, you can identify the array of desert plants that grow along the trail, including cheesebush, brittle-bush, catclaw (ouch!), and chuparosa. In about 0.5 mile, you're suddenly surprised by the sight of bright green, leafy palm trees up ahead. Borrego Palm Canyon is home to hundreds of mature native palms, the largest of more than 25 groves in the park. It's one of the largest oases in the United States. Head toward the palms, and in a few minutes, you'll be nestled in their shade, listening to the desert wind rustle their fronds. This first grove is not as large as it used to be, but it still has about 20 mature palms. Small, three- to five-foot palm trees are growing up in the aftermath of the destruction. Follow the trail a little farther, and you'll reach a 12-foot waterfall that streams over giant boulders and forms a large, sandy pool. For your return trip, follow the well-marked "Alternate Trail" back to the campground, which follows a slightly longer, more meandering route through the wash.

User Groups: Hikers only. No dogs, horses, or mountain bikes. No wheelchair facilities.

Permits: No permits are required. An $8 day-use fee is charged per vehicle.

Maps: Maps and brochures are available at the park visitor center, or by free download at www.parks.ca.gov. An Anza-Borrego Desert State Park map is also available from Tom

Harrison Maps or Wilderness Press. For a topographic map, ask the USGS for Borrego Palm Canyon.

Directions: From Julian, drive east on Highway 78 for approximately 19 miles to Highway S3/Yaqui Pass Road. Turn left (north) on Highway S3/Yaqui Pass Road and drive 12 miles to Borrego Springs. Turn left on Highway S22/Palm Canyon Drive and drive one mile to the signed junction just before the park visitors center. Turn right and drive one mile to Borrego Palm Canyon Campground. The trailhead is at the west end.

Contact: Anza-Borrego Desert State Park, 200 Palm Canyon Drive, Borrego Springs, CA 92004, 760/767-5311, www.parks.ca.gov; visitors center, 760/767-4205.

44 CACTUS LOOP AND YAQUI WELL

2.75 mi / 1.5 hr   🚶2 ⛰️8

in Anza-Borrego Desert State Park near Tamarisk Grove

Map page 789

The Cactus Loop and Yaqui Well Trails are two separate nature trails at Anza-Borrego Desert State Park, but since they're right beside each other, you might as well hike both. The Cactus Loop Trail is a 0.75-mile loop, and more hilly than you might expect from a nature trail. It shows off seven kinds of cacti, including barrel, hedgehog, fishhook, beavertail, and cholla. Visitors often spot chuckwallas and other lizards scurrying among the spiny plants. The Yaqui Well Trail climbs for one mile among cacti, ocotillo, and cholla to a mesquite grove and then reaches Yaqui Well. In a small circle around this seep, a tremendous variety of greenery grows, including mesquite and false desert willow, given life by the year-round presence of water. Desert birds show up here, particularly colorful hummingbirds. If you're in the mood for more desert education, drive five miles east of Tamarisk Grove to the short little loop trail at the Narrows. It's packed with

a lot of geologic punch; you'll get a big lesson in geological processes, from faulting and landslides to erosion and earthquakes.

User Groups: Hikers only. No dogs, horses, or mountain bikes. No wheelchair facilities.

Permits: No permits are required. Parking and access are free.

Maps: Maps and brochures are available at the park visitor center, or by free download at www.parks.ca.gov. An Anza-Borrego Desert State Park map is also available from Tom Harrison Maps or Wilderness Press. For a topographic map, ask the USGS for Borrego Sink.

Directions: From Julian, drive east on Highway 78 for 19 miles to Tamarisk Grove Campground at Road S3. The trailheads for the Cactus Loop and Yaqui Well Trails are opposite the camp entrance off Road S3.

Contact: Anza-Borrego Desert State Park, 200 Palm Canyon Drive, Borrego Springs, CA 92004, 760/767-5311; visitors center, 760/767-4205, www.parks.ca.gov.

45 THE SLOT

1.2 mi / 1.0 hr   🚶2 ⛰️10

in Anza-Borrego Desert State Park

Map page 789

This short hike is a winner for just about anybody—families, couples, photographers, and even people who don't really like to hike. This narrow siltsone canyon, simply called The Slot, is sheer entertainment of the type you'd expect to find at Disneyland, except that this place was made by Mother Nature. From the parking area, simply descend into the slot canyon—the large crevice that lies below you. There are usually plenty of footprints showing the best possible route to enter The Slot, and once you have accomplished this, the rest of the hike is extremely easy. Hike to your left (slightly downhill) and you'll soon notice the canyon becoming increasingly narrow. You will need to squeeze through walls that are sometimes no more than shoulder-width apart. The colors of the pink and tan siltstone, with the blue desert sky above, make for interesting photographs. About 0.5 mile from the start, you'll pass underneath a boulder bridge that is precariously lodged in a narrow gap. A few hundred yards beyond, the canyon widens and the trail meets up with a jeep road. Simply retrace your steps from here, enjoying the magic of this slot canyon all over again.

User Groups: Hikers only. No dogs, horses, or mountain bikes. No wheelchair facilities.

Permits: No permits are required. Parking and access are free.

Maps: Maps and brochures are available at the park visitor center, or by free download at www.parks.ca.gov. An Anza-Borrego Desert State Park map is also available from Tom Harrison Maps or Wilderness Press.

Directions: From Christmas Circle in Borrego Springs, drive 11.5 miles southwest on Borrego Springs Road. Turn left on Route 78 East and drive 1.5 miles to mile marker 87.2. Turn north on the unmarked Butte Pass Road (a dirt road that is very easy to miss). Drive one mile up this dirt road to a fork, where you bear left. Continue another mile to the parking area for The Slot. If the road is particularly rutted, low-clearance vehicles should stop and park 0.25 mile from the trailhead.

Contact: Anza-Borrego Desert State Park, 200 Palm Canyon Drive, Borrego Springs, CA 92004, 760/767-5311, www.parks.ca.gov; visitors center, 760/767-4205.

46 ELEPHANT TREE TRAIL
1.5 mi / 1.0 hr

in Anza-Borrego Desert State Park near Split Mountain

Map page 789

It's not just the odd-looking elephant tree that you get to see on this trail, but also many of the common flora of Anza-Borrego Desert—creosote bush, burroweed, indigo bush, barrel cactus, ocotillo, catclaw, cholla, smoke tree.... There's enough desert-plant identification to

do to keep you busy quizzing your hiking partner all day. But it's the single elephant tree on the loop that steals the show, with its crinkled, folded "skin" on its trunk. The tree is an odd patchwork of colors (yellowish bark, blue berries, and orange twigs) and its bark has a very evocative odor, something like a spicy air freshener. The Elephant Tree Trail used to feature several elephant trees, but all but this one lone specimen have died. It is located near the end of the loop. If possible, time your trip for late winter or early spring, when the ocotillos sprout brilliant red plumes and the pink sand verbenas bloom.

User Groups: Hikers only. No dogs, horses, or mountain bikes. No wheelchair facilities.

Permits: No permits are required. Parking and access are free.

Maps: Maps and brochures are available at the park visitor center, or by free download at www.parks.ca.gov. An Anza-Borrego Desert State Park map is also available from Tom Harrison Maps or Wilderness Press. For a topographic map, ask the USGS for Harper Canyon.

Directions: From Julian, drive east on Highway 78 for 35 miles to Ocotillo Wells. Turn south on Split Mountain Road and drive 5.8 miles to the right turnoff that is signed for Elephant Trees. Turn right and drive 0.8 mile on a rough, dirt road to the trailhead.

Contact: Anza-Borrego Desert State Park, 200 Palm Canyon Drive, Borrego Springs, CA 92004, 760/767-5311; visitors center, 760/767-4205, www.parks.ca.gov.

47 GHOST MOUNTAIN
2.0 mi / 1.0 hr

in Anza-Borrego Desert State Park near Blair Valley

Map page 789

When most people imagine a life of living off the land, they instinctively think of doing so in a place where water is plentiful. Not so with Marshal South, who in the 1930s chose Ghost Mountain, in the Anza-Borrego Desert. South and his wife built an adobe home atop the mountain and lived there with their children for more than 15 years. The family tried to live simply, attempting to survive in the spartan style of early Native Americans. Sadly, South's wife eventually tired of the rugged desert life and her husband's odd idealism, and the family split up.

The Ghost Mountain Trail climbs through a series of steep switchbacks to the remains of the South homesite, which includes a few partial walls, an old mattress frame, and some assorted cisterns and barrels used for storing precious water. The destination is worthwhile not just because the sight of it sparks your imagination, but also because of the lovely, 360-degree desert views you gain as you ascend Ghost Mountain. When you stand on the top on a clear, cool day, you can almost imagine why South chose this remote homesite.

Remember that Blair Valley and Ghost Mountain are higher in elevation than other parts of the park. Not only does this make them cooler spots for hiking, but it also means that a wide variety of desert plant life grows here. The ocotillos and yuccas put on a spectacular show in early spring.

User Groups: Hikers only. No dogs, horses, or mountain bikes. No wheelchair facilities.

Permits: No permits are required. Parking and access are free.

Maps: Maps and brochures are available at the park visitor center, or by free download at www.parks.ca.gov. An Anza-Borrego Desert State Park map is also available from Tom Harrison Maps or Wilderness Press. For a topographic map, ask the USGS for Earthquake Valley.

Directions: From Julian, drive east on Highway 78 for 12 miles to Road S2, turn south, and drive six miles to the left turnoff for Blair Valley Camp. Turn left (east), drive 1.4 miles on a dirt road, and then bear right at the fork. Drive another 1.6 miles, bear right again, and drive 0.5 mile to the Ghost Mountain/Marshal South Home trailhead.

Contact: Anza-Borrego Desert State Park,

200 Palm Canyon Drive, Borrego Springs, CA 92004, 760/767-5311; visitors center, 760/767-4205, www.parks.ca.gov.

48 PICTOGRAPH TRAIL
2.0 mi / 1.0 hr   👫2 🏔9

in Anza-Borrego Desert State Park near Blair Valley

Map page 789

Although a Native American rock-art site is the destination of this trip, the Pictograph Trail comes with a bonus: an inspiring overlook of the Vallecito Mountains from the brink of a dry waterfall. It's a desert vista that's hard to forget. The path begins at the Pictograph trailhead and wanders through huge granite boulders. First you head through a dry wash and then climb up a ridge. At 0.5 mile out, you begin to descend. At 0.75 mile, you'll find some pictographs, painted in red and yellow pigments by the nomadic Kumeyaay Indians. (Look for the pictographs on the side of a large boulder on the right side of the trail.) The slightly faded geometric designs were made with natural pigments and are estimated to be 2,000 years old. Continue farther on the trail, and the canyon narrows dramatically until its walls come together at the brink of a dry waterfall more than 150 feet tall. From its edge the panoramic view is stunning, both of the steep dropoff and the far-off mountains and valley.

User Groups: Hikers only. No dogs, horses, or mountain bikes. No wheelchair facilities.

Permits: No permits are required. Parking and access are free.

Maps: Maps and brochures are available at the park visitor center, or by free download at www.parks.ca.gov. An Anza-Borrego Desert State Park map is also available from Tom Harrison Maps or Wilderness Press. For a topographic map, ask the USGS for Earthquake Valley.

Directions: From Julian, drive east on Highway 78 for 12 miles to Road S2, turn south, and drive six miles to the left turnoff for Blair

Valley Camp. Turn left (east), drive 1.4 miles on a dirt road, and then bear right at the fork. Drive another 1.6 miles and bear left at the next fork. In 0.25 mile, bear left again. Continue two more miles to the end of the road, at the Pictograph trailhead.

Contact: Anza-Borrego Desert State Park, 200 Palm Canyon Drive, Borrego Springs, CA 92004, 760/767-5311; visitors center, 760/767-4205, www.parks.ca.gov.

49 MOUNTAIN PALM SPRINGS CANYON
2.6 mi / 2.0 hr

🏃1 ⛰9

in Anza-Borrego Desert State Park near Bow Willow

Map page 789

Although the groves of fan palms in Mountain Palm Springs Canyon are not as large as in Borrego Palm Canyon, they're still beautiful and popular with park visitors. The palm oases, fed by underground springs and shaded by the magnificent fan palms, create a haven for plants and wildlife, as well as for hikers looking for a cool and pleasant place to spend the day. Six distinct palm groves grow in Mountain Palm Springs Canyon, as well as occasional elephant trees; you can visit all of the groves in one walk. The trail doesn't look like much to start, just a rocky arroyo, but it gets more trail-like in short order. The first grove of trees, Pygmy Grove, has been burned. The second grove, Southwest Grove, is larger and prettier. Take the right fork just before you enter Southwest Grove and head uphill to an elephant tree and the one-mile path to the Surprise Canyon Grove. From Surprise Canyon, you can turn left to see Palm Grove Bowl—it's a natural bowl that is ringed with more than 100 palm trees. Return to Surprise Canyon and loop back to your starting point, passing by North Grove on the way. Or retrace your steps to Southwest Grove and take the short spur to the southwest to see Torote Bowl. There are

some good elephant tree specimens there. If you visit in early winter when the palms bear their fruit (dates), you may find so many birds singing in the palm trees that you can hardly hear yourself think. Look for the pretty hooded oriole in particular, which builds its nest on the underside of palm fronds.

User Groups: Hikers only. No dogs, horses, or mountain bikes. No wheelchair facilities.

Permits: No permits are required. Parking and access are free.

Maps: Maps and brochures are available at the park visitor center, or by free download at www.parks.ca.gov. An Anza-Borrego Desert State Park map is also available from Tom Harrison Maps or Wilderness Press. For a topographic map, ask the USGS for Sweeney Pass.

Directions: From Julian, drive east on Highway 78 for 12 miles to Road S2, turn south, and drive 29 miles to the Mountain Palm Springs Campground entrance road, on the right. Turn right and drive straight for 0.6 mile (don't take any of the campsite turnoffs) to the parking area by a stone marker for Mountain Palm Springs Canyon.

Contact: Anza-Borrego Desert State Park, 200 Palm Canyon Drive, Borrego Springs, CA 92004, 760/767-5311, www.parks.ca.gov; visitors center, 760/767-4205.

50 ROCK HILL TRAIL
2.0 mi / 1.5 hr

🏃1 ⛰8

on the east shore of the Salton Sea near Calipatria

Map page 787

If it's wintertime—anywhere from December to February—it's a good time to pay a visit to the Salton Sea National Wildlife Refuge (now called the Sonny Bono Salton Sea National Wildlife Refuge, after the 1970s singer-turned-politician), one of the lowest places in the United States, at 228 feet below sea level. Winter is the only season when the area isn't blistering hot, and it's also the time that peak populations of birds are gathered at the refuge. The place has one hiking trail, called the Rock Hill Trail, which gets hiked by approximately 40,000 bird-watchers a year. From the observation platform behind the visitors center, the path heads out along a levee and then abruptly climbs to a hill above the Salton Sea. It's a great place to watch the pelicans dive and to shake your head in wonder at the immense size of the saline Salton Sea. The sea was formed from 1905 to 1907, when a series of artificial dams on the Colorado River burst their seams. Its water has become increasingly saline over the years due to agricultural runoff, evaporation, and the lack of a replenishing freshwater supply.

Although fish do not fare well in the changing waters of the Salton Sea, bird lovers find plenty to cheer about. In addition to seeing the plentiful waterfowl that spend the winter in the saltwater and freshwater marshes—geese of many kinds, mergansers, widgeons, and teals—hikers might spot an endangered species such as the Yuma clapper rail or peregrine falcon. Migrating snow geese and Ross geese are also big attractions along this trail. They are seen in great numbers every December.

User Groups: Hikers only. No dogs, horses, or mountain bikes. No wheelchair facilities.

Permits: No permits are required. Parking and access are free.

Maps: A free map of the refuge is available at the visitors center. For a topographic map, ask the USGS for Niland.

Directions: From Indio, drive south on Highway 111 for approximately 50 miles to the turnoff for Sinclair Road, which is four miles south of Niland. (If you reach Calipatria, you've gone too far.) Turn right on Sinclair Road and drive six miles to the Salton Sea National Wildlife Refuge visitors center, located at the intersection of Sinclair Road and Gentry Road.

Contact: Sonny Bono Salton Sea National Wildlife Refuge, 906 W. Sinclair Road, Calipatria, CA 92233, 760/348-5278, http://pacific.fws.gov/salton.

51 NORTH ALGODONES DUNES WILDERNESS

1.0 mi / 1.0 hr   👣2 ⛰️8

east of Brawley and south of the Salton Sea

Map page 787

The Algodones Dunes could best be described as an ocean of sand. They are located in the far southeast corner of California, amid a whole lot of… well, to be honest, nothing. Still, this is a unique and fragile place, where a massive dune system covers more than 1,000 square miles. It's the largest (in breadth, not height) dune system in the United States. In between the dunes lie flat basins in which desert willow, smoke trees, and mesquite flourish. Rare reptiles, such as the desert tortoise and fringe-toed lizard, make their homes here. In fact, this is such a fragile environment that permits are required for all visitors. The only time to visit the dunes is between October and April, because it is as hot as Hades the rest of the year. Summer days are typically over 120 degrees. The dunes rise to heights of 350 feet and stretch over a five-mile-wide expanse. You can wander around as much as you like, but since walking in sand is a trying experience, you probably won't wander very far. (There are no formal trails across the dunes because of the continually shifting sands.) Mostly, this is a place to visit to gain a glimpse into a rare, special world comprised entirely of sand and sky.

User Groups: Hikers, dogs, and horses. No mountain bikes. No wheelchair facilities.

Permits: Permits are required for parking and access; visit www.blm.gov/ca/st/en/fo/elcentro.html for permit information.

Maps: A brochure and trail map are available from the Bureau of Land Management (BLM) office listed below. For a topographic map, ask the USGS for Niland.

Directions: From Brawley, drive east on Highway 78 for 26 miles. The wilderness area lies on the north side of the highway, but it is illegal to park alongside the road. Instead, park at the Watchable Wildlife Area north of Highway 78 on the Niland-Glamis Road (along the west side of the railroad tracks). If your visit will be 30 minutes or less, you can park at the Osborne Overlook on Highway 78 (a permit is not required if you park here).

Contact: Bureau of Land Management (BLM), El Centro Field Office, 1661 S. Fourth Street, El Centro, CA 92243, 760/337-4400, www.blm.gov/ca/st/en/fo/elcentro.html.

RESOURCES

NATIONAL FORESTS

The Forest Service provides access to many hikes—from the remote wilderness to public recreation lakes—and allows camping unless specifically prohibited. If you ever want to clear the cobwebs from your head and get away from it all, this is the way to go.

Many Forest Service campgrounds are quite remote and have no drinking water. You usually don't need to check in or make reservations, and sometimes, there is no fee. At many Forest Service campgrounds that provide drinking water, the camping fee is often only a few dollars, with payment made on the honor system. Because most of these campgrounds are in mountain areas, they are subject to winter closure due to snow or mud.

Dogs are permitted in national forests with no extra charge and no hassle. Leashes are required for all dogs in some places. Always carry documentation of current vaccinations.

National Forest Adventure Pass

Angeles, Cleveland, Los Padres, and San Bernardino National Forests require an Adventure Pass for each parked vehicle. Daily passes cost $5; annual passes are available for $30. You can buy Adventure Passes at national forest offices in Southern California and dozens of retail outlets and online vendors. The new charges are use fees, not entrance fees. Holders of Golden Age and Golden Access (not Golden Eagle) cards can buy the Adventure Pass at a 50 percent discount at national forest offices only, or at retail outlets for the retail price. A Golden Eagle passport is honored in lieu of an Adventure Pass.

When you buy an annual Adventure Pass, you can also buy an annual second-vehicle Adventure Pass for $5. Major credit cards are accepted at most retail and online outlets and at some forest service offices. You can buy Adventure Passes by telephone at 909/382-2622, -2623, -2621, or by mail at San Bernardino National Forest, Pass Program Headquarters, 602 S. Tippecanoe Avenue, San Bernardino, CA 92408-2607. Checks should be made payable to USDA Forest Service.

You will not need an Adventure Pass while traveling through these forests, nor when you've paid other types of fees such as camping or ski pass fees. However, if you are camping in these forests and you leave the campground in your vehicle and park outside the campground for recreation, such as at a trailhead, day-use area, near a fishing stream, etc., you will need an Adventure Pass for your vehicle. You also need an Adventure Pass if camping at a no-fee campground. More information about the Adventure Pass program, including a listing of retail and online vendors, can be obtained at www.fsadventurepass.org.

National Forest Reservations

Reservations at some of the more popular campgrounds, and most of the group camps, are made by a reservation system. Reservations can be made up to 240 days in advance, and up to 360 days in advance for groups. To reserve a site, call 877/444-6777 or visit www.reserveusa.com. There is a reservation fee of $9 (usually) for a campsite in a national forest; major credit cards are accepted. Holders of Golden Age or Golden Access passports receive a 50 percent discount for campground fees, except for group sites.

National Forest Maps

National Forest maps are among the best you can get for the price. They detail all backcountry streams, lakes, hiking trails, and logging roads for access. They cost $7 or more, and they can be obtained in person at forest service offices or by contacting U.S. Forest Service, Attn: Map Sales, P.O. Box 8268, Missoula, MT 59807, 406/329-3024, or www.fs.fed.us/recreation/nationalforeststore. Major credit cards are accepted if ordering by telephone.

Forest Service Information

Forest Service personnel are most helpful for obtaining camping or hiking trail information. Unless you are buying a map or Adventure Pass, it is advisable to phone in advance to get the best service. For specific information on a national forest, contact the following offices:

USDA Forest Service
Pacific Southwest Region
1323 Club Drive
Vallejo, CA 94592
707/562-USFS (707/562-8737)
fax 707/562-9130
www.fs.fed.us/r5

Angeles National Forest
701 N. Santa Anita Avenue
Arcadia, CA 91006
626/574-1613
fax 626/574-5233
www.fs.fed.us/r5/angeles

Cleveland National Forest
10845 Rancho Bernardo Road, No. 200
San Diego, CA 92127-2107
858/673-6180
fax 858/673-6192
www.fs.fed.us/r5/cleveland

Eldorado National Forest
100 Forni Road
Placerville, CA 95667
530/622-5061
fax 530/621-5297
www.fs.fed.us/r5/eldorado

Humboldt-Toiyabe National Forest
1200 Franklin Way
Sparks, NV 89431
775/331-6444
fax 775/355-5399
www.fs.fed.us/r4/htnf

Inyo National Forest
351 Pacu Lane, Suite 200
Bishop, CA 93514
760/873-2400
fax 760/873-2458
www.fs.fed.us/r5/inyo

Klamath National Forest
1312 Fairlane Road
Yreka, CA 96097-9549
530/842-6131
fax 530/841-4571
www.fs.fed.us/r5/klamath

Lake Tahoe Basin Management Unit
35 College Drive
South Lake Tahoe, CA 96150
530/543-2600
fax 530/543-2693
www.fs.fed.us/r5/ltbmu

Lassen National Forest
2550 Riverside Drive
Susanville, CA 96130
530/257-2151
fax 530/252-6448
www.r5.fs.fed.us/r5/lassen

Los Padres National Forest
6755 Hollister Avenue, Suite 150
Goleta, CA 93117
805/968-6640
fax 805/961-5729
www.fs.fed.us/r5/lospadres

Mendocino National Forest
825 N. Humboldt Avenue
Willows, CA 95988
530/934-3316
fax 530/934-7384
www.fs.fed.us/r5/mendocino

Modoc National Forest
800 W. 12th Street
Alturas, CA 96101
530/233-5811
fax 530/233-8709
www.fs.fed.us/r5/modoc

Plumas National Forest
P.O. Box 11500
159 Lawrence Street
Quincy, CA 95971
530/283-2050
fax 530/283-7746
www.fs.fed.us/r5/plumas

San Bernardino National Forest
602 S. Tippecanoe Avenue
San Bernardino, CA 92408-2607
909/382-2600
fax 909/383-5770
www.fs.fed.us/r5/sanbernardino

Sequoia National Forest
Giant Sequoia National Monument
1839 S. Newcomb Street
Porterville, CA 93257
559/784-1500
fax 559/781-4744
www.fs.fed.us/r5/sequoia

Shasta-Trinity National Forest
3644 Avtech Parkway
Redding, CA 96002
530/226-2500
fax 530/226-2470
www.fs.fed.us/r5/shastatrinity

Sierra National Forest
1600 Tollhouse Road
Clovis, CA 93611
559/297-0706
fax 559/294-4809
www.fs.fed.us/r5/sierra

Six Rivers National Forest
1330 Bayshore Way
Eureka, CA 95501
707/442-1721
fax 707/442-9242
www.fs.fed.us/r5/sixrivers

Stanislaus National Forest
19777 Greenley Road
Sonora, CA 95370
209/532-3671
fax 209/533-1890
www.fs.fed.us/r5/stanislaus

Tahoe National Forest
631 Coyote Street
Nevada City, CA 95959
530/265-4531
fax 530/478-6109
www.fs.fed.us/r5/tahoe

STATE PARKS

The California State Parks system provides many popular camping spots in spectacular settings. These campgrounds include drive-in numbered sites, tent spaces, and picnic tables, with showers and bathrooms provided nearby. Reservations are often necessary during the summer. Although many parks are well known, there are still some little-known gems in the state parks system where campers can enjoy seclusion, even in the summer.

State park fees have increased significantly since 2002, but camping in a state park is still a good deal. Many of the campgrounds along the California coastline are particularly popular in summer and require planning to secure a campsite.

State Park Reservations

Most of the state park campgrounds are on a reservation system, and campsites can be booked up to seven months in advance at these parks. There are also hike-in/bike-in sites at many of the parks, and these are available on a first-come, first-served basis. Reservations can be made by telephone at 800/444-PARK (800/444-7275) or online at www.reserveamerica.com. A reservation fee of $7.50 is charged for a campsite. Major credit cards are accepted for reservations but are generally not accepted in person at the parks.

Camping discounts of 50 percent are available for holders of the Disabled Discount Pass, and free camping is allowed for holders of the Disabled Veteran/Prisoner of War Pass.

For general information about California State Parks, contact:

California Department of Parks and Recreation
Public Information Office
P.O. Box 942896
1416 9th Street
Sacramento, CA 94296
916/653-6995 or 800/777-0369
fax 916/653-6995
www.parks.ca.gov

NATIONAL PARKS

California's national parks are natural wonders, varying from the spectacular yet crowded Yosemite Valley to the remote and rugged Lava Beds National Monument. Reservations for campsites are available five months in advance for many of the national parks in California. In addition to campground fees, expect to pay a park entrance fee ranging $10–20 per vehicle, or as low as $5 per person for hike-in/bike-in (you can buy an annual National Parks Pass that waives entrance fees). This entrance fee is valid for seven days. For an additional fee, a Golden Eagle sticker can be added to the National Parks Pass, thereby eliminating entrance fees at sites managed by the U.S. Fish and Wildlife Service, the U.S. Forest Service, and the Bureau of Land Management. Various discounts are available for holders of Golden Age and Golden Access passports, including a 50 percent reduction of camping fees (group camps not included) and a waiver of park entrance fees.

For Yosemite National Park reservations, call 800/436-PARK (800/436-7275) or visit http://reservations.nps.gov. Major credit cards are accepted.

For all other national parks, call 800/365-CAMP (800/365-2267) or visit http://reservations.nps.gov. Major credit cards are accepted.

National Park Service
Pacific West Region
One Jackson Center
1111 Jackson Street, Suite 700
Oakland, CA 94607
510/817-1304
www.nps.gov

Cabrillo National Monument
1800 Cabrillo Memorial Drive
San Diego, CA 92106-3601
619/557-5450
fax 619/226-6311
www.nps.gov/cabr

Channel Islands National Park
1901 Spinnaker Drive
Ventura, CA 93001
805/658-5730
fax 805/658-5799
www.nps.gov/chis

Death Valley National Park
P.O. Box 579
Death Valley, CA 92328-0579
760/786-3200
fax 760/786-3283
www.nps.gov/deva

Devils Postpile National Monument
P.O. Box 3999
Mammoth Lakes, CA 93546
760/934-2289 (summer only)
fax 760/934-8896 (summer only)
www.nps.gov/depo
For year-round information, contact Sequoia and Kings Canyon National Parks (see listing)

Golden Gate National Recreation Area
Fort Mason, Building 201
San Francisco, CA 94123-0022
415/561-4700
fax 415/561-4710
www.nps.gov/goga

Joshua Tree National Park
74485 National Park Drive
Twentynine Palms, CA 92277-3597
760/367-5500
fax 760/367-6392
www.nps.gov/jotr

Lassen Volcanic National Park
P.O. Box 100
Mineral, CA 96063-0100
530/595-4444
fax 530/595-3262
www.nps.gov/lavo

Lava Beds National Monument
1 Indian Well Headquarters
Tulelake, CA 96134
530/667-2282
fax 530/667-2737
www.nps.gov/labe

Mojave National Preserve
2701 Barstow Road
Barstow, CA 92311
760/733-4040 (information)
fax 760/252-6174
www.nps.gov/moja

Pinnacles National Monument
5000 Highway 146
Paicines, CA 95043
831/389-4485
fax 831/389-4489
www.nps.gov/pinn

Point Reyes National Seashore
Point Reyes Station, CA 94956-9799
415/464-5100
fax 415/464-5149
www.nps.gov/pore

Redwood National and State Parks
1111 2nd Street
Crescent City, CA 95531
707/464-6101
fax 707/464-1812
www.nps.gov/redw

Santa Monica Mountains National Recreation Area
401 West Hillcrest Drive
Thousand Oaks, CA 91360
805/370-2301
fax 805/370-1850
www.nps.gov/samo

Sequoia and Kings Canyon National Parks
47050 Generals Highway
Three Rivers, CA 93271-9651
559/565-3341
www.nps.gov/seki

Smith River National Recreation Area
P.O. Box 228
Gasquet, CA 95543
707/457-3131
fax 707/457-3794
www.fs.fed.us/r5/sixrivers

Whiskeytown National Recreation Area
P.O. Box 188
Whiskeytown, CA 96095
530/246-1225 or 530/242-3400
fax 530/246-5154
www.nps.gov/whis

Yosemite National Park
P.O. Box 577
Yosemite National Park, CA 95389
209/372-0200 for 24-hour recorded message
www.nps.gov/yose

U.S. ARMY CORPS OF ENGINEERS

Some of the family camps and most of the group camps operated by the U.S. Army Corps of Engineers are on a reservation system. Reservations can be made up to 240 days in advance, and up to 360 days in advance for groups. To reserve a site, call 877/444-6777 or visit www.reserveusa.com. The reservation fee is usually $9, and major credit cards are accepted. Holders of Golden Age or Golden Access passports receive a 50 percent discount for campground fees, except for group sites.

South Pacific Division
333 Market Street
San Francisco, CA 94105
415/977-8272
fax 415/977-8316
www.spn.usace.army.mil

Sacramento District
1325 "J" Street
Sacramento, CA 95814
916/557-5100
www.spk.usace.army.mil

Los Angeles District
915 Wilshire Boulevard, Suite 980
Los Angeles, CA 90017-3401
213/452-3908
fax 213/452-4209
www.spl.usace.army.mil

BUREAU OF LAND MANAGEMENT

Most of the Bureau of Land Management (BLM) campgrounds are primitive and in remote areas. Often, there is no fee charged for camping. Holders of Golden Age or Golden Access passports receive a 50 percent discount, except for group camps, at BLM fee campgrounds.

Bureau of Land Management
California State Office
2800 Cottage Way, Suite W-1834
Sacramento, CA 95825-1886
916/978-4400
fax 916/978-4416
www.blm.gov/ca

California Desert District Office
22835 Calle San Juan de los Lagos
Moreno Valley, CA 92553
951/697-5200
fax 951/697-5299
www.blm.gov/ca/cdd

Alturas Field Office
708 W. 12th Street
Alturas, CA 96101
530/233-4666
fax 530/233-5696
www.blm.gov/ca/alturas

Arcata Field Office
1695 Heindon Road
Arcata, CA 95521-4573
707/825-2300
fax 707/825-2301
www.blm.gov/ca/arcata

Bakersfield Field Office
3801 Pegasus Drive
Bakersfield, CA 93308
661/391-6000
fax 661/391-6040
www.blm.gov/ca/bakersfield

Barstow Field Office
2601 Barstow Road
Barstow, CA 92311
760/252-6000
fax 760/252-6099
www.blm.gov/ca/barstow

Bishop Field Office
351 Pacu Lane, Suite 100
Bishop, CA 93514
760/872-5000
fax 760/872-5050
www.blm.gov/ca/bishop

Eagle Lake Field Office
2950 Riverside Drive
Susanville, CA 96130
530/257-0456
fax 530/257-4831
www.blm.gov/ca/eaglelake

El Centro Field Office
1661 S. 4th Street
El Centro, CA 92243
760/337-4400
fax 760/337-4490
www.blm.gov/ca/elcentro

Folsom Field Office
63 Natoma Street
Folsom, CA 95630
916/985-4474
fax 916/985-3259
www.blm.gov/ca/folsom

Hollister Field Office
20 Hamilton Court
Hollister, CA 95023
831/630-5000
fax 831/630-5055
www.blm.gov/ca/hollister

Palm Springs/South Coast Field Office
P.O. Box 581260
North Palm Springs, CA 92258-1260
760/251-4800
fax 760/251-4899
www.blm.gov/ca/palmsprings

Redding Field Office
355 Hemsted Drive
Redding, CA 96002
530/224-2100
fax 530/224-2172
www.blm.gov/ca/redding

Ridgecrest Field Office
300 S. Richmond Road
Ridgecrest, CA 93555
760/384-5400
fax 760/384-5499
www.blm.gov/ca/ridgecrest

Ukiah Field Office
2550 N. State Street
Ukiah, CA 95482
707/468-4000
fax 707/468-4027
www.blm.gov/ca/ukiah

OTHER VALUABLE RESOURCES

State Forests
Jackson Demonstration State Forest
802 N. Main Street
Fort Bragg, CA 95437
707/964-5674
fax 707/964-0941

Mountain Home Demonstration State Forest
P.O. Box 517
Springville, CA 93265
559/539-2321 (summer)
559/539-2855 (winter)

County/Regional Park Departments
Del Norte County Parks
840 9th Street, Suite 11
Crescent City, CA 95531
707/464-7230
fax 707/464-5824
www.co.del-norte.ca.us

East Bay Regional Park District
P.O. Box 5381
Oakland, CA 94605-0381
510/562-PARK (510/562-7275)
fax 510/635-3478
www.ebparks.org

Humboldt County Parks
1106 2nd Street
Eureka, CA 95501
707/445-7651
fax 707/445-7409
www.co.humboldt.ca.us/

Marin Municipal Water District
220 Nellen Avenue
Corte Madera, CA 94925
415/945-1455
fax 415/927-4953
www.marinwater.org

Midpeninsula Regional Open Space District
330 Distel Circle
Los Altos, CA 94022-1404
650/691-1200
fax 650/691-0485
www.openspace.org

Pacific Gas and Electric Company
Corporate Real Estate/Recreation
5555 Florin-Perkins Road, Room 100
Sacramento, CA 95826
916/386-5164
fax 916/923-7044
www.pge.com/recreation

Sacramento County Regional Parks
3711 Branch Center Road
Sacramento, CA 95827
916/875-6961
fax 916/875-6050
www.sacparks.net

San Diego County Parks and Recreation Department
2454 Heritage Park Row
San Diego, CA 92110
858/694-3049
fax 619/260-6492
www.co.san-diego.ca.us/parks

San Luis Obispo County Parks Department
1087 Santa Rosa Street
San Luis Obispo, CA 93408
805/781-5930
fax 805/781-1102
www.slocountyparks.org

San Mateo County Parks and Recreation Department
455 County Center, 4th Floor
Redwood City, CA 94063-1646
650/363-4020
fax 650/599-1721
www.eparks.net

Santa Barbara County Parks and Recreation Department
610 Mission Canyon Road
Santa Barbara, CA 93105
805/568-2461
fax 805/568-2459
www.sbparks.com

Santa Clara County Parks Department
298 Garden Hill Drive
Los Gatos, CA 95032-7669
408/355-2200
fax 408/355-2290
www.parkhere.org

Sonoma County Regional Parks
2300 County Center Drive, Suite 120-A
Santa Rosa, CA 95404
707/565-2041
fax 707/579-8247
www.sonoma-county.org/parks

State and Federal Offices

U.S. Fish and Wildlife Service
1849 "C" Street NW
Washington, DC 20240
www.fws.gov

U.S. Geological Survey
Branch of Information Services
P.O. Box 25286, Bldg. 810, MS 306, Federal Center
Denver, CO 80225
888/ASK-USGS (888/275-8747) or
303/202-4700
www.usgs.gov

California Department of Fish and Game
1416 9th Street, 12th Floor
Sacramento, CA 95814
916/445-0411
www.dfg.ca.gov

Information Services

Lake County Visitor Information Center
P.O. Box 1025
6110 East Highway 20
Lucerne, CA 95458
707/274-5652 or 800/525-3743
fax 707/274-5664
www.lakecounty.com

Mammoth Lakes Visitors Bureau
P.O. Box 48
437 Old Mammoth Road, Suite Y
Mammoth Lakes, CA 93546
888/GO-MAMMOTH (888/466-2666) or
760/934-2712
fax 760/934-7066
www.visitmammoth.com

Mount Shasta Visitors Bureau
300 Pine Street
Mount Shasta, CA 96067
530/926-4865 or 800/926-4865
fax 530/926-0976
www.mtshastachamber.com

The Nature Conservancy of California
201 Mission Street, 4th Floor
San Francisco, CA 94105-1832
415/777-0487
fax 415/777-0244
www.nature.org/california

Plumas County Visitors Bureau
550 Crescent Street
P.O. Box 4120
Quincy, CA 95971
530/283-6345 or 800/326-2247
fax 530/283-5465
www.plumascounty.org

Shasta Cascade Wonderland Association
1699 Highway 273
Anderson, CA 96007
530/365-7500 or 800/474-2782
fax 530/365-1258
www.shastacascade.com

Map Sources

Map Link
30 S. La Patera Lane, Unit 5
Goleta, CA 93117
805/692-6777 or 800/962-1394
fax 805/692-6787 or 800/627-7768
www.maplink.com

Tom Harrison Maps
2 Falmouth Cove
San Rafael, CA 94901-4465
tel./fax 415/456-7940
www.tomharrisonmaps.com

U.S. Forest Service
Attn: Map Sales
P.O. Box 8268
Missoula, MT 59807
406/329-3024
fax 406/329-3030
www.fs.fed.us/recreation/nationalforeststore

U.S. Geological Survey
Branch of Information Services
P.O. Box 25286, Federal Center
Denver, CO 80225
303/202-4700 or
888/ASK-USGS (888/275-8747)
fax 303/202-4693
www.usgs.gov

Index

Acknowledgments

U.S. Forest Service

Debe Arndt, High Sierra Ranger District, Sierra National Forest
Mary August, Feather River Ranger District, Plumas National Forest
Paul Bailey, Devil's Garden Ranger District, Modoc National Forest
Cheryl Balle and Ann Wiltshire, Cannell Meadow Ranger District, Sequoia National Forest
Jim Barnhardt, Hat Creek Work Center, Lassen National Forest
Pamela Bierce, San Bernardino National Forest
Al Buchter, Salmon River Ranger District, Klamath National Forest
Kathy Burnett, Summit Ranger District, Stanislaus National Forest
Anne Carey, Descanso Ranger District, Cleveland National Forest
Joe Chavez, Downieville Ranger District, Tahoe National Forest
Maxine Chittender, Hume Lake Ranger District, Sequoia National Forest
Scott Clemons, Bridgeport Ranger District, Humboldt-Toiyabe National Forest
Pennie Custer, Inyo National Forest
Jim Fedderly, Calaveras Ranger District, Stanislaus National Forest
Anna Fiorella, Corning Work Center, Mendocino National Forest
Pat Garrahan, Happy Camp Ranger District, Klamath National Forest
Sharon Graham, Covelo Ranger District, Mendocino National Forest
Ken Graves, Hayfork Office, Shasta-Trinity National Forest
Jennifer Gray, Los Padres National Forest
Steve Hale, Carson Ranger District, Humboldt-Toiyabe National Forest
Bob Hemus, Orleans Ranger District, Klamath National Forest
Bob Hemus, Six Rivers National Forest
Charlie Kraus, Scott River Ranger District, Klamath National Forest
Ron Lawson, San Jacinto Ranger District, San Bernardino National Forest
Don Lee, Mount Shasta Ranger District, Shasta-Trinity National Forest
Mike LeFevre, Bass Lake Ranger Station, Sierra National Forest
John Louth, Ancient Bristlecone Pine Forest, Inyo National Forest
Dean Lutz, Truckee Ranger District, Tahoe National Forest
Patty Mahaffey, Nevada City Ranger District, Tahoe National Forest
Matt Mathes, Pacific Region Headquarters
Geneva May, Sierraville Ranger District, Tahoe National Forest
Marilyn Muse Meyer, Amador Ranger District, Eldorado National Forest
Joe Miranda, Stonyford Ranger Station, Mendocino National Forest
Deborah Nearing, Foresthill Ranger District, Tahoe National Forest
Liz Nelson, Mount Whitney Ranger Station, Inyo National Forest
Barbara Paolinetti, McCloud Ranger District, Shasta-Trinity National Forest
Del Pengilly, Tule River/Hot Springs Ranger District, Sequoia National Forest
Joyce Platt, Information Center, Eldorado National Forest
Robin Renteria, Lake Tahoe Basin Management Unit
Gerald Reponen, Angeles National Forest
John Sandstrom, Big Bar Ranger Station, Shasta-Trinity National Forest
Lisa Sedlacek, Almanor Ranger District, Lassen National Forest
Joseph Signorino, Ojai Ranger District, Los Padres National Forest

Jerry Snyder, Stanislaus National Forest
Cathy Southwick, Shasta Lake Ranger District, Shasta-Trinity National Forest
Jim Stout, Goosenest Ranger District, Klamath National Forest
Dustin Swan, Bridgeport Ranger District, Humboldt-Toiyabe National Forest
Nancy Upham, Inyo National Forest
Pandora Valle, Beckwourth Ranger District, Plumas National Forest
Keith Waterfall, Inyo National Forest
Beverly Way, Warner Mountain Ranger District, Modoc National Forest
Charlotte Wheeland, San Gabriel River Ranger District
Lorraine Worley, Doublehead Ranger District, Modoc National Forest
KC Wylie, Inyo National Forest
Alfredo Zarate Jr., Mill Creek Ranger Station, San Bernardino National Forest

National Parks

Nancy Bailey and Karen Haner, Lassen Volcanic National Park
Terry Baldino, Death Valley National Park
Richard Banuelos, Pinnacles National Monument
Phil Bono and Don Pass, Smith River National Recreation Area
Charlie Calligan, Death Valley National Park
Cathy Cook, Redwood National and State Parks
Ryan Cooper, Carrizo Plain National Monument
Malinee Crapsey, Sequoia and Kings Canyon National Parks
Tom Dore, Channel Islands National Park
Kris Fister, Sequoia and Kings Canyon National Parks
Trisha Ford, Whiskeytown National Recreation Area
Scott Gediman, Yosemite National Park
Philip Gomez, Mojave National Preserve
Ken Hires, Sequoia and Kings Canyon National Parks
B. G. Horvat, Pinnacles National Monument
Rick Jenkins, Cabrillo National Monument
Lauren Newman, Santa Monica Mountains National Recreation Area
Ruby Newton, Mojave National Preserve
Valerie Pillsbury, Sequoia and Kings Canyon National Parks
Cathy Purchis, Sequoia and Kings Canyon National Parks
Denise Robertson, Sequoia and Kings Canyon National Parks
Christian Slater, Salton Sea National Wildlife Refuge
Barney Stoffel, Lava Beds National Monument
Charles Taylor, Santa Monica Mountains National Recreation Area
Cindy VonHalle, Joshua Tree National Park

U.S. Army Corps of Engineers

Mary Ann Deeming, Black Butte Lake
Greg Volkman, Eastman Lake
Angie Wulsow, Lake Sonoma

Bureau of Land Management
Larry Ames, Ukiah Field Office
Stan Bell, Eagle Lake Field Office
Jenny Weiss, Arcata Field Office

State Parks
Greg Ahayes, Silverado District
Garratt Aitchison, Sugar Pine Point State Park
Jill Alford, Mendocino District
Jo Ann Allison, Big Sur Station (Big Sur state parks)
Kim Anbrychowicz, Prairie Creek Redwoods State Park
Jim Baird, Patrick's Point State Park
Katie Bernarding, Tomales Bay State Park
Becky Bradford, Butano State Park
Barry Breckling, Henry W. Coe State Park
Matthew Buonaguidi, Point Lobos State Reserve
James Burke and Tom Cline, Cuyamaca Rancho State Park
Brian Cahill, Colorado Desert District
Lori Castro, Castle Crags State Park
Trudy Ferris, Crystal Cove State Park
Sharon Galligan, Henry Cowell Redwoods State Park
Chuck Grennell, Calaveras Big Trees State Park
Bill Grummer, Bothe-Napa Valley State Park
Mike Hanes, Samuel P. Taylor State Park
David Horvitz, Sonoma Coast State Beach
Fred Jee, Anza Borrego Desert State Park
Allyn Kaye, Torrey Pines State Reserve
John Kolsrud, Armstrong Redwoods State Reserve
Bill Lindemann, Sierra District
John McGee, Point Lobos State Reserve
Susan McLaughlin, Richardson Grove State Park
Bill Mentzer, Mount Tamalpais State Park
Lynn Mochizuki, Point Mugu State Park, Leo Carrillo State Park, and Malibu Creek State Park
William Moffat, Tule Elk State Reserve
Jennifer Morgan, Pacheco State Park/San Luis Reservoir State Rec. Area
Ken Morse, Jedediah Smith Redwoods State Park
Roger Nelson, Half Moon Bay State Beach
Dean Oertly, Plumas-Eureka State Park
John O'Rourke, Humboldt Redwoods State Park
Alex Ott, Fremont Peak State Park
Paula Pennington, Grover Hot Spring State Park
Shannon Pulce, Chino Hills State Park
Richard Ranc, San Luis Reservoir State Recreation Area
Kay Robinson, Henry W. Coe State Park
Kelly Setters, Auburn State Recreation Area

John Trammer, Morro Bay State Park
Andrew Urlie, McArthur–Burney Falls State Park
Suzanne Westover, Salt Point State Park
Dan Winkelman, Angel Island State Park
Bill Wisehard, North Coast Redwoods District
Andy Zilke, Oceana Dunes State Vehicular Recreation Area

Other Parks and Preserves

Mark Andre, City of Arcata
Edward Arcetta, Santa Clara County Parks Department
Maryanne Bache, San Elijo Lagoon Conservancy
David Brooks, Loch Lomond Recreation Area
Linda Chaplin, Sequoya Challenge
Joe DiDonato, East Bay Regional Parks District
Kay Elliott, Santa Barbara County Parks and Recreation
Paula Forgi, Pacific Gas & Electric Company
John Fulton, San Luis National Wildlife Refuge Complex
Matt Gilbert, Jackson Demonstration State Forest
Margaret Harris, BLM Fieldcrest Office
Bill Hogan, Marin Open Space District
Denise Homer, Arcata Marsh Interpretive Center
Ed Hulme, Marin Municipal Water District
Paul Kilburg, Mission Trails Regional Park
Glenn Kinney, Wildwood Park, Conejo Rec. & Park District
Ken Klis, Lopez Lake Recreation Area
Donna LaGraffe, County of Sonoma
Nola Lamken, Silverwood Wildlife Sanctuary
Cory Linder, County of San Diego Parks and Recreation
Irene Lindsey, Kaweah Oaks Preserve
Barbara Lockwood, Dixon Lake/Escondido Parks and Recreation
Dave Lydick, County of Sacramento
Ned MacKay, East Bay Regional Parks District
Nancy McKay, East Bay Regional Parks District
Emily Messenger, TreePeople
Doug Miller, Toro County Park
Lauren Newman, Santa Monica Mountains National Recreation Area
David Numer, Devil's Punchbowl Natural Area
Olley Olsen, Santa Catalina Island Company
Dennis Parker, San Diego County Parks and Recreation
Sylvia Pelizza, Sonny Bono Salton Sea National Wildlife Refuge
Johanna Salomon, County of San Diego Parks and Recreation
Frances Scalvini, City of Ferndale
Kevin Smith, Santa Rosa Plateau Ecological Reserve
Tony Smock, Dixon Lake Recreation Area and Daley Ranch
Darrell Wanner, Placerita Canyon County Park

Roger Wilbur, Los Banos Wildlife Area
Jeff Wilson, Tilden Regional Park
Tricia Wilson, Elkhorn Slough National Estuarine Research Reserve
Helen Wong, Eaton Canyon Natural Area
Niki Woodard, Kaweah Oaks Preserve/Sequoia Riverlands Trust
Betty Zeller, Big Morongo Canyon Preserve

Field Scouts Providing Personal Updates

Bob Coomber, David Dayton, Phil Ford, Michael Furniss, John Hamilton, Doug Herbek, Jeremy Keyston, Kris Keyston, John King, Doug McConnell, Jim McDaniel, Paul McHugh, Ethel Mohler, John Reginato, Paul and Patty Sakuma, George Seifert, Peter Shyvers, Bob Simms, Marisa Solís, Bob and Eleanor Stienstra, Robert Stienstra Jr., John Thomas, Fritz Ward, Larry Yant.

www.moon.com

DESTINATIONS | ACTIVITIES | BLOGS | MAPS | BOOKS

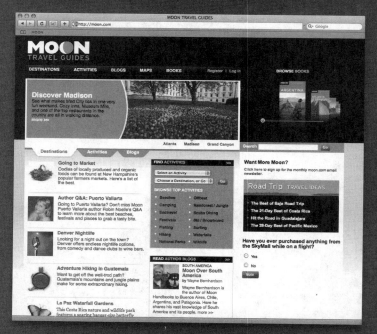

MOON.COM is ready to help plan your next trip! Filled with fresh trip ideas and strategies, author interviews, informative travel blogs, a detailed map library, and descriptions of all the Moon guidebooks, Moon.com is all you need to get out and explore the world—or even places in your own backyard. While at Moon.com, sign up for our monthly e-newsletter for updates on new releases, travel tips, and expert advice from our on-the-go Moon authors. As always, when you travel with Moon, expect an experience that is uncommon and truly unique.

KEEP UP WITH MOON ON FACEBOOK AND TWITTER
JOIN THE MOON PHOTO GROUP ON FLICKR

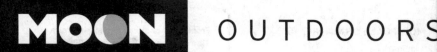

MOON OUTDOORS

YOUR ADVENTURE STARTS HERE

MINNESOTA CAMPING

CALIFORNIA HIKING

OREGON FISHING

NEW ENGLAND BIKING

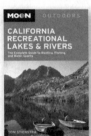

CALIFORNIA RECREATIONAL LAKES & RIVERS

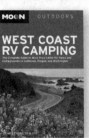

WEST COAST RV CAMPING

YELLOWSTONE & GRAND TETON CAMPING

TAKE A HIKE WASHINGTON DC

For campers, hikers, cyclists, anglers, boaters, and for those that like the comforts of an RV, Moon Outdoors guides are written by outdoor experts who offer well-researched info and insider tips.

For a complete list of guidebooks, visit Moon.com/books.

Moon Outdoors guidebooks are available through online booksellers, at bookstores, and at many outdoor retail stores.

MOON CALIFORNIA HIKING

Avalon Travel
a member of the Perseus Books Group
1700 Fourth Street
Berkeley, CA 94710, USA
www.moon.com

Editor and Series Manager: Sabrina Young
Production and Graphics Coordinators:
    Sean Bellows and Domini Dragoone
Cover Designer: Domini Dragoone
Interior Designer: Darren Alessi
Map Editor: Mike Morgenfeld
Cartographers: Mike Morgenfeld and
    Kaitlin Jaffe
Proofreader: Annie Blakely

ISBN-13: 978-1-61238-163-3
ISSN: 1078-960X

Printing History
1st Edition – 1994
9th Edition – March 2012
5 4 3 2 1

Keeping Current

We are committed to making this book the most accurate and enjoyable hiking guide to California. You can rest assured that every trail in this book has been carefully reviewed in an effort to keep this book as up-to-date as possible. However, by the time you read this book, some of the fees listed herein may have changed and trails may have closed unexpectedly.

If you have a favorite gem you'd like to see included in the next edition, or see anything that needs updating, clarification, or correction, please drop us a line. Send your comments via email to feedback@moon.com, or use the address above.